ICSE Exams 2026

AF814347

All in One®

MATHEMATICS

Class 10

ICSE Exams 2026

All in One®
MATHEMATICS
Class 10

Authors
Laxman Prasad
Brijesh Dwevedi

arihant
SUCCESS AND NOTHING LESS

ARIHANT PRAKASHAN
(School Division Series)

卐 *ADMINISTRATIVE & PRODUCTION OFFICES*

Regd. Office

'Ramchhaya' 4577/15, Agarwal Road, Darya Ganj, New Delhi -110002
Tele: 011- 47630600, 43518550; Fax: 011- 23280316

卐 *Head Office*

Kalindi, TP Nagar, Meerut (UP) - 250002, Tel: 0121-7156203, 7156204

卐 *SALES & SUPPORT OFFICES*

Agra, Ahmedabad, Bengaluru, Bareilly, Chennai, Delhi, Guwahati, Hyderabad, Jaipur, Jhansi, Kolkata, Lucknow, Nagpur & Pune.

PO No : TXT-XX-XXXXXXX-X-XX

Published By Arihant Publications (India) Ltd.

For further information about the books published by Arihant, log on to www.arihantbooks.com or e-mail at info@arihantbooks.com

Follow us on

卐 *PRICE* ₹555.00

PRODUCTION TEAM

Publishing Managers	*Cover Designer*	*Inner Designer*
Mahendra Singh Rawat & Keshav Mohan	Salman Shaikh	Ankit Tyagi
Project Head	*Page Layouting*	*Proof Reader*
Ashwani	Shivam Prajapati	Mukul Kaushik

Index *cum* Study Planner

One Book- Endless Features

to Help you Succeed

In This Chapter

At the start of each chapter, all the chapter topics have been listed , so that students may know what they are going to study.

5

Quadratic Equations in One Variable

SYLLABUS

- (a) Nature of Roots : (i) Two distinct real roots, if $b^2 - 4ac > 0$ (ii) Two equal real roots, if $b^2 - 4ac = 0$ (iii) No real roots, if $b^2 - 4ac < 0$ (b) Solving Quadratic equations by : (i) Factorisation (ii) Using Formula (c) Solving simple Quadratic equations problems

In earlier classes, we have already studied about the polynomial. The second degree polynomial in one variable is called quadratic polynomial and if we take it equal to zero, then it becomes a quadratic equation. In this chapter, we will study quadratic equations and various ways of finding their roots. We will also discuss some application of quadratic

Example 1. Check whether the following are quadratic equations or not.

(i) $(x-1)(x+2)=(x-3)(x+1)$

(ii) $(x+2)^2 = 4(x+3)$

Sol.

(i) Given, $(x-1)(x+2)=(x-3)(x+1)$ ...(i)

Here, in LHS, $(x-1)$ and $(x+2)$ are in product and in

Quadratic Equation

An equation of the form $ax^2 + bx + c = 0$ is called **quadratic equation** in variable x, where a, b and c are real numbers and $a \neq 0$. e.g. $2x^2 + x - 100 = 0$, $-x^2 + 300x + 1 = 0$, $4x - 3x^2 + 7 = 0$, $4x^2 - 25 = 0$ are quadratic equations.

The form $ax^2 + bx + c = 0$, $a \neq 0$, is called the **standard form of a quadratic equation**.

To express a quadratic equation in its standard form, write the equation in decreasing order of the degrees of variable. e.g. $3x^2 + x + 2 = 0$, $x^2 - 2x + 6 = 0$ are in standard form, whereas $x^2 - 3 + 4x = 0$, $x + x^2 + 8 = 0$ are not in standard form.

Simplified Theory

It contains the necessary study material well supported by Definitions, Facts, Figures, Flow Charts, etc.

Topical Exercises

To make students understand the chapter in a smooth part-by-part manner, Topical Exercises have been given in each chapter. These Exercises help students to assess the understanding of related concepts at regular interval.

Exercise 5.1

1. Check whether the following equations are quadratic or not.
   (i) $2x^2 - 5x = x^2 - 2x + 3$ (ii) $x^2 - 3x - \sqrt{x} + 4 = 0$
   (iii) $x(2x+3) = x + 2$ (iv) $x + \frac{3}{x} = x^2$
   (v) $x^2 - \frac{1}{x^2} = 5$
2. Is $x = -2$ a solution of the equation $x^2 - 2x + 8 = 0$?
3. Show that $x = -3$ is a solution of equation $x^2 + 6x + 9 = 0$.
4. Which of the following are the solutions of

10. $15y^2 = 41y - 14$
11. $6x^2 + 40 = 31x$
12. $21x^2 - 2x + \frac{1}{21} = 0$
13. $3x^2 + 2\sqrt{5}x - 5 = 0$
14. $2x^2 - 9x + 10 = 0$ when
    (i) $x \in N$ (ii) $x \in Q$

Directions (Q. Nos. 15-17) *Solve for x.*

15. $x^2 + 5x - (a^2 + a - 6) = 0$
16. $6a^2x^2 - 7abx - 3b^2 = 0, a \neq 0$

One Book- Endless Features

to Help you Succeed

Illustrative Figures

To make the concepts completely visible, illustrative diagrams have been given at various place.

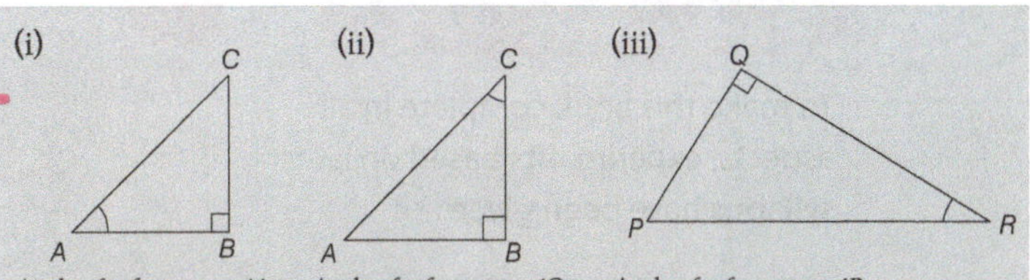

(i)	(ii)	(iii)
Angle of reference = $\angle A$	Angle of reference = $\angle C$	Angle of reference = $\angle R$
Perpendicular = BC	Perpendicular = AB	perpendicular = PQ
Base = AB	Base = BC	Base = QR
Hypotenuse = AC	Hypotenuse = AC	Hypotenuse = PR

Chapter Practice

a. 1 Mark Questions

1. Is -8 is a solution of the equation $3x^2 + 8x + 2 = 0$? [NCERT Exemplar]
   (a) Yes
   (b) No
   (c) Cannot be determined
   (d) None of the above
2. If $x = \frac{1}{\sqrt{3}}$ is root of the equation $px^2 + (\sqrt{3} - \sqrt{2})x - 1 = 0$, then the value of $p^2 + 1$ is [NCERT Exemplar]
   (a) $\sqrt{6}$ (b) 6 (c) 7 (d) 8
3. If 3 is a root of the quadratic equation $x^2 - px + 3 = 0$, then p is equal to [ICSE 2023]
   (a) 4 (b) 3 (c) 5 (d) 2
4. The sum of the squares of three consecutive integers is 110, then the smallest positive integer is [NCERT Exemplar]
   (a) 6 (b) 5 (c) 7 (d) 4

10. Solve the following quadratic equation:
    $$x^2 + 4x - 8 = 0$$
    Give your answer correct to one decimal place. (Use mathematical tables if necessary) [ICSE 2023]
11. Solve the quadratic equation $x^2 - 3x - 9 = 0$ for x and give your answer correct to two decimal places. [ICSE 2016, 2007]
12. Form a quadratic equation whose roots are
    (i) -5 and $\frac{5}{2}$ (ii) $2 + 2\sqrt{3}$
13. Find the quadratic equation, whose solution set is
    (i) $\{3, 5\}$ (ii) $\{-2, 3\}$
14. Solve the equation $4x^2 - 5x - 3 = 0$ and give your answer correct to two decimal places. [ICSE 2017]
15. Solve the quadratic equation $2x^2 + 5\sqrt{3}x + 6 = 0$ upto three decimal places. [take $\sqrt{3} = 1.732$]
16. Solve the quadratic equation $5x(x + 2) = 3$ and give your answer correct to two decimal places. [ICSE 2008]

Chapter Practice

To make students completely prepared for examination, this Exercise contains Exam Pattern Questions. This exercise covers all types of questions, like; 1 Mark, 2 Marks, 3 Marks, 4 Marks and 6 Marks. All the questions are fully explained helping students to understand, how to write the solutions to get full marks in the exam.

Olympiad Section

It includes some special questions based on the pattern of Olympiad and other competitions to give the students a taste of the questions asked in competitions. These are not meant for school examinations.

Olympiad Section

Brain Teasing Questions of Olympiad Pattern

1. The linear factors of the equation $x^2 + kx + 1 = 0$ exists, if
   (a) $k \geq 2$ (b) $k \leq -2$
   (c) Both (a) and (b) (d) $k = 2$
2. The root of the equation $2\sin\theta + \frac{3}{\sin\theta} + 7 = 0$ is
   (a) $\frac{1}{2}$ (b) $-\frac{1}{2}$
   (c) $\frac{1}{3}$ (d) $\frac{1}{7}$
3. The equation $x^2(a^2 + b^2) + 2x(ac + bd) + (c^2 + d^2) = 0$ has no real roots, if
   (a) $ad \neq bc$ (b) $ac \neq bd$
   (c) $ac \neq 2bd$ (d) None of these
4. A factory kept increasing its output by the same percentage every year. Then, the percentage, if it is known that the output is doubled in the last two years, will be
   (a) 44.1% (b) 14.4%
   (c) 44.4% (d) 41.4%
5. A trader bought a number of articles for ₹ 1200. Ten were damaged and he sold each of the rest at ₹ 2 more than what he paid for it, thus cleaning a profit of ₹ 60 on the whole transaction. If x denotes the number of articles he bought, then the value of x is
   (a) 100 (b) 60
   (c) 80 (d) 110
6. If the roots of the equation $x^2 + 2cx + ab = 0$ are real and unequal, then the equation $x^2 - 2(a + b)x + a^2 + b^2 + 2c^2 = 0$ has
   (a) real root (b) no real roots
   (c) equal root (d) real and equal
7. The values of x satisfying $p^2x^2 + (p^2 - q^2)x - q^2 = 0$ are
   (a) $\frac{q^2}{p^2}, -1$ (b) $\frac{p^2}{q^2}, 1$
   (c) $\frac{q^2}{p^2}, +1$ (d) $1, \frac{-q}{p}$
8. From a group of Saras birds, one-fourth of the number are moving about in lotus plants, one-ninth coupled with one-fourth as well as 7 times the square root of the total number are moving on a hill, while 56 birds are sitting in the Bakula trees. Then, what is the total number of birds?
   (a) 629 (b) 567
   (c) 675 (d) 576

One Book- Endless Features
to Help you Succeed

Internal Assessment of Practical Work

To make this book complete in all aspects, experiments based on latest syllabus have been given.

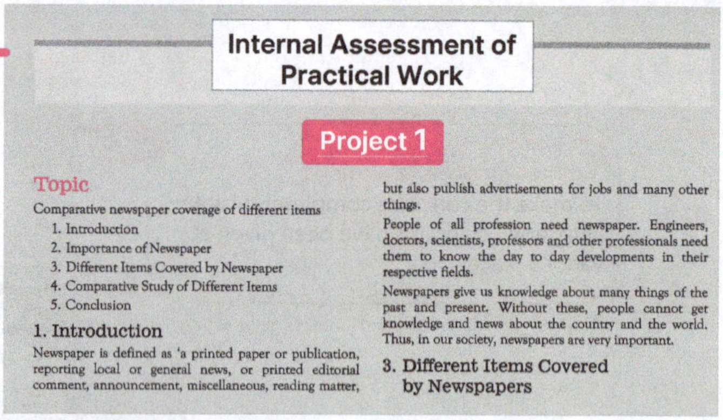

Internal Assessment of Practical Work

Project 1

Topic

Comparative newspaper coverage of different items

1. Introduction
2. Importance of Newspaper
3. Different Items Covered by Newspaper
4. Comparative Study of Different Items
5. Conclusion

1. Introduction

Newspaper is defined as 'a printed paper or publication, reporting local or general news, or printed editorial comment, announcement, miscellaneous, reading matter, but also publish advertisements for jobs and many other things.

People of all profession need newspaper. Engineers, doctors, scientists, professors and other professionals need them to know the day to day developments in their respective fields.

Newspapers give us knowledge about many things of the past and present. Without these, people cannot get knowledge and news about the country and the world. Thus, in our society, newspapers are very important.

3. Different Items Covered by Newspapers

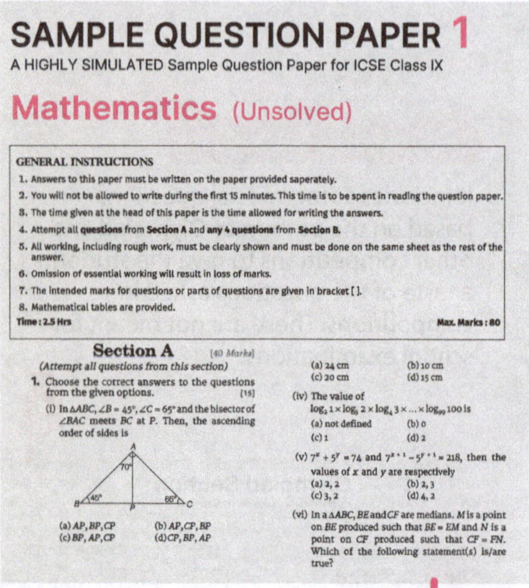

SAMPLE QUESTION PAPER 1

A HIGHLY SIMULATED Sample Question Paper for ICSE Class IX

Mathematics (Unsolved)

GENERAL INSTRUCTIONS

1. Answers to this paper must be written on the paper provided saperately.
2. You will not be allowed to write during the first 15 minutes. This time is to be spent in reading the question paper.
3. The time given at the head of this paper is the time allowed for writing the answers.
4. Attempt all **questions** from **Section A** and **any 4 questions** from **Section B.**
5. All working, including rough work, must be clearly shown and must be done on the same sheet as the rest of the answer.
6. Omission of essential working will result in loss of marks.
7. The intended marks for questions or parts of questions are given in bracket [ ].
8. Mathematical tables are provided.

Time : 2.5 Hrs | Max. Marks : 80

Section A [40 Marks]

(Attempt all questions from this section)

1. Choose the correct answers to the questions from the given options. [15]

(i) In ΔABC, $\angle B = 45°$, $\angle C = 65°$ and the bisector of $\angle BAC$ meets BC at P. Then, the ascending order of sides is

(a) AP, BP, CP (b) AP, CP, BP
(c) BP, AP, CP (d) CP, BP, AP

(a) 24 cm (b) 10 cm
(c) 20 cm (d) 15 cm

(iv) The value of $\log_2 1 \times \log_3 2 \times \log_4 3 \times \ldots \times \log_{99} 100$ is
(a) not defined (b) 0
(c) 1 (d) 2

(v) $7^x + 5^y = 74$ and $7^{x+1} - 5^{y+1} = 218$, then the values of x and y are respectively
(a) 2, 2 (b) 2, 3
(c) 3, 2 (d) 4, 2

(vi) In a ΔABC, BE and CF are medians. M is a point on BE produced such that $BE = EM$ and N is a point on CF produced such that $CF = FN$. Which of the following statement(s) is/are true?

Sample Question Papers

To make students practice of examination in real sense, there are 3 Sample Question Papers at the end. All these Sample Questions Papers are exactly prepared on the latest syllabus & pattern of examination.

Latest Course Structure

*There will be **one** paper of **two and a half** hours duration carrying 80 Marks and Internal Assessment of 20 Marks. The paper will be divided into two sections, **Section I** (40 Marks), **Section II** (40 Marks).*

***Section I** Will consists of compulsory short answer questions.*

***Section II** Candidates will be required to answer **four** out of **seven** questions.*

Commercial Mathematics

(i) Goods and Service Tax (GST)

Computation of tax including problems involving discounts, list-price, profit, loss, basic/cost price including inverse cases.

Candidates are also expected to find price paid by the consumer after paying State Goods and Service Tax (SGST) and Central Goods and Service Tax (CGST). The different rates as in vogue on different types of items will be provided. Problems based on corresponding inverse cases are also included.

(ii) Banking

Recurring Deposit Accounts : computation of interest and maturity value using the formula

$$I = P\frac{n(n+1)}{2\times 12}\times\frac{r}{100}$$

$$MV = P\times n + I$$

(iii) Shares and Dividends

(a) *Face/Nominal Value, Market Value, Dividend, Rate of Dividend, Premium.*

(b) *Formulae*

- *Income = Number of shares x Rate of dividend x FV.*
- *Return = (Income/Investment) x 100.*

Note : *Brokerage and fractional shares **not included.***

Algebra

(i) Linear Inequations

Linear Inequations in one unknown for $x \in N, W, Z, R$. Solving

- *Algebraically and writing the solution in set notation form.*
- *Representation of solution on the number line.*

(ii) Quadratic Equations in one variable.

(a) *Nature of roots*

- *Two distinct real roots, if $b^2 - 4ac > 0$.*
- *Two equal real roots, if $b^2 - 4ac = 0$.*
- *No real roots, if $b^2 - 4ac > 0$.*

(b) Solving Quadratic equations by

- *Factorisation.*
- *Using Formula.*

(c) Solving simple quadratic equation problems.

(iii) Ratio and Proportion

(a) *Proportion, Continued proportion, mean proportion*

(b) *Componendo, dividendo, alternendo, invertendo properties and their combinations.*

(c) *Direct simple applications on proportions only.*

(iv) Factorisation of polynomials

(a) *Factor Theorem.*

(b) *Remainder Theorem.*

(c) *Factorising a polynomial completely after obtaining one factor by factor theorem.*

Note : $f(x)$ not to exceed degree 3.

(v) Matrices

(a) *Order of a matrix. Row and column matrices.*

(b) *Compatibility for addition and multiplication.*

(c) *Null and Identity matrices.*

(d) *Addition and subtraction of 2×2 matrices.*

(e) *Multiplication of a 2×2 matrix by*

- *a non-zero rational number.*
- *a matrix.*

(vi) Arithmetic and Geometric Progression

- *Finding their General term.*
- *Finding sum of their first 'n' terms.*
- *Simple Applications.*

(vii) Coordinate Geometry

(a) *Reflection*

- *Reflection of a point in a line : $x = 0, y = 0, x = a, y = a$, the origin.*
- *Reflection of a point in the origin.*
- *Invariant points.*

(b) *Coordinates expressed as (x, y), Section formula, Mid-point formula, Concept of slope, equation of a line, Various forms of straight lines.*

(i) *Section and Mid-point formula (Internal section only, coordinates of the centroid of a triangle included).*

(ii) *Equation of a line*

- *Slope-intercept form $y = mx + c$.*

- Two-point form $(y - y_1) = m(x - x_1)$
- Geometric understanding of 'm' as slope/gradient/tan θ where θ is the angle the line makes with the positive direction of the X-axis.

  Geometric understanding of 'c' as the y-intercept/the ordinate of the point, where the line intercepts the Y-axis/the point on the line where x=0.
- Conditions for two lines to be parallel or perpendicular.

Simple applications of all the above.

Geometry

(a) Similarity

Similarity, conditions of similar triangles.

(i) As a size transformation.

(ii) Comparison with congruency, keyword being proportionality.

(iii) Three conditions : SSS, SAS, AA. Simple applications (proof not included).

(iv) Applications of Basic Proportionality Theorem.

(v) Areas of similar triangles are proportional to the squares of corresponding sides.

(vi) Direct applications based on the above including applications to maps and models.

(b) Loci

Loci : Definition, meaning, Theorems and constructions based on Loci.

(i) The locus of a point at a fixed distance from a fixed point is a circle with the fixed point as centre and fixed distance as radius.

(ii) The locus of a point equidistant from two intersecting lines is the bisector of the angles between the lines.

(iii) The locus of a point equidistant from two given points is the perpendicular bisector of the line joining the points.

Proofs not required

(c) Circles

(i) Angle Properties

- *The angle that an arc of a circle subtends at the centre is double that which it subtends at any point on the remaining part of the circle.*
- *Angles in the same segment of a circle are equal (without proof).*
- *Angle in a semi-circle is a right angle.*

(ii) Cyclic Properties

- *Opposite angle of a cyclic quadrilateral are supplementary.*
- *The exterior angles of a cyclic quadrilateral is equal to the opposite interior angle (without proof).*

(iii) Tangent and Secant Properties

- *The tangent at any point of a circle and the radius through the point are perpendicular to each other.*
- *If two circles touch, the point of contact lies on the straight line joining their centres.*
- *From any point outside a circle two tangents can be drawn and they are equal in length.*
- *If two chords intersect internally or externally, then the product of the lengths of the segments are equal.*
- *If a chord and a tangent intersect externally, then the product of the lengths of segments of the chord is equal to the square of the length of the tangent from the point of contact to the point of intersection.*
- *If a line touches a circle and from the point of contact, a chord is drawn, the angles between the tangent and the chord are respectively equal to the angles in the corresponding alternate segments.*

Note : Proofs of the theorems given above are to be taught unless specified otherwise.

(iv) Constructions

- *Construction of tangents to a circle from an external point.*
- *Circumscribing and inscribing a circle on a triangle and a regular hexagon.*

Mensuration

Area and volume of solids-Cylinder, Cone and Sphere.

Three-dimensional solids-right circular cylinder, right circular cone and sphere. Area (total surface and curved surface) and Volume. Direct application problems including cost, Inner and Outer volume and melting and recasting method to find the volume or surface area of a new solid. Combination of solids included.

Note : Problems on Frustum are not included.

Trigonometry

(a) Using Identities to solve/prove simple algebraic trigonometric expressions

$\sin^2 A + \cos^2 A = 1$

$1 + \tan^2 A = \sec^2 A$

$1 + \cot^2 A = \operatorname{cosec}^2 A ; 0 \le A \le 90^\circ$

(b) Heights and distances : Solving 2-D problems involving angles of elevation and depression using trigonometric tables.

Note : Cases involving more than two right angled triangles excluded.

Statistics

Statistics-basic concepts, Mean, Median, Mode. Histograms and Ogive.

(a) Computation of

Measures of Central Tendency : Mean, median, mode for raw and arrayed data. Mean, median class and modal class for grouped data. (both continuous and discontinuous).*

**Mean by all 3 methods included*

Direct : $\dfrac{\Sigma fx}{\Sigma f}$

Shortcut : $A + \dfrac{\Sigma fd}{\Sigma f}$, where $d = x - A$

Step-deviation : $A + \dfrac{\Sigma ft}{\Sigma f} \times i$, where $t = \dfrac{x-A}{i}$

(b) Graphical Representation, Histograms and Less than Ogive.

- *Finding the mode from the histogram, the upper quartile, lower quartile and median etc. from the ogive.*
- *Calculation of inter Quartile range.*

Probability

- *Random experiments*
- *Sample space*
- *Events*
- *Definition of probability*
- *Simple problems on single events*

Note : SI units, signs, symbols and abbreviations

1. Agreed conventions

(a) *Units may be written in full or using the agreed symbols, but no other abbreviation may be used.*

(b) *The letters' is never added to symbols to indicate the plural form.*

(c) *A full stop is not written after symbols for units unless it occurs at the end of a sentence.*

(d) *When unit symbols are combined as a quotient, e.g. metre per second it is recommended that it should be written as m/s or as ms^{-1}.*

(e) *Three decimal signs are in common international use : the full point, the mid-point and the comma. Since, the full point is sometimes used for multiplication and the comma for spacing digits in large numbers, it is recommended that the mid-point be used for decimals.*

2. Names and symbols

In general			
Implies that	$\Rightarrow$	is logically equivalent to	$\Leftrightarrow$
Identically equal to	$\equiv$	is approximately equal to	>>
In set language			
Belongs to	$\in$	does not belong to	$\notin$
is equivalent to	$\leftrightarrow$	is not equivalent to	$\not\leftrightarrow$
union	$\cup$	intersection	$\cap$
universal set	ξ	is contained in,	$\subset$
natural (counting) number	N	the empty set	ϕ
		whole numbers	W
integers	Z	real numbersR	R
In measures			
Kilometre	km	Metre	m
Centimetre	cm	Millimetre	mm
Kilogram	kg	Gram	g
Litre	L	Centilitre	cl
Square kilometre	km^2	Square metre	m^2
Square centimetre	cm^2	Hectare	ha
cubic metre	m^3	Cubic centimetre	cm^3
kilometres per hour	km/h	Metres per second	m/s

Internal Assessment

The minimum number of assignments :
Two assignments as prescribed by the teacher.

Suggested Assignments

- *Comparative newspaper coverage of different items.*
- Survey of various types of Bank accounts, rates of interest offered.
- Planning a home budget.

- Conduct a survey in your locality to study the mode of conveyance/Price of various essential commodities/favourite sports. Represent the data using a bar graph/histogram and estimate the mode.
- To use a newspaper to study and report on shares and dividends.
- Set up a dropper with ink in it vertical at a height say 20 cm above a horizontally placed sheet of plain paper. Release one ink drop; observe the pattern, if any, on the paper. Vary the vertical distance and repeat. Discover any pattern of relationship between the vertical height and the ink drop observed.
- You are provided (or you construct a model as shown)-three vertical sticks (size of a pencil) stuck to a horizontal board. You should also have discs of varying sizes with holes (like a doughnut). Start with one disc; place it on (in) stick *A*. Transfer it to another stick (*B* or *C*); this is one move (*m*). Now try with two discs placed in *A* such that the large disc is below and the smaller disc is above (number of discs = $n = 2$ now). Now transfer them one at a time in *B* or *C* to obtain similar situation (larger disc below). How many moves? Try with more discs ($n = 1, 2, 3$, etc.) and generalise.

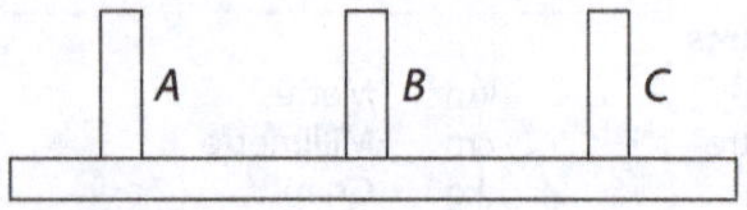

- The board has some holes to hold marbles, red on one side and blue on the other. Start with one pair. Interchange the positions by making one move at a time. A marble can jump over another to fill the hole behind. The move (*m*) equal 3. Try with 2 ($n = 2$) and more. Find the relationship between *n* and *m*.

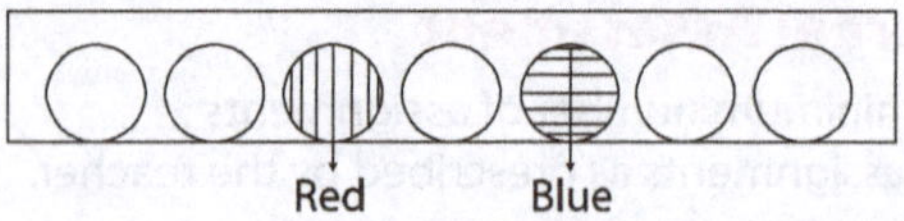

- Take a square sheet of paper of side 10 cm. Four small squares are to be cut from the corners of the square sheet and then the paper folded at the cuts to form an open box. What should be the size of the squares cut so that the volume of the open box is maximum?
- Take an open box, four sets of marbles (ensuring that marbles in each set are of the same size) and some water. By placing the marbles and water in the box, attempt to answer the question : do larger marbles or smaller marbles occupy more volume in a given space?
- An eccentric artist says that the best paintings have the same area as their perimeter (numerically). Let us not argue whether such sizes increase the viewer's appreciation, but only try and find what sides (in integers only) a rectangle must have if its area and perimeter are to be equal (Note there are only two such rectangles).
- Find by construction the centre of a circle, using only a 60-30 setsquare and a pencil.
- Various types of "cryptarithm".

Evaluation

The assignments/project work are to be evaluated by the subject teacher and by an External Examiner. (The External Examiner may be a teacher nominated by the Head of the school, who could be from the faculty, **but not teaching the subject in the section/class.** For example, a teacher of Mathematics of Class VIII may be deputed to be an External Examiner for class X, Mathematics projects).

The Internal Examiner and the External Examiner will assess the assignments independently.

Award of marks (20 Marks)

Subject Teacher (Internal Examiner)	:	10 Marks
External Examiner	:	10 Marks

The total marks obtained out of 20 are to be sent to the Council by the Head of the school.

The Head of the school will be responsible for the online entry of marks on Council's CAREERS portal by the due date.

Top tips to score highest marks in class 10th exam.
So, check out and apply these in your exams.

Top Tips
to Score the HIGHEST MARKS

1. ALWAYS FEEL POSITIVE

Positive attitude is the key to solve many of the problems which you face in your life. During exam time, this is an important feature to have in you for success and crack your exams with flying colours. Attitude is important for all students because it reflects your personality as well as your confidence or self-confidence. It always takes you to the top of everything, whether it is for exams or interviews or for your life. Positive attitude will take you through the door of success and make you feel full of self-confidence.

2. PLAN WELL FOR STUDYING

You must make a schedule for your studies followed by strict implementation of that schedule. Make that schedule detailing days or even hours when your exams are really close or it is high time for your exam.You must interact with your teachers for the important topics or topics which need more hard work or more time than other topics. Use last years' exam papers or sample papers for making a proper schedule for your studies.

You must study more or give more attention to the topics in which you feel you are not up to the mark or which your teachers recommended you to study more. You should study these topics first during your exam preparation.

3. JUST BEFORE THE EXAM

Never try to read anything or to study or cram just before the exam time, even if your friend asks you for some topic he has missed or left during preparation for the exams. Close your book an hour before the exam starts and feel relaxed and worry free and full of self-confidence. Also get up early in the morning and take another review of the important topics and make yourself filled with confidence, as confidence is the main key to score well. The night before the exam you should sleep as soon as possible to make your brain as well as body relax a bit and to be well prepared for the exams, as our brain too needs a rest to be fresh for the exam.

4. DISCUSS WHAT YOU LEARN

Find a friend or relative who has similar interests or who would enjoy hearing about your studies and let them know what's going on in your class.

5. CHART YOUR PROGRESS

Design your map of studying and you would see a certain satisfaction coming after watching your goals being accomplished. When times get hard, you can always turn to your chart and see how far you have reached.

6. DURING EXAM TIME

Check out all the things you require during exam time i.e., pen, pencil, sketch pens, rubber, sharpener. Each and every thing, whether it is small or big, matters a lot during your exam time. Read all the instructions carefully before starting the paper and keep them in your mind during exam time. Don't make any foolish mistake regarding your exam paper instructions.

7. ATTEMPTING THE EXAMINATION PAPER

Read out all the questions carefully before writing anything on the answer sheet and always start your answering from the questions which will carry maximum marks as well as which you think are tougher or need much time to think. When you start the exam from small questions, you will always feel the problem of questions left.

So, that's why time management is very much important during exams. You can write small questions even in the last 30 minutes but you will never be able to write enough for the large questions at the end, which will eventually result in sadness.

8. WHEN YOU FEEL STUCK DURING THE EXAM

There will also come a moment in your exam when you feel stuck with some questions or a single question. You just need to be relaxed and calm, don't panic in that situation and make yourself confident and try to think about the answer with a cool mind.

If you are not feeling like giving that answer at that time, make any sign or mark that question with pen and move on to the next question and try doing that question after you finish your paper but are still left with time. Never try to think about the 'stuck' question when you are writing the answer to any other question. This will reduce your concentration and when you feel no way out, just make a guess and attempt that question. This will leave you with something in the space you left for that question.

9. SOLUTION COPY SHOULD BE NEAT & CLEAN

Handwriting matters a lot for good or highest marks during your exam, as your writing makes the first impression on the checker's mind and makes your solution copy more filled with a glow for the examiner or checker of the answer sheet. Underline the lines you feel important and want to attract the examiner's attention towards so that he/she can be able to make a right mindset about the answer given and also reward you with the full or maximum marks.

10. AFTER COMPLETION OF EXAM PAPER

When you end the exam paper, don't feel like running out of the examination hall. Sit there and review each and every answer before depositing your answer book with the invigilator. Also, look for the questions you left during answering or in which you got stuck. Search for the mistakes you have done during writing and turn towards the hardest question you think and also feel uncomfortable in answering. Review it and look to add any other important lines you missed in that.

ART OF WRITING ANSWERS : GIVE YOUR BEST SHOT

- One can practice answering in previous test papers or sample papers to get used to the manner in which one has to write answers in the exams.
- Make sure that you answer the question asked and not answer what you hoped or wished the question would be.
- Examiners expect to the point and correct answers. Resist the temptation to write everything or writing beyond limits.
- Keep your answer stepwise. Some of you will be surprised to know that the board gives rather detailed dictates on how to evaluate the answer sheet. Try not to exceed the word limit.
- Write your answers in a logical systematic manner. Use examples, facts, figures, quotations, tables etc. wherever necessary to substantiate your answers. Give appropriate heading where necessary.
- Add a touch of class by putting extra information that indicate your being very knowledgeable and put this separately near the end, so that it is read just before giving the marks, especially in an essay type question like new trends etc.

CHAPTER

01

Goods and Service Tax

SYLLABUS

- **Goods and Services Tax** (GST) Computation of tax including problems involving discounts, list-price, profit, loss, basic/cost price including inverse cases. Candidates are also expected to find price paid by the consumer after paying State Goods and Service Tax (SGST) and Central Goods and Service Tax (CGST) - the different rates as in vogue on different types of items will be provided. Problems based on corresponding inverse cases are also included.

The Central (or State) Government provides various types of facilities to public, such as construction and maintenance of roads, schools, hospitals, etc. In order to provide above facilities, the government needs money which is collected by imposing different types of taxes on peoples and organisations such as, income tax, goods and service tax, etc.

Goods and Services Tax (GST)

It is an indirect tax levied by Central Government. In this tax there are so many tax merged such as Excise Duty, Custom Duty, Service Tax, Value Added Tax, Entertainment Tax and Lottery Tax etc. The purpose of GST is to make one nation and one tax.

Important Terms Related to GST

(i) **Manufacturer** The person who produce goods for sale, is called manufacturer.

(ii) **Dealer** The person, who purchases goods for resale, is known as a dealer (trader).

(iii) **Turnover** The total amount received from sale of goods (excluding tax) by a dealer during any fixed period, is called turnover.

(iv) **Intra-State Sales** Suppose a person do a business and they sales their goods (items) and provide their services in the same state (or union territory), then it is said to be Intra-state sales.

(v) **Inter-State Sales** Suppose a person do a business and they sales their goods (items) and provide their services outside the state (or union territory), then it is said to be Inter-state sales.

(vi) **Input GST** The tax paid by a dealer on his/her purchase of goods and providing services, is called Input GST.

(vii) **Output GST** The tax charged by a dealer on his/her sales of goods and providing services is called output GST.

Different Types of Taxes Used in GST

In this system, there are three taxes applicable, which are given below

(i) **State (or Union Territory) Goods and Service Tax** (SGST or UTGST) This tax is collected by the State (or union territory) Government on an intra-state sale.

e.g. Suppose some goods are manufactured in Uttar Pradesh and are sold in Uttar Pradesh, then tax on this transaction is said to be SGST.

(ii) **Central Goods and Services Tax (CGST)** This tax is collected by the Central Government on an intra-state sale.

Both SGST (or UTGST) and CGST are levied on intra-state (i.e. same state) sales of goods and services. In intra-state sales, GST is equally divided between Central and State Governments.

e.g. Suppose a dealer of Tamil Nadu sells some goods at the rate of ₹ 4000 to the consumer in the same state (i.e. Tamil Nadu). Suppose GST is charged at the rate of 18% on those goods, the GST will comprises of CGST at the rate 9% and SGST at the rate of 9%. Therefore, the seller will collect the CGST amount of ₹ 360 (i.e. 9% of ₹ 4000) and this amount goes to the account of Central Government and seller will also collect the SGST amount of ₹ 360 (i.e. 9% of ₹ 4000) which will go the account of State Government of Tamil Nadu. Hence, the dealer collects 18% GST amount on ₹ 4000 (i.e. ₹ 720), which will equally (i.e. 360 each) distribute in State (i.e. Tamil Nadu) and Central Government.

(iii) **Integrated Goods and Services Tax** (IGST) It is levied on inter-state sales of goods and services outside the state. This tax is also levied on import of goods and services from one country to another country.

This tax is collected only by the Central Government for inter state sale.

e.g. Suppose a dealer from Gujarat sells goods worth of ₹ 8000 to a another dealer of Rajasthan. Suppose rate of GST is 12% on the goods, then the seller will collect 12% of ₹ 8000 (i.e. 960) under as IGST and the whole amount of IGST will go the Central Government.

Rate Structure for GST

Generally, structure of goods and services are divided into 5 slabs, which are given below

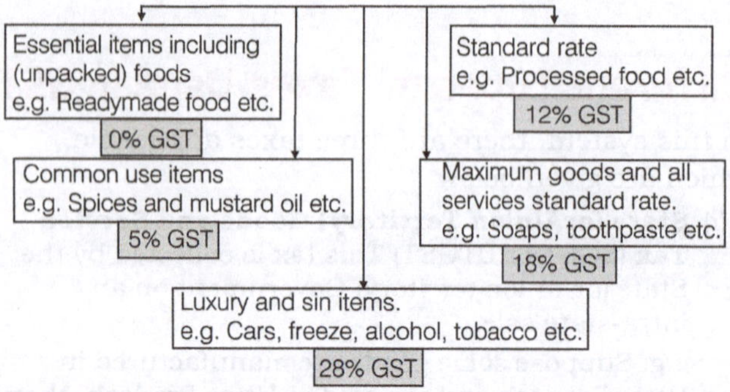

Please note that rates of GST given here are according to the latest information, these rates may be changed by the Government.

Input and Output GST Credit

When any supply of services or goods is supplied to a taxable person, then GST is charged, which is known as input tax, it is changed against of the output GST (i.e. GST collected) as follows

	Input GST credit	Output GST
(i)	CGST credit	First CGST, then IGST
(ii)	SGST/UTGST credit	First SGST/UTGST, then IGST
(iii)	IGST credit	First IGST, second CGST, then SGST/UTGST

CGST credit can't be set off against UTGST/SGST and vice-versa.

Both Central and State Government distribute the set off input GST against off output GST. While selling and purchasing of goods and services in each deal, dealer has to pay net GST (output GST – input GST).

Objectives and Advantages of GST

(i) The important advantage is that to reduce the multiplicity of taxes and make a unified common national market.

(ii) Through GST, the tax system becomes more transparent, regular and predictable.

(iii) **Ease of doing business** It means there are some administrative rules set up between the Central and State Governments, so that there is no interruption of doing business.

(iv) **Reduce Tax Evasion** Some of the persons are evading tax. So reduce tax evasion, use GST. In this procedure each tax payer registered under GST to make a GST return file electronically for each transaction (either purchase or sale) and this file should match with the input GST credit against the output GST and lastly paid net GST.

Basic Terms Required to Solve the Questions

There are various basic terms, which are as follow

(i) **Cost Price** (CP) The price, at which an article is bought, is called its cost price. All the overhead expenses in the transaction like freight, damage, etc., are added to the cost price.

(ii) **Selling Price** (SP) The price, at which an article is sold, is called its selling price.

(iii) **Profit** When, selling price of a commodity is more than its cost price, then we are in profit and it is given by Profit = SP − CP and Profit% = $\frac{\text{Profit}}{\text{CP}} \times 100$

(iv) **Loss** When, selling price of a commodity is less than its cost price, then we are in loss and it is given by

$$\text{Loss} = \text{CP} - \text{SP and Loss\%} = \frac{\text{Loss}}{\text{CP}} \times 100$$

(v) **Marked Price** (MP) The price of article excluding tax, is known as marked price. It is also, known as list price, quoted price, printed price, catalogue price and basic price.

(vi) **Discount** The reduction in price of object given by shopkeeper to the customer, is known as discount.

$$\therefore \quad \text{Discount} = \frac{\text{Rate of discount} \times \text{Marked price}}{100}$$

or Discount = Marked price − Selling price

Example 1. A dealer in a city buys some goods worth ₹ 8000 from the same city. If the rate of GST is 18%, find how much will the dealer pay for the goods bought.

Sol. Cost of goods = ₹ 8000 and GST = 18%

The dealer will pay GST = ₹ $\left(8000 \times \frac{18}{100}\right)$ = ₹ 1440

The dealer will pay = ₹ (8000 + 1440)
= ₹ 9440

Hence, the dealer will pay ₹ 9440.

Example 2. A manufacturer buys raw material worth ₹ 5000 paying GST at the rate of 5%. He sells the finished product to a shopkeeper at a profit of 30%, if the rate of GST for the finished product is 18%, find the tax liability of the manufacturer.

Sol. Given, value of raw material = ₹ 5000
Rate of GST = 5%

GST paid by the manufacturer for the raw material
= ₹ $\left(\frac{5}{100} \times 5000\right)$ = ₹ 250

GST of manufacturer = ₹ 250

Profit of the manufacturer = ₹ $\left(\frac{30}{100} \times 5000\right)$ = ₹ 1500

Selling price of the finished product = Cost price + Profit
= ₹ (5000 + 1500)
= ₹ 6500

Tax collected by the manufacturer from the shopkeeper for the finished product = ₹ $\left(\frac{18}{100} \times 6500\right)$ = ₹ 1170

Tax liability of the manufacturer = ₹ (1170 − 250) = ₹ 920

Hence, tax liability is ₹ 920.

Example 3. Mr. Sharma goes to a shop and buy a Jacket having cost ₹ 1180 (list price). The rate of GST 18%. He tells the shopkeeper to reduce the price is to such an extent that he has to pay ₹ 1180 inclusive of GST. Find the reduction needed in the price of the jacket.

Sol. Let the reduced price of jacket be ₹ x.

Then, amount of GST on ₹ x = 18% of ₹ x = ₹ $\left(\frac{18}{100} \times x\right)$

∴ Mr. Sharma pays the amount for jacket

$$= ₹\, x + ₹\, \frac{18}{100}x = ₹\left(1 + \frac{18}{100}\right)x$$

$$= ₹\left(1 + \frac{9}{50}\right)x = ₹\left(\frac{59}{50}\right)x$$

According to the given condition,

$$\frac{59}{50}x = 1180$$

$$\Rightarrow \quad x = \frac{1180 \times 50}{59}$$

$$= ₹\, 1000$$

∴ Reduced price of the jacket = ₹ 1000

Thus, the reduction needed in the price of jacket
= ₹ (1180 − 1000)
= ₹ 180

Example 4. A retailer buys an air-conditioner from a wholesaler for ₹ 35000 and sells it to a consumer at a profit of 8%. If the rate of GST is 28%, calculate the tax liability of the retailer.

Sol. Given, rate of the air-conditioner = ₹ 35000
Rate of GST = 28%

Retailer paid GST to the wholesalar = ₹ $\left(\frac{28}{100} \times 35000\right)$
= ₹ 9800

Retailer profit = ₹ $\left(\frac{8}{100} \times 35000\right)$ = ₹ 2800

Selling price of air-conditioner = Cost price + Profit
= ₹ (35000 + 2800)
= ₹ 37800

Amount of GST collected by the retailer from the consumer ₹ $\left(\frac{28}{100} \times 37800\right)$ = ₹ 10584

Tax liability of the retailer = ₹ (10584 − 9800)
= ₹ 784

Hence, the tax liability of retailer is ₹ 784.

Example 5. The price of a motorcycle is ₹ 44880 including tax (under GST) at the rate of 18% on its listed price. A buyer asks for a discount on the listed price, so that after charging GST, the selling price of motorcycle becomes equal to the listed price. Find the discount amount in which the seller has to allow for the deal.

Sol. Let the listed price of motorcycle be ₹ x and the discount be ₹ y.

Amount of GST on ₹ x = 18% of ₹ x

$$= \frac{18}{100} \times x = ₹ \frac{9}{50} x$$

Selling price of the motorcycle including tax

$$= ₹ \left(x + \frac{9}{50} x \right) = ₹ \left(\frac{59}{50} x \right)$$

According to the given condition,

$$\frac{59}{50} x = ₹ 44880$$

$$\Rightarrow \quad x = \frac{44880 \times 50}{59} = ₹ 38034$$

∴ List price of the motorcycle = ₹ 38034

Now, the reduced price of the motorcycle = ₹ (38034 − y)

Amount of GST on ₹ (38034 − y)

$$= 18\% \text{ of } ₹ (38034 - y)$$

$$= \frac{18}{100} \times (38034 - y) = ₹ \frac{9}{50} (38034 - y)$$

∴ New selling price of the motor cycle including GST

$$= ₹ \left[(38034 - y) + \frac{9}{50} (38034 - y) \right]$$

$$= ₹ \left[\left(1 + \frac{9}{50} \right) (38034 - y) \right]$$

$$= ₹ \left[\frac{59}{50} (38034 - y) \right]$$

According to the given condition,

Selling price of motorcycle including GST

= Listed price of motorcycle

$$\therefore \quad \frac{59}{50} (38034 - y) = 38034$$

$$\Rightarrow \quad 2244006 - 59y = 1901700$$

$$\Rightarrow \quad 59y = 342306 \Rightarrow y = ₹ 5802$$

Hence, the amount of discount is ₹ 5802.

Example 6. A shopkeeper buys a dining table whose list price is ₹ 30000 at some rate of discount from a wholesaler. He sells the article to a consumer at the list price and charges GST at the rate of 12%. If the sales are intra-state and the shopkeeper has to pay tax (under GST) of ₹ 36, to the State Government, find the rate of discount at which he bought the article from the wholesaler.

Sol. We have, sales are intra-state and rate of GST is 12%, so GST comprises of CGST at 6% and SGST at 6%.

Let the amount of discount be ₹ P. Then, selling price of the article (excluding tax) by the wholesaler

= Listed price − Discount = ₹(30000 − P)

Now, amount of GST received by the wholesaler from the shopkeeper,

$$\text{CGST} = 6\% \text{ of } ₹ (30000 - P) = \frac{6}{100} \times (30000 - P)$$

$$= \frac{3}{50} (30000 - P) = ₹ \left(1800 - \frac{3P}{50} \right)$$

$$\text{and SGST} = 6\% \text{ of } ₹ (30000 - P) = ₹ \left(1800 - \frac{3P}{50} \right)$$

Thus, input GST amount for shopkeeper,

$$\text{Input CGST} = ₹ \left(1800 - \frac{3P}{50} \right)$$

$$\text{and input SGST} = ₹ \left(1800 - \frac{3P}{50} \right)$$

The shopkeeper sells the article to a consumer at the list price i.e. ₹ 30000.

Amount of GST collected by the shopkeeper from the consumer,

$$\text{CGST} = 6\% \text{ of } ₹ 30000 = \frac{6}{100} \times 30000 = ₹ 1800$$

$$\text{and SGST} = 6\% \text{ of } ₹ 30000 = \frac{6}{100} \times 30000 = ₹ 1800$$

Output GST amount for shopkeeper,

Output CGST = ₹ 1800

and output SGST = ₹ 1800

∴ Amount of tax (under GST) paid by the shopkeeper to the State Government

= Output SGST − Input SGST

$$= ₹ 1800 - ₹ \left(1800 - \frac{3P}{50} \right) = ₹ \frac{3P}{50}$$

According to the given condition,

$$\frac{3P}{50} = 36 \Rightarrow P = ₹ 600$$

∴ Amount of discount = ₹ 600

Hence, the shopkeeper gets a discount of ₹ 600 from the wholesaler.

$$\therefore \text{Rate of discount} = \left(\frac{\text{Discount amount}}{\text{Article printed price}} \times 100 \right) \%$$

$$= \left(\frac{600}{30000} \times 100 \right) \%$$

$$= 2\%$$

Example 7. Manufacturer Suresh sells a television to a dealer Anil for ₹ 20000. The dealer Anil sells it to a consumer at a profit of ₹ 2000. If the sales are intra-state and the rate of GST is 12%, find

(i) the amount of tax (under GST) paid by the dealer Anil to the Central Government.

(ii) the amount of tax (under GST) received by the State Government.

(iii) the amount that the consumer pays for the television.

Sol. We have, sales are intra-state and the rate of GST is 12%, so GST comprises of CGST at 6% and SGST at 6%.

Also, given manufacturer Suresh sells the television to dealer Anil for ₹ 20000.

The GST amount collected by manufacturer Suresh from dealer Anil are

$$\text{CGST} = 6\% \text{ of } ₹ 20000 = \frac{6}{100} \times 20000 = ₹ 1200$$

$$\text{and SGST} = 6\% \text{ of } ₹ 20000 = \frac{6}{100} \times 20000 = ₹ 1200$$

∴ Amount of input GST for dealer Anil,

input CGST = ₹ 1200, input SGST = ₹ 1200

Thus, manufacturer Suresh will pay ₹ 1200 for CGST and ₹ 1200 for SGST.

As the dealer Anil sells the television to a consumer at a profit of ₹ 2000, the selling price of television by dealer Anil (or cost price of television for the consumer)

= ₹(20000 + 2000) = ₹ 22000

The amount of GST collected by dealer Anil (or paid by consumer)

$$CGST = 6\% \text{ of } ₹\,22000 = \frac{6}{100} \times 22000 = ₹\,1320$$

and $SGST = 6\% \text{ of } ₹\,22000 = \frac{6}{100} \times 22000 = ₹\,1320$

∴ Amount of output GST for dealer Anil,

Output CGST = ₹ 1320

Output SGST = ₹ 1320

(i) Amount of tax (under GST) paid by dealer Anil to the Central Government

= CGST paid by dealer Anil to the Central Government

= Output CGST – Input CGST

= ₹(1320 – 1200) = ₹ 120

(ii) The amount of tax (under GST) received by the State Government

= Manufactures pays SGST + Dealer pays SGST

= ₹ (1200 + 120) = ₹ 1320

(iii) Amount that the consumer pays for the television

= Cost price of television for consumer + CGST paid by consumer + SGST paid by consumer

= ₹(22000 + 1320 + 1320) = ₹ 24640

Example 8. A shopkeeper buys an item whose printed price is ₹ 3000 from a wholesaler at a discount of 15% and sells it to a consumer at the printed price. If the sales are intra-state and the rate of GST is 12%, find

(i) the price of the item inclusive of GST at which the shopkeeper bought it.

(ii) the amount of tax (under GST) paid by the shopkeeper to the State Government.

(iii) the amount of tax (under GST) received by the Central Government.

(iv) the amount which the consumer pays for the item.

Sol. We have, sales are intra-state and the rate of GST is 12%, so GST comprises of CGST at 6% and SGST at 6%.

(i) Also, given printed price of an item = ₹ 3000 and rate of discount = 15%

∴ Amount of discount = 15% of ₹ 3000

$$= \frac{15}{100} \times 3000 = ₹\,450$$

∴ Shopkeeper paid the amount to the wholesaler

= ₹(3000 – 450) = ₹ 2550

∴ Shopkeeper paid the amount of GST to the wholesaler,

$$CGST = 6\% \text{ of } ₹\,2550 = \frac{6}{100} \times 2550 = ₹\,153$$

and $SGST = 6\% \text{ of } ₹\,2550 = \frac{6}{100} \times 2550 = ₹\,153$

∴ Price of an item inclusive GST at which the shopkeeper bought it = ₹(2550 + 153 + 153) = ₹ 2856

(ii) Since, the wholesaler will pay ₹ 153 to the CGST and ₹ 153 to the SGST.

∴ Amount of input GST for shopkeeper, CGST = ₹ 153 and SGST = ₹ 153

Since, the shopkeeper sells the item to a consumer at printed price of ₹ 3000.

∴ Shopkeeper collect the GST amount (or paid by consumer),

$CGST = 6\% \text{ of } ₹\,3000 = \frac{6}{100} \times 3000 = ₹\,180$

and $SGST = 6\% \text{ of } ₹\,3000 = \frac{6}{100} \times 3000 = ₹180$

∴ The shopkeeper has amount for output GST,

CGST = ₹ 180 and SGST = ₹ 180

Thus, amount of tax (under GST) paid by the shopkeeper to the State Government = Shopkeeper paid the SGST amount to the State Government

= Output SGST – Input SGST

= ₹(180 – 153) = ₹ 27

(iii) Now, shopkeeper paid the CGST amount

= Output CGST – Input CGST

= ₹(180 – 153) = ₹ 27

∴ Amount of tax (under GST) received by the Central Government

= Wholesaler pays CGST + Shopkeeper pays CGST

= ₹(153 + 27) = ₹ 180

(iv) Now, amount which the consumer pays for the item

= Cost price of item for consumer + Consumer pays GST

= ₹ 3000 + Consumer pays CGST + Consumer pays SGST

= ₹(3000 + 180 + 180) = ₹ 3360

Example 9. The printed price of a panasonic air conditioner (PAC) is ₹ 35000. The wholesaler allows a discount of 14% to a dealer. The dealer sells the air conditioner to a consumer at a discount of 6% on the marked price. If the sales are intra-state and rate of GST is 18%, then find how much

(i) the dealer pays the amount of tax (under GST) to the Central and State Governments?

(ii) Central and State Governments receive the amount of tax (under GST)?

(iii) the consumer pays the total amount (inclusive of tax) for the panasonic AC?

Sol. We have, sales are intra-state and the rate of GST is 18%, so GST comprises of CGST at 9% and SGST at 9%.

Also given, the wholesaler sells the panasonic AC to a dealer at a discount of 14%.

∴ Selling price of panasonic AC by the wholesaler (excluding tax)

= ₹(1 – 14%) of ₹ 35000

$$= \left(1 - \frac{14}{100}\right) \times 35000 = \frac{86}{100} \times 35000$$

= ₹30100

It implies that, cost price of Panasonic AC to the dealer (excluding tax) = ₹ 30100

∴ The wholesaler collect the GST amount (or dealer pays to wholesaler),

$$CGST = 9\% \text{ of } ₹\, 30100 = \frac{9}{100} \times 30100 = ₹\, 2709$$

and $SGST = 9\% \text{ of } ₹\, 30100 = \frac{9}{100} \times 30100 = ₹\, 2709$

Therefore, the wholesaler will pay ₹ 2709 amount of CGST to the Central Government and ₹ 2709 amount of SGST to the State Government.

Amount of input GST of the dealer,

CGST = ₹ 2709 and SGST = ₹ 2709

Since, the dealer sells the Panasonic AC to a consumer at a discount of 6% on the marked price, therefore the dealer sales the panasonic AC (excluding tax)

$$= \left(1 - \frac{6}{100}\right) \times 35000 = \left(1 - \frac{3}{50}\right) \times 35000$$

$$= \frac{47}{50} \times 35000 = ₹\, 32900$$

∴ Cost price of panasonic AC to the consumer (excluding tax) = ₹ 32900

∴ Dealer collects the GST amount (or consumer pay the amount to the dealer)

$$CGST = 9\% \text{ of } ₹\, 32900$$

$$= \frac{9}{100} \times 32900 = ₹\, 2961$$

and $SGST = 9\% \text{ of } ₹\, 32900 = \frac{9}{100} \times 32900 = ₹\, 2961$

Amount of output GST for the dealer,

CGST = ₹ 2961 and SGST = ₹ 2961

(i) Dealer pays the amount of tax (under GST) to the Central Government = Output CGST – Input CGST

= ₹(2961 – 2709) = ₹ 252

and dealer pays the amount of tax (under GST) to the State Government = Output SGST – Input SGST

= ₹(2961 – 2709) = ₹ 252

(ii) Now, Central Government receive the amount of tax (under GST)

= Wholesaler pays CGST + Dealer pays CGST

= ₹(2709 + 252) = ₹ 2961

and the State Government receive the amount of tax (under GST)

= Wholesaler pays SGST + Dealer pays SGST

= ₹(2709 + 252) = ₹ 2961

(iii) The customer pays the total amount (inclusive of tax) for the panasonic AC

= Cost of panasonic AC + Consumer pays GST

= ₹ 32900 + Consumer pays CGST + Consumer pays SGST

= ₹(32900 + 2961 + 2961) = ₹ 38822

Example 10. The printed price of an item is ₹ 50000. The manufacturer allows a discount of 20% to a dealer Tarun. The dealer Tarun sells the item to another dealer Sachin at a discount of 5% on the marked price. The dealer Sachin sells it to a consumer at 2% above the printed price. Suppose all the sales are intra-state and the rate of GST is 12%.

(i) How much the dealer Tarun pays the price of the item inclusive tax (under GST)?

(ii) How much the dealer Sachin pays the price of an item inclusive tax (under GST)?

(iii) How much the consumer pays the amount for an item?

(iv) Find the amount of tax (under GST) paid by dealer Tarun to the Central Government.

(v) The amount of tax (under GST) paid by dealer Sachin to the State Government.

(vi) How much tax amount (under GST) collected by the Central Government?

Sol Here, sales are intra-state and rate of GST is 12%, so GST comprises of CGST at 6% and SGST at 6%.

(i) Also given, the printed price of an item is ₹ 50000.

Since, the manufacturer sells the item to the dealer Tarun at 20% discount. Therefore, the selling price of an item by manufacturer to the dealer Tarun

$$= ₹ \left(1 - \frac{20}{100}\right) \times 50000$$

$$= \left(1 - \frac{1}{5}\right) \times 50000 = \frac{4}{5} \times 50000 = ₹\, 40000$$

∴ Manufacturer collect the GST amount from dealer Tarun (or dealer Tarun pays to the manufacturer),

$$CGST = 6\% \text{ of } ₹\, 40000 = \frac{6}{100} \times 40000 = ₹\, 2400$$

and $SGST = 6\% \text{ of } ₹\, 40000 = \frac{6}{100} \times 40000 = ₹\, 2400$

∴ Dealer Tarun pays the price of the item inclusive tax (under GST) = Cost price of an item for dealer Tarun + Dealer Tarun pays GST (i.e. CGST and SGST)

= ₹(40000 + 2400 + 2400) = ₹ 44800

(ii) Since, dealer Tarun sells the item to dealer Sachin at a discount of 5% on the marked price. Therefore, the selling price of an item by dealer Tarun to dealer Sachin.

$$= ₹ \left(1 - \frac{5}{100}\right) \times 50000 = \left(1 - \frac{1}{20}\right) \times 50000$$

$$= \frac{19}{20} \times 50000 = ₹\, 47500$$

∴ GST amount collected by dealer Tarun from dealer Sachin (or dealer Sachin pays to dealer Tarun),

$$CGST = 6\% \text{ of } ₹\, 47500 = \frac{6}{100} \times 47500 = ₹\, 2850$$

and $SGST = 6\% \text{ of } ₹\, 47500 = \frac{6}{100} \times 47500 = ₹\, 2850$

∴ Dealer Sachin pays the price of an item inclusive tax (under GST) = Cost price of an item for dealer Sachin + Dealer Sachin pays GST (i.e. CGST and SGST)

= ₹(47500 + 2850 + 2850) = ₹ 53200

(iii) Since, the dealer Sachin sells the item to the consumer at 2% above the printed price. Therefore, the selling price of an item by dealer Sachin to a consumer

$$= ₹ \left(1 + \frac{2}{100}\right) \times 50000 = \left(1 + \frac{1}{50}\right) \times 50000$$

$$= \frac{51}{50} \times 50000 = ₹\, 51000$$

∴ Dealer Sachin collects the GST amount from consumer (or consumer pays the dealer Sachin)

CGST = 6% of ₹ 51000

$= \frac{6}{100} \times 51000$

= ₹ 3060

and SGST = 6% of ₹ 51000

$= \frac{6}{100} \times 51000 =$ ₹ 3060

∴ Consumer pays the amount for an item

= Cost price of an item for consumer + Consumer pays GST (i.e. SGST and CGST)

= ₹(51000 + 3060 + 3060)

= ₹ 57120

(iv) ∵ Dealer Tarun has input CGST = ₹ 2400 and dealer Tarun has output CGST = ₹ 2850

∴ Amount of tax (under GST) paid by dealer Tarun to the Central Government.

= Output CGST − Input CGST

= ₹(2850 − 2400)

= ₹ 450

(v) ∵ Dealer Sachin has input SGST = ₹ 2850 and dealer Sachin has output SGST = ₹ 3060

∴ Amount of tax (under GST) paid by dealer Sachin to the State Government

= Output SGST − Input SGST

= ₹(3060 − 2850)

= ₹ 210

(vi) Tax amount (under GST) collected by the Central Government.

= Manufacturer collects CGST amount + Dealer Tarun pays the CGST amount to the Central Government + Dealer Sachin pays the CGST amount to the Central Government

= ₹(2400 + 450 + 210)

= ₹ 3060

Example 11. A dealer buys a refrigerator from a wholesaler for ₹ 30000. He marks the price of the refrigerator 30% above his cost price and sells it to a customer at 15% discount on the marked price. If the sales are intra-state and rate of GST is 12%, determine

(i) the marked price of the refrigerator

(ii) the amount of tax (under GST) paid by the dealer to the Central Government

(iii) the amount of tax (under GST) received by the State Government

(iv) the amount which the customer pays for the refrigerator

Sol We have, sales are intra-state and rate of GST is 12%, so GST comprises of CGST at 6% and SGST at 6%.

Also, the cost price of the refrigerator which the retailer pays to the wholesaler is ₹ 30000.

(i) Since, the dealer marks the price of refrigerator 30% above his cost price.

The marked price of the refrigerator = ₹$\left(1+\frac{30}{100}\right) \times 30000$

= ₹$\left(\frac{130}{100} \times 30000\right)$

= ₹ 39000

(ii) The GST amount collected by the wholesaler from dealer are

CGST = 6% of 30000 $= \frac{6}{100} \times 30000 =$ ₹ 1800

and SGST = 6% of 30000 $= \frac{6}{100} \times 30000 =$ ₹ 1800

∴ Amount of input GST for dealer,

input CGST = ₹ 1800, input SGST = ₹ 1800

Thus, the wholesaler will pay ₹ 1800 for CGST and ₹ 1800 for SGST.

As the dealer sells the refrigerator to a customer at 15% discount on the marked price, the selling price of refrigerator by dealer (or cost price of refrigerator for the customer)

$= \left(1-\frac{15}{100}\right) \times 39000 = \left(1-\frac{3}{20}\right) \times 39000$

$= \frac{17}{20} \times 39000 =$ ₹ 33150

∴ Cost price of refrigerator to the customer (excluding tax)

= ₹ 33150

∴ Dealer collects the GST amount (or customer pay the amount to the dealer)

CGST = 6% of ₹ 33150

$= \frac{6}{100} \times 33150 =$ ₹ 1989

and SGST = 6% of ₹ 33150

$= \frac{6}{100} \times 33150 =$ ₹ 1989

Amount of output GST for the dealer,

CGST = ₹ 1989 and SGST = ₹ 1989

∴ Dealer pays the amount of tax (under GST) to the Central Government = Output CGST − Input CGST

= ₹ (1989 − 1800) = ₹ 189

(iii) The State Government receive the amount of tax (under GST)

= Wholesaler pays SGST + Dealer pays SGST

= ₹ (1800 + 189)

= ₹ 1989

(iv) The customer pays the total amount (inclusive of tax) for the refrigerator

= Cost of the refrigerator + Customer pays GST

= ₹ 33150 + Customer pays CGST + Customer pays SGST

= ₹(33150 + 1989 + 1989) = ₹ 37128

Example 12. The printed price of modular table is ₹ 2000. A wholesaler in Uttar Pradesh buys the modular table from a manufacturer in Rajasthan at a discount of 10% on the printed price. The wholesaler sells the modular table to a retailer in Madhya Pradesh at 20% above the marked price. Suppose, the rate of GST on modular table is 5%. Find

(i) the price of modular table inclusive tax (under GST) in which the wholesaler bought.

(ii) the price of modular table inclusive tax (under GST) in which the retailer bought.

(iii) how much the tax (under GST) paid by the wholesaler to the Central Government?

(iv) the total tax (under GST) collected by the Central Government.

Sol Given, printed price of modular table = ₹ 2000 and rate of GST on sales or purchase of modular table = 5%

Here, we see that both the given sales from manufacturer to wholesaler and wholesaler to retailer are inter-state, so IGST is levied on these sales at 5%.

(i) Also given, wholesaler buys the modular table from a manufacturer = 10% discount on the printed price.

∴ Cost price of the modular table to the wholesaler

$$= ₹\left(1-\frac{10}{100}\right)\times 2000=\left(1-\frac{1}{10}\right)\times 2000$$

$$=\frac{9}{10}\times 2000 = ₹\ 1800$$

Manufacturer collects the IGST amount from wholesaler (or wholesaler pays to manufacturer)

$$= 5\% \text{ of } ₹\ 1800 = \frac{5}{100}\times 1800$$

$$= ₹\ 90$$

It implies that input IGST for wholesaler is ₹ 90.

∴ Price of modular table inclusive tax (under GST) in which the wholesaler bought = Cost of modular table for wholesaler + Wholesaler pays IGST.

$$= ₹(1800 + 90) = ₹\ 1890$$

(ii) Since, the wholesaler sells the modular table to the retailer at 20% above the marked price. Therefore, the selling price of the modular table to the wholesaler

$$= ₹\left(1+\frac{20}{100}\right)\times ₹\ 2000$$

$$=\left(1+\frac{1}{5}\right)\times 2000$$

$$=\frac{6}{5}\times 2000$$

$$= ₹\ 2400$$

∴ Cost price (excluding tax) of the modular table to the retailer = ₹ 2400

∴ Wholesaler collects the IGST amount from retailer (or retailer pays to wholesaler)

$$= 5\% \text{ of } ₹\ 2400$$

$$=\frac{5}{100}\times 2400 = ₹\ 120$$

∴ Price of modular table inclusive tax (under GST) in which the retailer bought = Cost of modular table for retailer + Retailer pays IGST

$$= ₹(2400 + 120)$$

$$= ₹\ 2520$$

(iii) ∵ Wholesaler has output IGST = ₹ 120

∴ Tax paid by the wholesaler to the Central Government

= Output IGST − Input IGST

$$= ₹(120 - 90) = ₹\ 30$$

(iv) Total tax (under GST) collected by the Central Government = Manufacturer collects the IGST amount + Wholesaler collects the IGST amount

$$= ₹(90 + 30)$$

$$= ₹\ 120$$

Note In this transaction, none of the State Government gets any tax (under GST). The total tax goes to the Central Government.

Example 13. A shopkeeper who lives in Rajasthan buys an article at the printed price of ₹ 35000 from a wholesaler who lives in Gujarat. The shopkeeper sells the article to a consumer in Rajasthan at a profit of 22% on the basic cost price. If the rate of GST is 12%, find

(i) the price of an article inclusive tax (under GST) in which the shopkeeper bought it.

(ii) how much the amount of tax (under GST) paid by the shopkeeper to Governments?

(iii) the amount of tax (under GST) received by Gujarat Government.

(iv) the amount of tax (under GST) received by Central Government.

(v) the amount which the consumer pays for the article.

Sol. Given, shopkeeper buys an article from wholesaler

= ₹ 35000

and rate of GST = 12%

Here, transaction is from one state to another state, so IGST is levied on sale.

∴ Wholesaler collects the IGST amount from shopkeeper

$$= 12\% \text{ of } ₹\ 35000$$

$$=\frac{12}{100}\times 35000$$

$$= ₹\ 4200$$

(i) Price of an article inclusive tax (under GST) in which the shopkeeper bought = Cost price of article for shopkeeper + Shopkeeper pays GST amount

= ₹ 35000 + Shopkeeper pays the IGST amount to the wholesaler

$$= ₹\ (35000 + 4200)$$

$$= ₹\ 39200$$

(ii) Since, the wholesaler will pay IGST amount of ₹ 4200 to the Central government.

∴ Shopkeeper has input IGST amount = ₹ 4200

As the shopkeeper sells the article to a consumer at a profit of 22% on the basic cost price, therefore the selling price of the article by the shopkeeper

$$= \left(1+\frac{22}{100}\right)\times 35000$$

$$= \frac{122}{100}\times 35000 = ₹\,42700$$

Since, the shopkeeper sells the article to a consumer in Rajasthan, so this sale is intra-state. Therefore, GST comprises of CGST at 6% and SGST at 6%.

∴ Shopkeeper collects the GST amount from consumer,

CGST = 6% of ₹ 42700

$$= \frac{6}{100}\times 42700 = ₹\,2562$$

and SGST = 6% of ₹ 42700

$$= \frac{6}{100}\times 42700 = ₹\,2562$$

Amount of output GST for the shopkeeper,

CGST = ₹ 2562 and SGST = ₹ 2562

Amount of tax (under GST) paid by the shopkeeper to the Central Government;

First set of ₹ 4200 input IGST against ₹ 2562 output CGST. Then, set of the balance ₹ (4200 – 2562) i.e. ₹ 1638 input IGST against output SGST.

∴ SGST paid by the shopkeeper to the State Government (Rajasthan) = Output SGST – Balance of Input IGST

= ₹(2562 – 1638) = ₹ 924

∴ Net tax (under GST) paid by shopkeeper to the Central Government = No tax paid to the Central Government = 0

∴ Tax paid to Rajasthan Government = ₹ 924

(iii) Amount of tax (under GST) received by Gujarat Government is nil.

(iv) Amount of tax (under GST) received by the Central Government = IGST received from wholesaler + CGST received from shopkeeper

= ₹(4200 + Nil) = ₹ 4200

(v) Amount which the consumer pays for the article

= Cost price of article to consumer + Consumer pays GST (i.e. CGST and SGST)

= ₹(42700 + 2562 + 2562

= ₹ 47824

Chapter Practice

a. 1 Mark Questions

1. Which state became the first state of India to ractify GST bill?

(a) Bihar (b) Telangana
(c) Assam (d) Delhi

2. Which type of tax is GST?

(a) Direct tax (b) Indirect tax
(c) Both (a) and (b) (d) None of these

3. The taxable value of shoes is ₹ 700, rate of GST is 12%. What is the price of shoes?

(a) ₹ 784 (b) ₹ 800 (c) ₹ 616 (d) ₹ 900

4. How many slabs are there for collection of GST?

(a) 3 (b) 4 (c) 5 (d) 6

5. Mr. Ramesh paints sold 4 tins of lustre paint and taxable value of each tin is ₹ 3400, if the rate of GST is 12%, then find the amount of CGST charged in the tax invoice.

(a) ₹ 3400 (b) ₹ 816 (c) ₹ 972 (d) ₹ 1632

6. The printed price of an article is ₹ 3080. 1f the rate of GST is 10%, then the GST charged is **[ICSE 2023]**

(a) ₹ 154 (b) ₹ 308 (c) ₹ 30.80 (4) ₹ 15.40

7. The marked price of an article is ₹ 5000. The shopkeeper gives a discount of 10%. If the rate of GST is 12%, then the amount paid by the customer including GST is **[ICSE Semester I 2021]**

(a) ₹ 5040 (b) ₹ 6100 (c) ₹ 6272 (d) ₹ 6160

b. 3 Marks Questions

8. Miss Anjali goes to a mall to purchase a saree whose cost is ₹ 885 (list price). She tells the shopkeeper to reduce the price to such an extent that she has to pay ₹ 885, inclusive GST which is at the rate of 18%, find the reduction of price needed in the saree.

9. Sandeep purchased a digital camera for ₹ 25488, which includes 10% rebate on the list price and 18% tax (under GST) on the remaining price. Find the marked price of the digital camera.

10. The price of a spider toy is ₹ 3136 inclusive tax (under GST) at the rate of 12% on its listed price. A buyer asks for a discount on the listed price, so that after charging GST, the selling price becomes equal to the listed price. Find the amount of discount, which the seller has to allow for the deal.

11. A shopkeeper buys an item whose list price is ₹ 8000 at some rate of discount from a wholesaler. He sells the item to a consumer at the list price.

The sales are intra-state and the rate of GST is 18%. Suppose, the shopkeeper pay a tax (under GST) of ₹ 72 to the State government. Find the rate of discount in which he bought the item from the wholesaler.

12. Mrs. Arora bought the following articles from a departmental store

S.No.	Item	Price	Rate of GST	Discount
1	Hair Oil	₹ 1200	18%	₹ 100
2	Cashew nuts	₹ 600	12%	—

Find the

(a) total GST paid.

(b) total bill amount including GST. **[ICSE 2023]**

13. Mr. Bedi visits the market and buys the following articles. **[ICSE 2020]**

Medicines costing ₹ 950, GST @ 5%

A pair of shoes costing ₹ 3000, GST @ 18%

A laptop bag costing ₹ 1000 with a discount of 30%, GST @ 18%.

(i) Calculate the total amount of GST paid.

(ii) The total bill amount including GST paid by Mr. Bedi.

14. Manufacturer Anshul sells a LG fridge to a dealer Lalit for ₹ 12500. The dealer Lalit sells it to a consumer at a profit of ₹ 1500. If the sales are intra-state and the rate of GST is 12%, find

(i) the amount of tax (under GST), paid by the dealer Lalit to the Central Government.

(ii) how much the tax amount (under GST) received by the State Government?

(iii) the amount that the consumer pays for the LG fridge.

15. A manufacturer sells a Hercules cycle to a dealer for ₹ 18000 and the dealer sells it to a consumer at a profit of ₹ 1500. If the sales are intra-state and the rate of GST is 12%, find

(i) how much GST amount paid by the dealer to the State Government?

(ii) the GST amount received by the Central Government.

(iii) the GST amount received by the State Government.

(iv) the amount that the consumer pays for the Hercules cycle.

16. A shopkeeper buys an item whose printed price is ₹ 4000 from a wholesaler at a discount of 20% and sells it to a consumer at the printed price. If the sales are intra-state and the rate of GST is 12%, find
(i) the price of the article inclusive GST in which the shopkeeper bought it.
(ii) the amount of tax (under GST) paid by the shopkeeper to the State Government.
(iii) the amount of tax (under GST) received by the Central Government.
(iv) how much amount the consumer pays for the article?

17. A shopkeeper buys a dressing table at a discount of 20% from a wholesaler, the printed price of dressing table being ₹ 1600. The shopkeeper sells it to a consumer at the printed price. If the sales are intra-state and the rate of GST is 12%, find
(i) GST paid by the shopkeeper to the Central Government.
(ii) GST received by the Central Government.
(iii) GST received by the State Government.
(iv) the amount at which the consumer bought the dressing table.

18. A retailer buys a AC from a wholesaler for ₹ 40000. He marks the price of the AC 15% above his cost price and sells it to a consumer at 5% discount on the marked price. If the sales are intra-state and the rate of GST is 12%, find
(i) the marked price of the AC.
(ii) the amount of tax (under GST) paid by the retailer to the Central Government.
(iii) the amount of tax (under GST) received by the State Government.
(iv) the amount which the consumer pays for the AC.

c. 4/5 Marks Questions

19. A manufacturer marks an article at ₹ 5000. He sells it to a wholesaler at a discount of 25% on the marked price and the wholesaler sells it to a retailer at a discount of 15% on the marked price. The retailer sells it to a consumer at the marked price.
If all the sales are intra-state and the rate of GST is 12%, find
(i) the amount inclusive of tax (under GST) which the wholesaler pays for the article.
(ii) the amount inclusive of tax (under GST) which the retailer pays for the article.
(iii) the amount of tax (under GST) which the wholesaler pays to the Central Government.
(iv) the amount of tax (under GST) which the retailer pays to the State Government.

20. The printed price of a bedsheet is ₹ 2500. A wholesaler in Karnataka buys the bedsheet from a manufacturer in Punjab at a discount of 12% on the printed price. The wholesaler sells the bedsheet to a retailer in Jharkhand at 32% above the marked price. If the rate of GST on the bedsheet is 5%, find
(i) the price inclusive of tax (under GST) at which the wholesaler bought the bedsheet.
(ii) the price inclusive of tax (under GST) at which the retailer bought the bedsheet.
(iii) the tax (under GST) paid by the wholesaler to the Government.
(iv) the tax (under GST) received by the Central Government.

21. The printed price of a washing machine is ₹ 40000. A wholesaler in Chhattisgarh buys the washing machine from a manufacturer in Delhi at a discount of 10% on the printed price. The wholesaler sells the washing machine to a retailer in Haryana at 5% above the printed price. If the rate of GST on the washing machine is 18%, find
(i) the amount inclusive of tax (under GST) paid by the wholesaler for the washing machine.
(ii) the amount inclusive of tax (under GST) paid by the retailer for the washing machine.
(iii) the amount of tax (under GST) paid by the wholesaler to the Central Government.
(iv) the amount of tax (under GST) received by the Central Government.

d. 6 Marks Questions

22. The printed price of bicycle is ₹ 60000. The manufacturer allows a discount of 25% to a dealer Sanjeev. The dealer Sanjeev sells the article to another dealer Mohit at a discount of 12% on the marked price. The dealer Mohit sells it to a consumer at 5% above the printed price. If all the sales are intra-state and the rate of GST is 18%, find
(i) the price of bicycle inclusive of tax (under GST) paid by dealer Sanjeev.
(ii) the price of bicycle inclusive of tax (under GST) paid by dealer Mohit.
(iii) the amount which the consumer pays for the bicycle.
(iv) the amount of tax (under GST) paid by dealer Sanjeev to the Central Government.
(v) the amount of tax (under GST) paid by dealer Mohit to the State Government.
(vi) the amount of tax (under GST) received by the Central Government.

23. A shopkeeper in Tamil Nadu buys a bullet bike at the printed price of ₹ 40000 from a wholesaler in West Bengal. The shopkeeper sells the bullet bike to a consumer in Tamil Nadu at a profit of 25% on the basic cost price. If the rate of GST is 18%, find

(i) the price of the bullet bike inclusive of tax (under GST) at which the shopkeeper bought it.

(ii) how much tax the shopkeeper pays to the Central Government?

(iii) the amount of tax (under GST) received by West Bengal Government.

(iv) the amount of tax (under GST) received by Central Government.

(v) the amount which the consumer pays for the bullet bike.

24. A shopkeeper in Punjab buys scooty at the printed price of ₹ 24000 from a wholesaler in Himachal. The shopkeeper sells scooty to a consumer in Punjab at a profit of 15% on the basic cost price. If the rate of GST is 12%, find

(i) the price inclusive of tax (under GST) at which the shopkeeper bought the scooty.

(ii) the amount which the consumer pays for the scooty.

(iii) the amount of tax (under GST) received by the State Government of Punjab.

(iv) the amount of tax (under GST) received by the Central Government.

Hints and Answers

1. (c) **2.** (b)

3. (a) **4.** (c)

5. (b) **6.** (b)

7. (a)

8. **Hint** Do same as Example 3. **Ans.** ₹ 135

9. **Hint** Let the marked price be ₹ x.

Price after including 10% rebate and 18% GST in marked price $= x \times \frac{9}{10} \times \frac{59}{50}$

$\therefore \; x \times \frac{9}{10} \times \frac{59}{50} = 25488$ **Ans.** ₹ 24000

10. **Hint** Do same as Example 5. **Ans.** ₹ 300

11. **Hint** Do same as Example 6.

Ans. 10%

12.

S.No.	Item	Price	Rate of GST	Discount	Discounted Value
1	Hair Oil	₹ 1200	18%	₹ 100	₹ 1100
2	Cashew nuts	₹ 600	12%		₹ 600

(a) GST on Hair oil, = 18% of 1100

$= 1100 \times \frac{18}{100} = ₹\,198$

GST on cashew nuts = 12% of 600

$= 600 \times \frac{12}{100} = ₹\,72$

Total GST Paid = ₹ 198 + ₹ 72 = ₹ 270

(b) Total bill amount including GST

= Total discounted amount + Total paid GST

= (1100 + 600) + 270 = ₹ 1970

13. **Hint** Do same as Example 1.

(i) ₹ 713.50 (ii) 5363.5

14. **Hint** Do same as Example 7.

Ans. (i) ₹ 90 (ii) ₹ 840 (iii) ₹ 15680

15. **Hint** Do same as Example 8.

Ans. (i) ₹ 90 (ii) ₹ 1170 (iii) ₹ 1170 (iv) ₹ 21840

16. **Hint** Do same as Example 8.

Ans. (i) ₹ 3584 (ii) ₹ 48 (iii) ₹ 240 (iv) ₹ 4480

17. **Hint** Do same as Example 8.

Ans. (i) ₹19.20 (ii) ₹ 96 (iii) ₹ 96 (iv) ₹ 1792

18. **Hint** Do same as Example 11.

Ans. (i) ₹ 46000 (ii) ₹ 222 (iii) ₹ 2622 (iv) ₹ 48944

19. **Hint** Do same as Example 10.

Ans. (i) ₹ 4200 (ii) ₹ 4760 (iii) ₹ 30 (iv) ₹ 45

20. **Hint** Do same as Example 12.

Ans. (i) ₹ 2310 (ii) ₹ 3465 (iii) ₹ 55 (iv) ₹ 165

21. **Hint** Do same as Example 12.

Ans. (i) ₹ 42480 (ii) ₹ 49560 (iii) ₹ 1080 (iv) ₹ 7560

22. **Hint** Do same as Example 10.

Ans. (i) ₹ 53100 (ii) ₹ 62304 (iii) ₹ 74340 (iv) ₹ 702 (v) ₹ 918 (vi) ₹ 5670

23. **Hint** Do same as Example 13.

Ans. (i) ₹ 47200 (ii) ₹ 1800 (iii) ₹ Nil (iv) ₹ 7200 (v) ₹ 59000

24. **Hint** Do same as Example 13.

Ans. (i) ₹ 26880 (ii) ₹ 30912 (iii) ₹ 1656 (iv) ₹ 2880

CHAPTER

02

Banking

SYLLABUS

- **Banking** Recurring Deposit Accounts : Computation of interest and maturity value using the formula :

$$I = P\frac{n(n+1)}{2 \times 12} \times \frac{r}{100}$$

$$MV = P \times n + I$$

In simple words, banking can be defined as the business activity of accepting and safe guarding money owned by individuals and other entities and then lending out this money to other individuals or entities in order to earn a profit. In this activity, a sum paid (or charged) for the use of money (or for lending money), is called the interest and it is expressed as a percentage of the amount borrowed or lend over a given period.

Generally, the activity of banking is performed by banks. Banks can be defined as an institution that mainly carries on the business of getting deposits and lending money.

Different Types of Bank Accounts

Traditionally banks have four types of deposit account, which are discussed below.

1. Savings Bank Account

It is a bank account, which can be opened by any person with a minimum amount.

In this account, bank pay interest on the amount deposited by the person. The bank issues a passbook for the savings accounts, in which datewise entries regarding the deposits, withdrawls and the interest earned are recorded.

2. Current Account

It is a account, which is mainly used for business transactions. For the current account, there is no limit for number of transactions (deposits and withdrawls). No interest is payable on deposits made in this account. Bank issues passbook, debit card, credit card etc for current account.

3. Fixed Deposit Account

The account, which is opened for a fixed period (time) by depositing a particular amount, is known as fixed deposit account. In this account, the amount can be deposited only once.

The deposit is fixed and is repayable only after specific period is over.

4. Recurring (or Cumulative) Deposit Account

This is a special type of bank account, in which a depositor deposits fixed amount every month for a fixed period of time. At the end of the period, depositor gets all the principal sum, alongwith the fix interest earned during that period. This rate is fixed by Reserve Bank of India and is revised from time to time.

In this chapter, we will learn to calculate the interest and maturity value for recurring deposit.

Basic terms related to Recurring Deposit Account

(i) **Principal** The amount that the depositor deposits each month, is called principal amount.

(ii) **Maturity period** The fixed period, for which the recurring deposit account is opened, is called maturity period.

(iii) **Maturity value** Total amount (Deposited amount + Interest) received by the depositor at the end of the maturity period, is called maturity value.

Calculation of Interest and Maturity Value on Recurring Deposit

Let P be the principal, r be the annual rate of interest and n be the number of months. Then,

(i) Simple interest (or interest) $I = P \times \frac{n(n+1)}{2 \times 12} \times \frac{r}{100}$

$$= \frac{Pr\,n(n+1)}{2400}.$$

(ii) Maturity (or Matured) value

$$= \text{Total amount deposited} + \text{Interest}$$

$$= Pn + \frac{Pr\,n(n+1)}{2400} = Pn\left[1 + \frac{r(n+1)}{2400}\right]$$

or $\quad MV = P \times n + I$

Example 1. Katrina opened a Recurring Deposit Account with a nationalised bank for a period of 2 yr. If the bank pays interest at the rate of 6% per annum and the monthly installment is ₹ 1000, then find the

(i) interest earned in 2 yr.

(ii) matured value. **[ICSE 2015]**

Sol.

(i) Given, monthly installment (P) = ₹ 1000,

number of monthly installments $(n) = 2 \times 12 = 24$ months

and rate of interest (r) = 6% per annum

Now, $I = \frac{Pr\,n(n+1)}{2400}$

$$= \frac{1000 \times 6 \times 24 \times (24+1)}{2400} = ₹\ 1500$$

(ii) Matured value $= P \times n + I = 1000 \times 24 + 1500$

$$= 24000 + 1500 = ₹\ 25500$$

Alternate Method

In this recurring deposit account, ₹ 1000 will earn interest for 24 months, ₹ 1000 will earn interest for 23 months and so on.

∴ Equivalent principal for one month for whole deposit

$$= ₹\ 1000 \times (24 + 23 + 22 + \dots + 1)$$

$$= ₹\ 1000 \times (1 + 2 + 3 + \dots + 24)$$

$$= ₹\ 1000 \times \frac{24(24+1)}{2}$$

$$= ₹\ (1000 \times 12 \times 25) = ₹\ 300000.$$

(i) Interest on ₹ 300000 for 1 month at the rate of 6% per annum

$$= ₹\left(300000 \times \frac{1}{12} \times \frac{6}{100}\right) = ₹\ 1500$$

∴ Interest earned in 2 yrs = ₹ 1500.

(ii) Total amount deposited = ₹ (1000 × 24) = ₹ 24000

∴ Matured amount = Total money deposited + Interest earned

$$= ₹\ (24000 + 1500) = ₹\ 25500.$$

Example 2. Kiran deposited ₹ 200 for 36 months in a bank Recurring Deposit Account. If the bank pays interest at the rate of 11% per annum, then find the amount, she gets on maturity. **[ICSE 2012]**

Sol. Given, money deposited per month (P) = ₹ 200,

number of months (n) = 36 months

and rate of interest (r) = 11% per annum

∴ Maturity amount $= Pn\left[1 + \frac{r(n+1)}{2400}\right]$

$$= 200 \times 36\left[1 + \frac{11(36+1)}{2400}\right]$$

$$= 7200\left(\frac{2400 + 407}{2400}\right)$$

$$= 3(2807) = ₹\ 8421$$

Hence, Kiran will get the amount ₹ 8421 at the time of maturity.

Example 3. Mr. Sonu has a recurring deposit account and deposits ₹ 750 per month for 2 yr. If he gets ₹ 19125 at the time of maturity, then find the rate of interest.

Sol. Given, money deposit per month (P) = ₹ 750

Time $(n) = 2$ yr $= 2 \times 12 = 24$ months

and maturity value = ₹ 19125

Let the rate of interest be r% per annum.

∴ Maturity value $= Pn\left[1 + \frac{(n+1)r}{2400}\right]$

$$\Rightarrow \quad 19125 = 750 \times 24\left(1 + \frac{25r}{2400}\right)$$

$$\Rightarrow \quad 19125 = 18000\left(1 + \frac{r}{96}\right)$$

$$\Rightarrow \quad 1 + \frac{r}{96} = \frac{19125}{18000}$$

$$\Rightarrow \quad \frac{r}{96} = \frac{19125 - 18000}{18000}$$

$$\Rightarrow \quad \frac{r}{96} = \frac{1125}{18000}$$

$$\Rightarrow \quad r = \frac{1125}{18000} \times 96$$

$$\Rightarrow \quad r = 6$$

Hence, the required rate of interest is 6% per annum.

Example 4. Shahrukh opened a Recurring Deposit Account in a bank and deposited ₹ 800 per month for $1\frac{1}{2}$ yr. If he received ₹ 15084 at the time of maturity, then find the rate of interest per annum. [ICSE 2014]

Sol. Given, money deposited per month (P) = ₹ 800,

time $(n) = 1\frac{1}{2}$ yr = 18 months

and maturity value = ₹15084

Let the rate of interest be r% per annum.

$\because$ Maturity value $= Pn\left[1+\frac{(n+1)r}{2400}\right]$

$$\therefore \quad 15084 = 800 \times 18\left[1+\frac{(18+1)r}{2400}\right]$$

$$\Rightarrow \quad 15084 = 14400\left(\frac{2400+19r}{2400}\right)$$

$$\Rightarrow \quad 15084 = 6(2400+19r)$$

$$\Rightarrow \quad \frac{15084}{6} = 2400+19r$$

$$\Rightarrow \quad 2514 = 2400+19r$$

$$\Rightarrow \quad 19r = 114$$

$$\Rightarrow \quad r = \frac{114}{19} = 6$$

Hence, the required rate of interest is 6% per annum.

Example 5. Mr. Gupta opened a Recurring Deposit Account in a bank. He deposited ₹ 2500 per month for 2 yr. At the time of maturity, he got ₹ 67500. Find

(i) the total interest earned by Mr. Gupta.

(ii) the rate of interest per annum. [ICSE 2010]

Sol. Given, Mr. Gupta deposits per month (P) = ₹ 2500,

time period (n) = 2 yr = 2 × 12 = 24 months

and maturity value = ₹ 67500

(i) Now, total interest earned by Mr. Gupta

= Maturity value − Total deposit

= 67500 − nP

= 67500 − 24 × 2500

= 67500 − 60000

= ₹ 7500.

(ii) Let the rate of interest be r% per annum.

$$\because \quad I = \frac{Prn(n+1)}{2400}$$

$$\therefore \quad 7500 = \frac{2500 \times r \times 24\,(24+1)}{2400}$$

$$\Rightarrow \quad 7500 = 25r(25)$$

$$\Rightarrow \quad 625r = 7500$$

$$\Rightarrow \quad r = \frac{7500}{625} = 12$$

Hence, the rate of interest is 12% per annum.

Example 6. Rekha opened a Recurring Deposit Account for 20 months. The rate of interest is 9% per annum and Rekha receives ₹ 441 as interest at the time of maturity. Find the amount, Rekha deposited each month.

Sol. Let money deposit per month be P = ₹x.

Number of months (n) = 20,

rate of interest (r) = 9% per annum

and interest (I) = ₹ 441

$$\because \quad \text{Interest } (I) = \frac{P \times n(n+1) \times r}{2400}$$

$$\Rightarrow \quad 441 = \frac{x \times 20(20+1) \times 9}{2400}$$

$$\Rightarrow \quad 441 \times 2400 = x \times 20 \times 21 \times 9$$

$$x = \frac{441 \times 2400}{20 \times 21 \times 9} \Rightarrow x = \frac{441 \times 40}{63}$$

$$x = \frac{17640}{63} = ₹\ 280$$

Hence, Rekha deposited ₹ 280 each month.

Example 7. Mr. Sonu has a Recurring Deposit Account and deposits ₹ 750 per month for 2 yr. If he gets ₹ 19125 at the time of maturity, find the rate of interest.

Sol. Given, money deposit per month (P) = ₹ 750,

time (n) = 2 yr = 2 × 12 = 24 months

and maturity value = ₹ 19125

Let the rate of interest be r% per annum.

$\therefore$ Maturity value $= Pn\left[1+\frac{(n+1)r}{2400}\right]$

$$\Rightarrow \quad 19125 = 750 \times 24\left(1+\frac{25r}{2400}\right)$$

$$\Rightarrow \quad 19125 = 18000\left(1+\frac{r}{96}\right)$$

$$\Rightarrow \quad 1+\frac{r}{96} = \frac{19125}{18000} \Rightarrow \frac{r}{96} = \frac{19125-18000}{18000}$$

$$\Rightarrow \quad \frac{r}{96} = \frac{1125}{18000} \Rightarrow r = \frac{1125}{18000} \times 96$$

$$\Rightarrow \quad r = 6$$

Hence, the required rate of interest is 6% per annum.

Example 8. Priyanka has a Recurring Deposit Account of ₹1000 per month at 10% per annum. If she gets ₹5550 as interest at the time of maturity, find the total time, for which the account was held. [ICSE 2018]

Sol. Given, P = ₹ 1000, r = 10% per annum and I = ₹ 5550

Let the account be held for n months, then by using this formula,

$$I = P \times \frac{n(n+1)}{2 \times 12} \times \frac{r}{100}$$

$$\therefore \quad 5550 = 1000 \times \frac{n(n+1)}{24} \times \frac{10}{100}$$

$\Rightarrow \quad 5550 = 100 \times \frac{n(n+1)}{24}$

$\Rightarrow \quad 55.5 \times 24 = n(n+1)$

$\Rightarrow \quad n^2 + n - 1332 = 0$

$\Rightarrow \quad n^2 + 37n - 36n - 1332 = 0$

$\Rightarrow \quad n(n+37) - 36(n+37) = 0$

$\Rightarrow \quad (n+37)(n-36) = 0$

$\Rightarrow \quad n = -37 \text{ or } 36 \Rightarrow n = 36$

[since, months cannot be negative]

Hence, the account was held for 36 months i.e. 3 yr.

Example 9. Mr. Britto deposits a certain sum of money each month in a Recurring Deposit Account of a bank. If the rate of interest is 8% per annum and Mr. Britto gets ₹ 8088 from the bank after 3 yr, then find the value of his monthly installment. [ICSE 2013]

Sol. Given, rate of interest (r) = 8% per annum,

maturity value = ₹ 8088 and time (n) = 3 yr = 36 months

Let the monthly installment (P) be ₹ x.

$\because$ Maturity value $= Pn\left(1+\frac{r(n+1)}{2400}\right)$

$\therefore \quad 8088 = 36x\left(1+\frac{8\times 37}{2400}\right)$

$\Rightarrow \quad 8088 = 36x\left(\frac{2400+296}{2400}\right)$

$\Rightarrow \quad 8088 = 36x\left(\frac{2696}{2400}\right)$

$\Rightarrow \quad 8088 = \frac{97056\,x}{2400} \Rightarrow x = 200$

Hence, the monthly installment is ₹ 200.

Example 10. Mr. Amit opens a Recurring Deposit Account of ₹ 300 per month at 8% simple interest per annum. On maturity, he gets ₹ 9930. Find the period, for which he continued with the account.

Sol. Given, Mr. Amit deposits per month (P) = ₹ 300,

rate of interest (r) = 8% per annum

and maturity value = ₹ 9930

Let n be the number of months.

$\because$ Maturity value $= Pn\left(1+\frac{r(n+1)}{2400}\right)$

$\therefore \quad 9930 = 300n\left(1+\frac{8(n+1)}{2400}\right)$

$\Rightarrow \quad 9930 = 300n\left(1+\frac{(n+1)}{300}\right)$

$\Rightarrow \quad 9930 = 300n + (n^2 + n)$

$\Rightarrow \quad 9930 = 300n + n^2 + n$

$\Rightarrow \quad n^2 + 301n - 9930 = 0$

$\Rightarrow \quad n^2 + 331n - 30n - 9930 = 0$

$[\because -9930 = 331 \times (-30) \text{ and } 301 = 331 - 30]$

$\Rightarrow \quad n(n+331) - 30(n+331) = 0$

$\Rightarrow \quad (n+331)(n-30) = 0$

Either $n + 331 = 0$

$\Rightarrow \quad n = -331$ [which is not possible]

or $\quad n - 30 = 0 \Rightarrow n = 30$

$\therefore$ Period = 30 months = $2\frac{1}{2}$ yr.

Example 11. Ranjan started paying ₹ 500 per month in a 5 yr Recurring Deposit Account. After 3 yr, he started one more Recurring Deposit Account in which he deposited ₹ 1800 per month. If the bank pays 10% per annum simple interest in both the deposits, find at the end of 5 yr, which Recurring Deposit Account will give more money and by how much

Sol. **First RD**

Deposit per month P = ₹ 500, time = 5 yr

So, n = (5 × 12) months = 60 months

and rate = 10% per annum

$\therefore$ Amount received at the end = Total sum deposited + Interest received

$= P \times n + P \times \frac{n(n+1)}{24} \times \frac{r}{100}$

$= 500 \times 60 + \frac{500 \times 60\,(60+1)}{24} \times \frac{10}{100}$

$= 30000 + \frac{30000 \times 61}{24} \times \frac{10}{100}$

$= 30000 + 7625$

= ₹ 37625.

Second RD

Deposit per month P = ₹ 1800, time = 2 yr

So, n = 24 months and rate = 10% per annum

$\therefore$ Amount received at the end = Total sum deposited + Interest received

$= Pn + \frac{Pn(n+1)}{24} \times \frac{r}{100}$

$= 1800 \times 24 + \frac{1800 \times 24 \times 25}{24} \times \frac{10}{100}$

$= 43200 + 4500$

= ₹ 47700.

So, the second RD will give more money and the difference will be 47700 − 37625 = ₹(10075).

Chapter Practice

a. 1 Mark Questions

1. Mrs. Asha Mehta deposit ₹ 250 per month for one year in a bank's Recurring Deposit Account. If the rate of (simple) interest is 8% per annum, then the interest earned by her on this account is
(a) ₹ 65 (b) ₹ 120
(c) ₹ 130 (d) ₹ 260

2. If Shahrukh opened a Recurring Deposit Account in a bank and deposited ₹ 800 per month for $1\frac{1}{2}$ yr, then the total money deposited in the account is
(a) ₹ 11400 (b) ₹ 14400
(c) ₹ 13680 (d) None of these

3. Naveen deposits ₹ 800 every month in a Recurring Deposit Account for 6 months. If he receives ₹ 4884 at the time of maturity, then the interest he earns is [ICSE 2023]
(a) ₹ 84 (b) ₹ 42
(c) ₹ 24 (d) ₹ 284

4. Ramesh deposited ₹ 500 per month for 60 months in a bank's Recurring Deposit Account. If the bank pays interest at the rate of 6% per annum, then find the amount, he will get on maturity.
(a) ₹ 35486 (b) ₹ 34575
(c) ₹ 34880 (d) ₹ 35560

5. Mr. Sharma deposited ₹ 500 every month in a Cumulative Deposit Account for 2 yr. If the bank pays interest at the rate of 7% per annum, then the amount he gets on maturity is
(a) ₹ 875 (b) ₹ 6875
(c) ₹ 10875 (d) ₹ 12875

6. Mohit opened a Recurring Deposit Account in a bank for 2 yr. He deposits ₹ 1000 every month and receives ₹ 25500 on maturity. The interest he earned in 2 yr is [ICSE Semester I 2021]
(a) ₹ 13500 (b) ₹ 3000
(c) ₹ 24000 (d) ₹ 1500

b. 3 Marks Questions

7. Ashit had Recurring Deposit Account in a bank and deposited ₹ 950 per month for a period of 24 months. If the rate of interest was 9.5% per annum, then find the interest earned in 2 yr.

8. Sonia had a Recurring Deposit Account in a bank and deposited ₹600 per month for $2\frac{1}{2}$ yr. If the rate of interest was 10% per annum, then find the maturity value of this account. [ICSE 2018]

9. Mr. Mehta borrows ₹ 100000 from State Bank of India at 11% per annum compound interest. He repays ₹ 41000 at the end of first year and ₹ 47700 at the end of the second year. Find the amount outstanding at the beginning of the third year. [ICSE 2009]

10. If Mrs. Goswami deposits ₹ 1000 every month in a Recurring Deposit Account for 3 yr at 8% interest per annum, then find the matured value. [ICSE 2009]

11. Joseph deposits ₹ 600 per month in a Recurring Deposit Account in a post office for $4\frac{1}{2}$ yr. Find the amount payable to him on maturity, if the rate of interest is 9% per annum.

12. Nishita deposited ₹ 160 per month in her bank for $\frac{1}{2}$ yr under the Recurring Deposit Scheme. What will be the maturity of her deposit, if the rate of interest is 8% per annum and the interest is calculated at the end of every month?

13. Amit deposited ₹ 150 per month in a bank for 8 months under the Recurring deposit scheme. What will be the maturity value of his deposits, if the rate of interest is 8% per annum and interest is calculated at the end of every month? [ICSE 2001, 2007]

c. 4/5 Marks Questions

14. Sahil opened a Recurring Deposit Account in a bank and deposits ₹ 150 per month for 8 months. At the time of maturity, he received ₹ 1236. Find the rate of interest.

15. Mr. Aditya has a 4 yr Cumulative term Deposit Account in Axis Bank and deposits ₹ 650 per month. If he receives ₹ 36296 at the time of maturity, then find the rate of interest.

16. David opened a Recurring Deposit Account in a bank and deposited ₹ 300 per month for 2 yr. If he received ₹ 7725 at the time of maturity, then find the rate of interest per annum. [ICSE 2008]

17. Ahmed has a Recurring Deposit Account in a bank. He deposits ₹ 2500 per month for 2 yr. If he gets ₹ 66250 at the time of maturity, then find
(i) the interest paid by the bank.
(ii) the rate of interest. [ICSE 2011]

18. Mr. Anand opened a Cumulative Deposit Account of monthly installment ₹ 200 at 9% per annum simple interest. He earned a total interest of ₹ 1764. How many installments did he pay?

19. A man has a Recurring Deposit Account in a bank for $3\frac{1}{2}$ yr. If the rate of interest is 12% per annum and the man gets ₹ 30618 on maturity, then find the value of monthly installment.

20. Sangeeta gets ₹ 97076.25 at the end of five years at the rate of 8.5% per annum in a Reccuring Deposit Account. Find her monthly installment.

21. Kamal has a Recurring Deposit Account in a bank for $3\frac{1}{2}$ yr at 9.5% per annum. If he gets ₹ 58978, at the time of maturity, then find the monthly installment.

22. Mr. Bisla has a Recurring Deposit Account for 2 yr at 6% interest per annum. He receives ₹ 975 as interest on maturity. Find

(i) the monthly installment amount.

(ii) the maturity amount.

23. Mr. Malhotra deposits a certain sum of money every month in a Recurring Deposit Account for a period of 24 months. If the bank pays interest at the rate of 12% per annum and Mr. Malhotra gets ₹ 12484 as the maturity value of this account, what sum of money did he pay every month?

d. 6 Marks Questions

24. Ms. Arora deposits ₹ 100 per month in a Cumulative Deposit Account for a period of 5 yr. After the end of the period, she will receive ₹ 7220. (consider the interest rate to be simple). Find

(i) the total interest that Ms. Arora will earn.

(ii) the rate of interest per annum.

25. Ankita started paying ₹ 400 per month in a 3 yr Reccuring Deposit. After six months her brother Anshul started paying ₹ 500 per month in a $2\frac{1}{2}$ yr Reccuring Deposit. The bank paid 10% per annum simple interest for both. At maturity who will get more money and how much?

26. Salman deposits ₹ 1000 every month in a Recurring Deposit Account for 2 yr. If he receives ₹ 26000 on maturity, find

(i) the total interest Salman earns.

(ii) the rate of interest. **[ICSE 2023]**

27. Mohan has a Recurring Deposit Account in a bank for 2 yr at 6% per annum simple interest. If he gets ₹ 1200 as interest at the time of maturity, then find

(i) the monthly installment.

(ii) the amount of maturity. **[ICSE2016]**

28. Mr. Richard has a Recurring Deposit Account in a bank for 3 yr at 7.5% per annum simple interest. If he gets ₹ 8325 as interest at the time of maturity, then find

(i) the monthly deposit.

(ii) the maturity value. **[ICSE 2017]**

29. Mr. Rajiv Bhardwaj has a Recurring Deposit Account in a bank of ₹ 600 per month. If the bank pays simple interest of 7% per annum and he gets ₹ 15450 as maturity amount, then find the total time, for which the account was held.

30. Mrs. Sarkar deposits ₹ 1600 per month in a Recurring Deposit Account at 9% per annum simple interest. If she gets ₹ 65592 at the time of maturity, then find the total time for which the account was held.

31. Samita has a Recurring Deposit Account in a bank of ₹ 2000 per month at the rate of 10% per annum. If she gets ₹ 83100 at the time of maturity, then find the total time, for which the account was held.

32. Kiran started ₹ 400 per month in 3 yr Recurring Deposit Account. After 1 yr, he started one more Recurring Deposit Account, in which he deposited ₹ 1200 per month. If the bank pays 12% per annum simple interest in both the deposits, find at the end of 3 yr, which Recurring Deposit will give more money and by how much?

33. Rajshree deposited ₹ 600 per month for n months in a bank's Recurring Deposit Account. If the bank pays the rate of interest 10% annually and the maturity value is ₹ 24930, then find the value of n.

34. Mr. Sohit saves ₹ 10 daily and deposits ₹ 300 monthly in his Recurring Deposit Account in SBP for 2 yr. If the rate of interest is r% per annum, then he can get ₹ 10000 on maturity. Find the value of r.

35. Mr. Bajaj needs ₹ 30000 after 2 yr. What least money (in multiple of ₹ 5) must he deposit every month in a Recurring Deposit Account to get required money at the end of 2 yr, the rate of interest being 8% per annum?

36. Each of A and B opened a Reccuring Deposit Account in a bank. If A deposited ₹ 1200 per month for 3 yr and B deposited ₹ 1500 per month for $2\frac{1}{2}$ yr, then find on maturity, who will get more amount and by how much? The rate of interest paid by the bank is 10% per annum.

37. Joseph has a Recurring Deposit Account in a bank for 2 yr at the rate of 8% per annum simple interest. **[ICSE Semester-I 2021]**

(i) If at the time of maturity Joseph receives ₹ 2000 as interest, then the monthly installment is

(a) ₹ 1200
(b) ₹ 600
(c) ₹ 1000
(d) ₹ 1600

(ii) The total amount deposited in the bank

(a) ₹ 25000 (b) ₹ 24000
(c) ₹ 26000 (d) ₹ 23000

(iii) The amount Joseph receives on maturity is

(a) ₹ 27000 (b) ₹ 25000
(c) ₹ 26000 (d) ₹ 28000

(iv) If the monthly installment is ₹ 100 and the rate of interest is 8%, in how many months Joseph will receive ₹ 52 as interest?

(a) 18 (b) 30 (c) 12 (d) 6

Hints and Answers

1. (c) **2.** (b) **3.** (a)
4. (b) **5.** (b)

6. Hint Given, $P = ₹ 1000$

$n = 24$ months

and maturity value (MV) = ₹ 25500

$\therefore \quad MV = P \times n + I$

$\Rightarrow ₹ 25500 = ₹ 1000 \times 24 + I$

$\Rightarrow I = ₹ 25500 - ₹ 24000$

$\Rightarrow I = ₹ 1500$

7. Hint Use the formula, $I = \frac{Prn(n+1)}{2400}$.

Ans. ₹ 2256.25

8. Hint Do same as Example 1. **Ans.** ₹ 20325

9. Hint At the end of 1 yr,

$$\text{Interest} = \frac{PRT}{100} = \frac{100000 \times 11 \times 1}{100} = ₹ 11000$$

Amount = $P + I$ = ₹ 110000

Repaid amount = ₹ 41000

After 1 yr = 110000 − 41000 = ₹ 70000

Since, it is compound interest, principal will be outstanding of previous year,

$$I = \frac{PRT}{100} = ₹ 7700, A = ₹ 77700$$

Repaid amount = ₹ 47700

∴ Outstanding at start of 3 yr

= 77700 − 47700 = ₹ 30000

10. Hint Do same as Example 1. **Ans.** ₹ 40440

11. Hint Do same as Example 1. **Ans.** ₹ 39082.50

12. Hint Equivalent principal for 1 month

$$= \frac{160 \times 42}{2}$$

∴ Interest on this principal

$$= \frac{160 \times 42 \times 8}{2 \times 12 \times 100} = ₹ 22.4$$

Total money deposited by Nishita

= 160 × 6 = ₹ 960

Maturity value = ₹ 9824

13. Hint $MV = Pn + \frac{P \times n(n+1)}{24} \times \frac{r}{100}$

Ans. ₹ 1236

14. Hint Do same as Example 4. **Ans.** 8%

15. Hint Do same as Example 7. **Ans.** 8%

16. Hint Do same as Example 7. **Ans.** 7%

17. Hint Do same as Example 5. **Ans.** (i) ₹ 6250 (ii) 10%

18. Hint Let n be the number of installments.

Then, time period = n months

Now, use the formula

$$\text{Interest} = \frac{Prn(n+1)}{2400}$$

Ans. 48 months

19. Hint Do same as Example 9. **Ans.** ₹ 600

20. Hint Let monthly installment be ₹ P.

$n = 5$ yr = 60 months

$$\because \quad MV = \frac{n(n+1)}{2 \times 12} \times \frac{P \times R}{100} + P \cdot n$$

Ans. ₹ 1330.54

21. Hint Do same as Example 9. **Ans.** ₹ 1200

22. Hint

(i) Let the monthly installment be ₹ P.

Then, interest = $\frac{Prn(n+1)}{2400}$ **Ans.** ₹ 650

(ii) Maturity value = $P \times n$ + Interest = ₹ 1675

23. Hint Do same as Example 9. **Ans.** ₹ 462.37

24. Hint Do same as Example 5.

Ans. (i) ₹ 1220 (ii) 8%

25. Hint Case I (Ankita)

Amount received at the time of maturity be A,

$$\therefore \quad SI = \frac{P \times n(n+1)}{2 \times 12} \times \frac{r}{100}$$

$$= \frac{400 \times 36 \times 37}{24} \times \frac{10}{100} = 2220$$

Maturity value = 400 × 36 + 2220 = 16620

Case II (Anshul)

Amount received at the time of maturity be A_2,

$$\therefore \quad SI = \frac{P \times n(n+1)}{2400} \times r$$

$$= \frac{500 \times 30 \times 31}{24} \times \frac{10}{100} = 1937.5$$

Maturity value = 500 × 30 + 1937.5 = ₹ 16937.5

∴ Hence, Anshul will get more amount at maturity.

Difference = ₹ (16937.50 − 16620) = ₹ 317.50

26. **Hint** Do same as Example 5.

Ans. (i) ₹ 2000 (ii) 8% per annum

27. **Hint** Do same as Q. 22.

Ans. (i) ₹ 800 (ii) ₹ 20400

28. **Hint**

(i) Let monthly deposit be ₹ P.

Then, $I = \dfrac{Prn(n+1)}{2400}$

Ans. ₹ 2000

(ii) Maturity value $= 36P + 8325$

Ans. ₹ 80325

29. **Hint** Do same as Example 10.

Ans. 2 yr

30. **Hint** Do same as Example 10.

Ans. 3 yr

31. **Hint** Do same as Example 10.

Ans. 3 yr

32. **Hint** Do same as Example 11. **Ans.** ₹ 15336

33. **Hint** Do same as Example 10. **Ans.** 36 months

34. **Hint** Use the formula,

Maturity amount $= P \times n\left[1 + \dfrac{r(n+1)}{2400}\right]$

Ans. 37.3%

35. **Hint** $I = P \times \dfrac{n(n+1)r}{2400}$

$= P \times \dfrac{600}{24} \times \dfrac{8}{100} = 2P$

Then, $26P = 30000$

Ans. ₹ 1155 (multiple of 5).

36. **Hint** Installment per month $(P) =$ ₹ 1200

Number of months $(n) = 36$

Rate of interest $(r) = 10\%$ per annum

$\therefore \quad SI = \dfrac{P \times n(n+1)}{2 \times 12} \times \dfrac{r}{100}$

$= \dfrac{1200 \times 36(36+1)}{2 \times 12} \times \dfrac{10}{100}$

$=$ ₹ 6660

The amount that A will get at the time of maturity

$=$ ₹ $(1200 \times 36) +$ ₹ $6660 = 49860$

$\because \quad SI = \dfrac{P \times n(n+1)}{2 \times 12} \times \dfrac{r}{100}$

$= 1500 \times \dfrac{30(30+1)}{2 \times 12} \times \dfrac{10}{100}$

$=$ ₹ 5812.50

The amount that B will get at the time of maturity

$=$ ₹ $(1500 \times 30) +$ ₹ 5812.50

$=$ ₹ 50812.50

Difference between both amount

$=$ ₹ $(50812.50 - 49860) =$ ₹ 952.50

Hence, B will get more money than A by ₹ 952.50.

37. **Hint** Given, rate of interest $(r) = 8\%$ per annum

Number of month $(n) = 24$ months

(i) (c) Interest $(I) =$ ₹ 2000

$\therefore \quad SI = \dfrac{Pn(n+1)}{2400} \times r$

$\Rightarrow \quad 2000 = \dfrac{P \times 24 \times 25 \times 8}{2400}$

$\therefore \quad P = \dfrac{2000 \times 100}{25 \times 8} =$ ₹ 1000

(ii) (b) Monthly installment $=$ ₹ 1000

Time period 2 yr or 24 months

$\therefore$ Total amount deposit

$=$ Total month $\times$ monthly installment

$= 24 \times 1000 =$ ₹ 24000

(iii) (c) Maturity amount

$=$ Total amount deposit $+$ Interest

$=$ ₹ 24000 $+$ ₹ 2000

$=$ ₹ 26000

(iv) (c) Given, monthly installment $(P) =$ ₹ 100,

$r = 8\%$,

Months $(n) = ?$

and Interest $=$ ₹ 52

$\therefore \quad$ Interest $= \dfrac{Prn(n+1)}{2400}$

$\Rightarrow \quad 52 = \dfrac{100 \times 8 \times n(n+1)}{2400}$

$\Rightarrow \quad 52 \times 3 = n(n+1)$

$\Rightarrow \quad n^2 + n - 156 = 0$

$\Rightarrow \quad n^2 + 13n - 12n - 156 = 0$

$\Rightarrow \quad n(n+13) - 12(n+13) = 0$

$\Rightarrow \quad (n-12)(n+13) = 0$

$\Rightarrow \quad n = 12, -13$

Month can not be negative.

So, months $= 12$.

Olympiad Section

Brain Teasing Questions of Olympiad Pattern

1 Sneha opened a cumulative time deposit account with a bank and deposits ₹ 500 per month for $1\frac{1}{4}$ yr. If she receives ₹ 300 as interest, then find the rate of interest per annum.

(a) 6% (b) 8%
(c) 7.5% (d) 10%

2 Dinesh opened a Recurring Deposit Account with State Bank of India. He deposited ₹ 900 per month at 7.5% per annum. He received ₹ 1687.5 as interest. Then, the time period of his deposit will be

(a) 3 yr (b) 2 yr
(c) 5 yr (d) 3.5 yr

3 A Recurring Deposit Account of ₹ 1200 per month has a maturity value of ₹ 12440. If the rate of interest is 8% and the interest is calculated at the end of every month, then find the time of this Recurring Deposit Account.

(a) 10 months (b) 20 months
(c) 30 months (d) 50 months

4 Vishal has a Recurring Deposit Account in a finance company for 1 yr at 8% per annum. If he gets ₹ 9390 at the time of maturity, then how much amount per month has been invested by Vishal?

(a) ₹ 650 (b) ₹ 700
(c) ₹ 750 (d) ₹ 800

5 Ravi deposited ₹ 400 per month in a Recurring Deposit Account for 2 yr at 9% per annum. Sonu deposited ₹ 400 per month in a Recurring Deposit Account for $2\frac{1}{2}$ yr at 12% per annum. Which of the following can be concluded about the interests to be paid to them on maturities of their deposits?

(a) Ravi must be paid an interest of ₹ 860 less than that of Sonu
(b) Ravi must be paid an interest of ₹ 900 less than that of Sonu
(c) Ravi must be paid an interest of ₹ 916 less than that of Sonu
(d) Ravi must be paid an interest of ₹ 816 less than that of Sonu

Answers

1. (a) **2.** (b) **3.** (a) **4.** (c) **5.** (b)

* *These questions may or may not be asked in the examination, have been given just for additional practice required for olympiads Scholarship Exams etc. For detailed explanations refer Page No. 476.*

CHAPTER

03

Shares and Dividends

SYLLABUS

- (a) Face/Nominal Value, Market Value, Dividend, Rate of Dividend, Premium. (b) Formulae (i) Income = Number of shares × Rate of dividend × FV. (ii) Return = (Income/Investment) × 100.

Note Brokerage and fractional shares not included.

Share

While starting or establishing a company a large sum of money is required, generally it is not possible for a single/few person(s) to arrange such a huge amount of money on their own, so the company raises its capital from the public by issue of shares. A 'share' is one of the units into which the capital of the company is divided.

Some Basic Definitions

(i) **Nominal/Face value** The original value of a share is called its nominal (printed, register or face) value, which is fixed by the company.

(ii) **Shareholder** An individual who purchases/possesses the share(s) of the company is called a shareholder of the company.

(iii) **Market value/Cash value** The price of a share at any time in the market is called market value of the share. The market value of a share is not fixed, it varies from time-to-time.

(iv) **At par** When shares are issued at their face value, the shares are said to have been issued at par, e.g. shares with a face value of ₹10 is issued at ₹10.

(v) **At premium/above par** When shares are issued at a value which is higher than the face value of shares, the shares are said to have been issued at premium, i.e. issue price is more than face value, e.g. share with a face value of ₹10 is issued at ₹12, here ₹ 2 being premium.

(vi) **At discount/below par** When shares are issued at a value which is lower than the face value of shares, the shares are said to have been issued at discount, i.e. issue price is less than face value, e.g. share with a face value of ₹10 is issued at ₹8, here ₹2 being discount.

Important Formulae Related to Share

(i) Total face value = Number of shares × Nominal value of one share

(ii) Money invested = Number of shares × Market value of one share

(iii) When shares are purchased from the company, then

$$\text{Number of shares} = \frac{\text{Total investment}}{\text{Face value of a share}}$$

(iv) When shares are purchased from the market, then

$$\text{Number of shares} = \frac{\text{Total investment}}{\text{Market value of a share}}$$

Note In share market, share is purchased and sold on market value.

Example 1. A company issued shares at 10% premium. Lalit applied for 1000 shares, but was allotted 500 shares of this company. Find his investment, if the face value of a share is ₹ 100.

Sol. Given, face value of a share = ₹ 100

and premium percentage = 10%

∴ Premium on one share = ₹ 10

Now, market value of one share = 100 + 10 = ₹110

∴ Price of 500 shares = 500 × 110 = ₹ 55000

[∵ money invested = number of shares × market value of one share]

Hence, Lalit's investment in the company is ₹55000.

Example 2. A man invests ₹ 15840 in buying shares of face value ₹ 24 each and selling at 10% premium. Find the number of shares bought by him.

Sol. Given, total investment = ₹ 15840

and face value of one share = ₹ 24

Now, premium on one share = 10% of ₹ 24

$= \frac{10}{100} \times 24 =$ ₹ 2.40

and investment on one share = 24 + 2.40 = ₹ 26.40

$\therefore$ Number of shares bought $= \frac{\text{Total investment}}{\text{Investment on one share}}$

$= \frac{15840}{26.40} = 600$

Example 3. Akansha invested ₹ 8000 in buying ₹ 50 shares of a company. She sold half of these when they were at a premium of ₹ 10 and the remaining at a discount of ₹ 5. Find her gain or loss on the whole transaction.

Sol. Given, investment = ₹ 8000

and nominal value of one share = ₹ 50

$\therefore$ Number of shares $= \frac{\text{Investment}}{\text{Face value of one share}}$

$= \frac{8000}{50} = 160$

Selling price of a share at premium = 50 + 10 = ₹ 60

Number of shares sold at this rate $= \frac{1}{2}$ of 160 = 80

Amount received on selling 80 shares at ₹ 60 = 60 × 80

= ₹ 4800

Selling price of a share at discount = 50 − 5 = ₹ 45

Number of shares sold at this rate = 160 − 80 = 80

Amount received on selling 80 shares at ₹ 45

= 45 × 80 = ₹ 3600

Total amount obtained by selling all the shares

= 4800 + 3600 = ₹ 8400

$\because$ Amount invested = ₹ 8000

$\therefore$ Gain in total transaction = 8400 − 8000 = ₹ 400

Dividend

A part of profit of the company which a shareholder gets for his investment in shares from the company, is called dividend.

It is always expressed as the percentage of the face value of the share, which is called **rate of dividend**,

i.e. Dividend on one share $= \frac{d}{100} \times$ Nominal value

where, d is the rate of dividend.

The company always gives a dividend on the face value (nominal value) of the share irrespective of the market value of the share.

Annual Income

Total income received by a shareholder in a year, by way of dividend is referred to its annual income.

Yield Percentage

Yield percentage is the percentage return that a shareholder gets on the investment made by purchasing the shares of a company, with respect to the dividend declared by the company.

Some Useful Cases

20% of ₹ 100 shares at ₹ 140 means that

(i) the face value (nominal value) of 1 share = ₹ 100

(ii) the market value of 1 share = ₹ 140

(iii) the dividend on 1 share = 20% of ₹ 100

= ₹ 20 per annum

(iv) the income on ₹ 140 is ₹ 20 for one year

(v) the rate of return (or yield) per annum

$= \left(\frac{20}{140} \times 100\right)\%$

$= 14\frac{2}{7}\%$

Similarly, '10% of ₹ 50 shares at a discount of ₹ 10' means that

(i) the face value of 1 share = ₹ 50

(ii) the market value of 1 share = 50 − 10 = ₹ 40

(iii) the dividend on 1 share = 10% of 50

$= \frac{10}{100} \times 50 =$ ₹ 5 per annum

(iv) the income on ₹ 40 = ₹ 5 for one year

(v) the rate of return per annum

$= \left(\frac{5}{40} \times 100\right)\%$

$= 12.5\%$

Example 4. How much cash is obtained by selling shares

(i) 100, ₹ 25 shares at ₹ 3 premium?

(ii) 100, ₹ 25 shares at ₹ 2 discount?

(iii) 250, ₹ 250 shares at par?

Sol.

(i) Market value of one share = ₹ (25 + 3) = ₹ 28

$\therefore$ Cash obtained by selling 100 shares = 28 × 100 = ₹ 2800

(ii) Market value of one share = ₹ (25 − 2) = ₹ 23

$\therefore$ Cash obtained by selling 100 shares = 23 × 100 = ₹ 2300

(iii) Cash obtained by selling 250 shares of ₹ 250

= ₹ (250 × 250)

= ₹ 62500

Example 5. A man sells out a stock of ₹ 10000 when the price stands at ₹ 100 of ₹ 125 shares. Find the sale proceeds.

Sol. Given, stock of ₹ 10000

Stock of ₹ 125 is sold for amount = ₹ 100

Stock of ₹ 10000 is sold for amount $= \frac{100}{125} \times 10000 =$ ₹ 8000

Important Formulae Related to Dividend

(i) Annual income (or annual dividend) per share

$= \text{Nominal value of one share} \times \frac{\text{Rate of dividend}}{100}$

(ii) Total annual income = Number of shares

$\times \text{Nominal value of one share} \times \frac{\text{Rate of dividend}}{100}$

(iii) Number of shares $= \frac{\text{Annual income}}{\text{Income on one share}}$

Or $\frac{\text{Investment}}{\text{Market value of one share}}$

(iv) Rate of dividend (or income) on investment

$= \frac{\text{Dividend}}{\text{Investment}} \times 100\%$

(v) Rate of return (or yield) $= \left(\frac{\text{Annual income}}{\text{Total investment}} \times 100\right)\%$

(vi) Dividend percentage × Nominal value

= Percentage return × Market value

Example 6. A man bought 500 shares, each of face value ₹ 10, of a certain business concern and during the first year, after purchase, receives ₹ 400 as dividend on his shares. Find the rate of dividend on the shares.

Sol. Given, face value of each share = ₹ 10

Number of shares bought by man = 500

First year total dividend = ₹ 400

Total invested in shares = ₹ (500 × 10) = ₹ 5000

$\because$ Rate of dividend $= \frac{\text{Dividend}}{\text{Sum invested}} \times 100$

$= \left(\frac{400}{5000} \times 100\right)\%$

= 8%

Example 7. Mr. Prakash invested ₹ 52000 on ₹ 100 shares at a discount of ₹ 20, paying 8% dividend. At the end of one year, he sells the shares at a premium of ₹ 20. Find

(i) the total annual dividend.

(ii) the profit earned including his dividend. **[ICSE 2011]**

Sol. Given, money invested by Mr. Prakash = ₹ 52000

Nominal value of one share = ₹ 100 and dividend = 8%

Market value of one share = 100 − 20 = ₹ 80

$\therefore$ Number of shares $= \frac{\text{Total investment}}{\text{Market value of one share}}$

$= \frac{52000}{80} = 650$

(i) $\therefore$ Total annual dividend $= \frac{\text{Rate of dividend}}{100}$

× Number of shares × Nominal value of one share

$= \frac{8}{100} \times 650 \times 100 =$ ₹ 5200

(ii) As Mr. Prakash sells his shares at a premium of ₹ 20.

$\therefore$ Selling price of one share = 100 + 20 = ₹ 120

Now, selling value of his 650 shares

= 650 × Selling price of one share

= 650 × 120 = ₹ 78000

$\therefore$ Profit earned = Total selling value

+ Annual dividend − Money invested

= 78000 + 5200 − 52000 = ₹ 31200

Example 8. A man buys ₹ 10 share at a premium of ₹ 5 per share. If the company pays 9% dividend, then find the percentage return on his investment in buying 200 shares.

Sol. Given, face value of one share = ₹ 10

and premium = ₹ 5

Investment on one share = 10 + 5 = ₹ 15

$\therefore$ Investment in buying 200 shares = 200 × 15 = ₹ 3000

Also, given rate of dividend = 9%

Now, annual income on 1 share = 9% of ₹ 10

$= \frac{9}{100} \times 10 =$ ₹ $\frac{9}{10}$

$\therefore$ Annual income on 200 shares $= 200 \times \frac{9}{10} =$ ₹ 180

Now, percentage return on his investment

$= \left(\frac{\text{Annual income}}{\text{Total investment}} \times 100\right)\%$

$= \left(\frac{180}{3000} \times 100\right)\% = 6\%$

Example 9. Which is a better investment? 20% at 100 or 25% at 150?

Sol. **In First Case**

Income on ₹ 100 = 20% of ₹ 100 = ₹ 20

$\therefore$ Income of ₹ 1 = ₹ $\frac{20}{100}$

By investing ₹ 100 one's income $= \frac{20}{100} \times 100 =$ ₹ 20

In the Second Case

Income on ₹ 150 = 25% of ₹ 150 = ₹ 37.5

$\therefore$ Income of ₹ 1 = ₹ $\frac{37.5}{150}$

By investing ₹ 100 one's income $= \frac{37.5}{150} \times 100 =$ ₹ 25

The investment in second case is better than the investment in first case.

Example 10. At what price should a 10% ₹ 25 share be quoted when the money is worth 5%.

Sol. Given, rate of dividend = 10%

Face value = ₹ 25

Dividend on one share = $\frac{10 \times 25}{100}$ = ₹ 2.5

Rate of interest on investment = 5%

If interest is ₹ 5, then investment = ₹ 100

and if interest is ₹ 2.5 then investment = $\frac{100 \times 2.5}{5}$ = ₹ 50

Hence, the market value of each share is ₹ 50.

Example 11. A man invests ₹ 12800 in a company paying 18% dividend at a time when its ₹ 100 share can be bought at a premium of ₹ 60, find his annual income from these shares.

Sol. Given, face value of one share = ₹ 100

Premium for one share = ₹ 60

Rate of dividend = 18%

and total investment = ₹ 12800

Investment on one share = 100 + 60 = ₹ 160

Now, number of shares bought

$= \frac{\text{Total investment}}{\text{Investment on one share}}$

$= \frac{12800}{160} = 80$

Now, annual income on one share = 18% of ₹ 100

[∵ Annual income per share = Nominal value of a share $\times \frac{\text{Rate of dividend}}{100}$]

$= \frac{18}{100} \times 100$ = ₹ 18

∴ Annual income from 80 shares = 80 × 18 = ₹1440

Example 12. Salman invests a sum of money in ₹ 50 shares, paying 15% dividend and quoted at 20% premium. If his annual dividend is ₹ 600, then calculate

(i) the number of shares, he bought.

(ii) his total investment.

(iii) the rate of return on his investment. **[ICSE 2014]**

Sol. Given, nominal value of one share = ₹ 50

and rate of dividend = 15%

Now, dividend on one share

$= \frac{15}{100} \times 50$ = ₹ 7.50

Total dividend that Salman got from the company = ₹ 600

(i) ∴ Number of shares Salman bought

$= \frac{\text{Annual income}}{\text{Income on one share}}$

$= \frac{600}{7.50} = 80$

(ii) Premium on one share = 20% of ₹ 50 = $\frac{20}{100} \times 50$ = ₹ 10

∴ Market value of one share = 50 + 10 = ₹ 60

Total investment for 80 shares = 80 × 60 = ₹ 4800

(iii) ∴ Rate of return on his investment

$= \left(\frac{\text{Total dividend amount}}{\text{Total investment}} \times 100\right)\%$

$= \left(\frac{600}{4800} \times 100\right)\% = 12.5\%$

Example 13. Vivek invests ₹ 4500 in 8%, ₹ 10 shares at ₹ 15. He sells the shares, when the price rises to ₹ 30 and invests the proceeds in 12%, ₹ 100 shares at ₹ 125. Calculate **[ICSE 2010]**

(i) the sale proceeds.

(ii) the number of ₹ 125 shares, he buys.

(iii) the change in his annual income from dividend.

Sol. Given, money invested by Vivek = ₹ 4500

Nominal value of one share = ₹ 10

Market value of one share = ₹ 15

∴ Number of shares he bought

$= \frac{\text{Money invested}}{\text{Market value of one share}}$

$= \frac{4500}{15} = 300$

∴ Total nominal value = Number of shares × Nominal value of one share

= 300 × 10 = ₹ 3000

∴ Dividend = 8% of Total nominal value

$= \frac{8}{100} \times 3000$ = ₹ 240

(i) ∴ Sale proceeds = Amount received on selling 300 shares

= Number of shares × Market value

= 300 × 30 = ₹ 9000

(ii) If he bought a share at ₹ 125, then the number of shares he bought = $\frac{9000}{125} = 72$

(iii) Total nominal value of 72 shares

= 72 × 100 = ₹ 7200

∴ Dividend = 12% of total nominal value

$= \frac{12}{100} \times 7200$ = ₹ 864

∴ Change in his annual income

= 864 − 240 = ₹ 624

Example 14. Sachin invests ₹ 8500 in 10%, ₹ 100 shares at ₹ 170. He sells the shares when the price of each share rises by ₹ 30. He invests the proceeds in 12% ₹ 100 shares at ₹ 125. Find

(i) the sale proceeds.

(ii) the number of ₹ 125 shares he buys.

(iii) the change in his annual income. **[ICSE 2019]**

Sol. Given, money invested by Sachin = ₹ 8500

Nominal value of one share = ₹ 100

Market value of one share = ₹ 170

∴ Number of shares he bought

$$= \frac{\text{Money invested}}{\text{Market value of one share}} = \frac{8500}{170} = 50$$

∴ Total nominal value = Number of shares × Nominal value of one share

= 50 × 100 = ₹ 5000

∴ Dividend = 10% of ₹ 5000 = $\frac{10}{100} \times 5000$ = ₹ 500

(i) ∴ Sale proceeds = Amount received on selling 50 shares

= Number of shares × Market value

= 50 × 200

= ₹ 10000

(ii) If he bought a share at ₹ 125, then the number of shares he bought = $\frac{10000}{125} = 80$

(iii) Annual income of these shares = $\frac{12}{100} \times 100 \times 80$ = ₹ 960

∴ Change in his annual income = 960 − 500 = ₹ 460

Example 15. **Rohit invested ₹ 9600 on ₹ 100 shares at ₹ 20 premium paying 8% dividend. Rohit sold the shares, when the price rises to ₹ 160. He invested the proceeds (excluding dividend) in 10%, ₹ 50 shares at ₹ 40. Find**

(i) the original number of shares.

(ii) the sale proceeds.

(iii) the new number of shares.

(iv) the change in the two dividends. [ICSE 2015]

Sol. Given, money invested by Rohit = ₹ 9600

Nominal value of one share = 100

Premium on one share = ₹ 20

∴ Market value of one share = 100 + 20 = ₹ 120

(i) ∴ Original number of shares = $\frac{\text{Investment}}{\text{Market value}}$

$= \frac{9600}{120} = 80$

(ii) Sale proceeds = 80 × 160 = ₹ 12800

(iii) New number of shares = $\frac{12800}{40} = 320$

(iv) Change in two dividends

= 10% of (320 × 50) − 8% of (80 × 100)

= 1600 − 640

= ₹ 960

Example 16. **A man invests ₹ 8800 on buying shares of face value of ₹ 100 each at a premium of 10%. If he earns ₹ 1200 at the end of year as dividend, find**

(i) the number of shares he has in the company.

(ii) the dividend percentage per share. [ICSE 2001]

Sol. Given, investment = ₹ 8800

He earn by shares = ₹ 1200

Premium of each share = 10%

(i) Market value of each share = (100 + 10) = ₹ 110

∴ Number of shares purchased = $\frac{\text{Total investmenet}}{\text{Market value}}$

$= \frac{8800}{110} = 80$

(ii) ∴ Annual dividend = $\frac{\text{Rate of dividend}}{100}$ × Number of shares × Face value

$$\Rightarrow \quad 1200 = \frac{R}{100} \times 80 \times 100 \Rightarrow R = 15\%$$

Hence, the rate of dividend is 15%.

Example 17. **Ram has 450 shares of ₹ 200 of a company paying a dividend of 20% find his net income after paying an income tax of 16%.**

Sol. Given, number of shares = 450

Rate of dividend = 20%

Face value of one share = ₹ 200

∴ Total dividend = Number of shares × Face value of one share × Rate of dividend

Total dividend = 450 × 200 × $\frac{20}{100}$ = ₹ 18000

Income tax = 16% of ₹ 18000 = ₹ $\left(\frac{16}{100} \times 18000\right) = 2880$

∴ Net income = Total dividend − Income tax

= ₹ (18000 − 2880) = ₹ 15120

Example 18. **Mukul invests ₹ 9000 in a company paying a dividend of 6% per annum, when a share of face value ₹ 100 stands at ₹ 150. What is his annual income? He sells 50% of his shares when the price rises to ₹ 200. What is his gain on this transaction?**

Sol. Given, Mukul invested = ₹ 9000

Face value = ₹ 100

Market value of one share = ₹ 150

Mukul's number of shares bought

$$= \frac{\text{Mukul Invested Money}}{\text{Market value of a share}} = \frac{9000}{150} = 60$$

∴ Annual income = Number of shares × Face value a share × Rate of dividend

= 60 × 100 × $\frac{6}{100}$ = ₹ 360

Annual income = ₹ 360

Mukul sells shares = 50%

50% of his shares = $\frac{50}{100} \times 60 = 30$

Selling price of one share = ₹ 200

Selling price of 30 shates = ₹ (200 × 30) = ₹ 6000

Cost price of one share = ₹ 150

Cost price of 30 shares = ₹ (150 × 30) = ₹ 4500

He gain on this transaction = Selling price − Cost price

= ₹ (6000 − 4500) = ₹ 1500

Example 19. A company with 4000 shares of nominal value of ₹ 110 declares annual dividend of 15%. Calculate
(i) the total amount of dividend paid by the company.
(ii) the annual income of Shahrukh who holds 88 shares in the company.
(iii) if he received only 10% on his investment, find the price Shahrukh paid for each share. [ICSE 2008]

Sol.
(i) Given, nominal value of each share = ₹ 110
Number of shares = 4000
Annual dividend = 15%
∴ Total amount of dividend by the company
= Number of shares × Dividend on one share
$= ₹\left(4000 \times \frac{15}{100} \times 110\right) = ₹\ 66000$

(ii) ∴ Shahrukh's annual income
= Number of shares × Dividend on one share
$= ₹\left(88 \times \frac{15}{100} \times 110\right) = ₹\ 1452$

(iii) Let Shahrukh paid each share be ₹ x.
10% of x = 15% of ₹ 110
$\Rightarrow \frac{10x}{100} = \frac{15 \times 110}{100} \Rightarrow x = 165$
Hence, Shahrukh paid each share is ₹ 165.

Example 20. Ajay owns 560 shares of a company. The face value of each share is ₹ 25. The company declares a dividend of 9%. Calculate.
(i) the dividend that Ajay will get.
(ii) the rate of interest on his investment, if Ajay had paid ₹ 30 for each share. [ICSE 2007]

Sol. Given, number of shares = 560
Face value of each share = ₹ 25
Rate of divided = 9%
(i) Dividend on each share = 9% of ₹ 25
$= \left(\frac{9 \times 25}{100}\right) = ₹\frac{9}{4}$
Annual dividend that Ajay will get
= Dividend on 560 shares
$= \left(560 \times \frac{9}{4}\right) = ₹\ 1260$

(ii) Let rate of interest be x%.
$$\therefore \quad x = \left(\frac{\text{Annual dividend}}{\text{Market value each share} \times \text{Total number of share}} \times 100\right)\%$$
$$= \left(\frac{1260}{30 \times 560} \times 100\right)\%$$
$$= \frac{15}{2}\% = 7\frac{1}{2}\%$$

Example 21. Mr. Tiwari invested ₹ 29040 in 15% ₹ 100 shares at a premium of 20%. Calculate
(i) the number of shares bought by Mr. Tiwari.
(ii) Mr. Tiwari's income from the investment.
(iii) the percentage return on his investment. [ICSE 2005]

Sol.
(i) Given that, total invested = ₹ 29040
Market value of one share $= ₹\left(100 + \frac{20}{100} \times 100\right) = ₹\ 120$
Mr. Tiwari's number of shares
$= \frac{\text{Total investment}}{\text{Market value of one share}}$
$= \frac{29040}{120} = 242$

(ii) Nominal value of 242 shares = 100 × 242 = ₹ 24200
Dividend = 15%
Mr. Tiwari's income $= \frac{15}{100} \times 24200 = ₹\ 3630$

(iii) ∴ Percentage return $= \left(\frac{\text{Income}}{\text{Total investment}} \times 100\right)\%$
$= \left(\frac{3630}{29040} \times 100\right)\% = 12.5\%$

Example 22. A man wants to buy 62 shares available at ₹ 132 (par value of ₹ 100).
(i) How much should he invest?
(ii) If the dividend is 7.5%, what will be his annual income?
(iii) If he wants to increase his annual income by ₹150, how many extra shares should he buy? [ICSE 2002]

Sol.
(i) Market value of one share (par value ₹ 100) is ₹132.
∴ Market value of 62 shares = 132 × 62 = ₹ 8184
∴ The man should invest = ₹ 8184
(ii) ∴ Annual income = Face value of one share × Number of shares × Rate of dividend/100
$= 100 \times 62 \times \frac{7.5}{100} = ₹\ 465$
(iii) Since, income on one share is ₹ 7.5
∴ For income of ₹ 150, the number of shares $= \frac{150}{7.5} = 20$
Thus, to increase the income by ₹ 150, the number of extra shares to be purchased is 20.

Example 23. A person invested 20%, 30% and 40% of his savings in buying shares of three different companies A, B and C which declared dividends of 10%, 12% and 15%, respectively. If his total income from dividends is ₹ 1450, then find his savings and the amount which he invested in each company.

Sol. Let his savings be ₹ x.
Then, investment in company A = 20% of ₹ x = ₹ $\frac{20x}{100}$

Investment in company $B = 30\%$ of ₹ $x =$ ₹ $\frac{30x}{100}$

and investment in company $C = 40\%$ of ₹ $x =$ ₹ $\frac{40x}{100}$

Now, income from $A = \frac{20x}{100} \times \frac{10}{100} =$ ₹ $\frac{20x}{1000}$

Income from $B = \frac{30x}{100} \times \frac{12}{100} =$ ₹ $\frac{36x}{1000}$

and income from $C = \frac{40x}{100} \times \frac{15}{100} =$ ₹ $\frac{60x}{1000}$

∴ Total income $= \frac{20x}{1000} + \frac{36x}{1000} + \frac{60x}{1000} =$ ₹ $\frac{116x}{1000}$

But total income = ₹ 1450 [given]

∴ $\frac{116x}{1000} = 1450 \Rightarrow x = 1450 \times \frac{1000}{116} =$ ₹ 12500

∴ Investment in company $A = \frac{20}{100} \times 12500 =$ ₹ 2500

Investment in company $B = \frac{30}{100} \times 12500 =$ ₹ 3750

and investment in company $C = \frac{40}{100} \times 12500 =$ ₹ 5000

Example 24. **Mr. Ram Gopal invested ₹ 8000 in 7%, ₹ 100 shares at ₹ 80. After a year he sold these shares at ₹ 75 each and invested the proceeds (including his dividend) in 18%, ₹ 25 shares at ₹ 41. Find**

(i) his dividend for the first year.

(ii) his annual income in the second year.

(iii) the percentage increase in his return on his original investment. **[ICSE 2006]**

Sol.

(i) Given, Mr. Ram Gopal invested ₹ 8000

and per share = ₹ 80

The number of shares bought by Mr. Ram Gopal

$= \frac{8000}{80} = 100$

Dividend received on one share = 7% of ₹ 100 = ₹ 7

∴ The total dividend received after one years

$= 7 \times 100 =$ ₹ 700

∴ Mr. Ram Gopal dividend for the first year = ₹ 700

(ii) Mr. Ram Gopal sold his shares at ₹ 75 each.

The value of 100 shares $= 75 \times 100 =$ ₹ 7500

His investment in new shares i.e. his proceeds

= Sale value of shares + Dividend received

$= 7500 + 700 =$ ₹ 8200

Mr. Ram Gopal invested his proceeds i.e. ₹ 8200 in ₹ 25 shares at ₹ 41 each.

Mr. Ram Gopal purchased new shares $= \frac{8200}{41} = 200$

Dividend received on one share = 18% of ₹ 25

$= \left(\frac{18}{100} \times 25\right) =$ ₹ $\frac{9}{2}$

Total dividend received on his second investment

$= \left(\frac{9}{2} \times 200\right) =$ ₹ 900

Mr. Ram Gopal's annual second year income is ₹ 900.

(iii) The increase in return

= Dividend on second investment

− Dividend on first investment

= ₹ (900 − 700) = ₹ 200

The percentage increase in return on his investment

$= \left(\frac{200}{8000} \times 100\right)\% = \frac{5}{2}\% = 2.5\%$

Example 25. **Lalit invests ₹ 12500 partly in shares of face value ₹ 100 each paying 6% at ₹ 140 and the remaining in shares paying 5% at ₹ 125, if his total income is ₹ 520, how much has he invested in each?**

Sol. Given, total investment = ₹ 12500

Total income = ₹ 520

Case I Let the investment in shares paying 6% at ₹ 140 be ₹ x.

Case II Then, amount invested in shares paying 5% at ₹ 125 is ₹ $(12500 - x)$.

Total face value in Case I $= 100 \times \frac{x}{140} =$ ₹ $\frac{5}{7}x$

Face value of Case II $= \frac{100\,(12500 - x)}{125} =$ ₹ $\frac{4}{5}(12500 - x)$

Total income = ₹ 520

According to question,

6% of ₹ $\frac{5}{7}x$ + 5% of ₹ $\frac{4}{5}(12500 - x) = 520$

$\Rightarrow \frac{6}{100} \times \frac{5}{7}x + \frac{5}{100} \times \frac{4}{5}(12500 - x) = 520$

$\Rightarrow \frac{30x}{700} + \frac{4}{100}(12500 - x) = 520$

$\Rightarrow \frac{30x}{700} + 500 - \frac{4x}{100} = 520$

$\Rightarrow \frac{30x}{700} - \frac{4x}{100} = 520 - 500$

$\Rightarrow \frac{30x - 28x}{700} = 20 \Rightarrow \frac{2x}{700} = 20$

$\Rightarrow x = \frac{20 \times 700}{2} \Rightarrow x = 7000$

Investment in share paying 6% at 140 is ₹ 7000.

∴ Investment in share paying 5% at ₹ 125 is ₹ (12500 − 7000) = ₹ 5500

Example 26. **Mohit has a choice to invest in shares of two companies A and B. ₹ 100 shares of company A are available at 10% premium and its pays 8% dividend where as ₹ 50 shares of company B are available at 12% discount and its pays 7% dividend. If he invests equally in both the companies and the sum of his annual incomes from them is ₹ 1675, find how much in all, does he invest?**

Sol. Let Mohit invest ₹ x in each company.

For company A,

Nominal value of each share = ₹ 100

Market value of each share = 100 + 10% of ₹ 100 = ₹ 110

∴ The number of shares bought = $\frac{x}{110}$

Annual income = Number of share × Rate of dividend × Nominal value of one share

$$= \frac{x}{110} \times \frac{8}{100} \times ₹\,100 = ₹\,\frac{4x}{55}$$

For company B,

Nominal value of each share = ₹ 50

Market value of each share = 50 − 12% of ₹ 50 = 50 − 6 = ₹ 44

∴ The number of share bought = $\frac{x}{44}$

Annual income = Number of share × Rate of dividend × Nominal value of each share

$$= \frac{x}{44} \times \frac{7}{100} \times ₹\,50 = ₹\,\frac{7x}{88}$$

∴ Sum of annual income from both companies

$$= ₹\,\frac{4x}{55} + ₹\,\frac{7x}{88} = ₹\left(\frac{4x}{55} + \frac{7x}{88}\right) = ₹\,\frac{x}{11} \times \left(\frac{4}{5} + \frac{7}{8}\right) = ₹\,\frac{x}{11} \times \frac{(32+35)}{40} = ₹\,\frac{67x}{440}$$

According to the question,

$$₹\,\frac{67x}{440} = ₹\,1675$$

$$\Rightarrow \quad 67x = 440 \times 1675$$

$$\Rightarrow \quad x = \frac{440 \times 1675}{67} = 11000$$

Mohit invests ₹ 11000 in each company.

∴ Mohit invests in all = ₹ 11000 + ₹ 11000 = ₹ 22000

Example 27. **Ashok has a choice to invest in ₹ 100 shares of two companies at ₹ 120 each or at ₹ 130 each. The first company pays a dividend of 5% per annum and the second company pays divided of 6% per annum. How much more will his annual return be, if he invests ₹ 15600 with the company from which he gets a better return on his investment.**

Sol. Given, total investment = ₹ 15600

For first company, number of shares = $\frac{15600}{120} = 130$

Annual income = 130 × 5 = ₹ 650

For second company number of shares = $\frac{15600}{130} = 120$

Annual income = 120 × 6 = ₹ 720

Difference in his annual income = ₹ (720 − 650) = ₹ 70

Hence, the investment in second company is better than the investment in the first company.

Chapter Practice

a. 1 Mark Questions

1. Calculate the money required to buy 400 shares, ₹ 20 shares at a premium of ₹ 10.

   (a) ₹ 10000 (b) ₹ 12000
   (c) ₹ 8000 (d) ₹ 15000

2. How much should a man invest in ₹ 80 shares selling at ₹ 80 to obtain an annual income of ₹ 1280, if the dividend declared is 20%?

   (a) ₹ 7000 (b) ₹ 9600 (c) ₹ 6400 (d) ₹ 6000

3. What is the number of shares purchased formula?

   (a) Rate of dividend × Face value of one share × Market value of one share

   (b) $\frac{\text{Annual income}}{\text{Income on one share}}$

   (c) $\frac{\text{Annual income}}{\text{Investment}}$

   (d) None of the above

4. A man invests ₹ 4200 in shares of a company which pay 15% dividend at a time when a ₹ 25 shares cost ₹ 35, find the number of shares he bought.

   (a) 100 (b) 120 (c) 135 (d) 150

5. A man invests ₹ 4500 in 8%, ₹ 10 shares at ₹ 15. He sells the shares, when the price rises to ₹ 30 and invests the proceeds in 12%, ₹ 100 shares at ₹ 125. Calculate the sale proceeds.

   (a) ₹ 8000 (b) ₹ 9000 (c) ₹ 10000 (d) ₹ 15000

b. 3 Marks Questions

6. Find the dividend received on 60 shares of ₹ 20 each, if 9% dividend is declared.

7. A man buys shares at the par value of ₹ 10, yielding 8% dividend at the end of year. Find the number of shares bought, if he receives a dividend of ₹ 300.

8. A man bought 500 shares, each of face value ₹ 10 of a certain business concern and during the first year after purchase, received ₹ 400 as dividend on his shares. Find the rate of dividend on shares.

9. A man invests ₹ 8800 in a company paying 6% dividend, when a share of face value ₹ 100 is selling at ₹ 60 premium. What is the percentage return on his investment?

10. A man invests ₹ 4500 in shares of a company which is paying 7.5% dividend. If ₹ 100 shares are available at a discount of 10%.

    Find

    (i) number of shares he purchases.
    (ii) his annual income.

11. Sachin buys ₹ 100 shares at ₹ 20 premium in a company paying 15% dividend. Find

    (i) the market value of 200 shares.
    (ii) his annual income.
    (iii) his percentage return.

12. A man invests ₹ 22500 in ₹50 shares available at 10% discount. If the dividend paid by the company is 12%, then calculate

    (i) the number of shares purchased.
    (ii) the annual dividend received.
    (iii) the rate of return he gets on his investment. Give your answer correct to the nearest whole number. **[ICSE 2018]**

13. A company with 500 shares of nominal value ₹ 120 declares an annual dividend of 15%. Calculate

    (i) the total amount of dividend paid by the company.
    (ii) annual income of Mr. Sharma who holds 80 shares of the company.
    (iii) if the return percent of Mr. Sharma from his shares is 10%, find the market value of each share.

14. A man invests ₹ 9600 on ₹ 100 shares at ₹ 80. If the company pays him 18% dividend, then find

    (i) the number of shares, he buys.
    (ii) his total dividend.
    (iii) his percentage return on the shares.

    [ICSE 2012]

15. Amit Kumar invests ₹ 36000 in buying ₹ 100 shares at ₹ 20 premium. The dividend is 15% per annum. Find

    (i) the number of shares, he buys.
    (ii) his yearly dividend.
    (iii) the percentage return on his investment.

    Give your answer correct to the nearest whole number.

C. 4/5 Marks Questions

16. How much should a man invest in ₹ 50 shares selling at ₹ 60 to obtain an income of ₹ 450, if the rate of dividend declared is 10%. Also, find his yield percent, to the nearest whole number. [ICSE 2017]

17. What sum should a person invest in ₹ 25 shares, selling at ₹ 36, to obtain an income of ₹ 720, if the dividend declared is 12%? Find
   (i) the number of shares bought by him.
   (ii) the percentage return on his income.

18. Ashok invested ₹ 26400 on 12%, ₹ 25 shares of a company. If he receives a dividend of ₹ 2475, then find the
   (i) number of shares he bought.
   (ii) market value of each share. [ICSE 2016]

19. Mr. Jaipal invested a sum of money in ₹ 250 shares paying 24% dividend and quoted at 20% premium. If the annual dividend received by him is ₹ 6960, then calculate
   (i) total investment.
   (ii) the rate of return on his investment.

20. Karan buys 125 shares of ₹ 100 each of 'Reliance Technologies Ltd,' which pays a dividend of 6%. If his annual income is 4% of his total investment. Then, for what price did Karan buy all the shares?

21. Mr. Somil desires to have an annual income of ₹ 36000 from 18%, ₹ 125 shares available in the market at a premium of 20%. How much should he invest?

22. A company pays a dividend of 15% on its ₹ 10 shares, from which it deducts tax at the rate of 22%. Find the annual income of a man, who owns 1000 shares of this company.

23. Mahesh bought 600 shares of ₹ 50 each of 'Excel Computers'. He sold $\frac{1}{3}$rd of them when they were at a premium of ₹ 20 and the remaining when they were at a discount of ₹ 5. Find his gain or loss in the whole transaction.

24. By purchasing ₹ 25 shares, for ₹ 10 each, a man gets 4% profit on his investment. What rate percent is company paying? What is his dividend, if he buys 80 shares?

25. Smt. Shivangi sells 60, ₹ 15 shares of a company paying 12% dividend, at ₹ 21 each and invests the proceeds in ₹ 6 shares of another company at ₹ 9 each. Find her change in income, if the second company pays a dividend of 8%.

26. A man sells 100, ₹ 25 shares of a company paying 10% dividend, at ₹ 50 each and invests the proceeds in ₹ 5 shares of another company at ₹ 10 each. Find his change in income, if the second company pays a dividend of 6%.

27. Mr. Dubey has 60 shares of nominal value ₹100 and he decides to sell them when they are at a premium of 60%. He invests the proceeds in shares of nominal value ₹ 50, quoted at 4% discount, paying 18% dividend annually. Calculate
   (i) the sale proceeds.
   (ii) the number of shares he buys.
   (iii) his annual dividend from these shares.

28. A company with 10000 shares of nominal value of ₹ 100 declares an annual dividend of 8% to the shareholders. Calculate
   (i) the total amount of dividend paid by the company.
   (ii) Ramesh bought 90 shares of the company at ₹150 per share, then calculate the dividend.
   (iii) Find the percentage return on the investment of Ramesh.

29. Divide ₹ 40608 into two parts such that, if one part is invested in 8%, ₹ 100 shares at 8% discount and the other part is invested in 9%, ₹ 100 shares at 8% premium, annual incomes from both the investments are equal. Find each part of the investments.

30. Two person A and B invest ₹ 18000 each in buying share of two different companies. Person A buys 7.5%, ₹ 100 shares at a discount of 20%, whereas person B buys ₹ 50 shares at a premium of 20%. If both receive equal dividend at the end of the year, then find the rate of dividend received by person B.

31. Jai Prakash wants to invest ₹ 3600. He invests ₹750 in ₹ 100 shares of 3.5% at ₹ 75, ₹ 1050 in ₹ 100 shares of 3% at ₹ 70 and the remaining in ₹ 100 shares of 6%. If his total yield is $5\frac{5}{9}$% of his investment, at what price did he buy the shares of 6%?

32. Pramod wants to invest ₹35000 in shares, such that the percentage return on his investment is $8\frac{1}{7}$%. He invested ₹6000 in 6%, ₹50 shares of 'Lakme' at ₹40, ₹15000 in 8%, ₹100 shares of 'Volta' at ₹125 and the remaining in 12%, ₹150 shares of 'BPL'. At what rate did he buy the 'BPL' shares?

33. Mr. Ghosh sold a certain number of ₹ 20 shares paying 8% dividend at ₹ 18 and invested the proceeds in ₹ 10 shares, paying 12% dividend at 50% premium. If the change in his annual income is ₹ 120, then find the number of shares sold by Mr. Ghosh.

34. Ramesh had ₹100 shares of 'Bihar Steel' paying 8% dividend. He sold them at a market price of ₹130 and invested the proceeds in buying ₹ 50 shares of 'Jindal Steel' available at ₹ 75 and paying 12% dividend. He thus increased his annual income by ₹ 360. How many shares did Ramesh sell?

35. Mihir and Sameer both invested ₹ 90000 each in buying shares of two companies. Mihir invested in buying ₹150 shares of 'ABC Solutions' available at a 20% premium and paying a dividend of 18%. Sameer invested in buying ₹225 shares of 'Mphasis Ltd.' available at a 20% discount and paying a dividend of 16%. Whose investment is better?

36. Ahmad had 1000 shares of a company with a face value of ₹ 50 and paying 10% dividend. He sold some of these shares at a discount of 10% and invested the proceeds in ₹ 20 shares at a premium of 50% and paying 10% dividend. If the changes in his income is ₹ 200, then find the number of shares sold by Ahmad.

37. Mr. Gupta has a choice to invest in ₹ 10 shares of two firms at ₹13 or at ₹16. If the first firm pays 5% dividend and the second firm pays 6% dividend per annum, then find
(i) which firm is paying better?
(ii) how much, in all, does Mr. Gupta invest, if he invests equally in both the firms and the difference between the returns from them is ₹30?

d. 6 Marks Questions

38. Mamta and Sonia invested equal amounts in buying shares of two different companies. Mamta bought shares of Hindalco paying a dividend of 14% on its ₹125 share available in the market for ₹140, while Sonia bought shares of HLL paying a dividend of 13% on its ₹300 share available in the market for ₹260. If Sonia's annual income is ₹1820 more than that of Mamta, then find the amount invested by each of them.

39. Vishal wants to invest ₹ 27000 in buying shares. The shares of the following companies are available to him: ₹ 100 shares of company A at par value;
₹ 100 shares of company B at a premium of ₹ 25;
₹ 100 shares of company C at a discount of ₹ 10;
₹ 50 shares of company D at a premium of 20%.
Find how many shares will he get, if he buys shares of company
(i) A?
(ii) B?
(iii) C?
(iv) D?

40. Amit and Richa invest ₹ 12000 each in buying shares of two companies. Amit buys 15%, ₹100 shares at a discount of ₹ 20, while Richa buys ₹ 25 shares at a premium of 20%. If both receive equal dividends at the end of the year, then find the rate percent of the dividend declared by Richa's company.

41. Salman buys 50 shares of face value ₹ 100 available at ₹ 132.
(i) What is his investment?
(ii) If the dividend is 7.5%, then what will be his annual income?
(iii) If he wants to increase his annual income by ₹ 150, then how many extra shares should he buy? **[ICSE 2013]**

42. Bhavna invested ₹ 20000 and ₹ 25000 in buying shares of 'Bharti Telecom' and 'Satyam Infoways', which later declared dividends of 10% and 12.5%, respectively. After collecting the dividends, Bhavna sells all her shares at a loss of 4% and 5% respectively on her investments. Find her total earning.

43. Niharika invested her savings in the following manner:
25% of her savings in 12%, ₹ 100 shares available at 25% premium, 25% of her savings in 20%, ₹200 shares available at 25% premium and the balance in 18%, ₹ 50 shares available at 50% premium. If her total earning from all these shares is ₹ 26350, then calculate her total savings and the investment made in each.

Hints and Answers

1. (b) **Hint** Number of shares to be bought = 400

Market value of one share = ₹ 20 + ₹ 10 = ₹ 30

∴ Money required to buy 1 share = ₹ 30

Money required to buy 400 share = 400 × 30 = ₹ 12000

2. (c) **Hint** Dividend on one share 20% of ₹ 80 = ₹ 16

∴ Number of shares bought

$$= \frac{\text{Total dividend}}{\text{Dividend on one share}}$$

$$= \frac{1280}{16} = 80$$

Market value of each share = ₹ 80

Total invested by the man = 80 × 80 = ₹ 6400

3. (b) $\dfrac{\text{Annual income}}{\text{Income on one share}}$

4. (b) **Hint** The number of shares bought

$$= \frac{4200}{35} = 120$$

5. (b) **Hint** Given, money invested = ₹ 4500

Nominal value of one share = ₹ 10

Market value of one share = ₹ 15

∴ Number of shares he bought

$$= \frac{\text{Money invested}}{\text{Market value of one share}}$$

$$= \frac{4500}{15} = 300$$

∴ Total nominal value = Number of shares × Nominal value of one share = 300 × 10 = ₹ 3000

Annual dividend = $\dfrac{8}{100}$ × 3000 = ₹ 240

∴ Sale proceeds = Number of shares × Market value = 300 × 30 = ₹ 9000

6. **Hint** Dividend on one share = 9% of 20

Ans. ₹ 108

7. **Hint** Dividend = Number of shares × $\dfrac{8}{100}$ × 10

Ans. 375

8. **Hint** Here, total face value of shares = ₹ 5000 and dividend on 500 shares = ₹ 400

∴ Rate of dividend = $\left(\dfrac{400}{5000} \times 100\right)$%

Ans. 8%

9. **Hint** Market value of 1 share = 100 + 60 = ₹160

∴ Total number of shares bought

$$= \frac{\text{Total investment}}{\text{Investment on one share}}$$

Ans. 3.75%

10. **Hint** Given, total investment = ₹ 4500 and rate of dividend = 7.5%

(i) Nominal value of one share = ₹ 100 − 10% of 100 = 100 − 10 = ₹ 90

∴ Number of shares, he purchases = $\dfrac{4500}{90}$

Ans. 50

(ii) ∴ Annual income = Number of shares × Nominal value of share × Rate of dividend = 50 × 90 × 7.5 = ₹ 33750 **Ans.** ₹ 337.5

11. **Hint**

(i) Market value of one share = 100 + 20 = ₹120

(ii) ∴ Annual income = Number of shares × $\dfrac{\text{Rate of dividend}}{100}$ × Nominal value of one share

(iii) ∴ Percentage return = $\left(\dfrac{\text{Annual income}}{\text{Total investment}} \times 100\right)$%

Ans. (i) ₹ 24000 (ii) ₹ 3000 (iii) 12.5%

12. **Hint**

(i) Number of shares purchased = $\dfrac{\text{Total investment}}{\text{Issued price of each share}}$

(ii) Annual dividend = Number of shares purchased × Face value of a share × Rate of dividend/100

(iii) Rate of return = $\left(\dfrac{\text{Dividend}}{\text{Invested amount}} \times 100\right)$%

Ans. (i) 500 (ii) ₹ 3000 (iii) 13%

13. **Hint** Given, nominal value of one share = ₹ 120

Annual dividend = 15%

(i) Total amount of dividend = Number of shares × $\dfrac{\text{Rate of dividend}}{100}$ × Nominal value of one share

$$= 500 \times \frac{15}{100} \times 120$$

Ans. ₹ 9000

(ii) Annual income of Mr. Sharma = 80 × Dividend on one share

$$= 80 \times \frac{9000}{500}$$

Ans. ₹ 1440

(iii) Let the market value of one share be ₹ x.

The profit on one share = 10% of ₹ x = ₹ $\dfrac{x}{10}$

Since, the dividend paid on one share

$= ₹ \frac{9000}{500}$

$\therefore \frac{x}{10} = \frac{9000}{500}$

Ans. ₹ 180

14. Hint

(i) Number of shares

$= \frac{\text{Money invested}}{\text{Market value of one share}}$

(ii) Total dividend (annual income)

$= \text{Number of shares} \times \frac{\text{Rate of dividend}}{100} \times \text{Nominal value of one share}$

(iii) Percentage return

$= \left(\frac{\text{Annual income}}{\text{Investment}} \times 100\right)\%$

Ans. (i) 120 (ii) ₹ 2160 (iii) 22.5%

15. Hint (i) Number of shares

$= \frac{\text{Money invested}}{\text{Market value of one share}}$

(ii) Yearly dividend = Number of shares

$\times \frac{\text{Rate of dividend}}{100} \times \text{Nominal value of one share}$

(iii) Percentage return $= \left(\frac{\text{Annual dividend}}{\text{Investment}} \times 100\right)\%$

Ans. (i) 300 (ii) ₹ 4500 (iii) 12%

16. Hint

$\because$ Number of shares $= \frac{\text{Total dividend amount}}{\text{Dividend on one share}}$

$= \frac{450}{\frac{10}{100} \times 50} = 90$

$\therefore$ Total investment for 90 shares $= 90 \times 60$

Yield percent $= \left(\frac{\text{Annual income}}{\text{Investment}} \times 100\right)\%$

Ans. Total investment = ₹ 5400

and yield percent = 8%

17. Hint

(i) $\because$ Number of shares $= \frac{\text{Total dividend amount}}{\text{Dividend on one share}}$

(ii) Percentage return

$= \left(\frac{\text{Annual income}}{\text{Investment}} \times 100\right)\%$

Ans. (i) 240 (ii) $8\frac{1}{3}\%$

18. Hint

(i) Dividend = Number of shares $\times \frac{12}{100} \times 25$

(ii) Market price of share $= \frac{\text{Investment}}{\text{Number of shares}}$

Ans. (i) 825 (ii) ₹ 32

19. Hint Do same as Example 12.

Ans. (i) ₹ 34800 (ii) 20%

20. Hint Dividend $= 125 \times \frac{6}{100} \times 100 = ₹ 750$

$\because$ Annual income = 4% of total investment

$\therefore 750 = \frac{4}{100} \times \text{Total investment}$

Ans. ₹ 18750

21. Hint Do same as Example 12. **Ans.** ₹ 240000

22. Hint Dividend $= 1000 \times \frac{15}{100} \times 10 = ₹1500$

Annual income $= ₹\left(1500 - \frac{22}{100} \times 1500\right)$

Ans. ₹ 1170

23. Hint Number of shares = 600

Face value of one share = ₹ 50

$\Rightarrow$ Investment $= 600 \times 50 = ₹ 30000$

Selling price of a share at premium

$= 50 + 20 = ₹ 70$

Number of share sold at this rate $= \frac{1}{3}$ of 600

$= 200$

Amount received on selling 200 shares at ₹ 70

$= 70 \times 200 = ₹14000$

Selling price of a share at discount

$= 50 - 5 = ₹ 45$

Number of share sold at this rate

$= 600 - 200 = 400$

Amount received on selling 400 shares at ₹ 45

$= 45 \times 400 = ₹18000$

Total amount obtain $= 14000 + 18000 = ₹ 32000$

$\because$ Amount invested = ₹ 30000

$\therefore$ Gain in total transaction $= 32000 - 30000$

Ans. Gain of ₹ 2000

24. Hint Dividend on one share = 4% of ₹ 10

$= \frac{4}{100} \times 10$

$\therefore$ Rate of dividend $= \frac{\text{Dividend on one share}}{\text{Nominal value of one share}} \times 100$

Ans. 1.6% and ₹ 32

25. Hint Case I

Income on 1 share = 12% of ₹ 15 = ₹ 1.80

$\Rightarrow$ Total income $= 60 \times ₹1.80 = ₹108$

Now, she sells all the shares for ₹ 21 each.

$\therefore$ Money obtained by selling all the 60 shares

$= 60 \times ₹ 21 = ₹1260$

Case II

Sum invested = ₹ 1260

$\therefore$ Number of shares bought

$= \frac{\text{Sum invested}}{\text{Market value of 1 share}}$

$= \frac{1260}{90} = 140$

and dividend on 1 share = 8% of ₹ 6 = ₹ 0.48

Total income = 140 × ₹ 0.48 = ₹ 67.20

∴ Change in income = ₹ 108 − ₹ 67.20

Ans. ₹ 40.80

26. Hint Do same as Q. 25. **Ans.** ₹ 100

27. Hint Do same as Example 13.

Ans. (i) ₹ 9600 (ii) 200 (iii) ₹1800

28. Hint

(i) Total dividend = Number of shares $\times \frac{\text{Rate of dividend}}{100}$ × Nominal value of one share

(ii) Dividend on 90 shares = 90 × Dividend on one share

(iii) Percentage return

$$= \left(\frac{\text{Dividend}}{\text{Investment}} \times 100\right)\% = \left(\frac{720}{90 \times 150} \times 100\right)\%$$

Ans. (i) ₹ 8000 (ii) ₹ 720 (iii) $5\frac{1}{3}\%$

29. Hint Let the two parts be ₹ x and ₹ $(40608 - x)$.

For first part,

Market value of each share = ₹100 − 8% of ₹100 = ₹ 92

∴ Number of shares bought $= \frac{x}{92}$

⇒ Total dividend = Number of shares $\times \frac{\text{Rate of dividend}}{100}$ × Face value of one share

$$= \frac{2x}{23}$$

For second part,

Investment = ₹(40608 − x)

Market value of each share = ₹100 + 8% of ₹100 = ₹108

∴ Number of shares bought $= \frac{40608 - x}{108}$

⇒ Total dividend $= \frac{40608 - x}{108} \times \frac{9}{100} \times 100$

$$= ₹\left(\frac{40608 - x}{12}\right)$$

$$\therefore \quad \frac{2x}{23} = \frac{40608 - x}{12}$$

Ans. ₹19872 and ₹ 20736

30. Hint Market value of each shares = ₹ 100 − 20% of ₹ 100 = ₹ 80

∴ Number of share bought $= \frac{₹\,18000}{₹\,80} = 225$

∴ Dividend on one share = 7.5% of ₹ 100 = ₹ 7.50

∴ Total dividend received = 225 × ₹ 7.5 = ₹ 1687.50

Now, For person A

Nominal value of each share = ₹ 50

Market value of each share = ₹ 50 + 20% of ₹ 50 = ₹ 60

Number of shares bought $= \frac{₹\,18000}{₹\,60} = 300$

⇒ Total dividend received by A = Total dividend received by B = ₹ 1687.50

⇒ Dividend on 300 shares = ₹ 1687.50

Dividend on each share $= \frac{₹\,1687.50}{300} = ₹\,\frac{45}{8}$

⇒ Rate of dividend $= \frac{45}{8 \times 50} \times 100\%$ **Ans.** 11.25%

31. Hint

(i) Number of shares of 3.5% $= \frac{750}{75} = 10$

∴ Annual income from 3.5% shares $= 10 \times 100 \times \frac{3.5}{100} = ₹\,35$

(ii) Number of shares of 3% $= \frac{1050}{70} = 15$

∴ Annual income from 3% shares $= 15 \times 100 \times \frac{3}{100} = ₹\,45$

(iii) ∵ Annual income = Number of shares × Face value of one share $\times \frac{\text{Rate of dividend}}{100}$

∴ Number of shares of 6% = 20

Now, market price of 6% shares $= \frac{\text{Investment}}{\text{Number of shares}}$

Ans. ₹ 90 per share

32. Hint Do same as Q. 31.

Ans. ₹175 per share

33. Hint Let the number of shares sold by Mr. Ghosh be x.

∴ Total income on x shares = 8% of ₹ 20 × x.

As Mr. Ghosh invested the proceed, i.e. ₹$18x$ in ₹10 shares at 50% premium and market value of each share

= ₹(10 + 50% of ₹10) = ₹15

∴ Number of new shares bought $= \frac{18x}{15} = \frac{6x}{5}$

Now, change (loss) in income = Total income on x shares − Total income on new shares

Ans. 750

34. Hint Let the number of shares sold by Ramesh be x.

∴ Number of shares bought

$$= \frac{\text{Sum invested}}{\text{Market value of each share}} = \frac{26}{15}x$$

Now, total dividend received $= \frac{26}{15}x \times \frac{12}{100} \times 50 = ₹\,\frac{52}{5}x$

Given, change in income = ₹ 360

$$\Rightarrow \quad \frac{52}{5}x - 8x = 360$$ **Ans.** 150

35. **Hint** Income from 'ABC solution'

$= \text{Number of shares} \times \frac{\text{Rate of dividend}}{100} \times \text{Face value of one share}$

Income from 'Mphasis Ltd.'

$= \left(\frac{90000}{180}\right) \times \frac{16}{100} \times 225$

Ans. Sameer's investment is better.

36. **Hint** Let the number of shares sold by Ahmad be x.

Case I Dividend on each share = 10% of ₹ 50 = ₹ 5

∴ Dividend on x shares = ₹ $5x$

Selling price of each share = ₹ 50 − 10% of ₹ 50 = ₹ 45

Thus, money obtained by selling x shares = ₹ $45x$

Case II Sum invested = ₹ $45x$

Market value of each share = ₹ 20 + 50% of ₹ 20 = ₹ 30

∴ Number of shares bought

$= \frac{\text{Sum invested}}{\text{Market value of each share}} = \frac{45x}{30} = \frac{3x}{2}$

Now, total dividend received = Dividend on one share × Number of shares = ₹ $3x$

Given, change in income = ₹ 200

∴ $5x - 3x = 200$ **Ans.** 100

37. **Hint**

(i) Let the investment in each case be ₹(13 × 16).

Then, income from each firm

$= \text{Number of shares} \times \frac{\text{Rate of dividend}}{100} \times \text{Face value of one share}$

(ii) Let Mr. Gupta invest ₹ x in each firm.

Then, $\frac{x}{13} \times \frac{5}{100} \times 10 - \frac{x}{16} \times \frac{6}{100} \times 10 = 30$

Ans. (i) First firm (ii) ₹ 62400

38. **Hint** Let the investment in each case be ₹ x.

Then, Mamta's income $= \frac{x}{140} \times \frac{14}{100} \times 125 = \frac{x}{8}$

and Sonia's income $= \frac{x}{260} \times \frac{13}{100} \times 300 = \frac{3x}{20}$

According to given condition, we have

$\frac{3x}{20} = 1820 + \frac{x}{8}$ **Ans.** ₹ 72800

39. **Hint**

(i) Market value of a share of company A = ₹100

∴ Number of shares of company A

$= \frac{\text{Investment}}{\text{Market value of one share}}$

(ii) Market value of a share of company B

= 100 + 25 = ₹125

(iii) Market value of a share of company C

= 100 − 10 = ₹ 90

(iv) Market value of a share of company D

= ₹ 50 + 20% of ₹ 50 = ₹ 60

Ans. (i) 270 (ii) 216 (iii) 300 (iv) 450

40. **Hint** Annual dividend received by Amit

$= \text{Number of shares held by Amit} \times \frac{\text{Rate of dividend}}{100} \times \text{Face value of one share} = ₹\,2250$

∴ Annual dividend received by Richa = ₹ 2250

∴ Number of shares purchased by Richa

$= \frac{\text{Total invested amount by Richa}}{\text{Market value of one share purchased by Richa}}$

$= \frac{12000}{30} = 400$

Let r% be the rate of dividend declared by Richa company.

Then, $2250 = 400 \times \frac{r}{100} \times 25$

Ans. 22.5%

41. **Hint**

(i) Salman's investment in shares

= Market value of one share × Number of shares

= 132 × 50

(ii) Annual income

$= \text{Number of shares} \times \frac{\text{Rate of dividend}}{100} \times \text{Face value of one share}$

= ₹ 375

(iii) Let extra share he buys be x.

Then, total number of shares = 50 + x

According to the question, Salman's annual income increased by ₹150.

∴ $(50 + x) \times 7.5 = 375 + 150$

Ans. (i) ₹ 6600 (ii) ₹ 375 (iii) 20

42. **Hint** Dividend received at 10%

$= \frac{20000 \times 10}{100} = ₹\,2000$

Dividend received at 12.5%

$= \frac{25000 \times 12.5}{100} = ₹\,3125$

Amount at a loss of 4% $= \frac{20000 \times 4}{100} = ₹\,800$

Amount at a loss of 5% $= \frac{25000 \times 5}{100} = ₹\,1250$

Net earning = Total amount of dividends received − Total amount of loss

= [2000 + 3125] − [800 + 1250]

Ans. ₹ 3075

43. **Hint** Do same as Example 23.

Ans. Total savings = ₹ 212500

Investment in first company = ₹ 53125

Investment in second company = ₹ 53125

Investment in third company = ₹ 106250

Olympiad Section

Brain Teasing Questions of Olympiad Pattern

1. Which of the following is a better investment?
   (i) 10%, ₹ 100 shares at ₹ 120
   (ii) 9%, ₹ 100 shares at ₹ 110
   (a) Only (i) (b) Only (ii)
   (c) Both (i) and (ii) (d) Data insufficient

2. The total investment made in buying ₹ X shares at a premium of 25% is ₹ $125X$. The number of shares bought is
   (a) 500 (b) 250
   (c) 125 (d) 100

3. Ms. Shriya invested some amount buying ₹ 150 shares of a company which pays dividend at the rate of 8% per annum. If she gets back 10% per annum on his investment, then the value at which she bought the share, is
   (a) ₹ 100 (b) ₹ 120
   (c) ₹ 180 (d) ₹ 210

4. If ₹ 25000 more invested, then 400 more shares can be purchased. The market value of each share is
   (a) ₹ 62.50 (b) ₹ 77.50
   (c) ₹ 85.00 (d) Can't be determined

5. Mr. Anil bought ₹ 110 shares of a company at a discount of ₹ 10. If the company pays a dividend at the rate of x% per annum and Mr. Anil earns at the rate of y% per annum on his investment, then $x:y$ is
   (a) 10 : 9 (b) 9 : 10
   (c) 11 : 10 (d) 10 : 11

6. Ms. Neelam made an investment of ₹ 27000 in 10%, ₹ 100 shares at ₹ 90, while Mr. Ram made an investment of ₹ 30000 in 8%, ₹ 150 shares at ₹ 120. If both of them have sold their shares at the end of a year for ₹ 110 each, then their individual earnings are, respectively
   (a) ₹ 9000 and ₹ 500
   (b) ₹ 500 and ₹ 9000
   (c) ₹ 9000 and ₹ 9000
   (d) None of the above

7. Ram invested ₹ 54000 in 18%, ₹ 200 shares of Jindal Electronics. He bought them at a rate such that the percentage return on his investment is 16%. Later he sold them, when the market price was ₹ 275 and invested the proceeds in buying 24%, ₹ 100 shares of Golmal Entertainment. If his annual income increased by ₹ 1920, then the rate, at which he bought the Golmal Entertainment shares is
   (a) ₹ 120 (b) ₹ 180
   (c) ₹ 150 (d) ₹ 160

8. A man has choice to invest in ₹ 100 shares of two companies X and Y. Shares of company X are available at a premium of 20% and it pays 5% dividend whereas shares of company Y are available at a discount of 10% and it pays 7% dividend. If the man invests equally in both the companies and the sum of the returns from them is ₹1290, then find how much in all does he invest?
   (a) ₹ 20000 (b) ₹ 21000
   (c) ₹ 21500 (d) ₹ 21600

Answers

1. (a)	**2.** (d)	**3.** (b)	**4.** (a)	**5.** (d)	**6.** (a)	**7.** (c)	**8.** (d)

* *These questions may or may not be asked in the examination, have been given just for additional practice required for olympiads Scholarship Exams etc. For detailed explanations refer Page No. 476.*

CHAPTER

04

Linear Inequations

SYLLABUS

- **Linear Inequations in one unknown for $x \in N, W, Z, R$. Solving**
  (I) Algebraically and writing the solution in set notation form
  (ii) Representation of solution on the number line.

In earlier classes, we studied about such quantities, which are bigger (greater) or smaller (lesser) with respect to each other or any third quantity. Between any two quantities (say x and y) in the universe only three conditions hold, which are '<' (less than), '>' (greater than) and '=' (equal to) i.e. $x < y$, $x > y$ and $x = y$. The symbols '>', '<', '≥' and '≤' are called the sign of inequality or inequation.

In this chapter, we will study about the solution of inequations in one variable and their representation on number line.

Solving the Linear Inequations Algebraically

Inequality or Inequation

We can define inequations as a statement involving variable(s) and the sign of inequality <, >, ≤ or ≥.

Or

Two real numbers or two algebraic expressions related by the symbols < (less than), > (greater than), ≤ (less than or equal to) and ≥ (greater than or equal to) form an inequality.

Inequalities Among Real Numbers

Let x and y be any real numbers, then

(i) **'x is less than y'** is written as $x < y$. It is possible, if and only if $y - x$ is positive. e.g.,

(a) $5 < 8$. Here, $8 - 5 = 3$, which is positive.

(b) $-4 < -3$. Here, $-3-(-4) = -3+4 = 1$, which is positive.

(c) $\frac{3}{4} < \frac{6}{5}$. Here, $\frac{6}{5} - \frac{3}{4} = \frac{24-15}{20} = \frac{9}{20}$, which is positive.

(ii) **'x is less than or equal to y'** is written as $x \le y$. It is possible, if and only if $y - x$ is either positive or zero. For example,

(a) $-3 \le 5$. Here, $5-(-3) = 5+3 = 8$, which is positive.

(b) $\frac{3}{7} \le \frac{3}{7}$. Here, $\frac{3}{7} - \frac{3}{7} = 0$.

(iii) **'x is greater than y'** is written as $x > y$. It is possible, if and only if $x - y$ is positive. For example,

(a) $7 > 3$. Here, $7 - 3 = 4$, which is positive.

(b) $-3 > -4$. Here, $-3-(-4) = 1$, which is positive.

(iv) **'x is greater than or equal to y'** is written as $x \ge y$. It is possible, if and only if $x - y$ is either positive or zero. For example,

(a) $5 \ge -2$. Here, $5-(-2) = 7$, which is positive.

(b) $\frac{2}{7} \ge \frac{2}{7}$. Here, $\frac{2}{7} - \frac{2}{7} = 0$.

Example 1. Express the relation between the following numbers with the help of inequality and verify it.

(i) 5 and 7 (ii) $\frac{4}{5}$ and $\frac{1}{5}$

(iii) -7 and -3 (iv) 4 and -8

Sol.

(i) Given, numbers are 5 and 7.

We know that 7 is always greater than 5.

$\therefore \quad 7 > 5$

Verification $7 - 5 = 2$, which is positive.

(ii) Given, rational numbers are $\frac{4}{5}$ and $\frac{1}{5}$.

We know that if denominators of two fractions are same, then fraction having greater numerator is greater.

$\therefore \quad \frac{4}{5} > \frac{1}{5}$

Verification $\frac{4}{5} - \frac{1}{5} = \frac{4-1}{5} = \frac{3}{5}$, which is positive.

(iii) Given, numbers are -7 and -3.

We know that -3 is always greater than -7.

$\therefore \quad -3 > -7$

Verification $-3 - (-7) = -3 + 7 = 4$, which is positive.

(iv) Given, numbers are 4 and -8.

We know that 4 is always greater than -8.

$\therefore \quad 4 > -8$

Verification $4 - (-8) = 4 + 8 = 12$, which is positive.

Linear Inequality (Inequation)

An inequation is said to be linear, if and only if exponent of each variable occurring in it is one (or each variable occurs in first degree only) and there is no term involving the product of the variables.

e.g. $ax + b \le 0$, $ax + by + c > 0$, $ax \le 5$, $by \ge 10$, etc.

Linear Inequation in One Variable

A linear inequation, which has only one variable, is called linear inequation in one variable and can be written as

$ax + b < 0$ or $ax + b > 0$ or $ax + b \le 0$ or $ax + b \ge 0$, where a and b are real numbers and $a \ne 0$.

Example 2. Identify, which of the following is linear inequation in one variable?

(i) $ax + 4 \ge 3 + ay$ (ii) $4x + 7 \ge 2$

(iii) $3y + 8 > 5 + y$ (iv) $3x < 7y$

Sol.

(i) Given, $ax + 4 \ge 3 + ay$ is a linear inequation but it is not linear inequation in one variable because it has two variables i.e. x and y.

(ii) Given, $4x + 7 \ge 2$ is a linear inequation in one variable because it has only one variable i.e. x.

(iii) Given, $3y + 8 > 5 + y$ is a linear inequation in one variable because it has only one variable i.e. y.

(iv) Given, $3x < 7y$ is a linear inequation but it is not linear inequation in one variable because it has two variables i.e. x and y.

Replacement and Solution Sets

The set, from which values of the variable involved in the inequality are chosen, is called the **replacement set**. Generally, we use either N (set of natural numbers; 1, 2, 3, 4, ...) or W (set of whole numbers; 0, 1, 2, 3, ...) or I (set of integers; ... $-3, -2, -1, 0, 1, 2, 3$, ...) or R (real number) as the replacement set.

Also, the solution to an inequation is a number, which, when substituted for the variable, makes the inequation true and the set of all solutions of the given inequation is called the **solution set** of the inequation. Solution set is the subset of replacement set.

Example 3. If {1, 2, 3, 4, 5, 6, 7, 8, 9, 10, 11} is the replacement set, then find the solution set of the inequality $x > 5$.

Sol. Given, $x > 5$

$\therefore$ The solution set is {6, 7, 8, 9, 10, 11}.

Example 4. If {$-3, -2, -1, 0, 1, 2, 3, 4, 5$} is the replacement set, then find the solution set of $x \le 3$.

Sol. Given, $x \le 3$

$\therefore$ The solution set is {$-3, -2, -1, 0, 1, 2, 3$}.

Example 5. If {$-8, -7, -6, -5, -4, -3, -2, -1, 0, 1, 2, 3$} is the replacement set, then find the solution set of the inequality $x > 5$.

Sol. Given, $x > 5$

$\therefore$ The solution set is ϕ.

Rules for Solving Linear Inequations in One Variable

Some rules for solving linear inequations in one variable are given below

(i) **Addition** (or Subtraction) **Rule** Equal numbers or expressions may be added to or subtracted from both sides of an inequation, produces an equivalent inequation.

e.g. $x - 3 > 4$ is equivalent to $x - 3 + 2 > 4 + 2$

or $x + 3 > 5$ is equivalent to $x + 3 - 1 > 5 - 1$

(ii) **Multiplication** (or Division) **Rule** There are following two types of multiplication (or division) rule

(a) Multiplication (or division) on both sides of an inequation with same positive number produces an equivalent inequation.

e.g. $\frac{x}{7} > 2$ is equivalent to $\frac{x}{7} \times 7 > 2 \times 7$

or $5x < 6$ is equivalent to $\frac{5x}{5} < \frac{6}{5}$.

(b) Multiplication (or division) on both sides of an inequation with same negative number produces an equivalent inequation, if the symbol of inequality is reversed.

e.g. $x > 9$ is equivalent to $(-1) \cdot (x) < (9) \cdot (-1)$.

or $3x > 2$ is equivalent to $\frac{3x}{(-2)} < \frac{2}{(-2)}$

(iii) If $ax + b > c$, then it can be written as $c < ax + b$.

(iv) If $x > y$, then $\frac{1}{x} < \frac{1}{y}$ and if $x < y$, then $\frac{1}{x} > \frac{1}{y}$.

(v) The square root of any real number is always greater than or equal to zero.

(vi) If y and t are of same sign, then

$\frac{x}{y} > \frac{s}{t} \Rightarrow \frac{y}{x} < \frac{t}{s}$ or $xt > sy$

and $\frac{x}{y} < \frac{s}{t} \Rightarrow \frac{y}{x} > \frac{t}{s}$ or $xt < sy$.

(vii) If a, b, c and d are four real numbers such that

(a) $a > b$ and $c > d$, then $a \pm c > b \pm d$.

(b) $a < b$ and $c < d$, then $a \pm c < b \pm d$.

Example 6. Show that the sign of inequality remains same, if we add and subtract 3 and 2, respectively from the following inequalities.

(i) $7 < 10$ (ii) $-5 > -7$

Sol.

(i) Given, $7 < 10 \Rightarrow 7 + 3 < 10 + 3$ [adding 3 on both sides]

$\Rightarrow 10 < 13 \Rightarrow 10 - 2 < 13 - 2$ [subtracting 2 from both sides]

$\Rightarrow 8 < 11$, which is true.

Hence, the sign of the given inequality remains same.

(ii) Given, $-5 > -7$

$\Rightarrow -5 + 3 > -7 + 3$ [adding 3 on both sides]

$\Rightarrow -2 > -4$

$\Rightarrow -2 - 2 > -4 - 2$ [subtracting 2 from both sides]

$\Rightarrow -4 > -6$, which is true.

Hence, the sign of the given inequality remains same.

Example 7. Show that the sign of inequality remains same, if we multiply and divide the inequality $15 > 6$ by 2 and 6, respectively.

Sol. Given, inequality is

$15 > 6$

$\Rightarrow 15 \times 2 > 6 \times 2$ [multiplying both sides by 2]

$\Rightarrow 30 > 12$

$\Rightarrow \frac{30}{6} > \frac{12}{6}$ [dividing both sides by 6]

$\Rightarrow 5 > 2$, which is true.

Hence, this shows that the sign of inequality remains same, if we multiply or divide on both sides of inequality by same positive number.

Example 8. Check whether the sign of inequality $7 < 14$ changes, if divide by negative number (say) -7.

Sol. We have, $7 < 14$

On dividing both sides by -7, we get

$\frac{7}{(-7)} > \frac{14}{(-7)} \Rightarrow -1 > -2$, which is true.

Hence, this shows that the sign of inequality changes, when both sides of the inequality divided by same negative number.

Example 9. Check, which of the following inequalities are correct?

(i) If $a > b$, then $3a + 4 < 3b + 2$.

(ii) If $x > y$, then $2x + 5 > 2y + 4$.

(iii) If $5x \geq 4$ and $7y \leq 4$, then $5x = 7y$.

(iv) If $\frac{4}{x} > \frac{3}{y}$, then $\frac{x}{4} > \frac{y}{3}$.

Sol.

(i) Given, $a > b$

$\Rightarrow 3a > 3b$ [multiplying both sides by 3]

We know that, $4 > 2$

$\therefore 3a + 4 > 3b + 2$

But $3a + 4 < 3b + 2$ is given in the question.

Hence, the given statement is incorrect.

(ii) Given, $x > y \Rightarrow 2x > 2y$ [multiplying both sides by 2]

We know that $5 > 4$

$\therefore 2x + 5 > 2y + 4$

Hence, this statement is correct.

(iii) Given, $5x \geq 4$ and $7y \leq 4$

$\therefore 7y \leq 4 \leq 5x$

$\Rightarrow 7y \leq 5x$

Hence, the given statement is incorrect.

(iv) Given, $\frac{4}{x} > \frac{3}{y}$ and its reciprocal is $\frac{x}{4} < \frac{y}{3}$.

Hence, the given statement is not incorrect.

Example 10. Write the solution of the following inequation in the set notation form $5x - 10 \leq 2x + 2$.

Sol. Given, $5x - 10 \leq 2x + 2$

$\Rightarrow 5x - 10 + 10 \leq 2x + 2 + 10$ [adding 10 on both sides]

$\Rightarrow 5x \leq 2x + 12 \Rightarrow 5x - 2x \leq 2x + 12 - 2x$ [subtracting $2x$ from both sides]

$\Rightarrow 3x \leq 12 \Rightarrow \frac{3x}{3} \leq \frac{12}{3}$ [dividing both sides by 3]

$\Rightarrow x \leq 4$

Hence, the solution set is $\{x : x \leq 4, x \in R\}$ or $(-\infty, 4]$.

Example 11. Rohit needs a minimum of 360 marks in four tests in a Mathematics course to obtain an A grade. On his first three tests, he scored 88, 96, 79 marks. What should his score be in the fourth test, so that he can make an A grade?

Sol. Let Rohit score x marks in the fourth test. Then, the sum of Rohit's test scores should be greater than or equal to 360

i.e. $88 + 96 + 79 + x \geq 360 \Rightarrow 263 + x \geq 360$

$\Rightarrow \quad 263 + x - 263 \geq 360 - 263$ [subtracting 263 from both sides]

$\Rightarrow \quad x \geq 97$

Hence, Rohit should score 97 marks or more than 97 marks in the fourth test to obtain A grade.

Example 12. An integer is such that one-third of the next integer is atleast 2 more than one-fourth of the previous integer. Find the smallest value of the integer.

Sol. Let the integer be x, then one-third of the next integer is $\frac{x+1}{3}$ and one-fourth of the previous integer is $\frac{x-1}{4}$.

According to the question,

$$\frac{x+1}{3} \geq \frac{x-1}{4} + 2$$

$\Rightarrow \quad \frac{12(x+1)}{3} \geq \frac{12(x-1)}{4} + 2 \times 12$ [multiplying both sides by 12]

$\Rightarrow \quad 4(x+1) \geq 3(x-1) + 24$

$\Rightarrow \quad 4x + 4 \geq 3x - 3 + 24$

$\Rightarrow \quad 4x + 4 - (3x + 4) \geq 3x + 21 - (3x + 4)$ [subtracting $(3x + 4)$ from both sides]

$\Rightarrow \quad 4x + 4 - 3x - 4 \geq 3x + 21 - 3x - 4$

$\Rightarrow \quad x \geq 17$

Hence, the smallest value of x is 17.

Example 13. If P is the solution set of $8x - 1 > 5x + 2$ and Q is the solution set of $7x - 2 \geq 3(x + 6)$, where $x \in N$. Find the set $P \cap Q$.

Sol. Given, $8x - 1 > 5x + 2$

$\Rightarrow \quad 8x - 1 + (-5x + 1) > 5x + 2 + (-5x + 1)$ [adding $(-5x + 1)$ on both sides]

$\Rightarrow \quad 3x > 3 \Rightarrow x > 1$ [dividing both sides by 3]

But $x \in N$

$\therefore \quad P = \{2, 3, 4, 5, \ldots\}$

Also, $7x - 2 \geq 3(x + 6) \Rightarrow 7x - 2 \geq 3x + 18$

$\Rightarrow \quad 7x - 2 + (-3x + 2) \geq 3x + 18 + (-3x + 2)$ [adding $(-3x + 2)$ on both sides]

$\Rightarrow \quad 4x \geq 20 \Rightarrow x \geq 5$ [dividing both sides by 4]

But $x \in N$

$\therefore \quad Q = \{5, 6, 7, 8, \ldots\}$

Hence, the set $P \cap Q$ is $\{5, 6, 7, 8, \ldots\}$.

Representation of Solution Set of Linear Inequation in One Variable on the Number Line

We can represent the solution of a linear inequation in one variable on the number line.

(i) If the inequation involves $\geq$ or $\leq$, then draw filled circle or dark circle (•) on the number line to show that the number corresponding to the filled circle or dark circle is included in the solution set.

(ii) If the inequation involves $>$ or $<$, then draw unfilled circle or blank circle (◦) on the number line to show that the number corresponding to the unfilled circle or blank circle is excluded from the solution set.

Example 14. Solve the inequation $37 - (3x + 5) \geq 9x - 8(x - 3)$ and represent the solution set on the number line.

Sol. Given, $37 - (3x + 5) \geq 9x - 8(x - 3)$

$\Rightarrow \quad 37 - 3x - 5 \geq 9x - 8x + 24$

$\Rightarrow \quad 32 - 3x \geq x + 24$

$\Rightarrow \quad 32 - 3x - 32 \geq x + 24 - 32$ [subtracting 32 from both sides]

$\Rightarrow \quad -3x \geq x - 8$

$\Rightarrow \quad -3x - x \geq x - 8 - x$ [subtracting x from both sides]

$\Rightarrow \quad -4x \geq -8$

$\Rightarrow \quad \frac{-4x}{-4} \leq \frac{-8}{-4}$ [dividing both sides by -4]

$\Rightarrow \quad x \leq 2$

$\therefore$ Solution set $= (-\infty, 2]$

On the number line, it can be represented as

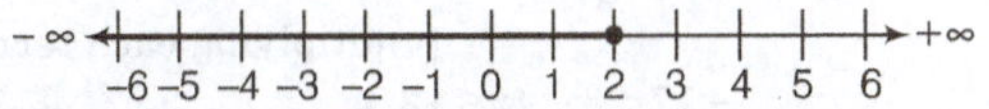

Here, the dark portion on the number line represents the solution of the given inequation.

Example 15. Solve the inequation $2x - 7 < 4$, $x \in \{1, 2, 3, 4, 5, 6, 7\}$ and represent the solution set on the number line.

Sol. Given, $2x - 7 < 4$

$\Rightarrow \quad 2x - 7 + 7 < 4 + 7$ [adding 7 on both sides]

$\Rightarrow \quad 2x < 11$

$\Rightarrow \quad \frac{2x}{2} < \frac{11}{2}$ [dividing both sides by 2]

$\Rightarrow \quad x < 5.5$

But it is given that $x \in \{1, 2, 3, 4, 5, 6, 7\}$.

Hence, the solution set is $\{1, 2, 3, 4, 5\}$.

On the number line, it can be represented as

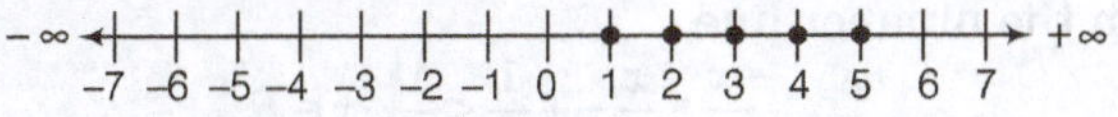

Example 16. Solve the following inequation and represent the solution set on a number line.

$$-8\frac{1}{2} < -\frac{1}{2} - 4x \le 7\frac{1}{2}, x \in I \quad \text{[ICSE 2017]}$$

Sol. Given, $-8\frac{1}{2} < -\frac{1}{2} - 4x \le 7\frac{1}{2}$

$\Rightarrow \quad -\frac{17}{2} < -\frac{1}{2} - 4x \le \frac{15}{2}$

$\Rightarrow \quad -\frac{17}{2} + \frac{1}{2} < \frac{-1}{2} - 4x + \frac{1}{2} \le \frac{15}{2} + \frac{1}{2}$

$\left[\text{adding } \frac{1}{2} \text{ on each term}\right]$

$\Rightarrow \quad -\frac{16}{2} < -4x \le \frac{16}{2}$

$\Rightarrow \quad -8 < -4x \le 8$

$\Rightarrow \quad \frac{-8}{-4} > \frac{-4x}{-4} \ge \frac{8}{-4}$ [dividing each term by (–4)]

$\Rightarrow \quad 2 > x \ge -2$ or $-2 \le x < 2$

But it is given that $x \in I$.

$\therefore$ The solution set $= \{x : -2 \le x < 2,\ x \in I\} = \{-2, -1, 0, 1\}$

$\therefore$ The graphical representation of the solution set is as follows

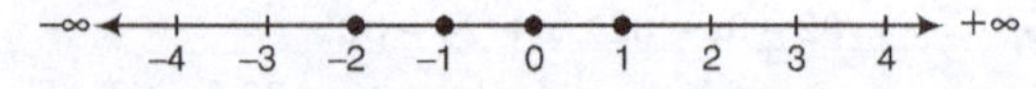

Example 17. Find the value of x, which satisfy the inequation $-2\frac{5}{6} < \frac{1}{2} - \frac{2x}{3} \le 2, \forall\ x \in W$ and also represent the solution set on the number line.

[ICSE 2014]

Sol. Given, $-2\frac{5}{6} < \frac{1}{2} - \frac{2x}{3} \le 2 \Rightarrow -\frac{17}{6} < \frac{3-4x}{6} \le 2$

$\Rightarrow \quad \frac{-17}{6} \times 6 < \frac{3-4x}{6} \times 6 \le 2 \times 6$

[multiplying each term by 6]

$\Rightarrow \quad -17 < 3 - 4x \le 12$

$\Rightarrow \quad -17 - 3 < 3 - 4x - 3 \le 12 - 3$

[subtracting 3 from each term]

$\Rightarrow \quad -20 < -4x \le 9$

$\Rightarrow \quad \frac{-20}{-4} > \frac{-4x}{-4} \ge \frac{9}{-4}$ [dividing each term by (– 4)]

$\Rightarrow \quad 5 > x \ge \frac{-9}{4} \Rightarrow \frac{-9}{4} \le x < 5$

$\Rightarrow \quad -2.25 \le x < 5$

Since, $x \in W$ i.e. $x \in \{0, 1, 2, 3, 4, \ldots\}$.

$\therefore$ The solution set is $\{0, 1, 2, 3, 4\}$.

On the number line, it can be represented as

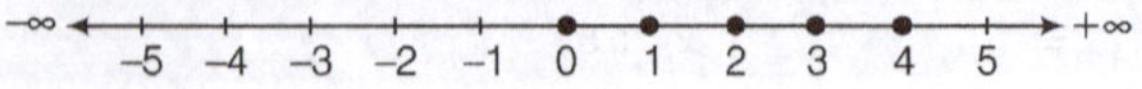

Example 18. Solve the following inequation and write the solution set. Also, represent the solution set on the number line.

$$\frac{-x}{3} \le \frac{x}{2} - 1\frac{1}{3} < \frac{1}{6}, x \in R \quad \text{[ICSE 2013]}$$

Sol. Given, inequation is $-\frac{x}{3} \le \frac{x}{2} - 1\frac{1}{3} < \frac{1}{6}$

On splitting the above inequation, we get

$\frac{-x}{3} \le \frac{x}{2} - 1\frac{1}{3}$ and $\frac{x}{2} - 1\frac{1}{3} < \frac{1}{6}$

Consider, $\frac{-x}{3} \le \frac{x}{2} - 1\frac{1}{3} \Rightarrow -\frac{x}{3} \le \frac{x}{2} - \frac{4}{3}$

$\Rightarrow \quad -\frac{x}{3} \times 6 \le \left(\frac{x}{2} - \frac{4}{3}\right) \times 6$ [multiplying both sides by 6]

$\Rightarrow \quad -2x \le 3x - 8 \Rightarrow -2x + 2x + 8 \le 3x - 8 + 2x + 8$

[adding $(2x + 8)$ on both sides]

$\Rightarrow \quad 8 \le 5x \Rightarrow \frac{8}{5} \le \frac{5x}{5}$ [dividing both sides by 5]

$\Rightarrow \quad \frac{8}{5} \le x$ ... (i)

and $\quad \frac{x}{2} - 1\frac{1}{3} < \frac{1}{6}$

$\Rightarrow \quad \frac{x}{2} - \frac{4}{3} < \frac{1}{6}$

$\Rightarrow \quad 6\left(\frac{x}{2} - \frac{4}{3}\right) < \frac{1}{6} \times 6$ [multiplying both sides by 6]

$\Rightarrow \quad 3x\ \ 8 < 1$

$\Rightarrow \quad 3x - 8 + 8 < 1 + 8$ [adding 8 on both sides]

$\Rightarrow \quad 3x < 9$

$\Rightarrow \quad \frac{3x}{3} < \frac{9}{3}$ [dividing both sides by 3]

$\Rightarrow \quad x < 3$ ...(ii)

From Eqs. (i) and (ii), we get $\frac{8}{5} \le x < 3$

$\therefore$ Solution set $= \left\{x : \frac{8}{5} \le x < 3, x \in R\right\} = x \in \left[\frac{8}{5}, 3\right)$

On the number line, it can be represented as

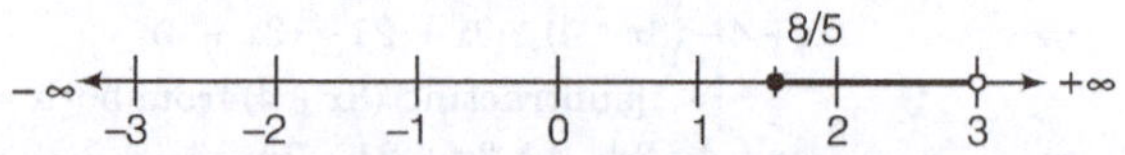

Here, the dark portion on the number line represents the solution set of the given inequation.

Example 19. Solve the following inequation, write the solution set and represent it on the number line.

$$-3(x-7) \ge 15 - 7x > \frac{x+1}{3}, x \in R \quad \text{[ICSE 2016]}$$

Sol. Given, inequation is $-3(x-7) \ge 15 - 7x > \frac{x+1}{3}, x \in R$

$\therefore \quad -3(x-7) \ge 15 - 7x$ and $15 - 7x > \frac{x+1}{3}$

[splitting into two inequations]

Consider, $-3(x-7) \ge 15 - 7x$

$\Rightarrow \quad -3x + 21 \ge 15 - 7x$

$-3x + 21 + 7x - 21 \ge 15 - 7x + 7x - 21$

[adding $(7x - 21)$ on both sides]

$\Rightarrow 4x \ge -6 \Rightarrow x \ge -\frac{6}{4} \Rightarrow x \ge -\frac{3}{2}$ [dividing both sides by 4]

$\Rightarrow \quad x \ge -1.5$ ...(i)

and $\quad 15 - 7x > \frac{x+1}{3}$

$\Rightarrow \quad 3(15 - 7x) > x + 1$ [multiplying both sides by 3]

$\Rightarrow \quad 45 - 21x > x + 1$

$\Rightarrow \quad 45 - 21x + 21x - 1 > x + 1 + 21x - 1$

[adding $(21x - 1)$ on both sides]

$\Rightarrow \quad 44 > 22x$ or $22x < 44$

$\Rightarrow \quad x < 2$ [dividing both sides by 22] ...(ii)

From Eqs. (i) and (ii), we get

$-1.5 \le x < 2$

$\therefore$ The solution set $= \{x : -1.5 \le x < 2, x \in R\} = x \in [-1.5, 2)$

Representation of the solution set on the number line is shown by dark line

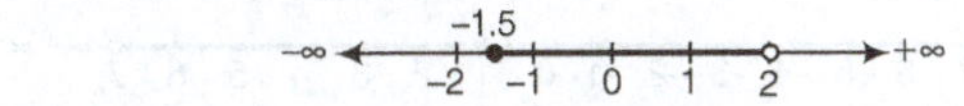

Example 20. Solve the following inequation and write down the solution set.

$$11x - 4 < 15x + 4 \le 13x + 14, x \in W$$

Represent the solution on a real number line.

[ICSE 2019]

Sol. We have, $11x - 4 < 15x + 4 \le 13x + 14, x \in W$

$\Rightarrow 11x - 4 < 15x + 4$ and $15x + 4 \le 13x + 14$

[splitting into two inequations]

Consider, $11x - 4 < 15x + 4$

$\Rightarrow \quad 11x - 4 - 4 < 15x + 4 - 4$

[subtracting 4 from both sides]

$\Rightarrow \quad 11x - 8 < 15x$

$\Rightarrow \quad 11x - 8 - 11x < 15x - 11x$

[subtracting $11x$ from both sides]

$\Rightarrow \quad -8 < 4x$

$\Rightarrow \quad \frac{-8}{4} < \frac{4x}{4}$ [dividing both sides by 4]

$-2 < x$

or $\quad x > -2$ ...(i)

and $\quad 15x + 4 \le 13x + 14$

$\Rightarrow 15x + 4 - 13x \le 13x + 14 - 13x$

[subtracting $13x$ from both sides]

$\Rightarrow \quad 2x + 4 \le 14$

$\Rightarrow \quad 2x + 4 - 4 \le 14 - 4$ [subtracting 4 from both sides]

$\Rightarrow \quad 2x \le 10$

$\Rightarrow \quad \frac{2x}{2} \le \frac{10}{2}$ [dividing both sides by 2]

$\Rightarrow \quad x \le 5$ ...(ii)

$\therefore$ From Eqs. (i) and (ii), we get

$-2 < x \le 5, x \in W$

$\therefore$ Solution set $= \{0, 1, 2, 3, 4, 5\}$

On the number line it can be represented as

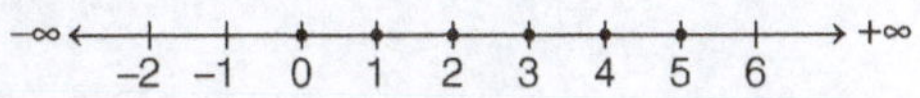

Example 21. Solve the following inequation and represent the solution set on the number line.

$$\frac{3x}{5} + 2 < x + 4 \le \frac{x}{2} + 5, x \in R$$

[ICSE 2020]

Sol. Given, $\frac{3x}{5} + 2 < x + 4 \le \frac{x}{2} + 5, x \in R$

$\Rightarrow \quad \frac{3x}{5} + 2 < x + 4$ and $x + 4 \le \frac{x}{2} + 5$

[splitting into two inequations]

Now, consider $\frac{3x}{5} + 2 < x + 4$

$\Rightarrow \quad \frac{3x}{5} + 2 - x < x + 4 - x$

[subtracting x from both sides]

$\Rightarrow \quad \frac{3x - 5x}{5} + 2 < 4$

$\Rightarrow \quad -\frac{2x}{5} + 2 - 2 < 4 - 2$ [subtracting 2 from both sides]

$\Rightarrow -\frac{2x}{5} < 2 \Rightarrow \frac{x}{5} > -1$ [dividing on both sides by -2, the sign of inequality reverse]

$\Rightarrow \quad x > -5$ [multiplying both sides by 5] ...(i)

and $\quad x + 4 \le \frac{x}{2} + 5$

$\Rightarrow \quad (x + 4) - \frac{x}{2} \le \frac{x}{2} + 5 - \frac{x}{2}$

[subtracting $\frac{x}{2}$ from both sides]

$\Rightarrow \quad \frac{x}{2} + 4 \le 5$

$\Rightarrow \quad \frac{x}{2} + 4 - 4 \le 5 - 4$ [subtracting 4 from both sides]

$\Rightarrow \quad \frac{x}{2} \le 1 \Rightarrow x \le 2$ [multiplying both sides by 2] ...(ii)

From Eqs. (i) and (ii), we get

$-5 < x \le 2$

$\therefore$ The solution set $= \{x : -5 < x \le 2, x \in R\} = (-5, 2]$

Representation of the solution set on the number line is shown by dark line.

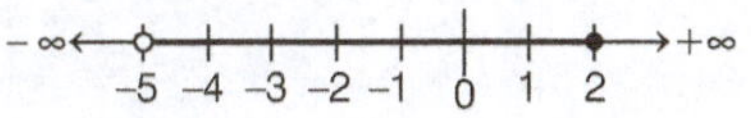

Example 22. Solve $\frac{2x + 1}{3x - 2} \ge \frac{3}{5}, x > \frac{2}{3}$.

Represent the solution set on the number line.

Sol. Given, $\frac{2x + 1}{3x - 2} \ge \frac{3}{5}$

$\Rightarrow \quad \frac{(2x + 1)(3x - 2)}{(3x - 2)} \ge \frac{3(3x - 2)}{5}$

[multiplying both sides by $(3x - 2)$, as $x > \frac{2}{3} \Rightarrow 3x - 2 > 0$]

$\Rightarrow \quad (2x + 1) \ge \frac{3(3x - 2)}{5}$

$\Rightarrow \quad 5(2x + 1) \ge \frac{5 \times 3(3x - 2)}{5}$

[multiplying both sides by 5]

$\Rightarrow \quad 5(2x + 1) \ge 3(3x - 2)$

$\Rightarrow \quad 10x + 5 \ge 9x - 6$

$\Rightarrow 10x + 5 - 9x \ge 9x - 6 - 9x$

[subtracting $9x$ from both sides]

$\Rightarrow \quad x + 5 \geq -6$

$\Rightarrow \quad x + 5 - 5 \geq -6 - 5$ [subtracting 5 from both sides]

$\Rightarrow \quad x \geq -11$

But $x > \frac{2}{3}$.

$\therefore$ Solution set $= \{x : x > \frac{2}{3}, \forall x \in R\} = x \in \left(\frac{2}{3}, \infty\right)$.

On the number line, it can be represented as

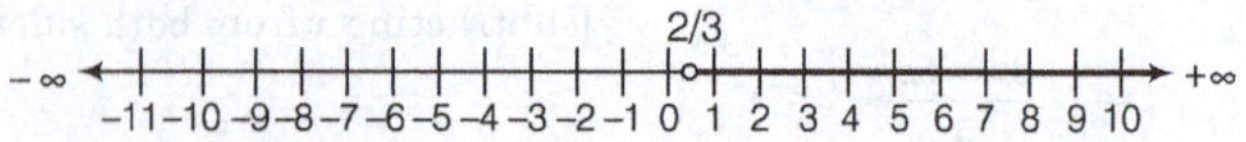

Here, the dark portion on the number line represents the solution of the given inequation.

Example 23. **If solution sets A and B are shown by two separate number lines**

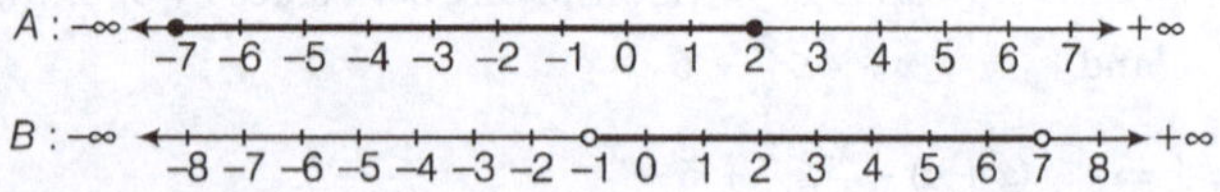

Then,

(i) Write down the set-builder form of A and B.

(ii) Represent each of the following sets on different number lines.

(a) $A \cup B$ (b) $A \cap B$ (c) $A' \cap B$ (d) $A \cap B'$

Sol. (i) From the figure,

Solution set $A = [-7, 2]$

and solution set $B = (-1, 7)$

$\therefore$ Set-builder form of $A = \{x : -7 \leq x \leq 2, \; x \in R\}$

and set-builder form of $B = \{x : -1 < x < 7, x \in R\}$

(ii) (a) $A \cup B = \{x : -7 \leq x < 7, \; x \in R\}$

Representation of $A \cup B$ on the number line is as

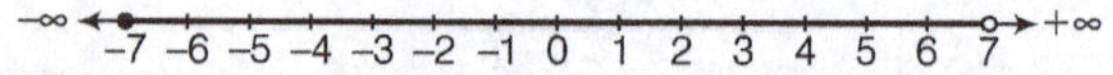

(b) $A \cap B = \{x : -1 < x \leq 2, \; x \in R\}$

Representation of $A \cap B$ on the number line is as

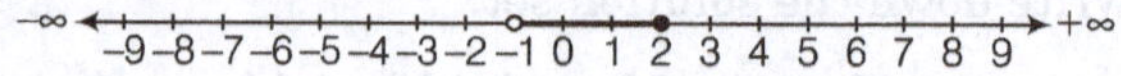

(c) $A' \cap B = B - A = \{x : 2 < x < 7, x \in R\}$

Representation of $A' \cap B$ on the number line is as

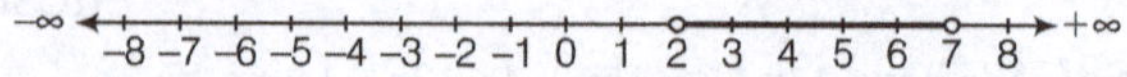

(d) $A \cap B' = A - B = \{x : -7 \leq x \leq -1, x \in R\}$

Representation of $A \cap B'$ on the number line is as

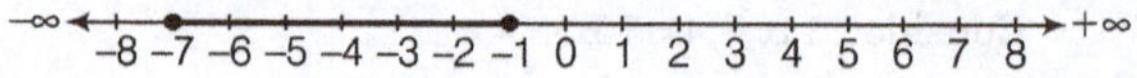

Chapter Practice

a. 1 Mark Questions

1. The solution of inequation $10t + 6 \leq 16 \;\forall\; x \in R$ is

(a) $(-\infty, 1)$ (b) $(-\infty, 1]$

(c) $\left[-\infty, \frac{1}{2}\right]$ (d) $[-\infty, 1)$

2. If P is the solution set of $-3x + 4 \leq 2x - 3$, $x \in N$ and Q is the solution set of $3x - 6 \leq 12$, $x \in W$, then $Q \cap P$ is equal to

(a) {1} (b) {3, 4, 5}

(c) {0, 1, 2, 3, 4} (d) {2, 3, 4, 5, 6}

3. Write the solution of the following inequation in the set notation form $5x - 10 \leq 2x + 2$.

(a) $(1, \infty)$ (b) $[1, \infty)$

(c) $[1, 5]$ (d) $(-\infty, 4]$

4. The solution set for the inequation $2x + 4 \leq 14$, $x \in W$ is **[ICSE 2023]**

(a) {1, 2, 3, 4, 5} (b) {0, 1, 2, 3, 4, 5}

(c) {1, 2, 3, 4} (d) {0,1, 2, 3, 4}

5. The smallest value of x for $x - 2(3 + x) < 3(2x - 1)$, when $x \in W$

(a) 3 (b) 2

(c) 0 (d) 1

6. Represent the solution set on the number line $2x - 3 \leq 3x - 10$, where $x \in I$.

(a) 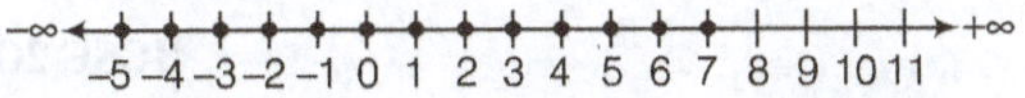

(b) 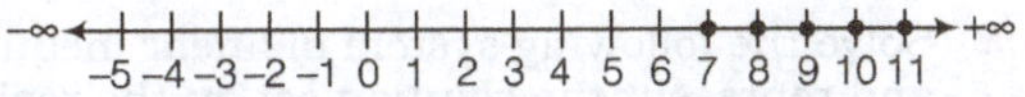

(c) 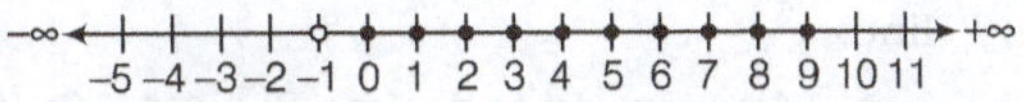

(d) 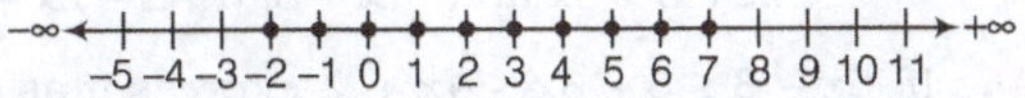

b. 3 Marks Questions

7. The solution set on the number line of the linear inequation $2y - 6 < y + 2 \leq 2y$, $y \in N$ is **[ICSE Semester-I 2021]**

(a) 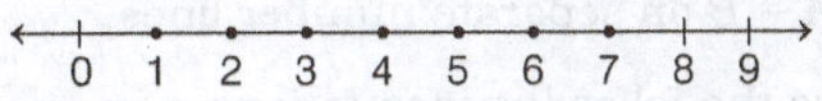

(b) 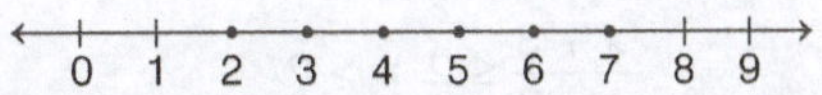

(c) 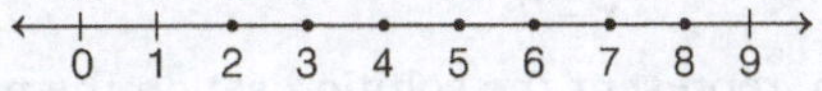

(d) 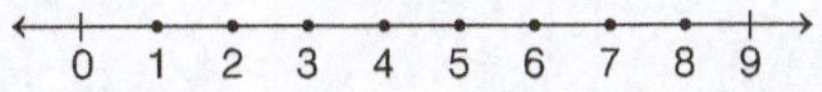

8. Express the relation between the following numbers with the help of the less than or greater than inequalities. Also, verify it.

(i) 7 and 10 (ii) -8 and 3 (iii) -11 and -9

(iv) $\frac{1}{5}$ and $\frac{3}{5}$ (v) $\frac{-7}{3}$ and $\frac{4}{3}$

9. Identify, which of the following is linear inequation in one variable?

(i) $2x + y \geq 4$ (ii) $3x + 11 \geq 5$

(iii) $x + 7 \geq 8 + 4y$ (iv) $10t + 3 \leq 7s + 10$

10. Check, which of the following inequations are correct?

(i) If $s > t$, then $3s + 5 > 3t + 2$.

(ii) If $\frac{1}{x} < \frac{2}{y}$, then $\frac{x}{5} < \frac{y}{2}$.

(iii) If $7x \geq 5$ and $3y \leq 5$, then $7x = 3y$.

(iv) If $x > y$, then $4x + 9 > 4y + 6$.

11. Given, $x \in \{-2, -3, -4, -5, -6, -7\}$ and $9 \leq 1 - 2x$, find the solution set of the given inequation.

12. Write the solution of inequation $13x + 3 \leq 16$, $\forall\; x \in R$ in the set notation form.

13. Write the solution of inequation $4x + 1 < 13$, $\forall\; x \in N$ in the set notation form.

14. Solve $-12x > 30$, when

(i) x is a natural number. (ii) x is an integer.

15. Solve $3x + 8 > 2$, when

(i) x is an integer. (ii) x is a real number.

16. If $25 - 4x \leq 16$, then find the smallest value of x.

(i) When x is a real number.

(ii) When x is an integer.

17. Find the largest value of x for which $3(x - 1) \leq 9 + x$, $x \in N$.

18. If P is the solution set of $-3x + 4 < 2x - 3$, $x \in N$ and Q is the solution set of $4x - 5 < 12$, $x \in W$, then find $Q \cap P$.

19. If $x \in R$, A is the solution set of $2(x - 1) < 3x - 1$ and B is the solution set of $4x - 4 \leq 8 + x$, then $A \cup B$.

20. Let $A = \{x : 11x - 5 > 7x + 3, x \in R\}$ and $B = \{x : 18x - 9 \geq 15 + 12x, x \in R\}$, then find the solution set of $A \cap B$. **[ICSE 2005]**

21. Consider the following figure

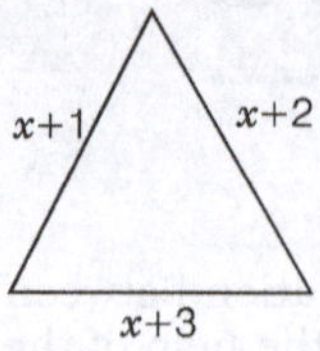

If the perimeter of triangle is less than equal to 33 and greater than equal to 24. Then, find the solution set, where $x \in N$.

22. One-third of a bamboo pole is buried in mud, one-sixth of it is in water and the part above the water is greater than or equal to 3 units. Find the length of the shortest pole.

23. Find the greatest integer, which is such that, if 7 is added to its double, then the resulting number becomes greater than three times the integer.

24. Find all pairs of consecutive even positive integers, both of which are larger than 5, such that their sum is less than 23.

25. The sum of three consecutive integer must not be more than 12. What is the minimum positive integer?

26. Find the largest three consecutive natural numbers such that the sum of one-third of first, one-fourth of second and one-fifth of the third is atmost 25.

C. 4/5 Marks Questions

27. In the first four examinations, each of 100 marks, Mohan got 94, 73, 72 and 84 marks. If average marks greater than or equal to 80 and less than 90 is needed in fifth examination to obtain a final grade B in a course, then what range of marks in fifth (last) examination will be required, if Mohan is receiving grade B in the course?

28. The marks obtained by Nilam in two tests were 60 and 80. Find the minimum marks, she should score in the third test to have an average of at least 70 marks.

29. The longest side of a triangle is twice the shortest side and the third side is 2 cm longer than the shortest side. If the perimeter of the triangle is more than 166 cm, then find the minimum length of the shortest side.

30. If the replacement set is the set of integers, lying between – 4 and 8, then find the solution set of $14 - 5x \geq 3x - 40$. Also, represent the solution set on the number line.

31. Solve the following linear inequation for the variable involved and also represent the solution set on the number line.

$$\frac{1}{4}(2t-1) - t < \frac{t}{6} - \frac{1}{3}, \forall\, t \in R$$

32. Solve the following inequation and represent the solution set on the number line.

$$x - 3 - \frac{1}{7}(5x - 17) > 0, \forall\, x \in R$$

33. Solve the inequation $1 - \frac{4}{25}(2x-1) < 1, \forall\, x \in N$ and $x < 5$. Also, represent the solution set on the number line.

34. Solve the following inequation and represent the solution set on the number line.

$$-3 < -\frac{1}{2} - \frac{2x}{3} \leq \frac{5}{6}, x \in R$$

35. Solve the following inequation and write the solution set. $13x - 5 < 15x + 4 < 7x + 12,\ x \in R$

Represent the solution on a real number line. **[ICSE 2015]**

36. Solve the following equation, write down the solution set and represent it on the real number line.

$$-2 + 10x \leq 13x + 10 < 24 + 10x,\ x \in Z$$

[ICSE 2018]

37. Solve the following inequation. Write down the solution set and represents it on the real number line.

$$-5(x-9) \geq 17 - 9x > x + 2,\ x \in R$$

[ICSE 2023]

38. Solve the following inequation and represent the solution set on the number line.

$$2x - 5 \leq 5x + 4 < 11, \text{ where } x \in I$$

[ICSE 2011, 2002]

39. Solve the following system of linear inequations and represent the solution set on the real number line.

$$4x + 5 > 3x \text{ and } -(x+3) + 4 \leq -2x + 5$$

40. If $5x - 3 \leq 5 + 3x \leq 4x + 2$, express it as $a \leq x \leq b$ and then state the values of a and b.

41. Given, $A = \{x : 7x - 2 > 4x + 1, \forall x \in R\}$ and $B = \{x : 9x - 45 \geq 5(x-5), \forall\, x \in R\}$.

Represent (i) $A \cap B$

(ii) $A - B$ on separate number lines.

42. Solve the following inequations

$$\frac{x+3}{x-2} \leq 2,\ x > 2.$$

Also, represent the solution set on the number line.

43. If solution sets P and Q are shown by two separate number lines

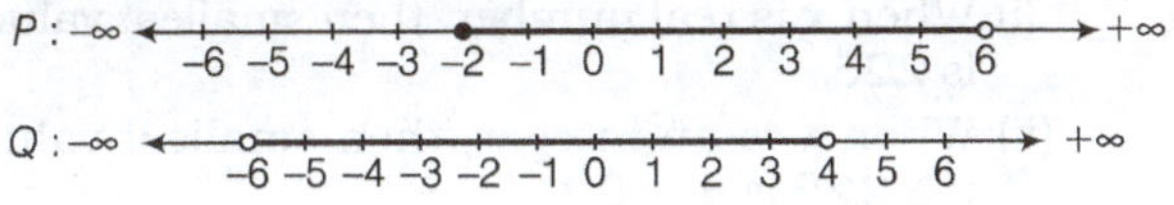

(i) Write down the set-builder form of P and Q.
(ii) Represent each of the following sets on different number lines
(a) $P \cup Q$ (b) $P \cap Q$ (c) $P' \cap Q$.

44. If P and Q are shown by two separate number lines

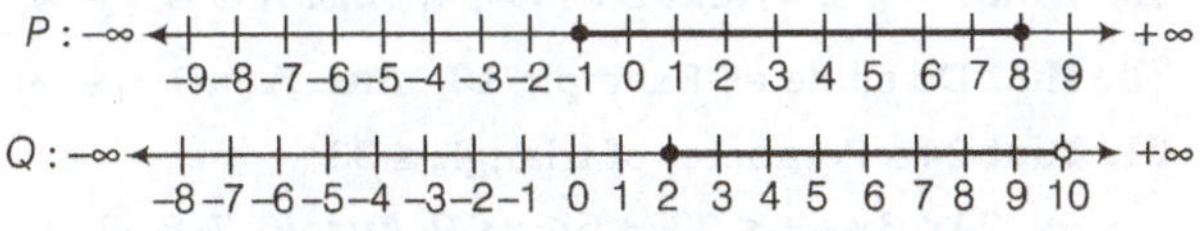

(i) Write down the set-builder form of P and Q.
(ii) Represent the solution set $P \cup Q$ and $P \cap Q$ on the number lines.

d. 6 Marks Questions

45. Solve the linear inequation $3x - 5 < x + 7$, when
(i) x is a natural number.
(ii) x is a whole number.
(iii) x is a positive odd integer.
(iv) x is a real number.
(v) x is a positive even integer.

46. Find the smallest value of x for $x - 3(2 + x) < 2(3x - 1)$, when
(i) $x \in W$ (ii) $x \in I$ (iii) $x \in N$

47. Solve the inequation $\frac{4}{x+1} \leq 3 \leq \frac{6}{x+1}$, $x > 0$ and represent the solution set on the number line.

48. Solve the inequation $-3 + x \leq \frac{8x}{3} + 2 \leq \frac{14}{3} + 2x$, $x \in I$ and represent the solution set on the number line. **[ICSE 2009]**

49. Solve the following inequation and represent the solution set on the number line.

$$4x - 19 < \frac{3x}{5} - 2 \leq \frac{-2}{5} + x, \ \forall \ x \in R$$

[ICSE 2012]

50. Given, $S = \{x : -(35 + 2x) < 4x - 5 \leq 7 - 2x, \forall \ x \in R\}$ and $T = \{x : 2 - 4x \leq 2 - 3x < 7 - 4x, \forall \ x \in R\}$.
(i) Represent solution set of S and T on the separate number lines.
(ii) Find $S \cup T$, $S \cap T$ and $S - T$.

51. The figure given below represents two solution sets P and Q on real number lines.

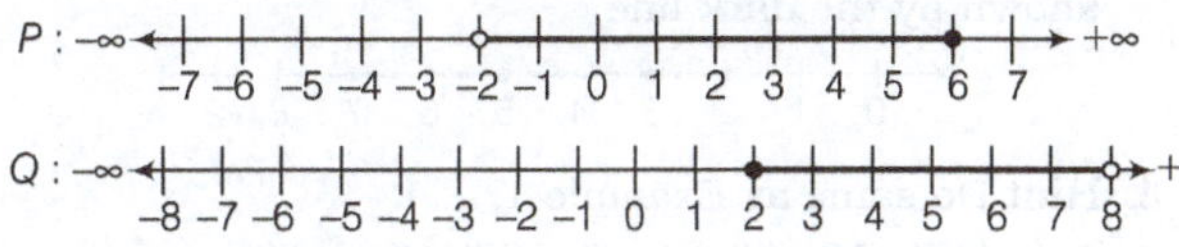

(i) Write down P and Q in set-builder form.
(ii) Represent each of the following sets on different number lines.
(a) $P \cap Q$ (b) $P' \cap Q$ (c) $P \cap Q'$

Hints and Answers

1. (b) Given, $10t + 6 \leq 16$

$\Rightarrow \quad 10t \leq 10 \Rightarrow t \leq 1$

$\Rightarrow \quad (-\infty, 1]$

2. (d) Given, $-3x + 4 \leq 2x - 3$

$\Rightarrow \quad -5x + 7 \leq 0 \Rightarrow -5x + 7 - 7 \leq 0 - 7$ [subtracting 7 from both sides]

$\Rightarrow \quad \frac{-5x}{-5} \geq \frac{-7}{-5}$ [dividing both sides by −5]

$\Rightarrow \quad x \geq \frac{7}{5} \Rightarrow x \geq 1.4$

$\therefore$ $P\{2, 3, 4, 5, \ldots\}$.

Also, $3x - 6 \leq 12$

$\Rightarrow \quad 3x - 6 + 6 \leq 12 + 6$ [adding 6 on both sides]

$\Rightarrow \quad x \leq 6$

$\therefore Q\{0, 1, 2, 3, 4, 5, 6\}$

Hence, the set $P \cap Q$ is $\{2, 3, 4, 5, 6\}$.

3. (d) Given, $5x - 10 \leq 2x + 2$

$\Rightarrow \quad 5x - 10 + 10 \leq 2x + 2 + 10$ [adding 10 on both sides]

$\Rightarrow \quad 5x \leq 2x + 12$

$\Rightarrow \quad 5x - 2x \leq 2x + 12 - 2x$ [subtracting $2x$ from both sides]

$\Rightarrow \quad 3x \leq 12 \Rightarrow \frac{3x}{3} \leq \frac{12}{3}$ [dividing both sides by 3]

$\Rightarrow \quad x \leq 4$

Hence, the solution set is $\{x : x \leq 4, x \in R\}$ or $(-\infty, 4]$.

4. (b) Given, expression is

$2x + 4 \leq 14$

$\Rightarrow \quad 2x \leq 14 - 4$

$\Rightarrow \quad 2x \leq 10$

$\Rightarrow \quad x \leq 5, x \in W$

Therefore, the solution set for this is $\{0, 1, 2, 3, 4, 5\}$.

5. (c) $x - 6 - 2x < 6x - 3$

$\Rightarrow \quad -x - 6 < 6x - 3$

$\Rightarrow \quad -x - 6 + x < 6x + x - 3$ [adding x on both sides]

$\Rightarrow \quad -6 < 7x - 3$

$\Rightarrow \quad -6 + 3 < 7x - 3 + 3$ [adding 3 on both sides]

$\Rightarrow \quad -3 < 7x$

$\Rightarrow \quad \frac{-3}{7} < \frac{7x}{7}$ [dividing both sides by 7]

$\Rightarrow \quad \frac{-3}{7} < x$

When $x \in W$, then the smallest value of x is 0.

6. (b) Given, inequation is $2x - 3 \le 3x - 10$

$\Rightarrow \quad 2x - 3 - 2x \le 3x - 2x - 10$ [subtracting $2x$ from both sides]

$\Rightarrow \quad -3 + 10 \le x - 10 + 10$ [adding 10 on both sides]

$\Rightarrow \quad 7 \le x$

$\Rightarrow \quad x \ge 7$

i.e. $x = \{7, 8, 9, ...\}$

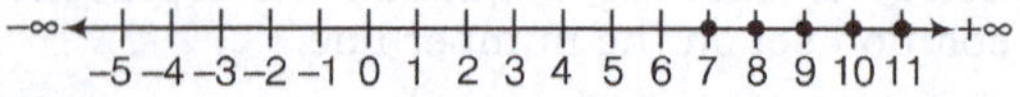

7. (b) We have, $2y - 6 < y + 2 \le 2y,\ y \in N$

$\therefore \quad 2y - 6 < y + 2$

$\Rightarrow \quad 2y - y < 2 + 6$

$\Rightarrow \quad y < 8$ ...(i)

Also, $\quad y + 2 \le 2y$

$\Rightarrow \quad 2 \le 2y - y$

$\Rightarrow \quad 2 \le y$ ...(ii)

From Eqs. (i) and (ii),

$2 \le y < 8$

i.e. $\{y : 2 \le y < 8,\ y \in N\}$

The graph of the solution set on the number line is shown by the dark line

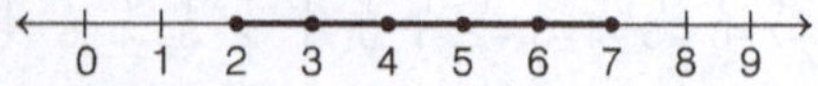

8. **Hint** Do same as Example 1.

Ans. (i) $7 < 10$ (ii) $-8 < 3$ (iii) $-11 < -9$

(iv) $\frac{1}{5} < \frac{3}{5}$ (v) $\frac{-7}{3} < \frac{4}{3}$

9. **Hint** Do same as Example 2.

Ans. Only (ii) is linear inequation in one variable.

10. **Hint** Do same as Example 9.

Ans. (i) Correct (ii) Incorrect (iii) Incorrect (iv) Correct

11. **Hint** Adding on both sides $2x - 9$ in $9 \le 1 - 2x$.

Ans. $\{-7, -6, -5, -4\}$

12. **Hint** Do same as Example 10.

Ans. The solution set is $\{x : x \le 1,\ x \in R\}$ or $(-\infty, 1]$.

13. **Hint** Given, $4x + 1 < 13$

$\Rightarrow \quad 4x + 1 - 1 < 13 - 1$

$\Rightarrow \quad 4x < 12$

$\Rightarrow \quad \frac{4x}{4} < \frac{12}{4}$

$\Rightarrow \quad x < 3$

Ans. The solution set is $\{x : x < 3,\ x \in N\}$ or $\{1, 2\}$.

14. **Hint** $-12x > 30 \Rightarrow x < -\frac{30}{12}$

Ans. (i) No solution

(ii) $\{...., -4, -3\}$

15. **Hint** $3x + 8 > 2$

$\Rightarrow \quad 3x + 8 - 8 > 2 - 8$

$\Rightarrow \quad 3x > -6$

$\Rightarrow \quad x > -2$

(i) $\{-1, 0, 1, 2, ...\}$ (ii) $(-2, \infty)$

16. **Hint** $25 - 4x \le 16 \Rightarrow x \ge 2.25$

Ans.

(i) When x is real number, then smallest value of x is 2.25.

(ii) When x is an integer, then smallest value of $x \ge 2.25$ is $x = 3$.

17. **Hint** $x \le 6$

$x \in \{1, 2, 3, 4, 5, 6\}$

Ans. Largest value of x is 6.

18. **Hint** Do same as Example 13. **Ans.** $Q \cap P = \{2, 3, 4\}$

19. **Hint** $A = (-1, \infty)$ and $B = (-\infty, 4]$ **Ans.** $A \cup B = (-\infty, \infty)$

20. **Hint** Do same as Example 13. **Ans.** $A \cap B = [4, \infty)$

21. **Hint** $24 \le$ Perimeter of triangle ≤ 33

$\Rightarrow \quad 24 \le 3x + 6 \le 33 \Rightarrow 6 \le x \le 9$ **Ans.** $\{6, 7, 8, 9\}$

22. **Hint** Let length of the bamboo pole = x units

Length of bamboo pole above water $= x - \left(\frac{x}{3} + \frac{x}{6}\right) = \frac{x}{2}$

According to the question, $\frac{x}{2} \ge 3$

Ans. Length of shortest pole = 6 units.

23. **Hint** Let greatest integer be x.

$\therefore \quad 7 + 2x > 3x$ **Ans.** 6

24. **Hint** Let pair of consecutive even positive integers be x and $x + 2$.

$\therefore \quad x > 5,\ x + 2 > 5$ and $2x + 2 < 23$

Now, find the values of x, which simultaneously satisfy all the inequations.

Ans. (6, 8) or (8, 10) or (10, 12)

25. **Hint** Let the three consecutive integers be x, $(x + 1)$ and $(x + 2)$.

Then, $\quad x + (x + 1) + (x + 2) \le 12$

$\therefore \quad x \le 3$ **Ans.** 1

26. **Hint** Let three consecutive natural numbers be x, $x + 1$ and $x + 2$, respectively.

$\therefore \quad \frac{x}{3} + \frac{x+1}{4} + \frac{x+2}{5} \le 25$

$\Rightarrow \quad x \le 31\frac{4}{47}$

Hence, the largest value of x is 31.

Ans. 31, 32 and 33

27. **Hint** Let x be the score obtained by Mohan in the last examination.

$\therefore \quad \frac{323 + x}{5} \ge 80 \Rightarrow 323 + x \ge 400$

[multiplying on both sides by 5]

$\Rightarrow \quad x \ge 77$ [subtracting 323 from both sides]

Ans. Required range is $77 \le x < 90$

28. **Hint** Let x be the marks obtained in the third test.

$\Rightarrow \quad 140 + x \ge 210$

Ans. $x \ge 70$, Nilam must obtain a minimum of 70 marks to get an average of atleast 70 marks.

29. Hint $\therefore$ $2x + x + (x+2) > 166 \Rightarrow 4x + 2 > 166$

Ans. $x > 41$. The length of the shortest side should be greater than 41 cm.

30. Hint We have, $14 - 5x \geq 3x - 40 \Rightarrow x \leq 6.75$

$\because$ Replacement set is the set of integer, lying between − 4 and 8.

$\therefore$ $x \in \{-3, -2, -1, 0, 1, 2, 3, 4, 5, 6\}$

Ans. The solution set is $\{-3, -2, -1, 0, 1, 2, 3, 4, 5, 6\}$.

31. Hint $\frac{t}{2} - \frac{1}{4} - t < \frac{t}{6} - \frac{1}{3} \Rightarrow \frac{t}{2} - t - \frac{t}{6} < -\frac{1}{3} + \frac{1}{4}$

$\Rightarrow \quad t > \frac{1}{8}$

Ans. $\{t : t > \frac{1}{8}, t \in R\}$ i.e. $\left(\frac{1}{8}, \infty\right)$

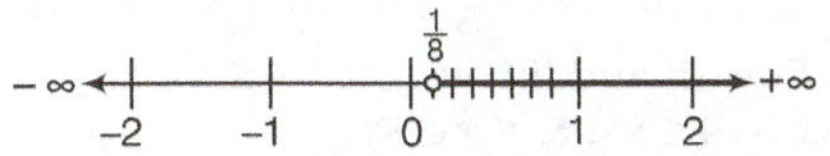

32. Hint $x - 3 - \frac{5x}{7} + \frac{17}{7} > 0$

$\Rightarrow \quad \frac{2x}{7} - \frac{4}{7} > 0 \Rightarrow x > 2$

Ans. $\{x : x > 2, x \in R\}$ i.e. $(2, \infty)$

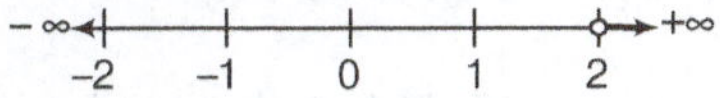

33. Hint $1 - \frac{8x}{25} + \frac{4}{25} < 1 \Rightarrow x > \frac{1}{2}$ and we have $x < 5$

$\therefore \quad \frac{1}{2} < x < 5$

Ans. $\{x : \frac{1}{2} < x < 5, x \in N\}$ or $\{1, 2, 3, 4\}$

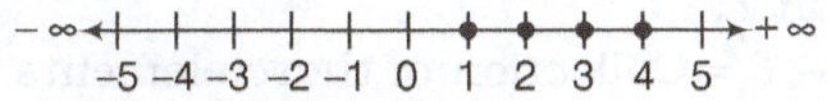

34. Hint Do same as Example 16.

Ans. $\{x : -2 \leq x < \frac{15}{4}, x \in R\}$

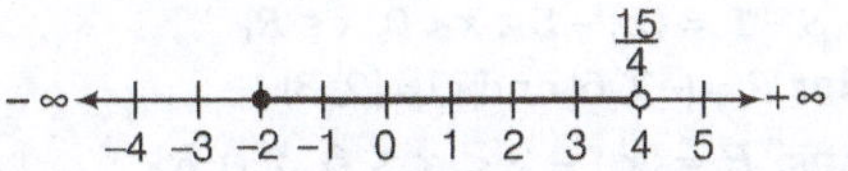

35. Hint $13x - 5 < 15x + 4$ and $15x + 4 < 7x + 12$

$\Rightarrow \quad x > -\frac{9}{2}$ and $x < 1$

Ans. $\{x : -\frac{9}{2} < x < 1, x \in R\}$

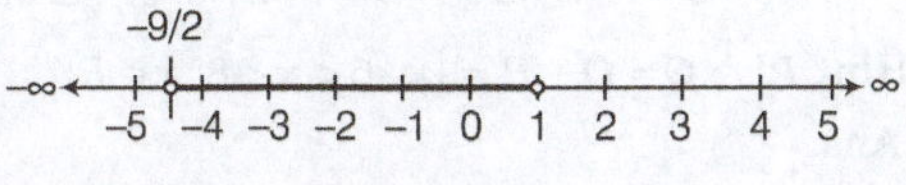

36. Hint $-2 + 10x \leq 13x + 10 < 24 + 10x, x \in Z$

$\therefore$ $-2 + 10x \leq 13x + 10$ and $13x + 10 < 24 + 10x$

$\therefore \quad -4 \leq x < 4\frac{2}{3}$

Ans. Solution set $= \{-4, -3, -2, -1, 0, 1, 2, 3, 4\}$

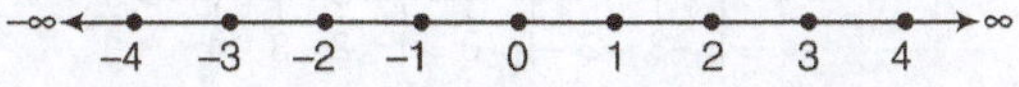

37. Given, equation is

$-5(x - 9) \geq 17 - 9x > x + 2, x \in R$

$\Rightarrow \quad (-5x + 45) \geq 17 - 9x > x + 2$

$\Rightarrow \quad -5x + 45 \geq 17 - 9x$ and $17 - 9x > x + 2$

[$\because$ Split into two inequalities]

$\Rightarrow \quad 4x \geq -28$ and $15 > 10x$

[$\because$ add $9x$ and subtract 17 from both sides of each inequality]

$\Rightarrow \quad x \geq -7$ and $x < 1.5$

[$\because$ divide both sides of each inequality by 4 and 10 respectively]

To satisfy both conditions, x must be a value that is greater than or equal to − 7 and less than 1.5.

Therefore, the solution set for x is $x \in [-7, 1.5]$

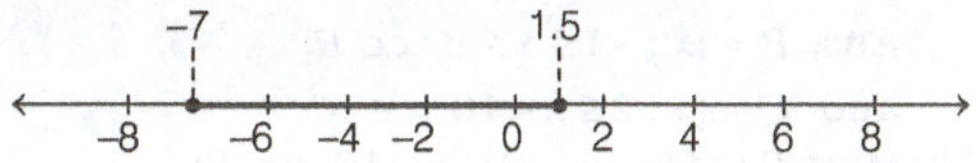

38. Hint Consider, $2x - 5 \leq 5x + 4 \Rightarrow x \geq -3$

and $\quad 5x + 4 < 11 \Rightarrow x < \frac{7}{5}$

Ans. The solution set is $\{-3, -2, -1, 0, 1\}$.

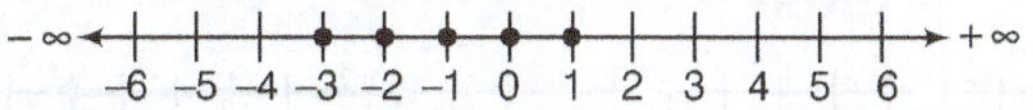

39. Hint First solve both linear inequations separately and find the intersection of solution set. Then, represents the solution set on the number line.

Ans. $\{x : -5 < x \leq 4, x \in R\}$

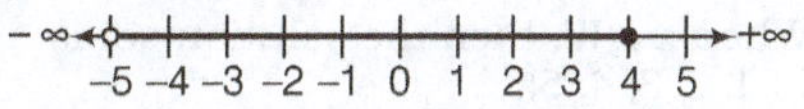

40. Hint Consider, $5x - 3 \leq 5 + 3x$

$\Rightarrow \quad x \leq 4$ ...(i)

and $\quad 5 + 3x \leq 4x + 2 \Rightarrow 3 \leq x$ ...(ii)

$\therefore \quad 3 \leq x \leq 4$

Now, compare the above inequation with $a \leq x \leq b$.

Ans. $a = 3$ and $b = 4$

41. Hint Consider, $7x - 2 > 4x + 1 \Rightarrow x > 1$

$\therefore \quad A = \{x : x > 1, x \in R\}$ ...(i)

and $\quad 9x - 45 \geq 5(x - 5)$

$\Rightarrow \quad 4x \geq 20 \Rightarrow x \geq 5$

$\therefore \quad B = \{x : x \geq 5, x \in R\}$ ...(ii)

Ans. (i) $A \cap B = \{x : x \geq 5, x \in R\}$

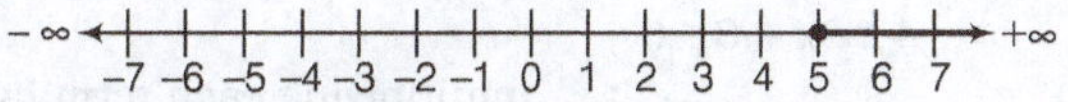

(ii) $A - B = \{x : 1 < x < 5, x \in R\}$

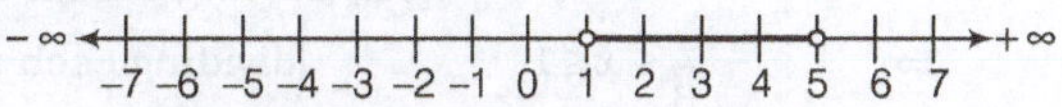

42. Hint Do same as Example 22. **Ans.** $\{x : x \geq 7, x \in R\}$

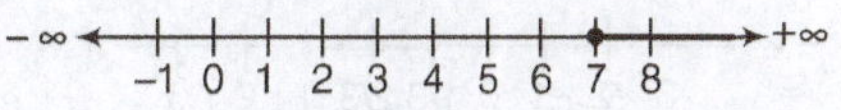

43. Hint Do same as Example 23.

Ans. (i) $P=\{x:-2\le x<6,\ x\in R\}$

and $Q=\{x:-6<x<4,\ x\in R\}$

(ii) (a) $P\cup Q=\{x:-6<x<6,\ x\in R\}$

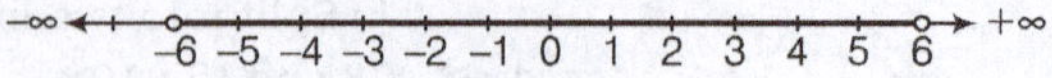

(b) $P\cap Q=\{x:-2\le x<4,\ x\in R\}$

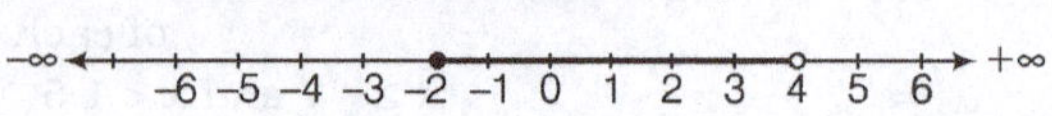

(c) $P'\cap Q=Q-P=\{x:-6<x<-2,\ x\in R\}$

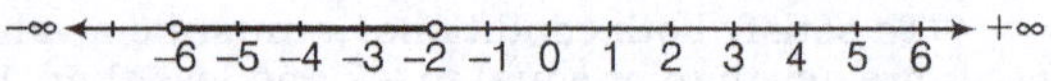

44. (i) **Hint** $P=[-1,8]$ and $Q=[2,10)$

Ans. $P=\{x:-1\le x\le 8,\ x\in R\}$

and $Q=\{x:2\le x<10,\ x\in R\}$

(ii) **Hint** $P\cup Q=\{x:-1\le x<10,\ x\in R\}$

and $P\cap Q=\{x:2\le x\le 8,\in R\}$

Ans.

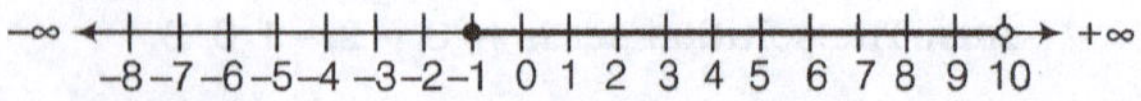

$P\cup Q$

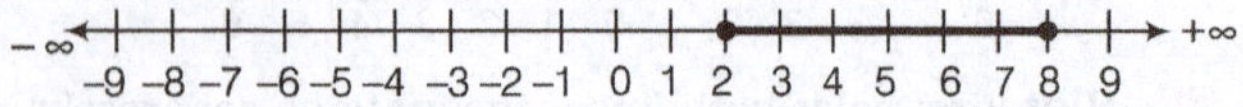

$P\cap Q$

45. Hint $3x-5<x+7\Rightarrow x<6$

Ans.

(i) When $x\in N$, then the solution set is $\{1, 2, 3, 4, 5\}$.

(ii) When $x\in W$, then the solution set is $\{0, 1, 2, 3, 4, 5\}$.

(iii) When $x\in$ positive odd integer, then the solution set is $\{1, 3, 5\}$.

(iv) When $x\in R$, then the solution set is $\{x:x<6,\ x\in R\}$.

(v) When $x\in$ positive even integer $\{2, 4\}$

46. Hint $x-6-3x<6x-2$

$\Rightarrow \qquad x>-\dfrac{1}{2}$

Ans.

(i) When $x\in W$, then the smallest value of x is 0.

(ii) When $x\in I$, then the smallest value of x is 0.

(iii) When $x\in N$, then the smallest value of x is 1.

47. Hint $\dfrac{4}{x+1}\le 3\le\dfrac{6}{x+1},\ x>0$

$\Rightarrow 4\le 3x+3\le 6$ [multiplying each term by $(x+1)$]

$1\le 3x\le 3$ [subtracting 3 from each term]

$\Rightarrow \qquad \dfrac{1}{3}\le x\le 1$ [dividing each term by 3]

Ans. ∴ The solution set is $\{x:\frac{1}{3}\le x\le 1,\ x\in R\}$.

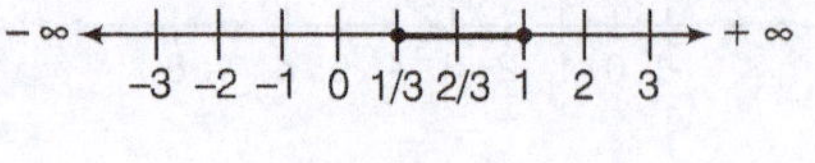

48. Hint Consider, $-3+x\le\dfrac{8x}{3}+2$

$\Rightarrow \qquad -3\le x$ ...(i)

and $\dfrac{8x}{3}+2\le\dfrac{14}{3}+2x\Rightarrow x\le 4$ ...(ii)

From Eqs. (i) and (ii), we get

$-3\le x\le 4$

Ans. The solution set is $\{-3,-2,-1,0,1,2,3,4\}$.

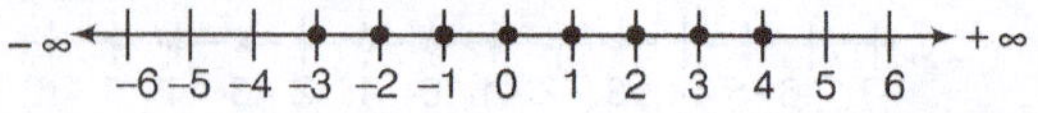

49. Hint Consider, $4x-19<\dfrac{3x}{5}-2\Rightarrow -17<\dfrac{3x-20x}{5}$

or $\qquad x<5$

$\left[\text{multiplying on both sides by } \dfrac{-5}{17}\right]$ ...(i)

and $\dfrac{3x}{5}-2\le-\dfrac{2}{5}+x\Rightarrow x\ge-4$ ...(ii)

From Eqs. (i) and (ii), we get $-4\le x<5$.

Ans. $\{x:-4\le x<5,\ \forall\ x\in R\}$

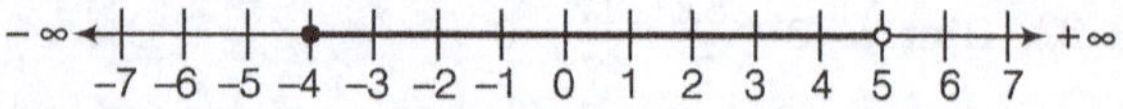

50. (i) **Hint** $S=\{x:-5<x\le 2,\ x\in R\}$

and $T=\{x:0\le x<5,\ \forall\ x\in R\}$

Ans.

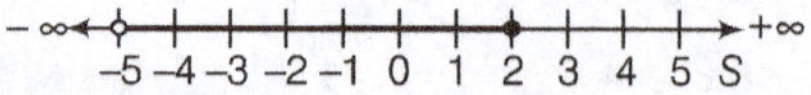

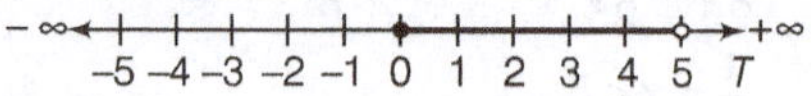

(ii) **Hint** $S\cup T$ = Collection of all elements of S and T.

$S\cap T$ = Collection of common elements of S and T.

$S-T$ = Collection of those elements of S, which are not in T.

Ans. $S\cup T=\{x:-5<x<5,\ x\in R\}$

$S\cap T=\{x:0\le x\le 2,\ x\in R\}$

$S-T=\{x:-5<x<0,\ x\in R\}$

51. (i) **Hint** $P=(-2,6]$ and $Q=[2,8)$

Ans. $P=\{x:-2<x\le 6,\ x\in R\}$

and $Q=\{x:2\le x<8,\ x\in R\}$

(ii) (a) **Hint** $P\cap Q=\{x:2\le x\le 6,\ x\in R\}$

Ans.

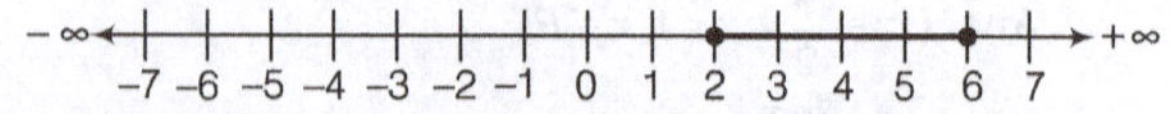

(b) **Hint** $P'\cap Q=Q-P=\{x:6<x<8,\ x\in R\}$

Ans.

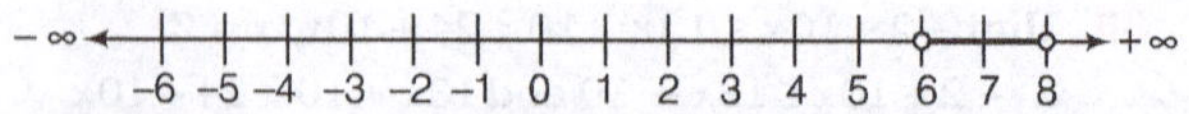

(c) **Hint** $P\cap Q'=P-Q=\{x:-2<x<2,\ x\in R\}$

Ans.

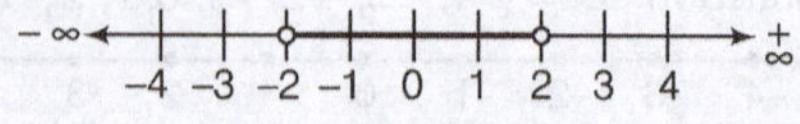

Olympiad Section

Brain Teasing Questions of Olympiad Pattern

1 Find the range of values of x which satisfy the inequation, $(x+1)^2 - (x-1)^2 < 6$.

(a) $\left(-\infty, -\frac{3}{2}\right) \cup \left(\frac{3}{2}, \infty\right)$

(b) $\left(\frac{3}{2}, \infty\right)$

(c) $\left(-\infty, \frac{3}{2}\right)$

(d) None of the above

2 The maximum value of $23 - |2x+3|$ is

(a) 20 (b) 26

(c) 17 (d) 23

3 The solution set of the inequation $\frac{1}{5+3x} \le 0$ is

(a) $\left(-\frac{5}{3}, \infty\right)$ (b) $\left(-\infty, \frac{5}{3}\right)$

(c) $\left(\frac{5}{3}, \infty\right)$ (d) $\left(-\infty, \frac{-5}{3}\right)$

4 Solve the inequation $\left|\frac{2}{x-4}\right| > 1, x \ne 4$

(a) $\{x : x \in (-2, 4) \cup (-4, 6), x \in R\}$

(b) $\{x : x \in [-2, 4) \cup (-4, 6], x \in R\}$

(c) $\{x : x \in (2, 4) \cup (4, 6), x \in R\}$

(d) $\{x : x \in [2, 4) \cup (4, 6), x \in R\}$

5 Solve for x: $|x+1| + |x| > 3$.

(a) $x \in (-\infty, -2) \cup (1, \infty)$

(b) $x \in (-2, \infty) \cup (-1, \infty)$

(c) $x \in (-\infty, -2] \cup [1, \infty)$

(d) $x \in [-2, \infty) \cup [-1, \infty)$

6 Graph the range of the inequation $-2\frac{2}{3} \le x + \frac{1}{3} \le 3\frac{1}{3}, \forall x \in R$ on the number line. If the solution set is consider as a diagonal of a square on the number line, then the area of obtained figure, is

(a) 11 sq units

(b) 14 sq units

(c) 17 sq units

(d) 18 sq units

7 Graph the solution set of $-2 < 2x - 6$ or $-2x + 5 \ge 13$, where $x \in R$. If we shift the origin at the position 1, then the new solution set, is

(a) $\{x : x < 1 \text{ or } x \ge -5, x \in R\}$

(b) $\{x : x > 1 \text{ or } x \le -5, x \in R\}$

(c) $\{x : x > 1 \text{ or } x \ge -5, x \in R\}$

(d) None of these

8 The solution sets P and Q on number line are given below

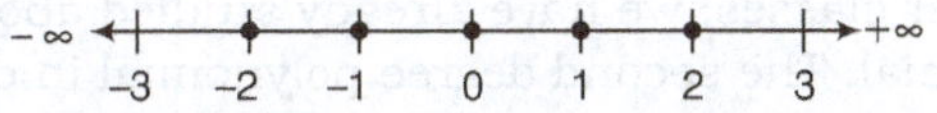

Consider the number line P on Y-axis and the number line Q on X-axis. Then, find the number of all the pairs of coordinates of the solution set.

(a) 25 (b) 24

(c) 23 (d) 22

Answers

1. (c) **2.** (d) **3.** (d) **4.** (c) **5.** (a) **6.** (d) **7.** (b) **8.** (a)

* *These questions may or may not be asked in the examination, have been given just for additional practice required for olympiads Scholarship Exams etc. For detailed explanations refer Page No. 477.*

CHAPTER 05

Quadratic Equations in One Variable

SYLLABUS

- (a) Nature of Roots : (i) Two distinct real roots, if $b^2 - 4ac > 0$ (ii) Two equal real roots, if $b^2 - 4ac = 0$ (iii) No real roots, if $b^2 - 4ac < 0$ (b) Solving Quadratic equations by : (i) Factorisation (ii) Using Formula (c) Solving simple Quadratic equations problems

In earlier classes, we have already studied about the polynomial. The second degree polynomial in one variable is called quadratic polynomial and if we take it equal to zero, then it becomes a quadratic equation. In this chapter, we will study quadratic equations and various ways of finding their roots. We will also discuss some application of quadratic equations based on daily life situations.

Quadratic Equation

An equation of the form $ax^2 + bx + c = 0$ is called **quadratic equation** in variable x, where a, b and c are real numbers and $a \neq 0$. e.g. $2x^2 + x - 100 = 0$, $-x^2 + 300x + 1 = 0$, $4x - 3x^2 + 7 = 0$, $4x^2 - 25 = 0$ are quadratic equations.

The form $ax^2 + bx + c = 0$, $a \neq 0$, is called the **standard form of a quadratic equation.**

To express a quadratic equation in its standard form, write the equation in decreasing order of the degrees of variable. e.g. $3x^2 + x + 2 = 0$, $x^2 - 2x + 6 = 0$ are in standard form, whereas $x^2 - 3 + 4x = 0$, $x + x^2 + 8 = 0$ are not in standard form.

Example 1. Check whether the following are quadratic equations or not.

(i) $(x-1)(x+2) = (x-3)(x+1)$

(ii) $(x+2)^2 = 4(x+3)$

Sol.

(i) Given, $(x-1)(x+2) = (x-3)(x+1)$ ...(i)

Here, in LHS, $(x-1)$ and $(x+2)$ are in product and in RHS, $(x-3)$ and $(x+1)$ are also in product. So, first we simplify their product.

LHS $= (x-1)(x+2) = x^2 + 2x - x - 2 = x^2 + x - 2$

RHS $= (x-3)(x+1) = x^2 + x - 3x - 3 = x^2 - 2x - 3$

On substituting these values in Eq. (i), we get

$$x^2 + x - 2 = x^2 - 2x - 3$$

$$\Rightarrow \quad x^2 - x^2 + x + 2x - 2 + 3 = 0 \Rightarrow 3x + 1 = 0$$

It is not of the form $ax^2 + bx + c = 0, a \neq 0$.

Hence, the given equation does not represent a quadratic equation.

Note In the above example, the given equation appears to be a quadratic equation, but it is not a quadratic equation. So, simplify the given equation before deciding whether it is quadratic or not.

(ii) Given, $(x+2)^2 = 4(x+3)$ ...(ii)

Here, term $(x+2)$ has power 2. So, first expand it.

LHS $= (x+2)^2 = x^2 + 4 + 4x$ $[\because (a+b)^2 = a^2 + b^2 + 2ab]$

On substituting this value in Eq. (ii), we get

$$x^2 + 4 + 4x = 4x + 12$$

$\Rightarrow \quad x^2 + 4x - 4x + 4 - 12 = 0$

$\Rightarrow \quad x^2 - 8 = 0$ or $x^2 + 0x - 8 = 0$

It is of the form $ax^2 + bx + c = 0, a \neq 0$.

Hence, the given equation represents a quadratic equation.

Solutions or Roots of a Quadratic Equation

All the values of variable which satisfy the given quadratic equation, are called **roots** or **solutions** of given quadratic equation.

In other words, a real number α is said to be a root or solution of a quadratic equation $ax^2 + bx + c = 0$, $a \neq 0$, if $a(\alpha)^2 + b(\alpha) + c = 0$.

Any quadratic equation can have atmost two roots.

Example 2. Determine whether $x = \frac{-1}{2}, x = \frac{1}{3}$ are the solutions of the given equation $6x^2 - x - 2 = 0$ or not.

Sol. Given, equation is in the form $p(x) = 0$, where

$$p(x) = 6x^2 - x - 2 \quad \text{...(i)}$$

On putting $x = \frac{-1}{2}$ in Eq. (i), we get

$$p\left(\frac{-1}{2}\right) = 6\left(\frac{-1}{2}\right)^2 - \left(\frac{-1}{2}\right) - 2$$

$$= \frac{6}{4} + \frac{1}{2} - 2 = \frac{6+2-8}{4} = \frac{8-8}{4} \Rightarrow p\left(\frac{-1}{2}\right) = 0$$

So, $x = \frac{-1}{2}$ is a solution of the given equation.

Now, putting $x = \frac{1}{3}$ in Eq. (i), we get

$$p\left(\frac{1}{3}\right) = 6\left(\frac{1}{3}\right)^2 - \left(\frac{1}{3}\right) - 2$$

$$= 6 \times \frac{1}{9} - \frac{1}{3} - 2 = \frac{6}{9} - \frac{1}{3} - 2$$

$$= \frac{6-3-18}{9} = \frac{-15}{9} \neq 0$$

$$\Rightarrow \quad p\left(\frac{1}{3}\right) \neq 0$$

So, $x = \frac{1}{3}$ is not a solution of the given equation.

Example 3. In each of the following equations, determine the value of k for which the given value is a solution of the equation.

(i) $kx^2 + 2x - 3 = 0, x = 2$

(ii) $x^2 + 2ax - k = 0, x = -a$

Sol.

(i) We have, $kx^2 + 2x - 3 = 0$, where k is unknown.

Since, $x = 2$ is a solution of given equation, so it will satisfy the given equation.

On putting $x = 2$ in the given equation, we get

$$k(2)^2 + 2(2) - 3 = 0$$

$$\Rightarrow \quad 4k + 4 - 3 = 0$$

$$\Rightarrow \quad 4k + 1 = 0 \Rightarrow k = \frac{-1}{4}$$

(ii) We have, $x^2 + 2ax - k = 0$, where k is unknown.

Since, $x = -a$ is a solution of given equation, so it will satisfy the given equation.

On putting $x = -a$ in the given equation, we get

$$(-a)^2 + 2a(-a) - k = 0$$

$$\Rightarrow \quad a^2 - 2a^2 - k = 0$$

$$\Rightarrow \quad -a^2 - k = 0$$

$$\Rightarrow \quad k = -a^2$$

Example 4. If $x = 2$ and $x = 3$ are roots of the equation $3x^2 - 2ax + 2b = 0$, then find the values of a and b.

Sol. Given, $\quad 3x^2 - 2ax + 2b = 0 \quad$ ...(i)

where, a and b are unknown constants.

Since, $x = 2$ and $x = 3$ are the solutions of given equation, so they will satisfy the given equation.

On putting $x = 2$ and $x = 3$ one-by-one, in Eq. (i), we get

$$3(2)^2 - 2a \times (2) + 2b = 0$$

$$\Rightarrow \quad 3 \times 4 - 4a + 2b = 0$$

$$\Rightarrow \quad 12 - 4a + 2b = 0$$

$$\Rightarrow \quad -2(2a - b - 6) = 0$$

$$\Rightarrow \quad 2a - b = 6 \qquad [\because -2 \neq 0] \text{ ...(ii)}$$

and $\quad 3(3)^2 - 2a \times 3 + 2b = 0$

$$\Rightarrow \quad 27 - 6a + 2b = 0$$

$$\Rightarrow \quad 6a - 2b = 27 \quad \text{...(iii)}$$

On multiplying Eq. (ii) by 2 and then subtract it from Eq. (iii), we get

$$6a - 2b - 4a + 2b = 27 - 12$$

$$\Rightarrow \quad 2a = 15$$

$$\Rightarrow \quad a = \frac{15}{2}$$

On substituting $a = \frac{15}{2}$ in Eq. (ii), we get

$$2 \times \frac{15}{2} - b = 6$$

$$\Rightarrow \quad 15 - b = 6$$

$$\Rightarrow \quad b = 15 - 6 = 9 \Rightarrow b = 9$$

Hence, the required values of a and b are 15/2 and 9, respectively.

Solution of a Quadratic Equation by Factorisation

A quadratic equation can be solved using two methods; by factorisation and by quadratic formula. Here, we will discuss the solution of quadratic equation by factorisation.

To find the solution of a quadratic equation by factorisation, we use the following steps

Step I Write the given equation in standard form i.e. $ax^2 + bx + c = 0$ (if not given in standard form) and find the values of a, b and c.

Step II Find the product of a and c and write it as a product of its two factors such that their sum is equal to b, i.e. write $ac = p \times q$ such that $p + q = b$, where p and q are factors of ac.

Step **III** Put the value of b obtained from Step II in given equation and then write its LHS as product of two linear factors.

Step **IV** Now, equate each factor to zero to get desired roots of given quadratic equation.

Note (i) In case of $ax^2 \pm bx + c = 0$, both p and q will be negative or positive.
(ii) In case of $ax^2 \pm bx - c = 0$, one of p and q will be negative.

Example 5. Solve the following quadratic equation by factorisation method.

(i) $x^2 - 14x + 24 = 0$ (ii) $4\sqrt{3}x^2 + 5x - 2\sqrt{3} = 0$

Sol.

(i) The given quadratic equation is $x^2 - 14x + 24 = 0$.
On comparing with standard form of quadratic equation
i.e. $ax^2 + bx + c = 0$
$\therefore$ $a = 1, b = -14$ and $c = 24$
Here, $ac = 1 \times 24 = 24$
Now, we need to find those factors of 24 whose sum is -14. So, let $p = -12$ and $q = -2$, as $p \times q = 24$ and $p + q = -14$

$\therefore$ $x^2 - 14x + 24 = 0$
$\Rightarrow$ $x^2 + (-12 - 2)x + 24 = 0$
$\Rightarrow$ $x^2 - 12x - 2x + 24 = 0$
$\Rightarrow$ $x(x - 12) - 2(x - 12) = 0$
$\Rightarrow$ $(x - 2)(x - 12) = 0$
$\Rightarrow$ $(x - 2) = 0$ or $(x - 12) = 0$
$\Rightarrow$ $x = 2$ or $x = 12$

Hence, the roots of the equation $x^2 - 14x + 24$ are 2 and 12.

(ii) Given $4\sqrt{3}x^2 + 5x - 2\sqrt{3} = 0$.
On comparing with standard form of quadratic equation
i.e $ax^2 + bx + c = 0$
$\therefore a = 4\sqrt{3}, \ b = 5$ and $c = -2\sqrt{3}$
Here, $ac = 4\sqrt{3} \times (-2\sqrt{3}) = -24$
Now, we need to find those factors of -24, whose sum is 5.
So, let $p = 8$ and $q = -3$, as $p \times q = -24$ and $p + q = 5$

$\Rightarrow$ $4\sqrt{3}x^2 + (8 - 3)x - 2\sqrt{3} = 0$
$\Rightarrow$ $4\sqrt{3}x^2 + 8x - 3x - 2\sqrt{3} = 0$
$\Rightarrow$ $4x(\sqrt{3}x + 2) - \sqrt{3}(\sqrt{3}x + 2) = 0$
$\Rightarrow$ $(4x - \sqrt{3})(\sqrt{3}x + 2) = 0$
$\Rightarrow$ $4x - \sqrt{3} = 0$ or $\sqrt{3}x + 2 = 0$
$\therefore$ $x = \frac{\sqrt{3}}{4}$ or $x = \frac{-2}{\sqrt{3}}$

Hence, the roots of equation $4\sqrt{3}x^2 + 5x - 2\sqrt{3} = 0$ are $\frac{\sqrt{3}}{4}$ and $\frac{-2}{\sqrt{3}}$.

Example 6. Find the roots of the quadratic equation $x^2 - 8x - 20 = 0$ by factorisation method.

Sol. Given, quadratic equation is $x^2 - 8x - 20 = 0$, which is already in standard form.

On comparing it with $ax^2 + bx + c = 0$, we get
$a = 1, b = -8$ and $c = -20$
Here, $ac = 1 \times (-20) = -20$
Now, let $p = -10$ and $q = 2$, as $p \times q = -20$ and $p + q = -8$

$\therefore$ $x^2 - 8x - 20 = 0$
$\Rightarrow$ $x^2 + (-10 + 2)x - 20 = 0$
$\Rightarrow$ $x^2 - 10x + 2x - 20 = 0$
$\Rightarrow$ $x(x - 10) + 2(x - 10) = 0$
$\Rightarrow$ $(x - 10)(x + 2) = 0$
$\Rightarrow$ $(x - 10) = 0$ or $x + 2 = 0$
$\Rightarrow$ $x = 10$ or $x = -2$

Thus, 10 and -2 are the required roots of the given quadratic equation.

Example 7. Solve the equation $x^2 + (3 - 2a)x - 6a = 0$ by factorisation method.

Sol. Given, equation is $x^2 + (3 - 2a)x - 6a = 0$.

$\Rightarrow$ $x^2 + 3x - 2ax - 6a = 0$
$\Rightarrow$ $x(x + 3) - 2a(x + 3) = 0$
$\Rightarrow$ $(x + 3)(x - 2a) = 0$ [factorising left side]
$\Rightarrow$ $x + 3 = 0$ or $x - 2a = 0$
$\therefore$ $x = -3$ or $x = 2a$

Hence, the roots of the given equation are -3 and $2a$.

Example 8. Solve the equation $\sqrt{3}x^2 + 11x + 6\sqrt{3} = 0$ by factorisation method.

Sol. Given, equation is $\sqrt{3}x^2 + 11x + 6\sqrt{3} = 0$.

$\Rightarrow$ $\sqrt{3}x^2 + 9x + 2x + 6\sqrt{3} = 0$
[$\because$ $9 + 2 = 11$ and $9 \cdot 2 = (6\sqrt{3})(\sqrt{3}) = 18$]
$\Rightarrow$ $\sqrt{3}x(x + 3\sqrt{3}) + 2(x + 3\sqrt{3}) = 0$
$\Rightarrow$ $(x + 3\sqrt{3})(\sqrt{3}x + 2) = 0$ [factorising left side]
$\Rightarrow$ $x + 3\sqrt{3} = 0$ or $\sqrt{3}x + 2 = 0$
$\therefore$ $x = -3\sqrt{3}$ or $x = \frac{-2}{\sqrt{3}} = \frac{-2\sqrt{3}}{3}$

Hence, the roots of the given equation are $-3\sqrt{3}$ and $-\frac{2\sqrt{3}}{3}$.

Example 9. Find the solution set of the equation $3x^2 - 8x - 3 = 0$ (using factorisation mathod)

(i) $x \in N$ (ii) $x \in Q$

Sol. Given, $3x^2 - 8x - 3 = 0$
$\Rightarrow$ $3x^2 - 9x + x - 3 = 0$
$\Rightarrow$ $3x(x - 3) + 1(x - 3) = 0$
$\Rightarrow$ $(3x + 1)(x - 3) = 0$
$x = -\frac{1}{3}$ or $x = 3$

(i) When $x \in N$
As $3 \in N$ and $-\frac{1}{3} \notin N$, therefore the given equation has 3 as its root.

(ii) When $x \in Q$
As $3, -\frac{1}{3} \in Q$, therefore the given equation has $\left\{3, -\frac{1}{3}\right\}$ as its roots.

Example 10. Solve the quadratic equation $\frac{x+3}{x-2} - \frac{1-x}{x} = \frac{17}{4}$ by factorisation method.

Sol. Given, equation is $\frac{x+3}{x-2} - \frac{1-x}{x} = \frac{17}{4}$.

$$\Rightarrow \frac{x(x+3) - (1-x)(x-2)}{x(x-2)} = \frac{17}{4}$$

$$\Rightarrow 4[x^2 + 3x - (x - 2 - x^2 + 2x)] = 17(x^2 - 2x)$$

$$\Rightarrow 4(x^2 + 3x - 3x + 2 + x^2) = 17x^2 - 34x$$

$$\Rightarrow 4(2x^2 + 2) = 17x^2 - 34x$$

$$\Rightarrow 8x^2 + 8 = 17x^2 - 34x$$

$$\Rightarrow 8x^2 - 17x^2 + 34x + 8 = 0$$

$$\Rightarrow -9x^2 + 34x + 8 = 0$$

$$\Rightarrow 9x^2 - 34x - 8 = 0 \quad \text{[multiplying by (-1)]}$$

$$\Rightarrow 9x^2 + (-36 + 2)x - 8 = 0$$

$$[\because (-36) \times 2 = -72 \text{ and } -36 + 2 = -34]$$

$$\Rightarrow 9x^2 - 36x + 2x - 8 = 0$$

$$\Rightarrow 9x(x-4) + 2(x-4) = 0$$

$$\Rightarrow (x-4)(9x+2) = 0$$

$$\Rightarrow x - 4 = 0 \text{ or } 9x + 2 = 0$$

$$\Rightarrow x = 4 \text{ or } x = -\frac{2}{9}$$

Hence, $x = 4$ and $x = -\frac{2}{9}$ are the required roots of given equation.

Solution of a Quadratic Equation by Quadratic Formula

Solution of quadratic equation by factorisation is somehow a lengthy process and also not applicable for all quadratic equations. So, there is a need of direct formula which can give the solution of any quadratic equation. This formula is called quadratic formula.

The roots/solutions of the quadratic equation $ax^2 + bx + c = 0$, by quadratic formula, are given by

$$x = \frac{-b \pm \sqrt{b^2 - 4ac}}{2a} = \frac{-b \pm \sqrt{D}}{2a}$$

where, $D = b^2 - 4ac$ is called the **discriminant**. This formula is also known as **Sridharacharya's formula**.

Example 11. Solve $12x^2 + 5x - 3 = 0$ by quadratic formula.

Sol. Given, quadratic equation is $12x^2 + 5x - 3 = 0$.

On comparing the given equation with $ax^2 + bx + c = 0$, we get $a = 12$, $b = 5$ and $c = -3$.

On substituting the values of a, b and c in quadratic formula $x = \frac{-b \pm \sqrt{b^2 - 4ac}}{2a}$, we get

$$x = \frac{-5 \pm \sqrt{(5)^2 - 4 \times 12 \times (-3)}}{2 \times 12}$$

$$\Rightarrow x = \frac{-5 \pm \sqrt{25 + 144}}{24} = \frac{-5 \pm \sqrt{169}}{24} = \frac{-5 \pm 13}{24}$$

Now, $x = \frac{-5+13}{24} = \frac{8}{24} = \frac{1}{3}$ [taking +ve sign]

or $x = \frac{-5-13}{24} = -\frac{18}{24} = -\frac{3}{4}$ [taking –ve sign]

Hence, the roots of the given equation are $\frac{1}{3}$ and $-\frac{3}{4}$.

Example 12. Using the quadratic formula, solve the quadratic equation $\sqrt{3}x^2 + 11x + 6\sqrt{3} = 0$.

Sol. Given, equation is $\sqrt{3}x^2 + 11x + 6\sqrt{3} = 0$.

On comparing it with $ax^2 + bx + c = 0$, we get

$$a = \sqrt{3},\ b = 11 \text{ and } c = 6\sqrt{3}$$

On substituting the values of a, b and c in the quadratic formula $x = \frac{-b \pm \sqrt{b^2 - 4ac}}{2a}$, we get

$$x = \frac{-11 \pm \sqrt{(11)^2 - 4(\sqrt{3})(6\sqrt{3})}}{2(\sqrt{3})}$$

$$= \frac{-11 \pm \sqrt{121 - 72}}{2\sqrt{3}} = \frac{-11 \pm \sqrt{49}}{2\sqrt{3}} = \frac{-11 \pm 7}{2\sqrt{3}}$$

$\Rightarrow x = \frac{-11+7}{2\sqrt{3}} = \frac{-4}{2\sqrt{3}} = \frac{-2}{\sqrt{3}}$ [taking +ve sign]

or $x = \frac{-11-7}{2\sqrt{3}} = \frac{-18}{2\sqrt{3}} = \frac{-9}{\sqrt{3}}$ [taking –ve sign]

Hence, $\frac{-2}{\sqrt{3}}$ and $\frac{-9}{\sqrt{3}}$ $\left(\text{or } \frac{-2\sqrt{3}}{3} \text{ and } -3\sqrt{3}\right)$ are the required solutions of the given equation.

Example 13. Solve the following quadratic equation.

$$x^2 - 7x + 3 = 0$$ **[ICSE 2020]**

and give your answer to two significant figure.

Sol. Given, quadratic equation $x^2 - 7x + 3 = 0$

On comparing with $ax^2 + bx + c = 0$, we get

$$a = 1,\ b = -7 \text{ and } c = 3$$

$\therefore x = \frac{-b \pm \sqrt{b^2 - 4ac}}{2a}$ [by quadratic formula]

$$= \frac{7 \pm \sqrt{(-7)^2 - 4 \times 1 \times 3}}{2 \times 1} = \frac{7 \pm \sqrt{49 - 12}}{2} = \frac{7 \pm \sqrt{37}}{2}$$

$$= \frac{7 \pm 6.08}{2} = \frac{7 + 6.08}{2}, \frac{7 - 6.08}{2} = \frac{13.08}{2}, \frac{0.92}{2}$$

$$\Rightarrow x = 6.54, 0.46$$

$x = 6.5, 0.46$ [correct to two significant numbers]

Example 14. Solve for x the quadratic equation $x^2 - 4x - 8 = 0$. Give your answer correct to three significant figures. **[ICSE 2019]**

Sol. Given, $x^2 - 4x - 8 = 0$

which is a quadratic equation of the form

$$ax^2 + bx + c = 0$$

Here, $a = 1, b = -4$ and $c = -8$

By using quadratic formula,

$$x = \frac{-b \pm \sqrt{b^2 - 4ac}}{2a} = \frac{+4 \pm \sqrt{(-4)^2 - 4 \times 1 \times (-8)}}{2 \times 1}$$

$$= \frac{4 \pm \sqrt{16 + 32}}{2} = \frac{4 \pm \sqrt{48}}{2}$$

$$= \frac{4 \pm 4\sqrt{3}}{2} = \frac{2(2 \pm 2\sqrt{3})}{2}$$

$$= 2 \pm 2\sqrt{3} = 2 + 2\sqrt{3}, 2 - 2\sqrt{3}$$

$$= 2 + 2(1.732), 2 - 2(1.732)$$

$$= 2 + 3.464, 2 - 3.464$$

$$= 5.464, -1.464$$

$$= 5.46, -1.46$$

[correct to three significant figures]

Example 15. Find the roots of the equation $x^2 + x - (a + 2)(a + 1) = 0$.

Sol. The given equation $x^2 + x - (a + 2)(a + 1) = 0$ ...(i)

On comparing Eq. (i) with $ax^2 + bx + c = 0$, we get

$$a = 1, b = 1, c = -(a + 2)(a + 1)$$

$$a = 1, b = 1, c = -(a^2 + 3a + 2)$$

We know that $x = \dfrac{-b \pm \sqrt{b^2 - 4ac}}{2a}$

$$x = \frac{-1 \pm \sqrt{1 + 4(a^2 + 3a + 2)}}{2 \times 1}$$

$$= \frac{-1 \pm \sqrt{4a^2 + 12a + 9}}{2}$$

$$x = \frac{-1 \pm \sqrt{(2a + 3)^2}}{2}$$

$\Rightarrow \dfrac{-1 \pm (2a + 3)}{2}$

$\Rightarrow x = \dfrac{-1 + 2a + 3}{2}, \dfrac{-1 - 2a - 3}{2}$

$\Rightarrow x = \dfrac{2a + 2}{2}, \dfrac{-(2a + 4)}{2}$

$\Rightarrow x = a + 1$ and $-(a + 2)$

Hence, the given roots of the given equation are $(a + 1)$ and $-(a + 2)$.

Example 16. Solve the following equation by using quadratic formula

(i) $x + \dfrac{1}{x} = 3, x \neq 0$

(ii) $\dfrac{1}{x} - \dfrac{1}{x - 2} = 3, x \neq 0, 2$

(iii) $\dfrac{1}{x + 1} + \dfrac{2}{x + 2} = \dfrac{4}{x + 4}$

Sol.

(i) Given that $x + \dfrac{1}{x} = 3$

$$x^2 - 3x + 1 = 0 \quad \text{...(i)}$$

On comparing Eq. (i) with $ax^2 + bx + c = 0$

$$a = 1, b = -3, c = 1$$

$\Rightarrow x = \dfrac{-(-3) \pm \sqrt{(-3)^2 - 4 \times 1 \times 1}}{2 \times 1} \Rightarrow \dfrac{3 \pm \sqrt{5}}{2}$

$\Rightarrow = \dfrac{3 + \sqrt{5}}{2}$ and $\dfrac{3 - \sqrt{5}}{2}$

Hence, the roots are $\dfrac{3 + \sqrt{5}}{2}$ and $\dfrac{3 - \sqrt{5}}{2}$.

(ii) Given, equation is $\dfrac{1}{x} - \dfrac{1}{x - 2} = 3, x \neq 0, 2$

$$\frac{(x - 2) - x}{x(x - 2)} = 3 \Rightarrow 3x^2 - 6x + 2 = 0 \quad \text{...(i)}$$

On comparing Eq. (i) with $ax^2 + bx + c = 0$

$$a = 3, b = -6, c = 2$$

$\therefore x = \dfrac{-(-6) \pm \sqrt{(-6)^2 - 4 \times 3 \times 2}}{2 \times 3} = \dfrac{6 \pm \sqrt{12}}{6}$

$$= \frac{6 \pm 2\sqrt{3}}{6} = \frac{3 \pm \sqrt{3}}{3}$$

$\Rightarrow x = \dfrac{3 + \sqrt{3}}{3}$ and $\dfrac{3 - \sqrt{3}}{3}$

Hence, the roots of the given equation are $\dfrac{3 + \sqrt{3}}{3}$ and $\dfrac{3 - \sqrt{3}}{3}$.

(iii) Given, equation is

$$\frac{1}{x + 1} + \frac{2}{x + 2} = \frac{4}{x + 4}$$

$\Rightarrow \dfrac{1(x + 2) + 2(x + 1)}{(x + 1)(x + 2)} = \dfrac{4}{x + 4}$

$\Rightarrow \dfrac{3x + 4}{(x + 1)(x + 2)} = \dfrac{4}{x + 4}$

$\Rightarrow (x + 4)(3x + 4) = 4[(x + 1)(x + 2)]$

$\Rightarrow 3x^2 + 12x + 4x + 16 = 4[x^2 + 2x + x + 2]$

$\Rightarrow 3x^2 + 16x + 16 = 4x^2 + 12x + 8$

$\Rightarrow x^2 - 4x - 8 = 0$ ...(i)

On comparing Eq. (i) with $ax^2 + bx + c = 0$, we get

$$a = 1, b = -4, c = -8$$

$\Rightarrow x = \dfrac{-(-4) \pm \sqrt{(-4)^2 - 4 \times 1 \times (-8)}}{2 \times 1}$

$\Rightarrow x = \dfrac{4 \pm \sqrt{48}}{2} \Rightarrow \dfrac{4 \pm 4\sqrt{3}}{2} = 2 \pm 2\sqrt{3}$

$\Rightarrow x = 2 + 2\sqrt{3}$ and $2 - 2\sqrt{3}$

Hence, the roots of the given equation are $2 + 2\sqrt{3}$ and $2 - 2\sqrt{3}$.

Exercise 5.1

1. Check whether the following equations are quadratic or not.
   (i) $2x^2 - 5x = x^2 - 2x + 3$ (ii) $x^2 - 3x - \sqrt{x} + 4 = 0$
   (iii) $x(2x + 3) = x + 2$ (iv) $x + \frac{3}{x} = x^2$
   (v) $x^2 - \frac{1}{x^2} = 5$
2. Is $x = -2$ a solution of the equation $x^2 - 2x + 8 = 0$?
3. Show that $x = -3$ is a solution of equation $x^2 + 6x + 9 = 0$.
4. Which of the following are the solutions of $2x^2 - 5x - 3 = 0$?
   (i) $x = 3$ (ii) $x = 4$
   (iii) $x = \frac{-1}{2}$ (iv) $x = -1$
   (v) $x = 2/3$ (vi) $x = 2$
5. In each of the following equations, determine whether the given values are a solution of the given equations or not.
   (i) $x^2 - x + 1 = 0; x = 1, x = -1$
   (ii) $x^2 + \sqrt{2}x - 4 = 0; x = \sqrt{2}, x = -2\sqrt{2}$
   (iii) $2x^2 - x + 9 = x^2 + 4x + 3; x = 2, x = 3$
   (iv) $\sqrt{5}x^2 - 8x + 3\sqrt{5} = 0; x = \sqrt{5}, x = \frac{3}{\sqrt{5}}$
6. In each of the following equations, find the value of unknown constant(s) for which the given value(s) is (are) solution of the equations.
   (i) $x^2 - k^2 = 0, x = 0.3$
   (ii) $3x^2 + 2ax - 3 = 0; x = \frac{-1}{2}$
   (iii) $7x^2 + kx - 3 = 0; x = \frac{2}{3}$
   (iv) $kx^2 + \sqrt{2}x - 4 = 0; x = \sqrt{2}$
   (v) $ax^2 + bx + 1 = 0; x = 1, x = 2$

Directions (Q. Nos. 7-14) *Solve each of the following equations by factorisation.*

7. $t^2 + 3t - 10 = 0$
8. $x^2 - 10x + 21 = 0$
9. $8x^2 - 22x - 21 = 0$
10. $15y^2 = 41y - 14$
11. $6x^2 + 40 = 31x$
12. $21x^2 - 2x + \frac{1}{21} = 0$
13. $3x^2 + 2\sqrt{5}x - 5 = 0$
14. $2x^2 - 9x + 10 = 0$ when
   (i) $x \in N$ (ii) $x \in Q$

Directions (Q. Nos. 15-17) *Solve for x.*

15. $x^2 + 5x - (a^2 + a - 6) = 0$
16. $6a^2x^2 - 7abx - 3b^2 = 0, a \neq 0$
17. $4x^2 - 4a^2x + (a^4 - b^4) = 0$
18. Solve $x^2 - 4x + 1 = 0$, by using quadratic formula.

Directions (Q. Nos. 19-21) *Find the roots of the following quadratic equations by applying the quadratic formula.*

19. $\frac{14}{x+3} - 1 = \frac{5}{x+1}; x \neq -3, -1$
20. $abx^2 + (b^2 - ac)x - bc = 0, a, b \neq 0$
21. $3a^2x^2 + 8abx + 4b^2 = 0, a \neq 0$
22. Solve $x^2 + 7x = 7$ and give your answer correct to two decimal places. **[ICSE 2018]**
23. Solve $(x - 1)^2 - 3x + 4 = 0$ for x, using the quadratic formula. Write your answer correct to two significant figures. **[ICSE 2014]**
24. Solve the following equation and give your answer correct to three significant figures.
   $5x^2 - 3x - 4 = 0$ **[ICSE 2012]**
25. $2x - \frac{1}{x} = 7$ give your answer two significant figure.
26. $\frac{1}{x} + \frac{1}{x-2} = 3, x \neq 0, 2$
27. $\frac{1}{x-2} + \frac{1}{x-3} + \frac{1}{x-4} = 0$
28. Find the roots of the equation
   $x^2 - 2x + (a + 3)(a + 1) = 0$

Nature of Roots of a Quadratic Equation

By quadratic formula, the roots of the quadratic equation $ax^2 + bx + c = 0, a \neq 0$ are given by

$$x = \frac{-b \pm \sqrt{b^2 - 4ac}}{2a} = \frac{-b \pm \sqrt{D}}{2a}$$

where, $D = b^2 - 4ac$ is called discriminant. The nature of roots depends upon the nature of the discriminant D. Since, D can be zero, positive or negative, so three cases arise.

Case I When $D = 0$, i.e. $b^2 - 4ac = 0$

If $D = b^2 - 4ac = 0$, then $x = \frac{-b \pm 0}{2a}$

$\Rightarrow x = -\frac{b}{2a}, -\frac{b}{2a}$

When $D = 0$, the quadratic equation has two equal real roots.

Case II When $D > 0$, i.e. $b^2 - 4ac > 0$

If $D = b^2 - 4ac > 0$, then

$$x = \frac{-b + \sqrt{D}}{2a}, \frac{-b - \sqrt{D}}{2a}$$

When $D > 0$, the quadratic equation has two distinct real roots.

Case III When $D < 0$, i.e. $b^2 - 4ac < 0$

If $D = b^2 - 4ac < 0$, then there is no real number, whose square is $b^2 - 4ac$. So, the quadratic equation has no real roots.

When $D > 0$, the quadratic equation has imaginary roots.

Points to be Remembered

For quadratic equation $ax^2 + bx + c = 0$,

Discriminant	Nature of roots	Roots
$b^2 - 4ac = 0$	Two equal real roots	$-\frac{b}{2a}, -\frac{b}{2a}$
$b^2 - 4ac > 0$	Two distinct real roots	$\frac{-b \pm \sqrt{b^2 - 4ac}}{2a}$
$b^2 - 4ac < 0$	Non-real roots imaginary	Cannot be determined in real number system.

Example 17. Find the discriminant in the following quadratic equations and state the nature of the roots.

(i) $3x^2 - 5x + 2 = 0$

(ii) $x^2 - \frac{1}{3}x + \frac{3}{2} = 0$

Sol.

(i) Given, quadratic equation is $3x^2 - 5x + 2 = 0$.

On comparing it with $ax^2 + bx + c = 0$, we get

$a = 3, b = -5$ and $c = 2$

Now, discriminant, $D = b^2 - 4ac = (-5)^2 - 4 \times 3 \times 2$

$= 25 - 24 = 1$

Since, $D > 0$, so the roots of the quadratic equation are real and distinct.

(ii) Given, quadratic equation is $x^2 - \frac{1}{3}x + \frac{3}{2} = 0$.

On comparing it with $ax^2 + bx + c = 0$, we get

$a = 1, b = -\frac{1}{3}$ and $c = \frac{3}{2}$

Now, discriminant, $D = b^2 - 4ac$

$= \left(\frac{-1}{3}\right)^2 - 4 \times 1 \times \left(\frac{3}{2}\right) = \frac{1}{9} - 6 = \frac{-53}{9}$

Since, $D < 0$, therefore the roots of the quadratic equation are imaginary.

Example 18. Determine the nature of the roots of the following equations.

(i) $2x^2 - 4x + 3 = 0$ (ii) $5x^2 - 2x - 3 = 0$

Sol.

(i) Given, quadratic equation is $2x^2 - 4x + 3 = 0$.

On comparing it with $ax^2 + bx + c = 0$, we get

$a = 2, b = -4$ and $c = 3$

Now, discriminant, $D = b^2 - 4ac$

$= (-4)^2 - 4 \times 2 \times 3 = 16 - 24 = -8 < 0$

$\therefore$ The roots of given quadratic equation are not real.

(ii) Given, quadratic equation is $5x^2 - 2x - 3 = 0$.

On comparing it with $ax^2 + bx + c = 0$, we get

$a = 5, b = -2$ and $c = -3$

Now, discriminant, $D = b^2 - 4ac = (-2)^2 - 4 \times 5 \times (-3)$

$= 4 + 60 = 64 > 0$

$\therefore$ The roots of given quadratic equation are real and distinct.

Example 19. Find the nature of roots of the following quadratic equations. If the real roots exist, then also find them.

(i) $2x^2 - 3x + 5 = 0$ (ii) $3x^2 - 4\sqrt{3}x + 4 = 0$

Sol.

(i) Given, equation is $2x^2 - 3x + 5 = 0$.

On comparing it with $ax^2 + bx + c = 0$, we get

$a = 2, b = -3$ and $c = 5$

Now, discriminant, $D = b^2 - 4ac$

$= (-3)^2 - 4 \times 2 \times 5 = 9 - 40 = -31 < 0$

$\therefore$ The given equation has no real roots.

(ii) Given, equation is $3x^2 - 4\sqrt{3}x + 4 = 0$. ...(i)

On comparing it with $ax^2 + bx + c = 0$, we get

$a = 3, b = -4\sqrt{3}$ and $c = 4$

Now, discriminant, $D = b^2 - 4ac$

$= (-4\sqrt{3})^2 - 4 \times 3 \times 4$

$= 48 - 48 = 0$

$\therefore$ The given equation has two equal real roots.

Now, Eq. (i) can be written as

$(\sqrt{3}x)^2 - 2(\sqrt{3}x)(2) + (2)^2 = 0$

$\Rightarrow (\sqrt{3}x - 2)^2 = 0$ $[\because a^2 - 2ab + b^2 = (a-b)^2]$

$\Rightarrow (\sqrt{3}x - 2)(\sqrt{3}x - 2) = 0$

$\Rightarrow \sqrt{3}x - 2 = 0$ and $\sqrt{3}x - 2 = 0$

$\therefore x = \frac{2}{\sqrt{3}}, \frac{2}{\sqrt{3}}$

Hence, the equal roots are $\frac{2}{\sqrt{3}}$ and $\frac{2}{\sqrt{3}}$.

Method to Determine the Value of Unknown, When Nature of Roots is Given

If nature of roots of a quadratic equation is given and quadratic equation involves an unknown, then to find the value of unknown, firstly we find the value of discriminant in terms of unknown and then take suitable condition $D > 0$ or $D = 0$ or $D < 0$, according to the given nature and simplify it.

Example 20. Find the values of k, for which the equation $x^2 + 5kx + 16 = 0$ has no real roots.

Sol. Given, equation is $x^2 + 5kx + 16 = 0$.

On comparing it with $ax^2 + bx + c = 0$, we get

$a = 1, b = 5k$ and $c = 16$

Now, discriminant, $D = b^2 - 4ac$

$= (5k)^2 - 4 \times 1 \times 16 = 25k^2 - 64$

Since, the given equation has no real roots.

$\therefore D < 0$

$\Rightarrow 25k^2 - 64 < 0$

$\Rightarrow 25\left(k^2 - \frac{64}{25}\right) < 0 \Rightarrow k^2 - \frac{64}{25} < 0$

$\Rightarrow k^2 < \frac{64}{25} \Rightarrow -\frac{8}{5} < k < \frac{8}{5}$

Example 21. Without solving the following quadratic equation, find the value of p, for which the roots are equal.

$px^2 - 4x + 3 = 0$ **[ICSE 2010]**

Sol. Given, quadratic equation is $px^2 - 4x + 3 = 0$.

On comparing it with $ax^2 + bx + c = 0$, we get

$a = p, b = -4$ and $c = 3$

Since, the given equation has equal roots.

So, the discriminant D will be zero.

i.e. $D = b^2 - 4ac = 0$

$\therefore (-4)^2 - 4 \times p \times 3 = 0$

$\Rightarrow 16 - 12p = 0 \Rightarrow 12p = 16$

$\therefore p = \frac{16}{12} = \frac{4}{3}$

Hence, the value of p is $\frac{4}{3}$.

Example 22. Without solving the following quadratic equation, find the value of m for which the given equation has real and equal roots.

$x^2 + 2(m-1)x + (m+5) = 0$ **[ICSE 2012]**

Sol. Given, quadratic equation is

$x^2 + 2(m-1)x + (m+5) = 0$

On comparing it with $ax^2 + bx + c = 0$, we get

$a = 1, b = 2(m-1)$ and $c = m + 5$

Since, the given equation has real and equal roots.

So, the discriminant will be zero. i.e. $b^2 - 4ac = 0$

$\Rightarrow [2(m-1)]^2 - 4 \times 1 \times (m+5) = 0$

$\Rightarrow 4(m-1)^2 - 4(m+5) = 0$

$\Rightarrow 4[m^2 + 1^2 - 2m - m - 5] = 0$ $[\because (a-b)^2 = a^2 + b^2 - 2ab]$

$\Rightarrow m^2 - 3m - 4 = 0$ [dividing by 4]

$\Rightarrow m^2 - 4m + m - 4 = 0$ [splitting the middle term]

$\Rightarrow m(m-4) + 1(m-4) = 0$

$\Rightarrow (m+1)(m-4) = 0$

$\Rightarrow m + 1 = 0$ or $m - 4 = 0$

$\therefore m = -1$ or $m = 4$

Hence, the values of m are -1 and 4.

Example 23. For what value of k, $(4-k)x^2 + (2k+4)x + (8k+1) = 0$ is a perfect square?

Sol. Given, equation is $(4-k)x^2 + (2k+4)x + (8k+1) = 0$

On comparing it with $ax^2 + bx + c = 0$, we get

$a = 4 - k, b = 2k + 4$ and $c = 8k + 1$

For perfect square, discriminant, $D = 0$.

$\therefore b^2 - 4ac = 0$

$\Rightarrow (2k+4)^2 - 4 \times (4-k)(8k+1) = 0$

$\Rightarrow 4k^2 + 16 + 16k - 4(32k + 4 - 8k^2 - k) = 0$

$\Rightarrow 4k^2 + 16 + 16k - 124k - 16 + 32k^2 = 0$

$\Rightarrow 36k^2 - 108k = 0 \Rightarrow 36k(k-3) = 0$

$\therefore k = 0, 3$

Example 24. Find the values of k, so that the equation $3x^2 + kx + 2 = 0$ has equal roots. Also, find the roots in each case.

Sol. Given, equation is $3x^2 + kx + 2 = 0$. ...(i)

On comparing it with $ax^2 + bx + c = 0$, we get

$a = 3, b = k$ and $c = 2$

Since, Eq. (i) will have equal roots.

$\therefore$ Discriminant, $D = 0 \Rightarrow b^2 - 4ac = 0$

$\Rightarrow (k)^2 - 4 \times 3 \times 2 = 0 \Rightarrow k^2 = 24 \Rightarrow k = \pm 2\sqrt{6}$

$\therefore$ The given equation has equal roots, if $k = 2\sqrt{6}$ or $-2\sqrt{6}$.

When $k = 2\sqrt{6}$, then Eq. (i) becomes $3x^2 + 2\sqrt{6}x + 2 = 0$ and its roots are given by

$$x = \frac{-2\sqrt{6} \pm \sqrt{(2\sqrt{6})^2 - 4 \times 3 \times 2}}{2 \times 3} = \frac{-2\sqrt{6} \pm 0}{6} = -\frac{\sqrt{6}}{3}, -\frac{\sqrt{6}}{3}$$

Thus, the required roots are $\frac{-\sqrt{6}}{3}$ and $-\frac{\sqrt{6}}{3}$.

When $k = -2\sqrt{6}$, then Eq. (i) becomes $3x^2 - 2\sqrt{6}x + 2 = 0$ and its roots are given by

$$x = \frac{-(-2\sqrt{6}) \pm \sqrt{(-2\sqrt{6})^2 - 4 \times 3 \times 2}}{2 \times 3}$$

$$= \frac{2\sqrt{6} \pm 0}{6} = \frac{\sqrt{6}}{3}, \frac{\sqrt{6}}{3}$$

Thus, the required roots are $\frac{\sqrt{6}}{3}$ and $\frac{\sqrt{6}}{3}$.

Example 25. Find the value of p, for which the quadratic equation $(p+1)x^2 - 6(p+1)x + 3(p+9) = 0$, $p \neq -1$ has equal roots. Hence, find the roots of the equation.

Sol. The given equation

$$(p+1)x^2 - 6(p+1)x + 3(p+9) = 0 \quad \ldots(i)$$

On comparing Eq. (i) with $ax^2 + bx + c = 0$

$a = p+1, b = -6(p+1)$

and $c = 3(p+9)$

Now, discriminant $b^2 - 4ac$

$= [-6(p+1)]^2 - 4(p+1)3(p+9)$

$= 36(p+1)^2 - 12(p+1)(p+9)$

$= 12(p+1)[3(p+1) - (p+9)]$

$= 12(p+1)(2p-6) = 24(p+1)(p-3)$

$\because$ For equal roots, discriminant = 0

$24(p+1)(p-3) = 0 \Rightarrow p+1 = 0$ or $p-3 = 0$

$p = -1$ or $p = 3$ but $p \neq -1$

$\therefore \quad p = 3$

$\Rightarrow \quad 4x^2 - 24x + 36 = 0 \Rightarrow x^2 - 6x + 9 = 0$

$\Rightarrow \quad (x-3)^2 = 0 \Rightarrow x = 3, 3$

Hence, the value of p is 3 and the roots are 3, 3.

Example 26. If -4 is a root of the quadratic equation $x^2 + px - 4 = 0$ and the quadratic equation $x^2 + px + k = 0$ has equal roots, then find the value of k.

Sol. Given, -4 is a root of the equation $x^2 + px - 4 = 0$.

So, -4 will satisfy the given equation.

$\therefore \quad (-4)^2 + p \times (-4) - 4 = 0$

$\Rightarrow \quad 16 - 4p - 4 = 0$

$\Rightarrow \quad 4p = 12$

$\Rightarrow \quad p = 3$

Now, the equation $x^2 + px + k = 0$ can be rewritten as $x^2 + 3x + k = 0$. Since, it has equal roots.

$\therefore$ Discriminant, $D = 0$

$\Rightarrow \quad b^2 - 4ac = 0$

$\Rightarrow \quad 3^2 - 4k = 0 \quad$ [here $a = 1$, $b = 3$ and $c = k$]

$\Rightarrow \quad 9 - 4k = 0$

$\therefore \quad k = \dfrac{9}{4}$

Example 27. If -4 is a root of the equation $x^2 + 2x + 4p = 0$, find the values of k, for which the equation $x^2 + p(1+3k)x + 7(3+2k) = 0$ has equal roots.

Sol. Given, -4 is a root of the equation

$$x^2 + 2x + 4p = 0.$$

So, -4 will satisfy the given equation.

$(-4)^2 + 2(-4) + 4p = 0$

$\Rightarrow \quad 16 - 8 + 4p = 0$

$\Rightarrow \quad 8 + 4p = 0$

$\Rightarrow \quad 2 + p = 0$

$\therefore \quad p = -2$

For $p = -2$, the equation $x^2 + p(1+3k)x + 7(3+2k) = 0$

$x^2 - 2(1+3k)x + 7(3+2k) + 0$

This quadratic equation has equal roots (given) its discriminant = 0

$\Rightarrow \quad [-2(1+3k)]^2 - 4 \times 1 \times 7(3+2k) = 0$

$\Rightarrow \quad 4(1 + 6k + 9k^2) - 28(3+2k) = 0$

$\Rightarrow \quad 1 + 6k + 9k^2 - 21 - 14k = 0$

$\Rightarrow \quad 9k^2 - 8k - 20 = 0$

$\Rightarrow \quad 9k^2 - 18k + 10k - 20 = 0$

$\Rightarrow \quad 9k(k-2) + 10(k-2) = 0$

$\Rightarrow \quad (k-2)(9k+10) = 0$

$\therefore \quad k = 2$

or $\quad k = -\dfrac{10}{9}$

Hence the value of k are 2 and $-\dfrac{10}{9}$.

Example 28. Determine the positive values of k, for which the equations $x^2 + kx + 64 = 0$ and $x^2 - 8x + k = 0$ will both have real roots.

Sol. Given, quadratic equations are

$$x^2 + kx + 64 = 0 \quad \ldots(i)$$

and $$x^2 - 8x + k = 0 \quad \ldots(ii)$$

Let D_1 and D_2 be the discriminants of Eqs. (i) and (ii), respectively.

Then, $\quad D_1 = k^2 - 4 \times 64 = k^2 - 256$

and $\quad D_2 = (-8)^2 - 4k = 64 - 4k$

Since, both the equations have real roots.

$\therefore \quad D_1 \geq 0$ and $D_2 \geq 0$

$\Rightarrow \quad k^2 - 256 \geq 0$ and $64 - 4k \geq 0$

$\Rightarrow \quad k^2 \geq 256$ and $4k \leq 64$

$\Rightarrow \quad k \geq 16$ and $k \leq 16 \quad [\because k > 0]$

$\therefore \quad k = 16$

Hence, for $k = 16$, both the equations will have real roots.

Example 29. Find the value of p, for which quadratic equation $px^2 - 8x + p = 0$ has real and distinct roots.

Sol. The given equation is $px^2 - 8x + p = 0 \quad \ldots(i)$

On comparing Eq. (i) with $ax^2 + bx + c = 0$

$a = p$, $b = -8$ and $c = p$

Discriminant $= b^2 - 4ac$

$= (-8)^2 - 4 \times p \times p = 64 - 4p^2$

For real and different roots discriminant > 0

$64 - 4p^2 > 0$

$\Rightarrow \quad 16 - p^2 > 0$

$\Rightarrow \quad p^2 - 16 < 0$

$\Rightarrow \quad (p+4)(p-4) < 0$

$\Rightarrow \quad -4 < p < 4$

Hence, the given equation has real and different roots, if $-4 < p < 4$.

Example 30. If k is a natural number and the roots of the equation $x^2 + 13x + 6k = 0$ are rational number, then find the smallest value of k.

Sol. The given equation $x^2 + 13x + 6k = 0$ ...(i)

On comparing Eq. (i) with $ax^2 + bx + c = 0$

$$a = 1, b = 13, c = 6k$$

$$\text{Discriminant} = b^2 - 4ac = (13)^2 - 4 \times 1 \times 6k = 169 - 24k$$

The coefficient of the given equation are rational numbers, therefore the given equation will have rational roots, if discriminant is a perfect square i.e. if $169 - 24k$ is a perfect square.

Given, k is a natural number.

For $k = 1$ discriminant $= 169 - 24 \times 1 = 145$, which is not a perfect square.

For $k = 2$ discriminant $= 169 - 24 \times 2 = 121$, which is a perfect square.

Hence, the smallest value of k for which the given equation has rational root is 2.

Exercise 5.2

1. Find the value of the discriminant in the following equations.
   (i) $x^2 + 2x + 4 = 0$
   (ii) $10x^2 - 1 = 3x$
   (iii) $x^2 - 5x + 1 = 0$
   (iv) $4x^2 - x - 3 = 0$
   (v) $4\sqrt{3}x^2 + 5x - 2\sqrt{3} = 0$
2. Determine the nature of the roots of the following quadratic equations.
   (i) $2x^2 + x - 1 = 0$ (ii) $x^2 - 4x + 4 = 0$
   (iii) $4x^2 - 8x + 5 = 0$ (iv) $7x^2 + 2x - 1 = 0$
   (v) $m^2 - 4m + 11 = 0$
3. Determine the nature of the roots of the following quadratic equations.
   (i) $2x^2 - 3x + 4 = 0$ (ii) $x^2 + 2\sqrt{3}x - 1 = 0$
   (iii) $(b + c)x^2 - (a + b + c)x + a = 0$
   (iv) $2x^2 - x - 3 = 0$ (v) $12x^2 = x + 1$
4. Find the value of k, for which the roots are real and equal, in each of the following equations.
   (i) $kx^2 - 2\sqrt{5}x + 4 = 0$
   (ii) $2kx^2 - 40x + 25 = 0$
   (iii) $(3k + 1)x^2 + 2(k + 1)x + k = 0$
   (iv) $x^2 - kx + 27 = 0$
   (v) $x^2 + 4kx + (k^2 - k + 2) = 0$ **[ICSE 2018]**
5. For the following equations determine the value of k, for which the given quadratic equation has real roots.
   (i) $2x^2 + kx + 3 = 0$
   (ii) $kx^2 + 6x + 1 = 0$
   (iii) $3x^2 + 2x + k = 0$
   (iv) $kx^2 + 2x - 7 = 0$
   (v) $3x^2 - kx - 4 = 0$
6. Find the value of k, for which the equation $5x^2 - kx + 1 = 0$ has real roots.
7. Find the values of k, for which the quadratic equation $9x^2 + kx + 1 = 0$ has equal roots. Also, find the roots in each case.
8. Find the value of p, for which the quadratic equation $(2p + 1)x^2 - (7p + 2)x + (7p - 3) = 0$ has equal roots, hence find the roots of the equation.
9. If the roots of the equation $(b - c)x^2 + (c - a)x + (a - b) = 0$ are equal, then prove that $2b = a + c$.
10. If the roots of the equations $ax^2 + 2bx + c = 0$ and $bx^2 - 2\sqrt{ac}\,x + b = 0$ are simultaneously real, then show that $b^2 = ac$.
11. If the roots of the equation $(c^2 - ab)x^2 - 2(a^2 - bc)x + (b^2 - ac) = 0$ are equal, prove that either $a = 0$ or $a^3 + b^3 + c^3 = 3abc$.
12. If -5 is a root of the quadratic equation $2x^2 + px + 5 = 0$ and the quadratic equation $p(x^2 + x) + k = 0$ has equal roots, then find the value of k.
13. If p, q, r and s are real numbers such that $pr = 2(q + s)$, then show that atleast one of the equations $x^2 + px + q = 0$ and $x^2 + rx + s = 0$ has real roots.
14. Prove that both the roots of the equation $(x-a)(x-b) + (x - b)(x - c) + (x - c)(x - a) = 0$ are real but they are equal only which $a = b = c$.
15. Find the value of p, for which the quadratic equation $px^2 - 6x + p = 0$ has real and distinct roots.
16. If k is a natural number and the roots of the equation $x^2 + 11x + 6k = 0$ are rational number, then find the smallest value of k.

Applications of Quadratic Equation

Many real life situations can be expressed as quadratic equations. The solution of such quadratic equations gives us the answer(s) to the problem. In this topic, we will discuss some simple applications of quadratic equations.

Different Types of Word Problems

Here, we will discuss various types of word problems and analyse, how to represent them as a quadratic equation.

1. Word Problems Based on Numbers

Some concepts that will be helpful in solving these types of problems are given below

(i) Two consecutive numbers can be chosen as x and $x+1$.

(ii) Two consecutive odd/even numbers can be chosen as x and $x+2$.

(iii) If sum of two numbers is given to us, say k, then the numbers can be chosen as x and $k-x$.

(iv) If difference of two numbers is given to us, say k, then the number can be chosen as x and $x+k$.

Example 31. The sum of the squares of two consecutive odd integers is 394. Find the integers.

Sol. Let two consecutive odd integers be x and $x+2$.

Then, according to the question,

$$x^2+(x+2)^2=394$$
$$\Rightarrow x^2+(x^2+4+4x)=394$$
$$\Rightarrow 2x^2+4x=390$$
$$\Rightarrow x^2+2x=195$$
$$\Rightarrow x^2+2x-195=0$$
$$\Rightarrow x^2+15x-13x-195=0$$
$$\Rightarrow x(x+15)-13(x+15)=0$$
$$\Rightarrow (x+15)(x-13)=0$$
$$\Rightarrow x=13 \text{ or } -15$$

When $x=13$, then other integer is 15 and when $x=-15$, then other integer is -13.

Thus, the integers are 13 and 15 or -13 and -15.

Example 32. Nine times a certain whole number is equal to five less than twice the square of the number. Find the number

Sol. Let the number be x.

Nine times the number = Twice the square of the number -5

$$\Rightarrow 9x=2x^2-5$$
$$\Rightarrow 2x^2-9x-5=0$$
$$\Rightarrow 2x^2-10x+x-5=0$$
$$\Rightarrow 2x(x-5)+1(x-5)=0$$
$$\Rightarrow (2x+1)(x-5)=0$$
$$x=5 \text{ or } x=-\frac{1}{2}$$

But x is a whole number, so

$$x=-\frac{1}{2} \text{ (reject).}$$

Hence, the required whole number is 5.

Example 33. The product of two consecutive natural numbers which are multiples of 3 is equal to 810. Find the two numbers.

Sol. Let two consecutive natural numbers having multiples of 3 are $3x$ and $3x+3$.

According to the given condition,

$$3x(3x+3)=810$$
$$\Rightarrow 9(x^2+x)=810$$
$$\Rightarrow x^2+x=90$$
$$\Rightarrow x^2+x-90=0$$
$$\Rightarrow x^2+10x-9x-90=0$$
$$\Rightarrow x(x+10)-9(x+10)=0$$
$$\Rightarrow (x-9)(x+10)=0$$
$$\Rightarrow x=9, x=-10$$

Since, numbers are natural, so we discard negative value.

$\therefore$ Required numbers are $3x=3\times 9=27$

and $3x+3=27+3=30$.

Example 34. The difference of two natural numbers is 4 and the difference of their reciprocals is 1/8. Find the numbers.

Sol. As the difference of two natural numbers is 4, let the numbers be x and $x+4$, where $x \in N$.

We know that $x+4>x$

$$\therefore \frac{1}{x+4}<\frac{1}{x}$$
$$\Rightarrow \frac{1}{x}-\frac{1}{x+4}>0$$

According to the question,

$$\frac{1}{x}-\frac{1}{x+4}=\frac{1}{8}$$
$$\Rightarrow \frac{(x+4)-x}{x(x+4)}=\frac{1}{8}$$
$$\Rightarrow \frac{4}{x(x+4)}=\frac{1}{8}$$
$$\Rightarrow x(x+4)=32$$
$$\Rightarrow x^2+4x-32=0$$
$$\Rightarrow x^2+8x-4x-32=0 \quad \text{[splitting the middle term]}$$
$$\Rightarrow x(x+8)-4(x+8)=0$$
$$\Rightarrow (x-4)(x+8)=0$$
$$\Rightarrow x-4=0 \text{ or } x+8=0$$
$$\Rightarrow x=4 \text{ or } x=-8$$

But $x \in N$

$$\therefore x=4$$

When $x=4$, then $x+4=4+4=8$

Hence, the required numbers are 4 and 8.

Example 35. The difference of two natural numbers is 7 and their product is 450. Find the numbers.

Sol. Let two natural numbers are respectively, x and y (such that $x > y$).

According to the question,

$$x - y = 7 \Rightarrow x = 7 + y \quad \text{...(i)}$$

and $xy = 450$

$\Rightarrow (7 + y)y = 450$ [using Eq. (i)]

$\Rightarrow 7y + y^2 = 450$

$\Rightarrow y^2 + 7y - 450 = 0 \Rightarrow y^2 + 25y - 18y - 450 = 0$

$\Rightarrow y(y + 25) - 18(y + 25) = 0 \Rightarrow (y - 18)(y + 25) = 0$

$\Rightarrow y = 18$ [$\because y \neq -25$]

$\therefore x = 7 + 18 = 25$

$\therefore$ Required natural number are 25 and 18.

Example 36. The sum of a number and its positive square root is $\frac{6}{25}$. Find the number.

Sol. Let the number be x. Then, its positive square root be $\sqrt{x}$.

$\therefore x + \sqrt{x} = \frac{6}{25}$ [by given condition]

$\Rightarrow 25x + 25\sqrt{x} = 6$ [multiplying both sides by 25]

$\Rightarrow 25x + 25\sqrt{x} - 6 = 0$

Put $\sqrt{x} = y \Rightarrow x = y^2$, then above equation becomes

$25y^2 + 25y - 6 = 0$

$\Rightarrow 25y^2 + 30y - 5y - 6 = 0$ [splitting the middle term]

$\Rightarrow 5y(5y + 6) - 1(5y + 6) = 0$

$\Rightarrow (5y - 1)(5y + 6) = 0$

$\Rightarrow y = \frac{1}{5}$ or $y = -\frac{6}{5}$

Again, substituting the values of y in $\sqrt{x} = y$, we get

$\sqrt{x} = \frac{1}{5}$ or $\sqrt{x} = -\frac{6}{5}$

But $\sqrt{x} = \frac{-6}{5}$ is not possible, because $\sqrt{x}$ is positive.

$\therefore \sqrt{x} = \frac{1}{5} \Rightarrow x = \frac{1}{25}$

Hence, the required number is $\frac{1}{25}$.

2. Word Problems Based on Digits

Some concepts that will be helpful in solving these types of problems, are given below

If the digit in unit's place is x and that in ten's place is y. Then, two-digit number is given by $10y + x$.

On interchanging the positions of the digits, the digit in unit's place becomes y and in ten's place becomes x and then two-digit number becomes $10x + y$.

Example 37. A two-digit positive number is such that the product of its digits is 6. If 9 is added to the number, then the digits interchange their places. Find the number. [ICSE 2014]

Sol. Let the required two-digit number be $10x + y$, where y is unit's digit and x is ten's digit.

According to the question,

$xy = 6$ and $10x + y + 9 = 10y + x$

$\Rightarrow y = \frac{6}{x}$ and $9x - 9y + 9 = 0$

Now, $9(x - y) = -9$

$\Rightarrow x - y = -1$ [dividing both sides by 9] ...(i)

$\Rightarrow x - \frac{6}{x} = -1$ $\left[\because y = \frac{6}{x}\right]$

$\Rightarrow \frac{x^2 - 6}{x} = -1$

$\Rightarrow x^2 - 6 = -x$

$\Rightarrow x^2 + x - 6 = 0$

$\Rightarrow x^2 + 3x - 2x - 6 = 0$ [splitting the middle term]

$\Rightarrow x(x + 3) - 2(x + 3) = 0$

$\Rightarrow (x + 3)(x - 2) = 0$ [factorising left side]

$\Rightarrow x = -3$ or $x = 2$

$\therefore x = 2$ [$\because$ digit cannot be negative]

On putting $x = 2$ in Eq. (i), we get

$2 - y = -1 \Rightarrow -y = -1 - 2 = -3 \Rightarrow y = 3$

$\therefore$ The required two-digit number

$= 10x + y = 10 \times 2 + 3 = 23$

Hence, the required number is 23.

3. Word Problems Based on Fractions

A concept that will be helpful in solving these types of problems is given below

If the numerator of the fraction is x and denominator is y, then the fraction is given by x / y.

Example 38. The denominator of a fraction is one more than twice the numerator. If the sum of fraction and its reciprocal is $2\frac{16}{21}$, then find the fraction.

Sol. Let the numerator of the fraction be $x (x \in I)$, then its denominator $= 2x + 1$ and so the fraction is $\frac{x}{2x+1}$.

According to the question,

$$\frac{x}{2x+1} + \frac{2x+1}{x} = 2\frac{16}{21}$$

$\Rightarrow \frac{x^2 + (2x+1)^2}{x(2x+1)} = \frac{58}{21}$

$\Rightarrow 58x(2x + 1) = 21(x^2 + 4x^2 + 4x + 1)$

$\Rightarrow 116x^2 + 58x = 105x^2 + 84x + 21$

$\Rightarrow 11x^2 - 26x - 21 = 0$

$\Rightarrow 11x^2 - 33x + 7x - 21 = 0$ [splitting the middle term]

$\Rightarrow 11x(x - 3) + 7(x - 3) = 0$

$\Rightarrow (x - 3)(11x + 7) = 0$

$\Rightarrow x - 3 = 0$ or $11x + 7 = 0$

$\Rightarrow x = 3$ or $x = -\frac{7}{11}$ [$\because x$ is an integer]

$\Rightarrow x = 3$

$\therefore$ Required fraction $= \frac{3}{2 \times 3 + 1} = \frac{3}{7}$

Example 39. The sum of the numerator and denominator of a certain fraction is 8. If 2 is added to both the numerator and denominator, the fraction is increased by $\frac{4}{35}$. Find the fraction.

Sol. Let the fraction be x/y. Then, according to the question,

$$x+y=8 \quad \text{...(i)}$$

and $$\frac{x+2}{y+2}=\frac{x}{y}+\frac{4}{35} \quad \text{...(ii)}$$

From Eq. (ii), we get

$$\frac{x+2}{y+2}-\frac{x}{y}=\frac{4}{35} \Rightarrow \frac{(x+2)y-x(y+2)}{y(y+2)}=\frac{4}{35}$$

$\Rightarrow$ $35(xy+2y-xy-2x)=4y(y+2)$

$\Rightarrow$ $35(2y-2x)=4y(y+2)$

$\Rightarrow$ $35(y-x)=2y(y+2)$ [dividing both sides by 2]

$\Rightarrow$ $35(y-(8-y))=2y(y+2)$ [from Eq. (i)]

$\Rightarrow$ $35(2y-8)=2y(y+2)$

$\Rightarrow$ $35(2(y-4))=2y(y+2)$

$\Rightarrow$ $35(y-4)=y(y+2)$ [dividing both sides by 2]

$\Rightarrow$ $35y-140=y^2+2y$

$\Rightarrow$ $y^2+2y-35y+140=0$

$\Rightarrow$ $y^2-33y+140=0$

$\Rightarrow$ $y^2-28y-5y+140=0$ [splitting the middle term]

$\Rightarrow$ $y(y-28)-5(y-28)=0$

$\Rightarrow$ $(y-28)(y-5)=0$

$\Rightarrow$ $y=28$ or $y=5$

$\Rightarrow$ $y=5$ [$\because y\neq 28$, as sum of fraction is 8]

On substituting $y=5$ in Eq. (i), we get

$$x+5=8 \Rightarrow x=3$$

Hence, the fraction is $\frac{3}{5}$.

4. Word Problems Based on Age

Some concepts that will be helpful in solving these types of problems, are given below

If the present age of a person is x yr, then

(i) 'a' yr ago, age of person was $(x-a)$ yr.

(ii) after 'b' yr, age of person will be $(x+b)$ yr.

Example 40. 7 yr ago, Varun's age was 5 times the square of Swati's age. 3 yr hence, Swati's age will be $\frac{2}{5}$th of Varun's age. Find their present ages.

Sol. Let 7 yr ago, Swati's age be x yr.

Then, Varun's age = $5x^2$ yr

$\therefore$ Swati's present age = $(x+7)$ yr

and Varun's present age = $(5x^2+7)$ yr

3 yr hence, i.e. after 3 yr from now,

Swati's age = $(x+7+3)=(x+10)$ yr

Varun's age = $(5x^2+7+3)=(5x^2+10)$ yr

According to the question,

$$x+10=\frac{2}{5}(5x^2+10)$$

$\Rightarrow$ $x+10=2x^2+4$

$\Rightarrow$ $2x^2-x-6=0$

$\Rightarrow$ $2x^2-4x+3x-6=0$ [splitting the middle term]

$\Rightarrow$ $2x(x-2)+3(x-2)=0 \Rightarrow (2x+3)(x-2)=0$

$\Rightarrow$ $x-2=0$ or $2x+3=0 \Rightarrow x=2$ or $x=\frac{-3}{2}$

But $x\neq\frac{-3}{2}$ [since, age cannot be negative]

$\therefore$ $x=2$

Hence, Swati's present age = 2 + 7 = 9 yr

and Varun's present age = $5\times 2^2+7=27$ yr

Example 41. 5 yr ago, a woman's age was the square of her son's age. 10 yr hence, her age will be twice that of her son's age. Find

(i) the age of the son 5 yr ago.

(ii) the present age of the woman. **[ICSE 2007]**

Sol. Let the age of the son 5 yr ago be x yr, then the age of the woman 5 yr ago be x^2 yr.

Now, the present age of the son = $(x+5)$ yr

and the present age of the woman = (x^2+5) yr

10 yr hence, i.e. after 10 yr from now,

the age of the son = $((x+5)+10)$ yr = $(x+15)$ yr

and the age of the woman = $((x^2+5)+10)$ yr = (x^2+15) yr

According to the question, $x^2+15=2(x+15)$

$\Rightarrow$ $x^2+15=2x+30 \Rightarrow x^2-2x-15=0$

$\Rightarrow$ $x^2-5x+3x-15=0$ [splitting the middle term]

$\Rightarrow$ $x(x-5)+3(x-5)=0$

$\Rightarrow$ $(x-5)(x+3)=0 \Rightarrow x-5=0$ or $x+3=0$

$\Rightarrow$ $x=5$ or $x=-3$ but x being age cannot be negative

$\therefore$ $x=5$

(i) The age of the son 5 yr ago = 5 yr

(ii) The present age of the woman = (x^2+5) yr = (5^2+5) yr = 30 yr

Example 42. The sum of the ages of Vivek and his younger brother Amit is 47 yr. The product of their ages in years is 550. Find their ages. **[ICSE 2017]**

Sol. Let the age of Vivek be x yr and age of younger brother be y yr.

According to the question,

$$x+y=47 \quad \text{...(i)}$$

and $$xy=550 \quad \text{...(ii)}$$

Now, $$x-y=\sqrt{(x+y)^2-4xy}=\sqrt{(47)^2-4\times 550}$$

$$=\sqrt{2209-2200}=\sqrt{9} \Rightarrow x-y=3 \quad \text{...(iii)}$$

On subtracting Eq. (iii) from Eq. (i), we get

$$2y=44 \Rightarrow y=\frac{44}{2}=22$$

On putting the value of y in Eq. (i), we get

$$x+22=47 \Rightarrow x=47-22=25$$

$\therefore$ Age of Vivek = 25 yr

and age of his younger brother = 22 yr

5. Word Problems Based on Time and Work

The concept that will be used for these types of problems, is given below

If a person can do a piece of work in n days, then he will do $1/n$ of the work in one day and *vice-versa*.

Example 43. B takes 16 days less than A to do a piece of work. If both, working together can do it in 15 days, then in how many days, will B alone complete the work?

Sol. Let A complete the work in x days. Then, B will complete it in $(x-16)$ days.

$\therefore$ A's one day work $= \frac{1}{x}$ and B's one day work $= \frac{1}{x-16}$

Since, A and B together can complete the work in 15 days.

$\therefore$ A's one day work + B's one day work $= \frac{1}{15}$

$$\Rightarrow \quad \frac{1}{x} + \frac{1}{x-16} = \frac{1}{15}$$
$$\Rightarrow \quad \frac{x-16+x}{x(x-16)} = \frac{1}{15}$$
$$\Rightarrow \quad x(x-16) = 15(2x-16)$$
$$\Rightarrow \quad x^2 - 16x = 30x - 240$$
$$\Rightarrow \quad x^2 - 46x + 240 = 0$$
$$\Rightarrow \quad x^2 - 40x - 6x + 240 = 0 \text{ [splitting the middle term]}$$
$$\Rightarrow \quad x(x-40) - 6(x-40) = 0 \Rightarrow (x-6)(x-40) = 0$$
$$\Rightarrow \quad x-6 = 0 \text{ or } x-40 = 0$$
$$\Rightarrow \quad x = 6 \text{ or } x = 40$$

If $x = 6$, then $x - 16 = 6 - 16 = -10$, which is not possible.

$$\therefore \quad x = 40$$

Hence, B alone will complete the work in $(40 - 16)$ days i.e. 24 days.

Example 44. To fill a swimming pool, two pipes are to be used. If the pipe of the larger diameter is used for 4 h and the pipe of the smaller diameter is used for 9 h, only half of the pool can be filled. Find how long it would take for each pipe to fill the pool separately, if the pipe of the smaller diameter takes 10 h more than the pipe of the larger diameter to fill the pool?

Sol. Let the time taken by the pipe of the larger diameter to fill the pool separately be x h, then the time taken by the pipe of the smaller diameter to fill the pool separately $= (x+10)$ h.

Then, the part of the pool filled by the pipe of larger diameter in 4 h $= \frac{4}{x}$ and the part of the pool filled by the pipe of the smaller diameter in 9 h $= \frac{9}{x+10}$.

According to the question, $\frac{4}{x} + \frac{9}{x+10} = \frac{1}{2}$

$$\Rightarrow \quad \frac{4(x+10)+9x}{x(x+10)} = \frac{1}{2} \Rightarrow \frac{13x+40}{x^2+10x} = \frac{1}{2}$$
$$\Rightarrow \quad x^2 + 10x = 26x + 80 \Rightarrow x^2 - 16x - 80 = 0$$
$$\Rightarrow \quad x^2 - 20x + 4x - 80 = 0 \text{ [splitting the middle term]}$$
$$\Rightarrow \quad x(x-20) + 4(x-20) = 0$$
$$\Rightarrow \quad (x-20)(x+4) = 0$$
$$\Rightarrow \quad x = 20 \text{ or } x = -4$$

But x being the time taken cannot be negative, so $x = 20$.

Hence, the time taken to fill the pool by the two pipes separately is 20 h and $(x+10)$ h i.e. 30 h.

6. Word Problems Based on Distance, Speed and Time

Some formulae that will be used for these types of problems, are given below

$$\text{Speed} = \frac{\text{Distance}}{\text{Time}} \Rightarrow \text{Distance} = \text{Speed} \times \text{Time}$$

$$\text{or Time} = \frac{\text{Distance}}{\text{Speed}}$$

If the problem is related to speed of boat going downstream and upstream and if the speed of boat in still water is x km/h and speed of stream is y km/h, then speed of boat downstream $= (x+y)$ km/h and speed of boat upstream $= (x-y)$ km/h.

Example 45. A car covers a distance of 400 km at a certain speed. Had the speed been 12 km/h more, the time taken for the journey would have been 1 h 40 min less. Find the original speed of the car. **[ICSE 2012]**

Sol. Let the original speed of the car be x km/h.

$\because$ Distance covered by a car = 400 km

$\therefore$ Original time taken, $T = \frac{400}{x}$ h $\quad \left[\because \text{time} = \frac{\text{distance}}{\text{speed}}\right]$

Further, speed is increased by 12 km/h.

$\therefore$ Speed $= (x+12)$ km/h

Now, new time taken $= \frac{400}{x+12}$ h

According to the question, $\frac{400}{x} - \frac{400}{x+12} = \frac{5}{3}$

$$\left[\because 1 \text{ h } 40 \text{ min} = 1 \text{ h} + 40 \text{ min} = 1 \text{ h} + \frac{40}{60}\text{ h} = 1\text{ h} + \frac{2}{3}\text{ h} = \left(1+\frac{2}{3}\right)\text{ h} = \frac{5}{3}\text{ h}\right]$$

$$\Rightarrow \quad 400\left(\frac{1}{x} - \frac{1}{x+12}\right) = \frac{5}{3} \Rightarrow 400\left[\frac{x+12-x}{x(x+12)}\right] = \frac{5}{3}$$
$$\Rightarrow \quad 80(12) \times 3 = x(x+12) \text{ [dividing both sides by 5]}$$
$$\Rightarrow \quad 2880 = x^2 + 12x$$
$$\Rightarrow \quad x^2 + 12x - 2880 = 0$$
$$\Rightarrow \quad x^2 + 60x - 48x - 2880 = 0 \text{ [splitting the middle term]}$$
$$\Rightarrow \quad x(x+60) - 48(x+60) = 0$$
$$\Rightarrow \quad (x+60)(x-48) = 0$$
$$\Rightarrow \quad x+60 = 0 \text{ or } x-48 = 0$$
$$\Rightarrow \quad x = 48 \text{ or } x = -60$$
$$\therefore \quad x = 48 \text{ km/h} \quad [\because \text{speed cannot be negative}]$$

Hence, the original speed of the car is 48 km/h.

Example 46. Sonal can row a boat at a speed of 5 km/h. If it takes her 1 h more to row the boat 5.25 km upstream than to return downstream, then find the speed of the stream.

Sol. Let the speed of the stream be x km/h, where $0 < x < 5$.

Then, speed of the boat upstream = $(5 - x)$ km/h

and speed of the boat downstream = $(5 + x)$ km/h

$\therefore$ Time taken for going 5.25 km upstream = $\frac{5.25}{5-x}$ h

and time taken for going 5.25 km downstream = $\frac{5.25}{5+x}$ h

According to the question,

$$\frac{5.25}{5-x} - \frac{5.25}{5+x} = 1$$

$$\Rightarrow \frac{21}{4}\left(\frac{1}{5-x} - \frac{1}{5+x}\right) = 1$$

$$\Rightarrow 21[(5+x) - (5-x)] = 4(5-x)(5+x)$$

$$\Rightarrow 42x = 4(25 - x^2) \quad [\because (a-b)(a+b) = a^2 - b^2]$$

$$\Rightarrow 4x^2 + 42x - 100 = 0$$

$$\Rightarrow 2x^2 + 21x - 50 = 0 \quad \text{[dividing both sides by 2]}$$

$$\Rightarrow 2x^2 + 25x - 4x - 50 = 0 \quad \text{[splitting the middle term]}$$

$$\Rightarrow x(2x + 25) - 2(2x + 25) = 0$$

$$\Rightarrow (2x + 25)(x - 2) = 0$$

$$\Rightarrow 2x + 25 = 0 \text{ or } x - 2 = 0$$

$$\Rightarrow x = \frac{-25}{2} \text{ or } x = 2$$

$$\therefore x = 2 \quad [\because \text{speed cannot be negative}]$$

Hence, the required speed is 2 km/h.

Example 47. In a flight of 600 km, an aircraft was slowed down due to bad weather. Its average speed for the trip was reduced by 200 km/h and the time of flight increased by 30 min. Find the duration of flight.

Sol. Let the original speed of the aircraft be x km/h. Then,

New speed = $(x - 200)$ km/h

Duration of flight at original speed = $\left(\frac{600}{x}\right)$ h

Duration of flight at reduced speed = $\left(\frac{600}{x-200}\right)$ h

According to the question,

$$\frac{600}{x-200} - \frac{600}{x} = 30 \text{ min} = \frac{1}{2} \text{ h}$$

$$\Rightarrow \frac{600}{x-200} - \frac{600}{x} = \frac{1}{2} \quad \left[\because 30 \text{ min} = \frac{30}{60} \text{ h} = \frac{1}{2} \text{ h}\right]$$

$$\Rightarrow \frac{600x - 600(x-200)}{x(x-200)} = \frac{1}{2} \Rightarrow \frac{120000}{x^2 - 200x} = \frac{1}{2}$$

$$\Rightarrow x^2 - 200x - 240000 = 0$$

$$\Rightarrow x^2 - 600x + 400x - 240000 = 0$$

[splitting the middle term]

$$\Rightarrow x(x - 600) + 400(x - 600) = 0$$

$$\Rightarrow (x - 600)(x + 400) = 0$$

$$\Rightarrow x - 600 = 0 \text{ or } x + 400 = 0$$

$$\Rightarrow x = 600 \text{ or } x = -400$$

$$\therefore x = 600 \quad [\because \text{speed cannot be negative}]$$

So, the original speed of the aircraft was 600 km/h.

Hence, the duration of flight = $\frac{600}{x}$ h = $\frac{600}{600}$ h = 1h

Example 48. A bus covers a distance of 240 km at a uniform speed. Due to heavy rain, its speed gets reduced by 10 km/h and as such it takes two hours longer to cover the total distance. Assuming the uniform speed to be 'x' km/h, form an equation and solve it to evaluate 'x'. **[ICSE 2016]**

Sol. Let the uniform speed of bus be x km/h.

$\therefore$ Time taken by bus to cover a distance of 240 km

$$T_1 = \frac{240}{x} \text{ h}$$

$\because$ Due to heavy rain, speed of bus is reduced by 10 km/h.

$\therefore$ Reduced speed = $(x - 10)$ km/h

Now, time taken by bus to cover a distance of 240 km with speed $(x - 10)$ km/h

$$T_2 = \left(\frac{240}{x-10}\right) \text{h}$$

According to the question,

$$T_2 - T_1 = 2$$

$$\Rightarrow \frac{240}{x-10} - \frac{240}{x} = 2$$

$$\Rightarrow 240\left[\frac{x - x + 10}{x(x-10)}\right] = 2 \Rightarrow \frac{2400}{x(x-10)} = 2$$

$$\Rightarrow 2x(x - 10) = 2400$$

$$\Rightarrow x(x - 10) = 1200$$

$$\Rightarrow x^2 - 10x - 1200 = 0$$

which is the required equation.

$$\therefore x = \frac{10 \pm \sqrt{100 + 4800}}{2}$$

[by Sridharacharya formula]

$$= \frac{10 \pm \sqrt{4900}}{2} = \frac{10 \pm 70}{2} = 40, -30$$

$$\therefore x = 40 \quad [\because \text{speed cannot be negative}]$$

Hence, the speed of bus is 40 km/h.

7. Word Problems Based on Monetary Transaction

Some concepts that will be helpful in solving these types of problems, are given below.

(i) If the cost of x articles is ₹ y, then the cost of each article is ₹ $\left(\frac{y}{x}\right)$.

(ii) Selling price of an article = Cost of an article + Profit *or* Cost of an article − Loss

Example 49. A dealer sells a toy for ₹ 24 and gains as much per cent as the cost price of the toy. Find the cost price of the toy.

Sol. Let the cost price of the toy be ₹ x.

Then, gain percent = x%

$\therefore$ Gain $= x \times \frac{x}{100} = ₹\ \frac{x^2}{100}$

Now, SP = CP + Gain $= x + \frac{x^2}{100}$

But SP = ₹ 24 [given]

$\therefore \quad x + \frac{x^2}{100} = 24$

$\Rightarrow \quad 100x + x^2 = 2400$

$\Rightarrow \quad x^2 + 100x - 2400 = 0$

$\Rightarrow \quad x^2 + 120x - 20x - 2400 = 0$ [splitting the middle term]

$\Rightarrow \quad x(x+120) - 20(x+120) = 0$

$\Rightarrow \quad (x+120)(x-20) = 0$

$\Rightarrow \quad x + 120 = 0$ or $x - 20 = 0$

$\Rightarrow \quad x = 20, -120$

$\therefore \quad x = 20$ [$\because$ cost cannot be negative]

Hence, the cost price of a toy is ₹ 20.

Example 50. ₹ 480 is divided equally among x children. If the number of children was 20 more than each would have got ₹ 12 less. Find the value of x. **[ICSE 2011]**

Sol. Given, total money = ₹ 480

and original number of children = x

Then, money received by each child = ₹ $\frac{480}{x}$

Since, number of children was 20 more.

$\therefore$ Total number of children = $x + 20$

and the money received by each child = ₹ $\frac{480}{x+20}$

According to the question, $\frac{480}{x} - \frac{480}{x+20} = 12$

$\Rightarrow \quad \frac{480(x+20) - 480x}{x(x+20)} = 12$

$\Rightarrow \quad \frac{480\,(x+20-x)}{x\,(x+20)} = 12$

$\Rightarrow \quad \frac{40\,(20)}{x\,(x+20)} = 1$ [dividing both sides by 12]

$\Rightarrow \quad x\,(x+20) = 800 \Rightarrow x^2 + 20x - 800 = 0$

$\Rightarrow \quad x^2 + 40x - 20\,x - 800 = 0$ [splitting the middle term]

$\Rightarrow \quad x\,(x+40) - 20\,(x+40) = 0$

$\Rightarrow \quad (x-20)(x+40) = 0$

$\Rightarrow \quad x = 20$ or $x = -40$

$\therefore \quad x = 20$ [$\because x$ cannot be negative]

Hence, the number of children is 20.

Example 51. A piece of cloth costs ₹ 200. If the piece was 5 m longer and each metre of cloth costs ₹ 2 less, the cost of the piece would have remained unchanged. How long is the piece and what is the original rate per metre?

Sol. Let the original length of piece be x m.

Then, rate = ₹ $\frac{200}{x}$ per m

$\therefore$ New length = $(x+5)$ m

Since, the cost remains same.

$\therefore$ New rate = ₹ $\frac{200}{x+5}$ per m

According to the question,

$\frac{200}{x+5} = \frac{200}{x} - 2 \Rightarrow \frac{200}{x} - \frac{200}{x+5} = 2$

$\Rightarrow \quad 200\left(\frac{1}{x} - \frac{1}{x+5}\right) = 2 \Rightarrow \frac{x+5-x}{x(x+5)} = \frac{2}{200}$

$\Rightarrow \quad \frac{5}{x^2+5x} = \frac{1}{100} \Rightarrow x^2 + 5x = 500$

$\Rightarrow \quad x^2 + 5x - 500 = 0$

$\Rightarrow \quad x^2 + 25x - 20x - 500 = 0$ [splitting the middle term]

$\Rightarrow \quad x(x+25) - 20(x+25) = 0$

$\Rightarrow \quad (x+25)(x-20) = 0$

$\Rightarrow \quad x + 25 = 0$ or $x - 20 = 0$

$\Rightarrow \quad x = -25$ or $x = 20$

$\Rightarrow \quad x = 20$ m [$\because$ length cannot be negative]

$\therefore \quad$ Rate $= \frac{200}{x} = \frac{200}{20} =$ ₹ 10 per m

Hence, the original length of the piece is 20 m and its original rate per metre is ₹ 10.

Example 52. A shopkeeper purchases a certain number of books for ₹ 960. If the cost per book was ₹ 8 less the number of books that could be purchased for ₹ 960, would be 4 more. Write an equation, taking the original cost of each book to be ₹ x and solve it to find the original cost of the books. **[ICSE 2013]**

Sol. Given, total cost of books purchased = ₹ 960

Let the original cost of one book purchased be ₹ x.

Then, the total number of books purchased = $\frac{960}{x}$

If the cost of per book is ₹ 8 less, then

Cost of one book purchased = ₹ $(x-8)$

and total number of books purchased = $\frac{960}{x-8}$

According to the question, $\frac{960}{x-8} = \frac{960}{x} + 4$

$\Rightarrow \quad \frac{960}{x-8} - \frac{960}{x} = 4 \Rightarrow 960\left(\frac{1}{x-8} - \frac{1}{x}\right) = 4$

$\Rightarrow \quad \frac{960\,(x-x+8)}{x(x-8)} = 4 \Rightarrow \frac{240 \times 8}{x\,(x-8)} = 1$ [dividing both sides by 4]

$\Rightarrow \quad x^2 - 8x = 1920$

$\Rightarrow \quad x^2 - 8x - 1920 = 0$

$\Rightarrow \quad x^2 - 48x + 40x - 1920 = 0$ [splitting the middle term]

$\Rightarrow \quad x\,(x-48) + 40\,(x-48) = 0 \Rightarrow (x-48)\,(x+40) = 0$

$\Rightarrow \quad x - 48 = 0$ or $x + 40 = 0$

$\Rightarrow \quad x = 48$ or $x = -40$

$\therefore \quad x = 48$ [$\because$ cost cannot be negative]

Hence, the original cost of each book is ₹ 48.

8. Word Problems Based on Geometry

Example 53. The hypotenuse of right angled triangle is 6 m more than twice the shortest side. If the third side is 2 m less than the hypotenuse, then find all sides of the triangle.

Sol. Let length of the shortest side be x m.

Then, hypotenuse $= (2x + 6)$m and third side $= (2x + 6 - 2)$m $= (2x + 4)$m

By Pythagoras theorem,

$$(2x+6)^2 = x^2 + (2x+4)^2 \quad [\because H^2 = P^2 + B^2]$$

$$\Rightarrow \quad 4x^2 + 24x + 36 = x^2 + 4x^2 + 16x + 16$$

$$[\because (a+b)^2 = a^2 + 2ab + b^2]$$

$$\Rightarrow \quad x^2 + 4x^2 + 16x + 16 - 4x^2 - 24x - 36 = 0$$

$$\Rightarrow \quad x^2 - 8x - 20 = 0 \quad \text{...(i)}$$

On comparing Eq. (i) with $ax^2 + bx + c = 0$, we get

$$a = 1, b = -8, c = -20$$

By quadratic formula,

$$x = \frac{-b \pm \sqrt{b^2 - 4ac}}{2a}$$

$$= \frac{-(-8) \pm \sqrt{(-8)^2 - 4 \times 1 \times (-20)}}{2 \times 1}$$

$$\Rightarrow \quad x = \frac{8 \pm \sqrt{64 + 80}}{2}$$

$$\Rightarrow \quad x = \frac{8 \pm \sqrt{144}}{2} \Rightarrow x = \frac{8 \pm 12}{2}$$

$$\Rightarrow \quad x = \frac{8+12}{2} \text{ or } x = \frac{8-12}{2}$$

$$\Rightarrow \quad x = \frac{20}{2} \text{ or } x = \frac{-4}{2}$$

$$\Rightarrow \quad x = 10 \text{ or } x = -2$$

But length of side cannot be negative.

$$\therefore \quad x = 10$$

Hence, the shortest side is 10 m, hypotenuse is $2 \times 10 + 6 = 26$ m and third side $= 2 \times 10 + 4 = 24$ m.

9. Word Problems Based on Mensuration

Example 54. A rectangular park is to be designed whose breadth is 3 m less than its length. Its area is to be 4 sq m more than the area of a park that has already been made in the shape of an isosceles triangle with its base as the breadth of the rectangular park and of altitude 12 m. Find its length and breadth of the rectangular park.

Sol. Let breadth of rectangular park be x m.

Then, length of rectangular park $= (x + 3)$ m

Now, area of rectangular park $= x(x+3) = (x^2 + 3x)$ m^2

[$\because$ area = length × breadth]

Given, base of triangular park = Breadth of the rectangular park

$\therefore$ Base of triangular park $= x$ m

and also it is given that altitude of triangular park $= 12$ m

$$\therefore \text{ Area of triangular park} = \frac{1}{2} \times x \times 12 = 6x \text{ m}^2$$

$$\left[\because \text{area of triangle} = \frac{1}{2} \times \text{base} \times \text{altitude}\right]$$

According to the question,

Area of rectangular park = 4 + Area of triangular park

$$\Rightarrow \quad x^2 + 3x = 4 + 6x$$

$$\Rightarrow \quad x^2 + 3x - 6x - 4 = 0$$

$$\Rightarrow \quad x^2 - 3x - 4 = 0$$

$$\Rightarrow \quad x^2 - 4x + x - 4 = 0 \quad \text{[by factorisation]}$$

$$\Rightarrow \quad x(x-4) + 1(x-4) = 0$$

$$\Rightarrow \quad (x-4)(x+1) = 0$$

$$\Rightarrow \quad x - 4 = 0 \text{ or } x + 1 = 0$$

$$\Rightarrow \quad x = 4 \text{ or } x = -1$$

Since, breadth cannot be negative, so neglect $x = -1$

$$\therefore \quad x = 4$$

Hence, the breadth of the rectangular park = 4 m and the length of the rectangular park $= x + 3 = 4 + 3 = 7$ m

Exercise 5.3

1. The sum of the squares of two consecutive natural numbers is 481. Find the numbers.
2. The sum of the squares of two consecutive odd positive integers is 290. Find them.
3. There are three consecutive positive integers such that the sum of the square of the first and the product of other two is 154. What are the integers?
4. Divide 25 into two parts, such that twice the square of the larger part exceeds thrice the square of the smaller part by 29. Find the smaller and larger part.
5. A natural number, when increased by 12 equals 160 times its reciprocal. Find the number
6. The sum of two numbers is 18. If the sum of their reciprocals is $\frac{1}{4}$, then find the numbers.
7. A two-digit number is such that the product of its digits is 18. When 63 is subtracted from the number, the digits interchange their places. Find the number.
8. A two-digit number contains the smaller of two digits in the unit's place .The product of the digits is 24 and the difference between the digits is 5. Find the number.

9. In a certain positive fraction, the denominator is greater than the numerator by 3. If 1 is subtracted from both the numerator and denominator, the fraction is decreased by $\frac{1}{14}$, then find the fraction.

10. The product of Shikha's age 5 yr ago and her age 8 yr later is 30, find her percentage.

11. The sum of the reciprocals of Rehman's ages (in years) 3 yr ago and 5 yr from now is 1/3. Find his present age.

12. A takes 10 days less than the time taken by B to finish a piece of work. If both A and B together can finish the work in 12 days, find the time taken by B to finish the work.

13. Two water pipes together can fill a tank in $9\frac{3}{8}$ h. The pipe of larger diameter takes 10 h less than the smaller one to fill the tank separately. Find the time in which each pipe can fill the tank separately.

14. A man covers a distance of 100 km, travelling with a uniform speed of x km/h. Had the speed been 5 km/h more it would have taken 1 h less. Find x the original speed. **[ICSE 2023]**

15. The speed of an express train is x km/h and the speed of an ordinary train is 12 km/h less than that of the express train. If the ordinary train takes one hour more than the express train to cover a distance of 240 km, then find the speed of the express train. **[ICSE 2009]**

16. An aeroplane flying with a wind of 30 km/h takes 40 min less to fly 3600 km than what it would to have taken to fly against the same wind. Find the aeroplane's speed of flying in still air.

17. A piece of cloth costs ₹ 300. If the piece was 5 cm longer and each metre of cloth costs ₹ 2 less, the cost of the piece would have remained unchanged. How long is the original piece of cloth and what is the rate per metre?

18. A peacock is sitting on pillar 9 m high. A snake at a distance of 27 m from the pillar, is coming to a hole at the base of the pillar. Seeing the snake, the peacock pounces upon it. If their speeds are equal, at what distance from the hole is snake caught?

19. Some students planned a picnic. The budget for the food was ₹ 480. As eight of them failed to join the party, the cost of the food for each member is increased by ₹ 10. Find how many students went for the picnic? **[ICSE 2008]**

20. The hotel bill for a number of persons for overnight stay is ₹ 4800. If there were 4 more persons, the bill each person had to pay, would have reduced by ₹ 200. Find the number of persons staying overnight. **[ICSE 2000]**

21. ₹7500 were divided equally among a certain number of children. Had there been 20 less children, each would have received ₹100 more. Find the original number of children. **[ICSE 2018]**

22. The hypotenuse of a right triangle is 25 cm. The difference between the lengths of the other two sides of the triangle is 5 cm. Find the lengths of these sides.

23. P and Q are centres of circles of radius 9 cm and 2 cm, respectively. $PQ = 17$ cm. R is the centre of a circle of radius X cm, which touches the above circles externally. Given that $\angle PRQ = 90°$. Write an equation in X and solve it.

24. Mohini wishes to fit three rods together in the shape of a right triangle. If the hypotenuse is 2 cm longer than the base and 4 cm longer than the shortest side, then find the lengths of the rods.

25. If the perimeter of a rectangular plot is 68 m and length of its diagonal is 26 m, then find its area.

26. The perimeter of a rectangular plot is 180 m and its area is 1800 m^2. Take the length of the plot as x m. Use the perimeter 180 m to write the value of the breadth in terms of x. Use the values of length, breadth and the area to write an equation in x. Solve the equation to calculate the length and breadth of the plot.

27. A grassy land is in the shape of a right triangle. The hypotenuse of the land is 1 m more than twice the shortest side. If the third side is 7 m more than the shortest side, find the sides of the grassy land.

28. A rectangular field is 20 m long and 14 m wide there is a path of equal width all around it. Having an area of 111 m^2. Find the width of the path.

Chapter Practice

a. 1 Mark Questions

1. Is – 8 is a solution of the equation $3x^2 + 8x + 2 = 0$? **[NCERT Exemplar]**

(a) Yes
(b) No
(c) Cannot be determined
(d) None of the above

2. If $x = \frac{1}{\sqrt{3}}$ is root of the equation $px^2 + (\sqrt{3} - \sqrt{2})\,x - 1 = 0$, then the value of $p^2 + 1$ is **[NCERT Exemplar]**

(a) $\sqrt{6}$ (b) 6 (c) 7 (d) 8

3. If 3 is a root of the quadratic equation $x^2 - px + 3 = 0$, then p is equal to **[ICSE 2023]**

(a) 4 (b) 3 (c) 5 (d) 2

4. The sum of the squares of three consecutive integers is 110, then the smallest positive integer is **[NCERT Exemplar]**

(a) 6 (b) 5 (c) 7 (d) 4

5. If α and β are roots of equation $ax^2 + bx + c = 0$, then $\frac{\alpha}{a\beta + b} + \frac{\beta}{a\alpha + b}$ equals **[NCERT Exemplar]**

(a) $\frac{2}{a}$ (b) $\frac{2}{b}$ (c) $\frac{2}{c}$ (d) $-\frac{2}{a}$

6. $(x^2 + 1)^2 - x^2 = 0$ has

(a) four real roots (b) two real roots
(c) no real roots (d) one real root

7. Which of the following quadratic equations has 2 and 3 as its roots? **[ICSE Semester I 2021]**

(a) $x^2 - 5x + 6 = 0$ (b) $x^2 + 5x + 6 = 0$
(c) $x^2 - 5x - 6 = 0$ (d) $x^2 + 5x - 6 = 0$

8. One of the roots of the quadratic equation $x^2 - 8x + 5 = 0$ is 7.3166. The root of the equation correct of 4 significant figures is **[ICSE Semester I 2021]**

(a) 7.3166 (b) 7.317
(c) 7.316 (d) 7.32

b. 3 Marks Questions

9. Solve the following quadratic equation by factorisation method.

$$(2x + 1)(x + 3) + 3 = 0$$

10. Solve the following quadratic equation:

$$x^2 + 4x - 8 = 0$$

Give your answer correct to one decimal place. (Use mathematical tables if necessary) **[ICSE 2023]**

11. Solve the quadratic equation $x^2 - 3x - 9 = 0$ for x and give your answer correct to two decimal places. **[ICSE 2016, 2007]**

12. Form a quadratic equation whose roots are

(i) -5 and $\frac{5}{2}$ (ii) $2 + 2\sqrt{3}$

13. Find the quadratic equation, whose solution set is

(i) {3, 5} (ii) {– 2, 3}

14. Solve the equation $4x^2 - 5x - 3 = 0$ and give your answer correct to two decimal places. **[ICSE 2017]**

15. Solve the quadratic equation $2x^2 + 5\sqrt{3}x + 6 = 0$ upto three decimal places. [take $\sqrt{3} = 1.732$]

16. Solve the quadratic equation $5x(x + 2) = 3$ and give your answer correct to two decimal places. **[ICSE 2008]**

17. Solve the equation $x - \frac{18}{x} = 6$. Give your answer correct to two significant figures. **[ICSE 2011]**

18. Find the value of k, for which $x = 3$ is a solution of the quadratic equation $(k + 2)x^2 - kx + 6 = 0$. Also, find the other root of the equation. **[ICSE 2015]**

19. Solve $2x - 3 = \sqrt{2x^2 - 2x + 21}$ by factorisation method.

20. Find the roots of equation

$$\sqrt{2x - 3} + \sqrt{3x - 5} - \sqrt{5x - 6} = 0.$$

21. Solve for x

$$\frac{2x}{x - 3} + \frac{1}{2x + 3} + \frac{3x + 9}{(x - 3)(2x + 3)} = 0,\ x \neq 3, -\frac{3}{2}$$

22. Solve for x :

$$4^x - 3(2^{x+3}) + 128 = 0$$

23. Solve for x :

$$x^4 - 3x^3 - 2x^2 + 3x + 1 = 0$$

24. Solve for x :

(i) $x(x - 1)(x + 2)(x - 3) + 8 = 0$
(ii) $(2x - 7)(x^2 - 9)(2x + 5) = 91$

25. Solve, $\frac{a}{ax-1}+\frac{b}{bx-1}=a+b$, where $a+b\neq 0$, $ab\neq 0$.

26. Solve the following quadratic equation for x.
$$x^2+\frac{a}{a+b}x+\frac{a+b}{a}x+1=0$$

27. Solve the following quadratic equation for x.
$$9x^2-9(a+b)x+2a^2+5ab+2b^2=0$$

28. Solve $\frac{1}{a+b+x}=\frac{1}{a}+\frac{1}{b}+\frac{1}{x}$, $a+b\neq 0$.

29. Find the nature of roots of each of the following equations.
(i) $x^2+2\sqrt{3}x-9=0$
(ii) $2x^2+8x+9=0$
(iii) $3x^2-2\sqrt{6}x+2=0$

c. 4/5 Marks Questions

30. Without solving the following quadratic equation, find the value of p for which the given equation has real and equal roots. **[ICSE 2013]**
$$x^2+(p-3)x+p=0$$

31. If the equation $(1+m^2)x^2+2mc\,x+(c^2-a^2)=0$ has equal roots, then prove that $c^2=a^2(1+m^2)$.

32. Find the values of k, for which the equation $(3k+1)x^2+2(k+1)x+1=0$ has equal roots. Also, find the roots.

33. Find the values of k, for which the quadratic equations $(k+4)x^2+(k+1)x+1=0$ has equal roots. Also, find the roots.

34. If -5 is a root of the quadratic equation $2x^2+px-15=0$ and the quadratic equation $p(x^2+x)+k=0$ has equal roots, then find the value of k.

35. If $x=-2$ is a root of the equation $3x^2+7x+p=0$, then find the value of k, so that the roots of the equation $x^2+k(4x+k-1)+p=0$ are equal.

36. If the product of two positive consecutive even integers is 288, then find the integers.

37. The product of two successive multiples of 4 is 28 more than the first multiple. Find them.

38. Divide 29 into two parts, such that the sum of the squares of the parts is 425.

39. The difference of squares of two numbers is 180. The square of the smaller number is 8 times the larger number. Find the two numbers.

40. Sum of two natural numbers is 8 and the difference of their reciprocals is $\frac{2}{15}$. Find the numbers. **[ICSE 2015]**

41. A number consists of two digits, whose product is 18. When 27 is subtracted from the number, the digits interchange their places. Find the number.

42. A two-digit number is such that, the product of its digits is 12. When 36 is added to this number, the digits interchange their places. Find the number.

43. The denominator of a fraction is 1 more than its numerator. The sum of the fraction and its reciprocal is 5/2. Find the fraction.

44. Two years ago, a man's age was three times the square of his son's age. In three years time, his age will be four times his son's age. Find their present ages.

45. A train travels a distance of 300 km at a constant speed. If the speed of the train is increased by 10 km/h, the journey would have taken 1 h less. Find the original speed of the train.

46. A train covers a distance of 600 km at x km/h. Had the speed been $(x+20)$ km/h, the time taken to cover the distance would have been reduced by 5 h. Write down an equation in x and solve it to evaluate x.

47. The speed of a boat in still water is 15 km/h. It can go 30 km upstream and return downstream to the original point in 4 h 30 min. Find the speed of the stream.

d. 6 Marks Questions

48. A positive number is divided into two parts, such that the sum of the squares of the two parts is 208. The square of the larger part is 18 times the smaller part. Taking x as the smaller part of the two parts, find the number. **[ICSE 2010]**

49. Three consecutive natural numbers are such that the square of the middle number exceeds the difference of the squares of the other two by 60. Assume the middle number to be x and form a quadratic equation satisfying the above statement. Hence, find the three numbers.

50. A takes 6 days less than the time taken by B to finish a work. If both can finish the work in 4 days, then find the time taken by B to finish the work.

51. Two pipes running together can fill a tank in $11\frac{1}{9}$ min. If one pipe takes 5 min more than the other to fill the tank separately, find the time in which each pipe would fill the tank separately.

52. Two pipes running together can fill a cistern in $2\frac{8}{11}$ min. If one pipe takes 1 min more than the other to fill the cistern, then find the time in which each pipe would fill the cistern.

53. A boat can cover 10 km up the stream and 5 km down the stream in 6 h. If the speed of the stream is 1.5 km/h, then find the speed of the boat in still water.

54. The speed of a boat in still water is 11 km/h. It can go 12 km upstream and return downstream to the original point in 2 h 45 min. Find the speed of the stream.

55. By increasing the speed of a car by 10 km/h, the time of journey for a distance of 72 km is reduced by 36 min. Find the original speed of the car. **[ICSE 2005]**

56. A scholarship amount of ₹ 75000 was distributed equally among a certain number of students. Had there been 10 students more, each would have got ₹ 250 less. Find the original number of students.

57. A shopkeeper buys a number of books of ₹ 80. If he had bought 4 more books for the same amount, each book would have cost ₹ 1 less. Taking the original number of books as x, form an equation in x and solve it.

58. A trader buys x articles for a total cost of ₹ 600.

(i) Write down the cost of one article in terms of x. If the cost per article were ₹ 5 more, the number of articles that can be bought for ₹ 600, would be four less.

(ii) Write down the equation in x for the above situation and solve it to find x.

59. A man on tour has ₹ 18000 for his daily expenses. If he extends his tour for 4 days, he has to cut down his daily expenses by ₹ 750, then find the original duration of the tour.

60. ₹ 6500 were divided equally among a certain number of persons. There had been 15 more persons, each would have got ₹ 30 less. Find the original number of persons.

61. In a class test, the sum of Shefali's marks in Mathematics and English is 30. Had she got 2 marks more in Mathematics and 3 marks less in English, the product of their marks would have been 210. Find her marks in the two subjects.

62. In an auditorium, seats are arranged in rows and columns. The number of rows was equal to the number of seats in each row. When the number of rows was doubled and the number of seats in each row was reduced by 10, the total number of seats increased by 300. Find

(i) the number of rows in the original arrangement.

(ii) the number of seats in the auditorium after re-arrangement. **[ICSE 2003]**

63. The sum of the areas of two squares is 468 m. If the difference of their perimeters is 24 m, then find the sides of the two squares.

64. The length of the sides forming right angles of a right angled triangle are $5x$ cm and $(3x - 1)$ cm. If the area of the triangle is 60 cm^2, then find its hypotenuse.

65. The perimeter of a rectangular field is 82 m and its area is 400 sq m. Find the length and breadth of the rectangle.

66. Two cars X and Y use 1 L of diesel to travel x km and $(x + 3)$ km, respectively. If both the cars covered a distance of 72 km, then **[ICSE Semester-I 2021]**

(i) The number of litres of diesel used by car X is

(a) $\frac{72}{x-3}$ L (b) $\frac{72}{x+3}$ L

(c) $\frac{72}{x}$ L (d) $\frac{12}{x}$ L

(ii) The number of litres of diesel used by car Y is

(a) $\frac{72}{x-3}$ L (b) $\frac{72}{x+3}$ L

(c) $\frac{72}{x}$ L (d) $\frac{12}{x+3}$ L

(iii) If car X used 4 L of diesel more than car Y in the journey, then

(a) $\frac{72}{x-3} - \frac{12}{x} = 4$ (b) $\frac{72}{x+3} - \frac{72}{x} = 4$

(c) $\frac{72}{x} - \frac{72}{x+3} = 4$ (d) $\frac{72}{x-3} - \frac{12}{x+3} = 4$

(iv) The amount of diesel used by the car X is

(a) 6 L (b) 12 L

(c) 18 L (d) 24 L

Hints and Answers

Exercise 5.1

1. **Hint** Do same as Example 1.
   Ans. (i) Yes (ii) No (iii) Yes (iv) No (v) No
2. **Hint** Do same as Example 2. **Ans.** No
3. **Hint** Do same as Example 2. **Ans.** Yes
4. **Hint** Do same as Example 2.
   Ans. (i) and (iii)
5. Do same as Example 2.
   Ans.
   (i) Both 1 and –1 are not the solution of the given equation.
   (ii) Both $\sqrt{2}$ and $-2\sqrt{2}$ are the solution of the given equation.
   (iii) Both 2 and 3 are the solution of the given equation.
   (iv) Both $\sqrt{5}$ and $3/\sqrt{5}$ are the solution of the given equation.
6. **Hint**
   (i) Do same as Example 3.
   Ans. $k = -0.3$ or 0.3
   (ii) Do same as Example 3. **Ans.** $a = -\frac{9}{4}$
   (iii) Do same as Example 3. **Ans.** $k = -\frac{1}{6}$
   (iv) Do same as Example 3. **Ans.** $k = 1$
   (v) Do same as Example 4.
   Ans. $a = \frac{1}{2}, b = -\frac{3}{2}$
7. **Hint** $ac = -10 = 5 \times (-2)$ and $5 + (-2) = 3$
   Ans. – 5, 2
8. **Hint** $ac = 21 = (-7)(-3)$ and $(-7) + (-3) = -10$
   Ans. 3, 7
9. **Hint** $ac = -168 = (-28)(6)$ and $(-28) + 6 = -22$
   Ans. $\frac{7}{2}, \frac{-3}{4}$
10. **Hint** $ac = 210 = (-35) \times (-6)$ and $(-35) + (-6) = -41$
    Ans. $\frac{7}{3}, \frac{2}{5}$
11. **Hint** $ac = 240 = (-16)(-15)$ and $(-16) + (-15) = -31$
    Ans. $\frac{8}{3}, \frac{5}{2}$
12. **Hint** First, multiply the equation with 21, to eliminate the denominator. Then, write $ac = 441 = (-21)(-21)$
    Ans. $\frac{1}{21}, \frac{1}{21}$
13. **Hint** $ac = -15$, take factors as $3\sqrt{5}$ and $-\sqrt{5}$.
    Ans. $-\sqrt{5}, \frac{\sqrt{5}}{3}$
14. **Hint** Do same as Example 9.
    Ans. (i) 3
    (ii) $\left(3, \frac{5}{2}\right)$
15. **Hint** First, factorise $a^2 + a - 6 = (a-2)(a+3)$, then factorise $x^2 + 5x - (a-2)(a+3) = 0$.
    Ans. $-(a+3), (a-2)$
16. **Hint** Do same as Example 7.
    Ans. $-\frac{b}{3a}, \frac{3b}{2a}$
17. **Hint** First, factorise $a^4 - b^4 = (a^2 - b^2)(a^2 + b^2)$, then factorise $4x^2 - 4a^2x + (a^2 - b^2)(a^2 + b^2) = 0$.
    Ans. $\frac{a^2 - b^2}{2}, \frac{a^2 + b^2}{2}$
18. **Hint** $x = \frac{-b \pm \sqrt{b^2 - 4ac}}{2a}$
    $$x = -\frac{(-4) \pm \sqrt{(-4)^2 - 4 \times 1 \times 1}}{2 \times 1}$$
    Ans. $2 + \sqrt{3}, 2 - \sqrt{3}$
19. **Hint** First, simplify the given equation, then do same as Example 16(iii).
    Ans. 1, 4
20. **Hint** $x = \frac{-(b^2 - ac) \pm \sqrt{(b^2 - ac)^2 + 4ab^2c}}{2ab}$
    Ans. $\frac{c}{b}, \frac{-b}{a}$
21. **Hint** $x = \frac{-8ab \pm \sqrt{64a^2b^2 - 4 \cdot 3a^2 \cdot 4b^2}}{6a^2}$
    Ans. $\frac{-2b}{a}, \frac{-2b}{3a}$
22. **Hint** Do same as Example 13.
    Ans. $x = 0.88$ or -7.88
23. **Hint** Do same as Example 13.
    Ans. 3.6 and 1.3
24. **Hint** Do same as Example 14.
    Ans. 1.243 and 0.643
25. **Hint** Do same as Example 16(i).
    Ans. 3.6 and 0.13
26. **Hint** Do same as Example 16(ii).
    Ans. $\frac{4 + \sqrt{10}}{3}$ and $\frac{4 - \sqrt{10}}{3}$
27. **Hint** Do same as Example 16(iii).
    Ans. $3 + \frac{1}{\sqrt{3}}$ and $3 - \frac{1}{\sqrt{3}}$.
28. **Hint** Do same as Example 15.
    Ans. $(a + 3)$ and $(-a - 1)$

Exercise 5.2

1. **Hint** Do same as Example 17.
Ans. (i) – 12 (ii) 49 (iii) 21 (iv) 49 (v) 121
2. **Hint** Do same as Example 18.
Ans. (i) Real and distinct
(ii) Real and equal (iii) Imaginary
(iv) Real and distinct (v) Imaginary
3. **Hint** Do same as Example 18.
Ans. (i) Imaginary
(ii) Real and distinct (iii) Real and distinct
(iv) Real and distinct (v) Real and distinct
4. **Hint** Do same as Example 21 and 22.
Ans. (i) $k = \frac{5}{4}$ (ii) $k = 8$
(iii) $k = \frac{-1}{2}, 1$ (iv) $k = \pm 6\sqrt{3}$
(v) $k = \frac{2}{3}, -1$
5. **Hint** First, find $D = b^2 - 4ac$ and then put $D \geq 0$, because for real roots, discriminant should be greater than or equal to zero.
Ans. (i) $k \leq -2\sqrt{6}$ or $k \geq 2\sqrt{6}$ (ii) $k \leq 9$
(iii) $k \leq \frac{1}{3}$ (iv) $k \geq \frac{-1}{7}$ (v) $-\infty < k < \infty$
6. **Hint** Put $D = b^2 - 4ac \geq 0$ **Ans.** $k \leq -\sqrt{20}$ or $k \geq \sqrt{20}$
7. **Hint** Do same as Example 24.
Ans. $k = 6, -6$, when $k = 6$, then roots are $\frac{-1}{3}, \frac{-1}{3}$ and when $k = -6$, then roots are $\frac{1}{3}, \frac{1}{3}$.
8. **Hint** Do same as Example 25.
Ans. $p = 4, -\frac{4}{7}$ and $\frac{5}{3}, 7$
9. **Hint** For equal roots, $D = b^2 - 4ac = 0$.
10. **Hint** $D_1 = 4b^2 - 4ac \geq 0$ and $D_2 = 4ac - 4b^2 \geq 0$
11. **Hint** $D = 4a(a^3 + b^3 + c^3 - 3abc)$
Put $D = 0$ as roots are equal.
12. **Hint** Do same as Example 26. **Ans.** $k = \frac{11}{4}$
13. **Hint** $D_1 + D_2 = p^2 - 4q + r^2 - 4s$
$$= (p^2 + r^2) - 4\left(\frac{pr}{2}\right) \quad [\because pr = 2(q + s)]$$
$$= (p - q)^2$$
$\Rightarrow (D_1 + D_2) \geq 0$
$\therefore$ Atleast one of D_1 and D_2 is greater than equal to zero.
14. **Hint** Given, equation can be rewritten as
$$3x^2 - 2x(a + b + c) + (ab + bc + ca) = 0$$
Now, find D and show it ≥ 0 and then put it equal zero for equal roots.
15. **Hint** Do same as Example 29.
Ans. $-3 < p < 3$
16. **Hint** Do same as Example 30.
Ans. $k = 3$

Exercise 5.3

1. **Hint** Let two consecutive natural numbers be p and $p + 1$, respectively.
Then, $p^2 + (p + 1)^2 = 481$. **Ans.** 15, 16
2. **Hint** Do same as Example 31.
Ans. 11, 13
3. **Hint** Let the integers be x, $x + 1$ and $x + 2$. Then, $x^2 + (x + 1) + (x + 2) = 154$
Ans. 8, 9, 10
4. **Hint** Let the smaller part be x and the larger part be $(25 - x)$.
According to the question, $2(25 - x)^2 = 3x^2 + 29$
Ans. 14, 11
5. **Hint** Let the number be x.
According to the given question,
$$x + 12 = \frac{160}{x}$$
$$\Rightarrow x^2 + 12x - 160 = 0 \Rightarrow (x + 20)(x - 8) = 0$$
$$\Rightarrow x = -20 \text{ or } 8$$
Ans. 8
6. **Hint** Let the numbers be x and $(18 - x)$, respectively.
According to the question, $\frac{1}{x} + \frac{1}{(18 - x)} = \frac{1}{4}$
$\Rightarrow x^2 - 18x + 72 = 0$
Ans. 6, 12
7. **Hint** Do same as Example 37.
Ans. 92
8. **Hint** Let the larger digit be x and smaller digit be y.
Then, the number is $10x + y$.
Also, $x - \frac{24}{x} = 5$
Ans. 83
9. **Hint** $\frac{x - 1}{(x + 3) - 1} = \frac{x}{x + 3} - \frac{1}{14}$ **Ans.** $\frac{4}{7}$
10. **Hint** Let Shikha's present age be x yr.
According to the question, $(x - 5)(x + 8) = 30$
Ans. 7 yr
11. **Hint** Let Rehman's age be x yr.
Then, we have $\frac{1}{x - 3} + \frac{1}{x + 5} = \frac{1}{3}$
Ans. 7 yr
12. **Hint** Do same as Example 43.
Ans. 30 days
13. **Hint** Let the time taken by the pipe of larger diameter to fill the tank separately be x h. Then, the time taken by the pipe of smaller diameter to fill the tank separately = $(x + 10)$ h.
According to the question,
$$\frac{1}{x} + \frac{1}{x + 10} = \frac{8}{75}$$
Ans. 15 h, 25 h

14. $\therefore$ The increased speed of the train $= (x + 5)$ km/h.

$\therefore$ Time taken by train under uniform speed to cover 100 km $= \frac{100}{x}$ h

$\Rightarrow$ Time taken by train under increased speed of cover 100 km $= \frac{100}{x+5}$ h

Then, according to question

$$\frac{100}{x} - \frac{100}{x+5} = 1$$

$$\Rightarrow \quad \frac{100(x+5) - 100x}{x(x+5)} = 1$$

$$\Rightarrow \quad x^2 + 5x = 500$$

$$\Rightarrow \quad x^2 + 5x - 500 = 0$$

$$\Rightarrow \quad x^2 + 25x - 20x - 500 = 0$$

$$\Rightarrow \quad x(x+25) - 20(x+25) = 0$$

$$\Rightarrow \quad (x+25)(x-20) = 0$$

$$\Rightarrow \quad x = -25 \text{ or } x = 20$$

[$\because$ Speed can never be negative]

Hence, the original speed of train is 20 km/h.

15. Hint Time taken by express train, $t_1 = \frac{240}{x}$ $\left[\because \text{time} = \frac{\text{distance}}{\text{speed}}\right]$

and time taken by ordinary train,

$$t_2 = \frac{240}{x-12}$$

According to the question,

$$\frac{240}{x-12} - \frac{240}{x} = 1$$

Ans. 60 km/h

16. Hint Let the speed of aeroplane in still air be x km/h.

Then, $\frac{3600}{x-30} - \frac{3600}{x+30} = \frac{2}{3}$ **Ans.** 570 km/h

17. Hint Do same as Example 51.

Ans. 25 m, ₹ 12 per m

18. Hint Let snake and peacock meet at B at a distance x from A (the hole).

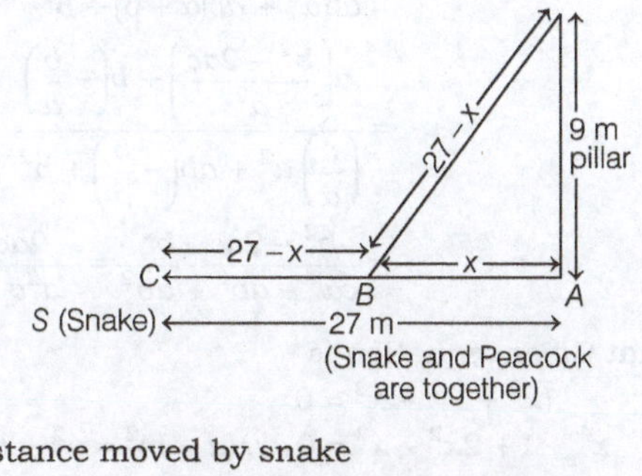

Distance moved by snake

= Distance moved by peacock

$= (27 - x)$ m [$\because$ they have the same speeds]

Clearly, $(27 - x^2) = x^2 + 9^2$

$\Rightarrow 729 + x^2 - 54x = x^2 + 81$ **Ans.** $x = 12$ m

19. Hint Let x be the number of students planned for the picnic.

According to the question, $\frac{480}{x-8} - \frac{480}{x} = 10$ **Ans.** 16

20. Hint Do same as Q. 19. **Ans.** 8

21. Hint Let the number of children be x.

According to question, $\frac{7500}{(x-20)} - \frac{7500}{x} = 100$

Ans. Original number of children = 50

22. Hint Let the other two sides of triangle be x and $(x + 5)$ cm.

Using Pythagoras theorem, we get

$$x^2 + (x+5)^2 = (25)^2$$

Ans. 15 cm, 20 cm

23. Hint By Pythagoras theorem

$$PQ^2 = PR^2 + QR^2$$

$$\Rightarrow \quad (17)^2 = (9+x)^2 + (2+x)^2$$

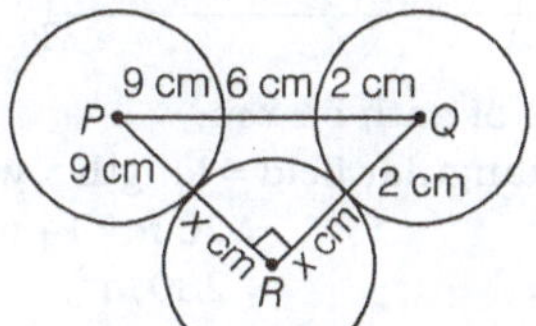

$$\Rightarrow \quad x^2 + 11x - 102 = 0$$

$$\Rightarrow \quad x^2 + 17x - 6x - 102 = 0$$

$$\Rightarrow \quad x(x+17) - 6(x+17) = 0$$

$$\Rightarrow \quad (x-6)(x+17) = 0$$

$$\Rightarrow \quad x = 6 \text{ or } x = -17$$

Ans. $x = 6$ cm

24. Hint Let the length of hypotenuse be x cm, then longer side is $(x - 2)$ cm and shortest side is $(x - 4)$ cm.

Applying Pythagoras theorem in right angled triangle.

$$(x-2)^2 + (x-4)^2 = x^2 \Rightarrow x = 2, x = 10$$

Ans. Length of hypotenuse = 10 cm

Longer side = 8 cm

Shortest side = 6 cm

25. Hint Perimeter of rectangle $= 2(l + b)$

and $(\text{diagonal})^2 = (\text{length})^2 + (\text{breadth})^2$

Let the length of rectangular plot be x m and breadth be y m.

Then, we have $\quad x + y = 34 \quad$ ...(i)

and $\quad (26)^2 = x^2 + y^2 \quad$ ...(ii)

On solving Eqs. (i) and (ii), we get the result.

Ans. 240 m^2

26. Hint The perimeter of a rectangular field = 180 m and area = 180 m^2

Let length of a rectangular field be x m

and breadth $= (90 - x)$ m

According to the condition,

$$x(90 - x) = 1800$$

$\Rightarrow 90x - x^2 - 1800 = 0$

$\Rightarrow (x-60)(x-30) = 0$

Ans. Length = 60 m and breadth = 30 m

Hence, length is greater than its breadth.

27. **Hint** Let the length of shortest side be x m.

According to the question,

$$(2x+1)^2 = x^2 + (x+7)^2$$

Ans. 8 m, 17 m and 15 m

28. **Hint** Given, length of rectangular field = 20 m

and width of rectangular field = 14 m

Area of path = 111 m^2

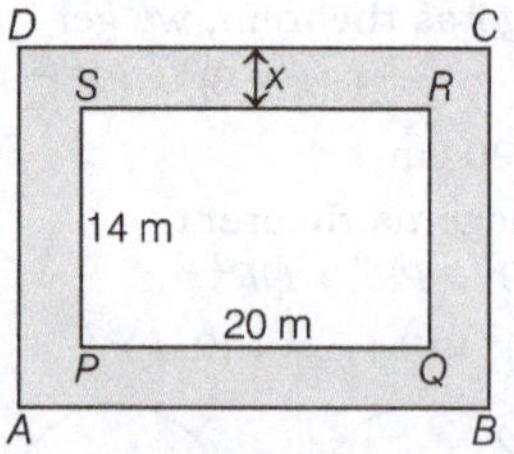

Let the width of path be x m.

$\therefore$ Area of rectangular field = length × width

$= 20 \text{ m} \times 14 \text{ m}$

$= 280 \text{ m}^2$

$\therefore$ Area of outer rectangle = length × width

$$= (20 + x + x)(14 + x + x)$$
$$= (20 + 2x)(14 + 2x)$$
$$= 280 + 40x + 28x + 4x^2$$
$$= 4x^2 + 68x + 280$$

$\therefore$ Area of path = Area of rectangle ($ABCD$) − Area of rectangle ($PQRS$)

$$111 = (4x^2 + 68x + 280) - 280$$
$$0 = 4x^2 + 68x - 111$$
$$= 4x^2 + 74x - 6x - 111$$
$$= 2x(2x+37) - 3(2x+37)$$
$$0 = (2x-3)(2x+37)$$
$$x = \frac{3}{2} \text{ and } x = -\frac{37}{2} \quad \text{[width cannot be – ve]}$$

Ans. $\frac{3}{2}$ or 1.5 m

Chapter Exercise

1. (b) **Hint** Given, equation is $3x^2 + 8x + 2 = 0$

Let $P(x) = 3x^2 + 8x + 2$ ...(i)

On putting $x = -8$ in Eq. (i), we get

$$P(-8) = 3(-8)^2 + 8(-8) + 2$$
$$= 3 \times 64 + (-64) + 2$$
$$= 192 - 64 + 2 = 130 \neq 0$$

Hence, − 8 is not a solution of the given equation.

2. (c) **Hint** Given, equation is

$$Px^2 + (\sqrt{3} - \sqrt{2})x - 1 = 0$$

and $x = \frac{1}{\sqrt{3}}$ is a root of the equation

$$\therefore \quad P\left(\frac{1}{\sqrt{3}}\right)^2 + (\sqrt{3} - \sqrt{2})\frac{1}{\sqrt{3}} - 1 = 0$$

$$\Rightarrow \quad \frac{P}{3} + \frac{\sqrt{3} - \sqrt{2} - \sqrt{3}}{\sqrt{3}} = 0 \Rightarrow \frac{P}{3} - \frac{\sqrt{2}}{\sqrt{3}} = 0$$

$$\Rightarrow \quad P = \frac{\sqrt{2}}{\sqrt{3}} \times 3 \Rightarrow P = \sqrt{2} \times \sqrt{3} = \sqrt{6}$$

$$\therefore \quad P^2 + 1 = (\sqrt{6})^2 + 1 = 6 + 1 = 7$$

3. (a) **Hint** The given quadratic equation is

$$x^2 - px + 3 = 0 \quad \text{...(i)}$$

$\because$ 3 is a root of this quadratic equation,

$x = 3$ will satisfy this quadratic equation

On putting $x = 3$ in Eq. (i), we get

$$3^2 - p(3) + 3 = 0$$
$$\Rightarrow \quad 9 - 3p + 3 = 0$$
$$\Rightarrow \quad 12 - 3p = 0$$
$$\Rightarrow \quad -3p = -12$$
$$\Rightarrow \quad p = 4$$

4. (b) **Hint** Let the smallest integer be x. Then, three consecutive integers are x, $x+1$, $x+2$.

From the question, $x^2 + (x+1)^2 + (x+2)^2 = 110$

$\Rightarrow 3x^2 + 6x - 105 = 0$

$$\therefore \quad x = \frac{-6 \pm \sqrt{6^2 - 4 \cdot 3 \cdot (-105)}}{2 \times 3} \quad \text{[using formula]}$$

$$= \frac{-6 \pm \sqrt{36 + 1260}}{6} = \frac{-6 \pm \sqrt{1296}}{6} = \frac{-6 \pm 36}{6}$$

$$= \frac{-6 + 36}{6}, \frac{-6 - 36}{6} = \frac{30}{6}, \frac{-42}{6} = 5, -7$$

Then, $x + 1 = 5 + 1, -7 + 1 = 6, -6$

and $x + 2 = 5 + 2, -7 + 2 = 7, -5$

$\therefore$ Three consecutive integers are 5, 6, 7 or − 7, − 6, − 5

Hence, the smallest positive integer is 5.

5. (d) **Hint** Here, $\alpha + \beta = -\frac{b}{a}$, $\alpha\beta = \frac{c}{a}$

and $\alpha^2 + \beta^2 = \frac{b^2 - 2ac}{a^2}$

$$\text{Now,} \quad \frac{\alpha}{a\beta + b} + \frac{\beta}{a\alpha + b} = \frac{\alpha(a\alpha + b) + \beta(a\beta + b)}{(a\beta + b)(a\alpha + b)}$$

$$= \frac{a(\alpha^2 + \beta^2) + b(\alpha + \beta)}{\alpha\beta a^2 + ab(\alpha + \beta) + b^2}$$

$$= \frac{a\left(\frac{b^2 - 2ac}{a^2}\right) + b\left(-\frac{b}{a}\right)}{\left(\frac{c}{a}\right)a^2 + ab\left(-\frac{b}{a}\right) + b^2}$$

$$= \frac{b^2 - 2ac - b^2}{ca^2 - ab^2 + ab^2} = \frac{-2ac}{a^2c} = \frac{-2}{a}$$

6. (c) **Hint** Given, equation is

$$(x^2 + 1)^2 - x^2 = 0$$

$$\Rightarrow \quad x^4 + 1 + 2x^2 - x^2 = 0 \quad [\because (a+b)^2 = a^2 + b^2 + 2ab]$$

$$\Rightarrow \quad x^4 + x^2 + 1 = 0$$

Let $x^2 = y$

$$\therefore \quad (x^2)^2 + x^2 + 1 = 0$$

$$\Rightarrow \quad y^2 + y + 1 = 0$$

On comparing with $ay^2 + by + c = 0$, we get

$$a = 1, b = 1 \text{ and } c = 1$$

Discriminant, $D = b^2 - 4ac$

$$= (1)^2 - 4(1)(1) = 1 - 4 = -3$$

Since, $D < 0$

$\therefore \quad y^2 + y + 1 = 0$ i.e. $x^4 + x^2 + 1 = 0$

or $(x^2 + 1)^2 - x^2 = 0$ has no real roots.

7. **Hint** Given, two roots of quadratic equation as $\alpha = 2$ and $\beta = 3$.

$\therefore$ Quadratic equation will be

$$x^2 - (\alpha + \beta)x + \alpha\beta = 0$$

$$\Rightarrow \quad x^2 - (2 + 3)x + (2)(3) = 0$$

Ans. $x^2 - 5x + 6 = 0$

8. **Hint** Given, root of the quadratic equation is 7.3166. Here, the significant figures are 7, 3, 1, 6, 6. Now, add 1 with the digit at 4th significant place because, digit at 5th significant place is greater than 5.

Ans. 7.317.

9. **Hint** $2x^2 + 7x + 6 = 0$

$$\Rightarrow 2x^2 + (3 + 4)x + 6 = 0$$

Ans. $-2, \frac{-3}{2}$

10. Given, quadratic equation is

$$x^2 + 4x - 8 = 0 \quad \text{...(i)}$$

On comparing Eq. (i) with $ax^2 + bx + c = 0$, we get

$$a = 1, b = 4, c = -8$$

Using quadratic formula,

$$x = \frac{-b \pm \sqrt{b^2 - 4ac}}{2a}$$

$$= \frac{-4 \pm \sqrt{(4)^2 - 4(1)(-8)}}{2(1)}$$

$$= \frac{-4 \pm \sqrt{16 + 32}}{2} = \frac{-4 \pm \sqrt{48}}{2}$$

$$= \frac{-4 \pm 4\sqrt{3}}{2} = -2 \pm 2\sqrt{3} = 2(-1 \pm \sqrt{3})$$

$\Rightarrow \quad x = 2(-1 + 1.73205)$ [taking '+ ve' sign]

$= 2(0.73205)$

$= 1.4641 = 1.4$

or $\quad x = 2(-1 - 1.73205)$ [taking '– ve' sign]

$x = 2(-2.73205)$

$= -5.4641$

$\Rightarrow \quad x = -5.5$

11. **Hint** Use quadratic formula. **Ans.** 4.85, – 1.85

12. **Hint**

(i) Sum of the roots $= \frac{5}{2} + \frac{3}{4} = \frac{13}{4}$

Product of the roots $= \frac{5}{2} \times \frac{3}{4} = \frac{15}{8}$

The required quadratic equation is

$$x^2 - \frac{13}{4}x + \frac{15}{8} = 0$$

Ans. $8x^2 - 26x + 15 = 0$

(ii) One root of the required quadratic equation is $2\sqrt{3} + 2$.

$\therefore$ Other root $= -2\sqrt{3} + 2$

Now, sum of the roots $= 2\sqrt{3} + 2 - 2\sqrt{3} + 2 = 4$

Product of the roots $= (2\sqrt{3} + 2)(-2\sqrt{3} + 2) = -8$

Ans. $x^2 - 4x - 8 = 0$

13. **Hint**

(i) Since, solution set = {3, 5}

Roots are 3 and 5.

$\Rightarrow \quad x = 3$ or $x = 5$

$\Rightarrow x - 3 = 0$ or $x - 5 = 0$

$\Rightarrow \quad (x - 3)(x - 5) = 0$

Ans. $x^2 - 8x + 15 = 0$

(ii) Do same as part (i)

Ans. $x^2 - x - 6 = 0$

14. **Hint** Use quadratic formula. **Ans.** – 0.44, 1.69

15. **Hint** Use quadratic formula.

Ans. – 0.866, – 3.464

16. **Hint** Use quadratic formula.

Ans. – 2.26, 0.26

17. **Hint** $\frac{x^2 - 18}{x} = 6 \Rightarrow x^2 - 6x - 18 = 0$

Ans. 8.20, – 2.20

18. **Hint** Put the value $x = 3$ in $(k + 2)x^2 - kx + 6 = 0$

Ans. $k = -4, x = -1$

19. **Hint** Squaring on both sides and solve.

Ans. 6, –1

20. **Hint** $\sqrt{2x - 3} + \sqrt{3x - 5} = \sqrt{5x - 6}$

On squaring both sides, we get

$$\sqrt{6x^2 - 19x + 15} = 1$$

Again, squaring both sides, we get

$$x = 2 \text{ or } \frac{7}{6}.$$

The value $x = \frac{7}{6}$ is not possible as

$$\sqrt{2x - 3} = \sqrt{2 \times \frac{7}{6} - 3} = \sqrt{\frac{-2}{3}} \text{ at } x = \frac{7}{6},$$

which is not defined.

Ans. 2

21. **Hint** Do same as Example 10.

Ans. – 1

22. **Hint** $4^x - 3(2^x \cdot 2^3) + 128 = 0$

$$(2^x)^2 - 24(2^x) + 128 = 0$$

Put $2^x = y$

$\therefore \quad y^2 - 24y + 128 = 0$

$\Rightarrow \quad (y - 8)(y - 16) = 0$

$\Rightarrow \quad y = 8$ or $y = 16$

$\Rightarrow \quad 2^x = 2^3$ or $2^x = 2^4$

Ans. 3, 4

23. Hint $x^4 - 3x^3 - 2x^2 + 3x + 1 = 0$

On dividing by x^2, we get

$$x^2 - 3x - 2 + \frac{3}{x} + \frac{1}{x^2} = 0$$

$$\Rightarrow \left(x^2 + \frac{1}{x^2}\right) - 3\left(x - \frac{1}{x}\right) = 0$$

Put $x - \frac{1}{x} = z \Rightarrow x^2 + \frac{1}{x^2} = z^2 + 2$

Ans. $1, -1, \frac{3 \pm \sqrt{13}}{2}$

24. Hint

(i) $x(x-1)(x+2)(x-3) + 8 = 0$

$(x^2 - x)(x^2 - x - 6) + 8 = 0$

Put $x^2 - x = y$

Ans. $x = 2, -1, \frac{1 \pm \sqrt{17}}{2}$

(ii) $\frac{1 \pm \sqrt{65}}{2}$

25. Hint $\frac{a}{ax-1} - a + \frac{b}{bx-1} - b = 0$

$$\Rightarrow \frac{a - abx + b}{ax - 1} + \frac{b - abx + a}{bx - 1} = 0$$

$$\Rightarrow (a + b - abx)\left[\frac{1}{ax-1} + \frac{1}{bx-1}\right] = 0$$

$$\Rightarrow a + b - abx = 0 \text{ or } \frac{1}{ax-1} + \frac{1}{bx-1} = 0$$

Ans. $x = \frac{a+b}{ab}$ or $x = \frac{2}{a+b}$

26. Hint $x\left(x + \frac{a}{a+b}\right) + \frac{a+b}{a}\left(x + \frac{a}{a+b}\right) = 0$

$$\Rightarrow \left(x + \frac{a}{a+b}\right)\left(x + \frac{a+b}{a}\right) = 0$$

Ans. $\frac{-a}{a+b}, \frac{-(a+b)}{a}$

27. Hint Consider, $2a^2 + 5ab + 2b^2 = (a + 2b)(2a + b)$

Hence, the equation will become

$9x^2 - 9(a+b)x + (a+2b)(2a+b) = 0$

$\Rightarrow [3x - (a+2b)][3x - (2a+b)] = 0$

Ans. $x = \frac{a+2b}{3}, \frac{2a+b}{3}$

28. Hint $\frac{1}{a+b+x} = \frac{1}{a} + \frac{1}{b} + \frac{1}{x}$

$\Rightarrow x^2 + (a+b)x + ab = 0 \qquad [\because (a+b) \neq 0]$

Ans. $-a, -b$

29. Hint Do same as Example 18.

Ans. (i) Real and distinct

(ii) Imaginary

(iii) Real and equal

30. Hint Do same as Example 22.

Ans. 1 or 9

31. Hint Since, the roots are equal.

$\therefore \quad D = b^2 - 4ac = 0$

32. Hint Do same as Example 25.

Ans. $k = 0, 1$ and $x = -1, -1$ or $\frac{-1}{2}, \frac{-1}{2}$

33. Hint We know that, for equal roots, $D = b^2 - 4ac = 0$.

Ans. $k = 5$ or -3; $x = 1, 1$ or $\frac{-1}{3}, \frac{-1}{3}$

34. Hint Do same as Example 27. **Ans.** $\frac{7}{4}$

35. Hint Do same as Example 27. **Ans.** $\frac{2}{3}, -1$

36. Hint Let two consecutive even positive integers be x and $x + 2$.

According to the question, $x(x+2) = 288$

Ans. 16, 18

37. Hint Let two successive multiples of 4 be $4k$ and $(4k + 4)$.

According to the question,

$$4k(4k+4) = 4k + 28$$

Ans. 4, 8

38. Hint Let two parts be x and $(29 - x)$.

Then, we have

$$x^2 + (29 - x)^2 = 425$$

Ans. 16, 13

39. Hint Let the larger number be x and smaller number be y.

Then, $x^2 - y^2 = 180$ ...(i)

and $y^2 = 8x$ ...(ii)

Ans. 18 and 12 or 18 and -12

40. Hint Let two natural numbers be x and y and also let $x < y$.

According to the question,

$$x + y = 8 \text{ and } \frac{1}{x} - \frac{1}{y} = \frac{2}{15}$$

Ans. 3 and 5

41. Hint Let ten's place digit be x and unit's place digit be y.

Then, $xy = 18$ ...(i)

and $(10x + y) - 27 = 10y + x$ ...(ii)

Ans. 63

42. Hint Do same as Q. 41. **Ans.** 26

43. Hint Let the numerator of the fraction be x.

Then, denominator $= x + 1$

According to the question,

$$\frac{x}{x+1} + \frac{x+1}{x} = \frac{5}{2}$$

Ans. $\frac{1}{2}$

44. Hint Do same as Example 40.

Ans. Father's age = 29 yr, Son's age = 5 yr

45. Hint Let the original speed be x km/h.

Then, $\frac{300}{x} - \frac{300}{x+10} = 1$ **Ans.** 50 km/h

46. **Hint** Do same as Q. 45. **Ans.** $x = 40$ km/h

47. **Hint** Do same as Example 46.
Ans. 5 km/h

48. **Hint** Let x and y be two numbers, in which x is smaller number. Then,
According to the question,
$$x^2 + y^2 = 208 \text{ and } y^2 = 18x$$
Ans. 20

49. **Hint** Let the middle number of the three consecutive numbers be x, therefore the other two numbers are $(x-1)$ and $(x+1)$.
Ans. 9, 10 and 11

50. **Hint** Let the time taken by $B = x$ days
Then, the time taken by $A = (x-6)$ days
According to the question,
$$\left(\frac{1}{x} + \frac{1}{x-6}\right) = \frac{1}{4}$$
Ans. 12 days

51. **Hint** Let time taken by pipe A be x min and time taken by pipe B be $(x+5)$ min.
In one minute, pipe A will fill $\frac{1}{x}$ tank.
In one minute, pipe B will fill $\frac{1}{x+5}$ tank.
According to the question,
$$\frac{1}{x} + \frac{1}{x+5} = \frac{9}{100}$$
Ans. Pipe $A = 20$ min and pipe $B = 25$ min

52. **Hint** Do same as Q. 51. **Ans.** 5 min, 6 min

53. **Hint** Let speed of the boat in still water
$= x$ km/h
Then, speed of the boat upstream
$= (x - 1.5)$ km/h
and speed of the boat downstream
$= (x + 1.5)$ km/h
Now, according to the question,
$$\frac{10}{x-1.5} + \frac{5}{x+1.5} = 6$$
Ans. 3.5 km/h

54. **Hint** Let speed of the stream be x km/h.
Relative speed of the boat when going upstream
$= (11 - x)$ km/h
Relative speed of the boat when going downstream
$= (11 + x)$ km/h
According to the question,
$$\frac{12}{11-x} + \frac{12}{11+x} = 2\frac{45}{60}$$
Ans. 5 km/h

55. **Hint** Let the original speed of car $= x$ km/h
According to the question,
$$\frac{72}{x} - \frac{72}{x+10} = \frac{36}{60}$$
Ans. 30 km/h

56. **Hint** Let the number of students be x.
According to the question,
$$\frac{75000}{x+10} = \frac{75000}{x} - 250$$ **Ans.** 50

57. **Hint** Do same as Example 52.
Ans. 16

58. **Hint** $\because$ Cost of x articles = ₹ 600
$\therefore$ Cost of 1 article = ₹ $\frac{600}{x}$
Ans. (i) ₹ $\frac{600}{x}$ (ii) $\frac{600}{x-4} - \frac{600}{x} = 5$; $x =$ ₹ 24

59. **Hint** Let the tour be of x days.
According to the question,
$$\frac{18000}{x} - \frac{18000}{x+4} = 750$$ **Ans.** 8 days

60. **Hint** Let the original number of persons be x.
Then, share of each person $= \frac{6500}{x}$
When the number of persons is increased by 15.
Then, new share $= \frac{6500}{x+15}$
Now, according to the question, we get
$$\frac{6500}{x} - \frac{6500}{x+15} = 30$$
Ans. 50

61. **Hint** Let Shefali's marks in Mathematics be x.
Then, Shefali's marks in English $= (30 - x)$.
According to the question,
(Marks in Mathematics + 2) × (Marks in English − 3)
= 210
Ans. When Shefali's marks in Mathematics are 12 and 13 respectively, then her marks in English are 18 and 17, respectively.

62. **Hint** Let the number of rows in the original arrangement be x.
Number of seats in the auditorium $= x^2$
In new arrangement, number of rows $= 2x$
Number of seats in each row $= x - 10$
$\therefore$ Number of seats after new arrangement $= 2x(x-10)$
Ans. (i) 30 (ii) 1200

63. **Hint** Let the sides of square be x and y.
Then, according to the question, $x^2 + y^2 = 468$
and $4(x-y) = 24 \Rightarrow x - y = 6$
Ans. 18 m, 12 m

64. Hint Use Pythagoras theorem and use the formula,

$$\text{Area of triangle} = \frac{1}{2} \times \text{Base} \times \text{Height}$$

Ans. 17 cm

65. Hint Let the length and breadth of the rectangle be x and y, respectively.
According to the question,

$$2(x + y) = 82 \Rightarrow x + y = 41$$

and $xy = 400$

Ans. 25, 16

66. Hint

(i) (c) To travel x km, diesel used by car $X = 1$ L

To travel 1 km, diesel used by car $X = \frac{1}{x}$ L

$\therefore$ To travel 72 km, diesel used by car $X = \frac{72}{x}$ L

(ii) (b) Similarly

To travel 72 km, diesel used by car $Y = \frac{72}{(x+3)}$ L

(iii) (c) Given, car X used 4 L of diesel more than car Y in the journey.

$$\therefore \quad \frac{72}{x} = \frac{72}{x+3} + 4$$

$$\Rightarrow \quad \frac{72}{x} - \frac{72}{x+3} = 4 \quad \text{...(i)}$$

(iv) (b) From Eq. (i), we have

$$\frac{72}{x} - \frac{72}{x+3} = 4$$

$$\Rightarrow \quad 72\left(\frac{x+3-x}{x(x+3)}\right) = 4$$

$$\Rightarrow \quad x^2 + 3x - 54 = 0$$

$$\Rightarrow \quad x^2 + 9x - 6x - 54 = 0$$

$$\Rightarrow \quad x(x+9) - 6(x+9) = 0$$

$$\Rightarrow \quad x = 6, x = -9 \text{ (neglected)}$$

$\therefore$ Required amount of diesel $= \frac{72}{x} = \frac{72}{6} = 12$ L

Olympiad Section

Brain Teasing Questions of Olympiad Pattern

1 The linear factors of the equation $x^2 + kx + 1 = 0$ exists, if

(a) $k \geq 2$ (b) $k \leq -2$
(c) Both (a) and (b) (d) $k = 2$

2 The root of the equation $2\sin\theta + \frac{3}{\sin\theta} + 7 = 0$ is

(a) $\frac{1}{2}$ (b) $-\frac{1}{2}$
(c) $\frac{1}{3}$ (d) $\frac{1}{7}$

3 The equation $x^2(a^2 + b^2) + 2x(ac + bd) + (c^2 + d^2) = 0$ has no real roots, if

(a) $ad \neq bc$ (b) $ac \neq bd$
(c) $ac \neq 2bd$ (d) None of these

4 A factory kept increasing its output by the same percentage every year. Then, the percentage, if it is known that the output is doubled in the last two years, will be

(a) 44.1% (b) 14.4%
(c) 44.4% (d) 41.4%

5 A trader bought a number of articles for ₹ 1200. Ten were damaged and he sold each of the rest at ₹ 2 more than what he paid for it, thus cleaning a profit of ₹ 60 on the whole transaction. If x denotes the number of articles he bought, then the value of x is

(a) 100 (b) 60
(c) 80 (d) 110

6 If the roots of the equation $x^2 + 2cx + ab = 0$ are real and unequal, then the equation $x^2 - 2(a + b)x + a^2 + b^2 + 2c^2 = 0$ has

(a) real root (b) no real roots
(c) equal root (d) real and equal

7 The values of x satisfying $p^2x^2 + (p^2 - q^2)x - q^2 = 0$ are

(a) $\frac{q^2}{p^2}, -1$ (b) $\frac{p^2}{q^2}, 1$
(c) $\frac{q^2}{p^2}, +1$ (d) $1, \frac{-q}{p}$

8 From a group of Saras birds, one-fourth of the number are moving about in lotus plants, one-ninth coupled with one-fourth as well as 7 times the square root of the total number are moving on a hill, while 56 birds are sitting in the Bakula trees. Then, what is the total number of birds?

(a) 629 (b) 567
(c) 675 (d) 576

Answers

1. (c) **2.** (b) **3.** (a) **4.** (d) **5.** (a) **6.** (b) **7.** (a) **8.** (d)

* *These questions may or may not be asked in the examination, have been given just for additional practice required for olympiads Scholarship Exams etc. For detailed explanations refer Page No. 479.*

CHAPTER

06

Ratio and Proportion

SYLLABUS

- (a) Proportion, Continued proportion, mean proportion. (b) Componendo, dividendo, alternendo, invertendo properties and their combinations. (c) Direct simple applications on proportions only.

In general, ratio is a relationship between two number (or similar quantities) indicating, how many times the first number (or quantity) is of the second? The equality of two ratios is called proportion. In this chapter, we will study properties, combinations and applications of ratio and proportion.

Ratio and Its Properties

A **ratio** is a comparison of two or more quantities of the same kind taken in the same unit.

If x and y are two quantities of same kind taken in the same unit, then fraction x/y is known as ratio of x and y. It is written as $x : y$ and read as 'x is to y'.

e.g. The ratio of $5l : 3l$ is $\frac{5}{3}$ or $5 : 3$.

In the expression $x : y$, the quantities x and y are called **terms of ratio**, where x is called the **first term** (or antecedent) and y is called the **second term** (or consequent).

Ratio is always expressed in numbers, that are coprimes. It can only be calculated, if the quantities involved are in the same unit.

The value of a ratio (say $x : y$) remains unchanged, if both the antecedent (x) and consequent (y) are multiplied by the same non-zero number (say a)

i.e. $x : y$ is the same as $ax : ay$. $\left[\because \frac{x}{y} = \frac{ax}{ay}\right]$

The value of a ratio (say $x : y$) remains unchanged, if both the antecedent (x) and consequent (y) are divided by the same non-zero number (say a)

i.e. $x : y$ is the same as $\frac{x}{a} : \frac{y}{a}$. $\left[\because \frac{x}{y} = \frac{x \div a}{y \div a}\right]$

Important Facts about Ratio

(i) The ratio between two or more unlike (or different) quantities does not exist.

(ii) Ratio is taken only between positive quantities.

(iii) The order of the terms in a ratio is important.

(iv) The ratio is always expressed in the lowest or simplest form.

(v) A ratio is a number, so it has no units.

(vi) Ratio $x : y$ is not equal to ratio $y : x$ i.e. $x : y \neq y : x$.

(vii) If the terms of the given ratio are in fractions, then convert the terms of the ratio in the whole numbers by multiplying each term by the LCM of their denominators.

e.g. $\frac{2}{5} : \frac{3}{4} = \frac{2}{5} \times 20 : \frac{3}{4} \times 20 = 2 \times 4 : 3 \times 5 = 8 : 15$

Example 1. Find the ratio between 7 months and 2 yr 4 months.

Sol. Clearly, 2 yr 4 months = 2×12 months + 4 months [$\because$ 1 yr = 12 months]

= 24 months + 4 months = 28 months

Ratio between 7 months and 2 yr 4 months

= Ratio between 7 months and 28 months

$= \frac{7}{28}$

Dividing both antecedent and consequent by 7, we get

$\therefore$ Required ratio $= \frac{1}{4}$ or 1 : 4

Example 2. Find the ratio of 50 min to $2\frac{1}{2}$ h.

Sol. Clearly, $2\frac{1}{2}\text{h} = \frac{5}{2}\text{h} = \frac{5}{2} \times 60\text{min}$ [$\because$ 1 h = 60 min]

= 150 min

$\therefore$ Ratio of 50 min to $2\frac{1}{2}$ h = Ratio of 50 min to 150 min

$= \frac{50}{150} = \frac{1}{3}$ [dividing numerator and denominator by 50]

$\therefore$ Required ratio = 1 : 3

Increase (or Decrease) a Quantity in Given Ratio

If a quantity increases (or decreases) in the ratio $x : y$.

Then, new quantity $= \frac{y}{x} \times$ Original quantity.

$\therefore$ Increase in quantity = Increased value − Original value

or Decrease in quantity = Original value − Decreased value

Example 3. When the fare of a certain journey by a train increase from ₹ 15 to ₹ 21 and the fare of original journey was ₹ 1015, then find the increase in the fare.

Sol. Given, original fare = ₹1015

and fare increases in the ratio 15 : 21 = 5 : 7

[dividing antecedent and consequent by 3]

$\therefore$ New fare of train $= \frac{7}{5} \times$ Original fare

[$\because$ new quantity $= \frac{y}{x} \times$ original quantity]

$= \frac{7}{5} \times 1015 = 7 \times 203$

= ₹ 1421

Increase in value = Increased value − Original value

$\therefore$ Increase in the fare = New fare − Original fare

= 1421 − 1015

= ₹ 406

Comparison of Ratios

1. When Two Ratios are Given

Let $x : y$ and $z : w$ be two ratios. Then,

(i) $(x : y) > (z : w)$, i.e. $\frac{x}{y} > \frac{z}{w}$, if $xw > yz$

(ii) $(x : y) = (z : w)$, i.e. $\frac{x}{y} = \frac{z}{w}$, if $xw = yz$

(iii) $(x : y) < (z : w)$, i.e. $\frac{x}{y} < \frac{z}{w}$, if $xw < yz$

Example 4. Compare 4/5 and 7/6. Also, write the relation between them.

Sol. We have, $\frac{4}{5}$ and $\frac{7}{6}$

Consider 4×6 and $7 \times 5 \Rightarrow 24$ and 35

Since, 24 < 35

$\therefore \frac{4}{5} < \frac{7}{6}$

2. When Three or More than Three Ratios are Given

In order to compare three or more than three ratios, we convert them into equivalent fractions with same denominator and then compare them.

Example 5. Compare the following ratios and write them in ascending order $\frac{4}{5}, \frac{3}{2}, \frac{1}{10}$.

Sol. We have, $\frac{4}{5}, \frac{3}{2}$ and $\frac{1}{10}$, which can be written as

$\frac{4 \times 2}{5 \times 2}, \frac{3 \times 5}{2 \times 5}$ and $\frac{1 \times 1}{10 \times 1}$ [$\because$ LCM of 5, 2 and 10 = 10]

$\Rightarrow \frac{8}{10}, \frac{15}{10}$ and $\frac{1}{10}$

Since, $1 < 8 < 15$

$\therefore \frac{1}{10} < \frac{8}{10} < \frac{15}{10}$ [divide each term by 10]

$\Rightarrow \frac{1}{10} < \frac{4}{5} < \frac{3}{2}$

Hence, the given ratios in ascending order of their magnitude are $\frac{1}{10}, \frac{4}{5}$ and $\frac{3}{2}$.

Example 6. Write the following ratios in descending order.

$\frac{1}{6}, \frac{2}{3}$ and $\frac{7}{12}$

Sol. Given, ratios are $\frac{1}{6}, \frac{2}{3}$ and $\frac{7}{12}$, which can be written as

$\frac{1 \times 2}{6 \times 2}, \frac{2 \times 4}{3 \times 4}$ and $\frac{7 \times 1}{12 \times 1}$ [$\because$ LCM of 6, 3 and 12 = 12]

$\Rightarrow \frac{2}{12}, \frac{8}{12}$ and $\frac{7}{12}$

Since, $8 > 7 > 2$

$\therefore \quad \frac{8}{12} > \frac{7}{12} > \frac{2}{12}$ [dividing each term by 12]

$\Rightarrow \quad \frac{2}{3} > \frac{7}{12} > \frac{1}{6}$

Hence, the given ratios in descending order of their magnitude are $\frac{2}{3}, \frac{7}{12}$ and $\frac{1}{6}$.

Example 7. If $A : B = 6 : 11$ and $B : C = 13 : 7$, then find the value of $A : B : C$.

Sol. Given, $A : B = 6 : 11$ and $B : C = 13 : 7$

The LCM of two value of B i.e. 11 and 13 is 143.

$A : B = 6 : 11 = 78 : 143$ and $B : C = 13 : 7 = 143 : 77$

$\therefore \quad A : B : C = 78 : 143 : 77$

Composition of Ratios

1. **Compounded ratio** When two or more ratios are multiplied with each other, then they are called compounded ratio.
   (i) Compounded ratio of $x : y$ and $z : w$ is $xz : yw$.
   (ii) Compounded ratio of $x : y$, $z : w$ and $s : t$ is $xzs : ywt$.
2. **Duplicate ratio** When ratio is multiplied with itself, then resulting ratio is called duplicate ratio of the given ratio.
   i.e. duplicate ratio of $x : y$ is $x^2 : y^2$.
3. **Triplicate ratio** When ratio is multiplied twice with itself, then the resulting ratio is called triplicate ratio of the given ratio.
   i.e. triplicate ratio of $x : y$ is $x^3 : y^3$.
4. **Sub-duplicate ratio** The square root of the ratio is called sub-duplicate ratio.
   i.e. sub-duplicate ratio of $x : y$ is $\sqrt{x} : \sqrt{y}$.
5. **Sub-triplicate ratio** The cube root of the ratio is called sub-triplicate ratio.
   i.e. sub-triplicate ratio of $x : y$ is $\sqrt[3]{x} : \sqrt[3]{y}$.
6. **Reciprocal ratio** The reciprocal ratio of $x : y$ is $y : x$.

Example 8. If $m : n = 3 : 4$, then find $(3m + 4n) : (9m - 5n)$

Sol. Given, $m : n = 3 : 4$

Let $m = 3x$ and $n = 4x$

and $\frac{3m + 4n}{9m - 5n} = \frac{3(3x) + 4(4x)}{9(3x) - 5(4x)} = \frac{9x + 16x}{27x - 20x} = \frac{25x}{7x} = 25 : 7$

Example 9. If $(2a + 3b) : (3a + 11b) = 11 : 29$, then find $a : b$.

Sol. Given, $(2a + 3b) : (3a + 11b) = 11 : 29$

$\Rightarrow \quad \frac{2a + 3b}{3a + 11b} = \frac{11}{29}$

$\Rightarrow \quad 29(2a + 3b) = 11(3a + 11b)$

$\Rightarrow \quad 58a + 87b = 33a + 121b$

$\Rightarrow \quad 58a - 33a = 121b - 87b$

$\Rightarrow \quad 25a = 34b$

$\Rightarrow \quad \frac{a}{b} = \frac{34}{25}$

Example 10. Find the compounded ratio of
(i) $2x : 3y$ and $2a : 5b$
(ii) $3x : 2y$, $4a : 5b$ and $z : t$.

Sol.
(i) $\therefore$ Required compounded ratio
$= (2x \times 2a) : (3y \times 5b) = 4ax : 15by$

(ii) $\therefore$ Required compounded ratio
$= (3x \times 4a \times z) : (2y \times 5b \times t)$
$= 12xaz : 10ybt$
$= 6xaz : 5ybt$
[dividing antecedent and consequent by 2]

Example 11. Find the following.
(i) The duplicate ratio of 2 : 5.
(ii) The triplicate ratio of 3 : 7.
(iii) The sub-duplicate ratio of 121 : 169.
(iv) The sub-triplicate ratio of 64 : 27.
(v) The reciprocal ratio of 13 : 17.

Sol.
(i) Duplicate ratio of 2 : 5 is $(2)^2 : (5)^2 = 4 : 25$
(ii) Triplicate ratio of 3 : 7 is $(3)^3 : (7)^3 = 27 : 343$
(iii) Sub-duplicate ratio of 121 : 169 is $\sqrt{121} : \sqrt{169} = 11 : 13$
(iv) Sub-triplicate ratio of 64 : 27 is $\sqrt[3]{64} : \sqrt[3]{27} = 4 : 3$
(v) Reciprocal ratio of 13 : 17 is 17 : 13.

Example 12. In a world war II, the ratio of number of Army officers to the number of Navy officers was 2 : 15 before a war. In the war, 5 Army officers and 13 Navy officers were killed. The ratio between the number of Army officers and the number of Navy officers, now is 1 : 11. Find the number of Army officers and Navy officers before the war.

Sol. **Before the war**

Let the number of Army officers be $2x$ and the number of Navy officers be $15x$.

After the war

The number of Army officers be $2x - 5$ and the number of Navy officers be $15x - 13$.

According to question,

$\frac{2x - 5}{15x - 13} = \frac{1}{11}$

$\Rightarrow \quad 11(2x - 5) = 1(15x - 13)$

$\Rightarrow \quad 22x - 55 = 15x - 13$

$\Rightarrow \quad 7x = 55 - 13$

$7x = 42 \Rightarrow x = 6$

Now, the number of Army officer before war $= 2 \times 6 = 12$

and the number of Navy officers before war $= 6 \times 15 = 90$

Example 13. In a mixture of 180 L of milk and water, milk and water are in the ratio 5 : 4. How much water required to be added to the mixture to make this ratio 2 : 3?

Sol. Given, mixture of 180 L of milk and water, milk and water are in the ratio 5 : 4.

So, quantity of milk $= \left(180 \times \frac{5}{5+4}\right) L = 100 L$

and quantity of water $= \left(180 \times \frac{4}{9}\right) L = 80 L$

Let x L water must be added

Now, total quantity of water $= (80 + x)$ L

Then, $\frac{100}{80+x} = \frac{2}{3}$

$\Rightarrow 300 = 2(80 + x)$

$\Rightarrow 300 = 160 + 2x$

$\Rightarrow 300 - 160 = 2x$

$\therefore x = \frac{140}{2} = 70 L$

Hence, 70 L water must be added to the mixture to make the ratio 2 : 3.

Example 14. There are 56 members on a student council in a school and the ratio of the number of boys to the number of girls is 5 : 2. How many more girls should be added to the council so that the ratio of number of boys to the number of girls may be 10 : 7.

Sol. Given, total members in a student council in a school = 56

$\therefore$ The number of boys in the council $= \frac{5}{7} \times 56 = 40$

and the number of girls in the council $= \frac{2}{7} \times 56 = 16$

Let x girls be added to the student council, then the number of girls in the council $= 16 + x$

According to the question,

$$\frac{40}{16+x} = \frac{10}{7}$$

$\Rightarrow 280 = 160 + 10x$

$\Rightarrow 28 - 16 = x$

$\therefore x = 12$

Hence, the number of girls to be added to the student council is 12.

Exercise 6.1

1. (i) If $A : B = 2 : 5$ and the value of A is 4, then what is the value of B?
   (ii) If $(3a + 2b) : (5a + 3b) = 18 : 29$, then find $a : b$.
2. Find the ratio between 7.8 cm and 8 km.
3. Find the ratio of 65 min to $1\frac{1}{5}$ h.
4. An alloy consists of $27\frac{1}{2}$ kg of copper and $2\frac{3}{4}$ kg of tin. Find the ratio by weight of tin to the alloy.
5. An alloy consists of $40\frac{1}{2}$ g of gold and $5\frac{1}{4}$ g of silver. Find the ratio by weight of the gold to the alloy.
6. The fare of a certain journey by an airline was increased in the ratio 5 : 7. Find the increase in the fare, if the original fare is ₹ 1050.
7. The current price of a box is ₹ 300. Find the original price of an article, if the price decreases from 15 to 9.
8. Arrange the ratios 3 : 4, 7 : 8, 10 : 12, 15 : 8 in ascending order of magnitude.
9. Compare the ratios $\frac{1}{7}, \frac{3}{4}$ and $\frac{9}{14}$ and write them in ascending order.
10. Compare the ratios $\frac{3}{8}, \frac{5}{24}$ and $\frac{7}{3}$ and write them in descending order.
11. Find the following :
    (i) The compounded ratio of $2a : 3b$, $mn : x^2$ and $x : n$.
    (ii) The duplicate ratio of $3\sqrt{3} : 2\sqrt{5}$.
    (iii) The triplicate ratio of $\frac{m}{2} : \frac{n}{3}$.
12. If $2X = 3Y = 5Z$, then find the value of $X : Y : Z$.
13. Find the following.
    (i) The sub-duplicate ratio of 9 : 16.
    (ii) The sub-duplicate ratio of $9p^2q^2 : 16r^2s^4$.
    (iii) The sub-duplicate ratio of 36 : 25
14. Find the following.
    (i) The sub-triplicate ratio of 216 : 512.
    (ii) The sub-triplicate ratio of $125a^3 : 1000b^6$
    (iii) The sub-triplicate ratio of 1 : 216.
15. Find the following.
    (i) The reciprocal ratio of 8 : 11.
    (ii) The reciprocal ratio of $13xyz : 4abc$
    (iii) The reciprocal ratio of $3x : \frac{1}{y}$.
16. If $(x - 9) : (3x + 6)$ is the duplicate ratio of 4 : 9, then find the value of x. [ICSE 2014]
17. Find the following
    (i) The compounded ratio of $(a - b) : (a + b)$, $(a + b)^2 : (a^2 + b^2)$ and $(a^4 - b^4) : (a^2 - b^2)^2$.

(ii) The duplicate ratio of $\sqrt{5}:7$.

(iii) The triplicate ratio of $\frac{1}{2}:\frac{1}{3}$.

18. In a business, A invest ₹ 50000 for 5 months, B ₹ 60000 for 4 months and C ₹ 70000 for 3 months. If they together earn ₹ 18800, then find the share of each.

19. The sides of a triangle are in the ratio 6 : 5 : 4 and its perimeter is 60 cm. Find the lengths of sides.

20. In an examination, the ratio of passes to failure was 3 : 1. If 20 less had appeared and 10 less passed, the ratio of passes to failures would have been 5 : 1. How many students appeared for the examination?

21. Divide ₹ 1870 into three parts in such a way that half of the first part, one-third of the second part and one-sixth of the third part are all equal.

22. A labourer earns ₹ 9000 per month and spends ₹ 6500 per month on his family and the rest he saves for the future needs. Find the ratio of his

(i) income to his expenditure.

(ii) income to his savings.

(iii) savings to his expenditure.

Proportion and Its Properties

An equality of two ratios is called the **proportion**. The four non–zero quantities x, y, z and t of the same kind taken in same unit are said to be in proportion, if and only if the product of **extremes** (i.e. first and fourth terms) is equal to the product of **means** (i.e. second and third terms).

Here, x and t are the extreme terms and y and z are the mean terms.

$\therefore$ x, y, z and t are in proportion, if $xt = yz$.

We can write $x : y = z : t$ as $x : y :: z : t$ and read as 'x is to y as z is to t'.

Example 15. Find the value of z, if $7 : z :: 5 : 20$.

Sol. We have, $7 : z :: 5 : 20$

$\Rightarrow \quad 5z = 7 \times 20$ [$\because$ product of means = product of extremes]

$\Rightarrow \quad z = \frac{7 \times 20}{5} = 28$

Hence, the required value of z is 28.

Example 16. The numbers $k + 3$, $k + 2$, $3k - 7$ and $2k - 3$ are in proportion. Find k. [ICSE 2019]

Sol. Given, numbers $k + 3, k + 2, 3k - 7$ and $2k - 3$ are in proprotion.

$\therefore \quad (k + 3) : (k + 2) :: (3k - 7) : (2k - 3)$

$\Rightarrow \quad \frac{k+3}{k+2} = \frac{3k-7}{2k-3}$

$\Rightarrow \quad (k + 3)(2k - 3) = (k + 2)(3k - 7)$

$\Rightarrow \quad 2k^2 + 3k - 9 = 3k^2 - k - 14$

$\Rightarrow \quad k^2 - 4k - 5 = 0$

$\Rightarrow \quad k^2 - 5k + k - 5 = 0$ [by splitting middle term]

$\Rightarrow \quad k(k - 5) + 1(k - 5) = 0$

$\Rightarrow \quad (k - 5)(k + 1) = 0$

$\Rightarrow \quad k = -1, 5$

Example 17. What number must be added to each of the numbers 7, 16, 43 and 79 to make them in proportion?

Sol. Let the required number be x.

According to the question,

$(7 + x) : (16 + x) :: (43 + x) : (79 + x)$

$\Rightarrow \quad \frac{7+x}{16+x} = \frac{43+x}{79+x}$

$\Rightarrow \quad (7 + x)(79 + x) = (16 + x)(43 + x)$ [by cross-multiplication]

$\Rightarrow \quad 553 + 7x + 79x + x^2 = 688 + 16x + 43x + x^2$

$\Rightarrow \quad 553 + 86x = 688 + 59x$

$\Rightarrow \quad 86x - 59x = 688 - 553$

$\Rightarrow \quad 27x = 135$

$\therefore \quad x = \frac{135}{27} = 5$

Hence, the required number is 5.

Example 18. If $(x^2 + z^2)(y^2 + t^2) = (xy + zt)^2$, then prove that x, y, z and t are in proportion.

Sol. We have,

$(x^2 + z^2)(y^2 + t^2) = (xy + zt)^2$

$\Rightarrow x^2y^2 + x^2t^2 + z^2y^2 + z^2t^2 = x^2y^2 + z^2t^2 + 2xyzt$ [$\because (a + b)^2 = a^2 + b^2 + 2ab$]

$\Rightarrow \quad x^2t^2 + z^2y^2 = 2xyzt$

$\Rightarrow x^2t^2 + z^2y^2 - 2xyzt = 0$

$\Rightarrow \quad (xt - zy)^2 = 0$ [$\because a^2 + b^2 - 2ab = (a - b)^2$]

$\Rightarrow \quad xt - zy = 0$ [$\because a^2 = 0 \Leftrightarrow a = 0$]

$\Rightarrow \quad xt = zy$

$\Rightarrow \quad \frac{xt}{yt} = \frac{zy}{yt}$ [dividing both sides by yt]

$\Rightarrow \quad \frac{x}{y} = \frac{z}{t}$

which shows that x, y, z and t are in proportion.

Example 19. If a, b, c and d are in proportion, then prove that $(ma + nb) : b = (mc + nd) : d$.

Sol. Given, a, b, c and d are in proportion.

$$\therefore \quad \frac{a}{b} = \frac{c}{d}$$

On multiplying both sides by m in numerator and by n in denominator, we get

$$\frac{ma}{nb} = \frac{mc}{nd}$$

On adding 1 both sides, we get

$$\frac{ma}{nb} + 1 = \frac{mc}{nd} + 1$$

$$\Rightarrow \quad \frac{ma + nb}{nb} = \frac{mc + nd}{nd}$$

$$\Rightarrow \quad \frac{ma + nb}{b} = \frac{mc + nd}{d} \quad \text{[multiplying both sides by } n]$$

$$\Rightarrow \quad (ma + nb) : b = (mc + nd) : d$$

Hence proved.

Continued Proportion

Three non-zero quantities x, y and z of same kind taken in same unit are said to be in continued proportion, if and only if the ratio of first term (i.e. x) and second term (i.e. y) is equal to the ratio of second term (i.e. y) and third term (i.e. z).

Thus, if x, y and z are in continued proportion, then

$$x : y :: y : z, \text{ i.e. } \frac{x}{y} = \frac{y}{z} \Rightarrow y^2 = xz$$

In general, the non–zero quantities x, y, z, t, s,..., etc., of same kind taken in same unit are said to be in continued proportion, if and only if

$$\frac{x}{y} = \frac{y}{z} = \frac{z}{t} = \frac{t}{s} = \dots .$$

First Proportional

If x, y and z are in continued proportion, then x is called first proportional.

Mean Proportional

If x, y and z are in continued proportion, then y is called the mean proportional.

i.e. $x : y :: y : z$

$$\Rightarrow \quad \frac{x}{y} = \frac{y}{z} \Rightarrow y^2 = xz \Rightarrow y = \sqrt{xz}$$

Thus, the mean proportion between two numbers is the positive square root of their product.

Third Proportional

If x, y and z are in continued proportion, then z is called third proportional.

Fourth Proportional

If x, y, z and t are in proportion, then t is called the fourth proportional.

Example 20. If $3 : x :: 2 : 18$, then find the value of x.

Sol. Given, $3 : x :: 2 : 18$

$$\frac{3}{x} = \frac{2}{18}$$

$$2x = 3 \times 18$$

$$x = \frac{3 \times 18}{2}$$

$$x = 27$$

Example 21. If a, 4, 12 and b are in continued proportion, then find the values of a and b.

Sol. Given, a, 4, 12 and b are in continued proportion.

$$\therefore \quad \frac{a}{4} = \frac{4}{12} = \frac{12}{b} \Rightarrow \frac{a}{4} = \frac{4}{12} \text{ and } \frac{4}{12} = \frac{12}{b}$$

$$\Rightarrow \quad a = \frac{16}{12} \text{ and } 4b = 12 \times 12$$

$$\therefore \quad a = \frac{4}{3} \text{ and } b = 36$$

Hence, the required values of a and b are 4/3 and 36, respectively.

Example 22. What is the mean proportional between $10 + 2\sqrt{3}$ and $15 - 3\sqrt{3}$?

Sol. Let the mean proportional between $(10 + 2\sqrt{3})$ and $(15 - 3\sqrt{3})$ be x.

Then, $(10 + 2\sqrt{3}) : x :: x : (15 - 3\sqrt{3})$

$$\Rightarrow \quad \frac{10 + 2\sqrt{3}}{x} = \frac{x}{(15 - 3\sqrt{3})}$$

$$\Rightarrow \quad x^2 = (10 + 2\sqrt{3})(15 - 3\sqrt{3})$$

$$\Rightarrow \quad x^2 = 2(5 + \sqrt{3}) \times 3(5 - \sqrt{3}) = 6(5 + \sqrt{3})(5 - \sqrt{3})$$

$$= 6[(5)^2 - (\sqrt{3})^2] \quad [\because (a - b)(a + b) = a^2 - b^2]$$

$$= 6(25 - 3) = 132$$

$$\Rightarrow \quad x = \sqrt{132} \quad \text{[taking positive square root]}$$

$$\therefore \quad x = 2\sqrt{33}$$

Hence, the required mean proportional is $2\sqrt{33}$.

Example 23. Find the mean proportional between $(a^3 - a^2 b)$ and $(a - b)$.

Sol. Let x be the mean proportional between $(a^3 - a^2 b)$ and $(a - b)$.

Then, $(a^3 - a^2 b) : x :: x : (a - b) \Rightarrow \frac{(a^3 - a^2 b)}{x} = \frac{x}{(a - b)}$

$$\Rightarrow \quad x^2 = (a^3 - a^2 b)(a - b) = a^2(a - b)(a - b)$$

$$\Rightarrow \quad x^2 = a^2(a - b)^2$$

Taking positive square root on both sides, we get

$$x = \sqrt{a^2(a - b)^2}$$

$$\therefore \quad x = a(a - b)$$

Hence, the required mean proportional is $a(a - b)$.

Example 24. If b is the mean proportion between a and c, then show that $\frac{a^4 + a^2b^2 + b^4}{b^4 + b^2c^2 + c^4} = \frac{a^2}{c^2}$. **[ICSE 2017]**

Sol. Given, b is the mean proportional between a and c.

$\therefore \quad \frac{a}{b} = \frac{b}{c} \Rightarrow b^2 = ac$

Now, LHS $= \frac{a^4 + a^2b^2 + b^4}{b^4 + b^2c^2 + c^4} = \frac{a^4 + a^2(ac) + (ac)^2}{(ac)^2 + (ac)c^2 + c^4}$ $[\because b^2 = ac]$

$= \frac{a^4 + a^3c + a^2c^2}{a^2c^2 + ac^3 + c^4}$

$= \frac{a^2(a^2 + ac + c^2)}{c^2(a^2 + ac + c^2)} = \frac{a^2}{c^2}$ = RHS **Hence proved.**

Example 25. If $x \neq y$ and $x : y$ is the duplicate ratio of $(x + z)$ and $(y + z)$, then prove that z is the mean proportional between x and y.

Sol. We have, $x : y$ = Duplicate ratio of $(x + z)$ and $(y + z)$

$\therefore \quad \frac{x}{y} = \frac{(x+z)^2}{(y+z)^2} \Rightarrow x(y+z)^2 = y(x+z)^2$

$\Rightarrow \quad x(y^2 + z^2 + 2yz) = y(x^2 + z^2 + 2xz)$

$[\because (a+b)^2 = a^2 + b^2 + 2ab]$

$\Rightarrow \quad xy^2 + xz^2 + 2xyz = x^2y + z^2y + 2xyz$

$\Rightarrow \quad xy^2 + xz^2 = x^2y + z^2y \Rightarrow xy^2 - x^2y + xz^2 - z^2y = 0$

$\Rightarrow \quad xy(y - x) - z^2(y - x) = 0 \Rightarrow (y - x)(xy - z^2) = 0$

$\Rightarrow \quad xy - z^2 = 0$ or $y - x = 0 \Rightarrow z^2 = xy$ $[\because y \neq x]$

$\therefore \quad z = \sqrt{xy}$ [taking positive square root]

Hence, z is the mean proportional between x and y.

Example 26. If x, y and z are in continued proportion, then prove that $\frac{(x+y)^2}{(y+z)^2} = \frac{x}{z}$. **[ICSE 2010]**

Sol. Since, x, y and z are in continued proportion, therefore

$\frac{x}{y} = \frac{y}{z} \Rightarrow y^2 = xz$

LHS $= \frac{(x+y)^2}{(y+z)^2} = \frac{x^2 + y^2 + 2xy}{y^2 + z^2 + 2yz} = \frac{x^2 + xz + 2xy}{xz + z^2 + 2yz}$ $[\because y^2 = xz]$

$= \frac{x(x + z + 2y)}{z(x + z + 2y)} = \frac{x}{z}$ = RHS **Hence proved.**

Example 27. If a, b and c are in continued proportion, then prove that

$(a + b + c)(a - b + c) = a^2 + b^2 + c^2$. **[ICSE 2015]**

Sol. If a, b and c are in continued proportion, then

$\frac{a}{b} = \frac{b}{c}$

or $\quad ac = b^2$

Now, LHS $= (a + b + c)(a - b + c)$

$= a^2 + ab + ac - ab - b^2 - bc + ac + bc + c^2$

$= a^2 - b^2 + c^2 + 2ac = a^2 - b^2 + c^2 + 2b^2$ $[\because ac = b^2]$

$= a^2 + b^2 + c^2$ = RHS **Hence proved.**

Example 28. Find the third proportional of 9 and 21.

Sol. Let the third proportional of 9 and 21 be x.

Then, $\quad 9 : 21 :: 21 : x$

$\Rightarrow \quad \frac{9}{21} = \frac{21}{x}$

$\Rightarrow \quad 9x = 21 \times 21$

$\Rightarrow \quad x = \frac{21 \times 21}{9} = 49$

Hence, the required third proportional is 49.

Example 29. What is the third proportional to $\frac{x}{y} + \frac{y}{x}$ and $\sqrt{(x+y)^2 - 2xy}$?

Sol. Let the third proportional be A.

Then, $\quad \frac{x}{y} + \frac{y}{x} : \sqrt{(x+y)^2 - 2xy} :: \sqrt{(x+y)^2 - 2xy} : A$

$\Rightarrow \quad \frac{\left(\frac{x}{y} + \frac{y}{x}\right)}{\sqrt{(x+y)^2 - 2xy}} = \frac{\sqrt{(x+y)^2 - 2xy}}{A}$

$\Rightarrow \quad \left(\frac{x}{y} + \frac{y}{x}\right)A = [\sqrt{(x+y)^2 - 2xy}]^2$

[by cross-multiplication]

$\Rightarrow \quad \left(\frac{x^2 + y^2}{xy}\right)A = (x+y)^2 - 2xy$

$\Rightarrow \quad \left(\frac{x^2 + y^2}{xy}\right)A = x^2 + y^2 + 2xy - 2xy$

$[\because (a+b)^2 = a^2 + b^2 + 2ab]$

$\Rightarrow \quad \left(\frac{x^2 + y^2}{xy}\right)A = x^2 + y^2$

$\Rightarrow \quad A = \frac{(x^2 + y^2)xy}{(x^2 + y^2)} = xy$

Hence, the required third proportional is xy.

Example 30. Find the fourth proportional to 9, 16 and 63.

Sol. Let the fourth proportional be x.

Then, $9 : 16 :: 63 : x$

$\Rightarrow \quad \frac{9}{16} = \frac{63}{x}$

$\Rightarrow \quad 9x = 63 \times 16$

$\therefore \quad x = \frac{63 \times 16}{9} = 112$

Hence, the required fourth proportional is 112.

Example 31. Find the fourth proportional to (a^3+8), $(a^4-2a^3+4a^2)$ and (a^2-4).

Sol. Let fourth proportional be x.

Then, $(a^3+8):(a^4-2a^3+4a^2)::(a^2-4):x$

$$\Rightarrow \frac{a^3+8}{a^4-2a^3+4a^2}=\frac{a^2-4}{x}$$

$$\Rightarrow x(a^3+8)=(a^2-4)(a^4-2a^3+4a^2)$$

[by cross-multiplication]

$$\therefore \quad x=\frac{(a^2-2^2)\times a^2(a^2-2a+4)}{(a^3+2^3)}$$

$$=\frac{a^2(a-2)(a+2)(a^2-2a+4)}{(a+2)(a^2-2a+4)}$$

$[\because a^3+b^3=(a+b)(a^2-ab+b^2)]$

$$=a^2(a-2)$$

Hence, the required value of fourth proportional is $a^2(a-2)$.

Properties and Combinations of Proportion

Some useful properties and combinations of proportion are given below

1. **Invertendo** If two ratios are equal, then their reciprocals are also equal,
   i.e. if $x:y::z:t$ or $\frac{x}{y}=\frac{z}{t}$, then $\frac{y}{x}=\frac{t}{z}$,
   i.e. $y:x::t:z$.
2. **Alternendo** If two ratios are equal, then the two ratios obtained by interchanging the consequent of first ratio and the antecedent of second ratio are also equal,
   i.e. if $x:y::z:t$ or $\frac{x}{y}=\frac{z}{t}$, then $\frac{x}{z}=\frac{y}{t}$,
   i.e. $x:z::y:t$.
3. **Componendo** If two ratios are equal, then the two ratios obtained on replacing the antecedent of both ratios by the sum of antecedent and consequent of given ratios are also equal,
   i.e. if $x:y::z:t$ or $\frac{x}{y}=\frac{z}{t}$, then $\frac{(x+y)}{y}=\frac{(z+t)}{t}$
   i.e. $(x+y):y::(z+t):t$.
4. **Dividendo** If two ratios are equal, then the two ratios obtained on replacing the antecedent of both ratios by the difference of antecedent and consequent of given ratios are also equal,
   i.e. if $x:y::z:t$ or $\frac{x}{y}=\frac{z}{t}$, then $\frac{x-y}{y}=\frac{z-t}{t}$,
   i.e. $(x-y):y::(z-t):t$.
5. **Componendo and Dividendo** If two ratios are equal, then the two ratios obtained on replacing the antecedent of both ratios by the sum of antecedent and consequent and replacing the consequent of both ratios by the difference of antecedent and consequent of given ratios are also equal,
   i.e. if $x:y::z:t$ or $\frac{x}{y}=\frac{z}{t}$, then $\frac{(x+y)}{(x-y)}=\frac{(z+t)}{(z-t)}$,
   i.e. $(x+y):(x-y)::(z+t):(z-t)$.
6. **Convertendo** If two ratios are equal, then the two ratios obtained on replacing the consequent of both ratios by difference of antecedent and consequent of given ratios are also equal,
   i.e. if $x:y::z:t$ or $\frac{x}{y}=\frac{z}{t}$, then $\frac{x}{(x-y)}=\frac{z}{(z-t)}$
   i.e. $x:(x-y)::z:(z-t)$.

Example 32. If $\frac{x}{y}=\frac{z}{t}$, then prove that $\frac{y-x}{x}=\frac{t-z}{z}$.

Sol. We have, $\frac{x}{y}=\frac{z}{t}\Rightarrow\frac{y}{x}=\frac{t}{z}$ [by invertendo property]

$\Rightarrow \frac{y-x}{x}=\frac{t-z}{z}$ [by dividendo property]

Hence proved.

Example 33. If $\frac{7m+2n}{7m-2n}=\frac{5}{3}$, then use the properties of proportion to find

(i) $m:n$. (ii) $\frac{m^2+n^2}{m^2-n^2}$. **[ICSE 2017]**

Sol. Given, $\frac{7m+2n}{7m-2n}=\frac{5}{3}$ ...(i)

(i) On applying componendo and dividendo property in Eq. (i), we get

$$\frac{7m+2n+7m-2n}{7m+2n-7m+2n}=\frac{5+3}{5-3}$$

$$\Rightarrow \frac{14m}{4n}=\frac{8}{2}\Rightarrow\frac{7m}{2n}=4\Rightarrow\frac{7m}{n}=8\Rightarrow\frac{m}{n}=\frac{8}{7}$$

(ii) From part (i), we get

$$\frac{m}{n}=\frac{8}{7}\Rightarrow\frac{m^2}{n^2}=\frac{64}{49}\Rightarrow\frac{m^2+n^2}{m^2-n^2}=\frac{64+49}{64-49}$$

[by componendo and dividendo property]

$$\Rightarrow \frac{m^2+n^2}{m^2-n^2}=\frac{113}{15}$$

Example 34. If $\frac{a^2+b^2}{a^2-b^2}=\frac{17}{8}$, then find the value of

(i) $a:b$ (ii) $(a^3+b^3):(a^3-b^3)$ **[ICSE 2014]**

Sol.

(i) We have, $\frac{a^2+b^2}{a^2-b^2}=\frac{17}{8}\Rightarrow\frac{(a^2+b^2)+(a^2-b^2)}{(a^2+b^2)-(a^2-b^2)}=\frac{17+8}{17-8}$

[by componendo and dividendo property]

$$\Rightarrow \frac{a^2+b^2+a^2-b^2}{a^2+b^2-a^2+b^2}=\frac{25}{9}\Rightarrow\frac{2a^2}{2b^2}=\frac{25}{9}\Rightarrow\left(\frac{a}{b}\right)^2=\left(\frac{5}{3}\right)^2$$

$\therefore \frac{a}{b}=\frac{5}{3}$ [taking positive square root]

Hence, $a:b$ is $5:3$.

(ii) From part (i), we get

$$\frac{a}{b}=\frac{5}{3} \Rightarrow \frac{a^3}{b^3}=\frac{125}{27} \quad \text{[cubing both sides]}$$

$$\Rightarrow \frac{a^3+b^3}{a^3-b^3}=\frac{125+27}{125-27}$$

[by componendo and dividendo property]

$$\Rightarrow \frac{a^3+b^3}{a^3-b^3}=\frac{152}{98}=\frac{76}{49}$$

Hence, $(a^3+b^3):(a^3-b^3)$ is 76 : 49.

Example 35. Given, $\frac{x^3+12x}{6x^2+8}=\frac{y^3+27y}{9y^2+27}$, using componendo and dividendo, find $x:y$. **[ICSE 2015]**

Sol. We have, $\frac{x^3+12x}{6x^2+8}=\frac{y^3+27y}{9y^2+27}$

Using componendo and dividendo property, we get

$$\frac{x^3+12x+6x^2+8}{x^3+12x-6x^2-8}=\frac{y^3+27y+9y^2+27}{y^3+27y-9y^2-27}$$

$$\Rightarrow \frac{(x+2)^3}{(x-2)^3}=\frac{(y+3)^3}{(y-3)^3}$$

$[\because (a+b)^3=a^3+3a^2b+3ab^2+b^3]$
$[\because (a-b)^3=a^3-3a^2b+3ab^2-b^3]$

Taking cube root on both sides, we get

$$\frac{x+2}{x-2}=\frac{y+3}{y-3}$$

Again, applying componendo and dividendo property, we get

$$\frac{(x+2)+(x-2)}{(x+2)-(x-2)}=\frac{(y+3)+(y-3)}{(y+3)-(y-3)}$$

$$\Rightarrow \frac{2x}{4}=\frac{2y}{6} \Rightarrow \frac{x}{y}=\frac{2}{3}$$

Hence, $x:y=2:3$

Example 36. Using properties of proportion find $x:y$, given $\frac{x^2+2x}{2x+4}=\frac{y^2+3y}{3y+9}$. **[ICSE 2020]**

Sol. We have, $\frac{x^2+2x}{2x+4}=\frac{y^2+3y}{3y+9}$

Using componendo and dividendo properties, we get

$$\frac{x^2+2x+2x+4}{x^2+2x-2x-4}=\frac{y^2+3y+3y+9}{y^2+3y-3y-9}$$

$$\Rightarrow \frac{(x+2)^2}{x^2-2^2}=\frac{(y+3)^2}{y^2-3^2} \quad [\because (a+b)^2=a^2+b^2+2ab]$$

$$\Rightarrow \frac{(x+2)(x+2)}{(x+2)(x-2)}=\frac{(y+3)(y+3)}{(y+3)(y-3)}$$

$[\because a^2-b^2=(a+b)(a-b)]$

$$\Rightarrow \frac{x+2}{x-2}=\frac{y+3}{y-3}$$

Again, applying componendo and dividendo property, we get

$$\frac{(x+2)+(x-2)}{(x-2)-(x-2)}=\frac{(y+3)+(y-3)}{(y+3)-(y-3)}$$

$$\Rightarrow \frac{2x}{4}=\frac{2y}{6} \Rightarrow \frac{x}{y}=\frac{2}{3}$$

Hence, $x:y=2:3$

Example 37. Using properties of proportion solve for x, given $\frac{\sqrt{5x}+\sqrt{2x-6}}{\sqrt{5x}-\sqrt{2x-6}}=4$. **[ICSE 2019]**

Sol. We have, $\frac{\sqrt{5x}+\sqrt{2x-6}}{\sqrt{5x}-\sqrt{2x-6}}=\frac{4}{1}$

Applying componendo and dividendo rule, we get

$$\frac{(\sqrt{5x}+\sqrt{2x-6})+(\sqrt{5x}-\sqrt{2x-6})}{(\sqrt{5x}+\sqrt{2x-6})-(\sqrt{5x}-\sqrt{2x-6})}=\frac{4+1}{4-1}$$

$$\Rightarrow \frac{2\sqrt{5x}}{2\sqrt{2x-6}}=\frac{5}{3}$$

$$\Rightarrow 3\sqrt{5x}=5\sqrt{2x-6}$$

On squaring both sides, we get

$$9(5x)=25(2x-6)$$

$$\Rightarrow 45x=50x-150$$

$$\Rightarrow 5x=150 \Rightarrow x=30$$

Exercise 6.2

1. (i) Find the value of n, if $n:15::4:30$.
   (ii) Find the value of a, if $8:a::4:20$.
   (iii) Find the value of a, if $7:28::5:a$.
2. What number must be added to each term of 2 : 5, so that it may be equal to 5 : 6?
3. Find whether the numbers 6, 10, 14 and 22 are in proportion or not. If not, what must be added to each of the numbers so that they become proportional?
4. What number must be added to each of the numbers 5, 11, 19 and 37, so that they are in proportion? **[ICSE 2009]**
5. Find the numbers which bears the same ratio to $\frac{7}{33}$ that $\frac{8}{21}$ does to $\frac{2}{7}$.
6. If $a+c=2b$ and $\frac{1}{b}+\frac{1}{d}=\frac{2}{c}$, then prove that a, b, c and d are in proportion.
7. If $p+r=mq$ and $\frac{1}{q}+\frac{1}{s}=\frac{m}{r}$, then prove that $p:q::r:s$.
8. If four quantities a, b, c and d are in proportion, then show that $(a-c)b^2:(b-d)cd=(a^2-b^2-ab):(c^2-d^2-cd)$.

9. If a, b, c and d are in proportion, then prove that $\frac{a-b}{c-d}=\sqrt{\frac{3a^2+8b^2}{3c^2+8d^2}}$.

10. If $(4x+5y)(4z-5u)=(4x-5y)(4z+5u)$, then prove that x, y, z and u are in proportion.

11. If $x:y::y:z$, prove that $x:z::x^2:y^2$.

12. (i) If (a^2+c^2), $(ab+cd)$ and (b^2+d^2) are in continued proportion, then prove that a, b, c and d are in proportion.

(ii) If x, 16, 48 and y are in continued proportion, then find the values of x and y.

13. If x, y and z are in continued proportion, then prove that $\frac{x}{z}=\frac{2x^2-5xy+7y^2}{2y^2-5yz+7z^2}$.

14. If a, b, c and d are in continued proportion, then prove that
$$\sqrt{ab}+\sqrt{bc}-\sqrt{cd}=\sqrt{(a+b-c)(b+c-d)}.$$

15. Find the mean proportional between the following.

(i) 5 and 80 (ii) $360x^4$ and $250x^2y^2$

(iii) $\sqrt{12}-\sqrt{8}$ and $\sqrt{12}+\sqrt{8}$

(iv) $\left(\frac{a-b}{a+b}\right)$ and $\left(\frac{a^2b^2}{a^2-b^2}\right)$.

16. If q is the mean proportional between p and r, then prove that $\frac{p^3+q^3+r^3}{p^2q^2r^2}=\frac{1}{p^3}+\frac{1}{q^3}+\frac{1}{r^3}$.

17. If x is the mean proportional between p and q, then prove that $p, q, (p^2+x^2)$ and (x^2+q^2) are in proportion.

18. If 6 is the mean proportional between two numbers x and y and 48 is the third proportional to x and y, then find the numbers. **[ICSE 2011]**

19. Find two numbers, such that the mean proportional between them is 18 and the third proportional to them is 144.

20. Find the third proportional to

(i) 25 and 15 (ii) $5+2\sqrt{3}$ and $37+20\sqrt{3}$

(iii) $\frac{x}{y}+\frac{y}{x}$ and $\frac{x}{y}$

21. Find the fourth proportional of the following.

(i) 8, 14 and 16 (ii) $2xy$, x^2 and y^2

(iii) (x^2-5x+4), (x^2+x-2) and (x^2-16)

(iv) x^3-y^3, $x^4+x^2y^2+y^4$ and $x-y$

22. Using the properties of proportion, solve for x, given $\frac{x^4+1}{2x^2}=\frac{17}{8}$. **[ICSE 2013]**

23. Using the properties of proportion, solve the following equation
$$\frac{5x+(x^2-1)}{5x-(x^2-1)}=\frac{7}{5}.$$

24. If $a:b::c:d$, then show that
$$(4a+5b):(4a-5b)::(4c+5d):(4c-5d).$$

25. If $\frac{4a^2+3b^2}{4a^2-3b^2}=\frac{7}{4}$, then find the value of $\frac{2a^4-11b^4}{2a^4+11b^4}$.

26. If $\frac{8a-5b}{8c-5d}=\frac{8a+5b}{8c+5d}$, then prove that $\frac{a}{b}=\frac{c}{d}$. **[ICSE 2008]**

27. If $x=\frac{\sqrt{2a+1}+\sqrt{2a-1}}{\sqrt{2a+1}-\sqrt{2a-1}}$, then prove that $x^2-4ax+1=0$. **[ICSE 2020]**

28. If $x=\frac{\sqrt{a+1}+\sqrt{a-1}}{\sqrt{a+1}-\sqrt{a-1}}$, then using the properties of proportion, then show that
$$x^2-2ax+1=0.$$ **[ICSE 2012]**

29. If $x=\frac{\sqrt{a+3b}+\sqrt{a-3b}}{\sqrt{a+3b}-\sqrt{a-3b}}$, then show that $3bx^2-2ax+3b=0$. **[ICSE 2007]**

30. Using properties of proportion, solve for x. Given that x is positive.
$$\frac{2x+\sqrt{4x^2-1}}{2x-\sqrt{4x^2-1}}=4$$ **[ICSE 2018]**

31. Using Componendo and Dividendo solve for x:
$$\frac{\sqrt{2x+2}+\sqrt{2x-1}}{\sqrt{2x+2}-\sqrt{2x-1}}=3$$ **[ICSE 2023]**

32. If $A=\frac{6xy}{x+y}$, then find the value of
$$\frac{A+3x}{A-3x}+\frac{A+3y}{A-3y}.$$

33. If $\frac{b+c-a}{y+z-x}=\frac{c+a-b}{z+x-y}=\frac{a+b-c}{x+y-z}$, then prove that each ratio is equal to $\frac{a}{x}=\frac{b}{y}=\frac{c}{z}$.

34. Solve : $\frac{1-px}{1+px}\sqrt{\frac{1+qx}{1-qx}}=1$

Chapter Practice

a. 1 Mark Questions

1. The ratio of 8 L of 1 L 600 mL is
(a) 1 : 5 (b) 5 : 2 (c) 5 : 1 (d) 2 : 5

2. Two numbers are in the ratio 5 : 3. If the sum of the numbers, is 128, then the smaller number is
(a) 80 (b) 48
(c) 45 (d) None of these

3. The mean proportional between 4 and 9 is **[ICSE 2023]**
(a) 4 (b) 6 (c) 9 (d) 36

4. The duplicate ratio of 5 : 6 is
(a) 25 : 36 (b) 5 : 36 (c) 25 : 6 (d) 25 : 30

5. If $A : B = 3 : 4$ and $B : C = 2 : 5$, then the value of $A : C$ is
(a) $\frac{3}{5}$ (b) $\frac{3}{11}$ (c) $\frac{3}{10}$ (d) $\frac{2}{1}$

6. If $A : B = 3 : 4$ and $B : C = 2 : 7$, then the value of $A : B : C$ is
(a) 3 : 8 : 14 (b) 3 : 4 : 14
(c) 4 : 6 : 7 (d) 3 : 5 : 9

7. If x, y, z are in continued proportion, then $(y^2 + z^2) : (x^2 + y^2)$ is equal to
(a) $z : x$ (b) $x : z$
(c) zx (d) $(y + z) : (x + y)$

8. If a, b, c and d are proportional, then $\frac{a+b}{a-b}$ is equal to
(a) $\frac{c}{d}$ (b) $\frac{c-d}{c+d}$ (c) $\frac{d}{c}$ (d) $\frac{c+d}{c-d}$

b. 3 Marks Questions

9. Arrange the ratios 5 : 6, 7 : 8 and 13 : 6 in descending order of magnitude.

10. Arrange the ratios 2 : 3, 17 : 21, 11 : 14 and 5 : 7 in descending order of magnitude.

11. If $x : y = 2 : 3$, $y : z = 4 : 5$ and $z : a = 6 : 7$, then find $x : a$.

12. If $(3a + 2b) : (5a + 3b) = 18 : 29$, then find $a : b$. **[ICSE 2016]**

13. If $X : Y = 3 : 2$, then find $(5X + 3Y) : (4X - 3Y)$.

14. If the ratio between 2 and 3 is the same as the ratio of $(m + n)$ to $(m + 3n)$, then find the value of $\frac{2n^2}{3m^2 + mn}$.

15. Two numbers are in the ratio 3 : 5. If 8 is added to each number, then the ratio becomes 2 : 3. Find the numbers. **[ICSE 2001]**

16. What quantity must be subtracted from each term of the ratio 9 : 17 to make it equal to 1 : 3?

17. A bag contains ₹ 140 in the form of 50 paise, ₹ 1 and ₹ 2 coins in the ratio of 6 : 3 : 7. Find the total number of coins.

18. The ages of A and B are in the ratio 7 : 8. 6 yr ago, their ages were in the ratio 5 : 6. Find their present ages.

19. Two positive numbers are in the ratio 3 : 5 and the difference between their squares is 400. Find the numbers.

20. The monthly pocket money of Ravi and Sanjeev are in the ratio 5 : 7. Their expenditures are in the ratio 3 : 5. If each save ₹ 80 every month, then find their monthly pocket money. **[ICSE 2012]**

21. The monthly income of P and Q are in the ratio 4 : 3 and their expenditures are in the ratio 3 : 2. If each of them saves ₹ 600 per month, then find the monthly income of each.

22. Find the following.
(i) The compounded ratio of $\sqrt{2} : 1$, $3 : \sqrt{5}$ and $\sqrt{20} : 9$.
(ii) The duplicate ratio of $5\sqrt{7} : 7\sqrt{5}$.
(iii) The triplicate ratio of $1 : 3xy$.

23. Find the following.
(i) The sub-duplicate ratio of $9x^2 : 49y^2$.
(ii) The sub-triplicate ratio of $64a^6 : 27b^3$.
(iii) The reciprocal ratio of $9x^2a^2 : 25z^2b^6$.

C. 4/5 Marks Questions

24. Find the following.
(i) The sub-duplicate ratio of $(x-y)^4 : (x+y)^6$.
(ii) The sub-triplicate ratio of
$$(a^3+b^3)^3 : (a^2+b^2-ab)^3 ab.$$
(iii) The reciprocal ratio of $\frac{x}{m} : \frac{y}{n}$.

25. If $(x+2y):(2x-y)$ is equal to the duplicate ratio of 3 : 2, then find $x:y$.

26. If $x:y$ is the duplicate ratio of $(x+a):(y+a)$, then show that $a^2 = xy$.

27. If $(p-x):(q-x)$ be the duplicate ratio of $p:q$, then show that $\frac{1}{p}+\frac{1}{q}=\frac{1}{x}$

28. If $(3a+1):(5a+3)$ is the triplicate ratio of 3 : 4, then find the value of a.

29. If $(a+2):(2a+10)$ is the triplicate ratio of 3 : 5, then find the value of a.

30. What number must be added to each of the numbers 4, 6, 8, 11 in order to get the four numbers in proportion? **[ICSE 2023]**

31. What number must be added to each of the numbers 6, 15, 20 and 43 to make them proportional? **[ICSE 2013, 2005]**

32. What must be subtracted from each of the four numbers 23, 40, 57 and 108 to make them in proportion?

33. If x, y, z and u are in proportion, then prove that
$$\frac{5x^2+12z^2}{5y^2+12u^2}=\sqrt{\frac{3x^4-7z^4}{3y^4-7u^4}}.$$

34. If $x:a=y:b$, then prove that
$$\frac{x^2+a^2}{x+a}+\frac{y^2+b^2}{y+b}=\frac{(x+y)^2+(a+b)^2}{(x+y)+(a+b)}.$$

35. If a, b, c, d are in proportion, then prove that
$$\frac{\sqrt{a^4+c^4}}{\sqrt{b^4+d^4}}=\frac{ma^2+nc^2}{mb^2+nd^2}.$$

36. If $ax=by=cz$, then prove that
$$\frac{x^2}{yz}+\frac{y^2}{zx}+\frac{z^2}{xy}=\frac{bc}{a^2}+\frac{ca}{b^2}+\frac{ab}{c^2}.$$

37. If $\frac{a}{b}=\frac{c}{d}=\frac{e}{f}$, then prove that
$$\left(\frac{a^2b^2+c^2d^2+e^2f^2}{ab^3+cd^3+ef^3}\right)^{3/2}=\sqrt{\frac{ace}{bdf}}.$$

38. If $\frac{x}{a}=\frac{y}{b}=\frac{z}{c}$, prove that
$$\frac{ax-by}{(a+b)(x-y)}+\frac{by-cz}{(b+c)(y-z)}+\frac{cz-ax}{(c+a)(z-x)}=3.$$

39. If $\frac{x}{a}=\frac{y}{b}=\frac{z}{c}$, then show that
$$\frac{x^3}{a^3}+\frac{y^3}{b^3}+\frac{z^3}{c^3}=\frac{3xyz}{abc}.$$ **[ICSE 2016]**

40. If a, b, c and d are in continued proportion, then prove that
(i) $\frac{a}{d}=\frac{a^3+b^3+c^3}{b^3+c^3+d^3}$
(ii) $abc(a+b+c)^3=(ab+bc+ca)^3$

41. If p, q, r, s are in continued proportion, then prove that
(i) $pqrs\left(\frac{1}{p^2}+\frac{1}{q^2}+\frac{1}{r^2}+\frac{1}{s^2}\right)=p^2+q^2+r^2+s^2$
(ii) $p^2q^2r^2(p^{-4}+q^{-4}+r^{-4})=q^{-2}(p^4+q^4+r^4)$
(iii) $\left(\frac{p-q}{r}+\frac{p-r}{q}\right)^2-\left(\frac{s-q}{r}+\frac{s-r}{q}\right)^2=(p-s)^2\left(\frac{1}{r^2}-\frac{1}{q^2}\right)$
(iv) $\sqrt{pq}+\sqrt{qr}-\sqrt{rs}=\sqrt{(p+q-r)(q+r-s)}$

42. Find the mean proportional between
(i) $\frac{x^2}{4ab}$ and $\frac{a}{by^2}$
(ii) $(\sqrt{27}-\sqrt{18})$ and $(\sqrt{27}+\sqrt{18})$.

43. Find the third proportional to
(i) $x^2-\frac{1}{x^2}$ and $x+\frac{1}{x}$
(ii) ab and ab^2

44. Find two numbers, such that the mean proportional between them is 28 and third proportional to them is 224.

45. Find the fourth proportional to (a^2-ab+b^2), (a^3+b^3) and $(a-b)$.

46. Show that, if $a>b>0$, then the ratio $(a^2-b^2):(a^2+b^2)$ is greater than $(a-b):(a+b)$.

47. If $(a-b):(a+b)=1:11$, then find the ratio $(5a+4b+15):(5a-4b+3)$.

48. Using componendo and dividendo, find the value of x in the equation $\frac{\sqrt{3x+4}+\sqrt{3x-5}}{\sqrt{3x+4}-\sqrt{3x-5}}=9$. **[ICSE 2011]**

49. Solve $\frac{1-px}{1+px}=\sqrt{\frac{1-qx}{1+qx}}$

d. 6 Marks Questions

50. The work done by $(3x+1)$ workers in $(2x-1)$ days and the work done by $(2x-1)$ workers in $(x+8)$ days are in the ratio $5:2$. Find the value of x.

51. Mr. Kamal reduces the number of workers of his factory in the ratio $9:7$ and increases their wages in the ratio $13:20$. In what ratio, the wages bill is increased or decreased?

52. An employer reduces the number of employees in the ratio $11:7$ and increases their wages in the ratio $10:13$. In what ratio, the wages bill is increased or decreased?

53. (i) If x, 9, y and 16 are in continued proportion, then find the values of x and y.

(ii) If a, b and c are in continued proportion, then prove that

$$\frac{a+b+c}{a-b+c}=\frac{(a+b+c)^2}{a^2+b^2+c^2}.$$

54. Find the mean proportional of $(a^4-b^4)^2$ and $[(a^2+b^2)(a+b)]^{-2}$.

55. Find the third proportional to

(i) 16 and 36

(ii) $(x^2+y^2+xy)^2$ and (x^3-y^3)

56. If y is the mean proportional between x and z, then prove that $(xy+yz)$ is the mean proportional between (x^2+y^2) and (y^2+z^2).

57. If b is the mean proportional between a and c, prove that $\frac{a^2-b^2+c^2}{a^{-2}-b^{-2}+c^{-2}}=b^4$.

58. Find the fourth proportional of the following.

(i) $3a^2b^2$, a^3 and b^3

(ii) a^2-5a+6, a^2+a-6 and a^2-9

59. What quantity should be added to the terms of the ratio $(p+q):(p-q)$ to make it equal to $(p+q)^2:(p-q)^2$?

60. What quantity must be added to each term of the ratio $(a+2b):(a-2b)$ to make it equal to the duplicate ratio of $(a+b):(a-b)$?

61. If $\frac{a^3+3ab^2}{3a^2b+b^3}=\frac{x^3+3xy^2}{3x^2y+y^3}$, then prove that $\frac{x}{a}=\frac{y}{b}$.

62. If $\frac{ay-bx}{c}=\frac{cx-az}{b}=\frac{bz-cy}{a}$, then show that $\frac{x}{a}=\frac{y}{b}=\frac{z}{c}$.

63. If $\frac{p}{q}=\frac{r}{s}=\frac{t}{u}$, then prove that

(i) $\frac{(p^3+r^3)^2}{(q^3+s^3)^2}=\frac{t^6}{u^6}$

(ii) $\frac{p^2}{q^2}+\frac{r^2}{s^2}+\frac{t^2}{u^2}=\frac{pr}{qs}+\frac{rt}{su}+\frac{pt}{qu}$

(iii) $qsu\left(\frac{p+q}{q}+\frac{r+s}{s}+\frac{t+u}{u}\right)^3$

$$=27(p+q)(r+s)(t+u)$$

64. If $7a-15b=4a+b$, then find the value of $\frac{3a^2+2b^2}{3a^2-2b^2}$.

65. If $\frac{ap+bq}{ar+bs}=\frac{ap-bq}{ar-bs}$, then show that $\frac{p}{q}=\frac{r}{s}$.

66. If x, y, z and u are in proportion, then prove that $(lx+my):(lz+mu)::(lx-my):(lz-mu)$.

67. If $p=\frac{4xy}{x+y}$, then find the value of $\frac{p+2x}{p-2x}+\frac{p+2y}{p-2y}$.

68. Solve $\frac{1+p+p^2}{1-p+p^2}=\frac{62(1+p)}{63(1-p)}$

69. Using the properties of proportion, solve the following equation for z, given

$$\frac{z^3+3z}{3z^2+1}=\frac{341}{91}$$

70. If $y=\frac{10ab}{a+b}$, then find the value of $\frac{y+5a}{y-5a}+\frac{y+5b}{y-5b}$.

71. If $\frac{x}{r^2-pq}=\frac{y}{p^2-qr}=\frac{z}{q^2-pr}$, then prove that $px+qy+rz=0$.

Hints and Answers

Exercise 6.1

1. **Hint**

(i) $A : B = 2 : 5$

$\therefore \frac{A}{B} = \frac{2}{5} \Rightarrow \frac{4}{B} = \frac{2}{5}$

Ans. $B = 10$

(ii) $\frac{3a + 2b}{5a + 3b} = \frac{18}{29}$

$3a = 4b$

Ans. 4 : 3

2. **Hint** 8 km = 8×1000 m, 8000 m $= 8000 \times 100$ cm

$\therefore$ Required ratio $= \frac{7.8}{800000}$

Ans. 39 : 4000000

3. **Hint** Do same as Example 2. **Ans.** 65 : 72

4. **Hint** Weight of alloy $= 27\frac{1}{2} + 2\frac{3}{4} = \frac{55}{2} + \frac{11}{4}$

$= \frac{121}{4}$ kg

$\therefore$ Ratio by weight of the tin to the alloy

$= 2\frac{3}{4} : \frac{121}{4} = \frac{11}{4} : \frac{121}{4}$

Ans. 1 : 11

5. **Hint** Do same as Q. 4. **Ans.** 54 : 61

6. **Hint** Do same as Example 3.

Ans. Increase in the fare is ₹ 420.

7. **Hint** Current price $= \frac{3}{5} \times$ Original price. **Ans.** ₹ 500

8. **Hint** Do same as Example 5. **Ans.** $\frac{3}{4}, \frac{10}{12}, \frac{7}{8}, \frac{15}{8}$

9. **Hint** Do same as Example 5. **Ans.** $\frac{1}{7}, \frac{9}{14}, \frac{3}{4}$

10. **Hint** Do same as Example 6. **Ans.** $\frac{7}{3}, \frac{3}{8}, \frac{5}{24}$

11. (i) **Hint** Do same as Example 10.

Ans. $2am : 3bx$

(ii) **Hint** Do same as Example 11 (i).

Ans. 27 : 20

(iii) **Hint** Do same as Example 11 (ii).

Ans. $27m^3 : 8n^3$

12. **Hint** Let $2X = 3Y = 5Z = k$

$2X = k, 3Y = k, 5Z = k$

$X = \frac{k}{2}, Y = \frac{k}{3}, Z = \frac{k}{5}$

Here, $X : Y : Z = \frac{k}{2} : \frac{k}{3} : \frac{k}{5} = \frac{1}{2} : \frac{1}{3} : \frac{1}{5}$

Take LCM of 2,3 and 5 which is 30,

$X : Y : Z = \frac{1}{2} \times \frac{15}{15} : \frac{1}{3} \times \frac{10}{10} : \frac{1}{5} \times \frac{6}{6} = 15 : 10 : 6$

Ans. 15 : 10 : 6

13. (i) **Hint** Do same as Example 11 (iii). **Ans.** 3 : 4

(ii) **Hint** Do same as Example 11 (iii).

Ans. $3pq : 4rs^2$

(iii) **Hint** Do same as Example 11 (iii). **Ans.** 6 : 5

14. (i) **Hint** Do same as Example 11 (iv). **Ans.** 6 : 8

(ii) **Hint** Do same as Example 11 (iv).

Ans. $5a : 10b^2$

(iii) **Hint** Do same as Example 11 (iv). **Ans.** 1 : 6

15. (i) **Hint** Do same as Example 11 (v). **Ans.** 11 : 8

(ii) **Hint** Do same as Example 11 (v).

Ans. $4abc : 13xyz$

(iii) **Hint** Do same as Example 11 (v). **Ans.** $\frac{1}{y} : 3x$

16. **Hint** We know that the duplicate ratio of $a : b$ is $a^2 : b^2$.

$\therefore \quad \frac{x - 9}{3x + 6} = \left(\frac{4}{9}\right)^2$ **Ans.** $x = 25$

17. (i) **Hint** Do same as Example 10. **Ans.** 1 : 1

(ii) **Hint** Do same as Example 11 (i). **Ans.** 5 : 49

(iii) **Hint** Do same as Example 11 (ii). **Ans.** 27 : 8

18. **Hint** In a business, A invests ₹ 50000 for 5 months, B invests ₹ 60000 for 4 months and C invests ₹ 70000 for 3 months.

Thus, ratio of share in profit of A, B and C respectively is

$= 50000 \times 5 : 60000 \times 4 : 70000 \times 3$

$= 5 \times 5 : 6 \times 4 : 7 \times 3 = 25 : 24 : 21$

So, let the share of A be $25x$, B be $24x$ and C be $21x$.

According to the question,

$25x + 24x + 21x = 18800$

$\Rightarrow \quad 70x = 18800$

$\Rightarrow \quad x = \frac{18800}{70}$

$= 268.57$

Ans. Share of each

$A = 25 \times 268.57 =$ ₹ 6714.25,

$B = 24 \times 268.57 =$ ₹ 6445.68

and $C = 21 \times 268.57 =$ ₹ 5639.97

19. **Hint** Given, perimeter of triangle = 60 cm

Ratio among their sides = 6 : 5 : 4

$\therefore$ Sum of ratio terms = 6 + 5 + 4 = 15

$\therefore$ Length of first side $= 60 \times \frac{6}{15} = 24$ cm

Length of second side $= 60 \times \frac{5}{15} = 20$ cm

and length of third side $= 60 \times \frac{4}{15} = 16$ cm

Ans. Sides of triangles are 24 cm, 20 cm and 16 cm.

20. Hint Let the number of candidates appeared be x.

$\therefore$ Number of passes $= \dfrac{x \times 3}{3+1} = \dfrac{3x}{4}$

According to the condition,

$$\frac{3x}{4} - \frac{(x-20)5}{6} = 10 \quad \textbf{Ans. } 80$$

21. Hint $\frac{1}{2}$ (1st part) $= \frac{1}{3}$ (2nd part)

$= \frac{1}{6}$ (3rd part) $= y$ (let)

$\Rightarrow$ 1st part $= 2y$, 2nd part $= 3y$

and 3rd part $= 6y$

According to the question, $2y + 3y + 6y = 1870$

Ans. ₹ 340, ₹ 510 and ₹1020

22. Hint Labourer's monthly income = ₹ 9000

and his monthly expenditure = ₹ 6500

$\therefore$ His monthly savings = 9000 − 6500 = ₹ 2500

Ans. (i) 18 : 13 (ii) 18 : 5 (iii) 5 : 13

Exercise 6.2

1. (i) **Hint** Do same as Example 15. **Ans.** $n = 2$

(ii) **Hint** Do same as Example 15. **Ans.** $a = 40$

(iii) **Hint** Do same as Example 15. **Ans.** $a = 20$

2. Hint Let the required number be x.

Then, $\dfrac{2+x}{5+x} = \dfrac{5}{6}$

Ans. $x = 13$

3. Hint Here, $6 \times 22 \neq 10 \times 14$

Now, do same as Example 17. **Ans.** 2

4. Hint Do same as Example 17. **Ans.** 2

5. Hint Let the required number be $\dfrac{x}{y}$.

Ratio of $\dfrac{8}{21}$ to $\dfrac{2}{7} = \dfrac{\frac{8}{21}}{\frac{2}{7}} = \dfrac{4}{3}$

Thus, we have $= \dfrac{\frac{x}{y}}{\frac{7}{33}} = \dfrac{4}{3}$

$\Rightarrow \dfrac{x}{y} = \dfrac{4}{3} \times \dfrac{7}{33}$

Ans. $\dfrac{28}{99}$

6. Hint Given, $\dfrac{d+b}{bd} = \dfrac{2}{c}$

$\Rightarrow c(d+b) = 2bd$ [by cross-multiplication]

$\Rightarrow cd + cb = (a+c)d$ [given, $a + c = 2b$]

$\Rightarrow \dfrac{ad}{bd} = \dfrac{cb}{bd}$ [dividing both sides by bd]

7. Hint Do same as Q. 6.

8. Hint Given, $a : b :: c : d \Rightarrow \dfrac{a}{b} = \dfrac{c}{d} = k$ (say)

$\Rightarrow a = bk$ and $c = dk$ [by cross-multiplication] ...(i)

Now, LHS $= \dfrac{(a-c)b^2}{(b-d)cd} = \dfrac{(bk-dk)b^2}{(b-d)(dk)d}$ [from Eq. (i)]

and RHS $= \dfrac{a^2-b^2-ab}{c^2-d^2-cd} = \dfrac{(bk)^2-b^2-(bk)b}{(dk)^2-d^2-(dk)d}$ [from Eq. (i)]

9. Hint Given, $\dfrac{a}{b} = \dfrac{c}{d} = k$ (say)

Now, LHS $= \dfrac{a-b}{c-d} = \dfrac{bk-b}{dk-d}$

RHS $= \sqrt{\dfrac{3a^2+8b^2}{3c^2+8d^2}} = \sqrt{\dfrac{3b^2k^2+8b^2}{3d^2k^2+8d^2}}$

10. Hint Simplify the expression of LHS and RHS.

11. Hint We have, $\dfrac{x}{y} = \dfrac{y}{z} \Rightarrow y^2 = xz$

Now, consider $\dfrac{x^2}{y^2} = \dfrac{x^2}{xz} = \dfrac{x}{z}$

12. (i) **Hint** Here, $(ab+cd)^2 = (a^2+c^2)(b^2+d^2)$

Now, do same as Example 18.

(ii) **Hint** Do same as Example 21.

Ans. $x = \dfrac{16}{3}, y = 144$

13. Hint Given, $\dfrac{x}{y} = \dfrac{y}{z} \Rightarrow y^2 = xz$ [by cross-multiplication]

$\Rightarrow y = \sqrt{xz}$ ...(i)

Now, RHS $= \dfrac{2x^2-5xy+7y^2}{2y^2-5yz+7z^2}$

$= \dfrac{2x^2-5x\sqrt{xz}+7xz}{2xz-5z\sqrt{xz}+7z^2}$ [from Eq. (i)]

14. Hint Given, $\dfrac{a}{b} = \dfrac{b}{c} = \dfrac{c}{d} = k$ (let)

$\Rightarrow c = dk, b = ck = dk^2$ and $a = bk = dk^3$ ...(i)

Now, LHS $= \sqrt{ab} + \sqrt{bc} - \sqrt{cd}$

$= \sqrt{(dk^3)(dk^2)} + \sqrt{(dk^2)(dk)} - \sqrt{(dk)d}$

$= dk^2\sqrt{k} + dk\sqrt{k} - d\sqrt{k}$ [from Eq. (i)]

and RHS $= \sqrt{(a+b-c)(b+c-d)}$

$= \sqrt{(dk^3+dk^2-dk)(dk^2+dk-d)}$

$= \sqrt{dk(k^2+k-1)\,d(k^2+k-1)}$ [from Eq. (i)]

15. Hint Do same as Example 22.

Ans. (i) 20 (ii) $300\,x^3y$

(iii) $\sqrt{(\sqrt{12}-\sqrt{8})(\sqrt{12}+\sqrt{8})}$ **Ans.** 2

(iv) **Hint** Do same as Example 23. **Ans.** $\dfrac{ab}{a+b}$

16. Hint Do same as Example 24.

17. Hint Do same as Example 24.

To prove, $\dfrac{p}{q} = \dfrac{p^2+x^2}{x^2+q^2}$

18. Hint Given, 6 is the mean proportional between two numbers x and y.

$\therefore \quad x:6::6:y$

$\Rightarrow \quad x=\dfrac{36}{y}$ ...(i)

Also, given 48 is the third proportional to x and y.

$\therefore \quad x:y::y:48$

$\Rightarrow \quad y^2=48x$

$\Rightarrow \quad y^2=48\times\dfrac{36}{y}$ [from Eq. (i)]

Ans. $x=3$ and $y=12$

19. Hint Let two numbers be x and y.

Then, $x:18::18:y$ and $x:y::y:144$

Ans. 9, 36

20. Hint Do same as Example 28.

Ans. (i) 9 (ii) $305+174\sqrt{3}$

(iii) **Hint** Do same as Example 29.

Ans. $\dfrac{x^3}{y(x^2+y^2)}$

21. (i) **Hint** Do same as Example 30. **Ans.** 28

(ii) **Hint** Let the fourth proportional be A.

Then, $2xy:x^2::y^2:A$ **Ans.** $\dfrac{xy}{2}$

(iii) **Hint** Let the fourth proportional be A.

Then, $(x^2-5x+4):(x^2+x-2)::(x^2-16):A$

$$\Rightarrow \quad \frac{x^2-5x+4}{x^2+x-2}=\frac{x^2-16}{A}$$

$$\Rightarrow \quad A=\frac{(x^2-16)(x^2+x-2)}{(x^2-5x+4)}=\frac{(x-4)(x+4)(x-1)(x+2)}{(x-1)(x-4)}$$

Ans. x^2+6x+8

(iv) **Hint** Let the fourth proportional be A.

Then, $x^3-y^3:x^4+x^2y^2+y^4::x-y:A$

$$A=\frac{(x-y)(x^4+x^2y^2+y^4)}{x^3-y^3}=\frac{(x-y)(x^4+x^2y^2+y^4)}{(x-y)(x^2+xy+y^2)}=\frac{(x^4+2x^2y^2+y^4-x^2y^2)}{(x^2+y^2+xy)}=\frac{[(x^2+y^2)^2-(xy)^2]}{(x^2+y^2+xy)}$$

Ans. x^2+y^2-xy

22. Hint On applying componendo and dividendo rule in the given proportion, we get

$$\frac{x^4+1+2x^2}{x^4+1-2x^2}=\frac{25}{9}$$

$$\Rightarrow \quad \frac{(x^2+1)^2}{(x^2-1)^2}=\left(\frac{5}{3}\right)^2$$

On taking square root both sides, we get

$$\frac{x^2+1}{x^2-1}=\frac{5}{3}\Rightarrow\frac{x^2+1+x^2-1}{x^2+1-(x^2-1)}=\frac{8}{2}$$

[by componendo and dividendo rule]

Ans. ± 2

23. Hint Do same as Q. 22. **Ans.** $\dfrac{3}{2},\dfrac{-2}{3}$

24. Hint We have, $\dfrac{a}{b}=\dfrac{c}{d}\Rightarrow\dfrac{4a}{5b}=\dfrac{4c}{5d}$

[multiplying numerator of both sides by 4 and denominator by 5]

Now, applying componendo and dividendo rule.

25. Hint We have, $\dfrac{4a^2+3b^2}{4a^2-3b^2}=\dfrac{7}{4}$

On applying componendo and dividendo rule, we get

$$\frac{8a^2}{6b^2}=\frac{11}{3}\Rightarrow\frac{a^2}{b^2}=\frac{11}{4}$$

$$\Rightarrow \quad \frac{a^4}{b^4}=\frac{11^2}{4^2}\Rightarrow\frac{2a^4}{11b^4}=\frac{2\times 11^2}{11\times 4^2}=\frac{11}{8}$$

Now, again applying componendo and dividendo rule.

Ans. $\dfrac{3}{19}$

26. Hint Given, $\dfrac{8a-5b}{8c-5d}=\dfrac{8a+5b}{8c+5d}$

$$\Rightarrow \quad \frac{8a-5b}{8a+5b}=\frac{8c-5d}{8c+5d}$$

[by alternendo property]

$$\Rightarrow \quad \frac{8a+5b}{8a-5b}=\frac{8c+5d}{8c-5d}$$

[by invertendo property]

On applying componendo and dividendo property, we get

$$\frac{8a+5b+8a-5b}{8a+5b-8a+5b}=\frac{8c+5d+8c-5d}{8c+5d-8c+5d}$$

27. Hint Given, $\dfrac{x}{1}=\dfrac{\sqrt{2a+1}+\sqrt{2a-1}}{\sqrt{2a+1}-\sqrt{2a-1}}$

On applying componendo and dividendo property, we get

$$\frac{x+1}{x-1}=\frac{\sqrt{2a+1}+\sqrt{2a-1}+\sqrt{2a+1}-\sqrt{2a-1}}{\sqrt{2a+1}+\sqrt{2a-1}-\sqrt{2a+1}+\sqrt{2a-1}}$$

$$\Rightarrow \quad \frac{x+1}{x-1}=\frac{\sqrt{2a+1}}{\sqrt{2a-1}}$$

On squaring both sides, we get

$$\frac{x^2+2x+1}{x^2-2x+1}=\frac{2a+1}{2a-1}$$

Again, applying componendo and dividendo property, we get

$$\frac{x^2+2x+1+x^2-2x+1}{x^2+2x+1-x^2+2x-1}=\frac{2a+1+2a-1}{2a+1-2a+1}$$

$$\Rightarrow \quad \frac{2x^2+2}{4x}=\frac{4a}{2}\Rightarrow\frac{x^2+1}{2x}=2a$$

$$\Rightarrow \quad x^2+1=4ax\Rightarrow x^2-4ax+1=0$$

Hence proved.

28. Hint On applying componendo and dividendo property, we get

$$\frac{x+1}{x-1}=\frac{\sqrt{a+1}+\sqrt{a-1}+\sqrt{a+1}-\sqrt{a-1}}{\sqrt{a+1}+\sqrt{a-1}-\sqrt{a+1}+\sqrt{a-1}}$$

$$\Rightarrow \quad \frac{x+1}{x-1}=\frac{\sqrt{a+1}}{\sqrt{a-1}}$$

On squaring both sides, we get

$$\frac{x^2+2x+1}{x^2-2x+1}=\frac{a+1}{a-1}$$

Again, applying componendo and dividendo property, and simplify to get the required result.

29. Hint Do same as Q. 28.

30. Hint Given, $\frac{2x+\sqrt{4x^2-1}}{2x-\sqrt{4x^2-1}}=\frac{4}{1}$

$$\Rightarrow \quad \frac{2x+\sqrt{4x^2-1}+2x-\sqrt{4x^2-1}}{2x+\sqrt{4x^2-1}-2x+\sqrt{4x^2-1}}=\frac{4+1}{4-1}$$

[using componendo and dividendo rule]

Ans. $x=\frac{5}{8}$

31. Hint On applying componendo and dividendo property.

Ans. 1

32. Hint Do same as Q. 31. **Ans.** 2

33. Hint Let each given ratio $=\frac{a+b+c}{x+y+z}$

Consider, $\frac{b+c-a}{y+z-x}=\frac{a+b+c}{x+y+z}$

$$\Rightarrow \quad \frac{b+c-a}{a+b+c}=\frac{y+z-x}{x+y+z} \quad \text{[by alternendo]}$$

$$\Rightarrow \quad \frac{-2a}{a+b+c}=\frac{-2x}{x+y+z} \quad \text{[by dividendo]}$$

$$\Rightarrow \quad \frac{a}{x}=\frac{a+b+c}{x+y+z}$$

Similarly, $\frac{a+b+c}{x+y+z}=\frac{b}{y}$

and $\frac{a+b+c}{x+y+z}=\frac{c}{z}$.

34. Hint $\sqrt{\frac{1+qx}{1-qx}}=\frac{1+px}{1-px}$

$$\Rightarrow \quad \frac{1+qx}{1-qx}=\frac{1+p^2x^2+2px}{1+p^2x^2-2px}$$

[on squaring both the sides]

On applying componendo and dividendo, we get

$$\frac{2}{2qx}=\frac{2+2p^2x^2}{4px}$$

Ans. $x=\frac{1}{p}\sqrt{\frac{2p-q}{q}}$

or $x=0$

Chapter Exercise

1. (c) **Hint** Clearly, 1 L 600 mL

$$=1\times1000 \text{ mL}+600 \text{ mL}$$
$$=1600 \text{ mL}=1.6 \text{ L}$$

Ratio between 8 L and 1.6 L $=\frac{8}{1.6}=5:1$

2. (b) **Hint** Let two numbers be $5x$ and $3x$.

According to the question,

$$5x+3x=128$$
$$\Rightarrow \quad 8x=128$$
$$\Rightarrow \quad x=\frac{128}{8}=16$$

$\therefore$ Two numbers are, $5\times16=80$

and $3\times16=48$

Hence, the smaller number is 48.

3. (b) **Hint** We know,

Mean proportional between two numbers = Square root of the product of the numbers

i.e. $M=\sqrt{x\times y}$

Let the given number, $x=4$ and $y=9$

$$M=\sqrt{4\times9}=\sqrt{36}=6$$

Hence, the mean proportional between 4 and 9 is 6.

4. (a) **Hint** The duplicate ratio of 5 : 6

$$=(5)^2:(6)^2=25:36$$

5. (c) **Hint** Given, $A:B=3:4 \Rightarrow \frac{A}{B}=\frac{3}{4}$

and $B:C=2:5 \Rightarrow \frac{B}{C}=\frac{2}{5}$

$$A:C=\frac{A}{B}\times\frac{B}{C}=\frac{3}{4}\times\frac{2}{5}=\frac{3}{10}$$

6. (b) **Hint** LCM of values corresponding to B i.e. 4 and 2 = 4

$$A:B=3:4 \quad \text{[given]}$$

An equivalent ratio of

$$B:C=2:7=2\times2:7\times2=4:14$$

Hence, $A:B:C=3:4:14$

7. (a) **Hint** If x, y, z are in continued proportion, then

$$\frac{x}{y}=\frac{y}{z}$$

$$\Rightarrow \quad xz=y^2 \quad \ldots\text{(i)}$$

$$\therefore \quad \frac{y^2+z^2}{x^2+y^2}=\frac{xz+z^2}{x^2+xz}=\frac{z(x+z)}{x(x+z)}=\frac{z}{x}$$

8. (d) **Hint** If a, b, c and d are porportional, then

$$\frac{a}{b}=\frac{c}{d}$$

$$\therefore \quad \frac{a+b}{a-b}=\frac{c+d}{c-d}$$

[by componendo and dividendo]

9. Hint Do same as Example 6.

Ans. $\frac{13}{6},\frac{7}{8},\frac{5}{6}$

10. Hint Do same as Example 6. **Ans.** $\frac{17}{21}, \frac{11}{14}, \frac{5}{7}, \frac{2}{3}$

11. Hint $x:a = \frac{x}{y} \times \frac{y}{z} \times \frac{z}{a}$. **Ans.** $\frac{16}{35}$

12. Hint Do same as Example 9. **Ans.** 4 : 3

13. Hint Given, $X:Y = 3:2$

Let $X = 3m$ and $Y = 2m$, where m is a variable.

and $\frac{5X+3Y}{4X-3Y} = \frac{5\times 3m + 3\times 2m}{4\times 3m - 3\times 2m}$

$= \frac{15m+6m}{12m-6m} = \frac{21m}{6m}$

Ans. 7 : 2

14. Hint $\frac{m+n}{m+3n} = \frac{2}{3} \Rightarrow 3m + 3n = 2m + 6n \Rightarrow \frac{m}{n} = \frac{3}{1}$

Also, $\frac{2n^2}{3m^2+mn} = \frac{2}{3\left(\frac{m^2}{n}\right)+\left(\frac{m}{n}\right)}$

Ans. 1 : 15

15. Hint Let two numbers be $3x$ and $5x$, respectively.

Then, $\frac{3x+8}{5x+8} = \frac{2}{3}$ **Ans.** 24, 40

16. Hint Let x must be subtracted from each term of 9 : 17 to make it equal to 1 : 3.

Then, $\frac{9-x}{17-x} = \frac{1}{3}$ **Ans.** 5

17. Hint Let number of 50 paise coins be $6x$, number of ₹ 1 coins be $3x$ and number of ₹ 2 coins be $7x$

According to the question,

$6x \times \frac{1}{2} + 3x \times 1 + 7x \times 2 = 140$ **Ans.** 112

18. Hint Let the present age of A be $7x$ and the present age of B be $8x$.

$\therefore \frac{7x-6}{8x-6} = \frac{5}{6}$ **Ans.** 21 yr and 24 yr

19. Hint Let two numbers be $3x$ and $5x$.

Then, $(5x)^2 - (3x)^2 = 400$ **Ans.** 15 and 25

20. Hint Let Ravi's monthly pocket money be ₹ $5x$ and Sanjeev's monthly pocket money be ₹ $7x$.

Again, let Ravi's expenditure be ₹ $3y$ and Sanjeev's expenditure be ₹ $5y$.

According to the question, each save ₹ 80.

∴ Pocket money − Expenditure = 80, which gives

$5x - 3y = 80$ ...(i)

and $7x - 5y = 80$ ...(ii)

On solving Eqs. (i) and (ii), we get the required value.

Ans. ₹ 200 and ₹ 280

21. Hint Do same as Q. 20. **Ans.** ₹ 2400, ₹ 1800

22. (i) **Hint** Do same as Example 10. **Ans.** $2\sqrt{2}:3$

(ii) **Hint** Do same as Example 11 (i). **Ans.** 5 : 7

(iii) **Hint** Do same as Example 11 (ii).

Ans. $1 : 27x^3y^3$

23. (i) **Hint** Do same as Example 11 (iii).

Ans. $3x:7y$

(ii) **Hint** Do same as Example 11 (iv).

Ans. $4a^2:3b$

(iii) **Hint** Do same as Example 11 (v).

Ans. $25z^2b^6: 9x^2a^2$

24. (i) **Hint** Do same as Example 11 (iii).

Ans. $(x-y)^2:(x+y)^3$

(ii) **Hint** Do same as Example 11 (iv) and use the formula $a^3 + b^3 = (a+b)(a^2 + b^2 - ab)$

Ans. $(a+b):\sqrt[3]{ab}$

(iii) **Hint** Do same as Example 11 (v).

Ans. $my:nx$

25. Hint $\frac{x+2y}{2x-y} = \frac{3^2}{2^2}$

Ans. 17 : 14

26. Hint $\frac{(x+a)^2}{(y+a)^2} = \frac{x}{y}$

27. Hint $\frac{p-x}{q-x} = \frac{p^2}{q^2}$

$pq^2 - xq^2 = qp^2 - xp^2$

Dividing throughout by xpq, we get

$\frac{1}{p} + \frac{1}{q} = \frac{1}{x}$ **Hence proved.**

28. Hint $\frac{3a+1}{5a+3} = \frac{(3)^3}{(4)^3}$ **Ans.** 17 : 57

29. Hint $\frac{a+2}{2a+10} = \frac{3^3}{5^3}$ **Ans.** $a = \frac{20}{71}$

30. Hint Do same as Example 17. **Ans.** 4

31. Hint Do same as Example 17. **Ans.** 3

32. Hint Let the required number be x.

According to the question,

$(23-x):(40-x)::(57-x):(108-x)$

Ans. 6

33. Hint Let $\frac{x}{y} = \frac{z}{u} = k$

$\Rightarrow x = yk$ and $z = uk$

Now, LHS $= \frac{5y^2k^2 + 12u^2k^2}{5y^2 + 12u^2} = k^2$

and RHS $= \sqrt{\frac{3y^4k^4 - 7u^4k^4}{3y^4 - 7u^4}} = k^2$

34. Hint Given $x : a = y : b$

$\Rightarrow \frac{x}{a} = \frac{y}{b} = k$ (say)

LHS $= \frac{x^2+a^2}{x+a} + \frac{y^2+b^2}{y+b} = \frac{a^2k^2+a^2}{ak+a} + \frac{b^2k^2+b^2}{bk+b}$

RHS $= \frac{(ak+bk)^2 + (a+b)^2}{(ak+bk)+(a+b)} = \frac{(k^2+1)(a+b)^2}{(k+1)(a+b)}$

LHS = RHS

35. Hint Let $\frac{a}{b}=\frac{c}{d}=k$ [say]

$\text{LHS}=\frac{\sqrt{a^4+c^4}}{\sqrt{b^4+d^4}}=\frac{\sqrt{k^4b^4+k^4d^4}}{\sqrt{b^4+d^4}}$

$\text{RHS}=\frac{ma^2+nc^2}{mb^2+nd^2}=\frac{m\cdot k^2b^2+n\cdot k^2d^2}{mb^2+nd^2}$

LHS = RHS

36. Hint $\text{LHS}=\left(\frac{x}{y}\right)\left(\frac{x}{z}\right)+\left(\frac{y}{z}\right)\left(\frac{y}{x}\right)+\left(\frac{z}{x}\right)\left(\frac{z}{y}\right)$

$=\left(\frac{b}{a}\right)\left(\frac{c}{a}\right)+\left(\frac{c}{b}\right)\left(\frac{a}{b}\right)+\left(\frac{a}{c}\right)\left(\frac{b}{c}\right)$

$\left[\because ax=by\Rightarrow\frac{x}{y}=\frac{b}{a},\ by=cz\Rightarrow\frac{y}{z}=\frac{c}{b}\right.$ and $\left.ax=cz\Rightarrow\frac{x}{z}=\frac{c}{a}\right]$

37. Hint $\frac{a}{b}=\frac{c}{d}=\frac{e}{f}=k$ (say)

$\Rightarrow\quad a=bk,\ c=dk$ and $e=fk$ ...(i)

Now, $\text{LHS}=\left(\frac{(bk)^2b^2+(dk)^2d^2+(fk)^2f^2}{(bk)b^3+(dk)d^3+(fk)f^3}\right)^{3/2}$ [from Eq. (i)]

and $\text{RHS}=\sqrt{\frac{(bk)(dk)(fk)}{bdf}}$ [from Eq. (i)]

38. Hint Let $\frac{x}{a}=\frac{y}{b}=\frac{z}{c}=k$

So, $x=ak$, $y=bk$ and $z=ck$

Taking LHS,

$\frac{ax-by}{(a+b)(x-y)}+\frac{by-cz}{(b+c)(y-z)}+\frac{cz-ax}{(c+a)(z-x)}$

$=\frac{a^2k-b^2k}{k(a^2-b^2)}+\frac{b^2k-c^2k}{k(b^2-c^2)}+\frac{c^2k-a^2k}{k(c^2-a^2)}$

$=1+1+1=3$

39. Hint Let $\frac{x}{a}=\frac{y}{b}=\frac{z}{c}=k$ (say)

$x=ak,\ y=bk$ and $z=ck$ ...(i)

Now, find LHS and RHS separately.

40. (i) **Hint** Let $\frac{a}{b}=\frac{b}{c}=\frac{c}{d}=k$ (say)

$\Rightarrow\quad c=dk,\ b=ck=dk^2$ and $a=bk=dk^3$ ...(i)

Now, $\text{LHS}=\frac{a}{d}=\frac{dk^3}{d}$ [from (i)]

and $\text{RHS}=\frac{(dk^3)^3+(dk^2)^3+(dk)^3}{(dk^2)^3+(dk)^3+d^3}$ [from (i)]

(ii) **Hint** Similar as part (i).

41. (i) **Hint** $\because p,q,r,s$ are in proportion.

$\therefore\quad\frac{p}{q}=\frac{r}{s}=k$ (say)

$\text{LHS}=qk\cdot q\cdot sk\cdot s\left[\frac{1}{q^2k^2}+\frac{1}{q^2}+\frac{1}{s^2k^2}+\frac{1}{s^2}\right]$

$\text{RHS}=q^2k^2+q^2+s^2k^2+s^2$

$\therefore$ LHS = RHS

(ii) **Hint** p,q,r are in proportion.

$\therefore\quad\frac{p}{q}=\frac{q}{r}=k$ [say]

$\text{LHS}=p^2q^2r^2\left[\frac{1}{p^4}+\frac{1}{q^4}+\frac{1}{r^4}\right]$

$=\frac{q^2r^2}{p^2}+\frac{r^2p^2}{q^2}+\frac{p^2q^2}{r^2}$

$\text{RHS}=\frac{1}{(rk)^2}[(rk^2)^4+(rk)^4+r^4]$

$\therefore$ LHS = RHS

(iii) **Hint** p,q,r,s are in continued proportion.

$\Rightarrow\frac{p}{q}=\frac{q}{r}=\frac{r}{s}=k$ (say)

$\Rightarrow r=sk,\ q=rk=sk^2,\ p=qk=sk^3$

$\text{LHS}=\left(\frac{p-q}{r}+\frac{p-r}{q}\right)^2-\left(\frac{s-q}{r}+\frac{s-r}{q}\right)^2$

$=\frac{(k^3-1)^2(k^2-1)}{k^4}$

$\text{RHS}=(p-s)^2\left(\frac{1}{r^2}-\frac{1}{q^2}\right)$

$=(sk^2-s)^2\left(\frac{1}{s^2k^2}-\frac{1}{s^2k^4}\right)$

$=\frac{(k^3-1)^2(k^2-1)}{k^4}$

(iv) **Hint** Do same as part (iii).

42. (i) **Hint** Let z be the required mean proportional between $\frac{x^2}{4ab}$ and $\frac{a}{by^2}$.

Then, $\frac{x^2}{4ab}:z::z:\frac{a}{by^2}$

Ans. $\frac{x}{2by}$

(ii) **Hint** Similar as part (i). **Ans.** 3

43. (i) **Hint** Let the required third proportional be z.

Then, $\left(x^2-\frac{1}{x^2}\right):\left(x+\frac{1}{x}\right)::\left(x+\frac{1}{x}\right):z$

$\Rightarrow\left(\frac{x^4-1}{x^2}\right):\left(\frac{x^2+1}{x}\right)=\left(\frac{x^2+1}{x}\right):z$

Ans. $\left(\frac{x^2+1}{x^2-1}\right)$

(ii) **Hint** Similar as part (i).

Ans. ab^3

44. Hint Let the required two numbers be x and y.

According to the question,

28 is mean proportional between x and y.

$\therefore\quad x:28::28:y\Rightarrow x=\frac{784}{y}$ ...(i)

and 224 is third proportional to x and y.

$\therefore\quad x:y::y:224\Rightarrow y^2=224x$

[by cross-multiplication] ...(ii)

Ans. 14 and 56

45. **Hint** Let the required fourth proportional be x.
Then, $(a^2 - ab + b^2):(a^3 + b^3)::(a-b):x$
Ans. $a^2 - b^2$

46. **Hint** $\frac{a}{b} > \frac{1}{1} \Rightarrow \frac{a^2}{b^2} > \frac{a}{b}$
Apply componendo and dividendo property.

47. **Hint** $\frac{a+b}{a-b} = \frac{11}{1}$

$$\Rightarrow \quad \frac{2a}{2b} = \frac{12}{10}$$
[by componendo and dividendo rule]
$$\Rightarrow \quad \frac{a}{b} = \frac{6}{5} \Rightarrow \frac{5a}{4b} = \frac{30}{20} = \frac{3}{2}$$
$$\Rightarrow \quad \frac{5a+4b}{5a-4b} = \frac{5}{1}$$
$$\Rightarrow \quad 5a + 4b = 5(5a - 4b)$$
Now, consider
$$\frac{5a+4b+15}{5a-4b+3} = \frac{5(5a-4b)+15}{(5a-4b+3)} = \frac{5[5a-4b+3]}{[5a-4b+3]}$$
Ans. 5 : 1

48. **Hint** On applying componendo and dividendo rule, we get
$$\frac{\sqrt{3x+4}}{\sqrt{3x-5}} = \frac{5}{4}$$
On squaring both sides, we get $\frac{3x+4}{3x-5} = \frac{25}{16}$
Ans. 7

49. **Hint** On squaring both sides, we get
$$\frac{1+p^2x^2-2px}{1+p^2x^2-2px} = \frac{1-qx}{1+qx}$$
By using componendo and dividendo rule, we have
$$\frac{1-qx+1+qx}{1-qx-1-qx} = \frac{1+p^2x^2+2px+1+p^2x^2-2px}{1+p^2x^2+2px-1-p^2x^2+2px}$$
Ans. $x = 0$ or $x = \pm\frac{1}{p}\sqrt{\frac{2p-q}{q}}$

50. **Hint** Let a man do A amount of work in one day.
Then, the quantity of work done by $(3x+1)$ workers in $(2x-1)$ days $= A(3x+1)(2x-1)$
and the quantity of work done by $(2x-1)$ workers in $(x+8)$ days $= A(2x-1)(x+8)$
According to the question,
$$\frac{A(3x+1)(2x-1)}{A(2x-1)(x+8)} = \frac{5}{2}$$
$$\Rightarrow \quad \frac{(3x+1)(2x-1)}{(2x-1)(x+8)} = \frac{5}{2}$$
Ans. 38

51. **Hint** Let the number of workers initially and at present be $9x$ and $7x$, respectively.
Again, let the wages per worker initially and at present be ₹ $13y$ and ₹ $20y$, respectively.
Then, total wages bill at initially $= 9x \times 13y$
$= ₹\,117xy$
and total wages bill at present $= 7x \times 20y$
$= ₹\,140xy$
Ans. Wages bill is increased in the ratio 117 : 140.

52. **Hint** Do same as Q. 51.
Ans. The wages bill is decreased in the ratio 110 : 91.

53. (i) **Hint** Do same as Example 21.
Ans. $x = \frac{27}{4}$ and $y = 12$
(ii) **Hint** Do same as Example 27.

54. **Hint** Do same as Example 23.
Ans. $(a - b)$

55. (i) **Hint** Do same as Example 28. **Ans.** 81
(ii) **Hint** Do same as Example 29.
Use the formula,
$$x^3 - y^3 = (x-y)(x^2 + y^2 + xy)$$
Ans. $(x - y)^2$

56. **Hint** As y is the mean proportion between two numbers x and z.
$$\therefore \quad x:y::y:z$$
$$\Rightarrow \quad y^2 = xz$$
To prove, $(xy + yz)^2 = (x^2 + y^2)(y^2 + z^2)$.

57. **Hint** a, b, c are in the continued proportion.
$$\Rightarrow \frac{a}{b} = \frac{b}{c} = k \text{ (say)}$$
$$= \frac{c^2k^4 - c^2k^2 + c^2}{c^{-2}k^{-4} - c^{-2}k^{-2} + c^{-2}} = \frac{c^2(k^4 - k^2 + 1)}{c^{-2}k^{-4}(1 - k^2 + k^4)}$$
$$= \frac{c^4k^4(k^4 - k^2 + 1)}{(k^4 - k^2 + 1)} = c^4k^4$$
$$= (ck)^4 = b^4 = \text{RHS}$$

58. **Hint** Do same as Example 31.
Ans. (i) $\frac{ab}{3}$ (ii) $(a+3)^2$

59. **Hint** Let the required added number be x.
According to the question,
$$(p+q+x):(p-q+x)::(p+q)^2:(p-q)^2$$
$$\Rightarrow \quad \frac{p+q+x}{p-q+x} = \frac{(p+q)^2}{(p-q)^2}$$
Now, on applying componendo and dividendo rule, we get the required value.
Ans. $\frac{q^2 - p^2}{2p}$

60. Let p be added to each term of the ratio $(a+2b):(a-2b)$,

$$\Rightarrow \frac{(a+2b+p)+(a-2b+p)}{(a+2b+p)-(a-2b+p)} = \frac{(a+b)^2+(a-b)^2}{(a+b)^2-(a-b)^2}$$

[by componendo and dividendo rule]

Ans. $\frac{b^2}{a}$

61. Hint On applying componendo and dividendo rule, we get

$$\frac{a^3+3ab^2+3a^2b+b^3}{a^3+3ab^2-3a^2b-b^3} = \frac{x^3+3xy^2+3x^2y+y^3}{x^3+3xy^2-3x^2y-y^3}$$

$$\Rightarrow \frac{(a+b)^3}{(a-b)^3} = \frac{(x+y)^3}{(x-y)^3}$$

$$\Rightarrow \frac{a+b}{a-b} = \frac{x+y}{x-y}$$

[taking cube root on both sides]

Again, applying componendo and dividendo rule, we get

$$\frac{a+b+a-b}{a+b-a+b} = \frac{x+y+x-y}{x+y-x+y} \Rightarrow \frac{a}{b} = \frac{x}{y}$$

62. Hint $\frac{c(ay-bx)}{c^2} = \frac{b(cx-az)}{b^2} = \frac{a(bz-cy)}{a^2}$

$$\Rightarrow \frac{cay-cbx}{c^2} = \frac{cbx-abz}{b^2} = \frac{abz-cay}{a^2}$$

Clearly, each ratio $= \frac{\text{Sum of antecedents}}{\text{Sum of consequents}}$

$$= \frac{cay-cbx+cbx-abz+abz-cay}{c^2+b^2+a^2} = 0$$

$$\therefore \frac{ay-bx}{c} = \frac{cx-az}{b} = \frac{bz-cy}{a} = 0$$

$\Rightarrow ay-bx=0,\ cx-az=0$ and $bz-cy=0$

63. (i) **Hint** $\frac{p}{q} = \frac{r}{s} = \frac{t}{u} = k$ (say)

$\therefore\ p=qk,\ r=sk$ and $t=uk$

(ii) **Hint** $p=qk,\ r=sk,\ t=uk$

$$\text{LHS} = \frac{p^2}{q^2}+\frac{r^2}{s^2}+\frac{t^2}{u^2} = \frac{q^2k^2}{q^2}+\frac{s^2k^2}{s^2}+\frac{u^2k^2}{u^2}$$

$$\text{RHS} = \frac{qk\cdot sk}{q\cdot s}+\frac{sk\cdot uk}{s\cdot u}+\frac{qk\cdot uk}{q\cdot u}$$

LHS = RHS

(iii) **Hint** Do same as part (i).

64. Hint $7a-15b=4a+b$

$$\Rightarrow \frac{a}{b} = \frac{16}{3} \Rightarrow \frac{a^2}{b^2} = \frac{256}{9} \Rightarrow \frac{3a^2}{2b^2} = \frac{768}{18}$$

Now, applying componendo and dividendo rule.

Ans. 131 : 125

65. Hint $\frac{ap+bq}{ap-bq} = \frac{ar+bs}{ar-bs}$.

Now, applying componendo and dividendo rule.

66. Hint Given, $\frac{x}{y} = \frac{z}{u}$

$$\Rightarrow \frac{lx}{my} = \frac{lz}{mu}$$

$$\Rightarrow \frac{lx+my}{lx-my} = \frac{lz+mu}{lz-mu}$$

[by componendo and dividendo rule]

67. Hint $p = \frac{(2x)(2y)}{(x+y)}$ ...(i)

Now, $\frac{p}{2x} = \frac{2y}{x+y}$ [from Eq. (i)]

On applying componendo and dividendo rule, we get

$$\frac{p+2x}{p-2x} = \frac{3y+x}{y-x} \quad \text{...(ii)}$$

Also, $\frac{p}{2y} = \frac{2x}{x+y}$ [from Eq. (i)]

On applying componendo and dividendo rule, we get

$$\frac{p+2y}{p-2y} = \frac{3x+y}{x-y} \quad \text{...(iii)}$$

On adding Eqs. (ii) and (iii), we get the required value.

Ans. 2

68. Hint $\frac{1+p+p^2}{1-p+p^2} = \frac{62(1+p)}{63(1-p)}$

$$\Rightarrow \frac{(1+p+p^2)(1-p)}{(1-p+p^2)(1+p)} = \frac{62}{63}$$

$$\Rightarrow \frac{1-p^3}{1+p^3} = \frac{62}{63}$$

[by componendo and dividendo rule]

Ans. $\frac{1}{5}$

69. Hint On applying componendo and dividendo rule, we get

$$\frac{z^3+3z+3z^2+1}{z^3+3z-3z^2-1} = \frac{341+91}{341-91}$$

Ans. $z=11$

70. Hint Do same as Q. 67.

Ans. 2

71. Hint Let $\frac{x}{r^2-pq} = \frac{y}{p^2-qr} = \frac{z}{q^2-pr} = k$.

Then,

$\text{LHS} = pk(r^2-pq)+qk(p^2-qr)+rk(q^2-pr)$

Olympiad Section

Brain Teasing Questions of Olympiad Pattern

1 The ratio of the price of coffee to that of tea, when coffee costs ₹ 24 per 100 g and the tea costs ₹ 80 per kg, is

(a) 1 : 2 (b) 2 : 1
(c) 1 : 3 (d) 3 : 1

2 If $2xy$ is subtracted from the antecedent and consequent of $(x^2 + y^2):(x^2 + y^2 + xy)$, then new ratio will be $(x^2 - y^2):1$. The value of $x:y$ is

(a) $(1+y^2):(1-x^2)$
(b) $(1-y^2):(1+x^2)$
(c) $(1-y^2):(1-x^2)$
(d) $(1+y^2):(1+x^2)$

3 The number of all possible proportions from the numbers 15, 18, 35 and 42 is

(a) 1 (b) 2
(c) 3 (d) 4

4 If $\frac{x+y}{a^3-b^3} = \frac{y+z}{b^3-c^3} = \frac{z+x}{c^3-a^3}$, then the value of $x+y+z$ is

(a) 1 (b) 0
(c) 2 (d) 3

5 If $\frac{3k+4l+6m+7n}{3k+4l-6m-7n} = \frac{3k-4l+6m-7n}{3k-4l-6m+7n}$, then k : $2m$ is proportional to

(a) $4l/7n$ (b) $5l/8n$
(c) $6l/7n$ (d) $4l/9n$

6 If a, b, c and d are in proportion, then $\frac{a^3+3ab^2}{3a^2b+b^3}$ is equal to

(a) $\frac{c^3-3cd^2}{3c^2d+d^3}$ (b) $\frac{c^3+3cd^2}{3c^2d+d^3}$
(c) $\frac{3c^2d-d^3}{c^3+3cd^2}$ (d) $\frac{3c^2d+d^3}{c^3+3cd^2}$

7 If $\frac{a}{b} = \frac{c}{d} = \frac{e}{f} = \frac{121}{125}$, then the value of $\frac{3a+4c+9e}{3b+4d+9f}$ is

(a) 120/125 (b) 125/120
(c) 121/125 (d) 125/121

8 If $x = \frac{\sqrt[3]{m+1}+\sqrt[3]{m-1}}{\sqrt[3]{m+1}-\sqrt[3]{m-1}}$, then the value of $x^3 - 3mx^2 + 3x$ is

(a) $-m$ (b) m
(c) $2m$ (d) $3m$

Answers

1. (d) **2.** (a) **3.** (d) **4.** (b) **5.** (a) **6.** (b) **7.** (c) **8.** (b)

* *These questions may or may not be asked in the examination, have been given just for additional practice required for olympiads Scholarship Exams etc. For detailed explanations refer Page No. 480.*

CHAPTER

7

Factorisation of Polynomials

SYLLABUS

• (a) Factor Theorem (b) Remainder Theorem (c) Factorising a polynomial completely after obtaining one factor by factor theorem
Note $f(x)$ not to exceed degree 3.

In this chapter, we will study the polynomial in one variable and their classification. Here, we also study about zero of a polynomial, remainder and factor theorems and their use in factorisation of a polynomial.

Polynomial

An algebraic expression which have only whole numbers or non-negative integers as the exponent of the variable(s), is called a polynomial. e.g. $x^2 + 1$; $x^2 + y^2 + xy$, xyz.

Polynomial in One Variable

An algebraic expression of the form

$a_0x^n + a_1x^{n-1} + a_2x^{n-2} + \dots + a_{n-1}x + a_n$, where $a_0, a_1, a_2, \dots, a_n$ are real numbers and n is a non-negative integer, is called a **polynomial** in the variable x.

Or

It is denoted by the symbols $f(x)$ or $g(x)$ or $p(x)$ or $q(x)$ etc.

Thus, $f(x) = a_0x^n + a_1x^{n-1} + a_2x^{n-2} + \dots + a_{n-1}x + a_n$.

Here, $a_0x^n, a_1x^{n-1}, a_2x^{n-2}, \dots, a_{n-1}x, a_n$ are **terms** of the polynomial $f(x)$; a_n is called the **constant term** and $a_0, a_1, a_2, \dots, a_n$ are **coefficients** of the polynomial.

e.g. (i) $p(x) = 3x^3 + 2x^2 - 7x + 5$ is a polynomial in one variable x.

(ii) $q(y) = 5y^2 + 3y$ is a polynomial in one variable y.

Important Terms Related to Polynomial

(i) **Constant polynomial** A polynomial containing only constant term, is called a **constant polynomial**, e.g. $f(x) = c$, where c is a constant.

(ii) **Zero polynomial** The constant polynomial 0 is called the **zero polynomial**.

Or

If all the coefficients of polynomial $f(x)$ are zero, then $f(x)$ is called the **zero polynomial**.

(iii) **Degree** The highest power of the variable in a polynomial, is known as **degree** of the polynomial.
e.g. (i) Degree of $f(x) = x^2 + 2x + 3$ is 2.
(ii) Degree of $g(x) = x^4 + x^3 + x$ is 4.

Polynomial Equation

If $f(x) = a_0x^n + a_1x^{n-1} + a_2x^{n-2} + \dots + a_{n-1}x + a_n$ is a polynomial of degree n, then $f(x) = 0$,
i.e. $a_0x^n + a_1x^{n-1} + a_2x^{n-2} + \dots + a_{n-1}x + a_n = 0$ is called a polynomial equation of degree n.

e.g. (i) $3x^2 - 5x + \sqrt{3} = 0$ is a polynomial equation of degree 2.

(ii) $4x^3 + \sqrt{2}x^2 + 7x - 8 = 0$ is a polynomial equation of degree 3.

Equality of Two Polynomials

Let two polynomials be

$$f(x) = a_0x^n + a_1x^{n-1} + a_2x^{n-2} + \dots + a_{n-1}x + a_n$$

and $g(x) = c_0x^m + c_1x^{m-1} + c_2x^{m-2} + \dots + c_{m-1}x + c_m$

Then, two polynomials $f(x)$ and $g(x)$ are equal, if and only if degree of $f(x)$ is equal to degree of $g(x)$ and corresponding elements are equal, i.e. $n = m$ and $a_i = c_i$ for all i.

Value of a Polynomial

The value obtained on putting a particular value of the variable in the polynomial is called the value of the polynomial. The value of a polynomial $f(x)$ at $x = a$ is denoted by $f(a)$.

e.g. Let $f(x) = 5x^3 - 2x^2 + 3x - 2$.

Then, at $x = 1$, $f(1) = 5(1)^3 - 2(1)^2 + 3(1) - 2$

$= 5 - 2 + 3 - 2 = 8 - 4 = 4$

So, 4 is the value of $f(x)$ at $x = 1$.

Example 1. Find the value of quadratic polynomial $f(x) = 8x^2 - 3x + 7$ at $x = -1$ and $x = 2$.

Sol. Given, $f(x) = 8x^2 - 3x + 7$

At $x = -1$, $f(-1) = 8(-1)^2 - 3(-1) + 7$

$= 8 \times 1 + 3 + 7 = 8 + 10 = 18$

At $x = 2$, $f(2) = 8(2)^2 - 3(2) + 7$

$= 8 \times 4 - 6 + 7 = 32 + 1 = 33$

Zero (Root) of a Polynomial

Zero of a polynomial $f(x)$ is a number α, such that $f(\alpha) = 0$. Zero of a polynomial $f(x)$ is also called a root of the polynomial equation $f(x) = 0$.

e.g. Let $f(x) = 5x + 7$.

Then, at $x = \frac{-7}{5}$, $f\left(\frac{-7}{5}\right) = 5\left(\frac{-7}{5}\right) + 7 = -7 + 7 = 0$

Hence, $x = -\frac{7}{5}$ is a zero of $f(x)$ and root of $f(x) = 0$.

Example 2. Prove that $x = 1$ is one of the root of $f(x) = 0$, where $f(x) = 3x^2 - 5x + 2$.

Sol. Given, $f(x) = 3x^2 - 5x + 2$

At $x = 1$, $f(1) = 3(1)^2 - 5(1) + 2 = 3 \times 1 - 5 + 2 = 3 - 3 = 0$

So, $x = 1$ is one of the root of quadratic equation $3x^2 - 5x + 2 = 0$.

Example 3. If one zero of the polynomial $2x^2 - 5x - (2k + 1)$ is twice the other, then find both the zeroes of the polynomial and the value of k.

Sol. Let α and 2α are the zeroes of the polynomial $2x^2 - 5x - (2k + 1)$.

Then, $2\alpha^2 - 5\alpha - (2k + 1) = 0$

and $2(2\alpha)^2 - 5(2\alpha) - (2k + 1) = 0$

$\Rightarrow$ $2\alpha^2 - 5\alpha = 2k + 1$ ...(i)

and $8\alpha^2 - 10\alpha = 2k + 1$ ...(ii)

From Eqs. (i) and (ii), we get

$2\alpha^2 - 5\alpha = 8\alpha^2 - 10\alpha$

$\Rightarrow$ $6\alpha^2 = 5\alpha \Rightarrow \alpha = \frac{5}{6}$ [$\because \alpha \neq 0$]

$\therefore$ $2\alpha = \frac{5}{6} \times 2 = \frac{5}{3}$

Thus, the zeroes of the polynomial are $\frac{5}{6}$ and $\frac{5}{3}$.

Now, substituting $\alpha = \frac{5}{6}$ in Eq. (i), we get

$2 \times \frac{25}{36} - \frac{25}{6} = 2k + 1$

$\Rightarrow$ $2k + 1 = \frac{50 - 150}{36}$

$\Rightarrow$ $2k + 1 = -\frac{100}{36}$

$\Rightarrow$ $2k = -\frac{100}{36} - 1$

$\Rightarrow$ $2k = -\frac{136}{36}$

$\Rightarrow$ $k = -\frac{68}{36} = \frac{-17}{9}$

Factor of a Polynomial

A non-zero polynomial $g(x)$ is said to be a factor of a polynomial $f(x)$, if and only if $f(x)$ is completely divisible by $g(x)$, i.e. remainder is 0.

e.g.

(i) As $2x^2 + 7x + 6 = (2x + 3)(x + 2)$

Therefore, $(2x + 3)$ is a factor of $2x^2 + 7x + 6$.

(ii) As $x^3 - 5x^2 + 7x - 3 = (x - 3)(x^2 - 2x + 1)$

Therefore, $(x - 3)$ is a factor of $(x^3 - 5x^2 + 7x - 3)$.

Example 4. Check whether $g(x) = x + 1$ be a factor of $f(x) = 3x + 3x^2 + x^3 + 1$.

Sol. Write the dividend and divisor in the standard form as

$f(x) = x^3 + 3x^2 + 3x + 1$ and $g(x) = x + 1$

$$\begin{array}{r|l} & x^2 + 2x + 1 \\ \hline x+1 & x^3 + 3x^2 + 3x + 1 \\ & \underline{x^3 + x^2} \\ & \quad - \quad - \\ & 2x^2 + 3x + 1 \\ & \underline{2x^2 + 2x} \\ & \quad - \quad - \\ & x + 1 \\ & \underline{x + 1} \\ & - \quad - \\ & 0 \end{array}$$

Here, the remainder is zero, so $g(x)$ be a factor of $f(x)$.

Remainder Theorem

Let $f(x)$ be a polynomial of degree n greater than or equal to 1 (i.e. $n \geq 1$) and a be any real number. If $f(x)$ is divided by the linear polynomial $(x - a)$, then the remainder is $f(a)$.

Note (i) If $f(x)$ is divided by $(x + a)$, then remainder is $f(-a)$.

(ii) If $f(x)$ is divided by $(ax - b)$, then remainder is $f\left(\frac{b}{a}\right), a \neq 0$.

(iii) If $f(x)$ is divided by $(ax + b)$, then remainder is $f\left(-\frac{b}{a}\right), a \neq 0$.

Example 5. Find the remainder (without division) on dividing $f(x)$ by $(x + 3)$ where $f(x) = 3x^2 - 7x + 1$.

Sol. Since, $x + 3 = x - (-3)$

$$\text{Remainder} = f(-3) = 3(-3)^2 - 7(-3) + 1 = 27 + 21 + 1 = 49$$

Example 6. Using remainder theorem, find the remainder when $x^3 - 5x^2 + 3x + 1$ is divided by $\left(x - \frac{1}{3}\right)$.

Sol. Let $f(x) = x^3 - 5x^2 + 3x + 1$.

Then, the remainder, when $f(x)$ is divided by $\left(x - \frac{1}{3}\right)$ is given by

$$f\left(\frac{1}{3}\right) = \left(\frac{1}{3}\right)^3 - 5\left(\frac{1}{3}\right)^2 + 3\left(\frac{1}{3}\right) + 1 \quad \text{[by remainder theorem]}$$

$$= \frac{1}{27} - 5\left(\frac{1}{9}\right) + \frac{3}{3} + 1 = \frac{1}{27} - \frac{5}{9} + 1 + 1$$

$$= \frac{1}{27} - \frac{5}{9} + 2 = \frac{1 - 15 + 54}{27} = \frac{55 - 15}{27} = \frac{40}{27}$$

Example 7. Using remainder theorem, find the value of x, if on dividing $7y^3 + 2y^2 - xy + 14$ by $y + 3$, leaves a remainder -49.

Sol. Let $f(y) = 7y^3 + 2y^2 - xy + 14$

Then, the remainder, when $f(y)$ is divided by $(y + 3)$, is given by

$$f(-3) = 7(-3)^3 + 2(-3)^2 - x(-3) + 14 \quad \text{[by remainder theorem]}$$

But its remainder $= -49$ [given]

$\therefore \quad 7(-27) + 2(9) + 3x + 14 = -49$

$\Rightarrow \quad -189 + 18 + 3x + 14 = -49$

$\Rightarrow \quad -157 + 3x = -49$

$\Rightarrow \quad 3x = -49 + 157 = 108$

$\Rightarrow \quad x = \frac{108}{3} = 36$

Hence, the value of x is 36.

Example 8. What must be added to the polynomial $2x^3 - 3x^2 - 8x$, so that it leaves a remainder 10 when divided by $2x + 1$? **[ICSE 2020]**

Sol. Let P be the required term to be added

$$f(x) = 2x^3 - 3x^2 - 8x + P$$

$\because f(x)$ when divided by $2x + 1$, then remainder 10

$\Rightarrow \quad f\left(-\frac{1}{2}\right) = 10$

$\Rightarrow \quad 2 \times \left(-\frac{1}{2}\right)^3 - 3 \times \left(-\frac{1}{2}\right)^2 - 8 \times \left(-\frac{1}{2}\right) + P = 10$

$\Rightarrow \quad 2\left(-\frac{1}{8}\right) - 3\left(\frac{1}{4}\right) - 8\left(-\frac{1}{2}\right) + P = 10$

$\Rightarrow \quad -\frac{1}{4} - \frac{3}{4} + 4 + P = 10$

$\Rightarrow \quad \frac{-1 - 3}{4} + 4 + P = 10$

$\Rightarrow \quad -1 + 4 + P = 10$

$\therefore \quad P = 7$

Hence, 7 is to be added.

Example 9. If the polynomials $ax^3 + 3x^2 + 5x - 4$ and $x^3 - 4x + a$ leave the same remainder, when divided by $(x - 2)$, then find the value of a.

Sol. Let $p_1(x) = ax^3 + 3x^2 + 5x - 4$ and $p_2(x) = x^3 - 4x + a$

Then, the remainders, when both $p_1(x)$ and $p_2(x)$ are divided by $(x - 2)$ are

$$p_1(2) = a(2)^3 + 3(2)^2 + 5(2) - 4 = 8a + 12 + 10 - 4 = 8a + 18$$

and $\quad p_2(2) = (2)^3 - 4(2) + a = 8 - 8 + a = a$ [by remainder theorem]

Now, according to the question,

$$p_1(2) = p_2(2) \Rightarrow 8a + 18 = a$$

$\Rightarrow \quad 8a - a = -18 \Rightarrow 7a = -18$

$\therefore \quad a = \frac{-18}{7}$

which is the required value of a.

Example 10. If r_1 and r_2 are the remainders when the polynomials $x^3 + 2x^2 - 5ax - 7$ and $x^3 + ax^2 - 12x + 6$ are divided by $(x - 1)$ and $(x + 2)$ respectively. Then, find the value of a. Given that $2r_1 + r_2 = 2$.

Sol. Let $f(x) = x^3 + 2x^2 - 5ax - 7$

and $\quad g(x) = x^3 + ax^2 - 12x + 6$

be the given polynomials.

Then, r_1 = remainder when $f(x)$ is divided by $(x - 1) = f(1)$

$\Rightarrow \quad r_1 = 1^3 + 2 \times 1^2 - 5a \times 1 - 7 = -5a - 4$

and r_2 = remainder when $g(x)$ is divided by $(x + 2)$ $= g(-2)$

$\Rightarrow \quad r_2 = (-2)^3 + a \times (-2)^2 - 12 \times (-2) + 6 = 22 + 4a$

According to the given question,

$$2r_1 + r_2 = 2$$

$\Rightarrow \quad 2(-5a - 4) + 22 + 4a = 2$

$\Rightarrow \quad -10a - 8 + 22 + 4a = 2$

$\Rightarrow \quad -6a = -12 \Rightarrow a = 2$

Hence, the value of a is 2.

Exercise 7.1

1. Write whether the following expressions are polynomials or not.
   (i) $x^3 + \frac{1}{x^3} + \frac{1}{x} + 1$ (ii) $\sqrt{2}\ y^3 + \sqrt{5}\ z$
   (iii) $z^{-1/2} - 13z + 11$
2. Write the degree of the following polynomials.
   (i) $5x^2 - 4x + 2$
   (ii) 7
   (iii) $13z^3 - 12z^2 + 11z + 5$
3. Find the value of the following polynomial at $x = -1$.
   (i) $2x^2 + 5x + 7$ (ii) $\frac{2}{5}x + 1 - x^2$
4. A function f is defined by $f(x) = 144 - 16x^2$, calculate $f(2)$. Also, find the value of x, when $f(x) = 0$.
5. Find the zeroes of the following polynomials.
   (i) $7y - 1$ (ii) $x^2 - 4x - 5$ (iii) $x^2 + 7x + 10$
6. Find the remainder (without division) when $2x^3 - 3x^2 + 7x - 8$ is divided by $x - 1$.
7. Find the remainder when $f(x) = 2x^3 - 3x^2 - 4x - 5$ is divided by $g(x) = 2x + 1$.
8. Find the remainder when $f(x) = 12x^3 - 13x^2 - 5x + 7$ is divided by $3x + 2$.
9. Use remainder theorem to factorize the polynomial $2x^3 + 3x^2 - 9x - 10$. **[ICSE 2018]**
10. Using remainder theorem, find the value of k, if on dividing $2x^3 + 3x^2 - kx + 5$ by $x - 2$, leaves a remainder 7. **[ICSE 2016]**
11. The polynomial $p(x) = kx^3 + 9x^2 + 4x - 8$, when divided by the polynomial $q(x) = x + 3$, leaves the remainder (-20). Find the value of k.
12. Find 'a', if the two polynomials $ax^3 + 3x^2 - 9$ and $2x^3 + 4x + a$ leave the same remainder when divided by $x + 3$. **[ICSE 2015]**
13. If $2x^3 + ax^2 - 11x + b$ leaves remainder 0 and 42 when divided by $(x - 2)$ and $(x - 3)$ respectively, find the values of a and b.
14. If r_1 and r_2 are remainders when the polynomials $x^3 + 2x^2 - 5ax - 7$ and $x^3 + ax^2 - 12x + 6$ are divided by $(x + 1)$ and $(x - 2)$ respectively. If $2r_1 + r_2 = 6$, then find the value of a.

Factor Theorem

Let $f(x)$ be a polynomial of degree $n \geq 1$ and a be any real number.

(i) If $f(a) = 0$, then $(x - a)$ is a factor of $f(x)$.
(ii) If $(x - a)$ is a factor of $f(x)$, then $f(a) = 0$.

Note (i) If $(x + a)$ is a factor of $f(x)$, then $f(-a) = 0$.
(ii) If $(ax - b)$ is a factor of $f(x)$, then $f\left(\frac{b}{a}\right) = 0$.
(iii) If $(ax + b)$ is a factor of $f(x)$, then $f\left(\frac{-b}{a}\right) = 0$.
(iv) If $(x - a)(x - b)$ is a factor of $f(x)$, then $f(a) = 0$ and $f(b) = 0$.

Example 11. Using factor theorem, show that
(i) $(x + 1)$ is a factor of $x^{19} + 1$.
(ii) $(x - 3)$ is a factor of $x^4 - 81$.

Sol.
(i) Let $f(x) = x^{19} + 1$
Clearly, $(x + 1)$ will be a factor of $f(x)$, if $f(-1) = 0$.
On putting $x = -1$ in $f(x)$, we get
$$f(-1) = (-1)^{19} + 1 = -1 + 1 = 0$$
Hence, by factor theorem, $(x + 1)$ is a factor of $x^{19} + 1$.

(ii) Let $f(x) = x^4 - 81$
Clearly, $(x - 3)$ will be a factor of $f(x)$, if $f(3) = 0$.
On putting $x = 3$ in $f(x)$, we get
$$f(3) = 3^4 - 81 = 81 - 81 = 0$$
Hence, by factor theorem, $(x - 3)$ is a factor of $f(x)$.

Example 12. Show that $(x - 5)$ and $(2x - 1)$ are factors of $2x^2 - 11x + 5$.

Sol. Let $f(x) = 2x^2 - 11x + 5$ ...(i)
Putting $x = 5$ in Eq. (i), we get
$$f(5) = 2 \times (5)^2 - 11 \times 5 + 5$$
$$= 50 - 55 + 5 = 0$$
$(x - 5)$ is a factor of $f(x)$
As, $2x - 1$, $x = \frac{1}{2}$
Putting $x = \frac{1}{2}$ in Eq. (i), we get
$$f\left(\frac{1}{2}\right) = 2\left(\frac{1}{2}\right)^2 - 11\left(\frac{1}{2}\right) + 5$$
$$= \frac{1}{2} - \frac{11}{2} + 5 = \frac{11}{2} - \frac{11}{2} = 0$$
Since, $(2x - 1)$ is a factor of $f(x)$.
Hence, $(x - 5)$ and $(2x - 1)$ are factors of $2x^2 - 11x + 5$.

Example 13. Using the factor theorem, factorise the polynomial $2x^2 + 10x + 12$.

Sol. Let $f(x) = 2x^2 + 10x + 12$

Using hit and trial method,

putting $x = 1$, we get

$$f(1) = 2(1)^2 + 10(1) + 12 = 2 + 10 + 12 = 24 \neq 0$$

putting $x = -1$, we get

$$f(-1) = 2(-1)^2 + 10(-1) + 12 = 2 - 10 + 12 = 4 \neq 0$$

putting $x = 2$, we get

$$f(2) = 2(2)^2 + 10(2) + 12 = 8 + 20 + 12 = 40 \neq 0$$

putting $x = -2$, we get

$$f(-2) = 2(-2)^2 + 10(-2) + 12$$
$$= 8 - 20 + 12 = 20 - 20 = 0$$

So, by factor theorem, $(x + 2)$ will be a factor of $f(x)$.

Now, to find other factor, let us divide $f(x)$ by $(x + 2)$ using long division method.

$$\begin{array}{r|l} & 2x + 6 \\ x + 2 & 2x^2 + 10x + 12 \\ & \underline{\overset{-}{2x^2} \overset{-}{+ 4x}} \\ & 6x + 12 \\ & \underline{\overset{-}{6x} \overset{-}{+ 12}} \\ & 0 \end{array}$$

Clearly, $(2x + 6)$ is another factor of $f(x)$.

Hence, $f(x) = (x + 2)(2x + 6)$.

Example 14. Use factor theorem to factorise $6x^3 + 17x^2 + 4x - 12$ completely. **[ICSE 2020]**

Sol. Let $f(x) = 6x^3 + 17x^2 + 4x - 12$

Using hit and trial method,

Putting $x = -2$, we get

$$f(-2) = 6(-2)^3 + 17(-2)^2 + 4(-2) - 12$$
$$= -48 + 68 - 8 - 12 = 0$$

So, by factor theorem, $(x + 2)$ will be a factor of $f(x)$. Now, to find other factor, let us divide $f(x)$ by $(x + 2)$ using long division method

$$\begin{array}{r|l|l} x + 2 & 6x^3 + 17x^2 + 4x - 12 & 6x^2 + 5x - 6 \\ & \underline{\overset{-}{6x^3} \overset{-}{+ 12x^2}} & \\ & 5x^2 + 4x & \\ & \underline{\overset{-}{5x^2} \overset{-}{+ 10x}} & \\ & -6x - 12 & \\ & \underline{\overset{+}{-6x} \overset{+}{- 12}} & \\ & 0 & \end{array}$$

Clearly, $6x^2 + 5x - 6$ is another factor of $f(x)$.

$\therefore\ f(x) = (x + 2)(6x^2 + 5x - 6)$

Now, factor of $6x^2 + 5x - 6$

$$= 6x^2 + 9x - 4x - 6$$
$$= 3x(2x + 3) - 2(2x + 3)$$
$$= (2x + 3)(3x - 2)$$

Hence, $f(x) = (x + 2)(2x + 3)(3x - 2)$.

Example 15. Using the factor theorem, factorise completely the polynomial

$$3x^3 + 2x^2 - 19x + 6$$ **[ICSE 2012]**

Sol. Let $f(x) = 3x^3 + 2x^2 - 19x + 6$

Using hit and trial method,

putting $x = 1$, we get

$$f(1) = 3(1)^3 + 2(1)^2 - 19(1) + 6$$
$$= 3 + 2 - 19 + 6$$
$$= -8 \neq 0$$

putting $x = -1$, we get

$$f(-1) = 3(-1)^3 + 2(-1)^2 - 19(-1) + 6$$
$$= -3 + 2 + 19 + 6$$
$$= -3 + 27 = 24 \neq 0$$

putting $x = 2$, we get

$$f(2) = 3(2)^3 + 2(2)^2 - 19(2) + 6$$
$$= 3 \times 8 + 2 \times 4 - 38 + 6$$
$$= 24 + 8 - 38 + 6$$
$$= 38 - 38 = 0$$

So, by factor theorem, $(x - 2)$ will be a factor of $f(x)$.

Now, to find other factor, let us divide $f(x)$ by $(x - 2)$ using long division method.

$$\begin{array}{r|l} & 3x^2 + 8x - 3 \\ x - 2 & 3x^3 + 2x^2 - 19x + 6 \\ & \underline{\overset{-}{3x^3} \overset{+}{- 6x^2}} \\ & 8x^2 - 19x + 6 \\ & \underline{\overset{-}{8x^2} \overset{+}{- 16x}} \\ & -3x + 6 \\ & \underline{-3x \overset{+}{+} 6} \\ & 0 \end{array}$$

Clearly, $(3x^2 + 8x - 3)$ is another factor of $f(x)$.

$\therefore\ f(x) = (x - 2)(3x^2 + 8x - 3)$ ...(i)

Now, factorise $3x^2 + 8x - 3 = 3x^2 + 9x - x - 3$

[by splitting the middle term]

$$= 3x(x + 3) - 1(x + 3)$$
$$= (3x - 1)(x + 3)$$

Hence, from Eq. (i), we get

$$f(x) = (x - 2)(3x - 1)(x + 3)$$

Example 16. Using the factor theorem, show that $(x - 2)$ is a factor of $x^3 + x^2 - 4x - 4$. Hence, factorise the polynomial completely. **[ICSE 2019]**

Sol. Let $f(x) = x^3 + x^2 - 4x - 4$ ...(i)

Using factor theorem, if $(x - 2)$ is a factor of $f(x)$, then

$$f(2) = 0$$

Now, put $x = 2$ in Eq. (i), we get

$$f(2) = (2)^3 + (2)^2 - 4 \times 2 - 4$$
$$= 8 + 4 - 8 - 4$$
$$= 0$$

Hence, factor theorem is satisfied.

Now, using long division divide $f(x)$ by $(x-2)$, we get

$$
\begin{array}{l}
x-2)\; x^3+x^2-4x-4\;(x^2+3x+2 \\
\quad\; x^3-2x^2 \\
\quad\; -\quad + \\
\hline
\qquad 3x^2-4x \\
\qquad 3x^2-6x \\
\qquad -\quad + \\
\hline
\qquad\quad 2x-4 \\
\qquad\quad 2x-4 \\
\qquad\quad -\quad + \\
\hline
\qquad\qquad 0
\end{array}
$$

$\therefore\; f(x) = (x-2)(x^2+3x+2)$

$= (x-2)[x^2+2x+x+2]$

$= (x-2)[x(x+2)+1(x+2)]$

$= (x-2)[(x+2)(x+1)]$

Example 17. Show that $(x-1)$ is a factor of $x^3-7x^2+14x-8$. Hence, completely factorise the above expression. **[ICSE 2007]**

Sol. Let $f(x) = x^3-7x^2+14x-8$ ...(i)

$\because f(x)$ is divisible by $(x-1)$

Putting $x = 1$ in Eq. (i),

$f(1) = 1^3 - 7\times(1)^2 + 14(1) - 8$

$= 1-7+14-8 = 0$

By factor theorem, $x-1$ is a factor of $f(x)$. Now, to find the other factor.

Let divide $f(x)$ by $(x-1)$ using long division method,

$$
\begin{array}{l}
x-1)\; x^3-7x^2+14x-8\;(x^2-6x+8 \\
\quad\; x^3-x^2 \\
\quad\; -\quad + \\
\hline
\qquad -6x^2+14x \\
\qquad -6x^2+6x \\
\qquad +\quad - \\
\hline
\qquad\quad 8x-8 \\
\qquad\quad 8x-8 \\
\qquad\quad -\quad + \\
\hline
\qquad\qquad 0
\end{array}
$$

The other factor of $f(x)$ are the factors of x^2-6x+8.

Now, factorise x^2-6x+8

$\Rightarrow\; x^2-2x-4x+8$

$\Rightarrow\; x(x-2)-4(x-2)$

$\Rightarrow\; (x-2)(x-4)$

Hence, $x^3-7x^2+14x-8 = (x-1)(x-2)(x-4)$.

Example 18. Find the value of 'a', if $x-a$ is a factor of the polynomial $3x^3+x^2-ax-81$. **[ICSE 2023]**

Sol. Given, $(x-a)$ is a factor of the polynomial

$3x^3+x^2-ax-81 = f(x)$ [say]

Then we have, by factor theorem

$f(a) = 0$

$x-a = 0 \Rightarrow x = a$

On substituting $x = a$ in given polynomial equation,

$\Rightarrow\; 3(a)^3+(a)^2-a(a)-81 = 0$

$\Rightarrow\; 3a^3+a^2-a^2-81 = 0$

$\Rightarrow\; 3a^3 = 81$

$\Rightarrow\; a^3 = 27 = (3)^3$

$\Rightarrow\; a = 3$

Example 19. Given that $x+2$ and $x+3$ are factors of $2x^3+ax^2+7x-b$. Determine the values of a and b. **[ICSE 2009]**

Sol. Let $f(x) = 2x^3+ax^2+7x-b$ ...(i)

Since, $(x+2)$ is a factor of $f(x)$.

$\therefore\; f(-2) = 0$ [by factor theorem]

$\Rightarrow\; 2(-2)^3+a(-2)^2+7(-2)-b = 0$ [putting $x = -2$ in Eq. (i)]

$\Rightarrow\; 2(-8)+4a-14-b = 0$

$\Rightarrow\; -16+4a-14-b = 0$

$\Rightarrow\; -30+4a-b = 0$

$\Rightarrow\; 4a-b = 30$ ...(ii)

Also, $(x+3)$ is a factor of $f(x)$.

$\therefore\; f(-3) = 0$ [by factor theorem]

$\Rightarrow\; 2(-3)^3+a(-3)^2+7(-3)-b = 0$ [putting $x = -3$ in Eq. (i)]

$\Rightarrow\; 2\times(-27)+9a-21-b = 0$

$\Rightarrow\; -54+9a-21-b = 0$

$\Rightarrow\; -75+9a-b = 0$

$\Rightarrow\; 9a-b = 75$ ...(iii)

On subtracting Eq. (ii) from Eq. (iii), we get

$$
\begin{array}{r}
9a-b = 75 \\
4a-b = 30 \\
-\quad+\quad- \\
\hline
5a = 45
\end{array}
$$

$\Rightarrow\; a = \frac{45}{5} = 9$

On putting $a = 9$ in Eq. (ii), we get

$4\times 9 - b = 30$

$\Rightarrow\; 36-b = 30$

$\Rightarrow\; -b = 30-36$

$\Rightarrow\; -b = -6 \Rightarrow b = 6$

Hence, $a = 9$ and $b = 6$.

Example 20. Without actual division, prove that $2x^4-6x^3+3x^2+3x-2$ is exactly divisible by x^2-3x+2.

Sol. Let $f(x) = 2x^4-6x^3+3x^2+3x-2$

and $g(x) = x^2-3x+2$

$g(x) = x^2-3x+2 = x^2-2x-x+2$

$= x(x-2)-1(x-2)$

$= (x-2)(x-1)$

$(x-2)$ and $(x-1)$ are factors of $g(x)$.

In order to prove that $f(x)$ is exactly divisible by $g(x)$, it is sufficient to prove that $x-2$ and $x-1$ are factors of $f(x)$ i.e. it is sufficient to show that

$f(1) = 0$ and $f(2) = 0$

Now, $f(1) = 2\times 1^4 - 6\times 1^3 + 3\times 1^2 + 3\times 1 - 2$

$= 2-6+3+3-2 = 0$

and now, $f(2) = 2\times 2^4 - 6\times 2^3 + 3\times 2^2 + 3\times 2 - 2$

$= 32-48+12+6-2$

$= 50-50 = 0$

$\therefore\; f(x)$ is divisible by $(x-2)$ and $(x-1)$

$f(x)$ is divisible by $(x-2)(x-1)$ i.e. x^2-3x+2

Hence, $f(x)$ is exactly divisible by $g(x)$.

Example 21. What number should be subtracted from $2x^3 - 5x^2 + 5x$, so that the resulting polynomial has a factor $2x - 3$?

Sol. Let the number to be subtracted from the given polynomial be k and let the resulting polynomial be $f(x)$, i.e.

$$f(x) = 2x^3 - 5x^2 + 5x - k \quad \text{...(i)}$$

Then, according to given condition, $(2x - 3)$ will be factor of $f(x)$.

So, by factor theorem, $f\left(\frac{3}{2}\right) = 0.$

Now, putting the value of $x = \frac{3}{2}$ in Eq. (i), we get

$$\Rightarrow \quad 2\left(\frac{3}{2}\right)^3 - 5\left(\frac{3}{2}\right)^2 + 5\left(\frac{3}{2}\right) - k = 0$$

$$\Rightarrow \quad 2 \times \frac{27}{8} - 5 \times \frac{9}{4} + \frac{15}{2} - k = 0$$

$$\Rightarrow \quad k = \frac{27}{4} - \frac{45}{4} + \frac{15}{2} = \frac{27 - 45 + 30}{4}$$

$$= \frac{27 - 15}{4} = \frac{12}{4} = 3$$

$$\therefore \quad k = 3$$

Hence, the required value of k is 3.

Example 22. The polynomial $px^3 + 4x^2 - 3x + q$ is completely divisible by $x^2 - 1$, find the values of p and q. Also, for these values of p and q factorise the given polynomial completely.

Sol. Let $f(x) = px^3 + 4x^2 - 3x + q$

$\because$ $f(x)$ is divisible by $x^2 - 1$

$\Rightarrow f(x)$ is divisible by $(x + 1)(x - 1)$

$\Rightarrow$ $(x + 1)$ and $(x - 1)$ both are factors of $f(x)$.

Now, by factor theorem, we get $f(-1) = 0$

$$\Rightarrow \quad p(-1)^3 + 4(-1)^2 - 3(-1) + q = 0$$

$$\Rightarrow \quad -p + 4 + 3 + q = 0$$

$$\Rightarrow \quad -p + q = -7 \quad \text{...(i)}$$

Also, we get $f(1) = 0$

$$\Rightarrow \quad p(1)^3 + 4(1)^2 - 3(1) + q = 0$$

$$\Rightarrow \quad p + 4 - 3 + q = 0$$

$$\Rightarrow \quad p + q = -1 \quad \text{...(ii)}$$

On adding Eqs. (i) and (ii), we get

$$-p + q = -7$$
$$p + q = -1$$
$$\overline{2q = -8}$$

$$\Rightarrow \quad q = -4$$

On putting $q = -4$ in Eq. (i), we get

$$-p + (-4) = -7 \Rightarrow -p = -7 + 4 \Rightarrow -p = -3 \Rightarrow p = 3$$

Hence, $p = 3$ and $q = -4$

$\therefore$ $f(x)$ becomes $3x^3 + 4x^2 - 3x - 4$.

Now, let us divide $f(x)$ by $(x^2 - 1)$ using long division method.

$$
\begin{array}{r|l}
 & 3x + 4 \\
x^2 - 1 & 3x^3 + 4x^2 - 3x - 4 \\
 & 3x^3 \quad\quad\; - 3x \\
 & - \quad\quad\quad\;\; + \\
\hline
 & 4x^2 - 4 \\
 & 4x^2 - 4 \\
 & - \quad + \\
\hline
 & 0
\end{array}
$$

Hence, $f(x) = (x^2 - 1)(3x + 4) = (x + 1)(x - 1)(3x + 4)$.

Example 23. Using the remainder and factor theorem, factorise the polynomial $2y^3 + y^2 - 2y - 1$.

Sol. Let $f(x) = 2y^3 + y^2 - 2y - 1$

By remainder theorem,

For $y = 1$, $f(1) = 2(1)^3 + (1)^2 - 2(1) - 1$

$$= 2 + 1 - 2 - 1 = 0$$

$\therefore$ By factor theorem,

$(y - 1)$ is a factor of $2y^3 + y^2 - 2y - 1$

$$
\begin{array}{r|l}
 & 2y^2 + 3y + 1 \\
y - 1 & 2y^3 + y^2 - 2y - 1 \\
 & 2y^3 - 2y^2 \\
 & - \quad + \\
\hline
 & 3y^2 - 2y \\
 & 3y^2 - 3y \\
 & - \quad + \\
\hline
 & y - 1 \\
 & y - 1 \\
 & - \quad + \\
\hline
 & 0
\end{array}
$$

$\Rightarrow 2y^2 + 3y + 1$ is another factor.

$$\Rightarrow 2y^3 + y^2 - 2y - 1 = (y - 1)(2y^2 + 3y + 1)$$
$$= (y - 1)(2y^2 + 2y + y + 1)$$
$$= (y - 1)[2y(y + 1) + 1(y + 1)]$$
$$= (y - 1)(y + 1)(2y + 1)$$

Example 24. $(x + 2)$ and $(x + 3)$ are two factors of the polynomial $x^3 + 6x^2 + 11x + 6$. If this polynomial is completely factorised the result is

[ICSE Semester I 2021]

Sol. (d) Let $f(x) = x^3 + 6x^2 + 11x + 6$

Given, $(x + 2)$ and $(x + 3)$ are two factors of $f(x)$.

$$\therefore \quad (x + 2)(x + 3) = x^2 + 3x + 2x + 6$$
$$= x^2 + 5x + 6$$

$\Rightarrow x^2 + 5x + 6$ is also a factor of $f(x)$.

Now, we divide $f(x)$ by $x^2 + 5x + 6$ using long division method.

$$
\begin{array}{r|l}
x^2 + 5x + 6 & x^3 + 6x^2 + 11x + 6 \; (x + 1 \\
 & x^3 + 5x^2 + 6x \\
 & - \quad - \quad - \\
\hline
 & x^2 + 5x + 6 \\
 & x^2 + 5x + 6 \\
 & - \quad - \quad - \\
\hline
 & \times
\end{array}
$$

Hence, $(x + 2)$, $(x + 3)$ and $(x + 1)$ is completely factorised the polynomial $f(x)$.

Exercise 7.2

1. Using factor theorem, check whether the polynomial $g(x) = x - 2$ is a factor of $f(x) = x^3 - 4x^2 + x + 6$ or not.
2. By factor theorem, show that $(x + 3)$ and $(2x - 1)$ are factors of $2x^2 + 5x - 3$.
3. Show that $(x - 2)$ is a factor of $7x^2 - 10x - 8$. Hence, factorise $7x^2 - 10x - 8$.
4. Show that $(2x + 7)$ is a factor of $2x^3 + 7x^2 - 4x - 14$. Hence, factorise $2x^3 + 7x^2 - 4x - 14$.
5. Use factor theorem to factorise completely $x^3 + x^2 - 4x - 4$.
6. Use factor theorem to factorise the polynomial $x^3 - 13x - 12$ completely. Hence, solve the corresponding polynomial equation.
7. If $(x + 2)$ and $(x + 3)$ are factors of $x^3 + ax + b$, find the values of 'a' and 'b'. [ICSE 2018]
8. Find the value of k, if $(x - 2)$ is a factor of $x^3 + 2x^2 - kx + 10$. Hence, determine whether $(x + 5)$ is also a factor. [ICSE 2011]
9. For what value of 'a', the polynomial $g(x)$ is a factor of $f(x)$.
$f(x) = x^3 + a(x^2 + 1) - 2x + 4, \ g(x) = x + a$
10. If $(x - 2)$ is a factor of the expression $2x^3 + ax^2 + bx - 14$ and when the expression is divided by $(x - 3)$, it leaves a remainder 52. Find the values of a and b. [ICSE 2013]
11. What must be subtracted from $16x^3 - 8x^2 + 4x + 7$, so that the resulting expression has $(2x + 1)$ as a factor? [ICSE 2017]

Chapter Practice

a. 1 Mark Questions

1. Find the value of 'k', if the division $kx^3 + 9x^2 + 4x - 10$ by $x + 3$ leaves the remainder 5.
(a) 1 (b) 2 (c) 3 (d) 4

2. Polynomial $x^3 - ax^2 + bx - 6$ leaves remainder -8, when divided by $x - 1$ and $x - 2$ is a factor of it. Find the value of a.
(a) 1 (b) 2 (c) -1 (d) -2

3. Show that $(x - 2)$ is a factor of $3x^2 - 5x - 2$ using the factor theorem.
(a) $(x + 1)(3x + 1)$ (b) $(x - 2)(3x - 1)$
(c) $(x - 2)(3x + 1)$ (d) $(x - 1)(3x - 1)$

4. What number should be added to $2x^3 - 3x^2 + x$, so that when the resulting polynomial is divided by $x - 2$, the remainder is 5?
(a) 1 (b) -1 (c) 2 (d) -2

5. If $x - 2$ is a factor of $x^3 - kx - 12$, then the value of k is **[ICSE 2023]**
(a) 3 (b) 2 (c) -2 (d) -3

6. If $(x + 2)$ is a factor of the polynomial $x^3 - kx^2 - 5x + 6$, then the value of k is **[ICSE Semester I 2021]**
(a) 1 (b) 2 (c) 3 (d) -2

7. The polynomial $x^3 - 2x^2 + ax + 12$ when divided by $(x + 1)$ leaves a remainder 20, then a is equal to **[ICSE Semester I 2021]**
(a) -31 (b) 9 (c) 11 (d) -11

b. 3 Marks Questions

8. Find the remainder (without division) on dividing $2x^3 + x^2 - 7x + 4$ by $(x - 2)$.

9. Without actual division, find the remainder, if $p(x) = 9x^2 - 6x + 2$ is divided by $(3x - 2)$.

10. Using remainder theorem, find the remainder when $f(x) = 3x^4 + 2x^3 - \frac{x^2}{3} - \frac{x}{9} + \frac{2}{27}$ is divided by $g(x) = x + \frac{2}{3}$.

11. When $x^3 - 3x^2 - kx + 4$ is divided by $(x - 3)$, then the remainder is k. Find the value of the constant k.

12. When divided by $(y - 2)$, the polynomials $py^3 + 3y^2 - 13$ and $2y^3 - 5y + p$ leaves the same remainder. Find the value of p.

13. The polynomials $3x^3 - ax^2 + 5x - 13$ and $(a + 1)x^2 - 7x + 5$ leaves the same remainder when divided by $(x - 3)$. Find the value of a.

14. What number must be added to $2x^3 - 7x^2 + 2x$, so that the resulting polynomial leaves the remainder -2 when divided by $2x - 3$?

15. Determine, whether the polynomial $g(x) = x - 7$ is a factor of $f(x) = x^3 - 6x^2 - 19x + 84$ or not.

16. Show that $(x - 5)$ is a factor of $2x^2 - 9x - 5$. Hence, factorise $2x^2 - 9x - 5$.

c. 4/5 Marks Questions

17. Show that $(x - 1)$ is a factor of $x^3 - 7x^2 + 14x - 8$. Hence, completely factorise the above expression. **[ICSE 2007]**

18. Use the factor theorem to factorise the following expression $2x^3 + x^2 - 13x + 6$. **[ICSE 2010]**

19. Factorise the expression
$$f(x) = 2x^3 - 7x^2 - 3x + 18$$
Hence, find all possible values of x for which $f(x) = 0$.

20. If $(y - p)$ is a common factor of the polynomials $f(y) = y^2 + ay + b$ and $g(y) = y^2 + my + n$, then show that $p = \frac{n - b}{a - m}$.

21. Find the value of the constants a and b, if $(x - 2)$ and $(x + 3)$ are both factors of the expression $x^3 + ax^2 + bx - 12$.

22. Find b and c such that $(y + 1)$ and $(y + 2)$ are the factors of the polynomial $y^3 + by^2 - cy + 10$.

23. $(x - 2)$ is a factor of expression $x^3 + ax^2 + bx + 6$. When this expression is divided by $(x - 3)$, it leaves the remainder 3. Find the values of a and b.

24. Using the remainder and factor theorem, factorise the following polynomial
$$x^3 + 10x^2 - 37x + 26$$ **[ICSE 2014]**

d. 6 Marks Questions

25. Factorise $x^3 - 23x^2 + 142x - 120$, using factor theorem.

26. By using factor theorem,

(i) Show that $(2x + 3)$ is a factor of $4x^3 + 20x^2 + 33x + 18$.

Hence, factorise the given polynomial completely.

(ii) Show that $(2x + 7)$ is factor of $2x^3 + 5x^2 - 11x - 14$.

Hence, factorise the given expression completely.

(iii) Show that $(3z + 10)$ is a factor of $9z^3 - 27z^2 - 100z + 300$. Factorise the given polynomial completely. $(3z + 10)$ is a factor of it.

27. Factorize completely using factor theorem

$$2x^3 - x^2 - 13x - 6$$ [ICSE 2023]

28. If $(-px^2 + qx + 6 + x^3)$ has $(x - 1)$ as a factor and leaves a remainder 4 when divided by $(x + 1)$, then find the values of p and q.

29. If $2y^3 + py^2 + qy - 6$ has a factor $(2y + 1)$ and leaves the remainder 12 when divided by $(y + 2)$. Calculate the values of p and q, hence factorise the expression completely.

30. Given $f(x) = px^2 + qx + 2$ and $g(x) = qx^2 + px + 1$. If $x - 2$ is a factor of $f(x)$ but leaves the remainder -15 when it divides $g(x)$, find the values of p and q with these values of p and q, factorise the expression.

$$f(x) + g(x) + 4x^2 + 7x.$$

Hints and Answers

Exercise 7.1

1. Hint In a polynomial, exponents of variable(s) are always a non-negative integer.

Ans. (i) Not a polynomial

(ii) Polynomial

(iii) Not a polynomial

2. Hint The highest power of the variable occurring in the polynomial, is called the degree of the polynomial.

Ans. (i) 2 (ii) 0 (iii) 3

3. Hint (i) Let $f(x) = 2x^2 + 5x + 7$

Then, $f(-1) = 2(-1)^2 + 5(-1) + 7$

(ii) Let $f(x) = \frac{2}{5}x + 1 - x^2$

Then, $f(-1) = \frac{2}{5}(-1) + 1 - (-1)^2$

Ans. (i) 4 (ii) $\frac{-2}{5}$

4. Hint Put $x = 2$ in $f(x)$

and $f(x) = 0$

$\Rightarrow \quad x^2 = \frac{144}{16} = 9$

Ans. $f(2) = 80$; $x = \pm 3$

5. Hint Equate the given polynomial to zero and then solve it.

Ans. (i) $\frac{1}{7}$ (ii) $-1, 5$ (iii) $-2, -5$

6. Given, $f(x) = 2x^3 - 3x^2 + 7x - 8$ ... (i)

$\Rightarrow f(x)$ is divided by $x - 1$.

$\Rightarrow \quad f(1) = 2(1)^3 - 3(1)^2 + 7(1) - 8$

$= 2 - 3 + 7 - 8 = -2$

Hence, the required remainder is -2.

7. Hint Required remainder $= f\left(-\frac{1}{2}\right)$ **Ans.** -4

8. Hint Required remainder $= f\left(\frac{-2}{3}\right)$ **Ans.** 1

9. Hint Let $f(x) = 2x^3 + 3x^2 - 9x - 10$

For $x = -1$,

$f(x) = f(-1) = 2(-1)^3 + 3(-1)^2 - 9(-1) - 10$

$= -2 + 3 + 9 - 10 = 12 - 12 = 0$

$\therefore \; 2x^3 + 3x^2 - 9x - 10 = (x + 1)(2x^2 + x - 10)$

Ans. $(x + 1)(x - 2)(2x + 5)$

10. Do same as Example 7. **Ans.** $k = 13$

11. Do same as Example 7. **Ans.** $k = 3$

12. Do same as Example 9. **Ans.** $a = 3$

13. Hint Let $f(x) = 2x^3 + ax^2 - 11x + b$.

Then, according to given conditions, we have

$f(2) = 0$ and $f(3) = 42$

$\Rightarrow \quad 4a + b = 6$ and $9a + b = 21$

On solving above equations, we get the required values of a and b.

Ans. $a = 3$ and $b = -6$.

14. Do same as Example 10.

Ans. $a = 2$

Exercise 7.2

1. Do same as Example 12.
Ans. Yes, $(x-2)$ is a factor of $f(x)$.

2. Do same as Example 12.

3. Hint Let $f(x) = 7x^2 - 10x - 8$. Then, show that $f(2) = 0$.
Further divide $f(x)$ by $(x-2)$ using long division method.
Ans. $(x-2)(7x+4)$.

4. Hint Let $f(x) = 2x^3 + 7x^2 - 4x - 14$.
Then, show that $f\left(-\frac{7}{2}\right) = 0$.
Further divide $f(x)$ by $(2x+7)$ using long division method.
Ans. $(x+\sqrt{2})(x-\sqrt{2})(2x+7)$

5. Do same as Example 15. **Ans.** $(x-2)(x+1)(x+2)$

6. Hint Do same as Example 15.
and consider, $x^3 - 13x - 12 = 0$
$\Rightarrow (x+1)(x+3)(x-4) = 0 \Rightarrow x = -1, -3, 4$
Ans. $(x+1)(x+3)(x-4)$; $-1, -3, 4$

7. Hint Let $f(x) = x^3 + ax + b$
Since, $(x+2)$ is a factor of $f(x)$, therefore $f(-2) = 0$
Also, $(x+3)$ is factor of $f(x)$, therefore $f(-3) = 0$
Ans. $a = -19$ and $b = -30$

8. Hint Let $f(x) = x^3 + 2x^2 - kx + 10$
Since, $x-2$ is a factor of $f(x)$ $\Rightarrow f(2) = 0$,
then $k = 13$

9. Hint Let $g(x)$ is factor of $f(x)$.
Then, $f(-a) = 0$.
$\Rightarrow -a^3 + a(a^2+1) + 2a + 4 = 0$ **Ans.** $a = -\frac{4}{3}$

10. Hint Here, we have $f(2) = 0$ and $f(3) = 52$
$\Rightarrow 2a + b + 1 = 0$ ...(i)
and $3a + b - 4 = 0$ ...(ii)
Ans. $a = 5$ and $b = -11$

11. Do same as Example 20. **Ans.** 1

Chapter Exercise

1. (b) Given, $x + 3 = 0 \Rightarrow x = -3$
Remainder = 5
$\therefore kx^3 + 9x^2 + 4x - 10 = 5$
$\Rightarrow k(-3)^3 + 9(-3)^2 + 4(-3) - 10 = 5 \Rightarrow k = 2$
Hence, the value of $k = 2$.

2. (d) $x - 1 = 0$
$x = 1$
$(1)^3 - a(1)^2 + b(1) - 6 = -8$
$a - b = 3$ ... (i)
and $x - 2 = 0$
$x = 2$
$(2)^3 - a(2)^2 + b(2) - 6 = 0$
$2a - b = 1$ ... (ii)
On solving Eqs. (i) and (ii), we get
$a - b = 3$
$2a - b = 1$
$-\quad+\quad-$
$-a = 2$
$a = -2$
Hence, the value of $a = -2$.

3. (c) Given, $x - 2 = 0 \Rightarrow x = 2$
and $3x^2 - 5x - 2 = 0$
$\Rightarrow 3(2)^2 - 5(2) - 2 = 0$ [$\because$ put $x = 2$]
Now, $(x-2)$ is a factor of $3x^2 - 5x - 2$.

$x-2)\ 3x^2 - 5x - 2\ (3x+1$
$3x^2 - 6x$
$-\quad+$
$x - 2$
$x - 2$
$-\quad+$
0

4. (b) Let the number added be t so the resulting polynomial is $2x^3 - 3x^2 + x + t$.
According to the question,
$x - 2$ is a factor of above polynomial.
i.e. $x - 2 = 0$ and remainder is 5
$\Rightarrow 2(2)^3 - 3(2)^2 + 2 + t = 5$
$\Rightarrow 16 - 12 + 2 + t = 5$
$\Rightarrow 18 - 12 + t = 5$
$\therefore t = -1$
Hence, the required number to be added is -1.

5. (c) Given, $(x-2)$ is a factor of $x^3 - kx - 12$.
$\Rightarrow x - 2 = 0$
$\Rightarrow x = 2$
On substituting $x = 2$ in given equation,
$2^3 - k \times 2 - 12 = 0$
$\Rightarrow 8 - 2k = 12 \Rightarrow -2k = 4$
$\Rightarrow k = -2$

6. (b) Let $f(x) = x^3 - kx^2 - 5x + 6$
Since, $(x+2)$ is a factor of $f(x)$.
$\therefore f(-2) = 0$ [by factor theorem]
$\Rightarrow (-2)^3 - k(-2)^2 - 5(-2) + 6 = 0$
$\Rightarrow -8 - 4k + 10 + 6 = 0$
$\Rightarrow -4k + 8 = 0$
$\Rightarrow 4k = 8 \Rightarrow k = 2$

7. (d) Let $f(x) = x^3 - 2x^2 + ax + 12$
Since, $f(x)$ is divided by $(x+1)$ leaves remainder 20.
$\therefore f(-1) = 20$
$\Rightarrow (-1)^3 - 2(-1)^2 + a(-1) + 12 = 20$
$\Rightarrow -1 - 2 - a + 12 = 20$
$\Rightarrow -3 - a + 12 = 20$
$\Rightarrow -a + 9 = 20$
$\Rightarrow -a = 11 \Rightarrow a = -11$

$\Rightarrow \quad -3-a+12=20$

$\Rightarrow \quad -a+9=20$

$\Rightarrow \quad -a=11 \Rightarrow a=-11$

8. **Hint** Put $x=2$ in $2x^3+x^2-7x+4$. **Ans.** 10

9. **Hint** If a polynomial $f(x)$ is divided by $ax-b$, $a \neq 0$, then remainder $= f\left(\frac{b}{a}\right)$. **Ans.** 2

10. **Hint** Required remainder $= f\left(-\frac{2}{3}\right)$ **Ans.** 0

11. **Hint** Here, we have $f(3)=k$ **Ans.** $k=1$

12. Do same as Example 9. **Ans.** $p=1$

13. Do same as Example 9. **Ans.** $a=5$

14. **Hint** Let $f(x)=2x^3-7x^2+2x+k$, where k is the required number.
Then, according to the questions $f\left(\frac{3}{2}\right)=-2$. **Ans.** 4

15. **Hint** Check whether $f(7)=0$ or not. **Ans.** Yes

16. **Hint** Let $f(x)=2x^2-9x-5$. Then, show that $f(5)=0$.
Further divide $f(x)$ by $(x-5)$ using long division method.
Ans. $(2x+1)(x-5)$

17. **Hint** Let $f(x)=x^3-7x^2+14x-8$.
Then, show that $f(1)=0$. Further, divide $f(x)$ by $(x-1)$ using long division method.
Ans. $(x-1)(x-2)(x-4)$

18. Do same as Example 14.
Ans. $(x-2)(2x-1)(x+3)$

19. **Hint** First, do same as Example 14.
Secondly, put each factor of $f(x)$ equal to zero, for obtaining the value of x.
Ans. $f(x)=(x-3)(x-2)(2x+3)$; $x=3, 2, \frac{-3}{2}$.

20. **Hint** Here, we have $f(p)=0$ and $g(p)=0$

$\Rightarrow \quad f(p)=g(p)$

21. Do same as Example 19.
Ans. $a=3$, $b=-4$

22. Do same as Example 19.
Ans. $b=8$, $c=-17$

23. **Hint** Let $f(x)=x^3+ax^2+bx+6$
Then, we have $f(2)=0$ and $f(3)=3$

$\Rightarrow \quad 2a+b+7=0 \quad \ldots(i)$

and $\quad 3a+b+10=0 \quad \ldots(ii)$

On solving Eqs. (i) and (ii), we get the required values.
Ans. $a=-3$, $b=-1$

24. Do same as Example 22.
Ans. $(x-1)(x-2)(x+13)$

25. Do same as Example 13.
Ans. $(x-1)(x-10)(x-12)$

26. (i) **Hint** Let $f(x)=4x^3+20x^2+33x+18$
Then, show that $f\left(-\frac{3}{2}\right)=0$.
Further, divide $f(x)$ by $(2x+3)$ using long division method.
Ans. $(x+2)(2x+3)(2x+3)$

(ii) Do same as part (i)
Ans. $(2x+7)(x-2)(x+1)$

(iii) Do same as part (i)
Ans. $(3z+10)(3z-10)(z-3)$

27. Given, expression is

$$2x^3-x^2-13x-6$$

$$= 2x^3+x^2-2x^2-x-12x-6$$

[$\because$ we can write $-x^2=x^2-2x^2$ and $-13x=-x-12x$]

$$= x^2(2x+1)-x(2x+1)-6(2x+1)$$

[$\because$ on taking x^2 common from first two terms and $(-x)$ common from mid two terms and -6 common from last two terms]

$$=(2x+1)(x^2-x-6)$$

[$\because (2x+1)$ is common in all three terms]

$$=(2x+1)(x^2-3x+2x-6)$$

$$=(2x+1)[x(x-3)+2(x-3)]$$

$$=(2x+1)[(x-3)(x+2)]$$

$$=(2x+1)(x-3)(x+2)$$

Hence, the factors of $2x^3-x^2-13x-6$ are $(2x+1)$, $(x-3)$ and $(x+2)$.

28. Do same as Q. 23. **Ans.** $p=4$, $q=-3$

29. **Hint** Let $f(y)=2y^3+py^2+qy-6$.
Then, we have

$$f\left(-\frac{1}{2}\right)=0 \text{ and } f(-2)=12$$

$\Rightarrow \quad p-2q=25$ and $2p-q=17$

On solving above equations, we get the required values of p and q.
Further, divide the given polynomial by $2y+1$.
Ans. $p=3$, $q=-11$; $(y-2)(2y+1)(y+3)$

30. **Hint** $f(2)=0$ and $g(2)=15$

$\Rightarrow \quad 4p+2q+2=0$ and $4q+2p+1=-15$

$\Rightarrow \quad 2p+q+1=0$ and $p+2q+8=0$

$$p=2, q=-5$$

$\therefore \quad f(x)+g(x)+4x^2+7x$

$$=(2x^2-5x+2) + (-5x^2+2x+1)+4x^2+7x$$

$$=x^2+4x+3$$

CHAPTER

08

Matrices

SYLLABUS

- (a) Order of a matrix. Row and column matrices. (b) Compatibility for addition and multiplication. (c) Null and Identity matrices. (d) Addition and subtraction of 2 × 2 matrices. (e) Multiplication of a 2 × 2 matrix by (I) a non-zero rational number (ii) a matrix

The evolution of concept of matrices is the result of an attempt to obtain compact and simple method of solving system of linear equations. It is compact notation for describing sets of data, sets of equations and electronic spreadsheet. The word 'Matrices' is plural of 'Matrix'. In this chapter, we will study the fundamentals of matrix and matrix algebra.

Matrix

A Matrix is an ordered **rectangular array** of numbers enclosed in [ ] or ( ). Each number (real or complex) or functions in a matrix is called an **element** or the **entry** of the matrix.

A matrix is represented by a single **capital letter** like A, B, X, Y, etc., and elements of a matrix are represented by the small letters a, b, c, ... etc.

In a matrix, horizontal lines are called **rows** and vertical lines are called **columns**.

e.g. $$A = \begin{bmatrix} 2 & -5 \\ 7 & 0 \\ 5 & 3 \end{bmatrix} \begin{array}{l} \rightarrow \text{First row } (R_1) \\ \rightarrow \text{Second row } (R_2) \\ \rightarrow \text{Third row } (R_3) \end{array}$$

↓ First column (C_1)   ↓ Second column (C_2)

Order of a Matrix

A matrix having m rows and n columns is called a matrix of order $m \times n$ and read as 'm by n'. By convention, number of rows are listed first and columns, second.

e.g. Order of matrix $A = \begin{bmatrix} 0 & 2 \\ 1 & 3 \end{bmatrix}$ is 2×2 means, matrix A with 2 rows and 2 columns.

Number of Elements in a Matrix

The total number of elements in a matrix is equal to the product of its number of rows and columns. In other words, the number of elements in an $m \times n$ matrix will be equal to mn.

e.g. if a matrix has 2 rows and 3 columns, then the number of elements $= 2 \times 3 = 6$.

Example 1. If a matrix has 30 elements, then what are the possible orders it can have?

Sol. Given, number of elements = 30

$\therefore \quad mn = 30$

All factors of 30 are 1, 2, 3, 5, 6, 10, 15 and 30.

Now, the possible ordered pairs whose element's product is 30, are (1, 30), (2, 15), (3, 10), (5, 6), (30, 1), (15, 2), (10, 3) and (6, 5).

Hence, all possible orders of matrix are

1×30, 2×15, 3×10, 5×6, 30×1, 15×2, 10×3 and 6×5.

Formation of a Matrix

Sometimes, a relation between the elements and its position is given to us. Then, to form a matrix, whose elements satisfies this relation, we put different values of i and j according to the given order and find all the elements of matrix and then write the matrix of given order.

Example 2. Construct a matrix of order 3×2, whose elements are determined by $a_{ij} = \dfrac{i+j}{2}$.

Sol. Let A be a matrix of order 3×2.

Then, $A = [a_{ij}]_{3 \times 2} = \begin{bmatrix} a_{11} & a_{12} \\ a_{21} & a_{22} \\ a_{31} & a_{32} \end{bmatrix}$ ...(i)

Given, $a_{ij} = \dfrac{i+j}{2}$ ...(ii)

On putting $i = 1, 2, 3$ and $j = 1, 2$ in Eq. (ii), we get

$$a_{11} = \frac{1+1}{2} = 1$$

$$a_{12} = \frac{1+2}{2} = \frac{3}{2}$$

$$a_{21} = \frac{2+1}{2} = \frac{3}{2}$$

$$a_{22} = \frac{2+2}{2} = 2$$

$$a_{31} = \frac{3+1}{2} = 2 \text{ and } a_{32} = \frac{3+2}{2} = \frac{5}{2}$$

On putting all the values in Eq. (i), we get

$$A = \begin{bmatrix} 1 & 3/2 \\ 3/2 & 2 \\ 2 & 5/2 \end{bmatrix}$$

which is the required 3×2 order matrix.

Types of Matrices

There are various types of matrices, which are as follows

1. **Row matrix** A matrix having only one row and some columns, is called a row matrix.
   e.g. $A = [1 \ 2 \ 3]_{1 \times 3}$ [one row and three columns]
2. **Column matrix** A matrix having only one column and some rows, is called a column matrix.
   e.g. $B = \begin{bmatrix} 1 \\ 2 \\ 3 \end{bmatrix}_{3 \times 1}$ [one column and three rows]
3. **Zero matrix or null matrix** A matrix of any $m \times n$ order whose all elements are zero, it is called a zero or null matrix and it is denoted by capital letter 'O'.
   e.g. $O = \begin{bmatrix} 0 & 0 & 0 \\ 0 & 0 & 0 \end{bmatrix}_{2 \times 3}$
4. **Square matrix** A matrix in which number of rows and number of columns are equal, is called a square matrix. e.g. $A = \begin{bmatrix} a & b \\ c & d \end{bmatrix}_{2 \times 2}$ [here, order is 2×2]
5. **Rectangular matrix** A matrix in which the number of rows are not equal to the number of columns is called a rectangular matrix
   e.g. $A = \begin{bmatrix} 1 & 3 & 5 \\ 2 & 3 & 4 \end{bmatrix}_{2 \times 3}$, $B = \begin{bmatrix} 1 & 3 \\ 2 & 5 \\ 7 & 9 \end{bmatrix}_{3 \times 2}$
6. **Diagonal matrix** A square matrix $A = [a_{ij}]_{n \times n}$ is said to be a diagonal matrix, if all the elements lying outside the diagonal elements are zero.
   e.g. $A = \begin{bmatrix} a & 0 & 0 \\ 0 & b & 0 \\ 0 & 0 & c \end{bmatrix}_{3 \times 3}$ ← Principal diagonal
7. **Scalar matrix** A diagonal matrix in which all diagonal elements are equal, is called a scalar matrix.
   e.g. $A = \begin{bmatrix} k & 0 & 0 \\ 0 & k & 0 \\ 0 & 0 & k \end{bmatrix}_{3 \times 3}$
8. **Identity matrix or Unit matrix** A square matrix having 1 (one) on its principal diagonal and 0 (zero) elsewhere, is called an identity matrix. Identity matrix of order n is denoted by I_n or simply I.
   e.g. $I_2 = \begin{bmatrix} 1 & 0 \\ 0 & 1 \end{bmatrix}_{2 \times 2}$

Note Identity matrix is always a scalar matrix.

Example 3. Classify the types of matrices and also write their orders.

(i) $\begin{bmatrix} 1 & -3 \\ 2 & 4 \end{bmatrix}$ (ii) $\begin{bmatrix} 4 & 0 & 0 \\ 0 & 2 & 0 \\ 0 & 0 & 1 \end{bmatrix}$ (iii) $\begin{bmatrix} 7 \\ 3 \\ -2 \end{bmatrix}$

(iv) $[1 \ 2 \ 3 \ 4]$ (v) $\begin{bmatrix} 1 & 0 & 0 \\ 0 & 1 & 0 \\ 0 & 0 & 1 \end{bmatrix}$ (vi) $\begin{bmatrix} 3 & 0 & 0 \\ 0 & 3 & 0 \\ 0 & 0 & 3 \end{bmatrix}$

(vii) $\begin{bmatrix} 0 & 0 & 0 \\ 0 & 0 & 0 \end{bmatrix}$ (viii) $\begin{bmatrix} 2 & 9 & 7 \\ 3 & 2 & 8 \end{bmatrix}$

Sol.

(i) The given matrix is a square matrix of order 2×2.
(ii) The given matrix is a diagonal matrix of order 3×3.
(iii) The given matrix is a column matrix of order 3×1.

(iv) The given matrix is a row matrix of order 1×4.
(v) The given matrix is an identity matrix of order 3×3.
(vi) The given matrix is a scalar matrix of order 3×3.
(vii) The given matrix is a null matrix of order 2×3.
(viii) The given matrix is a rectangular matrix of order 2×3.

Example 4. Write the null matrix denoted by each of the following.

(i) $O_{1\times 3}$ (ii) $O_{2\times 1}$ (iii) $O_{2\times 2}$

Sol. (i) $O_{1\times 3}=[0\ 0\ 0]$ (ii) $O_{2\times 1}=\begin{bmatrix}0\\0\end{bmatrix}$ (iii) $O_{2\times 2}=\begin{bmatrix}0&0\\0&0\end{bmatrix}$

Equality of Matrices

Two matrices $A=[a_{ij}]$ and $B=[b_{ij}]$ are said to be equal, if

(i) their orders are same
(ii) their corresponding elements are also equal, i.e. $a_{ij}=b_{ij}, \forall\, i, j$.

Symbolically, if two matrices A and B are equal, then we write it as $A=B$.

e.g. $\begin{bmatrix}1&2\\0&4\end{bmatrix}$ and $\begin{bmatrix}1&2\\0&4\end{bmatrix}$ are equal matrices, but $\begin{bmatrix}1&2\\0&4\end{bmatrix}$ and $\begin{bmatrix}2&1\\4&0\end{bmatrix}$ are not equal matrices.

Example 5. If $\begin{bmatrix}x-y&2x+z\\2x-y&3z+w\end{bmatrix}=\begin{bmatrix}-1&5\\0&13\end{bmatrix}$, then find the values of x, y, z and w.

Sol. Given, $\begin{bmatrix}x-y&2x+z\\2x-y&3z+w\end{bmatrix}=\begin{bmatrix}-1&5\\0&13\end{bmatrix}$

Here, both matrices are equal, so to find x, y, z and w, we equate the corresponding elements.

On equating the corresponding elements, we get

$$x-y=-1 \quad ...(i)$$
$$2x+z=5 \quad ...(ii)$$
$$2x-y=0 \quad ...(iii)$$
and $$3z+w=13 \quad ...(iv)$$

On solving Eqs. (i) and (iii), we get

$$x=1 \text{ and } y=2$$

On putting the value of x in Eq. (ii), we get

$$2\times 1+z=5 \Rightarrow z=5-2=3$$

On putting the value of z in Eq. (iv), we get

$$3\times 3+w=13 \Rightarrow w=13-9=4$$

Hence, $x=1$, $y=2$, $z=3$ and $w=4$.

Example 6. If $\begin{bmatrix}x+y&4\\-2+z&xy\end{bmatrix}=\begin{bmatrix}6&w\\1&8\end{bmatrix}$, then find the values of x, y, z and w.

Sol. Given, $\begin{bmatrix}x+y&4\\-2+z&xy\end{bmatrix}=\begin{bmatrix}6&w\\1&8\end{bmatrix}$

Here, both matrices are equal so to find x, y, z and w, we equate the corresponding elements.

On equating the corresponding elements, we get

$$x+y=6 \quad ...(i)$$
$$-2+z=1 \quad ...(ii)$$
$$w=4 \quad ...(iii)$$
and $$xy=8 \quad ...(iv)$$

Now, from Eq. (i),

$$x=6-y$$

Put the value of x in Eq. (iv),we get

$$(6-y)\,y=8$$
$$\Rightarrow \quad 6y-y^2=8$$
$$\Rightarrow \quad y^2-6y+8=0$$
$$\Rightarrow \quad (y-2)(y-4)=0$$
$$\therefore \quad y=2, 4$$

On putting the values of y in Eq. (i), we get

$$x=4, 2$$

On solving Eqs. (ii) and (iii), we get

$$z=3 \text{ and } w=4$$

Here, $x=4, 2$, $y=2, 4$, $z=3$ and $w=4$

Exercise 8.1

1. Identify the order of a matrix
   (i) $[2]$ (ii) $\begin{bmatrix}2\\1\end{bmatrix}$
   (iii) $[3\ 1]$ (iv) $\begin{bmatrix}1&2\\3&1\end{bmatrix}$

2. In the matrix $A=\begin{bmatrix}a&x^2\\y^2&b\end{bmatrix}$, write
   (i) the order of the matrix.
   (ii) the number of elements.
   (iii) the elements a_{21}, a_{12} and a_{22}.

3. If a matrix has 24 elements, then what are the possible orders it can have ?

4. If a matrix has 28 elements, then what are the possible orders it can have ? What, if it has 13 elements?

5. Construct a 2×2 matrix, whose elements are given by $a_{ij}=i\cdot j$.

6. Construct a 2×2 matrix, whose elements a_{ij} are given by $a_{ij}=\left(\dfrac{i-j}{i+j}\right)^2$.

7. Identify the types of matrices given below.

(i) $[1\ 5\ 7]$ (ii) $\begin{bmatrix}1&0\\0&1\end{bmatrix}$

(iii) $\begin{bmatrix}3\\2\\3\end{bmatrix}$ (iv) $\begin{bmatrix}1&2\\3&4\\7&9\end{bmatrix}$ (v) $\begin{bmatrix}0&0\\0&0\end{bmatrix}$

(vi) $\begin{bmatrix}1&0&0\\0&1&0\end{bmatrix}$ (vii) $\begin{bmatrix}5&0&0\\0&5&0\\0&0&5\end{bmatrix}$

8. Find the values of x, y, z and u, if

(i) $\begin{bmatrix}x+2&z-3\\y&3\end{bmatrix}=\begin{bmatrix}5&-7\\6&3\end{bmatrix}$

(ii) $\begin{bmatrix}x&-2\\y&7\end{bmatrix}=\begin{bmatrix}2&z\\3&z+u\end{bmatrix}$.

(iii) $\begin{bmatrix}x+y&u+z\\u-z&2x-3y\end{bmatrix}=\begin{bmatrix}5&-1\\3&-5\end{bmatrix}$

(iv) $\begin{bmatrix}2x+2&y^2+2\\5&y^2-5y\end{bmatrix}=\begin{bmatrix}x+4&3y\\5&-6\end{bmatrix}$

9. Find the value of each variable in the following matrix.

$$\begin{bmatrix}5-x\\y+6\end{bmatrix}=O_{2\times 1},$$

where O is a null matrix.

Operations on Matrices

Here, we will discuss certain operations on matrices, namely addition of matrices, subtraction of matrices, scalar multiplication of a matrix and multiplication of matrices.

Addition of Matrices

Two or more matrix can be added only, if they have same order.

The addition matrix of two or more matrix is simply the matrix obtain by adding the corresponding elements of different matrix.

e.g. $\begin{bmatrix}2&3\\0&-1\end{bmatrix}+\begin{bmatrix}6&9\\-4&1\end{bmatrix}=\begin{bmatrix}2+6&3+9\\0+(-4)&-1+1\end{bmatrix}=\begin{bmatrix}8&12\\-4&0\end{bmatrix}$

Compatibility for Addition

For addition of two matrices, both matrices should be of same order, otherwise we cannot add them.

e.g. If $A=\begin{bmatrix}2&3\\1&0\end{bmatrix}$ and $B=\begin{bmatrix}1&2&3\\1&0&1\end{bmatrix}$, then $A+B$ is not defined, because A and B are not of same order.

Properties of Addition of Matrices

Let A, B and C be the three matrices of same order $m\times n$. Then, the following properties hold

(i) **Commutative law** Matrix addition is commutative,

i.e. $A+B=B+A$.

(ii) **Associative law** Matrix addition is associative,

i.e. $A+(B+C)=(A+B)+C$.

(iii) **Existence of additive identity** For every matrix A, there exists zero matrix O, of same order such that

$$A+O=O+A=A.$$

Here, the matrix O is called the additive identity.

(iv) **Existence of additive inverse** For every matrix A, there exists another matrix $(-A)$, obtained by multiplying the elements of A by (-1), such that

$$A+(-A)=O=(-A)+A.$$

Here, the matrix $(-A)$ is called the additive inverse of A.

Example 7. If $A=\begin{bmatrix}-2&5\\3&4\end{bmatrix}$ and $B=\begin{bmatrix}4&-3\\1&5\end{bmatrix}$, then find $A+B$.

Sol. Given, $A=\begin{bmatrix}-2&5\\3&4\end{bmatrix}$ and $B=\begin{bmatrix}4&-3\\1&5\end{bmatrix}$

$$\therefore\ A+B=\begin{bmatrix}-2&5\\3&4\end{bmatrix}+\begin{bmatrix}4&-3\\1&5\end{bmatrix}$$

$$=\begin{bmatrix}(-2)+4&5+(-3)\\3+1&4+5\end{bmatrix}$$

$$=\begin{bmatrix}-2+4&5-3\\4&9\end{bmatrix}=\begin{bmatrix}2&2\\4&9\end{bmatrix}$$

Subtraction of Matrices

The difference can be possible only when they have same order.

The difference of two matrix is simply the matrix whose elements the difference of the corresponding elements of two matrices.

e.g. Let $A=\begin{bmatrix}a&b\\c&d\end{bmatrix}$ and $B=\begin{bmatrix}e&f\\g&h\end{bmatrix}$.

Then, $A-B=\begin{bmatrix}a-e&b-f\\c-g&d-h\end{bmatrix}$

Example 8. If $A = \begin{bmatrix} 3 & -2 \\ 1 & 4 \end{bmatrix}$ and $B = \begin{bmatrix} 2 & 4 \\ -3 & 1 \end{bmatrix}$, then find A − B.

Sol. Given, $A = \begin{bmatrix} 3 & -2 \\ 1 & 4 \end{bmatrix}$ and $B = \begin{bmatrix} 2 & 4 \\ -3 & 1 \end{bmatrix}$

$$\therefore \quad A - B = \begin{bmatrix} 3 & -2 \\ 1 & 4 \end{bmatrix} - \begin{bmatrix} 2 & 4 \\ -3 & 1 \end{bmatrix}$$

$$= \begin{bmatrix} 3-2 & -2-4 \\ 1-(-3) & 4-1 \end{bmatrix} = \begin{bmatrix} 1 & -6 \\ 1+3 & 3 \end{bmatrix} = \begin{bmatrix} 1 & -6 \\ 4 & 3 \end{bmatrix}$$

Scalar Multiplication [Multiplication of a Matrix by a Scalar (Number)]

When a matrix is multiply by a scalar (a number), then it is called scalar multiplication of matrix. Here, each element of matrix is multiply by the given scalar.

Properties of Scalar Multiplication

Let A and B be two matrices of same order. Then,

(i) $1 \cdot A = A$
(ii) $(-1)A = -A$
(iii) $0 \cdot A = O$
(iv) $l(kA) = k(lA)$, where k and l are scalars.
(v) $-kA = k(-A) = -(kA)$, where k is a scalar.
(vi) $k(A+B) = (A+B)k = kA + kB$, where k is a scalar.
(vii) $(k_1 + k_2)A = k_1A + k_2A$, where k_1 and k_2 are scalars.

Example 9. If $A = \begin{bmatrix} 2 & -1 \\ 0 & 3 \end{bmatrix}$, then find the following.

(i) $3A$ (ii) $(-2)A$

Sol. Given, $A = \begin{bmatrix} 2 & -1 \\ 0 & 3 \end{bmatrix}$

(i) $$3A = 3\begin{bmatrix} 2 & -1 \\ 0 & 3 \end{bmatrix} = \begin{bmatrix} 2\times 3 & -1\times 3 \\ 0\times 3 & 3\times 3 \end{bmatrix} = \begin{bmatrix} 6 & -3 \\ 0 & 9 \end{bmatrix}$$

(ii) $$(-2)A = (-2)\begin{bmatrix} 2 & -1 \\ 0 & 3 \end{bmatrix} = \begin{bmatrix} -2\times 2 & -2\times(-1) \\ -2\times 0 & -2\times 3 \end{bmatrix} = \begin{bmatrix} -4 & 2 \\ 0 & -6 \end{bmatrix}$$

Example 10. If $A = \begin{bmatrix} 1 & 2 \\ 3 & 4 \end{bmatrix}$ and $B = \begin{bmatrix} -2 & 3 \\ 0 & 4 \end{bmatrix}$, then show that $4(A+B) = 4A + 4B$.

Sol. Given, $A = \begin{bmatrix} 1 & 2 \\ 3 & 4 \end{bmatrix}$ and $B = \begin{bmatrix} -2 & 3 \\ 0 & 4 \end{bmatrix}$

Now, $$\text{LHS} = 4(A+B) = 4\left(\begin{bmatrix} 1 & 2 \\ 3 & 4 \end{bmatrix} + \begin{bmatrix} -2 & 3 \\ 0 & 4 \end{bmatrix}\right)$$

$$= 4\begin{bmatrix} 1-2 & 2+3 \\ 3+0 & 4+4 \end{bmatrix} = 4\begin{bmatrix} -1 & 5 \\ 3 & 8 \end{bmatrix}$$

$$= \begin{bmatrix} 4\times(-1) & 4\times 5 \\ 4\times 3 & 4\times 8 \end{bmatrix} = \begin{bmatrix} -4 & 20 \\ 12 & 32 \end{bmatrix} \quad \text{...(i)}$$

and $$\text{RHS} = 4A + 4B = 4\begin{bmatrix} 1 & 2 \\ 3 & 4 \end{bmatrix} + 4\begin{bmatrix} -2 & 3 \\ 0 & 4 \end{bmatrix}$$

$$= \begin{bmatrix} 4\times 1 & 4\times 2 \\ 4\times 3 & 4\times 4 \end{bmatrix} + \begin{bmatrix} 4\times(-2) & 4\times 3 \\ 4\times 0 & 4\times 4 \end{bmatrix}$$

$$= \begin{bmatrix} 4 & 8 \\ 12 & 16 \end{bmatrix} + \begin{bmatrix} -8 & 12 \\ 0 & 16 \end{bmatrix}$$

$$= \begin{bmatrix} 4-8 & 8+12 \\ 12+0 & 16+16 \end{bmatrix} = \begin{bmatrix} -4 & 20 \\ 12 & 32 \end{bmatrix} \quad \text{...(ii)}$$

From Eqs. (i) and (ii), we get
LHS = RHS **Hence proved.**

Example 11. Simplify

$$\sin A \begin{bmatrix} \sin A & -\cos A \\ \cos A & \sin A \end{bmatrix} + \cos A \begin{bmatrix} \cos A & \sin A \\ -\sin A & \cos A \end{bmatrix}.$$

Sol. $$\sin A \begin{bmatrix} \sin A & -\cos A \\ \cos A & \sin A \end{bmatrix} + \cos A \begin{bmatrix} \cos A & \sin A \\ -\sin A & \cos A \end{bmatrix}$$

$$= \begin{bmatrix} \sin^2 A & -\sin A\cos A \\ \sin A\cos A & \sin^2 A \end{bmatrix} + \begin{bmatrix} \cos^2 A & \cos A\sin A \\ -\sin A\cos A & \cos^2 A \end{bmatrix}$$

$$= \begin{bmatrix} \sin^2 A + \cos^2 A & -\sin A\cos A + \cos A\sin A \\ \sin A\cos A - \sin A\cos A & \sin^2 A + \cos^2 A \end{bmatrix}$$

$$= \begin{bmatrix} 1 & 0 \\ 0 & 1 \end{bmatrix} \quad [\because \cos^2\theta + \sin^2\theta = 1]$$

Multiplication of Matrices by a Matrix

Two matrices are preferred to multiply only on following conditions

(i) The number of columns in A is equal to the number of rows in B.

(ii) $A_{m\times n} \times B_{n\times p} = (AB)_{m\times p}$
If A of order $m\times n$ and B is of order $n \times p$, then AB is of order $m \times p$ and defined as
$$A_{m\times n} \times B_{n\times p} = (AB)_{m\times p}$$
(i, k)th element of AB = {sum of the products of element of ith row of A with the corresponding elements of kth column of B.}

Compatibility for Multiplication of Matrices

We can multiply two matrices, if the number of columns of first matrix is equal to the number of rows of second matrix, otherwise we cannot multiply them.

e.g. If $A = \begin{bmatrix} 3 \\ 4 \end{bmatrix}$ and $B = \begin{bmatrix} 3 & 4 \\ 5 & 6 \end{bmatrix}$, then AB is not defined, because number of columns of first matrix is not same as the number of rows of second matrix. But BA is defined.

Example 12. Find AB, if $A=\begin{bmatrix}6&9\\2&3\end{bmatrix}$ and $B=\begin{bmatrix}2&0\\7&8\end{bmatrix}$.

Sol. Given, $A=\begin{bmatrix}6&9\\2&3\end{bmatrix}_{2\times2}$ and $B=\begin{bmatrix}2&0\\7&8\end{bmatrix}_{2\times2}$

Here, number of columns in A = number of rows in $B = 2$. So, the product of A and B is possible and it will be of order 2×2.

$$\therefore \quad AB=\begin{bmatrix}6&9\\2&3\end{bmatrix}\begin{bmatrix}2&0\\7&8\end{bmatrix}$$
$$=\begin{bmatrix}6\times2+9\times7 & 6\times0+9\times8\\2\times2+3\times7 & 2\times0+3\times8\end{bmatrix}$$
$$=\begin{bmatrix}12+63&0+72\\4+21&0+24\end{bmatrix}=\begin{bmatrix}75&72\\25&24\end{bmatrix}$$

Example 13. If $A=\begin{bmatrix}3&7\\2&4\end{bmatrix}$, $B=\begin{bmatrix}0&2\\5&3\end{bmatrix}$ and $C=\begin{bmatrix}1&-5\\-4&6\end{bmatrix}$, then find $AB-5C$. **[ICSE 2015]**

Sol. Given, $A=\begin{bmatrix}3&7\\2&4\end{bmatrix}$, $B=\begin{bmatrix}0&2\\5&3\end{bmatrix}$ and $C=\begin{bmatrix}1&-5\\-4&6\end{bmatrix}$

Now, $AB=\begin{bmatrix}3&7\\2&4\end{bmatrix}\begin{bmatrix}0&2\\5&3\end{bmatrix}$
$$=\begin{bmatrix}0+35&6+21\\0+20&4+12\end{bmatrix}=\begin{bmatrix}35&27\\20&16\end{bmatrix}$$

and $5C=5\begin{bmatrix}1&-5\\-4&6\end{bmatrix}=\begin{bmatrix}5&-25\\-20&30\end{bmatrix}$

$$\therefore AB-5C=\begin{bmatrix}35&27\\20&16\end{bmatrix}-\begin{bmatrix}5&-25\\-20&30\end{bmatrix}=\begin{bmatrix}30&52\\40&-14\end{bmatrix}$$

Example 14. If $A=\begin{bmatrix}2&1\\0&-2\end{bmatrix}$, $B=\begin{bmatrix}4&1\\-3&-2\end{bmatrix}$ and $C=\begin{bmatrix}-3&2\\-1&4\end{bmatrix}$, then find $A^2+AC-5B$. **[ICSE 2014]**

Sol. Given, $A=\begin{bmatrix}2&1\\0&-2\end{bmatrix}$, $B=\begin{bmatrix}4&1\\-3&-2\end{bmatrix}$ and $C=\begin{bmatrix}-3&2\\-1&4\end{bmatrix}$

Now, $A^2=\begin{bmatrix}2&1\\0&-2\end{bmatrix}\begin{bmatrix}2&1\\0&-2\end{bmatrix}$
$$=\begin{bmatrix}2\times2+1\times0 & 2\times1+1\times(-2)\\0\times2+(-2)\times0 & 0\times1+(-2)\times(-2)\end{bmatrix}$$
[multiplying row by column]
$$=\begin{bmatrix}4+0&2-2\\0-0&0+4\end{bmatrix}=\begin{bmatrix}4&0\\0&4\end{bmatrix} \quad ...(i)$$

$$AC=\begin{bmatrix}2&1\\0&-2\end{bmatrix}\begin{bmatrix}-3&2\\-1&4\end{bmatrix}$$
$$=\begin{bmatrix}2\times(-3)+1\times(-1) & 2\times2+1\times4\\0\times(-3)+(-2)\times(-1) & 0\times2+(-2)\times4\end{bmatrix}$$
[multiplying row by column]
$$=\begin{bmatrix}-6-1&4+4\\0+2&0-8\end{bmatrix}=\begin{bmatrix}-7&8\\2&-8\end{bmatrix} \quad ...(ii)$$

and $5B=5\begin{bmatrix}4&1\\-3&-2\end{bmatrix}=\begin{bmatrix}5\times4&5\times1\\5\times(-3)&5\times(-2)\end{bmatrix}$
[multiplying each element of matrix by 5]
$$=\begin{bmatrix}20&5\\-15&-10\end{bmatrix} \quad ...(iii)$$

$$\therefore \; A^2+AC-5B=\begin{bmatrix}4&0\\0&4\end{bmatrix}+\begin{bmatrix}-7&8\\2&-8\end{bmatrix}-\begin{bmatrix}20&5\\-15&-10\end{bmatrix}$$
$$=\begin{bmatrix}4-7-20&0+8-5\\0+2+15&4-8+10\end{bmatrix}=\begin{bmatrix}-23&3\\17&6\end{bmatrix}$$

Example 15. If $A=\begin{bmatrix}3&x\\0&1\end{bmatrix}$ and $B=\begin{bmatrix}9&16\\0&-y\end{bmatrix}$, then find x and y, when $A^2=B$. **[ICSE 2015]**

Sol. Given, $A=\begin{bmatrix}3&x\\0&1\end{bmatrix}$ and $B=\begin{bmatrix}9&16\\0&-y\end{bmatrix}$

It is given that, $A^2=B$ ...(i)

Here, $A^2=A\cdot A=\begin{bmatrix}3&x\\0&1\end{bmatrix}\begin{bmatrix}3&x\\0&1\end{bmatrix}$
$$=\begin{bmatrix}9+0&3x+x\\0+0&0+1\end{bmatrix}=\begin{bmatrix}9&4x\\0&1\end{bmatrix}$$

Now, from Eq. (i), we get $A^2=B$
$$\Rightarrow \begin{bmatrix}9&4x\\0&1\end{bmatrix}=\begin{bmatrix}9&16\\0&-y\end{bmatrix}$$

On comparing the corresponding elements, we get
$$4x=16 \text{ and } 1=-y$$
$$\Rightarrow x=\frac{16}{4} \text{ and } y=-1$$
$$\Rightarrow x=4 \text{ and } y=-1$$

Example 16. If $A=\begin{bmatrix}2&0\\-1&7\end{bmatrix}$, $I=\begin{bmatrix}1&0\\0&1\end{bmatrix}$ and $A^2=9A+mI$, then find m. **[ICSE 2016]**

Sol. Given, $A=\begin{bmatrix}2&0\\-1&7\end{bmatrix}$ and $I=\begin{bmatrix}1&0\\0&1\end{bmatrix}$

Also, it is given that $A^2=9A+mI$ ...(i)

Here, $A^2=A\cdot A=\begin{bmatrix}2&0\\-1&7\end{bmatrix}\begin{bmatrix}2&0\\-1&7\end{bmatrix}$
$$=\begin{bmatrix}2\times2+0\times(-1) & 2\times0+0\times7\\-1\times2+7\times(-1) & -1\times0+7\times7\end{bmatrix}=\begin{bmatrix}4&0\\-9&49\end{bmatrix}$$

Now, from Eq. (i), we get
$$\begin{bmatrix}4&0\\-9&49\end{bmatrix}=9\begin{bmatrix}2&0\\-1&7\end{bmatrix}+m\begin{bmatrix}1&0\\0&1\end{bmatrix}$$
$$\Rightarrow \begin{bmatrix}4&0\\-9&49\end{bmatrix}=\begin{bmatrix}18&0\\-9&63\end{bmatrix}+\begin{bmatrix}m&0\\0&m\end{bmatrix}$$
$$\Rightarrow \begin{bmatrix}4&0\\-9&49\end{bmatrix}=\begin{bmatrix}18+m&0\\-9&63+m\end{bmatrix}$$

On comparing corresponding elements both sides, we get
$$18+m=4 \Rightarrow m=4-18=-14$$
and $$63+m=49 \Rightarrow m=49-63=-14$$
$$\therefore \quad m=-14$$

Example 17. If $A=\begin{bmatrix}1&3\\2&4\end{bmatrix}, B=\begin{bmatrix}1&2\\2&4\end{bmatrix}, C=\begin{bmatrix}4&1\\1&5\end{bmatrix}$ and $I=\begin{bmatrix}1&0\\0&1\end{bmatrix}$. Find $A(B+C)-14I$ [ICSE 2023]

Sol. Given, $A=\begin{bmatrix}1&3\\2&4\end{bmatrix}, B=\begin{bmatrix}1&2\\2&4\end{bmatrix}, C=\begin{bmatrix}4&1\\1&5\end{bmatrix}$

$$\because B+C=\begin{bmatrix}1&2\\2&4\end{bmatrix}+\begin{bmatrix}4&1\\1&5\end{bmatrix}=\begin{bmatrix}1+4&2+1\\2+1&4+5\end{bmatrix}=\begin{bmatrix}5&3\\3&9\end{bmatrix}$$

Now, $A(B+C)=\begin{bmatrix}1&3\\2&4\end{bmatrix}\begin{bmatrix}5&3\\3&9\end{bmatrix}$

$$=\begin{bmatrix}(1\times5)+(3\times3)&(1\times3)+(3\times9)\\(2\times5)+(4\times3)&(2\times3)+(4\times9)\end{bmatrix}$$

$$=\begin{bmatrix}14&30\\22&42\end{bmatrix}$$

and $14I=14\begin{bmatrix}1&0\\0&1\end{bmatrix}=\begin{bmatrix}14&0\\0&14\end{bmatrix}$

Therefore, $A(B+C)-14I=\begin{bmatrix}14&30\\22&42\end{bmatrix}-\begin{bmatrix}14&0\\0&14\end{bmatrix}$

$$=\begin{bmatrix}14-14&30-0\\22-0&42-14\end{bmatrix}$$

$$\Rightarrow \quad A(B+C)-14I=\begin{bmatrix}0&30\\22&28\end{bmatrix}$$

Properties of Multiplication of Matrices

Multiplication of matrices have following properties

(i) **Associative law** Matrix multiplication is associative, i.e. if A, B and C are three matrices, then $A(BC)=(AB)C$, whenever both sides are defined.

(ii) **Distributive law** Distributive law holds in matrix multiplication, i.e. if A, B and C are three matrices, then $A(B+C)=AB+AC$
or $(A+B)C=AC+BC$,
whenever both sides are defined.

(iii) **Existence of multiplicative identity** For every square matrix A, there exists identity matrix I of same order, such that $AI=A=IA$.
Here, the identity matrix I is called the multiplicative identity.

(iv) **Non-commutativity** Generally, matrix multiplication is not commutative, i.e. if A and B are two matrices such that AB and BA both exist, then it is not necessary that $AB=BA$.

(v) **Zero matrix as the product of two non-zero matrices** If the product of two matrices is a zero matrix, then it is not necessary that one of the matrices is zero matrix.

e.g. $A=\begin{bmatrix}0&-1\\0&2\end{bmatrix}\neq O$ and $B=\begin{bmatrix}3&5\\0&0\end{bmatrix}\neq O$.

But $AB=\begin{bmatrix}0&-1\\0&2\end{bmatrix}\begin{bmatrix}3&5\\0&0\end{bmatrix}=\begin{bmatrix}0&0\\0&0\end{bmatrix}=O$.

Note Multiplication of diagonal matrices of same order will be commutative.

Example 18. If $A=\begin{bmatrix}1&-2\\-4&2\end{bmatrix}$ and $B=\begin{bmatrix}2&3\\4&5\end{bmatrix}$, then show that $AB\neq BA$.

Sol. Given, $A=\begin{bmatrix}1&-2\\-4&2\end{bmatrix}$

and $B=\begin{bmatrix}2&3\\4&5\end{bmatrix}$

Now, $AB=\begin{bmatrix}1&-2\\-4&2\end{bmatrix}\begin{bmatrix}2&3\\4&5\end{bmatrix}$

$$=\begin{bmatrix}1\times2+(-2)\times4&1\times3+(-2)\times5\\(-4)\times2+2\times4&(-4)\times3+2\times5\end{bmatrix}$$

[multiplying row by column]

$$=\begin{bmatrix}2-8&3-10\\-8+8&-12+10\end{bmatrix}$$

$$\Rightarrow \quad AB=\begin{bmatrix}-6&-7\\0&-2\end{bmatrix} \quad \text{...(i)}$$

and $BA=\begin{bmatrix}2&3\\4&5\end{bmatrix}\begin{bmatrix}1&-2\\-4&2\end{bmatrix}$

$$=\begin{bmatrix}2\times1+3\times(-4)&2\times(-2)+3\times2\\4\times1+5\times(-4)&4\times(-2)+5\times2\end{bmatrix}$$

[multiplying row by column]

$$=\begin{bmatrix}2-12&-4+6\\4-20&-8+10\end{bmatrix}$$

$$\Rightarrow \quad BA=\begin{bmatrix}-10&2\\-16&2\end{bmatrix} \quad \text{...(ii)}$$

From Eqs. (i) and (ii), we get

$AB\neq BA$ **Hence proved.**

Solving the Matrix Equation

In order to solve equation of the type $A+kX=B$, where k is a scalar and A, B, X (unknown) are matrices of same order, take the unknown matrix on LHS with unity coefficient and shift rest of the matrices to the RHS of the equation. Simplify the RHS, to get the unknown matrix.

Example 19. If $A=\begin{bmatrix}1 & 3\\ 3 & 4\end{bmatrix}, B=\begin{bmatrix}-2 & 1\\ -3 & 2\end{bmatrix}$ and $A^2-5B^2=5C$, then find matrix C, where C is a 2×2 matrix. **[ICSE 2017]**

Sol. Given, $A=\begin{bmatrix}1 & 3\\ 3 & 4\end{bmatrix}$ and $B=\begin{bmatrix}-2 & 1\\ -3 & 2\end{bmatrix}$

Also, we have $A^2-5B^2=5C$

$$\therefore \quad C=\frac{1}{5}A^2-B^2$$

Here, $A^2=A\cdot A=\begin{bmatrix}1 & 3\\ 3 & 4\end{bmatrix}\begin{bmatrix}1 & 3\\ 3 & 4\end{bmatrix}=\begin{bmatrix}1+9 & 3+12\\ 3+12 & 9+16\end{bmatrix}=\begin{bmatrix}10 & 15\\ 15 & 25\end{bmatrix}$

$$\Rightarrow \frac{1}{5}A^2=\frac{1}{5}\begin{bmatrix}10 & 15\\ 15 & 25\end{bmatrix}=\begin{bmatrix}2 & 3\\ 3 & 5\end{bmatrix}$$

and $B^2=B\cdot B=\begin{bmatrix}-2 & 1\\ -3 & 2\end{bmatrix}\begin{bmatrix}-2 & 1\\ -3 & 2\end{bmatrix}$

$$=\begin{bmatrix}4-3 & -2+2\\ 6-6 & -3+4\end{bmatrix}=\begin{bmatrix}1 & 0\\ 0 & 1\end{bmatrix}$$

$$\therefore \quad C=\frac{1}{5}A^2-B^2=\begin{bmatrix}2 & 3\\ 3 & 5\end{bmatrix}-\begin{bmatrix}1 & 0\\ 0 & 1\end{bmatrix}$$

$$=\begin{bmatrix}2-1 & 3-0\\ 3-0 & 5-1\end{bmatrix}=\begin{bmatrix}1 & 3\\ 3 & 4\end{bmatrix}$$

Example 20. Given matrix $B=\begin{bmatrix}1 & 1\\ 8 & 3\end{bmatrix}$. Find the matrix X, if $X=B^2-4B$. Hence, solve for a and b, given that $X\begin{bmatrix}a\\ b\end{bmatrix}=\begin{bmatrix}5\\ 50\end{bmatrix}$. **[ICSE 2017]**

Sol. Given, $B=\begin{bmatrix}1 & 1\\ 8 & 3\end{bmatrix}$

We have, $X=B^2-4B$

Now, $B^2=B\cdot B=\begin{bmatrix}1 & 1\\ 8 & 3\end{bmatrix}\begin{bmatrix}1 & 1\\ 8 & 3\end{bmatrix}=\begin{bmatrix}1+8 & 1+3\\ 8+24 & 8+9\end{bmatrix}$

$$=\begin{bmatrix}9 & 4\\ 32 & 17\end{bmatrix}$$

and $4B=4\begin{bmatrix}1 & 1\\ 8 & 3\end{bmatrix}=\begin{bmatrix}4 & 4\\ 32 & 12\end{bmatrix}$

$$\therefore \quad X=B^2-4B=\begin{bmatrix}9 & 4\\ 32 & 17\end{bmatrix}-\begin{bmatrix}4 & 4\\ 32 & 12\end{bmatrix}$$

$$=\begin{bmatrix}9-4 & 4-4\\ 32-32 & 17-12\end{bmatrix}=\begin{bmatrix}5 & 0\\ 0 & 5\end{bmatrix}$$

Given, $X\begin{bmatrix}a\\ b\end{bmatrix}=\begin{bmatrix}5\\ 50\end{bmatrix}$

$$\therefore \quad \begin{bmatrix}5 & 0\\ 0 & 5\end{bmatrix}\begin{bmatrix}a\\ b\end{bmatrix}=\begin{bmatrix}5\\ 50\end{bmatrix}$$

$$\Rightarrow \quad \begin{bmatrix}5a+0\\ 0+5b\end{bmatrix}=\begin{bmatrix}5\\ 50\end{bmatrix}$$

$$\begin{bmatrix}5a\\ 5b\end{bmatrix}=\begin{bmatrix}5\\ 50\end{bmatrix}$$

On comparing corresponding elements both sides, we get

$$5a=5\Rightarrow a=1 \text{ and } 5b=50\Rightarrow b=10$$

Example 21. Given $\begin{bmatrix}4 & 2\\ -1 & 1\end{bmatrix}M=6I$, where M is a matrix and I is unit matrix of order 2×2.

(i) State the order of matrix M.

(ii) Find the matrix M.

Sol. We have,

$$\begin{bmatrix}4 & 2\\ -1 & 1\end{bmatrix}M=6I \quad \text{...(A)}$$

(i) Since, $\begin{bmatrix}4 & 2\\ -1 & 1\end{bmatrix}$ is a order of 2×2 and right side of the equation I is also a 2×2 order. So, the matrix M should be the order of 2×2.

(ii) Let $M=\begin{bmatrix}a & b\\ c & d\end{bmatrix}$

From Eq. (A), we get

$$\begin{bmatrix}4 & 2\\ -1 & 1\end{bmatrix}\begin{bmatrix}a & b\\ c & d\end{bmatrix}=6\begin{bmatrix}1 & 0\\ 0 & 1\end{bmatrix}$$

$$\Rightarrow \quad \begin{bmatrix}4a+2c & 4b+2d\\ -a+c & -b+d\end{bmatrix}=\begin{bmatrix}6 & 0\\ 0 & 6\end{bmatrix}$$

On comparing corresponding elements both sides, we get

$$4a+2c=6 \quad \text{...(i)}$$

$$4b+2d=0 \quad \text{...(ii)}$$

$$-a+c=0 \quad \text{...(iii)}$$

and $$-b+d=6 \quad \text{...(iv)}$$

On solving Eqs. (i) and (iii), we get

$$a=1 \text{ and } c=1$$

Now, on solving Eqs. (ii) and (iv), we get

$$b=-2 \text{ and } d=4$$

$$\therefore \quad M=\begin{bmatrix}1 & -2\\ 1 & 4\end{bmatrix}$$

Example 22. Given matrices $A=\begin{bmatrix}4\sin 30^\circ & \cos 0^\circ\\ \cos 0^\circ & 4\sin 30^\circ\end{bmatrix}$ and $B=\begin{bmatrix}4\\ 5\end{bmatrix}$. If $AX=B$, then

(i) write the order of matrix X.

(ii) find the matrix X. **[ICSE 2016]**

Sol.

(i) Given, $A=\begin{bmatrix}4\sin 30^\circ & \cos 0^\circ\\ \cos 0^\circ & 4\sin 30^\circ\end{bmatrix}_{2\times 2}$ and $B=\begin{bmatrix}4\\ 5\end{bmatrix}_{2\times 1}$

Also, we have

$$AX=B$$

Since, product of matrices A and X are possible.

$\therefore$ Number of columns in A = Number of rows in X

$\Rightarrow$ Number of rows in X is 2.

Since, product of matrices A and X results a matrix B, which have order 2×1.

$\because$ Number of columns in matrix X should be same as in matrix B.

$\therefore$ Number of columns in matrix $X=1$

Thus, order of matrix X is 2×1.

(ii) We have, $A = \begin{bmatrix} 4\sin 30^\circ & \cos 0^\circ \\ \cos 0^\circ & 4\sin 30^\circ \end{bmatrix} = \begin{bmatrix} 2 & 1 \\ 1 & 2 \end{bmatrix}$

$\left[\because \sin 30^\circ = \frac{1}{2}, \cos 0^\circ = 1\right]$

Let $X = \begin{bmatrix} x_1 \\ x_2 \end{bmatrix}_{2\times 1}$.

Then, $AX = B \Rightarrow \begin{bmatrix} 2 & 1 \\ 1 & 2 \end{bmatrix}\begin{bmatrix} x_1 \\ x_2 \end{bmatrix} = \begin{bmatrix} 4 \\ 5 \end{bmatrix} \Rightarrow \begin{bmatrix} 2x_1 + x_2 \\ x_1 + 2x_2 \end{bmatrix} = \begin{bmatrix} 4 \\ 5 \end{bmatrix}$

On comparing corresponding elements both sides, we get

$2x_1 + x_2 = 4$ ...(i)

and $x_1 + 2x_2 = 5$ ...(ii)

On solving Eqs. (i) and (ii), we get

$x_1 = 1$ and $x_2 = 2$

$\therefore X = \begin{bmatrix} 1 \\ 2 \end{bmatrix}$

Exercise 8.2

1. If $A = \begin{bmatrix} 2 & 3 \\ 2 & 1 \end{bmatrix}$, $B = \begin{bmatrix} 6 & -5 \\ -1 & 2 \end{bmatrix}$ and $C = \begin{bmatrix} 4 & 0 \\ 2 & 1 \end{bmatrix}$, then find

(i) $A + B$ (ii) $C + A$

2. If $C = \begin{bmatrix} 4 & 7 \\ 9 & 8 \end{bmatrix}$, $D = \begin{bmatrix} 3 & 0 \\ 0 & 3 \end{bmatrix}$ and $E = \begin{bmatrix} 0 & 1 \\ 0 & 2 \end{bmatrix}$, then find

(i) $C - D$ (ii) $D - E$

3. Find the values of 'x' and 'y', if

$2\begin{bmatrix} x & 7 \\ 9 & y-5 \end{bmatrix} + \begin{bmatrix} 6 & -7 \\ 4 & 5 \end{bmatrix} = \begin{bmatrix} 10 & 7 \\ 22 & 15 \end{bmatrix}$ **[ICSE 2018]**

4. If $C = \begin{bmatrix} 1 & 2 \\ 0 & 5 \end{bmatrix}$ and $D = \begin{bmatrix} 1 & -2 \\ -1 & 3 \end{bmatrix}$, then find the product CD.

5. If $A = \begin{bmatrix} 3 & 5 \\ 4 & -2 \end{bmatrix}$ and $B = \begin{bmatrix} 2 \\ 4 \end{bmatrix}$. Is the product AB possible? Give reason. If yes, then find their product. **[ICSE 2011]**

6. Evaluate $\begin{bmatrix} 4\sin 30^\circ & 2\cos 60^\circ \\ \sin 90^\circ & 2\cos 0^\circ \end{bmatrix}\begin{bmatrix} 4 & 5 \\ 5 & 4 \end{bmatrix}$. **[ICSE 2010]**

7. Evaluate

$\begin{bmatrix} 2\cos 60^\circ & -2\sin 30^\circ \\ -\tan 45^\circ & \cos 0^\circ \end{bmatrix}\begin{bmatrix} \cot 45^\circ & \operatorname{cosec} 30^\circ \\ \sec 60^\circ & \sin 90^\circ \end{bmatrix}$.

8. If $A = \begin{bmatrix} 1 & 2 \\ 2 & -1 \end{bmatrix}$ and $B = \begin{bmatrix} 1 & 0 \\ 2 & 1 \end{bmatrix}$, then find the value of $(A + B)(A - B)$.

9. Given, $A = \begin{bmatrix} 3 & -2 \\ -1 & 4 \end{bmatrix}$, $B = \begin{bmatrix} 6 \\ 1 \end{bmatrix}$, $C = \begin{bmatrix} -4 \\ 5 \end{bmatrix}$ and $D = \begin{bmatrix} 2 \\ 2 \end{bmatrix}$.

Find $AB + 2C - 4D$. **[ICSE 2010]**

10. Find the value of x, given that $A^2 = B$, $A = \begin{bmatrix} 2 & 12 \\ 0 & 1 \end{bmatrix}$ and $B = \begin{bmatrix} 4 & x \\ 0 & 1 \end{bmatrix}$. **[ICSE 2005]**

11. If $X = \begin{bmatrix} -1 & 1 \\ x & y \end{bmatrix}$ and $X^2 = I$, then find the values of x and y.

12. If $X = \begin{bmatrix} \sin^2\theta & -1 \\ -\sec^2\theta & 2 \end{bmatrix}$ and $Y = \begin{bmatrix} -\cos^2\theta & 0 \\ -\tan^2\theta & 2 \end{bmatrix}$, then find the value of matrix A, if $A + X = Y$.

13. If $A = \begin{bmatrix} 3 & 0 \\ 5 & 1 \end{bmatrix}$ and $B = \begin{bmatrix} -4 & 2 \\ 1 & 0 \end{bmatrix}$. Find $A^2 - 2AB + B^2$.

14. Given, $\begin{bmatrix} 2 & 1 \\ -3 & 4 \end{bmatrix} X = \begin{bmatrix} 7 \\ 6 \end{bmatrix}$, then find

(i) the order of the matrix X.

(ii) the matrix X. **[ICSE 2012]**

Chapter Practice

a. 1 Mark Questions

1. If $\begin{bmatrix} m+3 & 4 \\ n-4 & m+n \end{bmatrix} = \begin{bmatrix} 5 & 4 \\ 3 & 9 \end{bmatrix}$, then the values of m and n are

(a) $m = 2$ and $n = 7$ (b) $m = 7$ and $n = 2$
(c) $m = 3$ and $n = 6$ (d) $m = -2$ and $n = 7$

2. If $\begin{bmatrix} 2 & 0 \\ 0 & 4 \end{bmatrix}\begin{bmatrix} x \\ y \end{bmatrix} = \begin{bmatrix} 2 \\ -8 \end{bmatrix}$, then the values of x and y respectively, are **[ICSE 2023]**

(a) 1, – 2 (b) – 2, 1
(c) 1, 2 (d) – 2, – 1

3. If $A = \begin{bmatrix} 0 & 2 \\ 2 & 0 \end{bmatrix}$, then A^2

(a) $\begin{bmatrix} 2 & 2 \\ 0 & 0 \end{bmatrix}$ (b) $\begin{bmatrix} 0 & 0 \\ 2 & 2 \end{bmatrix}$ (c) $\begin{bmatrix} 4 & 0 \\ 0 & 4 \end{bmatrix}$ (d) $\begin{bmatrix} 0 & 4 \\ 4 & 0 \end{bmatrix}$

4. If $A = \begin{bmatrix} 3 & 1 \\ -1 & 2 \end{bmatrix}$, then A^3

(a) $\begin{bmatrix} 18 & 19 \\ 1 & -18 \end{bmatrix}$ (b) $\begin{bmatrix} 19 & 18 \\ -18 & 1 \end{bmatrix}$

(c) $\begin{bmatrix} 1 & 18 \\ 19 & -18 \end{bmatrix}$ (d) None of these

5. If $X = \begin{bmatrix} 2 & -2 \\ -2 & 2 \end{bmatrix}$ and $X^2 = \alpha X$, then value of α is

(a) 2 (b) 4 (c) –2 (d) –4

6. If $A = \begin{bmatrix} 3 & 5 \\ 1 & 4 \end{bmatrix}$, $B = \begin{bmatrix} 2 & 4 \\ 0 & 3 \end{bmatrix}$ and $C = \begin{bmatrix} 1 & -1 \\ 2 & 1 \end{bmatrix}$, then $5A - BC$ is equal to **[ICSE Semester-I 2021]**

(a) $\begin{bmatrix} -5 & -23 \\ 1 & 17 \end{bmatrix}$ (b) $\begin{bmatrix} 5 & 23 \\ 1 & 17 \end{bmatrix}$

(c) $\begin{bmatrix} -2 & 8 \\ -3 & 3 \end{bmatrix}$ (d) $\begin{bmatrix} 5 & 23 \\ -1 & 17 \end{bmatrix}$

7. If $A = \begin{bmatrix} 5 & 10 \\ 3 & -4 \end{bmatrix}$ and $I = \begin{bmatrix} 1 & 0 \\ 0 & 1 \end{bmatrix}$, then AI is equal to **[ICSE Semester-I 2021]**

(a) $\begin{bmatrix} 1 & 0 \\ 0 & 1 \end{bmatrix}$ (b) $\begin{bmatrix} 5 & 10 \\ -3 & 4 \end{bmatrix}$ (c) $\begin{bmatrix} 5 & 10 \\ 3 & -4 \end{bmatrix}$ (d) $\begin{bmatrix} 15 & 15 \\ -1 & -1 \end{bmatrix}$

8. The product AB of two matrices A and B is possible if **[ICSE Semester I 2021]**

(a) A and B have the same number of rows
(b) the number of columns of A is equal to the number of rows of B
(c) the number of rows of A is equal to the number of columns of B
(d) A and B have the same number of columns

b. 3 Marks Questions

9. If the matrix $A = \begin{bmatrix} a & 1 & x \\ 2 & \sqrt{3} & x^2 - y \\ 0 & 5 & -2/5 \end{bmatrix}$, then write

(i) the order of the matrix A.
(ii) the number of elements.
(iii) elements a_{23}, a_{31} and a_{12}.

10. Write the order of the following matrix.

$$A = \begin{bmatrix} 3 & 1 \\ 1 & 2 \end{bmatrix}$$

Also, find the elements a_{11}, a_{12}, a_{21} and a_{22}. Show that $a_{11} \times a_{22} = 3(a_{12} + a_{21})$.

11. If a matrix has 32 elements, then what are the possible orders it can have?

12. If a matrix has 40 elements, then what are the possible orders it can have? What, if it has 41 elements?

13. Construct a 1×3 order matrix, whose elements are given by $c_{ij} = 4i - 3j$.

14. Construct a 3×3 matrix, whose elements are given by $a_{ij} = \sin ix \operatorname{cosec} jx$.

15. Find the values of a, b, c and d, if

$$\begin{bmatrix} a & -2 \\ b & 7 \end{bmatrix} = \begin{bmatrix} 2 & c \\ 3 & 2c + d \end{bmatrix}.$$

16. Find the values of a, b, c and d, if

$$\begin{bmatrix} a+b & 3 \\ 4 & c \end{bmatrix} = \begin{bmatrix} 2 & d \\ b & 1 \end{bmatrix}.$$

17. If $\begin{bmatrix} x-3 & x-z-4 \\ z & x+y+z \end{bmatrix} = I$, where I is the identity matrix of same order, then find the values of x, y and z.

18. Find the values of x, y, a and b, when

$$\begin{bmatrix} x+y & a-b \\ a+b & 2x-3y \end{bmatrix} = \begin{bmatrix} 5 & 3 \\ -1 & -5 \end{bmatrix}.$$

19. $\begin{bmatrix} m^2 \\ n^2 \end{bmatrix} - 2\begin{bmatrix} m \\ 3n \end{bmatrix} = \begin{bmatrix} 3 \\ 12 \end{bmatrix}$, find the values of m and n.

20. If $\begin{bmatrix} 39 & 5x + 7y \\ 2x - 5y & 41 \end{bmatrix} = \begin{bmatrix} 7u + 9v & 1 \\ 16 & 9u + 7v \end{bmatrix}$, then find the value of $x + y + u + v$.

21. If $A=\begin{bmatrix}7 & 2\\-5 & 5\end{bmatrix}$, $B=\begin{bmatrix}0 & 1\\1 & 0\end{bmatrix}$ and $C=\begin{bmatrix}-9 & 1\\0 & -7\end{bmatrix}$, then find

(i) $A+B$ (ii) $B+C$ (iii) $C+A$

22. If $P=\begin{bmatrix}4 & 0\\-10 & 7\end{bmatrix}$, $Q=\begin{bmatrix}3 & 10\\0 & 1\end{bmatrix}$ and $R=\begin{bmatrix}8 & 5\\7 & 1\end{bmatrix}$, then find the value of each of the following.

(i) $P-Q$ (ii) $Q-R$ (iii) $R-P$

23. If $E=\begin{bmatrix}3 & 1\\4 & 1\end{bmatrix}$, $F=\begin{bmatrix}-1 & 2\\-4 & 0\end{bmatrix}$ and $G=\begin{bmatrix}3 & 0\\0 & 3\end{bmatrix}$, then find

(i) $E+F+G$ (ii) $E-F-G$

24. If $A=\begin{bmatrix}2 & 0\\-1 & 2\end{bmatrix}$, $B=\begin{bmatrix}-3 & 1\\-2 & 2\end{bmatrix}$ and $C=\begin{bmatrix}4 & 7\\0 & 0\end{bmatrix}$, then find

(i) $2A-3B$

(ii) $3A+2B-C$

25. If $2\begin{bmatrix}3 & 4\\5 & x\end{bmatrix}+\begin{bmatrix}1 & y\\0 & 1\end{bmatrix}=\begin{bmatrix}7 & 0\\10 & 5\end{bmatrix}$, then find the values of x and y.

26. If $A=\begin{bmatrix}1 & 3\\2 & -1\end{bmatrix}$, find $f(A)$, where $f(x)=x^3+2x^2-x$.

C. 4/5 Marks Questions

27. Find x, y, z and t, if

$$2\begin{bmatrix}x & z\\y & t\end{bmatrix}+3\begin{bmatrix}1 & -1\\0 & 2\end{bmatrix}=3\begin{bmatrix}3 & 5\\4 & 6\end{bmatrix}.$$

28. If $A=\begin{bmatrix}ab & b^2\\-a^2 & -ab\end{bmatrix}$, then prove that $A^2=\begin{bmatrix}0 & 0\\0 & 0\end{bmatrix}$.

29. If $A=\begin{bmatrix}1 & 2\\2 & 3\end{bmatrix}$, $B=\begin{bmatrix}2 & 1\\3 & 2\end{bmatrix}$

and $C=\begin{bmatrix}1 & 3\\3 & 1\end{bmatrix}$, then find $C(B-A)$.

30. If $P=\begin{bmatrix}4 & 1\\-1 & 2\end{bmatrix}$, then prove that $6P-P^2=9I_2$.

31. If $P=\begin{bmatrix}2 & -2\\-3 & 4\end{bmatrix}$, then evaluate $(-P^2+6P)$.

32. If $A=\begin{bmatrix}3 & 1\\-1 & 2\end{bmatrix}$ and $I=\begin{bmatrix}1 & 0\\0 & 1\end{bmatrix}$, then find $A^2-5A+7I$. **[ICSE 2012]**

33. If $A=\begin{bmatrix}2 & 3\\5 & 7\end{bmatrix}$, $B=\begin{bmatrix}0 & 4\\-1 & 7\end{bmatrix}$ and $C=\begin{bmatrix}1 & 0\\-1 & 4\end{bmatrix}$, find $AC+B^2-10C$. **[ICSE 2018]**

34. Let $A=\begin{bmatrix}1 & 0\\2 & 1\end{bmatrix}$, $B=\begin{bmatrix}2 & 3\\-1 & 0\end{bmatrix}$, then find A^2+AB+B^2. **[ICSE 2007]**

35. If $A=\begin{bmatrix}8 & 6\\-2 & 4\end{bmatrix}$ and $B=\begin{bmatrix}-3 & 5\\1 & 0\end{bmatrix}$, then solve for 2×2 matrix X, such that $X-B=A$.

36. If $[A\ B]\begin{bmatrix}A\\B\end{bmatrix}=[25]$ and $[-A\ B]\begin{bmatrix}2A\\B\end{bmatrix}=[-2]$, find the values of A and B, if

(i) $A, B \in W$ (whole number)

(ii) $A, B \in Z$ (integers)

37. If $\begin{bmatrix}1 & 4\\-2 & 3\end{bmatrix}+2M=3\begin{bmatrix}3 & 2\\0 & -3\end{bmatrix}$, then find the matrix M. **[ICSE 2008]**

38. Given, $A=\begin{bmatrix}2 & -1\\2 & 0\end{bmatrix}$, $B=\begin{bmatrix}-3 & 2\\4 & 0\end{bmatrix}$ and $C=\begin{bmatrix}1 & 0\\0 & 2\end{bmatrix}$, then find a matrix X, such that $A+X=2B+C$.

39. Solve the matrix equation $\begin{bmatrix}2 & 1\\5 & 0\end{bmatrix}-2X=\begin{bmatrix}-7 & 4\\2 & 6\end{bmatrix}$.

40. Given, $A=\begin{bmatrix}2 & -6\\2 & 0\end{bmatrix}$, $B=\begin{bmatrix}-3 & 2\\4 & 0\end{bmatrix}$ and $C=\begin{bmatrix}4 & 0\\0 & 2\end{bmatrix}$. Find the matrix X, such that $A+2X=2B+C$. **[ICSE 2013]**

41. Find a and b, if $\begin{bmatrix}1 & 0\\-2 & 4\end{bmatrix}\begin{bmatrix}1\\a\end{bmatrix}=\begin{bmatrix}b\\-3\end{bmatrix}$.

42. Find x and y, if $\begin{bmatrix}-2 & 0\\3 & 1\end{bmatrix}\begin{bmatrix}-1\\2x\end{bmatrix}+3\begin{bmatrix}-2\\1\end{bmatrix}=2\begin{bmatrix}y\\3\end{bmatrix}$. **[ICSE 2014]**

43. Find x and y, if $\begin{bmatrix}3 & -2\\-1 & 4\end{bmatrix}\begin{bmatrix}2x\\1\end{bmatrix}+2\begin{bmatrix}-4\\5\end{bmatrix}=4\begin{bmatrix}2\\y\end{bmatrix}$. **[ICSE 2003]**

44. If $A=\begin{bmatrix}3 & 0\\0 & 2\end{bmatrix}$, $B=\begin{bmatrix}x & y\\0 & z\end{bmatrix}$ and $AB=(A+B)$, then find the values of x, y and z.

45. If $A=\begin{bmatrix}1 & -1\\2 & -1\end{bmatrix}$, $B=\begin{bmatrix}x & 1\\4 & -1\end{bmatrix}$ and $(A+B)^2=A^2+B^2$, then find the value of x.

46. If A, B and C are matrices of the same order, then state with reason, whether the following are true or false.

(i) Addition of matrices is associative

(ii) Addition of matrices is commutative

(iii) Multiplication of matrices is commutative

(iv) Multiplication of matrices is associative

(v) Multiplication of matrices is distributive with respect to addition.

47. Let $X = \begin{bmatrix} 3 & 2 \\ 0 & 5 \end{bmatrix}$ and $Y = \begin{bmatrix} 1 & 0 \\ 1 & 2 \end{bmatrix}$. Find
(i) $(X + Y)(X - Y)$
(ii) $X^2 - Y^2$
(iii) Is $(X + Y)(X - Y) = X^2 - Y^2$

d. 6 Marks Questions

48. Find x and y, if $\begin{bmatrix} x & 3x \\ y & 4y \end{bmatrix}\begin{bmatrix} 2 \\ 1 \end{bmatrix} = \begin{bmatrix} 5 \\ 12 \end{bmatrix}$. **[ICSE 2013, 02]**

49. Find x and y, if $\begin{bmatrix} 2x & x \\ y & 3y \end{bmatrix}\begin{bmatrix} 3 \\ 2 \end{bmatrix} = \begin{bmatrix} 16 \\ 9 \end{bmatrix}$. **[ICSE 2009]**

50. If $A = \begin{bmatrix} \cot 45^\circ & 0 \\ -1 & 1 \end{bmatrix}$ and $B = \begin{bmatrix} 1 & \cos 0^\circ \\ 4 & 5 \end{bmatrix}$, then find the value of the following.
(i) AB
(ii) $B^2 - A^2$

51. If $X = \begin{bmatrix} 1 & -2 \\ 2 & -1 \end{bmatrix}$ and $Y = \begin{bmatrix} 3 & 2 \\ -2 & 1 \end{bmatrix}$, find $2Y - X^2$.

52. If $A = \begin{bmatrix} 1 & -1 \\ 2 & -2 \end{bmatrix}$, $B = \begin{bmatrix} 4 & 5 \\ 3 & 3 \end{bmatrix}$ and $C = \begin{bmatrix} 2 & 7 \\ 1 & 5 \end{bmatrix}$, then show that $AB = AC$. What conclusion can you find?

53. If $A = \begin{bmatrix} 3 & 0 \\ 0 & -3 \end{bmatrix}$, find A^2 and A^3.

54. If $X = \begin{bmatrix} 1 & 3 \\ -2 & 0 \end{bmatrix}$, $Y = \begin{bmatrix} 2 & 4 \\ 5 & 1 \end{bmatrix}$ and $Z = \begin{bmatrix} -3 & 4 \\ 6 & 0 \end{bmatrix}$, verify that
(i) $(XY)Z = X(YZ)$
(ii) $X(Y + Z) = XY + XZ$

55. If $A = \begin{bmatrix} 6 & 2 \\ 5 & -4 \end{bmatrix}$ and $B = \begin{bmatrix} 1 & 2 \\ -5 & 1 \end{bmatrix}$, then find a matrix X, such that $2A + 3B - 5X = O$.

56. Find the matrix A of order 2×2 which satisfies the equation
$$\begin{bmatrix} 3 & 7 \\ 2 & 4 \end{bmatrix}\begin{bmatrix} 0 & 2 \\ 5 & 3 \end{bmatrix} + 2A = \begin{bmatrix} 1 & -5 \\ -4 & 6 \end{bmatrix}$$

57. If $A = \begin{bmatrix} 2 & 3 \\ 1 & 2 \end{bmatrix}$, then show that $A^3 - 4A^2 + A = O$.

58. If $A = \begin{bmatrix} 2 & x \\ -3 & 5 \end{bmatrix}$, $B = \begin{bmatrix} -2 & 3 \\ 7 & y \end{bmatrix}$ and $C = \begin{bmatrix} z & 9 \\ -1 & -11 \end{bmatrix}$ and $5A + 2B = C$, then the values of x, y and z.

59. If $\begin{bmatrix} x^2 \\ y^2 \end{bmatrix} - 3\begin{bmatrix} x \\ 2y \end{bmatrix} = \begin{bmatrix} -2 \\ 9 \end{bmatrix}$, find the values of x and y.

60. If $A = \begin{bmatrix} p & 0 \\ 0 & 2 \end{bmatrix}$, $B = \begin{bmatrix} 0 & -q \\ 1 & 0 \end{bmatrix}$, $C = \begin{bmatrix} 2 & -2 \\ 2 & 2 \end{bmatrix}$ and $BA = C^2$, then find the values of p and q. **[ICSE 2008]**

61. If $A = \begin{bmatrix} \alpha & 0 \\ 1 & 1 \end{bmatrix}$ and $B = \begin{bmatrix} 1 & 0 \\ 5 & 1 \end{bmatrix}$, then find the value of α, for which $A^2 = B$.

62. If $A = \begin{bmatrix} 2 & -3 \\ p & q \end{bmatrix}$, then find p and q, so that $A^2 = I$.

63. If $X = \begin{bmatrix} 2 & 6 \\ 3 & 9 \end{bmatrix}$ and $Y = \begin{bmatrix} 3 & m \\ n & 2 \end{bmatrix}$, find m and n such that XY is null matrix.

64. Let $A = \begin{bmatrix} 3 & 2 \\ -1 & 1 \end{bmatrix}$ and $B = \begin{bmatrix} 14 & 3 \\ 2 & 4 \end{bmatrix}$, then find the matrix C, such that $AC = B$.

65. If I is the unit matrix of order 2×2. Find the matrix X, such that
(i) $X - 2I = 3\begin{bmatrix} -1 & 0 \\ 4 & 1 \end{bmatrix}$
(ii) $5X + 3I = 4\begin{bmatrix} 2 & -5 \\ 0 & -3 \end{bmatrix}$

66. State with reason, whether the following are true or false X, Y and Z are matrices of order 2×2
(i) $X \cdot Y = Y \cdot X$
(ii) $X \cdot (Y \cdot Z) = (X \cdot Y) \cdot Z$
(iii) $(X + Y)^2 = X^2 + 2XY + Y^2$
(iv) $X \cdot (Y + Z) = X \cdot Y + X \cdot Z$

67. If $A = \begin{bmatrix} 1 & 0 \\ -1 & 7 \end{bmatrix}$ and I is the unit matrix of same order as A, then find the value of k, so that $A^2 = 8A + kI$.

68. Solve the following matrix equation.
$$\begin{bmatrix} x & 1 \end{bmatrix}\begin{bmatrix} 1 & 0 \\ -2 & -3 \end{bmatrix}\begin{bmatrix} x \\ 5 \end{bmatrix} = 0$$

69. If $A = \begin{bmatrix} 0 & 1 \\ -1 & 0 \end{bmatrix}$, then find the real values of x and y, such that $(xI + yA)^2 = A$.

70. If $A = \begin{bmatrix} 0 & 1 \\ 0 & 0 \end{bmatrix}$, show that $(aI + bA)^3 = a^3I + 3a^2bA$, where I is the unit matrix of order 2.

Hints and Answers

Exercise 8.1

1. (i) 1×1 (ii) 2×1
(iii) 1×2 (iv) 2×2

2. (i) **Hint** Here, A has two rows and two columns.
Ans. 2×2
(ii) **Hint** Number of elements in an $m \times n$ matrix $= mn$.
Ans. 4
(iii) **Hint** a_{21} = Element of second row and first column.
a_{12} = Element of first row and second column.
a_{22} = Element of second row and second column.
Ans. $a_{21} = y^2$, $a_{12} = x^2$ and $a_{22} = b$

3. **Hint** Do same as Example 1.
Ans. $1 \times 24, 2 \times 12, 3 \times 8, 4 \times 6, 6 \times 4, 8 \times 3, 12 \times 2, 24 \times 1$.

4. **Hint** Do same as Example 1.
Ans. $1 \times 28, 2 \times 14, 4 \times 7, 7 \times 4, 14 \times 2$ and 28×1; 1×13 and 13×1

5. **Hint** Do same as Example 2.
Ans. $\begin{bmatrix} 1 & 2 \\ 2 & 4 \end{bmatrix}_{2 \times 2}$

6. **Hint** Do same as Example 2.
Ans. $\begin{bmatrix} 0 & 1/9 \\ 1/9 & 0 \end{bmatrix}_{2 \times 2}$

7. (i) **Hint** Do same as Example 3 (iv).
Ans. Row matrix
(ii) **Hint** Do same as Example 3 (v).
Ans. Identity matrix
(iii) **Hint** Do same as Example 3 (iii).
Ans. Column matrix
(iv) **Hint** Do same as Example 3 (viii).
Ans. Rectangular matrix
(v) **Hint** Do same as Example 3 (vii).
Ans. Null matrix
(vi) **Hint** Do same as Example 3 (viii).
Ans. Rectangular matrix
(vii) **Hint** Do same as Example 3 (vi).
Ans. Scalar matrix

8. **Hint** Do same as Example 5.
Ans. (i) $x = 3$, $y = 6$ and $z = -4$
(ii) $x = 2$, $y = 3$, $z = -2$ and $u = 9$
(iii) $x = 2$, $y = 3$, $u = 1$ and $z = -2$
(iv) $x = 2$ and $y = 2$

9. **Hint** $\begin{bmatrix} 5-x \\ y+6 \end{bmatrix} = \begin{bmatrix} 0 \\ 0 \end{bmatrix}$.
Now, proceed as in Example 5.
Ans. $x = 5$, $y = -6$

Exercise 8.2

1. **Hint** Do same as Example 7.
Ans. (i) $\begin{bmatrix} 8 & -2 \\ 1 & 3 \end{bmatrix}$ (ii) $\begin{bmatrix} 6 & 3 \\ 4 & 2 \end{bmatrix}$

2. **Hint** Do same as Example 8.
Ans. (i) $\begin{bmatrix} 1 & 7 \\ 9 & 5 \end{bmatrix}$ (ii) $\begin{bmatrix} 3 & -1 \\ 0 & 1 \end{bmatrix}$

3. **Hint** Given that,

$$2\begin{bmatrix} x & 7 \\ 9 & y-5 \end{bmatrix} + \begin{bmatrix} 6 & -7 \\ 4 & 5 \end{bmatrix} = \begin{bmatrix} 10 & 7 \\ 22 & 15 \end{bmatrix}$$

$$\Rightarrow \begin{bmatrix} 2x & 14 \\ 18 & 2y-10 \end{bmatrix} + \begin{bmatrix} 6 & -7 \\ 4 & 5 \end{bmatrix} = \begin{bmatrix} 10 & 7 \\ 22 & 15 \end{bmatrix}$$

$$\Rightarrow \begin{bmatrix} 2x+6 & 7 \\ 22 & 2y-5 \end{bmatrix} = \begin{bmatrix} 10 & 7 \\ 22 & 15 \end{bmatrix}$$

Here, both matrices are equal, so we equate the corresponding elements.

$2x + 6 = 10 \Rightarrow 2x = 4$
and $2y - 5 = 15 \Rightarrow 2y = 20$
Ans. $x = 2$ and $y = 10$

4. **Hint** Do same as Example 12. **Ans.** $\begin{bmatrix} -1 & 4 \\ -5 & 15 \end{bmatrix}$

5. **Hint** Number of columns in A = Number of rows in B.
Ans. Yes; $AB = \begin{bmatrix} 26 \\ 0 \end{bmatrix}$

6. **Hint** Given, matrices can be written as

$$\begin{bmatrix} 4 \times \frac{1}{2} & 2 \times \frac{1}{2} \\ 1 & 2 \times 1 \end{bmatrix} \begin{bmatrix} 4 & 5 \\ 5 & 4 \end{bmatrix}$$

Ans. $\begin{bmatrix} 13 & 14 \\ 14 & 13 \end{bmatrix}$

7. **Hint** Write the given product as

$$\begin{bmatrix} 2 \times \frac{1}{2} & -2 \times \frac{1}{2} \\ -1 & 1 \end{bmatrix} \begin{bmatrix} 1 & 2 \\ 2 & 1 \end{bmatrix}$$ **Ans.** $\begin{bmatrix} -1 & 1 \\ 1 & -1 \end{bmatrix}$

8. **Hint** $(A + B)(A - B) = \begin{bmatrix} 2 & 2 \\ 4 & 0 \end{bmatrix} \begin{bmatrix} 0 & 2 \\ 0 & -2 \end{bmatrix}$ **Ans.** $\begin{bmatrix} 0 & 0 \\ 0 & 8 \end{bmatrix}$

9. **Hint** Do same as Example 14. **Ans.** $\begin{bmatrix} 0 \\ 0 \end{bmatrix}$

10. **Hint** Do same as Example 15. **Ans.** $x = 36$

11. **Hint** $X^2 = X \cdot X = \begin{bmatrix} -1 & 1 \\ x & y \end{bmatrix} \begin{bmatrix} -1 & 1 \\ x & y \end{bmatrix}$

$$= \begin{bmatrix} 1+x & -1+y \\ -x+xy & x+y^2 \end{bmatrix} = \begin{bmatrix} 1 & 0 \\ 0 & 1 \end{bmatrix}$$

Ans. $x = 0$, $y = 1$

12. **Hint** $A = Y - X$ **Ans.** $\begin{bmatrix} -1 & 1 \\ 1 & 0 \end{bmatrix}$

13. **Hint** Do same as Example 14.

Ans. $\begin{bmatrix} 51 & -20 \\ 54 & -17 \end{bmatrix}$

14. **Hint** Do same as Example 21.

Ans. (i) Order = 2×1 (ii) $X = \begin{bmatrix} 2 \\ 3 \end{bmatrix}$

Chapter Exercise

1. (a) $\begin{bmatrix} m+3 & 4 \\ n-4 & m+n \end{bmatrix} = \begin{bmatrix} 5 & 4 \\ 3 & 9 \end{bmatrix}$

On comparing both sides, we get

$$m + 3 = 5$$
$$\Rightarrow \quad m = 5 - 3 = 2$$
and $$n - 4 = 3$$
$$\Rightarrow \quad n = 3 + 4 = 7$$
$$\therefore \quad m = 2 \text{ and } n = 7$$

2. (a) $\because\ 2x + 0y = 2$

$$\Rightarrow \quad 2x = 2$$
$$\Rightarrow \quad x = 1 \quad \ldots\text{(i)}$$
$$\because \quad 0x + 4y = -8$$
$$\Rightarrow \quad 4y = -8$$
$$\Rightarrow \quad y = -2$$

Hence, $x = 1,\ y = -2$

3. (c) $A^2 = A \times A = \begin{bmatrix} 0 & 2 \\ 2 & 0 \end{bmatrix}\begin{bmatrix} 0 & 2 \\ 2 & 0 \end{bmatrix}$

$$A^2 = \begin{bmatrix} 0+4 & 0+0 \\ 0+0 & 4+0 \end{bmatrix} = \begin{bmatrix} 4 & 0 \\ 0 & 4 \end{bmatrix}$$

4. (b) $A = \begin{bmatrix} 3 & 1 \\ -1 & 2 \end{bmatrix}$

$$A^2 = \begin{bmatrix} 3 & 1 \\ -1 & 2 \end{bmatrix}\begin{bmatrix} 3 & 1 \\ -1 & 2 \end{bmatrix}$$
$$= \begin{bmatrix} 9-1 & 3+2 \\ -3-2 & -1+4 \end{bmatrix} = \begin{bmatrix} 8 & 5 \\ -5 & 3 \end{bmatrix}$$
$$A^3 = A^2 \cdot A = \begin{bmatrix} 8 & 5 \\ -5 & 3 \end{bmatrix}\begin{bmatrix} 3 & 1 \\ -1 & 2 \end{bmatrix}$$
$$= \begin{bmatrix} 24-5 & 8+10 \\ -15-3 & -5+6 \end{bmatrix}$$
$$A^3 = \begin{bmatrix} 19 & 18 \\ -18 & 1 \end{bmatrix}$$

5. (b) $X = \begin{bmatrix} 2 & -2 \\ -2 & 2 \end{bmatrix}$ and $X^2 = \alpha X$

$$X \cdot X = X^2 = \begin{bmatrix} 2 & -2 \\ -2 & 2 \end{bmatrix}\begin{bmatrix} 2 & -2 \\ -2 & 2 \end{bmatrix}$$
$$X^2 = \begin{bmatrix} 4+4 & -4-4 \\ -4-4 & 4+4 \end{bmatrix} = \begin{bmatrix} 8 & -8 \\ -8 & 8 \end{bmatrix}.$$

According to the question,

$$X^2 = \alpha X$$
$$\therefore \quad \begin{bmatrix} 8 & -8 \\ -8 & 8 \end{bmatrix} = \alpha \begin{bmatrix} 2 & -2 \\ -2 & 2 \end{bmatrix}$$

On comparing both sides, we get

$$\alpha = 4$$

6. (d) Given, $A = \begin{bmatrix} 3 & 5 \\ 1 & 4 \end{bmatrix}$, $B = \begin{bmatrix} 2 & 4 \\ 0 & 3 \end{bmatrix}$

and $C = \begin{bmatrix} 1 & -1 \\ 2 & 1 \end{bmatrix}$

$$\therefore \quad 5A - BC = 5\begin{bmatrix} 3 & 5 \\ 1 & 4 \end{bmatrix} - \begin{bmatrix} 2 & 4 \\ 0 & 3 \end{bmatrix}\begin{bmatrix} 1 & -1 \\ 2 & 1 \end{bmatrix}$$
$$= \begin{bmatrix} 15 & 25 \\ 5 & 20 \end{bmatrix} - \begin{bmatrix} 10 & 2 \\ 6 & 3 \end{bmatrix}$$
$$= \begin{bmatrix} 5 & 23 \\ -1 & 17 \end{bmatrix}$$

7. (c) Given, $A = \begin{bmatrix} 5 & 10 \\ 3 & -4 \end{bmatrix}$ and $I = \begin{bmatrix} 1 & 0 \\ 0 & 1 \end{bmatrix}$

$$\therefore \quad AI = \begin{bmatrix} 5 & 10 \\ 3 & -4 \end{bmatrix}\begin{bmatrix} 1 & 0 \\ 0 & 1 \end{bmatrix}$$
$$= \begin{bmatrix} 5 & 10 \\ 3 & -4 \end{bmatrix}$$

8. (b)

9. **Hint** Do same as Q. 2 of Exercise 8.1.

Ans. (i) 3×3 (ii) 9

(iii) $a_{23} = x^2 - y$, $a_{31} = 0$ and $a_{12} = 1$.

10. **Hint** Do same as Q. 2 of Exercise 8.1.

Ans. Order = 2×2;

$a_{11} = 3$, $a_{12} = 1$, $a_{21} = 1$ and $a_{22} = 2$

11. **Hint** Do same as Example 1.

Ans. $1 \times 32,\ 2 \times 16,\ 4 \times 8,\ 8 \times 4,\ 16 \times 2,\ 32 \times 1$

12. Do same as Example 1.

Ans. $1 \times 40,\ 2 \times 20,\ 4 \times 10,\ 5 \times 8,\ 8 \times 5,\ 10 \times 4,\ 20 \times 2,\ 40 \times 1$ and $1 \times 41,\ 41 \times 1$

13. **Hint** Do same as Example 2. **Ans.** $[1 \quad -2 \quad -5]$

14. **Hint** Do same as Example 2.

Ans. $\begin{bmatrix} 1 & \sin x \operatorname{cosec} 2x & \sin x \operatorname{cosec} 3x \\ \sin 2x \operatorname{cosec} x & 1 & \sin 2x \operatorname{cosec} 3x \\ \sin 3x \operatorname{cosec} x & \sin 3x \operatorname{cosec} 2x & 1 \end{bmatrix}$

15. **Hint** Do same as Example 5.

Ans. $a = 2,\ b = 3,\ c = -2$ and $d = 11$

16. **Hint** Do same as Example 5.

Ans. $a = -2,\ b = 4,\ c = 1$ and $d = 3$

17. **Hint** $\begin{bmatrix} x-3 & x-z-4 \\ z & x+y+z \end{bmatrix} = \begin{bmatrix} 1 & 0 \\ 0 & 1 \end{bmatrix}$

Now, proceed as in Example 5.

Ans. $x = 4,\ y = -3,\ z = 0$

18. **Hint** Do same as Example 5.

Ans. $x=2,\ y=3,\ a=1,\ b=-2$

19. **Hint** $\begin{bmatrix} m^2-2m \\ n^2-6n \end{bmatrix}=\begin{bmatrix} 3 \\ 12 \end{bmatrix}$

Ans. $m=-1$, 3 and $n=3\pm\sqrt{21}$

20. **Hint** Do same as Example 5.

Ans. $x+y+u+v=6$

21. **Hint** Do same as Example 7.

Ans. (i) $A+B=\begin{bmatrix} 7 & 3 \\ -4 & 5 \end{bmatrix}$ (ii) $B+C=\begin{bmatrix} -9 & 2 \\ 1 & -7 \end{bmatrix}$

(iii) $C+A=\begin{bmatrix} -2 & 3 \\ -5 & -2 \end{bmatrix}$

22. **Hint** Do same as Example 8.

Ans. (i) $P-Q=\begin{bmatrix} 1 & -10 \\ -10 & 6 \end{bmatrix}$

(ii) $Q-R=\begin{bmatrix} -5 & 5 \\ -7 & 0 \end{bmatrix}$ (iii) $R-P=\begin{bmatrix} 4 & 5 \\ 17 & -6 \end{bmatrix}$

23. (i) **Hint** $E+F+G=\begin{bmatrix} 3-1+3 & 1+2+0 \\ 4-4+0 & 1+0+3 \end{bmatrix}$

Ans. $E+F+G=\begin{bmatrix} 5 & 3 \\ 0 & 4 \end{bmatrix}$

(ii) **Hint** $E-F-G=\begin{bmatrix} 3-(-1)-3 & 1-2-0 \\ 4-(-4)-0 & 1-0-3 \end{bmatrix}$

Ans. $E-F-G=\begin{bmatrix} 1 & -1 \\ 8 & -2 \end{bmatrix}$

24. (i) **Hint** $2A=\begin{bmatrix} 2\times 2 & 2\times 0 \\ 2\times(-1) & 2\times 2 \end{bmatrix}$

and $3B=\begin{bmatrix} 3\times(-3) & 3\times 1 \\ 3\times(-2) & 3\times 2 \end{bmatrix}$

Ans. $2A-3B=\begin{bmatrix} 13 & -3 \\ 4 & -2 \end{bmatrix}$

(ii) $3A=\begin{bmatrix} 3\times 2 & 3\times 0 \\ 3\times(-1) & 3\times 2 \end{bmatrix}$

and $2B=\begin{bmatrix} 2\times(-3) & 2\times 1 \\ 2\times(-2) & 2\times 2 \end{bmatrix}$

Ans. $3A+2B-C=\begin{bmatrix} -4 & -5 \\ -7 & 10 \end{bmatrix}$

25. **Hint** $\begin{bmatrix} 7 & 8+y \\ 10 & 2x+1 \end{bmatrix}=\begin{bmatrix} 7 & 0 \\ 10 & 5 \end{bmatrix}$

Ans. $x=2$ and $y=-8$

26. **Hint** $A=\begin{bmatrix} 1 & 3 \\ 2 & -1 \end{bmatrix}$ and $f(x)=x^3+2x^2-x$

Then, $f(A)=A^3+2A^2-A$

$A^2=A\cdot A=\begin{bmatrix} 1 & 3 \\ 2 & -1 \end{bmatrix}\begin{bmatrix} 1 & 3 \\ 2 & -1 \end{bmatrix}=\begin{bmatrix} 7 & 0 \\ 0 & 7 \end{bmatrix}$

$A^3=A^2\cdot A=\begin{bmatrix} 7 & 0 \\ 0 & 7 \end{bmatrix}\begin{bmatrix} 1 & 3 \\ 2 & -1 \end{bmatrix}=\begin{bmatrix} 7 & 21 \\ 14 & -7 \end{bmatrix}$

Now, A^3+2A^2-A

$=\begin{bmatrix} 7 & 21 \\ 14 & -7 \end{bmatrix}+2\begin{bmatrix} 7 & 0 \\ 0 & 7 \end{bmatrix}-\begin{bmatrix} 1 & 3 \\ 2 & -1 \end{bmatrix}$

$=\begin{bmatrix} 7 & 21 \\ 14 & -7 \end{bmatrix}+\begin{bmatrix} 14 & 0 \\ 0 & 14 \end{bmatrix}-\begin{bmatrix} 1 & 3 \\ 2 & -1 \end{bmatrix}$

$=\begin{bmatrix} 21 & 21 \\ 14 & 7 \end{bmatrix}-\begin{bmatrix} 1 & 3 \\ 2 & -1 \end{bmatrix}=\begin{bmatrix} 20 & 18 \\ 12 & 8 \end{bmatrix}$

27. **Hint** $\begin{bmatrix} 2x+3 & 2z-3 \\ 2y & 2t+6 \end{bmatrix}=\begin{bmatrix} 9 & 15 \\ 12 & 18 \end{bmatrix}$

Ans. $x=3,\ y=6,\ z=9$ and $t=6$

28. **Hint** $A^2=\begin{bmatrix} ab & b^2 \\ -a^2 & -ab \end{bmatrix}\begin{bmatrix} ab & b^2 \\ -a^2 & -ab \end{bmatrix}$

29. **Hint** $C(B-A)=\begin{bmatrix} 1 & 3 \\ 3 & 1 \end{bmatrix}\left(\begin{bmatrix} 2 & 1 \\ 3 & 2 \end{bmatrix}-\begin{bmatrix} 1 & 2 \\ 2 & 3 \end{bmatrix}\right)$

Ans. $\begin{bmatrix} 4 & -4 \\ 4 & -4 \end{bmatrix}$

30. **Hint** $6P-P^2=6P-P\cdot P=\begin{bmatrix} 24 & 6 \\ -6 & 12 \end{bmatrix}-\begin{bmatrix} 15 & 6 \\ -6 & 3 \end{bmatrix}$

31. **Hint** $-\left(\begin{bmatrix} 2 & -2 \\ -3 & 4 \end{bmatrix}\begin{bmatrix} 2 & -2 \\ -3 & 4 \end{bmatrix}\right)+6\begin{bmatrix} 2 & -2 \\ -3 & 4 \end{bmatrix}=\begin{bmatrix} 2 & 0 \\ 0 & 2 \end{bmatrix}$

Ans. $2I_2$

32. **Hint** $A^2=A\times A=\begin{bmatrix} 3 & 1 \\ -1 & 2 \end{bmatrix}\begin{bmatrix} 3 & 1 \\ -1 & 2 \end{bmatrix}=\begin{bmatrix} 8 & 5 \\ -5 & 3 \end{bmatrix}$

$A^2-5A+7I=\begin{bmatrix} 8 & 5 \\ -5 & 3 \end{bmatrix}-5\begin{bmatrix} 3 & 1 \\ -1 & 2 \end{bmatrix}+7\begin{bmatrix} 1 & 0 \\ 0 & 1 \end{bmatrix}$

Ans. $\begin{bmatrix} 0 & 0 \\ 0 & 0 \end{bmatrix}=O$

33. **Hint** Do same as Example 14.

Ans. $\begin{bmatrix} -15 & 40 \\ 1 & 33 \end{bmatrix}$

34. **Hint** $A^2+AB+B^2=A\cdot A+A\cdot B+B\cdot B$

$=\begin{bmatrix} 1 & 0 \\ 4 & 1 \end{bmatrix}+\begin{bmatrix} 2 & 3 \\ 3 & 6 \end{bmatrix}+\begin{bmatrix} 1 & 6 \\ -2 & -3 \end{bmatrix}$

Ans. $\begin{bmatrix} 4 & 9 \\ 5 & 4 \end{bmatrix}$

35. **Hint** $X=A+B$

Ans. $X=\begin{bmatrix} 5 & 11 \\ -1 & 4 \end{bmatrix}$

36. **Hint** $[A\ B]\begin{bmatrix} A \\ B \end{bmatrix}=[25]$

$\Rightarrow\quad A^2+B^2=25$ ...(i)

$[-A\ B]\begin{bmatrix} 2A \\ B \end{bmatrix}=[-2]$

$\Rightarrow\ -2A^2+B^2=-2$ ...(ii)

From Eqs. (i) and (ii),

$A=\pm 3$ and $B=\pm 4$

Ans. (i) $A=3$ and $B=4$ (ii) $A=\pm 3$ and $B=\pm 4$

37. Hint $2M = 3\begin{bmatrix}3 & 2\\0 & -3\end{bmatrix} - \begin{bmatrix}1 & 4\\-2 & 3\end{bmatrix}$ **Ans.** $M = \begin{bmatrix}4 & 1\\1 & -6\end{bmatrix}$

38. Hint $X = 2B + C - A$ **Ans.** $X = \begin{bmatrix}-7 & 5\\6 & 2\end{bmatrix}$

39. Hint $2X = \begin{bmatrix}2 & 1\\5 & 0\end{bmatrix} - \begin{bmatrix}-7 & 4\\2 & 6\end{bmatrix}$ **Ans.** $\frac{3}{2}\begin{bmatrix}3 & -1\\1 & -2\end{bmatrix}$

40. Hint $2X = 2B + C - A$ **Ans.** $X = \begin{bmatrix}-2 & 5\\3 & 1\end{bmatrix}$

41. Hint $\begin{bmatrix}1\\-2+4a\end{bmatrix} = \begin{bmatrix}b\\-3\end{bmatrix}$ **Ans.** $a = -\frac{1}{4}$ and $b = 1$

42. Hint $\begin{bmatrix}-2\times(-1)+0\times 2x\\3\times(-1)+1\times 2x\end{bmatrix} + \begin{bmatrix}-2\times 3\\1\times 3\end{bmatrix} = \begin{bmatrix}2\times y\\2\times 3\end{bmatrix}$

$$\Rightarrow \begin{bmatrix}-4\\2x\end{bmatrix} = \begin{bmatrix}2y\\6\end{bmatrix}$$

On comparing the corresponding elements both sides, we get the required result.

Ans. $x = 3$ and $y = -2$

43. Hint We have,

$$\begin{bmatrix}3\times 2x+(-2)\times 1\\-1\times 2x+4\times 1\end{bmatrix} + \begin{bmatrix}-4\times 2\\5\times 2\end{bmatrix} = \begin{bmatrix}4\times 2\\4\times y\end{bmatrix}$$

$$\begin{bmatrix}6x-10\\-2x+14\end{bmatrix} = \begin{bmatrix}8\\4y\end{bmatrix}$$

On comparing the corresponding elements both sides, we get the required result.

Ans. $x = 3$ and $y = 2$

44. Hint $\begin{bmatrix}3x & 3y\\0 & 2z\end{bmatrix} = \begin{bmatrix}3+x & y\\0 & 2+z\end{bmatrix}$

Now, proceed as in Example 5.

Ans. $x = \frac{3}{2}$, $y = 0$ and $z = 2$

45. Hint $\left(\begin{bmatrix}1 & -1\\2 & -1\end{bmatrix} + \begin{bmatrix}x & 1\\4 & -1\end{bmatrix}\right)^2 = \begin{bmatrix}1 & -1\\2 & -1\end{bmatrix}\begin{bmatrix}1 & -1\\2 & -1\end{bmatrix} + \begin{bmatrix}x & 1\\4 & -1\end{bmatrix}\begin{bmatrix}x & 1\\4 & -1\end{bmatrix}$

$$\Rightarrow \begin{bmatrix}(1+x)^2 & 0\\6x-6 & 4\end{bmatrix} = \begin{bmatrix}x^2+3 & x-1\\4x-4 & 4\end{bmatrix}$$

On comparing the corresponding elements both sides, we get the required result.

Ans. $x = 1$

46. Ans. (i) True (ii) True

(iii) False (iv) True

(v) True

47. Hint

(i) $\therefore (X+Y)(X-Y) = \begin{bmatrix}4 & 2\\1 & 7\end{bmatrix}\begin{bmatrix}2 & 2\\-1 & 3\end{bmatrix}$

(ii) $\therefore X^2 = \begin{bmatrix}3 & 2\\0 & 5\end{bmatrix}\begin{bmatrix}3 & 2\\0 & 5\end{bmatrix}$

and $Y^2 = \begin{bmatrix}1 & 0\\1 & 2\end{bmatrix}\begin{bmatrix}1 & 0\\1 & 2\end{bmatrix}$

Ans. (i) $\begin{bmatrix}6 & 14\\-5 & 23\end{bmatrix}$ (ii) $\begin{bmatrix}8 & 16\\-3 & 21\end{bmatrix}$

(iii) From the results of part (i) and (ii) it is clear that.

$$(X+Y)(X-Y) \neq X^2 - Y^2$$

48. Hint $\begin{bmatrix}x\times 2+3x\times 1\\y\times 2+4y\times 1\end{bmatrix} = \begin{bmatrix}5\\12\end{bmatrix}$

Ans. $x = 1$ and $y = 2$

49. Hint Do same as Q. 48.

Ans. $x = 2$ and $y = 1$

50. (i) **Hint** $AB = \begin{bmatrix}1 & 0\\-1 & 1\end{bmatrix}\begin{bmatrix}1 & 1\\4 & 5\end{bmatrix}$ **Ans.** $\begin{bmatrix}1 & 1\\3 & 4\end{bmatrix}$

(ii) **Hint** $B^2 - A^2 = \begin{bmatrix}1 & 1\\4 & 5\end{bmatrix}\begin{bmatrix}1 & 1\\4 & 5\end{bmatrix} - \begin{bmatrix}1 & 0\\-1 & 1\end{bmatrix}\begin{bmatrix}1 & 0\\-1 & 1\end{bmatrix}$

Ans. $\begin{bmatrix}4 & 6\\26 & 28\end{bmatrix}$

51. Hint $2Y - X^2 = \begin{bmatrix}6 & 4\\-4 & 2\end{bmatrix} - \begin{bmatrix}-3 & 0\\0 & -3\end{bmatrix}$

Ans. $\begin{bmatrix}9 & 4\\-4 & 5\end{bmatrix}$

52. Hint $A \cdot B = \begin{bmatrix}1 & 2\\2 & 4\end{bmatrix} = AC$

Ans. The conclusion is cancellation law may not hold for multiplication of matrices, i.e. $AB = AC$ may not imply $B = C$, $A \neq O$.

53. Hint $\therefore A^2 = A \times A = \begin{bmatrix}3 & 0\\0 & -3\end{bmatrix}\begin{bmatrix}3 & 0\\0 & -3\end{bmatrix}$

$$A^2 = \begin{bmatrix}9 & 0\\0 & 9\end{bmatrix}$$

$$A^3 = A^2 \times A = \begin{bmatrix}9 & 0\\0 & 9\end{bmatrix}\begin{bmatrix}3 & 0\\0 & -3\end{bmatrix}$$

$$A^3 = \begin{bmatrix}27 & 0\\0 & -27\end{bmatrix}$$

Ans. $A^2 = \begin{bmatrix}9 & 0\\0 & 9\end{bmatrix}$ and $A^3 = \begin{bmatrix}27 & 0\\0 & -27\end{bmatrix}$

54. Hint

(i) $XY = \begin{bmatrix}17 & 7\\-4 & -8\end{bmatrix}$

$\therefore (XY)Z = \begin{bmatrix}17 & 7\\-4 & -8\end{bmatrix}\begin{bmatrix}-3 & 4\\6 & 0\end{bmatrix}$

(ii) $Y + Z = \begin{bmatrix}-1 & 8\\11 & 1\end{bmatrix}$

$\therefore X(Y+Z) = \begin{bmatrix}1 & 3\\-2 & 0\end{bmatrix}\begin{bmatrix}-1 & 8\\11 & 1\end{bmatrix}$

55. Hint $5X = 2A + 3B$ **Ans.** $X = \begin{bmatrix}3 & 2\\-1 & -1\end{bmatrix}$

56. Hint $2A = \begin{bmatrix}1 & -5\\-4 & 6\end{bmatrix} - \begin{bmatrix}35 & 27\\20 & 16\end{bmatrix}$

Ans. $A = \begin{bmatrix}-17 & -16\\-12 & -5\end{bmatrix}$

57. Hint $A^3 - 4A^2 + A = A \cdot A \cdot A - 4A \cdot A + A$

$= A^2 \cdot A - 4A \cdot A + A$

$= \begin{bmatrix} 7 & 12 \\ 4 & 7 \end{bmatrix}\begin{bmatrix} 2 & 3 \\ 1 & 2 \end{bmatrix} - 4\begin{bmatrix} 7 & 12 \\ 4 & 7 \end{bmatrix} + \begin{bmatrix} 2 & 3 \\ 1 & 2 \end{bmatrix}$

58. Hint $5A + 2B = C$

$\begin{bmatrix} 10 & 5x \\ -15 & 25 \end{bmatrix} + \begin{bmatrix} -4 & 6 \\ 14 & 2y \end{bmatrix} = \begin{bmatrix} z & 9 \\ -1 & -11 \end{bmatrix}$

Ans. $x = \frac{3}{5}$, $y = -18$ and $z = 6$

59. Hint $\begin{bmatrix} x^2 - 3x \\ y^2 - 6y \end{bmatrix} = \begin{bmatrix} -2 \\ 9 \end{bmatrix}$

Ans. $x = 1, 2$ and $y = 3 \pm 3\sqrt{2}$

60. Hint $\begin{bmatrix} 0 & -q \\ 1 & 0 \end{bmatrix}\begin{bmatrix} p & 0 \\ 0 & 2 \end{bmatrix} = \begin{bmatrix} 2 & -2 \\ 2 & 2 \end{bmatrix}\begin{bmatrix} 2 & -2 \\ 2 & 2 \end{bmatrix}$

$\Rightarrow \begin{bmatrix} 0 & -2q \\ p & 0 \end{bmatrix} = \begin{bmatrix} 0 & -8 \\ 8 & 0 \end{bmatrix}$

Ans. $p = 8$ and $q = 4$

61. Hint $\begin{bmatrix} \alpha & 0 \\ 1 & 1 \end{bmatrix}\begin{bmatrix} \alpha & 0 \\ 1 & 1 \end{bmatrix} = \begin{bmatrix} 1 & 0 \\ 5 & 1 \end{bmatrix}$

Ans. There is no value of α for which $A^2 = B$ is true.

62. Hint $\begin{bmatrix} 2 & -3 \\ p & q \end{bmatrix}\begin{bmatrix} 2 & -3 \\ p & q \end{bmatrix} = \begin{bmatrix} 1 & 0 \\ 0 & 1 \end{bmatrix}$

Ans. $p = 1$ and $q = -2$

63. Hint

$\therefore \quad XY = 0$

$\therefore \begin{bmatrix} 6 + 6n & 2m + 12 \\ 9 + 9n & 3m + 18 \end{bmatrix} = \begin{bmatrix} 0 & 0 \\ 0 & 0 \end{bmatrix}$

Ans. $m = -6$ and $n = -1$

64. Hint Let the matrix $C = \begin{bmatrix} a & b \\ c & d \end{bmatrix}$

$\begin{bmatrix} 3 & 2 \\ -1 & 1 \end{bmatrix}\begin{bmatrix} a & b \\ c & d \end{bmatrix} = \begin{bmatrix} 14 & 3 \\ 2 & 4 \end{bmatrix}$

$\Rightarrow \begin{bmatrix} 3a + 2c & 3b + 2d \\ -a + c & -b + d \end{bmatrix} = \begin{bmatrix} 14 & 3 \\ 2 & 4 \end{bmatrix}$

Now, proceed as in Example 21 (ii).

Ans. $C = \begin{bmatrix} 2 & -1 \\ 4 & 3 \end{bmatrix}$

65. Hint

(i) $X = \begin{bmatrix} -3 & 0 \\ 12 & 3 \end{bmatrix} + \begin{bmatrix} 2 & 0 \\ 0 & 2 \end{bmatrix}$

$X = \begin{bmatrix} -1 & 0 \\ 12 & 5 \end{bmatrix}$

(ii) $X = \frac{1}{5}\begin{bmatrix} 5 & -20 \\ 0 & -15 \end{bmatrix}$

$X = \begin{bmatrix} 1 & -4 \\ 0 & -3 \end{bmatrix}$

Ans. (i) $\begin{bmatrix} -1 & 0 \\ 12 & 5 \end{bmatrix}$ (ii) $\begin{bmatrix} 1 & -4 \\ 0 & -3 \end{bmatrix}$

66. (i) False (ii) True
(iii) False (iv) True

67. Hint $\begin{bmatrix} 1 & 0 \\ -1 & 7 \end{bmatrix}\begin{bmatrix} 1 & 0 \\ -1 & 7 \end{bmatrix} = \begin{bmatrix} 8 + k & 0 \\ -8 & 56 + k \end{bmatrix}$

Ans. $k = -7$

68. Hint $[x \;\; 1]\begin{bmatrix} x \\ -2x - 15 \end{bmatrix} = 0$

$\Rightarrow \quad x^2 - 2x - 15 = 0$

$\Rightarrow \quad (x - 5)(x + 3) = 0$

Ans. $x = 5, -3$

69. Hint $\begin{bmatrix} x & y \\ -y & x \end{bmatrix}\begin{bmatrix} x & y \\ -y & x \end{bmatrix} = \begin{bmatrix} 0 & 1 \\ -1 & 0 \end{bmatrix}$

$\begin{bmatrix} x^2 - y^2 & 2xy \\ -2xy & x^2 - y^2 \end{bmatrix} = \begin{bmatrix} 0 & 1 \\ -1 & 0 \end{bmatrix}$

Ans. $x = \frac{1}{\sqrt{2}}$, $y = \frac{1}{\sqrt{2}}$ or $x = \frac{-1}{\sqrt{2}}$, $y = \frac{-1}{\sqrt{2}}$

70. Hint Given, $A = \begin{bmatrix} 0 & 1 \\ 0 & 0 \end{bmatrix}$

Now, $aI + bA = \begin{bmatrix} a & 0 \\ 0 & a \end{bmatrix} + \begin{bmatrix} 0 & b \\ 0 & 0 \end{bmatrix} = \begin{bmatrix} a & b \\ 0 & a \end{bmatrix}$

$(aI + bA)^2 = \begin{bmatrix} a & b \\ 0 & a \end{bmatrix}\begin{bmatrix} a & b \\ 0 & a \end{bmatrix} = \begin{bmatrix} a^2 & 2ab \\ 0 & a^2 \end{bmatrix}$

and $(aI + bA)^3 = \begin{bmatrix} a^2 & 2ab \\ 0 & a^2 \end{bmatrix}\begin{bmatrix} a & b \\ 0 & a \end{bmatrix}$

$= \begin{bmatrix} a^3 & 3a^2b \\ 0 & a^3 \end{bmatrix}$ ...(i)

Now, $a^3I + 3a^2bA = a^3\begin{bmatrix} 1 & 0 \\ 0 & 1 \end{bmatrix} + 3a^2b\begin{bmatrix} 0 & 1 \\ 0 & 0 \end{bmatrix}$

$= \begin{bmatrix} a^3 & 0 \\ 0 & a^3 \end{bmatrix} + \begin{bmatrix} 0 & 3a^2b \\ 0 & 0 \end{bmatrix}$

$= \begin{bmatrix} a^3 & 3a^2b \\ 0 & a^3 \end{bmatrix}$ ...(ii)

From Eqs. (i) and (ii), we get

$(aI + bA)^3 = a^3I + 3a^2bA$

Olympiad Section

Brain Teasing Questions of Olympiad Pattern

1 If α and β are the roots of the equation $x^2 + x - 6 = 0$ such that $\beta > \alpha$, then the product of the matrices $\begin{bmatrix} 0 & \alpha \\ \alpha & \beta \end{bmatrix}$ and $\begin{bmatrix} \beta+1 & 0 \\ -\beta & \alpha \end{bmatrix}$ is

(a) $\begin{bmatrix} 6 & 9 \\ -13 & -6 \end{bmatrix}$ (b) $\begin{bmatrix} 5 & 4 \\ 9 & 2 \end{bmatrix}$

(c) $\begin{bmatrix} 6 & 13 \\ 9 & 6 \end{bmatrix}$ (d) $\begin{bmatrix} -5 & 4 \\ -9 & -2 \end{bmatrix}$

2 The matrices A and B, such that $AB = O$, but $A \neq O$ and $B \neq O$, are

(a) $A = \begin{bmatrix} 2 & 2 \\ 2 & 2 \end{bmatrix}$, $B = \begin{bmatrix} 1 & 1 \\ -1 & -1 \end{bmatrix}$

(b) $A = \begin{bmatrix} -2 & -2 \\ -2 & -2 \end{bmatrix}$, $B = \begin{bmatrix} -1 & -1 \\ -1 & -1 \end{bmatrix}$

(c) $A = \begin{bmatrix} 2 & 2 \\ 2 & 2 \end{bmatrix}$, $B = \begin{bmatrix} 1 & 1 \\ 1 & 1 \end{bmatrix}$

(d) $A = \begin{bmatrix} -2 & -2 \\ 2 & 2 \end{bmatrix}$, $B = \begin{bmatrix} 1 & 1 \\ 1 & 1 \end{bmatrix}$

3 If $A = \begin{bmatrix} 3 & 1 \\ -1 & 2 \end{bmatrix}$, then the value of matrix A^5 is

(a) $\begin{bmatrix} 62 & 149 \\ -149 & -87 \end{bmatrix}$ (b) $\begin{bmatrix} 87 & 149 \\ 149 & 62 \end{bmatrix}$

(c) $\begin{bmatrix} -62 & -149 \\ 149 & 87 \end{bmatrix}$ (d) $\begin{bmatrix} 87 & 149 \\ 149 & -62 \end{bmatrix}$

4 If both $A + B$ and AB are defined, then which one of the following is true?

(a) A and B are rectangular matrices of same order
(b) A and B are square matrices of same order
(c) A and B are rectangular matrices of different order
(d) A and B are square matrices of different order

5 If $A = \begin{bmatrix} 3 & 0 \\ 0 & 3 \end{bmatrix}$, then A^n (where, n is a natural number) is equal to

(a) $\begin{bmatrix} 3n & 0 \\ 0 & 3n \end{bmatrix}$ (b) $\begin{bmatrix} 3 & 0 \\ 0 & 3 \end{bmatrix}$

(c) $3^n \begin{bmatrix} 1 & 0 \\ 0 & 1 \end{bmatrix}$ (d) $I_{2 \times 2}$

6 If $\begin{bmatrix} a^x \\ a^{-x} \end{bmatrix} [1 \;\; 2] = \begin{bmatrix} p & a^{-2} \\ q & \log_2 2 \end{bmatrix}$, $a > 0$, then a^{p-q} is equal to

(a) $2^{3/2}$ (b) $2^{-3/2}$
(c) 1 (d) $4^{3/2}$

7 If $A = \begin{bmatrix} 5 & 5 \\ 0 & 0 \end{bmatrix} \begin{bmatrix} 0 & 0 \\ 5 & 5 \end{bmatrix}$ and $A^n = \begin{bmatrix} 5^{200} & 5^{200} \\ 0 & 0 \end{bmatrix}$, then the value of n is

(a) 100
(b) 50
(c) 25
(d) None of the above

8 If $\begin{bmatrix} 7 & -6 \\ 8 & -7 \end{bmatrix}^{2016} = \begin{bmatrix} 7 & -6 \\ 8 & -7 \end{bmatrix}^{2018}$, then $\begin{bmatrix} 7 & -6 \\ 8 & -7 \end{bmatrix}^{2017}$ equals

(a) $\begin{bmatrix} 7 & -6 \\ 8 & -7 \end{bmatrix}^{2016} + \begin{bmatrix} 7 & -6 \\ 8 & -7 \end{bmatrix}^{2018}$

(b) $\begin{bmatrix} 1 & 0 \\ 0 & 1 \end{bmatrix}$

(c) $\begin{bmatrix} 7 & -6 \\ 8 & -7 \end{bmatrix}$

(d) None of the above

Answers

1. (a) **2.** (a) **3.** (a) **4.** (b) **5.** (c) **6.** (b) **7.** (a) **8.** (c)

* *These questions may or may not be asked in the examination, have been given just for additional practice required for olympiads Scholarship Exams etc. For detailed explanations refer Page No. 482.*

CHAPTER

09

Arithmetic and Geometric Progression

SYLLABUS

- (a) Arithmetic Progression (AP) (b) Sum of First n Terms of an AP (c) Geometric Progression (GP) (d) Sum of First n Terms of an GP

In this chapter, we will study the sequence (list of numbers) in which succeeding terms are obtained by adding or multiplying a fixed number to the preceding term. We will also study the formulae to find the value of its nth term and the sum of terms of these types of sequence.

Sequence

A list of numbers arranged in a definite order according to some definite rule, is called a **sequence**.

e.g.

(i) 1, 10, 12, 16, 100, ... In this sequence, numbers are arranged in ascending order.

(ii) 1, 2, 3, 4, 5, 6, ... In this sequence, each number is 1 more than the number preceding it, except first number.

(iii) 2, 4, 8, 16, ... In this sequence, each number is obtained on multiplying the preceding number by 2, except first number.

The various numbers occurring in a sequence are called its **terms**. Consider a sequence $a_1, a_2, a_3, a_4, \ldots$. Here, a_1 is called **first term**, a_2 is called **second term** and so on. Its nth term can be written as a_n, which is known as the **general term** of a sequence. A sequence is said to be **finite** or **infinite** accordingly it has **finite** or **infinite** number of terms.

Series

When the numbers or terms in a sequence are connected to each other by positive or negative signs, then the sequence becomes series. A series is finite or infinite, according as the number of terms in the series is finite or infinite.

e.g.

(i) $2 + 4 + 6 + 8 + \ldots + 102$ is finite series.

(ii) $-3 - 9 - 27 - \ldots$ is infinite series.

Progression

Those sequences whose terms always follow certain pattern are called **progressions**. e.g.

(i) The sequence 3, 5, 7, 9, ... is a progression, as each term can be found by adding 2 to the term preceding it.

(ii) The sequence 3, 10, 18, 21, 35, ... is not a progression as its terms are not following any certain pattern.

Note All progressions are sequences but all sequences need not be progressions.

In this chapter, we will study about two types of progressions, **arithmetic** and **geometric progression.**

Arithmetic Progression (AP)

An **Arithmetic Progression** (AP) is a list of numbers in which each term is obtained by adding a fixed number to the preceding term, except the first term. This fixed number is called the **common difference** (d) of the AP. It can be positive, negative or zero.

Thus, a list of numbers $a_1, a_2, a_3, \ldots, a_n, \ldots$ is called an arithmetic progression (AP), if there exists a constant number d (called common difference) such that

$$a_2 = a_1 + d$$
$$a_3 = a_2 + d$$
$$a_4 = a_3 + d$$
$$\vdots \quad \vdots \quad \vdots$$
$$a_n = a_{n-1} + d \text{ and so on.}$$

In other words, a list of numbers is called an arithmetic progression (AP), if and only if the difference of any term from its preceding term is constant. Thus, $a_1, a_2, a_3, a_4, \ldots$ is an AP, if and only if $a_{n+1} - a_n = d$, a constant (independent of n).

In general, $a, a+d, a+2d, a+3d, \ldots$ represent an arithmetic progression, where a is the first term and d is the common difference. This is called **general form of AP.**

If number of terms in an AP is finite, then it is called a **finite AP**, otherwise it is called an **infinite AP**.

Example 1. Examine that the sequence 13, 10, 7, 4,... is an AP.

Sol. Here, $a_2 - a_1 = 10 - 13 = -3$, $a_3 - a_2 = 7 - 10 = -3$,

$a_4 - a_3 = 4 - 7 = -3$ and so on.

Since, difference of any term from its preceding term is constant. So, the given sequence is an AP.

Example 2. Examine that the list of numbers obtained from following situation, will be in the form of an AP.

"Amount left with Sandeep (in ₹) out of the total amount of ₹ 12000 which he had in the beginning, when he spends ₹ 500 in the beginning of every month."

Sol. Given, total amount Sandeep had = ₹ 12000

In the beginning of every month, he spend = ₹ 500

So, in the beginning of 1st month, he had amount,

$t_1 =$ ₹ 12000

In the beginning of 2nd month, he had amount,

$t_2 = 12000 - 500 =$ ₹ 11500

In the beginning of 3rd month, he had amount,

$t_3 = 11500 - 500 =$ ₹ 11000

In the beginning of 4th month, he had amount,

$t_4 = 11000 - 500 =$ ₹ 10500 and so on.

Now, the list of amounts is 12000, 11500, 11000, 10500, ...

Here, $t_2 - t_1 = t_3 - t_2 = t_4 - t_3 = -500$

i.e. the difference of any term from its preceding term is constant. So, the above list of numbers forms an AP.

Method to Find the Common Difference of an AP

Let an AP $a_1, a_2, a_3, a_4, \ldots$ be given. Then, common difference of this AP will be the difference of any term from its preceding term, i.e. common difference

$(d) = a_2 - a_1$ or $a_3 - a_2$ or $a_4 - a_3$ and so on.

If the common difference of an AP is zero, i.e. $d = 0$, then each term of the AP will be same as the first term of the AP.

Example 3. Find the common difference of the following AP.

(i) $3, -2, -7, -12, \ldots$

(ii) 11, 11, 11, 11, ...

(iii) $5\frac{1}{2}, 9\frac{1}{2}, 13\frac{1}{2}, 17\frac{1}{2}, \ldots$

Sol.

(i) Given, AP is $3, -2, -7, -12, \ldots$

Here, $a_1 = 3$, $a_2 = -2$, $a_3 = -7$, $a_4 = -12$ and so on.

$\therefore$ Common difference $(d) = a_2 - a_1 = -2 - 3 = -5$

(ii) Given, AP is 11, 11, 11, 11, ...

Here, $a_1 = 11, a_2 = 11, a_3 = 11, a_4 = 11$ and so on.

$\therefore$ Common difference $(d) = a_2 - a_1 = 11 - 11 = 0$

(iii) Given, AP is $5\frac{1}{2}, 9\frac{1}{2}, 13\frac{1}{2}, 17\frac{1}{2}, \ldots$

Here, $a_1 = 5\frac{1}{2}$, $a_2 = 9\frac{1}{2}$, $a_3 = 13\frac{1}{2}$, $a_4 = 17\frac{1}{2}$ and so on.

$\therefore$ Common difference $(d) = a_2 - a_1$

$$= 9\frac{1}{2} - 5\frac{1}{2}$$

$$= \frac{19}{2} - \frac{11}{2} = \frac{8}{2} = 4$$

Method to Write an AP, When First Term and Common Difference are Given

To write an AP, the minimum information required is to know the first term a and the common difference d of the arithmetic progression.

Then, put the values of a and d in

$a, a+d, a+2d, a+3d, \ldots$ to get required AP.

Example 4. Write an AP having 4 as the first term and –3 as the common difference.

Sol. Given, first term $(a) = 4$ and common difference $(d) = -3$

On putting the values of a and d in general form of AP, i.e. $a, a+d, a+2d, a+3d, \ldots$, we get

$4, 4-3, 4+2(-3), 4+3(-3), \ldots$

or $4, 1, 4-6, 4-9, \ldots$

or $4, 1, -2, -5, \ldots$ which is the required AP.

Example 5. Which of the following are AP's? If they form an AP, then find the common difference d and write three more terms.

(i) $2, 4, 8, 16, \ldots$ (ii) $2, \frac{5}{2}, 3, \frac{7}{2}, \ldots$

(iii) $-1.2, -3.2, -5.2, -7.2, \ldots$

Sol.

(i) Here, $a_2 - a_1 = 4 - 2 = 2$ and $a_3 - a_2 = 8 - 4 = 4$

Since, $a_2 - a_1 \neq a_3 - a_2$. Therefore, the given list of numbers does not form an AP.

(ii) Here, $a_2 - a_1 = \frac{5}{2} - 2 = \frac{5-4}{2} = \frac{1}{2}$,

$a_3 - a_2 = 3 - \frac{5}{2} = \frac{6-5}{2} = \frac{1}{2}$,

$a_4 - a_3 = \frac{7}{2} - 3 = \frac{7-6}{2} = \frac{1}{2}$ and so on.

Since, the difference of any term from its preceding term constant. Therefore, the given list of numbers forms an AP and its common difference (d) is $\frac{1}{2}$.

Now, next three terms of this AP are

$a_5 = a_4 + d = \frac{7}{2} + \frac{1}{2} = \frac{7+1}{2} = \frac{8}{2} = 4$

$a_6 = a_5 + d = 4 + \frac{1}{2} = \frac{8+1}{2} = \frac{9}{2}$

and $a_7 = a_6 + d = \frac{9}{2} + \frac{1}{2} = \frac{9+1}{2} = \frac{10}{2} = 5$

(iii) Here, $a_2 - a_1 = -3.2 - (-1.2) = -3.2 + 1.2 = -2$,

$a_3 - a_2 = -5.2 - (-3.2) = -5.2 + 3.2 = -2$,

$a_4 - a_3 = -7.2 - (-5.2) = -7.2 + 5.2 = -2$

and so on.

Since, the difference of any term from its preceding term is constant. Therefore, the given list of numbers forms an AP and its common difference, d is -2.

Now, the next three terms of this AP are

$a_5 = a_4 + d = -7.2 + (-2) = -9.2$

$a_6 = a_5 + d = -9.2 + (-2) = -11.2$

and $a_7 = a_6 + d = -11.2 + (-2) = -13.2$

Properties of AP

(i) If a fixed number is added or subtracted from each term of an AP, then the resulting sequence is also an AP.

(ii) If each term of an AP is multiplied or divided by a fixed non-zero number, then the resulting sequence is also an AP.

General Term or *n*th Term of an AP

If the first term of an AP is 'a' and its common difference is 'd', then its nth term is given by the formula

$$a_n = a + (n-1)d$$

The nth term of an AP is also called its **general term.** If there are n terms in an AP, then nth term is known as last term of an AP and it is denoted by l, which is given by the formula

$$l = a + (n-1)d$$

where, a is first term and d is common difference.

Example 6. Find the 20th term of the sequence $7, 3, -1, -5, \ldots$.

Sol. Given, sequence is $7, 3, -1, -5, \ldots$.

Here, $3 - 7 = -4$, $-1 - 3 = -4$, $-5 + 1 = -4$

So, given sequence is an AP, in which $a = 7$ and $d = -4$.

$\because$ nth term, $a_n = a + (n-1)d$

On putting $n = 20$, we get

$a_{20} = a + (20-1)d = 7 + 19(-4)$ $[\because a = 7, d = -4]$

$= 7 - 19 \times 4 = 7 - 76$

$= -69$

Hence, 20th term of the given sequence is -69.

Example 7. Find the AP whose nth term is $2n - 3$.

Sol. Given, $a_n = 2n - 3$ ...(i)

Putting $n = 1, 2, 3, 4 \ldots\ldots$ in Eq. (i), we get

$a_1 = 2 \times 1 - 3 = -1$,

$a_2 = 2 \times 2 - 3 = 1$,

$a_3 = 2 \times 3 - 3 = 3$,

and $a_4 = 2 \times 4 - 3 = 5$

Hence, the AP is $-1, 1, 3, 5 \ldots$.

Example 8. Find the nth term and the 20th term of the sequence $9, 5, 1, -3 \ldots$

Sol. The given list of number is $9, 5, 1, -3 \ldots$

Here, $a_2 - a_1 = 5 - 9 = -4$,

$a_3 - a_2 = 1 - 5 = -4$

$a_4 - a_3 = -3 - 1 = -4$ and so on.

The given sequence is an AP with first term $a = 9$ and common difference $d = -4$.

$\therefore$ nth term $= a_n = a + (n-1)d$

$= 9 + (n-1)(-4)$

$= 9 - 4n + 4$

nth term $= 13 - 4n$

20th term $= a_{20} = 9 + (20-1) \times (-4)$

$= 9 + 19 \times (-4)$

$= 9 - 76$

$= -67$

Hence, the 20th term is -67.

Example 9. How many terms are there in the sequence 3, 6, 9, 12, ..., 111?

Sol. Given, sequence is 3, 6, 9, 12, ..., 111.

Here, $6 - 3 = 9 - 6 = 12 - 9 = 3$

So, it is an AP with first term, $a = 3$ and common difference, $d = 3$.

Let there be n terms in the given sequence.

Then, nth term $(a_n) = 111$

$\Rightarrow \quad a + (n-1)d = 111 \quad [\because a_n = a + (n-1)d]$

$\Rightarrow \quad 3 + (n-1) \times 3 = 111 \quad [\because a = d = 3]$

$\Rightarrow \quad 3(1 + n - 1) = 111$

$\therefore \quad n = \dfrac{111}{3} = 37$

Hence, the given sequence contains 37 terms.

Example 10. Which term of an AP 21, 18, 15,... is –81?

Sol. Given, AP is 21, 18, 15, ...

Here, $a = 21$ and $d = 18 - 21 = -3$

Let nth term of the given AP be -81.

Then, $a_n = -81 \Rightarrow a + (n-1)d = -81 \quad [\because a_n = a + (n-1)d]$

On putting the values of a and d, we get

$21 + (n-1)(-3) = -81$

$\Rightarrow \quad 21 - 3n + 3 = -81$

$\Rightarrow \quad 24 - 3n = -81$

$\Rightarrow \quad -3n = -81 - 24 = -105$

$\Rightarrow \quad n = \dfrac{-105}{-3} = 35$

Hence, 35th term of the given AP is -81.

Example 11. Find the value of the middle most term(s) of the AP –11, –7, –3, ...49.

Sol. First term $= a = -11$

and common difference $= d = -7 - (-11) = -7 + 11 = 4$

If the given AP consists of n terms,

then $a_n = 49$

$a + (n-1)d = 49$

$\Rightarrow \quad -11 + (n-1) \times 4 = 49$

$\Rightarrow \quad 4(n-1) = 60$

$\Rightarrow \quad n - 1 = 15$

$\Rightarrow \quad n = 16$

The given AP consists of 16 terms. So, we will get two terms in the middle of AP and their position will be $\dfrac{n}{2}$, $\dfrac{n}{2} + 1$, we get $\dfrac{16}{2}, \dfrac{16}{2} + 1$ the term 8th term and 9th term

Now, 8th term $= a + (8-1)d = -11 + 7 \times 4 = -11 + 28 = 17$

and 9th term $= a + (9-1)d = -11 + 8 \times 4 = -11 + 32 = 21$

Hence, the value of two middle most term are 17 and 21.

Example 12. Determine the general term of an AP whose 7th term is – 1 and 16th term is 17.

Sol. Let a be the first term and d be the common difference of the AP, whose 7th term is –1 and 16th term is 17.

Thus, $\quad a_7 = -1$ and $a_{16} = 17$

Now, $\quad a + (7-1)d = -1 \Rightarrow a + 6d = -1 \quad$ ...(i)

and $\quad a + (16-1)d = 17 \Rightarrow a + 15d = 17 \quad$ ...(ii)

$[\because a_n = a + (n-1)d]$

On subtracting Eq. (i) from Eq. (ii), we get

$a + 15d - a - 6d = 17 + 1$

$\Rightarrow \quad 9d = 18$

$\Rightarrow \quad d = 2$

On substituting $d = 2$ in Eq. (i), we get

$a + 6 \times 2 = -1$

$\Rightarrow \quad a + 12 = -1$

$\Rightarrow \quad a = -13$

Hence, general term, $a_n = a + (n-1)d$

$= -13 + (n-1)2 \quad [\because a = -13$ and $d = 2]$

$= -13 + 2n - 2 = 2n - 15$

Example 13. An AP consists of 50 terms of which the third term is 12 and the last term is 106. Find the 29th term.

Sol. Let a be the first term and d be the common difference of the AP.

Given, $a_3 = 12$ and $a_{50} = 106$

$a + (3-1)d = 12$

$a + 2d = 12 \quad$ ...(i)

and $\quad a + (50-1)d = 106$

$a + 49d = 106 \quad$ ...(ii)

On subtracting Eq. (i) from Eq. (ii), we get

$47d = 94$

$\Rightarrow \quad d = 2$

On putting $d = 2$ in Eq. (i), we get

$a + 2 \times 2 = 12$

$\Rightarrow \quad a + 4 = 12$

$\Rightarrow \quad a = 8$

$\therefore$ 29th term of the AP $= a + (29-1)d$

$= 8 + 28 \times 2$

$= 8 + 56 = 64$

Example 14. The 26th, 11th and the last term of an AP are 0, 3 and $-\dfrac{1}{5}$, respectively. Find the common difference and the number of terms.

Sol. Let a be the first term, d be the common difference and n be the total number of terms of the AP.

Given, $a_{11} = 3$, $a_{26} = 0$ and $a_n = -\dfrac{1}{5}$

Now, $a_{26} = 0 \Rightarrow a + 25d = 0 \quad$ ...(i)

$a_{11} = 3 \Rightarrow a + 10d = 3 \quad$ ...(ii)

$a_n = -\dfrac{1}{5} \Rightarrow a + (n-1)d = -\dfrac{1}{5} \quad$ ...(iii)

On subtracting Eq. (ii) from Eq. (i), we get

$15d = -3 \Rightarrow d = -\dfrac{1}{5}$

On putting $d = -\dfrac{1}{5}$ in Eq. (i), we get

$a + 25\left(-\dfrac{1}{5}\right) = 0 \Rightarrow a = 5$

On putting $a = 5$ and $d = -\frac{1}{5}$ in Eq. (iii), we gt

$$5 + (n-1)\left(-\frac{1}{5}\right) = -\frac{1}{5} \Rightarrow 25 + (n-1)(-1) = -1$$

$\Rightarrow$ $25 - n + 1 = -1$

$\Rightarrow$ $n = 27$

Hence, the common difference is $-\frac{1}{5}$ and the number of terms is 27.

Example 15. The sum of the 5th and 9th terms of an AP is 30. If its 25th term is three times its 8th term, find the AP.

Sol. Let a be the first term and d be the common difference of the AP.

According to the question,

$a_5 + a_9 = 30$

$\Rightarrow (a + 4d) + (a + 8d) = 30$

$\Rightarrow$ $2a + 12d = 30$

$\Rightarrow$ $a + 6d = 15$ ...(i)

$\Rightarrow$ $a_{25} = 3a_8$

$\Rightarrow$ $a + 24d = 3(a + 7d)$

$\Rightarrow$ $a + 24d = 3a + 21d$

$\Rightarrow$ $2a = 3d$

$\Rightarrow$ $d = \frac{2}{3}a$ [put in Eq. (i)]

$\Rightarrow$ $a + 6 \times \frac{2}{3}a = 15$

$\Rightarrow$ $a + 4a = 15$

$\Rightarrow$ $5a = 15$

$\Rightarrow$ $a = 3$

$\therefore$ $d = \frac{2}{3} \times 3 = 2$

So, the AP is $a, a + d, a + 2d, a + 3d$

i.e. $3, 3 + 2, 3 + 2 \times 2, \ldots\ldots$

$= 3, 5, 7, 9, \ldots$

Example 16. Show that the sum $f(m + n)$ th term and $(m - n)$th term of an AP is equal to twice the mth term.

Sol. Let a be the first term and d be the common difference of the AP, then

$a_{m+n} = a + [(m + n) - 1]d$ ...(i)

and $a_{m-n} = a + [(m - n) - 1]d$ ...(ii)

On adding Eqs. (i) and (ii), we get

$a_{m+n} + a_{m-n} = [a + (m + n - 1)d] + [a + (m - n - 1)d]$

$= 2a + (m + n - 1 + m - n - 1)d$

$= 2a + 2(m - 1)d$

$= 2[a + (m - 1)d] = 2a_m.$ **Hence proved.**

Example 17. If the 9th term of an AP is zero, prove that its 29th term is twice its 19th term.

Sol. Let a be the first term and d be the common difference of the AP.

Given, $a_9 = 0$

$\Rightarrow$ $a + 8d = 0$

$\Rightarrow$ $a = -8d$ ...(i)

$\Rightarrow$ $a_{29} = a + 28d$ [put the value of a from Eq. (i)]

$= -8d + 28d$

$= 20d$

Now, $a_{19} = a + 18d$ [put the value of a from Eq. (i)]

$= -8d + 18d$

$= 10d$

$\Rightarrow$ $2a_{19} = 20d$

$\therefore$ $a_{29} = 2a_{19}$ **Hence proved.**

Example 18. If m times the mth term of an AP is equal to n times its nth term, then find its $(m + n)$th term.

Sol. Let a be the first term and d be the common difference of the AP.

Given, $ma_m = na_n$

$\Rightarrow m[a + (m - 1)d] = n[a + (n - 1)d]$

$\Rightarrow$ $(m - n)a + (m^2 - m - n^2 + n)d = 0$

$\Rightarrow$ $(m - n)a + (m^2 - n^2 - m + n)d = 0$

$\Rightarrow (m - n)a + ((m - n)(m + n) - 1(m - n))d = 0$

$\Rightarrow$ $(m - n)a + (m - n)(m + n - 1)d = 0$

$\Rightarrow$ $(m - n)[a + (m + n - 1)d] = 0$ $[\because m \neq n]$

$\Rightarrow$ $a + (m + n - 1)d = 0$

$\Rightarrow$ $a_{m+n} = 0$

Hence, $(m + n)$th term is zero.

Example 19. In an AP, the pth term is $\frac{1}{q}$ and the qth term is $\frac{1}{p}$. Find its (pq)th term.

Sol. Let a be the first term and d be the common difference of the AP, then

$a_p = \frac{1}{q}$ and $a_q = \frac{1}{p}$

$\Rightarrow$ $a + (p - 1)d = \frac{1}{q}$ ...(i)

$\Rightarrow$ $a + (q - 1)d = \frac{1}{p}$ ...(ii)

On subtracting Eq. (ii) from Eq. (i), we get,

$d = \frac{1}{pq}$

On putting $d = \frac{1}{pq}$ in Eq. (i), we get

$$a + (p - 1) \times \frac{1}{pq} = \frac{1}{q} = a + \frac{1}{q} - \frac{1}{pq} = \frac{1}{q}$$

$\Rightarrow$ $a - \frac{1}{pq} = 0 \Rightarrow a = \frac{1}{pq}$

Now, (pq)th term $= a + (pq - 1)d$

$= \frac{1}{pq} + (pq - 1)\frac{1}{pq}$

$= \frac{1}{pq} + 1 - \frac{1}{pq} = 1$

Hence, (pq)th term is 1.

Example 20. For what value of n, the nth term of two AP's 63, 65, 67, 69, ... and 3, 10, 17, 19 ..... are equal? Also, find that term.

Sol. In the given AP 63, 65, 67, 69 ......

$a = 63, d = 2,$

$n\text{th term} = a + (n-1)d$
$= 63 + (n-1)2$
$= 2n + 61$ ...(i)

and in given AP 3, 10, 17, ...

$a = 3, d = 7$

$n\text{th term} = a + (n-1)d$
$= 3 + (n-1)7$
$= 7n - 4$ ...(ii)

Since, the nth term of both AP's are same from Eqs. (i) and (ii), we get

$2n + 61 = 7n - 4$

$\Rightarrow -5n = -65 \Rightarrow n = 13$

To find the term put $n = 13$ in $2n + 61$

$\therefore$ The term is $2 \times 13 + 61 = 26 + 61 = 87$

Hence, the 13th term of both AP's are equal and this term is 87.

Example 21. Which term of the AP 121, 117, 113, ... is the first negative term?

Sol. $a = 121$ and $d = 117 - 121 = -4$

Let nth term, i.e. a_n be the first negative term

$a_n < 0 \Rightarrow a + (n-1)d < 0$

$\Rightarrow 121 + (n-1)(-4) < 0$

$\Rightarrow 121 < 4(n-1)$

$\Rightarrow \frac{121}{4} < n - 1$

$\Rightarrow \frac{121}{4} + 1 < n$

$\Rightarrow \frac{125}{4} < n$

$\Rightarrow n > \frac{125}{4}$

The least positive integer value of n which satisfies $n > \frac{125}{4}$ is 32.

Hence, 32th is the first negative term of the given AP.

Example 22. How many numbers of two-digits are divisible by 7?

Sol. Two-digits numbers are 10, 11, 12, 13, 14, 15, ..., 97, 98, 99 in which only 14, 21, 28, ..., 98 are divisible by 7.

Here, $21 - 14 = 28 - 21 = 7$

So, the list of numbers 14, 21, 28, ..., 98 forms an AP, whose first term $(a) = 14$ and common difference $(d) = 7$.

Let there are n terms in the above sequence, then

$a_n = 98$

$\Rightarrow a + (n-1)d = 98$ $[\because a_n = a + (n-1)d]$

$\Rightarrow 14 + (n-1)7 = 98$ $[\because a = 14 \text{ and } d = 7]$

$\Rightarrow 14 + 7n - 7 = 98 \Rightarrow 7n = 91$

$\Rightarrow n = \frac{91}{7} = 13$

Hence, 13 numbers of two digits are divisible by 7.

Example 23. A sum of ₹ 2000 is invested at 7% simple interest per year. Calculate the interest at the end of each year. Do these interest form an AP? If so, then find the interest at the end of 20 yr making use of this fact.

Sol. Given, initial money P = ₹ 2000

Rate of interest, $R = 7\%$ per year; Time, $T = 1, 2, 3, 4, \ldots$

We know that simple interest is given by the formula

$$\text{SI} = \frac{PRT}{100}$$

$\therefore$ SI at the end of 1st year $= \frac{2000 \times 7 \times 1}{100} =$ ₹ 140

SI at the end of 2nd year $= \frac{2000 \times 7 \times 2}{100} =$ ₹ 280

SI at the end of 3rd year $= \frac{2000 \times 7 \times 3}{100} =$ ₹ 420

Thus, required list of numbers is 140, 280, 420, ...

Here, $280 - 140 = 420 - 280 = 140$

So, above list of numbers forms an AP, whose first term $(a) = 140$ and common difference $(d) = 140$.

Now, SI at the end of 20 yr will be equal to 20th term of the above AP.

$\because a_{20} = a + (20-1)d = 140 + 19 \times 140$ $[\because a_n = a + (n-1)d]$

$= 140 + 2660 = 2800$

Hence, the interest at the end of 20 yr will be ₹ 2800.

*n*th Term from the End of an AP

Let 'a' be the first term, 'd' be the common difference and 'l' be the last term of an AP, then nth term from the end can be found by the formula

nth term from the end $= l - (n-1)d$

Example 24. Determine the 10th term from the end of an AP 4, 9, 14, ..., 254.

Sol. Given, AP is 4, 9, 14,..., 254.

Here, l = last term = 254

and d = common difference $= 9 - 4 = 5$

$\because$ nth term from the end $= l - (n-1)d$

$\therefore$ 10th term from the end $= l - (10-1)d = l - 9d$
$= 254 - 9 \times 5$
$= 254 - 45 = 209$

Alternate Method

On reversing the given AP, new AP is 254, ..., 14, 9, 4.

Here, first term $(a) = 254$

and common difference $(d) = -5$

Now, 10th term of new AP $= a_{10} = 254 + (10-1)(-5)$ $[\because a_n = a + (n-1)d]$

$= 254 - 9 \times 5 = 209$

Hence, 10th term from the end of the given AP is 209.

Selection of Terms in an AP

Sometimes, we have to select certain number of terms in an AP. The convenient way of selecting terms is given below

Number of terms	Terms	Common difference
3	$a-d, a, a+d$	d
4	$a-3d, a-d, a+d, a+3d$	$2d$
5	$a-2d, a-d, a, a+d, a+2d$	d

Note If the terms of an AP are not given, then the terms can be chosen as $a, a+d, a+2d, \ldots$.

Example 25. The sum of three numbers in AP is 15 and their product is 105. Find the numbers.

Sol. Let three numbers in AP be $a-d, a$ and $a+d$.

According to the question,

Sum of numbers = 15

$\therefore \quad (a-d)+a+(a+d)=15 \Rightarrow 3a=15 \Rightarrow a=5$

and the product of numbers = 105

$\therefore \quad (a-d)(a)(a+d)=105$

$\Rightarrow \quad (5-d)(5)(5+d)=105$ [put $a=5$]

$\Rightarrow \quad (25-d^2)5=105$ [$\because (A-B)(A+B)=A^2-B^2$]

$\Rightarrow \quad 25-d^2=21$ [dividing both sides by 5]

$\Rightarrow \quad d^2=4 \Rightarrow d=\pm 2$

When $d=2$, then numbers in AP are $5-2$, 5 and $5+2$ i.e. 3, 5, 7.

When $d=-2$, then terms in AP are $5+2$, 5, $5-2$, i.e. 7, 5, 3.

Example 26. The sum of the first three terms of an AP is 42 and the product of the first and third term is 52. Find the first term and the common difference. **[ICSE 2019]**

Sol. Let a and d be the first term and common difference of an AP and first three terms of an AP are

$$a, a+d \text{ and } a+2d.$$

According to the question,

$$a+(a+d)+(a+2d)=42$$

$\Rightarrow \quad 3a+3d=42$

$\Rightarrow \quad a+d=14$

Also, $\quad a\times(a+2d)=52$

$\Rightarrow \quad a\times[a+2(14-a)]=52$

$\Rightarrow \quad a\times(28-a)=52$

$\Rightarrow \quad 28a-a^2=52$

$\Rightarrow \quad a^2-28a+52=0$

$\Rightarrow \quad a^2-26a-2a+52=0$

$\Rightarrow \quad a(a-26)-2(a-26)=0$

$\Rightarrow \quad (a-2)(a-26)=0$

$\Rightarrow \quad a=2, a=26$

When $a=2$, then

$$d=14-a$$
$$=14-2=12$$

When $a=26$, then

$$d=14-26=-12$$

Exercise 9.1

1. Write first three terms of the following sequences.

(i) $a_n=5n+3$ (ii) $a_n=3n^2-2$ (iii) $a_n=\dfrac{n-3}{2}$

2. Write the first four terms in each of the list of numbers defined by

(i) $a_n=2n+3$ (ii) $a_n=(-1)^{n-1}n^4$ (iii) $a_n=\dfrac{(n-1)^2}{3}$

3. Which of the following form an AP? Justify your answer.

(i) 1, 1, 2, 2, 3, 3, ... (ii) $\sqrt{3}, \sqrt{12}, \sqrt{27}, \sqrt{48}, \ldots$

(iii) $-1, \frac{1}{4}, \frac{3}{2}, \frac{11}{4}, \ldots$ (iv) 0.5, 0.8, 1.1, ...

(v) $-3, -5, -6, -8, \ldots$

4. Check that the list of numbers defined by the following nth term is an AP or not. Also, give the reason.

(i) $a_n=3n+5$ (ii) $a_n=9-11n^2$

(iii) $a_n=8n^2+n$ (iv) $a_n=4n^3+3$

5. Show that the sequence defined by $a_n=3n^2-5$ is not an AP.

6. Write the common difference of the following AP's.

(i) $\sqrt{3}, 2\sqrt{3}, 3\sqrt{3}, \ldots$ (ii) $\frac{1}{6}, \frac{1}{3}, \frac{1}{2}, \ldots$

(iii) $20, 19\frac{1}{4}, 18\frac{1}{2}, 17\frac{3}{4}, \ldots$

7. Examine that the sequence 7, 13, 19, 25, ... is an AP. Also, find the common difference.

8. Show that the sequence, defined by its nth term $\dfrac{3+n}{4}$, forms an AP. Also, find the common difference of it.

9. In the following, find the first four terms of an AP, whose

(i) first term is -2 and the common difference is -2.

(ii) first term is $-\frac{1}{2}$ and the common difference is -1.

(iii) first term is 0.5 and the common difference is 1.2.

10. Find the common difference and the next two terms of the following AP's.
(i) 6, 12, 18, ... (ii) $\frac{1}{3}, \frac{4}{3}, \frac{7}{3}, \ldots$ (iii) −15, −13, −11, ...

11. If $(k-3), (2k+1), (4k+3)$ are three consecutive terms of an AP, find the value of k. [ICSE 2018]

12. Find the following terms of an AP.
(i) 10th term of the sequence − 5, − 5/2, 0, 5/2, ...
(ii) 11th term of the sequence −3, − 1/2, 2, ...
(iii) 23rd term of the sequence 7, 5, 3, 1, ...

13. If $d = -4$, $n = 7$ and $a_n = 4$, then find the value of a.

14. Find the nth term and the 25th term of the sequence 11, 7, 3, −1, −5, ...

15. The first term of an AP is 5, common difference is 3 and the last term is 80. Find the number of terms.

16. Find the value of the middle most term of the AP −7, −3, 1 ...... 53.

17. Check 0 is a term of an AP : 31, 28, 25, ...

18. Find p, if the given value of x is the pth term of an AP 25, 50, 75, 100, ... ; $x = 1000$.

19. The 11th term of an AP is 80 and the 16th term is 110. Find the 31st term.

20. Which term of AP : 3, 8, 13, 18, ... will be 130 more than its 31st term?

21. An AP consists of 20 terms of which the fourth term is 8 and the last term is 40, then find the 12th term.

22. If 8th term of an AP is zero, prove that its 38th term is triple of its 18th term.

23. If the nth term of the two AP's 9, 7, 5 ...... and 24, 21, 18 ...... are the same, find the value of n. Also, find that term.

24. Find the value of x, if
$$-4 + (-1) + 2 + \ldots + x = 437$$

25. Which term of the AP 53, 48, 43 ...... is the first negative term?

26. How many numbers lie between 10 and 300, which divided by 4 leave a remainder 3?

27. In a flower bed, there are 43 rose plants in the first row, 41 in the second, 39 in the third and so on. There are 11 rose plants in the last row. How many rows are there in the flower bed?

28. A man starts repaying a loan as first installment of ₹ 100. If he increases the installment by ₹ 5 every month, then what amount he will pay in the 30th installment?

29. A sum of ₹ 5000 is invested at 8% simple interest per annum. Calculate the interest at the end of each year. Do these interests form an AP? Find the interest at the end of 30 yr.

30. Find the 6th term from the end of an AP 17, 14, 11, ..., − 40.

31. In an AP, if $a = 10$, $d = 5$ and $n = 100$, then find the value of a_{100} and also find the 50th term from the end.

32. Split 207 into three parts such that these are in AP and the product of two smaller parts is 4623.

33. The angles of a triangle are in AP. The greatest angle is twice the least. Find all the angles of the triangle.

Sum of First n Terms of an AP

If first term of an AP is 'a' and its common difference is 'd', then the sum of its first n terms S_n, is given by the formula

$$S_n = \frac{n}{2}[2a + (n-1)d]$$

This formula can also be written as

$$S_n = \frac{n}{2}(a + a_n)$$

where, a_n = nth term of the AP

If l is the last term of an AP of n terms, then sum of all the terms is given by the formula

$$S_n = \frac{n}{2}(a + l)$$

Example 27. Find the sum of the first 22 terms of the AP 8, 3, − 2, ...

Sol. Given, AP is 8, 3, − 2, ...

Here, first term $(a) = 8$,
common difference $(d) = 3 - 8 = -5$ and $n = 22$

$\because$ Sum of first n terms $(S_n) = \frac{n}{2}[2a + (n-1)d]$

$\therefore$ Sum of first 22 terms $(S_{22}) = \frac{22}{2}[2 \times 8 + (22-1) \times (-5)]$
$= 11[16 + 21 \times (-5)]$
$= 11(16 - 105)$
$= 11(-89)$
$= -979$

Hence, the sum of first 22 terms of an AP is − 979.

Example 28. Find the sum of first 20 terms of an AP in which $a = 1$ and 20th term = 58.

Sol. Given, $a = 1, l = 58$ and $n = 20$

Now, sum of 20 terms, $S_{20} = \frac{20}{2}(1 + 58)$ $\left[\because S_n = \frac{n}{2}(a + l)\right]$

$= 10(59) = 590$

Example 29. In an AP the fourth and sixth terms are 8 and 14, respectively.
Find the
(i) first term
(ii) common difference
(iii) sum of the first 20 terms. [ICSE 2019]

Sol. Let a and d be the first term and common difference of an AP.

Then, $T_4 = 8$ and $T_6 = 14$

$\Rightarrow \quad a + (4-1)d = 8$

and $\quad a + (6-1)d = 14$ $\quad [\because T_n = a + (n-1)d]$

$\Rightarrow \quad a + 3d = 8$ ...(i)

and $\quad a + 5d = 14$ ...(ii)

On solving Eqs. (i) and (ii), we get

$a = -1$ and $d = 3$

(i) first term $(a) = -1$
(ii) common difference $(d) = 3$
(iii) sum of first 20 terms $= S_{20} = \frac{20}{2}[2\times(-1) + (20-1)3]$

$\left[\because S_n = \frac{n}{2}[2a + (n-1)d]\right]$

$= 10[-2 + 57] = 10 \times 55 = 550$

Example 30. Find the sum of first 24 terms of an AP, whose nth term is given by $a_n = 3 + 2n$.

Sol. Given, nth term of an AP, $a_n = 3 + 2n$

Clearly, sum of first 24 terms

$S_{24} = \frac{24}{2}(a_1 + a_{24})$ $\left[\because S_n = \frac{n}{2}(a + a_n) \text{ and } a = a_1\right]$

$= \frac{24}{2}[(3 + 2\times 1) + (3 + 2\times 24)]$

$= \frac{24}{2}(3 + 2 + 3 + 48)$

$= 12 \times 56 = 672$

Hence, the required sum of first 24th terms of an AP is 672.

Problems Based on Sum of First n Terms of an AP

Some types of these problems are given below

Example 31. The 4th term of an AP, is 22 and 15th term is 66. Find the first term and the common difference. Hence, find the sum of the series to 8 terms. [ICSE 2018]

Sol. Given, $\quad T_4 = 22$

$\Rightarrow \quad a + 3d = 22$ ...(i)

and $\quad T_{15} = 66$

$\Rightarrow \quad a + 14d = 66$ ...(ii)

On subtracting Eq. (i) from Eq. (ii), we get

$a + 14d - (a + 3d) = 66 - 22$

$\Rightarrow \quad 11d = 44$

$\Rightarrow \quad d = \frac{44}{11} = 4$

On putting the value of d in Eq. (i), we get

$a + 3 \times 4 = 22$

$\Rightarrow \quad a + 12 = 22$

$\Rightarrow \quad a = 22 - 12 = 10$

$\because \quad S_n = \frac{n}{2}[2a + (n-1)d]$

$\therefore \quad S_8 = \frac{8}{2}[2\times 10 + (8-1)\times 4]$

$= 4[20 + 28] = 4 \times 48 = 192$

Example 32. Find the sum of the last 10 terms of an AP 8, 10, 12, ... 126

Sol. We have, 8, 10, 12 is an AP.
with common difference $10 - 8 = 2$
If we write the terms of an AP in the reverse order, then it is an AP with $a = 126$ and $d = -2$.
$\therefore$ Sum of the last 10 terms of the given AP

$S_{10} = \frac{10}{2}[2\times 126 + (10-1)\times(-2)] = 5[252 - 18]$

$= 5 \times 234 = 1170$

Hence, the sum of the last 10 terms sum is 1170.

Example 33. Find the sum of all the 11 terms of an AP, whose middle most term is 30.

Sol. Given, number of terms $(n) = 11$

Let the AP $a, a + d, a + 2d$

$\therefore$ Middle term $\left(\frac{n+1}{2}\right)$th term

$= \left(\frac{11+1}{2}\right)$th term

$= 6$th term

Given, middle most term $= 30 = a + 5d = 30$

$\because$ Sum of all the 11th terms

$S_{11} = \frac{11}{2}[2a + (11-1)d]$ $\left[\because S_n = \frac{n}{2}\{2a + (n-1)d\}\right]$

$= \frac{11}{2}[2a + 10d]$

$= 11[a + 5d]$

$= 11 \times 30 = 330$

Hence, the sum of all the 11 terms of an AP is 330.

Example 34. How many terms of an AP $20, 19\frac{1}{3}, 18\frac{2}{3}, \ldots$ must be taken, so that their sum is 300?

Sol. Given AP is $20, 19\frac{1}{3}, 18\frac{2}{3}, \ldots$.

Here, $\quad a = 20$

and $\quad d = 19\frac{1}{3} - 20 = \frac{58}{3} - 20 = \frac{58-60}{3} = \frac{-2}{3}$

Let n terms of the given AP be required to get the sum 300.

We know that, $S_n = \frac{n}{2}[2a + (n-1)d]$

$$\Rightarrow \quad 300 = \frac{n}{2}\left[2(20) + (n-1)\left(\frac{-2}{3}\right)\right]$$

[$\because a = 20$ and $d = -2/3$]

$$\Rightarrow \quad 600 = n\left(40 - \frac{2}{3}n + \frac{2}{3}\right)$$

$$\Rightarrow \quad 600 = \frac{1}{3}(120n - 2n^2 + 2n)$$

$$\Rightarrow \quad 600 \times 3 = 122n - 2n^2$$

$$\Rightarrow \quad 1800 + 2n^2 - 122n = 0$$

$$\Rightarrow \quad 2(n^2 - 61n + 900) = 0$$

$$\Rightarrow \quad n^2 - 61n + 900 = 0 \quad [\because 2 \neq 0]$$

$$\Rightarrow \quad n^2 - 36n - 25n + 900 = 0$$

$$\Rightarrow \quad n(n-36) - 25(n-36) = 0$$

$$\Rightarrow \quad (n-36)(n-25) = 0$$

$$\Rightarrow \quad n = 36 \text{ or } 25$$

Since, a is positive and d is negative, so both values of n are possible.

Hence, sum of first 25 terms of given AP = Sum of first 36 terms of given AP = 300.

Example 35. If the mth term of an AP is $\frac{1}{n}$ and nth term is $\frac{1}{m}$, show that the sum of mn terms is $\frac{1}{2}(mn+1)$.

Sol. Let the first term of an AP be a and the common difference of the given AP be d.

Now, according to the question

$$a_m = \frac{1}{n} \Rightarrow a + (m-1)d = \frac{1}{n} \quad \text{...(i)}$$

$$a_n = \frac{1}{m} \Rightarrow a + (n-1)d = \frac{1}{m} \quad \text{...(ii)}$$

On subtracting Eq. (ii) from Eq. (i), we get

$$(m-n)d = \frac{1}{n} - \frac{1}{m}$$

$$\Rightarrow \quad (m-n)d = \frac{m-n}{mn}$$

$$\Rightarrow \quad d = \frac{1}{mn}$$

On substituting $d = \frac{1}{mn}$ in Eq. (i), we get

$$a + (m-1)\frac{1}{mn} = \frac{1}{n}$$

$$a + \frac{1}{n} - \frac{1}{mn} = \frac{1}{n} \Rightarrow a = \frac{1}{mn}$$

$$\therefore \text{Sum of } mn \text{ terms} = \frac{mn}{2}[2a + (mn-1)d]$$

$$= \frac{mn}{2}\left[2 \times \frac{1}{mn} + (mn-1) \times \frac{1}{mn}\right]$$

$$= \frac{1}{2}[2 + (mn-1)] = \frac{1}{2}(mn+1)$$

Hence Proved.

Example 36. The ratio of the 11th term to the 18th term of an AP is 2 : 3, find the ratio of the 5th term to the 21st term, and also the ratio of the sum of first five terms to the sum of first 21 terms.

Sol. Let the first term of AP be a and common difference be d, then

$$\frac{a_{11}}{a_{18}} = \frac{2}{3} \Rightarrow \frac{a + 10d}{a + 17d} = \frac{2}{3}$$

$$\Rightarrow \quad 3a + 30d = 2a + 34d$$

$$\Rightarrow \quad a = 4d \quad \text{...(i)}$$

Now, $\frac{a_5}{a_{21}} = \frac{a + 4d}{a + 20d} = \frac{4d + 4d}{4d + 20d} = \frac{8d}{24d} = \frac{1}{3}$ [using Eq. (i)]

Therefore, ratio of 5th and 21st term of an AP = 1: 3

Also, $\frac{S_5}{S_{21}} = \frac{\frac{5}{2}(2a + 4d)}{\frac{21}{2}(2a + 20d)} = \frac{5}{21} \times \frac{a + 2d}{a + 10d}$

$= \frac{5}{21} \times \frac{4d + 2d}{4d + 10d}$ [using Eq. (i)]

$= \frac{5}{21} \times \frac{6}{14} = \frac{5}{49}$

Example 37. Show that $a_1, a_2, a_3 \ldots$ form an AP, where a_n is defined as $a_n = 9 - 5n$. Also, find the sum of the first 15 terms.

Sol. Given, $a_n = 9 - 5n$

Putting $n = 1$, we get $a_1 = 9 - 5 \times 1 = 4$

Now, $a_{n+1} - a_n = [9 - 5(n+1)] - [9 - 5n] = -5$

i.e. any term − Preceding term = − 5, a fixed number.

$\therefore$ The numbers a_1, a_2, a_3 ...... form an AP with $a = 4$ and $d = -5$.

$\therefore$ The sum of first 15 terms $= \frac{15}{2}(2a + 14d)$

[using, $S_n = \frac{n}{2}[2a + (n-1)d]$]

$= 15(a + 7d)$

$= 15[4 + 7(-5)]$

$= 15(4 - 35)$

$= 15(-31)$

$= -465$

Example 38. If S_n denotes the sum of first n term of an AP. Prove that $S_{12} = 3(S_8 - S_4)$.

Sol. Let a be the first term and d be the common difference of AP.

$$S_{12} = \frac{12}{2}[2a + (12-1)d] = 6[2a + 11d] \Rightarrow 12a + 66d$$

$$S_8 = \frac{8}{2}[2a + (8-1)d] = 4[2a + 7d] = 8a + 28d$$

$$S_4 = \frac{4}{2}[2a + (4-1)d] = 2(2a + 3d) = 4a + 6d$$

Now, $3(S_8 - S_4) = 3(8a + 28d - 4a - 6d)$

$= 3(4a + 22d) = 12a + 66d = S_{12}$

Hence, $S_{12} = 3(S_8 - S_4)$

Example 39. Find the sum of first 40 positive integers divisible by 6.

Sol. 6, 12, 18 ...., 40 terms

The first term AP is 6 and the common difference of AP is 6 and $l = 240$

Sum of these number $= \frac{40}{2}(6 + 240) = 20 \times 246 = \underline{4920}$

Hence, the 40 positive integers divisible by 6 will be $\underline{4920}$.

If S_n is the sum of first n terms of an AP, then its nth term is given by

$$\boxed{a_n = S_n - S_{n-1}}$$

It can be easily understood with the help of following example.

Example 40. If the sum of first n terms of an AP is given by $S_n = 6n + 7n^2$, then find the nth term of the AP. Also, find 10th term of an AP.

Sol. We have, $S_n = 6n + 7n^2$ ...(i)

On replacing n by $(n-1)$ in Eq. (i), we get

$S_{n-1} = 6(n-1) + 7(n-1)^2 = 6n - 6 + 7(n^2 + 1 - 2n)$

$[\because (a-b)^2 = a^2 + b^2 - 2ab]$

$= 6n - 6 + 7n^2 + 7 - 14n = 7n^2 - 8n + 1$ ...(ii)

Clearly, nth term, $a_n = S_n - S_{n-1}$

$= 6n + 7n^2 - 7n^2 + 8n - 1 = 14n - 1$

Now, 10th term of an AP, [from Eqs. (i) and (ii)]

$a_{10} = 14 \times 10 - 1$

$= 140 - 1 = 139.$

Applications of Arithmetic Progression (AP)

To solve word problems, first we form the list of numbers with the help of given information and check that this list is an AP or not. If it is an AP, then use the formula of sum of first n terms and calculate the missing value.

Example 41. A man repays a loan of ₹ 3250 by ₹ 20 in the first month and then increases the payment by ₹ 15 every month. How long will it take him to clear the loan?

Sol. Given, total amount of loan = ₹ 3250

Amount paid in first month = ₹ 20

and amount increases every month = ₹ 15

Clearly, the amounts of repayment form an AP with first term $(a) = 20$ and common difference $(d) = 15$.

Let the loan be cleared in n months.

Then, $S_n = 3250$

$\Rightarrow \frac{n}{2}[2a + (n-1)d] = 3250 \quad \left[\because S_n = \frac{n}{2}\{2a + (n-1)d\}\right]$

$\Rightarrow \frac{n}{2}[2(20) + (n-1)15] = 3250$

$\Rightarrow n(40 + 15n - 15) = 3250 \times 2$

$\Rightarrow 25n + 15n^2 = 6500$

$\Rightarrow 3n^2 + 5n - 1300 = 0$ [dividing both sides by 5]

$\Rightarrow 3n^2 + 65n - 60n - 1300 = 0$

$\Rightarrow n(3n + 65) - 20(3n + 65) = 0$

$\Rightarrow (n - 20)(3n + 65) = 0$

$\Rightarrow n = 20$ or $n = \frac{-65}{3}$

Since, n should be a positive integer, so neglect $n = \frac{-65}{3}$.

Thus, $n = 20$

Hence, the loan will clear in 20 months.

Example 42. Kanika was given her pocket money on Jan 1st, 2018. She puts ₹ 1 on day 1, ₹ 2 on day 2, ₹ 3 on day 3 and continued doing so till the end of the month, from this money into her piggy bank. She also spent ₹ 204 of her pocket money and found that at the end of the month she still had ₹ 100 with her. How much was her pocket money for the month?

Sol. Let her pocket money be ₹ x.

Given, she puts ₹ 1 on day 1, ₹ 2 on day 2, ₹ 3 on day 3 and so on till the end of the month, into her piggy bank.

Clearly, the amounts that she puts everyday of the month, form an AP, in which number of terms is 31, first term $(a) = 1$ and common difference $(d) = 2 - 1 = 1$.

Now, sum of first 31 terms,

$S_{31} = \frac{31}{2}[2 \times 1 + (31 - 1) \times 1] \quad \left[\because S_n = \frac{n}{2}\{2a + (n-1)d\}\right]$

$= \frac{31}{2}(2 + 30) = \frac{31 \times 32}{2}$

$= 31 \times 16 = 496$

So, Kanika puts ₹ 496 into her piggy bank.

Also, it is given that, she spent ₹ 204 of her pocket money and found that at the end of the month, she still had ₹100 with her.

According to the condition,

$(x - 496) - 204 = 100$

$\Rightarrow x - 700 = 100$

$\Rightarrow x = ₹\ 800$

Hence, ₹ 800 was her pocket money for the month.

Exercise 9.2

1. Find the sum of the following AP.
   (i) 50, 46, 42, ... upto 10 terms.
   (ii) 2, 4, 6, ... upto 100 terms.
   (iii) −37, −33, −29, ... upto 12 terms.
   (iv) 0.6, 1.7, 2.8, ... upto 100 terms.
   (v) $\frac{1}{15}, \frac{1}{12}, \frac{1}{10}, \ldots$ upto 11 terms.
2. Find the sum of first 25 terms of an AP, whose nth term is $1 - 4n$.
3. Find the sum of first 21 terms of an AP, whose 2nd term is 8 and 4th term is 4.
4. Find the sum of first 17 terms of an AP, where 4th and 9th terms are − 15 and − 30, respectively.
5. If the sum of first p terms of an AP is q and the sum of first q terms is p, then find the sum of first $(p+q)$ terms.
6. If sum of first 6 terms of an AP is 36 and that of the first 16 terms is 256, then find the sum of first 10 terms.
7. The sum of the first five terms and the sum of the first seven terms of an AP is 167. If the sum of the first ten terms of this AP is 235, then find the sum of its first twenty terms.
8. Find the number of terms of the following AP.
   (i) 64, 60, 56, ... having sum 544.
   (ii) 9, 17, 25, ... having sum 636.
   (iii) − 7, − 4, − 1, ... having sum 210.
   (iv) 0.6, 0.9, 1.2, ... having sum 69.
9. Find the sum of the last 12 terms of an AP 2, 4, 6, ... 100.
10. Find the sum of all the 13 terms of an AP, whose middle most term is 20.
11. The sum of the first n terms of an AP is given by $S_n = 2n^2 + 5n$. Find the nth term of an AP.
12. If the sum of first n terms of an AP is given by $S_n = n(4n+1)$, then find the nth term of an AP. Also, find an AP.
13. Show that $a_1, a_2, a_3, \ldots\ldots$ form an AP, where a_n is defined as $a_n = 3 + 4n$. Also, find the sum of first 15 terms.
14. If S_n denotes the sum of first n terms of an AP prove that $S_{30} = 3(S_{20} - S_{10})$.
15. Find the sum of all natural numbers less than 100 which are divisible by 6.
16. The sum of first six terms of an arithmetic progression is 42. The ratio of its 10th term to its 30th term is 1 : 3. Calculate the first and the 13th terms of an AP.
17. Prove that the sum of later half of $2n$ terms of an AP is equal to one-third of the sum of the first $3n$ terms.
18. In an AP of 50 terms, the sum of first 10 terms is 210 and the sum of its last 15 terms is 2565. Find an AP.
19. If the 6th term of an AP is equal to four times its first term and the sum of first six terms is 75, find the first term and the common difference.
20. If the sum of first m terms of an AP is the same as the sum of its first n terms $(m \neq n)$, show that the sum of its first $(m+n)$ terms is zero.
21. Yasmeen saves ₹ 32 during the first month, ₹ 36 in the second month and ₹ 40 in the third month. If she continues to save in this manner, in how many months will she save ₹ 2000?
22. 228 logs are to be stacked in a store in the following manner: 30 logs in the bottom, 28 in the next row, then 26 and so on, in how many rows can these 228 logs be stacked? How many logs are there in the last row?
23. The ages of the students in a class are in AP, whose common difference is 4 months. If the youngest student is 8 yr old and the sum of the ages of all the students is 168 yr, then find the number of students in the class.
24. A man arranges to pay off a debt of ₹ 3600 by 40 annual installments which are in AP. When 30 of the installments are paid, he dies leaving one-third of the debt unpaid. Find the value of the 8th installment.

Geometric Progression (GP)

A sequence of non-zero numbers is said to be a geometric progression, if the ratio of each term, except the first one, by its preceding term is always constant.

In other words, we can say that a sequence $a_1, a_2, \ldots, a_n$ is called **geometric progression** (geometric sequence), if it follows the relation

$$\frac{a_{k+1}}{a_k} = r \text{ (constant) for all } k \in N.$$

The constant ratio is called **common ratio** of the GP and it is denoted by r. In a GP, we usually denote the first term by a and the nth term by T_n or a_n.

The general form of GP can be written as $a, ar, ar^2, ar^3, \ldots$ and so on.

e.g. The sequence 4, 12, 36, 108, ... is a GP.

Here, $a = 4$ and $r = \frac{12}{4} = \frac{36}{12} = \frac{108}{36} = \ldots = 3$

Example 43. Examine that the sequence $2, 2\sqrt{2}, 4, 4\sqrt{2}, \ldots$ is a GP.

Sol. Here, $\frac{a_2}{a_1} = \frac{2\sqrt{2}}{2} = \sqrt{2}$

$$\frac{a_3}{a_2} = \frac{4}{2\sqrt{2}} \times \frac{\sqrt{2}}{\sqrt{2}} = \frac{4\sqrt{2}}{2 \times 2} = \sqrt{2},$$

$$\frac{a_4}{a_3} = \frac{4\sqrt{2}}{4} = \sqrt{2} \text{ and so on.}$$

Since, ratio of any term by its preceding term is constant, so the given sequence is a GP.

Example 44. Examine that the list of numbers obtained from the following situation, will be in the form of a GP. An insect starts from a point and travels in a straight path 1 mm in first second and half of the distance covered in previous second in the succeeding second.

Sol. Given, distance moved by the insect in 1st second = 1mm

$\therefore$ Distance moved by the insect in 2nd second = 1/2 mm

and so on distance moved by the insect in 3rd second = 1/4 mm

Here, $\frac{a_2}{a_1} = \frac{1/2}{1} = \frac{1}{2}$

$\Rightarrow \frac{a_3}{a_2} = \frac{1/4}{1/2} = \frac{1}{2}$ and so on

i.e. $\frac{a_{k+1}}{a_k}$ is same for all $k \in N$.

So, the above list of numbers forms a GP.

Example 45. Find the common ratio of the following GP.

(i) $1, \sqrt{3}, 3, 3\sqrt{3}, \ldots$ (ii) $12, 4, 1\frac{1}{3}, \ldots$

(iii) $17, 17, 17, 17, \ldots$

Sol.

(i) Given, GP is $1, \sqrt{3}, 3, 3\sqrt{3}, \ldots$
Here, $a_1 = 1, a_2 = \sqrt{3}, a_3 = 3, a_4 = 3\sqrt{3}$ and so on.

$\therefore$ Common ratio $(r) = \frac{a_2}{a_1} = \frac{\sqrt{3}}{1} = \sqrt{3}$

(ii) Given, GP is $12, 4, 1\frac{1}{3}, \ldots$
Here, $a_1 = 12, a_2 = 4, a_3 = 1\frac{1}{3}$ and so on.

$\therefore$ Common ratio $(r) = \frac{a_2}{a_1} = \frac{4}{12} = \frac{1}{3}$

(iii) Given, GP is 17, 17, 17, 17, ...
Here, $a_1 = 17, a_2 = 17, a_3 = 17, a_4 = 17$ and so on.

$\therefore$ Common ratio $(r) = \frac{a_2}{a_1} = \frac{17}{17} = 1.$

Method to Write a GP, When First Term and Common Ratio are Given

To write a GP, the minimum information required is to know the first term a and the common ratio r of the geometric progression. Then, put the values of a and r in $a, ar, ar^2, ar^3, \ldots$ to get required GP.

Example 46. Write a GP having 2 as the first term and $\frac{1}{2}$ as the common ratio.

Sol. Given, first term $(a) = 2$ and common ratio $(r) = \frac{1}{2}$

On putting the values of a and r in the general form of GP, i.e. $a, ar, ar^2, ar^3, \ldots$, we get

$$2, 2 \times \frac{1}{2}, 2 \times \left(\frac{1}{2}\right)^2, 2 \times \left(\frac{1}{2}\right)^3, \ldots \text{ or } 2, 1, \frac{1}{2}, \frac{1}{4}, \ldots,$$

which is the required GP.

Example 47. If the sum of the first two terms of a GP is –4 and the fifth term is 4 times the third term, find the GP.

Sol. Let a be the first term and r is the common ratio of the GP

Given, $a_1 + a_2 = -4 \Rightarrow a + ar = -4$

$$a(1 + r) = -4 \quad \ldots(i)$$

and $a_5 = 4a_3 \Rightarrow ar^4 \Rightarrow 4 \times ar^2$

$$r^2 = 4 \Rightarrow r = \pm 2$$

When, $r = 2$, from Eq. (i), we get

$$a(1 + 2) = -4 \Rightarrow a = -\frac{4}{3}$$

GP is $-\frac{4}{3}, -\frac{8}{3}, -\frac{16}{3}$

When, $r = -2$ from Eq. (i), we get

$$a(1-2) = -4 \Rightarrow a = 4$$

GP is 4, –8, 16 ......

Hence, the required GP is $-\frac{4}{3}, -\frac{8}{3}, -\frac{16}{3}$, ... or 4, –8, 16 ....

Properties of GP

(i) If a, b and c are in GP, then

$$\frac{b}{a} = \frac{c}{b},$$

i.e. $b^2 = ac$

$\therefore$ a, b and c are in GP

$\Rightarrow$ $b^2 = ac$

Conversely, $b^2 = ac$

$\Rightarrow$ a, b and c are in GP.

(ii) If each term of a GP is multiplied or divided by a fixed non-zero number, the resulting sequence is also a GP.

(iii) The sequence obtained by taking the reciprocals of the terms of a GP is also a GP.

e.g. 6, 24, 96, 384, ... is a GP.

$\Rightarrow$ $\frac{1}{6}, \frac{1}{24}, \frac{1}{96}, \frac{1}{384}, \ldots$ is also a GP.

Example 48. For what values of k, the numbers $-\frac{2}{7}, k, -\frac{7}{2}$ are in GP ?

Sol. If $-\frac{2}{7}, k, -\frac{7}{2}$ are in GP, then $k^2 = \left(-\frac{2}{7}\right)\left(-\frac{7}{2}\right)$

[$\because$ if a, b and c are in GP, then $\Rightarrow b^2 = ac$]

$\Rightarrow$ $k^2 = 1 \Rightarrow k = \pm 1$

Example 49. If a, b and c are in GP, then find the value of $\frac{a-b}{b-c}$.

Sol. Given that, a, b and c are in GP.

Then, $\frac{b}{a} = \frac{c}{b} = r$ (constant) ...(i)

$\Rightarrow$ $b = ar$ and $c = br$

$\Rightarrow$ $b = ar$ and $c = (ar)r = ar^2$

Now, $\frac{a-b}{b-c} = \frac{a-ar}{ar-ar^2} = \frac{a(1-r)}{ar(1-r)} = \frac{1}{r}$

$\Rightarrow$ $\frac{a-b}{b-c} = \frac{1}{r} = \frac{a}{b}$ or $\frac{b}{c}$ [using Eq. (i)]

General Term of a GP

If a is the first term of a GP and r its common ratio, then general term or nth term,

$$a_n \text{ or } T_n = ar^{n-1}$$

Problems Based on General Term of a GP

Some types of these problems are given below

Example 50. Find the nth term and the 12th term of the sequence – 6, 18, – 54, ...

Sol. Given, sequence is – 6, 18, – 54, ...

Clearly, the ratio of each term by its preceding term is same.

So, the given sequence forms a GP with

first term, $a = -6$ and common ratio, $r = \frac{18}{-6} = -3$.

Now, nth term,

$$a_n = ar^{n-1} = -6(-3)^{n-1} = (-1)^n 6 \cdot 3^{n-1}$$

and $a_{12} = (-1)^{12} 6 \cdot 3^{12-1} = (1) \cdot 6 \cdot 3^{11}$

$= 2 \cdot 3 \cdot 3^{11} = 2 \cdot 3^{12}$

Hence, the nth term of given GP is $(-1)^n 6 \cdot 3^{n-1}$ and 12th term is $2 \cdot 3^{12}$.

Example 51. Which term of the GP 5, 10, 20, 40, ... is 5120?

Sol. Given GP is 5, 10, 20, 40, ...

Here, $a = 5$ and $r = \frac{10}{5} = 2$

Let nth term of given GP = 5120, i.e. $a_n = 5120$

Now, $a_n = ar^{n-1} = 5120$

$\Rightarrow$ $5(2)^{n-1} = 5120$ [$\because a = 5, r = 2$]

$\Rightarrow$ $2^{n-1} = \frac{5120}{5} = 1024$

$\Rightarrow$ $2^{n-1} = 1024 \Rightarrow 2^{n-1} = 2^{10}$

On equating the powers, we get

$$n - 1 = 10 \Rightarrow n = 10 + 1 = 11$$

Hence, 11th term of given GP is 5120.

Example 52. The 4th, 6th and last term of a geometric progression are 10, 40 and 640 respectively. If the common ratio is positive, find the first term, common ratio and the number of terms of the series. **[ICSE 2020]**

Sol. Let the first term and common ratio of GP be a and r, respectively and total number of terms be n.

According to the question,

4th term $= ar^{4-1} = 10 \Rightarrow ar^3 = 10$ ... (i)

6th term $= ar^{6-1} = 40 \Rightarrow ar^5 = 40$ ... (ii)

and last term $= ar^{n-1} = 640$ ... (iii)

On dividing Eq. (ii) by Eq. (i), we get

$$\frac{ar^5}{ar^3} = \frac{40}{10} \Rightarrow r^2 = 4$$

$\Rightarrow$ $r = 2$ [since common ratio is positive]

Now, from Eq. (i),

$$a(2)^3 = 10 \Rightarrow a = \frac{10}{8} = \frac{5}{4}$$

On putting values of a and r in Eq. (iii), we get

$$\left(\frac{5}{4}\right)(2)^{n-1} = 640$$

$$\Rightarrow \quad 2^{n-1} = 640 \times \frac{4}{5} = 512$$

$$\Rightarrow \quad 2^{n-1} = 2^9$$

$$\Rightarrow \quad n - 1 = 9 \Rightarrow n = 10$$

$\therefore$ First term $= \frac{5}{4}$, Common ratio $= 2$

and number of terms of the series = 10.

Example 53. If the 4th and 9th terms of a GP are 54 and 13122 respectively, then find the GP.

Sol. Let a be the first term and r be the common ratio of GP.

Given, 4th term, $a_4 = 54$

$$\Rightarrow \quad ar^{4-1} = 54$$

$$\Rightarrow \quad ar^3 = 54 \quad \text{...(i)}$$

and 9th term, $a_9 = 13122$

$$\Rightarrow \quad ar^{9-1} = 13122$$

$$\Rightarrow \quad ar^8 = 13122 \quad \text{...(ii)}$$

On dividing Eq. (ii) by Eq. (i), we get

$$\frac{ar^8}{ar^3} = \frac{13122}{54}$$

$$\Rightarrow \quad r^5 = 243 \Rightarrow r^5 = (3)^5$$

$$\therefore \quad r = 3$$

On putting the value of r in Eq. (i), we get

$$a(3)^3 = 54 \Rightarrow 27a = 54 \Rightarrow a = \frac{54}{27} = 2$$

$\therefore$ Required GP is $a, ar, ar^2, ar^3, \ldots$, i.e. 2, 6, 18, 54, ...

Example 54. If the pth and qth terms of a GP are q and p respectively, then show that its $(p+q)$th term is $\left(\frac{q^p}{p^q}\right)^{\frac{1}{p-q}}$.

Sol. Let the first term and common ratio of GP be a and r, respectively.

According to the question, pth term $= q$

$$\Rightarrow \quad ar^{p-1} = q \quad \text{...(i)}$$

and qth term $= p$

$$\Rightarrow \quad ar^{q-1} = p \quad \text{...(ii)}$$

On dividing Eq. (i) by Eq. (ii), we get

$$\frac{ar^{p-1}}{ar^{q-1}} = \frac{q}{p} \Rightarrow r^{p-1-q+1} = \frac{q}{p}$$

$$\Rightarrow \quad r^{p-q} = \frac{q}{p} \Rightarrow r = \left(\frac{q}{p}\right)^{\frac{1}{p-q}}$$

On substituting the value of r in Eq. (i), we get

$$a\left(\frac{q}{p}\right)^{\frac{p-1}{p-q}} = q \Rightarrow a = \frac{q}{\left(\frac{q}{p}\right)^{\frac{p-1}{p-q}}} = q \cdot \left(\frac{p}{q}\right)^{\frac{p-1}{p-q}}$$

Now, $(p+q)$th term, $a_{p+q} = a \cdot r^{p+q-1}$

$$= q \cdot \left(\frac{p}{q}\right)^{\frac{p-1}{p-q}} \cdot (r)^{p+q-1}$$

$$= q \cdot \left(\frac{p}{q}\right)^{\frac{p-1}{p-q}} \times \left(\frac{q}{p}\right)^{\frac{p+q-1}{p-q}}$$

$$= \frac{q^{1-\frac{p-1}{p-q}+\frac{p+q-1}{p-q}}}{p^{\frac{p+q-1}{p-q}-\frac{p-1}{p-q}}} = \frac{q^{\frac{p-q-p+1+p+q-1}{p-q}}}{p^{\frac{p+q-1-p+1}{p-q}}}$$

$$= \frac{q^{\frac{p}{p-q}}}{p^{\frac{q}{p-q}}} = \left(\frac{q^p}{p^q}\right)^{\frac{1}{p-q}}$$

Hence proved.

Example 55. Three numbers whose sum is 21 are in AP. If 2, 2, 14 are added to them respectively, the resulting numbers are in GP, find the numbers.

Sol. Let an AP $a-d, a, a+d$ (given three numbers)

Their sum $3a = 21 \Rightarrow a = 7$

Therefore, the numbers are $7-d, 7, 7+d$

According to the question,

Adding 2, 2, 14 respectively, we get the numbers $9-d$, 9, $21+d$. Since, these are in GP.

$$\therefore \quad (9)^2 = (9-d)(21+d)$$

$$\Rightarrow \quad d^2 + 12d - 108 = 0 \Rightarrow (d+18)(d-6) = 0$$

$$d = 6 \text{ or } -18$$

Using $d = -18$, we get three numbers 25, 7, −11.

Using $d = 6$, we get three numbers 1, 7, 13.

Hence, the numbers are 1, 7, 13 or 25, 7, −11.

Example 56. The $(m+n)$th and $(m-n)$th terms of a GP are p and q, respectively. Show that the mth and nth terms are $\sqrt{pq}$ and $p\left(\frac{q}{p}\right)^{m/2n}$, respectively.

Sol. Let a be the first term and r be the common ratio.

Then, $\quad a_{m+n} = p$ and $a_{m-n} = q$

$$\Rightarrow \quad ar^{m+n-1} = p \text{ and } ar^{m-n-1} = q \quad [\because n\text{th term} = ar^{n-1}]$$

$$\Rightarrow \quad \frac{ar^{m+n-1}}{ar^{m-n-1}} = \frac{p}{q}$$

$$\Rightarrow \quad r^{2n} = \frac{p}{q}$$

$$\Rightarrow \quad r = \left(\frac{p}{q}\right)^{1/2n} \Rightarrow \frac{1}{r} = \left(\frac{q}{p}\right)^{1/2n}$$

Now, $a_m = ar^{m-1}$

$$\Rightarrow \quad a_m = ar^{(m-1)} \cdot r^n \cdot \frac{1}{r^n}$$

$$\Rightarrow \quad a_m = ar^{(m+n-1)}\left(\frac{1}{r}\right)^n$$

$$\Rightarrow \quad a_m = a_{m+n}\left(\frac{1}{r}\right)^n \quad [\because a_{m+n} = ar^{m+n-1}]$$

$$\Rightarrow \quad a_m = p\left(\frac{q}{p}\right)^{n/2n} \quad \left[\because a_{m+n} = p \text{ and } \frac{1}{r} = \left(\frac{q}{p}\right)^{1/2n}\right]$$

$$\Rightarrow \quad a_m = p\left(\frac{q}{p}\right)^{1/2} = \sqrt{pq}$$

and $\quad a_n = ar^{n-1}$

$$\Rightarrow \quad a_n = ar^{m+n-1}\left(\frac{1}{r}\right)^m$$

$$= a_{m+n}\left(\frac{1}{r}\right)^m \quad [\because a_{m+n} = ar^{m+n-1}]$$

$$\Rightarrow \quad a_n = p\left(\frac{q}{p}\right)^{m/2n} \quad \left[\because a_{m+n} = p \text{ and } \frac{1}{r} = \left(\frac{q}{p}\right)^{1/2n}\right]$$

Hence proved.

Example 57. If x, $2x+2$, $3x+3$ are first three terms of a geometric progression, find its fourth term.

Sol. Since x, $2x+2$, $3x+3$ are in GP

$\therefore \quad (2x+2)^2 = x \times (3x+3)$

$\Rightarrow \quad 4x^2 + 8x + 4 = 3x^2 + 3x$

$\Rightarrow \quad x^2 + 5x + 4 = 0$

$\Rightarrow \quad (x+1)(x+4) = 0$

$\Rightarrow \quad x = -1$ or $x = -4$

Using $x = -1$, we get first three terms as $-1, 0, 0$ which is not possible, as in a GP all terms are non-zero.

Using $x = -4$, we get first three terms as $-4, -6, -9$, which is a GP with common ratio

$$r = \frac{3}{2}$$

Hence, the 4th term = Common ratio × (3rd term)

$$= \frac{3}{2} \times (-9) = -\frac{27}{2}$$

nth Term of a GP from the End

Let a be the first term and r be the common ratio of a GP having m terms. Then, nth term from the end is $(m-n+1)$th term from the beginning.

$\therefore$ **nth term from the end** $= ar^{m-n+1-1} = ar^{m-n}$

$\therefore$ where, $m > n$.

Also, nth term from the end $= l\left(\frac{1}{r}\right)^{-1}$, where l is the last term of the GP.

Example 58. Find the 8th term from the end of the sequence 3, 6, 12, ... 25th term.

Sol. Here, $a = 3$, $r = \frac{6}{3} = 2$, $m = 25$ and $n = 8$.

Now, 8th term from the end of sequence is equal to the $(25 - 8 + 1)$, i.e. 18th term from the beginning,

and $\quad a_{18} = ar^{18-1} = 3(2)^{18-1} \quad [\because a = 3, r = 2]$

$$= 3(2)^{17} = 3 \times 131072 = 393216$$

Hence, the 8th term from the end is 393216.

Selection of Terms in GP

Sometimes we have to select certain number of terms in GP. The convenient way of selecting terms is given below

Number of terms	Terms	Common ratio
3	$\frac{a}{r}, a, ar$	r
4	$\frac{a}{r^3}, \frac{a}{r}, ar, ar^3$	r^2
5	$\frac{a}{r^2}, \frac{a}{r}, a, ar, ar^2$	r

Note If the terms of the GP are not given, then the terms can be chosen as $a, ar, ar^2, ar^3, \ldots$.

Example 59. Find four numbers forming a GP in which the third term is greater than the first term by 9 and the second term is greater than 4th by 18.

Sol. Let the GP be $a, ar, ar^2, ar^3, \ldots$

Given, third term = first term + 9

$\Rightarrow \quad ar^2 = a + 9$

$\Rightarrow \quad ar^2 - a = 9 \quad \ldots(i)$

Also, it is given that, second term = fourth term + 18

$\Rightarrow \quad ar = ar^3 + 18$

$\Rightarrow \quad ar - ar^3 = 18 \quad \ldots(ii)$

On dividing Eq. (i) by Eq. (ii), we get

$$\frac{ar^2 - a}{ar - ar^3} = \frac{9}{18} \Rightarrow \frac{a(r^2-1)}{ar(1-r^2)} = \frac{1}{2}$$

$$\Rightarrow \quad \frac{-1(1-r^2)}{r(1-r^2)} = \frac{1}{2} \Rightarrow -\frac{1}{r} = \frac{1}{2}$$

$\Rightarrow \quad r = -2$

On putting $r = -2$ in Eq. (i), we get

$$a(-2)^2 - a = 9 \Rightarrow 4a - a = 9$$

$\Rightarrow \quad 3a = 9 \Rightarrow a = 3$

$\therefore$ GP is $3, 3(-2), 3(-2)^2, 3(-2)^3, \ldots$

Hence, the required four numbers are 3, – 6, 12 and – 24.

Note Here, 'greater than' word stands for excess in term.

Example 60. If pth, qth and rth terms of a GP are themselves in GP. Show that p, q, r in AP.

Sol. Let A be the first term and R be the common ratio of the given GP.

Now, $\quad a_p = AR^{p-1}$

$\quad a_q = AR^{q-1}$

and $\quad a_r = AR^{r-1}$

$\therefore \quad (AR^{q-1})^2 = (AR^{p-1})(AR^{r-1})$

$\Rightarrow \quad A^2 . R^{2q-2} = A^2 . R^{p+r-2}$

$\Rightarrow \quad 2q - 2 = p + r - 2 \Rightarrow 2q = p + r$

$\because \quad r - q = q - p$

Hence, proved that p, q, r in AP.

Exercise 9.3

1. Show that the following progressions is a GP. Also, find the common ratio in each case.
   (i) $4, -2, 1, -1/2, \ldots$ (ii) $a, \frac{3a^2}{4}, \frac{9a^3}{16}, \ldots$
2. For what value of x, the numbers $(x+9), (x-6)$ and 4 are in GP?
3. Find the term of the following GP's.
   (i) 11th term of the GP : 3, 6, 12, 24, ...
   (ii) 10th term of the GP : $12, 4, \frac{4}{3}, \frac{4}{9}, \ldots$
   (iii) 17th term of the GP : $2, 2\sqrt{2}, 4, 8\sqrt{2}, \ldots$
   (iv) 8th term of the GP : 0.3, 0.06, 0.012, ...
   (v) 12th term of the GP $\frac{1}{a^3x^3}, ax, a^5x^5, \ldots$
4. Find the 20th and nth terms of the following GP.
   $\frac{5}{2}, \frac{5}{4}, \frac{5}{8}, \ldots$
5. Find the 10th term of the geometric series $5 + 25 + 125 + \ldots$. Also, find its nth term.
6. Find 12th term of a GP, whose 8th term is 192 and common ratio is 2.
7. Which term of the following sequences
   (i) $\sqrt{3}, 3, 3\sqrt{3}, \ldots$ is 729?
   (ii) $\frac{1}{3}, \frac{1}{9}, \frac{1}{27}, \ldots$ is $\frac{1}{19683}$?
   (iii) $-3, -27, -243, \ldots$ is -1594323?
   (iv) 0.2, 0.4, 0.8, ... is 204.8?
8. Three numbers are in AP and their sum is 15. If 1, 4 and 19 are added to these numbers respectively, the resulting numbers are in GP. Find the numbers.
9. The 4th term of a GP is 16 and 7th term is 128. Find the first term and common ratio of the series. [ICSE 2018]
10. Find the GP whose 5th and 8th terms are 80 and 640, respectively.
11. The first term of a GP is 1. Sum of the third term and fifth term is 90. Find the common ratio of GP.
12. Find a GP for which sum of the first two terms is -4 and fifth term is 4 times the third term.
13. If the 4th, 10th and 16th terms of a GP are x, y, z respectively. Prove that x, y, z are in GP.
14. If $x, 2y, 3z$ are in AP, where the distinct numbers x, y, z are in GP, then find the common ratio of the GP.
15. If the pth, qth and rth terms of a GP are a, b and c respectively. Prove that $a^{q-r} b^{r-p} c^{p-q} = 1$.
16. If p, q, r in AP, then show that pth, qth and rth terms of a GP are themselves in GP.
17. If the first and nth terms of a GP are a and b respectively and P is the product of n terms, then prove that $P^2 = (ab)^n$.
18. Find the term of the following GP's.
    (i) 6th term from the end of the GP $8, 4, 2, \ldots, \frac{1}{1024}$.
    (ii) 4th term from the end of the GP $8, 4, 2, \ldots, \frac{1}{1024}$.
19. Prove that in a finite GP the product of the terms equidistant from the beginning and the end is always same and equal to the product of first and last term.
20. If the sum of three numbers in GP is 13/12 and their product is -1, then find the numbers.
21. The sum of first three terms of a GP is 39/10 and their product is 1. Find the first three terms of the GP, if terms of GP are real numbers.
22. The product of first three terms of a GP is 1000. If 6 is added to its second term and 7 added to its third term, the terms become in AP. Find the GP.
23. The lengths of the sides of a triangle form a GP. If the perimeter of the triangle is 37 cm and the shortest side is of length 9 cm, then find the lengths of the other two sides.

Sum of First n Terms of a GP

If a and r are the first term and common ratio of a GP respectively, then sum of first n terms of this GP is given by

$$S_n = \frac{a(1-r^n)}{1-r} \text{ when } r<1$$

and $$S_n = \frac{a(r^n-1)}{r-1} \text{ when } r>1\ (r \neq 1)$$

Note (i) If $r=1$ in GP $a, ar, ar^2 \ldots$, then $S_n = a + a + \ldots + n$ terms $= na$

(ii) Suppose a GP contains n terms with first term $= a$, common ratio $= r$ and last term $= l$. Then, sum of GP is given by $S_n = \frac{a-lr}{1-r}$, when $r<1$ and $S_n = \frac{lr-a}{r-1}$, when $r>1$.

Problems Based on Sum of Terms of a GP

There are so many problems which can be solved by using the sum formula of a GP.

Some types of these problems are given below

Example 61. Find the sum of the following sequences.

(i) $\frac{1}{2}, \frac{3}{2}, \frac{9}{2}, \ldots$ upto 10 terms

(ii) $2, -\frac{1}{2}, \frac{1}{8}, \ldots$ upto 12 terms

Sol.

(i) Given, sequence is $\frac{1}{2}, \frac{3}{2}, \frac{9}{2}, \ldots$

Clearly, the ratio of any term by its preceding is same.

So, the above sequence forms a GP, with first term, $a = \frac{1}{2}$ and common ratio, $r = \frac{3}{2} \div \frac{1}{2} = 3 > 1$

$$\therefore \quad S_{10} = \frac{\frac{1}{2}(3^{10}-1)}{3-1} \qquad \left[\because S_n = \frac{a(r^n-1)}{r-1}, \text{ as } r>1\right]$$

$$= \frac{1}{2} \cdot \frac{(3^{10}-1)}{2} = \frac{1}{4}(3^{10}-1) = 14762$$

(ii) Given, sequence is $2, -\frac{1}{2}, \frac{1}{8}, \ldots$

Clearly, the ratio of any term by its preceding term is same. So, the above sequence forms a GP with first term, $a = 2$ and common ratio, $r = -\frac{1}{2} \div 2 = \frac{-1}{4} < 1$

$$\therefore \quad S_{12} = \frac{2\left[1-\left(\frac{-1}{4}\right)^{12}\right]}{1-\left(\frac{-1}{4}\right)} \qquad \left[\because S_n = \frac{a(1-r^n)}{1-r}, \text{ as } r<1\right]$$

$$= \frac{2\left[1-\frac{1}{(4)^{12}}\right]}{1+\frac{1}{4}} = \frac{2\left[1-\left(\frac{1}{4}\right)^{12}\right]}{\left(\frac{5}{4}\right)} = \frac{8}{5}\left[1-\left(\frac{1}{4}\right)^{12}\right]$$

Example 62. Find the sum of the series

$$2 + 6 + 18 + 54 + \ldots + 4374$$

Sol. Given, series is $2+6+18+54+\ldots+4374$

Clearly, the ratio of any term by its preceding term is same.

So, the above series forms a GP with first term, $a = 2$, common ratio, $r = \frac{6}{2} = 3 > 1$ and last term, $l = 4374$.

$$\therefore \text{Required sum} = \frac{(lr-a)}{(r-1)} = \frac{(4374 \times 3 - 2)}{(3-1)}$$

$$= \frac{13120}{2} = 6560$$

Hence, the sum of the given series is 6560.

Example 63. Find the sum to n terms of the sequence given by $a_n = 2^n + 3n$, $n \in N$.

Sol. Let S_n denotes the sum to n terms of the given sequence.

Then, $S_n = a_1 + a_2 + a_3 + \ldots + a_n$

$$\Rightarrow \quad S_n = (2^1 + 3\times 1) + (2^2 + 3\times 2) + (2^3 + 3 \times 3) + \ldots + (2^n + 3 \times n)$$

$$\Rightarrow S_n = (2^1 + 2^2 + 2^3 + \ldots + 2^n) + (3\times 1 + 3 \times 2 + 3 \times 3 + \ldots + 3 \times n)$$

$$= (2^1 + 2^2 + 2^3 + \ldots + 2^n) + 3(1 + 2 + 3 + \ldots + n)$$

$$= 2\left(\frac{2^n-1}{2-1}\right) + 3\left\{\frac{n}{2}(1+n)\right\}$$

[$\because 2 + 2^2 + 2^3 + 2^n$ is a GS and $1 + 2 + 3 + \ldots + n$ is an AS]

$$= 2(2^n - 1) + \frac{3n}{2}(n+1)$$

Example 64. The first and last term of a Geometric Progression (GP) are 3 and 96, respectively. If the common ratio is 2, then find

(i) n, the number of terms of the GP.

(ii) sum of the n terms. **[ICSE 2019]**

Sol. Given, $a = 3$, $l = a_n = 96$ and $r = 2$

(i) nth term of a GP is $a_n = ar^{n-1}$

$$\therefore \quad 96 = 3(2)^{n-1}$$

$$\Rightarrow \quad 32 = 2^{n-1}$$

$$\Rightarrow \quad 2^5 = 2^{n-1}$$

On equating the power of 2, we get

$$5 = n - 1$$

$$\Rightarrow \quad n = 6$$

Hence, the number of terms in a GP is 6.

(ii) Now, sum of n terms of a GP is

$$S_n = \frac{a(r^n-1)}{(r-1)}, r > 1 = \frac{3(2^6-1)}{2-1}$$

$$= \frac{3 \times (64-1)}{1} = 3 \times 63 = 189$$

Example 65. Find the sum of series

$$\frac{3}{5} + \frac{4}{5^2} + \frac{3}{5^3} + \frac{4}{5^4} + \ldots \text{ to } 2n \text{ terms.}$$

Sol. Let $S = \frac{3}{5} + \frac{4}{5^2} + \frac{3}{5^3} + \frac{4}{5^4} + \ldots$ to $2n$ terms

$$= \left[\frac{3}{5} + \frac{3}{5^3} + \ldots \text{ to } n \text{ terms}\right] + \left[\frac{4}{5^2} + \frac{4}{5^4} + \ldots \text{ to } n \text{ terms}\right]$$

$$= \frac{\frac{3}{5}\left[1-\left(\frac{1}{5^2}\right)^n\right]}{\left[1-\left(\frac{1}{5^2}\right)\right]} + \frac{\frac{4}{5^2}\left[1-\left(\frac{1}{5^2}\right)^n\right]}{\left[1-\left(\frac{1}{5^2}\right)\right]} \quad \left[\because S_n = \frac{a(1-r^n)}{1-r}, r<1\right]$$

$$= \frac{\frac{3}{5}\left(1-\frac{1}{5^{2n}}\right)}{1-\frac{1}{25}} + \frac{\frac{4}{25}\left(1-\frac{1}{5^{2n}}\right)}{1-\frac{1}{25}}$$

$$= \frac{\frac{3}{5}\left(1-\frac{1}{5^{2n}}\right)}{\frac{24}{25}} + \frac{\frac{4}{25}\left(1-\frac{1}{5^{2n}}\right)}{\frac{24}{25}}$$

$$= \frac{5}{8}\left(1-\frac{1}{5^{2n}}\right) + \frac{1}{6}\left(1-\frac{1}{5^{2n}}\right)$$

$$= \left(1-\frac{1}{5^{2n}}\right)\left(\frac{5}{8}+\frac{1}{6}\right)$$

$$= \left(1-\frac{1}{5^{2n}}\right)\left(\frac{15+4}{24}\right)$$

$$= \frac{19}{24}\left(1-\frac{1}{5^{2n}}\right).$$

Example 66. Find the sum of the products of the corresponding terms of the sequences 2, 4, 8, 16, 32 and 128, 32, 8, 2, $\frac{1}{2}$.

Sol. Given, sequences are 2, 4, 8, 16, 32 ...(i)

and 128, 32, 8, 2, $\frac{1}{2}$ ...(ii)

On multiplying the corresponding terms of Eqs. (i) and (ii), we get a new sequence 256, 128, 64, 32, 16

Let $S = 256 + 128 + 64 + 32 + 16$

Clearly, the ratio of any term by its preceding term is same. So, the above obtained series forms a GP, with first term, $a = 256$ and common ratio, $r = \frac{128}{256} = \frac{1}{2} < 1$

$$\therefore \text{ Required sum, } S_5 = \frac{256\left[1-\left(\frac{1}{2}\right)^5\right]}{1-\frac{1}{2}} \quad \left[\because S_n = \frac{a(1-r^n)}{1-r}, r<1\right]$$

$$= 256 \times 2\left(1-\frac{1}{2^5}\right)$$

$$= 512 \times \left(1-\frac{1}{32}\right) = 512\left(\frac{32-1}{32}\right)$$

$$= 16 \times 31 = 496$$

Example 67. How many terms of the GP 3, $\frac{3}{2}$, $\frac{3}{4}$, ... are needed to give the sum of $\frac{3069}{512}$?

Sol. Let the number of terms be 'n', the first term of GP = $a = 3$ and common ratio $r = \frac{1}{2}$

$$\therefore \quad S_n = \frac{a(1-r^n)}{1-r} = \frac{3069}{512}$$

$$\Rightarrow \quad \frac{3\left[1-\left(\frac{1}{2}\right)^n\right]}{1-\frac{1}{2}} = \frac{3069}{512}$$

$$\Rightarrow \quad 6\left[1-\left(\frac{1}{2}\right)^n\right] = \frac{3069}{512}$$

$$\Rightarrow \quad 1-\left(\frac{1}{2}\right)^n = \frac{3069}{6\times 512}$$

$$\Rightarrow \quad 1-\left(\frac{1}{2}\right)^n = \frac{1023}{1024}$$

$$\Rightarrow \quad \left(\frac{1}{2}\right)^n = 1-\frac{1023}{1024}$$

$$\Rightarrow \quad \left(\frac{1}{2}\right)^n = \frac{1}{1024}$$

$$\Rightarrow \quad \left(\frac{1}{2}\right)^n = \left(\frac{1}{2}\right)^{10}$$

$$\Rightarrow \quad n = 10$$

Hence, the required number of terms = 10

Example 68. A GP consists of an even number of terms. If the sum of all the terms is 5 times the sum of terms occupying odd places, then find its common ratio.

Sol. Let the GP be $a, ar, ar^2, ar^3, ar^4, \ldots, ar^{2n-2}, ar^{2n-1}$, where $a, ar^2, ar^4, ar^6, \ldots$ occupy odd places and $ar, ar^3, ar^5, ar^7, \ldots$ occupy even places.

According to the question,

Sum of all terms = 5 × Sum of terms occupying odd places

$$\Rightarrow a + ar + ar^2 + \ldots + ar^{2n-1} = 5 \times (a + ar^2 + ar^4 + \ldots + ar^{2n-2})$$

$$\Rightarrow \frac{a(r^{2n}-1)}{r-1} = \frac{5a[(r^2)^n - 1]}{r^2-1} \quad \left[\because S_n = \frac{a(r^n-1)}{r-1}, r>1\right]$$

$$\Rightarrow \frac{r^{2n}-1}{r-1} = \frac{5(r^{2n}-1)}{(r-1)(r+1)}$$

$$\Rightarrow 1 = \frac{5}{r+1}$$

$$\Rightarrow r + 1 = 5 \Rightarrow r = 4$$

Example 69. The sum of the first three terms of a GP is 16 and the sum of next three terms is 128. Determine the first term, the common ratio and the sum to n terms of the GP.

Sol. Let the GP be $a, ar, ar^2, ar^3, \dots$.

According to the given condition,

Sum of first three terms $= a + ar + ar^2 = 16$ ...(i)

and sum of next three terms $= ar^3 + ar^4 + ar^5 = 128$ ...(ii)

On dividing Eq. (i) by Eq. (ii), we get

$$\frac{a + ar + ar^2}{ar^3 + ar^4 + ar^5} = \frac{16}{128}$$

$$\Rightarrow \frac{a(1 + r + r^2)}{ar^3(1 + r + r^2)} = \frac{1}{8}$$

$$\Rightarrow \left(\frac{1}{r}\right)^3 = \left(\frac{1}{2}\right)^3$$

On comparing the base of power 3 from both sides, we get

$$\frac{1}{r} = \frac{1}{2} \Rightarrow r = 2$$

On putting $r = 2$ in Eq. (i), we get

$$a + 2a + 4a = 16$$

$$\Rightarrow 7a = 16$$

$$\Rightarrow a = \frac{16}{7}$$

Now, sum to n terms, $S_n = \frac{a(r^n - 1)}{r - 1}$ $[\because r = 2 > 1]$

$$= \frac{\frac{16}{7}(2^n - 1)}{2 - 1}$$

$$= \frac{16}{7}(2^n - 1)$$

Hence, $a = \frac{16}{7}$, $r = 2$ and $S_n = \frac{16}{7}(2^n - 1)$.

Example 70. If S_1, S_2 and S_3 are respectively the sum of n, $2n$ and $3n$ terms of a GP, then prove that

$$S_1(S_3 - S_2) = (S_2 - S_1)^2.$$

Sol. Let a be the first term and r be the common ratio of the given GP. Then,

$$S_1(S_3 - S_2) = \frac{a(1 - r^n)}{(1 - r)} \cdot \left\{\frac{a(1 - r^{3n})}{(1 - r)} - \frac{a(1 - r^{2n})}{(1 - r)}\right\} \quad [\text{let } r < 1]$$

$$= \frac{a(1 - r^n)}{(1 - r)} \cdot \frac{(a - ar^{3n} - a + ar^{2n})}{(1 - r)}$$

$$= \frac{a(1 - r^n)}{(1 - r)} \cdot \frac{ar^{2n}(1 - r^n)}{(1 - r)} = \frac{a^2r^{2n}(1 - r^n)^2}{(1 - r)^2} \quad \text{...(i)}$$

and $$(S_2 - S_1)^2 = \left\{\frac{a(1 - r^{2n})}{(1 - r)} - \frac{a(1 - r^n)}{(1 - r)}\right\}^2$$

$$= \frac{(a - ar^{2n} - a + ar^n)^2}{(1 - r)^2}$$

$$= \frac{\{ar^n(1 - r^n)\}^2}{(1 - r)^2} = \frac{a^2r^{2n}(1 - r^n)^2}{(1 - r)^2} \quad \text{...(ii)}$$

Now, from Eqs. (i) and (ii), we get

$$S_1(S_3 - S_2) = (S_2 - S_1)^2$$

Example 71. Let S be the sum, P be the product and R be the sum of reciprocals of n terms in a GP. Prove that $P^2R^n = S^n$.

Sol. Let the GP be $a, ar, ar^2, ar^3, \dots, ar^{n-1}$.

Given, $S =$ Sum of n terms

$$= a + ar + ar^2 + ar^3 + \dots + ar^{n-1}$$

$$= \frac{a(r^n - 1)}{r - 1} \quad [\text{let } r > 1] \quad \text{...(i)}$$

$R =$ Sum of the reciprocals of n terms

$$= \frac{1}{a} + \frac{1}{ar} + \frac{1}{ar^2} + \dots + \frac{1}{ar^{n-1}} \quad \left[\because \frac{1}{r} < 1\right]$$

$$= \frac{\frac{1}{a}\left[1 - \left(\frac{1}{r}\right)^n\right]}{1 - \frac{1}{r}}$$

$$= \frac{1}{a}\left(\frac{1}{1} - \frac{1}{r^n}\right) \times \frac{1}{\frac{r - 1}{r}} = \frac{1}{a}\left(\frac{r^n - 1}{r^n}\right) \times \frac{r}{r - 1}$$

$$\Rightarrow R = \frac{(r^n - 1)r}{ar^n(r - 1)} \quad \text{...(ii)}$$

and $P =$ Product of n terms

$$= a \times ar \times ar^2 \times ar^3 \times \dots \times ar^{n-1}$$

$$= a^{1 + 1 + 1 + \dots + n \text{ terms}} \cdot r^{1 + 2 + 3 + \dots + (n - 1) \text{ terms}}$$

$$= a^n r^{\frac{n(n-1)}{2}} \quad \left[\because \Sigma n = \frac{n(n + 1)}{2}\right]$$

$$\Rightarrow P^2 = a^{2n} r^{n(n-1)} \quad \text{...(iii)}$$

Now, we have to prove $P^2R^n = S^n$

or $P^2 = \frac{S^n}{R^n}$ or $P^2 = \left(\frac{S}{R}\right)^n$

$$\text{RHS} = \left(\frac{S}{R}\right)^n$$

$$= \left[\frac{a(r^n - 1)}{r - 1} \times \frac{ar^n(r - 1)}{(r^n - 1)r}\right]^n \quad [\text{using Eqs. (i) and (ii)}]$$

$$= [a^2r^nr^{-1}]^n = (a^2r^{n-1})^n$$

$$= a^{2n}r^{n(n-1)} = P^2 = \text{LHS} \quad [\text{from Eq. (iii)}]$$

Hence proved.

Example 72. Find the least value of n for which the sum $1 + 3 + 3^2 + \dots$ to n terms is greater than 7000. [use log 14001 = 4.1461 and log 3 = 0.4771]

Sol. We have, $S_n = 1 + 3 + 3^2 + \dots$ to n terms

Clearly, the ratio of any terms by its preceding term is same. So, the above series forms a GP, with first term, $a = 1$ and common ratio, $\frac{3}{1} = 3 > 1$

$$\therefore S_n = 1 \times \left(\frac{3^n - 1}{3 - 1}\right) = \frac{3^n - 1}{2} \quad \left[\because S_n = a\left(\frac{r^n - 1}{r - 1}\right), r > 1\right]$$

Now, $S_n > 7000$

$$\Rightarrow \frac{3^n - 1}{2} > 7000$$

$\Rightarrow \quad 3^n - 1 > 14000$

$\Rightarrow \quad 3^n > 14001$

$\Rightarrow \quad n \log 3 > \log 14001$

$\Rightarrow \quad n > \dfrac{\log 14001}{\log 3} \Rightarrow n > \dfrac{4.1461}{0.4771} = 8.69$

Hence, the least value of n is 9.

Example 73. Sum of series $(x + y) + (x^2 + xy + y^2) + (x^3 + x^2y + xy^2 + y^3)$ + ... upto n terms

Sol. $S_n = (x+y) + (x^2 + xy + y^2) + (x^3 + x^2y + xy^2 + y^3) + ...n$

[multiply and divide with $(x - y)$]

$$= \frac{1}{x-y}[(x^2 - y^2) + (x^3 - y^3) + (x^4 - y^4) + ... \text{ upto } n \text{ terms}]$$

$$= \frac{1}{x-y}[(x^2 + x^3 + x^4 + ... \text{ upto } n \text{ terms}) - [y^2 + y^3 + y^4 + ... \text{ upto } n \text{ terms}]$$

$$= \frac{1}{x-y}\left[\frac{x^2(1-x^n)}{1-x} - \frac{y^2(1-y^n)}{1-y}\right]$$

Example 74. Find the sum of first n terms of the series 7 + 77 + 777 + ...

Sol. Let S_n be the required sum, then

$$S_n = 7 + 77 + 777 + ... \text{ upto } n \text{ terms}$$

$$= 7(1 + 11 + 111 + ... \text{ upto } n \text{ terms})$$

$$= \frac{7}{9}[9 + 99 + 999 + ... \text{ upto } n \text{ terms})$$

$$= \frac{7}{9}[(10-1) + (100-1) + (1000-1) + ... \text{ upto } n \text{ terms}]$$

$$= \frac{7}{9}[(10 + 100 + 1000 + ... \text{ upto } n \text{ terms}) - (1 + 1 + 1 + ... \text{ upto } n \text{ terms})]$$

$$= \frac{7}{9}[10 + 10^2 + 10^3 + ... \text{ upto } n \text{ terms}] - [1 + 1 + 1 ...... \text{ upto } n \text{ terms}]$$

$$= \frac{7}{9}\left[10\left(\frac{10^n - 1}{10 - 1}\right) - n\right] = \frac{7}{9}\left[\frac{10^{n+1} - 10 - 9n}{9}\right]$$

$$= \frac{7}{81}[10^{n+1} - 10 - 9n].$$

Applications of GP

Sometimes we can solve some real life problems by using the concept of GP. Some of them are given below

Example 75. At the end of each year, the value of a certain machine has depreciated by 20% of its value at the beginning of that year. If its initial value was ₹ 1250, then find the value at the end of 5 yr.

Sol. Given, every year depreciation in value of machine = 20%

After each year, the value of the machine is 80% (100 − 20)% of its value of the previous year.

So at the end of 1st year value of machine will be 1250 (0.8), at the end of 2nd year value of machine will be 1250 (0.8) (0.8) = 1250 $(0.8)^2$ and so on.

Thus, we have to find the 6th term of the GP whose first term a_1 is 1250 and common ratio r is 0.8.

Hence, value at the end of 5 yr

$$= a_6 = a_1 r^5 = 1250(0.8)^5 = 409.6$$

Example 76. The lengths of three unequal edges of a rectangular solid block are in GP. If the volume of the block is 216 cm^3 and the total surface area is 252 cm^2, then find the length of its edges.

Sol. Let the length, breadth and height of rectangular solid block be $\frac{a}{r}$, a and ar, respectively.

$\therefore$ Volume $= \dfrac{a}{r} \times a \times ar = 216 \text{ cm}^3$

[∵ volume of a cuboid = length × breadth × height]

$\Rightarrow \quad a^3 = 216$

$\Rightarrow \quad a^3 = 6^3$

$\therefore \quad a = 6 \text{ cm}$

Now, surface area $= 2\left(\dfrac{a^2}{r} + a^2 r + a^2\right) = 252$

[∵ surface area of cuboid = $2(lb + bh + hl)$]

$\Rightarrow \quad 2a^2\left(\dfrac{1}{r} + r + 1\right) = 252$

$\Rightarrow \quad 2 \times 36\left(\dfrac{1 + r^2 + r}{r}\right) = 252$

$\Rightarrow \quad \dfrac{1 + r^2 + r}{r} = \dfrac{252}{2 \times 36}$

$\Rightarrow \quad 1 + r^2 + r = \dfrac{126}{36}$

$\Rightarrow \quad 1 + r^2 + r = \dfrac{21}{6} r$

$\Rightarrow \quad 6 + 6r^2 + 6r = 21r$

$\Rightarrow \quad 6r^2 - 15r + 6 = 0$

$\Rightarrow \quad 2r^2 - 5r + 2 = 0$

$\Rightarrow \quad (2r - 1)(r - 2) = 0$

$\Rightarrow \quad r = \dfrac{1}{2}$ or 2

For $r = \dfrac{1}{2}$,

length $= \dfrac{a}{r} = \dfrac{6 \times 2}{1} = 12$ cm,

breadth $= a = 6$ cm

and height $= ar = 6 \times \dfrac{1}{2} = 3$ cm

For $r = 2$, length $= \dfrac{a}{r} = \dfrac{6}{2} = 3$ cm

breadth $= a = 6$ cm

and height $= ar = 6 \times 2 = 12$ cm

Exercise 9.4

1. Find the sum of following geometric progressions.
   (i) $\sqrt{7}, \sqrt{21}, 3\sqrt{7}, \ldots$ n terms
   (ii) $1, -a, a^2, -a^3, \ldots$ n terms (if $a \neq -1$)
   (iii) 2, 6, 18, ... upto 7 terms
   (iv) $1, \sqrt{3}, 3, 3\sqrt{3}, \ldots$ upto 10 terms
   (v) 0.15, 0.015, 0.0015, ... 20 terms
2. The sum of some terms of GP is 315, whose first term and common ratio are 5 and 2, respectively. Find the last term and number of terms.
3. The first term of a GP is 27 and its 8th term is 1/81. Find the sum of its first 10 terms.
4. Find the sum of first 12 terms of a GP whose 8th term is 192 and the common ratio is 2.
5. The 2nd and 5th terms of a GP are $\frac{-1}{2}$ and $\frac{1}{16}$, respectively. Find the sum of the GP upto 8 terms.
6. How many terms of the series $1 + 3 + 3^2 + 3^3 + \ldots$ must be taken to make 3280?
7. How many terms of the sequence $\sqrt{3}, 3, 3\sqrt{3}, \ldots$ must be taken to make the sum $39 + 13\sqrt{3}$?
8. How many terms of the GP $1, \sqrt{2}, 2, 2\sqrt{2} \ldots$ are required to give a sum of $1023(\sqrt{2} + 1)$?
9. Given, a GP with $a = 729$ and 7th term is 64, determine S_7.
10. In a GP, if $T_1 = 3, T_n = 96$ and $S_n = 189$, then find n.
11. The ratio of the sum of first three terms to that of first 6 terms of a GP is 125 : 152. Find the common ratio.
12. Show that the ratio of the sum of the first n terms of a GP to the sum of terms from $(n + 1)$th to $(2n)$th term is $1/r^n$.
13. Find the sum of n terms of the nubmers
    $$\left(x + \frac{1}{x}\right)^2, \left(x^2 + \frac{1}{x^2}\right)^2, \left(x^3 + \frac{1}{x^3}\right)^2, \ldots\ldots$$
14. Sum of series $x(x + y) + x^2(x^2 + y^2) + x^3(x^3 + y^3) + \ldots\ldots\ldots$ upto n terms.
15. Find the sum of first n terms of the series $5 + 55 + 555 + \ldots\ldots$
16. A person has 2 parents, 4 grandparents and so on. Find the numbers of his ancestors during the ten generations preceding his own.
17. The inventor of the chessboard suggested a reward of one grain of wheat for the first square; 2 grains for the second; 4 grains for the third and so on, doubling the number of grains for subsequent squares. How many grains would have to be given to the inventor? (Note that there are 64 squares in the chessboard.)
18. A man writes a letter to four of his friends. He asks each one of them to copy the letter and mail to four different persons with the instruction that they move the chain similarly. Assuming that the chain is not broken and it costs ₹ 2 to mail one letter, find the amount spent on postage when 8th set of letters is mailed.
19. Let a_n be the nth term of the GP of positive numbers. Let $\sum_{n=1}^{100} a_{2n} = \alpha$ and $\sum_{n=1}^{100} a_{2n-1} = \beta$, such that $\alpha \neq \beta$. Prove that the common ratio of the GP is $\frac{\alpha}{\beta}$.

Chapter Practice

a. 1 Mark Questions

1. In an AP, if $a = 3.5$, $d = 0$ and $n = 101$, then a_n will be

(1) 0 (b) 3.5
(c) 103.5 (d) 104.5

2. The first four terms of an AP, whose first term is 4 and common difference is – 6, are **[ICSE Semester I 2021]**

(a) 4, – 10, – 16, – 22 (b) 4, 10, 16, 22
(c) 4, – 2, – 8, – 14 (d) 4, 2, 8, 14

3. In an AP, if $d = -4$, $n = 7$ and $a_n = 4$, then a is equal to

(a) 6 (b) –1 (c) 1 (d) 28

4. The nth term of an Arithmetic Progression (AP) is $2n + 5$. The 10th term is **[ICSE 2023]**

(a) 7 (b) 15 (c) 25 (d) 45

5. In an AP, if first term is 5, common difference is –3 and the nth term is –7, then n is equal to **[ICSE Semester I 2021]**

(a) 5 (b) 17 (c) –13 (d) 7

6. In an AP have 8 as the first term and –5 as the common difference and its first three terms are 8, A and B, then $(A + B)$ is equal to

(a) 0 (b) –1 (c) 1 (d) 6

7. If the common difference of an AP is 5, then what is the value of $a_{18} - a_{13}$?

(a) 2 (b) 20 (c) 25 (d) 30

8. The sum of the first 20 terms of an AP 2, 4, 6, 8, ... is

(a) 400 (b) 840 (c) 420 (d) 800

9. Find the sum of the series $1 - \frac{1}{2} + \frac{1}{4} - \frac{1}{8} + ...$ upto 8 terms.

(a) $\frac{255}{384}$ (b) $\frac{286}{395}$
(c) $\frac{385}{282}$ (d) None of these

b. 3 Marks Questions

10. If the numbers $2n - 1$, $3n + 2$ and $6n - 1$ are in AP, then find n and hence find the numbers.

11. If 21, a, b and – 3 are in AP, then find the value of $(a + b)$.

12. Determine k, so that $k^2 + 4k + 8$, $2k^2 + 3k + 6$ and $3k^2 + 4k + 4$ are three consecutive terms of an AP.

13. Which term of the AP, 120, 116, 112, ... is first negative term?

14. If the nth term of the two AP's, 9, 7, 5, ... and 24, 21, 18,... are the same, then find the value of n. Also, find that term.

15. The 4th term of an AP is zero. Prove that the 25th term of the AP is three times its 11th term.

16. If the 2nd term of an AP is 13 and 5th term is 25, then what is its 7th term?

17. The fourth term of an AP is 11. The sum of the fifth and seventh terms of the AP is 24. Find its common difference.

18. The 16th term of an AP is 1 more than twice its 8th term. If the 12th term of an AP is 47, then find its nth term.

19. The eighth term of an AP is half of its second term and the eleventh term exceeds one-third of its fourth term by 1. Find the 15th term.

20. The sum of 5th and 9th terms of an AP is 72 and sum of 7th and 12th terms is 97. Find the AP.

21. The sum of the first three terms of an AP is 42 and the product of the first and third term is 52. Find the first term and the common difference.

22. How many two-digit numbers are divisible by 6?

23. How many multiples of 9 lie between 10 and 300?

24. Find the number of natural numbers between 101 and 999 which are divisible by both 2 and 5.

25. Split 210 into three parts such that these are in AP and the product of the two greatest parts is 5110.

26. The sum of the first three terms of an AP is 33. If the product of the first and the third terms exceeds the second term by 29, then find the AP.

27. The angles of a triangle are in AP. The greatest angle is thrice the least. Find all the angles of the triangle.

28. If four numbers are in AP such that their sum is 50 and the greatest number is 4 times the least, then find the numbers.

29. If a, b and c are in AP, show that $(b + c)$, $(c + a)$ and $(a + b)$ are also in AP.

30. Find the sum of the series $\frac{3}{\sqrt{5}} + \frac{4}{\sqrt{5}} + \sqrt{5} + \ldots$ upto 25 terms.

31. Find the sum of the first 25 terms of an AP, whose nth term is given by $a_n = 7 - 3n$.

32. If the nth term of an AP is $a_n = 2n + 1$, find its sum.

33. If an AP has $a = 1$, $a_n = 20$ and $S_n = 399$, then find the value of n.

34. The sum of first, third and seventeenth terms of an AP is 216. Find the sum of the first 13 terms of the AP.

35. The 5th term and the 9th term of an Arithmetic Progression are 4 and – 12 respectively. Find [ICSE 2023]

(i) the first term
(ii) common difference
(iii) sum of 16 terms of the AP.

36. If a, b and c are the 1st, 3rd and nth terms respectively of an AP, then prove that the sum to n terms is $\frac{c + a}{2} + \frac{c^2 - a^2}{b - a}$.

c. 4/5 Marks Questions

37. If the number of terms of an AP is $2n + 1$, then find the ratio of sum of the odd terms of sum of even terms.

38. Find the sum of all multiple of 7 lying between 500 and 900.

39. Find the sum of all three-digit natural numbers, which are multiples of 11.

40. Find the sum of all two-digit numbers greater than 50, when divided by 7 leaves remainder 4.

41. The fourth term of a GP is the square of its second term and the first term is – 3. Determine its 7th term.

42. If 5th and 8th terms of a GP are 48 and 384, respectively. Find the GP, if terms of GP are real numbers.

43. If $a^x = b^y = c^z$ and x, y, z are in GP, then show that $\log_b a = \log_c b$.

44. Find the sum of n terms of the series $(a + b) + (a^2 + 2b) + (a^3 + 3b) + \ldots$.

d. 6 Marks Questions

45. Which term of the Arithmetic Progression (AP) 15, 30, 45, 60... is 300? Hence, find the sum of all the terms of the Arithmetic Progression (AP). [ICSE 2023]

46. Find the common difference of an AP whose first term is 5 and the sum of its first 4 terms is half the sum of the next 4 terms.

47. The sum of the first term and the fifth term of an ascending AP is 26 and the product of the second term by the fourth term is 160. Find the sum of the first seven terms of this AP.

48. Sum of the first n terms of an AP is $5n^2 - 3n$. Find the AP and also find its 16th term.

49. Solve the equation $-4 + (-1) + 2 + \ldots + x = 437$.

50. Find the sum of all two-digit odd positive numbers.

51. Jaspal Singh repays his total loan of ₹ 118000 by paying every month starting with the first installment of ₹ 1000. If he increases the installment by ₹ 100 every month, then what amount will he paid by him in the 30th installment? What amount of loan does he still have to pay after 30th installment?

52. Each year, a tree grows 5 cm less than it did the preceding year. If it grew by 1m in the first year, then in how many years will it have ceased growing?

53. Komal decides to solve two questions of Mathematics first day and doubles the number everyday. In how many days will she able to solve the total questions 2046 in the book?

54. Rohit borrows ₹ 10000 from his friend, Mohit. Mohit asks him to return the money just by repaying ₹ 10 at first day and double the amount in the subsequent days than the each previous day continuously for only ten days. Rohit thanks Mohit for his help. Now, determine whether Mohit was in loss or profit.

55. 150 workers were engaged to finish a job in a certain number of days, 4 workers dropped out on second day, 4 more workers dropped out an third day and so on. It took 8 more days of finish the work. Find the number of days in which the work was completed.

56. A person writes a letter to four of his friends. He asks each one of them to copy the letter and mail to four different persons with the instruction that they move the chain similarly. Assuming that the chain is not broken and that it costs 25 paise to mail one letter, determine the amount spent on postage when the 8th set of letters is mailed.

Hints and Answers

Exercise 9.1

1. Hint To find the first three terms of the sequence, put $n = 1, 2$ and 3.

Ans. (i) 8, 13 and 18 (ii) 1, 10, 25 (iii) $-1, -\frac{1}{2}, 0$

2. Hint To find the first four terms of the sequence, put $n = 1, 2, 3$ and 4.

Ans. (i) 5, 7, 9, 11 (ii) 1, −16, 81, −256 (iii) $0, \frac{1}{3}, \frac{4}{3}, 3$

3. (i) **Hint** Here, $a_2 - a_1 \neq a_3 - a_2$ **Ans.** No

(ii) **Hint** Here, $a_2 - a_1 = a_3 - a_2 = a_4 - a_3$ **Ans.** Yes

(iii) **Hint** Do same as part (ii). **Ans.** Yes

(iv) **Hint** Do same as part (ii). **Ans.** Yes

(v) **Hint** Do same as part (i). **Ans.** No

4. (i) **Hint** Here, $a_{n+1} - a_n = [3(n+1) + 5] - [3n + 5]$
$= 3n + 3 + 5 - 3n - 5 = 3$

Ans. Yes, because $a_{n+1} - a_n$ is independent of n.

(ii) **Hint** Here,
$a_{n+1} - a_n = [a - 11(n+1)^2] - [a - 11n^2]$
$= 11n^2 - 11(n+1)^2 = -11(2n+1)$

Ans. No, because $a_{n+1} - a_n$ is not independent of n.

(iii) **Hint** Do same as part (ii). **Ans.** No, because $a_{n+1} - a_n$ is not independent of n.

(iv) **Hint** Do same as part (ii). **Ans.** No, because $a_{n+1} - a_n$ is not independent of n.

5. Hint Here, $a_{n+1} - a_n$ is not independent of n.

6. (i) **Hint** Here, $d = a_2 - a_1 = 2\sqrt{3} - \sqrt{3}$. **Ans.** $\sqrt{3}$

(ii) **Hint** Here, $d = a_2 - a_1 = \frac{1}{3} - \frac{1}{6}$. **Ans.** $\frac{1}{6}$

(iii) **Hint** Here, $d = a_2 - a_1 = 19\frac{1}{4} - 20 = \frac{77}{4} - 20$.

Ans. $-3/4$

7. Hint $a_2 - a_1 = a_3 - a_2 = \ldots = 6$. **Ans.** Yes, 6

8. Hint Here, $a_{n+1} - a_n$ is independent of n.

Ans. 1/4

9. Hint $a_2 = a_1 + d;\ a_3 = a_2 + d$ and $a_4 = a_3 + d$

Ans. (i) −2, −4, −6, −8 (ii) $-\frac{1}{2}, -\frac{3}{2}, -\frac{5}{2}, -\frac{7}{2}$

(iii) 0.5, 1.7, 2.9, 4.1

10. Hint Do same as Example 5.

Ans. (i) 6; 24, 30(ii) 1; $\frac{10}{3}, \frac{13}{3}$ (iii) 2; −9, −7

11. Hint $\therefore 2k + 1 = \frac{k - 3 + 4k + 3}{2}$ **Ans.** $k = 2$

12. Hint Do same as Example 6.

Ans. (i) 17.5 (ii) 22 (iii) −37

13. Hint Use the formula, $a_n = a + (n-1)d$. **Ans.** 28

14. Hint Do same as Example 8.

Ans. $a_n = 15 - 4n, -85,$

15. Hint Let the number of terms be n.

Then, $l = a + (n-1)d$. **Ans.** 26

16. Hint Do same as Example 11. **Ans.** 21, 25.

17. Hint Let $a_n = 0$, then by using the formula, $a_n = a + (n-1)d$, we get fractional value of n, which is not possible. **Ans.** No

18. Hint Here, $a_p = 1000$. **Ans.** 40

19. Hint Do same as Example 12. **Ans.** 200

20. Hint Let $a_n = a_{31} + 130$

$\Rightarrow \quad a + (n-1)d = a + (31-1)d + 130$

$\Rightarrow \quad 3 + (n-1)(5) = 3 + 30 \times 5 + 130$. **Ans.** 57th

21. Hint Do same as Example 13. **Ans.** 24

22. Hint Do same as Example 17.

23. Hint Do same as Example 20.

Ans. $n = 16$, term −21

24. Hint The given numbers form an AP with $a = -4$ and $d = (-1) - (-4) = 3$ and $S = 437$

Let the number of terms in the AP be n, then using

$S = \frac{n}{2}[2a + (n-1)d]$, we get

$\frac{n}{2}[2 \times (-4) + (n-1) \times 3] = 437$

$\Rightarrow \quad n(3n - 11) = 874$

$\Rightarrow \quad 3n^2 - 11n\ 874 = 0$

$n = \frac{11 \pm \sqrt{(-11)^2 - 4 \times 3 \times (-874)}}{2 \times 3}$

$= \frac{11 \pm \sqrt{10609}}{6}$

$\Rightarrow \quad n = \frac{11 \pm 103}{6} = \frac{114}{6}, \frac{-92}{6} = 19, -\frac{46}{3}$

but n being the number of terms,

$n \neq -\frac{46}{3} \Rightarrow n = 19$

Now, $x = n$th term $= 19$th term $= a + 18d$
$= -4 + 18 \times 3 = 50$

Ans. The value of x is 50.

25. Hint Do same as Example 21. **Ans.** 12th term

26. Hint The required numbers are 11, 15, ..., 299.

Now, let there be n numbers.

Then, $a_n = 299 \Rightarrow 299 = 11 + (n-1)4$ **Ans.** 73

27. Hint Here, $a = 43$, $d = 41 - 43 = -2$ and $a_n = 11$.

Now, use the formula, $a_n = a + (n-1)d$. **Ans.** 17

28. Hint Here, $a = 100$, $d = 105 - 100 = 5$ and $n = 30$.

Now, find, $a_{30} = a + (30-1)d$. **Ans.** ₹ 245

29. Hint Do same as Example 23. **Ans.** Yes, ₹ 12000

30. **Hint** Do same as Example 24. **Ans.** –25

31. **Hint** Use the formulae, nth term from the beginning, $a_n = a + (n-1)d$ and nth term from the end $= l - (n-1)d$. **Ans.** 505, 260

32. **Hint** Let three parts be $a-d, a, a+d$.

Then, $(a-d) + a + (a+d) = 207$

and $a(a-d) = 4623$ **Ans.** 67, 69, 71

33. **Hint** Let three angles be $(a-d)°, a°, (a+d)°$.

Then, we have $(a-d)° + a° + (a+d)° = 180°$

and $(a+d) = 2(a-d)$ **Ans.** 40°, 60°, 80°

Exercise 9.2

1. **Hint** Do same as Example 27.

Ans. (i) 320 (ii) 10100 (iii) – 180 (iv) 5505 (v) 33/20

2. **Hint** Do same as Example 30. **Ans.** – 1275

3. **Hint** Here, we have $a_2 = 8$ and $a_4 = 4$

$\Rightarrow \quad a + d = 8$ and $a + 3d = 4$

On solving these equations, we get the values of a and d.

Now, S_{21} can be obtained by using

$$S_n = \frac{n}{2}[2a + (n-1)d] \quad \textbf{Ans. } -210$$

4. **Hint** Do same as Q. 3. **Ans.** – 510

5. **Hint** We have, $S_p = q$ and $S_q = p$.

$$\Rightarrow \quad S_p - S_q = q - p$$

$$2a + (p+q-1)d = -2$$

Now, $S_{p+q} = \frac{p+q}{2}[2a + (p+q-1)d]$

$$= \left(\frac{p+q}{2}\right)[-2] = -(p+q)$$

Ans. – $(p+q)$

6. **Hint** Given, $S_6 = 36$

$$\Rightarrow \quad \frac{6}{2}[2a + (6-1)\cdot d] = 36 \quad \left[\because S_n = \frac{n}{2}[2a + (n-1)d]\right]$$

$$\Rightarrow \quad 2a + 5d = 12 \quad \ldots(i)$$

and $S_{16} = 256$

$$\Rightarrow \quad \frac{16}{2}[2a + (16-1)\cdot d] = 256$$

$$\Rightarrow \quad 2a + 15d = 32 \quad \ldots(ii)$$

From Eq. (i) and Eq. (ii), we get

$$d = 2 \text{ and } a = 1$$

Now, sum of first 10 terms

$$S_{10} = \frac{10}{2}[2 \times 1 + (10-1) \times 2]$$

$$= 5[2 + 18] = 100$$

Ans. 100

7. **Hint** Given, $S_5 + S_7 = 167$ and $S_{10} = 235$

$\therefore$ $12a + 31d = 167$ and $2a + 9d = 47$

Now, find a and d, and then S_{20}. **Ans.** $S_{20} = 970$

8. **Hint** Do same as Example 34.

Ans. (i) 16, 17 (ii) 12 (iii) 15 (iv) 20

9. **Hint** Do same as Example 32. **Ans.** 1068

10. **Hint** Do same as Example 33. **Ans.** 260.

11. **Hint** Do same as Example 40. **Ans.** $4n + 3$

12. **Hint** Do same as Example 40.

Ans. $8n - 3$; 5, 13, 21, ...

13. **Hint** Do same as Example 37. **Ans.** 525

14. **Hint** Do same as Example 38.

15. **Hint** Do same as Example 39. **Ans.** 816

16. **Hint** Given, $S_6 = 42$ and $\frac{a_{10}}{a_{30}} = \frac{1}{3}$.

This implies $2a + 5d = 14$ and $a = d$, respectively.

Ans. $a_1 = 2$ and $a_{13} = 26$

17. **Hint** To prove, $S_{2n} - S_n = \frac{1}{3}S_{3n}$

18. Let a is the first term and d is common difference of the AP.

Given, it consists of 50 terms i.e., $n = 50$

Sum of n terms of AP is

$$S_n = \frac{n}{2}[2a + (n-1)d]$$

$$S_{10} = 210 = \frac{10}{2}[2a + 9d]$$

$$2a + 9d = 42 \quad \ldots(i)$$

Also, 15th term from last

$= (50 - 15 + 1)$th term from beginning

$= 36$th term from beginning

$$S_{50} - S_{35} = 2565$$

$$= \frac{50}{2}(2a + 49d) - \frac{35}{2}(2a - 34d) = 2565$$

$$= 10(2a + 49d) - 7(2a + 34d)$$

$$= 2565 \times \frac{2}{5} = 6a + 252d = 1026$$

$$= 2a + 84d = 342 \quad \ldots(ii)$$

Subtracting Eq. (i) from Eq. (ii), we get

$$2a + 9 \times 4 = 42$$

$$\Rightarrow \quad 2a = 6 \Rightarrow a = 3$$

The A.P. is $a, a+d, a+2d, a+3d$ ...

i.e. 3, 7, 11, 15 ...

19. **Hint** Let a be the first term and d be the common difference of an AP.

According to the question,

$$T_6 = 4a$$

$$\Rightarrow \quad a + (6-1)d = 4a \quad [\because T_n = a + (n-1)d]$$

$$\Rightarrow \quad 3a = 5d \quad \ldots(i)$$

and $S_6 = 75$

$$\Rightarrow \quad \frac{6}{2}[2a + (6-1)d] = 75 \quad \left[\because S_n = \frac{n}{2}[2a + (n-1)d]\right]$$

$$\Rightarrow \quad 3(2a + 5d) = 75$$

$$\Rightarrow \quad 2a + 5d = 25 \quad \ldots(ii)$$

From Eqs. (i) and (ii), we get

$$2a + 3a = 25$$

$$\Rightarrow \quad 5a = 25 \Rightarrow a = 5$$

and putting $a = 5$ in Eq. (i), we get

$$5d = 3 \times 5 = 15 \Rightarrow d = 3$$

Ans. $a = 5$ and $d = 3$

20. Let first term of series be a, and common difference be d

Given, $S_m = S_n = \frac{m}{2}[2a + (m-1)d]$

$= \frac{n}{2}[2a + (n-1)d]$

$= 2ma + m(m-1)d = 2an + n(n-1)d$

$= 2a(m-n) + (m^2 - n^2 - m + n)d = 0$

$= 2a(m-n) + [(m-n)(m+n) - 1(m-n)]d = 0$

$= (m-n)(2a + (m+n-1)d) = 0 \quad [\because m - n \neq 0]$

$= 2a + (m+n-1)d = 0$

The sum of first $(m+n)$ terms of the AP

$S_{m+n} = \frac{m+n}{2}[2a + (m+n-1)d]$

$= \frac{m+n}{2} \times 0 = 0$

Hence, the sum of first $(m+n)$ terms of the AP is zero

21. Hint Here, $a = 32$, $d = 36 - 32 = 4$ and $S_n = 2000$

Use the formula, $S_n = \frac{n}{2}[2a + (n-1)d]$

Ans. 25 months

22. Hint Here, $a = 30$, $d = 28 - 30 = -2$ and $S_n = 228$

To find, n and l

Use the formula, $S_n = \frac{n}{2}[2a + (n-1)d]$

and $l = a + (n-1)d$

Ans. 12 and 8

23. Hint Here, $a = 8$, $d = \frac{1}{3}$ yr and $S_n = 168$

$\left[\because 4 \text{ months} = \frac{4}{12} \text{ yr} = \frac{1}{3} \text{ yr}\right]$

Use the formula, $S_n = \frac{n}{2}[2a + (n-1)d]$

Ans. Number of students in the class = 16.

24. Hint Let the amount of installments are

$a, a+d, a+2d, \ldots$

Then, according to given condition,

$S_{40} = 3600$ and $S_{30} = 3600 - \frac{1}{3} \times 3600 = 2400$

$\Rightarrow 2a + 39d = 180$ and $2a + 29d = 160$

Now, find a and d and then find a_8.

Ans. $a_8 = ₹\,65$

Exercise 9.3

1. Do same as Examples 43 and 45.

Ans. (i) $-\frac{1}{2}$ (ii) $\frac{3a}{4}$

2. Hint For GP, $\frac{x-6}{x+9} = \frac{4}{x-6}$. **Ans.** 0 or 16

3. (i) **Hint** Here, $a = 3$ and $r = 2$. Now, use the formula $a_n = ar^{n-1}$, to find the required term.

Ans. 3072

(ii) **Hint** Do same as part (i). **Ans.** $\frac{4}{6561}$

(iii) **Hint** Do same as part (i). **Ans.** 512

(iv) **Hint** Do same as part (i). **Ans.** $(0.3)(0.2)^7$

(v) **Hint** Do same as part (i). **Ans.** $(ax)^{41}$

4. Hint Here, a = first term $= \frac{5}{2}$

and common ratio $(r) = \frac{5/4}{5/2} = \frac{2}{4} = \frac{1}{2}$

Use the formula, $a_n = ar^{n-1}$ to find the required terms.

Ans. $a_{20} = \frac{5}{2^{20}}$ and $a_n = \frac{5}{2^n}$

5. Hint Here, $a = 5$ and $r = 5$. Now, find a_{10} and a_n

Ans. 5^{10}, 5^n

6. Hint Here, $a_8 = 192$ and $r = 2$

$\because \quad a_8 = ar^{8-1} = ar^7$

$\therefore \quad a = \frac{3}{2}$

Ans. $a_{12} = 3072$

7. Hint Do same as Example 51.

Ans. (i) 12 (ii) 9 (iii) 7 (iv) 11

8. Hint Do same as Example 55.

Ans. 2, 5, 8 and 26, 5, –16

9. Hint Do same as Example 52.

Ans. $a = 2$ and $r = 2$

10. Hint Find GP as in Example 53.

Find the corresponding geometric series by replacing comma (,) by + sign.

Ans. 5 + 10 + 20 + 40 + ...

11. Hint Given, $a = 1$ and $a_3 + a_5 = 90$

$\therefore \quad ar^2 + ar^4 = 90$

$\Rightarrow \quad r^2 + r^4 = 90$

$\Rightarrow \quad r^4 + r^2 - 90 = 0 \quad [\text{as } a = 1]$

$\Rightarrow \quad (r^2 + 10)(r^2 - 9) = 0$

$\Rightarrow \quad r = \pm 3$

$[\because r^2 = -10 \text{ is not real number}]$

Ans. ± 3

12. Hint Given, $a + ar = -4 \quad \ldots(i)$

and $a_5 = 4a_3 \Rightarrow ar^{5-1} = 4ar^{3-1} \Rightarrow r = \pm 2$

If $r = 2$, then from Eq. (i),

$a + a(2) = -4$

$\Rightarrow \quad 3a = -4 \Rightarrow a = -\frac{4}{3}$

If $r = -2$, then from Eq. (i),

$a + a(-2) = -4$

$\Rightarrow \quad -a = -4$

$\therefore \quad a = 4$

Ans. GP is ... $-\frac{4}{3}, -\frac{8}{3}, -\frac{16}{3}, \ldots$ or $4, -8, 16, \ldots$

13. Hint Here, we have $ar^3 = x$ ...(i)

$ar^9 = y$ ...(ii)

and $ar^{15} = z$ ...(iii)

To prove $y^2 = xz$

Now, multiply Eqs. (i) and (iii) to get the result.

14. Given, $x, 2y, 3z$ are in AP and x, y, z are in GP.

$2(2y) = x + 3z$

i.e. $4y = x + 3z$ ...(i)

Let r be the common ratio of the GP, then

$y = xr$ and $z = xr^2$

substituting these values of y and z in Eq. (i), we get

$4(xr) = x + 3(xr^2)$

$\Rightarrow 4r = 1 + 3r^2$

$\Rightarrow 3r^2 - 4r + 1 = 0$

$\Rightarrow (3r-1)(r-1) = 0$

$r = \frac{1}{3}, 1$ but $r \neq 1$

Since, x, y, z are distinct

$r = \frac{1}{3}$

Hence, the common ratio of the GP is $\frac{1}{3}$.

15. Hint Let A be the first term and R be the common ratio.

Then, we have $AR^{p-1} = a$ ...(i)

$AR^{q-1} = b$ ...(ii)

$AR^{r-1} = c$ ...(iii)

Now, substitute the value of a, b and c in LHS, $a^{q-r}b^{r-p}c^{p-q}$ and simplify it to get the result.

16. Hint Do same as Example 60.

17. Hint nth term, $ar^{n-1} = b$ ...(i)

Now, P = Product of n terms

$\Rightarrow P = a \times ar^1 \times ar^2 \times ar^3 \times \dots$ to n terms

$\Rightarrow P = a^{1+1+1+\dots+n \text{ terms}} \cdot r^{1+2+3+\dots+(n-1) \text{ terms}}$

$\Rightarrow P = a^n r^{\frac{n(n-1)}{2}}$

$\Rightarrow P^2 = a^n a^n r^{n(n-1)} = (a \cdot ar^{n-1})^n$

18. Hint Do same as Example 58. **Ans.** (i) $\frac{1}{32}$ (ii) $\frac{1}{128}$

19. Hint Let the GP consist n terms.

Then, a_k = kth term from the beginning $= a_1 r^{k-1}$

a_{n-k+1} = kth term from the end $= a_n\left(\frac{1}{r}\right)^{k-1}$, where

$1 < k < n$, $a_k\, a_{n-k+1} = (a_1 r^{k-1})\, a_n\left(\frac{1}{r}\right)^{k-1} = a_1 a_n$

for all k satisfying $1 < k < n$.

20. Hint Let $\frac{a}{r}, a, ar$ be three numbers which are in GP.

According to the question,

$\frac{a}{r} + a + ar = \frac{13}{12}$ ...(i)

and $\frac{a}{r} \times a \times ar = -1$

$\Rightarrow a = -1$

On substituting $a = -1$ in Eq. (i), we get

$\frac{-1}{r} + (-1) + (-1)r = \frac{13}{12}$

$\Rightarrow 12r^2 + 25r + 12 = 0$

$\Rightarrow (3r+4)(4r+3) = 0$

$\Rightarrow r = -\frac{4}{3}$ or $-\frac{3}{4}$

Ans. $\frac{3}{4}, -1, \frac{4}{3}$ or $\frac{4}{3}, -1, \frac{3}{4}$

21. Do same as Q. 20. **Ans.** $\frac{5}{2}, 1, \frac{2}{5}$ or $\frac{2}{5}, 1, \frac{5}{2}$

22. Hint Let the terms of given GP be $\frac{a}{r}, a, ar$.

According to question, $\frac{a}{r} \cdot a \cdot ar = 1000$

$\Rightarrow a^3 = 1000 \Rightarrow a = 10$

Also, it is given that $\frac{a}{r}, a+6, ar+7$ are in AP

$\therefore 2(a+6) = \frac{a}{r} + ar + 7$

$\Rightarrow r = 2, \frac{1}{2}$

Ans. 5, 10, 20, ... or 20, 10, 5, ...

23. Hint Let lengths of the sides of triangle be $\frac{a}{r}, a, ar$, which forms a GP.

Given, shortest side = 9 cm

$\therefore \frac{a}{r} = 9$

$\Rightarrow a = 9r$ ...(i)

Also, given perimeter of the triangle = 37

$\therefore \frac{a}{r} + a + ar = 37$ ...(ii)

On solving Eqs. (i) and (ii), we get the required values.

Ans. 12 cm, 16 cm

Exercise 9.4

1. Hint Use the formula, $S_n = \frac{a(r^n - 1)}{r-1}, r > 1$

or $\frac{a(1-r^n)}{1-r}, r < 1$

(i) $\frac{\sqrt{7}}{2}(\sqrt{3}+1)(3^{n/2}-1)$ (ii) $\frac{1-(-a)^n}{1+a}$

(iii) 2186 (iv) $121(\sqrt{3}+1)$ (v) $\frac{1}{6}[1-(0.1)^{20}]$

2. Hint Here, $a = 5$ and $r = 2$

$\because \frac{a(r^n-1)}{r-1} = 315$

$\Rightarrow \frac{5(2^n-1)}{2-1} = 315$

Ans. Number of terms = 6 and last term = 160.

3. Hint $\frac{1}{81} = 27(r)^{8-1} \Rightarrow r = \frac{1}{3}$

Ans. $\frac{81}{2}\left(1 - \frac{1}{3^{10}}\right)$

4. Hint $ar^{8-1} = 192 \Rightarrow a \times (2)^7 = 192$

$\Rightarrow \quad a = \dfrac{3}{2}$

Ans. $S_{12} = 6142.5$

5. Hint Here, $ar = -\dfrac{1}{2}$ ...(i)

and $ar^4 = \dfrac{1}{16}$ ...(ii)

On dividing Eq. (ii) by Eq. (i), we get r

Then, find a using Eq. (i).

Ans. $\dfrac{85}{128}$

6. Hint Here, $a = 1, r = \dfrac{3}{1} = 3$

$\therefore \dfrac{1\cdot(3^n - 1)}{3-1} = 3280$ **Ans.** $n = 8$

7. Hint Let the required number of terms be n.

Then, we have

$\sqrt{3}\dfrac{[(\sqrt{3})^n - 1]}{[\sqrt{3}-1]} = 39 + 13\sqrt{3} \qquad \left[\because S_n = \dfrac{a(r^n-1)}{(r-1)}, r > 1\right]$

Ans. $n = 6$

8. Hint Do same as Example 67. **Ans.** $n = 20$

9. Hint $ar^{7-1} = 64 \Rightarrow r^6 = \left(\dfrac{2}{3}\right)^6 \Rightarrow r = \dfrac{2}{3}$

$\therefore \quad S_7 = \dfrac{729\left[1-\left(\dfrac{2}{3}\right)^7\right]}{1-2/3}$

Ans. 2059

10. Hint Here, $T_1 = a = 3, T_n = 96$ and $S_n = 189$

Now, find r, using

$S_n = \dfrac{a(r^n-1)}{r-1} = \dfrac{ar^n - a}{r-1} = \dfrac{r\cdot T_n - a}{r-1}$

After finding r, use $ar^{n-1} = 96$ to find n.

Ans. $n = 6$

11. Hint $\dfrac{a + ar + ar^2}{a + ar + ar^2 + ar^3 + ar^4 + ar^5} = \dfrac{125}{152}$

$\Rightarrow \dfrac{1 + r + r^2}{(1 + r + r^2)(1 + r^3)} = \dfrac{125}{152}$

$\Rightarrow r^3 = \dfrac{27}{125}$

Ans. $r = \dfrac{3}{5}$

12. Hint Let the GP be

$\underbrace{a, ar, ar^2, ar^3, ar^4, ar^5, \ldots, ar^{n-1}}_{n \text{ terms}}, \underbrace{ar^n, ar^{n+1}, \ldots, ar^{2n-1}}_{n \text{ terms}}$

Now, required ratio $= \dfrac{\dfrac{a(r^n-1)}{r-1}}{\dfrac{ar^n(r^n-1)}{r-1}}$

13. Hint Given, $S_n = \left(x + \dfrac{1}{x}\right)^2 + \left(x^2 + \dfrac{1}{x^2}\right)^2 + \left(x^3 + \dfrac{1}{x^3}\right)^2$ ....

$S_n = \left(x + \dfrac{1}{x}\right)^2 + \left(x^2 + \dfrac{1}{x^2}\right)^2 + \left(x^3 + \dfrac{1}{x^3}\right)^2 + \ldots\ldots + \left(x^n + \dfrac{1}{x^n}\right)^2$

$= \left(x^2 + \dfrac{1}{x^2} + 2\right) + \left(x^4 + \dfrac{1}{x^4} + 2\right) + \left(x^6 + \dfrac{1}{x^6}\right) + \ldots\ldots + \left(x^{2n} + \dfrac{1}{x^{2n}} + 2\right)$

$= (x^2 + x^4 + x^6 + \ldots\ldots + x^{2n}) + \left(\dfrac{1}{x^2} + \dfrac{1}{x^4} + \dfrac{1}{x^6} + \ldots\ldots \dfrac{1}{x^{2n}}\right) + (2 + 2 + 2 + \ldots\ldots \text{ utpo } n \text{ terms})$

$= x^2 \times \dfrac{(x^2)^n - 1}{x^2 - 1} + \dfrac{1}{x^2} \times \dfrac{1 - \left(\dfrac{1}{x^2}\right)^n}{1 - \dfrac{1}{x^2}} + 2n$

$= x^2 \times \left(\dfrac{x^{2n}-1}{x^2-1}\right) + \dfrac{1}{x^2} \times \left(\dfrac{x^{2n}-1}{x^2-1}\right) + 2n$

$= \dfrac{x^{2n}-1}{x^2-1}\left(x^2 + \dfrac{1}{x^2}\right) + 2n$

14. Hint Do same as Example 73.

Ans. $\dfrac{x^2(1 - x^{2n})}{1 - x^n} + \dfrac{xy(1 - x^n y^n)}{1 - xy}$

15. Hint Do same as Example 74.

Ans. $\dfrac{5}{81}(10^{n+1} - 10 - 9n)$

16. Hint Here, $a = 2, r = \dfrac{4}{2} = 2$ and $n = 10$

$\because S_{10} = \dfrac{2(2^{10}-1)}{2-1} = 2(2^{10}-1) = 2(1024-1)$

Ans. 2046

17. Hint Required number of grains

$= 1 + 2 + 2^2 + \ldots$ to 64 terms

$= 1 + (2 + 2^2 + 2^3 + \ldots + 2^{63}) = \left\{1 + \dfrac{2(2^{63}-1)}{(2-1)}\right\}$

Ans. $(2^{64} - 1)$

18. Hint Successive number of letters are 4, 16, 64, ...

This is a GP with $a = 4$ and $r = 4$.

Now, the total number of letters, when 8th set of letters is mailed $= S_8 = \dfrac{4(4^8-1)}{4-1} = 87380$

Ans. Cost of postage = ₹ (87380 × 2) = ₹ 174760

19. Hint According to the question,

$a_2 + a_4 + \ldots + a_{200} = \alpha$

and $a_1 + a_3 + \ldots + a_{199} = \beta$

$\Rightarrow ar + ar^3 + \ldots + ar^{199} = \alpha$

and $a + ar^2 + \ldots + ar^{198} = \beta$

$\Rightarrow ar\left[\dfrac{1-(r^2)^{100}}{1-r^2}\right] = \alpha$ and $a\left\{\dfrac{1-(r^2)^{100}}{1-r^2}\right\} = \beta$

Now, finding the value of $\dfrac{\alpha}{\beta}$, we get the result.

Chapter Exercise

1. (b) For an AP, $a_n = a + (n-1)d$

$3.5 + (101-1) \times 0 = 3.5$

2. (c) **Hint** Given, $a = 4$ and $d = -6$

$\therefore$ First four terms of an AP are

$a, a+d, a+2d, a+3d$
$= 4, 4-6, 4-2(6), 4-3(6)$
$= 4, -2, -8, -14$

3. (d) In an AP, $a_n = a + (n-1)d$

$\Rightarrow \quad 4 = a + 6(-4) \Rightarrow 4 + 24 = a$

$\therefore \quad a = 28$

4. (c) Given, the nth term of an Arithmetic Progression $= 2n + 5$

$\therefore \quad t_n = 2n + 5$

For 10th term, put $n = 10$

$\Rightarrow \quad t_{10} = 2(10) + 5 = 20 + 5$

$\Rightarrow \quad t_{10} = 25$

5. (a) Given, $a = 5$, $d = -3$ and $T_n = -7$

Now, $T_n = a + (n-1)d$

$\Rightarrow \quad -7 = 5 + (n-1)(-3)$

$-7 = 5 - 3n + 3$

$\Rightarrow \quad -7 = 8 - 3n$

$\Rightarrow \quad 3n = 15 \Rightarrow n = 5$

6. (c) Given, first term, $a = 8$

and common difference, $d = -5$

On putting the value of a and d is general form $a, a+d, a+2d, a+3d, \ldots\ldots$, we get

$8, 8-5, 8+2(-5), 8+3(-5), \ldots$

$8, 3, -2, -7 \ldots\ldots$

On comparing with given terms $8, A, B, \ldots\ldots$, we get

$A = 3, B = -2$

$\therefore \quad A + B = 3 + (-2) = 3 - 2 = 1$

7. (c) Given, common difference of AP i.e.

$d = 5$

Now, $a_{18} - a_{13} = a + (18-1)d - [a + (13-1)d]$

$= a + 17 \times 5 - a - 12 \times 5$

$= 85 - 60 = 25$

8. (c) Given AP is 2, 4, 6, 8, ...

$\therefore \quad a = 2$ and $d = 4 - 2 = 2$

Now, $S_n = \frac{n}{2}[2a + (n-1)d]$

$\therefore \quad S_{20} = \frac{20}{2}[2 \times 2 + (20-1) \times 2]$

$= 10[4 + 38] = 10 \times 42 = 420$

9. (d) We have, $S_8 = \frac{a(1-r^8)}{1-r} = \frac{1\left[1-\left(-\frac{1}{2}\right)^8\right]}{1-\left(-\frac{1}{2}\right)}$ [from formula]

$= \frac{1-\frac{1}{256}}{\frac{3}{2}} = \frac{255}{256} \times \frac{2}{3} = \frac{85}{128}$

10. **Hint** Here, $a_2 - a_1 = a_3 - a_2$

$\Rightarrow \quad 3n + 2 - 2n + 1 = 6n - 1 - 3n - 2$

Ans. $n = 3$ and the numbers are 5, 11, 17.

11. **Hint** Here, $a - 21 = b - a$

$\Rightarrow \quad 2a - b = 21 \quad \ldots(i)$

and $\quad -3 - b = b - a \Rightarrow a - 2b = 3 \quad \ldots(ii)$

On solving Eqs. (i) and (ii), we get

$a = 13$ and $b = 5$

Ans. 18

12. **Hint** Let $k^2 + 4k + 8$, $2k^2 + 3k + 6$ and $3k^2 + 4k + 4$ are in AP. Then, we have $(2k^2 + 3k + 6) - (k^2 + 4k + 8) = (3k^2 + 4k + 4) - (2k^2 + 3k + 6)$

Now, simply to find the required value of k.

Ans. $k = 0$

13. **Hint** Do same as Example 21. **Ans.** 32nd term

14. **Hint** $9 + (n-1) \times (-2) = 24 + (n-1) \times (-3)$

Ans. $n = 16$ and 16th term is -21.

15. **Hint** $a + 3d = 0 \Rightarrow a = -3d \quad \ldots(i)$

To prove $a_{25} = 3a_{11}$

Proof Clearly, $a_{25} = a + 24d$ [from Eq. (i)]

Also, $\quad a_{11} = a + 10d$

$\Rightarrow \quad a_{11} = 7d$ [from Eq. (i)]

16. **Hint** Here, $a_2 = 13$ and $a_5 = 25$

$a + d = 13$ and $a + 4d = 25$

On solving the above equations, we get

$a = 9$ and $d = 4$.

Ans. 33

17. **Hint** Given, $a_4 = 11 \Rightarrow a + 3d = 11 \quad \ldots(i)$

and $\quad a_5 + a_7 = 24 \Rightarrow a + 5d = 12 \quad \ldots(ii)$

Now, solving Eqs. (i) and (ii) and then get the value of d.

Ans. $d = \frac{1}{2}$

18. **Hint** Here, $a_{16} = 1 + 2a_8$

$\Rightarrow \quad a - d = -1 \quad \ldots(i)$

and $\quad a + 11d = 47 \quad \ldots(ii)$

On solving Eqs. (i) and (ii), we get

$d = 4$ and $a = 3$

Ans. $a_n = 4n - 1$

19. **Hint** We have, $a_8 = \frac{1}{2}a_2$ and $a_{11} = \frac{1}{3}a_4 + 1$

$\Rightarrow \quad a + 13d = 0$ and $2a + 27d = 3$

Now, solving above equations, we get

$a = -39$ and $d = 3$ **Ans.** 3

20. **Hint** $a_5 + a_9 = 72$ and $a_7 + a_{12} = 97$

Ans. 6, 11, 16, 21, 26, ...

21. **Hint** Let a and d be the first term and common difference of an AP and first three terms of an AP are $a, a+d$ and $a+2d$.

According to the question,

$a + (a+d) + (a+2d) = 42$

$\Rightarrow \quad 3a + 3d = 42 \Rightarrow a + d = 14$

Also, $a \times (a + 2d) = 52$

$\Rightarrow a \times [a + 2(14 - a)] = 52$

$\Rightarrow a \times (28 - a) = 52$

$\Rightarrow 28a - a^2 = 52$

$\Rightarrow a^2 - 28a + 52 = 0$

$\Rightarrow a^2 - 26a - 2a + 52 = 0$

$\Rightarrow a(a - 26) - 2(a - 26) = 0$

$\Rightarrow (a - 2)(a - 26) = 0$

$\Rightarrow a = 2, a = 26$

When $a = 2$, then $d = 14 - a = 14 - 2 = 12$

When $a = 26$, then $d = 14 - 26 = -12$

Ans. First term is 2 or 26 and common difference is 12 or 12

22. Hint 12, 18, 24, ..., 96

Now, proceed same as Example 22. **Ans.** 15

23. Hint 18, 27, 36, ..., 297

Now, proceed same as Example 22. **Ans.** 32

24. Hint Natural numbers between 101 and 999 divisible by both 2 and 5, i.e. divisible by 10, are 110, 120, 130, ..., 990.

Here, common difference,

$d = 120 - 110 = 130 - 120 = \ldots = 10.$

Let $l = a_n = a + (n - 1)d$

Then, $990 = 110 + (n - 1) \times 10$

Ans. $n = 89$

25. Hint Let the three parts be $a - d, a, a + d$, where $d > 0$.

$\therefore a - d + a + a + d = 210 \Rightarrow a = 70$

and product of two greatest parts = 5110

$\Rightarrow a(a + d) = 5110$

$\Rightarrow 70(70 + d) = 5110$ $[\because a = 70]$

$\Rightarrow d = 3$

Ans. 67, 70, 73

26. Hint Let the three terms in AP be $a - d, a, a + d$.

Then, $(a - d) + a + (a + d) = 33 \Rightarrow a = 11$

By the second condition,

$(a - d)(a + d) = a + 29 \Rightarrow d = \pm 9$

Ans. 2, 11, 20, ... and 20, 11, 2, ...

27. Hint Let the angles be $(a - d)°, a°, (a + d)°$.

Then, $(a - d)° + a° + (a + d)° = 180°$

and $(a + d)° = 3(a - d)° \Rightarrow a° = 2d$

Ans. 30°, 60°, 90°

28. Hint Let four numbers be $a - 3d, a - d, a + d, a + 3d$ which are in AP.

Then, $a - 3d + a - d + a + d + a + 3d = 50$

$\Rightarrow a = \frac{25}{2}$

and $a + 3d = 4(a - 3d)$

$\Rightarrow d = \frac{a}{5} = \frac{25}{2 \times 5} = \frac{5}{2}$

Ans. 5, 10, 15 and 20

29. Hint Given, a, b and c are in AP.

$\Rightarrow a - (a + b + c), b - (a + b + c)$ and $c - (a + b + c)$ are in AP.

[subtracting same quantity $(a + b + c)$ from each term of the AP]

$\Rightarrow -(b + c), -(c + a)$ and $-(a + b)$ are in AP.

$\Rightarrow (b + c), (c + a)$ and $(a + b)$ are in AP.

30. Hint Here, $a = \frac{3}{\sqrt{5}}$

and common difference, $d = \frac{4}{\sqrt{5}} - \frac{3}{\sqrt{5}} = \frac{1}{\sqrt{5}}$.

$\therefore S_{25} = \frac{25}{2}\left[2 \times \frac{3}{\sqrt{5}} + (25 - 1)\frac{1}{\sqrt{5}}\right]$

Ans. $75\sqrt{5}$

31. Hint Do same as Example 30. **Ans.** -800

32. Hint We have, $a_n = 2n + 1$

Clearly, $S_n = \frac{n}{2}(a_1 + a_n) = \frac{n}{2}[2(1) + 1 + (2n + 1)]$

Ans. $n(n + 2)$

33. Hint $1 + (n - 1)d = 20$ ...(i)

and $\frac{n}{2}[2 + (n - 1)d] = 399 \Rightarrow \frac{n}{2}(1 + 20) = 399$ [from Eq. (i)]

Ans. 38

34. Hint Here, $a_1 + a_3 + a_{17} = 216$

$\Rightarrow a + 6d = 72$ ...(i)

Now, $S_{13} = \frac{13}{2}[2a + (13 - 1)d] = \frac{13}{2}[2(a + 6d)]$

Ans. 936

35. Let a be the first term and d be the common difference of the AP.

Given,

5th term = 4

$\Rightarrow t_5 = a + 4d = 4$ ...(i)

and 9th term = -12

$\Rightarrow t_9 = a + 8d = -12$ ...(ii)

On subtracting Eq. (i) from Eq. (ii), we get

$4d = -16 \Rightarrow d = -4$ ...(iii)

On putting $d = -4$ in Eq. (i), we get

$a + 4(-4) = 4 \Rightarrow a = 20$

(a) First term = 20

(b) Common difference = -4

(c) Sum of 16 terms can be given by

$S_{16} = \frac{16}{2}[2 \times 20 + 15(-4)]$ $\left[\because S_n = \frac{n}{2}[(2a + (n - 1)d]\right]$

$\Rightarrow S_{16} = 8[40 - 60]$

$\Rightarrow S_{16} = -160$

36. Hint Let A be the first term and D be the common difference of the given AP.

According to the question,

$a_1 = A = a$ ...(i)

$a_3 = A + 2D = b$ ...(ii)

and $a_n = A + (n - 1)D = c$ ...(iii)

On solving Eqs. (i) and (ii), we get

$D = \frac{b - a}{2}$

On putting $A = a$ and $D = \left(\frac{b-a}{2}\right)$ in Eq. (iii), we get

$$a + (n-1)\left(\frac{b-a}{2}\right) = c$$

$$\Rightarrow \quad (n-1) = \frac{2(c-a)}{b-a}$$

$$\Rightarrow \quad n = \frac{2c - 3a + b}{b-a}$$

Now, $S_n = \frac{n}{2}(A + a_n) = \frac{(2c - 3a + b)}{2(b-a)}(a+c)$

$$= \frac{1}{2(b-a)}[2ac - 3a^2 + ab + 2c^2 - 3ac + bc]$$

$$= \frac{1}{2(b-a)}[(b-a)(c+a) + 2(c^2 - a^2)]$$

37. Hint Sum of odd terms

$$= \frac{(n+1)}{2}[2a + (n+1-1)(2d)] = (n+1)(a+nd)$$

Sum of even terms

$$= \frac{n}{2}[2(a+d) + (n-1)(2d)] = n(a+nd)$$

$$\therefore \quad \frac{S_{odd}}{S_{even}} = \frac{(n+1)(a+nd)}{n(a+nd)}$$

Ans. $(n+1) : n$

38. Hint The multiples of 7 lying between 500 and 900 are 504, 511, 518, ..., 896.

Clearly, it forms an AP.

Here, $a = 504$ and $d = 511 - 504 = 7$

Let there are n terms, i.e. $a_n = 896$

$\Rightarrow \quad a + (n-1)d = 896 \Rightarrow n = 57$

Now, $\quad S_{57} = \frac{n}{2}(a + a_n) = \frac{57}{2}(504 + 896)$

Ans. 39900

39. Hint All three-digit natural numbers, multiple of 11 are 110, 121, 132, ..., 990.

Here, common difference,

$$d = 121 - 110 = 132 - 121 = \ldots = 11.$$

Let $l = a_n = a + (n-1)d$

Then, $\quad 990 = 110 + (n-1) \times 11 \Rightarrow n = 81$

$$\because \quad S_n = \frac{n}{2}(a + l)$$

$$\therefore \quad S_{81} = \frac{81}{2}(110 + 990)$$

Ans. $S_{81} = 44550$

40. Hint All two-digit numbers greater than 50 which when divided by 7 leaves remainder 4, are 53, 60, 67, ..., 95.

Now, proceed same as Q. 39.

Ans. 518

41. Hint $a_4 = (a_2)^2$ and $a = -3$

$$\because \quad a_4 = (a_2)^2 \Rightarrow ar^3 = (ar)^2$$

$$\Rightarrow -3r^3 = (-3)^2 r^2 \qquad [\because a = -3]$$

$$\Rightarrow \quad r = -3$$

Now, $\quad a_7 = ar^6 = -3(-3)^6 = -3 \times 729$

Ans. -2187

42. Hint Here, $a_5 = 48 \Rightarrow ar^4 = 48$ ...(i)

and $\quad a_8 = 384 \Rightarrow ar^7 = 384$ ...(ii)

On dividing Eq. (ii) by Eq. (i), we get

$$\frac{ar^7}{ar^4} = \frac{384}{48}$$

$$\Rightarrow \quad r^3 = 8 \Rightarrow r = 2$$

On putting $r = 2$ in Eq. (i), we get $a = 3$

Ans. 3, 6, 12, ... are in GP.

43. Hint Let $a^x = b^y = c^z = k$

$\therefore x = \log_a k,\ y = \log_b k,\ z = \log_c k$

Since, x, y and z are in GP.

$$\therefore \quad \frac{\log_b k}{\log_a k} = \frac{\log_c k}{\log_b k} \Rightarrow \frac{\log_k a}{\log_k b} = \frac{\log_k b}{\log_k c}$$

$$\Rightarrow \quad \log_b a = \log_c b$$

44. Hint Let $S_n = (a+b) + (a^2 + 2b) + (a^3 + 3b) + \ldots$ upto n terms

$= (a + a^2 + a^3 + \ldots$ upto n terms$)$ $+ (b + 2b + 3b + \ldots$ upto n terms$)$

$$= a\left(\frac{a^n - 1}{a-1}\right) + \frac{n}{2}[2b + (n-1)b]$$

$$\left[\because S_{n(GP)} = \frac{A(R^n - 1)}{R-1},\ R > 1 \text{ and } S_{n(AP)} = \frac{n}{2}\{2A + (n-1)D\}\right]$$

Ans. $\frac{a(1-a^n)}{1-a} + \frac{bn(n+1)}{2}$

45. We have, by formula for nth term of an AP.

$$t_n = a + (n-1)d \qquad \ldots(i)$$

where t_n is the nth term of the AP.

a is the first term, n is the number of terms and d is the common difference.

Given, AP is 15, 30, 45, 60, ... is 300

Here, $a = 15$, $d = 30 - 15 = 15$, $t_n = 300$

Then, $300 = 15 + (n-1)15 \Rightarrow (n-1)15 = 285$

$\Rightarrow \quad (n-1) = 19 \Rightarrow n = 20$

Therefore, the 20th term of the AP is 300.

For sum of all term, we have by formula

$$S_n = \frac{n}{2}(a + t_n),$$

where S_n is the sum of first n terms of AP.

$$\Rightarrow \quad S_{20} = \frac{20}{2}(15 + 300)$$

$$\Rightarrow \quad S_n = 10 \times 315 = 3150$$

Therefore, the sum of all terms of the AP is 3150.

46. Hint $S_4 = \frac{1}{2}(\text{Sum of } a_5, a_6, a_7, a_8) = \frac{1}{2}(S_8 - S_4)$

$$\Rightarrow \quad 2S_4 = S_8 - S_4 \Rightarrow 3S_4 = S_8$$

$$\Rightarrow \quad 3\left\{\frac{4}{2}[2a + (4-1)d]\right\} = \frac{8}{2}[2a + (8-1)d]$$

$$\left[\because S_n = \frac{n}{2}[2a + (n-1)d]\right]$$

$$\Rightarrow \quad 6[2(5) + 3d] = 4[2(5) + 7d]$$

$$\Rightarrow \quad 60 + 18d = 40 + 28d$$

Ans. $d = 2$

47. **Hint** Here, $a_1 + a_5 = 26$

$\Rightarrow \quad a + 2d = 13 \quad \text{...(i)}$

Also, we have $a_2 \times a_4 = 160$

$\Rightarrow (a + d) \times (a + 3d) = 160$

$\Rightarrow (13 - 2d + d)(13 - 2d + 3d) = 160$ [from Eq. (i)]

$\Rightarrow \quad (13)^2 - (d)^2 = 160$

$\therefore \quad d = \pm 3$

When $d = 3$, then from Eq. (i) $a = 7$

and when $d = -3$, then from Eq. (i), $a = 19$

Now, the sum of first seven terms,

when $a = 7$ and $d = 3$

$$S_7 = \frac{7}{2}[2 \times 7 + (7 - 1) 3]$$

Again, sum of first seven terms,

when $a = 19$ and $d = -3$

$$S_7 = \frac{7}{2}[2 \times 19 + (7 - 1) \times -3]$$

Ans. 112, 70

48. **Hint** Do same as Example 40.

Ans. 2, 12, 22, ... and 152

49. **Hint** $-4, -1, 2, \ldots, x$ forms an AP with first term, $a = -4$ and common difference $d = -1 - (-4) = 3$

Also, last term, say $a_n = x$

$\because$ nth term of an AP, $a_n = a + (n - 1) d$

$\Rightarrow \quad x = -4 + (n - 1) 3$

$\Rightarrow \quad n = \frac{x + 7}{3} \quad \text{...(ii)}$

$\because$ Sum of first n terms, $S_n = \frac{n}{2}[2a + (n - 1) d]$

$$\therefore \quad S_{\left(\frac{x+7}{3}\right)} = \frac{x + 7}{2 \times 3}\left[2(-4) + \left(\frac{x + 4}{3}\right) \cdot 3\right]$$

$\Rightarrow \quad x^2 + 3x - 2650 = 0$ **Ans.** 50, – 53

50. **Hint** 11, 13, 15, ..., 99

$\therefore \quad 99 = 11 + (n - 1) \times 2$

$\Rightarrow \quad n = 45$

Now, $S_{45} = \frac{45}{2}[2 \times 11 + (45 - 1) \times 2]$ **Ans.** 2475

51. **Hint** Here, first term, $a = 1000$ and common difference, $d = 100$.

Now, amount paid in 30th installment,

$a_{30} = 1000 + (30 - 1)100 = ₹ 3900$

Amount paid in 30 installments,

$$S_{30} = \frac{30}{2}[2 \times 1000 + (30 - 1)100]$$

$= ₹ 73500$

Hence, remaining amount of loan that he has to pay

$= ₹ 118000 - ₹ 73500$

Ans. ₹ 44500

52. **Hint** Given that, tree grow 5 cm or 0.05 m less than preceding year.

The following sequence can be formed.

$1, (1 - 0.05), (1 - 2 \times 0.05), \ldots, 0$

i.e. $\quad 1, 0.95, 0.90, \ldots, 0$ which is an AP.

Here, $\quad a = 1, d = 0.95 - 1 = -0.05$ and $l = 0$

Let $l = a_n = a + (n - 1)d$.

Then, $\quad 0 = 1 + (n - 1)(-0.05)$

Ans. 21 yr

53. **Hint** The sequence of solved questions is given as

$2 + 4 + 8 + 16 + \ldots n$ days $= 2046$

By using, $S_n = \frac{a(r^n - 1)}{r - 1}$, we have

$$2046 = \frac{2(2^n - 1)}{2 - 1}$$

Ans. 10 days

54. **Hint** Total amount repaid in ten days

$= (10 + 20 + 40 + 80 + \ldots$ upto to 10 days)

$= \frac{10\{2^{10} - 1\}}{2 - 1}, r > 1$

$= 10(2^{10} - 1) = 10(1024 - 1)$

$= ₹ 10230$

Ans. Hence, there is a profit of 230.

55. **Hint** Let the number of days in which the work is completed, be n.

Now, according to the question, 4 workers dropped on everyday. So, number of workers present on successive days are 150, 146, 142, 138, ...

If the workers not dropped, then the work would have finished in $(n - 8)$ days with 150 workers working on each day.

Hence, the total number of workers who would have worked for all the n days, is $150(n - 8)$.

Clearly, the work done in both conditions is same.

i.e. $\quad 150(n - 8) = \frac{n}{2}[2 \times 150 + (n - 1)(-4)]$

Ans. The work will be completed in 25 days.

56. **Hint** Amount spent on first set

$= ₹ 1 \; (4 \times 25$ paise)

Amount spent on second set $= ₹ 4 \times 1 = ₹ 4$

[$\because$ each time the number of letters is multiplied by 4]

$\therefore$ Amount spent on all the eight sets

$= \{1 + 4 \times 1 + 4 \times 4 \times 1 + 4 \times 4 \times 4 \times 1 + \ldots$ upto 8 terms$\}$

$$= \frac{1(4^8 - 1)}{4 - 1} = \left(\frac{65536 - 1}{3}\right) = \frac{65535}{3}$$

Ans. ₹ 21845

Olympiad Section

Brain Teasing Questions of Olympiad Pattern

1 Five distinct positive integers are in arithmetic progression with a positive common difference. If their sum is 10020, then the smallest possible value of the last term is

(a) 2002 (b) 2004
(c) 2006 (d) 2007

2 The sum of series $1 + (1+2) + (1+2+3) + (1+2+3+4) + \dots + (1+2+3+\dots+20)$ is

(a) 1470 (b) 1540
(c) 1610 (d) 1370

3 An AP starts with a positive fraction and every alternate term is an integer. If the sum of the first 11 terms is 33, then the fourth term is

(a) 2 (b) 3
(c) 5 (d) 6

4 The sum of the series

$45^2 - 43^2 + 44^2 - 42^2 + 43^2 - 41^2 + 42^2 - 40^2 + \dots$

upto 30 terms is

(a) 1110 (b) 2220
(c) 3330 (d) 4440

5 Take a point $A(3, 4)$ on the graph and draw two lines from it, one is parallel to X-axis and another parallel to Y-axis. Again, take four points on both lines on both sides of A, such that their x-coordinates and y-coordinates form an AP with common difference 2. Then, the area of circle, passing through these four points, is

(a) 12 sq units
(b) 13 sq units
(c) 12.56 sq units
(d) 13.56 sq units

6 If a, b, c and d are in GP, then $(a^2 + b^2 + c^2)(b^2 + c^2 + d^2)$ is equal to

(a) $(ab + bc + cd)$ (b) $(ab + bc + cd)^2$
(c) $a^2 + b^2 + c^2$ (d) $b^2 + c^2 + d^2$

7 If a, b and c are respectively the pth, qth and rth terms of a GP, then the value of $(q - r)\log a + (r - p)\log b + (p - q)\log c$ is

(a) $\log abc$ (b) $\log ab$
(c) $\log bc$ (d) 0

Answers

1. (c) **2.** (b) **3.** (a) **4.** (b) **5.** (c) **6.** (b) **7.** (d)

* *These questions may or may not be asked in the examination, have been given just for additional practice required for olympiads Scholarship Exams etc. For detailed explanations refer Page No. 483.*

CHAPTER

10

Reflection

SYLLABUS

- (a) Reflection of a point in a line: x = 0, y = 0, x = a, y = a, the origin. (b) Reflection of a point in the origin. (c) Invariant points.

In this chapter, we will study about an important concept of coordinate geometry, i.e. 'reflection'. **Reflection** is an image or duplication of an object that appears identical but in opposite direction. Here, we will find the reflection of a point about the lines and axes and invariant points.

Reflection of a Point in a Line

When an object is placed in front of a plane mirror, then the image is formed at the same distance behind the mirror as the object is in front of it and the mirror is perpendicular to the line joining the object and its image.

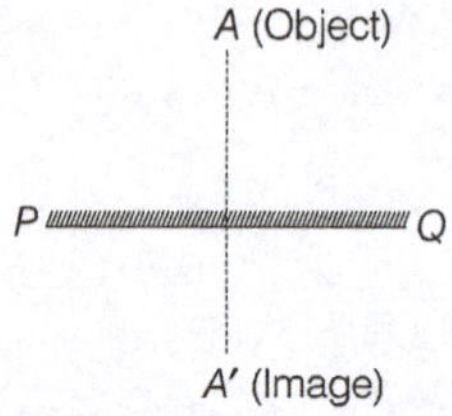

Definition The reflection (or image) of a point A in a line PQ is a point A' such that PQ is perpendicular bisector of the line segment AA'. Here, the line PQ is called the **axis of reflection** (or mediator).

Reflection of a Point in the X-axis ($y = 0$)

Let $A(x, y)$ be any point in the coordinate plane, then $A'(x, -y)$ is the reflection of $A(x, y)$ in the X-axis, if and only if the perpendicular distance from A to X-axis is equal to the perpendicular distance from A' to X-axis, i.e. $MA = MA'$.

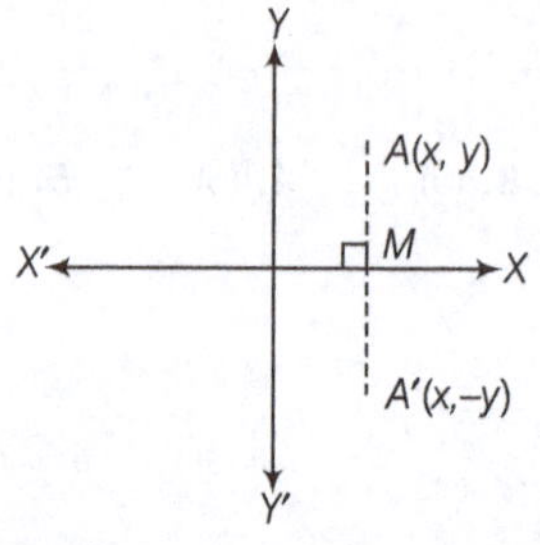

Rule to find the reflection of a point (x, y) in the X-axis ($y = 0$)

(i) Keep the sign of abscissa or x-coordinate unchanged.

(ii) Change the sign of ordinate or y-coordinate.

Example 1. Find the reflection of the following points in the X-axis.

(i) (5, 3) (ii) (– 1, 2)

(iii) (3, 0) (iv) (– 2, – 5)

Sol.

(i) The reflection of the point (5, 3) in the X-axis, is the point (5, –3).

(ii) The reflection of the point (– 1, 2) in the X-axis, is the point (– 1, – 2).

(iii) The reflection of the point (3, 0) in the X-axis, is the point (3, 0).

(iv) The reflection of the point (– 2, – 5) in the X-axis, is the point (– 2, 5).

Reflection of a Point in the Y-axis ($x = 0$)

Let $A(x, y)$ be any point in the coordinate plane, then $A'(-x, y)$ is the reflection of $A(x, y)$ in the Y-axis, if and only if the perpendicular distance from A to Y-axis is equal to the perpendicular distance from A' to Y-axis, i.e. $NA = NA'$.

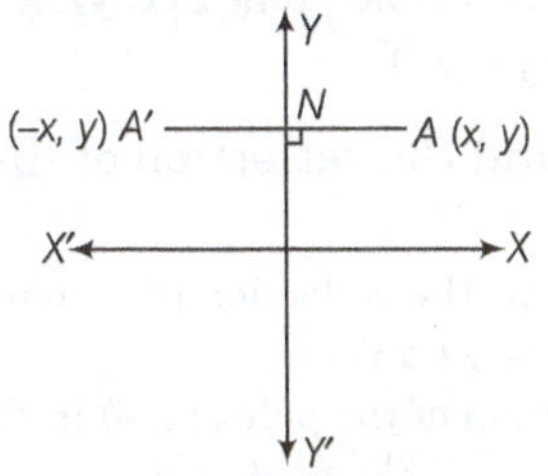

Rule to find the reflection of a point (x, y) in the Y-axis ($x = 0$)

(i) Keep the sign of ordinate or y-coordinate unchanged.
(ii) Change the sign of abscissa or x-coordinate.

Example 2. Find the reflection of the following points in the Y-axis.

(i) (1, 0) (ii) (– 3, 2.5)
(iii) (4.5, – 7) (iv) (0, – 1.5)

Sol. (i) The reflection of the point (1, 0) in the Y-axis is (– 1, 0).
(ii) The reflection of the point (– 3, 2.5) in the Y-axis is (3, 2.5).
(iii) The reflection of the point (4.5, – 7) in the Y-axis is (– 4.5, – 7).
(iv) The reflection of the point (0, – 1.5) in the Y-axis is (0, – 1.5).

Example 3. Find the reflection of the following points in the line $x = 0$.

(i) (– 2.5, 3.5) (ii) (0, 7)
(iii) (3, – 1.5) (iv) (– 1, 0)

Sol. The line $x = 0$ means Y-axis, i.e. reflection of points is to found in Y-axis.
(i) The reflection of the point (– 2.5, 3.5) in the line $x = 0$ is (2.5, 3.5).
(ii) The reflection of the point (0, 7) in the line $x = 0$ is (0, 7).
(iii) The reflection of the point (3, – 1.5) in the line $x = 0$ is (–3, –1.5).
(iv) The reflection of the point (– 1, 0) in the line $x = 0$ is (1, 0).

Example 4. Use a graph paper for this question. (Take 2 cm = 1 unit on both X and Y-axes)

(i) Plot the following points.
$A(0, 4)$, $B(2, 3)$, $C(1, 1)$ and $D(2, 0)$
(ii) Reflect points B, C, D in the Y-axis and write down their coordinates.
Name the images as B', C' and D', respectively.

[ICSE 2017]

Sol.
(i) We can plot the points $A(0, 4)$, $B(2, 3)$, $C(1, 1)$ and $D(2, 0)$ on graph paper as follows

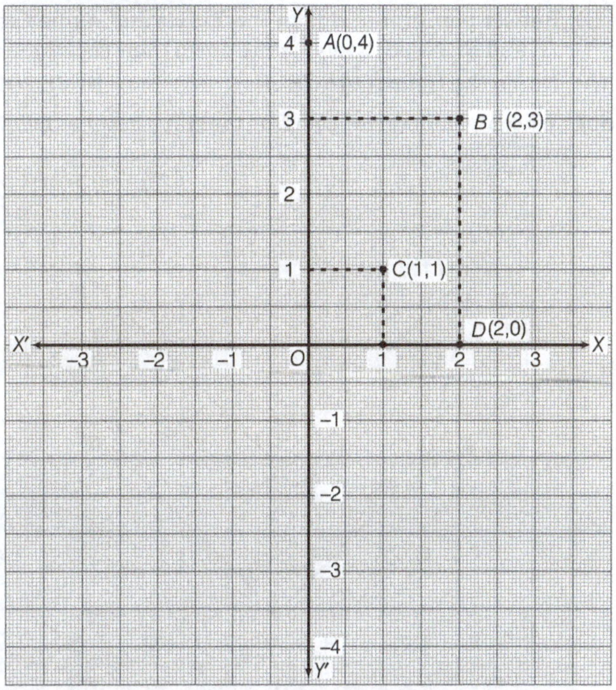

(ii) We know that, the image of point (x, y) on Y-axis has the coordinates $(-x, y)$.
Image of $B(2, 3)$ on Y-axis has the coordinates $B'(-2, 3)$.
Image of $C(1, 1)$ on Y-axis has the coordinates $C'(-1, 1)$.
Image of $D(2, 0)$ on Y-axis has the coordinates $D'(-2, 0)$.

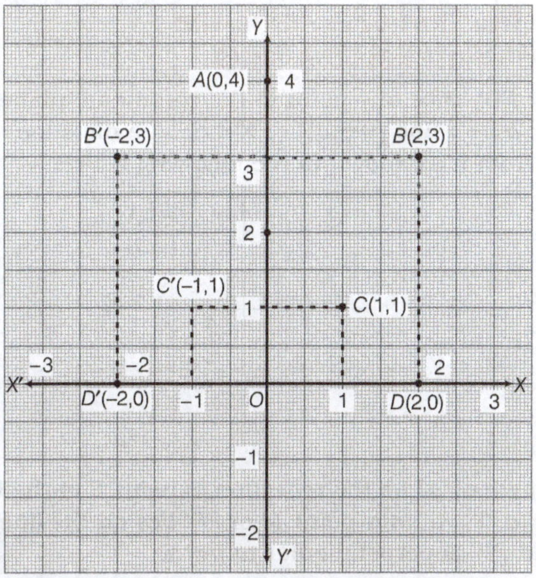

Example 5. Use graph paper for this question. (Take 2 cm = 1 unit along both X and Y-axes).
Plot the points $O(0, 0)$, $A(-4, 4)$, $B(-3, 0)$ and $C(0, -3)$

(i) Reflect points A and B on the Y-axis and name them A' and B', respectively. Write down their coordinates.

(ii) Name the figure $OABCB'A'$. [ICSE 2016]

Sol. We can plot the given points on the graph paper as follows

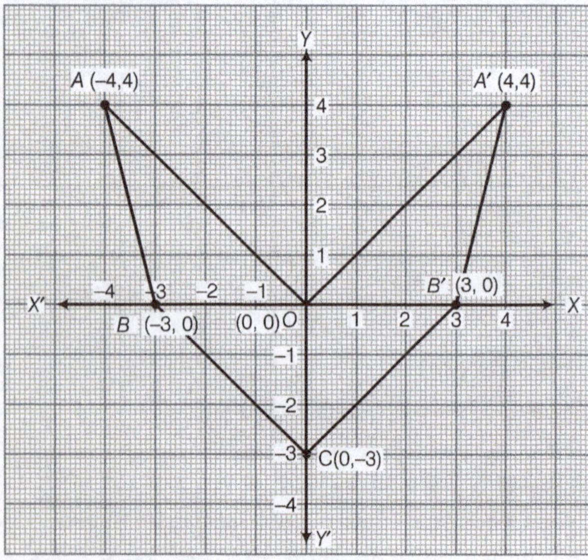

(i) When points $A(-4, 4)$ and $B(-3, 0)$ are reflected in Y-axis. Then, the image of points $A(-4, 4)$ and $B(-3, 0)$ are $A'(4, 4)$ and $B'(3, 0)$, respectively.

(ii) $OABCB'A'$ is a hexagon.

Reflection of a Point in a Line Parallel to X-axis

Let $P(x, y)$ be any point in the coordinate plane and $y = a$ be a line parallel to X-axis at a distance 'a' from it as shown in the following figure.

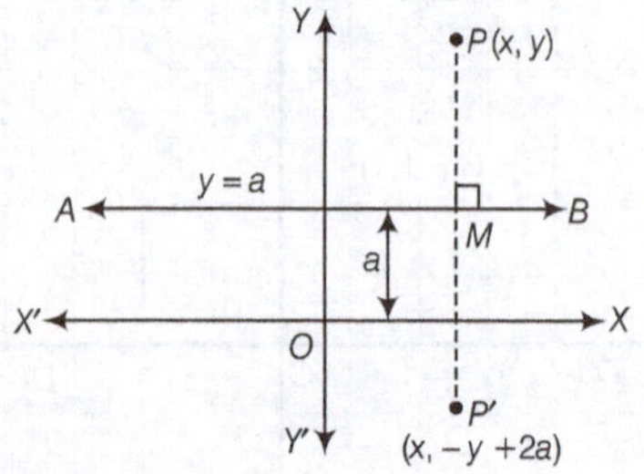

Let $P'(x_1, y_1)$ be the reflection of point P in the line $y = a$. Then, mid-point M of PP' lies on the line $y = a$ and PP' is perpendicular to $y = a$.

$\therefore$ Coordinates of $M = \left(\dfrac{x + x_1}{2}, \dfrac{y + y_1}{2}\right)$

Since, M lies on the line $y = a$.

$\therefore \dfrac{y + y_1}{2} = a \Rightarrow y + y_1 = 2a \Rightarrow y_1 = -y + 2a$

Also, x-coordinate of P', M and P are same.

$\therefore \quad x_1 = x$

So, the coordinates of $P' = (x, -y + 2a)$

Thus, the reflection of the point $P(x, y)$ in the line $y = a$ is the point $P'(x, -y + 2a)$.

Example 6. Find the reflection of the point (4, 5) in the line $y = 2$.

Sol. We know that, the reflection of a point $P(x, y)$ in the line $y = a$ is $P'(x, -y + 2a)$.

$\therefore$ The reflection of the point (4, 5) in the line $y = 2$ is the point $(4, -5 + 2 \times 2)$, i.e. $(4, -1)$.

[$\because x = 4$, $y = 5$ and $a = 2$]

Reflection of a Point in a Line Parallel to Y-axis

Let $P(x, y)$ be any point and $x = a$ be a line parallel to Y-axis at a distance 'a' from it as shown in the following figure. Let $P'(x_1, y_1)$ be the reflection of P in the line $x = a$.

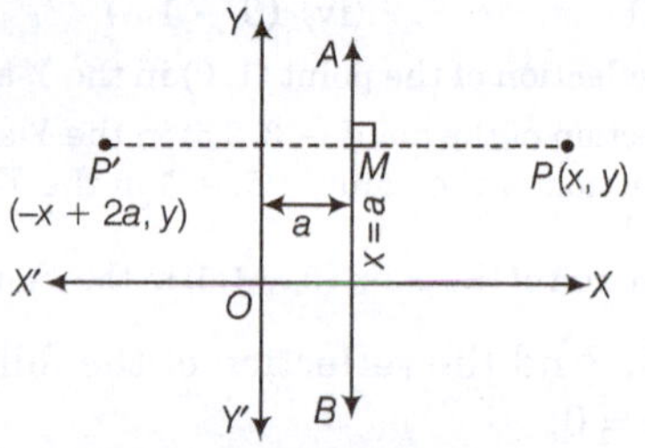

Then, the mid-point M of PP' lies on the line $x = a$ and PP' is perpendicular to $x = a$.

$\therefore$ Coordinates of $M = \left(\dfrac{x + x_1}{2}, \dfrac{y + y_1}{2}\right)$

Clearly, M lies on the line $x = a$.

$\therefore \quad \dfrac{x + x_1}{2} = a \Rightarrow x + x_1 = 2a$

$\Rightarrow \quad x_1 = -x + 2a$

Also, y-coordinate of P', M and P are same.

$\therefore \quad y_1 = y$

So, the coordinates of $P' = (-x + 2a, y)$.

Thus, the coordinates of the reflection of the point $P(x, y)$ in the line $x = a$, is $(-x + 2a, y)$.

Example 7. Find the reflection of the point (3, 2) in the line $x = 2$.

Sol. We know that, the reflection of a point $P(x, y)$ in the line $x = a$ is $(-x + 2a, y)$.

$\therefore$ The reflection of the point (3, 2) in the line $x = 2$ is $(-3 + 2 \times 2, 2)$, i.e. $(1, 2)$. [$\because x = 3$, $y = 2$ and $a = 2$]

Reflection of a Point in a Given Point

The reflection of a point P in a given point M, is the point P' such that M is the mid-point of the line segment PP'.

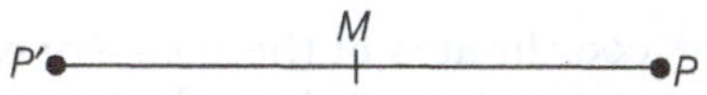

Example 8. Find the reflection of the point (– 1, 5) in the given point (2, 3).

Sol. Let $P'(x, y)$ be the reflection of the point $P(-1, 5)$ in the given point $M(2, 3)$. Then, M is the mid-point of the line segment PP'.

$\therefore$ Coordinates of $M = \left(\frac{-1+x}{2}, \frac{5+y}{2}\right)$

But coordinates of $M = (2, 3)$ [given]

$\therefore \quad (2, 3) = \left(\frac{-1+x}{2}, \frac{5+y}{2}\right)$

On comparing both sides, we get

$\frac{-1+x}{2} = 2$ and $\frac{5+y}{2} = 3 \Rightarrow -1+x = 4$ and $5+y = 6$

$\Rightarrow \quad x = 4+1$ and $y = 6-5 \Rightarrow x = 5$ and $y = 1$

$\therefore$ The coordinates of $P' = (5, 1)$

Thus, the reflection of the point (– 1, 5) in the given point (2, 3) is (5, 1).

Reflection of a Point in the Origin

Let $P(x, y)$ be any point in the coordinate plane as shown in the following figure.

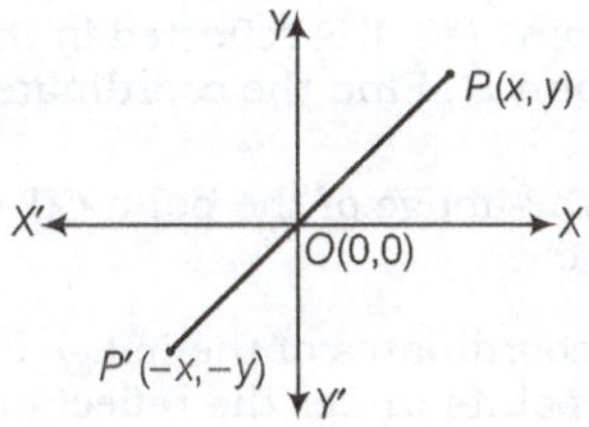

In order to find the reflection of P in the origin O, let us join OP and extend it to a point P' in such a way that $OP = OP'$. Clearly, point P' is the reflection of point P in the origin O. Let (x_1, y_1) be the coordinates of P'.

Then, coordinates of the mid-point of PP'

$$= \left(\frac{x + x_1}{2}, \frac{y + y_1}{2}\right)$$

But origin is the mid-point of PP'.

$$\therefore \quad \frac{x + x_1}{2} = 0 \Rightarrow \frac{y + y_1}{2} = 0$$

$$\Rightarrow \quad x_1 = -x, y_1 = -y$$

So, the coordinates of $P' = (-x, -y)$. Thus, the reflection of point $P(x, y)$ in the origin, is $P'(-x, -y)$.

Example 9. Find the reflection of (2, 3) in the origin.

Sol. We know that, the reflection of a point $P(x, y)$ in the origin $O(0, 0)$ is $P'(-x, -y)$.

$\therefore$ The reflection of the point (2, 3) in the origin, is the point (– 2, – 3).

Some Important Points about Reflection

(i) If three points A, B and C are clockwise, then their images A', B' and C' are anti-clockwise.

(ii) The image of a figure under reflection is congruent to the original figure.

(iii) Reflection in the X-axis, followed by the reflection in the Y-axis is equivalent to reflection in the origin.

Invariant Point

Any point that remains unaltered under a given transformation is called an **invariant point**.

Or

Reflection of a point in the point itself is called invariant point.

Or

A point is called an invariant point with respect to a given line, if and only if it lies on the reflection line.

e.g. If AB is a reflection line and a point P lies on it, then P is the invariant point, as the image of P is P itself.

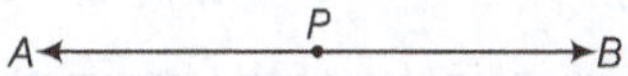

Example 10. The point $P(a, b)$ is invariant, when the reflected in the origin. Find the values of a and b.

Sol. The image of point P in the origin is $P'(-a, -b)$.

Now, as P is invariant

$\therefore \quad (a, b) = (-a, -b)$

$\Rightarrow \quad a = -a$ and $b = -b$

$\Rightarrow \quad 2a = 0$ and $2b = 0$

$\Rightarrow \quad a = 0$ and $b = 0$

Chapter Practice

a. 1 Mark Questions

1. The reflection of the point $A(-4, 3)$ in the Y-axis is

(a) (4, 3) (b) (4, – 3) (c) (– 4, – 3) (d) (0, 3)

2. The coordinates of the point $P(-3, 5)$ on reflecting on the X-axis are **[ICSE Semester II 2022]**

(a) (3, 5) (b) (– 3, – 5) (c) (3, – 5) (d) (– 3, 5)

3. If the image of the point P under reflection in the X-axis is (– 6, 2), then the coordinates of the point P are

(a) (6, 2) (b) (– 6, – 2) (c) (6, – 2) (d) (– 6, 0)

4. The reflection of the point $A(5, -2)$ in the line $x = 2$ is

(a) (– 1, – 2) (b) (8, – 1)
(c) (0, 1) (d) None of these

5. The reflection of the point $P(1, 2)$ in the line $y = -1$ is

(a) (– 3, – 2) (b) (1, – 4) (c) (1, 4) (d) (1, 0)

6. The reflection of the point (– 6, 0) in the origin is the point

(a) (0, – 6) (b) (0, 6)
(c) (6, 0) (d) None of these

b. 3 Marks Questions

7. Find the coordinates of the image of each of the following points under the reflection in X-axis.

(i) (5, 2) (ii) (– 2, 3)
(iii) (4, –6) (iv) (0, – 1)
(v) (7, 0) (vi) (– 5, – 3)

8. Find the coordinates of the image of each of the following points under the reflection in the line $y = 0$.

(i) (3, – 6) (ii) (1, – 2)
(iii) (– 3, – 1) (iv) (0, – 2)
(v) (3, 0) (vi) $\left(\frac{1}{2}, \frac{3}{4}\right)$

9. Find the coordinates of the image of each of the following points under the reflection in the line $x = 0$.

(i) $\left(\frac{3}{2}, \frac{5}{2}\right)$ (ii) (2, – 1)
(iii) (0, – 3) (iv) (– 7, 0)
(v) (– 5, – 3) (vi) (2, 8)

10. Find the coordinates of the image of each of the following points under the reflection in Y-axis.

(i) $\left(-\frac{1}{2}, \frac{4}{5}\right)$ (ii) (3, 7)
(iii) (3, 0) (iv) (– 3, – 8)
(v) $\left(0, \frac{7}{2}\right)$ (vi) (– 6, 7)

11. The point (– 8, 0) on reflection in a line is mapped as (8, 0)

(i) Name the mirror line.
(ii) Write the coordinates of the image of (– 3, – 4) in the mirror line.

12. The point (– 6, 0) on reflection in a line is mapped as (6, 0)

(i) Name the line of reflection.
(ii) Write the coordinates of the image of (5, – 8) in the line obtained in (i).

13. (i) The point $T(-3, 5)$ is reflected in the line $y = 3$ to the point T'. Find the coordinates of the point T'.
(ii) Find the image of the point $S(1, 4)$ in the line $y = -3$.

14. (i) The point $P(3, 1)$ is reflected in the line $x = 2$ to the point P'. Find the coordinates of the point P'.
(ii) Find the image of the point $Q(1, -2)$ in the line $x = -1$.

15. Find the coordinates of the image of each of the following points under the reflection in the origin.

(i) (2, – 5) (ii) (0, – 1)
(iii) (0, 0) (iv) (7, 8)
(v) $\left(\frac{1}{2}, \frac{3}{2}\right)$ (vi) $\left(\frac{1}{5}, 0\right)$

16. A, B have coordinates (– 1, 2) and (6, 4), respectively. Reflect A in the X-axis to A'. Calculate the length of the segment $A'B$. [Leave your answer in square root form]

17. A point S is reflected in the origin and the coordinates of its image are (2, – 5).

(i) Find the coordinates of S.
(ii) Find the coordinates of the image of S under the reflection in the X-axis.
(iii) Find the coordinates of the image of S under the reflection in the Y-axis.

18. A point P is reflected in the $x = 0$ and the coordinates of its image are $(-1, 2)$.
 (i) Find the coordinates of P.
 (ii) Find the coordinates of the image of P under the reflection in the line $y = 0$.
 (iii) Find the coordinates of the image of P under the reflection in the origin.

19. The point $A(-4, -5)$ on reflection in Y-axis is mapped on A'. The point A' on reflection in the origin is mapped on A''. Find the coordinates of A' and A''. Write down a single transformation that maps A onto A''.

20. The point $B(1, 7)$ on the reflection in the line $y = 0$ is mapped on B'. The point B' on reflection in the origin is mapped on B''. Find the coordinates of B' and B''. Also, write down a single transformation that maps B onto B''.

21. A point $P(h, k)$ is reflected in X-axis to $P'(2, -3)$, write down the values of h and k. P'' is the image of P, when reflected in the Y-axis. Write down the coordinates of P''. Find the coordinates of P''', when P is reflected in the origin.

22. (i) A point $Q(a, b)$ is reflected in the line $x = 0$ to $Q'(-5, 2)$. Write down the values of a and b.
 (ii) Q'' is the image of Q, when reflected in the line $y = 0$. Write down the coordinates of Q''.
 (iii) Find the coordinates of Q''', when Q is reflected in the origin.

23. Points P and Q have coordinates $(2, 5)$ and $(0, 3)$. Find
 (i) the image P' of P under the reflection in the X-axis.
 (ii) the image Q' of Q under the reflection in the line PP'.

C. 4/5 Marks Questions

24. A and B have coordinates $(0, 4)$ and $(-2, 3)$.
 (i) A is invariant when reflected in an axis. Name the axis.
 (ii) Find the image of B on reflection in the axis found in (i).
 (iii) $(0, k)$ on reflection in the origin is invariant. Write the value of k.
 (iv) Write the coordinate of the image of B, obtained by reflecting it in the origin followed by reflection in X-axis.

25. Points A and B have coordinates $(1, -3)$ and $(2, 4)$. Find the following.
 (i) The image A' of A under the reflection in the line $x = 0$.
 (ii) The image B' of B under the reflection of the line AA'.

26. Given, two points A and B, and that (1) the image of A on reflection in Y-axis is the point B and (2) the mid-point of AB is invariant on reflection in X-axis. Locate
 (i) the X-axis (ii) the Y-axis and
 (iii) the origin.

27. Use a graph paper for this question.
 Take 2 cm = 1 unit along both the axes.
 (i) Plot the points $A(0, 4)$, $B(2, 2)$, $C(5, 2)$, $D(4, 0)$ and $E(0, 0)$ is the origin.
 (ii) Reflect B, C, D on the Y-axis and name them as B', C' and D', respectively.
 (iii) Join the points $ABCDD'C'B'$ and A in order and give a geometrical name to the closed figure. **[ICSE Semester II 2022]**

28. Use a graph paper for this question. (Take 10 small divisions = 1 unit on both axes). P and Q have coordinates $(0, 5)$ and $(-2, 4)$.
 (i) P is invariant when reflected in an axis. Name the axis.
 (ii) Find the image of Q on reflection in the axis found in (i).
 (iii) $(0, k)$ on reflection in the origin is invariant. Write the value of k.
 (iv) Write the coordinates of the image of Q, obtained by reflecting it in the origin followed by reflection in X-axis. **[ICSE 2005]**

29. The points $P(4, -11)$, $Q(5, 3)$, $R(2, 15)$ and $S(1, 1)$ are the vertices of a parallelogram. If the parallelogram is reflected in the Y-axis and then in the origin, find the coordinates of the final images. Check whether it remains a parallelogram. Write a single transformation that brings the above change.

30. A point P is its own image under the reflection in a line l. Describe the position of the point P with respect to the line l.

31. Use a graph paper for this question. (Take 1 box = 1 unit on both the axes)
 S and R have coordinates $(0, -3)$ and $(-1, 6)$, respectively.
 (i) S is invariant when reflected in an axis. Name the axis.
 (ii) $(a, 0)$ on the reflection in the origin is invariant. Write the value of a.
 (iii) Write the coordinates of the image of R under the reflection in the line $x = 0$.

32. The points $A(2, 3)$, $B(4, 5)$ and $C(7, 2)$ are the vertices of ΔABC.
 (i) Write down the coordinates of A_1, B_1, C_1, if $\Delta A_1B_1C_1$ is the image of ΔABC when reflected in the origin.

(ii) Write down the coordinates of A_2, B_2, C_2, if $\Delta A_2B_2C_2$ is the image of ΔABC when reflected in the X-axis.

(iii) Assign the special name of the quadrilateral BCC_2B_2 and find its area. [ICSE 2006]

33. The ΔEFG, where E is $(1, 2)$, $F(-3, 5)$ and G is $(4, 7)$, is reflected in the line $x = 0$ to $\Delta E'F'G'$. $\Delta E'F'G'$ is then reflected in the origin to $\Delta E''F''G''$.

(i) Write down the coordinates of $E''F''G''$

(ii) Write down a single transformation that maps ΔEFG onto $\Delta E''F''G''$.

(iii) Are the two triangles congruent?

34. Use graph paper for this question (Take 10 small divisions = 1 unit on both axes).

Plot points $P(3, 2)$ and $Q(-3, -2)$. From P and Q, draw perpendiculars PM and QN on the X-axis.

(i) Name the image of P on reflection in the origin.

(ii) Assign the special name to the geometrical figure $PMQN$ and find its area.

(iii) Write the coordinates of the point to which M is mapped on reflection in

(a) X-axis (b) Y-axis (c) origin.

d. 6 Marks Questions

35. Use graph paper for this question.

Take 1 cm = 1 unit on both X and Y-axes.

(i) Plot the following points on your graph sheets $A(-4, 0)$, $B(-3, 2)$, $C(0, 4)$, $D(4, 1)$ and $E(7, 3)$

(ii) Reflect the points B, C, D and E on the X-axis and name them as B', C', D' and E', respectively.

(iii) Join the points $A, B, C, D, E, E', D', C', B'$ and A' in order.

(iv) Name the closed figure formed. [ICSE 2020]

36. Use a graph sheet for this question.

Take 1 cm = 1 unit along both X and Y-axes.

(i) Plot the following points.

$A(0, 5)$, $B(3, 0)$, $C(1, 0)$ and $D(1, -5)$

(ii) Reflect the points B, C and D on the Y-axis and name them as B', C' and D', respectively.

(iii) Write down the coordinates of B', C' and D'.

(iv) Join the points A, B, C, D, D', C', B' and A' in order and give a name to the closed figure $ABCDD'C'B'$. [ICSE 2019]

37. Use graph paper for this question.

(Take 2 cm = 1 unit along both X and Y-axes)

$ABCD$ is a quadrilateral whose vertices are $A(2, 2)$, $B(2, -2)$, $C(0, -1)$, and $D(0, 1)$.

(i) Reflect quadrilateral $ABCD$ on the Y-axis and name it as $A'B'CD$.

(ii) Write down the coordinates of A' and B'.

(iii) Name two points which are invariant under the above reflection.

(iv) Name the polygon $A'B'CD$. [ICSE 2018]

38. Use graph sheet to answer this question. Take 2 cm = 1 unit along both the axes.

(i) Plot A, B, C where $A(0, 4)$, $B(1, 1)$ and $C(4, 0)$

(ii) Reflect A and B on the X-axis and name them as E and D, respectively.

(iii) Reflect B through the origin and name it F. Write down the coordinates of F.

(iv) Reflect B and C on the Y-axis and name them as H and G respectively.

(v) Join points A, B, C, D, E, F, G, H and A in order and name the closed figure formed. [ICSE 2023]

39. Use graph paper for this question.

(i) The point $P(2, -4)$ is reflected about the line $x = 0$ to get the image Q. Find the coordinates of Q.

(ii) Point Q is reflected about the line $y = 0$ to get the image R. Find the coordinates of R.

(iii) Name the figure PQR.

(iv) Find the area of the figure PQR. [ICSE 2007]

40. Using graph paper and taking 1 cm = 1 unit along with X-axis and Y-axis.

(i) Plot the point $A(-4, 4)$ and $B(2, 2)$.

(ii) Reflect A and B in the origin to get the images A' and B', respectively.

(iii) Write down the coordinates of A' and B'.

(iv) Give the geometrical name for the figure $ABA'B'$. [ICSE 2012]

41. Use a graph paper to answer the following questions. (Take 1 cm = 1 unit on both axes)

(i) Plot $A(4, 4)$, $B(4, -6)$ and $C(8, 0)$, the vertices of a ΔABC.

(ii) Reflect ABC on the Y-axis and name it as $A'B'C'$.

(iii) Write the coordinates of the images A', B' and C'.

(iv) Give a geometrical name for the figure $AA'C'B'BC$. [ICSE 2011]

42. Use a graph paper for this question.

(Taking 1cm = 1 unit along both the X and Y-axes)

(i) Plot the points $A(0, 5)$, $B(2, 5)$, $C(5, 2)$, $D(5, -2)$, $E(2, -5)$ and $F(0, -5)$.

(ii) Reflect the points B, C, D and E on the Y-axis and name them respectively as B', C', D' and E'.

(iii) Write the coordinates of B', C', D' and E'.

(iv) Name the figure formed by $BCDEE'D'C'B'$. [ICSE 2015]

43. Point (2, 0) and (– 2, 0) are invariant points under reflection in the line L_1; points (0, – 3) and (0, 1) are invariant points on reflection in the line L_2.
(i) Names the lines L_1 and L_2.
(ii) Write down the images of points $P(3, 4)$ and $Q(-5, -2)$ on reflection in L_1. Name the images as P' and Q', respectively.
(iii) Write down the images of P and Q on reflection in L_2. Name the images as P'' and Q'' respectively.
(iv) State or describe a single transformation that maps P' onto P''.

44. Using a graph paper, plot the points $A(6, 4)$ and $B(0, 4)$.
(i) Reflect A and B in the origin to get the images A' and B'.
(ii) Write the coordinates of A' and B'.
(iii) State the geometrical name for the figure $ABA'B'$.
(iv) Find its perimeter. **[ICSE 2013]**

45. Use a graph paper to answer the following questions. (Take 2 cm = 1 unit on both axes)
(i) Plot the points $A(-4, 2)$ and $B(2, 4)$.
(ii) A' is the image of A, when reflected in the Y-axis. Plot it on the graph paper and write the coordinates of A'.
(iii) B' is the image of B, when reflected in the line AA'. Write the coordinates of B'.
(iv) Write the geometric name of the figure $ABA'B'$. **[ICSE 2014]**

46. The point $A(6, 3)$ was reflected in the origin to get the image A'.
(i) Write down the coordinates of A'.
(ii) If B is the foot of the perpendicular from A to the X-axis, find the coordinate of B.
(iii) If C is the foot of the perpendicular from A' to the X-axis, find the coordinates of C.
(iv) Name the figure $ABA'C$.
(v) Find the area of the figure $ABA'C$.

Hints and Answers

1. (a) The reflection of the point $A(-4, 3)$ in the Y-axis is (4, 3).

2. (b) The reflection of the point (– 3, 5) in the X-axis, is the point (– 3, – 5).

3. (b) Given, the image of point P under reflection in the X-axis is (– 6, 2), then the co-ordinate of the point P are (– 6, – 2).

4. (a) We know that the reflection of a point $P(x, y)$ in the line $x = 2$ is $(-5 + 2 \times 2, -2)$ i.e. (– 1, – 2).

5. (b) We know that the reflection of a point $P(x, y)$ in the line $y = a$ is $P'(x, -y + 2a)$.
$\therefore$ The reflection of the point $P(1, 2)$ in the line $y = -1$ is the point $(1, -2 + 2 \times -1)$, i.e. (1, – 4).

6. (c) We know that the reflection of point $P(x, y)$ in the origin is $P'(-x, -y)$.
$\therefore$ The reflection of the point (– 6, 0) in the origin is the point (6, 0).

7. **Hint** The image of a point $P(x, y)$ under the reflection in X-axis is $P'(x, -y)$, i.e. only the sign of y-coordinate will be changed.
Ans. (i) (5, –2) (ii) (– 2, –3) (iii) (4, 6) (iv) (0, 1) (v) (7, 0) (vi) (– 5, 3)

8. **Hint** Do same as Q. 7.
Ans. (i) (3, 6) (ii) (1, 2) (iii) (– 3, 1) (iv) (0, 2) (v) (3, 0) (vi) $\left(\frac{1}{2}, \frac{-3}{4}\right)$

9. **Hint** The image of a point $P(x, y)$ under the reflection in the line $x = 0$ (i.e. Y-axis) is $P'(-x, y)$, i.e. only the sign of x-coordinate will be changed.
Ans (i) $\left(-\frac{3}{2}, \frac{5}{2}\right)$ (ii) (– 2, – 1) (iii) (0, – 3) (iv) (7, 0) (v) (5, – 3) (vi) (– 2, 8)

10. **Hint** Do same as Q. 9.
Ans. (i) $\left(\frac{1}{2}, \frac{4}{5}\right)$ (ii) (– 3, 7) (iii) (– 3, 0) (iv) (3, – 8) (v) $\left(0, \frac{7}{2}\right)$ (vi) (6, 7)

11. **Ans.** (i) Y-axis (ii) (3, – 4)

12. **Ans.** (i) Y-axis; equation is $x = 0$ (ii) (–5, – 8)

13. **Hint** We know that the reflection of the point (x, y) in the line $y = a$ is the point $(x, -y + 2a)$.
Ans. (i) (– 3, 1) (ii) (1, – 10)

14. **Hint** We know that the reflection of the point (x, y) in the line $x = a$ is the point $(-x + 2a, y)$.
Ans. (i) (1, 1) (ii) (– 3, – 2)

15. **Hint** The image of a point $P(x, y)$ under the reflection of origin is $P'(-x, -y)$, i.e. the sign of both coordinates will be changed.
Ans (i) (– 2, 5) (ii) (0, 1) (iii) (0, 0) (iv) (– 7, – 8) (v) $\left(-\frac{1}{2}, -\frac{3}{2}\right)$ (vi) $\left(-\frac{1}{5}, 0\right)$

16. **Hint** Length of $A'B = \sqrt{(6+1)^2 + (4+2)^2}$ where $A' = (-1, -2)$ **Ans.** $\sqrt{85}$ units

17. (i) **Hint** The sign of the both coordinates will be changed. **Ans.** $(-2, 5)$

(ii) **Hint** Do same as Example 1. **Ans.** $(-2, -5)$

(iii) **Hint** Do same as Example 2. **Ans.** $(2, 5)$

18. (i) **Hint** Do same as Q. 9. **Ans.** $(1, 2)$

(ii) **Hint** Do same as Q. 7. **Ans.** $(1, -2)$

(iii) **Hint** Do same as Example 9. **Ans.** $(-1, -2)$

19. Ans. $A'(4, -5)$, $A''(-4, 5)$, Reflection of A in X-axis.

20. Hint

(i) The reflection of a point (x, y) in the line $y = 0$ is the point $(x, -y)$.

(ii) The reflection of a point (x, y) in the origin is $(-x, -y)$.

Ans. $B'(1, -7)$, $B''(-1, 7)$, Reflection of B in Y-axis.

21. Hint

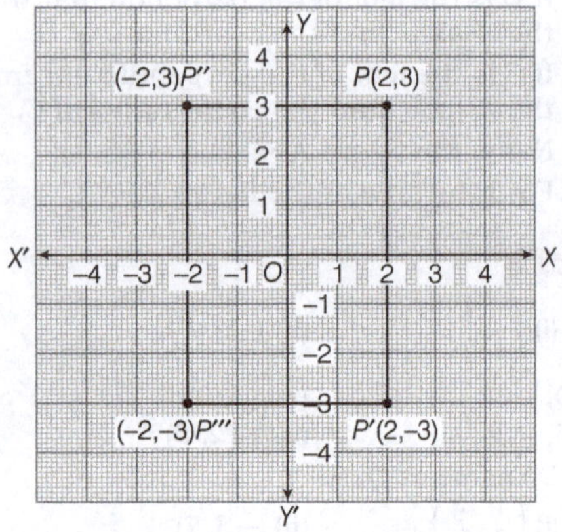

Ans. $h = 2$, $k = 3$, $P'' \equiv (-2, 3)$, $P''' = (-2, -3)$

22. Hint (i) $a = 5$, $b = 2$ (ii) $(5, -2)$ (iii) $(-5, -2)$

23. Hint Here, $x = 2$

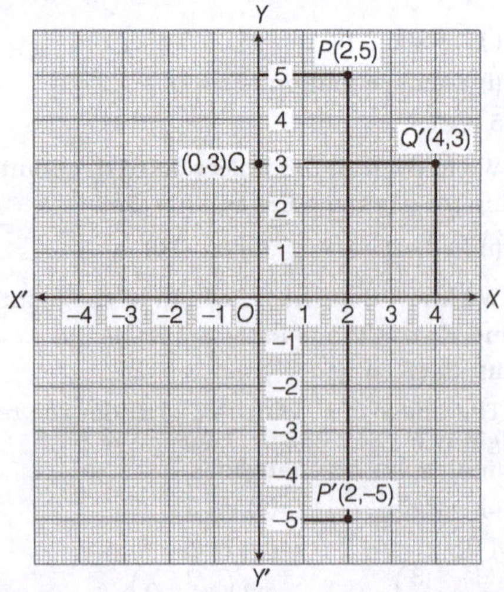

Ans. (i) $(2, -5)$ (ii) $(4, 3)$

24. (i) **Hint** A point is called an invariant point with respect to a given line, if and only if it lies on the reflection line. **Ans.** Y-axis

(ii) **Hint** The reflection of a point (x, y) in the Y-axis is the point $(-x, y)$. **Ans.** $(2, 3)$

(iii) **Hint** Reflection of a point in the point itself is called invariant point. **Ans.** $k = 0$

(iv) **Hint** The reflection of point (x, y) in the X-axis is the point $(x, -y)$. **Ans.** $(2, 3)$.

25. (i) **Hint** The reflection of a point (x, y) in the line $x = 0$ is the point $(-x, y)$. **Ans.** $(-1, -3)$

(ii) **Hint** Do same as Example 6. (here, $y = -3$)

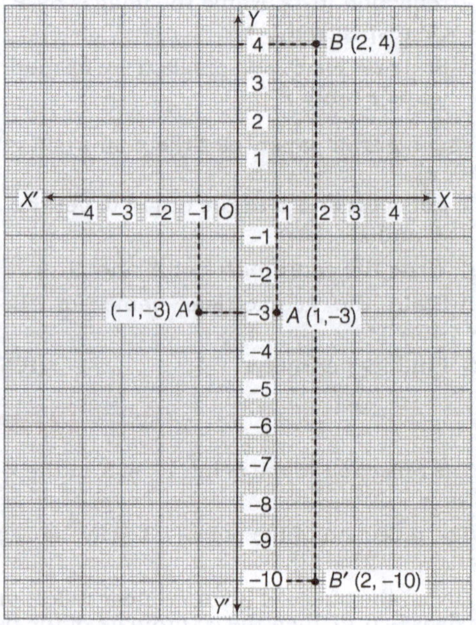

Ans. $(2, -10)$

26. Hint (i) X-axis is the line AB.

(ii) Y-axis is the right bisector of the line segment AB.

(iii) Origin is the mid-point of AB.

Ans. (i) AB (ii) right bisector (iii) mid-point

27. Hint Do same as Example 5.

Let XOX' and YOY' are two perpendicular axes meet at origin on a graph paper and mark 2 cm = 1 unit on both coordinate axes.

(i) **Ans.**

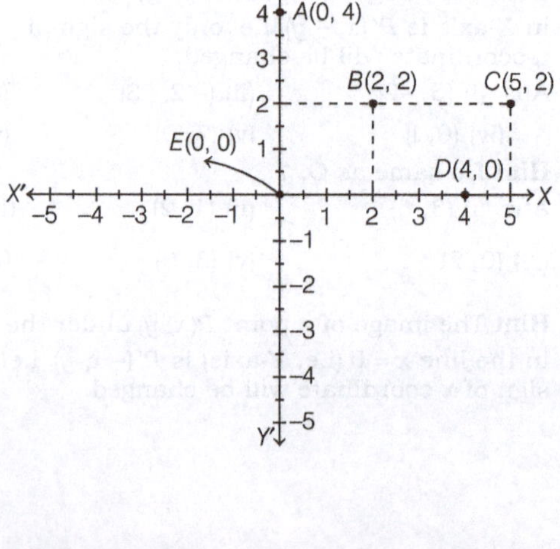

(ii) **Ans.**

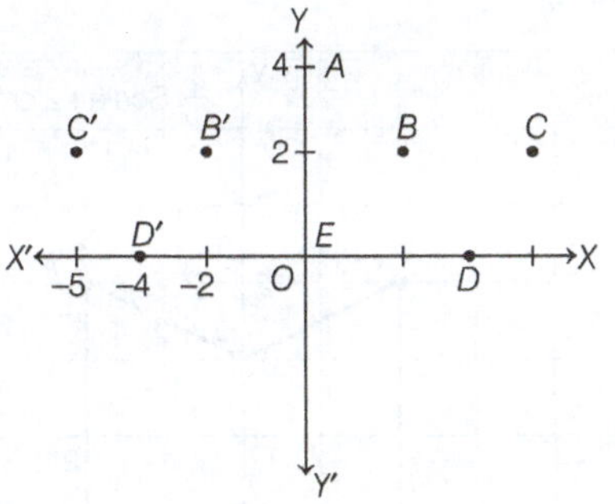

(iii) **Ans.**

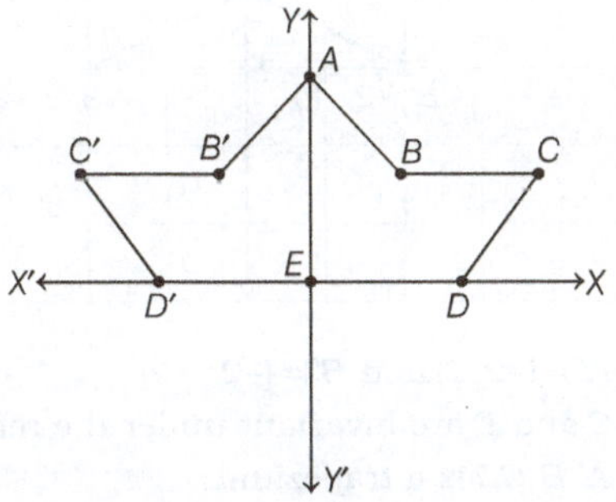

(Irregular Heptagon)

28. (i) **Hint** We know that a point is invariant when line of reflection passing through it.
Ans. Y-axis.

(ii) **Hint** Reflect the point $(-2, 4)$ in Y-axis.
Ans. $(2, 4)$

(iii) **Hint** The reflection of $(0, k)$ in the origin has coordinates $(0, -k)$. But, it is given that $(0, k)$ on reflection in the origin is invariant.
$\therefore$ $(0, k) = (0, -k)$ **Ans.** $k = 0$

(iv) **Hint** The reflection of Q in the origin is Q'' $(2, -4)$. Now, the reflection of Q'' $(2, 4)$ as shown in the graph below.

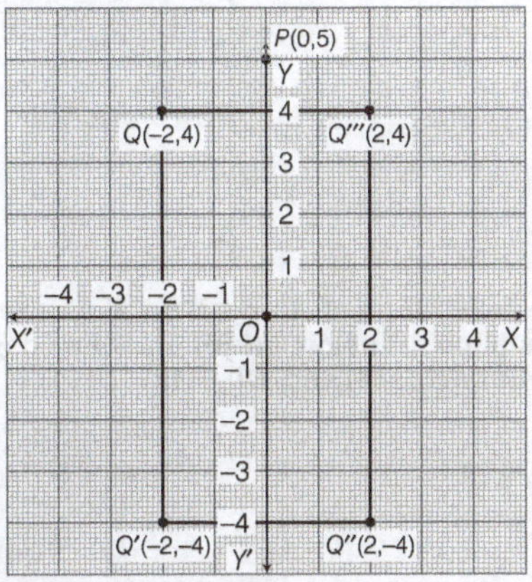

Ans. $(2, 4)$

29. **Hint** The reflection of a point (x, y) in the Y-axis is the point $(-x, y)$.
The reflection of a point (x, y) in the origin, is $(-x, -y)$.
The reflection of a point (x, y) in the X-axis is the point $(x, -y)$.
Ans. $(4, 11)$, $(5, -3)$, $(2, -15)$ and $(1, -1)$ respectively; yes; reflection in the X-axis.

30. **Hint** Point P is an invariant point.
Ans. Point P is on the line L.

31. **Hint** Do same as Q. 28.
Ans. (i) Y-axis (ii) $a = 0$ (iii) $(1, 6)$

32. (i) **Hint** Image of any point (x, y) in the origin is $(-x, -y)$.
Ans. $A_1(-2, -3)$, $B_1(-4, -5)$, $C_1(-7, -2)$

(ii) **Hint** The reflection of the point (x, y) in the X-axis is $(x, -y)$.
Ans. $A_2(2, -3)$, $B_2(4, -5)$, $C_2(7, -2)$

(iii) **Hint** Plot the points B, C, C_2 and B_2 on a graph paper.

$\therefore$ Area of trapezium $= \frac{1}{2}$ (Sum of parallel sides) $\times$ (Perpendicular distance between parallel sides)

$= \frac{1}{2}(4 + 10) \times 3$

Ans. Trapezium; 21 sq units

33. (i) **Hint** The reflection of a point (x, y) in the line $x = 0$ is the point $(-x, y)$.
The reflection of a point (x, y) in the origin, is $(-x, -y)$.
Ans. $(1, -2)$, $(-3, -5)$, $(4, -7)$

(ii) **Hint** The reflection of a point (x, y) in the X-axis is the point $(x, -y)$.
Ans. Reflection in the X-axis.

(iii) **Hint** $\Delta EFG \cong E''F''G''$ (by SSS congruence rule)
Ans. Yes

34. (i) **Hint**

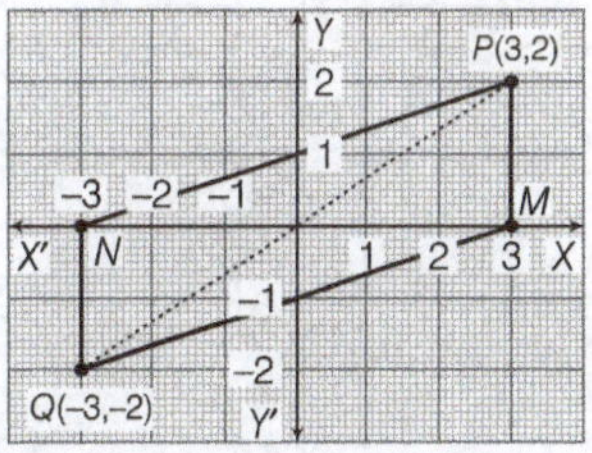

Ans. Point Q

(ii) **Hint** Clearly, $PMQN$ is a parallelogram.
Area of parallelogram $PMQN$
$= 2$ (Area of ΔNMP)
$= 2 \times \frac{1}{2}(NM \times MP)$

Ans. 12 sq units

(iii) **Hint** Reflect the point $(3, 0)$ in X-axis, Y-axis and origin, respectively.
Ans. (a) $(3, 0)$ (b) $(-3, 0)$ (c) $(-3, 0)$

35. (i) **Hint** We plot the given points on the graph paper as shown below

Ans.

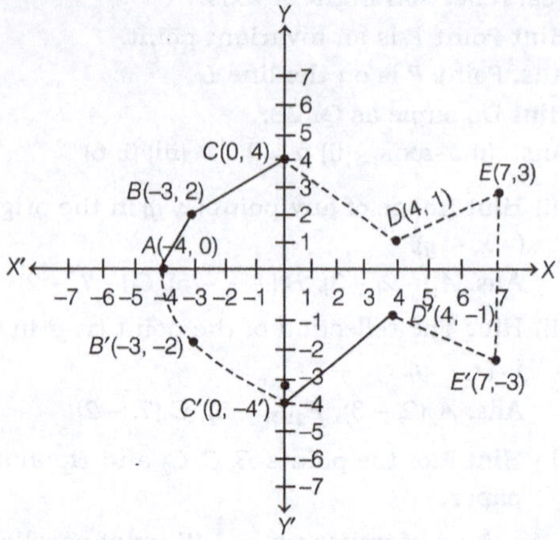

(ii) **Ans.** The reflection of the points *B*, *C*, *D* and *E* on the *X*-axis are the points *B*′(− 3, − 2), *C*′(0, − 4), *D*′(4, − 1) and *E*′(7, − 3).

(iii) **Ans.** See figure

(iv) **Ans.** irregular decagon

36. Hint

(i) We can plot the points *A* (0, 5), *B*(3, 0), *C*(1, 0) and *D* (1, − 5).

(ii) The reflection of the points *B*, *C* and *D* on the *Y*-axis are *B*′, *C*′ and *D*′ which are shown below

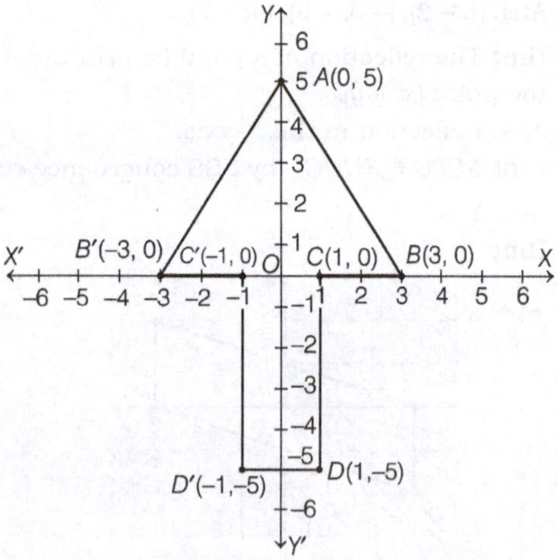

(iii) **Ans.** *B*′(−3, 0), *C*′(−1, 0), *D*′(−1, − 5).

(iv) **Ans.** arrow.

37. Ans. (i)

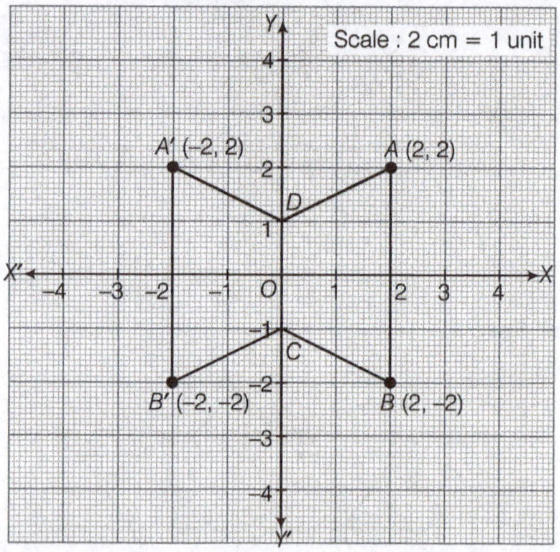

(ii) *A*′ = (−2, 2) and *B*′ = (−2, − 2)

(iii) *C* and *D* are invariant under the reflection.

(iv) *A*′ *B*′ *CD* is a trapezium.

38. (i) On graph sheet the given coordinates *A* (0, 4) will be located 4 units up the *Y*-axis, *B*(1, 1) will be located 1 unit up the *Y*-axis and 1 unit to the right of the origin, and *C*(4, 0) will be located 4 units of the right to the origin.

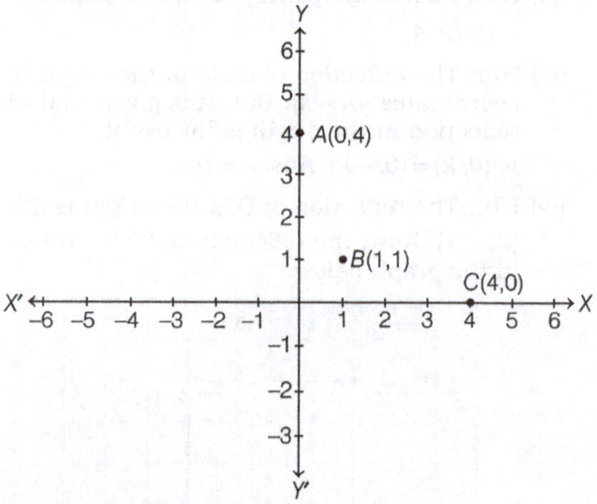

(ii) The reflections of *A* and *B* on *X*-axis will be *E* and *D* as show in below graph and the coordinates of *E* will be (0, − 4) and *D*(1, − 1).

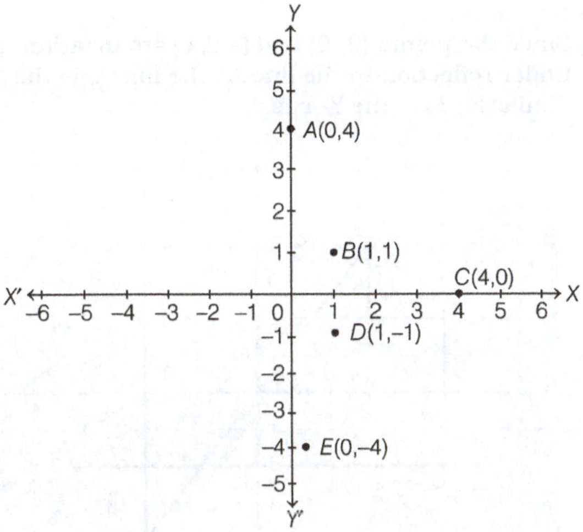

(iii) The reflection of B through the origin will be F. The coordinates of F will be $(-1, -1)$.

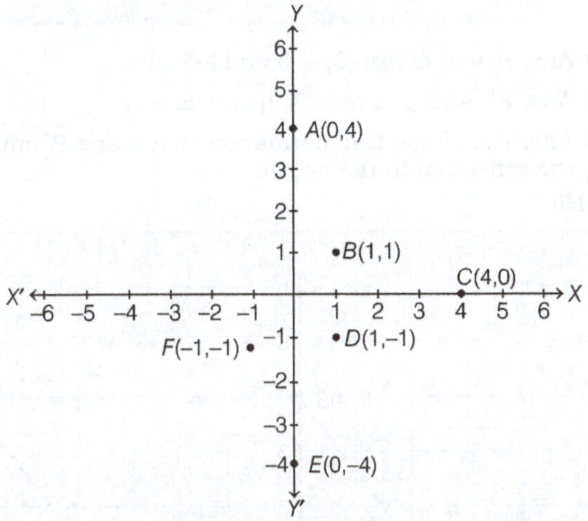

(iv) The reflection of B and C on Y-axis will be H and G. The coordinates of H will be $(-1, 1)$, and the coordinates of G will be $(-4, 0)$.

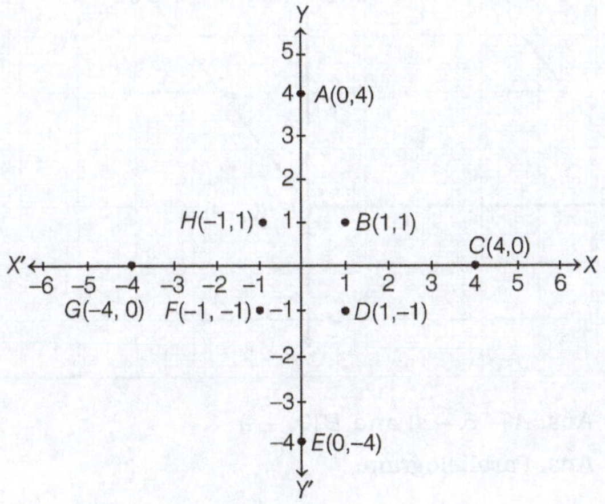

(v) On joining points A, B, C, D, E, F, G, H and A in order to form a closed figure.
The closed figure formed is a concave octagon as show in below graph.

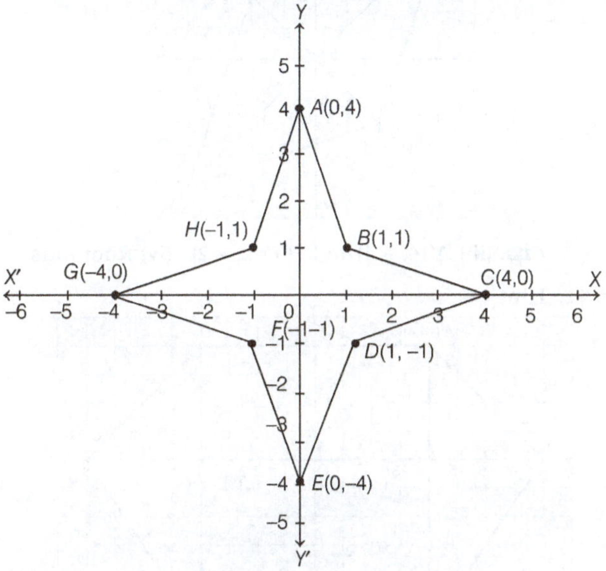

39. **Hint** Let us take 10 small divisions = 1 unit on both the axes.

(i) **Hint** Do same as Example 3. **Ans.** $(-2, -4)$

(ii) **Hint** Do same as Q. 7. **Ans.** $(-2, 4)$

(iii) **Hint**

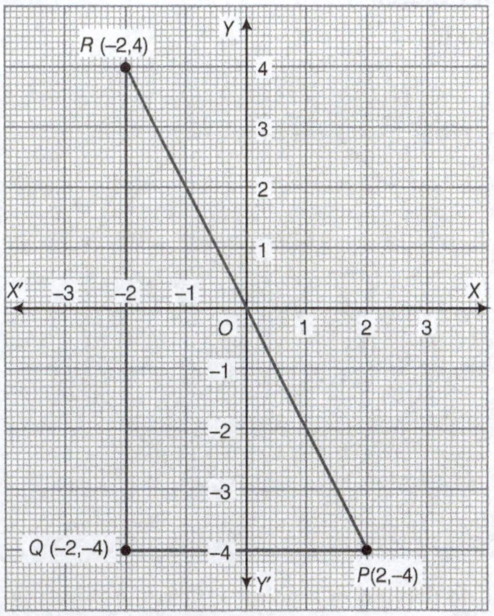

Ans. Right angled triangle

(iv) **Hint** We have, $PQ = 2 + 2 = 4$ units

and $QR = 4 + 4 = 8$ units

$\therefore$ Area of $\Delta PQR = \frac{1}{2}(PQ \times QR) = \frac{1}{2} \times 4 \times 8$

Ans. 16 sq units

40. Hint

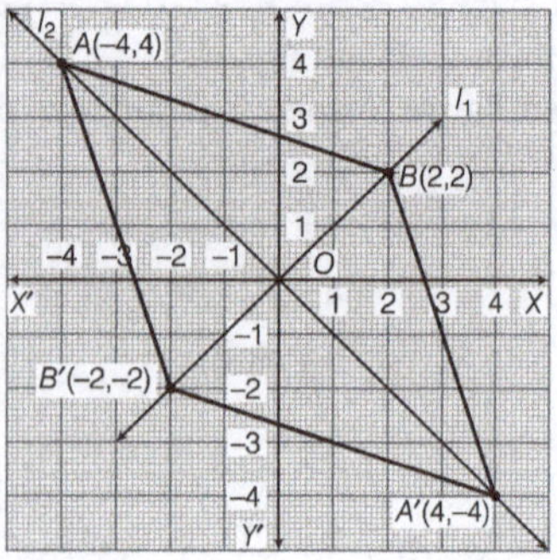

Ans. (iii) $A'(4, -4)$ and $B'(-2, -2)$ (iv) Rhombus

41. Hint

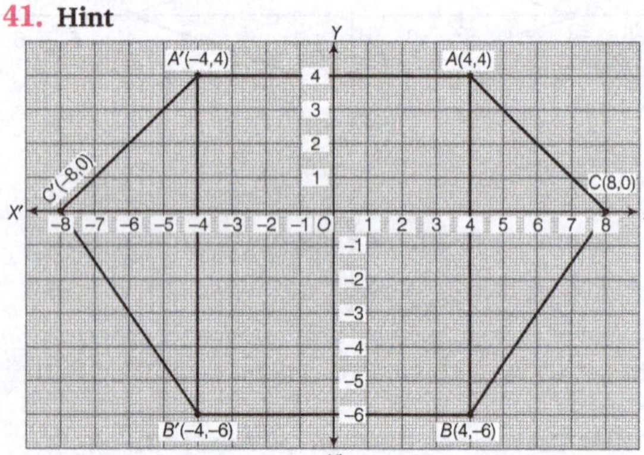

Ans. (iii) $A'(-4, 4)$, $B'(-4, -6)$ and $C'(-8, 0)$

(iv) Hexagon

42. Hint (i)

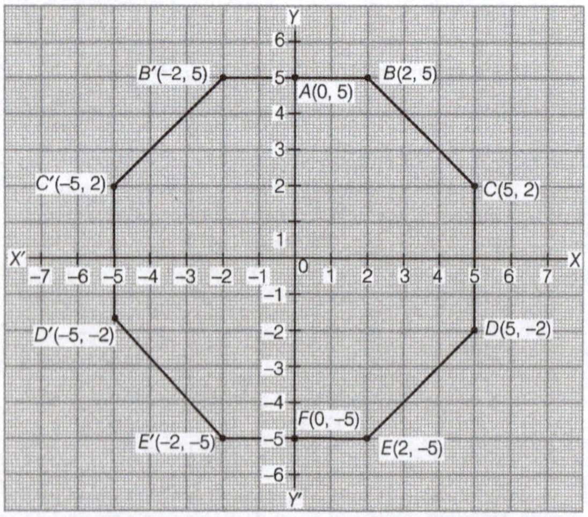

(ii) Reflection of a point (x, y) in the Y-axis is $(-x, y)$.

Ans. (iii) $B'(-2, 5)$, $C'(-5, 2)$, $D'(-5, -2)$ and $E'(-2, -5)$

(iv) Octagon

43. Hint

(i) Since the points (2, 0) and (– 2, 0) are invariant points under reflection in the line L_1, the line L_1 is the X-axis. Similarly, L_2 is the Y-axis.

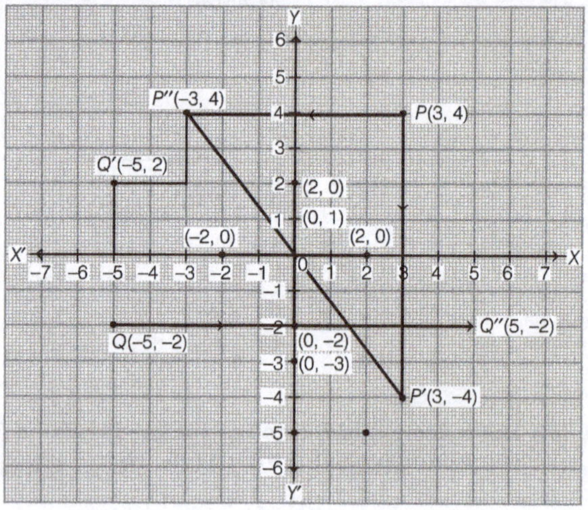

(ii) **Ans.** P' and Q' are (3, – 4) and (–5, 2)

(iii) **Ans.** P'' and Q'' are (– 3, 4) and (5, – 2)

(iv) **Ans.** The single transformation that maps P' onto P'' is the reflection in the origin.

44. (i) **Hint**

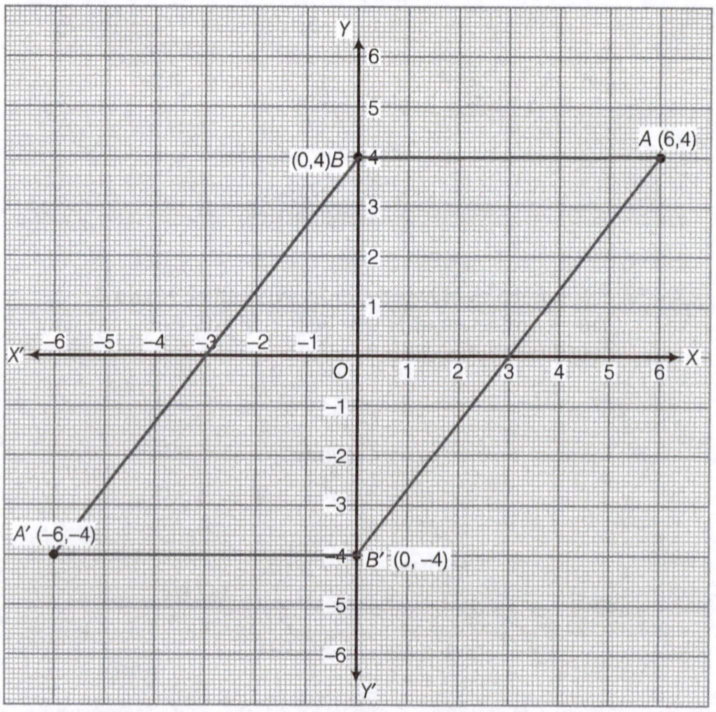

(ii) **Ans.** $A'(-6, -4)$ and $B'(0, -4)$

(iii) **Ans.** Parallelogram

(iv) **Hint** Perimeter of a parallelogram $ABA'B'$

$= 2(AB + AB') = 2(6 + 10)$

[$\because$ in right angled $\Delta ABB'$,

$AB' = \sqrt{AB^2 + BB'^2} = \sqrt{6^2 + 8^2} = \sqrt{100} = 10$ units]

Ans. 32 units

45. Hint (i)

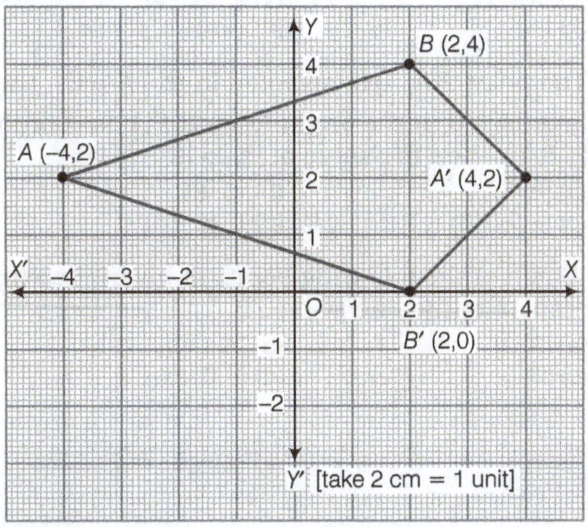

(ii) **Ans.** (4, 2)

(iii) **Hint** B' is the image of B, when reflected in the line $y = 2$. **Ans.** (2, 0)

(iv) **Ans.** Kite

46. Hint

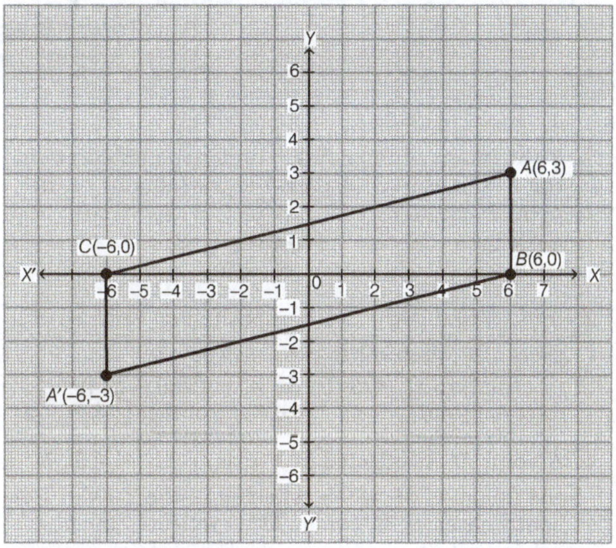

(i) **Ans.** (– 6, – 3)

(ii) **Ans.** B (6, 0)

(iii) **Ans.** (– 6, 0)

(iv) **Ans.** Parallelogram

(v) **Ans.** Area = 36 sq units

Olympiad Section

Brain Teasing Questions of Olympiad Pattern

1 If the image of the point P under the reflection in the X-axis is (– 3, 2), then the coordinates of the point P are

(a) (3, 2) (b) (– 3, – 2)
(c) (3, – 2) (d) (–3, 0)

2 If (4, 3) and (–4, – 3) are opposite two vertices of a rectangle, then other two vertices are

(a) (4, – 3) and (– 4, 3) (b) (4, – 3) and (– 3, 4)
(c) (– 4, 4) and (– 3, 4) (d) None of these

3 A point M is reflected in X-axis to M' (4, – 5). M'' is the image of M, when reflected in the Y-axis. The coordinates of M''' when M'' is reflected in the origin, is

(a) (4, 5) (b) (– 4, – 5)
(c) (4, – 5) (d) None of these

4 The point $P(h, k)$ is reflected in the X-axis, then it is reflected in the origin to P'. If P' has coordinate (– 8, 5), then the value of (h, k) is

(a) (8, 5) (b) (5, 8)
(c) (– 5, – 8) (d) (– 8, – 5)

5 Which of the following points is invariant with respect to the line $y = -2$?

(a) (3, 2) (b) (3, – 2)
(c) (2, 3) (d) (– 2, 3)

Answers

1. (b) **2.** (a) **3.** (c) **4.** (a) **5.** (b)

* *These questions may or may not be asked in the examination, have been given just for additional practice required for olympiads Scholarship Exams etc. For detailed explanations refer Page No. 484.*

CHAPTER

11

Section and Mid-point Formulae

SYLLABUS

- **Section and Mid-point formula** (Internal section only, coordinates of the centroid of a triangle included.)

In class IX, we used the concepts of coordinate geometry to find the distance between two points whose coordinates are given. Here, we will extend our study and will find the coordinates of a point which divides the line segment joining two points in a given ratio. Alongwith it, we will also learn to find the coordinates of mid-point of a line segment and the coordinates of centroid of a triangle whose vertices are given.

Section Formula for Internal Division

Let $A(x_1, y_1)$ and $B(x_2, y_2)$ be the two points and $P(x, y)$ is a point on the line segment joining A and B such that $AP : BP = m_1 : m_2$.

i.e. $\frac{AP}{BP} = \frac{m_1}{m_2}$

To find The coordinates of point P.

Let $P = (x, y)$

Draw AR, PS and BT perpendicular on the X-axis.

Also, draw $AQ \perp PS$ and $PU \perp BT$.

It is clear that $AR \parallel PS \parallel BT$

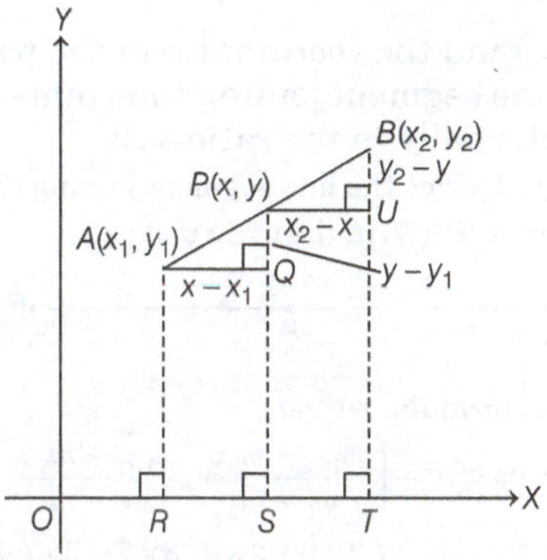

Also, $AQ = RS = OS - OR = x - x_1$;

$PQ = PS - QS = PS - AR = y - y_1$;

$PU = ST = OT - OS = x_2 - x$

and $BU = BT - UT = BT - PS = y_2 - y$

Now, ΔAPQ and ΔPBU are similar.

$\therefore \quad \frac{AQ}{PU} = \frac{PQ}{BU} = \frac{AP}{BP}$

[corresponding sides of similar triangles are in proportion]

Consider, $\frac{AQ}{PU} = \frac{AP}{BP}$

$\Rightarrow \quad \frac{x - x_1}{x_2 - x} = \frac{m_1}{m_2}$

$\Rightarrow m_2x - m_2x_1 = m_1x_2 - m_1x$

$\Rightarrow \quad m_1x + m_2x = m_1x_2 + m_2x_1$

$\Rightarrow x(m_1 + m_2) = m_1x_2 + m_2x_1$

$$\Rightarrow \quad x = \frac{m_1x_2 + m_2x_1}{m_1 + m_2}$$

Now consider, $\frac{PQ}{BU} = \frac{AP}{BP}$

$$\Rightarrow \quad \frac{y - y_1}{y_2 - y} = \frac{m_1}{m_2} \Rightarrow y = \frac{m_1y_2 + m_2y_1}{m_1 + m_2}$$

Thus, the coordinates of point P are

$$\left(\frac{m_1x_2 + m_2x_1}{m_1 + m_2}, \frac{m_1y_2 + m_2y_1}{m_1 + m_2}\right).$$

This formula is known as section formula for internal division.

Note Trisection means a line divided into three equal parts

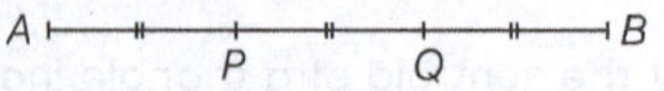

i.e. $AP = PQ = QB$

Here, P and Q trisect AB in the ratio of 1 : 2 and 2 : 1, respectively.

Example 1. **Find the coordinates of the point which divides the line segment joining the points (4, – 3) and (9, 7) internally in the ratio 3 : 2.**

Sol. Let $P(x, y)$ divides the line segment joining the points $A(4, -3)$ and $B(9, 7)$ in the ratio of 3 : 2.

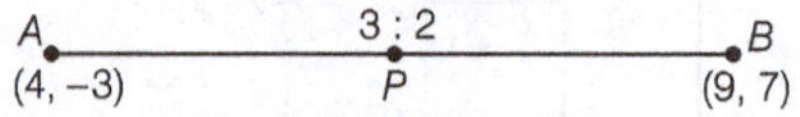

By section formula, we get

$$\text{Coordinates of } P = \left(\frac{m_1x_2 + m_2x_1}{m_1 + m_2}, \frac{m_1y_2 + m_2y_1}{m_1 + m_2}\right)$$

$$= \left(\frac{3\times 9 + 2\times 4}{3+2}, \frac{3\times 7 + 2\times(-3)}{3+2}\right)$$

$[\because (x_1, y_1) \equiv (4, -3), (x_2, y_2) \equiv (9, 7) \text{ and } m_1 = 3, m_2 = 2]$

$$= \left(\frac{27+8}{5}, \frac{21-6}{5}\right) = P\left(\frac{35}{5}, \frac{15}{5}\right) = P\ (7, 3)$$

Therefore, (7, 3) is the required point.

Example 2. **In what ratio, does the point $P(-4, 1)$ divide the line segment joining the points $A(2, -2)$ and $B(-14, 6)$? Also, verify the ratio.**

Sol. Let point $P(-4, 1)$ divides the line segment joining the points $A(2, -2)$ and $B(-14, 6)$ in the ratio $m_1 : m_2$.

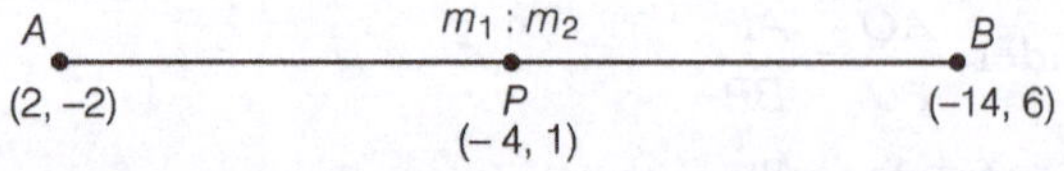

By section formula, we get

$$\text{Coordinates of } P = \left(\frac{-14m_1 + 2m_2}{m_1 + m_2}, \frac{6m_1 - 2m_2}{m_1 + m_2}\right)$$

$[\because (x_1, y_1) \equiv (2, -2) \text{ and } (x_2, y_2) \equiv (-14, 6)]$

But coordinates of P is given, i.e. (– 4, 1).

$$\therefore \quad (-4, 1) = \left(\frac{-14m_1 + 2m_2}{m_1 + m_2}, \frac{6m_1 - 2m_2}{m_1 + m_2}\right)$$

On equating the x-coordinates both sides of Eq. (i), we get

$$-4 = \frac{-14m_1 + 2m_2}{m_1 + m_2} \Rightarrow -4m_1 - 4m_2 = -14m_1 + 2m_2$$

$$\Rightarrow \quad -4m_1 + 14m_1 = 4m_2 + 2m_2 \Rightarrow 10m_1 = 6m_2$$

$$\Rightarrow \quad \frac{m_1}{m_2} = \frac{6}{10} \Rightarrow \frac{m_1}{m_2} = \frac{3}{5}$$

or $\quad m_1 : m_2 = 3 : 5$

On equating the y-coordinates both sides of Eq. (i), we get

$$1 = \frac{6m_1 - 2m_2}{m_1 + m_2} \Rightarrow 1 = \frac{6\frac{m_1}{m_2} - 2}{\frac{m_1}{m_2} + 1}$$

[dividing the numerator and denominator of RHS by m_2]

$$\Rightarrow \quad 1 = \frac{6\left(\frac{3}{5}\right) - 2}{\frac{3}{5} + 1} \quad \left[\because \frac{m_1}{m_2} = \frac{3}{5}\right]$$

$$\Rightarrow \quad 1 = \frac{\frac{18}{5} - 2}{\frac{3+5}{5}} = \frac{18-10}{8}$$

$$\Rightarrow \quad 1 = \frac{8}{8} \Rightarrow 1 = 1$$

Hence, the point (– 4, 1) divides the line segment joining the points $A(2, -2)$ and $B(-14, 6)$ in the ratio 3 : 5.

Example 3. **$P(1, -2)$ is a point on the line segment joining $A(3, -6)$ and $B(x, y)$ such that $AP : PB$ is equal to 2 : 3. Find the coordinates of B.** **[ICSE 2017]**

Sol. Given, a line segment joining $A(3, -6)$ and $B(x, y)$ such that

$$AP : PB = 2 : 3$$

i.e. P divides AB in the ratio 2 : 3 internally.

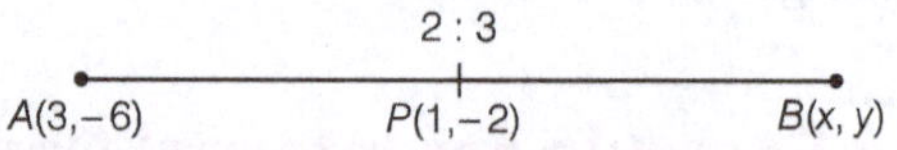

By section formula, we get

Coordinates of P

$$= \left[\frac{(2x) + (3\times 3)}{2+3}, \frac{2y + 3\times(-6)}{2+3}\right] = \left(\frac{2x+9}{5}, \frac{2y-18}{5}\right)$$

$[\because (x_1, y_1) \equiv (3, -6), (x_2, y_2) \equiv (x, y) \text{ and } m_1 = 2, m_2 = 3]$

But given coordinates of $P \equiv (1, -2)$

$$\therefore \quad (1, -2) = \left(\frac{2x+9}{5}, \frac{2y-18}{5}\right)$$

On equating x and y-coordinates both sides, we get

$$\therefore \quad \frac{2x+9}{5} = 1 \text{ and } \frac{2y-18}{5} = -2$$

$\Rightarrow \quad 2x + 9 = 5$ and $2y - 18 = -10$

$\Rightarrow \quad 2x = 5 - 9$ and $2y = -10 + 18$

$\Rightarrow \quad 2x = -4$ and $2y = 8$

$\Rightarrow \quad x = -2$ and $y = 4$

Thus, coordinates of $B \equiv (-2, 4)$.

Example 4. If the line joining the points $A(4, -5)$ and $B(4, 5)$ is divided by the point P, such that $\frac{AP}{AB} = \frac{2}{5}$, then find the coordinates of P. **[ICSE 2007]**

Sol. Given, a line segment joining $A(4, -5)$ and $B(4, 5)$ such that $\frac{AP}{AB} = \frac{2}{5} \Rightarrow \frac{AB}{AP} = \frac{5}{2} \Rightarrow \frac{AB}{AP} - 1 = \frac{5}{2} - 1$

[subtracting 1 from both sides]

$$\Rightarrow \frac{AB - AP}{AP} = \frac{5-2}{2} \Rightarrow \frac{PB}{AP} = \frac{3}{2}, \text{ i.e. } m_1 : m_2 = 2 : 3$$

i.e. P divides AB is the ratio 2 : 3 internally.

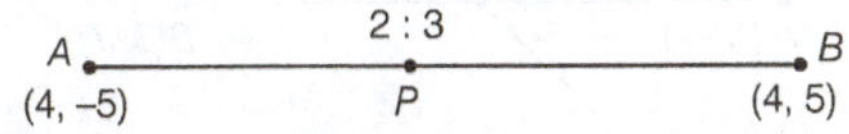

By section formula, we get

$$\text{Coordinates of } P = \left(\frac{2 \times 4 + 3 \times 4}{2+3}, \frac{2 \times 5 + 3 \times (-5)}{2+3} \right)$$

$[\because (x_1, y_1) \equiv (4, -5), (x_2, y_2) \equiv (4, 5) \text{ and } m_1 = 2, m_2 = 3]$

$$= \left(\frac{8+12}{2+3}, \frac{10-15}{2+3} \right) = \left(\frac{20}{5}, \frac{-5}{5} \right) = (4, -1)$$

Hence, the coordinates of P are $(4, -1)$.

Example 5. The line segment joining $A(2, 3)$ and $B(6, -5)$ is intersected by the X-axis at the point k. Write the coordinates of the point k. Hence, find the ratio in which k divides AB. **[ICSE 2006]**

Sol. Let K divides the line segment joining the points A (2, 3) and B (6, – 5) in the ratio $m_1 : m_2$.

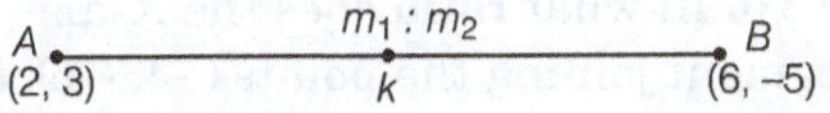

By section formula, we get

$$\therefore \text{ Coordinates of } K \text{ are } \left(\frac{6m_1 + 2m_2}{m_1 + m_2}, \frac{-5m_1 + 3m_2}{m_1 + m_2} \right)$$

$[\because (x_1, y_1) \equiv (2, 3) \text{ and } (x_2, y_2) \equiv (6, -5)]$

But line segment AB intersected at point K by the X-axis, so coordinates of K will be $(x, 0)$.

$$\therefore \quad (x, 0) = \left(\frac{6m_1 + 2m_2}{m_1 + m_2}, \frac{-5m_1 + 3m_2}{m_1 + m_2} \right) \quad \text{...(i)}$$

On equating y-coordinates both sides of Eq. (i), we get

$$\frac{-5m_1 + 3m_2}{m_1 + m_2} = 0 \Rightarrow -5m_1 + 3m_2 = 0 \Rightarrow 5m_1 = 3m_2 \Rightarrow \frac{m_1}{m_2} = \frac{3}{5}$$

Hence, the required ratio is 3 : 5.

On equating x-coordinates both sides, we get

$$x = \frac{6m_1 + 2m_2}{m_1 + m_2} = \frac{6 \cdot \frac{m_1}{m_2} + 2}{\frac{m_1}{m_2} + 1} = \frac{6 \times \frac{3}{5} + 2}{\frac{3}{5} + 1}$$

$$= \frac{18+10}{8} = \frac{28}{8} = \frac{7}{2} \qquad \left[\because \frac{m_1}{m_2} = \frac{3}{5} \right]$$

So, coordinates of point K is $\left(\frac{7}{2}, 0 \right)$.

Example 6. Find the ratio in which the point $(2, a)$ divides the line segment joining $(-4, 3)$ and $(6, 3)$. Hence, find a.

Sol. Let the point $P(2, a)$ divides the line joining the points $A(-4, 3)$ and $B(6, 3)$ in the ratio k : 1.

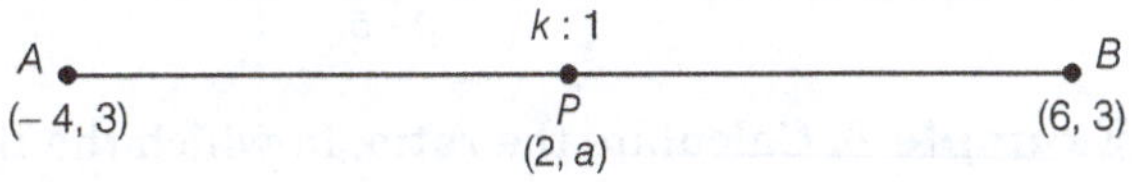

By section formula, we get

$$\text{Coordinates of } P = \left(\frac{6 \times k + 1 \times -4}{k+1}, \frac{3 \times k + 1 \times 3}{k+1} \right)$$

$[\because (x_1, y_1) \equiv (-4, 3), (x_2, y_2) \equiv (6, 3) \text{ and } m_1 = k, m_2 = 1]$

But coordinates of P is given, i.e. $(2, a)$.

$$\therefore \quad (2, a) = \left(\frac{6k-4}{k+1}, \frac{3k+3}{k+1} \right) \quad \text{...(i)}$$

On equating x-coordinates both sides of Eq. (i), we get

$$2 = \frac{6k-4}{k+1} \Rightarrow 2k + 2 = 6k - 4$$

$$\Rightarrow \quad 4k = 6 \Rightarrow k = \frac{6}{4} \Rightarrow k = \frac{3}{2}$$

Hence, the point P divides the line joining the points $(-4, 3)$ and $(6, 3)$ in the ratio 3 : 2.

On equating y-coordinates both sides of Eq. (i), we get

$$a = \frac{3k+3}{k+1} = \frac{3 \times \frac{3}{2} + 3}{\frac{3}{2} + 1} = \frac{\frac{9}{2} + 3}{\frac{3}{2} + 1}$$

$$= \frac{9+6}{3+2} = \frac{15}{5} = 3 \qquad \left[\because k = \frac{3}{2} \right]$$

Example 7. M and N are two points on the X-axis and Y-axis, respectively. If $P(3, 2)$ divides the line segment MN in the ratio 2 : 3. **[ICSE 2019]**

Find

(i) the coordinates of M and N.

(ii) slope of the line MN.

Sol. Let the coordinates of M and N be $(x, 0)$ and $(0, y)$.

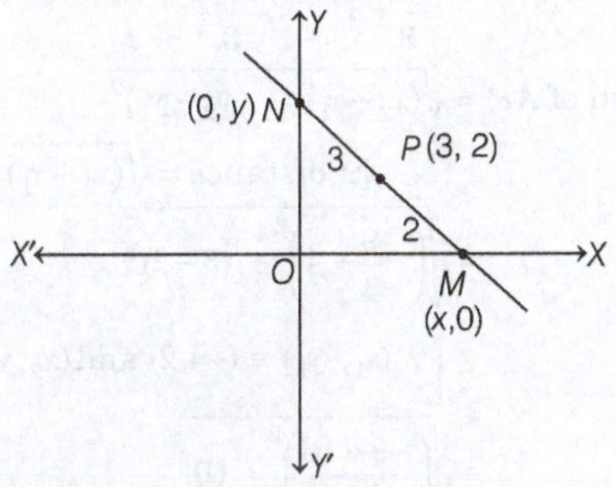

(i) Using internal section formula,

$$P(3, 2) = \left(\frac{3x + 0}{2+3}, \frac{0 + 2y}{2+3} \right)$$

$$\Rightarrow \quad (3, 2) = \left(\frac{3x}{5}, \frac{2y}{5} \right)$$

$\therefore \quad \frac{3x}{5} = 3$ and $\frac{2y}{5} = 2$

$\Rightarrow \quad x = 5$ and $y = 5$

Hence, the coordinates of M and N are (5,0) and (0, 5), respectively.

(ii) Slope of line $MN = \frac{y_2 - y_1}{x_2 - x_1} = \frac{5-0}{0-5} = \frac{5}{-5} = -1$

Example 8. Calculate the ratio, in which the line joining $A(-4,2)$ and $B(3,6)$ is divided by $P(x,3)$. Also, find

(i) x. (ii) length of AP. [ICSE 2014]

Sol. Let $P(x,3)$ divides the line segment joining the points $A(-4,2)$ and $B(3,6)$ in the ratio $k:1$.

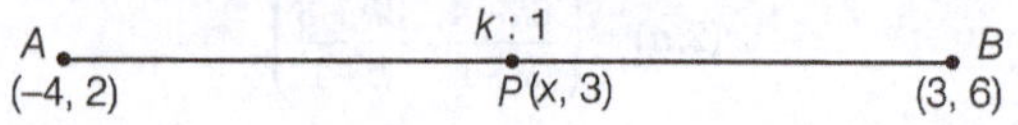

By section formula, we get

Coordinates of P

$$=\left[\frac{3\times k+1\times -4}{k+1}, \frac{k\times 6+1\times 2}{k+1}\right] = \left(\frac{3k-4}{k+1}, \frac{6k+2}{k+1}\right)$$

$[\because (x_1, y_1) \equiv (-4, 2), (x_2, y_2) \equiv (3, 6)$ and $m_1 = k, m_2 = 1]$

But coordinates of P is given, i.e. $(x, 3)$.

$$\therefore \quad (x, 3) = \left(\frac{3k-4}{k+1}, \frac{6k+2}{k+1}\right) \quad \text{...(i)}$$

On equating y-coordinates both sides of Eq. (i), we get

$$3 = \frac{6k+2}{k+1}$$

$\Rightarrow \quad 3(k+1) = 6k+2$

$\Rightarrow \quad 3k+3 = 6k+2 \Rightarrow 6k - 3k = 3-2$

$\Rightarrow \quad 3k = 1 \Rightarrow k = \frac{1}{3}$

Hence, the required ratio is $\frac{1}{3}$.

(i) On equating x-coordinates both sides of Eq. (i), we get

$$x = \frac{3k-4}{k+1}$$

$$\Rightarrow \quad x = \frac{3\left(\frac{1}{3}\right)-4}{\frac{1}{3}+1} = \frac{\frac{3-12}{3}}{\frac{1+3}{3}} = \frac{-9}{4} \quad \left[\because k = \frac{1}{3}\right]$$

(ii) $\therefore$ Length of $AP = \sqrt{(x_2-x_1)^2 + (y_2-y_1)^2}$

$\left[\because \text{distance} = \sqrt{(x_2-x_1)^2+(y_2-y_1)^2}\right]$

$$= \sqrt{\left(-\frac{9}{4}+4\right)^2 + (3-2)^2}$$

$\left[\because (x_1, y_1) \equiv (-4,2) \text{ and } (x_2, y_2) \equiv \left(\frac{-9}{4}, 3\right)\right]$

$$= \sqrt{\left(\frac{-9+16}{4}\right)^2 + (1)^2}$$

$$= \sqrt{\left(\frac{7}{4}\right)^2 + 1^2} = \sqrt{\frac{49}{16}+1}$$

$$= \sqrt{\frac{49+16}{16}} = \frac{\sqrt{65}}{4} \text{ units}$$

Example 9. Determine the ratio in which the line $2x + y - 4 = 0$ divides the line segment joining the points $A(2, -2)$ and $B(3, 7)$.

Sol. Given, points are $A(2, -2)$ and $B(3, 7)$ and given line is

$$2x + y - 4 = 0 \quad \text{...(i)}$$

Let the given line Eq. (i) divide the line segment joining the points $A(2, -2)$ and $B(3, 7)$ in the ratio $k:1$ at the point P i.e. $AP : PB = k : 1$.

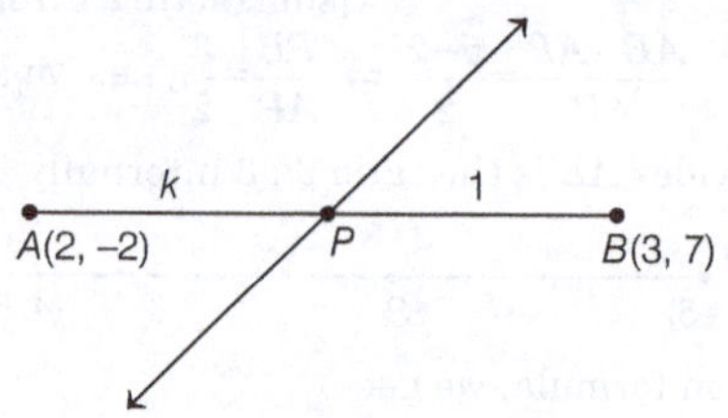

$\therefore$ Coordinates of P are $\left(\frac{3k+2}{k+1}, \frac{7k-2}{k+1}\right)$

The point P lies on the line Eq. (i), we have

$$2\times\frac{3k+2}{k+1} + \frac{7k-2}{k+1} - 4 = 0$$

$\Rightarrow \quad 2(3k+2) + (7k-2) - 4(k+1) = 0$

$\Rightarrow \quad 6k + 4 + 7k - 2 - 4k - 4 = 0$

$\Rightarrow \quad 9k = 2$

$\Rightarrow \quad k = \frac{2}{9}$

Hence, the required ratio is $\frac{2}{9} : 1$ i.e. $2 : 9$.

Example 10. In what ratio does the X-axis divide the line segment joining the points $(-4, -6)$ and $(-1, 7)$? Also, find the coordinates of the point of division.

Sol. Let the line segment joining the points $A(-4, -6)$ and $B(-1, 7)$ be divided by the X-axis in the ratio $k:1$ at the point P

i.e. $AP : PB = k : 1$, then the point P is $\left(\frac{-k-4}{k+1}, \frac{7k-6}{k+1}\right)$

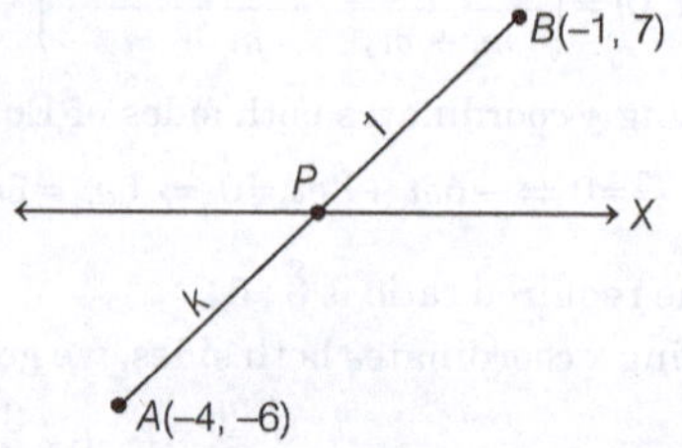

But P lies on the X-axis, therefore y-coordinates of P is 0

$$\frac{7k-6}{k+1} = 0$$

$\Rightarrow \quad 7k - 6 = 0$

$\Rightarrow \quad k = \frac{6}{7}$ i.e. $6 : 7$

$\therefore$ The required ratio is $6 : 7$.

The coordinates of the point of division P are $\left(\dfrac{-\frac{6}{7}-4}{\frac{6}{7}+1}, 0\right)$

i.e. $\left(-\dfrac{34}{13}, 0\right)$.

Example 11. In what ratio is the line joining $P(5, 3)$ and $Q(-5, 3)$ divided by the Y-axis? Also, find the coordinates of the point of intersection.

Sol. Let the line segment joining $P(5, 3)$ and $Q(-5, 3)$ divided by the Y-axis in the ratio $k:1$ at the point A.

$\therefore$ Coordinates of A are $\left(\dfrac{-5k+5}{k+1}, \dfrac{3k+3}{k+1}\right)$

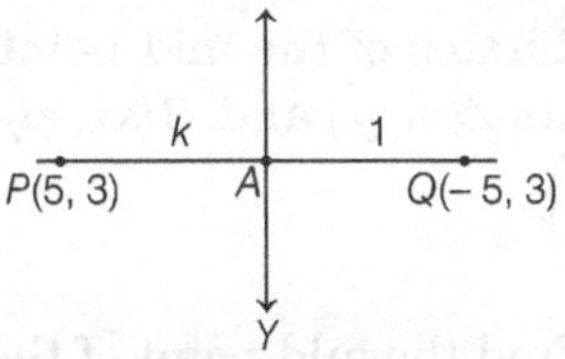

Since, A lies on the Y-axis, therefore, x-coordinates of A is 0.

$$\Rightarrow \quad \frac{-5k+5}{k+1} = 0 \Rightarrow -5k+5 = 0$$

$$\Rightarrow \quad -5k = -5 \Rightarrow k = 1$$

$\therefore$ Required ratio $= k:1 = 1:1$

$\therefore$ The coordinates of the point of intersection A are

$$\left(\frac{-5\times1+5}{1+1}, \frac{3\times1+3}{1+1}\right) = (0, 3).$$

Example 12. Given a line segment AB joining the points $A(-4, 6)$ and $B(8, -3)$. Find

(i) the ratio in which AB is divided by the Y-axis.

(ii) the coordinates of the point of intersection.

(iii) the length of AB. **[ICSE 2012]**

Sol. Given, coordinates of A and B are $(-4, 6)$ and $(8, -3)$, respectively.

(i) Let AB is divided by the Y-axis at point $M(0, y)$ in the ratio $m_1 : m_2$.

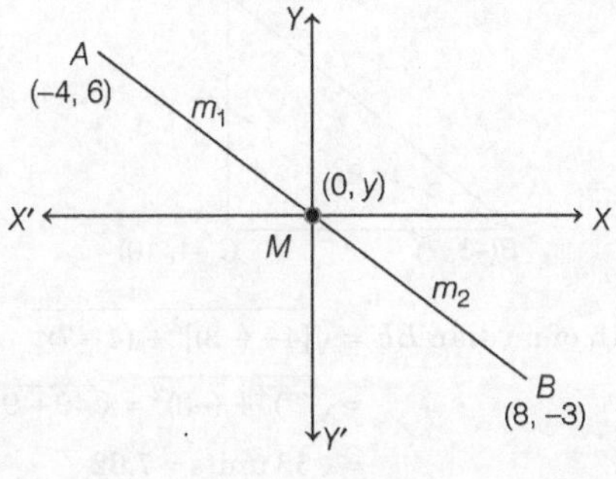

Then, coordinates of $M = \left(\dfrac{m_1x_2 + m_2x_1}{m_1+m_2}, \dfrac{m_1y_2 + m_2y_1}{m_1+m_2}\right)$

$$= \left(\frac{m_1\times8 + m_2\times(-4)}{m_1+m_2}, \frac{m_1\times(-3) + m_2\times6}{m_1+m_2}\right)$$

$[\because (x_1, y_1) \equiv (-4, 6) \text{ and } (x_2, y_2) \equiv (8, -3)]$

But x-coordinate of M is 0.

$$\therefore \quad 0 = \frac{m_1\times8 + m_2\times(-4)}{m_1+m_2}$$

$$\Rightarrow \quad 0 = 8m_1 - 4m_2$$

$$\Rightarrow \quad 4m_2 = 8m_1$$

$$\Rightarrow \quad \frac{4}{8} = \frac{m_1}{m_2} \Rightarrow \frac{m_1}{m_2} = \frac{1}{2}$$

(ii) At the point of intersection, $x = 0$

and $\quad y = \dfrac{-3m_1 + 6m_2}{m_1+m_2}$

$$= \frac{-3\frac{m_1}{m_2} + 6}{\frac{m_1}{m_2} + 1} = \frac{-3\left(\frac{1}{2}\right) + 6}{\frac{1}{2} + 1} \quad \left[\because \frac{m_1}{m_2} = \frac{1}{2}\right]$$

$$= \frac{-3+12}{3} = \frac{9}{3} = 3$$

Hence, the coordinates of M are $(0, 3)$.

(iii) Length of $AB = \sqrt{(x_2-x_1)^2 + (y_2-y_1)^2}$

$$= \sqrt{(8+4)^2 + (-3-6)^2}$$

$[\because (x_1, y_1) = (-4, 6) \text{ and } (x_2, y_2) = (8, -3)]$

$$= \sqrt{(12)^2 + (-9)^2}$$

$$= \sqrt{144+81} = \sqrt{225} = 15 \text{ units}$$

Example 13. Find the coordinates of the points of trisection of the line segment joining $(2, -3)$ and $(4, -1)$.

Sol. Let P and Q be the points of trisection as shown below

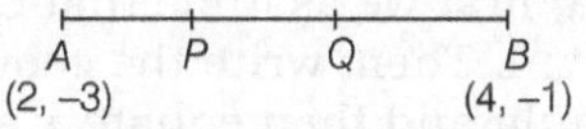

Then, $AP : PB = 1:2$ and $AQ : QB = 2:1$

(i) Let P divides AB in the ratio 1:2, then $\dfrac{m_1}{m_2} = \dfrac{1}{2}$.

Here, $A(x_1, y_1) \equiv (2, -3)$ and $B(x_2, y_2) \equiv (4, -1)$

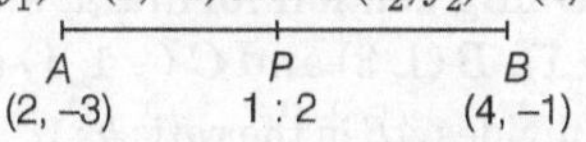

Now, $\quad P(x, y) \equiv P\left(\dfrac{m_1x_2 + m_2x_1}{m_1+m_2}, \dfrac{m_1y_2 + m_2y_1}{m_1+m_2}\right)$

[by section formula]

$$= P\left[\frac{1\times4 + 2\times2}{1+2}, \frac{1\times(-1) + 2\times(-3)}{1+2}\right]$$

$$= P\left(\frac{4+4}{3}, \frac{-1-6}{3}\right) = P\left(\frac{8}{3}, \frac{-7}{3}\right)$$

(ii) Let Q divide AB in the ratio 2:1, then $\dfrac{m_1}{m_2} = \dfrac{2}{1}$.

Here, $A(x_1, y_1) \equiv (2, -3)$ and $B(x_2, y_2) \equiv (4, -1)$

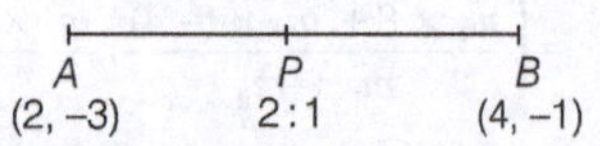

Now, $Q(x, y) \equiv Q\left(\dfrac{m_1x_2+m_2x_1}{m_1+m_2}, \dfrac{m_1y_2+m_2y_1}{m_1+m_2}\right)$

$$= Q\left[\frac{2\times4+1\times2}{2+1}, \frac{2\times(-1)+1\times(-3)}{2+1}\right]$$

$$= Q\left(\frac{8+2}{3}, \frac{-2-3}{3}\right)$$

$$= Q\left(\frac{10}{3}, \frac{-5}{3}\right)$$

Example 14. The line segment joining the points $A(2, 1)$ and $B(5, -8)$ is trisected at the points P and Q such that P is nearer to A. If P lies on the line $2x - y + k = 0$, find the value of k.

Sol. Let $A(2, 1)$ and $B(5, -8)$.

As, AB is trisected at P and Q and P is nearest of the A, so $AP : PB = 1 : 2$, therefore

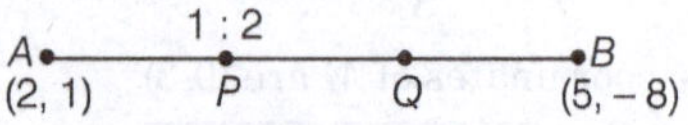

$\therefore P\left(\dfrac{1\times5+2\times2}{1+2}, \dfrac{1\times(-8)+2\times1}{1+2}\right)$ i.e. $P(3, -2)$

$\because P$ lies on the line $2x - y + k = 0$

$$2\times3-(-2)+k=0$$

$$8+k=0$$

$$k=-8$$

To Show Collinearity using Section Formula

To show collinearity of points, say A, B and C by section formula, first we assume that C divides AB in the ratio of $k : 1$. Then, write the coordinates of C by section formula and then equate x and y-coordinates both sides separately. If value of k from both equations are same, then A, B and C are collinear, otherwise not.

Example 15. Using section formula, show that the points $A(-3, -1)$, $B(1, 3)$ and $C(-1, 1)$ are collinear.

Sol. Let $C(-1, 1)$ divides AB in the ratio $k : 1$.

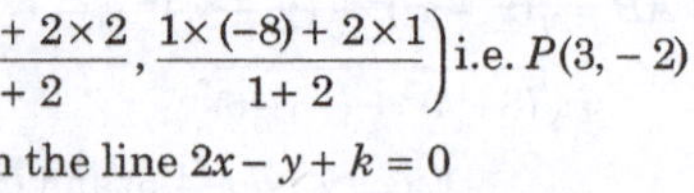

Then, by section formula, we get

$$C(-1, 1) = C\left(\frac{k-3}{k+1}, \frac{3k-1}{k+1}\right)$$

On equating x-coordinates both sides, we get

$$-1 = \frac{k-3}{k+1} \Rightarrow -k-1 = k-3$$

$$\Rightarrow \quad -2k = -3+1 \Rightarrow -2k = -2 \Rightarrow k = 1$$

On equating y-coordinates both sides, we get

$$1 = \frac{3k-1}{k+1} \Rightarrow k+1 = 3k-1$$

$$\Rightarrow \quad 2k = 2 \Rightarrow k = 1$$

Since, in both cases value of k is same. So, C divides AB in the ratio 1 : 1.

Hence, A, B and C are collinear.

Mid-point Formula

If a point divides the line segment joining the points $A(x_1, y_1)$ and $B(x_2, y_2)$ internally in the ratio 1:1, then we get mid–point of this line segment which bisect the line joining two points.

Thus, the coordinates of the mid-point P of the line joining the points $A(x_1, y_1)$ and $B(x_2, y_2)$ are $\left(\dfrac{x_1+x_2}{2}, \dfrac{y_1+y_2}{2}\right)$.

Example 16. Find the mid-point of the line segment joining the points $(3, -1)$ and $(7, 9)$.

Sol. Let $C(x, y)$ be the mid-point of the line joining the points $A(3, -1)$ and $B(7, 9)$.

$\therefore$ Coordinates of mid-point of AB, i.e.

$$C(x, y) = \left(\frac{x_1+x_2}{2}, \frac{y_1+y_2}{2}\right)$$

Here, $x_1 = 3$, $x_2 = 7$ and $y_1 = -1$, $y_2 = 9$.

$$\therefore \quad C(x, y) = \left(\frac{3+7}{2}, \frac{-1+9}{2}\right) = \left(\frac{10}{2}, \frac{8}{2}\right) = (5, 4)$$

Hence, the mid-points of line segment joining $(3, -1)$ and $(7, 9)$ is $(5, 4)$.

Example 17. Find the length of the median through the vertex B of the ΔABC with vertices $A(9, -2)$, $B(-3, 7)$ and $C(-1, 10)$.

Sol. Let E be the mid-point of AC, then BE is the median through B and E is the mid-point of AC.

Coordinates of E are $\left[\dfrac{9+(-1)}{2}, \dfrac{-2+10}{2}\right]$ i.e. $(4, 4)$

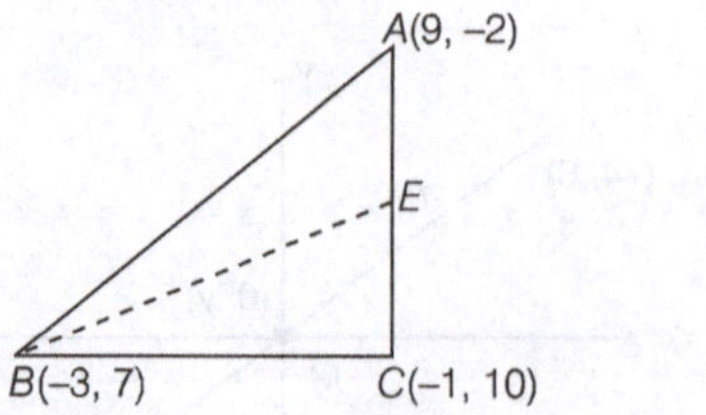

$\therefore$ Length of median $BE = \sqrt{[4-(-3)]^2+(4-7)^2}$

$$= \sqrt{(7)^2+(-3)^2} = \sqrt{49+9}$$

$$= \sqrt{58} \text{ units} = 7.62$$

Hence, the length of median BE is 7.62 units.

Example 18. Find the fourth vertex of a parallelogram $ABCD$, if the three consecutive vertices are $A(10,-6)$, $B(2,-6)$ and $C(-4,-2)$.

Sol. Given, in parallelogram $ABCD$, the three consecutive vertices are $A(10,-6)$, $B(2,-6)$ and $C(-4,-2)$.

Let the coordinates of fourth vertex be $D(x, y)$.

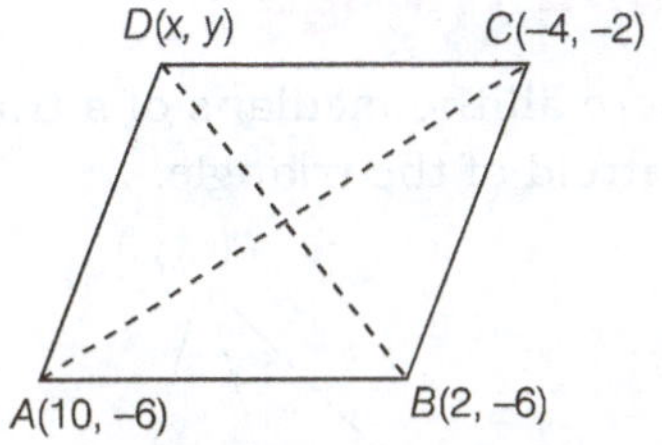

We know that the diagonals of a parallelogram bisect each other.

$\therefore$ Coordinates of mid-point of diagonal AC

= Coordinates of mid-point of diagonal BD

$$\Rightarrow \left(\frac{10+(-4)}{2}, \frac{-6+(-2)}{2}\right) = \left(\frac{2+x}{2}, \frac{-6+y}{2}\right)$$

$$\left[\because \text{mid-point} = \left(\frac{x_1+x_2}{2}, \frac{y_1+y_2}{2}\right)\right]$$

$$\Rightarrow \left(\frac{6}{2}, -\frac{8}{2}\right) = \left(\frac{2+x}{2}, \frac{-6+y}{2}\right)$$

$$\Rightarrow (3,-4) = \left(\frac{2+x}{2}, \frac{-6+y}{2}\right)$$

On equating x and y-coordinates both sides, we get

$$\frac{2+x}{2} = 3 \text{ and } \frac{-6+y}{2} = -4$$

$$\Rightarrow 2+x = 6 \text{ and } -6+y = -8$$

$$\Rightarrow x = 4 \text{ and } y = -2$$

Hence, the fourth vertex of the parallelogram $ABCD$ is $D(4,-2)$.

Example 19. If the points $A(6,1)$, $B(8,2)$, $C(9,4)$ and $D(p,3)$ are the vertices of a parallelogram, taken in order, then find the value of p.

Sol. Given, vertices of a parallelogram are $A(6,1)$, $B(8,2)$, $C(9,4)$ and $D(p,3)$.

We know that diagonals of a parallelogram bisect each other.

$\therefore$ Coordinates of mid-point of diagonal AC

= Coordinates of mid-point of diagonal BD

$$\Rightarrow \left(\frac{6+9}{2}, \frac{1+4}{2}\right) = \left(\frac{8+p}{2}, \frac{2+3}{2}\right)$$

$$\left[\because \text{mid-point} = \left(\frac{x_1+x_2}{2}, \frac{y_1+y_2}{2}\right)\right]$$

$$\Rightarrow \left(\frac{15}{2}, \frac{5}{2}\right) = \left(\frac{8+p}{2}, \frac{5}{2}\right)$$

On equating x-coordinates both sides, we get

$$\frac{15}{2} = \frac{8+p}{2} \Rightarrow 15 = 8+p \Rightarrow p = 15-8 \Rightarrow p = 7$$

Hence, the required value of p is 7.

Example 20. AB is a diameter of a circle with centre $C(-2,5)$ and $A(3,-7)$. Find

(i) the length of radius AC.

(ii) the coordinates of B. [ICSE 2013]

Sol. (i) Let $A(3,-7) = (x_1, y_1)$ and $C(-2,5) = (x_2, y_2)$

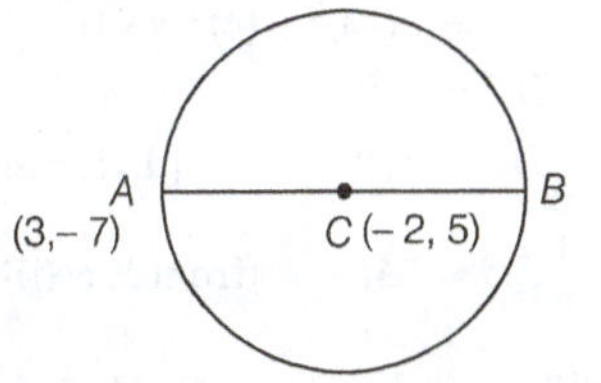

$\therefore$ Length of radius, $AC = \sqrt{(x_2-x_1)^2 + (y_2-y_1)^2}$

$= \sqrt{(-2-3)^2 + (5+7)^2}$

$= \sqrt{(-5)^2 + (12)^2}$

$= \sqrt{25+144} = \sqrt{169} = 13$ units

(ii) Let the coordinates of B be (x_3, y_3).

Since, C is the centre of circle. Then, C is the mid-point of diameter AB.

$$\Rightarrow \text{Coordinates of } C \left(\frac{3+x_3}{2}, \frac{-7+y_3}{2}\right)$$

$$\left[\because \text{mid-point} = \left(\frac{x_1+x_2}{2}, \frac{y_1+y_2}{2}\right)\right]$$

But coordinates of C is given, i.e. $(-2,5)$.

$$\therefore \quad (-2,5) = \left(\frac{3+x_3}{2}, \frac{-7+y_3}{2}\right)$$

On equating x and y-coordinates both sides, we get

$$-2 = \frac{3+x_3}{2} \text{ and } 5 = \frac{-7+y_3}{2}$$

$$\Rightarrow -2\times 2 = 3+x_3 \text{ and } 5\times 2 = -7+y_3$$

$$\Rightarrow x_3 = -4-3 \text{ and } y_3 = 10+7$$

$$\Rightarrow x_3 = -7 \text{ and } y_3 = 17$$

Hence, the coordinates of B are $(-7, 17)$.

Example 21. If $A(10,5)$, $B(6,-3)$ and $C(2,1)$ are the vertices of a ΔABC. L is the mid-point of AB and M is the mid-point of AC. Write down the coordinates of L and M. Show that $LM = \frac{1}{2}BC$.

Sol. Given, vertices of a triangle are $A(10,5)$, $B(6,-3)$ and $C(2,1)$.

$\therefore$ Coordinates of L = Mid-point of $AB = \left(\frac{10+6}{2}, \frac{5-3}{2}\right)$

$= \left(\frac{16}{2}, \frac{2}{2}\right) = (8,1)$

$$\left[\because \text{coordinates of mid-point} = \left(\frac{x_1+x_2}{2}, \frac{y_1+y_2}{2}\right)\right]$$

Coordinates of M = Mid-point of AC

$= \left(\frac{10+2}{2}, \frac{5+1}{2}\right) = \left(\frac{12}{2}, \frac{6}{2}\right) = (6,3)$

Now, length of $LM = \sqrt{(x_2-x_1)^2 + (y_2-y_1)^2}$

$= \sqrt{(6-8)^2 + (3-1)^2}$

$[\because (x_1, y_1) = (8,1) \text{ and } (x_2, y_2) = (6,3)]$

$$= \sqrt{(-2)^2 + (2)^2} = \sqrt{4+4}$$

$$= \sqrt{8} = 2\sqrt{2} \text{ units} \quad \ldots\text{(i)}$$

and length of $BC = \sqrt{(x_2 - x_1)^2 + (y_2 - y_1)^2}$

$$= \sqrt{(2-6)^2 + (1+3)^2}$$

$$[\because (x_1, y_1) = (6, -3) \text{ and } (x_2, y_2) = (2, 1)]$$

$$= \sqrt{(-4)^2 + (4)^2} = \sqrt{16+16} = 4\sqrt{2} \text{ units}$$

Now, $BC = 4\sqrt{2}$

$\Rightarrow \frac{1}{2}BC = 2\sqrt{2}$ [dividing both sides by 2]

$\Rightarrow \frac{1}{2}BC = LM$ [from Eq. (i)] **Hence proved.**

Example 22. The mid-points D, E and F of the sides AB, BC and CA of a triangle are (3, 4), (8, 9) and (6, 7), respectively. Find the coordinates of the vertices of the triangle.

Sol. Let $A(x_1, y_1)$, $B(x_2, y_2)$ and $C(x_3, y_3)$ be the vertices of the ΔABC such that $D(3, 4)$, $E(8, 9)$ and $F(6, 7)$ are mid-points of the sides AB, BC and CA, respectively.

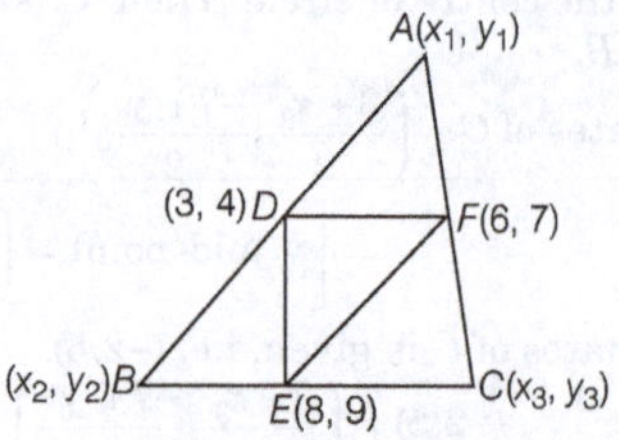

Since, $D(3, 4)$ is the mid-point of AB.

$$\therefore \quad (3, 4) = \left(\frac{x_1 + x_2}{2}, \frac{y_1 + y_2}{2}\right)$$

On equating x and y-coordinates both sides, we get

$$\frac{x_1 + x_2}{2} = 3 \text{ and } \frac{y_1 + y_2}{2} = 4$$

$\Rightarrow \quad x_1 + x_2 = 6 \quad \ldots\text{(i)}$

and $\quad y_1 + y_2 = 8 \quad \ldots\text{(ii)}$

As, $E(8, 9)$ is the mid-point of BC.

$$\therefore \quad \frac{x_2 + x_3}{2} = 8 \text{ and } \frac{y_2 + y_3}{2} = 9$$

$\Rightarrow \quad x_2 + x_3 = 16 \quad \ldots\text{(iii)}$

and $\quad y_2 + y_3 = 18 \quad \ldots\text{(iv)}$

Also, $F(6, 7)$ is the mid-point of AC.

$$\therefore \quad \frac{x_3 + x_1}{2} = 6 \text{ and } \frac{y_3 + y_1}{2} = 7$$

$\Rightarrow \quad x_3 + x_1 = 12 \quad \ldots\text{(v)}$

and $\quad y_3 + y_1 = 14 \quad \ldots\text{(vi)}$

On adding Eqs. (i), (iii) and (v), we get

$$2(x_1 + x_2 + x_3) = 34 \Rightarrow x_1 + x_2 + x_3 = 17 \quad \ldots\text{(vii)}$$

On subtracting one-by-one Eqs. (i), (iii) and (v) from Eq. (vii), we get

$$x_3 = 11, x_1 = 1 \text{ and } x_2 = 5$$

On adding Eqs. (ii), (iv) and (vi), we get

$$2(y_1 + y_2 + y_3) = 40$$

$\Rightarrow \quad y_1 + y_2 + y_3 = 20 \quad \ldots\text{(viii)}$

On subtracting one-by-one Eqs. (ii), (iv) and (vi) from Eq. (viii), we get

$$y_3 = 12, y_1 = 2 \text{ and } y_2 = 6$$

Hence, the vertices of the triangle are $A(1, 2)$, $B(5, 6)$ and $C(11, 12)$.

Centroid of a Triangle

The point where all the medians of a triangle meet is called the centroid of the triangle.

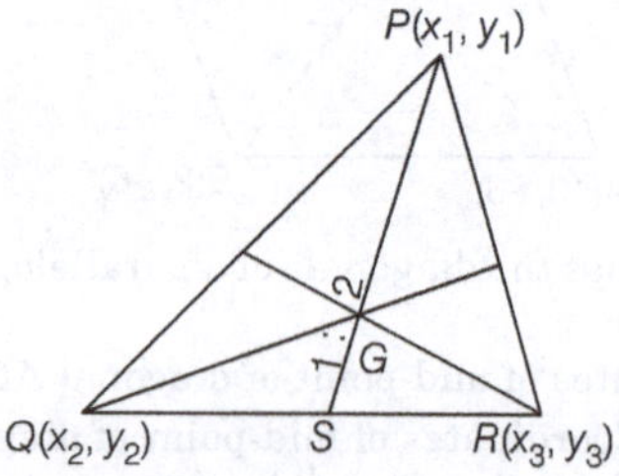

Let $P(x_1, y_1)$, $Q(x_2, y_2)$ and $R(x_3, y_3)$ be the given vertices of a ΔPQR and let G be the centroid of ΔPQR, then coordinates of G are $\left(\frac{x_1 + x_2 + x_3}{3}, \frac{y_1 + y_2 + y_3}{3}\right)$.

Example 23. Find the coordinates of the centroid of a triangle with vertices (3, 5), (2, – 1) and (6, 12).

Sol. Let the given coordinates be $A(3, 5)$, $B(2, -1)$ and $C(6, 12)$.

Now, we know that coordinates of centroid of a triangle are $\left(\frac{x_1 + x_2 + x_3}{3}, \frac{y_1 + y_2 + y_3}{3}\right)$.

Here, $x_1 = 3$, $x_2 = 2$, $x_3 = 6$, $y_1 = 5$, $y_2 = -1$ and $y_3 = 12$

$$\text{Coordinates of centroid} = \left[\frac{3 + 2 + 6}{3}, \frac{5 + (-1) + 12}{3}\right] = \left(\frac{11}{3}, \frac{16}{3}\right)$$

Example 24. The centroid of ΔABC is the origin. If the coordinates of A and B are respectively, (1, 3) and (2, – 4), then find the coordinates of C.

Sol. Let the centroid and the third vertex of the triangle be $G(0, 0)$ and $C(x_3, y_3)$, respectively.

Also, let $A(x_1, y_1) = (1, 3)$ and $B(x_2, y_2) = (2, -4)$

$\because$ Coordinates of the centroid of a triangle

$$= \left(\frac{x_1 + x_2 + x_3}{3}, \frac{y_1 + y_2 + y_3}{3}\right)$$

$$\therefore \quad (0, 0) = \left(\frac{1 + 2 + x_3}{3}, \frac{3 - 4 + y_3}{3}\right)$$

On equating x and y-coordinates both sides, we get

$$0 = \frac{3 + x_3}{3} \text{ and } 0 = \frac{-1 + y_3}{3}$$

$\Rightarrow \quad x_3 = -3$ and $y_3 = 1$

Hence, the coordinates of third vertex be $C(-3, 1)$.

Example 25. ABC is a triangle and $G(4, 3)$ is the centroid of the triangle. If $A(1, 3)$, $B(4, b)$ and $C(a, 1)$, then find a and b. Find the length of side BC.

[ICSE 2011]

Sol. Given, vertices and centroid of a triangle are $A(1, 3)$, $B(4, b)$, $C(a, 1)$ and $G(4, 3)$.

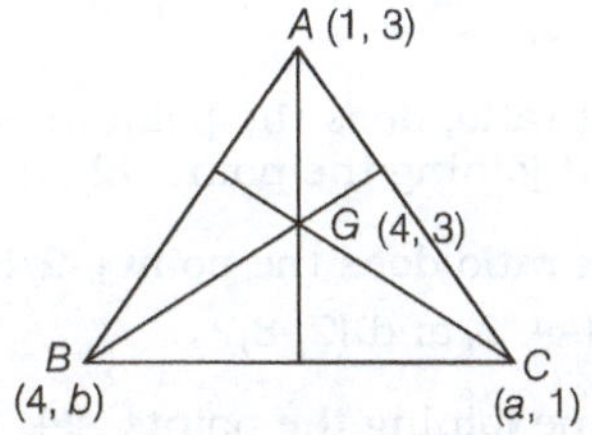

We know that

Coordinates of centroid of the triangle,

$$G = \left(\frac{x_1 + x_2 + x_3}{3}, \frac{y_1 + y_2 + y_3}{3}\right)$$

Here, $(x_1, y_1) = (1, 3)$, $(x_2, y_2) = (4, b)$ and $(x_3, y_3) = (a, 1)$

$\therefore$ Centroid of the triangle,

$$G = \left(\frac{1 + 4 + a}{3}, \frac{3 + b + 1}{3}\right) = \left(\frac{5 + a}{3}, \frac{4 + b}{3}\right)$$

But centroid is given by $G(4, 3)$.

$$\therefore \quad (4, 3) = \left(\frac{5 + a}{3}, \frac{4 + b}{3}\right)$$

On equating x and y-coordinates both sides, we get

$$4 = \frac{5 + a}{3} \text{ and } 3 = \frac{4 + b}{3}$$

$$\Rightarrow \quad 4 \times 3 = 5 + a \text{ and } 3 \times 3 = 4 + b$$

$$\Rightarrow \quad 12 = 5 + a \text{ and } 9 = 4 + b$$

$$\Rightarrow \quad a = 12 - 5 \text{ and } b = 9 - 4$$

$$\Rightarrow \quad a = 7 \text{ and } b = 5$$

$\therefore$ Coordinates of B and C are $(4, 5)$ and $(7, 1)$, respectively.

Now, the length of side BC

$$= \sqrt{(7 - 4)^2 + (1 - 5)^2}$$

$$[\because \text{distance} = \sqrt{(x_2 - x_1)^2 + (y_2 - y_1)^2}]$$

$$= \sqrt{(3)^2 + (-4)^2}$$

$$= \sqrt{9 + 16} = \sqrt{25} = 5 \text{ units}$$

Chapter Practice

a. 1 Mark Questions

1. The point which divides the line segment joining the points (7, – 6) and (3, 4) in ratio 1 : 2 internally lies in the **[NCERT Exemplar]**

(a) I quadrant (b) II quadrant
(c) III quadrant (d) IV quadrant

2. The mid-point of the line segment joining the points $A(-2, 8)$ and $B(-6, -4)$ is

(a) (–4, – 6) (b) (2, 6)
(c) (–4, 2) (d) (4, 2)

3. If $P\left(\frac{a}{3}, 4\right)$ is the mid-point of the line segment joining the points $Q(-6, 5)$ and $R(-2, 3)$, then the value of a is

(a) –4 (b) –6
(c) 12 (d) –12

4. The fourth vertex D of a parallelogram $ABCD$ whose three vertices are $A(-2, 3)$, $B(6, 7)$ and $C(8, 3)$ is

(a) (0, 1) (b) (0, –1)
(c) (–1, 0) (d) (1, 0)

5. If $x - 2y + k = 0$ is a median of the triangle whose vertices are at points $A(-1, 3)$, $B(0, 4)$ and $C(-5, 2)$, then the value of k is

(a) 2 (b) 4
(c) 6 (d) 8

6. The coordinates of the vertices of ΔABC are respectively (– 4, – 2), (6, 2) and (4, 6). The centroid G of ΔABC is **[ICSE 2023]**

(a) (2, 2) (b) (2, 3)
(c) (3, 3) (d) (0, – 1)

b. 3 Marks Questions

7. Find a point P which divides internally the line segment joining the points $A(-3, 9)$ and $B(1, -3)$ in the ratio 1 : 3.

8. Find the coordinates of the point which divides the line segment joining of (– 1, 7) and (4, – 3) in the ratio 2 : 3.

9. If P divides the distance between $A(-2, 1)$ and $B(1, 4)$ in the ratio 2 : 1. Calculate the coordinates of the point P.

10. What will be the value of y, if the point $\left(\frac{23}{5}, y\right)$ divides the line segment joining the points (5, 7) and (4, 5) in the ratio 2 : 3 internally?

11. Find the ratio, in which the line segment joining the points (– 3, 10) and (6, –8) is divided by (– 1, 6).

12. In what ratio, does the point (5, 4) divide the line segment joining the points (2, 1) and (7, 6)?

13. In what ratio does the point (–2/5, 6) divide the join of (–4, 3) and (2, 8)?

14. If the line joining the points $A(4, -5)$ and $B(4, 5)$ is divided by the point C such that $\frac{AC}{AB} = \frac{3}{5}$, then find the coordinates of C.

15. Find the ratio, in which Y-axis divides the line joining

(i) (1, – 2) and (– 3, – 4)
(ii) (3, 4) and (–2, 1)

16. The line segment joining the points $A(3, 2)$ and $B(5, 1)$ is divided at the point P in the ratio 1 : 2 and it lies on the line $3x - 18y + k = 0$, then find the value of k.

17. Find the ratio in which Y-axis divides the line segment joining the points $A(5, -6)$ and $B(-1, -4)$. Also, find the coordinates of the point of division.

18. Find the ratio in which the point $(-3, k)$ divides the line segment joining the points (–5, – 4) and (–2, 3). Also, find the value of k.

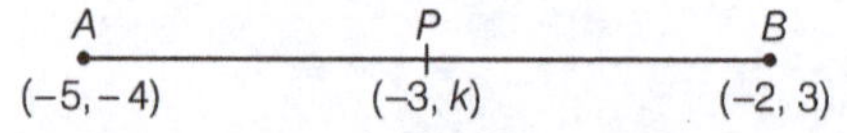

19. A point P divides the line joining $A(-4, 1)$ and $B(17, 10)$ in the ratio 1 : 2.

(i) Calculate the distance OP, where O is the origin.
(ii) In what ratio, does the Y-axis divide the line AB?

20. Find the coordinates of the points of trisection of the line segment joining

(i) (4, – 1) and (– 2, – 3)
(ii) (5, – 6) and (– 7, 5)
(iii) (5, – 3) and (2, – 9)

21. Let P and Q be the points of trisection of the line segment joining the points $A(2, -2)$ and $B(-7, 4)$ such that P is nearer to A. Find the coordinates of P and Q.

22. The line segment joining the points $P(3, 3)$ and $Q(6, -6)$ is trisected at the points A and B such that A is nearer to P. If A also lies on the line given by $2x + y + k = 0$, then find the value of k.

23. If the line segment joining the points $A(-1, 3)$ and $B(3, 9)$ into four equal segments by the points P, Q and R. Determine the coordinates of the points P, Q and R.

24. Find the value of p, if $(p, -2)$, $(-5, 6)$ and $(1, 2)$ are collinear.

25. The line segment joining $A(-3, 1)$ and $B(5, -4)$ is a diameter of a circle, whose centre is C. Find the coordinates of the point C.

26. Find the image of the point $P(-2, 4)$ under reflection in the point $O(-2, 3)$.

27. Find the third vertex of a triangle, if its two vertices are $(-1, 4)$ and $(5, 2)$, and mid-point of one side is $(0, 3)$.

28. Show that $A(-1, 0)$, $B(3, 1)$, $C(2, 2)$ and $D(-2, 1)$ are the vertices of a parallelogram $ABCD$.

29. Calculate the length of the median through the vertex A of the ΔABC with vertices
    (i) $A(5, -1)$, $B(-3, -2)$ and $C(-1, 8)$
    (ii) $A(-5, 2)$, $B(3, -6)$ and $C(7, 4)$
    (iii) $A(7, -3)$, $B(5, 3)$ and $C(3, -1)$

30. Find the value of a and b.
    (i) The mid-point of the line joining $(3a, 4)$ and $(-2, 2b)$ is $(2, 2a + 2)$.
    (ii) The mid-point of the line segment joining $(2a, 4)$ and $(-2, 2b)$ is $(1, 2a + 1)$. [ICSE 2007]

31. If two adjacent vertices of a parallelogram are $(3, 2)$ and $(-1, 0)$, and the diagonals intersect at $(2, -5)$, then find the other two vertices.

32. A and B are two points on the X-axis and Y-axis respectively. [ICSE 2023]

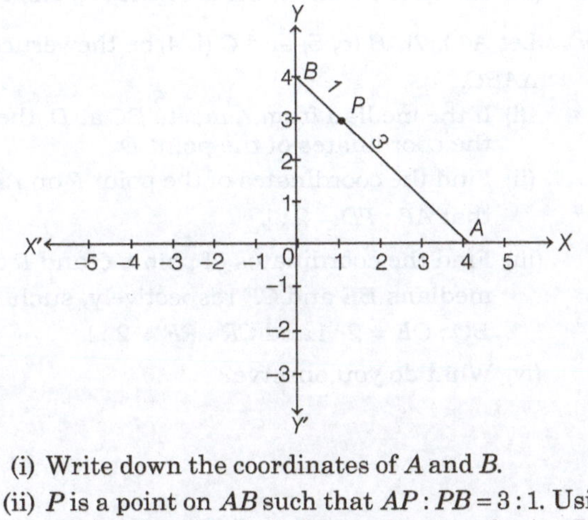

    (i) Write down the coordinates of A and B.
    (ii) P is a point on AB such that $AP : PB = 3 : 1$. Using section formula find the coordinates of point P.

33. In the figure given below, the line segment AB meets X-axis at A and Y-axis at B. The point $P(-3, 4)$ on AB divides it in the ratio $2 : 3$. Find the coordinates of A and B. [ICSE 2013]

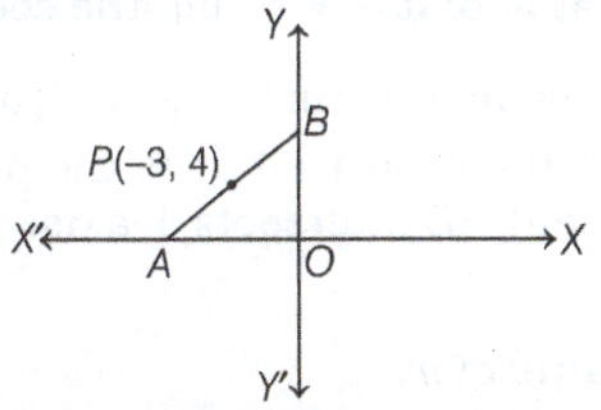

34. Find the centroid of a triangle, whose vertices are $(3, -5)$, $(-7, 4)$ and $(10, -2)$.

35. Find the third vertex of the triangle.
    (i) If the centroid of a triangle is at $(0, -3)$ and two of its vertices are $(-1, 4)$ and $(5, 2)$.
    (ii) If the centroid of a triangle is the point $(6, -1)$ and two of its vertices are $(3, 4)$ and $(-2, 5)$.
    (iii) If the centroid of a triangle is at $(2, -1)$ and two of its vertices are $(3, -5)$ and $(7, -4)$.

C. 6 Marks Questions

36. (i) Write down the coordinates of the point P, that divides the line joining $A(2, 1)$ and $B(-7, 10)$ in the ratio $2 : 1$.
    (ii) Calculate the distance OP, where O is the origin.
    (iii) In what ratio, does the Y-axis divide the line AB?

37. The line segment joining $A(-1, 3)$ and $B(6, 2)$ is intersected by the Y-axis at point k. Write down the coordinates of k. Also, find the ratio in which k divides.

38. Find the ratio in which the line segment joining the points $A(3, -3)$ and $B(-2, 7)$ is divided by X-axis. Also, find the coordinates of the point of division.

39. If $R(x, y)$ is a point on the line segment joining the points $P(a, b)$ and $Q(b, a)$, then prove that $x + y = a + b$.

40. Find the ratio in which the line joining points $(a + b, b + a)$ and $(a - b, b - a)$ is divided by the point (a, b).

41. If $P(9a - 2, -b)$ divides the line segment joining $A(3a + 1, -3)$ and $B(8a, 5)$ in the ratio $3 : 1$. Find the values of a and b.

42. If $A(-3, 4)$, $B(3, -1)$ and $C(-2, 4)$ are the vertices of ΔABC. Find the length of line segment AP, where P lies inside BC such that $BP : PC = 2 : 3$.

43. The line segment joining $A\left(-1, \frac{5}{3}\right)$ and $B(a, 5)$ is divided in the ratio 1 : 3 at P, the point where the line segment AB intersects Y-axis. Calculate

(i) the value of a. (ii) the coordinates of P.

44. The line segment joining $A(-2, 3)$ and $B(m, 4)$ is divided in the ratio 1 : 4 at P, the point where the line segment AB intersects Y-axis.

Calculate

(i) the value of m.
(ii) the coordinates of P.

45. If $A(-4, 3)$ and $B(8, -6)$. Find

(i) the length of AB.
(ii) the ratio is the line joining AB divided by the X-axis? [ICSE 2008]

46. The line joining $P(-4, 5)$ and $Q(3, 2)$ intersect the Y-axis at R. PM and QN are perpendicular from P and Q on the X-axis. Find

(i) the ratio $PR : PQ$.
(ii) the coordinates of R.
(iii) the area of the quadrilateral $PMNQ$.

47. The centre O of a circle has the coordinates (4, 5) and one point on the circumference is (8, 10). Find the coordinates of the other end of the diameter of the circle through this point.

48. If the coordinates of the mid-points of the sides of a triangle are (3, – 2), (– 3, 1) and (4 – 3), then find the coordinates of its vertices.

49. If two vertices of a parallelogram are (2, 3) and (0, – 1) and the diagonals cut at (– 5, 2), then find the other vertices of the parallelogram.

50. If a vertex of a triangle be (1, 1) and the mid-points of the sides through it be (– 2, 3) and (5, 2). Find the other vertices.

51. The coordinates of the vertices of ΔABC are $A(7, 2)$, $B(9, 10)$ and $C(1, 4)$. If E and F are the mid-points of AB and AC respectively, prove that $EF = \frac{1}{2} BC$.

52. If $A(2, 5)$, $B(-1, 2)$ and $C(5, 8)$ are the vertices of a ΔABC. P and Q are points on AB and AC respectively, such that $AP : PB = AQ : QC = 1 : 2$.

(i) Find the coordinates of P and Q.
(ii) Show that $PQ = \frac{1}{3} BC$.

53. Find coordinates of vertices of the triangle, the middle points of whose sides are $\left(0, \frac{1}{2}\right)$, $\left(\frac{1}{2}, \frac{1}{2}\right)$ and $\left(\frac{1}{2}, 0\right)$.

54. Prove that the diagonals of a rectangle $ABCD$, with vertices $A(2, -1)$, $B(5, -1)$, $C(5, 6)$ and $D(2, 6)$ are equal and bisect each other.

55. The vertices of ΔABC are $A(6, -2)$, $B(0, -6)$ and $C(4, 8)$. Find the coordinates of mid-points of AB, BC and AC.

56. If (a, b) is the mid-point of the segment joining the points $A(10, -6)$, $B(k, 4)$ and $a - 2b = 18$, find the value of k, (a, b) and the distance AB.

57. Given, $O(0, 0)$, $A(1, 2)$, $B(-3, 0)$. A divides OE in the ratio 1 : 2 and $OACB$ is a parallelogram.

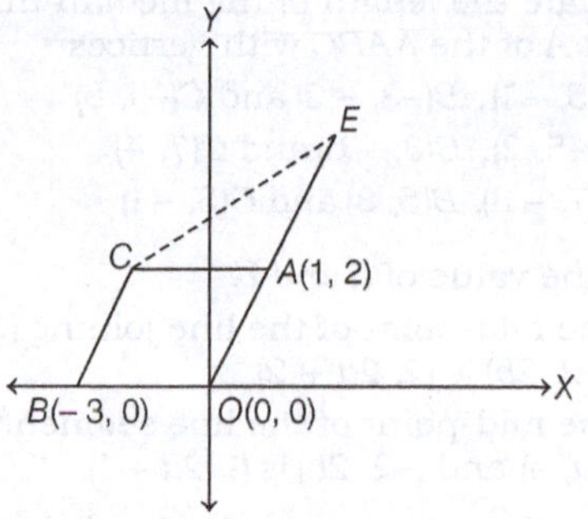

Determine

(i) the coordinates of E.
(ii) the coordinates of C.
(iii) the ratio in which CE is divides by the Y-axis.

58. Let $A(4, 2)$, $B(6, 5)$ and $C(1, 4)$ be the vertices of ΔABC.

(i) If the median from A meets BC at D, then find the coordinates of the point D.
(ii) Find the coordinates of the point P on AD such that $AP : PD = 2 : 1$.
(iii) Find the coordinates of points Q and R on medians BE and CF respectively, such that $BQ : QE = 2 : 1$ and $CR : RF = 2 : 1$.
(iv) What do you observe?

Hints and Answers

1. (d) If $P(x, y)$ divides the line segment joining $A(x_1, y_1)$ and $B(x_2, y_2)$ internally in the ratio $m:n$,

then $x = \dfrac{mx_2 + nx_1}{m+n}$ and $y = \dfrac{my_2 + ny_1}{m+n}$

Given that,

$$x_1 = 7,\ y_1 = -6,\ x_2 = 3,\ y_2 = 4,\ m = 1 \text{ and } n = 2$$

$$\therefore \quad x = \frac{1(3) + 2(7)}{1+2},\ y = \frac{1(4) + 2(-6)}{1+2}$$

[by section formula]

$$\Rightarrow \quad x = \frac{3+14}{3},\ y = \frac{4-12}{3}$$

$$\Rightarrow \quad x = \frac{17}{3},\ y = -\frac{8}{3}$$

So, $(x, y) = \left(\dfrac{17}{3}, -\dfrac{8}{3}\right)$ lies in IV quadrant.

[since, in IV quadrant, x-coordinate is positive and y-coordinate is negative]

2. (c) Let the mid-point be (x, y)

Let $A(x_1, y_1) = A(-2, 8)$ and $B(x_2, y_2) = B(-6, -4)$

$$x_1 = -2,\ y_1 = 8,\ x_2 = -6 \text{ and } y_2 = -4$$

$$\therefore \quad x = \frac{x_1 + x_2}{2} = \frac{-2-6}{2} = \frac{-8}{2} = -4$$

$$\therefore \quad y = \frac{y_1 + y_2}{2} = \frac{8-4}{2} = \frac{4}{2} = 2$$

$$\therefore \quad (x, y) = (-4, 2)$$

3. (d) Mid-point of line segment joining two points (x_1, y_1) and (x_2, y_2)

$$\left(\frac{x_1 + x_2}{2}, \frac{y_1 + y_2}{2}\right)$$

Given, mid-point of line segment joining the points

$$Q(-6, 5) \text{ and } R(-2, 3) = P\left(\frac{a}{3}, 4\right)$$

$$= \left(\frac{-6-2}{2}, \frac{5+3}{2}\right) = \left(\frac{a}{3}, 4\right)$$

$$= \left(\frac{-8}{2}, \frac{8}{2}\right) = \left(\frac{a}{3}, 4\right)$$

On equating x-coordinates both sides,we get

$$\frac{-8}{2} = \frac{a}{3}$$

$$\Rightarrow \quad 2a = -24$$

$$\Rightarrow \quad a = -12$$

4. (b)

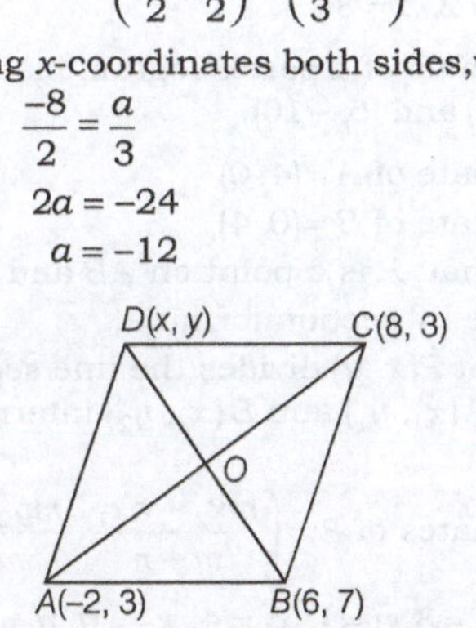

Given, in parallelogram $ABCD$, the three consecutive vertices are $A(-2, 3)$, $B(6, 7)$ and $C(8, 3)$.

Let the coordinates of fourth vertex be $D(x, y)$.

We know that, the diagonals of a parallelogram bisect each other.

$$O\left(\frac{x+6}{2}, \frac{y+7}{2}\right)$$

Also, $O\left(\dfrac{8-2}{2}, \dfrac{3+3}{2}\right)$ i.e. $O(3, 3)$

So, $\dfrac{x+6}{2} = 3$ and $\dfrac{y+7}{2} = 3$

$$x + 6 = 6 \text{ and } y + 7 = 6$$

$$x = 0 \text{ and } y = -1$$

Hence, the fourth vertex is $D(0, -1)$.

5. (d) Coordinate of the centroid G of ΔABC

$$= \left(\frac{-1+0-5}{3}, \frac{3+4+2}{3}\right) = (-2, 3)$$

Since, G lies on the median $x - 2y + k = 0$.

So, G satisfy the equation $x - 2y + k = 0$.

$$\therefore \quad -2 - 6 + k = 0 \Rightarrow k = 8$$

6. (a) Given, coordinates of vertices of ΔABC are $(-4, -2)$, $(6, 2)$ and $(4, 6)$.

Let $(x_1, y_1) = (-4, -2)$, $(x_2, y_2) = (6, 2)$ and $(x_3, y_3) = (4, 6)$

We have by centroid formula,

Centroid G of ΔABC

$$= \left(\frac{x_1 + x_2 + x_3}{3}, \frac{y_1 + y_2 + y_3}{3}\right)$$

$$= \left(\frac{-4+6+4}{3}, \frac{-2+2+6}{3}\right) = (2, 2)$$

7. Let coordinates of the point P be (x, y).

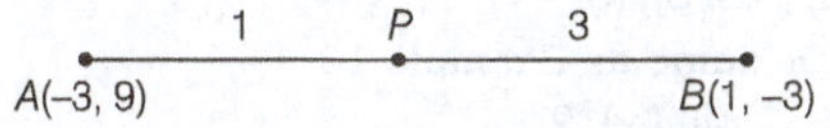

$$P(x, y) = \left(\frac{1 \times 1 + 3(-3)}{1+3}, \frac{1(-3) + 3 \times 9}{1+3}\right)$$

$$= \left(\frac{1-9}{4}, \frac{-3+27}{4}\right)$$

$$= (-2, 6)$$

8. **Hint** Do same as Example 1. **Ans.** (1, 3)

9. **Hint** Do same as Example 1. **Ans.** (0, 3)

10. **Hint** By section formula,

y-coordinate of internally division,

$$y = \frac{2 \times 5 + 3 \times 7}{2+3}.$$

Ans. $\dfrac{31}{5}$

11. **Hint** Do same as Example 2. **Ans.** 2 : 7

12. **Hint** Do same as Example 2. **Ans.** 3 : 2

13. **Hint** Do same as Example 2. **Ans.** 3 : 2

14. **Hint** Do same as Example 4. **Ans.** (4, 1)

15. **Hint** Do same as Example 12 (i).

Ans. (i) 1 : 3 (ii) 3 : 2

16. **Hint** By section formula,

$$P\left(\frac{mx_2+nx_1}{m+n}, \frac{my_2+ny_1}{m+n}\right)$$

$$=\left(\frac{1\times5+2\times3}{1+2}, \frac{1\times1+2\times2}{1+2}\right)=P\left(\frac{11}{3}, \frac{5}{3}\right)$$

$P\left(\frac{11}{3}, \frac{5}{3}\right)$ lies on the line $3x-18y+k=0$

$$\Rightarrow \quad 3\left(\frac{11}{3}\right)-18\left(\frac{5}{3}\right)+k=0 \Rightarrow k=19$$

17. **Hint** Apply section formula and then put the x-coordinate equal to zero. **Ans.** $5:1, \left(0, -\frac{13}{3}\right)$

18. **Hint** $(-3, k)=\left(\frac{-2m_1-5m_2}{m_1+m_2}, \frac{3m_1-4m_2}{m_1+m_2}\right)$

Ans. $2:1, k=\frac{2}{3}$

19. **Hint** First, use section formula

i.e. $\left(\frac{m_1x_2+m_2x_1}{m_1+m_2}, \frac{m_1y_2+m_2y_1}{m_1+m_2}\right)$

(i) Using distance formula,

$OP=\sqrt{(x_2-x_1)^2+(y_2-y_1)^2}$ **Ans.** 5 units

(ii) In section formula, put the x-coordinate equals to zero.

Ans. 4 : 17

20. **Hint** Do same as Example 13.

Ans. (i) $\left[\left(2, -\frac{5}{3}\right) \text{ and } \left(0, -\frac{7}{3}\right)\right]$

(ii) $\left(1, \frac{-7}{3}\right), \left(-3, \frac{4}{3}\right)$

(iii) $(4, -5), (3, -7)$

21. **Hint** Do same as Example 13.

Ans. $(-1, 0), (-4, 2)$

22. **Hint** Do same as Example 14. **Ans.** $k=-8$

23. **Hint** Use mid-point formula,

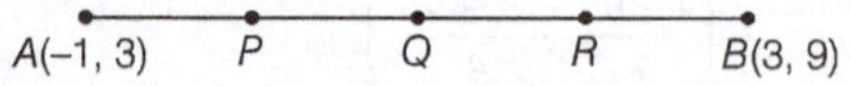

Ans. $P\left(0, \frac{9}{2}\right), Q(1, 6), R\left(2, \frac{15}{2}\right)$

24. **Hint** Let the given points be $A(p, -2)$, $B(-5, 6)$ and $C(1, 2)$.

Also, suppose the point $C(1, 2)$ divides the line joining the points $A(P, -2)$ and $B(-5, 6)$ in the ratio $k:1$.

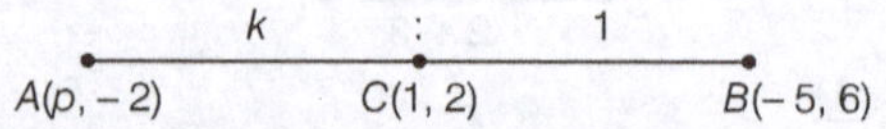

On applying section formula, we have

$$C\left(\frac{-5k+p}{k+1}, \frac{6k-2}{k+1}\right)=C(1, 2)$$

Now, equate x and y-coordinates both sides separately to get the required result.

Ans. $p=7$

25. **Hint** Use the mid-point formula. **Ans.** $\left(1, \frac{-3}{2}\right)$

26. **Hint** Let image of the point $P(-2, 4)$ be $I(x, y)$.

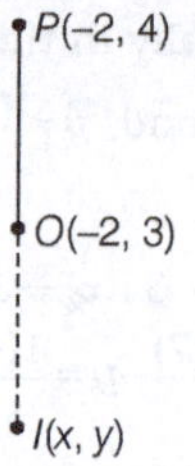

It is clear that O is the mid-point of P and I. So, use mid-point formula to determine the coordinates of I.

Ans. $(-2, 2)$.

27. **Hint** There are following two cases arise

Case I Suppose mid-point (0, 3) between A and C.

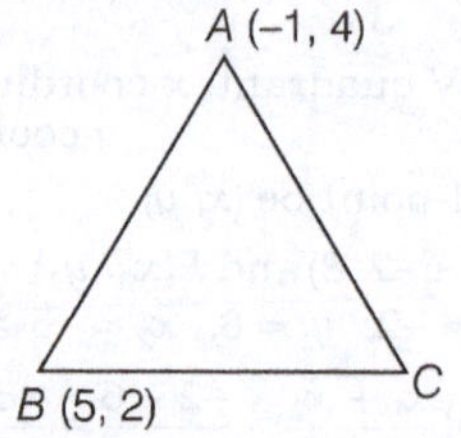

Case II Suppose mid-point (0, 3) between B and C.

Ans. $(-5, 4)$ or $(1, 2)$

28. **Hint** Show that $AB=CD$, $BC=DA$ and mid-point of AC and BD coincide.

29. (i) **Hint** First, find coordinates of D, which is the mid-point of BC. Then, use the distance formula, $AD=\sqrt{(x_2-x_1)^2+(y_2-y_1)^2}$. **Ans.** $\sqrt{65}$ units

(ii) **Hint** Do same as part (i). **Ans.** $\sqrt{109}$ units

(iii) **Hint** Do same as part (i). **Ans.** 5

30. (i) **Hint** $(2, 2a+2)=\left(\frac{3a-2}{2}, \frac{4+2b}{2}\right)$

Ans. $a=2, b=4$

(ii) **Hint** Do same as part (i).

Ans. $a=2, b=3$

31. **Hint** Diagonals of a parallelogram bisects each other.

Ans. $(1, -12)$ and $(5, -10)$

32. (i) Coordinate of $A=(4, 0)$

Coordinate of $B=(0, 4)$

(ii) Given that, P is a point on AB and $AP:PB=3:1$.

We have by section formula,

Let point $P(x, y)$ divides the line segment joining points $A(x_1, y_1)$ and $B(x_2, y_2)$ internally in ratio $m:n$.

$$\text{Coordinates of } P=\left(\frac{mx_2+nx_1}{m+n}, \frac{my_2+ny_1}{m+n}\right)$$

Here, $m=3, n=1, x_1=4, x_2=0, y_1=0, y_2=4$

∴ Coordinates of

$$P(x, y) = \left(\frac{3\times 0 + 1\times 4}{3+1}, \frac{3\times 4 + 1\times 0}{3+1}\right)$$

$$= \left(\frac{4}{4}, \frac{12}{4}\right) = (1, 3)$$

33. Hint $P(-3, 4) = P\left(\frac{3x}{5}, \frac{2y}{5}\right)$ **Ans.** (–5, 0), (0, 10)

34. Hint Do same as Example 23. **Ans.** (2, – 1)

35. Hint Do same as Example 24.
Ans. (i) (–4, – 15) (ii) (17, – 12) (iii) (– 4, 6)

36. (i) **Hint** Do same as Example 1. **Ans.** (–4, 7)
(ii) **Hint** Do same as Q. 19. **Ans.** $\sqrt{65}$ units
(iii) **Hint** Do same as Q. 19. **Ans.** 2 : 7

37. Hint Let the coordinates of point k be $(0, y)$ and let the point k divides AB in the ratio $p:1$.
On applying section formula, we have

$$\left(\frac{6p-1}{p+1}, \frac{2p+3}{p+1}\right) = (0, y)$$

Ans. $\left(0, \frac{20}{7}\right)$, 1 : 6

38. Hint Do same as Example 5.
Ans. 3 : 7, $\left(\frac{3}{2}, 0\right)$

39. Hint Let point R divides the line joining P and Q in the ratio $\lambda:1$.

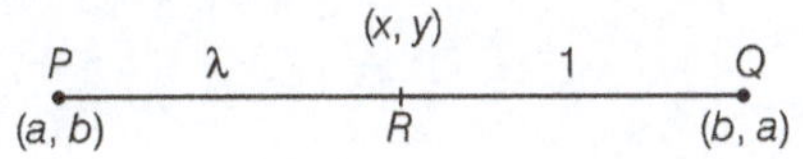

$$x = \frac{\lambda b + a}{\lambda + 1} \text{ and } y = \frac{\lambda a + b}{\lambda + 1}$$

On adding, we get $x + y = \frac{\lambda b + a + \lambda a + b}{\lambda + 1}$

40. Hint Let $A(a+b, b+a)$, $B(a-b, b-a)$ and $P(a, b)$ and P divides AB in $k:1$, then

$$a = \frac{k(a-b) + 1(a+b)}{k+1}$$ **Ans.** 1 : 1

41. Hint $(9a - 2, -b) = \left[\frac{3\times 8a + 1(3a+1)}{3+1}, \frac{3\times 5 + 1\times(-3)}{3+1}\right]$

Equating the x-coordinate and y-coordinate both side and further simplify to get the values of a and b.
Ans. $a = 1, b = -3$

42. Hint First use section formula to find the coordinates of P. Further, use distance formula,

$$AP = \sqrt{(x_2 - x_1)^2 + (y_2 - y_1)^2}$$

Ans. 5 units

43. Hint
(i) First, put the x-coordinate of internally division is equal to zero. Then, determine the value of a.
(ii) Using section formula.
Ans. (i) $a = 3$ (ii) $\left(0, \frac{5}{2}\right)$

44. Hint Using section formula,

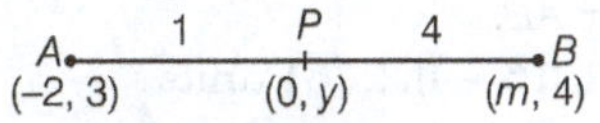

Ans. (i) 8 (ii) $\left(0, \frac{16}{5}\right)$

45. Hint (i) Use distance formula,

$$d = \sqrt{(x_2 - x_1)^2 + (y_2 - y_1)^2}$$

(ii) After applying section formula, put the y-coordinate equals to zero.
Ans. (i) 15 units (ii) 1 : 2

46. Hint

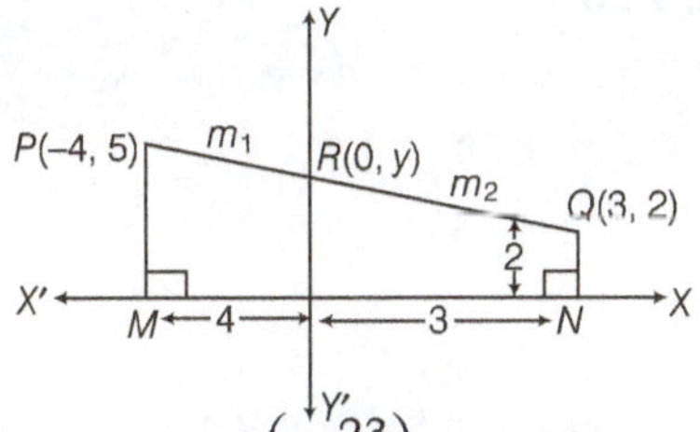

Ans. (i) 4 : 7 (ii) $\left(0, \frac{23}{7}\right)$ (iii) 24.5 sq units

47. Hint Use mid-point formula.
Ans. (0, 0)

48. Hint Do same as Example 22.
Ans. (10, – 6), (–4, 2), (–2, 0)

49. Hint Diagonals of a parallelogram bisect each other. Apply mid-point formula.
Ans. (– 12, 1), (– 10, 5)

50. Hint Use mid-point formula in AB and AC.

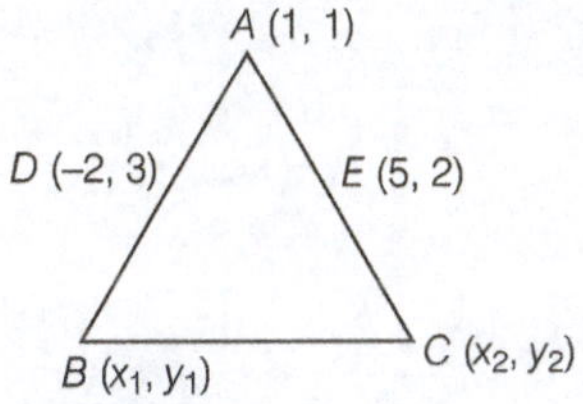

Ans. (–5, 5) and (9, 3)

51. Hint Do same as Example 21.

52. Hint (i) To find the coordinates of P and Q use section formula.
(ii) Use distance formula.
Ans. (i) $P = (1, 4)$, $Q = (3, 6)$

53. Hint Do same as Example 22.
Ans. (0, 0), (1, 0) and (0, 1)

54. Hint Use distance and mid-point formulae to prove that the diagonals of a rectangle are equal and bisect each other, respectively.

55. Hint Using mid-point formula in AB, BC, CA.
Ans. (3, – 4), (2, 1), (5, 3)

56. Hint First use mid-point formula and then distance formula for *AB*.

Ans. $k = 22$, $(16, -1)$, $2\sqrt{61}$ units

57. (i) **Hint** Use section formula. **Ans.** (3, 6)

(ii) **Hint** Diagonals of a parallelogram bisect each other. Mid-point of diagonal AB = mid-point of diagonal OC. **Ans.** $(-2, 2)$

(iii) **Hint** Coordinate of the point where Y-axis divides CE is $(0, y)$. On applying section formula, we have

$$\left(\frac{3m-2n}{m+n}, \frac{6m+2n}{m+n}\right) = (0, y).$$

Ans. 2 : 3

58. Hint

(i) Use mid-point formula.

(ii) Use internal section formula.

(iii) BE is the median of ΔABC. So, E is the mid-point of AC and its coordinate are $E\left(\frac{5}{2}, 3\right)$.

Similarly for F.

Ans. (i) $\left(\frac{7}{2}, \frac{9}{2}\right)$ (ii) $\left(\frac{11}{3}, \frac{11}{3}\right)$ (iii) $Q\left(\frac{11}{3}, \frac{11}{3}\right)$, $R\left(\frac{11}{3}, \frac{11}{3}\right)$

(iv) We observe that the points P, Q and R coincide at the point $\left(\frac{11}{3}, \frac{11}{3}\right)$.

Olympiad Section

Brain Teasing Questions of Olympiad Pattern

1 Join two points $P(2, 2)$ and $Q(4, 2)$ in a plane. Fixed the point P and rotate the line PQ in anti-clockwise direction at an angle of 270°. Then, the new coordinates of point Q and the area formed by this figure will be

(a) (4, 2); 4.92 sq units (b) (2, 4); 9.42 sq units
(c) (2, 0); 9.42 sq units (d) (2, 4); 2.94 sq units

2 If G be the centroid of a ΔABC and P be any other point in the plane, then $GA^2 + GB^2 + GC^2 + 3GP^2$ is equal to

(a) $PA^2 + PC^2 - PB^2$ (b) $PB^2 + PC^2 - PA^2$
(c) $PA^2 + PB^2 - PC^2$ (d) $PA^2 + PB^2 + PC^2$

3 A figure is shown below

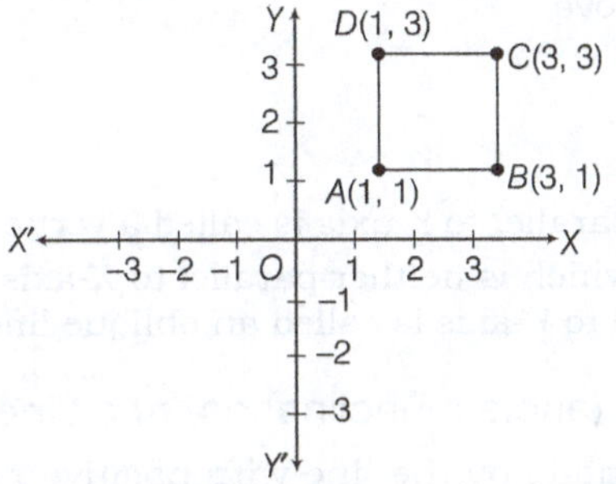

If we rotate this graph about O at an angle of 180° in anti-clockwise direction, then the intersection point of diagonals will be

(a) (3, 2) (b) (2, 2) (c) (2, 3) (d) (2, 1)

4 If (– 4, 3) and (4, 3) are two vertices of an equilateral triangle and the origin lies in the interior of the triangle, then the coordinates of the third vertex will be

(a) (0, 1) (b) (1, 0)
(c) $(0, 3 - 4\sqrt{3})$ (d) $(1, 3 - 4\sqrt{3})$

5 Suppose there are four points $A(2, 4)$, $B(6, 4)$, $C(6, 6)$ and $D(2, 6)$, which lie in the first quadrant. If we rotate only the axes at an angle of 90° in anti-clockwise direction, then what will be the new coordinates of the point C and what will be the name of the figure, when we join adjacent points.

(a) (–6, 6); square
(b) (6, – 6); rectangle
(c) (6, 4); square
(d) (2, – 6); rectangle

6 Suppose PQ be a pole, whose coordinates are $P(1, 3)$ and $Q(3, 3)$ and A be the position of a man whose coordinates are (1, 1).

(i) If a pole makes an angle of elevation to the point A, then the angle θ is

(ii) Also, if we shift the origin at (1, 1), then the angle θ is

(a) 45°, 45° (b) 45°, 60°
(c) 45°, 90 (d) 75, 45°

7 The sum of the squares of the distances of a moving point (x, y) from two fixed points $(a, 0)$ and $(-a, 0)$ is equal to a constant quantity $2b^2$. The value of $x^2 + y^2 + a^2$ is equal to

(a) ab (b) $-b^2$
c) $-a^2$ (d) b^2

8 A point (x, y) moves, so that the sum of its distances from $(ae, 0)$ and $(-ae, 0)$ is $2a$. If $b^2 = a^2(1 - e^2)$, then $\frac{x^2}{a^2} + \frac{y^2}{b^2}$ is equal to

(a) 0 (b) – 1
(c) 1 (d) 2

Answers

1. (c) **2.** (d) **3.** (b) **4.** (c) **5.** (b) **6.** (a) **7.** (d) **8.** (c)

* *These questions may or may not be asked in the examination, have been given just for additional practice required for olympiads Scholarship Exams etc. For detailed explanations refer Page No. 484.*

CHAPTER 12

Equation of a Straight Line

SYLLABUS

- **Equation of a line** (I) Slope-intercept form (ii) Two point form $(y - y_1) = m(x - x_1)$ Geometric understanding of 'm' as slope/gradient/tan q where q is the angle the line makes with the positive direction of the X-axis. Geometric understanding of 'c' as the y-intercept/ the ordinate of the point where the line intercepts they Y-axis/the point on the line where x = 0. (iii) Conditions for two lines to be parallel or perpendicular. Simple applications of all the above.

In earlier classes, we studied about coordinate axes, coordinate plane, plotting of points in a plane, distance between two points, etc., all these are the basics concepts of coordinate geometry. In this chapter we will study about straight line and its slope (gradient) along with equation of a straight line in different forms and the conditions for two lines to be parallel or perpendicular.

Straight Line and Its Equation in Different Forms

Straight Line

A **straight line** is a curve, such that all the points on the line segment joining any two points of it lies on it.

Every first degree equation in x and y represents a straight line, i.e. equation of the form $ax + by + c = 0$ represent a straight line.

e.g. $x + y = 0$, $3x - y + 2 = 0$ are straight lines.

There are three types of straight line

(i) A line parallel to X-axis is called a horizontal line.

(ii) A line parallel to Y-axis is called a vertical line.

(iii) A line which is neither parallel to X-axis nor parallel to Y-axis is called an oblique line.

Inclination (angle of inclination) of a Line

The angle made by the line with positive X-axis in anti-clockwise direction, is called inclination (angle of inclination) of a line. The inclination is usually denoted by θ. Thus, $0° \le \theta < 180°$.

An inclination of a line is either acute or obtuse, as shown in the following figures.

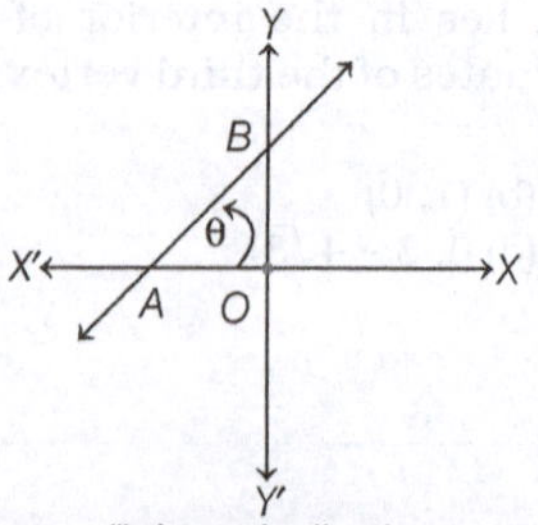

(i) Acute inclination

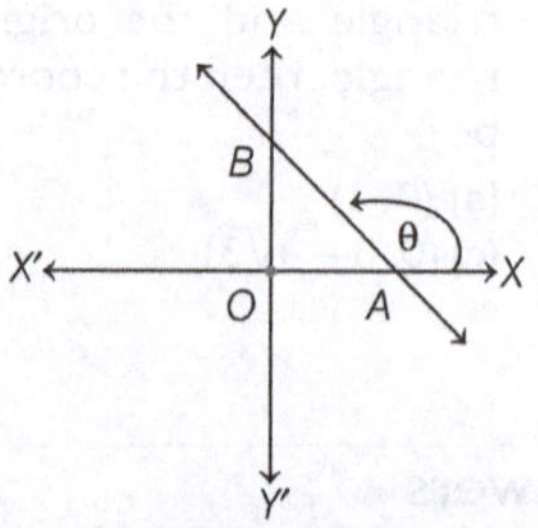

(ii) Obtuse inclination

Inclination of Axes

(i) The inclination of X-axis and lines parallel to it, is $0°$.

(ii) The inclination of Y-axis and lines parallel to it, is $90°$.

Example 1. Find the inclination of a line l in the following figure.

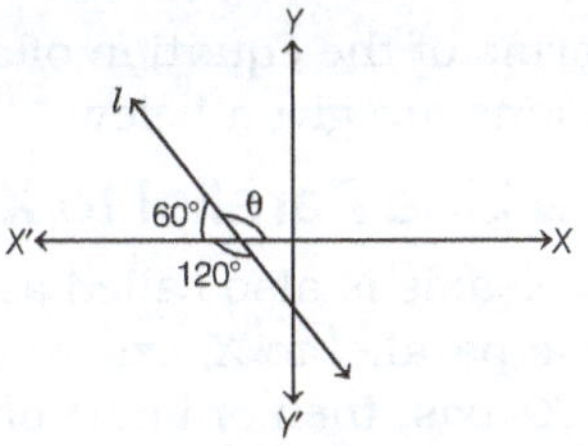

Sol. From the figure, we see that $\theta = 120°$ [vertically opposite angles]

Hence, inclination of a line l is 120°.

Slope (or Gradient) of a Line

If θ is the angle of inclination of a line l, then $\tan\theta$ is called the slope or gradient of the line l and it is denoted by m, i.e. $m = \tan\theta$.

Thus, slope of a line is the tangent of the angle made by the line in the anti-clockwise direction with the positive X-axis.

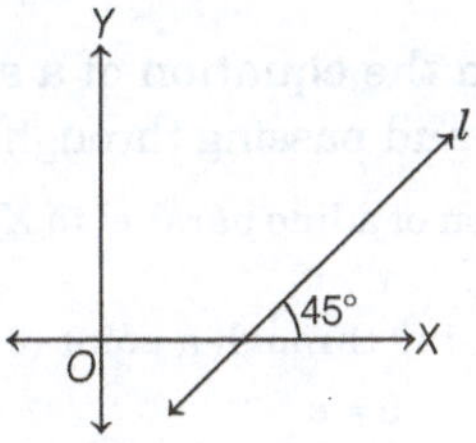

e.g. from the figure, slope of line $l = m = \tan 45° = 1$

(i) The slope of X-axis is $m = \tan 0° = 0$

(ii) The slope of Y-axis is not defined (as $\tan 90°$ is not defined).

(iii) The slope of a line is positive, if it makes an acute angle in the anti-clockwise direction with X-axis.

(iv) The slope of a line is negative, if it makes an obtuse angle in the anti-clockwise direction with the X-axis.

Example 2. Find the slope of a line, whose inclination is 60°.

Sol. Let θ be the inclination of a line, then its slope $= \tan\theta$.

At $\theta = 60°$, slope of a line $= \tan 60° = \sqrt{3}$

Example 3. Find the inclination of the line whose slope is $\sqrt{3}$.

Sol. Given, slope $= \sqrt{3}$

$\Rightarrow \quad \tan\theta = \sqrt{3}$

$\therefore \quad \theta = 60°$

Example 4. The equation of straight line is $x - y - 6 = 0$. Find

(i) gradient of the line

(ii) the inclination of the line.

(iii) the y-intercept of the line

Sol. The equation of the line is $x - y - 6 = 0$

$\Rightarrow \quad y = x - 6$

Comparing with $y = mx + c$, then we get

$m = 1$ and $c = -6$

(i) The gradient of the line $= m = 1$

(ii) Let θ be the inclination of the line

$\therefore \tan\theta = 1 \Rightarrow \theta = 45°$

(iii) y-intercept $= c = -6$

Slope of a Line Passing through Two Points

The slope of a line passing through two points $P(x_1, y_1)$ and $Q(x_2, y_2)$ is given by

$$m = \frac{y_2 - y_1}{x_2 - x_1} \text{ or } \frac{y_1 - y_2}{x_1 - x_2}.$$

Example 5. Find the slope of a line joining following two points.

(i) $A(1, 2)$ and $B(3, -4)$ (ii) $(3, -2)$ and $(7, -2)$.

Sol. We know that slope of a line joining two points (x_1, y_1) and (x_2, y_2) is $m = \dfrac{y_2 - y_1}{x_2 - x_1}$.

(i) Given, $A(1, 2) = (x_1, y_1)$ and $B(3, -4) = (x_2, y_2)$

$\therefore$ Slope of a line joining the points A and B is

$$m = \frac{-4 - 2}{3 - 1} = \frac{-6}{2} = -3$$

(ii) Slope of a line joining the points $(3, -2)$ and $(7, -2)$ is

$$m = \frac{-2 - (-2)}{7 - 3} = \frac{0}{4} = 0$$

Example 6. The slope of a line joining $P(6, k)$ and $Q(1 - 3k, 3)$ is 1/2. Find

(i) the value of k.

(ii) mid-point of PQ, using the value of 'k' found in part (i). **[ICSE 2016]**

Sol. Given, points are $P(6, k)$ and $Q(1 - 3k, 3)$.

(i) Slope of a line joining these two points $= \dfrac{1}{2}$

$$\Rightarrow \quad \frac{3 - k}{1 - 3k - 6} = \frac{1}{2} \qquad \left[\because \text{slope} = \frac{y_2 - y_1}{x_2 - x_1}\right]$$

$$\Rightarrow \quad \frac{3 - k}{-3k - 5} = \frac{1}{2}$$

$\Rightarrow \quad 6 - 2k = -3k - 5$

$\Rightarrow \quad 3k - 2k = -5 - 6$

$\therefore \quad k = -11$

(ii) When $k = -11$, the coordinates of points P and Q are respectively $(6, -11)$ and $(34, 3)$.

$\therefore$ Mid-point of $PQ = \left(\frac{6+34}{2}, \frac{-11+3}{2}\right)$ $\left[\because \text{mid-point } \left(\frac{x_1+x_2}{2}, \frac{y_1+y_2}{2}\right)\right]$

$= \left(\frac{40}{2}, \frac{-8}{2}\right) = (20, -4)$

Hence, the mid-point of PQ is $(20, -4)$.

Intercept Made by a Line on the Axes

If a line intersect X-axis at a distance of a units from the origin and Y-axis at a distance of b units from the origin, then a is called the **x-intercept** and b is called the **y-intercept**.

Consider the figure, in which OA is called x-intercept and OB is called y-intercept.

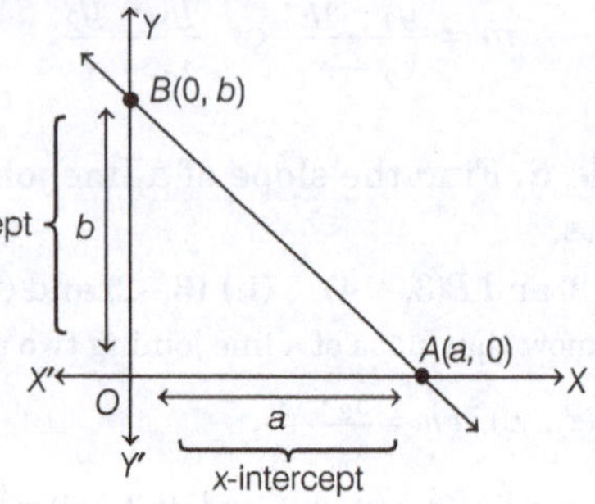

Convention for the Signs of Intercepts

(i) We considered x-intercept as positive, if it is measured to the right of origin; and negative, if it is measured to the left of origin.

(ii) We considered y-intercept as positive, if it is measured above the origin; and negative, if it is measured below the origin.

Example 7. Find the intercepts made by a line passing through the following points.

(i) $A(2, 0)$ and $B(0, 3)$

(ii) $P(5, 0)$ and $Q(0, -3)$

Sol.

(i) Given, points are $A(2, 0)$ and $B(0, 3)$.

In coordinates $A(2, 0)$, x-coordinate is $+2$ and y-coordinate is 0, so x-intercept is 2. In coordinates $B(0, 3)$, x-coordinate is 0 and y-coordinate is $+3$, so y-intercept is 3.

Hence, the intercepts made by a line passing through A and B are 2 and 3, respectively.

(ii) Given, points are $P(5, 0)$ and $Q(0, -3)$.

In coordinates $P(5, 0)$, x-coordinate is $+5$ and y-coordinate is 0, so x-intercept is 5. In coordinates $Q(0, -3)$, x-coordinate is 0 and y-coordinate is -3, so y-intercept is -3.

Hence, the intercepts made by a line passing through P and Q are 5 and -3, respectively.

Equation of a Straight Line in Different Forms

The different forms of the equation of a line under different conditions are given below

Equation of a Line Parallel to X-axis

Line parallel to X–axis is also called as **horizontal line.** If a line L is parallel to X–axis at a distance of a units from the X–axis, then ordinate of every point lying on the line is either a or $-a$.

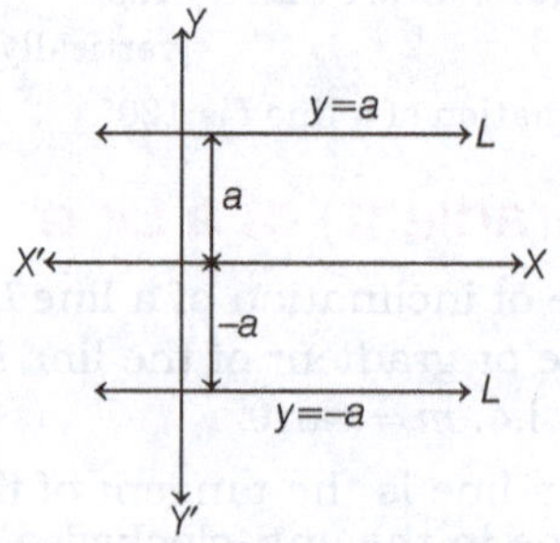

$\therefore$ **Equation of a line L is either $y = a$ or $y = -a$.**

Example 8. Find the equation of a straight line parallel to X-axis and passing through the point $(3, -5)$.

Sol. Let the equation of a line parallel to X-axis is

$$y = a \quad \text{...(i)}$$

Since, it is passing through a point $(3, -5)$.

$\therefore$ $-5 = a$

$\Rightarrow$ $a = -5$

On putting $a = -5$ in Eq. (i), we get

$$y = -5$$

Hence, the required equation of a straight line is $y + 5 = 0$.

Equation of a Line Parallel to Y-axis

Line parallel to Y-axis is also called as **vertical line.** If a line L is parallel to Y-axis at a distance of b units from the Y-axis, then abscissa of every point lying on this line is either b or $-b$.

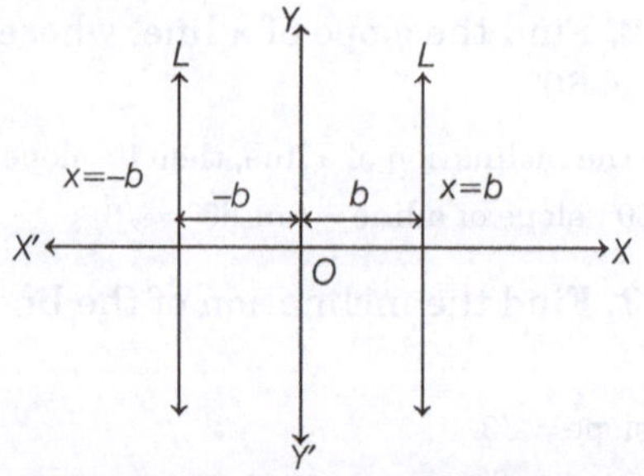

$\therefore$ **Equation of a line L is either $x = b$ or $x = -b$.**

Note (i) Equation of X-axis is $y = 0$. (ii) Equation of Y-axis is $x = 0$.

Example 9. Find the equation of a straight line parallel to Y-axis and passing through the point $(-4, 7)$.

Sol. Let the equation of a line parallel to Y-axis is

$$x = b \quad \text{...(i)}$$

Since, it is passing through a point $(-4, 7)$.

$\therefore \quad -4 = b$

Now, putting $b = -4$ in Eq. (i), we get $x = -4$

Hence, the required equation of line parallel to Y-axis is $x + 4 = 0$.

Equation of a Line in Slope-Intercept Form

Suppose, the line L with slope m, makes an intercept c on Y-axis, i.e. the line L with the slope m passes through the point $(0, c)$. Then, the equation of the line L is given by

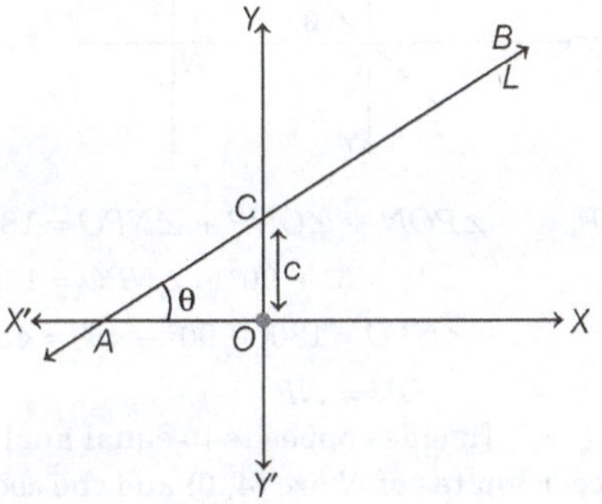

$$\boxed{y = mx + c}$$

Geometrical Understanding of c As per the equation $y = mx + c$, the constant c is called the y-intercept. It is the ordinate of the point, where the line intercepts the Y-axis. Also, it is the point on the line where $x = 0$.

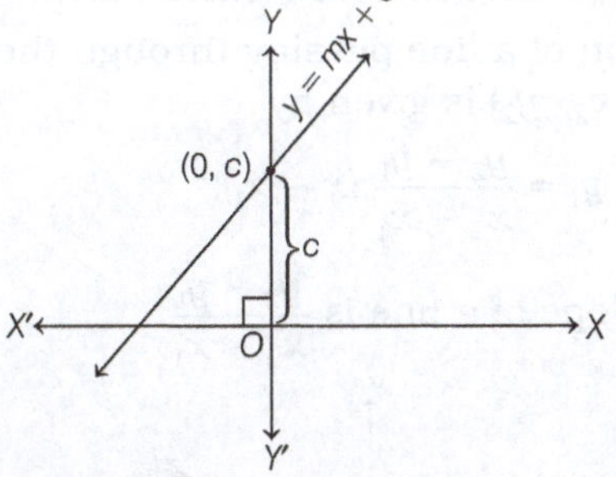

(i) If the line passes through the origin, then $0 = m(0) + c \Rightarrow c = 0$.

Thus, the equation of line passing through the origin is $y = mx$, where m is the slope of the line.

(ii) If the line is parallel to X-axis, then $m = 0$.

Therefore, the equation of a line parallel to X-axis is $y = c$.

Example 10. Find the equation of a line, whose inclination is 30° and y-intercept is 2.

Sol. Given, inclination, $\theta = 30°$ and y-intercept, $c = 2$

Now, slope of a line, $m = \tan\theta = \tan 30° = \frac{1}{\sqrt{3}}$ $\quad [\because \theta = 30°]$

$\therefore$ The equation of line having slope $m = \frac{1}{\sqrt{3}}$ and y-intercept $c = 2$ is $y = mx + c$

$$\Rightarrow \quad y = \frac{1}{\sqrt{3}}x + 2 \Rightarrow \sqrt{3}\,y = x + 2\sqrt{3}$$

which is the required equation of a line.

Example 11. Find the equation of the line through $(1, 3)$ and making an intercept of 5 on the Y-axis.

Sol. Since, y-intercept of the line, $c = 5$, therefore its equation is

$$y = mx + 5 \quad [\because y = mx + c] \text{ ...(i)}$$

where, m is unknown constant.

As the line (i) passes through the point $(1, 3)$, we get

$$3 = m \cdot 1 + 5 \Rightarrow m = -2$$

On substituting $m = -2$ in Eq. (i), we get

$$y = -2x + 5,$$

which is the required equation.

Example 12. Find the slope and y-intercept of the lines $\frac{x}{4} + \frac{y}{5} = 1$.

Sol. Given, equation of the line is $\frac{x}{4} + \frac{y}{5} = 1$

It can be rewritten as $\frac{y}{5} = 1 - \frac{x}{4} \Rightarrow y = -\frac{5x}{4} + 5$ $\quad$ ...(i)

On comparing Eq. (i) with $y = mx + c$, we get

$$m = -5/4 \text{ and } c = 5$$

Hence, the slope of a line is $-5/4$ and y-intercept is 5.

Example 13. The equation of a line is $4x - 3y + 12 = 0$. It meets the X-axis at point A and the Y-axis at point B. Find

(i) the coordinates of points A and B;

(ii) the length of intercept AB, cut by the line within the coordinate axes.

Sol.

(i) For A (the point on the X-axis); the value of $y = 0$

$\therefore \quad 4x - 3y + 12 = 0 \Rightarrow 4x - 3 \times 0 + 12 = 0$

$$x = -3 \text{ and } A(-3, 0)$$

and for B (the points on the Y-axis); the value of $x = 0$.

$\therefore \quad 4x - 3y + 12 = 0 \Rightarrow 4 \times 0 - 3y + 12 = 0$

$$y = 4 \text{ and } B(0, 4)$$

(ii) Let $A(-3, 0) = (x_1, y_1)$ and $B(0, 4) = (x_2, y_2)$

$\therefore \quad AB = \sqrt{(x_2 - x_1)^2 + (y_2 - y_1)^2}$

$= \sqrt{(0 + 3)^2 + (4 - 0)^2}$

$= \sqrt{25} = 5$ units

Equation of a Line in Point-Slope Form

The equation of a straight line having slope m and passes through the point $Q(x_1, y_1)$ is given by

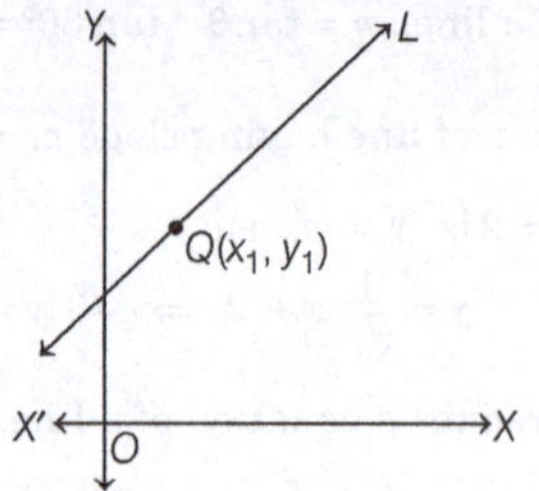

$$y - y_1 = m(x - x_1)$$

Example 14. Find the equation of the line passing through the point (3, 8) and having slope 2.

Sol. We know that equation of line passing through the point (x_1, y_1) and having slope m is given by

$$y - y_1 = m(x - x_1)$$

$\therefore$ Equation of line passing through the point (3, 8) and having slope 2 is

$$y - 8 = 2(x - 3)$$

$[\because m = 2, (x_1, y_1) = (3, 8)]$

$\Rightarrow \quad y - 8 = 2x - 6$

$\Rightarrow \quad 2x - y + 2 = 0$

which is the required equation.

Example 15. Find the equation of a straight line with slope -3 and which intersect X-axis at a distance of 5 units to the left of origin.

Sol. Given, slope of the line, $m = -3$

Since, the line intersect X-axis at a distance of 5 units to the left of origin, it passes through the point $(-5, 0)$.

So, clearly, the equation of the line passing through the point $(-5, 0)$ and with slope -3 is $y - 0 = -3(x - (-5))$

$\Rightarrow \quad y = -3x + (-15)$

$\Rightarrow \quad y + 3x + 15 = 0$

Example 16. Given, equation of line L_1 is $y = 4$.

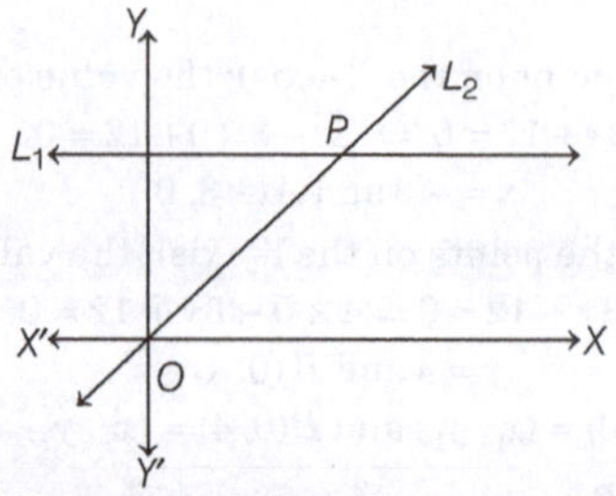

(i) Write the slope of line L_2, if L_2 is bisector of $\angle O$.

(ii) Write the coordinates of point P.

(iii) Find the equation of L_2. [ICSE 2011]

Sol.

(i) Given, L_2 is the bisector of $\angle O$.

Since, $\angle XOY = 90°$

$\therefore \quad \angle POX = \angle POY$

$$= \frac{90°}{2} = 45° = \theta \text{ (say)}$$

Now, slope of $L_2 = \tan 45° = 1$ $[\because \theta = 45°]$

(ii) Let line L_1 intersects Y-axis at M. Through P, draw a line parallel to Y-axis which intersect X-axis at N.

Then, clearly $PN = OM = 4$

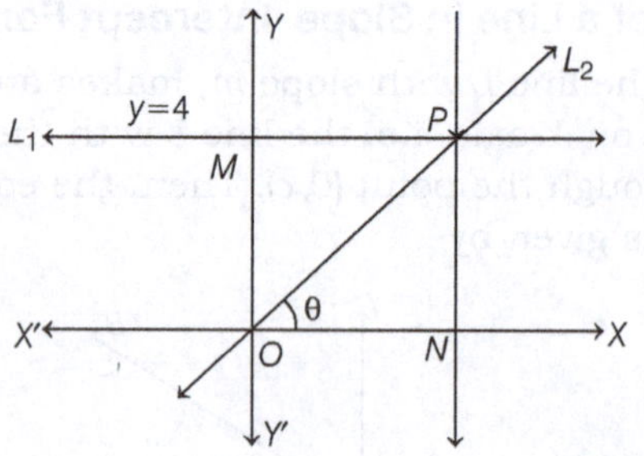

In ΔONP, $\angle PON + \angle ONP + \angle NPO = 180°$

$\Rightarrow \quad 45° + 90° + \angle NPO = 180°$

$\Rightarrow \quad \angle NPO = 180° - 90° - 45° = 45°$

$\Rightarrow \quad ON = NP$

[$\because$ sides opposite to equal angles are equal]

So, the coordinates of N are (4, 0) and the coordinates of M are (0, 4).

Hence, the coordinates of P are (4, 4).

(iii) Equation of line L_2, which is passing through origin (0, 0) and having slope 1, is

$$y - 0 = 1(x - 0) \quad [\because y - y_1 = m(x - x_1)]$$

$\Rightarrow \quad y = x$

Hence, the required equation of L_2 is $y = x$.

Equation of a Line in Two Points Form

The equation of a line passing through the points (x_1, y_1) and (x_2, y_2) is given by

$$y - y_1 = \frac{y_2 - y_1}{x_2 - x_1}(x - x_1).$$

Here, the slope of a line is $\dfrac{y_2 - y_1}{x_2 - x_1}$.

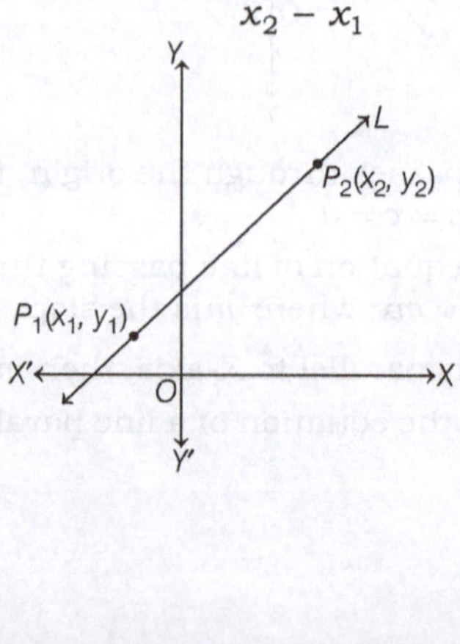

Example 17. Find the equation of line, which is passing through the points (1, 1) and (2, 4).

Sol. We know that equation of a line passing through the two points (x_1, y_1) and (x_2, y_2) is given by

$$y - y_1 = \frac{y_2 - y_1}{x_2 - x_1}(x - x_1)$$

Here, $(x_1, y_1) = (1, 1)$ and $(x_2, y_2) = (2, 4)$

$\therefore$ Equation of a line is $y - 1 = \frac{4-1}{2-1}(x-1)$

$\Rightarrow \quad y - 1 = 3(x-1) \Rightarrow 3x - y - 2 = 0$

Example 18. Find the equation of the line passing through the point (0, – 4) and the point of intersection of the lines $3x + 4y = 1$ and $-3x + 4y = -9$.

Sol. The given lines are $3x + 4y = 1$ ...(i)

and $-3x + 4y = -9$ ...(ii)

We solve these equations, simultaneously.

Add Eqs. (i) and (ii), we get

$$y = -1 \text{ and } x = \frac{5}{3}$$

$\therefore$ The point of intersection of the given lines is $\left(\frac{5}{3}, -1\right)$.

The slope of the line passing the points $\left(\frac{5}{3}, -1\right)$ and (0, – 4)

$$= \frac{-4-(-1)}{0-\frac{5}{3}} \qquad \left[\because m = \frac{y_2 - y_1}{x_2 - x_1}\right]$$

$$= \frac{-3\times 3}{-5} = \frac{9}{5}$$

The equation of the line passing through (0, – 4) and with slope $\frac{9}{5}$.

$\Rightarrow \quad y - (-4) = \frac{9}{5}(x - 0) \Rightarrow 5y + 20 = 9x$

$\therefore \quad 9x - 5y - 20 = 0$

Example 19. *ABC* is a triangle whose vertices are $A(1, -1)$, $B(0, 4)$ and $C(-6, 4)$. *D* is the mid-point of *BC*. Find the **[ICSE 2023]**

(i) coordinates of *D*.

(ii) equation of the median *AD*.

Sol. Given, vertices are $A(1, -1)$, $B(0, 4)$ and $C(-6, 4)$.

(i) Mid-point of $BC = \left(\frac{0-6}{2}, \frac{4+4}{2}\right) = (-3, 4)$

$\Rightarrow$ Coordinates of *D* are (– 3, 4).

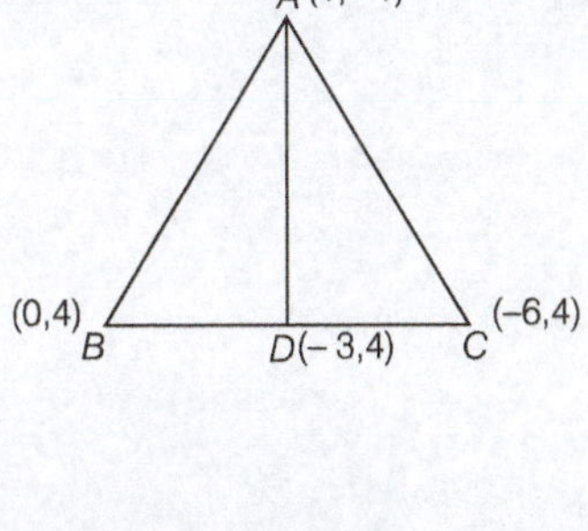

(ii) Equation of the median *AD*

$\therefore$ Equation of the line passing through two points $A(1, -1)$ and $D(-3, 4)$.

$$\frac{y - y_1}{y_2 - y_1} = \frac{(x - x_1)}{(x_2 - x_1)}$$

$\Rightarrow \quad \frac{y-(-1)}{4-(-1)} = \frac{x-1}{-3-(1)} \Rightarrow \frac{y+1}{5} = \frac{x-1}{-4}$

$\Rightarrow \quad -4y - 4 = 5x - 5 \Rightarrow 5x + 4y = 1$

Hence, equation of median *AD* is $5x + 4y = 1$

Example 20. Three vertices of a parallelogram *ABCD* taken in order are *A*(3, 6), *B*(5, 10) and *C*(3, 2). Find

(i) the coordinates of the fourth vertex *D*.

(ii) the length of diagonal *BD*.

(iii) the equation of side *AB* of the parallelogram *ABCD*. **[ICSE 2015]**

Sol.

(i) Let the coordinates of vertex *D* be (x, y).

Since, *ABCD* is a parallelogram and we know that diagonals bisect each other in a parallelogram. So, the mid-point of *AC* and mid-point of *BD* are same.

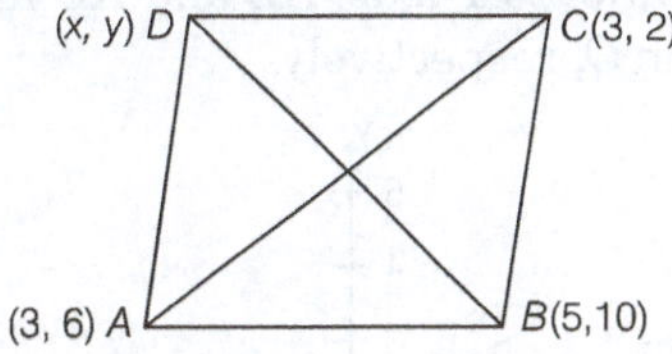

Now, the mid-point of $AC = \left(\frac{3+3}{2}, \frac{6+2}{2}\right) = (3, 4)$

and the mid-point of $BD = \left(\frac{5+x}{2}, \frac{10+y}{2}\right)$

$\therefore \quad \left(\frac{5+x}{2}, \frac{10+y}{2}\right) = (3, 4)$

On comparing both sides, we get

$$\frac{5+x}{2} = 3 \text{ and } \frac{10+y}{2} = 4 \Rightarrow 5 + x = 6 \text{ and } 10 + y = 8$$

$\therefore \quad x = 1$ and $y = -2$

Hence, the coordinates of *D* are (1, – 2).

(ii) Length of diagonal $BD = \sqrt{(x_2 - x_1)^2 + (y_2 - y_1)^2}$ [by distance formula]

$= \sqrt{(5-1)^2 + (10+2)^2}$ $[\because x_1 = 1, x_2 = 5, y_1 = -2 \text{ and } y_2 = 10]$

$= \sqrt{(4)^2 + (12)^2} = \sqrt{16 + 144}$

$= \sqrt{160} = 4\sqrt{10}$ units

(iii) Equation of side *AB* having points $(x_1, y_1) = (3, 6)$ and $(x_2, y_2) = (5, 10)$ is given by

$$y - y_1 = \frac{y_2 - y_1}{x_2 - x_1}(x - x_1)$$

$\therefore \quad y - 6 = \frac{10-6}{5-3}(x-3) \Rightarrow y - 6 = \frac{4}{2}(x-3)$

$\Rightarrow \quad y - 6 = 2(x-3) \Rightarrow y - 6 = 2x - 6 \Rightarrow 2x - y = 0$

Example 21. The vertices of a ΔABC are $A(3, 8)$, $B(-1, 2)$ and $C(6, -6)$. Find the

(i) slope of BC.

(ii) equation of a line perpendicular to BC and passing through A. **[ICSE 2019]**

Sol. Given, vertices of a ΔABC are

$A(3, 8)$, $B(-1, 2)$ and $C(6, -6)$.

(i) Now, slope of BC, $m = \dfrac{y_2 - y_1}{x_2 - x_1}$

$$= \frac{-6-2}{6-(-1)} = \frac{-8}{7}$$

(ii) Now, equation of a line passing through $A(3, 8)$ and perpendicular to BC is

$$y - 8 = -\frac{1}{m}(x-3)$$

$$\Rightarrow \quad y - 8 = +\frac{7}{8}(x-3)$$

$$\Rightarrow \quad 8y - 64 = 7x - 21$$

$$\Rightarrow \quad 7x - 8y + 43 = 0$$

Example 22. In the given figure, ABC is a triangle and BC is parallel to Y-axis. AB and AC intersect the Y-axis at P and Q, respectively.

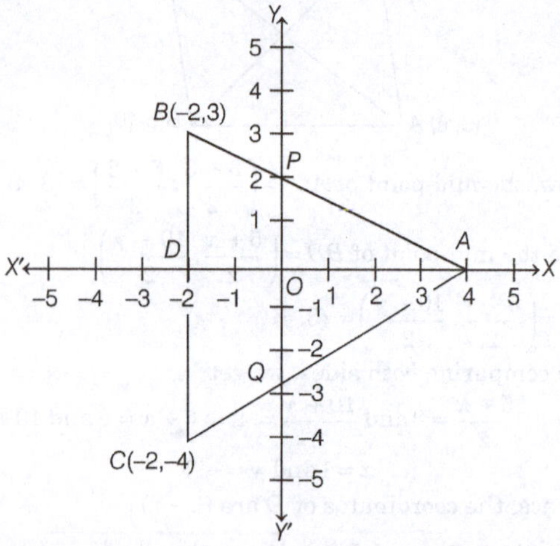

(i) Write the coordinates of A.

(ii) Find the length of AB and AC.

(iii) Find the ratio, in which Q divides AC.

(iv) Find the equation of the line AC. **[ICSE 2015]**

Sol. Given, points are $B(-2, 3)$ and $C(-2, -4)$.

(i) Coordinates of $A = (4, 0)$ [from figure]

(ii) Length of $AB = \sqrt{(x_2 - x_1)^2 + (y_2 - y_1)^2}$ [by distance formula]

$$= \sqrt{(-2-4)^2 + (3-0)^2}$$

$$= \sqrt{(-6)^2 + (3)^2}$$

$$= \sqrt{36+9}$$

$$= \sqrt{45} \text{ units}$$

Length of $AC = \sqrt{(-2-4)^2 + (-4-0)^2}$

$$= \sqrt{(-6)^2 + (-4)^2}$$

$$= \sqrt{36+16}$$

$$= \sqrt{52} \text{ units}$$

(iii) Let Q divides AC in $\lambda : 1$.

Using section formula,

$$\text{Coordinates of } Q = \left(\frac{-2\lambda + 4}{\lambda + 1}, \frac{-4\lambda + 0}{\lambda + 1}\right)$$

$$= \left(\frac{4 - 2\lambda}{\lambda + 1}, \frac{-4\lambda}{\lambda + 1}\right)$$

Since, Q lies on Y-axis, therefore x-coordinate will be 0.

$$\therefore \quad \frac{4 - 2\lambda}{\lambda + 1} = 0$$

$$\Rightarrow \quad 2\lambda = 4$$

$$\Rightarrow \quad \lambda = 2$$

So, $\lambda : 1 = 2 : 1$

Hence, the required ratio is $2 : 1$.

(iv) Equation of AC having points $A(4, 0)$ and $C(-2, -4)$, is given by

$$(y - y_1) = \frac{y_2 - y_1}{x_2 - x_1}(x - x_1)$$

$$\Rightarrow \quad y - 0 = \frac{-4-0}{-2-4}(x-4)$$

$$\Rightarrow \quad y = \frac{2}{3}(x-4)$$

$$\Rightarrow \quad 3y = 2x - 8$$

$$\Rightarrow \quad 2x - 3y - 8 = 0$$

Exercise 12.1

1. Find the inclination of a line l in the following figure.

(i)

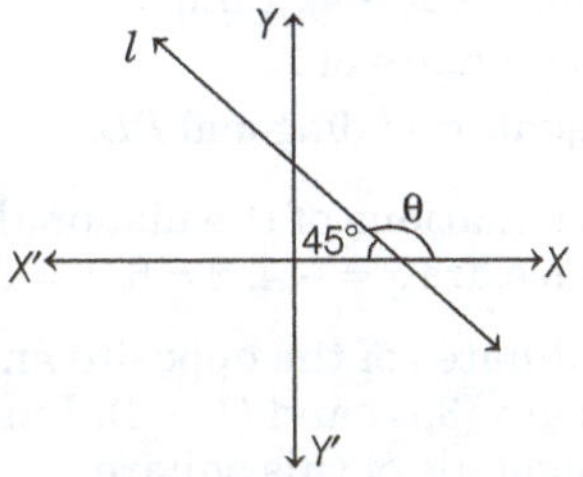

(ii)

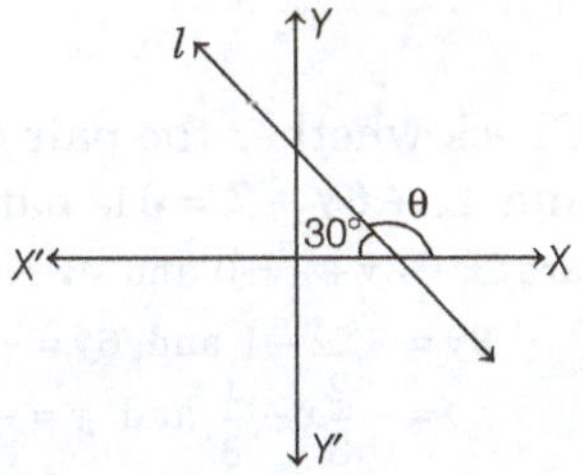

(iii)

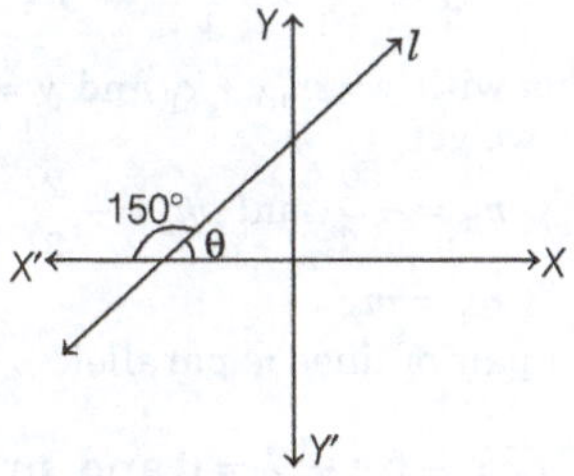

(iv)

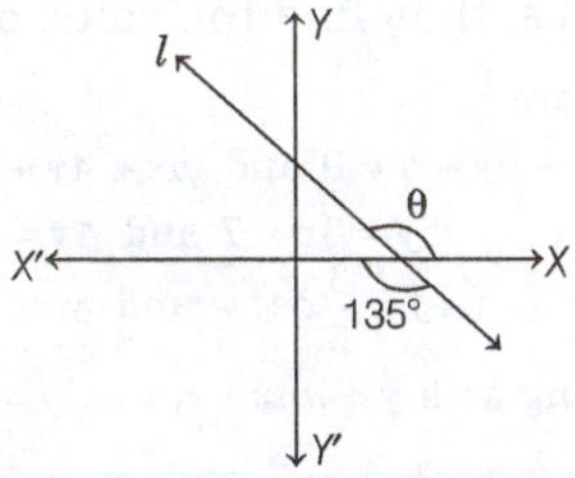

2. Find the slope of line, whose inclination is
   (i) 0° (ii) 90° (iii) 30°
3. A line whose gradient is 1.28. Find the inclination of a line. (Given, $\tan 52° = 1.28$)
4. Find the slope of the line which passes through the points $A(4, -6)$ and $B(-2, -5)$.
5. Determine x so that 2 is the slope of the line joining points (2, 5) and (x, 3).
6. Find the intercept made by a line passing through the following points.
   (i) $A(3, 0)$ and $B(0, 3)$
   (ii) $P(-2, 0)$ and $P(0, -3)$
   (iii) $A(-5, 0)$ and $B(1, 0)$
7. Find the value of P, given that the line $y = 2x - P$ passes through the point $(-3, 3)$.
8. Find the equation of a straight line parallel to X-axis and passing through the point $(-2, 7)$.
9. Find the equation of the line parallel to the Y-axis and 3 units to the right of it.
10. Find the equation of a line, which is equidistant from the lines $x = -6$ and $x = 12$.
11. Find the equation of a straight line whose inclination is 60° and y-intercept is -3.
12. Find the equation of a line, whose gradient is $1/\sqrt{3}$ and y-intercept is 3.
13. Find the equation of the line whose x-intercept is 6 and y-intercept is -8.
14. Find the equation of a line passing through the point $(3, -1)$ and making an intercept of -4 on Y-axis.
15. Find the slope and y-intercept of the following lines.
    (i) $4x - 5y - 6 = 0$ (ii) $\frac{x}{2} + \frac{y}{7} = 1$
16. The equation of a line AB is $4y - 4x + 8 = 0$.
    (i) Write down the slope of the line AB.
    (ii) Calculate the angle that the line AB makes with the positive direction of X-axis.
17. The line passes through the point $P(5, 3)$ and intersects Y-axis at Q.

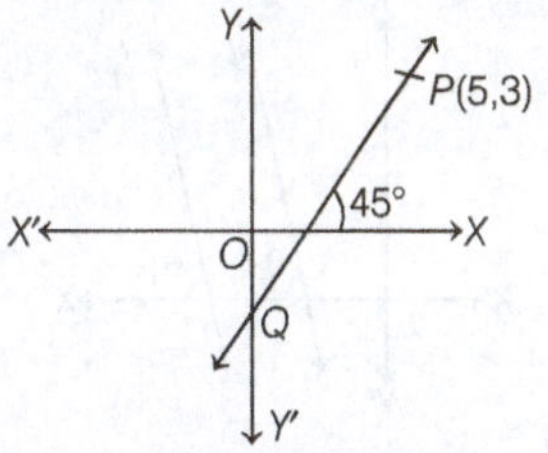

    (i) Write the slope of the line.
    (ii) Write the equation of the line.
    (iii) Find the coordinates of Q. **[ICSE 2012]**
18. Find the equation of the line passing through the point (2, 3) and having slope 3.
19. Find the equation of a line passing through (4, 8) and equally inclined to the coordinate axes in the first quadrant.
20. A line passes through the point $P(1, 2)$ and cuts of positive intercepts, on the X-axis and Y-axis in the ratio 3 : 5. Find the equation of the line.

21. Find the equation of a line passing through the point (2, 4) and intersecting the line $2x + 3y + 6 = 0$ on the X-axis.
22. In ΔABC, if $A(3,5)$, $B(7,8)$ and $C(1,-10)$, then find the equation of the median through A. **[ICSE 2013]**
23. Suppose, $P(3, 4)$, $Q(7, -2)$ and $R(-2, -1)$ are the vertices of ΔPQR. Write down the equation of the median of the triangle through R. **[ICSE 2004]**
24. $OABC$ is a square, O is the origin and the points A and B are (4, 0) and (p, q). If $OABC$ lies in the first quadrant, find the values of p and q. Also, write down the equations of AB and BC.
25. If two opposite vertices of a square are (1, 2) and (5, 8). Find the coordinates of its other two vertices and the equations of its sides.
26. $ABCD$ is a parallelogram, where $A(x, y)$, $B(5, 8)$, $C(4, 7)$ and $D(2, -4)$. Find
    (i) the coordinates of A.
    (ii) the equation of diagonal BD. **[ICSE 2011]**
27. Find the equations of the diagonals of a rectangle whose sides are $x = -4$, $x = 6$, $y = 2$ and $y = -6$.
28. The coordinates of the opposite angular points of a square are (3, 4) and (1, − 1). Find the equations of the diagonals of this square.

Conditions for Two Lines to be Parallel and Perpendicular

Conditions for Two Lines to be Parallel

Two (non-vertical) lines are parallel, if and only if (iff) their slopes are equal.

Proof Let l_1, l_2 be two (non-vertical) lines; m_1, m_2 be their slopes and θ_1, θ_2 be the inclinations of these lines.

(i) First, consider lines l_1 and l_2 are parallel. Then, their corresponding angles are equal.

i.e. $\theta_1 = \theta_2$

On taking tangent both sides, we get

$\tan\theta_1 = \tan\theta_2$

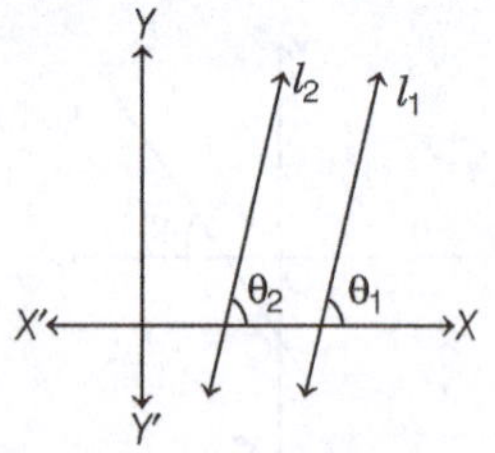

$\Rightarrow \quad m_1 = m_2 \quad [\because m_1 = \tan\theta_1 \text{ and } m_2 = \tan\theta_2]$

Thus, if **two lines are parallel, then their slopes are equal.**

(ii) Second, consider lines l_1 and l_2 have equal slopes,

i.e. $m_1 = m_2 \Rightarrow \tan\theta_1 = \tan\theta_2 \Rightarrow \theta_1 = \theta_2$ [converse of part (i)]

Thus, lines l_1 and l_2 are parallel.

Hence, two lines are parallel, if and only if their slopes are equal (i.e. $m_1 = m_2$).

Note The slope of every horizontal line is same and it is equal to zero.

Example 23. Check whether the pair of lines $2x + 3y + 1 = 0$ and $4x + 6y + 7 = 0$ is parallel or not.

Sol. Given lines are $2x + 3y + 1 = 0$ and $4x + 6y + 7 = 0$

$$\Rightarrow \quad 3y = -2x - 1 \text{ and } 6y = -4x - 7$$

$$\Rightarrow \quad y = -\frac{2}{3}x - \frac{1}{3} \text{ and } y = -\frac{4}{6}x - \frac{7}{6}$$

$$\Rightarrow \quad y = -\frac{2}{3}x - \frac{1}{3} \text{ and } y = -\frac{2}{3}x - \frac{7}{6}$$

On comparing with $y = m_1x + c_1$ and $y = m_2x + c_2$ respectively, we get

$$m_1 = -\frac{2}{3} \text{ and } m_2 = -\frac{2}{3}$$

$$\because \quad m_1 = m_2$$

Hence, given pair of lines is parallel.

Example 24. If $3x - 5y + 7 = 0$ and $px + 4y + 6 = 0$ are parallel lines, then find the value of p.

Sol. Given lines are

$$3x - 5y + 7 = 0 \text{ and } px + 4y + 6 = 0$$

$$\Rightarrow \quad 5y = 3x + 7 \text{ and } 4y = -px - 6$$

$$\Rightarrow \quad y = \frac{3}{5}x + \frac{7}{5} \text{ and } y = -\frac{p}{4}x - \frac{6}{4}$$

On comparing with $y = m_1x + c_1$ and $y = m_2x + c_2$ respectively, we get $m_1 = \frac{3}{5}$ and $m_2 = -\frac{p}{4}$

Since, the lines are parallel.

$$\therefore \quad m_1 = m_2 \Rightarrow \frac{3}{5} = -\frac{p}{4} \Rightarrow p = \frac{-4 \times 3}{5} = -\frac{12}{5}$$

Example 25. Find the equation of the line through the point $P(-5, 1)$ and parallel to the line joining the points $A(7, -1)$ and $B(0, 3)$.

Sol. Slope of the line joining the points $A(7, -1)$ and $B(0, 3)$ is

$$m_1 = \frac{3-(-1)}{0-7} = -\frac{4}{7} \quad \left[\because m = \frac{y_2 - y_1}{x_2 - x_1}\right] \quad \ldots\text{(i)}$$

$\therefore$ Slope of a line parallel to line $AB = -\frac{4}{7}$ $[\because m_1 = m_2]$

Now, the equation of line passing through $P(-5,1)$ and having slope $-\frac{4}{7}$, is

$$y-1=-\frac{4}{7}(x-(-5)) \quad [\because y-y_1=m(x-x_1)]$$

$$\Rightarrow \quad 7y-7=-4x-20 \Rightarrow 4x+7y+13=0$$

Example 26. $A(-1, 3)$, $B(4, 2)$ and $C(3, -2)$ are the vertices of a triangle.

(i) Find the coordinates of the centroid G of the triangle.

(ii) Find the equation of the line through G and parallel to AC. **[ICSE 2017]**

Sol. Given, $A(-1, 3)$, $B(4, 2)$ and $C(3, -2)$ are the vertices of the triangle.

(i) We know that coordinates of centroid of a triangle, whose vertices are (x_1, y_1), (x_2, y_2) and (x_3, y_3), is given by $\left(\frac{x_1+x_2+x_3}{3}, \frac{y_1+y_2+y_3}{3}\right)$.

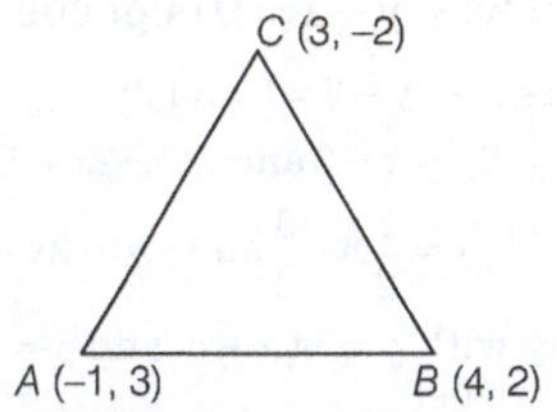

$\therefore$ Coordinates of centroid G of

$$\Delta ABC=\left(\frac{-1+3+4}{3}, \frac{3-2+2}{3}\right)=(2, 1)$$

(ii) We know that the slope of line passing through points (x_1, y_1) and (x_2, y_2) is given by $m=\frac{y_2-y_1}{x_2-x_1}$

$\therefore$ Slope of line $AC=\frac{-2-3}{3-(-1)}=-\frac{5}{4}$

We know that slope of parallel lines are equal.

$\therefore$ Slope of line parallel to $AC=-\frac{5}{4}$

Now, equation of the line through $G(2, 1)$ and parallel to AC is

$$y-1=-\frac{5}{4}(x-2)$$

[$\because$ equation of line passing through (x_1, y_1) having slope m is $y-y_1=m(x-x_1)$]

$$\Rightarrow \quad 4y-4=-5x+10 \Rightarrow 5x+4y-14=0$$

Collinearity of Three Points in a Plane

Three points are said to be collinear, if they lie on a straight line.

Suppose, A, B and C are three points in a plane, then these three points are said to be collinear, if and only if AB is

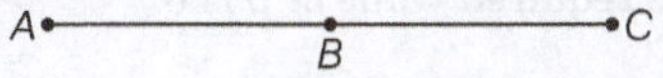

parallel to BC, i.e. slope (Gradient) of AB = slope (Gradient) of BC

Example 27. Show that the points $A(-6, -1)$, $B(0, 2)$ and $C(8, 6)$ are collinear.

Sol. Given points are $A(-6, -1)$, $B(0, 2)$ and $C(8, 6)$.

Now, slope of AB is $m_1=\frac{2+1}{0+6}=\frac{3}{6}=\frac{1}{2}$

and slope of BC is

$$m_2=\frac{6-2}{8-0}=\frac{4}{8}=\frac{1}{2} \quad \left[\because \text{slope of a line}=\frac{y_2-y_1}{x_2-x_1}\right]$$

Here, $m_1=m_2$ and B is common point.

Hence, points A, B and C are collinear.

Example 28. The points $P(2,3)$, $Q(0,-5)$ and $R(-2,k)$ are collinear, then find the value of k.

Sol. Given, $P(2,3)$, $Q(0,-5)$ and $R(-2,k)$ are collinear points.

$\therefore$ Slope of PQ = Slope of QR

$$\Rightarrow \quad \frac{-5-3}{0-2}=\frac{k+5}{-2-0} \quad \left[\because \text{slope of the line}=\frac{y_2-y_1}{x_2-x_1}\right]$$

$$\Rightarrow \quad \frac{-8}{-2}=\frac{k+5}{-2}$$

$$\Rightarrow \quad 4=\frac{k+5}{-2}$$

$$\Rightarrow \quad -8=k+5$$

$$\Rightarrow \quad k=-8-5=-13$$

Hence, the required value of k is -13.

Example 29. Find the value of a, for which the points $A(a, 3)$, $B(2, 1)$ and $C(5, a)$ are collinear. Also, find the equation of the line. **[ICSE 2014]**

Sol. Given, points $A(a, 3)$, $B(2, 1)$ and $C(5, a)$ are collinear.

$\therefore$ Slope of AB = Slope of BC

$$\Rightarrow \quad \frac{1-3}{2-a}=\frac{a-1}{5-2} \quad \left[\because \text{slope}=\frac{y_2-y_1}{x_2-x_1}\right]$$

$$\Rightarrow \quad \frac{-2}{2-a}=\frac{a-1}{3}$$

$$\Rightarrow \quad -2\times 3=(a-1)(2-a)$$

$$\Rightarrow \quad -6=2a-a^2-2+a$$

$$\Rightarrow \quad a^2-3a-4=0$$

$$\Rightarrow \quad a^2-4a+a-4=0 \quad \text{[splitting the middle term]}$$

$$\Rightarrow \quad a(a-4)+1(a-4)=0 \Rightarrow (a+1)(a-4)=0$$

$$\therefore \quad a=-1, 4$$

Now, the given points become $A(-1, 3)$, $B(2, 1)$ and $C(5, -1)$ or $A(4, 3)$, $B(2, 1)$ and $C(5, 4)$.

Now, we have to find equation of a line.

***Case I* When collinear points are $A(-1, 3)$, $B(2, 1)$ and $C(5, -1)$.**

Then, the equation of a line passing through the points $A(-1, 3)$ and $B(2, 1)$ is given by

$$y-y_1=\frac{y_2-y_1}{x_2-x_1}(x-x_1)$$

$$\Rightarrow \quad y-3=\frac{1-3}{2+1}(x+1)$$

$$\Rightarrow \quad y - 3 = -\frac{2}{3}(x+1)$$
$$\Rightarrow \quad 3(y-3) = -2(x+1)$$
$$\Rightarrow \quad 3y - 9 = -2x - 2$$
$$\Rightarrow \quad 2x + 3y - 7 = 0$$

***Case* II When collinear points are A (4, 3), B (2, 1) and C (5, 4).**

Then, the equation of a line passing through the points $A(4, 3)$ and B (2, 1) is given by

$$y - y_1 = \frac{y_2 - y_1}{x_2 - x_1}(x - x_1)$$
$$\Rightarrow \quad y - 3 = \frac{1-3}{2-4}(x-4) \Rightarrow y - 3 = \frac{-2}{-2}(x-4)$$
$$\Rightarrow \quad y - 3 = 1(x-4)$$
$$\Rightarrow \quad y - 3 = x - 4 \Rightarrow x - y - 1 = 0$$

Hence, the required equations of the line are

$$2x + 3y - 7 = 0 \text{ and } x - y - 1 = 0.$$

Conditions for Two Lines to be Perpendicular

Two (non–vertical) lines are perpendicular, if and only if (iff) the product of their slopes is –1.

Proof Let l_1, l_2 be two (non–vertical) lines; m_1, m_2 be their slopes and θ_1, θ_2 be the inclinations of these lines.

(i) First, consider lines l_1 and l_2 are perpendicular.

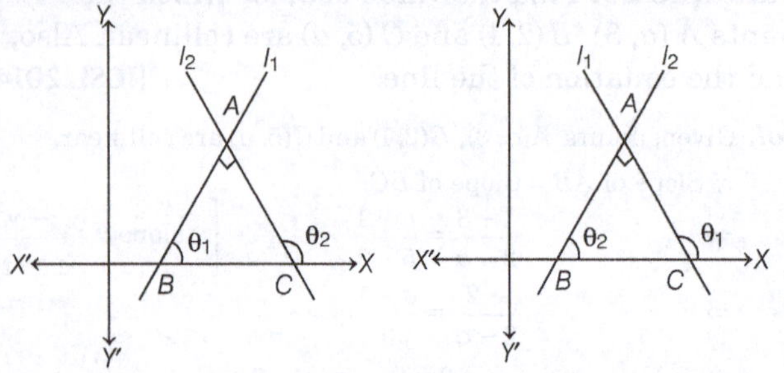

Then, $\theta_2 = \theta_1 + 90°$ or $\theta_1 = 90° + \theta_2$

[$\because$ exterior angle of a ΔABC is equal to the sum of opposite interior angles]

On taking tangent on both sides, we get

$$\tan\theta_2 = \tan(90° + \theta_1)$$
$$\text{or} \quad \tan\theta_1 = \tan(90° + \theta_2)$$
$$\Rightarrow \quad \tan\theta_2 = -\cot\theta_1$$
$$\text{or} \quad \tan\theta_1 = -\cot\theta_2$$
$$\Rightarrow \quad \tan\theta_2 = -\frac{1}{\tan\theta_1}$$
$$\text{or} \quad \tan\theta_1 = -\frac{1}{\tan\theta_2}$$
$$\Rightarrow \quad \tan\theta_1 \tan\theta_2 = -1$$

Therefore, in either cases, $m_1 \cdot m_2 = -1$

(ii) Second, consider the lines l_1 and l_2 such that the product of their slopes is – 1,

i.e. $\quad m_1 \cdot m_2 = -1 \quad$ [converse of part (i)]

$$\Rightarrow \quad \tan\theta_1 \tan\theta_2 = -1$$
$$\Rightarrow \quad \tan\theta_1 = -\frac{1}{\tan\theta_2}$$
$$\Rightarrow \quad \tan\theta_1 = -\cot\theta_2$$
$$\Rightarrow \quad \tan\theta_1 = \tan(90° + \theta_2)$$
$$\Rightarrow \quad \theta_1 = 90° + \theta_2$$

Thus, lines l_1 and l_2 are perpendicular.

Hence, two lines are perpendicular, if and only if product of their slopes is – 1 (i.e. $m_1 \cdot m_2 = -1$).

Note The slope of a perpendicular line is the negative reciprocal of the slope of given line.

Example 30. Check whether the pair of lines $x - 2y - 3 = 0$ and $2x + y - 1 = 0$ is perpendicular or not.

Sol. Given lines are $x - 2y - 3 = 0$ and $2x + y - 1 = 0$

$$\Rightarrow \quad 2y = x - 3 \text{ and } y = -2x + 1$$
$$\Rightarrow \quad y = \frac{1}{2}x - \frac{3}{2} \text{ and } y = -2x + 1$$

On comparing with $y = m_1x + c_1$ and $y = m_2x + c_2$ respectively, we get

$$m_1 = \frac{1}{2} \text{ and } m_2 = -2$$

Now, $\quad m_1 \cdot m_2 = \frac{1}{2} \times (-2) = -1$

Hence, the given pair of lines is perpendicular.

Example 31. Find the value of p, for which the lines $2x + 3y - 7 = 0$ and $4y - px - 12 = 0$ are perpendicular to each other. **[ICSE 2009]**

Sol. Given lines are $2x + 3y - 7 = 0$ and $4y - px - 12 = 0$

$$\Rightarrow \quad 3y = -2x + 7 \text{ and } 4y = px + 12$$
$$\Rightarrow \quad y = -\frac{2}{3}x + \frac{7}{3} \text{ and } y = \frac{p}{4}x + \frac{12}{4}$$

On comparing with equation $y = m_1x + c_1$ and $y = m_2x + c_2$ respectively, we get

$$m_1 = -\frac{2}{3} \text{ and } m_2 = \frac{p}{4}$$

Since, the given lines are perpendicular to each other.

$$\therefore \quad m_1 \cdot m_2 = -1$$
$$\Rightarrow \quad -\frac{2}{3} \times \frac{p}{4} = -1$$
$$\Rightarrow \quad p = \frac{3 \times 4}{2} = 3 \times 2$$
$$\Rightarrow \quad p = 6$$

Hence, the required value of p is 6.

Example 32. Find the equation of the perpendicular from the point $A(-1, -3)$ on the line $3x + 4y - 12 = 0$. Also, find the coordinates of the foot of perpendicular.

Sol. The given line is $3x + 4y - 12 = 0$ ...(i)

$\Rightarrow \quad 4y = -3x + 12 \Rightarrow y = -\frac{3}{4}x + 3$

$\therefore$ The slope of the line (i) $= -\frac{3}{4}$

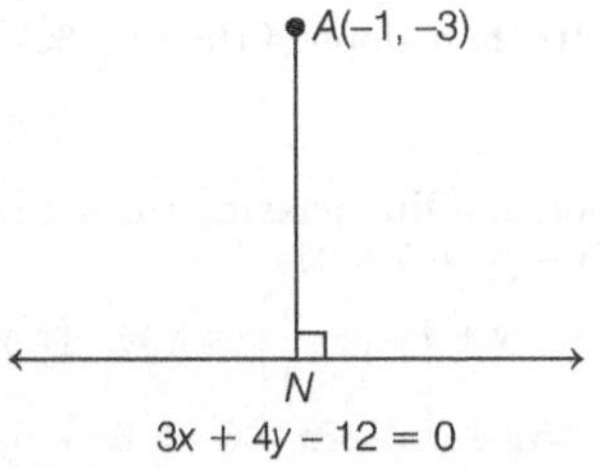

From $A(-1, -3)$, draw AN perpendicular to the given line.

$\therefore$ The slope of the line $AN = \frac{4}{3}$ $\quad \left| m_2 = -\frac{1}{m_1} \right.$

The equation of the line through $A(-1, -3)$ and having slope $\frac{4}{3}$ is $y - (-3) = \frac{4}{3}(x - (-1)) \Rightarrow 3y + 9 = 4x + 4$

$\Rightarrow 4x - 3y - 5 = 0$ ...(ii)

which is the required equation of the perpendicular from A to the given line.

The coordinates of O (the foot of perpendicular), solve Eqs. (i) and (ii) simultaneously.

Multiplying Eq. (i) by 3 and Eq. (ii) by 4 and on adding, we get

$$x = \frac{56}{25} \text{ and } y = \frac{33}{25}$$

Hence, the coordinates of the foot of perpendicular are $\left(\frac{56}{25}, \frac{33}{25}\right)$.

Example 33. Find the equation of a line passing through the intersection of lines $4x + 3y = 1$ and $3x - y + 9 = 0$ and perpendicular to the line $3x - 2y + 5 = 0$.

Sol. Consider the equation, $3x - 2y + 5 = 0$ ...(i)

$\Rightarrow \quad 2y = 3x + 5 \Rightarrow y = \frac{3}{2}x + \frac{5}{2}$

On comparing it with $y = m_1 x + c$, we get $m_1 = \frac{3}{2}$ ...(ii)

Now, the slope (m) of line perpendicular to the line (i) is given by $m = \frac{-1}{m_1} = \frac{-2}{3}$ [using Eq. (ii)]

i.e. the slope of required line $= m = \frac{-2}{3}$. ...(iii)

Now, let us find the intersection point of

$4x + 3y = 1$ ...(iv)

and $\quad 3x - y = -9$ ...(v)

On multiplying Eq. (v) by 3 and adding with Eq. (iv), we get

$9x - 3y + 4x + 3y = -27 + 1$

$\Rightarrow \quad 13x = -26 \Rightarrow x = -2$

On putting $x = -2$ in Eq. (iv), we get

$4(-2) + 3y = 1 \Rightarrow 3y = 1 + 8 = 9 \Rightarrow y = 3$

Thus, the intersection point is $(-2, 3)$.

Hence, the equation of line passing through $(-2, 3)$ and having slope $\frac{-2}{3}$ is $(y - 3) = \frac{-2}{3}(x + 2)$

$\Rightarrow \quad 3y - 9 = -2x - 4$

$\Rightarrow \quad 2x + 3y - 5 = 0$, which is the required equation.

Example 34. A line AB meets X-axis at A and Y-axis at B. $P(4, -1)$ divides AB in the ratio $1 : 2$.

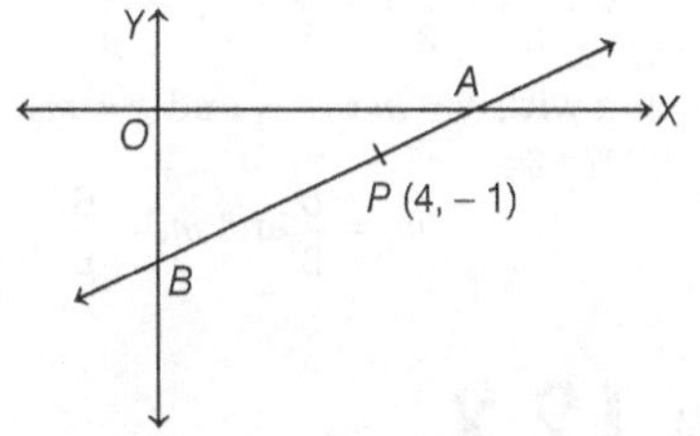

(i) Find the coordinates of A and B.

(ii) Find the equation of the line through P and perpendicular to AB. [ICSE 2016]

Sol.

(i) Let the coordinates of point A lying on X-axis be $(x, 0)$ and the coordinates of point B lying on Y-axis be $(0, y)$.

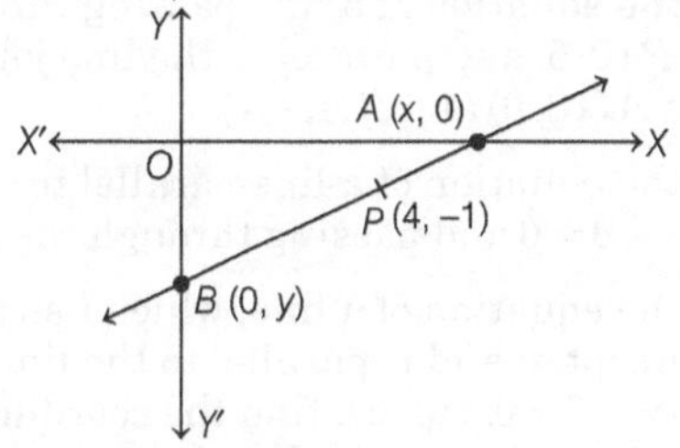

By using section formula,

$4 = \frac{1 \times 0 + 2 \times x}{1 + 2}$ $\quad \left[\because x = \frac{m_1 x_2 + m_2 x_1}{m_1 + m_2}\right]$

$\Rightarrow \quad 4 = \frac{2x}{3} \Rightarrow x = \frac{12}{2} = 6$

and $\quad -1 = \frac{1 \times y + 2 \times 0}{1 + 2}$ $\quad \left[\because y = \frac{m_1 y_2 + m_2 y_1}{m_1 + m_2}\right]$

$\Rightarrow \quad -1 = \frac{y}{3}$

$\Rightarrow \quad y = -3$

Hence, the coordinates of points A and B are $(6, 0)$ and $(0, -3)$, respectively.

(ii) Slope of line $AB = \frac{y_2 - y_1}{x_2 - x_1} = \frac{-3 - 0}{0 - 6} = \frac{1}{2}$

Let m be the slope of desired line, then

$\frac{1}{2} \times m = -1 \Rightarrow m = -2$

[$\because$ both lines are perpendicular to each other, $m_1 m_2 = -1$]

Now, equation of a line passes through $(4, -1)$ having slope -2 is $(y + 1) = -2(x - 4)$ $\quad [\because y - y_1 = m(x - x_1)]$

$\Rightarrow \quad y + 1 = -2x + 8$

$\Rightarrow \quad 2x + y - 7 = 0$

Example 35. Find the value of 'p' if the lines, $5x - 3y + 2 = 0$ and $6x - py + 7 = 0$ are perpendicular to each other. Hence, find the equation of a line passing through $(-2, -1)$ and parallel to $6x - py + 7 = 0$.

Sol. Given, equation of lines are **[ICSE 2020]**

$$5x - 3y + 2 = 0 \text{ and } 6x - py + 7 = 0$$

$$\Rightarrow \quad -3y = -5x - 2 \text{ and } -py = -6x - 7$$

$$\Rightarrow \quad y = \frac{5}{3}x + \frac{2}{3} \text{ and } y = \frac{6}{p}x + \frac{7}{p}$$

On comparing with $y = m_1x + c_1$ and $y = m_2x + c_2$ respectively, we get

$$m_1 = \frac{5}{3} \text{ and } m_2 = \frac{6}{p}$$

Since, given lines are perpendicular.

$\therefore \quad m_1 \times m_2 = -1$

$\Rightarrow \quad \frac{5}{3} \times \frac{6}{p} = -1 \Rightarrow \frac{10}{p} = -1$

$\Rightarrow \quad p = -10$

When $p = -10$, then slope of the line $6x - py + 7 = 0$ is $\frac{6}{-10}$ or $\frac{-3}{5}$.

$\therefore$ The equation of a line passing through $(-2, -1)$ and parallel to $6x - py + 7 = 0$ is

$$y + 1 = \left(-\frac{3}{5}\right)(x + 2) \quad [\because y - y_1 = m(x - x_1)]$$

$$\Rightarrow \quad 5y + 5 = -3x - 6 \Rightarrow 3x + 5y + 11 = 0$$

Exercise 12.2

1. Check whether the pair of lines $7x + y + 3 = 0$ and $14x + 2y + 5 = 0$ is parallel or not.
2. If the lines $3(\alpha - 1)y - 6x = 2$ and $4y - 8x + 10 = 0$ are parallel, then find the value of α.
3. Find the equation of a line passing through the point $P(0, 5)$ and parallel to the line joining the points $A(18, 0)$ and $B(1, -1)$.
4. Find the equation of a line parallel to $x - 2y + 8 = 0$ and passing through the point $(1, 2)$.
5. Find the equation of a line, which has the y-intercept 4; and is parallel to the line $2x - 3y - 7 = 0$. Hence, find the coordinates of the point, where it cuts the X-axis.
6. Find the equation of a straight line passing through the intersection of $2x + 5y - 4 = 0$ with X-axis and parallel to the line $3x - 7y + 8 = 0$.
7. $A(1, 4)$, $B(3, 2)$ and $C(7, 5)$ are the vertices of a ΔABC. Find
   (i) the coordinates of the centroid G of ΔABC.
   (ii) the equation of a line passing through G and parallel to AB. **[ICSE 2002]**
8. Without using the distance formula, show that the points $P(5, 6)$, $Q(2, 3)$, $R(5, 4)$ and $S(8, 7)$ are the vertices of a parallelogram.
9. Check whether the points $(-2, 9/7)$, $(-5, 0)$ and $(2, 3)$ are collinear or not.
10. Find a, if $A(2a + 2, 3)$, $B(7, 4)$ and $C(2a + 5, 2)$ are collinear. **[ICSE Semester II 2022]**
11. If the three points $(k, 3)$, $(2, -4)$ and $(-k + 1, -2)$ are collinear, then find the value of k.
12. Check whether the pair of lines $x + 3y - 7 = 0$ and $3x - y - 21 = 0$ is perpendicular or not.
13. If the straight lines $3x - 5y = 7$ and $4x + ay + 9 = 0$ are perpendicular to one another, find the value of a. **[ICSE 2018]**
14. The line passing through $A(-2, 3)$ and $B(4, b)$ is perpendicular to the line $2x - 4y = 5$. Find the value of b. **[ICSE 2012]**
15. Find the equation of a line which is perpendicular to the line joining $(5, 3)$ and $(4, 6)$ and cuts off an intercept of length 3 on Y-axis.
16. Find the equation of a line, that has y-intercept 4 and is perpendicular to the line joining $(2, -3)$ and $(4, 2)$.
17. Find the equation of the perpendicular bisector of the line joining the points $(1, 3)$ and $(3, 1)$.
18. Find the image of the point $P(-2, 1)$ in the line $2x - 3y = 4$.
19. Find the equation of the perpendicular dropped from the point $(-1, 2)$ onto the line joining $(1, 5$ and $(3, 3)$.
20. Without using Pythagoras theorem, show that $A(4, 4)$, $B(3, 5)$ and $C(-1, -1)$ are the vertices of a right angled triangle.
21. Line AB is perpendicular to CD. Coordinates of B, C and D are respectively, $(4, 0)$, $(0, -1)$ and $(4, 3)$. Find
   (a) slope of CD.
   (b) equation of AB. **[ICSE Semester II 2022]**

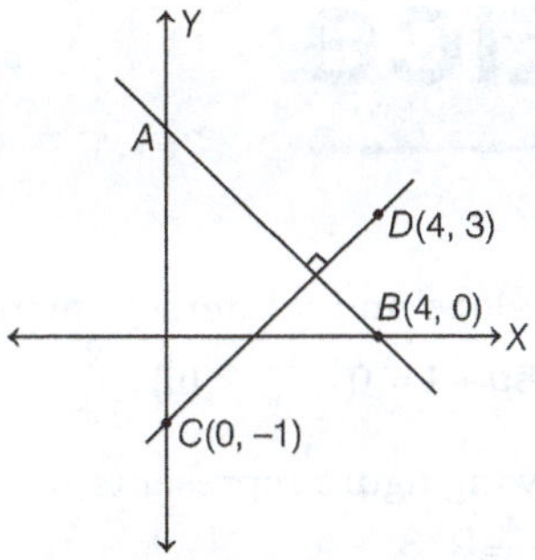

22. The equation of a line is $3x + 4y - 7 = 0$. Find

(i) the slope of the line.

(ii) the equation of a line perpendicular to the given line and passing through the intersection of the lines $x - y + 2 = 0$ and $3x + y - 10 = 0$.

23. In the given figure,

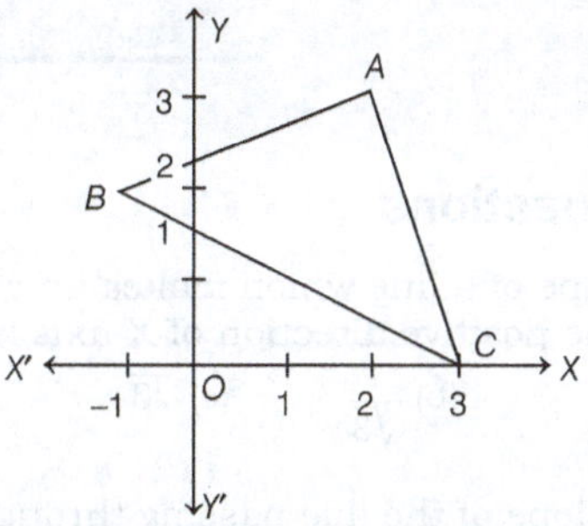

write

(i) the coordinates of A, B and C.

(ii) the equation of a line passing through A and perpendicular to BC. **[ICSE 2005]**

Chapter Practice

a. 1 Mark Questions

1. The slope of a line which makes an angle of 60° with the positive direction of X-axis is

(a) 1 (b) $\frac{1}{\sqrt{3}}$ (c) $\sqrt{3}$ (d) $-\frac{1}{\sqrt{3}}$

2. If the slope of the line passing through the points (3, 5) and (k, 3) is 2, then the value of k is

(a) 3 (b) 2 (c) 4 (d) 5

3. The slope of a line parallel to the line passing through the points (0, 8) and (9, 5) is

(a) $\frac{3}{7}$ (b) $-\frac{3}{7}$ (c) $-\frac{1}{3}$ (d) $-\frac{7}{3}$

4. The slope of a line perpendicular to the line passing through the points (3, 5) and (– 3, 6) is

(a) $\frac{1}{6}$ (b) 6 (c) –6 (d) 9

5. If the line $3x + 2y = 5$ and $kx - 6y = 7$ are parallel, then the value of k is

(a) – 9 (b) 9 (c) 8 (d) 12

6. If two lines are perpendicular to one another, then the relation between their slopes m_1 and m_2 is **[ICSE Semester II 2022]**

(a) $m_1 = m_2$ (b) $m_1 = \frac{1}{m_2}$

(c) $m_1 = -m_2$ (d) $m_1 \times m_2 = -1$

7. If the line $4x - 3y + 7 = 0$ and $2x + ky + 5 = 0$ are perpendicular to each other, then the value of k is

(a) 8/3 (b) 9/4 (c) 6/7 (d) 3/2

b. 3 Marks Questions

8. If the side BC of an equilateral ΔABC is parallel to above X-axis, then find the slope of lines along sides BC, CA and AB. [Given, $\tan(90° + \theta) = -\cot\theta$]

9. Find the slope of a line, which passes through the origin and mid-point of the line segment joining the points P (0, – 4) and B (8, 0).

10. Find the intercepts made by the line $2x - 3y + 12 = 0$ on the coordinates axes.

11. Find the equation of the straight lines parallel to
(i) X-axis and passing through the point (–8, – 7).
(ii) Y-axis and passing through the point (1.8, 0.9).

12. Find the equation of the line passing through (2, – 5) and making an intercept of –3 on the Y-axis.

13. Find the slope and y-intercept made by the line
(i) $7x - 8y + 1 = 0$ (ii) $\frac{x}{1.5} + \frac{y}{0.5} = 1.$

14. The following figure represents the lines $y = x - 2$ and $y = \frac{x}{\sqrt{3}} + 3$.

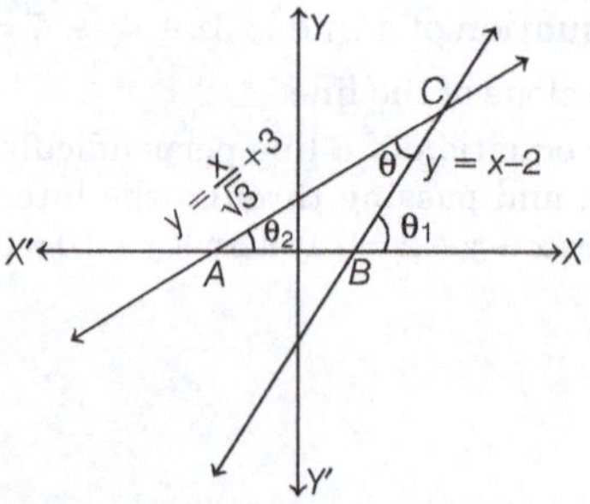

(i) Find the angles which the lines make with the positive direction of X-axis.
(ii) Determine the value of θ.

15. Find the equation of the line passing through the point $\left(9, \frac{1}{2}\right)$ and having slope $-\frac{3}{2}$.

16. Using the point-slope form, find the equation of the line AB.

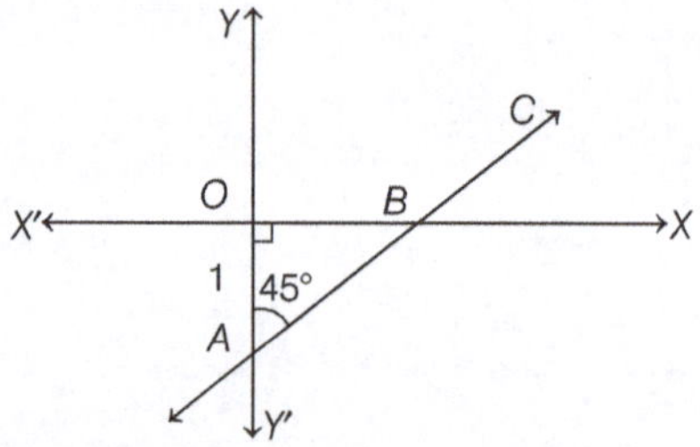

c. 4/5 Marks Questions

17. Find the equation of the line intersecting the X-axis at a distance of three units to the left of origin with slope –2.

18. Find the equation of the line, which is passing through the points (–1, 0) and (0, – 10).

19. Find the equation of a line with x-intercept = 5 and passing through the point (4, – 7). **[ICSE 2009]**

20. (i) Write down the coordinates of the point P, that divides the line joining A (– 4, 1) and B (17, 10) in the ratio 1 : 2.
(ii) Calculate the distance OP, where O is origin.
(iii) Find the equation of a line AB.

21. In the given figure, a straight line passes through the points $P(-1, 4)$ and $Q(5, -2)$. It intersects the coordinate axes at points A and B. If M is the mid-point of the segment AB, then find

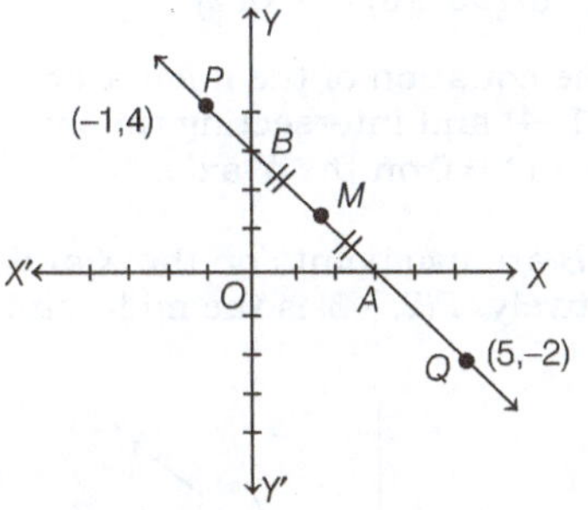

(i) the equation of the line.
(ii) the coordinates of A and B.
(iii) the coordinates of M. **[ICSE 2003]**

22. Show that the pair of lines $x + 9y - 7 = 0$ and $3x + 27y + 19 = 0$ is parallel.

23. Show that the line through (0, 0) and (1, 2) is parallel to the line through (2, 4) and (3, 6).

24. Suppose, two straight lines $3x - 2y = 5$ and $2x + ky + 7 = 0$. Find the value of k for which the given lines are parallel to each other.

25. Find the equation of the line through the point $A(0, -3)$ and parallel to the line joining the points $M(3, 2)$ and $N(-1, 0)$.

26. In the following diagram, write down the equation of line through A and parallel to BC.

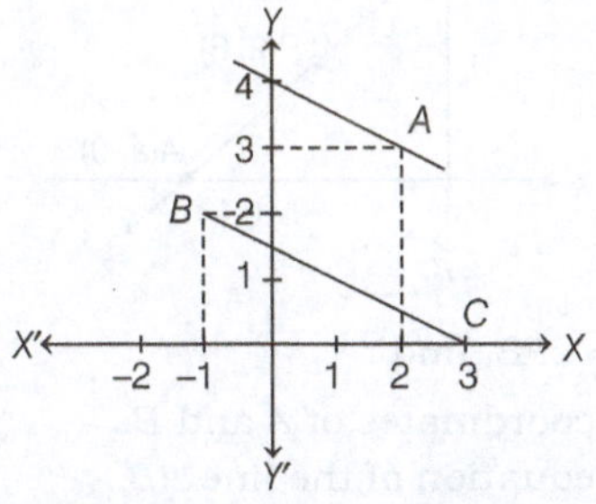

27. Find the equation of the diagonal of a rectangle whose sides are $x = -1$, $x = 4$, $y = -1$ and $y = 2$.

28. Find the equation of a line parallel to the line $2x + y - 7 = 0$ and passing through the intersection of the lines $x + y - 4 = 0$ and $2x - y = 8$. **[ICSE Semester II 2022]**

29. A quadrilateral has the vertices at the points (– 4, 2), (2, 6), (8, 5) and (9, – 7). Show that the mid-points of the sides of this quadrilateral are the vertices of a parallelogram by using slope formula.

30. In the given figure, $OABC$ is a parallelogram. Inclination of OC is 60° and the point B has coordinates (4, 3). Find the equations of all the sides of parallelogram $OABC$.

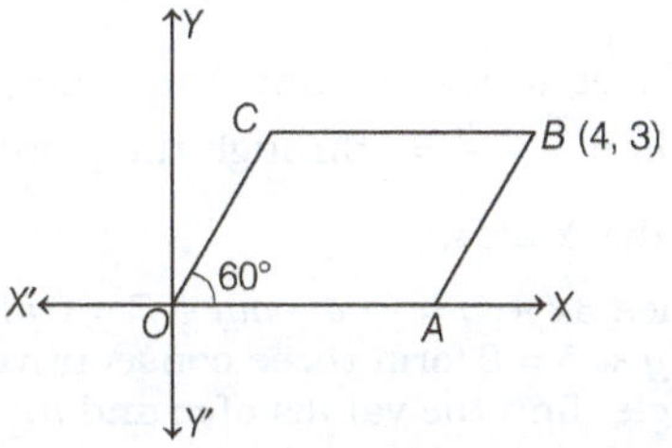

31. Show that the points (– 3, 2), (2, – 1) and $\left(-\frac{19}{4}, 4\right)$ are collinear.

32. If the points (2, – 5), $(p - 1, p + 4)$ and (4, 3) are collinear, then the value of p.

33. Write down the equation of the line perpendicular to $3x + 8y = 12$ and passing through the point (–1, – 2).

34. Show that the pair of lines $3x - y = 0$ and $x + 3y - 3 = 0$ is perpendicular.

35. Show that the line through the points (– 2, 6) and (4, 8) is perpendicular to the line through the points (14, 24) and (10, 36).

36. Given, two straight lines $kx - 2y = 5$ and $2x + 3y + 7 = 0$. If the given pair of lines is perpendicular, then find the value of k.

37. Find the value of p, if the lines $y = 3x + 7$ and $y + px = 3$ are
(i) parallel to each other.
(ii) perpendicular to each other.

38. Find the value of a, if the lines $\frac{y}{2} = x - p$ and $ax + 5 = 3y$ are
(i) parallel to each other.
(ii) perpendicular to each other.

39. Lines $2x - ny + 5 = 0$ and $mx + 3y = 2$ are parallel. Find the relation connecting m and n.

40. Lines $mx + 3y + 7 = 0$ and $5x - ny - 3 = 0$ are perpendicular to each other. Find the relation connecting m and n.

41. Find the equation of the line passing through the point of intersection of $7x + 6y = 71$ and $5x - 8y = -23$ and perpendicular to the line $4x - 2y = 1$.

42. Without using distance formula show that the triangle formed by the points $A(1, 3)$, $B(3, -1)$ and $C(-5, -5)$ is a right angled triangle (by using slopes).

43. Find the value of p if the lines, $5x - 3y + 2 = 0$ and $6x - py + 7 = 0$ are perpendicular to each other. Hence, find the equation of a line passing through $(-2, -1)$ and parallel to $6x - py + 7 = 0$. **[ICSE 2020]**

44. Find the equation of a line drawn perpendicular to the line $\frac{x}{4} + \frac{y}{6} = 1$ through the point, where it meets the Y-axis.

45. The lines $3x + y = 4$, $x - my + 7 = 0$ and $nx + 2y + 5 = 0$ form three consecutive sides of a rectangle, find the values of m and n.

46. Show that the perpendicular drawn from the point (4, 1) on the line segment joining (6, 5) and (2, − 1) divides it internally in the ratio 8 : 5.

47. Points A (9, 2), B (1, 10) and C (− 7, − 6) are the vertices of a ΔABC. Find the equation of
(i) the median of the triangle through A.
(ii) the altitude of the triangle through B.

d. 6 Marks Questions

48. The side AB of a square $ABCD$ is parallel to the Y-axis as shown in the given figure.

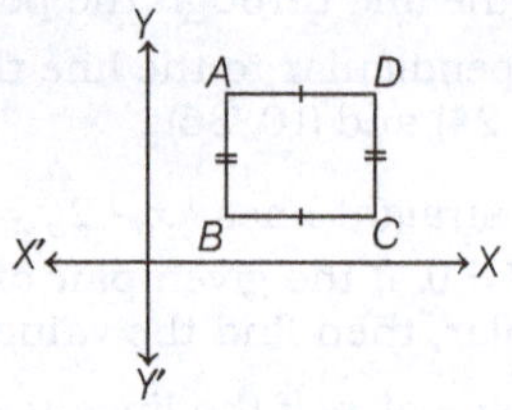

Calculate
(i) the slope of AD. (ii) the slope of BD.
(iii) the slope of AC.
[given, $\tan(90° + \theta) = -\cot\theta$]

49. The equation of a line α_1 is $y = -8$.

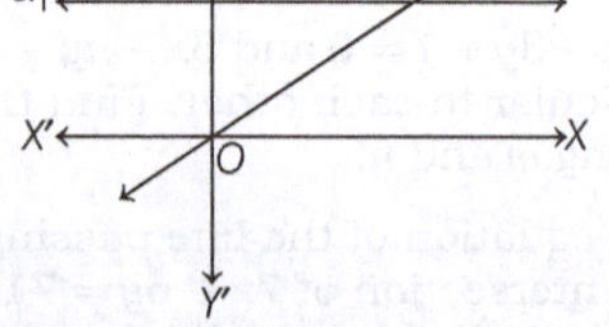

(i) Write the slope of the line α_2 if α_2, is the bisector of $\angle O$.
(ii) Write the coordinates of point P.
(iii) Find the equation of α_2.

50. If a line passes through the point (2,3) and cuts-off equal positive intercepts on the two axes of reference, then find the slope and equation of the line.
[given, $\tan(90° + \theta) = -\cot\theta$]

51. Find the equation of the line passing through the point (1, 4) and intersecting the line $x - 2y - 11 = 0$ on the Y-axis.

52. A and B are two points on the X and Y-axes, respectively. $P(2, -3)$ is the mid-point of AB. Find the

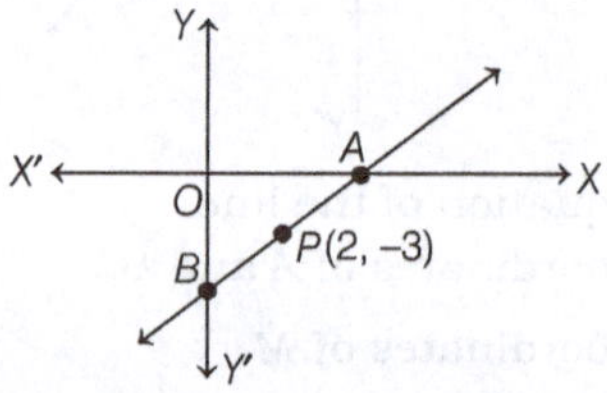

(i) coordinate of A and B. (ii) slope of line AB.
(iii) equation of line AB.

53. The points P (5, 0), Q (− 2, 2) and R (3, 4) are the vertices of a ΔPQR. Find the equation of the median through P, Q and R, respectively.

54. The line passes through the point $P(2, 3)$ and meets the coordinated axes at the points A and B (in fig).

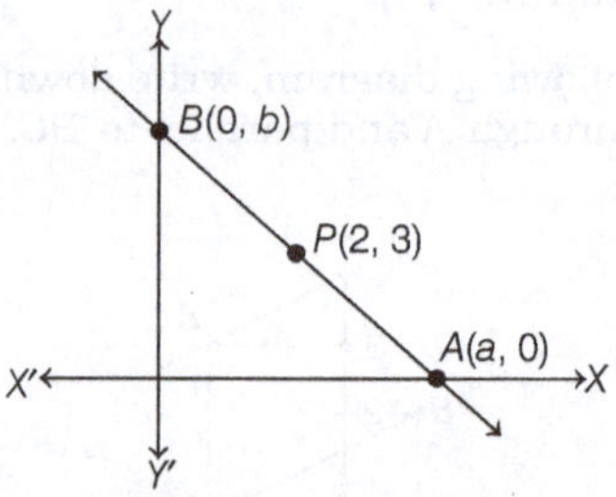

If $3PA = 2PB$, find
(i) the coordinates of A and B.
(ii) the equation of the line AB.

55. Find the equation of the line, which passes through the point (3, 4) and the sum of its intercepts on the axes is 14.

56. Find the equation of the line passing through the points P (5, 1) and Q (1, − 1). Hence, show that the points P, Q and R (11, 4) are collinear.

57. Match the equations A, B, C, D and E with the lines L_1, L_2, L_3, L_4 and L_5 whose graphs are roughly drawn in the given diagram.

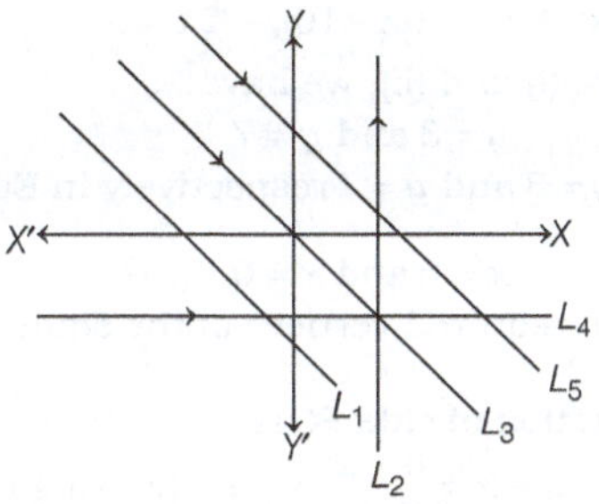

$A = 3x + 2y = 0$, $B = 3x + 2y = 20$

$C = x = 6$, $D = y = -8$, $E = 3x + 2y + 12 = 0$

58. If the line $x - 4y - 6 = 0$ is the perpendicular bisector of the line segment AB and the coordinates of A are (1, 3), find the coordinates of B.

59. The equation of a line is $y = 3x - 5$. Write down the slope of this line and the intercept made by its on the Y-axis. Hence or otherwise, write down the equation of a line, which is parallel to the line and which passes through the point (0, 5).

60. $A(2,5)$, $B(-1, 2)$ and $C(5, 8)$ are the vertices of a ΔABC, 'M' is a point on AB such that $AM : MB = 1:2$. Find the coordinates of 'M'. Hence, find the equation of the line passing through the points C and M. **[ICSE 2018]**

Hints and Answers

Exercise 12.1

1. (i) **Hint** Use linear pair property of angles. **Ans.** 135°

(ii) **Hint** Do same as part (i). **Ans.** 150°

(iii) **Hint** Do same as part (i). **Ans.** 30°

(iv) **Hint** Do same as Example 1. **Ans.** 135°

2. Do same as Example 2.

Ans. (i) 0 (ii) not defined (iii) $\frac{1}{\sqrt{3}}$

3. **Hint** Given, slope = 1.28

$\Rightarrow \tan\theta = 1.28 \Rightarrow \theta = 52°$

Ans. The inclination of a line 52°.

4. **Hint** Do same as Example 5. **Ans.** $-\frac{1}{6}$

5. **Hint** Do same as Example 6(i). **Ans.** 1

6. **Hint** Do same as Example 7.

Ans. (i) 3, 3 (ii) $-2, -3$ (iii) $-5, 1$

7. **Hint** Satisfies the point $(-3, 3)$ in equation of line

$y = 2x - p$

$3 = 2(-3) - p$ **Ans.** $p = -9$

8. **Hint** Do same as Example 8. **Ans.** $y - 7 = 0$

9. **Hint** Let the equation of line parallel to Y-axis is $x = b$.

Now, as it given that line is 3 units to the right of Y-axis, therefore $b = 3$. **Ans.** $x = 3$

10. **Hint** Since, the lines $x = 12$ and $x = -6$ cut X-axis at A (12, 0) and B (−6, 0), respectively. Therefore, a line equidistant from these two lines will pass through the mid-point of AB.

Now, coordinates of the mid-point of AB

$$= \left(\frac{-6+12}{2}, \frac{0+0}{2}\right) = (3, 0)$$

Ans. $x = 3$

11. **Hint** Do same as Example 10. **Ans.** $\sqrt{3}x - y - 3 = 0$

12. **Hint** Put $m = 1/\sqrt{3}$ and $c = 3$ in the equation $y = mx + c$.

Ans. $\sqrt{3}y = x + 3\sqrt{3}$

13. **Hint** Let $(6, 0) = (x_1, y_1)$ and $(0, -8) = (x_2, y_2)$

$$\Rightarrow \quad \text{Slope} = \frac{y_2 - y_1}{x_2 - x_1}$$

Ans. $4x - 3y - 24 = 0$

14. **Hint** Do same as Example 11.

Ans. $y = x - 4$

15. **Hint** Do same as Example 12.

Ans. (i) $\frac{4}{5}, -\frac{6}{5}$ (ii) $-\frac{7}{2}, 7$

16. (i) **Hint** Do same as Example 12. **Ans.** 1

(ii) **Hint** Slope of a line = $\tan\theta$. **Ans.** 45°.

17. (i) **Hint** From the given figure, $\theta = 45°$.

$\therefore$ Slope of the line PQ is $m = \tan\theta$. **Ans.** 1

(ii) **Hint** The equation of line passing through P (5, 3) and having slope 1, is $y - 3 = 1(x - 5)$.

Ans. $y = x - 2$

(iii) **Hint** Since, the coordinates of Q lie on Y-axis, so put $x = 0$ in the equation obtained in part (ii).

Ans. (0, −2)

18. **Hint** Do same as Example 14.

Ans. $3x - y - 3 = 0$

19. **Hint** We know that a line equally inclined to the coordinate axes in the first quadrant makes angle 45° with the positive direction of X-axis.

$\therefore \quad m$ = Slope of the line = $\tan 45° = 1$

Ans. $x - y + 4 = 0$

20. **Hint** According to the question,

$$\frac{a}{b} = \frac{3}{5}$$

Slope of the line $AB = \frac{-b}{a} = \frac{-5}{3}$

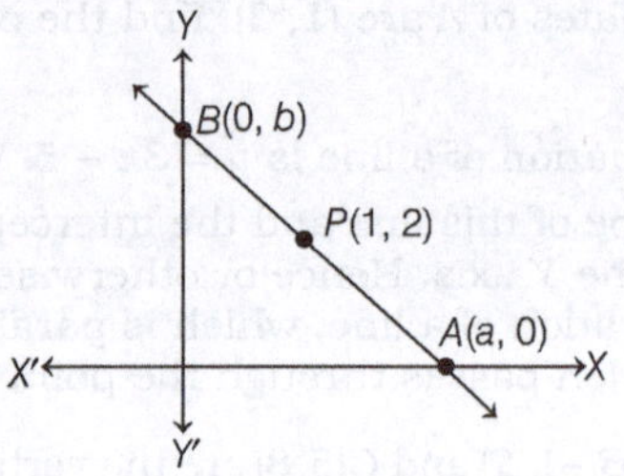

Ans. $3y + 5x - 11 = 0$

21. **Hint** Since, the line $2x + 3y + 6 = 0$ intersects the X-axis, put $y = 0$, we get $x = -3$

$\therefore$ The point of intersection on X-axis is $(-3, 0)$.

The equation of line passes through $(2, 4)$ and $(-3, 0)$ is

$$y - 4 = \frac{0-4}{-3-2}(x - 2)$$

Ans. $4x - 5y + 12 = 0$

22. **Hint** Do same as Example 19. **Ans.** $6x + y - 23 = 0$

23. **Hint** Do same as Example 19. **Ans.** $2x - 7y = 3$

24. **Hint**

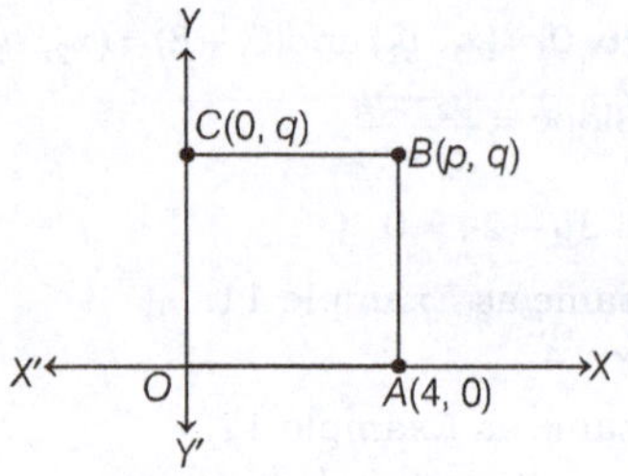

$OA = AB = BC = OC$ and $OA = OC = 4$ units

Ans. $p = 4, q = 4$

equation of line AB, $x = 4$ and equation of line BC, $y = 4$.

25. **Hint**

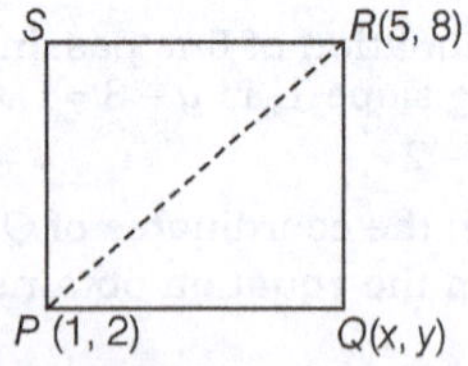

Let $PQRS$ be a square.

Suppose $Q(x, y)$ be the unknown vertex, then

$$PQ = QR \Rightarrow PQ^2 = QR^2$$

Using distance formula,

$$(x-1)^2 + (y-2)^2 = (5-x)^2 + (8-y)^2$$

On solving it,we get

$$x = \frac{21-3y}{2} \quad \text{...(i)}$$

Now, in right angle ΔPQR,

$$PQ^2 + QR^2 = PR^2$$

$$\Rightarrow \quad (x-1)^2 + (y-2)^2 + (5-x)^2 + (8-y)^2 = (5-1)^2 + (8-2)^2$$

$$\Rightarrow \quad x^2 + y^2 - 6x - 10y + 21 = 0 \quad \text{...(ii)}$$

From Eqs. (i) and (ii), we have

$$y = 3 \text{ and } y = 7$$

Putting $y = 3$ and $y = 7$ respectively in Eq. (i), we have

$$x = 6 \text{ and } x = 0$$

Thus, two required vertices of the square are $Q(6, 3)$ and $S(0, 7)$.

Now, equation of side PQ is

$$y - 2 = \frac{3-2}{6-1}(x - 1) \quad [\because \text{using two point form}]$$

$$= x - 5y + 9 = 0$$

Similarly, find equations of side QR, RS and SP.

Ans. Equation of sides are $x - 5y + 9 = 0$, $5x + y - 33 = 0$, $x - 5y + 35 = 0$, $5x + y - 7 = 0$ and coordinates of its other vertices are $(6, 3)$ and $(0, 7)$.

26. **Hint** Do same as Example 20.

Ans. (i) $(3, -3)$ (ii) $4x - y - 12 = 0$

27. **Hint**

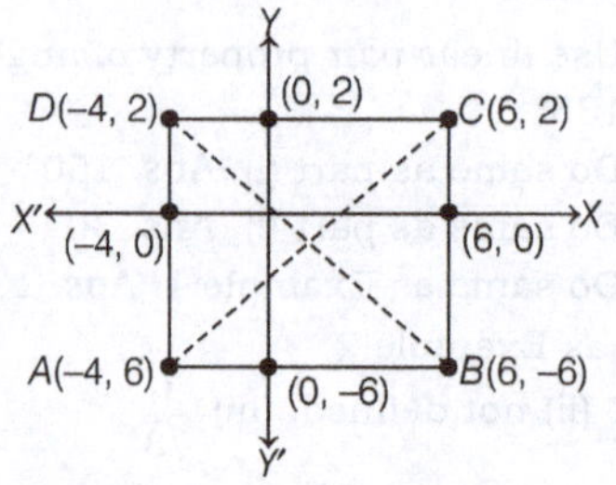

Slope of diagonal $AC = \frac{2-6}{6-(-4)} = -\frac{4}{10}$

and slope of diagonal $BD = \frac{-6-2}{6-(-4)} = -\frac{8}{10}$

Ans. Equation of diagonal AC, $2x + 5y - 22 = 0$

Equation of diagonal BD, $4x + 5y + 6 = 0$

28. **Hint** Apply two points slope form,

$$y - y_1 = \frac{y_2 - y_1}{x_2 - x_1}(x - x_1)$$

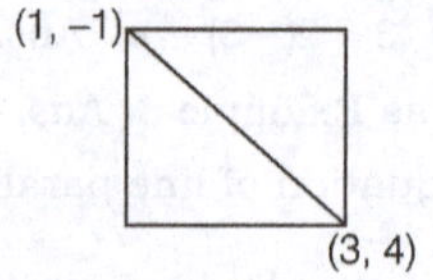

Ans. $5x - 2y - 7 = 0$

Exercise 12.2

1. **Hint** Do same as Example 23. **Ans.** Yes

2. **Hint** Do same as Example 24. **Ans.** $\alpha = 2$

3. **Hint** Do same as Example 25.

Ans. $x - 17y + 85 = 0$

4. **Hint** Let the equation of line parallel to given line is $x - 2y + \lambda = 0$.

Put $x = 1$ and $y = 2$ in the equation, then determine λ.

Ans. $x - 2y + 3 = 0$

5. **Hint** Equation of line $y = mx + c$ in $c = 4$ and $m = \frac{2}{3}$.

Ans. $2x - 3y + 12 = 0$ and $(-6, 0)$

6. **Hint** The intersection point of given line on X-axis is $(2, 0)$.

$\therefore$ Equation of line passing through $(2, 0)$ and slope $3/7$ is $y - 0 = \frac{3}{7}(x - 2)$.

Ans. $3x - 7y - 6 = 0$

7. **Hint** Do same as Example 26.

Ans. (i) $\left(\frac{11}{3}, \frac{11}{3}\right)$

(ii) $3x + 3y = 22$

8. **Hint**

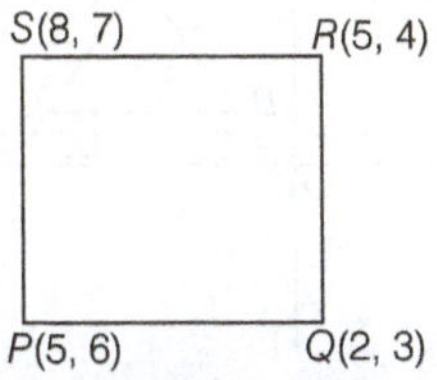

In parallelogram, opposite sides are parallel.

Slope of PQ, $m_1 = 1$, Slope of RS, $m_2 = 1$

$$m_1 = m_2 = 1$$

Similarly, Slope of QR = Slope of PS

$\therefore$ $PQ \parallel RS$ and $QR \parallel PS$.

9. **Hint** Do same as Example 27. **Ans.** Collinear

10. **Hint** Given, three points $A(2a + 2, 3)$, $B(7, 4)$ and $C(2a + 5, 2)$ are collinear.

$\therefore$ Slope of AB = Slope of BC.

$$\Rightarrow \quad \frac{4 - 3}{7 - 2a - 2} = \frac{2 - 4}{2a + 5 - 7}$$

$$\Rightarrow \quad \frac{1}{5 - 2a} = \frac{-2}{2a - 2}$$

$$\Rightarrow \quad 2a - 2 = -10 + 4a$$

$$\Rightarrow \quad 2a = 8$$

$$\Rightarrow \quad a = 4$$

11. Do same as Example 28. **Ans.** $-\frac{1}{3}$

12. Do same as Example 30. **Ans.** Yes

13. Do same as Example 31. **Ans.** $a = \frac{12}{5}$

14. **Hint** Slope of AB, $m_1 = \frac{b - 3}{6}$

and slope of line $2x - 4y = 5$, $m_2 = \frac{1}{2}$

We know that, if the lines having slopes m_1 and m_2 are perpendicular, then $m_1 \cdot m_2 = -1$.

Ans. -9

15. **Hint** Slope of line joining the points $(5, 3)$ and $(4, 6)$ is -3.

$\therefore$ Slope of line perpendicular to it is $\frac{1}{3}$.

$\because$ The perpendicular line cuts-off an intercept of length 3 on Y-axis. **Ans.** $x - 3y + 9 = 0$

16. **Hint** Slope of required line,

$$m = \frac{-1}{\left(\frac{2 + 3}{4 - 2}\right)} = -\frac{2}{5} \text{ and } c = 4 \quad \textbf{Ans. } 2x + 5y - 20 = 0$$

17. **Hint** The mid-point of line joining given point is $M(2, 2)$

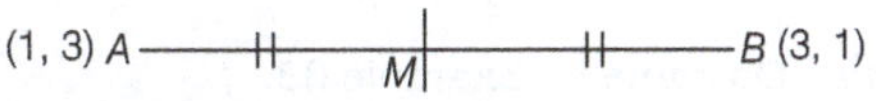

Ans. $y - x = 0$

18. **Hint** From P, draw PM perpendicular to the line $2x - 3y + 4$ and produce it to a point P' such that $P'M = MP$, then P' is the image of P in the line $2x - 3y + 4$ and the line $2x - 3y + 4$ is the right bisector of the segment PP'.

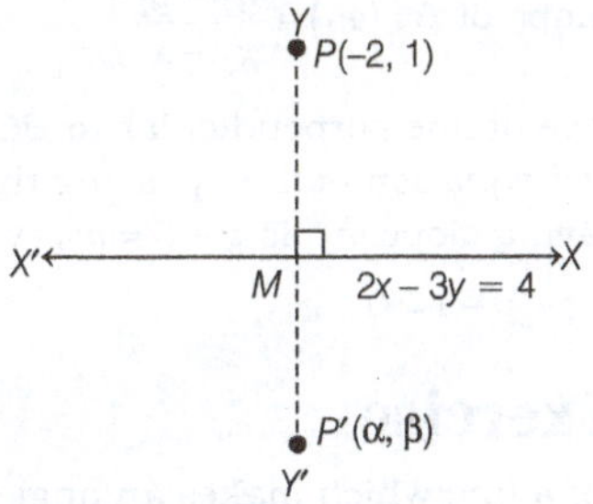

Let P' be (α, β)

Then, slope of $PP' = \frac{\beta - 1}{\alpha + 2}$

Also, the mid-point of PP' is $M\left(\frac{\alpha - 2}{2}, \frac{\beta + 1}{2}\right)$

Ans. The image of P in the given line is $P'\left(\frac{18}{13}, \frac{-53}{13}\right)$.

19. **Hint** Slope of the line joining the points $A(1, 5)$ and $B(3, 3) = \frac{3 - 5}{3 - 1} = -1$ $\left|\ m = \frac{y_2 - y_1}{x_2 - x_1}\right.$

The equation of the line through $(-1, 2)$ and having slope 1 is $\left|\ m_2 = \frac{-1}{m_1}\right.$.

Ans. $x - y + 3 = 0$

20. **Hint** Slope of AB is $m_1 = \frac{5 - 4}{3 - 4} = -1$

and slope of AC is $m_2 = \frac{(-1) - 4}{(-1) - 4} = 1$

Here, $m_1 \cdot m_2 = -1$

Ans. This shows that $AB \perp AC$, i.e. $\angle CAB = \frac{\pi}{2}$.

21. (i) Slope of CD, $m = \frac{y_2 - y_1}{x_2 - x_1}$

$$m = \frac{3 + 1}{4 - 0} = \frac{4}{4} = 1$$

Slope of CD is 1.

(ii) Equation of AB

$$y - y_1 = \frac{-1}{m}(x - x_1)$$

$y - 0 = \frac{-1}{1}(x - 4)$

$\Rightarrow \quad y = -x + 4 \quad \Rightarrow x + y - 4 = 0$

$x + y - 4 = 0$

22. (i) **Hint** Compare the given equation with $y = mx + c$. **Ans.** $-\frac{3}{4}$

(ii) **Hint** Do same as Example 33.

Ans. $4x - 3y + 4 = 0$

23. (i) **Hint** Measures the perpendicular distance from given points to the Y and X-axes.

Ans. $A(2, 3)$, $B(-1, 2)$ and $C(3, 0)$

(ii) **Hint** Slope of $BC(m_1) = \frac{y_2 - y_1}{x_2 - x_1}$

Let slope of line perpendicular to BC be m_2. Then, required equation of line, passing through A (2, 3) and having slope m_2, is $y - 3 = m_2(x - 2)$.

Ans. $2x - y - 1 = 0$

Chapter Exercise

1. (c) Slope of a line which makes an angle of 60° with positive direction of X-axis = $\tan 60° = \sqrt{3}$.

2. (b) Slope of line $= \frac{3-5}{k-3} = 2$

$\Rightarrow 3 - 5 = 2(k - 3) \Rightarrow -2 = 2(k - 3) \Rightarrow k = 3 - 1 = 2$

3. (c) Slope of the line passing through (0, 8) and (9, 5)

$= \frac{5-8}{9-0} = \frac{-3}{9} = -\frac{1}{3}$

We know that slope of parallel lines are equal.

4. (b) Slope of the line passing through (3, 5) and (– 3, 6)

$= \frac{6-5}{-3-3} = -\frac{1}{6}$

When two lines are perpendicular, if and only if the product of their slope is – 1.

Slope of the line perpendicular to this line = 6

5. (a) Given, $3x + 2y = 5 \Rightarrow 2y = 5 - 3x$

$\Rightarrow \quad y = -\frac{3}{2}x + 5$

$\therefore$ The slope of line $m_1 = -\frac{3}{2}$

and $\quad kx - 6y = 7 \Rightarrow kx - 7 = 6y$

$y = \frac{k}{6}x - \frac{7}{6}$

$\therefore$ The slope of line $m_2 = \frac{k}{6}$

$\therefore$ Lines are parallel, $m_1 = m_2$; $\frac{k}{6} = -\frac{3}{2}$

$\Rightarrow \quad k = -9$

6. (d) If two lines having slopes m_1 and m_2 are perpendicular to each other, then the angle θ between them is 90°.

Also, $m_1 \times m_2 = 1$

7. (a) Given, $4x - 3y + 7 = 0 \Rightarrow y = \frac{4x}{3} + \frac{7}{3}$

$\therefore$ The slope of line, $m_1 = \frac{4}{3}$ and $2x + ky + 5 = 0$

$y = -\frac{2x}{k} - \frac{5}{k}$

$\therefore$ The slope of line, $m_2 = -\frac{2}{k}$

Lines are perpendicular, $m_1 \cdot m_2 = -1 \Rightarrow \frac{4}{3} \times -\frac{2}{k} = -1$

$\therefore \quad k = \frac{8}{3}$

8. **Hint** Clearly, $\angle ABC = \angle ACB = \angle BAC = 60°$

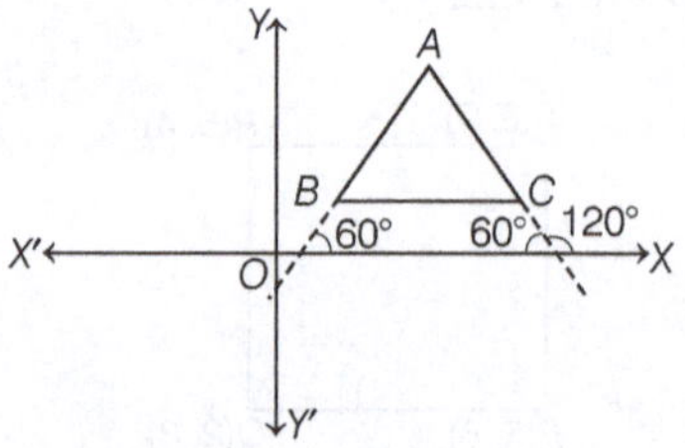

Since, BC is parallel to X-axis.Therefore, inclinations of lines along the sides AB, BC and CA are 60°, 0° and 120°, respectively.

$\therefore$ Slope of line along $BC = \tan 0°$.

Slope of line along $AB = \tan 60°$.

Slope of line along $CA = \tan 120°$

$= \tan(90° + 30°) = -\cot 30°$

Ans. 0°, $-\sqrt{3}$, $\sqrt{3}$

9. **Hint** Mid-point of P and $B = \left(\frac{0+8}{2}, \frac{-4+0}{2}\right) = (4, -2)$

and origin (0, 0)

$\left[\text{for slope of line apply formula, } m = \frac{y_2 - y_1}{x_2 - x_1}\right]$

$\therefore$ Slope of a line $= \frac{-2-0}{4-0}$ **Ans.** $-\frac{1}{2}$

10. **Hint** x-intercept is the x-coordinate, of the point, where it cut the X-axis. For this put $y = 0$.

and y-intercept is the y-coordinate, of the point, where it cut the Y-axis. For this put $x = 0$.

Ans. x-intercept = – 6, y-intercept = 4

11. (i) **Hint** Do same as Example 8. **Ans.** $y + 7 = 0$

(ii) **Hint** Do same as Example 9. **Ans.** $x - 1.8 = 0$

12. **Hint** Do same as Example 11. **Ans.** $x + y + 3 = 0$

13. **Hint** Do same as Example 12.

Ans. (i) $\frac{7}{8}$ and $\frac{1}{8}$ (ii) $-\frac{1}{3}$ and $\frac{1}{2}$

14. (i) **Hint** On comparing with $y = mx + c$, we get

$m_1 = 1$ and $m_2 = \frac{1}{\sqrt{3}}$ **Ans.** 45°, 30°

(ii) **Hint** In ΔABC, $\theta_1 = \theta_2 + \theta$

[$\because$ exterior angle of a triangle is equal to the sum of opposite interior angles]

Ans. 15°

15. Hint Do same as Example 14.

Ans. $3x + 2y - 28 = 0$

16. Hint $\because \angle OAB = 45°$

and $\angle AOB + \angle OBA + \angle OAB = 180°$

$\therefore \quad 90° + \angle OBA + 45° = 180°$

$\Rightarrow \quad \angle OBA = 45° = \angle XBC$

[$\because$ vertically opposite angles]

$\therefore$ Slope of a line AB is $m = \tan 45° = 1$

It is clear from the figure that the coordinates of point A is $(0, -1)$.

Now, the equation of line AB passing through $A(0, -1)$ and having slope 1 is $y - y_1 = m(x - x_1)$.

Ans. $x - y - 1 = 0$

17. Hint Clearly, line passes through the point $(-3, 0)$ and having slope, $m = -2$.

Equation of line in point-slope form is

$y - y_1 = m(x - x_1)$. **Ans.** $2x + y + 6 = 0$

18. Hint Do same as Example 17.

Ans. $10x + y + 10 = 0$

19. Hint Given, points are $(5, 0)$ and $(4, -7)$.

Now, using the formula of straight line,

$y - y_1 = \frac{y_2 - y_1}{x_2 - x_1}(x - x_1)$ **Ans.** $7x - y - 35 = 0$

20. (i) **Hint** Coordinates of P

$$= \left(\frac{1 \times 17 + 2 \times (-4)}{1 + 2}, \frac{1 \times 10 + 2 \times 1}{1 + 2}\right).$$

Ans. $(3, 4)$

(ii) **Hint** The distance between $O(0, 0)$ and $P(3, 4)$ is

$OP = \sqrt{(3 - 0)^2 + (4 - 0)^2}$ **Ans.** 5

(iii) **Hint** The equation of a line passing through $A(-4, 1)$ and $B(17, 10)$ is

$$y - 1 = \frac{10 - 1}{17 + 4}[x - (-4)].$$

Ans. $3x - 7y + 19 = 0$

21. (i) **Hint** Equation of line passing through two points is

$y - y_1 = \frac{y_2 - y_1}{x_2 - x_1}(x - x_1)$. **Ans.** $x + y - 3 = 0$

(ii) **Hint** Here, the line $x + y - 3 = 0$ meets the X and Y-axes, respectively.

On putting $y = 0$ in $x + y - 3 = 0$, we get

$x = 3$.

Now, putting $x = 0$ in $x + y - 3 = 0$, we get

$y = 3$.

Ans. $(3, 0)$ and $(0, 3)$

(iii) **Hint** Coordinates of mid-point of $A(3, 0)$ and $B(0, 3) = \left(\frac{3 + 0}{2}, \frac{0 + 3}{2}\right)$ **Ans.** $\left(\frac{3}{2}, \frac{3}{2}\right)$

22. Hint Do same as Example 23.

23. Hint Slope of line through $(0, 0)$ and $(1, 2)$ i.e.

$m_1 = 2$

and slope of line through $(2, 4)$ and $(3, 6)$ i.e.

$m_2 = 2$

$m_1 = m_2$

24. Hint Do same as Example 24. **Ans.** $k = -4/3$

25. Hint Do same as Example 25.

Ans. $x - 2y - 6 = 0$

26. Hint Coordinate of $C = (3, 0)$

and coordinate of $B(-1, 2)$

Apply two point slope form

$$= y - y_1 = \frac{y_2 - y_1}{x_2 - x_1}(x - x_1)$$

Ans. $2x + 4y - 6 = 0$

27. Hint

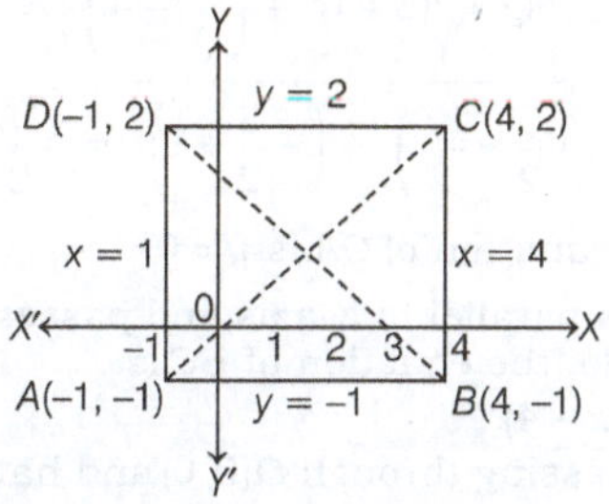

Clearly, the vertices of rectangle $ABCD$ are $A(-1, -1)$, $B(4, -1)$, $C(4, 2)$ and $D(-1, 2)$.

Slope of the diagonal

$$AC = \frac{2 - (-1)}{4 - (-1)} = \frac{3}{5}$$

$\therefore$ The equation of AC is $y - (-1) = \frac{3}{5}(x - (-1))$

$\Rightarrow \quad 5y + 5 = 3x + 3$

$\Rightarrow \quad 3x - 5y - 2 = 0$

Slope of the diagonal $BD = \frac{2 - (-1)}{-1 - 4} = \frac{-3}{5}$,

$\therefore$ The equation of BD is $y - (-1) = \frac{-3}{5}(x - 4)$

$\Rightarrow \quad 5y + 5 = -3x + 12$

Ans. $3x - 5y - 2 = 0$, $3x + 5y - 7 = 0$

28. Hint Given, lines are

$2x + y - 7 = 0$ ...(i)

$x + y - 4 = 0$ ...(ii)

$2x - y - 8 = 0$ ...(iii)

From Eq. (i), $y = -2x + 7$

$\Rightarrow$ Slope, $m = -2$

Now, solving Eqs. (ii) and (iii), we get

$x_1 = 4$ and $y_1 = 0$

Now, the equation of a line parallel to the line $2x + y - 7 = 0$ and passing through the intersection of the lines $x + y - 4 = 0$ and $2x - y - 8 = 0$ is given by

$y - y_1 = m(x - x_1)$

$y - 0 = -2(x - 4)$

$\Rightarrow \quad y = -2x + 8$

$\Rightarrow \quad 2x + y = 8$

Ans. $2x + y = 8$

29. **Hint** Let $A(-4, 2)$, $B(2, 6)$, $C(8, 5)$ and $D(9, -7)$ be the vertices of the given quadrilateral. Let P, Q, R and S be the mid-points of AB, BC, CD and DA, respectively. Then, the coordinates of P, Q, R and S are $P(-1, 4)$, $Q\left(5, \frac{11}{2}\right)$, $R\left(\frac{17}{2}, -1\right)$ and $S\left(\frac{5}{2}, -\frac{5}{2}\right)$, respectively.

In order to prove that $PQRS$ is a parallelogram, it is sufficient to show that PQ is parallel to RS and $PQ = RS$.

Here, slope of PQ, $m_1 = \frac{11/2 - 4}{5-(-1)} = \frac{1}{4}$

slope of RS, $m_2 = \frac{-5/2 + 1}{5/2 - 17/2} = \frac{1}{4}$,

$$PQ = \sqrt{(5+1)^2 + \left(\frac{11}{2} - 4\right)^2} = \frac{\sqrt{153}}{2}$$

and $RS = \sqrt{\left(\frac{5}{2} - \frac{17}{2}\right)^2 + \left(-\frac{5}{2} + 1\right)^2} = \frac{\sqrt{153}}{2}$

30. **Hint** The equation of OA is $y = 0$.

Side BC is parallel to X-axis and passes through $B(4, 3)$. So, the equation of BC is $y - 3 = 0\,(x - 4)$.

Side OC passing through $O(0, 0)$ and having slope $\tan 60° = \sqrt{3}$. So, its equation is $y - 0 = \sqrt{3}(x - 0)$.

Now, slope of AB = slope of $OC = \sqrt{3}$

So, equation of side AB having point $B(4, 3)$ and the slope $\sqrt{3}$ is $y - 3 = \sqrt{3}(x - 4)$.

Ans. Equation of OA is $y = 0$, equation of AB is $\sqrt{3}x - y - 4\sqrt{3} + 3 = 0$, equation of BC is $y = 3$ and equation of OC is $y = \sqrt{3}x$.

31. **Hint** Do same as Example 27.

32. **Hint** Do same as Example 28.
Ans. $p = 7$

33. **Hint** Slope of line $3x + 8y = 12$, $m_1 = -\frac{3}{8}$

Apply point slope form, $y - y_1 = m(x - x_1)$

Ans. $3y = 8x + 2$

34. **Hint** Do same as Example 30.

35. **Hint** Slope of line through $(-2, 6)$ and $(4, 8)$

i.e. $m_1 = \frac{1}{3}$ $\quad\left[\because \text{by using formula } m = \frac{y_2 - y_1}{x_2 - x_1}\right]$

and slope of line through $(14, 24)$ and $(10, 36)$,

i.e. $m_2 = -3$

$m_1 m_2 = -1$

36. **Hint** Do same as Example 31. **Ans.** $k = 3$

37. (i) **Hint** Do same as Example 24. **Ans.** $p = -3$

(ii) **Hint** Do same as Example 31. **Ans.** $p = \frac{1}{3}$

38. (i) **Hint** Do same as Example 24. **Ans.** $a = 6$

(ii) **Hint** Do same as Example 31. **Ans.** $a = -\frac{3}{2}$

39. Slope of line $2x - ny + 5 = 0$

$$m_1 = \frac{2}{n}$$

and slope of line $mx + 3y = 2$

$$m_2 = -\frac{m}{3}$$

$\because$ For parallel, $m_1 = m_2$

$$mn = -6$$

40. **Hint** Slope of line $mx + 3y + 7 = 0$

$$m_1 = \frac{-m}{3}$$

Slope of line $5x - ny - 3 = 0$

$$m_2 = \frac{5}{n}$$

Given, lines are perpendicular to each other.

$\Rightarrow \quad m_1 \cdot m_2 = -1$

$\Rightarrow \quad \frac{-m}{3} \times \frac{5}{n} = -1$

$\Rightarrow \quad \frac{-5m}{3n} = -1$

$\Rightarrow \quad -5m = -3n$

$\Rightarrow \quad 5m = 3n$

Ans. $5m = 3n$

41. **Hint** Do same as Example 33. **Ans.** $x + 2y - 17 = 0$

42. **Hint** Slope of $AB = -2$ and slope of $BC = \frac{1}{2}$

Slope of $AB \times$ Slope of $BC = -1$

So, clearly $AB \perp BC$, $\angle ABC = 90°$.

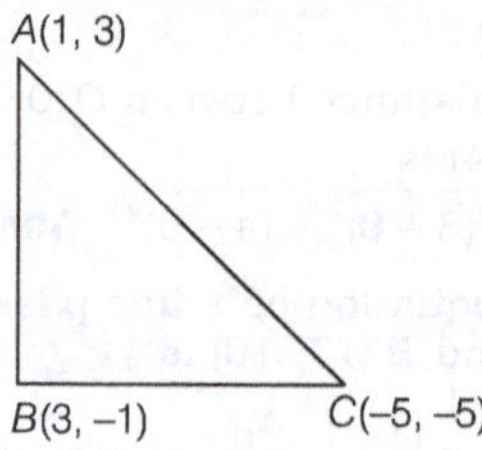

43. Given, equation of lines are

$5x - 3y + 2 = 0$

and $\quad 6x - py + 7 = 0$

$\Rightarrow \quad -3y = -5x - 2$

and $\quad -py = -6x - 7$

$\Rightarrow \quad y = \frac{5}{3}x + \frac{2}{3}$

and $\quad y = \frac{6}{p}x + \frac{7}{p}$

On comparing with $y = m_1x + c_1$ and $y = m_2x + c_2$ respectively, we get

$$m_1 = \frac{5}{3} \text{ and } m_2 = \frac{6}{p}$$

Since, given lines are perpendicular.

$\therefore \quad m_1 \times m_2 = -1$

$\Rightarrow \quad \frac{5}{3} \times \frac{6}{p} = -1 \Rightarrow \frac{10}{p} = -1 \Rightarrow p = -10$

When $p = -10$, then slope of the line $6x - py + 7 = 0$ is $\frac{6}{-10}$ or $\frac{-3}{5}$.

$\therefore$ The equation of a line passing through (– 2, – 1) and parallel to $6x - py + 7 = 0$ is

$$y + 1 = \left(-\frac{3}{5}\right)(x + 2) \qquad [\because y - y_1 = m(x - x_1)]$$

$\Rightarrow \quad 5y + 5 = -3x - 6 \Rightarrow 3x + 5y + 11 = 0$

44. **Hint** $\frac{x}{4} + \frac{y}{6} = 1 \Rightarrow 3x + 2y = 12$ ...(i)

If line (i) meets the Y-axis, then putting $x = 0$ in Eq. (i), we get $y = 6$

So, the point is (0, 6).

Slope of line (i) is $m_1 = \frac{-3}{2}$.

Now, the equation of line having slope $\frac{2}{3}$ and passing through (0, 6) is given by $y - 6 = \frac{2}{3}(x - 0)$.

Ans. $2x - 3y + 18 = 0$

45. **Hint** Clearly, $AB \perp BC$

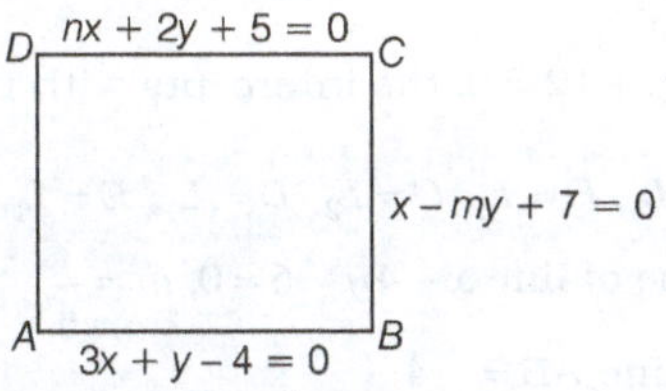

m_1 = Slope of line $AB = -3$

m_2 = Slope of line $BC = \frac{1}{m}$

$\therefore m_1 m_2 = -1$

Similarly, m_3 = Slope of line $CD = \frac{-n}{2}$

$\therefore m_2 \cdot m_3 = -1$

Ans. $m = 3$ and $n = 6$

46. Let m be the slope of PM.

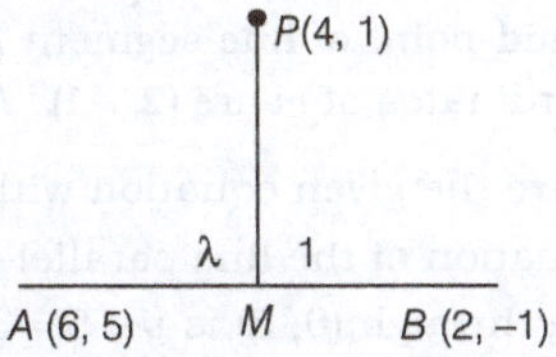

Since, as $PM \perp AB$

$\therefore$ Slope of $PM \times$ Slope of $AB = -1$

$\Rightarrow \quad m \times \frac{-1-5}{2-6} = -1 \Rightarrow m = \frac{-2}{3}$

Equation of line PM is $y - 1 = \frac{-2}{3}(x - 4)$

$\Rightarrow \quad 2x + 3y - 11 = 0$ ...(i)

Let line PM divide the line AB in ratio $\lambda : 1$.

The coordinates of M are $\left(\frac{2\lambda + 6}{\lambda + 1}, \frac{-\lambda + 5}{\lambda + 1}\right)$.

Since, M lies on line PM, so it will satisfies Eq. (i).

$$\therefore 2\left(\frac{2\lambda + 6}{\lambda + 1}\right) + 3\left(\frac{-\lambda + 5}{\lambda + 1}\right) - 11 = 0.$$

$$\Rightarrow \quad \frac{4\lambda + 12 - 3\lambda + 15}{\lambda + 1} = \frac{11}{1}$$

$$\Rightarrow \quad \frac{\lambda + 27}{\lambda + 1} = \frac{11}{1}$$

$\Rightarrow \quad \lambda + 27 = 11\lambda + 11$

$\Rightarrow \quad 16 = 10\lambda$

Dividing by 2 on both sides,

$8 = 5\lambda$

$\Rightarrow \quad \frac{\lambda}{1} = \frac{8}{5} \Rightarrow \lambda : 1 = 8 : 5$

47. (i) **Hint** First, determine the mid-point of BC, then find the equation of line passing through two points using the formula,

$$y - y_1 = \frac{y_2 - y_1}{x_2 - x_1}(x - x_1).$$ **Ans.** $y = 2$

(ii) **Hint** Now, determine the slope m of line AC, then find the equation of altitude through B.

i.e. $y - y_1 = -\frac{1}{m}(x - x_1)$

Ans. $2x + y - 12 = 0$

48. (i) **Hint** Line parallel to X-axis. **Ans.** 0

(ii) **Hint** Since, the diagonals of a square bisect the angles, therefore $\angle CBD$, i.e. $\theta = 45°$.

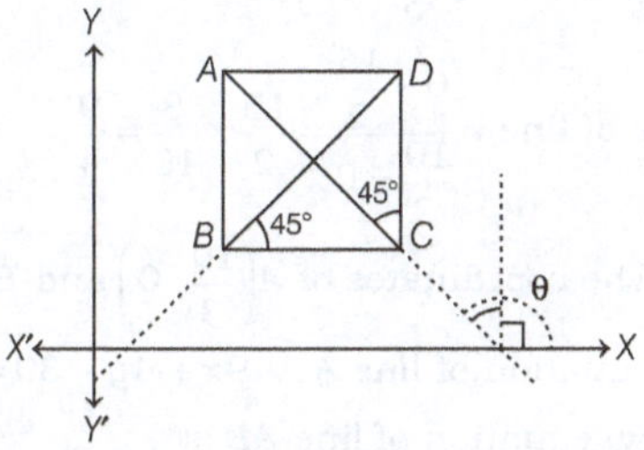

Ans. 1

(iii) **Hint** $\theta = 135°$ **Ans.** –1

49. Do same as Example 16.

Ans. (i) $m = 1$ (ii) (–8, – 8) (iii) $y = x$

50. **Hint** Slope of a line, $m = \tan 135°$

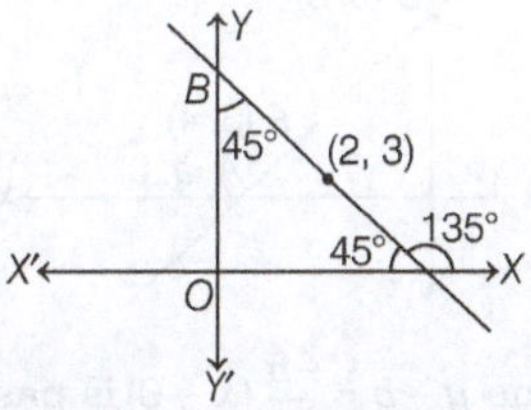

Now, equation of line AB is $y - 3 = -1(x - 2)$.

Ans. Slope = –1; Equation of line is $x + y = 5$

51. **Hint** Since, line $x - 2y - 11 = 0$ intersect the Y-axis, putting $x = 0$, we get $y = -\frac{11}{2}$.

$\therefore$ Coordinates on Y-axis is $\left(0, -\frac{11}{2}\right)$.

Use two-points form of equation of line formula.

Ans. $19x - 2y - 11 = 0$

52. (i) **Hint** Do same as Example 34.

Ans. $A(4, 0)$ and $B(0, -6)$

(ii) **Hint** Use the formula, slope $= \dfrac{y_2 - y_1}{x_2 - x_1}$.

Ans. $1\dfrac{1}{2}$

(iii) $\because$ Slope, $m = 1\dfrac{1}{2} = \dfrac{3}{2}$

and coordinates of points A and B are

$A(4, 0)$ and $B(0, -6)$

Now, equation of AB by using point slope form

$$(y - 0) = \frac{3}{2}(x - 4)$$

$[\because$ point slope form is $(y - y_1) = m(x - x_1)]$

$$\Rightarrow \quad 2y = 3x - 12$$

$$2y = 3x - 12$$

53. Hint Do same as Example 19.

Ans. $2x + 3y = 10$, $y = 2$, $2x - y = 2$

54. Hint (i) $PA : PB = \dfrac{2}{3}$ $\left[\text{by using section formula, } (x, y) = \dfrac{m_1x_2 + m_2x_1}{m_1 + m_2}, \dfrac{m_1y_2 + m_2y_1}{m_1 + m_2}\right]$

$\therefore$ The coordinate of the point

$$\left(\frac{3 \cdot a + 2 \cdot 0}{5}, \frac{3 \cdot 0 + 2 \cdot b}{5}\right)$$

(ii) Slope of line $= \dfrac{0 - \frac{15}{2}}{\frac{10}{3} - 0} = \dfrac{15}{2} \times \dfrac{3}{10} = \dfrac{9}{4}$

Ans. (i) The coordinates of $A\left(\dfrac{10}{3}, 0\right)$ and $B\left(0, \dfrac{15}{2}\right)$.

(ii) The equation of line AB, $9x + 4y - 30 = 0$

55. Hint Now, equation of line AB is

$$y - b = \frac{0 - b}{a - 0}(x - 0)$$

$$\Rightarrow \quad y - b = \frac{-b}{a}(x - 0) \quad \text{...(i)}$$

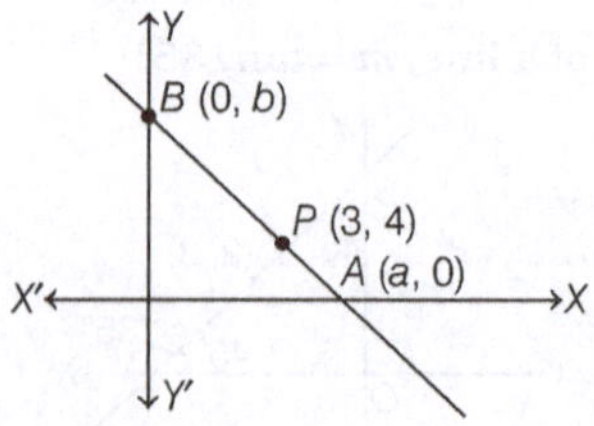

Since, the line $y - b = \dfrac{-b}{a}(x - 0)$ is passing through the point (3, 4).

$$\therefore \quad 4 - b = \frac{-b}{a}(3 - 0) \quad \text{...(ii)}$$

Also, given $a + b = 14$ ...(iii)

Now, simplify Eqs. (ii) and (iii), we have two values of a and b

$a = 6, 7$, when $a = 6$, then $b = 8$

and when $a = 7$, then $b = 7$

On putting the values of a and b in Eq. (i), we have

$$x + y = 7 \text{ and } 4x + 3y = 24$$

Ans. $x + y = 7$ and $4x + 3y = 24$

56. Hint First, use the formula,

$$y - y_1 = \frac{y_2 - y_1}{x_2 - x_1}(x - x_1).$$

To prove collinear, show that R satisfy the equation of line.

Ans. $x - 2y - 3 = 0$

57. Hint $A = 3x + 2y = 0$ passes through origin;

B. Now, slope of $3x + 2y = 0$ and $3x + 2y = 20$ are equal.

C. The equation of a line parallel to Y-axis is of the form $x = a$.

D. The equation of a line parallel to X-axis is of the form $y = a$

E. $3x + 2y + 12 = 0$, the intercepts with the axes are negative.

Ans. $A = L_3$, $B = L_5$, $C = L_2$, $D = L_4$, $E = L_1$

58. Hint Slope of line $x - 4y - 6 = 0$, $m = \dfrac{1}{4}$

Slope of line $AB = -4$

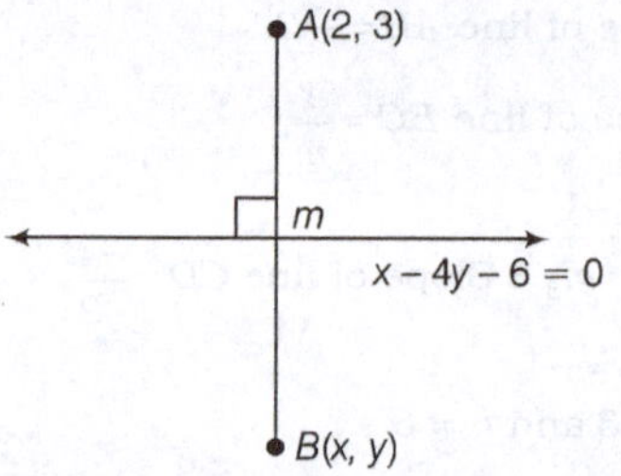

Now, equation of line AB, $4x + y = 7$

$\therefore$ m is the mid-point of line segment AB

and the coordinates of m are $(2, -1)$. **Ans.** $(2, -5)$

59. Hint Compare the given equation with $y = mx + c$.

Further, equation of the line parallel to given line and passing through (0, 5) is $y - 5 = 3(x - 0)$.

Ans. 3, – 5 and $y = 3x + 5$

60. Hint

By using section formula,

Coordinate of $M = \left(\dfrac{1 \times -1 + 2 \times 2}{1 + 2}, \dfrac{1 \times 2 + 2 \times 5}{1 + 2}\right)$

$\therefore$ Equation of line joining C and M is

$$y - 4 = \frac{8 - 4}{5 - 1}(x - 1)$$

$$\Rightarrow \quad y - 4 = \frac{4}{4}(x - 1)$$

Ans. $M = (1, 4)$; $y = x + 3$

Olympiad Section

Brain Teasing Questions of Olympiad Pattern

1 The coordinates of the orthocentre of the triangle, whose vertices are $(-1, 3)$, $(2, -1)$ and $(0, 0)$, is

(a) $(4, 3)$ (b) $(-4, -3)$
(c) $(3, 4)$ (d) $(-3, -4)$

2 The point $P(-2, 4)$ is reflected in the line parallel to Y-axis at a distance 3 units to the left of Y-axis onto the point P'. The point Q is reflected in the origin onto the point $Q'(4, -1)$. The equation the line $P'Q$ is

(a) $x + 4 = 0$ (b) $x - 4 = 0$
(c) $y + 4 = 0$ (d) $y - 4 = 0$

3 If the slope of a line passing through the point $A(3, 2)$ is $3/4$, then the point on the line, which are 5 units away from the point A is

(a) $(-1, -1)$ (b) $(7, 5)$
(c) $(7, -5)$ (d) Both (a) and (b)

4 A ray of light coming from the point $(1, 2)$ is reflected at a point A on the X-axis and then passes through the point $(5, 3)$, then the coordinates of the point A is

(a) $(0, 1)$ (b) $(0, 13/5)$
(c) $(13/5, 0)$ (d) $(1, 0)$

5 A line passes through the point $(3, -2)$. The locus of the middle point of the portion of the line intercepted between axes is

(a) $2x - 3y = 2xy$ (b) $3y + 2x = -2xy$
(c) $2x + 3y = 2xy$ (d) $3y - 2x = 2xy$

6 If the image of the point $(2, 1)$ with respect to the line mirror be $(5, 2)$, then the equation of the mirror is

(a) $3x + y - 12 = 0$
(b) $3x - y + 12 = 0$
(c) $3x + y + 12 = 0$
(d) None of the above

7 Suppose the equation of the line through the point $(0, 2)$ making an angle $\frac{2\pi}{3}$ with the positive X-axis. Find the equation of line parallel to the given line and below the origin, which is equidistant from origin. [Given $\tan(\pi - \theta) = -\tan\theta$]

(a) $\sqrt{3}x - y - 2 = 0$ (b) $\sqrt{3}x + y + 2 = 0$
(c) $\sqrt{3}x - y + 2 = 0$ (d) $\sqrt{3}x + y - 2 = 0$

8 Suppose ABC be a triangle, whose centroid is G. If the coordinates of B, C and G are $(-2, 0)$, $(3, 1)$ and $(1, 5)$, then the equations of the sides AB and AC are respectively.

(a) $7x - 2y + 14 = 0, 13x + y - 40 = 0$
(b) $7x + 2y + 14 = 0, x + 13y - 40 = 0$
(c) $7x - 2y - 14 = 0, 13x + 13y - 40 = 0$
(d) None of these

Answers

1. (b) **2.** (a) **3.** (d) **4.** (c) **5.** (d) **6.** (a) **7.** (b) **8.** (a)

* *These questions may or may not be asked in the examination, have been given just for additional practice required for olympiads Scholarship Exams etc.* *For detailed explanations refer Page No. 486.*

CHAPTER

13

Similarity

SYLLABUS

- **Similarity, conditions of similar triangles.**
  (I) Comparison with congruency, keyword being proportionality.
  (ii) Three conditions SSS, SAS, AA. Simple applications (proof not included).

Two geometrical figures are said to be similar figures, if they have same shape but not necessarily the **same size**. A shape is said to be similar to other, if the ratios of their corresponding sides are equal and the corresponding angles are equal.

Some examples of similar figures are given below

(i)  and  (ii)  and 

(iii) 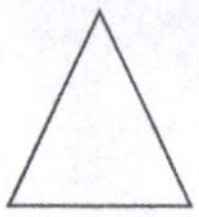 and 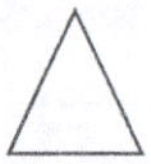 (iv) 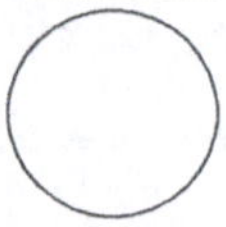 and 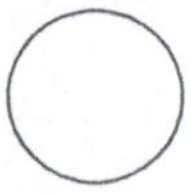

Two polygons of same number of sides are similar, if

(i) all the corresponding angles are equal.
(ii) all the corresponding sides are in the same ratio or proportion.

Comparison between Congruency and Similarity

If two figures are congruent, then it means their shape and size (area) both are equal, but for two similar figures, shape will necessarily be same but their sizes will not be same, rather their sizes will be proportional, i.e. one figure similar to other can be smaller or greater than to other. A figure similar to a given figure can be obtained by enlarging or reducing the given figure in a uniform manner.

e.g. All circles are similar (because the shape of all the circles are same) and can be obtained by reducing or enlarging the given circle.

Scale Factor

The ratio that compares the measurements of two similar shapes, is called the scale factor or representative fraction. It is equal to the ratio of corresponding sides of two figures. We can use the ratio of corresponding sides to find unknown sides of similar shapes.

Example 1. State whether the given quadrilaterals are similar or not.

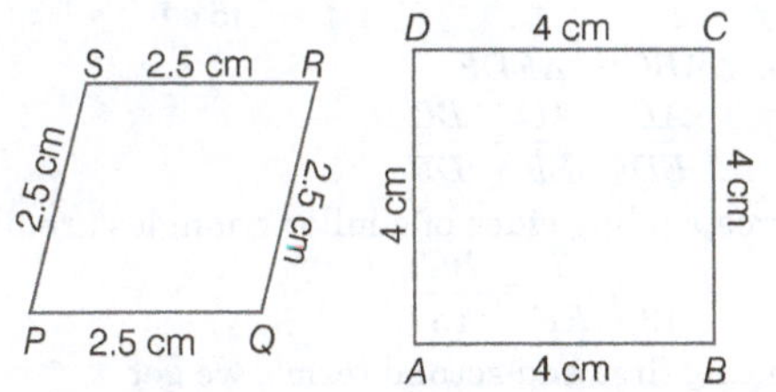

Sol. Here, $\frac{PQ}{AB} = \frac{2.5}{4} = \frac{25}{10 \times 4} = \frac{5}{8}$ and $\frac{RQ}{BC} = \frac{2.5}{4} = \frac{25}{10 \times 4} = \frac{5}{8}$

Clearly, the corresponding sides of quadrilaterals *ABCD* and *PQRS* are proportional but their corresponding angles are not equal.

Hence, quadrilaterals *ABCD* and *PQRS* are not similar.

Similarity as a Size Transformation

Size transformation is the process, in which a geometrical figure is enlarged or reduced by a scale factor k, such that the resulting figure (the image) is similar to the given figure.

Consider a ΔABC having sides of length 4 cm, 3 cm and 5 cm.

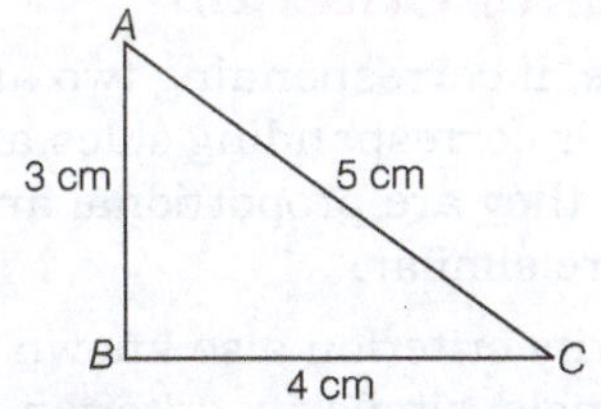

From the figure it is clear that ΔABC is a right angle triangle, right angled at *B*.

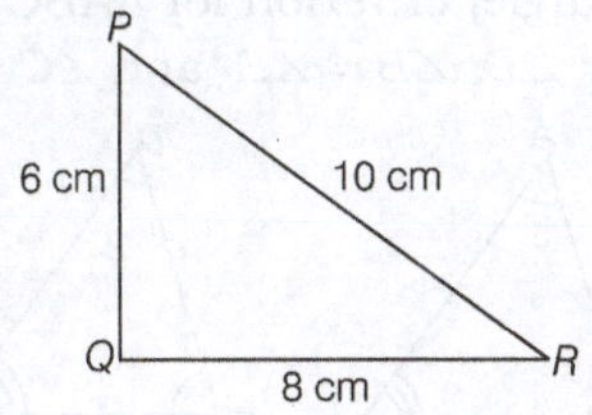

Now, we make one or more right angled triangle *PQR* by taking the sides double to the given triangle i.e. 6 cm, 8 cm and 10 cm.

We see that shapes of ΔABC and ΔPQR are similar but they have different sizes.

Thus, we can say that, two figures are similar, if one can be obtained from the other by size transformation.

Example 2. A ΔABC has been enlarged by a scale factor $k = 2$ to the ΔPQR. Calculate

(i) the length of *AB*, if $PQ = 6$ cm.

(ii) the length of *PR*, if $AC = 8$ cm.

Sol. As we know that, if k is a scale factor, then each side of the resulting figure = k times the corresponding side of given figure. Therefore, we have

$$PQ = kAB \text{ and } PR = kAC \quad \text{...(i)}$$

(i) Now, as $PQ = 6$ cm, therefore

$$AB = \frac{1}{k} PQ = \frac{1}{2} \times 6 = 3 \text{ cm} \quad \text{[using Eq. (i)]}$$

(ii) As $AC = 8$ cm, therefore

$$PR = kAC = 2 \times 8 = 16 \text{ cm} \quad \text{[using Eq. (i)]}$$

Similar Triangles and Criteria for Similarity of Two Triangles

Similar Triangles

A triangle is a plane figure bounded by three lines. It has three sides and three angles.

Two triangles are said to be similar, if

(i) their corresponding angles are equal.

(ii) their corresponding sides are proportional (i.e. the ratios between the lengths of corresponding sides are equal).

e.g. In ΔABC and ΔPQR, if

$$\angle A = \angle P, \quad \angle B = \angle Q, \quad \angle C = \angle R$$

and $\frac{AB}{PQ} = \frac{BC}{QR} = \frac{AC}{PR}$.

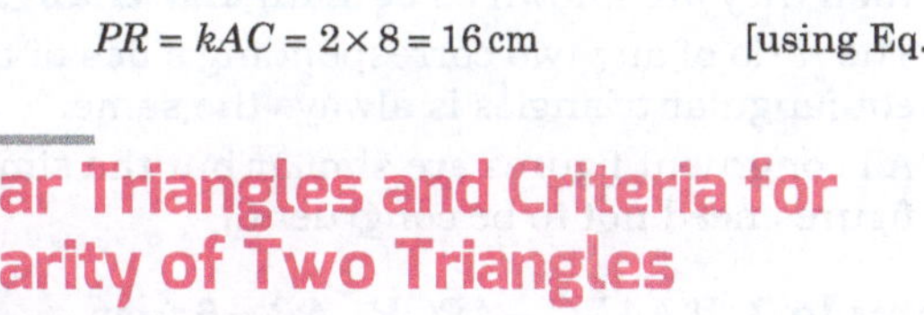

Then, $\Delta ABC \sim \Delta PQR$, where symbol '~' is read as 'is similar to'.

Symbolic Expression of Two Similar Triangles

Similarity of two triangles should be expressed symbolically using correct correspondence of their vertices.

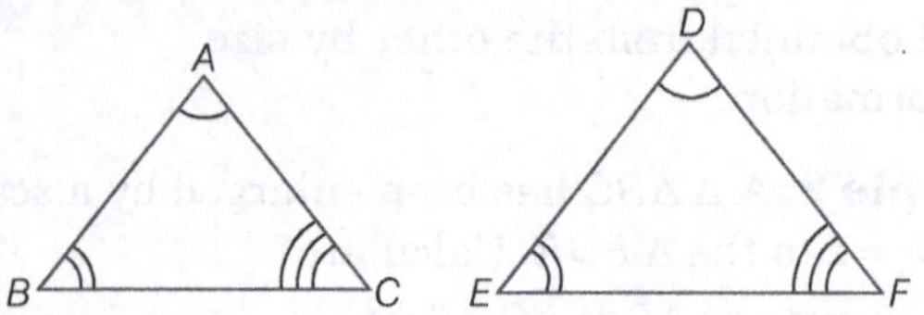

e.g. In ΔABC and ΔDEF, $\angle A = \angle D$, $\angle B = \angle E$ and $\angle C = \angle F$, then we should write $\Delta ABC \sim \Delta DEF$, we cannot write $\Delta ABC \sim \Delta EDF$ or $\Delta BAC \sim \Delta DEF$.

Conversely (Converse of Similar Triangles),
If ΔABC is similar to ΔPQR, then $\angle A = \angle P$, $\angle B = \angle Q$, $\angle C = \angle R$ and $\frac{AB}{PQ} = \frac{BC}{QR} = \frac{AC}{PR}$.

(i) If corresponding angles of two triangles are equal, then they are known as **equiangular triangles.**

(ii) The ratio of any two corresponding sides of two equiangular triangles is always the same.

(iii) All congruent figures are similar but the similar figures need not to be congruent.

Example 3. If $\Delta ABC \sim \Delta PQR$, $AB = 6.5$ cm, $PQ = 10.4$ cm and perimeter of $\Delta ABC = 60$ cm, find the perimeter of ΔPQR.

Sol. Given, $AB = 6.5$ cm and $PQ = 10.4$ cm

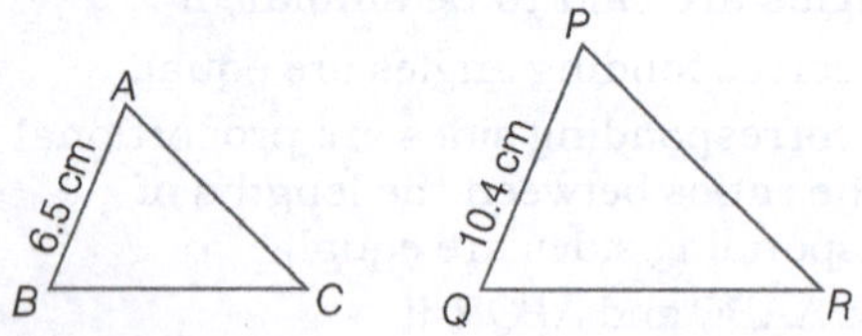

Since, $\Delta ABC \sim \Delta PQR$.

$$\therefore \quad \frac{AB}{PQ} = \frac{BC}{QR} = \frac{AC}{PR} = \frac{6.5}{10.4} = \frac{65}{104}$$

[$\because$ corresponding sides of similar triangles are proportional]

i.e. $AB = \frac{65}{104} PQ$, $BC = \frac{65}{104} QR$, $AC = \frac{65}{104} PR$

Also given, perimeter of $\Delta ABC = 60$ cm

$$\therefore \quad AB + BC + AC = 60 \Rightarrow \frac{65}{104}(PQ + QR + PR) = 60$$

$$\Rightarrow \quad PQ + QR + PR = \frac{60 \times 104}{65} = 96 \text{ cm}$$

Hence, the perimeter of ΔPQR is 96 cm.

Example 4. It is given that $\Delta ABC \sim \Delta EDF$ such that $AB = 5$ cm, $AC = 7$ cm, $DF = 15$ cm and $DE = 12$ cm. Find the lengths of the remaining sides of the triangles.

Sol. Given, $\Delta ABC \sim \Delta EDF$

Also, $AB = 5$ cm, $AC = 7$ cm, $DF = 15$ cm, $DE = 12$ cm ...(i)

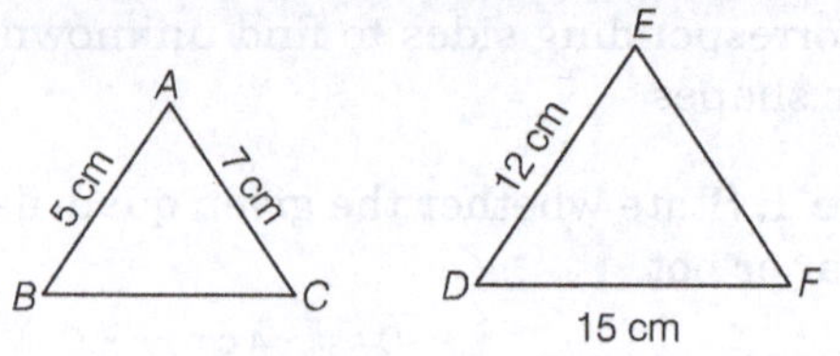

Since, $\Delta ABC \sim \Delta EDF$

$$\therefore \quad \frac{AB}{ED} = \frac{AC}{EF} = \frac{BC}{DF}$$

[$\because$ corresponding sides of similar triangles are proportion]

$$\Rightarrow \quad \frac{5}{12} = \frac{7}{EF} = \frac{BC}{15}$$

On taking first and second terms, we get

$$\frac{5}{12} = \frac{7}{EF} \Rightarrow EF = \frac{7 \times 12}{5} = 16.8 \text{ cm}$$

On taking first and third terms, we get

$$\frac{5}{12} = \frac{BC}{15} \Rightarrow BC = \frac{5 \times 15}{12} = 6.25 \text{ cm}$$

Hence, the lengths of remaining sides of the triangles are $EF = 16.8$ cm and $BC = 6.25$ cm.

Criteria for Similarity of Triangles

We have some criteria for similarity of two triangles involve relationship between less number of pairs of corresponding parts of two triangles instead of all the six pairs of corresponding parts. These criteria are discussed below

1. AA Similarity Criterion

In two triangles, if corresponding two angles are equal, then their corresponding sides are in the same ratio, i.e. they are proportional and hence, the two triangles are similar.

This AA similarity criterion also known as AAA (Angle-Angle-Angle) similarity criterion.

AA (Angle-Angle)

In AA (Angle-Angle) criterion for ΔABC and ΔDEF,

$$\angle A = \angle D, \angle B = \angle E \text{ and } \angle C = \angle F$$

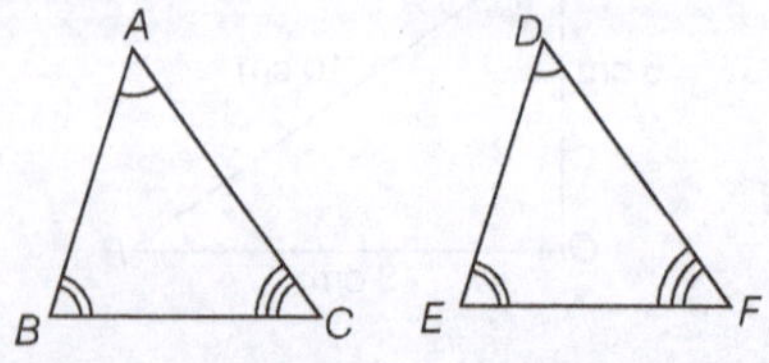

Hence, $\Delta ABC \sim \Delta DEF$.

If two angles of a triangle are respectively equal to two angles of another triangle, then by angle sum property of a triangle, their third angle will also be equal and the two triangles will be similar, it is called **AA similarity criterion**.

2. SSS Similarity Criterion

If in two triangles, sides of one triangle are proportional (i.e. in the same ratio) to the sides of the other triangle, then their corresponding angles are equal and hence, the two triangles are similar.

In SSS (Side-Side-Side) criterion,

$$\frac{AB}{DE} = \frac{AC}{DF} = \frac{BC}{EF}$$

Hence, $\Delta ABC \sim \Delta DEF$.

In case of similarity of two triangles, it is not necessary to check both the conditions (AAA and SSS), because one condition implies the other.

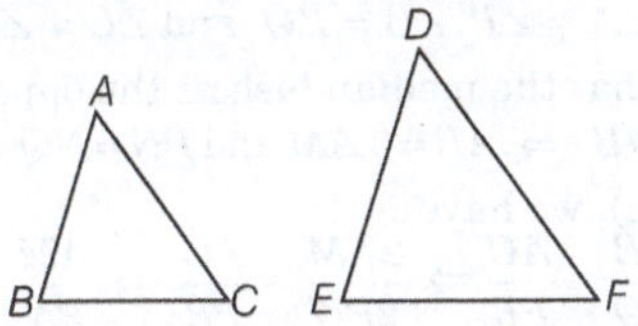

3. SAS Similarity Criterion

If one angle of a triangle is equal to one angle of the other triangle and the sides including these angles are proportional, then the two triangles are similar.

In SAS (Side-Angle-Side) criterion,

$$\frac{AB}{DE} = \frac{AC}{DF} \text{ and } \angle A = \angle D$$

or $$\frac{AB}{DE} = \frac{BC}{EF} \text{ and } \angle B = \angle E$$

or $$\frac{AC}{DF} = \frac{BC}{EF} \text{ and } \angle C = \angle F$$

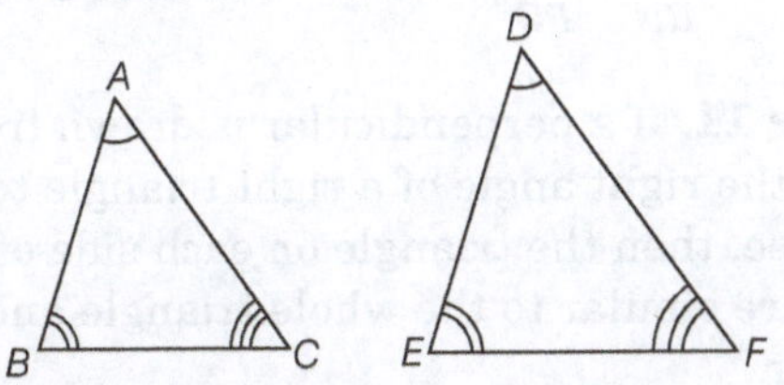

Hence, $\Delta ABC \sim \Delta DEF$.

For proving (or finding) the similarity, we use the criteria, AA, SAS and SSS. While proving (or finding) the congruency, we use the rule SAS, ASA, SSS and RHS.

Problems Based on Similarity of Triangles

There are many problems which can be solved or proved by using these three criterion of similarity. Some of such kind of problems are given below

Example 5. State which pairs of triangles in the given figure are similar? Also, state the similarity criterion used.

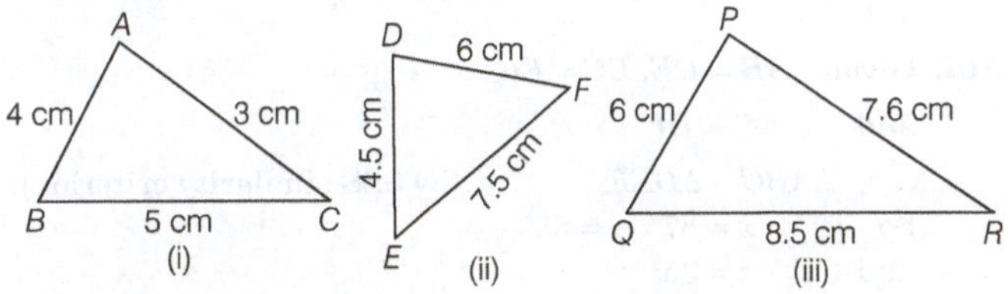

Sol. Here, $\frac{AB}{DF} = \frac{4}{6} = \frac{2}{3}$,

$$\frac{BC}{EF} = \frac{5}{7.5} = \frac{2}{3}$$

and $$\frac{AC}{DE} = \frac{3}{4.5} = \frac{2}{3}$$

As, $$\frac{AB}{DF} = \frac{BC}{EF} = \frac{AC}{DE}$$

So, $\Delta ABC \sim \Delta DFE$ [by SSS similarity criterion]

Hence, figures (i) and (ii) are similar triangles, but no other pairs of triangles in the given figure are similar.

Example 6. State which of the two triangles given in the figure are similar. Also, state the similarity criterion used.

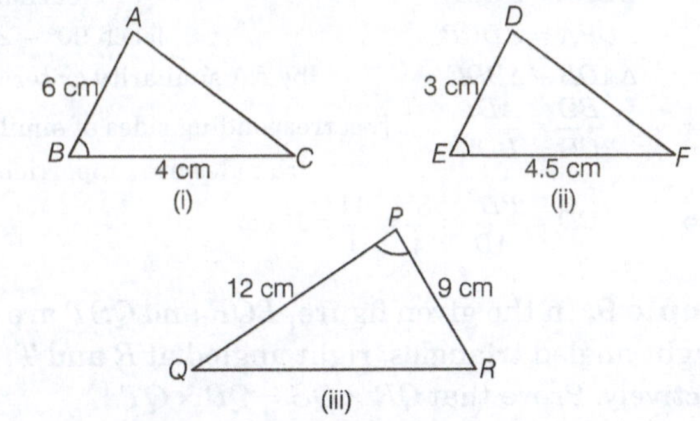

Sol. Here, $\frac{AB}{EF} = \frac{6}{4.5} = \frac{60}{45} = \frac{4}{3}$,

$$\frac{BC}{DE} = \frac{4}{3}$$

So, $$\frac{AB}{EF} = \frac{BC}{DE}$$

and $\angle ABC = \angle FED$ [given]

$\therefore$ $\Delta ABC \sim \Delta FED$ [by SAS similarity criterion]

Hence, figures (i) and (ii) are similar triangles, but no other pairs of triangles in the given figure are similar.

Example 7. Find the value of each of the pronumerals in the given pair of triangles. Give reason for your answer.

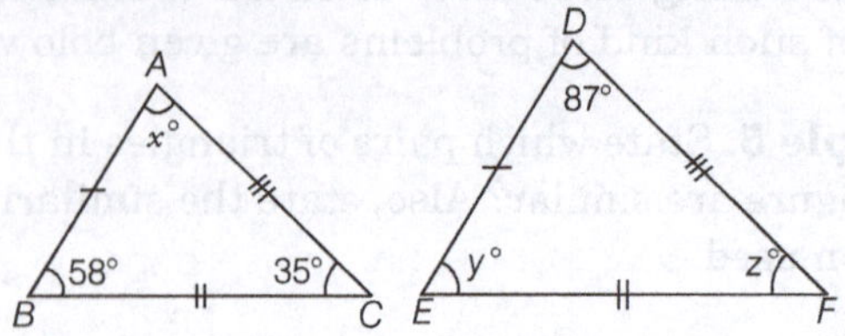

Sol. Given, $AB = DE, BC = EF$

and $AC = DF$

$\therefore$ $\Delta ABC \sim \Delta DEF$ [by SSS similarity criterion]

So, $x = 87°, y = 58°$

and $z = 35°$

[$\because$ corresponding angles of similar triangles are equal]

Example 8. In the given figure, $\angle ABC = 90°$ and $BD \perp AC$. If $BD = 8$ cm and $AD = 4$ cm, then find the value of CD.

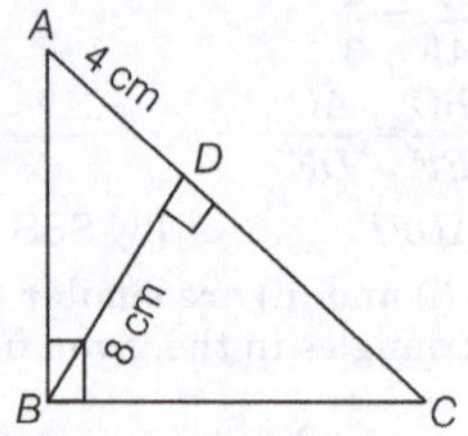

Sol. Given, $BD = 8$ cm and $AD = 4$ cm

In ΔADB and ΔBDC,

$\angle BDA = \angle CDB$ [each 90°]

$\angle DBA = \angle DCB$ [each $90° - \angle A$]

$\therefore$ $\Delta ADB \sim \Delta BDC$ [by AA similarity criterion]

$\Rightarrow$ $\frac{BD}{CD} = \frac{AD}{BD}$ [$\because$ corresponding sides of similar triangles are proportional]

$\Rightarrow$ $CD = \frac{BD^2}{AD} = \frac{8^2}{4} = \frac{64}{4} = 16$ cm

Example 9. In the given figure, PQR and QST are two right angled triangles, right angled at R and T, respectively. Prove that $QR \times QS = QP \times QT$.

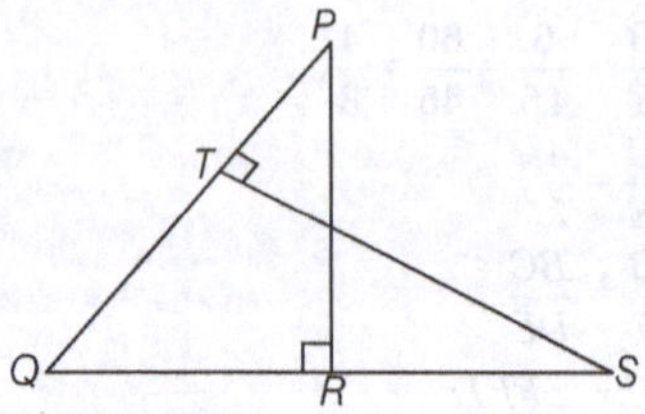

Sol. In ΔPRQ and ΔSTQ,

$\angle PRQ = \angle STQ$ [each 90°]

$\angle PQR = \angle SQT$ [common angle]

So, $\Delta PRQ \sim \Delta STQ$ [by AA similarity criterion]

Then, $\frac{QR}{QT} = \frac{QP}{QS}$

[$\because$ corresponding sides of similar triangles are proportional]

$\Rightarrow$ $QR \times QS = QP \times QT$ **Hence proved.**

Example 10. In the following figure, CM and RN are respectively the medians of ΔABC and ΔPQR. If $\Delta ABC \sim \Delta PQR$, prove that

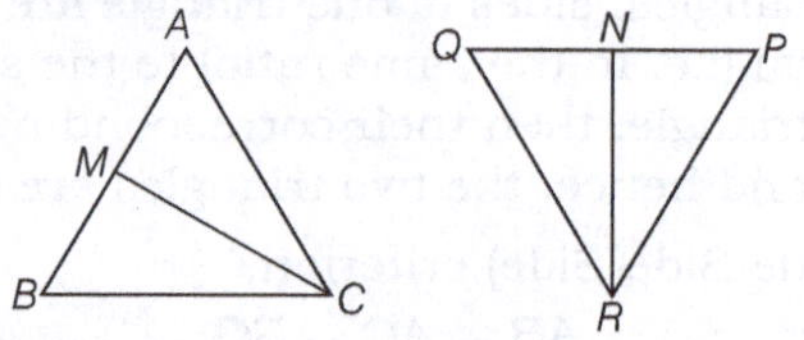

(i) $\Delta AMC \sim \Delta PNR$ (ii) $\frac{CM}{RN} = \frac{AB}{PQ}$

Sol.

(i) Given, $\Delta ABC \sim \Delta PQR$

$\therefore$ $\frac{AB}{PQ} = \frac{BC}{QR} = \frac{AC}{PR}$ ...(i)

and $\angle A = \angle P, \angle B = \angle Q$ and $\angle C = \angle R$ ...(ii)

We know that the median bisects the opposite side.

$\therefore$ $AM = MB \Rightarrow AB = 2AM$ and $PN = NQ \Rightarrow PQ = 2PN$

From Eq. (i), we have

$\frac{AB}{PQ} = \frac{AC}{PR} \Rightarrow \frac{2AM}{2PN} = \frac{AC}{PR} \Rightarrow \frac{AM}{PN} = \frac{AC}{PR}$ ...(iii)

In ΔAMC and ΔPNR, $\angle A = \angle P$ [from Eq. (ii)]

and $\frac{AM}{PN} = \frac{AC}{PR}$ [from Eq. (iii)]

So, $\Delta AMC \sim \Delta PNR$ [by SAS similarity criterion]

(ii) We have, $\Delta AMC \sim \Delta PNR \Rightarrow \frac{AM}{PN} = \frac{AC}{PR} = \frac{CM}{RN}$

[$\because$ triangles are similar, hence corresponding sides will be proportional]

$\therefore$ $\frac{CM}{RN} = \frac{AC}{PR} \Rightarrow \frac{CM}{RN} = \frac{AM}{PN}$ [from Eq. (iii)]

$\Rightarrow$ $\frac{CM}{RN} = \frac{2AM}{2PN}$

[multiplying numerator and denominator by 2 in RHS]

$\Rightarrow$ $\frac{CM}{RN} = \frac{AB}{PQ}$ [$\because AB = 2AM$ and $PQ = 2PN$]... (iv)

Example 11. If a perpendicular is drawn from the vertex of the right angle of a right triangle to the hypotenuse, then the triangle on each side of the altitude are similar to the whole triangle and also to each other.

Sol. Given, a right angle ΔPQR in which $\angle P = 90°$ and $PS \perp QR$.

To prove

(i) $\Delta QSP \sim \Delta PQR$

(ii) $\Delta PSR \sim \Delta PQR$

(iii) $\Delta QSP \sim \Delta SPR$

Proof Mark the angles as shown in the figure.

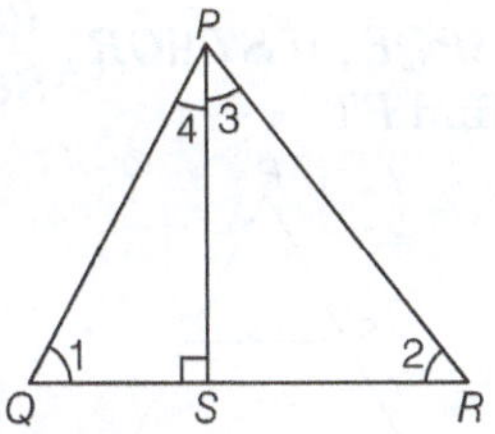

(i) In ΔQSP and ΔPQR,

$\angle PSQ = \angle QPR$ [right angle]

$\angle PQS = \angle PQR$ [common]

By AA similarity criterion $\Delta QSP \sim \Delta PQR$.

(ii) In ΔSPR and ΔPQR

$\angle PSR = \angle RPS$ [right angle]

$\angle PRS = \angle PRQ$ [common]

By AA similarity criterion

$\Delta SPR \sim \Delta PQR$

(iii) Now, $\angle 1 + \angle 4 = 90^\circ \Rightarrow \angle 3 + \angle 4 = 90^\circ$

$\Rightarrow \angle 1 + \angle 4 = \angle 3 + \angle 4 \Rightarrow \angle 1 = \angle 3$

In ΔQSP and ΔPSR, $\angle 1 = \angle 3$

$\angle PSQ = \angle PSR$

$\therefore \Delta QSP \sim \Delta SPR$

Example 12. A girl of height 90 cm is walking away from the base of a lamp-post at a speed of 1.2 m/s. If the lamp is 3.6 m above the ground, then find length of her shadow after 4s.

Sol. Let AB be the lamp-post, CD be the girl and D be the position of girl after 4 s.

Again, let $DE = x$ m be the length of shadow of the girl.

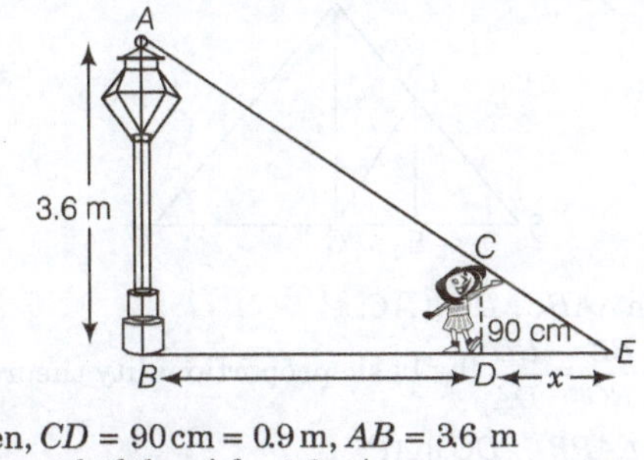

Given, $CD = 90\,\text{cm} = 0.9\,\text{m}$, $AB = 3.6$ m and speed of the girl $= 1.2\,\text{m/s}$

$\therefore$ Distance of the girl from lamp-post after 4 s,

$BD = 1.2 \times 4 = 4.8$ m [$\because$ distance = speed × time]

In ΔABE and ΔCDE, $\angle B = \angle D$ [each 90°]

$\angle E = \angle E$ [common angle]

$\therefore \Delta ABE \sim \Delta CDE$ [by AA similarity criterion]

$\Rightarrow \dfrac{BE}{DE} = \dfrac{AB}{CD}$ ...(i)

[$\because$ corresponding sides of similar triangles are proportional]

On putting all the values in Eq. (i), we get

$\dfrac{4.8 + x}{x} = \dfrac{3.6}{0.9}$ [$\because BE = BD + DE = 4.8 + x$]

$\Rightarrow \dfrac{4.8 + x}{x} = 4 \Rightarrow 4.8 + x = 4x$

$\Rightarrow 3x = 4.8 \Rightarrow x = \dfrac{4.8}{3} = 1.6\,\text{m}$

Hence, the length of her shadow after 4s is 1.6 m.

Basic Proportionality Theorem (BPT)

Here, we shall learn Basic Proportionality Theorem (BPT), its converse and their applications.

Theorem 1 (Basic Proportionality Theorem) *If a line is drawn parallel to one side of a triangle to intersect the other two sides in distinct points, then the other two sides are divided in the same ratio. This theorem is also known as Thales Theorem.*

In the following figure $DE \parallel BC$, so $\dfrac{AD}{DB} = \dfrac{AE}{EC}$

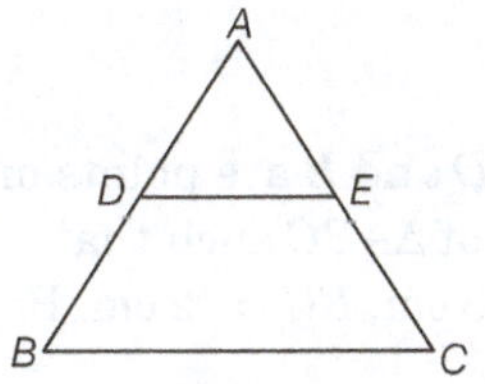

Theorem 2 (Converse of Basic Proportionality Theorem) *If a line divides any two sides of a triangle in the same ratio, then the line must be parallel to the third side.*

In the following figure, $\dfrac{AD}{DB} = \dfrac{AE}{EC}$

So, $DE \parallel BC$

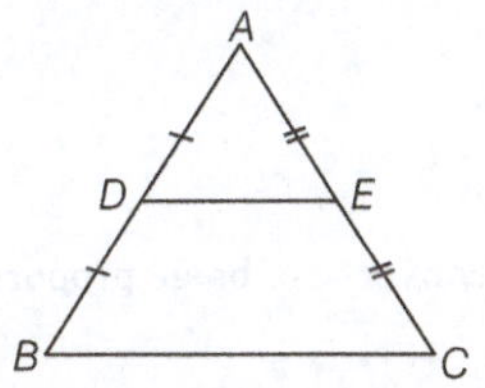

Theorem 3 (Internal bisector of an angle of a triangle) *The internal bisector of an angle of a triangle divides the opposite side internally in the ratio of the sides containing the angle.*

In the following figure AD is the bisector of $\angle A$.

So, $\dfrac{BD}{DC} = \dfrac{AB}{AC}$

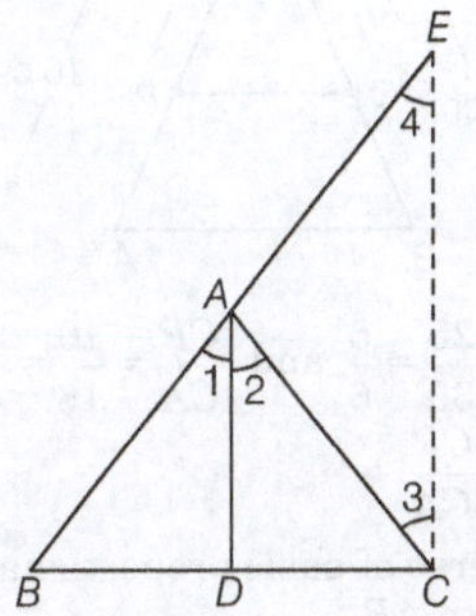

Example 13. In the given figure, $DE \parallel BC$. If $AD = 3$ cm, $DB = 4$ cm and $AE = 6$ cm, find EC.

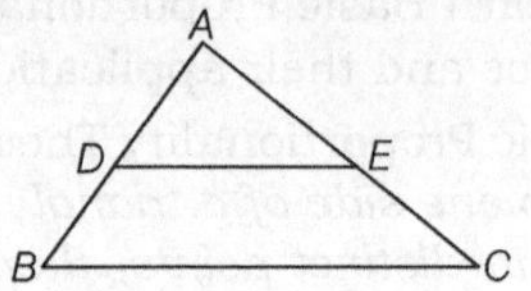

Sol. Given, in ΔABC, $DE \parallel BC$

$\therefore \quad \frac{AD}{DB} = \frac{AE}{EC}$ [by basic proportionality theorem]

$\Rightarrow \quad \frac{3}{4} = \frac{6}{EC}$ [given, $AD = 3$cm, $DB = 4$cm and $AE = 6$cm]

$\therefore \quad EC = 8$cm

Example 14. If D and E are points on the respective sides AB and AC of ΔABC such that $AD = 6$ cm, $BD = 9$ cm, $AE = 8$ cm, $EC = 12$ cm. Prove that $DE \parallel BC$.

Sol. In ΔABC, $\frac{AD}{DB} = \frac{6}{9} = \frac{2}{3}$ and $\frac{AE}{EC} = \frac{8}{12} = \frac{2}{3}$

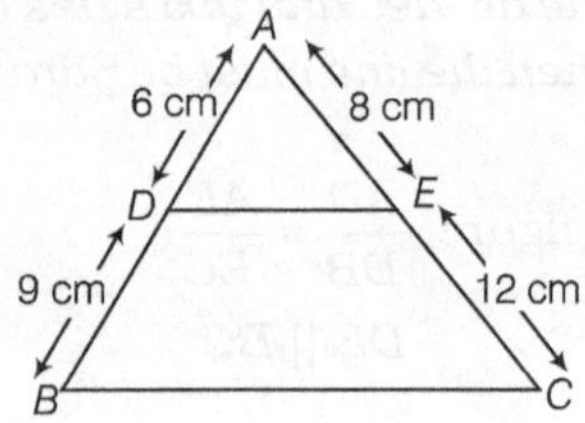

So, $\frac{AD}{DB} = \frac{AE}{EC}$

Hence, $DE \parallel BC$.

[by converse of basic proportionality theorem]

Hence proved.

Example 15. In ΔABC, points P and Q are on CA and CB, respectively such that $CA = 16$ cm, $CP = 10$ cm, $CB = 30$ cm and $CQ = 25$ cm. Is $PQ \parallel AB$?

Sol. Given, $CQ = 25$cm, $CB = 30$cm, $CP = 10$cm and $CA = 16$ cm.

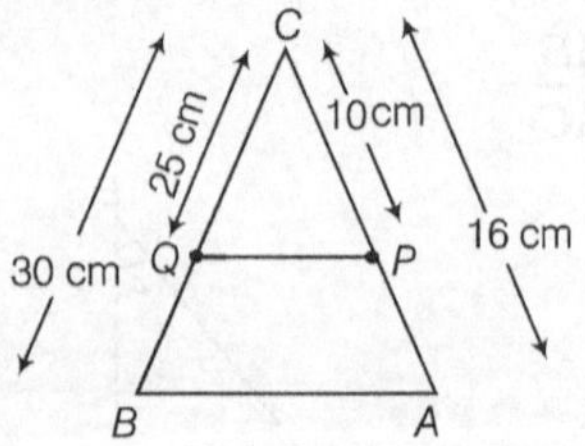

Now, $\frac{CQ}{CB} = \frac{25}{30} = \frac{5}{6}$ and $\frac{CP}{CA} = \frac{10}{16} = \frac{5}{8}$

$\Rightarrow \quad \frac{CQ}{CB} \neq \frac{CP}{CA}$

Then, by converse of basic proportionality theorem, PQ is not parallel to AB.

Example 16. In ΔPQR, if $ST \parallel QR$, $\frac{PS}{SQ} = \frac{3}{5}$ and $PR = 28$ cm then find PT.

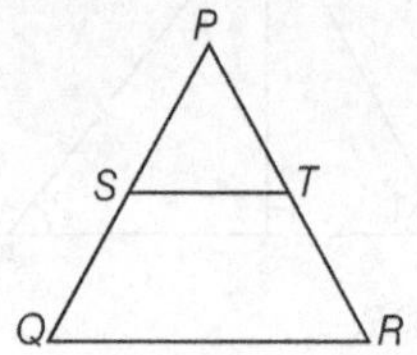

Sol. Given, $ST \parallel QR$, $PS/SQ = 3/5$ and $PR = 28$cm

By using basic proportionality theorem, we get

$$\frac{PS}{SQ} = \frac{PT}{TR}$$

$$\Rightarrow \quad \frac{PS}{SQ} = \frac{PT}{PR - PT}$$

$$\Rightarrow \quad \frac{3}{5} = \frac{PT}{28 - PT}$$

$$\Rightarrow \quad 3(28 - PT) = 5PT$$

$$\Rightarrow \quad 84 = 5PT + 3PT$$

$$\Rightarrow \quad PT = \frac{84}{8}$$

$$\Rightarrow \quad PT = 10.5 \text{ cm}$$

Hence, the length of PT is 10.5 cm.

Example 17. In the given figure, $DE \parallel AC$. If $DC \parallel AP$, where point P lies on BC produced, then prove that $\frac{BE}{EC} = \frac{BC}{CP}$.

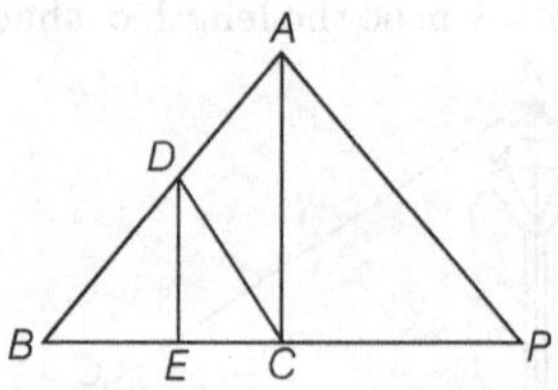

Sol. Given, in ΔABC, $DE \parallel AC$.

So, $\frac{BE}{EC} = \frac{BD}{DA}$ [by basic proportionality theorem] ...(i)

Also, in ΔAPB, $DC \parallel AP$ [given]

So, $\frac{BC}{CP} = \frac{BD}{DA}$ [by basic proportionality theorem] ...(ii)

From Eqs. (i) and (ii), we get

$\frac{BE}{EC} = \frac{BC}{CP}$ **Hence proved.**

Example 18. If the bisector of an angle of a triangle bisects the opposite side, prove that the triangle is isosceles.

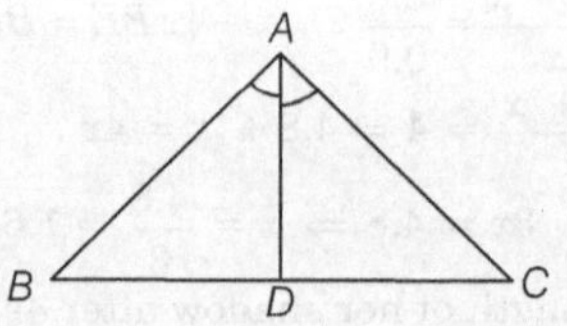

Sol. Let AD be the bisector of $\angle A$ of ΔABC such that AD bisects BC, i.e. $BD = DC$. We want to prove that ΔABC is isosceles.

As AD is bisector of $\angle A$.

$$\therefore \quad \frac{BD}{DC} = \frac{AB}{AC}$$

But $BD = DC \Rightarrow \dfrac{BD}{DC} = 1 \Rightarrow \dfrac{AB}{AC} = 1 \Rightarrow AB = AC$

$\Rightarrow \Delta ABC$ is isosceles.

Example 19. In the given figure, AD is bisector of $\angle BAC$. If $AB = 12$ cm, $AC = 8$ cm and $BD = 6$ cm, find BC.

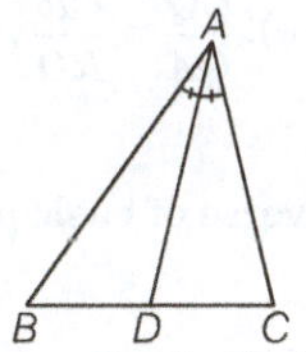

Sol. Since angular bisector divide the base in the ratio of other two sides.

So, $\dfrac{BD}{DC} = \dfrac{AB}{AC} \Rightarrow \dfrac{6}{DC} = \dfrac{12}{8}$

$$DC = \frac{8 \times 6}{12} = 4 \text{ cm}$$

So, $BC = BD + DC = 6 + 4 = 10$ cm

Example 20. In the given figure, the median BD and CE of a ΔABC meet at the point G. Prove that

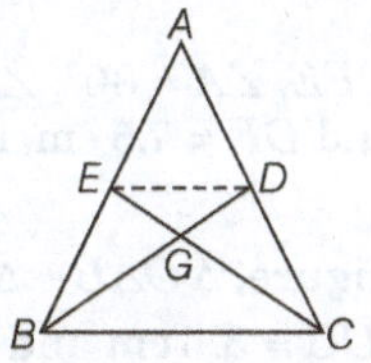

(i) $\Delta EGD \sim \Delta CGB$ (ii) $BG = 2GD$

Sol. Given, the median BD and CE of a ΔABC meet at point G.

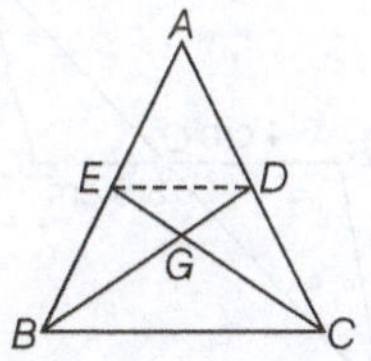

(i) In ΔEGD and ΔCGB

$ED \parallel BC$ and $ED = \frac{1}{2} BC$ [by mid-point theorem]

We have, $\angle EGD = \angle BGC$ [vertically opposite angle]

$\angle EDG = \angle CBG$ [alternate angles]

and $\angle GED = \angle GCB$ [alternate angles]

$\therefore$ $\Delta EGD \sim \Delta CGB$ [by AAA similarity criterion]

(ii) Since, BD is a median.

$$\therefore \quad \frac{BG}{GD} = \frac{2}{1}$$

[$\because$ centroid of a ΔABC divides the median in ratio 2 : 1]

$\Rightarrow$ $BG = 2GD$ **Hence proved.**

Example 21. In the given figure, $ABCD$ is a trapezium with $AB \parallel DC$. E and F are two points on non-parallel sides AD and BC respectively, such that EF is parallel to AB. Show that $\dfrac{AE}{ED} = \dfrac{BF}{FC}$.

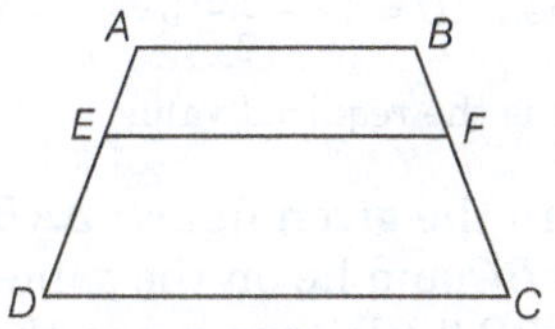

Sol. **Given** In trapezium $ABCD$, $AB \parallel DC$ and $EF \parallel AB$

To prove $\dfrac{AE}{ED} = \dfrac{BF}{FC}$

Construction Join AC to intersect EF at G.

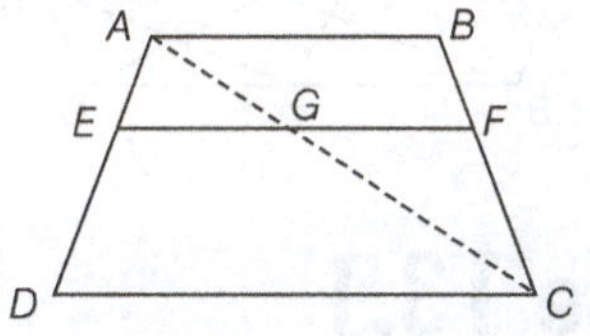

Proof Since, $AB \parallel DC$ and $EF \parallel AB$

$\therefore$ $EF \parallel DC$ [$\because$ lines parallel to the same line are also parallel to each other]

In ΔADC, $EG \parallel DC$ [$\because EF \parallel DC$]

By using basic proportionality theorem, $\dfrac{AE}{ED} = \dfrac{AG}{GC}$ ...(i)

In ΔABC, $GF \parallel AB$ [$\because EF \parallel AB$]

By using basic proportionality theorem,

$\dfrac{CG}{AG} = \dfrac{CF}{BF}$ or $\dfrac{AG}{GC} = \dfrac{BF}{CF}$ [reciprocal the terms] ...(ii)

From Eqs. (i) and (ii), we get $\dfrac{AE}{ED} = \dfrac{BF}{FC}$ **Hence proved.**

Example 22. In ΔABC, D and E are points on the sides AB and AC respectively, such that $DE \parallel BC$. If $AD = 4x - 3$, $AE = 8x - 7$, $BD = 3x - 1$ and $CE = 5x - 3$, then find the value of x.

Sol. Given, in ΔABC, $DE \parallel BC$

By Thales theorem, we get

$$\frac{AD}{DB} = \frac{AE}{EC} \Rightarrow \frac{4x-3}{3x-1} = \frac{8x-7}{5x-3}$$

[$\because AD = 4x - 3$, $DB = 3x - 1$, $AE = 8x - 7$, $EC = 5x - 3$]

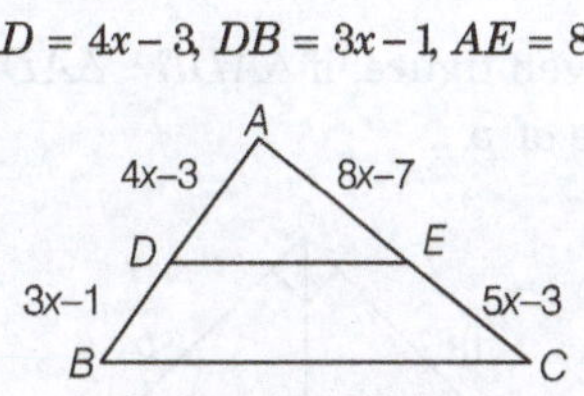

$\Rightarrow$ $(4x - 3)(5x - 3) = (8x - 7)(3x - 1)$

$\Rightarrow$ $20x^2 - 12x + 9 - 15x = 24x^2 - 21x - 8x + 7$

$\Rightarrow$ $4x^2 - 2x - 2 = 0$

$\Rightarrow$ $2x^2 - x - 1 = 0$ [dividing both sides by 2]

$\Rightarrow \quad 2x^2 - 2x + x - 1 = 0$ [by splitting the middle term]

$\Rightarrow \quad 2x(x-1) + 1(x-1) = 0$

$\Rightarrow \quad (2x+1)(x-1) = 0$

$\therefore \quad x = -\frac{1}{2}$ or $x = 1$

If $x = -\frac{1}{2}$, then $AD = 4 \times -\frac{1}{2} - 3 = -5 < 0$ [not possible]

Hence, $x = 1$ is the required value.

Example 23. In the given figure, ΔABC and ΔDBC have same base BC and lie on the same side of BC. If $PQ \parallel BA$ and $PR \parallel BD$, then prove that $QR \parallel AD$.

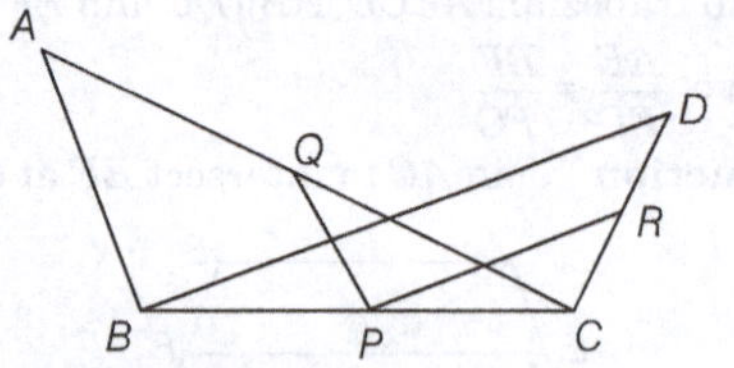

Sol. **Given** ΔABC and ΔDBC have same base BC and lie on the same side of BC.

To prove $QR \parallel AD$

Construction Join QR and AD.

Proof In ΔABC, $PQ \parallel AB$

So, $\frac{CP}{PB} = \frac{CQ}{QA}$ [by basic proportionality theorem]...(i)

In ΔBCD, $PR \parallel BD$

So, $\frac{CP}{PB} = \frac{CR}{RD}$ [by basic proportionality theorem]...(ii)

From Eqs. (i) and (ii), $\frac{CQ}{QA} = \frac{CR}{RD}$

Hence, $QR \parallel AD$.

[by converse of basic proportionality theorem]

Hence proved.

Exercise 13.1

1. State whether the given pairs of triangles are similar or not. In case of similarity, mention the criterion.

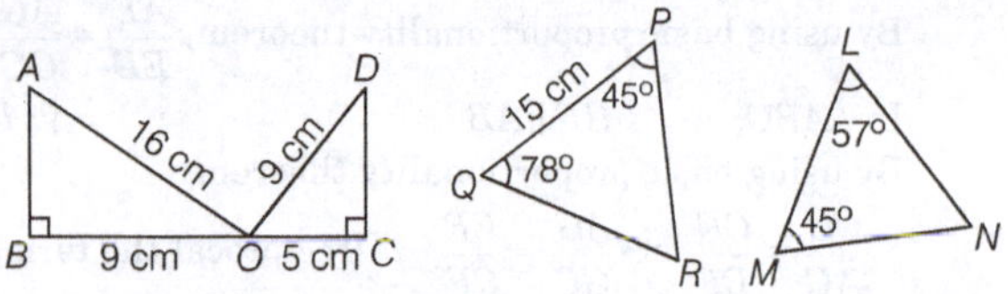

(i) (ii)

2. In the given figure, AB and DE are perpendiculars to BC. If $AB = 9$ cm, $DE = 3$ cm and $AC = 24$ cm, find the length of AD.

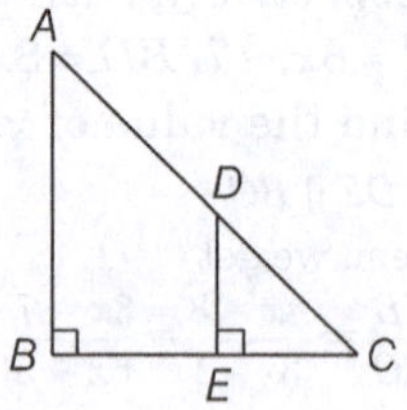

3. In the given figure, if $\Delta ADB \sim \Delta ADC$, then find the value of p.

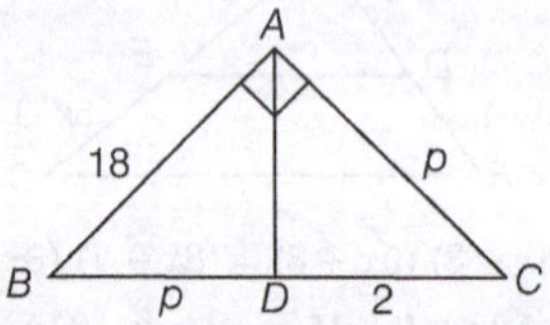

4. Find the value of unknown variables, if ΔABC and ΔPQR are similar.

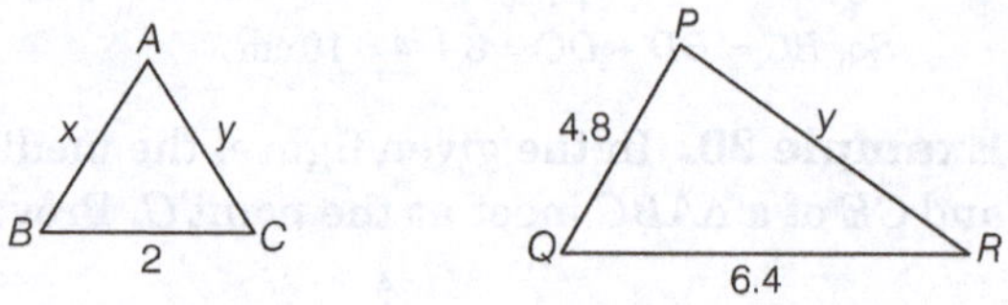

5. If $\Delta ABC \sim \Delta DFE$, $\angle A = 30°$, $\angle C = 50°$, $AB = 5$ cm, $AC = 8$ cm and $DF = 7.5$ cm, then find DE and $\angle F$.

6. In the given figure, $\Delta OAB \sim \Delta OCD$. If $AB = 8$ cm, $BO = 6.4$ cm, $OC = 3.5$ cm and $CD = 5$ cm, then find the values of OA and DO.

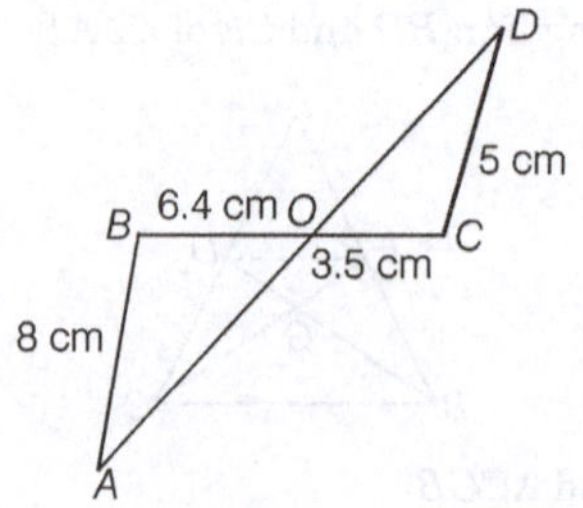

7. In the given figures, find $\angle MLN$.

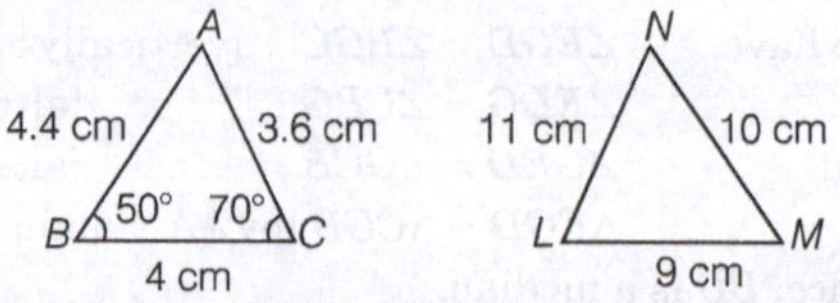

8. In the given figure, two line segments AC and BD intersect each other at the point P such that $PA = 6$ cm, $PB = 3$ cm, $PC = 2.5$ cm, $PD = 5$ cm, $\angle APB = 50°$ and $\angle CDP = 30°$. Then, find $\angle PBA$.

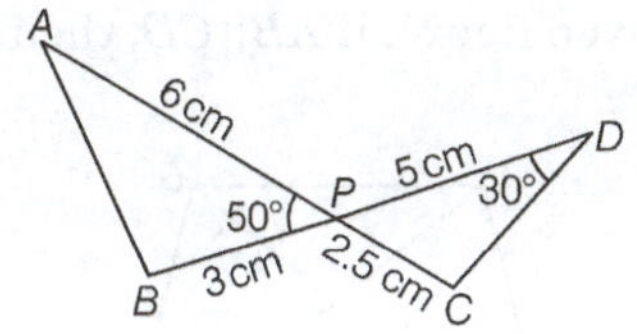

9. In the given figure, $\angle ABC = 90°$ and $BD \perp AC$. If $AB = 5.7$ cm, $BD = 3.8$ cm and $CD = 5.4$ cm, find the value of BC.

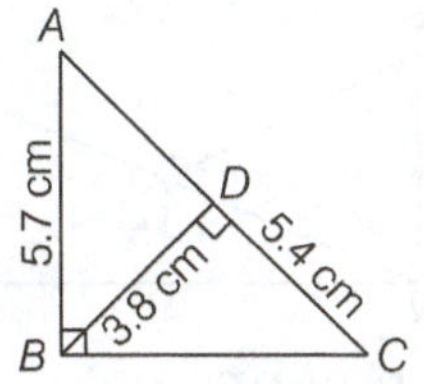

10. In the given figure, if $\angle A = \angle C$, $AB = 6$ cm, $BP = 15$ cm, $AP = 12$ cm and $CP = 4$ cm, find the lengths of PD and CD.

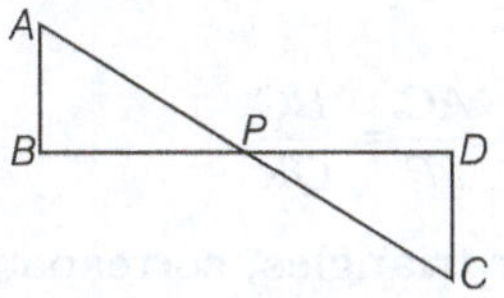

11. In the given figure, $\angle M = \angle N = 46°$. Express x in terms of a, b and c, where a, b and c are the lengths of LM, MN and NK, respectively.

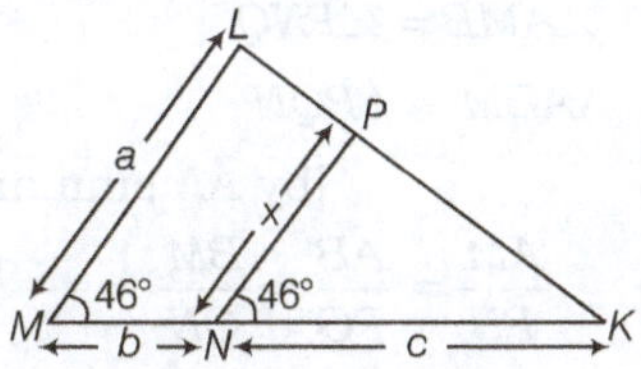

12. In the given figure, if $\angle BAC = 90°$ and $AD \perp BC$, prove that $AD^2 = BD \cdot CD$.

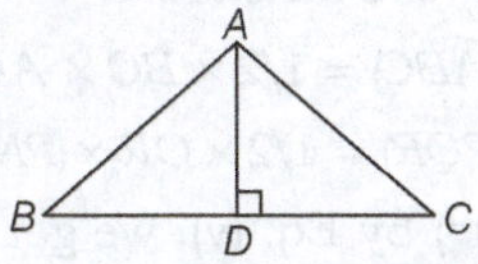

13. In the given figure, $MN \parallel DO$. If OM and PQ intersect each other at Z, prove that $ZM \times OQ = ZO \times MP$.

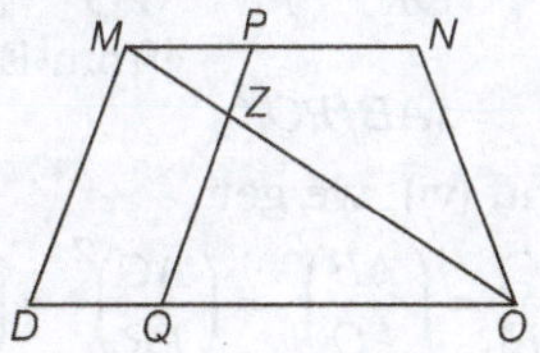

14. A 15 m high tower casts a shadow 24 m long at a certain time and at the same time, telephone pole casts a shadow 16 m long. Find the height of the telephone pole.

15. P and Q are the points on sides AB and AC, respectively of ΔABC. If $AP = 3$ cm, $PB = 6$ cm, $AQ = 5$ cm and $QC = 10$ cm, show that $BC = 3PQ$.

16. ΔABC and ΔAMP are two right angled triangles, right angled at B and M, respectively. Prove that $CA \times MP = PA \times BC$.

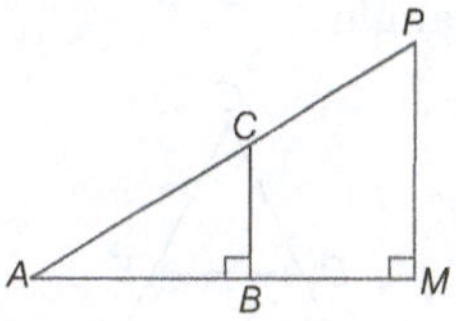

17. In a ΔABC, P and Q are points in AB and AC, respectively and $PQ \parallel BC$. Prove that the median bisects PQ.

18. In the given figure, find the value of x, if $DE \parallel BC$.

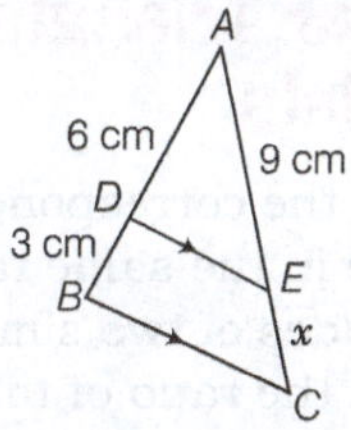

19. In ΔABC, P and Q are points on AB and AC such that $PQ \parallel BC$. If $AP = 4$ cm, $AQ = 3$ cm and $PB = 2$ cm, then find the value of AC.

20. What value of a will make $DE \parallel AB$ in the figure given below?

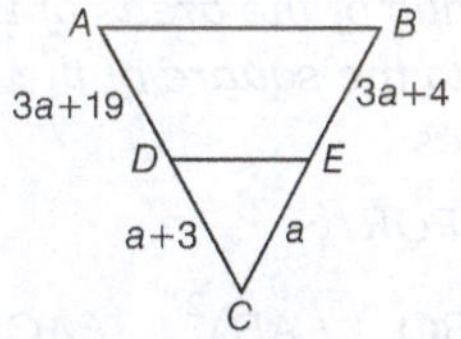

21. In the given figure, $LM \parallel CB$ and $LN \parallel CD$:

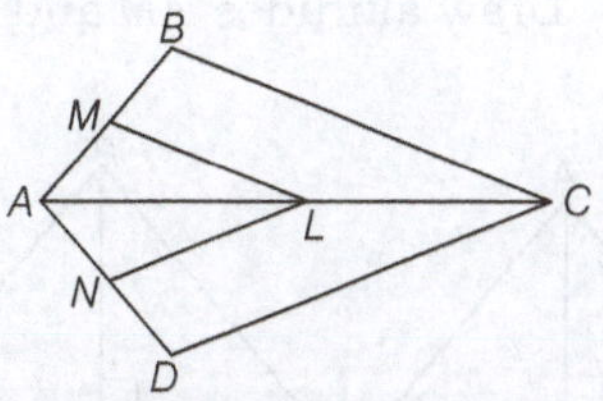

Prove that $\frac{AM}{AB} = \frac{AN}{AD}$.

22. $ABCD$ is a parallelogram, P is a point on the side BC and DP when produced meets AB produced at Q. Prove that

(i) $\dfrac{DP}{PQ}=\dfrac{DC}{BQ}$

(ii) $\dfrac{DQ}{DP}=\dfrac{AQ}{DC}$

23. In the given figure, if $\dfrac{AD}{DC}=\dfrac{BE}{EC}$ and $\angle CDE=\angle CED$, then prove that ΔCAB is an isosceles triangle.

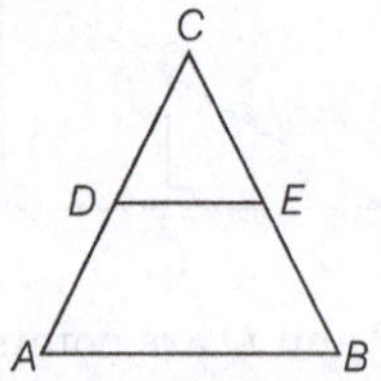

24. In the given figure, if $AB \| CD$, then find the value of x.

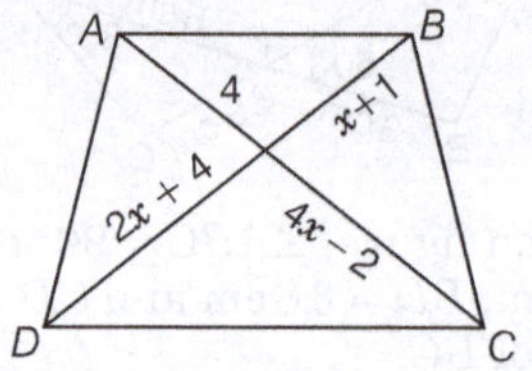

25.

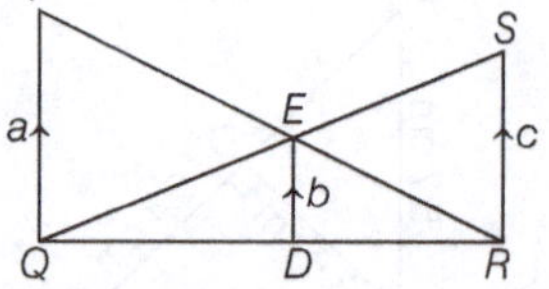

Given that $PQ \| DE \| RS$.

Show that $\dfrac{1}{a}+\dfrac{1}{c}=\dfrac{1}{b}$.

Areas of Similar Triangles, Maps and Models

We have learnt that the corresponding sides of two similar triangles are in the same ratio and corresponding altitudes of two similar triangles are in the same ratio as the ratio of their corresponding sides.

So, the ratio of the areas of two similar triangles is the same as the ratio of the squares of their corresponding sides.

Now, we discuss about this theorem given below.

Theorem 1 *The ratio of the areas of two similar triangles is equal to the square of the ratio of their corresponding sides.*

Given $\Delta ABC \sim \Delta PQR$

To prove $\dfrac{\text{ar}(\Delta ABC)}{\text{ar}(\Delta PQR)}=\left(\dfrac{AB}{PQ}\right)^2=\left(\dfrac{AC}{PR}\right)^2=\left(\dfrac{BC}{QR}\right)^2$

Construction Draw altitudes AM and PN of ΔABC and ΔPQR.

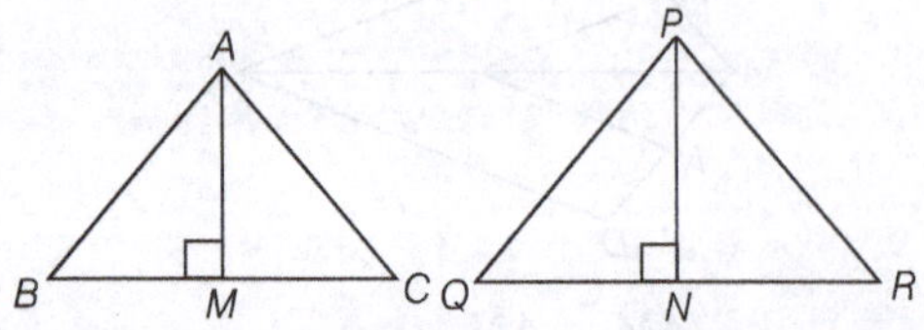

Proof Since, $\Delta ABC \sim \Delta PQR$

$\therefore \quad \angle A=\angle P,\ \angle B=\angle Q$ and $\angle C=\angle R$ ...(i)

Also, $\dfrac{AB}{PQ}=\dfrac{AC}{PR}=\dfrac{BC}{QR}$ ...(ii)

[$\because$ in similar triangles, corresponding angles are equal and corresponding sides are in the same ratio]

In ΔABM and ΔPQN,

$\angle B=\angle Q$ [from Eq. (i)]

$\angle AMB=\angle PNQ$ [each 90°]

$\therefore \quad \Delta ABM \sim \Delta PQN$

[by AA similarity criterion]

So, $\dfrac{AM}{PN}=\dfrac{AB}{PQ}=\dfrac{BM}{QN}$ ...(iii)

[$\because$ in similar triangles, corresponding sides are in the same ratio]

Since, AM and PN are altitudes.

$\therefore \quad \text{ar}(\Delta ABC)=1/2\times BC\times AM$ ...(iv)

and $\text{ar}(\Delta PQR)=1/2\times QR\times PN$ ...(v)

On dividing Eq. (iv) by Eq. (v), we get

$$\frac{\text{ar}(\Delta ABC)}{\text{ar}(\Delta PQR)}=\frac{BC\times AM}{QR\times PN}$$

$$=\frac{BC}{QR}\times\frac{AM}{PN}=\frac{AB}{PQ}\times\frac{AB}{PQ}$$

[from Eqs. (ii) and (iii)]

$=(AB/PQ)^2$ ...(vi)

From Eqs. (ii) and (vi), we get

$$\frac{\text{ar}(\Delta ABC)}{\text{ar}(\Delta PQR)}=\left(\frac{AB}{PQ}\right)^2=\left(\frac{AC}{PR}\right)^2=\left(\frac{BC}{QR}\right)^2$$

Hence proved.

Example 24. If $\Delta ABC \sim \Delta QRP$, $\dfrac{ar(\Delta ABC)}{ar(\Delta QRP)} = \dfrac{9}{4}$, $AB = 18$ cm and $BC = 15$ cm, then find PR.

Sol. Given, $\Delta ABC \sim \Delta QRP$, $AB = 18$ cm, $BC = 15$ cm

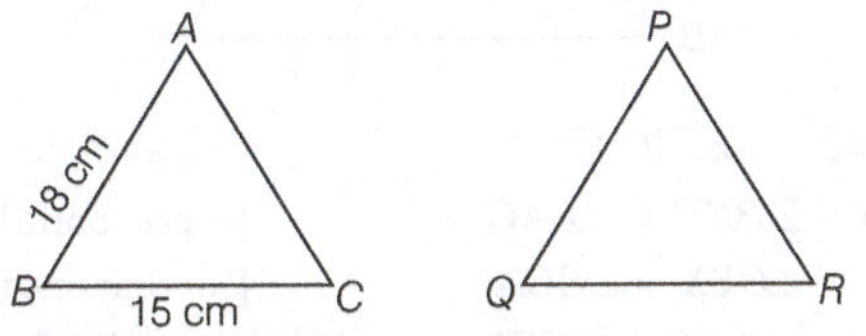

We know that the ratio of areas of two similar triangles is equal to the ratio of squares of their corresponding sides.

$$\therefore \quad \frac{ar(\Delta ABC)}{ar(\Delta QRP)} = \frac{BC^2}{RP^2}$$

But $\dfrac{ar(\Delta ABC)}{ar(\Delta QRP)} = \dfrac{9}{4}$ [given]

$\therefore \quad \dfrac{(15)^2}{RP^2} = \dfrac{9}{4}$ [$\because BC = 15$ cm]

$\Rightarrow \quad RP^2 = \dfrac{225 \times 4}{9} = 100$

$\therefore \quad RP = 10$ cm [taking positive square root]

Example 25. In the given figure, if $DE \parallel BC$, find the ratio of ar (ΔADE) and ar $(DECB)$.

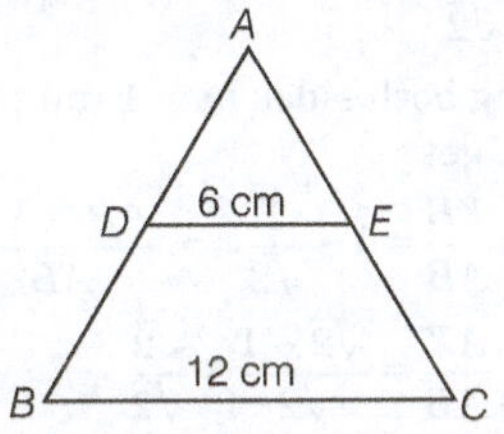

Sol. Given, $DE \parallel BC$, $DE = 6$ cm $BC = 12$ cm.

In ΔABC and ΔADE,

$\angle ABC = \angle ADE$ [corresponding angles]

$\angle ACB = \angle AED$ [corresponding angles]

and $\angle A = \angle A$ [common angle]

$\therefore \quad \Delta ABC \sim \Delta ADE$ [by AAA similarity criterion]

We know that the ratio of areas of two similar triangles is equal to the ratio of squares of their corresponding sides.

$$\therefore \quad \frac{ar(\Delta ADE)}{ar(\Delta ABC)} = \frac{DE^2}{BC^2} = \frac{(6)^2}{(12)^2} = \left(\frac{1}{2}\right)^2$$

$$\Rightarrow \quad \frac{ar(\Delta ADE)}{ar(\Delta ABC)} = \frac{1}{4}$$

Let ar $(\Delta ADE) = k$, then ar $(\Delta ABC) = 4k$

Now, ar $(DECB)$ = ar (ΔABC) − ar(ΔADE)

$= 4k - k = 3k$

$\therefore$ Required ratio = ar (ΔADE) : ar $(DECB)$

$= k : 3k = 1 : 3$

Example 26. D, E and F are the mid-points of the sides BC, CA and AB, respectively of ΔABC. Determine the ratio of the area of ΔDEF and ΔABC.

Sol. Since, D and E are the mid-points of the sides BC and CA, respectively of ΔABC.

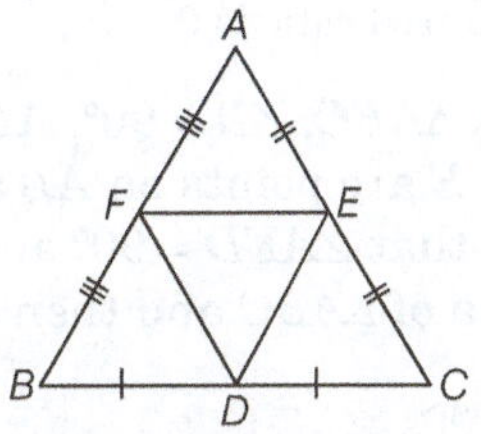

Therefore, $DE \parallel BA \Rightarrow DE \parallel BF$

[by mid-point theorem] ...(i)

Since, F and E are the mid-points of AB and AC, respectively of ΔABC.

$\therefore \quad FE \parallel BC \Rightarrow FE \parallel BD$ ...(ii)

From Eqs. (i) and (ii), we conclude that $BDEF$ is a parallelogram.

$\therefore \angle B = \angle DEF$ [opposite angles of a parallelogram] ...(iii)

Similarly, $AFDE$ is a parallelogram.

$\therefore \angle A = \angle FDE$ [opposite angles of a parallelogram]...(iv)

In ΔABC and ΔDEF, we have

$\angle B = \angle DEF$ [from Eq. (iii)]

$\angle A = \angle FDE$ [from Eq. (iv)]

$\therefore \quad \Delta ABC \sim \Delta DEF$ [by AA similarity criterion]

Since, the ratio of the area of two similar triangles is equal to the ratio of the square of any two corresponding sides.

$$\therefore \quad \frac{ar(\Delta DEF)}{ar(\Delta ABC)} = \frac{DE^2}{AB^2} = \frac{\left(\frac{AB}{2}\right)^2}{AB^2} = \frac{1}{4}$$

[$\because$ mid-point theorem, $DE = \frac{1}{2}AB$]

Hence, ar (ΔDEF): ar (ΔABC) = 1: 4.

Example 27. Diagonals of a trapezium $PQRS$ intersect each other at the point O, $PQ \parallel RS$ and $PQ = 3RS$. Find the ratio of the areas of ΔPOQ and ΔROS.

Sol. Given, $PQRS$ is a trapezium in which $PQ \parallel RS$ and $PQ = 3RS$.

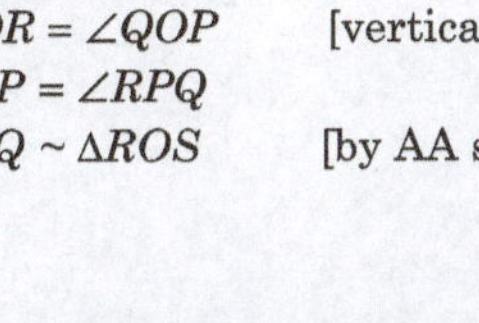

$\Rightarrow \quad \dfrac{PQ}{RS} = \dfrac{3}{1}$ ...(i)

In ΔPOQ and ΔROS,

$\angle SOR = \angle QOP$ [vertically opposite angles]

$\angle SRP = \angle RPQ$ [alternate angles]

$\therefore \quad \Delta POQ \sim \Delta ROS$ [by AA similarity criterion]

By property of area of similar triangle,

$$\frac{\text{ar}(\Delta POQ)}{\text{ar}(\Delta ROS)} = \frac{PQ^2}{RS^2} = \left(\frac{3}{1}\right)^2 \quad \text{[from Eq. (i)]}$$

$$\Rightarrow \frac{\text{ar}(\Delta POQ)}{\text{ar}(\Delta ROS)} = \frac{9}{1}$$

Hence, the required ratio is 9 : 1.

Example 28. In ΔABC, $\angle B = 90°$, $AB = 3$ cm and $AC = 5$ cm, D and E are points on AB and AC, respectively such that $\angle AED = 90°$ and $DE = 2$ cm. Calculate the area of ΔABC and then the area of ΔADE.

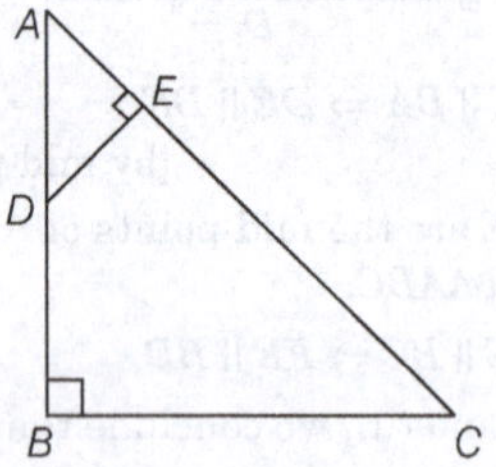

Sol. In ΔABC, $\angle B = 90°$

$$AB^2 + BC^2 = AC^2 \quad \text{[Pythagoras theorem]}$$

$$\Rightarrow BC^2 = 5^2 - (3)^2 = 25 - 9 = 16$$

$$BC = 4 \text{ cm}$$

$$\therefore \text{Area of } \Delta ABC = \frac{1}{2} \times \text{base} \times \text{height}$$

$$= \frac{1}{2} \times BC \times AB = \left(\frac{1}{2} \times 4 \times 3\right) \text{cm}^2 = 6 \text{ cm}^2$$

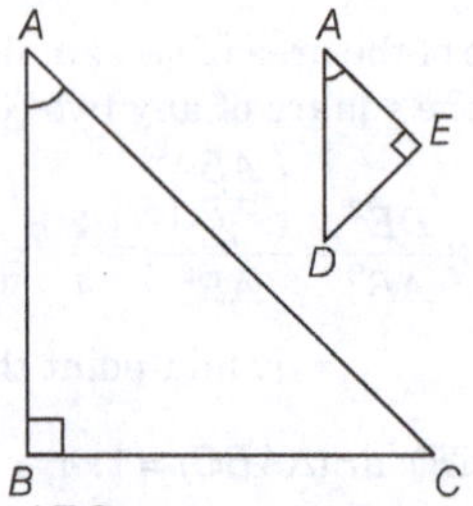

In ΔADE and ΔABC,

$$\angle ABC = \angle AED = 90°$$

and $\angle A$ is common to both.

$$\therefore \Delta ADE \sim \Delta ABC \quad \text{[by AA similarity criterion]}$$

$$\Rightarrow \frac{\Delta ADE}{\Delta ABC} = \frac{DE^2}{BC^2}$$

$$\Rightarrow \frac{\Delta ADE}{} = \frac{(2)^2}{(4)^2}$$

$$\Rightarrow \text{Area of } \Delta ADE = \frac{4}{16} \times 6 = \frac{6}{4} = 1.5 \text{ cm}^2$$

Example 29. In the given figure, the line segment XY is parallel to side AC of ΔABC and it divides the triangle into two parts of equal areas. Find the ratio $\frac{AX}{AB}$.

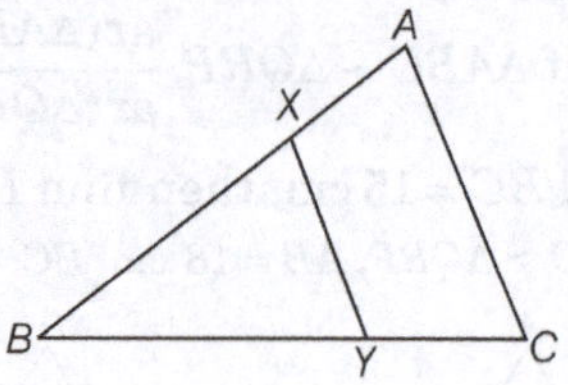

Sol. Given, $XY \parallel AC$

Then, $\angle BXY = \angle BAC$ [corresponding angles]

and $\angle BYX = \angle BCA$ [corresponding angles]

$\therefore \Delta ABC \sim \Delta XBY$ [by AA similarity criterion]

$$\text{Then, } \frac{\text{ar}(\Delta ABC)}{\text{ar}(\Delta XBY)} = \left(\frac{AB}{XB}\right)^2 \quad \text{...(i)}$$

[$\because$ ratio of the areas of two similar triangles is equal to the square of the ratio of their corresponding sides]

Also, given that XY divides the triangle into two parts of equal areas.

$$\therefore \frac{\text{ar}(\Delta ABC)}{\text{ar}(\Delta XBY)} = \frac{2}{1} \quad \text{...(ii)}$$

From Eqs. (i) and (ii),

$$\left(\frac{AB}{XB}\right)^2 = \frac{2}{1}$$

$$\Rightarrow \frac{AB}{XB} = \sqrt{\left(\frac{2}{1}\right)} = \frac{\sqrt{2}}{1} \quad \text{[taking positive square root]}$$

$$\Rightarrow \frac{XB}{AB} = \frac{1}{\sqrt{2}} \quad \text{[reciprocal the terms]}$$

On multiplying both sides by -1 and then adding 1 on both sides, we get

$$1 - \frac{XB}{AB} = 1 - \frac{1}{\sqrt{2}} \Rightarrow \frac{AB - XB}{AB} = \frac{\sqrt{2} - 1}{\sqrt{2}}$$

$$\Rightarrow \frac{AX}{AB} = \frac{\sqrt{2} - 1}{\sqrt{2}} \times \frac{\sqrt{2}}{\sqrt{2}}$$

[multiplying numerator and denominator by $\sqrt{2}$ in RHS]

$$\Rightarrow \frac{AX}{AB} = \frac{2 - \sqrt{2}}{2}$$

which is the required ratio.

Example 30. Prove that the area of the equilateral triangle described on the side of an isosceles right angled triangle is half the area of the equilateral triangle described on its hypotenuse.

Sol. Given A ΔABC in which $\angle ABC = 90°$ and $AB = BC$.

ΔABD and ΔCEA are equilateral triangles.

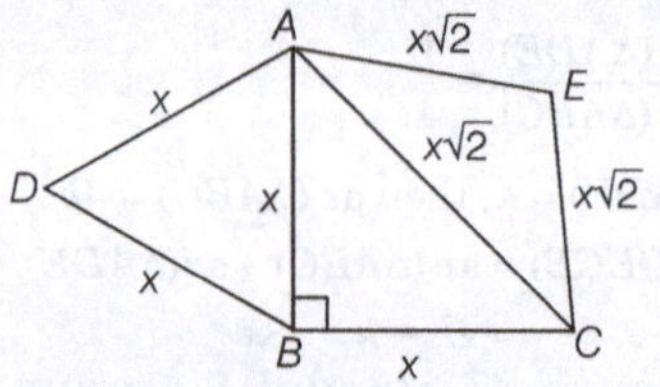

To prove ar $(\Delta ABD) = \frac{1}{2}$ ar (ΔCEA)

Proof Let $AB = BC = x$ units

Now, $CA = \sqrt{AB^2 + BC^2} = \sqrt{x^2 + x^2} = x\sqrt{2}$ units

[by Pythagoras theorem]

In ΔABD and ΔCEA, each angle is 60° as they are equilateral triangle.

$\therefore \quad \Delta ABD \sim \Delta CEA$

Since, the ratio of the area of two similar triangles is equal to the ratio of the squares of their corresponding sides.

$$\therefore \quad \frac{\text{ar}(\Delta ABD)}{\text{ar}(\Delta CEA)} = \frac{AB^2}{CE^2} = \frac{x^2}{(x\sqrt{2})^2} = \frac{x^2}{2x^2} = \frac{1}{2}$$

Hence, ar $(\Delta ABD) = \frac{1}{2}$ ar (ΔCEA).

Example 31. In ΔABC, $\angle ABC = \angle DAC$, $AB = 8$ cm, $AC = 4$ cm and $AD = 5$ cm.

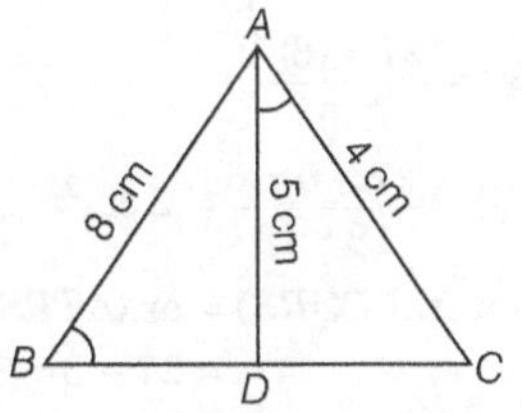

(i) Prove that ΔACD is similar to ΔBCA.

(ii) Find BC and CD.

(iii) Find area of ΔACD : area of ΔBCA. **[ICSE 2014]**

Sol. Given $\angle ABC = \angle DAC$, $AB = 8$ cm, $AC = 4$ cm, $AD = 5$ cm

(i) **To prove** $\Delta ACD \sim \Delta BCA$

Proof In ΔACD and ΔBCA,

$\angle ACD = \angle BCA$ [common angle]

and $\angle ABC = \angle DAC$ [given]

$\therefore \quad \Delta ACD \sim \Delta BCA$ [by AA similarity criterion]

Hence proved.

(ii) Since, $\Delta ACD \sim \Delta BCA$

$$\therefore \quad \frac{AC}{BC} = \frac{CD}{CA} = \frac{AD}{BA}$$

[∵ if two triangles are similar, then their corresponding sides are proportional]

$$\Rightarrow \quad \underset{\text{I}}{\frac{4}{BC}} = \underset{\text{II}}{\frac{CD}{4}} = \underset{\text{III}}{\frac{5}{8}}$$

On taking I and III terms, we get

$$\frac{4}{BC} = \frac{5}{8} \Rightarrow BC = \frac{4 \times 8}{5} = \frac{32}{5} = 6.4 \text{ cm}$$

On taking II and III terms, we get

$$\frac{CD}{4} = \frac{5}{8} \Rightarrow CD = \frac{4 \times 5}{8} = \frac{5}{2} = 2.5 \text{ cm}$$

(iii) Since, $\Delta ACD \sim \Delta BCA$

$$\therefore \quad \frac{\text{ar}(\Delta ACD)}{\text{ar}(\Delta BCA)} = \frac{(AC)^2}{(BC)^2} = \frac{(4)^2}{(6.4)^2} = \frac{16}{40.96} = \frac{1600}{4096} = \frac{25}{64}$$

[∵ ratio of the areas of two triangles is equal to the squares of the ratio of their corresponding sides]

Hence, area of ΔACD : area of $\Delta BCA = 25 : 64$.

Example 32. PQR is a triangle. S is a point on the side QR of ΔPQR such that $\angle PSR = \angle QPR$. Given $QP = 8$ cm, $PR = 6$ cm and $SR = 3$ cm.

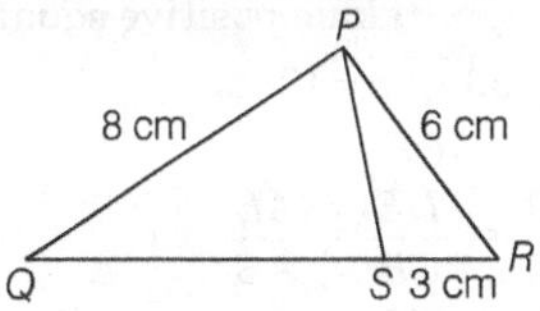

(i) Prove that $\Delta PQR \sim \Delta SPR$.

(ii) Find the length of QR and PS.

(iii) Find $\frac{\text{area of } \Delta PQR}{\text{area of } \Delta SPR}$. **[ICSE 2017]**

Sol.

(i) In ΔPQR and ΔSPR, we have

$\angle PSR = \angle QPR$ [given]

$\angle SRP = \angle PRQ$ [common angle]

So, by AA similarity criterion,

$\Delta PQR \sim \Delta SPR$

(ii) ∵ $\Delta PQR \sim \Delta SPR$

$$\therefore \quad \frac{QR}{PR} = \frac{RP}{RS} \Rightarrow \frac{QR}{6} = \frac{6}{3} \Rightarrow QR = \frac{6 \times 6}{3} = 12 \text{ cm}$$

$$\text{Also,} \quad \frac{PQ}{PS} = \frac{RP}{RS} \Rightarrow \frac{8}{PS} = \frac{6}{3} \Rightarrow PS = \frac{8 \times 3}{6} \Rightarrow PS = 4 \text{ cm}$$

(iii) We know that the ratio of areas of two similar triangle is equal to the ratio of the squares of their corresponding sides.

$$\therefore \quad \frac{\text{area of } \Delta PQR}{\text{area of } \Delta SPR} = \frac{RP^2}{RS^2} = \frac{(6)^2}{(3)^2} = \frac{36}{9} = 4$$

Example 33. ABC is a right angled triangle with $\angle ABC = 90°$. D is any point on AB and DE is perpendicular to AC.

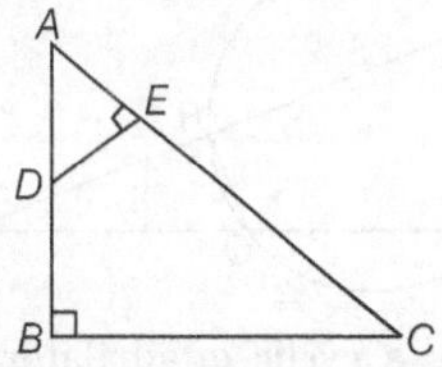

(i) Prove that $\Delta ADE \sim \Delta ACB$.

(ii) If $AC = 13$ cm, $BC = 5$ cm and $AE = 4$ cm, find DE and AD.

(iii) Find area of ΔADE : area of quadrilateral $BCED$. **[ICSE 2015]**

Sol.

(i) In ΔADE and ΔACB,

$\angle AED = \angle B$ [90° each]

$\angle DAE = \angle BAC$ [common angle]

$\therefore \quad \Delta ADE \sim \Delta ACB$ [by AA similarity criterion]

(ii) In ΔABC,

$AC = 13$ cm, $BC = 5$ cm

Using Pythagoras theorem in ΔABC,

$$AC^2 = AB^2 + BC^2$$

$$\Rightarrow \quad AB = \sqrt{AC^2 - BC^2} = \sqrt{(13)^2 - (5)^2}$$

[taking positive square root both sides]

$$= \sqrt{169 - 25} = 12 \text{ cm}$$

Since, $\Delta ADE \sim \Delta ACB$

$$\therefore \quad \frac{AD}{AC} = \frac{DE}{CB} = \frac{AE}{AB}$$

$$\Rightarrow \quad \frac{AD}{13} = \frac{DE}{5} = \frac{4}{12} \qquad [\because AE = 4 \text{ cm, given}]$$

On taking, $\dfrac{AD}{13} = \dfrac{4}{12} \Rightarrow AD = \dfrac{13}{3} = 4.33 \text{ cm}$

On taking, $\dfrac{DE}{5} = \dfrac{4}{12} \Rightarrow DE = \dfrac{5}{3} = 1.66 \text{ cm}$

(iii) Area of $\Delta ADE = \dfrac{1}{2} \times \text{Base} \times \text{Height}$

$$= \frac{1}{2} \times AE \times DE = \frac{1}{2} \times 4 \times \frac{5}{3} = \frac{10}{3} = 3.33 \text{ cm}^2$$

Area of $\Delta ABC = \dfrac{1}{2} \times 12 \times 5 = 30 \text{ cm}^2$

Area of quadrilateral $BCED$

$= \text{Area of } \Delta ABC - \text{Area of } \Delta AED$

$= (30 - 3.33) \text{ cm}^2 = 26.67 \text{ cm}^2$

Hence, area of ΔADE : area of quadrilateral $BCED$

$= 3.33 : 26.67 \text{ cm}^2$

Example 34. In the given figure, $PQRS$ is a cyclic quadrilateral, PQ and SR produced to meet at T.

(i) Prove $\Delta TPS \sim \Delta TRQ$.

(ii) Find SP, if $TP = 18$ cm, $RQ = 4$ cm and $TR = 6$ cm.

(iii) Find area of quadrilateral $PQRS$, if area of $\Delta PTS = 27 \text{ cm}^2$.

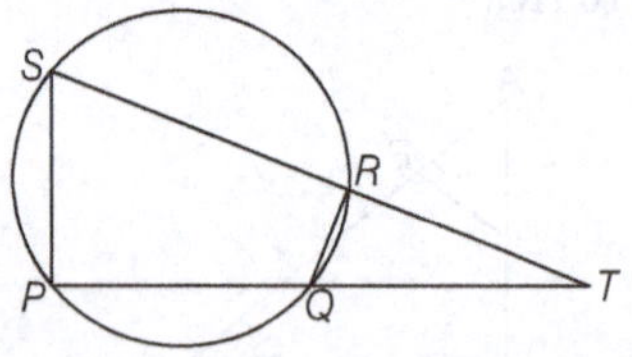

[ICSE 2016]

Sol. Given $PQRS$ is a cyclic quadrilateral, PQ and RS are produced such that it intersect at T.

To prove $\Delta TPS \sim \Delta TRQ$

Proof In cyclic quadrilateral $PQRS$,

$$\angle SPQ + \angle SRQ = 180° \qquad \text{... (i)}$$

[$\because$ sum of opposite angles of a cyclic quadrilateral is 180°]

$$\angle SRQ + \angle QRT = 180° \qquad \text{[linear pair] ...(ii)}$$

On subtracting Eq. (ii) from Eq. (i), we get

$$(\angle SPQ + \angle SRQ) - (\angle SRQ + \angle QRT) = 180° - 180°$$

$$\Rightarrow \quad \angle SPQ - \angle QRT = 0 \Rightarrow \angle SPQ = \angle QRT$$

Now, in ΔTPS and ΔTRQ,

$$\angle SPQ = \angle QRT \qquad \text{[proved above]}$$

and $\qquad \angle PTS = \angle RTQ \qquad$ [common]

$$\Rightarrow \quad \Delta TPS \sim \Delta TRQ \qquad \text{[by AA similarity criterion]}$$

Hence proved.

(ii) Since, ΔTPS and ΔTRQ are similar.

$$\therefore \quad \frac{TP}{TR} = \frac{PS}{RQ}$$

[$\because$ in similar triangles, corresponding sides are proportional]

$$\Rightarrow \quad \frac{18}{6} = \frac{PS}{4}$$

$$\therefore \quad PS = \frac{18 \times 4}{6} = 12 \text{ cm}$$

(iii) Since, ΔTPS and ΔTRQ are similar.

$$\therefore \quad \frac{\text{ar}(\Delta TPS)}{\text{ar } \Delta TRQ} = \left(\frac{TP}{TR}\right)^2$$

[$\because$ ratio of the areas of two similar triangles is equal to the square of the ratio of their corresponding sides]

$$\Rightarrow \quad \frac{27}{\text{ar}(\Delta TRQ)} = \left(\frac{18}{6}\right)^2 \qquad \left[\begin{array}{l}\because TP = 18 \text{ cm, } TR = 6 \text{ cm and} \\ \text{ar}(\Delta TPS) = 27 \text{ cm}^2\text{, given}\end{array}\right]$$

$$\Rightarrow \quad \text{ar}(\Delta TRQ) = \frac{27 \times (6)^2}{(18)^2}$$

$$\Rightarrow \quad \text{ar } \Delta TRQ) = \frac{27 \times 6 \times 6}{18 \times 18} = 3 \text{ cm}^2$$

$$\therefore \quad \text{ar (quadrilateral } PQRS) = \text{ar}(\Delta TPS) - \text{ar}(\Delta TRQ)$$

$$= 27 - 3 = 24 \text{ cm}^2$$

Maps

The maps of a plane figure and the actual figure are similar to one another. If the map of a plane figure is drawn to the scale $1 : x$, then scale factor $k = \dfrac{1}{x}$.

(i) Length of the map = $k \times$ (Length of the actual figure)

(ii) Breadth of the map

= $k \times$ (Breadth of the actual figure)

(iii) Area of the map = $k^2 \times$ (Area of the actual figure)

The ratio that compares the measurements of two similar shapes, is called the scale factor or representative fraction. It is equal to the ratio of corresponding sides of two figures.

Example 35. The scale of map is 1 : 50000. In the map, a triangular plot ABC of land has the following dimensions $AB = 2$ cm, $BC = 3.5$ cm and $\angle ABC = 90°$. Calculate

(i) the actual length of the side BC (in km) of the land.

(ii) the area of the plot (in km^2).

Sol. Given, scale factor, $k = \dfrac{1}{50000}$, $AB = 2$ cm

and $BC = 3.5$ cm $\qquad$ ...(i)

(i) Length BC of triangular plot on the map

= k (Length BC of actual triangular plot)

$\Rightarrow$ Length BC of triangular plot on the map = $\left(\dfrac{1}{50000}\right)$

(Length BC of actual triangular plot)

$= 50000$ (Length BC of triangular plot on the map)

$= 50000 \times 3.5 = 175000\,\text{cm}$

$= \dfrac{175000}{10^5}\,\text{km}$ $\left[\because 1\,\text{cm} = \dfrac{1}{10^5}\,\text{km}\right]$

$= \dfrac{1.75 \times 10^5}{10^5} = 1.75\,\text{km}$

(ii) Area of ΔABC in map $= \dfrac{1}{2} \times AB \times BC = \dfrac{1}{2} \times 2 \times 3.5 = 3.5\,\text{cm}^2$

$\because$ Area of ΔABC in the map $= k^2$ (Area of actual ΔABC)

$\therefore$ Area of ΔABC in the map

$= \left(\dfrac{1}{50000}\right)^2$ (Area of actual ΔABC)

Area of the actual ΔABC

$= 50000$ (Area of ΔABC on the map)

$= (50000)^2 \times 3.5 = 2500000000 \times 3.5$

$= 25 \times 35 \times 10^7 = 875 \times 10^7\,\text{km}^2$

$= \dfrac{875 \times 10^7}{10^5 \times 10^5}\,\text{km}^2$ $\left[\because 1\,\text{cm} = \dfrac{1}{10^5}\,\text{km}\right]$

$= \dfrac{875}{10^3}\,\text{km}^2 = 0.875\,\text{km}^2$

Models

The models of a solid and the actual solid are similar to one another.

If the model of a solid is drawn to the scale $1 : x$, then scalar factor $k = \dfrac{1}{x}$

(i) Each side of the model

$= k \times$ (Corresponding side of the actual solid)

(ii) Surface area of the model

$= k^2 \times$ (Surface area of the actual solid)

(iii) Volume of the model

$= k^3 \times$ (Volume of the actual solid)

Example 36. The dimensions of the model of a multistoried building are $1\,\text{m} \times 60\,\text{cm} \times 1.25\,\text{m}$. If the model is drawn to a scale $1 : 60$, then find the actual dimension of the building in metres.

Sol. Given, scale factor, $k = \dfrac{1}{60}$

$\therefore$ Length of building on the model

$= k$ (Length of actual building)

$\Rightarrow$ Length of building on the model

$= \dfrac{1}{60}$ (Length of actual building)

Length of actual building

$= 60$ (Length of building on the model) $= 60 \times 1\,\text{m}$

$\therefore$ Length of actual building $= 60\,\text{m}$

Similarly, breadth of actual building

$= \dfrac{1}{k}$ (Breadth of building on the model)

$= 60 \times 60 = 3600\,\text{cm}$

$= \dfrac{3600}{100}\,\text{m} = 36\,\text{m}$ $\left[\because 1\,\text{cm} = \dfrac{1}{100}\,\text{m}\right]$

$\therefore$ Breadth of actual building $= 36\,\text{m}$

and height of actual building

$= \dfrac{1}{k}$ (Height of building on the model)

$= 60 \times 1.25\,\text{m} = 75\,\text{m}$

Hence, the actual dimensions of the building are $60\,\text{m} \times 36\,\text{m} \times 75\,\text{m}$.

Example 37. A model of a ship is made to a scale of 1 : 250. Find

(i) the length of the ship, if the length of its model is 1.2 m.

(ii) the area of the deck of the ship, if the area of the deck of its model is $1.6\,\text{m}^2$.

(iii) the volume of its model, when the volume of the ship is $1\,\text{km}^3$.

Sol. Given, scale factor, $k = \dfrac{1}{250}$

$\therefore \quad \dfrac{1}{k} = 250$

(i) Actual length of the ship

$= \dfrac{1}{k}$ (Length of the model of the ship)

$= 250 \times 1.2$

$= 300\,\text{m}$

(ii) Actual area of deck of the ship

$= \dfrac{1}{k^2}$ (area of the deck of model of ship)

$= (250)^2 \times 1.6\,\text{m}^2$

$= 62500 \times 1.6\,\text{m}^2$

$= 100000\,\text{m}^2$

(iii) Volume of the model of ship

$= k^3$ (Volume of the actual ship)

$= \dfrac{(1000)^3}{(250)^3} = \left(\dfrac{1000}{250}\right)^3$

$= (4)^3 = 64\,\text{m}^3$

Exercise 13.2

1. Suppose, ΔABC and ΔDEF are similar. Area of ΔABC is 9 cm^2 and area of ΔDEF is 64 cm^2. If $DE = 5.1$ cm, then find the value of AB.

2. Suppose, ΔABC and ΔDEF are similar and $AB = \frac{1}{3} DE$, then find ar (ΔABC) : ar (ΔDEF).

3. In the given figure, S and T are points on the sides PQ and PR, respectively of ΔPQR, such that $PT = 2$ cm, $TR = 4$ cm and $ST \parallel QR$. Find the ratio of the areas of ΔPST and ΔPQR.

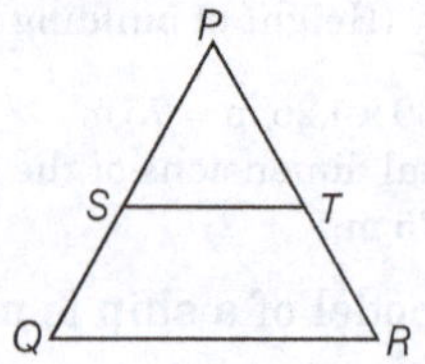

4. The areas of two similar triangles are 25 cm^2 and 81 cm^2, respectively. Find the ratio of their corresponding sides.

5. In the given figure, $DE \parallel BC$. $DE = 4$ cm, $BC = 8$ cm, area of $\Delta ADE = 25$ sq cm. Find the area of ΔABC.

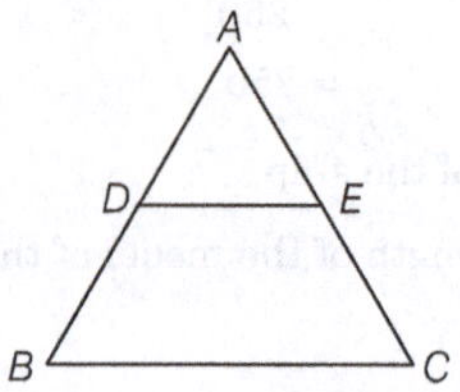

6. If the areas of two similar triangles are 81 cm^2 and 49 cm^2 respectively, then find the ratio of their corresponding medians.

7. Two isosceles right angled triangles have equal vertical angles and their areas are in the ratio 36 : 25. Find the ratio of their corresponding heights.

8. In ΔPQR, MN is parallel to QR and $\frac{PM}{MQ} = \frac{2}{3}$.

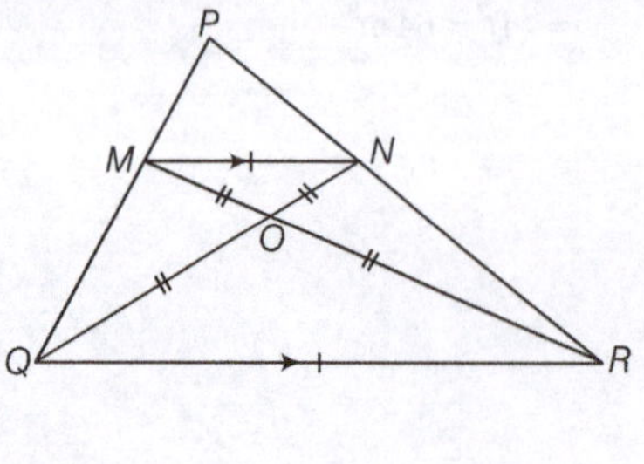

(i) Find $\frac{MN}{QR}$.

(ii) Prove that ΔOMN and ΔORQ are similar.

(iii) Find area of ΔOMN : area of ΔORQ. **[ICSE 2018]**

9. In the given figure, ΔAED and trapezium $EBCD$ are such that the area of trapezium is three times the area of the triangle. Find the ratio $\frac{AE}{AB}$.

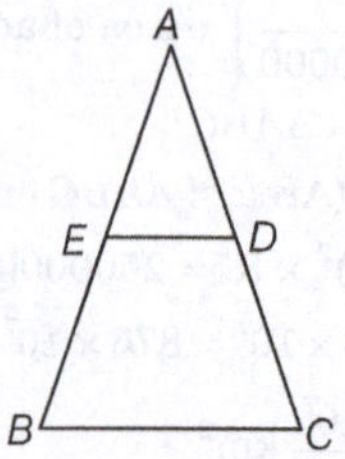

10. In an isosceles ΔABC, if $AB = AC = 25$ cm and altitude from A on BC is 24 cm, then find BC.

11. In the given figure, AB and DE are perpendicular to BC.

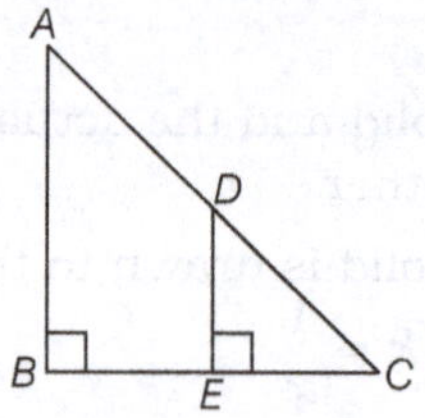

(i) Prove that $\Delta ABC \sim \Delta DEC$.

(ii) If $AB = 6$ cm, $DE = 4$ cm and $AC = 15$ cm, then calculate CD.

(iii) Find the ratio of area of ΔABC : area of ΔDEC. **[ICSE 2013]**

12. In the given figure, $PQ \parallel RS$, area of $\Delta POS = 4$ sq cm and area of $\Delta QRS = 7$ sq cm.

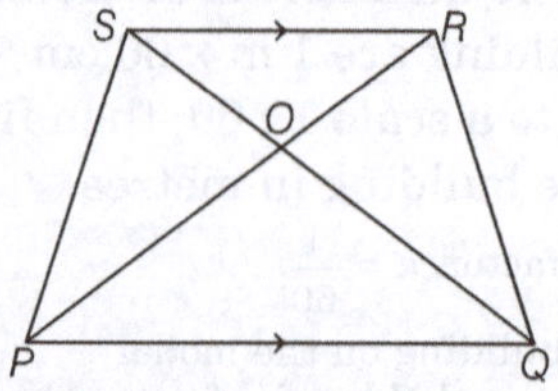

Calculate

(i) Area of ΔROS

(ii) The ratio $QO : OS$

(iii) Area of ΔOPQ

13. In the given figure, ABC and CEF are two triangles, where BA is parallel to CE and $AF : AC = 5 : 8$.

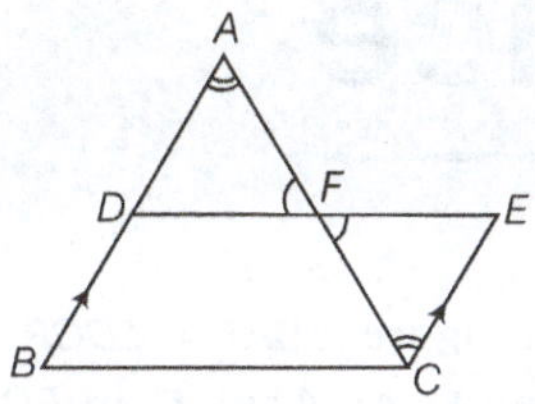

(i) Prove that $\Delta ADF \sim \Delta CEF$.

(ii) Find AD, if $CE = 6$ cm .

(iii) If DE is parallel to BC, then find area of ΔADF : area of ΔABC. **[ICSE 2009]**

14. Prove that the area of the equilateral triangle described on the side of a square is half of area of the equilateral triangle described on its diagonal.

15. The area of two similar triangles are 81 cm^2 and 144 cm^2. Find the ratio of their corresponding heights. What is the ratio of their corresponding median?

16. On a map drawn to a scale of 1 : 50000, a rectangular plot of land $ABCD$ has dimensions $AB = 6$ cm, $BC = 8$ cm and all angles are right angles. Find

(i) the actual length of the diagonal distance AC of the plot in km.

(ii) the actual area of the plot in sq km. **[ICSE 2018]**

17. A model of a square $PQRS$ is made to a scale of 0.006. If the area of the square on the model is 150 cm^2, then find the actual area of the square.

18. A model of a ship is made to a scale of 1 : 200.

(i) If the length of the model is 4 m. Calculate the length of the ship.

(ii) If the area of the deck of the ship is 160000 m^2, then find the area of the deck of the model.

(iii) The volume of the model is 100 L. Calculate the volume of the ship (in m^3).

Chapter Practice

a. 1 Mark Questions

1. In the given figure, $\Delta ABC \sim \Delta PQR$. Then, $\angle R$ is

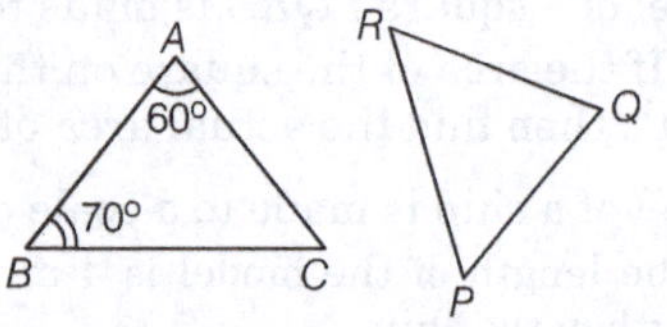

(a) 60° (b) 50° (c) 70° (d) 80°

2. In the given figure, $AB = 24$ cm, $AC = 18$ cm, $DE = 12$ cm, $DF = 9$ cm and $\angle BAC = \angle EDF$.

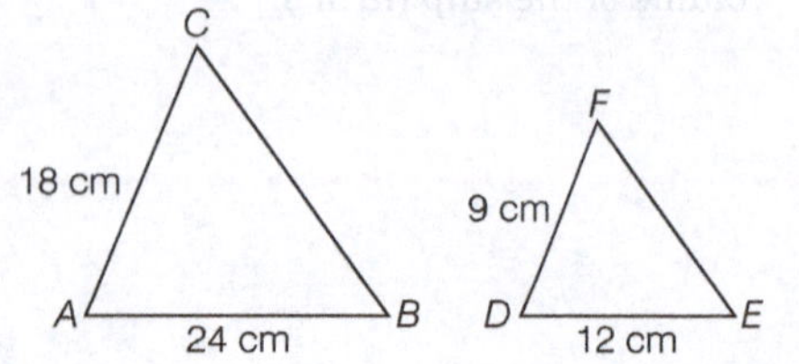

Then, $\Delta ABC \sim \Delta DEF$ by the condition

[ICSE Semester I 2021]

(a) AAA (b) SAS (c) SSS (d) AAS

3. In the given figure, $\Delta ABC \sim \Delta PQR$. The value of x is

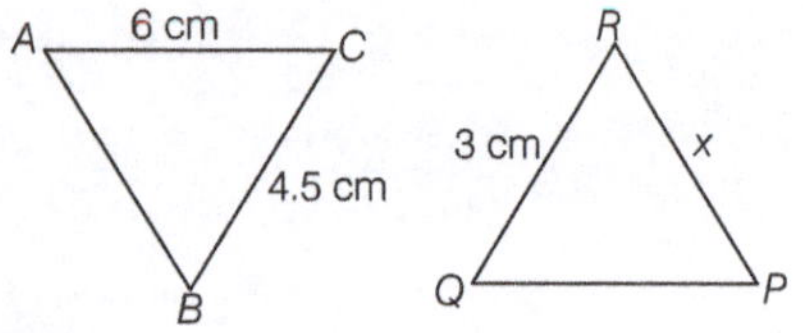

(a) 2.25 cm (b) 4 cm
(c) 4.5 cm (d) 5.25 cm

4. If $\Delta PQR \sim \Delta ABC$, $PQ = 6$ cm, $AB = 8$ cm and perimeter of ΔABC is 36 cm, then perimeter of ΔPQR is

(a) 20.25 cm (b) 27 cm
(c) 48 cm (d) 64 cm

5. In the given figure, $DE \parallel BC$. If $AD = 6$ cm, $DB = 8$ cm and $AE = 12$ cm, then the value of EC is

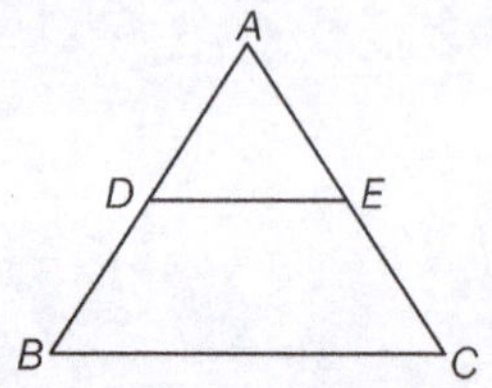

(a) 18 cm (b) 12 cm (c) 16 cm (d) 6 cm

6. In the given figure $\angle BAP = \angle DCP = 70°$, $PC = 6$ cm and $CA = 4$ cm, then $PD : DB$ is

[ICSE 2023]

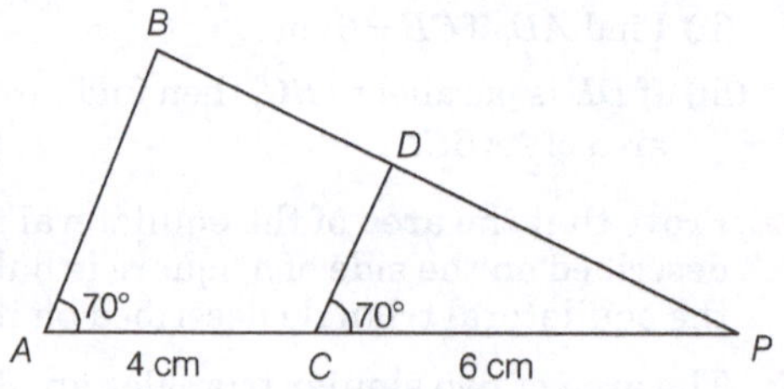

(a) 5 : 3 (b) 3 : 5
(c) 3 : 2 (d) 2 : 3

7. If the areas of two similar triangles are 144 cm^2 and 64 cm^2 respectively, then the ratio of their corresponding medians is

(a) 8 : 12 (b) 12 : 8
(c) 3 : 5 (d) 4 : 5

b. 3 Marks Questions

8. In the given figure, $\angle CAB = 90°$, $AD \perp BC$ and $\Delta BDA \sim \Delta BAC$. If $AC = 75$ cm, $AB = 1$ m and $BC = 1.25$ m, then find the value of AD.

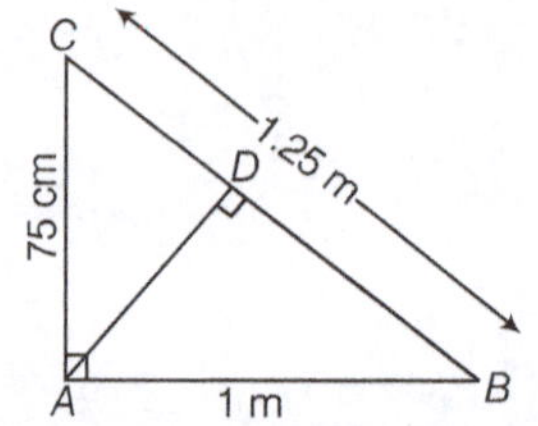

9. A vertical stick 1 m long casts a shadow 80 cm long. At the same time a tower casts a shadow 30 m long. Determine the height of the tower.

10. The perimeters of two similar ΔABC and ΔPQR are 18 cm and 12 cm, respectively. If $PQ = 5$ cm, then find AB.

11. In ΔABC, if $\angle ADE = \angle B$, then prove that $\Delta ADE \sim \Delta ABC$. Also, if $AD = 7.6$ cm, $AE = 7.2$ cm, $BE = 4.2$ cm and $BC = 8.4$ cm, find DE.

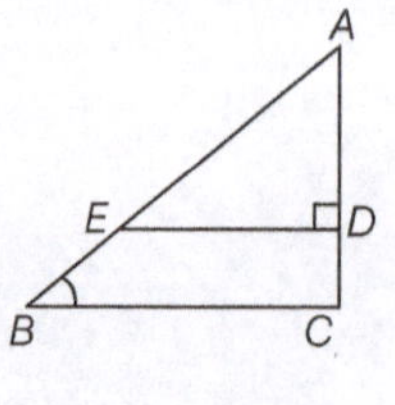

12. In the given figure, alongside,

$\angle QPS = \angle RPT$ and $\angle PRQ = \angle PTS$.

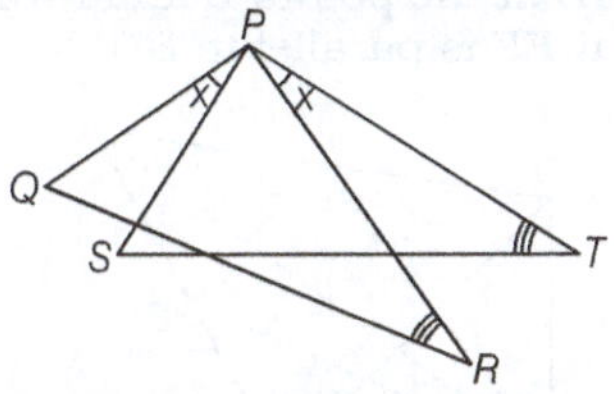

(i) Prove that ΔPQR and ΔPST are similar.

(ii) If $PT : ST = 3 : 4$, then find the ratio between $QR : PR$.

13. In the given figure, $\angle ACB = 90°$ and $CD \perp AB$.

Prove that $\frac{BC^2}{AC^2} = \frac{BD}{AD}$.

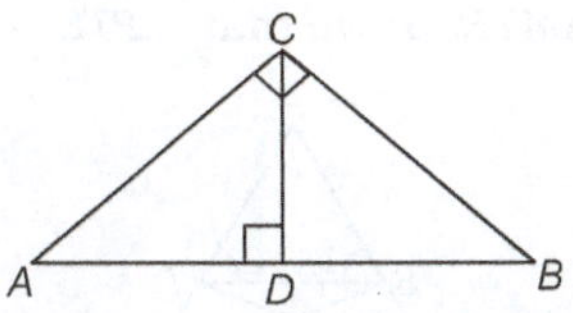

14. In the given figure, ABC is a right angled triangle, right angled at C and $DE \perp AB$. Prove that $\Delta ABC \sim \Delta ADE$ and hence find the lengths of AE and DE.

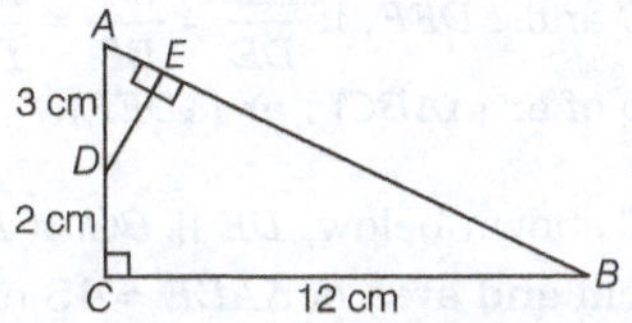

15. In the given figure, ΔABC and ΔAMP are right angled at B and M, respectively. Given, $AC = 10$ cm, $AP = 15$ cm and $PM = 12$ cm.

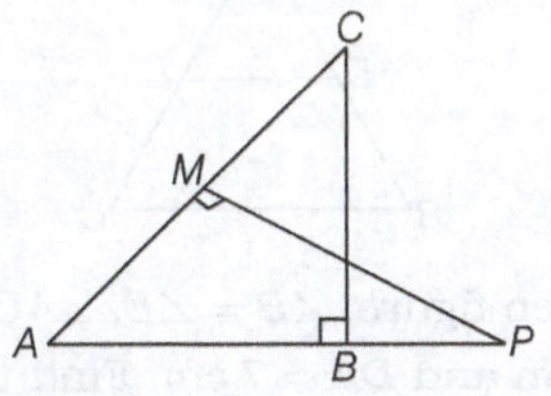

(i) Prove that $\Delta ABC \sim \Delta AMP$.

(ii) Find AB and BC. **[ICSE 2012]**

16. In ΔABC, $\angle A$ is obtuse, $PB \perp PC$ and $QC \perp QB$. Prove that $AB \times AQ = AC \times AP$.

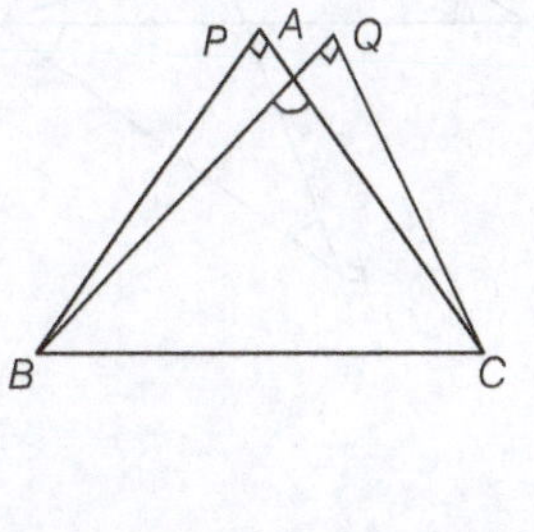

17. In ΔABC, AD is perpendicular to side BC and $AD^2 = BD \times CD$.

Show that angle $BAC = 90°$.

18. In the given figure, if $AB \perp BC$, $DE \perp AC$ and $GF \perp BC$, then prove that $\Delta ADE \sim \Delta GCF$.

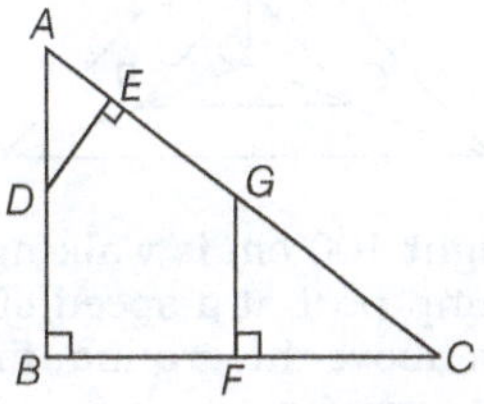

19. In the given figure, $DB \perp BC$ and $DE \perp AB$.

Prove that $\frac{BE}{DE} = \frac{AC}{BC}$.

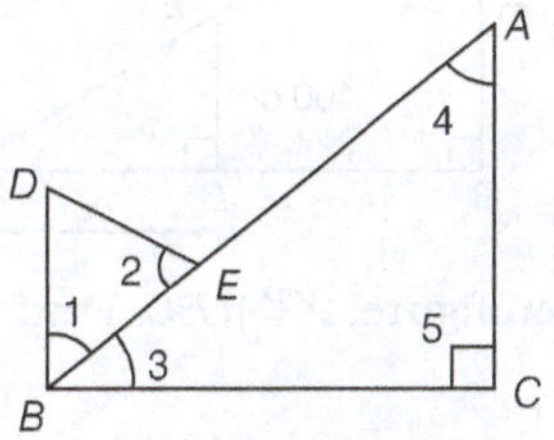

20. In the given figure, T is the exterior point on the diagonal PR of a parallelogram $PQRS$. SR produced meets QT at N and QR produced meets ST at M. Prove that $MN \parallel SQ$.

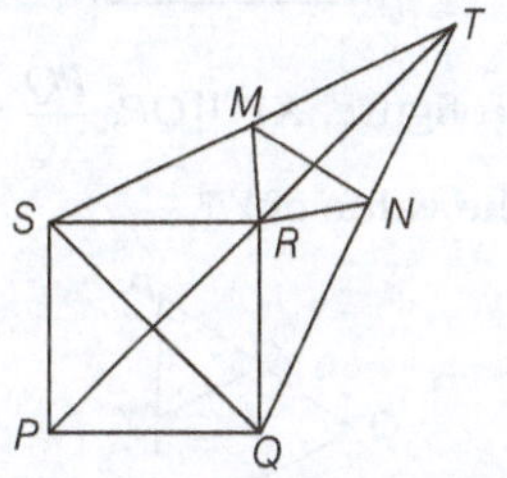

21. In the given figure, lines l and m are parallel. Three concurrent lines through point O meet line l at points A, B and C and line m at points P, Q and R as shown.

Prove that $\frac{AB}{BC} = \frac{QR}{PQ}$.

C. 4/5 Marks Questions

22. In the given figure, $\frac{OP}{OA} = \frac{OR}{OC}$ and $QR \parallel BC$. Prove that $PQ \parallel AB$.

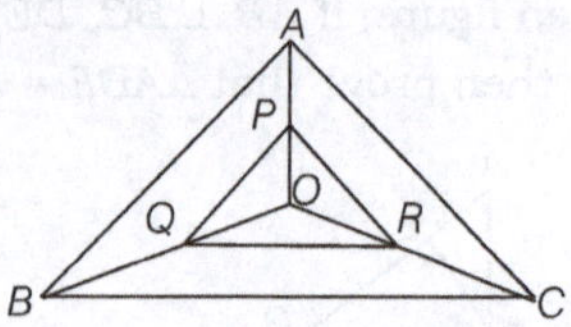

23. A girl of height 100 cm is walking away from the base of a lamp-post at a speed of 1.9 m/s. If the lamp is 5 m above the ground, find the length of her shadow after 4 s.

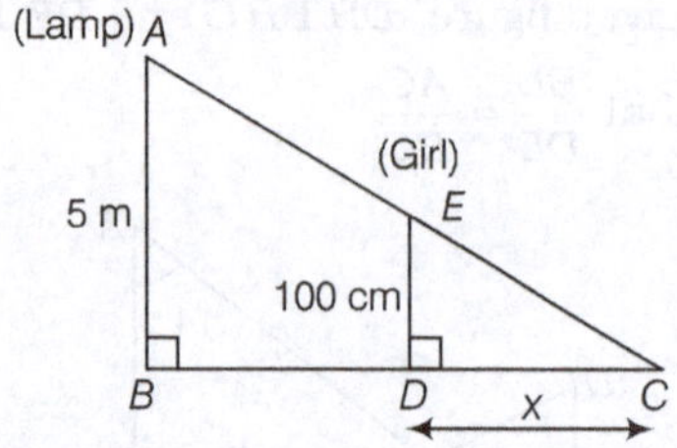

24. In the given figure, $XY \parallel BC$. Find the length of YC.

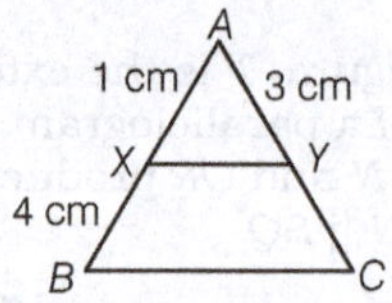

25. In the given figure, $XY \parallel QR$, $\frac{PQ}{XQ} = \frac{7}{3}$ and $PR = 6.3$ cm. Find the value of YR.

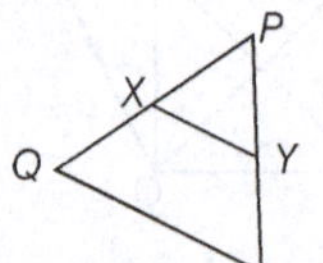

26. In ΔABC, $DE \parallel BC$, so that $AD = (7x - 4)$ cm, $AE = (5x - 2)$ cm, $DB = (3x + 4)$ cm and $EC = 3x$ cm. Then, find the value of x.

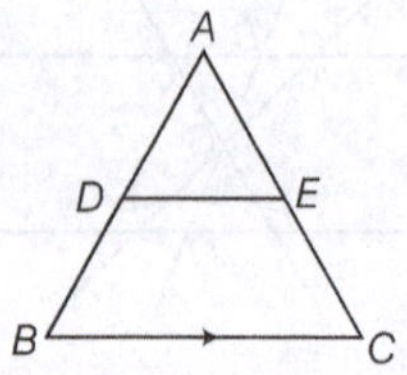

27. $ABCD$ is a trapezium in which $AB \parallel DC$. P and Q are points on sides AD and BC, respectively such that $PQ \parallel AB$. If $PD = 18$ cm, $BQ = 35$ cm and $QC = 15$ cm, find the value of AD.

28. In the adjoining quadrilateral $ABCD$, $AB = AD$. The bisectors of $\angle BAC$ and $\angle CAD$ meet the sides BC and CD at the points E and F respectively. Prove that EF is parallel to BD.

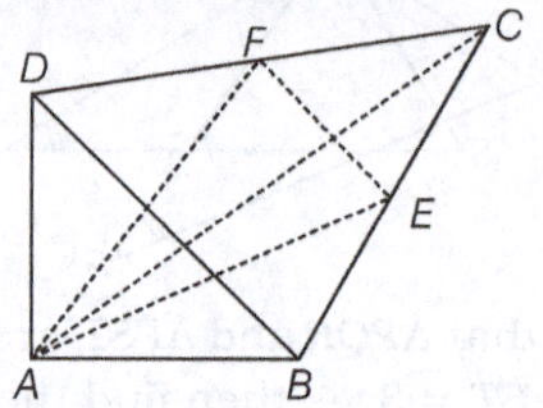

29. AD is median of ΔABC. The bisectors of $\angle ADB$ and $\angle ADC$ meet AB and AC in points E and F respectively. Prove that $EF \parallel BC$.

30. In the given figure, if $\angle 1 = \angle 2$ and $\Delta NSQ \cong \Delta MTR$, prove that $\Delta PTS \sim \Delta PRQ$.

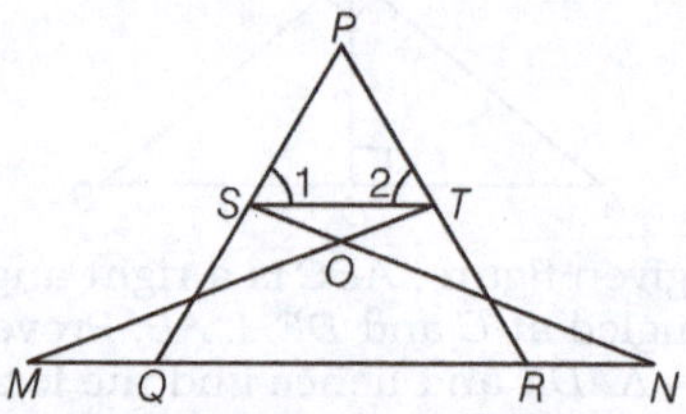

31. In ΔABC and ΔDEF, if $\frac{AB}{DE} = \frac{BC}{EF} = \frac{AC}{DF} = \frac{5}{9}$, find the ratio of ar (ΔABC) : ar (ΔDEF).

32. In ΔABC shown below, $DE \parallel BC$. If $BC = 8$ cm, $DE = 6$ cm and area of $\Delta ADE = 45$ cm^2, what is the area of ΔABC?

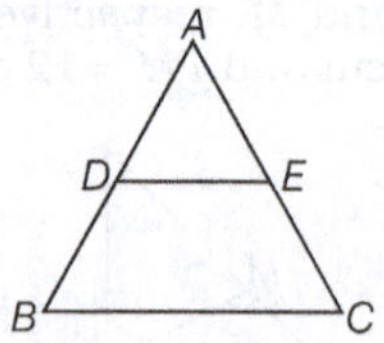

33. In the given figure, $\angle B = \angle E$, $\angle ACD = \angle BCE$, $AB = 10$ cm and $DE = 7$ cm. Find the ratio between areas of the ΔABC and ΔDEC.

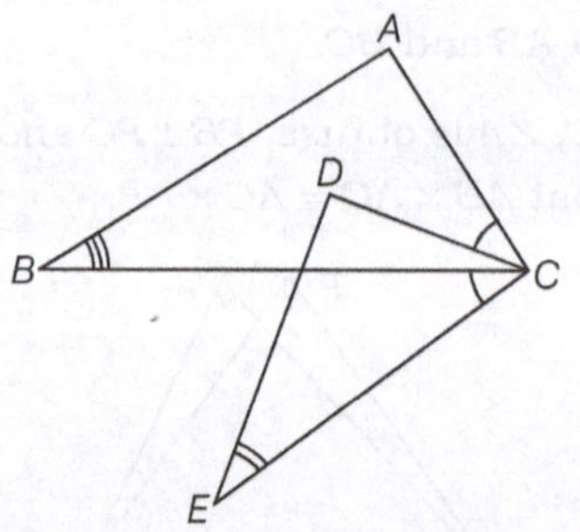

34. ABC is a triangle in which $\angle A = 90°$, $AN \perp BC$, $BC = 12$ cm and $AC = 5$ cm. Find the ratio of the areas of ΔANC and ΔABC.

35. If $\Delta ABC \sim \Delta DEF$, such that $AB = 1.2$ cm and $DE = 1.4$ cm, then find the ratio of areas of ΔABC and ΔDEF.

36. P, Q and R are respectively, the mid-points of the sides AB, BC and CA of ΔABC. Find the ratio of areas of ΔPQR and ΔABC.

37. Prove that the area of the ΔBCE described on one side BC of a square $ABCD$ as base, is one-half the area of the similar ΔACF described on the diagonal AC as base.

38. In ΔABC, $AP : PB = 2 : 3$, PO is parallel to BC and is extended to Q, so that CQ is parallel to BA.

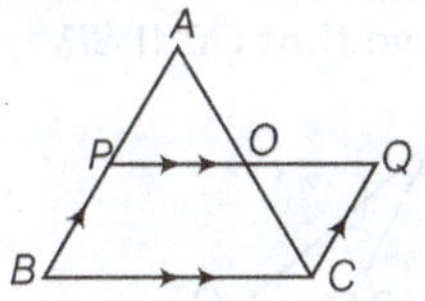

Find
(i) area of ΔAOP : area of ΔABC.
(ii) area of ΔAPO : area of ΔCQO. **[ICSE 2008]**

39. In the given figure, $ABCD$ is a trapezium, which DC is parallel to AB.
$AB = 16$ cm and $DC = 8$ cm, $OD = 5$ cm, $OB = (y + 3)$ cm, $OA = 11$ cm and $OC = (x - 1)$ cm. **[ICSE Semester I 2021]**

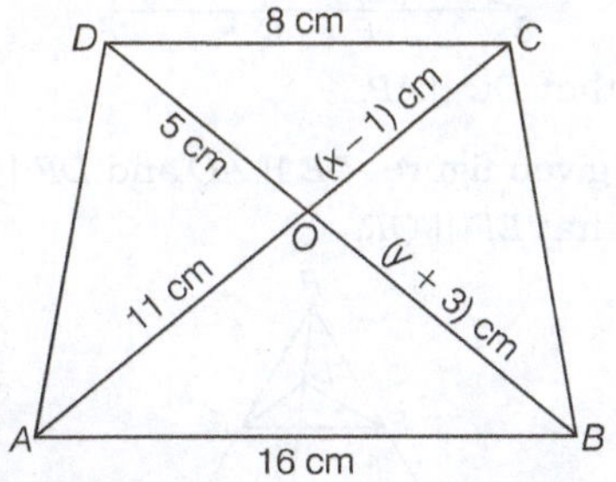

Using the given information answer the following questions.
(i) From the given figure name the pair of similar triangles.
(a) ΔOAB, ΔOBC (b) ΔCOD, ΔAOB
(c) ΔADB, ΔACB (d) ΔCOD, ΔCOB
(ii) The corresponding proportional sides with respect to the pair of similar triangles obtained in (i).
(a) $\frac{CD}{AB} = \frac{OC}{OA} = \frac{OD}{OB}$ (b) $\frac{AD}{BC} = \frac{OC}{OA} = \frac{OD}{OB}$
(c) $\frac{AD}{BC} = \frac{BD}{AC} = \frac{AB}{DC}$ (d) $\frac{OD}{OB} = \frac{CD}{CB} = \frac{OC}{OA}$
(iii) The ratio of the sides of the pair of similar triangles is
(a) 1 : 3 (b) 1 : 2 (c) 2 : 3 (d) 3 : 1
(iv) Using the ratio of sides of the pair of similar triangles the values of x and y are respectively.
(a) $x = 4.6$, $y = 7$ (b) $x = 7$, $y = 7$
(c) $x = 6.5$, $y = 7$ (d) $x = 6.5$, $y = 2$

40. In the given figure, PS, SQ, PT and TR are 4 cm, 1 cm, 6 cm and 1.5 cm, respectively. Prove that $ST \parallel QR$. Also, find $\frac{\text{ar}(\Delta PST)}{\text{ar (trapezium } QRTS)}$.

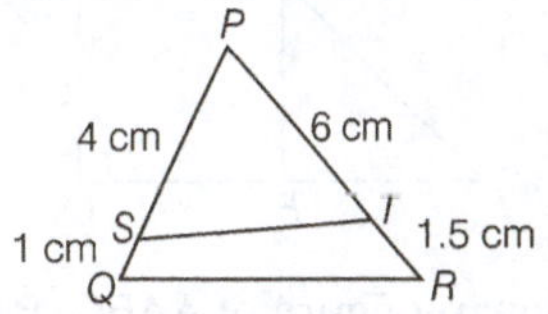

41. In the given figure, in ΔABC, $XY \parallel AC$ and XY divides the ΔABC into two regions such that ar $(\Delta BXY) = 2$ar (ΔCYX).
Determine $\frac{AX}{AB}$.

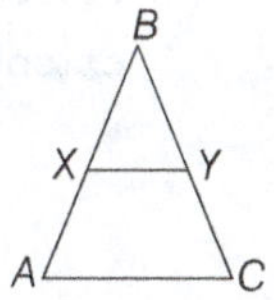

42. The model of a building is constructed with scale factor 1 : 30.
(i) If the height of the model is 80 cm, then find the actual height of the building in metres.
(ii) If the actual volume of a tank at the top of the building is 27 m^3, then find the volume of the tank on the top of the model. **[ICSE 2009]**

d. 6 Marks Questions

43. In the given figure, $AB \parallel EF \parallel DC$: $AB = 67.5$ cm, $DC = 40.5$ cm and $AE = 52.5$ cm.

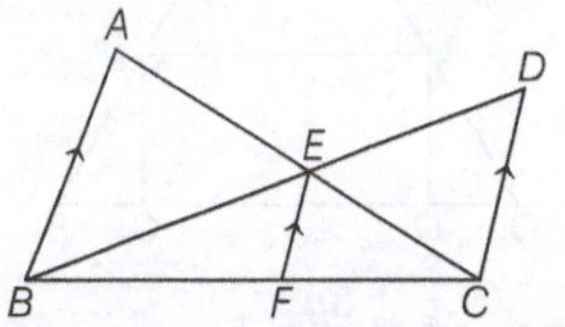

(i) Name the three pairs of similar triangles.
(ii) Find the lengths of EC and EF.

44. In the given figure, $ABCD$ and $AEFG$ are two squares.

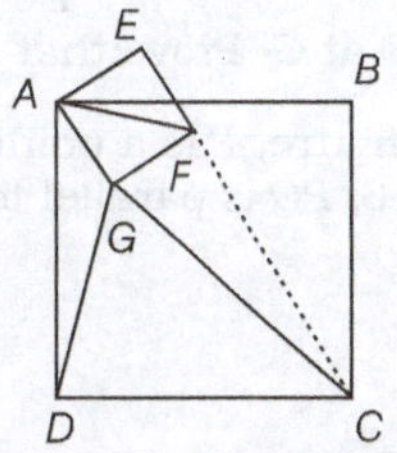

Prove that

(i) $\dfrac{AF}{AG} = \dfrac{AC}{AD}$

(ii) $\Delta ACF \sim \Delta ADG$

45. Legs (sides other than the hypotenuse) of a right triangle are of lengths 12 cm and 6 cm. Find the length of the side of the largest square that can be inscribed in the triangle.

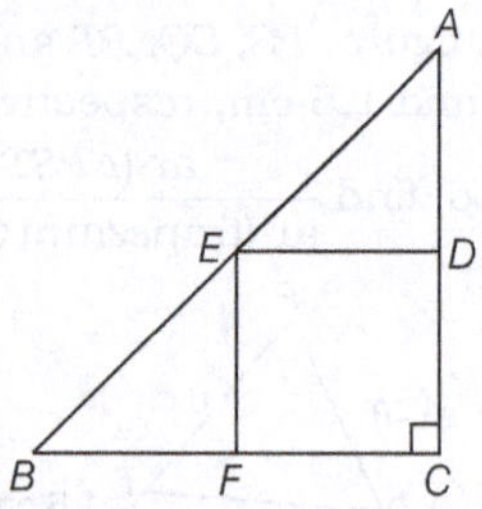

46. In the following figure of ΔABC, P is the mid-point of BC and 'Q' is the middle point of AP. If extended BQ meets AC at R, prove that $RA = \dfrac{1}{3} CA$.

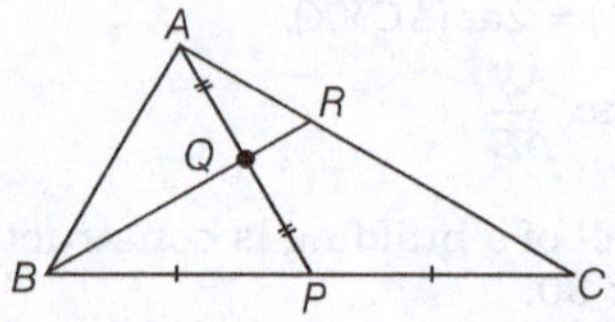

47. PQR is an isosceles triangle in which $PQ = PR = 10$ cm, $QR = 12$ cm. $ABCD$ is a rectangle inside the isosceles triangle. Given, $AB = CD = y$ cm, $AD = BC = 2x$ cm.

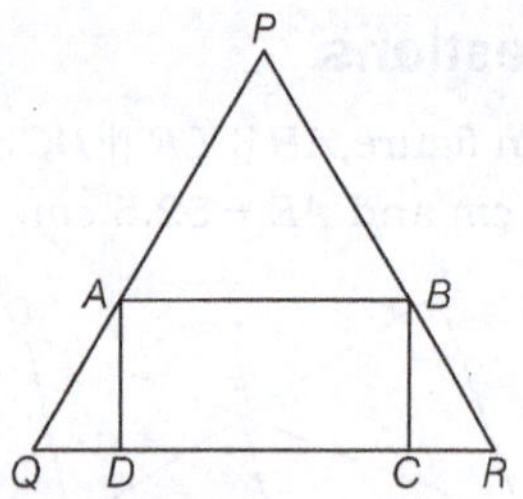

Prove that $x = 6 - \dfrac{3y}{4}$.

48. In a trapezium $ABCD$, $AB \parallel DC$ and $DC = 2AB$. $EF \parallel AB$, where E and F lie on BC and AD respectively, such that $\dfrac{BE}{EC} = \dfrac{4}{3}$. Diagonal DB intersects EF at G. Prove that $7EF = 11AB$.

49. In the given figure, P is a point on AB such that $AP : PB = 4 : 3$, PQ is parallel to AC.

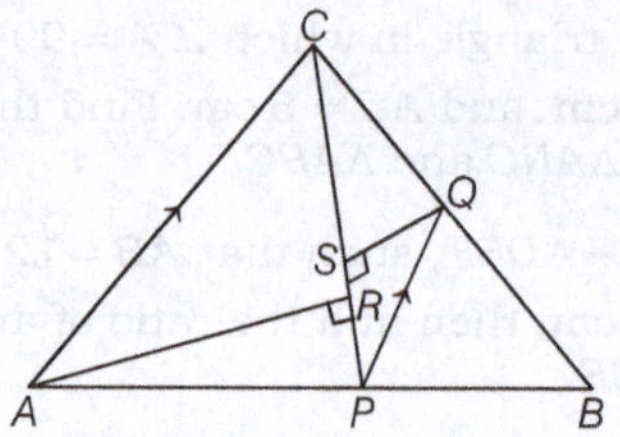

(i) Calculate the ratio $PQ : AC$, given reason for your answer.

(ii) In ΔARC, $\angle ARC = 90°$ and in ΔPQS, $\angle PSQ = 90°$. Given, $QS = 6$ cm, calculate the length of AR.

50. D is the mid-point of side BC of a ΔABC. AD is bisected at the point E and BE produced cuts AC at the point X. Prove that $BE : EX = 3 : 1$.

51. In the given figure, if $PQRS$ is a parallelogram and $AB \parallel PS$, prove that $OC \parallel SR$.

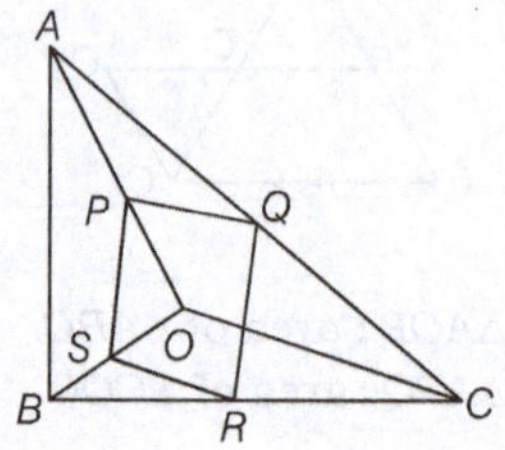

52. In the given figure, $DE \parallel AC$ and $\dfrac{BE}{EC} = \dfrac{BC}{CP}$.

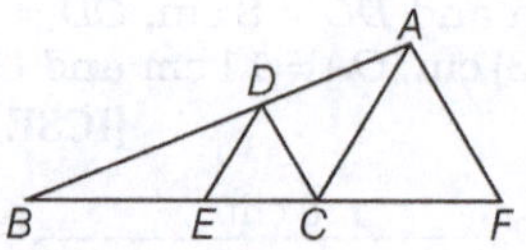

Prove that $DC \parallel AP$.

53. In the given figure, $DE \parallel AQ$ and $DF \parallel AR$. Prove that $EF \parallel QR$.

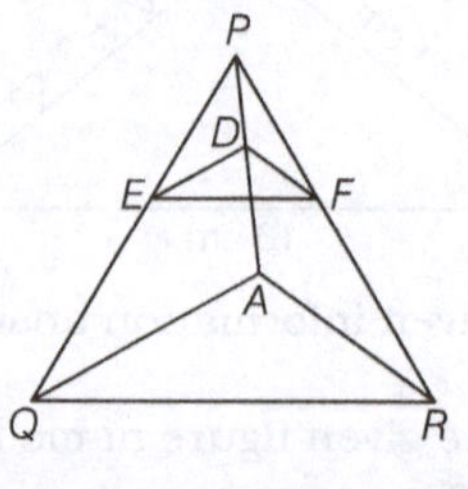

54. In the given figure, ABC is a right angled triangle with $\angle BAC = 90°$.

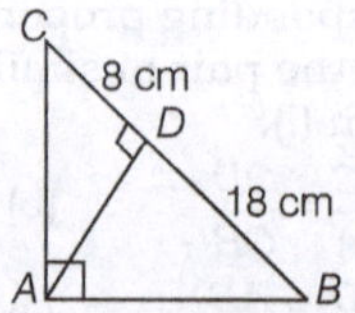

(i) Prove that $\Delta ADB \sim \Delta CDA$.

(ii) If $BD = 18$ cm and $CD = 8$ cm, then find AD.

(iii) Find the ratio of the area of ΔADB to the area of ΔCDA. **[ICSE 2011]**

55. In the given figure, ABC is a triangle with $\angle EDB = \angle ACB$. Prove that $\Delta ABC \sim \Delta EBD$. If $BE = 6$ cm, $EC = 4$ cm, $BD = 5$ cm and area of $\Delta BED = 9\,\text{cm}^2$, then calculate

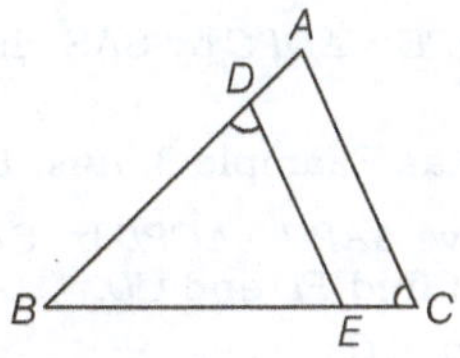

(i) the length of AB.

(ii) the area of ΔABC. **[ICSE 2010]**

56. In the given figure, $AC \parallel DE \parallel BF$.
If $AC = 24$ cm, $EG = 8$ cm, $GB = 16$ cm, $BF = 30$ cm.

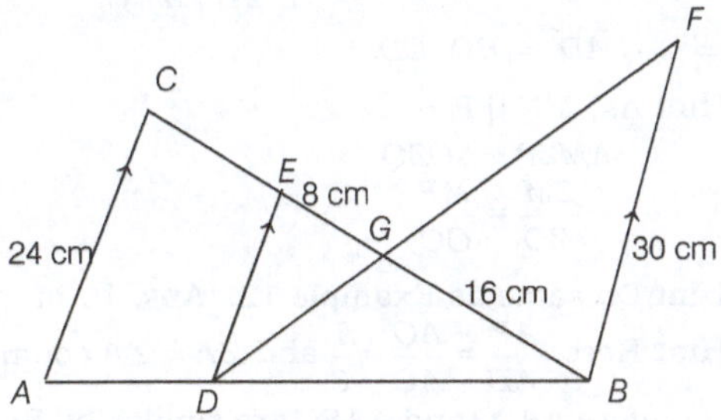

(i) Prove $\Delta GED \sim \Delta GBF$

(ii) Find DE

(iii) $DB : AB$ **[ICSE 2023]**

57. In the given figure, PB and QA are perpendiculars to the line segment AB. If $PO = 6$ cm, $QO = 9$ cm and the area of $\Delta POB = 120\,\text{cm}^2$, then find the area of ΔAOQ.

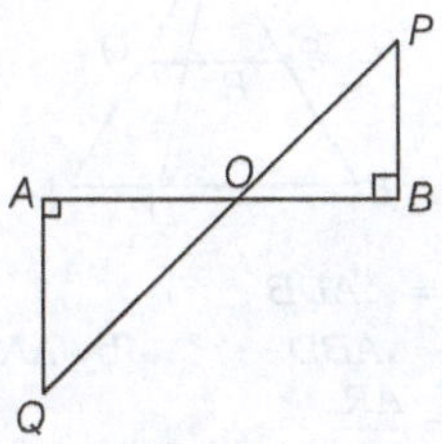

58. In the given figure, BC is parallel to DE, area of $\Delta ABC = 25\,\text{cm}^2$, area of trapezium $BCED = 24\,\text{cm}^2$ and $DE = 14$ cm. Calculate the length of BC.

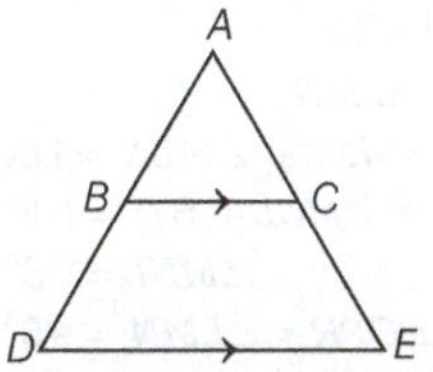

59. The ratio between the areas of two similar triangle is 9 : 16. Find the ratio between their

(i) perimeters

(ii) corresponding altitudes

(iii) corresponding medians

60. In the given figure, if $DE \parallel BC$ and $AD : DB = 5 : 4$, then find $\dfrac{\text{ar}\,(\Delta DFE)}{\text{ar}\,(\Delta CFB)}$.

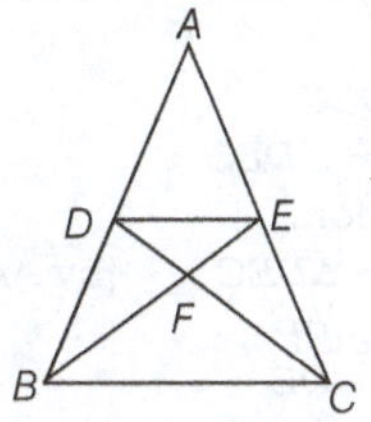

61. A rectangular tank has length = 4 m, width = 3 m and capacity = 30 m^3. A small model of the tank is made with capacity 240 cm^3. Find

(i) the dimensions of the model

(ii) the ratio between the total surface area of the tank and its model.

62. The scale of a map is 1 : 200000. A plot of land of area 20 km^2 is to be represented on the map. Find

(i) the number of kilometres on the ground, which is represented by 1 cm on the map.

(ii) the area (in km^2), that can be represented by 1 cm^2.

(iii) the area on the map, that represents the plot of land.

63. In a size transformation, the area of the image of an object of area 6 m^2 is 37.5 cm^2. Calculate

(i) the scale factor.

(ii) the volume of an object, if the volume of its image is 360 cm^3.

Hints and Answers

Exercise 13.1

1. (i) **Hint** Corresponding sides are not in proportion.
   Ans. Not similar

   (ii) **Hint** From ΔLMN,

$$\angle LMN + \angle MNL + \angle MLN = 180°$$
$$\Rightarrow \quad 45° + \angle MNL + 57° = 180°$$
$$\Rightarrow \quad \angle MNL = 78°$$
$$\therefore \quad \angle QPR = \angle LMN = 45°$$
$$\text{and} \quad \angle PQR = \angle MNL = 78°$$

   So, $\Delta PQR \sim \Delta MNL$ [by AA similarity criterion]

   Ans. Yes similar

2. **Hint**

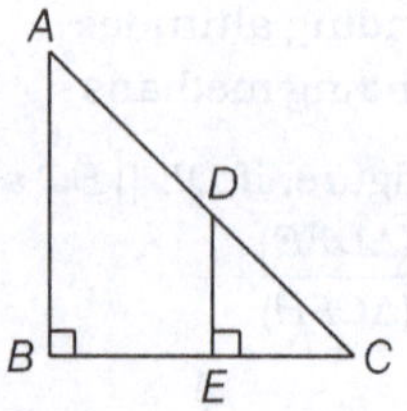

   In ΔABC and ΔDEC

$$\angle ABC = \angle DEC \quad \text{[each 90°]}$$

   and $\angle C$ is common.

$$\therefore \quad \Delta ABC \sim \Delta DEC \quad \text{[by AA similarity criterion]}$$
$$\Rightarrow \quad \frac{AC}{DC} = \frac{AB}{DE}$$
$$\Rightarrow \quad DC = \frac{24 \times 3}{9} = 8 \text{ cm}$$
$$\text{and} \quad AD = AC - DC$$

   Ans. 16 cm

3. **Hint** As, $\Delta ADB \sim \Delta ADC$

$$\Rightarrow \quad \frac{AB}{AC} = \frac{DB}{DC} \Rightarrow \frac{18}{p} = \frac{p}{2}$$

   Ans. $p = 6$ cm

4. **Hint** As, ΔABC and ΔPQR are similar,

$$\text{i.e.} \quad \frac{AB}{PQ} = \frac{BC}{QR} \Rightarrow \frac{x}{4.8} = \frac{2}{6.4} \Rightarrow x = 1.5$$
$$\text{and} \quad \frac{AC}{PR} = \frac{BC}{QR} \Rightarrow \frac{4}{y} = \frac{2}{6.4} \Rightarrow y = 12.8$$

   Ans. $x = 1.5$ cm and $y = 12.8$ cm

5. **Hint** As $\Delta ABC \sim \Delta DFE$

$$\angle D = \angle A = 30°, \quad \angle C = \angle E = 50°$$
$$\therefore \quad \angle B = \angle F = 180° - (50° + 30°) = 100°$$
$$\text{Now,} \quad \frac{AB}{DF} = \frac{AC}{DE}$$
$$\Rightarrow \quad \frac{5}{7.5} = \frac{8}{DE}$$
$$\Rightarrow \quad DE = 12 \text{ cm}$$

   Ans. $DE = 12$ cm, $\angle F = 100°$

6. **Hint** As $\Delta OAB \sim \Delta OCD$,

$$\frac{OA}{OC} = \frac{AB}{CD} = \frac{BO}{OD} \Rightarrow \frac{OA}{3.5} = \frac{8}{5} = \frac{6.4}{DO}$$

   Ans. $OA = 5.6$ cm, $DO = 4$ cm

7. **Hint** First prove $\Delta ABC \sim \Delta LNM$ by SSS similarity criterion, then find $\angle MLN$. **Ans.** 60°.

8. **Hint** Prove $\Delta APB \sim \Delta DPC$ by SAS similarity criterion. **Ans.** 100°.

9. **Hint** Do same as Example 8. **Ans.** $BC = 8.1$ cm

10. **Hint** First prove $\Delta APB \sim \Delta CPD$ by SAS similarity criterion, then find PD and CD.
    Ans. $PD = 5$ cm, $CD = 2$ cm

11. **Hint** ΔPNK and ΔLMK, are similar by AA similarity criterion.

$$\frac{NK}{MK} = \frac{PN}{LM} \Rightarrow \frac{c}{b+c} = \frac{x}{a} \Rightarrow x = \frac{ac}{b+c}$$

12. **Hint** $\Delta ADB \sim \Delta ADC$, then $\frac{BD}{AD} = \frac{AD}{CD}$

$$\Rightarrow \quad AD^2 = BD \cdot CD.$$

13. **Hint** As, $MN \parallel PO$

$$\Delta MZP \sim \Delta OZQ$$
$$\frac{ZM}{ZO} = \frac{MP}{OQ}$$

14. **Hint** Do same as Example 12. **Ans.** 10 m

15. **Hint** Here, $\frac{AP}{AB} = \frac{AQ}{AC} = \frac{1}{3}$ and $\angle A = \angle A$ common,

    therefore ΔAPQ and ΔABC are similar by SAS similarity criterion,

$$\text{i.e.} \quad \frac{AP}{AB} = \frac{AQ}{AC} = \frac{PQ}{BC} = \frac{1}{3} \Rightarrow BC = 3PQ$$

16. **Hint** Prove ΔABC and ΔAMP are similar by AA similarity criterion, take ratio $\frac{AC}{AP} = \frac{BC}{MP}$.

17. **Hint** In ΔAPR and ΔABD, $\angle APR = \angle ABD$

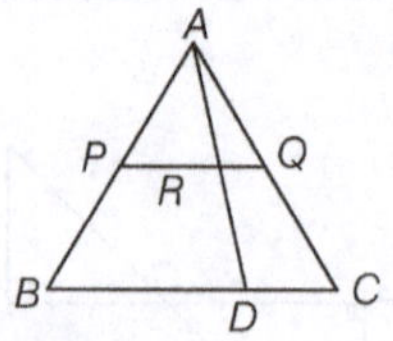

$$\angle ARP = \angle ADB$$
$$\therefore \quad \Delta APR \sim \Delta ABD \quad \text{[by AA similarity criterion]}$$
$$\frac{PR}{BD} = \frac{AR}{AD} \quad \text{...(i)}$$

   Similarly, we can prove $\frac{AR}{AD} = \frac{RQ}{DC}$ ...(ii)

   From Eqs. (i) and (ii), we get

$$\frac{PR}{BD} = \frac{RQ}{DC}$$
$$\Rightarrow \quad PR = RQ$$

18. **Hint** Do same as Example 13. **Ans.** $x = 4.5$ cm

19. **Hint** Do same as Example 13. **Ans.** $AC = 4.5$ cm

20. **Hint** Do same as Example 22. **Ans.** $a = 2$

21. $\therefore LM \parallel CB, \dfrac{AM}{AB} = \dfrac{AL}{LC}$ ...(i) [by BPT theorem]

Similarly, $LN \parallel CD, \dfrac{AN}{ND} = \dfrac{AL}{LC}$ ...(ii)

From Eqs. (i) and (ii), we get

$$\frac{AM}{AB} = \frac{AN}{AD}$$

22. **Hint**

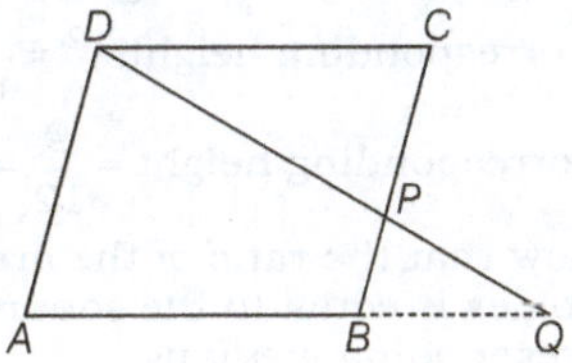

$\therefore BP \parallel AD, \dfrac{PQ}{DP} = \dfrac{BQ}{AB} \Rightarrow \dfrac{DP}{PQ} = \dfrac{DC}{BQ} [AB = DC]$ ...(i)

$\because \dfrac{DP}{PQ} + 1 = \dfrac{DC}{BQ} + 1 \Rightarrow \dfrac{DP+PQ}{PQ} = \dfrac{DC+BQ}{BQ}$ ...(ii)

Dividing Eq. (ii) by Eq. (i), as required

$$\frac{DQ}{DP} = \frac{AQ}{DC}$$

23. **Hint** In $\Delta ABC, \dfrac{AD}{DC} = \dfrac{BE}{EC}$

$\Rightarrow DE \parallel AB$ [by converse of BPT]

$\therefore \angle CDE = \angle A$ and $\angle CED = \angle B$

Since, $\angle CDE = \angle CED$

$\angle A = \angle B \Rightarrow CB = CA$

$\therefore \Delta CAB$ is an isosceles triangle.

24. **Hint** Use the result 'the diagonals of a trapezium divide each other proportionally.' **Ans.** $x = 3$

25. **Hint** Let $QD = x$ units and $DR = y$ units,

Then, $QR = (x + y)$ units

$\therefore \Delta EDR \sim \Delta PRQ$

$\Rightarrow \dfrac{ED}{PQ} = \dfrac{DR}{QR} \Rightarrow \dfrac{b}{a} = \dfrac{y}{(x+y)}$ units ...(i)

Similarly, $\Delta EDQ \sim \Delta SRQ$

$\Rightarrow \dfrac{ED}{SR} = \dfrac{QD}{QR} \Rightarrow \dfrac{b}{c} = \dfrac{x}{(x+y)}$ units ...(ii)

On adding Eqs. (i) and (ii), $\dfrac{1}{a} + \dfrac{1}{c} = \dfrac{1}{b}$

Exercise 13.2

1. **Hint** Do same as Example 24. **Ans.** $AB = 1.91$ cm

2. **Hint** $\dfrac{\text{ar } \Delta ABC}{\text{ar } \Delta DEF} = \dfrac{AB^2}{DE^2}$ **Ans.** $\dfrac{1}{9}$

3. **Hint** $\dfrac{\text{ar } \Delta PST}{\text{ar } \Delta PQR} = \dfrac{PT^2}{PR^2}$ **Ans.** $\dfrac{1}{9}$

4. **Hint** Use the fact that the ratio of area of two similar triangles is equal to the ratio of the square of its corresponding sides. **Ans.** $\dfrac{5}{9}$

5. **Hint** $\dfrac{\text{ar } \Delta ADE}{\text{ar } \Delta ABC} = \dfrac{DE^2}{BC^2}$ **Ans.** 100 cm^2

6. **Hint** The ratio of areas of two similar triangles is equal to the ratio of the square of their median. **Ans.** 9 : 7

7. **Hint** Use the fact that ratio of area of two similar triangles is equal to the ratio of the square of its corresponding sides. **Ans.** $\dfrac{6}{5}$

8. **Hint**

(i) Here, $\Delta PMN \sim \Delta PQR$ [by AA similarity criteria]

$\therefore \dfrac{MN}{QR} = \dfrac{PM}{PQ} = \dfrac{2}{5}$ ...(i)

We have, $\dfrac{PM}{MQ} = \dfrac{2}{3} \Rightarrow \dfrac{MQ}{PM} = \dfrac{3}{2}$

$\Rightarrow \dfrac{MQ}{PM} + 1 = \dfrac{3}{2} + 1$ **Ans.** $\dfrac{MN}{QR} = \dfrac{2}{5}$

(ii) In ΔOMN and ΔORQ,

$\angle OMN = \angle ORQ$ [alternate interior angles]

$\angle ONM = \angle OQR$ [alternate interior angles]

$\therefore$ By AA similarity criteria, $\Delta OMN \sim \Delta ORQ$

(iii) Clearly, $\dfrac{(\Delta OMN)}{(\Delta ORQ)} = \left(\dfrac{MN}{QR}\right)^2$

Ans. 4 : 25

9. **Hint** $\Delta AED \sim \Delta ABC$

So, $\dfrac{\text{ar }(\Delta AED)}{\text{ar }(ABC)} = \dfrac{\text{ar }(\Delta AED)}{\text{ar }(\Delta AED) + \text{ar (trapezium } EBCD)}$

$= \dfrac{AE^2}{AB^2}$

Ans. 1 : 2

10. **Hint** Do same as Example 31 (ii). **Ans.** 16 cm

11. (i) **Hint** In ΔABC and ΔDEC,

$\angle ABC = \angle DEC = 90°$

and $\angle ACB = \angle DCE$ [common angle]

$\therefore \Delta ABC \sim \Delta DEC$ [by AA at similarity criterion]

(ii) **Hint** Since, $\Delta ABC \sim \Delta DEC$ [proved above]

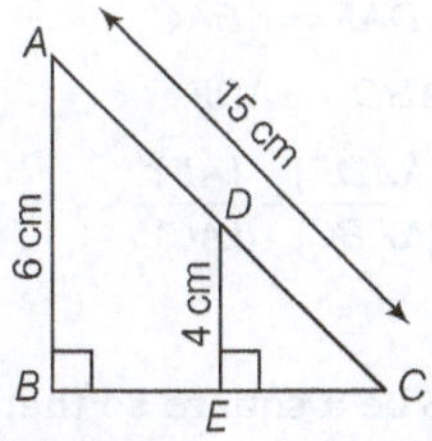

$\therefore \dfrac{AB}{DE} = \dfrac{AC}{DC}$

$\Rightarrow \dfrac{6}{4} = \dfrac{15}{DC}$

Ans. 10 cm

(iii) **Hint** Since, $\Delta ABC \sim \Delta DEC$

$\therefore \dfrac{\text{ar }(\Delta ABC)}{\text{ar }(\Delta DEC)} = \dfrac{(AB)^2}{(DE)^2}$

Ans. 9 : 4

12. **Hint**

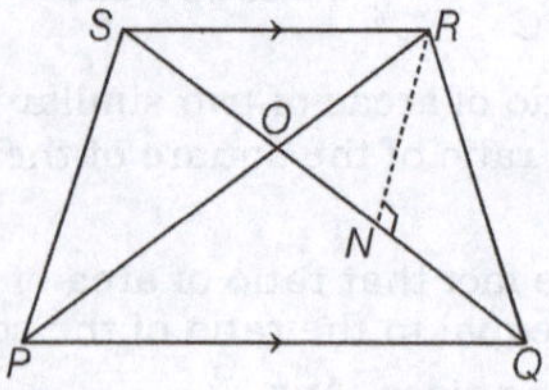

(i) Area of ΔPRS = Area of ΔQRS

$\Rightarrow$ Area of ΔORS + Area of ΔPOS = 7 sq cm

(ii) From R, draw $RN \perp SQ$.

Area of ΔOQR = Area of ΔQRS − Area of ΔORS = 4 sq cm

Now, $\dfrac{\Delta OQR}{\Delta ORS} = \dfrac{\frac{1}{2} \times QO \times RN}{\frac{1}{2} \times OS \times RN}$

(iii) In ΔOPQ and ΔORS,

$$\frac{\Delta OPQ}{\Delta ORS} = \frac{OQ^2}{OS^2}$$

Ans. (i) 3 sq cm (ii) 4 : 3 (iii) $5\frac{1}{3}$ sq cm

13. (i) **Hint** In ΔADF and ΔCEF, we have

$\angle AFD = \angle CFE$, $\angle DAF = \angle FCE$

$\therefore \quad \Delta ADF \sim \Delta CEF$ [by AA at similarity criterion]

(ii) **Hint** Since, $\Delta ADF \sim \Delta CEF$

$\therefore \quad \dfrac{AD}{CE} = \dfrac{AF}{CF}$

$$\left[\because \frac{AC}{AF} = \frac{8}{5} \Rightarrow \frac{AC}{AF} - 1 = \frac{8}{5} - 1 \Rightarrow \frac{CF}{AF} = \frac{3}{5}\right]$$

$\Rightarrow \quad \dfrac{AD}{6} = \dfrac{5}{3} \Rightarrow AD = \dfrac{5 \times 6}{3}$

$\therefore \quad AD = 10$ cm

(iii) **Hint** Here, $\dfrac{AF}{AC} = \dfrac{AD}{AB}$ ...(i)

and $\angle DAF = \angle BAC$ [common angle]

$\therefore \quad \Delta ABC \sim \Delta ADF$

Then, $\dfrac{\text{ar}(\Delta ADF)}{\text{ar}(\Delta ABC)} = \dfrac{(AF)^2}{(AC)^2}$

Ans. 25 : 64

14. **Hint** Let $PQRS$ be a square so that,

$PQ = QR = RS = SP$

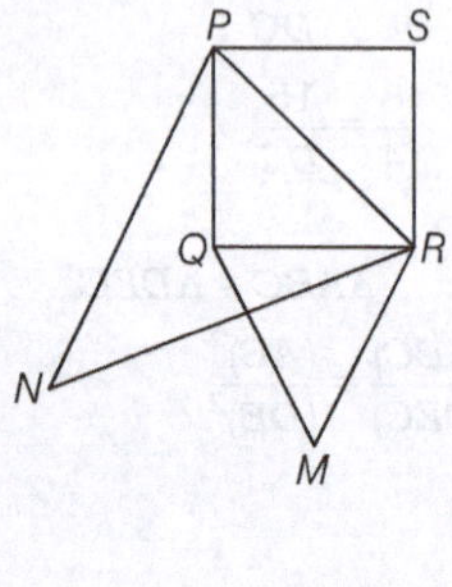

By Pythagoras theorem,

$$PR^2 = PQ^2 + QR^2 = 2QR^2$$

As ΔQRM and ΔPRN are equilateral,

$$\Delta QRM \sim \Delta PRN$$

$$\therefore \quad \frac{\Delta QRM}{\Delta PRN} = \frac{QR^2}{PR^2}$$

$\Rightarrow$ Area of $\Delta QRM = \dfrac{1}{2}$ Area of ΔPRN

15. **Hint** We know, the ratio of the areas of two similar triangles is equal to the square of the ratios of their corresponding altitudes i.e. height.

$\therefore$ (ratio of corresponding heights)$^2 = \dfrac{81}{144}$

$\Rightarrow$ ratio of corresponding height $= \dfrac{9}{12} = \dfrac{3}{4} = 3:4$

Also, we know that the ratio of the areas of two similar triangles is equal to the square of the ratios of their corresponding medians.

$\therefore$ (ratio of corresponding medians)$^2 = \dfrac{81}{144}$

$$= \frac{9}{12} = \frac{3}{4} = 3:4$$

Ans. 3 : 4, 3 : 4

16. **Hint** Do same as Example 35.

Ans. (i) 5 km (ii) 12 km^2

17. **Hint** Do same as Example 37 (ii).

Ans. 25000 cm^2

18. **Hint** Do same as Example 37.

Ans. (i) 800 m (ii) 4 m^2 (iii) 800000 m^3

Chapter Exercise

1. (b) Given, $\Delta ABC \sim \Delta PQR$,

$\therefore \quad \angle A + \angle B = 180° - \angle C$

Similarly, $\angle R = 180° - (p + q)$

where, $\angle A = \angle P$ and $\angle B = \angle Q$

$\angle R = 180° - (60° + 70°) = 50°$

2. (b) $\Delta ABC \sim \Delta DEF$, then $\dfrac{AB}{AC} = \dfrac{DE}{DF}$ is true and $\angle BAC = \angle DEF$.

3. (b) Given $\Delta ABC \sim \Delta PQR$,

$\therefore \quad \dfrac{AC}{PR} = \dfrac{BC}{QR} = \dfrac{AB}{PQ}$

$\Rightarrow \quad \dfrac{6}{x} = \dfrac{4.5}{3} \Rightarrow x = \dfrac{6 \times 3}{4.5} = 4$ cm

4. (c) Given, $\Delta PQR \sim \Delta ABC$

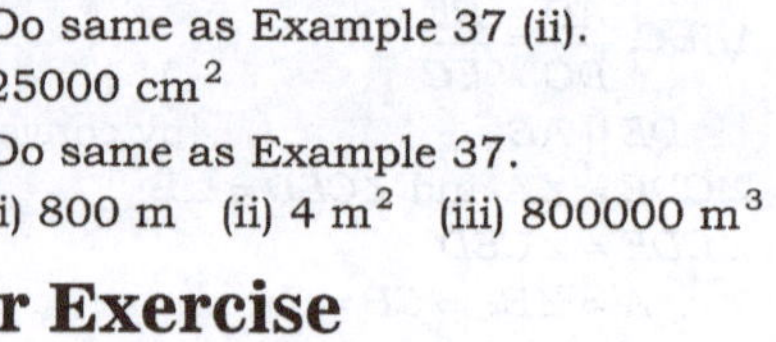

$$\frac{AB}{PQ} = \frac{BC}{QR} = \frac{AC}{PR} = \frac{6}{8} = \frac{3}{4}$$

[$\because$ Corresponding sides of similar triangles are proportional]

$$AB = \frac{3}{4}PQ,\ BC = \frac{3}{4}QR,\ AC = \frac{3}{4}PR$$

Also given perimeter of $\Delta ABC = 36$ cm

$\therefore\ AB + BC + AC = 36$ cm

$\therefore AB + BC + AC = \frac{3}{4}(PQ + QR + PR)$

$36 = \frac{3}{4}$ (perimeter of ΔPQR)

$\therefore$ Perimeter of $\Delta PQR = \frac{36 \times 4}{3} = 48$ cm

5. (c) Given, in ΔABC, $DE \parallel BC$,

$\therefore\ \frac{AD}{DB} = \frac{AE}{EC}$ [by BPT Theorem]

$\Rightarrow\ \frac{6}{8} = \frac{12}{EC}$

$\Rightarrow\ EC = \frac{12 \times 8}{6} = 16$ cm

6. (c) In the given figure,

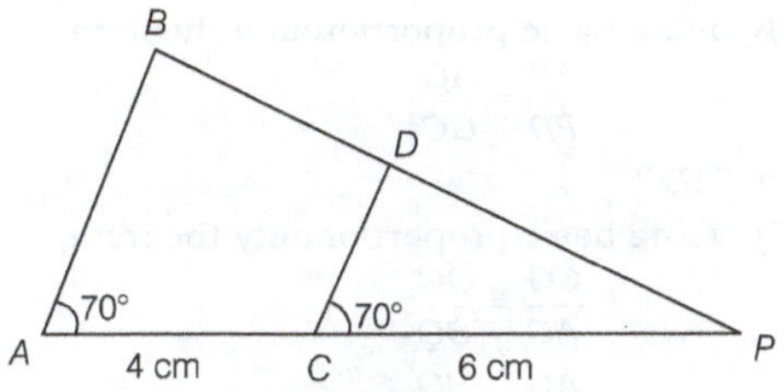

$\angle BAP = \angle DCP$

$\therefore\ AB \parallel CD$ {corresponding angles are equal}

$\Rightarrow\ \frac{PC}{CA} = \frac{PD}{DB}$ [$\because$ By basic Proportionality Theorem]

$\Rightarrow\ \frac{PD}{DB} = \frac{6}{4} = \frac{3}{2}$

7. (b) The ratio of areas of two similar triangles is equal to the ratio of the square of their median.

$$\frac{\text{Area of first triangle}}{\text{Area of second triangle}} = \left[\frac{\text{Median of 1st triangle}}{\text{Median of 2nd triangle}}\right]^2$$

$\Rightarrow\ \frac{144}{64} = (\text{ratio of median})^2$

$\Rightarrow\ 12 : 8 =$ ratio of median

8. Hint Since, $\Delta BDA \sim \Delta BAC$

$\therefore\ \frac{AD}{AC} = \frac{BA}{BC}$ **Ans.** 60cm

9. Hint Let h be the height of the tower.

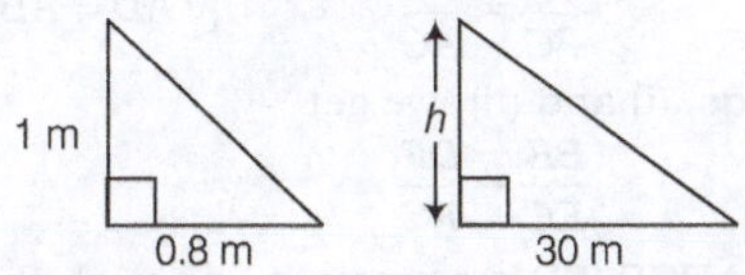

[$\because$ 80 cm = 0.8 m]

Since, it is clear that both the triangles will be similar.

$\therefore\ \frac{1}{h} = \frac{0.8}{30}$

Ans. 37.5 m

10. Hint Since, $\Delta ABC \sim \Delta PQR$

$\therefore\ \frac{AB}{PQ} = \frac{18}{12} \Rightarrow AB = \frac{18 \times 5}{12} = 7.5$ cm **Ans.** 7.5 cm

11. Hint In ΔADE and ΔABC,

$\angle ADE = \angle ABC$ [given]

$\Rightarrow\ \angle DAE = \angle BAC$ [common angle]

So, $\Delta ADE \sim \Delta ABC$ [by AA similarity criterion]

Then, $\frac{AD}{AB} = \frac{AE}{AC} = \frac{DE}{BC}$

$\Rightarrow\ \frac{7.6}{7.2 + 4.2} = \frac{DE}{8.4}$ **Ans.** $DE = 5.6$ cm

12. (i) In ΔPQR and ΔPST,

$\therefore \Delta PQR \sim \Delta PST$ [AA postulate]

(ii) Since the corresponding sides of similar triangles are proportional.

$\therefore$ In similar ΔPQR and ΔPST,

$$\frac{QR}{ST} = \frac{PR}{PT}$$

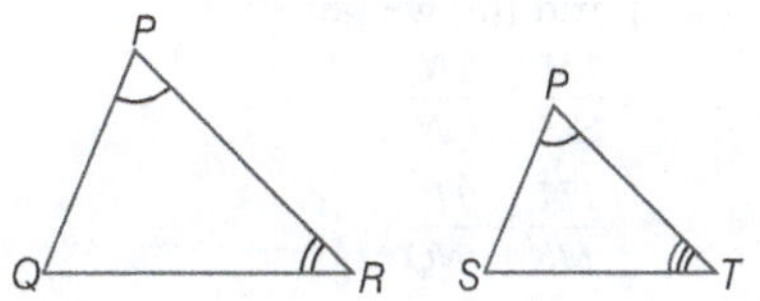

Ans. $QR : PR = 4 : 3$

13. Hint Here, $\Delta ADC \sim \Delta ACB$ and $\Delta BDC \sim \Delta BCA$

$\therefore\ \frac{AD}{AC} = \frac{AC}{BA}$ and $\frac{BD}{BC} = \frac{BC}{AB}$

$\Rightarrow\ AC^2 = AB \times AD$ and $BC^2 = AB \times BD$

14. Hint Use AA similarity criterion to prove $\Delta ABC \sim \Delta ADE$.

Ans. $AE = \frac{15}{13}$ cm and $DE = \frac{36}{13}$ cm

15. (i) **Hint** In ΔABC and ΔAMP,

$\angle ABC = \angle AMP = 90°$ [given]

$\angle BAC = \angle PAM$ [common angles]

$\therefore\ \Delta ABC \sim \Delta AMP$ [by AA similarity criterion]

(ii) **Hint** Since, $\Delta ABC \sim \Delta AMP$ [prove above]

Now, taking $\frac{AC}{AP} = \frac{BC}{MP}$

$\therefore\ \frac{10}{15} = \frac{BC}{12} \Rightarrow BC = 8$ cm

In ΔABC, right angled at B, using Pythagoras theorem,

$$AB = \sqrt{AC^2 - BC^2} = \sqrt{(10)^2 - (8)^2}$$

Ans. 8 cm, 6 cm

16. Hint Prove that $\Delta APB \sim \Delta AQC$. [by AA similarity criterion]

17. Hint

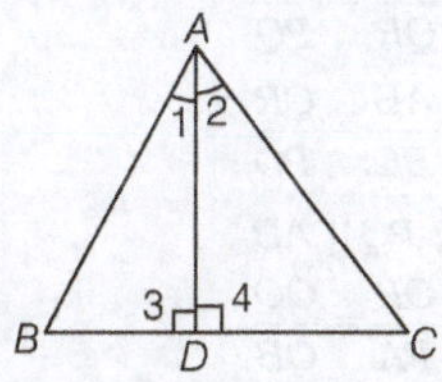

$AD^2 = BD \times DC$ [given]

$\Rightarrow \quad \frac{AD}{BD} = \frac{DC}{AD}$

$\therefore \quad \Delta ADB \sim \Delta ADC$ [SAS similarity]

$\therefore \angle B + \angle C = \angle BAC$ [$\because \angle 2 = \angle B$ and $\angle 1 = \angle C$]

$\angle A = \frac{180^\circ}{2} = 90^\circ$

18. Hint Since, $AB \perp BC$ and $GF \perp BC$, therefore $AB \parallel GF$ and hence $\angle BAC = \angle FGC$ (corresponding angles).
Now, use AA similarity criteria in ΔADE and ΔGCF.

19. Hint Since, $DB \perp BC$ and $AC \perp BC$, therefore $DB \parallel AC$ and hence $\angle 1 = \angle 4$ (alternate angles).
Now, use AA similarity criteria in ΔBDE and ΔABC.

20. Hint In ΔSTP,

$\frac{TR}{PR} = \frac{TM}{SM}$ [by using BPT] ...(i)

In ΔQTP,

$\frac{TR}{PR} = \frac{TN}{QN}$ [by using BPT] ...(ii)

From Eqs. (i) and (ii), we get

$\frac{TM}{SM} = \frac{TN}{QN}$

or $\frac{TM}{MS} = \frac{TN}{NQ}$

Thus, in ΔSTQ,

$\frac{TM}{MS} = \frac{TN}{NQ}$

$\Rightarrow \quad MN \parallel SQ$ [by converse of BPT]

21. Hint Since, line l is parallel to line m and AR is transversal.

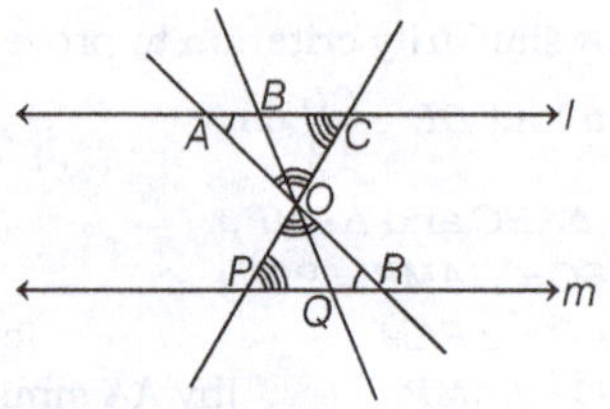

$\therefore \quad \Delta OAB \sim \Delta ORQ$ [by AA postulate]

$\Rightarrow \quad \frac{AB}{QR} = \frac{OB}{OQ}$ ...(i)

[Corresponding sides of similar triangle are in proportion]

$\therefore \quad \Delta BOC \sim \Delta QOP$ [by AA postulate]

$\Rightarrow \quad \frac{BC}{PQ} = \frac{OB}{OQ}$ ...(ii)

[Corresponding sides of similar triangles]

From Eqs. (i) and (ii), we get

$\frac{AB}{QR} = \frac{BC}{PQ}$

$\Rightarrow \quad \frac{AB}{BC} = \frac{QR}{PQ}$ **Hence proved.**

22. Hint In ΔAOB, $PQ \parallel AB$

$\frac{OP}{PA} = \frac{OQ}{QB}$

[by basic proportionality theorem]

23. Hint Do same as Example 12. **Ans.** 190 cm

24. Hint Do same as Example 13. **Ans.** 12 cm

25. Hint Do same as Example 16. **Ans.** 2.7 cm

26. Hint Do same as Example 22. **Ans.** 4 cm

27. Hint

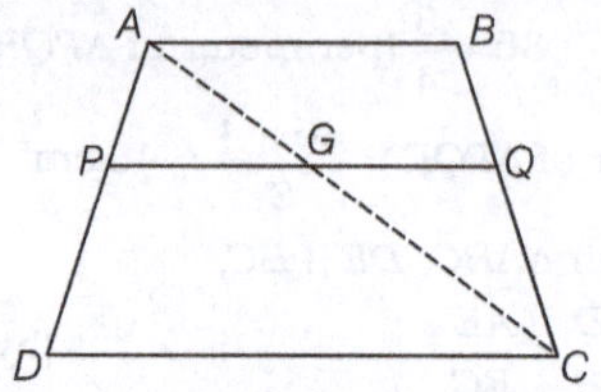

$ABCD$ is a trapezium in which $AB \parallel DC$ and $PQ \parallel AB$.
Also, given

$PD = 18$ cm, $BQ = 35$ cm and $QC = 15$ cm

Join AC to intersect PQ at G.
In ΔADC,
By using basic proportionality theorem,

$\frac{AP}{PD} = \frac{AG}{GC}$ ...(i)

In ΔABC,
By using basic proportionality theorem,

$\frac{CG}{AG} = \frac{QC}{BQ}$

$\Rightarrow \quad \frac{AG}{GC} = \frac{BQ}{QC}$ ...(ii)

From Eqs. (i) and (ii), we get

$\frac{AP}{PD} = \frac{BQ}{QC}$

$\Rightarrow \quad \frac{AP}{18} = \frac{35}{15}$

$\Rightarrow \quad 15 \times AP = 18 \times 35$

$\Rightarrow \quad AP = 42$ cm

$\therefore \quad AD = AP + PD$
$= 42 + 18$
$= 60$ cm

Ans. 60 cm

28. In ΔBAC, AE is the (internal) bisector of $\angle BAC$.

$\therefore \quad \frac{BE}{EC} = \frac{AB}{AC}$ ...(i)

In ΔCAD, AF is the (internal) bisector of $\angle CAD$.

$\therefore \quad \frac{DF}{FC} = \frac{AD}{AC}$

$\Rightarrow \quad \frac{DF}{FC} = \frac{AB}{AC}$ [$\because AD = AB$ given] ...(ii)

From Eqs. (i) and (ii), we get

$\frac{BE}{EC} = \frac{DF}{FC}$ ...(iii)

Now in ΔBCD, EF is a straight line such that

$\frac{BE}{EC} = \frac{DF}{FC}$ [using Eq. (iii)]

i.e. EF divides two sides of ΔBCD in the same ratio, therefore, EF is parallel to BD (by converse of BPT).

29. In ΔABD, DE is bisector of $\angle ADB$.

$$\therefore \quad \frac{AE}{EB} = \frac{DA}{DB} \quad \ldots(i)$$

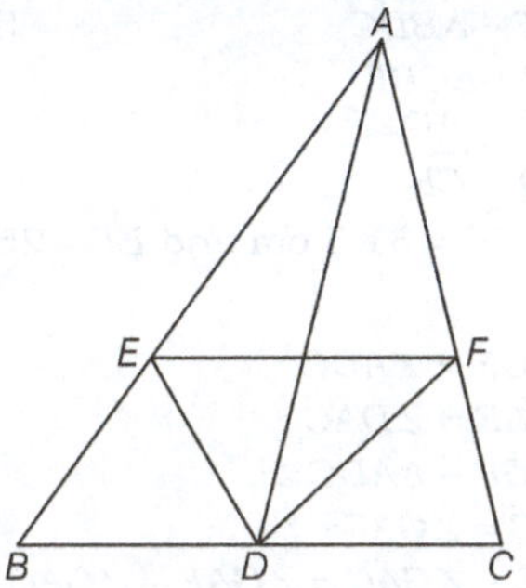

In ΔACD, DF is bisector of $\angle ADC$.

$$\therefore \quad \frac{AF}{FC} = \frac{DA}{DC} \Rightarrow \frac{AF}{FC} = \frac{DA}{DB} \quad \ldots(ii)$$

[$\because AD$ is median of ΔABC, so $BD = DC$]

From Eqs. (i) and (ii), we get

$$\frac{AE}{EB} = \frac{AF}{FC} \Rightarrow EF \parallel BC \quad \text{[by converse of BPT]}$$

30. Hint Since, $\Delta NSQ \cong \Delta MTR$

$\therefore \quad SQ = TR \quad \ldots(i)$

Also, $\quad \angle 1 = \angle 2$

$\Rightarrow \quad PT = PS \quad \ldots(ii)$

From Eqs. (i) and (ii), $\dfrac{PS}{SQ} = \dfrac{PT}{TR} \Rightarrow ST \parallel QR$

Hence, $\Delta PTS \sim \Delta PRQ$ by AAA similarity criterion.

31. Hint $\Delta ABC \sim \Delta DEF$, $\dfrac{\text{ar}(\Delta ABC)}{\text{ar}(\Delta DEF)} = \left(\dfrac{AB}{DE}\right)^2$

Ans. 25 : 81

32. Hint $\Delta ADE \sim \Delta ABC$ [by AA similarity criterion]

$$\Rightarrow \quad \frac{\text{ar}(\Delta ADE)}{\text{ar}(\Delta ABC)} = \left(\frac{DE}{BC}\right)^2$$

Ans. 80 cm^2

33. $\angle ACD + \angle BCD = \angle BCE + \angle BCD$

$\Rightarrow \quad \angle ACB = \angle DCE$

$\therefore \quad \Delta ABC \sim \Delta DEC$ [from AA similarity]

$$\therefore \quad \frac{\Delta ABC)}{\Delta DEC)} = \left(\frac{AB}{DE}\right)^2 = \left(\frac{10}{7}\right)^2$$

$$= \frac{100}{49} = 100:49$$ **Ans.** 100 : 49

34. Hint Here, $\Delta ANC \sim \Delta BAC$

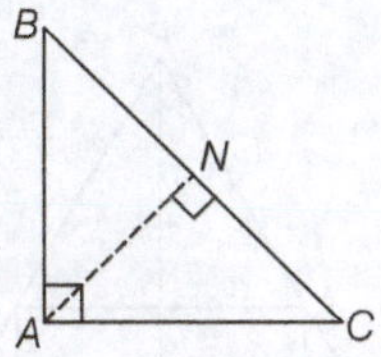

$$\Rightarrow \quad \frac{\text{ar}(\Delta ANC)}{\text{ar}(\Delta ABC)} = \left(\frac{AC}{BC}\right)^2$$

Ans. 25 : 144

35. Hint We know that the ratio of areas of two similar triangles is equal to square of the ratio of their corresponding sides.

$$\therefore \quad \frac{\text{ar}(\Delta ABC)}{\text{ar}(\Delta DEF)} = \left(\frac{AB}{DE}\right)^2 = \left(\frac{1.2}{1.4}\right)^2$$

Ans. 36 : 49

36. Hint $QR \parallel AB$ and $QR = \dfrac{1}{2} AB$

$\Rightarrow \quad QR \parallel AP$

So, clearly $RAPQ$ is a parallelogram.

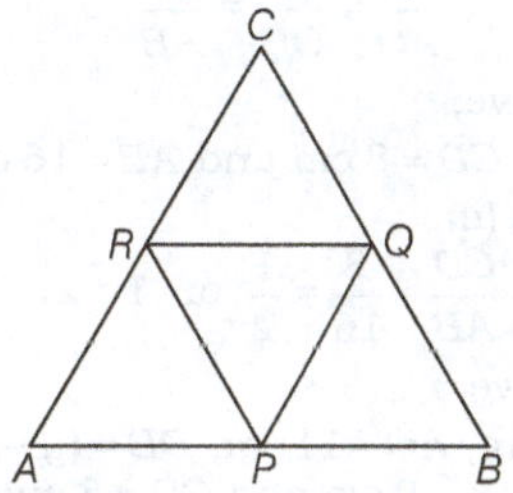

Similarly, $\angle B$ of $\Delta ABC = \angle R$ of ΔPQR

$\therefore \quad \Delta PQR \sim \Delta ABC$

$$\therefore \quad \frac{\Delta PQR}{\Delta ABC} = \frac{QR^2}{AB^2}$$

Ans. 1 : 4

37. Hint Here, $AB = BC = CD = DA$ and $AC = \sqrt{2}\, BC$

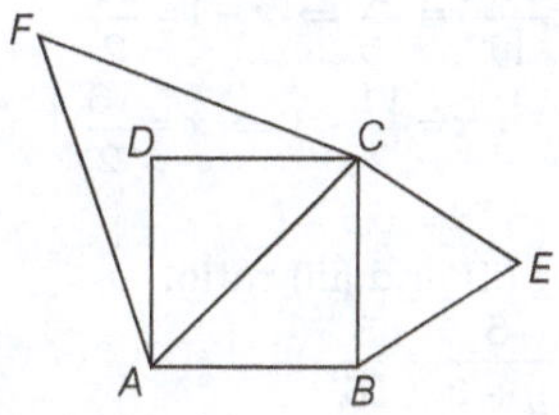

Since, $\Delta BCE \sim \Delta ACF$ [given]

$$\therefore \quad \frac{\text{ar}(\Delta BCE)}{\text{ar}(\Delta ACF)} = \left(\frac{BC}{AC}\right)^2$$

$$\Rightarrow \quad \frac{\text{ar}(\Delta BCE)}{\text{ar}(\Delta ACF)} = \left(\frac{BC}{\sqrt{2}BC}\right)^2$$

38. (i) **Hint** Here, $\dfrac{AP}{PB} = \dfrac{2}{3} \quad \ldots(i)$

$$\Rightarrow \quad \frac{AP}{AP + PB} = \frac{2}{2+3}$$

Also, given $\quad PO \parallel BC$

i.e. $\quad PQ \parallel BC$ and $PB \parallel QC$

So, $PBCQ$ is a parallelogram.

$\therefore \quad BP = CQ$

From Eq. (i), we get

$$\frac{AP}{PB} = \frac{2}{3} \Rightarrow \frac{AP}{CQ} = \frac{2}{3} \quad \ldots(iii)$$

Also, $\Delta APO \sim \Delta ABC$ by AA similarity criterion

Then, $\dfrac{\text{ar}(\Delta APO)}{\text{ar}(\Delta ABC)} = \dfrac{(AP)^2}{(AB)^2}$

Ans. 4 : 25

(ii) **Hint** Here, $\Delta AOP \sim \Delta CQO$ by AA similarity criterion.

Then, $\frac{\text{ar}(\Delta APO)}{\text{ar}(\Delta CQO)} = \frac{AP^2}{CQ^2}$

Ans. 4 : 9

39. Hint

(i) (b) $\Delta COD \sim \Delta AOB$ [$\because CD \parallel AB$ and by AA similarity]

(ii) (a) We have,

$\Delta COD \sim \Delta AOB$, then

$$\frac{CO}{AO} = \frac{OD}{OB} = \frac{CD}{AB}$$

(iii) (b) We have,

$CD = 8$ cm and $AB = 16$ cm

$\therefore$ By part (ii),

$$\frac{CD}{AB} = \frac{8}{16} = \frac{1}{2} \text{ or } 1:2.$$

(iv) (c) We have,

$AB = 16$ cm, $AO = 11$ cm, $DB = (y+3)$ cm, $OD = 5$ cm, $OC = (x-1)$ cm and $CD = 8$ cm

By part (ii),

$$\frac{CO}{AO} = \frac{OD}{OB} = \frac{CD}{AB}$$

$$\Rightarrow \frac{x-1}{11} = \frac{5}{y+3} = \frac{8}{16}$$

By taking (i) and (iii) ratio,

$$\frac{x-1}{11} = \frac{8}{16} \Rightarrow x-1 = \frac{11}{2}$$

$$\Rightarrow x = \frac{11}{2} + 1 \Rightarrow x = \frac{13}{2}$$

$$\Rightarrow x = 6.5$$

By taking (ii) and (iii) ratio,

$$\frac{5}{y+3} = \frac{8}{16}$$

$$\Rightarrow \frac{5}{y+3} = \frac{1}{2}$$

$$\Rightarrow 10 = y + 3 \Rightarrow y = 7$$

40. Hint Here, $\frac{PS}{SQ} = \frac{PT}{TR} = \frac{4}{1}$

By converse of BPT, $ST \parallel QR$. **Ans.** $\frac{16}{9}$

41. Hint Do same as Example 6. **Ans.** $\frac{\sqrt{3}-\sqrt{2}}{\sqrt{3}}$

42. Hint Here, $k = \frac{1}{30}$

(i) Actual height of the building

$= \frac{1}{k} \times$ (Height of the model)

$= 30 \times 80 = 2400$ cm

Ans. 24 m [$\because$ 1 m = 100 cm]

(ii) Volume of the model tank = k (Volume of the tank)

$$= \left(\frac{1}{30}\right)^3 \times 27 \text{ m}^3$$

Ans. 1 L [$\because 1 \text{ L} = 0.001 \text{ m}^3$]

43. Hint

(i) $\Delta ABE \sim \Delta CDE$ [by AAA similarity]

$\Rightarrow \Delta CFE \sim \Delta CBA$ [by AAA similarity]

$\Rightarrow \Delta BEF \sim \Delta BDC$ [by AA similarity]

$\Rightarrow \Delta ABE \sim \Delta CDE$

$$\Rightarrow \frac{AB}{CD} = \frac{AE}{CE}$$

Ans. (ii) $EC = 31.5$ cm and $EF = 25.31$ cm

44. Hint

(i) $\angle AGF = \angle ADC$ [each 90°]

and $\angle GAF = \angle DAC$ [each 45°]

$\therefore \Delta AGF \sim \Delta ADC$

(ii) $\angle DAC = \angle GAF$

$\Rightarrow \angle DAC - \angle GAC = \angle GAF - \angle GAC$

$\Rightarrow \angle DAG = \angle CAF$

and $\frac{AG}{AD} = \frac{AF}{AC}$ [from part (i)]

45. Hint Let side of square be x cm, then $ED = CD = x$ cm

and $AD = (6 - x)$ cm

$\therefore \Delta ADE \sim \Delta ACB$

$$\frac{6-x}{6} = \frac{x}{12}$$

Ans. The side of the largest inscribed square is 4 cm.

46. Hint

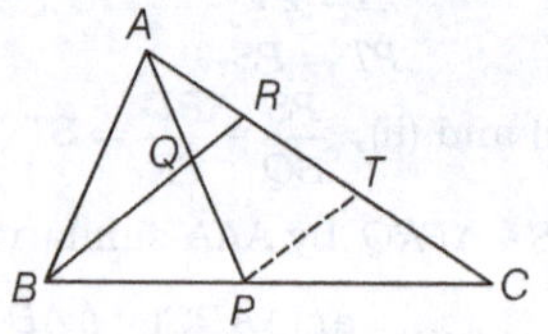

In ΔCBR, $PT \parallel BR$

$$\therefore \frac{CT}{TR} = \frac{CP}{BP}$$

$\Rightarrow \frac{CT}{TR} = 1$ [$\because P$ is mid-point of BC]

$\Rightarrow CT = TR$ ...(i)

In ΔAPT, $QR \parallel PT$

$$\therefore \frac{AQ}{QP} = \frac{AR}{RT}$$

$\Rightarrow 1 = \frac{AR}{RT}$ [$\because Q$ is mid-point of AP]

$\Rightarrow AR = RT$ ...(ii)

From Eqs. (i) and (ii), we get $AR = RT = CT$

$$\therefore AR = \frac{1}{3} AC$$

47. Hint

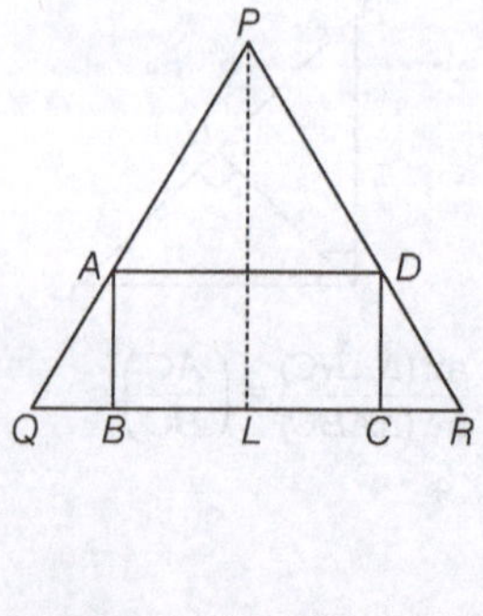

Draw $PL \perp QR$, L is mid-point of QR.

$\therefore \quad \Delta ABQ \sim \Delta PLQ$ [by AA similarity]

$$\frac{AB}{PL} = \frac{BQ}{QL}$$

$$\Rightarrow \quad \frac{y}{8} = \frac{6-x}{y} \quad [\because PQ^2 = QL^2 + PL^2]$$

48. **Hint** $\frac{AF}{FD} = \frac{BE}{EC} = \frac{4}{3} \Rightarrow \frac{AD}{FD} = \frac{7}{3}$

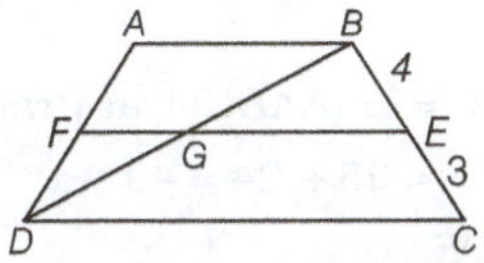

Also, $\Delta DFG \sim \Delta DAB$ and $\Delta BGE \sim \Delta BDC$

$$\Rightarrow \quad \frac{DF}{DA} = \frac{FG}{AB} \text{ and } \frac{GE}{DC} = \frac{BE}{BC}$$

$$\Rightarrow \quad \frac{3}{7} = \frac{FG}{AB} \text{ and } \frac{GE}{2AB} = \frac{4}{7}$$

Now, $\quad EF = FG + GE = \frac{3}{7}AB + \frac{8}{7}AB$

49. (i) $\therefore \quad BPQ \sim \Delta BAC$ [AA similarity]

$$\frac{BP}{BA} = \frac{PQ}{AC} = \frac{BQ}{BC} \quad \left[\because \text{given } \frac{AP}{PB} = \frac{4}{3}\right]$$

$$\Rightarrow \quad \frac{PQ}{AC} = \frac{PB}{AP + BP} = \frac{3}{3+4} = \frac{3}{7}$$

$$\Rightarrow \quad \frac{PQ}{AC} = \frac{3}{7} \quad \textbf{Ans. } \frac{3}{7}$$

(ii) **Hint** In ΔABC, P is a point on AB such that

$$PA : AB = 4 : 3$$

$$PQ \parallel AC$$

$$\Delta ARC \sim \Delta PQS$$

$$\because \quad AR = \frac{AC}{PQ} \times QS$$

Ans. 14 cm

50. **Hint** Draw $DY \parallel BX$. Then, $\Delta BCX \sim \Delta DCY$

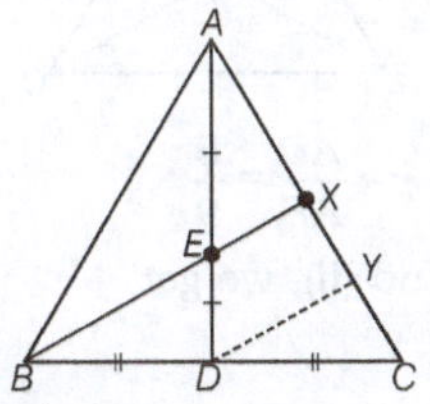

$$\Rightarrow \quad \frac{BX}{DY} = \frac{BC}{DC}$$

$$\Rightarrow \quad \frac{BX}{DY} = 2 \quad \text{...(i)}$$

Similarly, $\Delta AEX \sim \Delta ADY$

$$\Rightarrow \quad \frac{EX}{DY} = \frac{1}{2} \quad \text{...(ii)}$$

From Eqs. (i) and (ii), we get

$$\frac{BX}{EX} = 4$$

$$\Rightarrow \quad BE + EX = 4EX$$

51. **Hint** In ΔOPS and ΔOAB,

$$PS \parallel AB$$

$\angle POS = \angle AOB$ [common angle]

$\angle OSP = \angle OBA$ [corresponding angles]

$\therefore \quad \Delta OPS \sim \Delta OAB$ [by AA similarity criterion]

Then, $\quad \frac{PS}{AB} = \frac{OS}{OB}$ ...(i)

In ΔCQR and ΔCAB,

$$QR \parallel PS \parallel AB$$

$\angle QCR = \angle ACB$ [common angle]

$\angle CRQ = \angle CBA$ [corresponding angle]

$\therefore \quad \Delta CQR \sim \Delta CAB$ [by AA similarity criterion]

Then, $\quad \frac{QR}{AB} = \frac{CR}{CB}$

$\Rightarrow \quad \frac{PS}{AB} = \frac{CR}{CB}$ ...(ii)

From Eqs. (i) and (ii), we get

$$\frac{OS}{OB} = \frac{CR}{CB} \text{ or } \frac{OB}{OS} = \frac{CB}{CR}$$

On subtracting 1 from both sides, we get

$$\frac{OB}{OS} - 1 = \frac{CB}{CR} - 1$$

$$\Rightarrow \quad \frac{OB - OS}{OS} = \frac{CB - CR}{CR} \Rightarrow \frac{BS}{OS} = \frac{BR}{CR}$$

By converse of basic proportionality theorem, we get the result.

52. **Hint** In ΔABC, $DE \parallel AC$

$\therefore \quad \frac{BE}{EC} = \frac{BD}{DA}$ [by BPT]

But $\quad \frac{BE}{EC} = \frac{BC}{CP}$ (given)

$\Rightarrow \quad \frac{BD}{DA} = \frac{BC}{CP} \Rightarrow DC \parallel AP$ [converse of BPT]

53. In ΔPQA, $DE \parallel AQ$

$\therefore \quad \frac{PE}{EQ} = \frac{PD}{DA}$ ...(i)

Similarly, $\quad \frac{PD}{DA} = \frac{PF}{FR}$ ...(ii)

$\Rightarrow \quad \frac{PE}{EQ} = \frac{PF}{FR}$ [from Eqs. (i) and (ii)]

Thus, in ΔPQR, $\frac{PE}{EQ} = \frac{PF}{FR}$

$EF \parallel QR$ [converse of BPT]

54. (i) **Hint** In ΔADB and ΔCDA, we have

$$\angle DAB = \angle DCA = \theta \text{ and } \angle CAD = \angle ABD = 90° - \theta$$

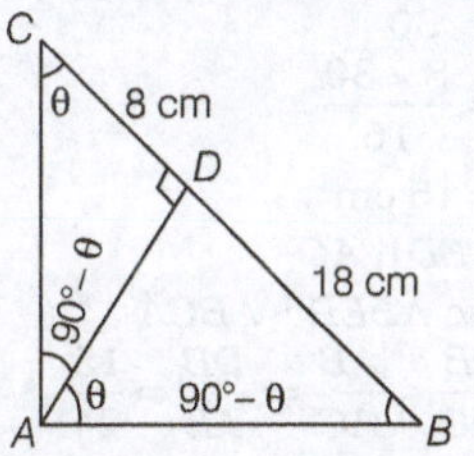

$\therefore \quad \Delta ADB \sim \Delta CDA$ [by AA similarity criterion]

(ii) **Hint** Since, $\Delta ADB \sim \Delta CDA$

$\therefore \quad \dfrac{AD}{CD} = \dfrac{BD}{AD}$

$\Rightarrow \quad AD^2 = BD \times CD$ **Ans.** 12 cm

(iii) **Hint** $\dfrac{\text{ar}(\Delta ADB)}{\text{ar}(\Delta CDA)} = \dfrac{(AD)^2}{(CD)^2}$ **Ans.** 9 : 4

55. Hint In ΔABC and ΔEBD, we have

$\angle ACB = \angle EDB$ [given]

$\angle ABC = \angle EBD$ [common angle]

$\therefore \quad \Delta ABC \sim \Delta EBD$ [by AA similarity criterion]

(i) Since, $\Delta ABC \sim \Delta EBD$

$\therefore \quad \dfrac{AB}{EB} = \dfrac{BC}{BD} = \dfrac{AC}{ED}$

Now, taking first two terms, we get

$\dfrac{AB}{EB} = \dfrac{BC}{BD}$

$\Rightarrow \quad \dfrac{AB}{6} = \dfrac{BE + EC}{5}$

Ans. 12 cm

(ii) Since, $\Delta ABC \sim \Delta EBD$

$\therefore \quad \dfrac{\text{ar}(\Delta ABC)}{\text{ar}(\Delta EBD)} = \dfrac{AB^2}{EB^2}$ **Ans.** 36 cm^2

56. Given, $AC \parallel DE \parallel BF$

$AC = 24$ cm, $EG = 8$ cm, $GB = 16$ cm, $BF = 30$ cm

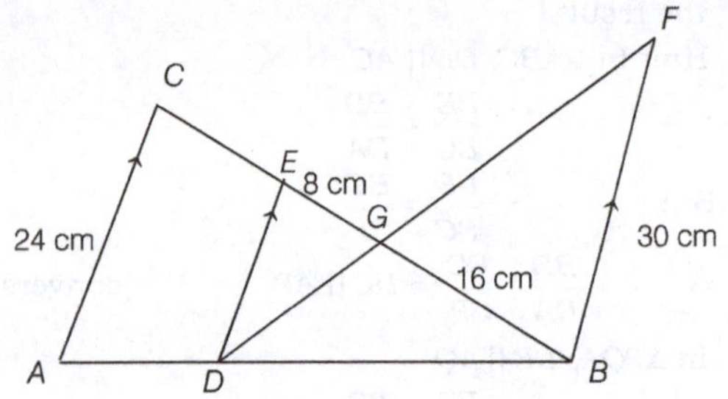

(i) From figure, we have

$\angle EGD = \angle BGF$

[vertically opposite angles]

$\angle DEG = \angle FBG$

[alternate interior angles]

$\therefore \quad \Delta GED \sim \Delta GBF$ [AA similarity criterion]

Hence proved.

(ii) $\because \Delta GED \sim \Delta GBF$

$\Rightarrow \quad \dfrac{GE}{GB} = \dfrac{DE}{FB}$

$\Rightarrow \quad \dfrac{8}{16} = \dfrac{DE}{30}$

$\Rightarrow \quad DE = \dfrac{8 \times 30}{16}$

$\Rightarrow \quad DE = 15$ cm

(iii) We have, $ED \parallel AC$,

$\because$ We have $\Delta BED \sim \Delta BCA$ [$\because$ AA similarity]

$\Rightarrow \quad \dfrac{DB}{DE} = \dfrac{AB}{AC} \Rightarrow \dfrac{DB}{AB} = \dfrac{15}{24}$

$\Rightarrow \quad DB : AB = 5 : 8$

57. Hint In ΔAOQ and ΔBOP, we have

$\angle QAO = \angle OBP = 90°$

and $\quad \angle AOQ = \angle POB$

$\therefore \quad \Delta AOQ \sim \Delta BOP$ [by AA similarity criterion]

Then, $\quad \dfrac{\text{ar}(\Delta AOQ)}{\text{ar}(\Delta BOP)} = \dfrac{OQ^2}{PO^2}$

$\therefore \quad \text{ar}(\Delta AOQ) = \left(\dfrac{9}{6}\right)^2 \times 120$

Ans. 270 cm^2

58. Hint ar (ΔADE) = ar (ΔABC) + ar (trapezium $BCED$)

$= 25 + 24 = 49$ cm^2

Since, $BC \parallel DE$

In ΔABC and ΔADE, we have

$\angle BAC = \angle DAE$ and $\angle ABC = \angle ADE$

So, $\quad \Delta ABC \sim \Delta ADE$

$\therefore \quad \dfrac{\text{ar}(\Delta ABC)}{\text{ar}(\Delta ADE)} = \dfrac{BC^2}{DE^2}$

Ans. $BC = 10$ cm

59. Hint

(i) $\dfrac{\text{Area of first triangle}}{\text{Area of second triangle}} = \dfrac{S_1^2}{S_2^2}$, where S_1 and S_2 are the corresponding sides.

(ii) The ratio between the altitudes of two similar triangles is same as the ratio between their sides.

(iii) The ratio between the medians of two similar triangle is same as the ratio between their sides.

Ans. (i) 3 : 4 (ii) 3 : 4 (iii) 3 : 4

60. Hint $\Delta ADE \sim \Delta ABC$

$\Rightarrow \quad \dfrac{AD}{AB} = \dfrac{DE}{BC}$ ...(i)

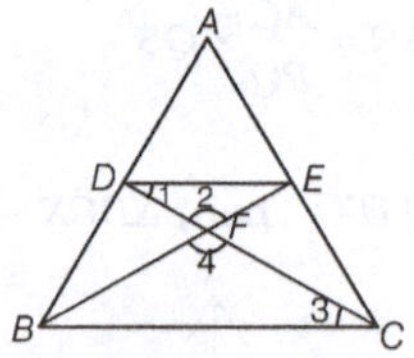

and $\quad \dfrac{AD}{DB} = \dfrac{5}{4} \Rightarrow \dfrac{AD}{AB} = \dfrac{5}{9}$ ...(ii)

From Eqs. (i) and (ii), we get

$\dfrac{DE}{BC} = \dfrac{5}{9}$

Here, $\quad \angle 1 = \angle 3$ and $\angle 2 = \angle 4$

$\therefore \quad \Delta DFE \sim \Delta CFB$

$\Rightarrow \quad \dfrac{\text{ar}(\Delta DFE)}{\text{ar}(\Delta CFB)} = \left(\dfrac{DE}{BC}\right)^2$

Ans. 25 : 81

61. Hint For tank :

Volume = length × breadth × height

$\Rightarrow \quad 4\text{ m} \times 3\text{ m} \times \text{height} = 30\text{ m}^3$

$\Rightarrow \quad$ Height = 2.5 m

Let the scale factor for reduction = k

$\Rightarrow$ Volume of the model

$= k^3 \times$ volume of the tank

$\Rightarrow 240 \text{ cm}^3 = k^3 \times 30 \times 100 \times 100 \times 100 \text{ cm}^3$

$\Rightarrow \quad k = \dfrac{1}{125000}$

$\Rightarrow$ Scale factor, $k = \dfrac{1}{50}$

(i) $\therefore$ Length of the model $= k \times$ length of the tank

$= \dfrac{1}{50} \times 4 \text{ m} = 8 \text{ cm}$

Breadth of the model $= k \times$ breadth of the tank

$= \dfrac{1}{50} \times 3 \text{ m} = 6 \text{ cm}$

And height of the model $= \dfrac{1}{50} \times 2.5 \text{ m} = 5 \text{ cm}$

(ii) Total surface area of the model

$= k^2 \times$ total surface area of the tank.

Ans. (i) Dimensions of the model

$= 8 \text{ cm} \times 6 \text{ cm} \times 5 \text{ cm}$

(ii) 2500 : 1

62. (i) **Hint** Given, scale factor,

$k = \dfrac{1}{200000}$

[$\because$ 1 cm on map represents 200000 cm on the ground]

$\Rightarrow$ 200000 cm = 2 km **Ans.** 2 km

(ii) **Hint** Since, 1 cm on the map represents 2 km on the ground. **Ans.** 4 km^2

(iii) **Hint** Area of plot on the map $= k^2$ (Area of plot on the ground)

Area of plot on the map $= \dfrac{20}{(200000)^2} \text{ km}^2$

$= \dfrac{20 \times 10^5 \times 10^5}{(2 \times 10^5)^2} \text{ cm}^2$

[$\because 1 \text{ km} = 10^5 \text{ cm}$]

Ans. 5 cm^2

63. (i) **Hint** Area of the model

$= k^2$ (Area of the object)

$\Rightarrow \quad 37.5 \text{ m}^2 = k^2 \times 6 \text{ cm}^2$

$\Rightarrow \quad \dfrac{1}{k^2} = \dfrac{6 \text{ m}^2}{37.5 \text{ cm}^2}$

$= \dfrac{6 \times 100 \times 100 \text{ cm}^2}{37.5 \text{ cm}^2}$

$= \dfrac{6 \times 100 \times 100 \times 10}{375}$

Ans. $\dfrac{1}{40}$

(ii) **Hint** Volume of an object

$= \dfrac{1}{k^3}$ (Volume of the model)

$= (40)^3 \times 360$

Ans. 23040000 cm^3

Olympiad Section

Brain Teasing Questions of Olympiad Pattern

1 A boy of height 90 cm is walking away from the base of a lamp-post at a speed of 1.2 m/s. If the lamp is 3.6 m above the ground, then the length of his shadow after 6 s is

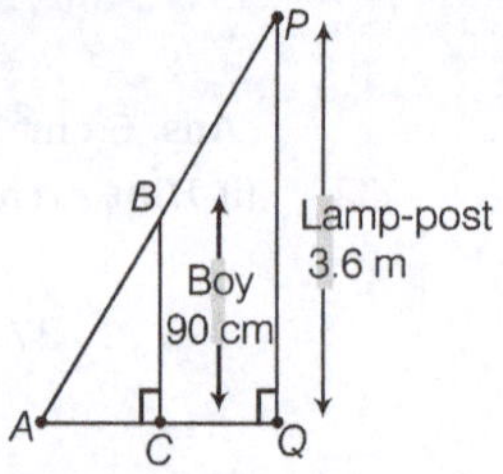

(a) 1.2 m (b) 2.4 m (c) 3.6 m
(d) None of these

2 In the figure given below, $AM : MC = 3 : 4$, $BP : PM = 3 : 2$ and $BN = 12$ cm. Then, AN equals to

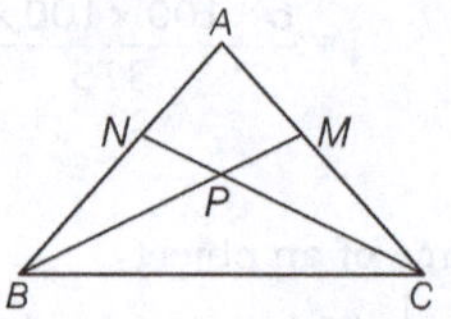

(a) 10 cm (b) 12 cm (c) 14 cm (d) 16 cm

3 Diagonal AC of a rectangle $ABCD$ is produced to the point E such that $AC : CE = 2 : 1$, $AB = 8$ cm and $BC = 6$ m. The length of DE is

(a) $2\sqrt{19}$ cm (b) 15 cm (c) $3\sqrt{17}$ cm (d) 13 cm

4 In the given figure, $DE \parallel BC$ and $AD : DB = 5 : 4$. Find the ratio of areas of ΔDEF and ΔCFB.

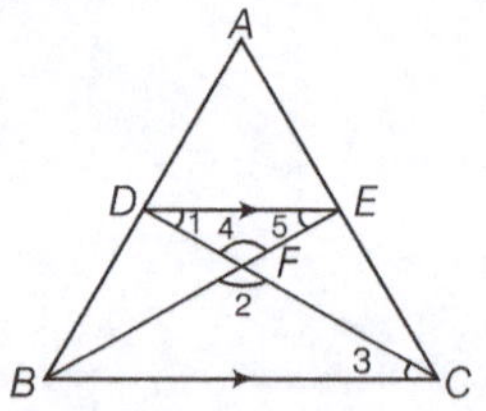

(a) 25 : 81 (b) 81 : 25 (c) 16 : 25 (d) 25 : 16

5 Through the mid-point M of the side CD of a parallelogram $ABCD$, the line BM is drawn intersecting AC at L and AD produced at E. The values of EL and ar (ΔAEL) are respectively

(a) BL and ar (ΔCBL) (b) ar (ΔCBL) and BL
(c) $2BL$ and 4 ar (ΔCBL) (d) 4 ar (ΔCBL) and $2BL$

6 Radhika wants to visit her friend who recently moved to a new house. The road map between Radhika's home and her friend's as well as the distance known to Radhika are as shown in the figure given below

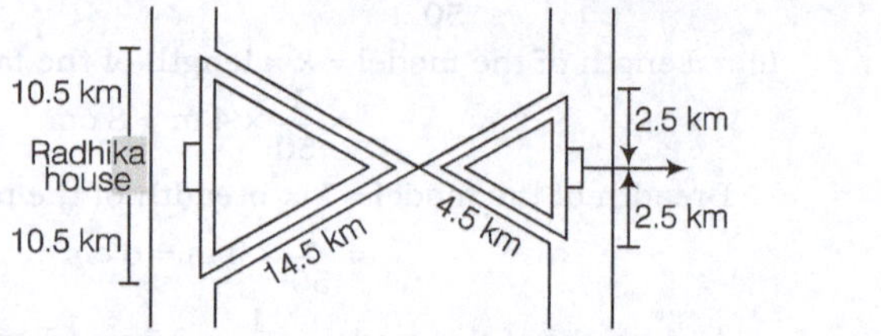

To reach the friend's house, the shortest distance which Radhika has to travel, is

(a) 30.95 km (b) 32.5 km
(c) 28.5 km (d) 35.35 km

7 In the given figure, PA, QB and RC are each perpendicular to AC. The value of

$$\frac{[\text{ar}(\Delta PAC)\text{ar}(\Delta QBA) + \text{ar}(\Delta RCA)\text{ar}(\Delta QBC)]}{\text{ar}(\Delta QBC)\text{ar}(\Delta QBA)} \text{ is}$$

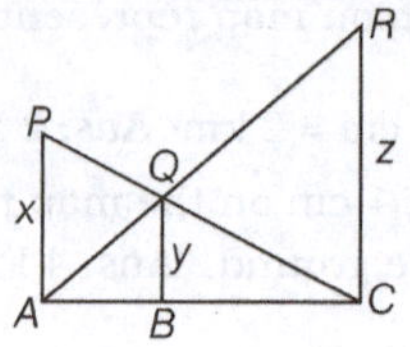

(a) $\frac{x^2 + y^2}{z^2}$ (b) $\frac{x^2 + z^2}{y^2}$ (c) $\frac{z^2 + y^2}{x^2}$ (d) None of these

8 O is the point of intersection of the diagonals AC and BD of a trapezium $ABCD$ with $AB \parallel DC$. Through O, a line segment PQ is drawn parallel to AB meeting AD in P and BC in Q, then OP is equal to

(a) $OP = OQ$ (b) $OP = 2OQ$
(c) $OQ = 2\,OP$ (d) $OP = \frac{1}{3}OQ$

9 In a ΔPQR, L and M are two points on base QR, such that $\angle LPQ = \angle QRP$ and $\angle RPM = \angle RQP$. Then, which of the following is/are true

(i) $\Delta PQL \sim \Delta RPM$
(ii) $QL \times RM = PL \times PM$
(iii) $PQ^2 = QR \cdot QL$

(a) Both (i) and (ii) (b) Both (ii) and (iii)
(c) Both (i) and (iii) (d) All the three

Answers

1. (b)	**2.** (c)	**3.** (c)	**4.** (a)	**5.** (c)
6. (a)	**7.** (b)	**8.** (a)	**9.** (d)	

* *These questions may or may not be asked in the examination, have been given just for additional practice required for olympiads Scholarship Exams etc. For detailed explanations refer Page No. 489.*

CHAPTER

14

Locus

SYLLABUS

- **Loci : Definition, Meaning, Theorems and Constructions based on Loci.** (i) The locus of a point at a fixed distance from a fixed point is a circle with the fixed point as centre and fixed distance as radius. (ii) The locus of a point equidistant from two intersecting lines is the bisector of the angles between the lines. (iii) The locus of a point equidistant from two given points is the perpendicular bisector of the line joining the points.

Locus is a Latin word which means 'Location' or 'Place'. The locus of a point is the path travelled by it moving under given geometrical conditions.

Or

Locus is the set of all those points, which satisfy one or more geometrical conditions.

The concept (or meaning) of 'Locus' is best explained as

1. When a point A moves in the plane, such that it is always equidistant from the fixed point O in the same plane, then the path followed by A is a circle.

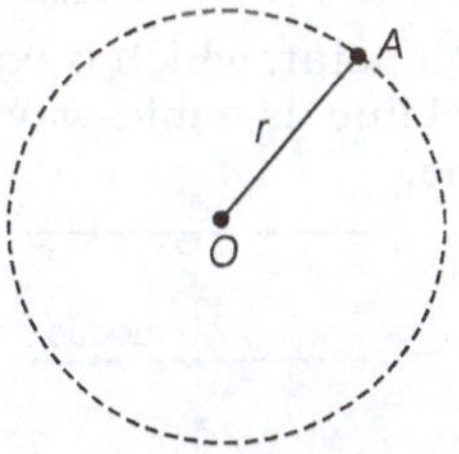

Thus, the locus of point A is a circle.

2. Let a point Q moves such that its distance from a fixed line is always equal to d. Then, point Q will trace out a straight line AB parallel to the fixed line. Thus, the locus of a point Q is the straight line AB.

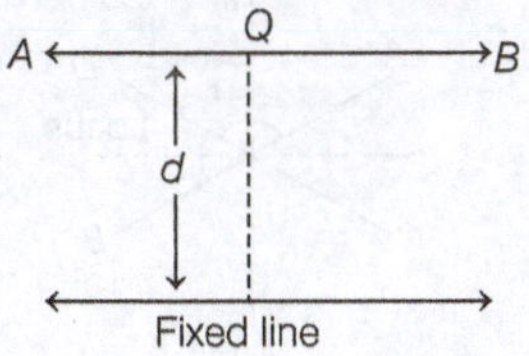

Some important point related to locus are as follow

(i) Every point which satisfies one or more geometrical conditions, lies on the locus and *vice-versa.*

(ii) A point which does not satisfy the one or more geometrical conditions, cannot lie on the locus and *vice-versa.*

(iii) The locus of a point moving in a plane under a given geometrical condition (or conditions), is always a straight or curved line.

(iv) To find the locus of a moving point, take few points which satisfy the given geometrical conditions and then join them.

Theorems Based on Locus

There are various theorems based on locus, which are as follow

Theorem 1 *The locus of a point equidistant from a fixed point, is a circle with the fixed point as centre and fixed distance as radius.*

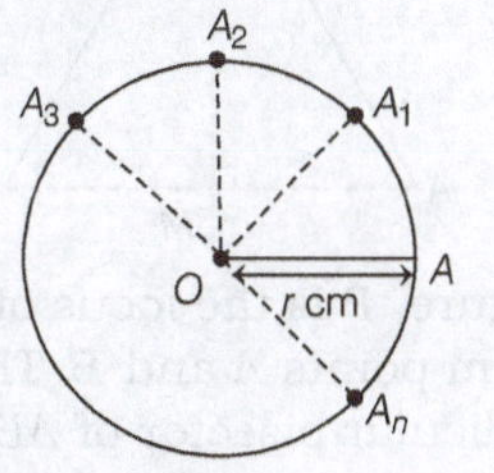

In the given figure, O is a fixed points and OA_1, $OA_2,\ldots,OA_n$ all are equidistance. Then, path traced by points $A_1, A_2, \ldots, A_n$ is the circle.

Theorem 2 *Locus of a point equidistant from two intersecting straight lines, is the bisector of the angles between the lines.*

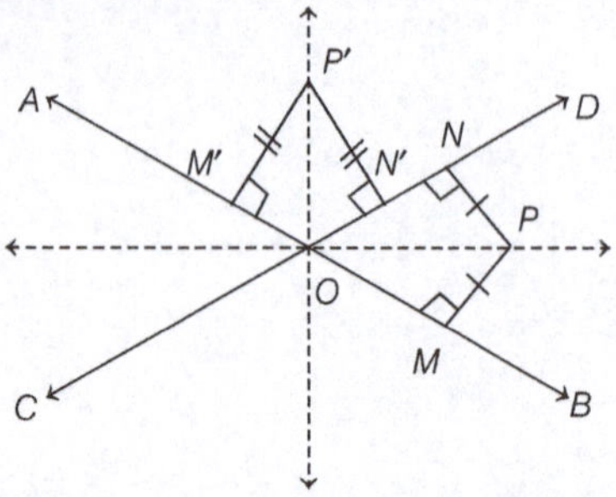

In the given figure, P is the locus of a point which is equidistant from lines OD and OB. Then, line OP will be the bisector of intersecting lines.

Theorem 3 (Converse of Theorem 2) *Any point on the bisector of an angle is equidistant from the arms of that angle.*

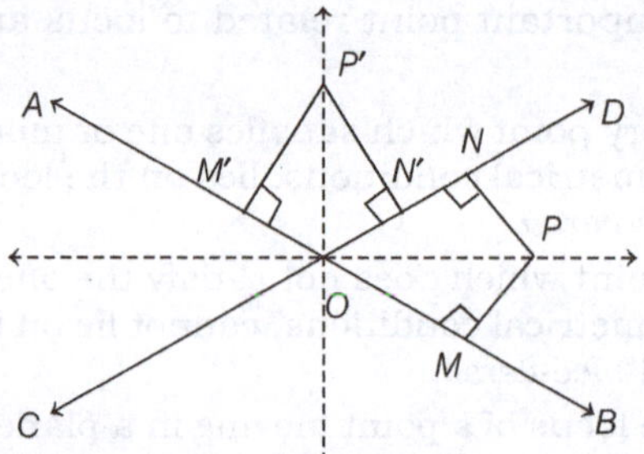

In the given figure, line OP is the angle bisector of lines OD and OB. Then, point P will be the equidistant from OD and OB.

Theorem 4 *The locus of a point equidistant from two given fixed points is the perpendicular bisector of the line joining the two fixed points.*

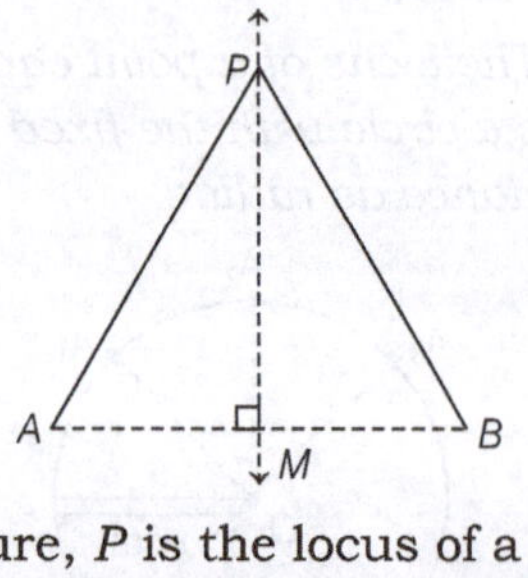

In the given figure, P is the locus of a point, which is equidistant from points A and B. Then, line PM will be the perpendicular bisector of AB.

Theorem 5 (Converse of Theorem 4) *Any point on the perpendicular bisector of a line segment joining two fixed points is equidistant from the fixed points.*

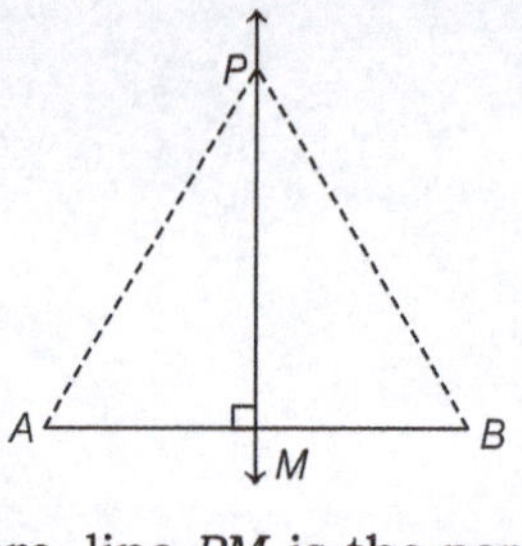

In the given figure, line PM is the perpendicular bisector of AB. Then, the distances from point P to the fixed points are equal, i.e. $AP = BP$.

Locus in Some Standard Cases

There are various cases, which are given below

1. The locus of a point, which is equidistant from two fixed points, is the perpendicular bisector of the joining two fixed points.

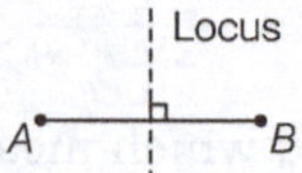

2. The locus of a point, which is equidistant from a given straight line, is the straight lines parallel to the given line (i.e. above or below it).

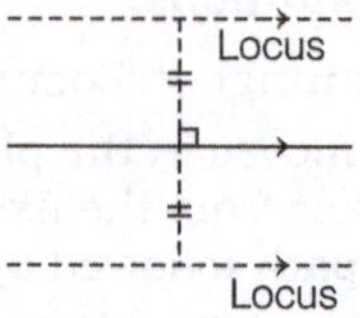

3. The locus of a point, which is equidistant from two given parallel line, is a mid-way line between the two given line.

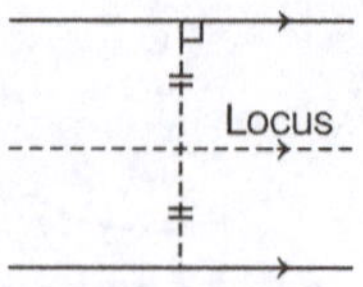

4. The locus of a point, which is equidistant from two intersecting straight lines, is angular bisector of the angles formed by the two intersecting straight lines.

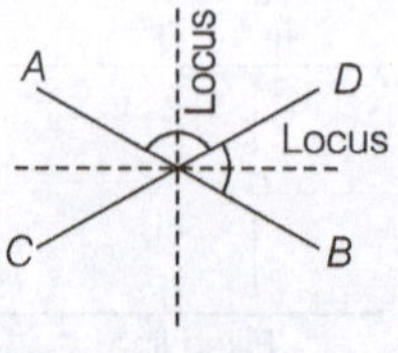

5. The locus of inside point of a circle, which is equidistant from two given points on the circle, is diameter of the circle perpendicular to the chord formed by the two fixed points.

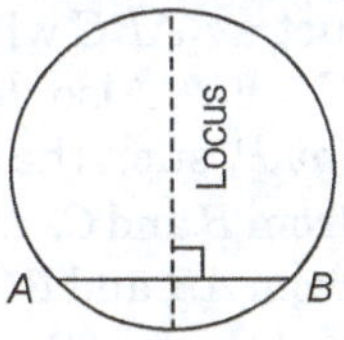

6. The locus of a point, which is equidistant from concentric circles, is the circumference of the circle concentric to the two given circles and lying mid-way between them.

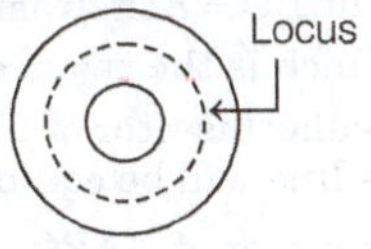

7. The locus of a mid-points of all parallel chords is a diameter of the circle, which is perpendicular to the given chords.

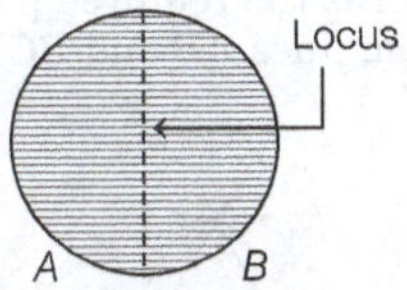

8. The locus of centre of a wheel, which is moving on a horizontal road is a straight line parallel to the road and at a distance equal to the radius of wheel.

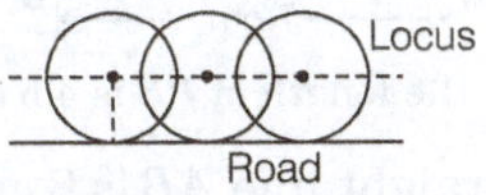

9. The locus of a point, which is equidistant from a given circle, is a pair of circles concentric with the given circle.

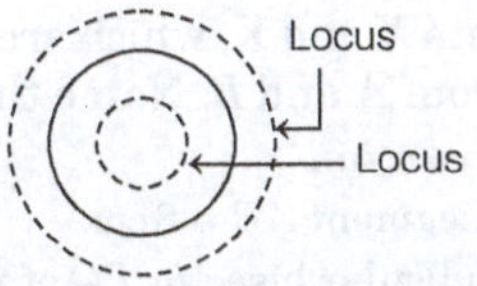

10. The locus of a centres of a circles, which is touching a given line at a given point, is a straight line perpendicular to the given line at the given point.

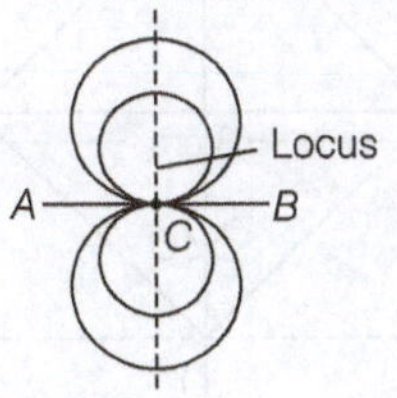

Example 1. Find a point M which is equidistant from three given non-collinear points.

Sol. Let A, B and C be three non-collinear points. Join AB and BC. Let M be a moving point. Since, M is equidistant from A and B, it follows that M lies on the perpendicular bisector of AB.

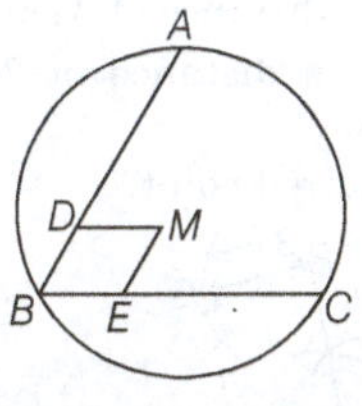

Again M is equidistant from B and C. So, M lies on the perpendicular bisector of BC. Thus, M is point of intersection of the perpendicular bisector of AB and BC. So, M coincides with the centre which passing through three given non-collinear points. Hence, the required locus is the centre of the circle passing through three given non-collinear points.

Example 2. Draw an $\angle PQR = 60°$, having $PQ = 5$ cm and $QR = 7$ cm. Find a point A equidistant from PQ and QR and also equidistant from P and Q.

Sol. Steps of construction

1. Draw a line segment $QR = 7$ cm.
2. Take Q as centre and draw an $\angle XQR = 60°$.
3. From Q, mark an arc of 5 cm, which intersects XQ at P.
4. Draw the bisector QY of $\angle PQR$.

Draw the perpendicular bisector AB of PQ, so that it intersects QY at A.

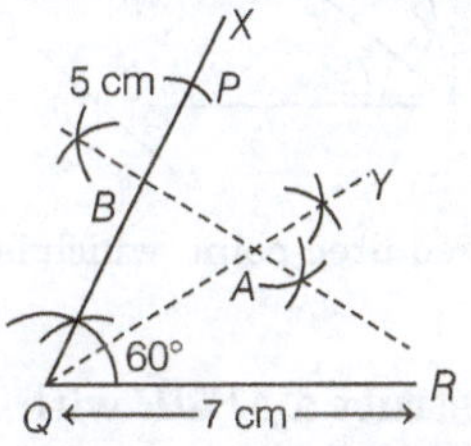

Thus, A is the required point, which is equidistant from PQ and QR, and also from P and Q.

Example 3. Find the locus of a point on the base of an isosceles triangle equidistant from its sides.

Sol. Let the given isosceles triangle be ΔPQR, whose base is QR. Now, draw the bisector of $\angle QPR$, which meets base QR at A.

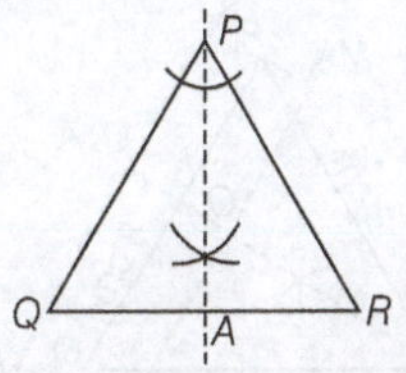

Thus, A is the required locus of a point, which is equidistant from the sides PQ, and PR of an isosceles triangle.

Example 4. Draw an $\angle PQR = 75°$. Find a point A, such that A is at a distance of 3 cm from PQ and 2 cm from QR.

Sol. Steps of construction

1. Draw $\angle PQR = 75°$.
2. Draw $EF \parallel PQ$ at a distance of 3 cm from PQ.
3. Draw $GH \parallel QR$ at a distance of 2 cm from QR, which intersects EF at A.

   Thus, A is the required point.

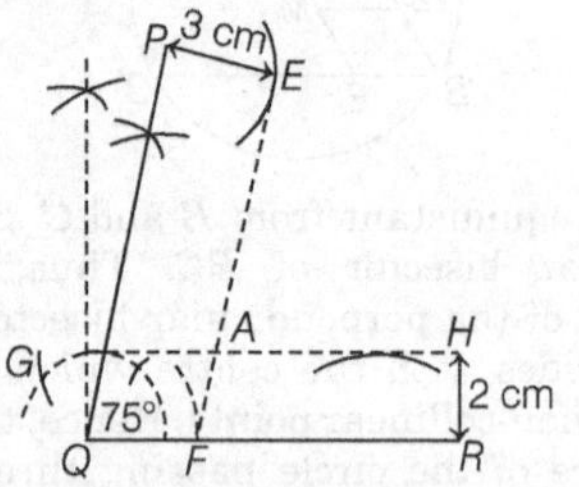

Example 5. Construct $\angle EFG = 75°$. Mark a point P equidistant from EF and FG, such that distance from another line AB is 4 cm.

Sol. Steps of construction

1. Draw $\angle EFG = 75°$.
2. Draw a bisector of $\angle EFG$ and take any point P on it.
3. Draw $AB \parallel FP$ at a distance of 4 cm.

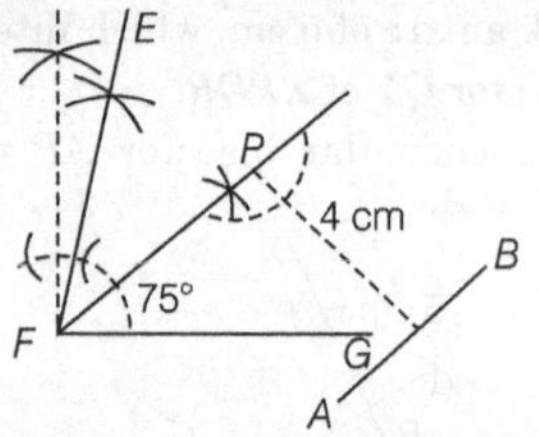

Thus, P is the required point, which is equidistant from EF and FG.

Example 6. Construct a ΔPQR with $PQ = 6$ cm and $PR = QR = 8$ cm. Find the points equidistant from PQ and PR, and also 4 cm from QR. Measure the distance between the two points obtained.

Sol. Steps of construction

1. Draw a line segment $PQ = 6$ cm.
2. Draw arcs of radii 8 cm each from P and Q to intersect at R.
3. Join PR and QR. Thus, ΔPQR is formed.

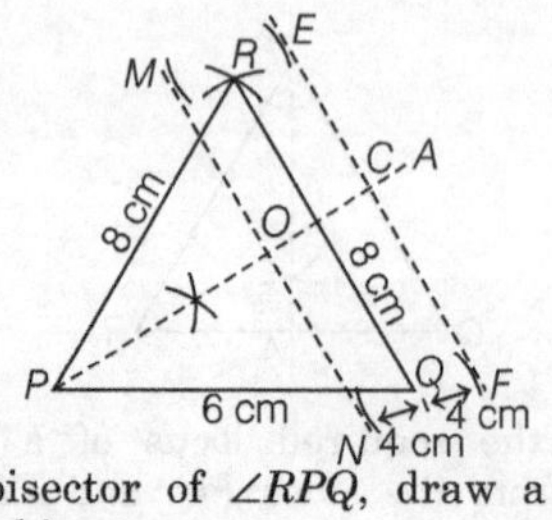

4. Draw the bisector of $\angle RPQ$, draw a line PA passing through this bisector.
5. Draw $MN \parallel QR$ and $EF \parallel QR$ at a distance of 4 cm each, which intersects PA at O and C, respectively. Measure OC.

   Thus, O and C are the required points and distance OC is 8.2 cm (approx.).

Example 7. Construct a ΔABC with $AB = 7$ cm, $BC = 8$ cm and $\angle ABC = 60°$. Also, locate by construction, the point P, such that

(i) P is equidistant from B and C.

(ii) P is equidistant from AB and BC.

(iii) Measure and record the length of PB. **[ICSE 2000]**

Sol. Steps of construction

(i) 1. Draw a line segment $AB = 7$ cm.

2. Draw an $\angle XBA = 60°$, with the help of pair of compasses.
3. From point B, cut $BC = 8$ cm from BX.
4. Join A and C, which is the required ΔABC.
5. Draw perpendicular bisector of line BC. The point P situated on this line will be equidistant from B and C.

(ii) 6. Draw angular bisector of $\angle ABC$. Any point situated on this angular bisector is equidistant from lines AB and BC.

7. The intersection point of perpendicular bisector and angular bisector is the required point P, which is equidistant from lines AB and BC and also from points B and C.

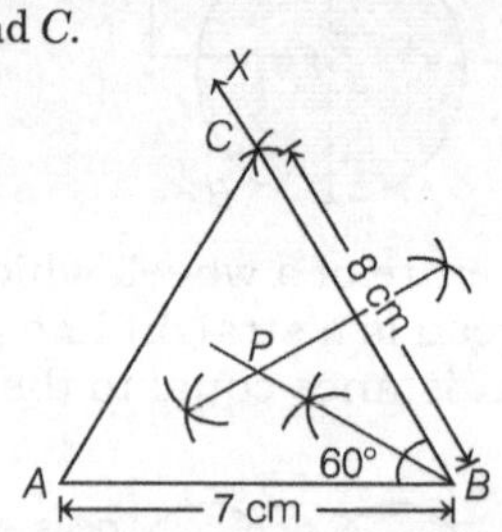

(iii) On measuring, the length of PB is 4.5 cm.

Example 8. A straight line AB is 8 cm long. Locate, by construction the locus of a point, which is

(i) equidistant from A and B. **[ICSE 2008]**

(ii) always 4 cm long from the line AB.

(iii) Mark two points X and Y, which are 4 cm from AB and equidistant from A and B. Name the figure $AXBY$.

Sol. Steps of construction

(i) 1. Draw a line segment $AB = 8$ cm.

2. Draw perpendicular bisector PQ of AB, which is the locus of a point, equidistant from A and B.

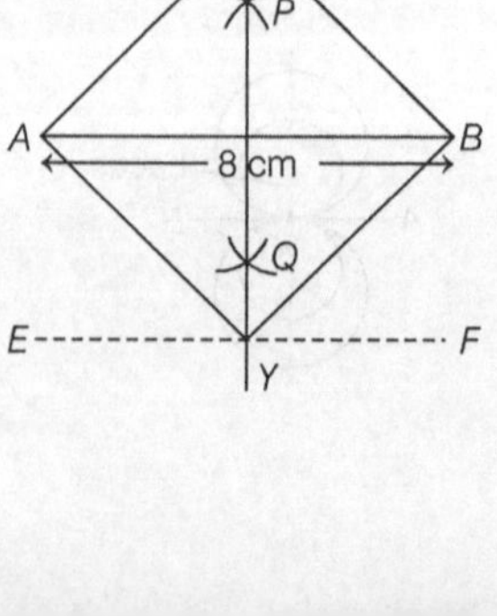

(ii) 3. Draw CD and EF both parallel to opposite sides of AB and each at a distance of 4 cm from AB. Thus, CD and EF are the required loci.

(iii) 4. Extends PQ on both sides, which meets the lines CD and EF at X and Y respectively, which are at a distance 4 cm from AB.

5. Join AX, XB, BY and YA.

Hence, the formed figure $AXBY$ is a square.

Example 9. Use ruler and compass only for this question.

(i) Construct ΔABC, where $AB = 3.5$ cm, $BC = 6$ cm and $\angle ABC = 60°$.

(ii) Construct the locus of points inside the triangle, which are equidistant from BA and BC.

(iii) Construct the locus of points inside the triangle, which are equidistant from B and C.

(iv) Mark the point P, which is equidistant from AB and BC; and also equidistant from B and C. Measure and record the length of PB. **[ICSE 2010]**

***Sol.* Steps of construction**

(i) 1. Draw a line segment $BC = 6$ cm.

2. From the point B, draw $\angle XBC = 60°$.

3. Taking B as centre, cut $BA = 3.5$ cm from BX.

4. Join AC. Thus, we get the required ΔABC.

(ii) 5. Draw angle bisector of $\angle ABC$, which is the locus of points inside the triangle, which are equidistant from BA and BC.

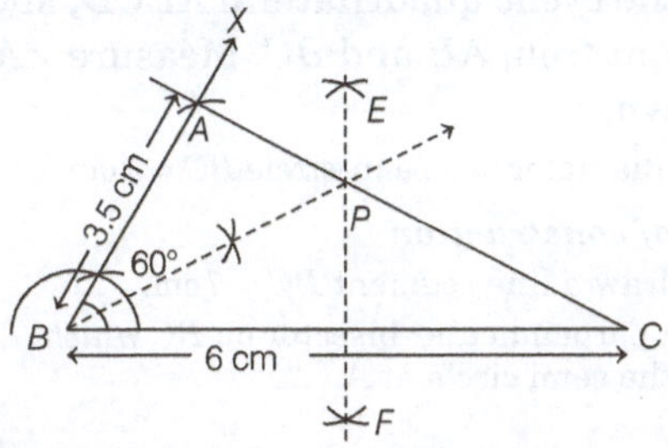

(iii) 6. Draw perpendicular bisector EF of BC, which intersects the angular bisector at point P. Then, EF is the locus of points inside the triangle, which are equidistant from B and C.

(iv) 7. The intersection point of angle bisector and EF is the required point P, which is equidistant from AB, BC, B and C. On measuring, the length of PB is 3.5 cm.

Example 10. If the bisectors of $\angle A$ and $\angle B$ of a quadrilateral $ABCD$ intersect each other at the point P, prove that P is equidistant from AD and BC.

Sol. From P, draw $PM \perp AB$, $PN \perp BC$ and $PL \perp AD$.

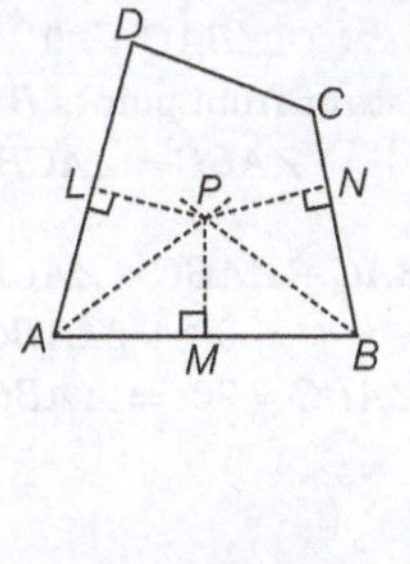

Since, P lies on the bisector of $\angle A$, $MP = LP$ ...(i)

Also, P lies on the bisector of $\angle B$, $MP = NP$ ...(ii)

From Eqs. (i) and (ii), we get $LP = NP$

So, P is equidistant from AD and BC.

Example 11. Construct a ΔBCP, given $BC = 5$ cm, $BP = 4$ cm and $\angle CBP = 45°$.

(i) Complete the rectangle $ABCD$, such that

(a) P is equidistant from AB and BC.

(b) P is equidistant from C and D.

(ii) Measure and record the length of AB. **[ICSE 2007]**

***Sol.* Steps of construction**

(i) (a) 1. Draw a line segment $BC = 5$ cm.

2. Draw a ray making $\angle XBC = 45°$ at B.

3. Cut $BP = 4$ cm from BX and join PC. Then, ΔBCP is the required triangle.

4. Draw $BQ \perp BC$ and $CR \perp BC$. Here, PB is the bisector of $\angle QBC$, so it is equidistant from BC and QB.

(b) 5. Now, cut BQ at A, such that $PA = PC$ and cut CR at D, such that $PC = PD$.

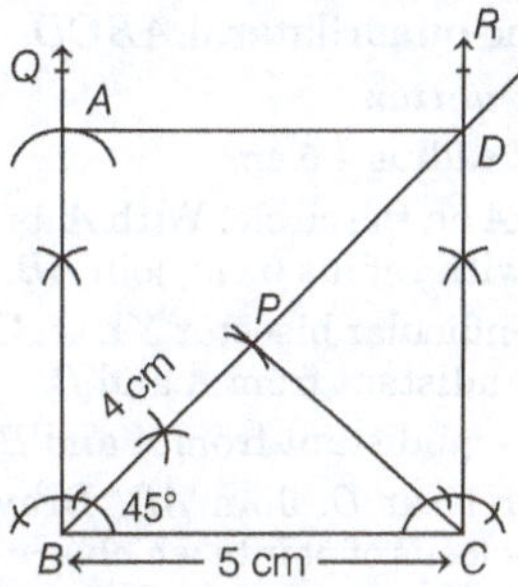

6. Join AD. Thus, the rectangle $ABCD$. is the required rectangle.

(ii) On measuring, the length of AB is 5.7 cm (approx.).

Example 12. Construct a ΔABC, in which base $BC = 6$ cm, $AB = 5.5$ cm and $\angle ABC = 120°$.

(i) Construct a circle circumscribing the ΔABC.

(ii) Draw a cyclic quadrilateral $ABCD$, so that D is equidistant from B and C. **[ICSE 2012]**

***Sol.* Steps of construction**

(i) 1. Draw a line segment $BC = 6$ cm.

2. From the point B, draw $\angle XBC = 120°$.

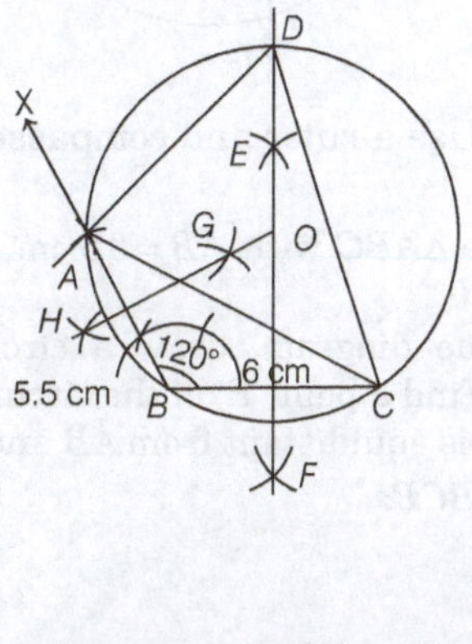

3. Taking radius 5.5 cm with B as centre, cut $BA = 5.5$ cm from BX.
4. Join AC, which is the required ΔABC.
5. Draw perpendicular bisectors EF of BC and GH of AB. They both intersect at point O.
6. Draw a circle with O as centre and OA or OC or OB as radius. Then, we get the required circumcircle.

(ii) 7. Extend line FE in the direction of E, which meets the circle at point D and which is equidistant from B and C.
8. Join AD and CD.
Hence, $ABCD$ is the required cyclic quadrilateral.

Example 13. Use ruler and compass for this question. Construct a circle of radius 4.5 cm. Draw a chord $AB = 6$ cm.

(i) Find the locus of points equidistant from A and B. Mark the point where it meets the circle as D.

(ii) Join AD and find the locus of points which are equidistant from AD and AB. Mark the point where it meets the circle as C.

(iii) Join BC and CD. Measure and write down the length of side CD of the quadrilateral $ABCD$.

Sol. Steps of construction

(a) Draw a circle of radius 4.5 cm.

(b) Take any point A on the circle. With A as a centre draw an arc B on circle with radius 6 cm, join AB.

(c) Draw the perpendicular bisector XY of AB to get the locus of the points equidistant from A and B.
Locus of points equidistant from A and B is the line DM.

(d) XY cuts the circle at D. Join AD. Draw the bisector of $\angle BAD$ to get the locus of points which are equidistant from AD and AB. This bisector meets at C on the circle.
Locus of points equidistant from AB and AD is the line AC.

(e) Joing BC and CD and get the required quadrilateral $ABCD$.
On measuring, the length $CD = 5.2$ cm.

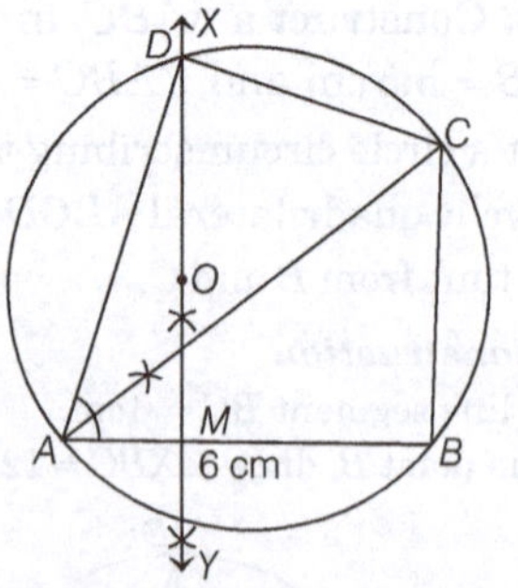

Example 14. Use a ruler and compasses only for this question.

(i) Construct a ΔABC with $AB = 3.5$ cm, $BC = 6$ cm and $\angle ABC = 120°$.

(ii) In the same diagram, draw a circle with BC as diameter. Find a point P on the circumference of the circle, that is equidistant from AB and BC.

(iii) Measure $\angle BCP$. **[ICSE 2013, 05]**

Sol. Steps of construction

(i) 1. Draw a line segment $BC = 6$ cm.
2. From the point B, draw $\angle XBC = 120°$.
3. Taking length 3.5 cm with B as centre, cut $BA = 3.5$ cm from BX.
4. Join A to C. Thus, we get the required ΔABC.

(ii) 5. Draw perpendicular bisector MN of BC, which meets BC at point O.

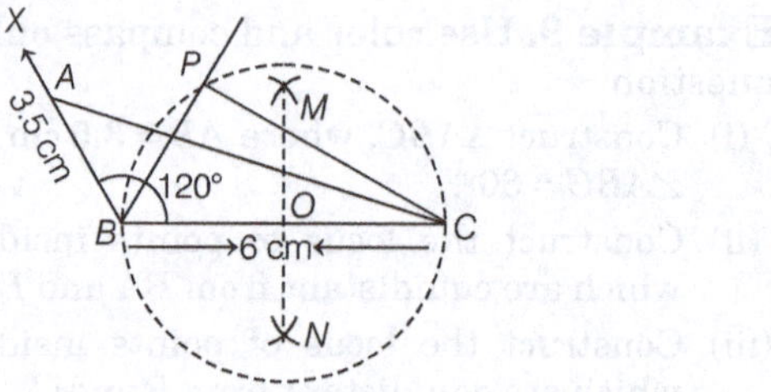

6. Draw a circle with O as centre and OC or OB as radius.
7. Draw angle bisector of $\angle ABC$, which intersects the circumference of the circle at P. Then, point P is equidistant from AB and BC.
8. Join BP and CP.

(iii) On measuring, we get $\angle BCP = 30°$.

Example 15. Using ruler and a compass only construct a semi-circle with diameter $BC = 7$ cm. Locate a point A on the circumference of the semi-circle such that A is equidistant from B and C. Complete the cyclic quadrilateral $ABCD$, such that D is equidistant from AB and BC. Measure $\angle ADC$ and write it down.

Sol. Given, diameter of a semi-circle $BC = 7$ cm

Steps of construction

(i) First, draw a line segment $BC = 7$ cm.

(ii) Draw a perpendicular bisector on BC which meets the semi circle at A.

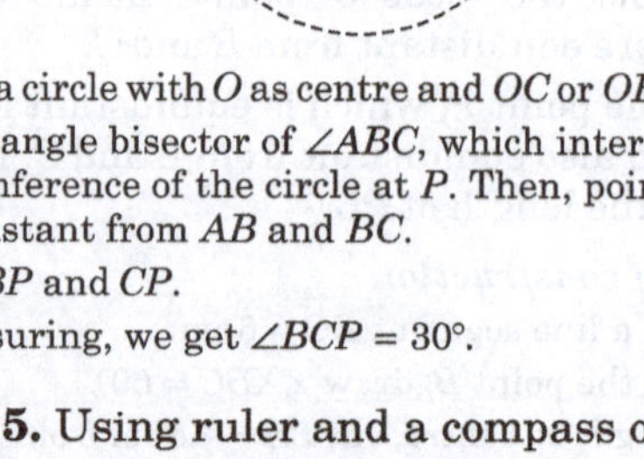

(iii) Since, D is equidistant from A and C, therefore D lies on the bisector of $\angle ABC$.
As point A is on semi-circle, therefore

$$\angle BAC = 90°$$

Also, A is equidistant from points B and C

$$\therefore \quad \angle ABC = \angle ACB$$

In ΔABC,

$$\angle BAC + \angle ABC + \angle ACB = 180°$$

$$\Rightarrow \quad 90° + 2\angle ABC = 180°$$

$$\Rightarrow \quad 2\angle ABC = 90° \Rightarrow \angle ABC = 45°$$

Since, $ABCD$ is a cyclic quadrilateral.

$\therefore \quad \angle ABC + \angle ADC = 180^\circ$

[sum of opposite angles of a cyclic quadrilateral is 180°]

$\Rightarrow \quad \angle ADC = 180^\circ - 45^\circ = 135^\circ$

Example 16. Using a ruler and a compass construct a ΔABC in which $AB = 7$ cm, $\angle CAB = 60^\circ$ and $AC = 5$ cm. Construct the locus of

(i) points equidistant from AB and AC.

(ii) points equidistant from BA and BC.

Hence, construct a circle touching the three sides of the triangle internally. **[ICSE 2017]**

Sol. ***Steps of construction***

Step I Draw a line segment $AB = 7$ cm.

Step II Taking A as centre and some radius, draw an arc of a circle which intersect AB, say at P.

Step III Taking P as centre and with the same radius as before drawn an arc intersecting previously draw an arc, say at a point Q.

Step IV Draw the ray AX passing through Q, then $\angle XAB = 60^\circ$

Step V With A as centre and radius equal to 5 cm, draw an arc cutting AX at C.

Step VI Join CB.

Thus, ΔABC is obtained.

(i) **Locus is the bisector of $\angle BAC$**

Step VII Taking P and Q as centre and with the radius more than $\frac{1}{2}PQ$, draw arcs to intersect each other, say at M.

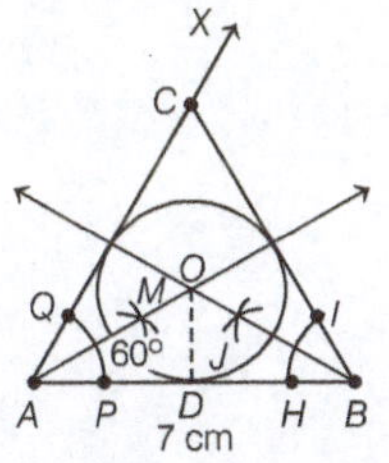

Step VIII Join MA, which is required locus of point equidistant from AB and AC.

[$\because$ any point on the angle bisector of an angle is equidistant from its arms]

(ii) **Locus is the bisector of $\angle ABC$**

Step IX Taking B as centre and draw an arc of a circle, which intersects BA at H and BC at I.

Step X Taking H and I as centres and with the radius more than $\frac{1}{2}HI$, draw two arcs intersect each other say at J.

Step XI Join JB, which is required locus of points equidistant from BA and BC.

Step XII Suppose both bisectors AM and BJ intersect at a point say O.

Step XIII Draw perpendicular from point O on any side of the triangle, say OD on AB.

Step XIV Taking O as centre and OD as radius, draw a circle, which is required incircle.

Example 17. Use ruler and compass only for the following question. All construction lines and arcs must be clearly shown. **[ICSE 2016]**

(i) Construct a ΔABC in which $BC = 6.5$ cm, $\angle ABC = 60^\circ$, $AB = 5$ cm.

(ii) Construct the locus of points at a distance of 3.5 cm from A.

(iii) Construct the locus of points equidistant from AC and BC.

(iv) Mark 2 points X and Y which are at a distance of 3.5 cm from A and also equidistant from AC and BC. Measure XY.

Sol. Given, $BC = 6.5$ cm, $\angle ABC = 60^\circ$ and $AB = 5$ cm.

Steps of construction

(i) **Step I** Draw $BC = 6.5$ cm.

Step II At point B, make $\angle ZBC = 60^\circ$ with the help of compass.

Step III Taking radius 5 cm, with B as centre cut $BA = 5$ cm from BZ.

Step IV Join A to C.

Thus, ΔABC is the required triangle.

(ii) Draw a circle with A as centre and radius equal to 3.5 cm, which cut the ΔABC at point X and Y. Also, it is the locus of a point equidistant from point A.

(iii) Draw angle bisector of $\angle ACB$, which is the locus of points equidistant from AC and BC.

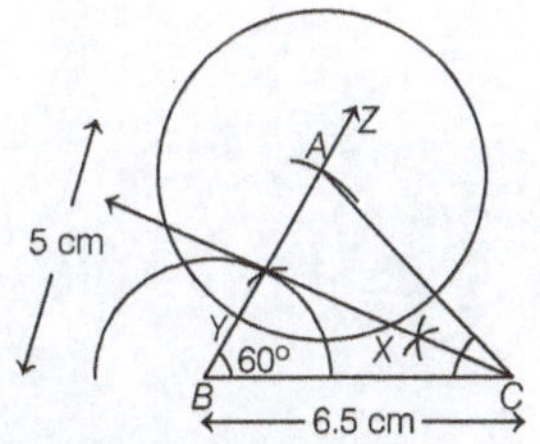

(iv) Since, the points are equidistant from point A and also equidistant from AC and BC.

Therefore, the required point will be the point of intersection of angle bisector of $\angle ACB$ and circle.

On measuring, we get

$$XY = 5.2 \text{ cm}$$

Example 18. Use graph paper for this question. (Take 1 cm = 1 unit on both axes.)

(i) Plot the points $A(1, 1)$, $B(5, 3)$ and $C(2, 7)$.
(ii) Construct the locus of points equidistant from A and B.
(iii) Construct the locus of points equidistant from AB and AC.
(iv) Locate the point P such that $PA = PB$ and P is equidistant from AB and AC.
(v) Measure and record the length PA (in cm).

Sol. Take 1 cm = 1unit on both axes.

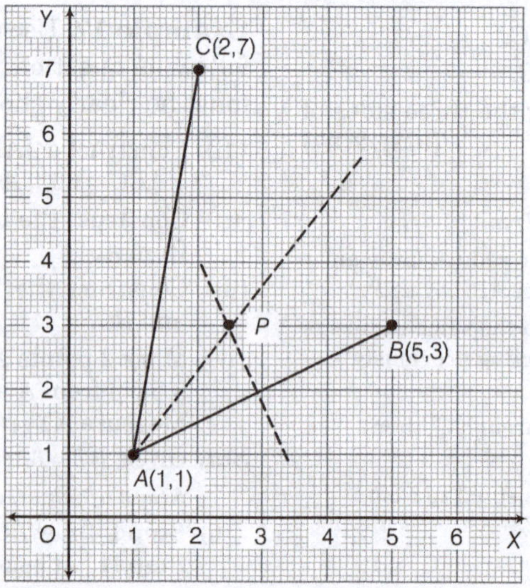

(i) Plot the given points $A(1,1)$, $B(5,3)$ and $C(2,7)$.
(ii) As the locus of points equidistant from A and B is the right bisector of AB, so construct the right bisector of segment AB.
(iii) As the locus of the points equidistant from AB and AC is the bisector of $\angle BAC$, so construct the bisector of $\angle BAC$.
(iv) P is the point of intersection of the right bisector of the segment AB and the bisector of $\angle BAC$, where $PA = PB$.
(v) Length $PA = 2.5$ cm approx.

Chapter Practice

a. 1 Mark Questions

1. What will be the locus of mid-points of equal chords of a circle?

(a) circle
(b) chord
(c) distance of centre from chord
(d) centre point

2. The locus of points located at equal distance from two fixed points is called

(a) line segment
(b) perpendicular bisector of line segment
(c) two points
(d) circle

3. Locus of swinging in swing wheel will be

(a) perpendicular bisector
(b) line segment
(c) semi-circle
(d) circle

b. 3 Marks Questions

4. The speed of sound is 332 m/s. A gun is fired. Describe the locus of all the people on the earth's surface, who hear the sound exactly after one second?

5. Find the locus of a point at a distance 3 cm from a fixed line *AB*.

6. A point *P* moves such that its distance from a fixed line *AB* is always the same. What is the relation between *AB* and the path travelled by *P*?

7. Draw a line segment and construct the locus of a point, that is equidistant from the ends of the line segment $EF = 7$ cm.

8. Draw a line segment and construct the locus of a point, that is equidistant from the ends of the line segment $AB = 4$ cm.

9. Construct $\angle ABC = 135°$ with $AB = 4$ cm and $BC = 6$ cm. Also, construct the locus of a point, that is equidistant from the arms of the angle.

10. Construct $\angle PQR = 150°$ with $PQ = 5$ cm and $QR = 6.5$ cm. Also, construct the locus of a point, that is equidistant from the arms of the angle.

11. Draw two straight lines *PQ* and *RS*, intersecting at *C*, such that $\angle PCR = 70°$. Construct the loci of a point, that is equidistant from the lines.

12. Draw two straight lines *AB* and *CD*, intersecting at *P*, such that $\angle APC = 45°$. Construct the loci of a point, that is equidistant from the lines.

13. In the figure given below, find a point *P* on *CD* equidistant from points *A* and *B*.

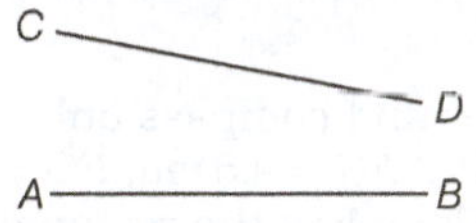

14. Construct $\angle ABC = 60°$. Mark a point *O* equidistant from *AB* and *BC*, such that distance from another line *PQ* is 2 cm.

15. Construct a ΔEFG, in which $EF = 5$ cm, $FG = 6$ cm and $GE = 5.5$ cm. Find the point *O* equidistant from *F* and *G* and also equidistant from *EF* and *FG*.

16. Construct a ΔABC, in which $AB = 7$ cm, $BC = 5.5$ cm and $CA = 4$ cm. Find the point *P* equidistant from *B* and *C*, and also equidistant from *AB* and *BC*.

c. 4/5 Marks Questions

17. *l* is the perpendicular bisector of the line segment *AB* and *C* is a point on the same side of *l*, as *A*. The line segment *BC* intersects *l* at *X*.

Prove that $AX + XC = BC$

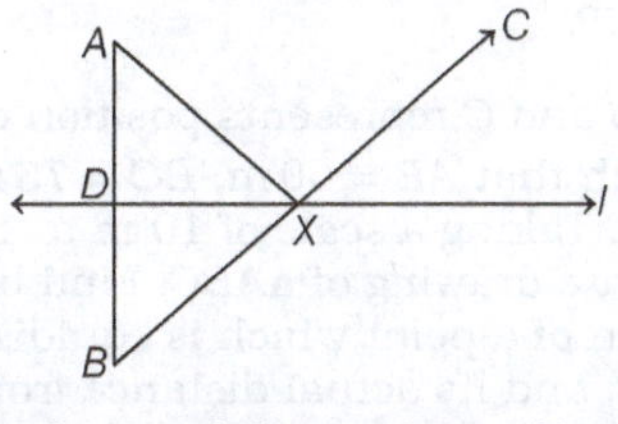

18. What is the locus of the vertices of isosceles triangles having a common base?

19. What is the locus of the vertices of an equilateral triangle having common base?

20. What is the locus of point *A*, which is equidistant from four given non-collinear points?

21. Draw an angle of 105°. Find a point *B*, such that *B* is at a distance of 5 cm from the base and 3 cm from the arm of the given angle.

d. 6 Marks Questions

22. Construct a ΔABC, having given $AB = 4.8$ cm, $AC = 4$ cm and $\angle A = 75°$.

(i) Find a point P inside the ΔABC

(ii) Find a point P' outside the ΔABC equidistant from B and C and at a distance of 1.2 cm from BC.

23. Construct a ΔMNO with $MN = 4$ cm and $MO = NO = 7$ cm. Find the points equidistant from MN and MO and also 5 cm from NO. Measure the distance between the two points obtained.

24. If ΔPBC, ΔQBC and ΔRBC are three isosceles triangles on the same base BC. Show that P, Q, R are collinear.

25. Using the ruler and compass only, construct a ΔFGO, such that $FG = 4.5$ cm, $FO = 3$ cm and $\angle GFO = 45°$. Complete the rectangle $EFGH$, such that

(i) O is equidistant from EF and FG.

(ii) O is equidistant from G and H.

26. Using only ruler and compass, construct $\angle ABC = 120°$, where $AB = BC = 5$ cm.

(i) Mark two points D and E, which satisfy the condition that they are equidistant from both BA and BC.

(ii) In the figure obtained in part (i), join AE and EC. Describe the figures **[ICSE 2002]**

(a) $ABCD$ (b) $\angle ABD$

(c) ABE

27. Without using set square or a protractor, construct a ΔABC, in which $AB = 4$ cm, $BC = 5$ cm and $\angle ABC = 120°$. Locate the point P, such that $\angle BAP = 90°$ and $BP = CP$. Also, measure the length of BP.

28. Points A, B and C represents position of three towers such that $AB = 60$ m, $BC = 73$ m and $CA = 52$ m. Taking a scale of 10 m to 1 cm, make and accurate drawing of ΔABC. Find by drawing, the location of a point which is equidistant from A, B and C, and its actual distance from any of the towers.

29. Use a ruler and a pair of compass only for this question.

(i) Construct a ΔPQR with $PQ = 4.5$ cm, $QR = 7$ cm and $\angle PQR = 135°$.

(ii) In the same diagram, draw a circle with QR as diameter. Find a point P on the circumference of the circle, that is equidistant from PQ and QR.

(iii) Measure $\angle QRP$.

30. Using ruler and compass, construct

(i) a ΔABC in which $AB = 5.5$ cm, $BC = 3.4$ cm and $CA = 4.9$ cm.

(ii) the locus of points equidistant from A and C.

(iii) a circle touching AB at A and passing through C. **[ICSE 2009]**

31. Use ruler and compasses, construct

(i) a ΔLMN, in which $LM = 3.5$ cm, $MN = 4$ cm and $NL = 5$ cm.

(ii) the locus of points equidistant from L and N.

(iii) a circle touching LM at L and passing through N.

32. Construct a ΔABC with $AB = 5.5$ cm, $AC = 6$ cm and $\angle BAC = 105°$. Hence,

(i) construct the locus of points equidistant from BA and BC.

(ii) construct the locus of points equidistant from B and C.

(iii) mark the point which satisfies the above two loci as P. Measure and write the length of PC. **[ICSE 2015]**

33. In parallelogram $ABCD$, side AB is greater than side BC and P is a point in AC such that PB bisects angle B.

Prove that P is equidistant from AB and BC.

34. Construct a ΔABC, such that $AB = 7$ cm, $AC = 5$ cm and $BC = 6$ cm. Construct a point which is equidistant from all the three sides of the triangle. Name the point.

35. In ΔABC, bisectors of interior angles at A and C intersect each other at point O.

Prove that

(i) point O is equidistant from all the three sides of the triangle.

(ii) OA bisects $\angle ABC$.

36. Construct a rhombus $ABCD$ with each sides equal to 5 cm and $\angle A = 60°$

(i) Construct the locus of a point equidistant from vertices A and C and describe it in relation to the rhombus.

(ii) Construct the locus of a point equidistant from the points B and D.

(iii) Is there a point in the rhombus which is equidistant from all the four vertices?

37. Construct a kite $ABCD$, such that $BD = 10$ cm, $AD = 7$ cm and $AB = 5$ cm.

(i) Construct the locus of a point equidistant from the vertices A and C.

(ii) Construct the locus of a point equidistant from B and D.

38. Without using set square or protractor, construct rhombus $ABCD$ with sides of length 4 cm and diagonal AC of length 5 cm. Measure $\angle ABC$. Find the point R on AD such that $RB = RC$. Measure the length of AR.

39. Prove that the locus of a point equidistant from the arms of an angle is the bisector of the angle.

40. What is the locus of the following?

(i) The centre of a wheel of a cycle.

(ii) The door-handle as the door opens.

41. Show that the locus of the centres of all circles, passing through two given points A and B is the perpendicular bisector of line segment AB.

42. Find the locus of centres of circles, which touch two intersecting lines.

43. P and Q are two different points. Prove that the locus of a point R, such that $\angle PRQ = 90°$, is a circle with mid-point O of PQ as centre and OP as radius.

44. Use ruler and a pair of compasses only for this question. Draw a circle of radius 4 cm and mark two chords AB and AC of the circle of length 6 cm and 5 cm, respectively.

(i) Construct the locus of points inside the circle, that are equidistant from A and C. Prove your construction.

(ii) Construct the locus of points inside the circle, that are equidistant from AB and AC.

45. A is a fixed point on the circumference of a circle of radius 4 cm with centre O. M is the mid-point of a variable chord AB. State the locus of M and justify your answer.

46. Attempt this question on the graph paper. [Take 2 boxes = 1 unit]

(i) Draw the line $x = 7$. Now, the same graph paper, draw the locus of the point, which moves in such a way that its distance from the given line is always equal to 2 units.

(ii) Draw the line $y = 3$ in the different graph paper. Now, draw the locus of the point on this graph, which moves in such a way that its distance from the given line is always equal to 3 units.

47. Use graph paper for this question.

Take 10 small divisions = 1 unit on both the axes.

(i) Plot the points P (2,2), Q (6,4) and R (3,8).

(ii) Construct the locus of points equidistant from P and Q.

(iii) Construct the locus of points equidistant from and PR.

(iv) Locate the point A, such that $AP = AQ$ and A is equidistant from PQ and PR.

(v) Measure and record the length AP (in cm).

48. Plot the points E (2,9), F (−1, 3) and C (6, 3) on a graph paper. On same graph paper, draw the locus of point E, so that area of ΔEFG remains same as E moves.

Hints and Answers

1. (a) The locus of mid-points of equal chords is a circle of radius equal to the perpendicular drawn to it from centre. The locus of mid-points of parallel chords is the diameter.

2. (b) A point is said to be equidistant from a set of objects, if the distances between that point and each object in the set are equal. The locus of points equidistant from two given points is their perpendicular bisector.

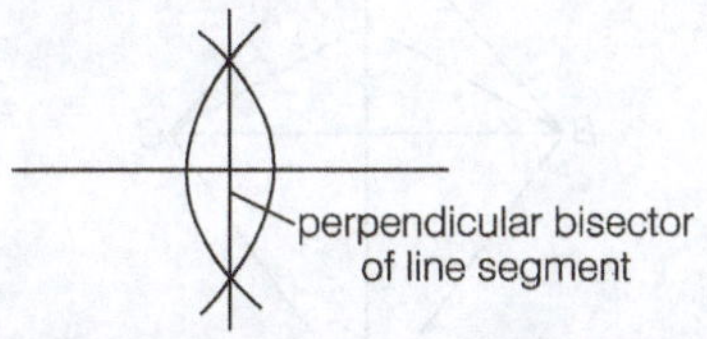

3. (d) Locus of swinging in swing wheel will be circle. Let the locus of point P is a circle which has its centre at O and has a radius equal to r. Similarly, locus of swinging will have the same point.

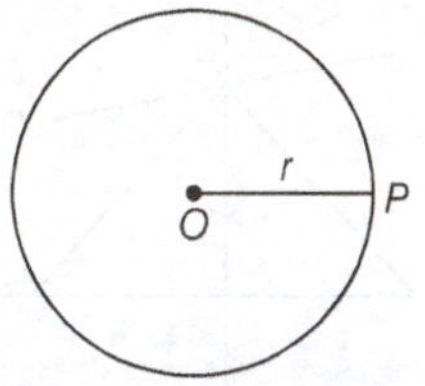

4. Hint Circumference of the circle of radius 332 m with centre at the point from where the gun is fired.

5. Hint

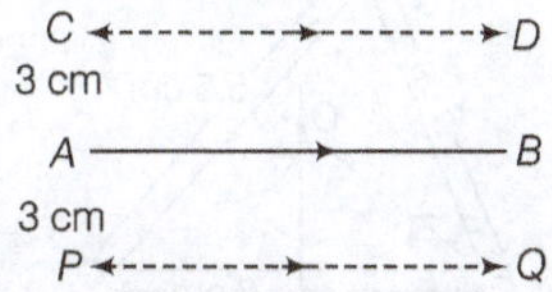

The locus of the points at a distance 3 cm from a fixed line is a pair of straight lines parallel to the given fixed line.

6. Hint Do same as Q. 5.

Ans. A pair of straight lines parallel to AB.

7. Hint

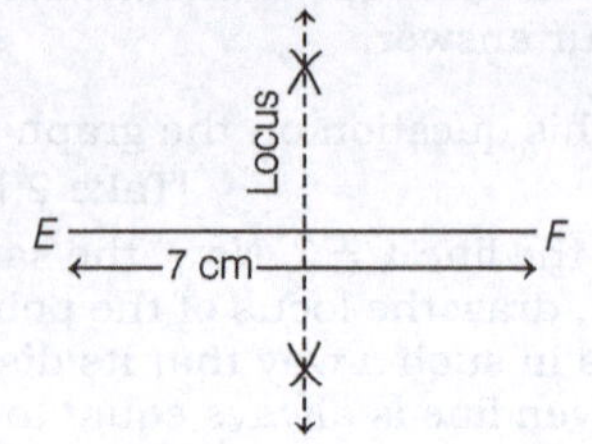

8. Hint Do same as Q. 7.

9. Hint

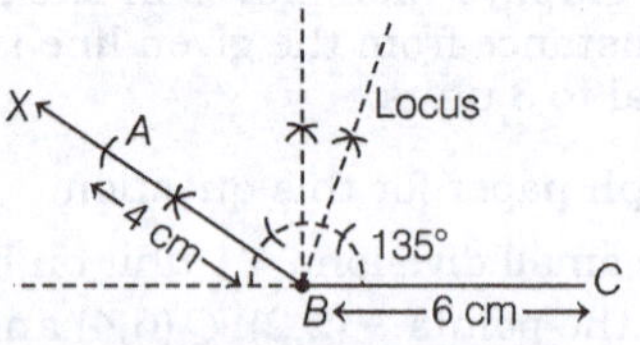

The locus of a point equidistant from AB and BC is the bisector of $\angle ABC$.

10. Hint Do same as Q. 9.

11. Hint

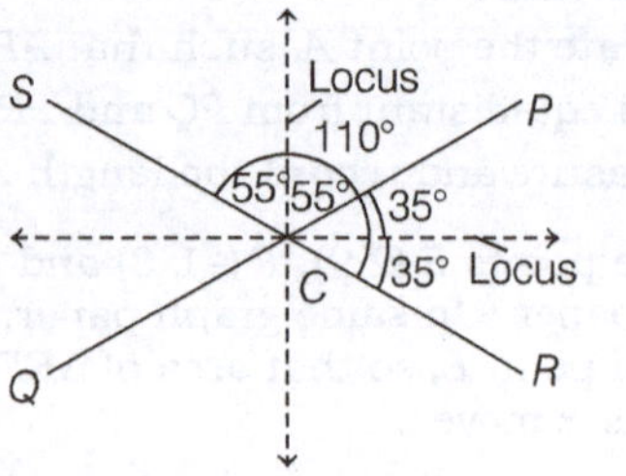

12. Hint Do same as Q. 11.

13. Hint

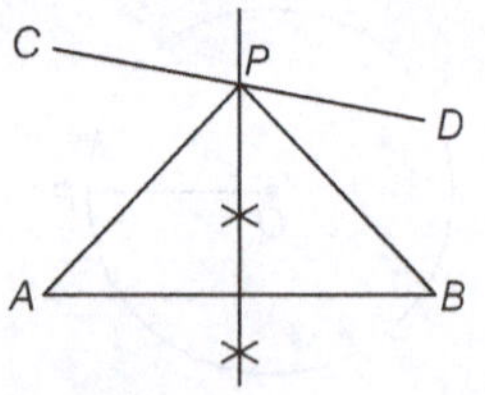

14. Hint Do same as Example 5.

15. Hint

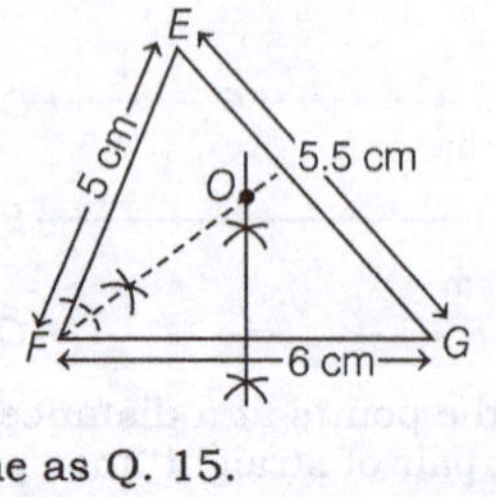

16. Hint Do same as Q. 15.

17. Hint Since, l is the perpendicular bisector of line segment AB, D is any point on l is equidistant from the two points A and B, in view of converse of Theorem 2.

$$AX = XB$$

18. Hint

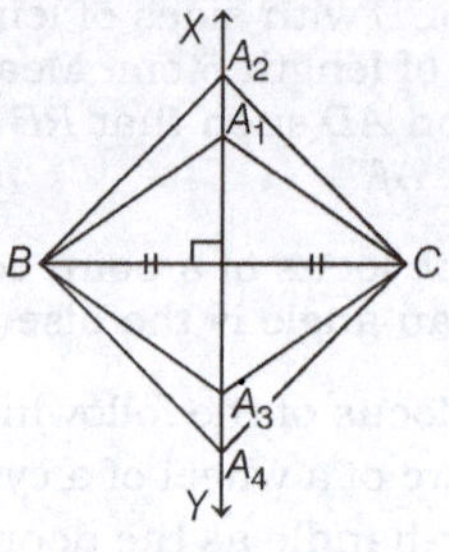

19. Hint Do same as Q. 18.

20. Hint Let four given non-collinear points be A, B, C and D. Now, draw perpendicular bisector of each side.

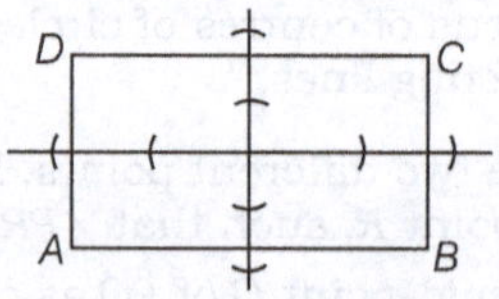

21. Hint Do same as Example 4.

22. Hint (i)

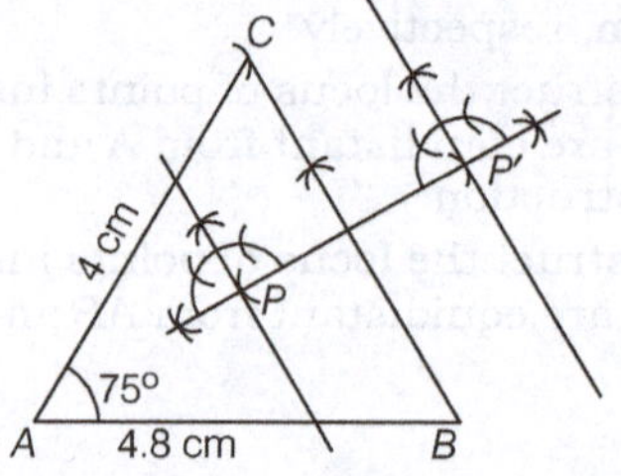

(ii) P and P' are the required points which are inside and outside the given ΔABC.

23. Hint Do same as Example 6.

24. Hint

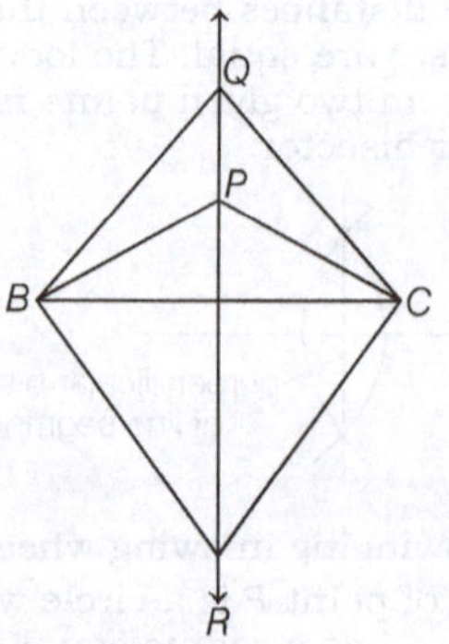

In ΔPBC, $PB = PC$ [given]

Since, the locus of a point P equidistant from B and C is the perpendicular bisector of line segment BC.

Hence, PQR are collinear.

25. Hint Do same as Example 11.

26. Hint

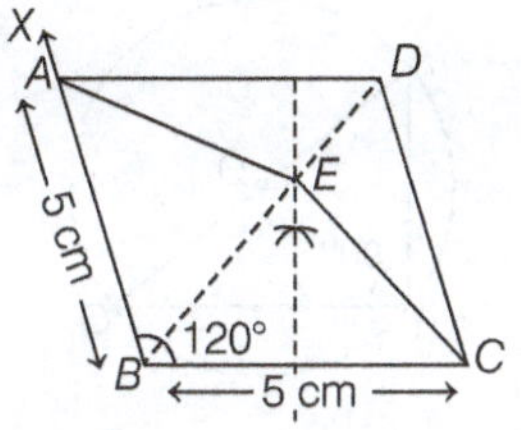

Ans. (a) Rhombus
(b) Bisector of $\angle ABC$
(c) Triangle

27. Hint

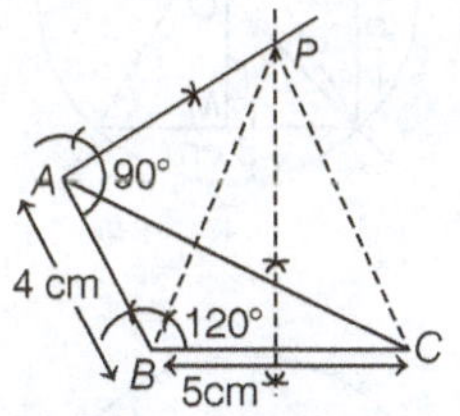

Ans. Measure of $BP = 6.8$ cm.

28. Hint

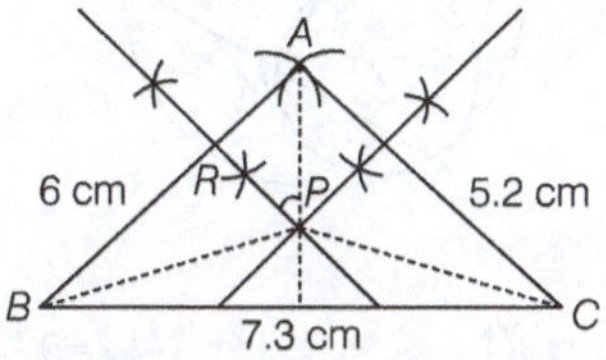

29. Hint Do same as Example 14.
Ans. (iii) $\angle QRP = 22°$

30. Hint

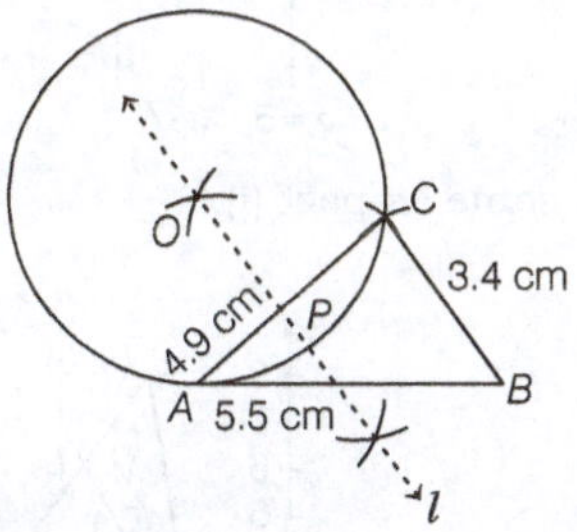

(ii) Point P.

31. Hint Do same as Q. 30.

32. Hint

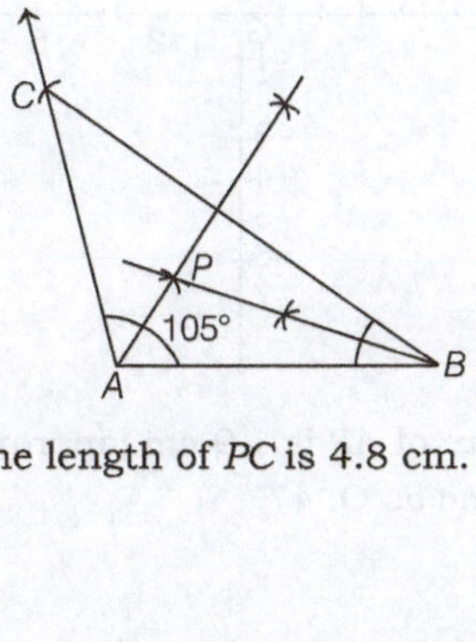

Ans. (iii) The length of PC is 4.8 cm.

33. Hint

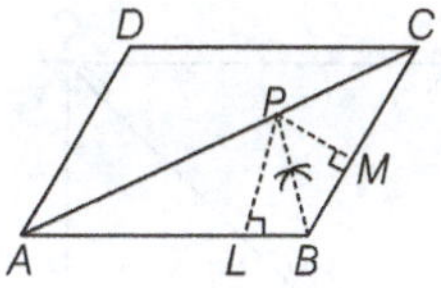

From P, draw $PL \perp AB$ and $PM \perp BC$.

$\Delta PLB \cong \Delta PMB$ (AAS postulate)

$\therefore$ $PL = PM$ (CPCT)

34. Hint

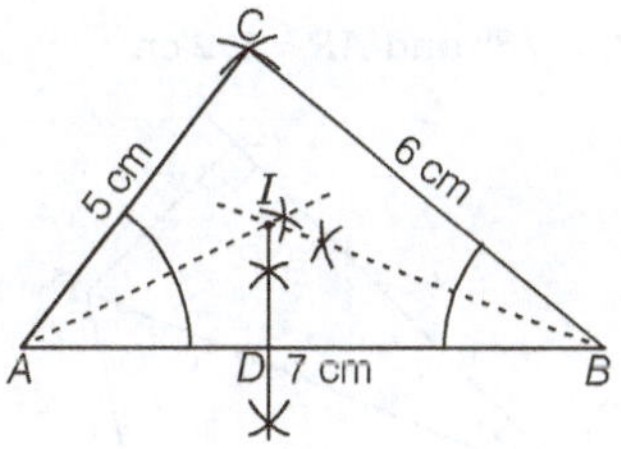

Ans. The point is I.

35. Hint Do same as Q. 34.

36. Hint

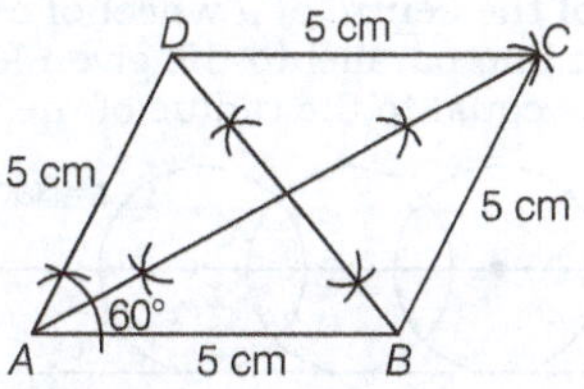

37. Hint

(i)

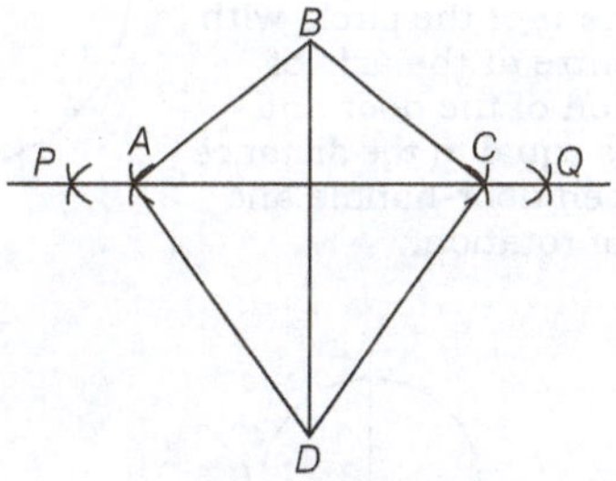

(ii)

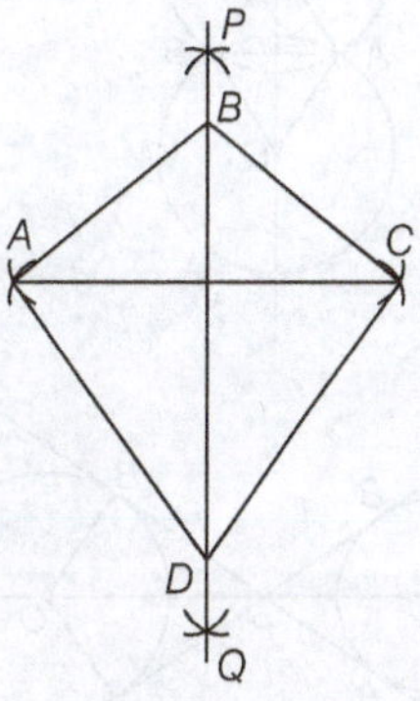

38. Hint

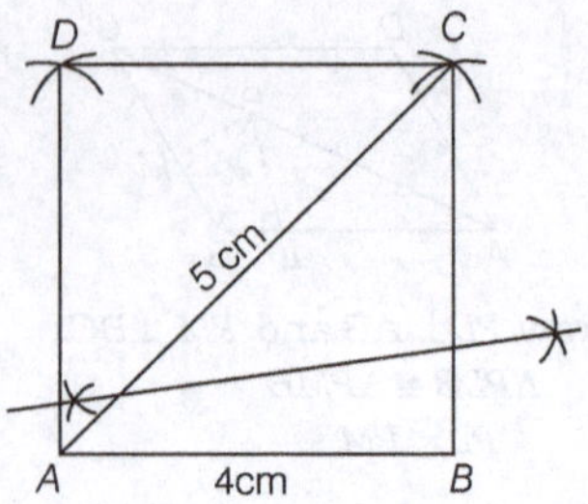

Ans. $\angle ABC = 78°$ and $AR = 1.2$ cm

39. Hint

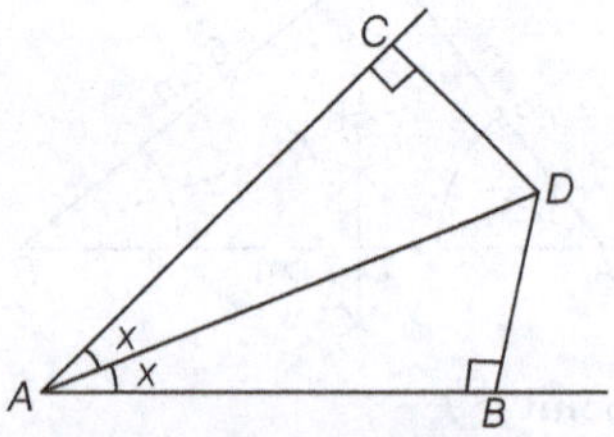

$\angle BAC = \angle BAD + \angle DAC$

40. Hint

(i) **Locus of the centre of a wheel of a cycle is a straight line parallel to the given level of road at a distance equal to the radius of the wheel.**

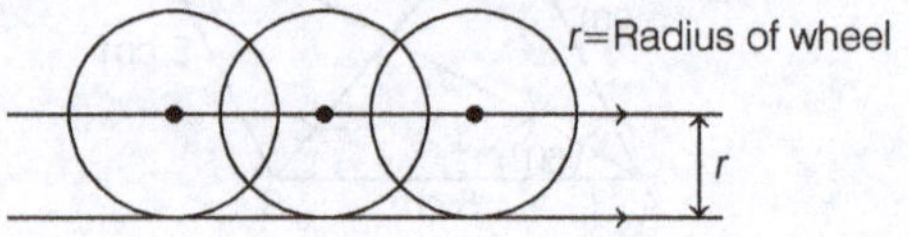

(ii) **Locus of the door-handle as the door opens, is the quadrant of the circle with its centre at the axis of rotation of the door and radius equal to the distance between door-handle and axis of rotation.**

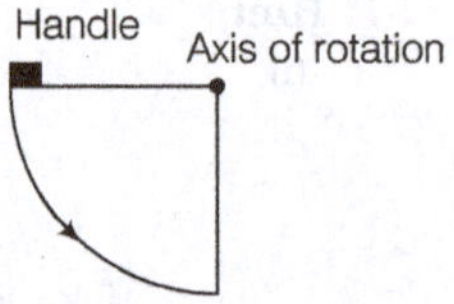

41. Hint

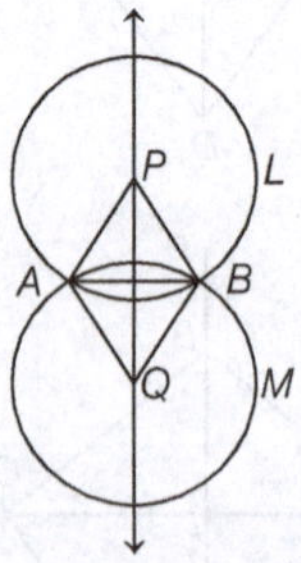

42. Hint

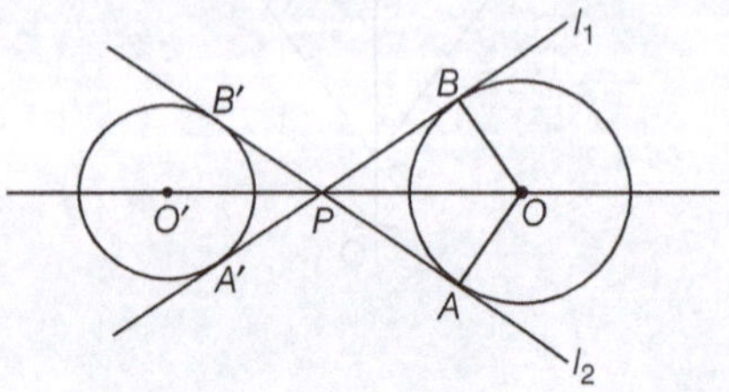

43. Hint

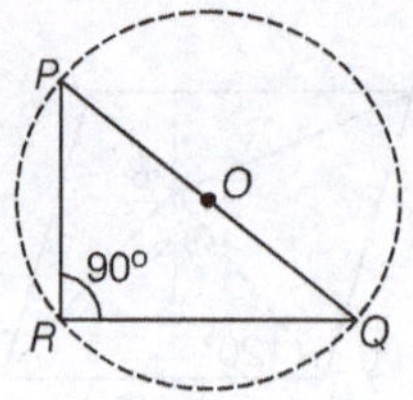

44. Hint

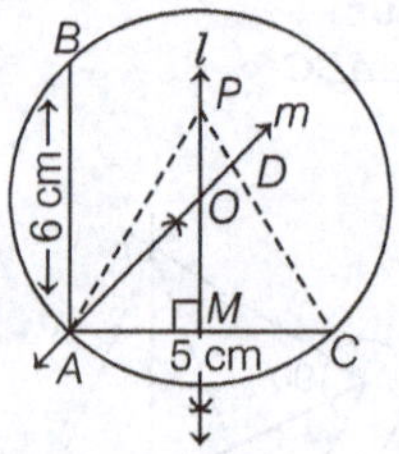

45. Hint

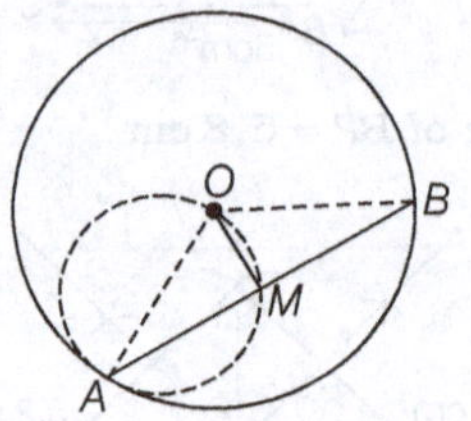

46. Hint (i)

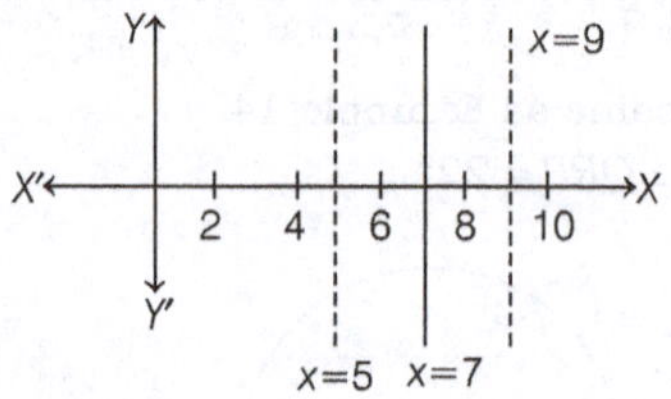

(ii) **Hint** Do same as part (i).

47. Hint

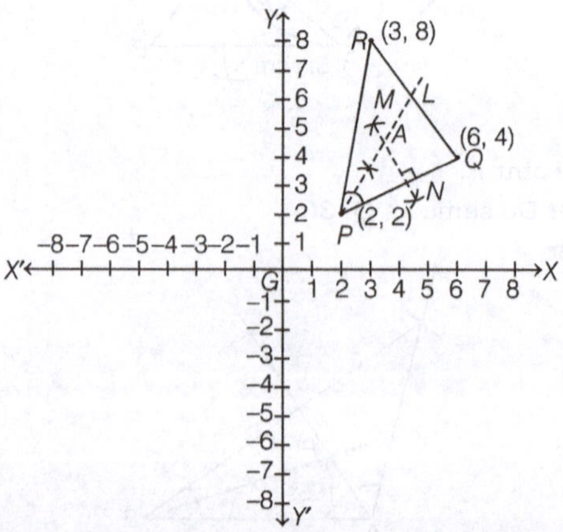

Ans. Measure of AP is 1.9 cm (approx.).

48. Hint Do same as Q. 47.

Olympiad Section

Brain Teasing Questions of Olympiad Pattern

1 $ABCD$ is a quadrilateral in which $AB = BC$. E is the point of intersection of the perpendicular bisectors of AD and CD. Then, $\angle ABC$ is

(a) $2\angle ABE$ (b) $2\angle AEB$
(c) $2AEC$ (d) $2\angle AED$

2 If a point moves so that the sum of its distances from two intersecting straight lines is always constant, then the locus of the moving point is

(a) $\angle FGO$
(b) $2\angle FGO$
(c) thrice of $\angle FGO$
(d) bisector of $\angle FGO$

3 The locus of the vertex of a triangle of given base AB and height h, is a pair of lines

(a) parallel to the base
(b) perpendicular to the base
(c) Both (a) and (b)
(d) None of the above

4 In the given figures, AX bisects $\angle BAC$ and PQ is perpendicular bisector of AC, which meets AX at point Y.

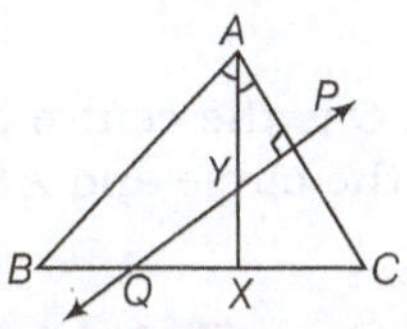

The following statements are given below

I. X is equidistant from AB and AC.

II. Y is equidistant from A and C.

(a) I is true
(b) II is true
(c) I and II are true
(d) None of the above

5 We construct a ΔABC, in which $AB = 4.2$ cm, $BC = 6.3$ cm and $AC = 5$ cm, and draw perpendicular bisector of BC, which meets AC at point D. The point D is equidistant from

(a) A and C
(b) B and C
(c) A and B
(d) None of the above

6 We construct a right angled ΔPQR, in which $\angle Q = 90°$, hypotenuse $PR = 8$ cm and $QR = 4.5$ cm, and draw bisector of $\angle PQR$ which meets PR at point T. Then,

(a) $BT = AT$
(b) $BT > AT$
(c) $BT < AT$
(d) None of the above

7 We construct a ΔABC, in which $\angle ABC = 75°$, $AB = 5$ cm and $BC = 6.4$ cm. Draw perpendicular bisector of side BC and also the bisector of $\angle ACB$. If these bisectors intersect each other at point P. Which of the following statements is/are true?

I. P is equidistant from B and C.

II. P is equidistant from AC and BC.

(a) I is true
(b) II is true
(c) Both I and II are true
(d) None of the above

Answers

1. (a) **2.** (d) **3.** (a) **4.** (c) **5.** (b) **6.** (a) **7.** (c)

* *These questions may or may not be asked in the examination, have been given just for additional practice required for olympiads Scholarship Exams etc. For detailed explanations refer Page No. 491.*

CHAPTER

15

Circles

SYLLABUS

- (a) **Angle Properties** (I) The angle that an arc of a circle subtends at the centre is double that which it subtends at any point on the remaining part of the circle. (ii) Angles in the same segment of a circle are equal (without proof). (iii) Angle in a semi-circle is a right angle. (b) **Cyclic Properties** (I) Opposite angles of a cyclic quadrilateral are supplementary. (ii) The exterior angle of a cyclic quadrilateral is equal to the opposite interior angle (without proof). (c) **Tangent and Secant Properties** (I) The tangent at any point of a circle and the radius through the point are perpendicular to each other. (ii) If two circles touch, the point of contact lies on the straight line joining their centres. (iii) From any point outside a circle, two tangents can be drawn, and they are equal in length. (iv) If two chords intersect internally or externally, then the product of the lengths of the segments are equal. (v) If a chord and a tangent intersect externally, then the product of the lengths of segments of the chord is equal to the square of the lengths of the tangent from the point of contact to the point of intersection. (vi) If a line touches a circle and from the point of contact a chord is drawn, the angles between the tangent and the chord are respectively equal to the angles in the corresponding alternate segments.

In class IX, we have already studied about circle and its related terms like chord, segments, sectors, arcs and chord properties. Here in this chapter, we will extend our knowledge to some more properties related to circle, like angle properties, cyclic properties, tangent and secant properties.

Circle

A circle is a collection of all points in a plane, which are at a constant distance from a fixed point. Here, fixed point is called **centre** and constant distance is called **radius** of circle.

Or

A circle is the locus of a point, which moves in a plane in such a way that its distance from a given fixed point in the plane is always constant.

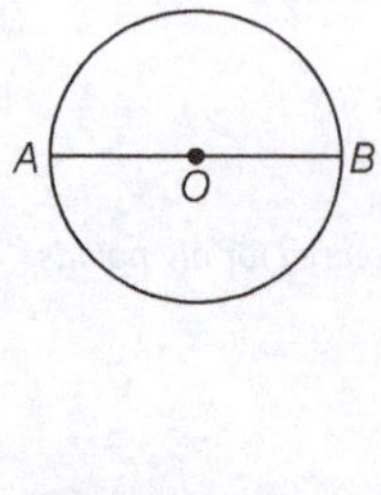

In the given figure, O is the centre of circle, OA and OB are the radii of the circle and AB is the diameter of the circle.

Some Basic Terms Related to Circle

There are various terms related to circle, which are as follow

(i) **Interior of a circle** A point P lies inside a circle, if and only if its distance from the centre of the circle is less than the radius of the circle.

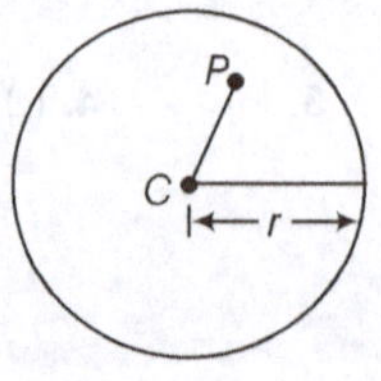

i.e. $CP < r$

The set of all such points P forms the interior of the circle.

(ii) **Exterior of a circle** A point P lies outside a circle, if and only if its distance from the centre of the circle is greater than the radius of the circle.

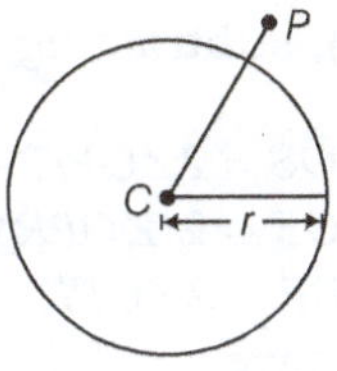

i.e. $CP > r$.

The set of all such points P forms the exterior of the circle.

(iii) **Concentric circles** Two or more circles are called concentric circles, if and only if they have same centre and different radii.

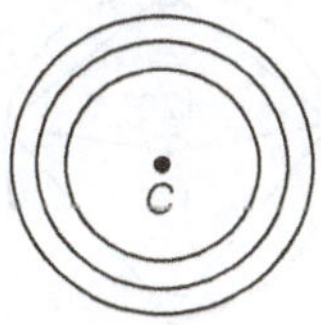

(iv) **Equal** (Congruent) **circles** Two or more circles are called equal (or congruent) circles, if and only if they have same radii.

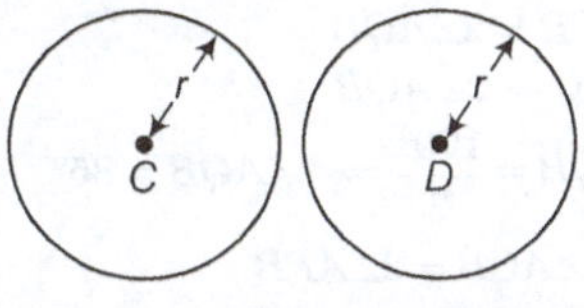

(v) **Chord of a circle** A line segment which join any two points on a circle, is called a chord of the circle.

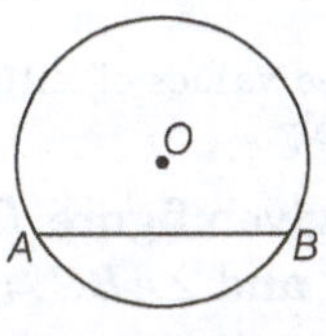

The maximum length of the chord is equal to the length of the diameter.

(vi) **Diameter of a circle** If a chord of a circle passing through its centre, then it is called a diameter of a circle.

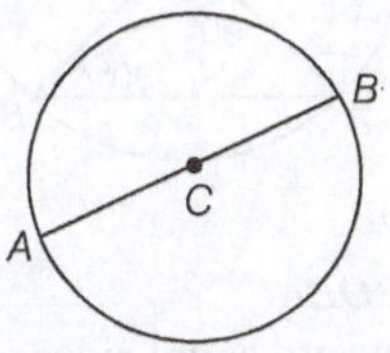

(vii) **Secant of a circle** A line which intersects the circle in two points, is called secant of the circle.

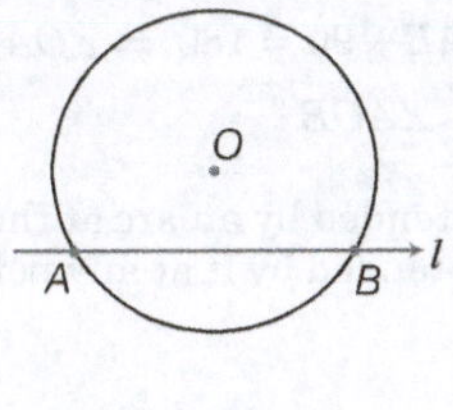

(viii) **Arc of a circle** A piece of a circle between two points is called an arc.

In figure, there are two pieces, one longer and the other smaller.

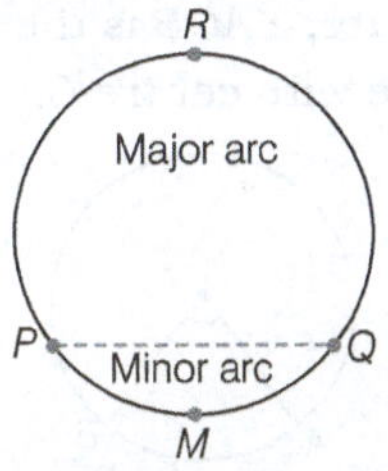

The longer one is called the **major arc** ($\widehat{PRQ}$) and the smaller one is called the **minor arc** ($\widehat{PMQ}$).

(ix) **Semi–circle** A diameter of a circle divides it into two equal parts, which are two equal arcs. Each of these two arcs is called a semi–circle.

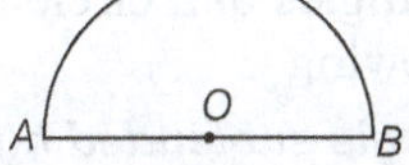

(x) **Circumference of a circle** The whole arc of a circle is called the circumference of a circle.

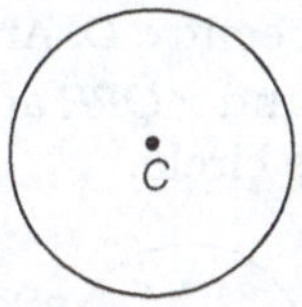

(xi) **Segment of a circle** The region between a chord and either of its arcs, is called a segment of the circular region or simply a segment of the circle.

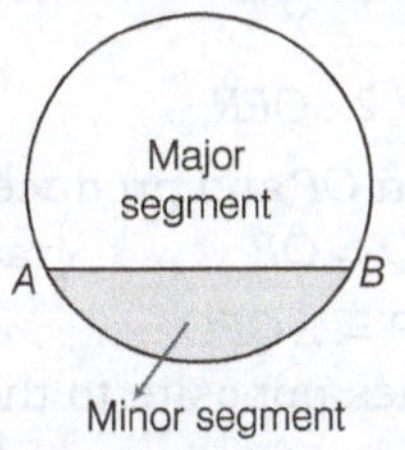

The segment formed by minor arc alongwith chord, is called minor segment and the segment formed by major arc, is called the major segment.

(xii) **Sector of a circle** The region between an arc and the two radii, is called a sector.

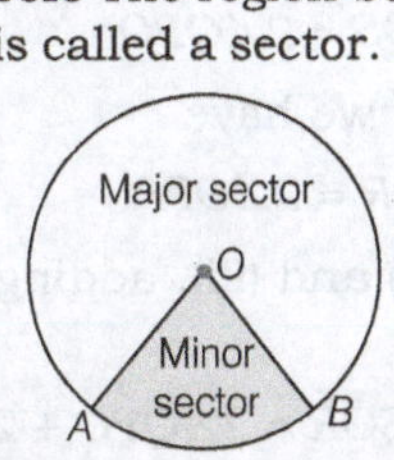

Minor sector is the sector formed by the minor arc and **major sector** is the sector formed by the major arc.

(xiii) **Angle subtended by an arc** The angle formed by the two bounding radii of an arc of a circle at the centre of the circle, is called the angle subtended by an arc.

In the given figure, $\angle AOB$ is the angle subtended by $\overset{\frown}{AB}$ of a circle with centre O.

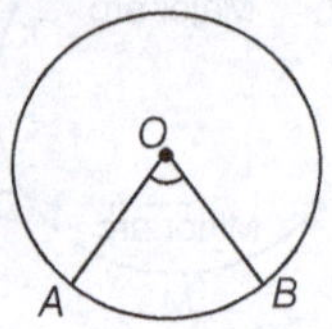

The measurement of $\angle AOB$ in degree is called degree measurement of $\overset{\frown}{AB}$.

Angle Properties of a Circle

The properties of angles of a circle in the form of theorems, are following

Theorem 1 *The angle subtended by an arc of a circle at the centre is double the angle subtended by it at any point on the remaining part of the circle.*

Given A circle with centre O. Arc QR subtends $\angle QOR$ at the centre and $\angle QPR$ at any point P on the remaining part of the circle.

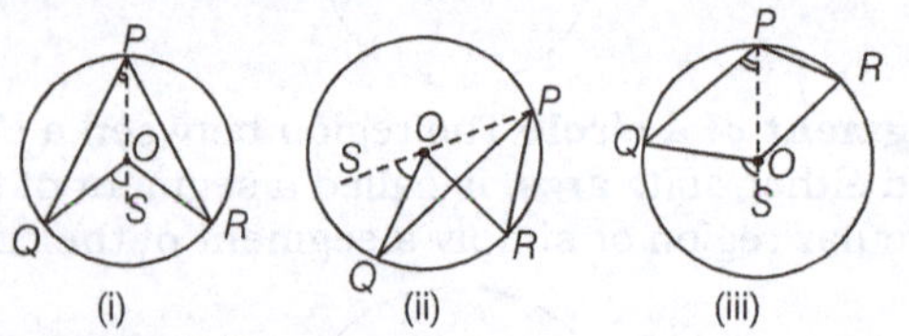

To prove $\angle QOR = 2\angle QPR$

Construction Join OP and produce it to any point S.

Proof In ΔPOQ, $OQ = OP$ [radii of same circle]

$\Rightarrow \quad \angle OQP = \angle QPO$ ...(i)

[$\because$ angles opposite to the equal sides of a triangle are equal]

Now, $\quad \angle QOS = \angle OQP + \angle QPO$

[$\because$ exterior angle = sum of opposite interior angles]

$\Rightarrow \quad \angle QOS = \angle QPO + \angle QPO$ [from Eq. (i)]

$\Rightarrow \quad \angle QOS = 2\angle QPO$ ...(ii)

Similarly, in ΔPOR, we have

$\angle SOR = 2\angle OPR$ ...(iii)

Case I From Fig. (i) and (iii), adding Eqs. (ii) and (iii), we get

$\Rightarrow \quad \angle QOS + \angle SOR = 2\angle QPO + 2\angle OPR$

$\Rightarrow \quad \angle QOR = 2(\angle QPO + \angle OPR)$

$\Rightarrow \quad \angle QOR = 2\angle QPR$

Case II From Fig. (ii), subtracting Eq. (ii) from Eq. (iii), we get

$\angle SOR - \angle QOS = 2\angle OPR - 2\angle QPO$

$\Rightarrow \quad \angle QOR = 2(\angle OPR - \angle QPO)$

$\Rightarrow \quad \angle QOR = 2\angle QPR$

In all the cases, we have

$\angle QOR = 2\angle QPR$ **Hence proved.**

Example 1. In the following figure, C be the centre of the circle and $\angle ACB = 170°$, then find the value of $\angle AQB$ and $\angle APB$.

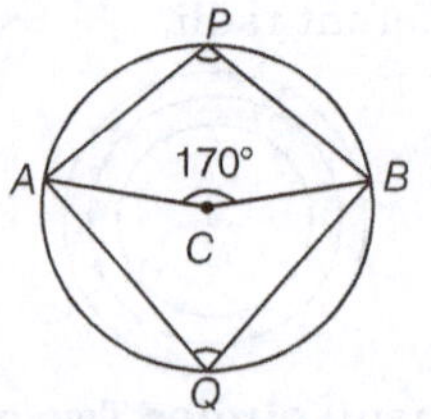

Sol. Given, $\angle ACB = 170°$ ...(i)

Since, angle at the centre of a circle is twice the angle at the remaining part of the circumference of the circle.

$\therefore \quad \angle ACB = 2\angle AQB$

$\Rightarrow \quad 170° = 2\angle AQB$ [from Eq. (i)]

$\Rightarrow \quad \angle AQB = \dfrac{170°}{2} \Rightarrow \angle AQB = 85°$

Also, reflex $\angle ACB = 2\angle APB$

$\therefore \quad 360° - \angle ACB = 2\angle APB$

$\Rightarrow \quad 360° - 170° = 2\angle APB$ [from Eq. (i)]

$\Rightarrow \quad 190° = 2\angle APB \Rightarrow \angle APB = \dfrac{190°}{2} = 95°$

Hence, the required values of $\angle AQB$ and $\angle APB$ are 85° and 95°, respectively.

Example 2. In the given figure, O is the centre of the circle. If $\angle AOB = 90°$ and $\angle ABC = 30°$, then find the measure of $\angle CAO$.

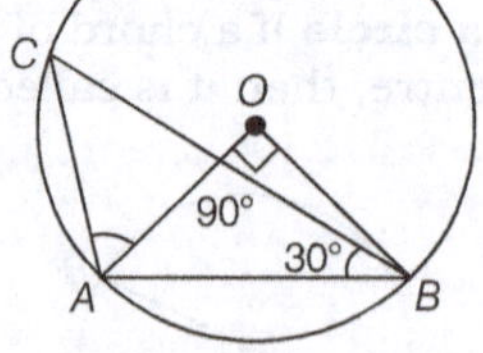

Sol. In ΔOAB, $OA = OB$ [radii of same circle]

$\Rightarrow \quad \angle OAB = \angle OBA$

[$\because$ opposite equal sides of a triangle are equal]

In ΔOAB, $\angle OAB + \angle OBA + \angle AOB = 180°$

[sum of angles of a triangle]

$\Rightarrow \angle OAB + \angle OAB + 90° = 180° \Rightarrow \angle OAB = 45°$

Now, $\angle ACB = \dfrac{1}{2}\angle AOB$

[$\because$ angle subtended by an arc at the centre = double the angle subtended by it at any point on the remaining part of the circle]

$\Rightarrow \angle ACB = \frac{1}{2} \times 90° = 45°$

In ΔABC, $\angle CAB + \angle CBA + \angle ACB = 180°$ [angle sum property of a triangle]

$\Rightarrow \angle CAB + 30° + 45° = 180° \Rightarrow \angle CAB = 105°$

From the figure, $\angle CAO + \angle OAB = \angle CAB$

$\Rightarrow \angle CAO + 45° = 105° \Rightarrow \angle CAO = 60°$

Example 3. In the given figure, O is the circumcentre of ΔABC. If $OD \perp BC$, prove that $\angle BOD = \angle BAC$.

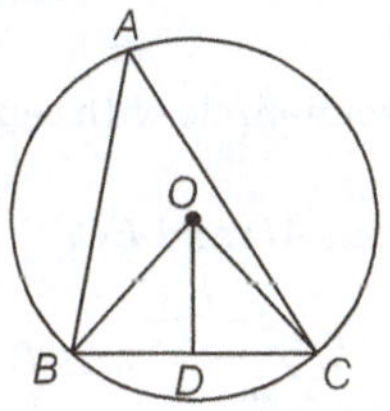

Sol. In ΔOBD and ΔOCD,

$OB = OC$ [radii of same circle]

$OD = OD$ [common]

$\angle ODB = \angle ODC$ [each angle = 90°, as $OD \perp BC$]

$\therefore \Delta OBD \cong \Delta OCD$ [RHS rule of congruency]

$\Rightarrow \angle BOD = \angle COD$ [by CPCT]

$\Rightarrow \angle BOC = 2\angle BOD$ ...(i)

Now, $\angle BOC = 2\angle BAC$

[$\because$ angle subtended by an arc at the centre = double the angle subtended by it at any point on the remaining part of the circle]

$\Rightarrow 2\angle BOD = 2\angle BAC$ [using Eq. (i)]

$\therefore \angle BOD = \angle BAC$ **Hence proved.**

Theorem 2 *Angles in the same segment of a circle are equal,*

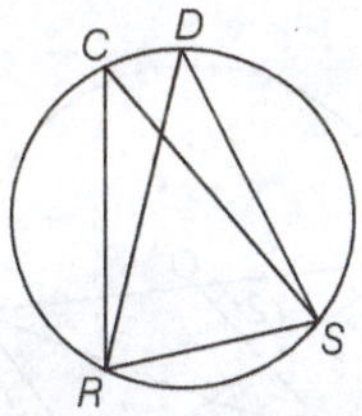

i.e. $\angle C = \angle D$ [$\because \angle C$ and $\angle D$ lie in the same segment]

Example 4. In the following figure, $CB = CD$ and $\angle CDB = 85°$, then find $\angle BAD$.

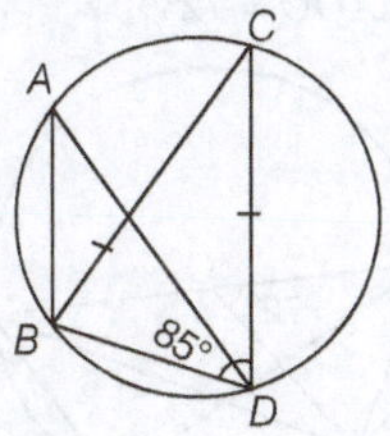

Sol. Given, $CB = CD$ and $\angle CDB = 85°$.

Now, in ΔCBD, we have

$CB = CD$ [given]

$\therefore \angle CBD = \angle CDB = 85°$ ...(i)

[$\because$ angles opposite to equal sides of a triangle are equal]

Also, $\angle CDB + \angle CBD + \angle BCD = 180°$

[by angle sum property of a triangle]

$\Rightarrow 85° + 85° + \angle BCD = 180°$ [from Eq. (i)]

$\Rightarrow 170° + \angle BCD = 180°$

$\Rightarrow \angle BCD = 180° - 170°$

$\Rightarrow \angle BCD = 10°$ ...(ii)

Now, $\angle BAD = \angle BCD$

[$\because$ angles of same segment are equal]

$\Rightarrow \angle BAD = 10°$ [from Eq. (ii)]

Hence, the required value of $\angle BAD$ is 10°.

Example 5. Bisectors of angles A, B and C of a ΔABC intersect its circumcircle at points D, E and F, respectively. Prove that the angles of the ΔDEF are $90° - \frac{1}{2}\angle A$, $90° - \frac{1}{2}\angle B$ and $90° - \frac{1}{2}\angle C$.

Sol. Here, $\angle ADE = \angle ABE$ [angles in same segment]

and $\angle ADF = \angle ACF$ [angles in same segment]

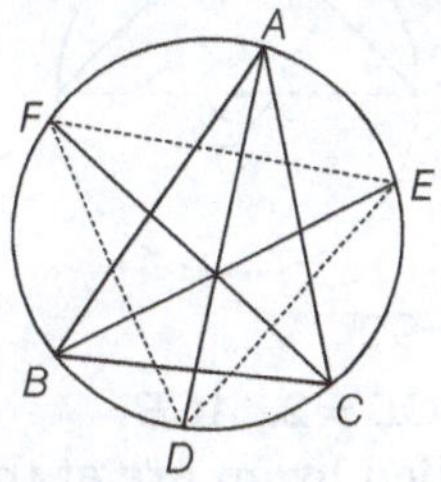

But $\angle ABE = \frac{1}{2}\angle B$ [$\because BE$ is bisector of $\angle B$]

and $\angle ACF = \frac{1}{2}\angle C$ [$\because CF$ is bisector of $\angle C$]

$\therefore \angle ADE = \frac{1}{2}\angle B$ and $\angle ADF = \frac{1}{2}\angle C$

$\therefore \angle EDF = \angle ADE + \angle ADF = \frac{1}{2}(\angle B + \angle C)$

$= \frac{1}{2}(180° - \angle A)$ [$\because \angle A + \angle B + \angle C = 180°$]

$= 90° - \frac{1}{2}\angle A$

Similarly, $\angle DEF = 90° - \frac{1}{2}\angle B$ and $\angle EFD = 90° - \frac{1}{2}\angle C$.

Hence proved.

Example 6. In the given figure, O is the centre of the circle. Prove that $a = b + c$.

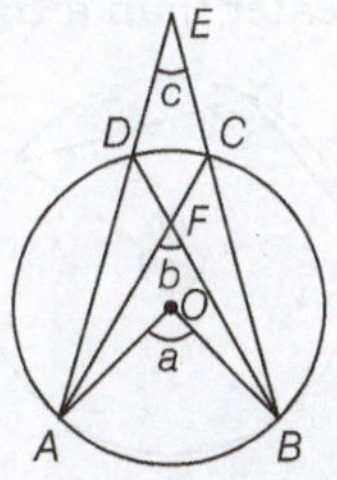

Sol. We have, $a = 2\angle ADB$

[$\because$ angle subtended by an arc at the centre is double the angle subtended by it at any other point on the remaining part of the circle]

$= 2\angle ACB$

[$\because$ angles in the same segment are equal]

$\Rightarrow \quad \angle ADB = \angle ACB = \frac{a}{2}$

Also, $\quad \angle BDE = 180° - \frac{a}{2} = \angle ACE \quad$ [$\because$ linear pair axiom]

and $\quad \angle CFD = b \quad$ [vertically opposite angles]

In quadrilateral $DECF$,

$\angle DEC + \angle ECF + \angle CFD + \angle FDE = 360°$

[$\because$ sum of all angles of a quadrilateral is 360°]

$\Rightarrow \quad c + 180° - \frac{a}{2} + b + 180° - \frac{a}{2} = 360°$

$\Rightarrow \quad c + b - a = 0 \Rightarrow a = b + c$ **Hence proved.**

Theorem 3 *The angle in a semi-circle is a right angle.*

Given A semi-circle ACB of a circle with centre O.

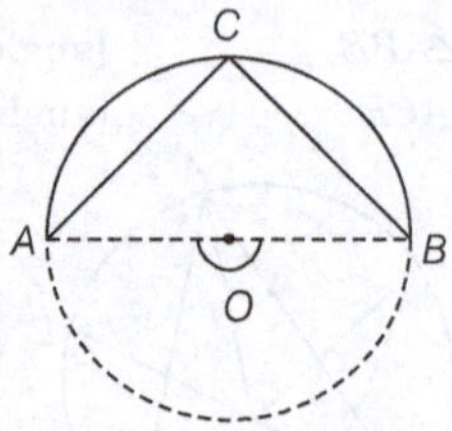

To prove $\angle ACB = 90°$

Proof Clearly, $\angle AOB = 2\angle ACB$

[$\because$ angle subtended by an arc at the centre is twice the angle subtended at the remaining circumference]

But $\quad \angle AOB = 180°$ [$\because$ AOB is a straight line]

$\therefore \quad 2\angle ACB = 180° \Rightarrow \angle ACB = 90°$

Hence, the angle in a semi-circle is 90°.

(i) In a circle, the angle in a segment greater than a semi-circle, is less than a right angle.

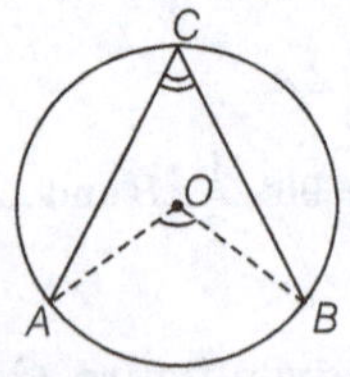

(ii) In a circle, the angle in a segment less than a semi-circle, is greater than a right angle.

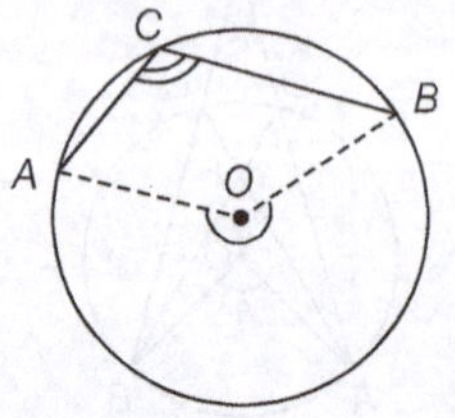

Theorem 4 **(Converse of Theorem 3)** *If an arc of a circle subtends a right angle at any point on the remaining part of the circle, then the arc is a semi-circle.*

A circle drawn with hypotenuse of a right angled triangle as diameter, passes through its opposite vertex.

Example 7. In the given figure, ABC is a semi-circle with centre O. Find the values of $\angle DEC$ and $\angle DAC$, if $\angle AED = 124°$.

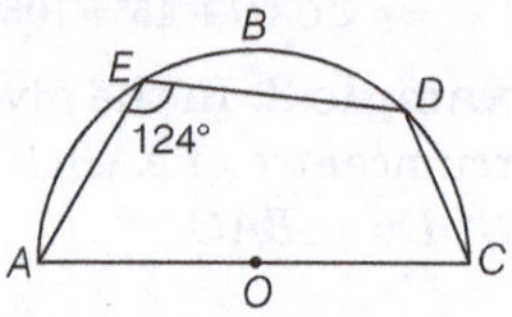

Sol. Given ABC is a semi-circle with centre O and $\angle AED = 124°$.

Construction Join AD and EC.

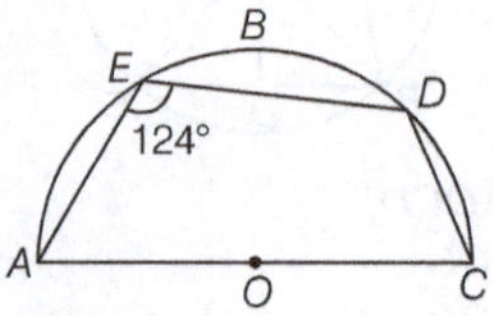

Since, the angle in a semi-circle is a right angle.

$\therefore \quad \angle AEC = 90°$

Now, $\quad \angle DEC = \angle AED - \angle AEC$

$\Rightarrow \quad \angle DEC = 124° - 90°$ [given]

$\Rightarrow \quad \angle DEC = 34°$ ...(i)

$\therefore \quad \angle DAC = \angle DEC$

[$\because$ angles in the same segment are equal]

$\Rightarrow \quad \angle DAC = 34°$ [from Eq. (i)]

Hence, the required values of $\angle DEC$ and $\angle DAC$ are 34° and 34°, respectively.

Example 8. In the figure below, O is the centre of the circle and AB is diameter. If $AC = BD$ and $\angle AOC = 72°$. Find **[ICSE 2020]**

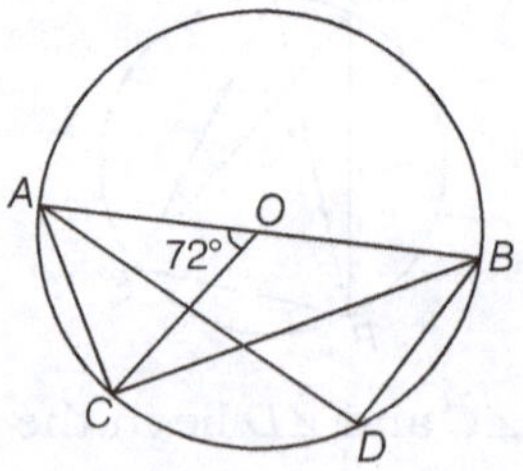

(i) $\angle ABC$ (ii) $\angle BAD$ (iii) $\angle ABD$

Sol. (a) Given, O is the centre of the circle and AB is a diameter.

If $AC = BD$ and $\angle AOC = 72°$

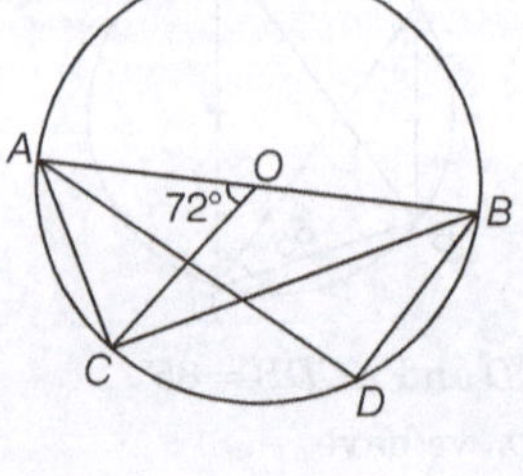

(i) $\angle ABC = \frac{1}{2} \times \angle AOC = \frac{1}{2} \times 72° = 36°$

[∵ angle subtended by an arc at the remaining circumference is half the angle subtended at the centre]

(ii) $\angle BAD = \angle ABC = 36°$

[equal chords $AC = BD$ of a circle subtend equal angles at any point on the major (or minor) arcs of the circle]

(iii) In ΔABD, $\angle ABD + \angle ADB + \angle BAD = 180°$

[angle sum property of triangle]

$\Rightarrow \quad \angle ABD + 90° + 36° = 180°$

[$\angle ADB = 90°$, angle in a semi-circle is a right angle]

$\Rightarrow \quad \angle ABD + 126° = 180°$

$\Rightarrow \quad \angle ABD = 180° - 126° \Rightarrow \angle ABD = 54°$

Example 9. In the given circle with diameter AB, find the value of x.

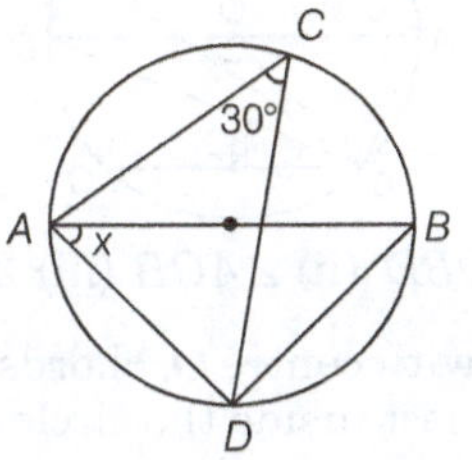

Sol. We have, $\angle ABD = \angle ACD$

[∵ angles in same segment are equal]

$\Rightarrow \quad \angle ABD = 30° \qquad$ [∵ $\angle ACD = 30°$, given]

Since, AB is a diameter of the given circle, $\angle ADB = 90°$

[∵ angle in a semi-circle = 90°]

In ΔABD, $\angle DAB + \angle ADB + \angle ABD = 180°$

[by angle sum property of a triangle]

$\Rightarrow x + 90° + 30° = 180° \Rightarrow x = 180° - 90° - 30° = 60°$

Example 10. In the given figure, O is the centre of the circle. Find the measure of $\angle BOC$.

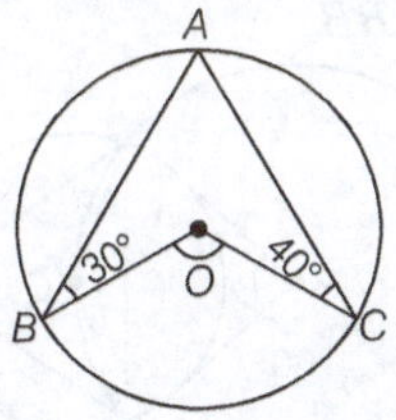

Sol. Join OA

In ΔOAC, $OC = OA$ [radii of semi-circle]

$\therefore \angle OAC = \angle ACO$

[angles opposite to equal sides of a triangle are equal]

$\angle OAC = 40°$ [∵ $\angle ACO = 40°$ given]

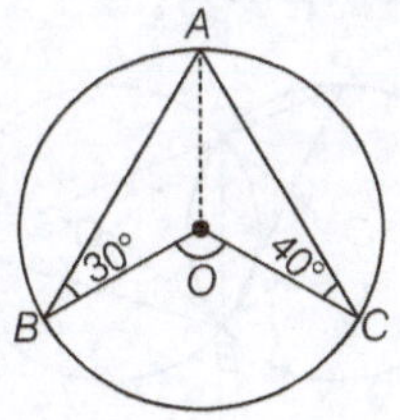

In ΔOAB, $OB = OA$ (radius of same circle)

$\therefore \angle OAB = \angle ABO$

[$\angle S$ opposite equal sides of a triangle are qual]

$\angle OAB = 30° \qquad$ [∵ $\angle ABO = 30°$, given]

$\therefore \angle BAC = \angle OAB + \angle OAC = 30° + 40° = 70°$

Now, $\angle BOC = 2\angle BAC$

(∵ angle subtended by an arc at the centre = double the angle subtended by it at any point on the remaining part of circle).

$\angle BOC = 2 \times 70° = 140°$

Example 11. In the given figure, O is the centre of the circle, $BD = OD$ and $CD \perp AB$. Find $\angle CAB$.

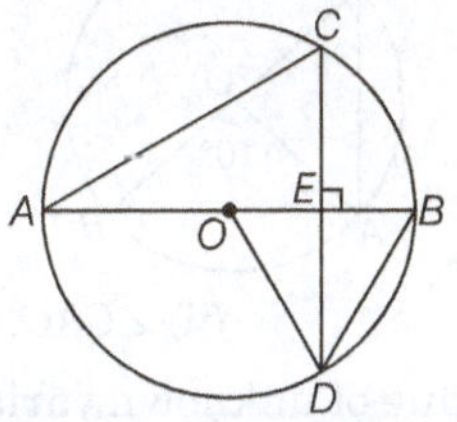

Sol. In ΔODB, we have

$BD = OD$ (given)

$\angle DOB = \angle DBO$

[∵ angles opposite to equal sides of a triangle are equal]

In ΔODB is equilateral, $\angle OBD = 60°$

Also $CD \perp AB$, so $\angle BED = 90°$

In ΔEBD, $\angle BED + \angle EBD + \angle BDE = 180°$

$\Rightarrow \quad 90° + 60° + \angle BDE = 180°$

$\Rightarrow \quad \angle BDE = 30°$

$\Rightarrow \quad \angle BDC = 30°$

But $\angle CAB = \angle BDC \qquad$ [∵ angles in same arc are equal]

$\angle CAB = 30°$

Example 12. In the adjoining figure, AB is a diameter of a circle with centre O and CD is a chord equal to the radius of the circle. AC and BD when extended intersect at E. Prove that $\angle AEB = 60°$.

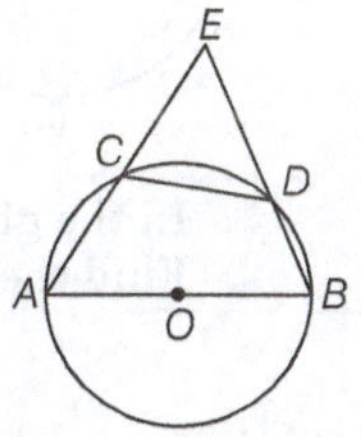

Sol. Join OC, OD and CB.

As $CD = OC = OD$ [given]

$\therefore \Delta OCD$ is an equilateral triangle.

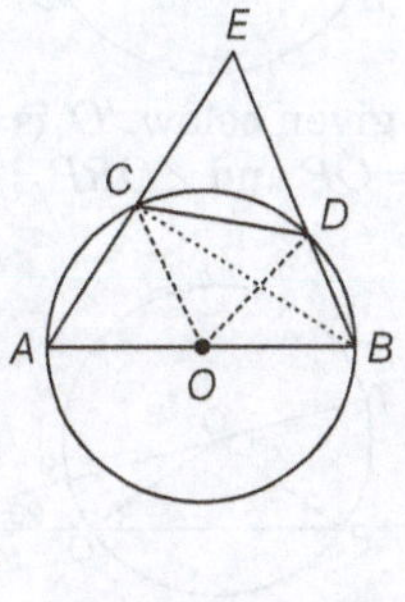

$\Rightarrow \angle COD = 60°$

$\therefore \quad \angle CBD = \frac{1}{2} \times \angle COD = \frac{1}{2} \times 60° = 30°$

[∵ the angle subtended by an arc at the centre is double the angle subtended by it at any point on the remaining part of the circle.]

As, AB is a diameter, $\angle ACB = 90°$ [∵ angle in a semi-circle]

Since, $\angle ACB$ is an exterior angle of ΔCBE.

$\therefore \quad \angle ACB = \angle CEB + \angle CBE$

[∵ exterior angle = sum of two interior opposite angles]

$\Rightarrow \quad 90° = \angle CEB + 30° \quad$ [∵ $\angle CBE = \angle CBD = 30°$]

$\Rightarrow \quad \angle CEB = 60°$

$\Rightarrow \quad \angle AEB = 60°$ **Hence proved.**

Exercise 15.1

1. In the given figure, O is the centre of circle and $\angle AOB = 110°$. Calculate

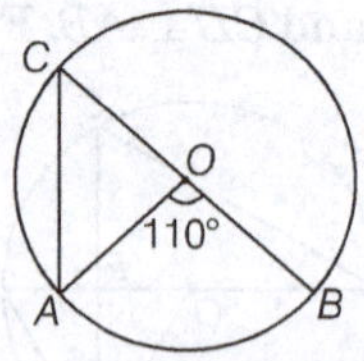

(i) $\angle ACO$ (ii) $\angle CAO$.

2. Find the value of unknown variables in the following

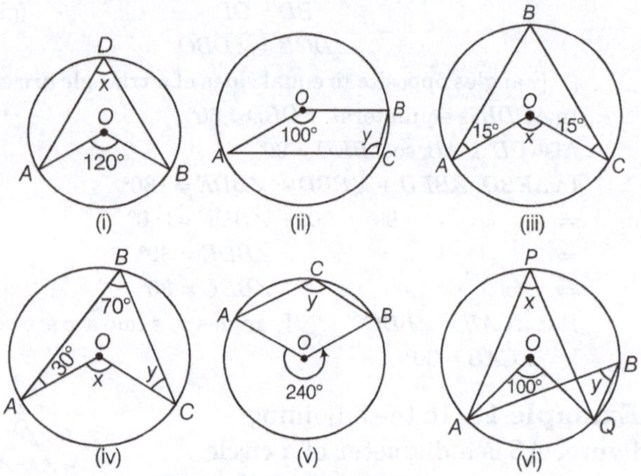

3. In the given figure, O is the centre of the circle. Find the measure of $\angle BOC$.

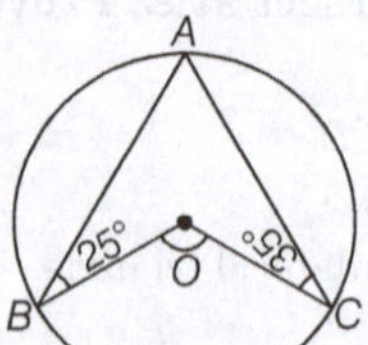

4. In the figure given below, 'O' is the centre of the circle. If $QR = OP$ and $\angle ORP = 20°$. Find the value of 'x'. **[ICSE 2018]**

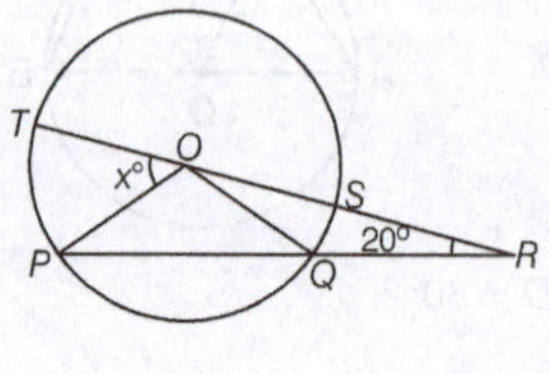

5. In the given figure, AD is a diameter and O is the centre of the circle AD is parallel to BC and $\angle CBD = 32°$.

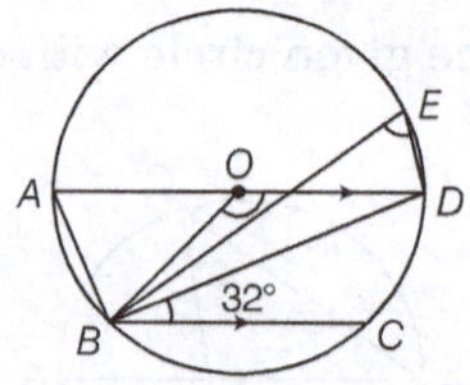

Find (i) $\angle OBD$ (ii) $\angle AOB$ (iii) $\angle BED$ **[ICSE 2016]**

6. In a circle with centre O, chords AB and CD of the circle intersect inside the circle at E. Prove that: $\angle AOC + \angle BOD = 2\angle AEC$

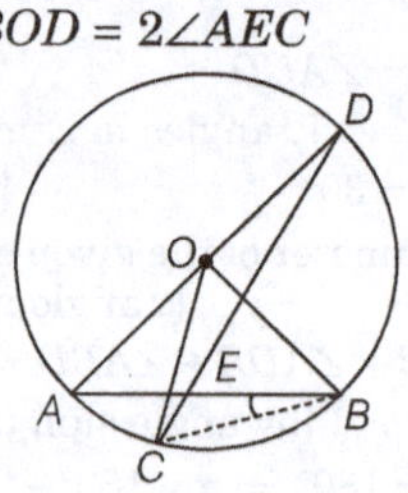

7. In the given figure, the two circles with centres P and Q intersect at A and B. Q lies on the circumference of the bigger circle. If $\angle APB = 60°$, then find $\angle ARB$.

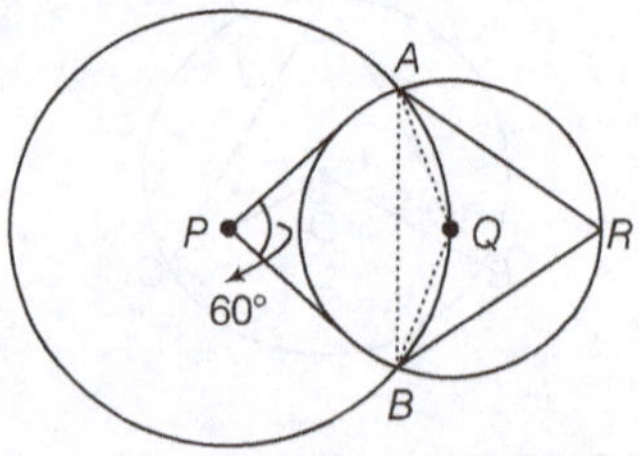

8. Two congruent circles intersect each other at points A and B. Through A, any line segment PAQ is drawn so that P, Q lie on the two circles. Prove that $BP = BQ$.

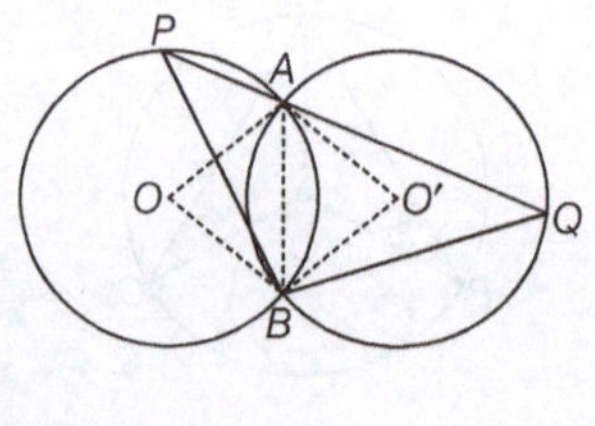

9. In the given figure, AB is a diameter of the circle with centre O and $CD \parallel BA$. If $\angle CAB = x$, find the values of
(i) $\angle COB$
(ii) $\angle ODC$
(iii) $\angle DAC$
(iv) $\angle ADC$

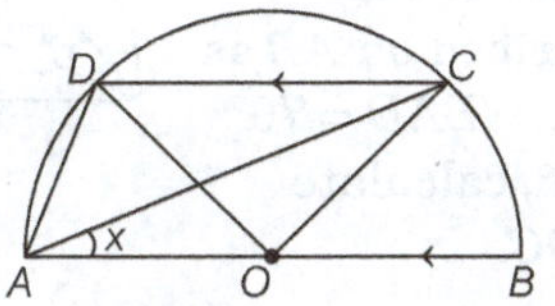

10. Given that $\angle AEC = 50°$, $AB = BC$, AOE is the diameter, find $\angle AOB$. Hence, show that $BO \parallel CE$.

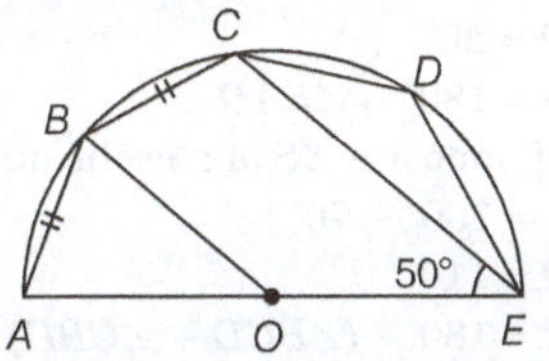

11. AC and BD are chords of a circle that bisect each other. Prove that
(i) AC and BD are diameters.
(ii) $ABCD$ is a rectangle.

12. In the given figure, ABC is a triangle in which $\angle BAC = 30°$. Show that BC equals the radius of the circumcircle of ΔABC, whose centre is O.

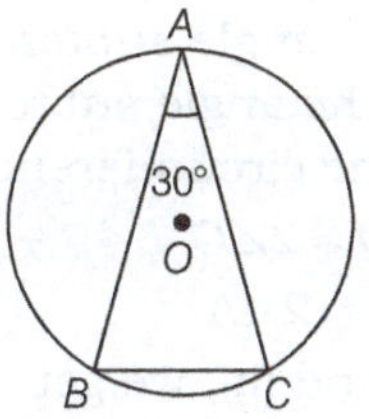

13. In the following figure, A, B, C and D are four points on a circle. AC and BD intersect at a point E. If $\angle BEC = 130°$ and $\angle ECD = 20°$, find $\angle BAC$.

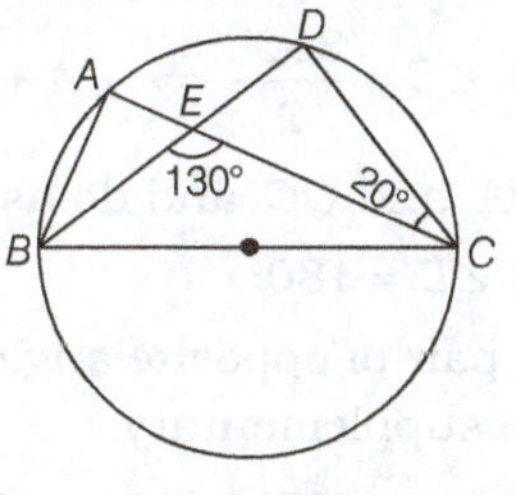

(i) Show that AC is the diameter. (ii) Find $\angle ACB$.

14. In the given figure, $\angle BAD = 65°$, $\angle ABD = 70°$ and $\angle BDC = 45°$.

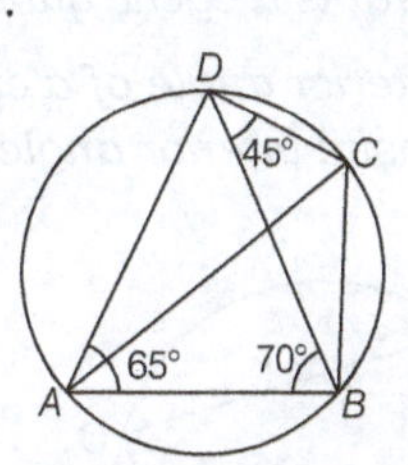

(i) Show that AC is the diameter. (ii) Find $\angle ACB$.

Cyclic Properties of Circles

Cyclic Quadrilateral

A quadrilateral inscribed in a circle, is called cyclic quadrilateral.

Or

A quadrilateral is called cyclic quadrilateral, if and only if its all vertices lie on the circumference of a circle.

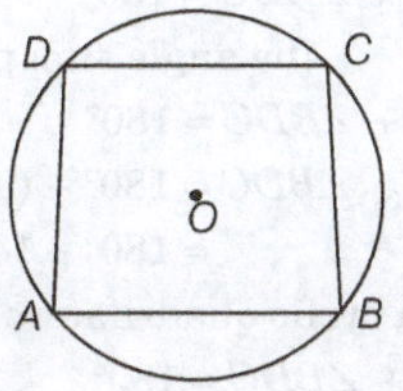

Concyclic Points

The points which lie on the circumference of the same circle, are called concyclic points.

In the above figure, A, B, C and D are the concyclic points.

Note The cyclic quadrilateral $ABCD$ (say) has two pairs of opposite angles $\angle A$, $\angle C$ and $\angle B$, $\angle D$.

Properties of Cyclic Quadrilateral

Its properties are shown in terms of theorems as follow

Theorem 1 *The opposite angles of a cyclic quadrilateral are supplementary.*

Given $ABCD$ is a cyclic quadrilateral in a circle with centre O.

To prove $\angle A + \angle C = 180°$ and $\angle B + \angle D = 180°$.

Construction Join OB and OD.

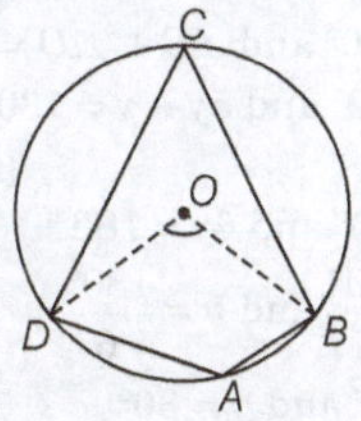

Proof We know that, angle subtended by an arc at the centre is twice the angle subtended at the remaining part of the circumference of the circle.

$\therefore \quad \angle BOD = 2\angle C \quad \text{...(i)}$

and $\quad$ reflex $\angle BOD = 2\angle A \quad \text{...(ii)}$

On adding Eqs. (i) and (ii), we get

$$\angle BOD + \text{Reflex } \angle BOD = 2\angle C + 2\angle A$$

$$\Rightarrow \quad 360° = 2(\angle A + \angle C)$$

[$\because$ sum of angles around a point is 360°]

$$\Rightarrow \quad \angle A + \angle C = \frac{360°}{2} \Rightarrow \angle A + \angle C = 180°$$

Similarly, join OA and OC and do as above, we get

$$\angle B + \angle D = 180°$$

Hence, the each pair of opposite angles of a cyclic quadrilateral are supplementary.

Theorem 2 *(Converse of Theorem 1) If a pair of opposite angles of a quadrilateral is supplementary, then the quadrilateral is a cyclic quadrilateral.*

Theorem 3 *The exterior angle of a cyclic quadrilateral is equal to the opposite interior angle, i.e.* $\angle CBE = \angle ADC$.

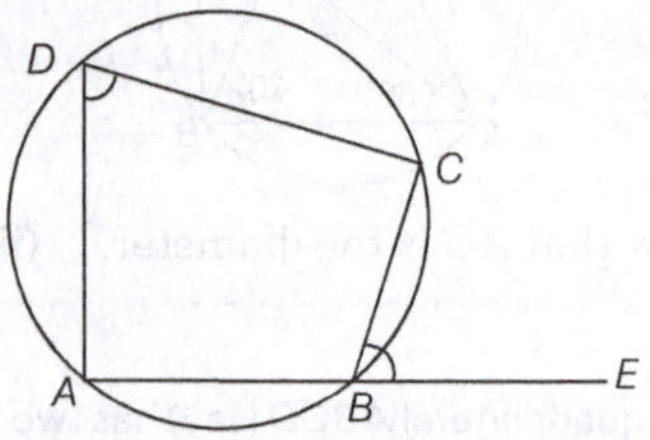

Example 13. In the given figure, if $ABCD$ is a cyclic quadrilateral, then find the measure of each of its angles.

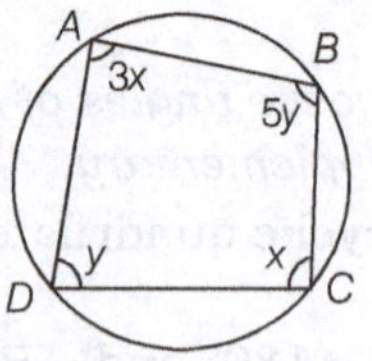

Sol. We know that the opposite angles of a cyclic quadrilateral are supplementary.

$\therefore \quad \angle A + \angle C = 180°$ and $\angle B + \angle D = 180°$

$\Rightarrow \quad 3x + x = 180°$ and $5y + y = 180°$

[from the given figure]

$\Rightarrow \quad 4x = 180°$ and $6y = 180°$

$\Rightarrow \quad x = \frac{180°}{4}$ and $y = \frac{180°}{6}$

$\therefore \quad x = 45°$ and $y = 30°$

Now, $\quad \angle A = 3x = 3 \times 45° = 135°$

$\angle B = 5y = 5 \times 30° = 150°$

$\angle C = x = 45°$ and $\angle D = y = 30°$

Hence, the required angles of the cyclic quadrilateral are 135°, 150°, 45° and 30°.

Example 14. In the given figure, C and D are points on the circumference of the semi-circle described on AB as diameter. Given, $\angle BAD = 70°$ and $\angle DBC = 30°$, calculate $\angle ABD$ and $\angle BDC$.

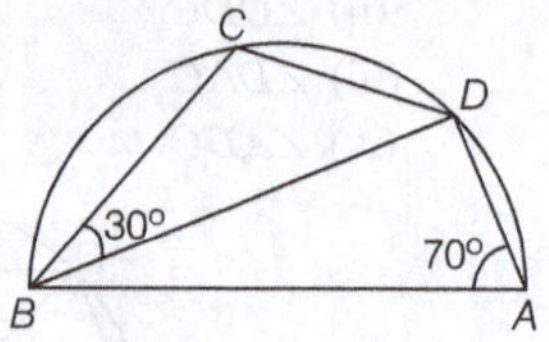

Sol. $\angle BDA = 90°$ [angle in a semi-circle = 90°]

Again $\angle ABD = 180° - (\angle ADB + \angle BAD)$

$= 180 - 90 - 70$

$\angle ABD = 20°$

$\angle BCD = 180° - \angle BAD$

[sum of opposite $\angle S$ of a cyclic quadrilateral = 180°]

$= 180° - 70°$

$\angle BCD = 110°$

$\angle BDC = 180° - (\angle BCD + \angle CBD)$

$= 180° - (110° + 30°) = 40°$

Hence, $\angle ABD = 20°$ and $\angle BDC = 40°$

Example 15. In the given figure, $\angle DBC = 58°$. BD is a diameter of the circle.

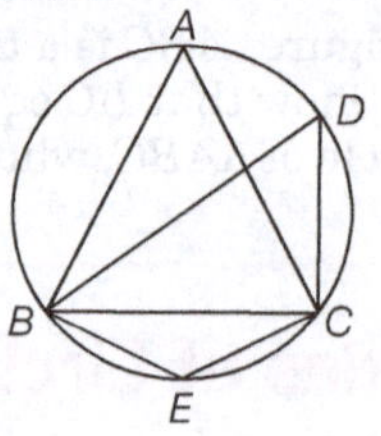

Calculate

(i) $\angle BDC$ (ii) $\angle BEC$ (iii) $\angle BAC$. **[ICSE 2014]**

Sol. Given, $\angle DBC = 58°$

(i) Since, BD is a diameter of a circle.

$\therefore \quad \angle BCD = 90°$ [$\because$ angle in a semi-circle is 90°]

In ΔBCD, we have

$\angle DBC + \angle BCD + \angle BDC = 180°$

[by angle sum property of a triangle]

$\Rightarrow \quad 58° + 90° + \angle BDC = 180°$

$\therefore \quad \angle BDC = 180° - (90° + 58°)$

$= 180° - 148° = 32°$

(ii) Since, $BECD$ is a cyclic quadrilateral.

$\therefore \quad \angle BEC + \angle BDC = 180°$

[$\because$ sum of opposite angles in a cyclic quadrilateral is 180°]

$\Rightarrow \quad \angle BEC = 180° - 32° = 148°$

(iii) Now, $\quad \angle BAC = \angle BDC$

[$\because$ angles in a same segment are equal]

$\therefore \quad \angle BAC = 32°$ [$\because \angle BDC = 32°$]

Example 16. In the given figure, O is the centre of the circle. If $\angle BOC = 126°$, then find $\angle BAC$, $\angle BDC$ and $\angle OBC$.

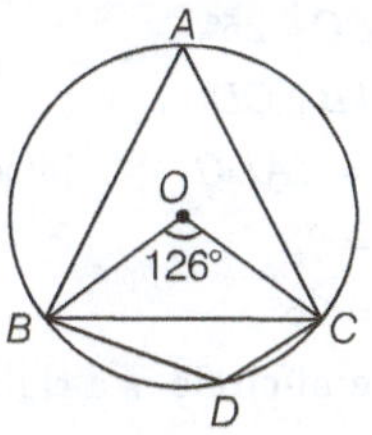

Sol. Given, $\angle BOC = 126°$

$\therefore \quad \angle BAC = \frac{1}{2}\angle BOC$

[$\because$ angle subtended by an arc at the remaining circumference is half the angle subtended at the centre]

$\Rightarrow \quad \angle BAC = \frac{1}{2} \times 126° = 63°$

Also, $\angle BDC + \angle BAC = 180°$

[$\because$ sum of opposite angles of a cyclic quadrilateral is 180°]

$\Rightarrow \quad \angle BDC = 180° - 63° = 117°$

In ΔOBC, we have $OB = OC$ [radii of same circle]

$\therefore \quad \angle OBC = \angle OCB$ ...(i)

Now, $\angle BOC + \angle OBC + \angle OCB = 180°$

[by angle sum property of a triangle]

$\Rightarrow \quad \angle OBC + \angle OCB = 180° - 126° = 54°$

$\Rightarrow \quad 2\angle OBC = 54°$ [from Eq. (i)]

$\therefore \quad \angle OBC = 27°$

Hence, $\angle BAC = 63°$, $\angle BDC = 117°$ and $\angle OBC = 27°$.

Example 17. In the given figure, $ABCD$ is a cyclic quadrilateral, O is the centre of the circle. If $\angle BOD = 160°$, then find the measure of $\angle BPD$ and $\angle BCD$.

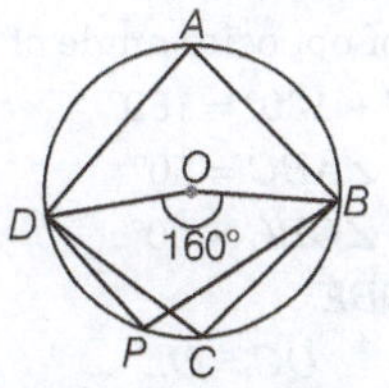

Sol. Consider the arc BCD of the circle. This arc makes an angle $\angle BOD = 160°$ at the centre of the circle and $\angle BAD$ at a point A on the circumference.

$\therefore \angle BAD = \frac{1}{2}\angle BOD = \frac{160°}{2} = 80°$

Since, $ABPD$ is a cyclic quadrilateral.

$\therefore \quad \angle BAD + \angle BPD = 180°$

$\Rightarrow \quad 80° + \angle BPD = 180°$

$\Rightarrow \quad \angle BPD = 100°$

$\Rightarrow \quad \angle BCD = 100°$

[$\because \angle BPD$ and $\angle BCD$ are angles in the same segment, therefore $\angle BCD = \angle BPD$]

Example 18. In the given figure, O is the centre of the circle. The angle subtended by the arc SRQ at the centre is 140°. If SR is produced to T, then determine the values of $\angle SPQ$ and $\angle QRT$.

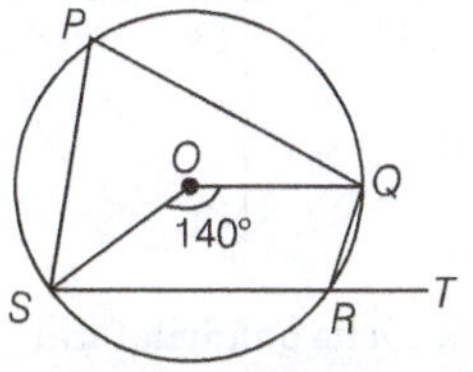

Sol. Given, $\angle SOQ = 140° \Rightarrow \angle SPQ = \frac{1}{2}\angle SOQ$

[$\because$ angle subtended by an arc at the centre is twice the angle subtended at the remaining part of the circumference of the circle]

$\Rightarrow \quad \angle SPQ = \frac{1}{2} \times 140° \Rightarrow \angle SPQ = 70°$ ...(i)

We know that, exterior angle of a cyclic quadrilateral is equal to the opposite interior angle.

$\therefore \quad \angle QRT = \angle SPQ = 70°$ [from Eq. (i)]

Hence, the required value of $\angle SPQ$ and $\angle QRT$ are 70° and 70°.

Example 19. In the given figure, $ABCDE$ is a pentagon inscribed in a circle such that AC is a diameter and side $BC \parallel AE$. If $\angle BAC = 50°$, then find giving reasons

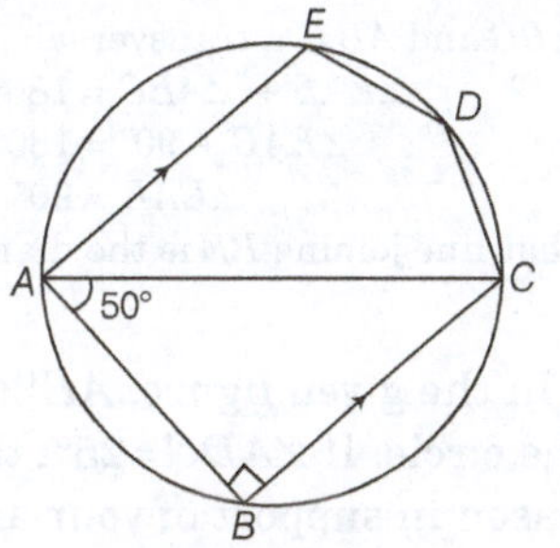

(i) $\angle ACB$ (ii) $\angle EDC$

(iii) $\angle BEC$ [ICSE 2019]

Hence, prove that BE is also a diameter.

Sol.

(i) Given, $\angle BAC = 50°$ and AC is a diameter of a circle.

$\therefore \Delta ABC$ is a right angled triangle at B,

i.e. $\angle ABC = 90°$.

We know that the sum of all angles of a triangle is 180°.

$\therefore \quad \angle CAB + \angle ABC + \angle BCA = 180°$

$\Rightarrow \quad 50° + 90° + \angle BCA = 180°$

$\Rightarrow \quad \angle BCA = 180° - (90° + 50°)$

$= 180° - 140° = 40°$

(ii) Also, $BC \parallel AE$

$\therefore \quad \angle EAB + \angle ABC = 180°$

$\Rightarrow \quad \angle EAO + 50° + 90° = 180°$

$\Rightarrow \quad \angle EAO = 180° - 140° = 40°$

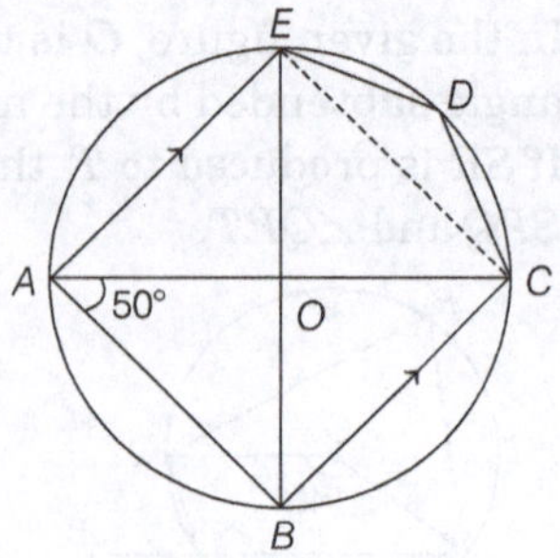

Here, $AEDC$ is a cyclic quadrilateral.

$\therefore \quad \angle EAO + \angle EDC = 180°$

$\Rightarrow \quad 40° + \angle EDC = 180°$

$\Rightarrow \quad \angle EDC = 140°$

(iii) Since, AC is a diameter of a circle.

Therefore, $\angle AEC = 90° \Rightarrow \angle ECB = 90°$

[$\because$ sum of all angle of a quadrilateral is 360°]

It is clear that $ABCE$ is a square.

$\angle BOC = 180° - \angle AOB$ [linear pair]

Now, $\angle AOB = 2\angle ACB$

$\angle BOC = 180° - 80° = 100°$

$\angle BEC = \frac{1}{2} \times \angle BOC$

$= \frac{1}{2} \times 100° = 50°$

[angle at the centre is double the angle at the circumference]

Since, $AE \parallel BC$ and AB is a transversal.

$\therefore \quad \angle EAB + \angle ABC = 180°$

$\Rightarrow \quad \angle EAB + 90° = 180°$

$\Rightarrow \quad \angle EAB = 90°$

It implies that line joining BE is the diameter of the circle. **Hence proved.**

Example 20. In the given figure, $AB \parallel CD$ and O is the centre of the circle. If $\angle ADC = 25°$, then find $\angle AEB$. Give reason in support of your answer.

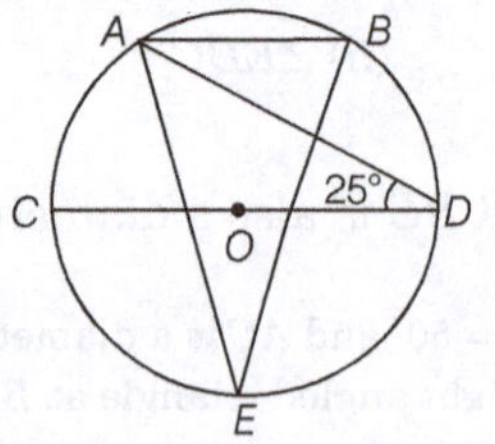

Sol. Given, $AB \parallel CD$, O is the centre of the circle and $\angle ADC = 25°$.

Join AC and CE.

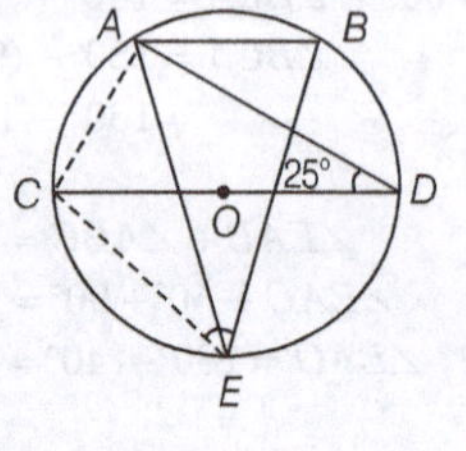

We know that, angles in the same segment are equal.

$\therefore \quad \angle AEC = \angle ADC$

But $\quad \angle ADC = 25°$ [given]

$\therefore \quad \angle AEC = 25°$

$\because \quad AB \parallel CD$ [given]

$\therefore \quad \angle BAD = \angle ADC$ [alternate interior angles]

But $\quad \angle ADC = 25°$ [given]

$\therefore \quad \angle BAD = 25°$

Also, angle in a semi-circle is a right angle.

$\therefore \quad \angle CAD = 90°$

In cyclic quadrilateral $ABEC$, $\angle CAB + \angle CEB = 180°$

[$\because$ sum of opposite angles in a cyclic quadrilateral is 180°]

$\Rightarrow \angle CAD + \angle BAD + \angle AEC + \angle AEB = 180°$

$\Rightarrow \quad 90° + 25° + 25° + \angle AEB = 180°$

$\Rightarrow \quad 140° + \angle AEB = 180°$

$\therefore \quad \angle AEB = 180° - 140°$

$= 40°$

Example 21. In the given figure, AB is a diameter of the circle with centre O. If $\angle ADC = 130°$ and chord BC = chord BE, then find $\angle CBE$.

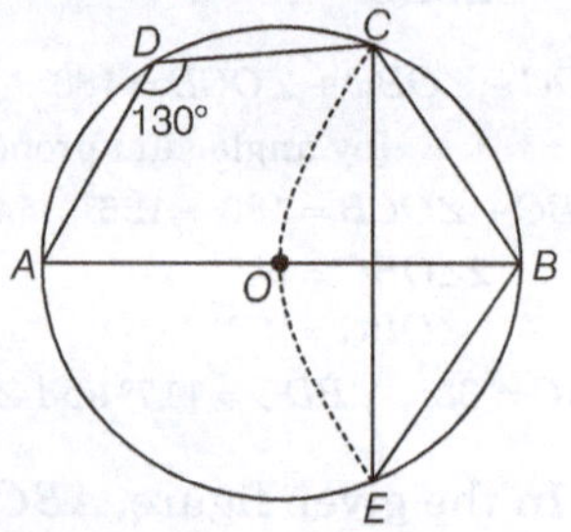

Sol. Joint OC and OE.

$ABCD$ is a cyclic quadrilateral,

$\angle ABC + \angle ADC = 180°$

[sum of opposite angle of a cyclic quadrilateral]

$\angle ABC + 130° = 180°$

$\angle ABC = 50°$

i.e. $\quad \angle OBC = 50°$

In ΔOBC and ΔOBE,

$OC = OE$ [radii of same circle]

$BC = BE$ [given]

$OB = OB$ [common]

$\therefore \quad \Delta OBC \cong \Delta OBE$ [SSS rule of congruency]

$\angle OBC = \angle OBE$

$\angle OBC = 50°$

$\therefore \quad \angle CBE = \angle OBC + \angle OBE$

$= 50 + 50 = 100°$

Example 22. In the given figure, AD is the diameter of the circle with centre O. Chords AB, BC and CD are equal.

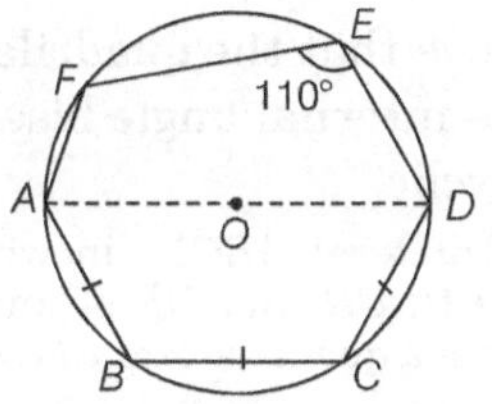

If $\angle DEF = 110°$, then calculate

(i) $\angle AEF$ (ii) $\angle FAB$.

Sol. Join AE, OB and OC.

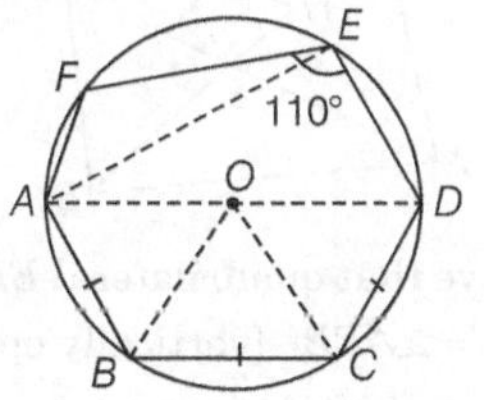

(i) Since, angle in a semi-circle is a right angle.

$\therefore \quad \angle AED = 90°$

Now, $\angle AEF = \angle DEF - \angle AED = 110° - 90° = 20°$

(ii) As, $AB = BC = CD$

$\therefore$ arc AB = arc BC = arc CD

$\Rightarrow \quad \angle AOB = \angle BOC = \angle COD$

[$\because$ equal arcs subtend equal angles at centre]

But AOD is a straight line.

$\therefore \quad \angle AOB = \frac{1}{3}\angle AOD$

$\therefore \quad \angle AOB = \frac{1}{3} \times 180° = 60°$

$\because \quad OA = OB$ [radii of same circle]

$\therefore \quad \angle OAB = \angle OBA$

[$\because$ angles opposite to equal sides of a triangle are equal]

$\therefore \quad \angle OAB = \frac{1}{2}(180° - \angle AOB)$

[by angle sum property of a triangle]

$= \frac{1}{2}(180° - 60°) = \frac{1}{2} \times 120° = 60°$

In a cyclic quadrilateral $ADEF$,

$\angle FAD + \angle DEF = 180° \Rightarrow \angle FAD + 110° = 180°$

$\Rightarrow \quad \angle FAD = 180° - 110°$

$\therefore \quad \angle FAD = 70°$

Now, $\angle FAB = \angle FAD + \angle OAB = 70° + 60° = 130°$

Example 23. In the given figure, if $\angle ACE = 43°$ and $\angle CAF = 62°$, then find the values of a, b and c.

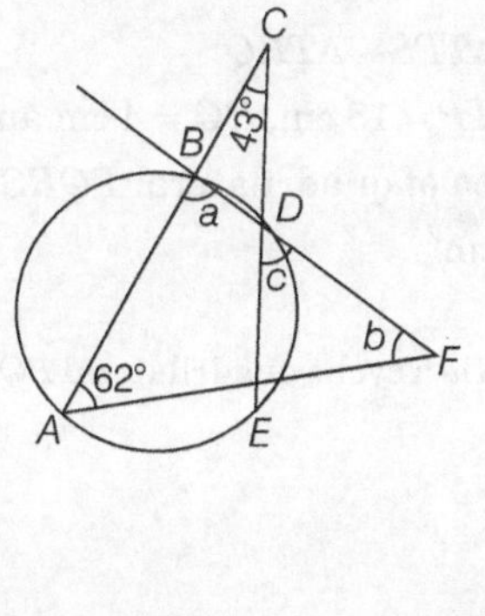

Sol. In ΔACE, we have

$\angle AEC + \angle EAC + \angle ACE = 180°$

[by angle sum property of a triangle]

$\Rightarrow \quad \angle AEC + 62° + 43° = 180°$

$\Rightarrow \quad \angle AEC = 180° - 105° = 75°$

Since, points A, B, D and E are the points on a circle, so quadrilateral $ABDE$ is a cyclic quadrilateral.

We know that, sum of opposite angles of a cyclic quadrilateral is 180°.

$\therefore \quad \angle EAB + \angle EDB = 180°$

$\therefore \quad \angle EDB = 180° - 62° = 118°$

and $\quad \angle ABD + \angle AED = 180°$

$\Rightarrow \quad a = 180° - 75° = 105°$ [$\because \angle AEC = \angle AED = 75°$]

Since, BF is a straight line.

$\therefore \quad \angle BDE + \angle EDF = 180°$

$\Rightarrow \quad 118° + c = 180°$

$\Rightarrow \quad c = 180° - 118° = 62°$

In ΔDEF, we have

$\angle DEF + \angle EFD + \angle FDE = 180°$ [by angle sum property]

$\Rightarrow \quad 105° + b + 62° = 180°$

[$\because$ exterior angle of a cyclic quadrilateral is equal to the opposite interior angle, i.e. $\angle DEF = a = 105°$]

$\Rightarrow \quad b = 180° - (105° + 62°) = 180° - 167° = 13°$

Hence, $a = 105°$, $b = 13°$ and $c = 62°$.

Example 24. The given figure shows a pentagon, inscribed in a circle with centre O. Given, $AB = BC = CD$ and $\angle ABC = 132°$.

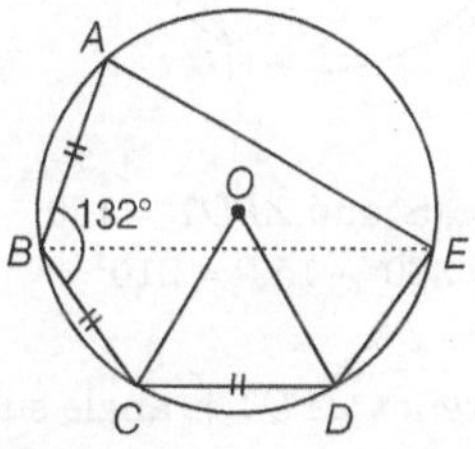

Calculate the value of

(i) $\angle AEB$ (ii) $\angle AED$ (iii) $\angle COD$.

Sol.

(i) Join CE.

Since, $ABCE$ is a cyclic quadrilateral,

$\angle AEC + 132° = 180°$

[$\because$ sum of opposite angles of a cyclic quadrilateral is 180°]

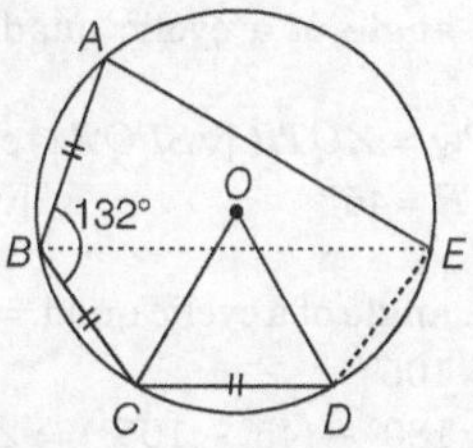

$\Rightarrow \quad \angle AEC = 180° - 132° = 48°$

$\Rightarrow \quad \angle AEB + \angle BEC = 48°$ ...(i) [from figure]

$\therefore \quad \angle AOB = \angle BOC$

[$\because AB = BC$ and equal chords subtend equal angles at the centre]

$\Rightarrow \quad \frac{1}{2}\angle AOB = \frac{1}{2}\angle BOC \Rightarrow \angle AEB = \angle BEC$

[$\because$ angle subtended by an arc at the center is double the angle subtended by it any point on remaining part of circle]

$\therefore \quad 2\angle AEB = 48°$

$\Rightarrow \quad \angle AEB = \frac{1}{2} \times 48° = 24°$

(ii) $\angle CED = \angle AEB$

[$\because CD = AB$ and equal chords subtend equal angles in the same segment]

$\Rightarrow \angle CED = 24°$

$\therefore \angle AED = \angle AEC + \angle CED = 48° + 24° = 72°$

(iii) $\angle COD = 2\angle CED$ [$\because$ angle at the centre = double the angle at the remaining part of the circle]

$\therefore \angle COD = 2 \times 24° = 48°$

Example 25. In the given figure, O is the centre of the circle. If $\angle SPQ = 45°$ and $\angle POT = 150°$, then find the measures of

(i) $\angle PST$ (ii) $\angle PUT$ (iii) $\angle QTR$ (iv) $\angle QRT$

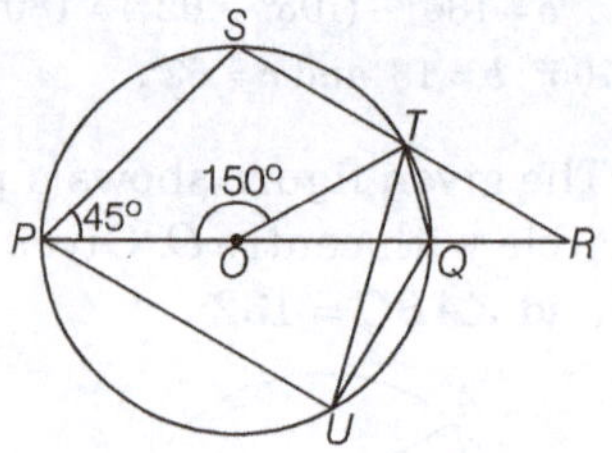

Sol.

(i) Given, $\angle SPQ = 45°$ and $\angle POT = 150°$

Reflex $\angle POT = 360° - 150° = 210°$

$\therefore \angle PST = \frac{1}{2}$ of reflex $\angle POT$ [$\because$ angle subtended by major arc POT at the center = double the angle subtended by it at any point on the remaining part of circle]

$\Rightarrow \quad \angle PST = \frac{1}{2} \times 210 = 105°$

(ii) The sum of opposite angles of a cyclic quadrilateral is 180°,

$\angle PST + \angle PUT = 180°$

$\Rightarrow \quad \angle PUT = 180° - 105°$

$\Rightarrow \quad \angle PUT = 75°$

(iii) As an exterior angle of a cyclic quadrilateral = interior opposite angle

$\Rightarrow \quad \angle SPQ = \angle QTR$ [$\because SPQT$ is cyclic quadrilateral]

$\Rightarrow \quad \angle QTR = 45°$ [$\because \angle SPQ = 45°$ given]

(iv) $\angle TQR = \angle PST$

[ext. angle of a cyclic quad. = interior opp angle]

$\Rightarrow \quad \angle TQR = 105°$ [$\because \angle PST = 105°$]

$\therefore \quad \angle QRT = 180° - (45° + 105°) \Rightarrow \angle QRT = 30°$

Example 26. Prove that the quadrilateral formed (if possible) by the internal angle bisectors of any quadrilateral is cyclic.

Sol. Given, a quadrilateral $ABCD$ in which internal angle bisectors AF, BH, CH and DF of angles A, B, C and D respectively form a quadrilateral $EFGH$.

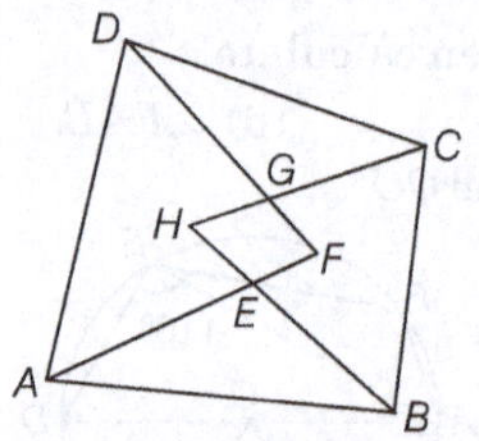

We need to prove that quadrilateral $EFGH$ is cyclic.

$\angle HEF = \angle AEB$ [vertically opposite angles] ...(i)

In ΔAEB,

$\angle AEB + \frac{1}{2}\angle A + \frac{1}{2}\angle B = 180°$

[$\because AE$ is bisector of $\angle A$ and BE is bisector of $\angle B$]

$\Rightarrow \quad \angle AEB = 180° - \frac{1}{2}(\angle A + \angle B)$ ...(ii)

From Eqs. (i) and (ii), we get

$\angle HEF = 180° - \frac{1}{2}(\angle A + \angle B)$ ...(iii)

Similarly, $\angle HGF = 180° - \frac{1}{2}(\angle C + \angle D)$ ...(iv)

On adding Eqs. (iii) and (iv), we get

$\angle HEF + \angle HGF = 360° - \frac{1}{2}(\angle A + \angle B + \angle C + \angle D)$

$= 360° - \frac{1}{2} \times 360°$ [sum of angles of a quadrilateral]

$= 360° - 180° = 180°$

Therefore, $EFGH$ is a cyclic quadrilateral.

[$\because$ sum of a pair of opposite angles is 180°]

Hence proved.

Example 27. In the given figure, $PQRS$ is a cyclic quadrilateral. PQ and SR produced meet at T.

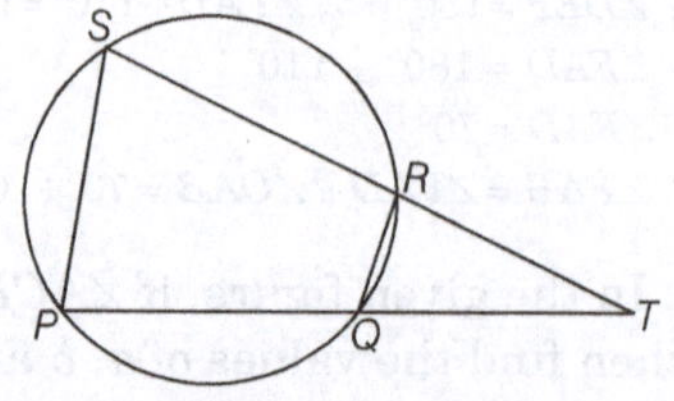

(i) Prove that $\Delta TPS \sim \Delta TRQ$

(ii) Find SP, if $TP = 18$ cm, $RQ = 4$ cm and $TR = 6$ cm.

(iii) Find the area of quadrilateral $PQRS$, if area of $\Delta PTS = 27 \text{ cm}^2$. **[ICSE 2016]**

Sol.

(i) Given, $PQRS$ is a cyclic quadrilateral PQ and SR meet at T on product.

In ΔTPS and ΔTRQ,

$\angle PSR = \angle RQT$ [$\because$ $PQRS$ is a cyclic quadrilateral, exterior angle is equal to the oppoiste interior angle]

$\Rightarrow$ $\angle PTS = \angle QTR$ [common in both triangles]

$\Rightarrow$ $\Delta TPS \sim \Delta TRQ$

(ii) As $\Delta TPS \sim \Delta TRQ$

$$\frac{SP}{QR} = \frac{TP}{TR} = \frac{SP}{4} = \frac{18}{6} \Rightarrow SP = 12\,\text{cm}$$

(iii) As the ratio of the areas of two similar triangles is equal to the ratio of the squares of any two corresponding sides,

$$\frac{\text{Area of } \Delta TRQ}{\text{Area of } \Delta TPS} = \frac{TR^2}{TP^2}$$

$$\Rightarrow \left(\frac{TR}{TP}\right)^2 = \left(\frac{6}{18}\right)^2 \Rightarrow \frac{\text{Area of } \Delta TRQ}{27\text{ cm}^2} = \left(\frac{1}{3}\right)^2$$

Area of $\Delta TRQ = 3\,\text{cm}^2$

$\therefore$ Area of quadrilateral $PQRS$ = Area of ΔTPS − Area of ΔTRQ

$= 27\text{cm}^2 - 3\text{ cm}^2 = 24\text{ cm}^2$

Exercise 15.2

1. In the given figure, AB is the diameter of a circle with centre O and $\angle BCD = 120°$.

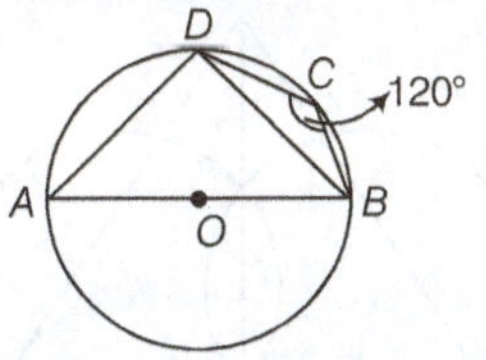

Find (i) $\angle BAD$ (ii) $\angle DBA$

2. If O is the centre of the circle, find the value of x in the following figures (using the given information)

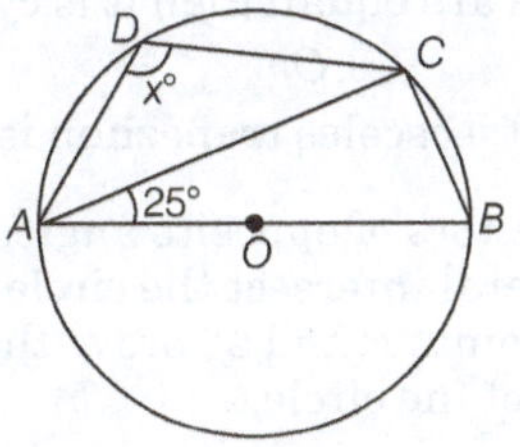

3. In the given figure, if $\angle BAD = 65°$, $\angle ABD = 70°$ and $\angle BDC = 45°$. [ICSE 2013]

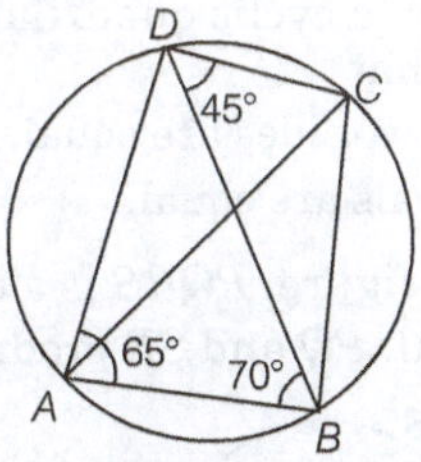

Prove that AC is a diameter of the circle and find $\angle ACB$.

4. In the given figure, AB is a diameter of the circle and C, D, E are any three points on the semi-circle. Find the value of $\angle ACD + \angle BED$.

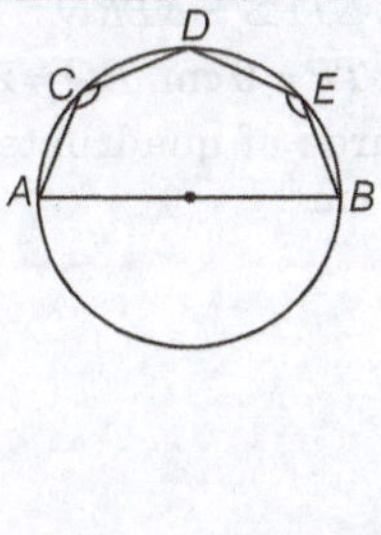

5. In the given figure, AC is a diameter of the circle. If $AB = BC$ and $\angle AED = 118°$, then find
(i) $\angle DEC$ (ii) $\angle DAB$

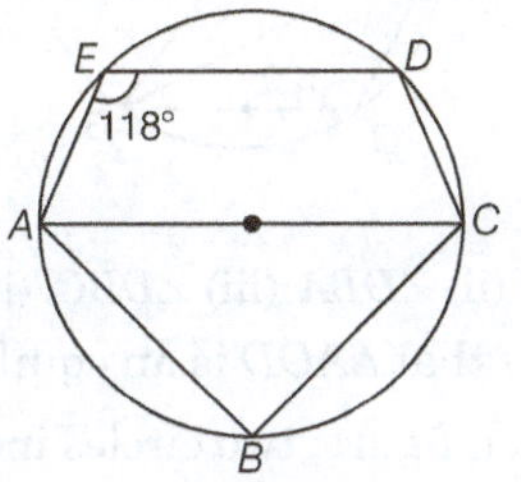

6. $PQRS$ is a cyclic quadrilateral. Given $\angle QPS = 73°$, $\angle PQS = 55°$ and $\angle PSR = 82°$, calculate

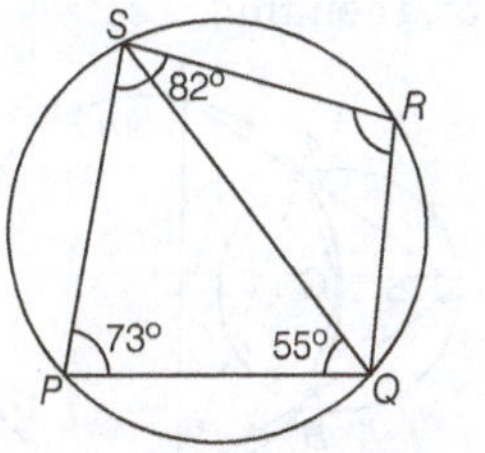

(i) $\angle QRS$ (ii) $\angle RQS$ (iii) $\angle PRQ$ [ICSE 2018]

7. In the given figure, O is centre of the circle. If $\angle BAD = 75°$ and $BC = CD$, then find

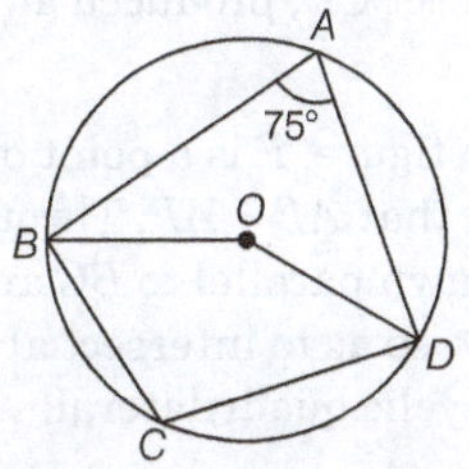

(i) $\angle BOD$ (ii) $\angle BCD$
(iii) $\angle BOC$ (iv) $\angle OBD$

8. In the given figure, AB is parallel to DC, $\angle BCE = 80°$ and $\angle BAC = 25°$.

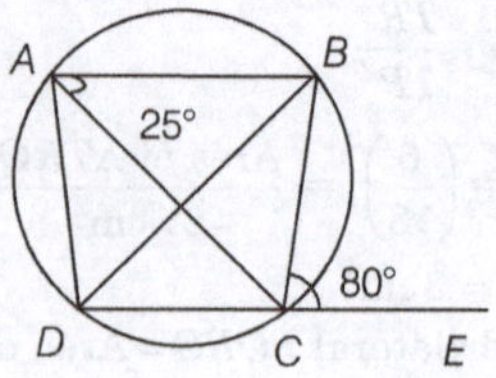

Find
(i) $\angle CAD$ (ii) $\angle CBD$ (iii) $\angle ADC$

9. In the given figure, AB is a diameter of the circle with centre O, $DO \parallel CB$ and $\angle DCB = 120°$.

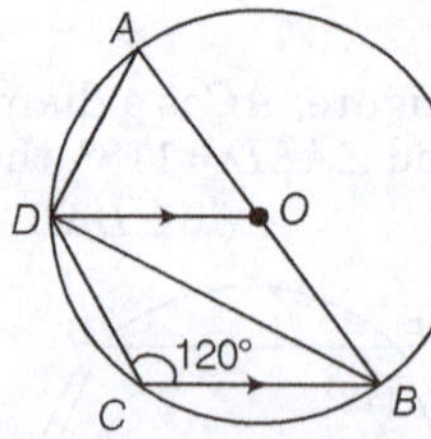

Calculate
(i) $\angle DAB$ (ii) $\angle DBA$ (iii) $\angle DBC$ (iv) $\angle ADC$
Also, show that ΔAOD is an equilateral triangle.

10. In the given figure, two circles intersect each other at A and B. The centre of the smaller circle is O and lies on the circumference of the larger circle. If PAC and PBD are straight lines and $\angle APB = 75°$, then find

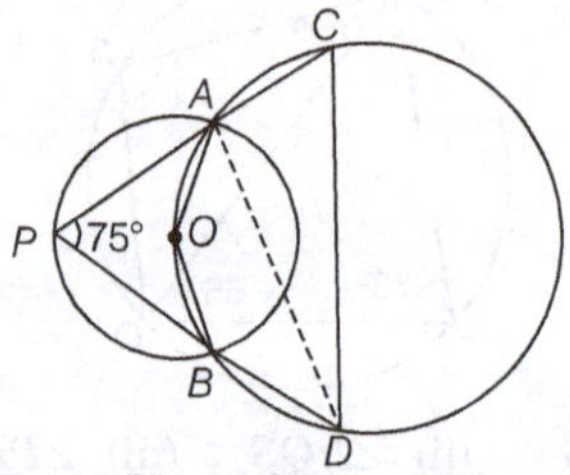

(i) $\angle AOB$ (ii) $\angle ACB$ (iii) $\angle ADB$

11. $ABCD$ is a parallelogram. The circle through A, B and C intersect CD, produced at E. Prove that $AE = AD$.

12. In the given figure, P is a point on the side BC of ΔABC, such that $AB = AP$. Through A and C, lines are drawn parallel to BC and PA respectively, so as to intersect at D. Show that $ABCD$ is a cyclic quadrilateral.

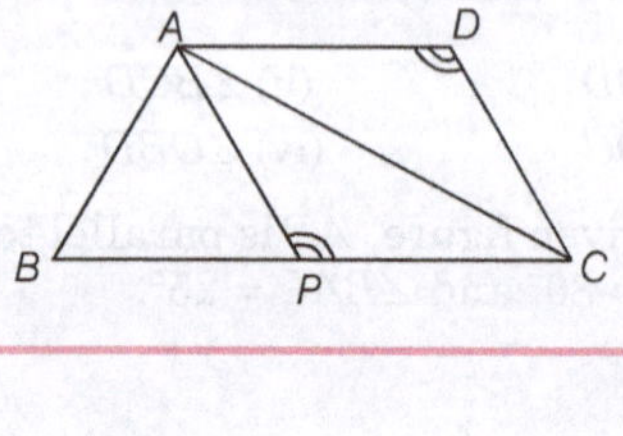

13. In the given figure, SP is bisector of $\angle RPT$ and $PQRS$ is a cyclic quadrilateral. Prove that $SQ = SR$.

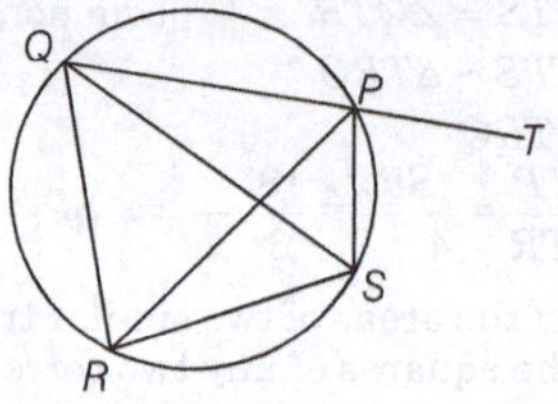

14. In the given figure, two circles intersect at S and T. STP, BSC and BAP are straight lines. Prove that $PATD$ is a cyclic quadrilateral.

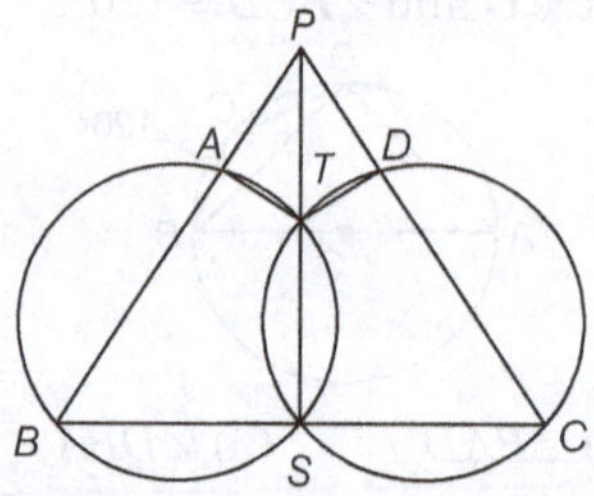

15. Prove that, if two non-parallel sides of a trapezium are equal, then it is cyclic.

Or

Prove that isosceles trapezium is always cyclic.

16. If the bisectors of opposite angles of a cyclic quadrilateral intersect the circle circumscribing it at the points P and Q, prove that PQ is a diameter of the circle.

17. Prove that, in a cyclic quadrilateral, if one pair of opposite sides is equal, the other pair is parallel.

18. If two sides of a cyclic quadrilateral are parallel, then prove that
(i) its other two sides are equal.
(ii) its diagonals are equal.

19. In the given figure, $PQRS$ is a cyclic quadrilateral. PQ and SR produced meet at T.

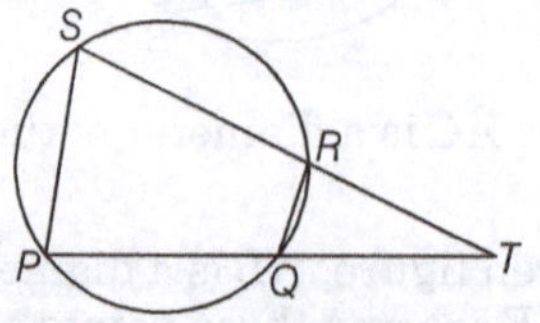

(i) Prove that $\Delta TPS \sim \Delta TRQ$.
(ii) Find SP, if $TP = 9$ cm, $RQ = 2$ cm and $TR = 3$ cm.
(iii) Find the area of quadrilateral $PQRS$, if area of $\Delta PTS = 27 \text{ cm}^2$.

Tangent and Secant Properties of Circles

Tangent of a Circle

The word 'Tangent' has been derived from the Latin word 'Tangere', which means 'To touch' and it was introduced by the Danish Mathematician Thomas Fineke in 1583. Thus, a tangent to a circle is a line that intersects or touch the circle at only one point.

This point, i.e. the common point of the tangent and the circle is called the point of contact.

Also, we can say that the tangent to a circle is a special case of the secant, when two end points of its corresponding chord are coincide.

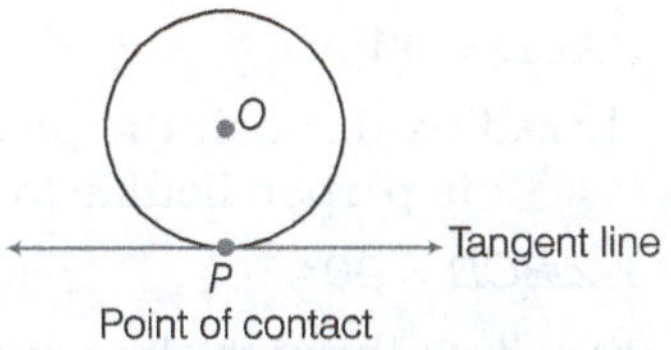

(i) There is only one tangent at a point of the circle.

(ii) A circle can have maximum two parallel tangents which can be drawn to the opposite side of the centre.

Properties of a Tangent

The properties of a tangent in the form of theorems are given below

Theorem 1 *The tangent at any point of a circle and the radius through the point of contact are perpendicular to each other.*

Given A circle with centre O and a tangent AB at a point P of the circle.

To prove $OP \perp AB$

Construction Take any point Q, other than P on the tangent AB and join OQ.

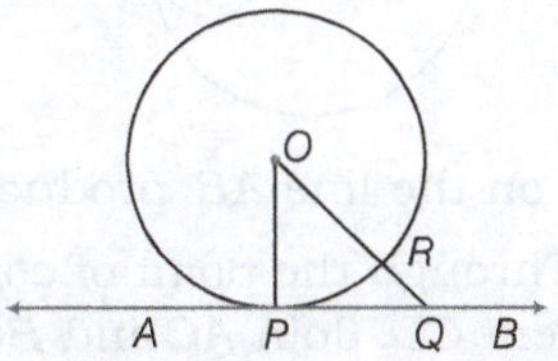

Proof Here, Q is a point on the tangent AB, other than the point of contact P. So, Q lies outside the circle [if Q lies inside the circle, then AB becomes a secant and not a tangent to the circle].

Let OQ intersects the circle at R.

$\because$ $OP = OR$ [radii of the same circle]

Now, $OQ = OR + RQ$

$\Rightarrow$ $OQ > OR$

$\Rightarrow$ $OQ > OP$ [$\because OP = OR$]

or $OP < OQ$

Thus, OP is shorter than any other segment joining O to any point of AB. Also, we know that, the shortest distance between a point and a line is perpendicular distance from the point to the line. So, OP is perpendicular to AB.

i.e. $OP \perp AB$. Hence proved.

Theorem 2 *(Converse of Theorem 1) A line drawn through the end of a radius and perpendicular to it, is a tangent to the circle.*

Example 28. A line through the centre O of a circle of radius 5 cm cuts the tangent at a point P on the circle at Q such that $PQ = 12$ cm. Find the length of OQ.

Sol. We know that, tangent at a point on a circle is perpendicular to the radius through the point of contact.

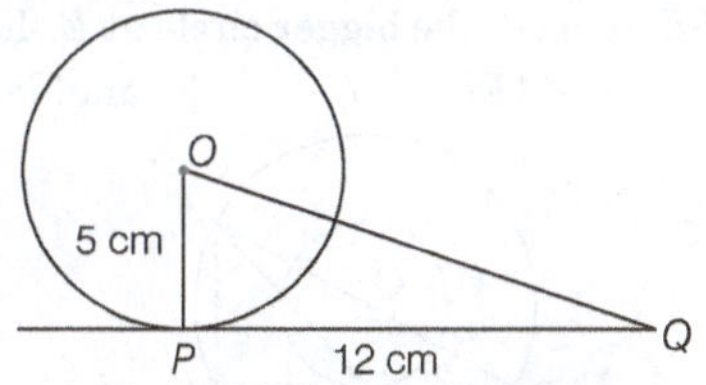

Therefore, OP is perpendicular to PQ.

In right angled ΔOPQ, we have

$OQ^2 = OP^2 + PQ^2$ [by Pythagoras theorem]

$\Rightarrow$ $OQ^2 = 5^2 + 12^2$

$\Rightarrow$ $OQ^2 = 25 + 144 \Rightarrow OQ^2 = 169$

$\therefore$ $OQ = 13$ cm [taking positive square root]

Example 29. In the given figure, O is the centre of the circle and SP is a tangent. If $\angle SRT = 65°$, then find the values of x, y and z. [ICSE 2015]

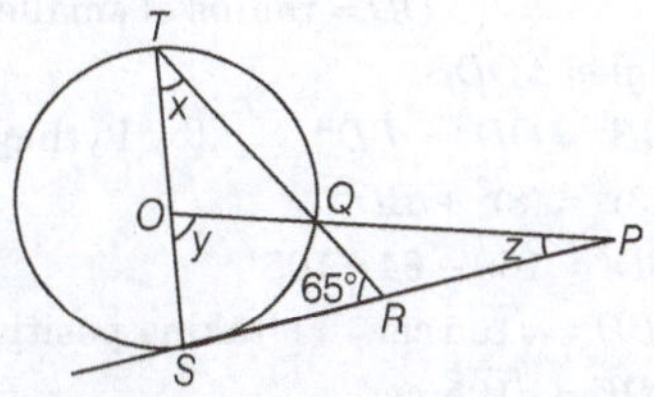

Sol. Given, $\angle TRS = 65°$

Join SQ. Here, SP is a tangent.

$\therefore$ $\angle OSR = 90°$

[$\because$ tangents at any point of a circle and radius through the point of contact are perpendicular to each other]

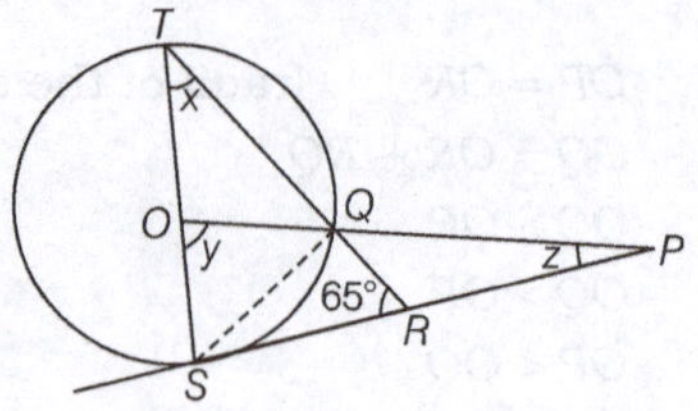

In ΔSTR, $\angle STR + \angle TRS + \angle TSR = 180°$

[by angle sum property of a triangle]

$\Rightarrow x + 65° + 90° = 180° \Rightarrow x = 180° - 155°$

$\therefore \quad x = 25°$

We know that, angle made by a chord at centre is double the angle made by it at remaining part.

$\therefore \quad y = 2x = 2 \times 25° = 50°$

In ΔOPS, $\angle SOP + \angle OPS + \angle OSP = 180°$

[by angle sum property of a triangle]

$\Rightarrow \quad 50° + z + 90° = 180°$

$\therefore \quad z = 180° - 140° = 40°$

Example 30. The radii of two concentric circles are 13 cm and 8 cm. *AB* is a diameter of the bigger circle. *BD* is a tangent to the smaller circle touching it at *D*. Find the length of *AD*.

Sol. Produce *BD* to meet the bigger circle at *E*. Join *AE*.

Then, $\angle AEB = 90°$ [$\because$ angle in semi-circle]

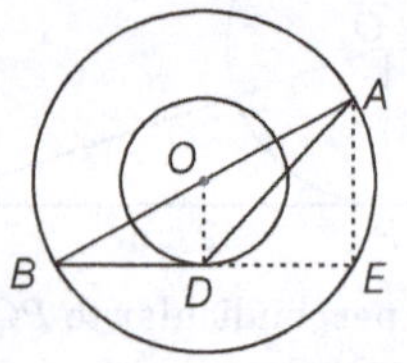

Here, $OD \perp BE$ [$\because$ *BE* is tangent to the smaller circle at *D* and *OD* is its radius]

and $BD = DE$

[$\because$ *BE* is chord of the bigger circle and $OD \perp BE$]

$\therefore \quad OD \parallel AE$ [$\because \angle AEB = \angle ODB = 90°$]

In ΔAEB, *O* and *D* are the mid-points of *AB* and *BE*.

Therefore, by mid-point theorem, we have

$OD = \frac{1}{2}AE \Rightarrow AE = 2 \times 8 = 16$ cm

[$\because$ *OD* = radius of smaller circle = 8 cm]

In right angled ΔODB,

$OB^2 = OD^2 + BD^2$ [by Pythagoras theorem]

$\Rightarrow (13)^2 = (8)^2 + BD^2$

$\Rightarrow BD^2 = 169 - 64 = 105$

$\Rightarrow BD = \sqrt{105}$ cm [taking positive square root]

$\Rightarrow DE = \sqrt{105}$ cm [$\because BD = DE$]

Now, in ΔAED, we have

$AD^2 = AE^2 + ED^2$ [by Pythagoras theorem]

$\Rightarrow AD^2 = 16^2 + (\sqrt{105})^2 = 256 + 105$

$\Rightarrow AD^2 = 361$

$\Rightarrow AD = \sqrt{361} = 19$ cm

Hence, the length of *AD* is 19 cm.

Theorem 3 *If two circles touch each other, then the point of contact lies on the straight line through their centres.*

Case I When two circles touch each other externally.

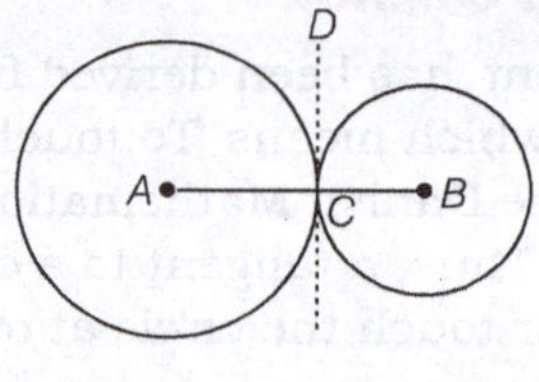

Given Two circles with centres *A* and *B* touching each other externally at *C*.

To prove *C* lies on the line *AB*.

Construction Through the point of contact *C*, draw a common tangent *CD*. Join *AC* and *BC*.

Proof Here, $\angle ACD = 90°$ ...(i)

[$\because$ radius through the point of contact is perpendicular to the tangent]

and $\angle BCD = 90°$ ...(ii)

[$\because$ radius through the point of contact is perpendicular to the tangent]

On adding Eqs. (i) and (ii), we get

$\angle ACD + \angle BCD = 90° + 90°$

$\Rightarrow \quad \angle ACD + \angle BCD = 180° \Rightarrow \angle ACB = 180°$

$\Rightarrow$ *ACB* is a straight line.

[$\because$ 180° is the angle of straight line]

$\therefore$ *C* lies on the line *AB*.

Case II When the given two circles touch each other internally.

Given Two circles with centres *A* and *B*, touching each other internally at point *C*.

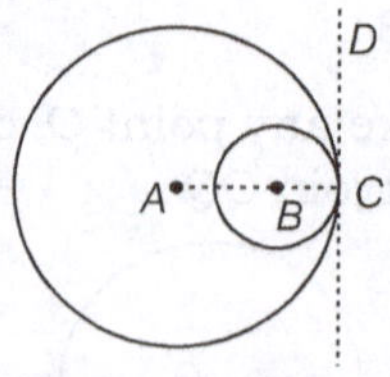

To prove *C* lies on the line *AB* produced.

Construction Through the point of contact *C*, draw a common tangent *CD*. Join *AC* and *BC*.

Proof Here, $\angle ACD = 90°$ ...(i)

[$\because$ radius through the point of contact is perpendicular to the tangent]

and $\angle BCD = 90°$ ...(ii)

[$\because$ radius through the point of contact is perpendicular to the tangent]

Thus, AC and BC both are perpendicular to the tangent CD at the same point C.
[from Eqs. (i) and (ii)]

$\Rightarrow$ AC and BC lie in the same line AC.
[$\because$ only one perpendicular can be drawn, to a line through a point on it]

$\Rightarrow$ ABC is a straight line.

$\therefore$ C lies on the line AB produced. **Hence proved.**

Let r_1, r_2 be the radii of the bigger and smaller circles respectively, and d be the distance between their centres, i.e. $d = AB$, then

(i) the circles touch externally, if and only if $r_1 + r_2 = d$.
(ii) the circles touch internally, if and only if $r_1 - r_2 = d$.

Theorem 4 *The lengths of two tangents drawn from an external point to a circle, are equal.*

Given AP and AQ are two tangents from a point A to a circle, with centre O.

To prove $AP = AQ$

Construction Join OP, OQ and OA.

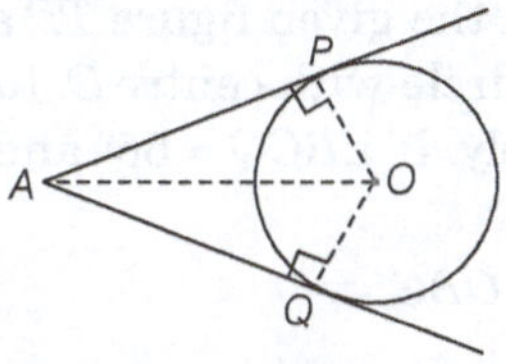

Proof We know that, a tangent at any point of a circle is perpendicular to the radius through the point of contact.

Here, AP is a tangent and OP is the radius of the circle through P.

$\therefore$ $OP \perp AP$

Similarly, $OQ \perp AQ$

$\Rightarrow$ $\angle OPA = \angle OQA = 90°$ ...(i)

First method In $\Delta\, OPA$ and ΔOQA, we have

$OP = OQ$ [radii of a circle]

$\angle OPA = \angle OQA$ [from Eq. (i)]

$OA = OA$ [common side]

So, by RHS criterion of congruence, we get

$\Delta OPA \cong \Delta OQA$

Then, $AP = AQ$ [by CPCT]

Second method In right angled ΔOPA,

$OA^2 = OP^2 + AP^2$ [by Pythagoras theorem]

$\Rightarrow$ $AP^2 = OA^2 - OP^2$

$\Rightarrow$ $AP^2 = OA^2 - OQ^2$ [$\because$ $OP = OQ$ = radii of a circle]

$\Rightarrow$ $AP^2 = AQ^2$ [$\because$ in $\Delta\, OQA$, $OA^2 = OQ^2 + AQ^2$ $\Rightarrow AQ^2 = OA^2 - OQ^2$]

$\Rightarrow$ $AP = AQ$ **Hence proved.**

From the above theorem, $\angle OAP = \angle OAQ$ [$\because$ $\Delta OPA \cong \Delta OQA$]

$\Rightarrow$ OP is the angle bisector of $\angle PAQ$.

Thus, the centre of the circle lies on the bisector of the angle between the two tangents.

Example 31. Two circles with centres O and O' touch each other externally at point D. If A is a point on the common tangent through D, then prove that the tangents AB and AC are equal.

Sol. **Given** Two circles with centres O and O' touch each other externally at point D. AB and AC are the tangents to the circles with centres O and O', respectively from point A, which lie on the common tangent AD.

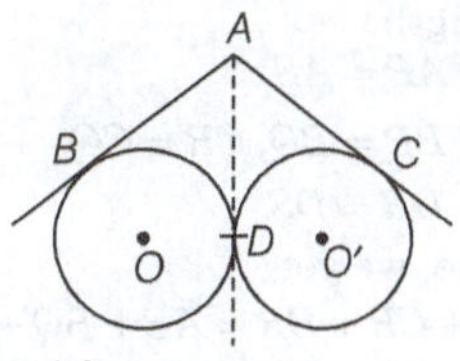

To prove $AB = AC$

Proof AB and AD are the tangents to the circle (with centre O) from point A.

$\therefore$ $AB = AD$ ...(i)
[$\because$ lengths of two tangents drawn from an external point to a circle are equal]

Again, AC and AD the tangents to the circle (with centre O') from point A.

$\therefore$ $AC = AD$ ...(ii)
[$\because$ lengths of two tangents drawn from an external point to a circle are equal]

From Eqs. (i) and (ii), we get $AB = AC$ **Hence proved.**

Example 32. In the given figure, if two circles touch each other externally at C, then prove that common tangent at C bisects the other two common tangents.

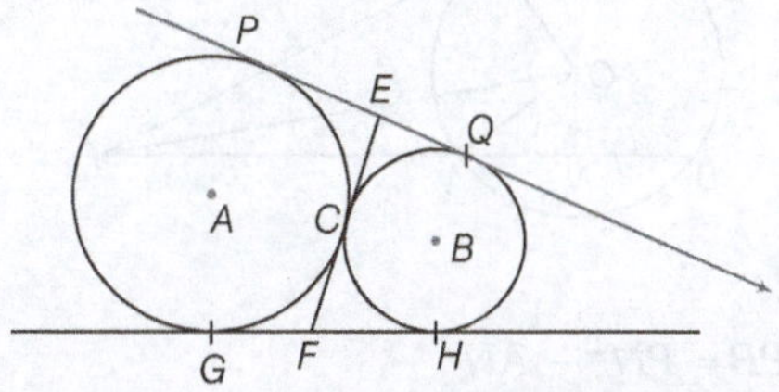

Sol. **Given** PQ and GH are the common tangents to both circles and common tangent at C meets PQ at E and GH at F.

To prove EF bisects PQ and GH.

Proof We know that, tangents drawn from an external point to a circle are equal in length.

$\therefore$ $EP = EC$ and $EQ = EC \Rightarrow EP = EQ$

$\Rightarrow$ PQ is bisected by EF at E.

Similarly, $GF = FC$ and $HF = FC \Rightarrow GF = HF$

$\Rightarrow$ GH is bisected by EF at F.

Hence, the common tangent EF drawn at point C bisects the other two common tangents. **Hence proved.**

Example 33. **If the sides of a parallelogram touch a circle, then prove that the parallelogram is a rhombus.**

Sol. **Given** A parallelogram $ABCD$ in which a circle touches the sides at P, Q, R and S, respectively.

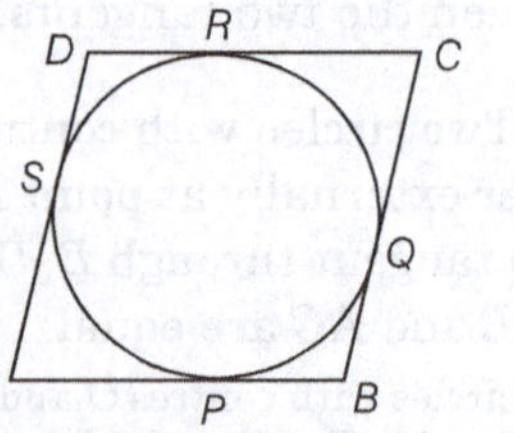

To prove $ABCD$ is a rhombus.

Proof Since, tangents from an external point to a circle are equal in length.

$\therefore$ $AP = AS$

Similarly, $BP = BQ$, $CR = CQ$

and $DR = DS$

On adding these, we get

$$AP + BP + CR + DR = AS + BQ + CQ + DS$$

$$\Rightarrow (AP + BP) + (CR + DR) = (AS + DS) + (BQ + CQ)$$

$$\Rightarrow AB + CD = AD + BC$$

But $ABCD$ is a parallelogram.

$\therefore$ $AB = CD$ and $AD = BC$

$\therefore$ $AB + AB = BC + BC$

$\Rightarrow$ $2AB = 2BC$

$\Rightarrow$ $AB = BC$

$\Rightarrow$ $AB = BC = CD = AD$

Hence, $ABCD$ is a rhombus. **Hence proved.**

Example 34. **In the given figure, from an external point P, a tangent PT and a line segment PAB drawn to a circle with centre O. ON is perpendicular on the chord AB.**

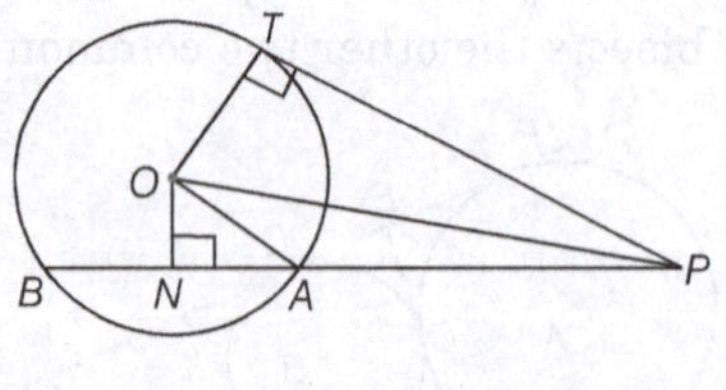

Prove that

(i) $PA \cdot PB = PN^2 - AN^2$

(ii) $PN^2 - AN^2 = OP^2 - OT^2$

(iii) $PA \cdot PB = PT^2$.

Sol. **Given** PT is a tangent drawn from an external point P and a line segment PAB is drawn to a circle with centre O. ON is perpendicular on the chord AB.

To prove

(i) $PA \cdot PB = PN^2 - AN^2$

(ii) $PN^2 - AN^2 = OP^2 - OT^2$

(iii) $PA \cdot PB = PT^2$

Proof

(i) $PA \cdot PB = (PN - AN)(PN + BN)$

$= (PN - AN)(PN + AN)$

[$\because AN = BN$ as $ON \perp AB$ and bisect it]

$= PN^2 - AN^2$

(ii) $PN^2 - AN^2 = (OP^2 - ON^2) - AN^2$

[$\because$ in right angled ΔONP by Pythagoras theorem $OP^2 = ON^2 + PN^2 \Rightarrow PN^2 = OP^2 - ON^2$]

$= OP^2 - ON^2 - AN^2$

$= OP^2 - (ON^2 + AN^2)$

$= OP^2 - OA^2$ [$\because$ in ΔONA, $OA^2 = ON^2 + AN^2$]

$= OP^2 - OT^2$ [$\because OA = OT$ = radii]

(iii) From parts (i) and (ii), we get

$PA \cdot PB = OP^2 - OT^2 \Rightarrow PA \cdot PB = PT^2$

[$\because$ in ΔOTP, $OP^2 = OT^2 + PT^2 \Rightarrow PT^2 = OP^2 - OT^2$]

Hence proved.

Example 35. **In the given figure TP and TQ are two tangents to the circle with centre O, touching at A and C, respectively. If $\angle BCQ = 55°$ and $\angle BAP = 60°$, find**

(i) $\angle OBA$ and $\angle OBC$

(ii) $\angle AOC$

(iii) $\angle ATC$ **[ICSE 2020]**

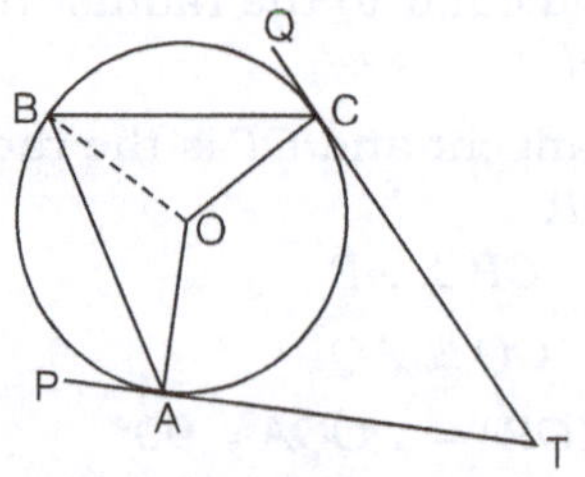

Sol. Given, TP and TQ are two tangents to the circle with centre O touching at A and C, respectively.

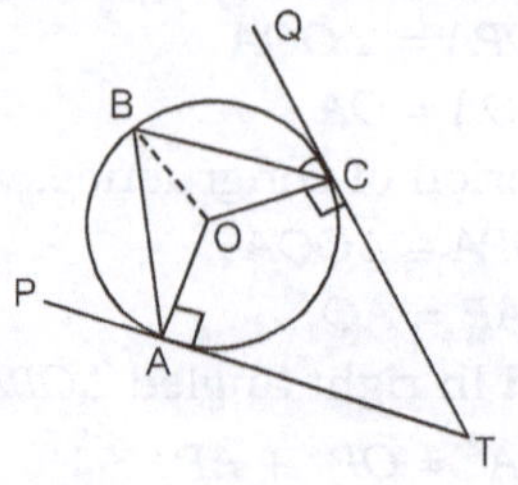

Since, $\angle BCO = 90° - \angle BCQ = 90° - 55° = 35°$ ...(i)

[$\because$ radius $\perp$ tangent]

and $\angle BAP = 60°$

$\therefore$ $\angle BAO = 90° - \angle BAP = 90° - 60° = 30°$ ...(ii)

[$\because$ radius $\perp$ tangent]

(i) In ΔBOC, $OC = OB$ [radii]

$\Rightarrow \angle OBC = \angle OCB = 35°$ [using Eq. (i)]

[$\because$ angles opposite to equal sides are equal]

In ΔAOB, $OA = OB$ [radii]

$\Rightarrow \angle OBA = \angle OAB = 30°$ [using Eq. (ii)]

[$\because$ angles opposite to equal sides are equal]

(ii) $\angle ABC = \angle ABO + \angle CBO = 30° + 35° = 65°$

$\therefore \angle AOC = 2 \times ABC = 2 \times 65° = 130°$

(iii) In quadrilateral $AOCT$,

$$\angle AOC + \angle OAT + \angle OCT + \angle ATC = 360°$$

[$\because$ sum of all the angles of a quadrilateral is 360°]

$\Rightarrow 130° + 90° + 90° + \angle ATC = 360°$

$\Rightarrow \angle ATC = 360° - 310° = 50°$

Example 36. In the given figure, $PQ = 24$ cm, $QR = 7$ cm and $\angle PQR = 90°$. Find the radius of the inscribed circle.

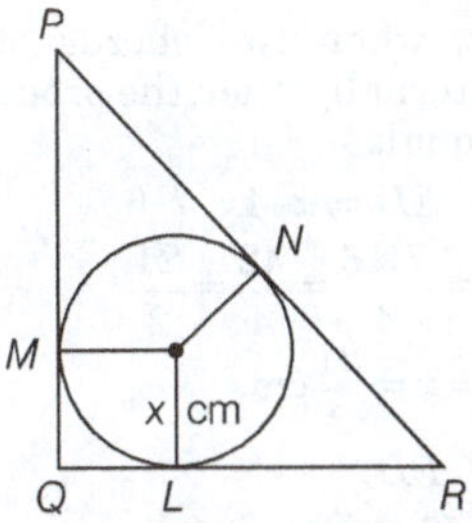

[ICSE 2012]

Sol. Given, $PQ = 24$ cm, $QR = 7$ cm and $\angle PQR = 90°$.

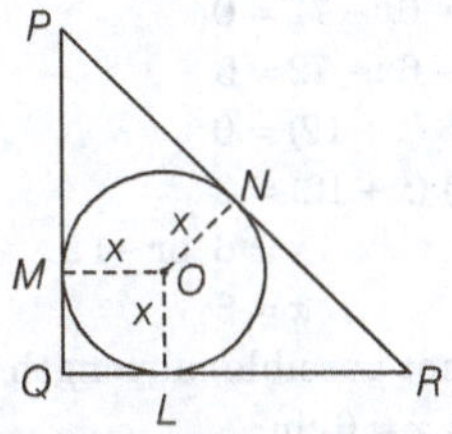

In right angled ΔPQR,

$PR^2 = PQ^2 + QR^2$ [by Pythagoras theorem]

$= (24)^2 + (7)^2 = 576 + 49 = 625$

$\Rightarrow PR^2 = (25)^2 \Rightarrow PR = 25$ cm

[taking positive square root as length cannot be negative]

Here, PQ, QR and PR are the tangents of inscribed circle.

The tangent at any point of a circle and the radius through the point are perpendicular to each other.

$\therefore \angle OMQ = \angle OLQ = \angle ONR = 90°$

Since, all the angles of a quadrilateral $OLQM$ are 90° and $QL = QM$. [$\because$ tangents drawn from an external point to the circle are equal in length]

So, $OLQM$ is a square.

$\Rightarrow QL = QM = x$ (say)

Now, $LR = QR - QL = 7 - x = RN$

[$\because$ tangents drawn from an external point to the circle are equal in length]

and $MP = PQ - QM = 24 - x = PN$

$\because PR = PN + NR$

$\therefore 25 = 24 - x + 7 - x \Rightarrow 25 = 31 - 2x$

$\Rightarrow 2x = 31 - 25 \Rightarrow 2x = 6 \Rightarrow x = \frac{6}{2}$

Hence, the radius of the inscribed circle is 3 cm.

Example 37. If a, b and c are the sides of a right triangle, where c is hypotenuse, then prove that the radius r of the circle which touches the sides of the triangle, is given by $r = \frac{a+b-c}{2}$.

Sol. Let a, b and c be the sides of right angled ΔABC, such that $BC = a$, $CA = b$ and $AB = c$.

Let the circle touches the sides BC, CA, AB at D, E and F, respectively.

Then, $AE = AF$ and $BD = BF$

[$\because$ tangents drawn from an external point to the circle are equal in length]

Also, $CE = CD = r$

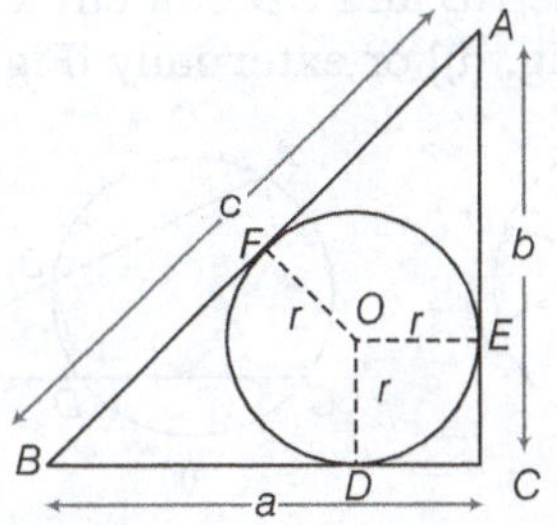

$\therefore AF = AE = AC - EC = b - r$ and $BF = a - r$

Now, $AB = c$

$\Rightarrow AF + BF = (b - r) + (a - r)$

$\Rightarrow AB = b - r + a - r$

$\Rightarrow c = a + b - 2r$

$\Rightarrow 2r = a + b - c$

$\therefore r = \frac{a+b-c}{2}$ **Hence proved.**

Example 38. In the given figure, ΔABC is drawn to circumscribe a circle of radius 3 cm, such that the segments BD and DC are, respectively of lengths 6 cm and 9 cm. If the area of ΔABC is 54 cm^2, then find the lengths of the sides AB and AC.

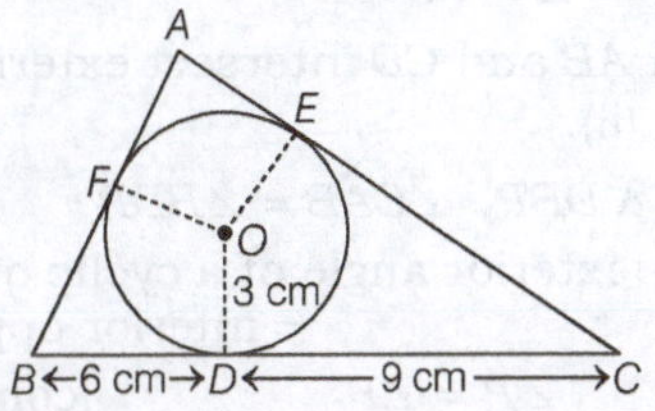

Sol. As the length of tangents drawn from an external point to circle are equal.

$CE = CD = 9$m, $BF = BD = 6$cm

Let $AE = AF = x$ cm (say), then

$$AC = AE + CE = (x + 9)\text{ cm}$$
$$AB = AF + BF = (x + 6)\text{ cm}$$

$\therefore$ Area of triangle $= \frac{1}{2} \times \text{base} \times \text{height}$

Given area of $\Delta ABC = 54\text{ cm}^2$

$\Rightarrow$ ar (ΔOBC) + ar (ΔOAB) + ar $(\Delta OCA) = 54\text{ cm}^2$

$\Rightarrow \frac{1}{2}(BC \times OD) + \frac{1}{2}(AB \times OF) + \frac{1}{2}(AC + OE) = 54$

$\Rightarrow BC \times 3 + AB \times 3 + AC \times 3 = 108$

$\Rightarrow (6 + 9) + (x + 6) + (x + 9) = 36$

$\Rightarrow 2x + 30 = 36$

$\Rightarrow x = 3$

$\therefore$ Length of side $AC = (x + 9)$ cm $= (3 + 9)$ cm $= 12$ cm

$\therefore$ Length of side $AB = (x + 6)$ cm $= (3 + 6)$ cm $= 9$ cm

Theorem 5 *If two chords of a circle intersect internally or externally, then the product of the lengths of segments are equal.* **[ICSE 2015]**

Given Two chords AB and CD of a circle intersecting at P internally [Fig. (i)] or externally [Fig. (ii)].

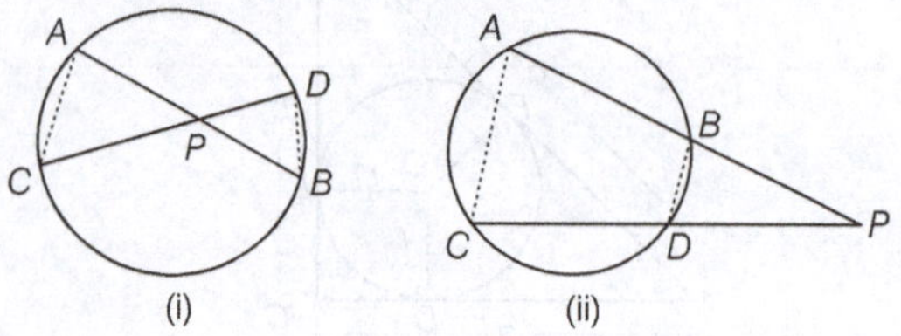

To prove $PA \cdot PB = PC \cdot PD$

Construction Join AC and BD.

Proof

Case I When AB and CD intersect internally as shown in Fig. (i).

In ΔACP and ΔDBP,

$\angle APC = \angle BPD$ [vertically opposite angles]

$\angle CAP = \angle PDB$ [angles in same segment]

$\therefore \Delta ACP \sim \Delta DBP$ [by AA similarity criterion]

$\Rightarrow \frac{PA}{PD} = \frac{PC}{PB}$

[$\because$ corresponding sides of similar triangles are proportional]

$\Rightarrow PA \cdot PB = PC \cdot PD$

Case II When AB and CD intersect externally as shown in Fig. (ii).

In ΔACP and ΔDBP, $\angle CAB = \angle BDP$

[exterior angle of a cyclic quadrilateral = interior opposite angle]

$\angle P = \angle P$ [common angle]

$\therefore \Delta ACP \sim \Delta DBP$

[by AA similarity criterion]

$\Rightarrow \frac{PA}{PD} = \frac{PC}{PB}$

[$\because$ corresponding sides of similar triangles are proportional]

$\Rightarrow PA \cdot PB = PC \cdot PD$

Hence, in both the cases,

$PA \cdot PB = PC \cdot PD$ **Hence proved.**

Example 39. Find the length of the unknown part of the chord in the given figures.

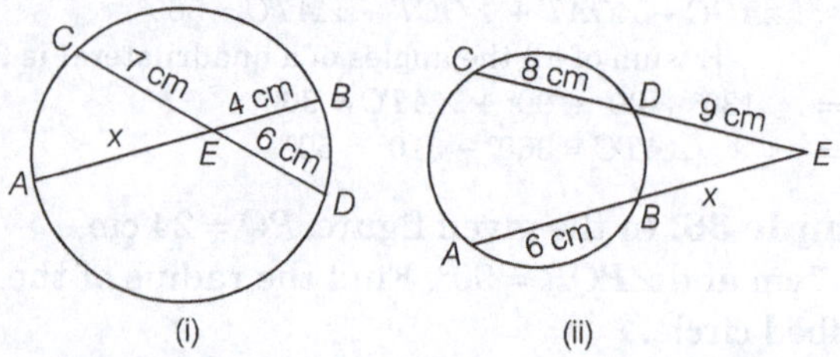

Sol. We know that, when two chords of a circle intersect internally or externally, then the products of the lengths of segments are equal.

(i) $\because EA \cdot EB = EC \cdot ED \Rightarrow x \cdot 4 = 7 \cdot 6$

$\Rightarrow x = \frac{7 \times 6}{4} = \frac{42}{4} = \frac{21}{2}$

Therefore, $EA = x = \frac{21}{2}$ cm.

(ii) $\because EA \cdot EB = EC \cdot ED$

$\Rightarrow (6 + x)\, x = 8 \cdot 9$

$\Rightarrow 6x + x^2 = 72$

$\Rightarrow x^2 + 6x - 72 = 0$

$\Rightarrow x^2 + 12x - 6x - 72 = 0$

$\Rightarrow x(x + 12) - 6(x + 12) = 0$

$\Rightarrow (x - 6)(x + 12) = 0$

$\Rightarrow x = 6$ or -12

$\therefore x = 6$

[$\because x = -12$ (not possible) as length cannot be negative]

Therefore, $EB = x = 6$ cm.

Example 40. In the given figure $AB = 9$ cm, $PA = 7.5$ cm and $PC = 5$ cm.

Chords AD and BC intersect at P. **[ICSE 2020]**

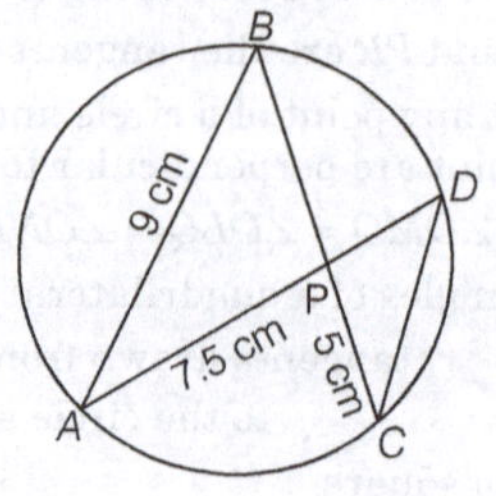

(i) Prove that $\Delta PAB \sim \Delta PCD$.

(ii) Find the length of CD.

(iii) Find area of ΔPAB : area of ΔPCD.

Sol. Given, $AB = 9\,cm$, $PA = 7.5\,cm$ and $PC = 5\,cm$

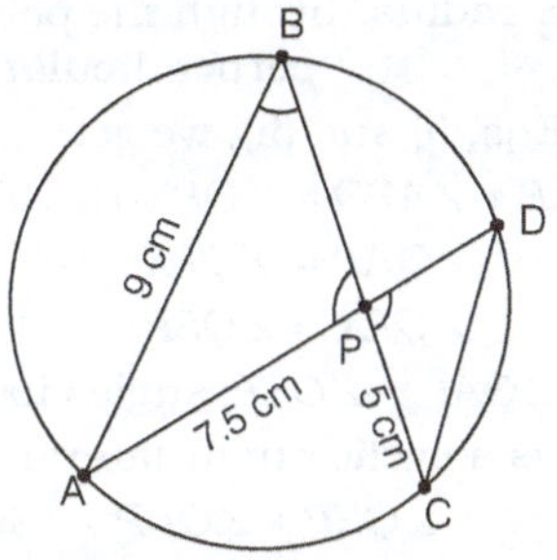

(i) In ΔPAB and ΔPCD,

$\angle PBA = \angle PDC$

[∵ angle in the same segment of a circle are equal]

and $\angle APB = \angle CPD$ [vertically opposite angles]

By AA similarity criterion,

$\Delta PAB \sim \Delta PCD$ **Hence proved.**

(ii) $\dfrac{AP}{CP} = \dfrac{AB}{CD}$ [Since, $\Delta PAB \sim \Delta PCD$ corresponding sides of similar triangles are proportional]

$\Rightarrow \dfrac{7.5}{5} = \dfrac{9}{CD} \Rightarrow CD = \dfrac{5 \times 9}{7.5} = 6\,cm$

(iii) $\dfrac{\text{ar}(\Delta PAB)}{\text{ar}(\Delta PCD)} = \left(\dfrac{AB}{CD}\right)^2$

[∵ the ratio of areas of two similar triangles in equal to the square of the ratio of their corresponding sides]

$= \left(\dfrac{9}{6}\right)^2 = \dfrac{9}{4}$

$\Rightarrow$ ar (ΔPAB) : ar $(\Delta PCD) = 9 : 4$

Theorem 6 *If a chord and a tangent intersect externally, then the product of the lengths of the segments of the chord is equal to the square of the length of the tangent from the point of contact to the point of intersection.*

Given Let AB be the chord of a circle with centre C and tangent to the circle at F meets the chord AB produced at E.

To prove $EA \times EB = EF^2$

Construction Draw $CD \perp AB$ and join AC, BC, CE and CF.

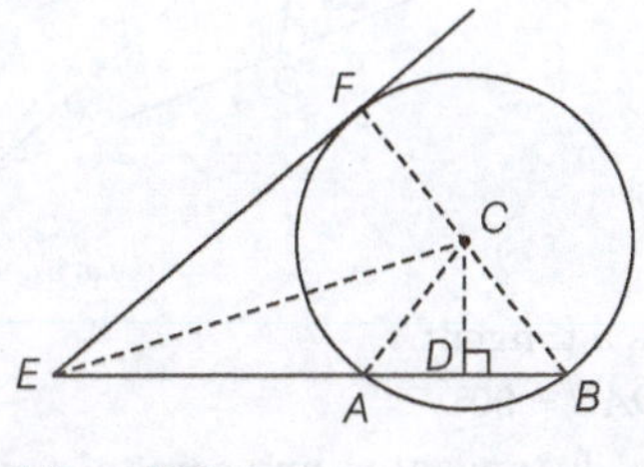

Proof Here, $AD = DB$ ...(i)

[∵ perpendicular from the centre bisects the chord]

Now, $EA \times EB = (ED - AD)(ED + DB)$

$= (ED - AD)(ED + AD)$ [from Eq. (i)]

$EA \times EB = ED^2 - AD^2$ [∵ $(a - b)(a + b) = a^2 - b^2$]

$= ED^2 - [AC^2 - CD^2]$

[by Pythagoras theorem in ΔADC, $AD^2 = AC^2 - CD^2$]

$= ED^2 - AC^2 + CD^2$

$= ED^2 + CD^2 - AC^2 = EC^2 - AC^2$

[by Pythagoras theorem in ΔEDC, $ED^2 + CD^2 = EC^2$]

$= EC^2 - CF^2$

[∵ $AC = CF$, radii of the same circle]

$= EF^2$

[by Pythagoras theorem in ΔEFC, $EC^2 - CF^2 = EF^2$]

∴ $EA \times EB = EF^2$ **Hence proved.**

Example 41. In the given figure, O is the centre of the circle and PQ is a tangent at Q. If $PQ = 20$ cm and $PR = 8$ cm. Calculate the radius of the circle.

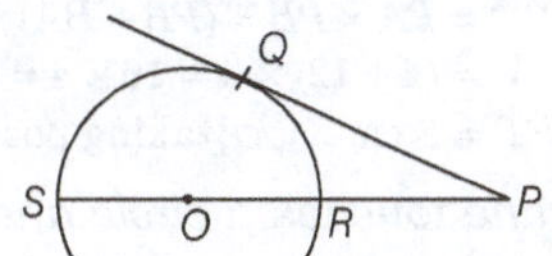

Sol. Given, PQ is the tangent to the circle with centre O.

Also, $PQ = 20\,cm$ and $PR = 8\,cm$ ...(i)

Since, $PQ^2 = PR \times PS$

[∵ product of the lengths of the segments of the chord = square of the length of the tangent]

$\Rightarrow (20)^2 = 8 \times PS$ [from Eq. (i)]

$\Rightarrow 400 = 8 \times PS \Rightarrow PS = \dfrac{400}{8} = 50$ ...(ii)

∴ Diameter, $SR = PS - PR = 50 - 8$ [from Eqs. (i) and (ii)]

$= 42\,cm$

∴ Radius of a circle $= \dfrac{\text{Diameter}}{2} = \dfrac{42}{2} = 21\,cm$

Hence, the required radius of a circle is 21 cm.

Example 42. In the given figure, diameter AB and chord CD of a circle meet at P. PT is a tangent to the circle at T and $CD = 7.8$ cm, $PD = 5$ cm, $PB = 4$ cm.

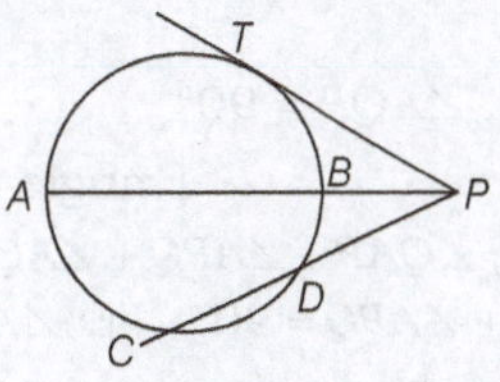

Find

(i) AB. (ii) the length of tangent PT. [ICSE 2014]

Sol. Given, $CD = 7.8$ cm, $PD = 5$ cm, $PB = 4$ cm.

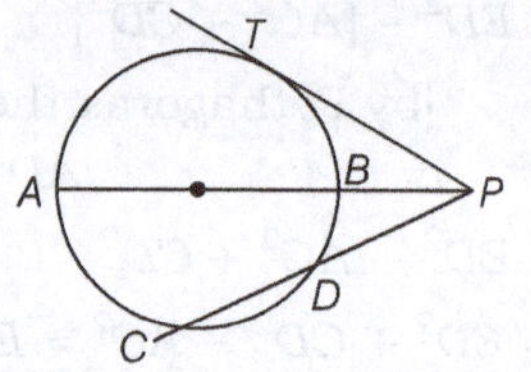

(i) Since, the chord CD and tangent at point T intersect each other at P.

$$\therefore \quad PC \times PD = PT^2 \quad \text{...(i)}$$

Since, the chord AB and tangent at point T intersect each other at P.

$$\therefore \quad PA \times PB = PT^2 \quad \text{...(ii)}$$

From Eqs. (i) and (ii), we get

$$PC \times PD = PA \times PB \quad \text{...(iii)}$$

Now, $PA = PB + BA = 4 + AB$

and $PC = PD + DC = 5 + 7.8 = 12.8$ cm

From Eq. (iii), we get

$$12.8 \times 5 = (4 + AB) \times 4 \Rightarrow 4 + AB = \frac{12.8 \times 5}{4}$$

$$\Rightarrow \quad AB = 16 - 4 = 12 \text{ cm}$$

(ii) From Eq. (ii), we get

$$PT^2 = PA \times PB = (PB + BA) \times PB$$
$$= (4 + 12) \times 4 = 16 \times 4 = 64$$

$$\Rightarrow \quad PT = 8 \text{ cm} \quad \text{[taking positive square root]}$$

Theorem 7 *If a line touches a circle and from the point of contact, a chord is drawn then the angles between the tangent and the chord are respectively, equal to the angle in the corresponding alternate segments.*

Given A tangent to a circle at a point P and PQ is a chord. S and R are the points in the alternate segments.

To prove (i) $\angle QPX = \angle QSP$ (ii) $\angle QPX' = \angle QRP$

Construction Let O be the centre of circle. Join OP and produce it to meet the circle at A. Join AQ.

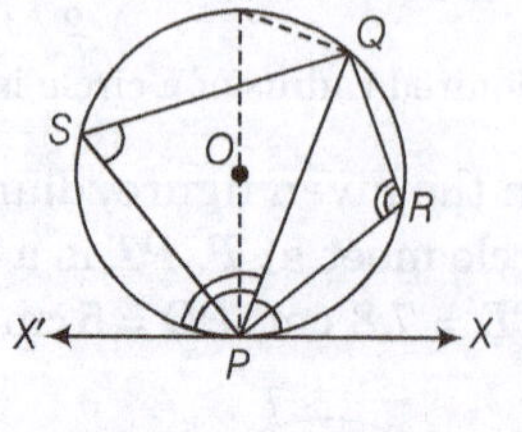

Proof (i) Clearly, $\angle AQP = 90°$

[∵ angle in a semi-circle]

and In ΔAPQ, $\angle QAP + \angle APQ + \angle AQP = 180°$

$$\Rightarrow \quad \angle QAP + \angle APQ = 90° \quad [\because \angle AQP = 90°] \quad \text{...(i)}$$

Also, $\angle QPX + \angle APQ = 90°$ ...(ii)

[∵ radius through the point of contact is perpendicular to the tangent]

Now, from Eqs. (i) and (ii), we get

$$\angle QAP + \angle APQ = \angle QPX + \angle APQ$$

$$\Rightarrow \quad \angle QAP = \angle QPX \quad \text{...(iii)}$$

$$\Rightarrow \quad \angle QPX = \angle QSP$$

[∵ $\angle QAP = \angle QSP$; angles in same segment]

(ii) Now, $PQRS$ is a cyclic quadrilateral, therefore

$$\angle QSP + \angle QRP = 180° \quad \text{...(iv)}$$

Also, $\angle QPX + \angle QPX' = 180°$ ...(v)

[by linear pair axiom]

From Eqs. (iii) and (iv), we get

$$\angle QSP + \angle QRP = \angle QPX + \angle QPX'$$

$$\Rightarrow \quad \angle QRP = \angle QPX' \quad [\because \angle QPX = \angle QSP]$$

Hence proved.

Example 43. In the given figure AC is a tangent to the circle with centre O. If $\angle ADB = 55°$, find x and y. Give reasons for your answers. [ICSE 2019]

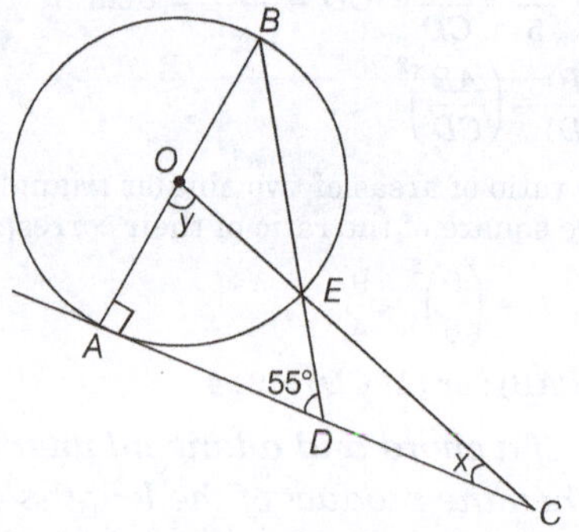

Sol. (a) Given, $\angle ADB = 55°$

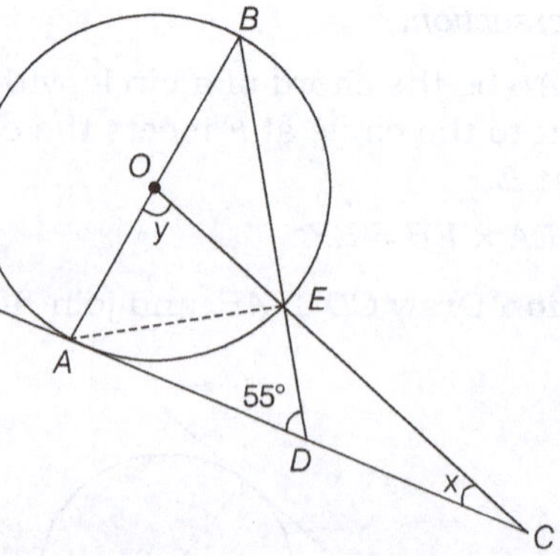

Join AE.

Here, AC is a tangent.

$$\therefore \quad \angle OAC = 90°$$

[∵ tangent at any point of a circle and radius through the point of contact are perpendicular to each other]

In ΔABD,

$$\angle ABD + \angle BAD + \angle ADB = 180^\circ$$

[by angle sum property of a triangle]

$\Rightarrow \quad \angle ABD + 90^\circ + 55^\circ = 180^\circ$

$\Rightarrow \quad \angle ABD = 180^\circ - (90^\circ + 55^\circ) = 35^\circ$

We know that angle made by a chord at centre is double the angle made by it any remaining part

$\therefore \quad y = 2\angle ABD = 2 \times 35^\circ = 70^\circ$.

In ΔOAC,

$$y + \angle OAC + \angle ACO = 180^\circ$$

$\Rightarrow \quad 70^\circ + 90^\circ + x^\circ = 180^\circ$

$\Rightarrow \quad x^\circ = 180^\circ - (70^\circ + 90^\circ) = 20^\circ$

Example 44. In the given figure, $AB = 7$ cm and $BC = 9$ cm.

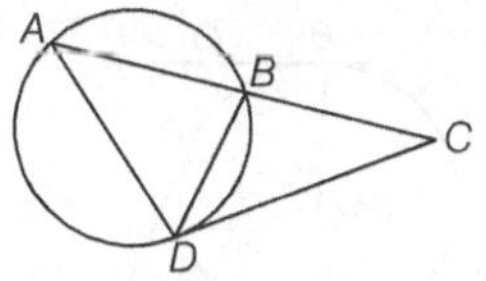

(i) Prove that $\Delta ACD \sim \Delta DCB$.

(ii) Find the length of CD.

Sol. Given, $AB = 7\text{cm}$ and $BC = 9\text{cm}$

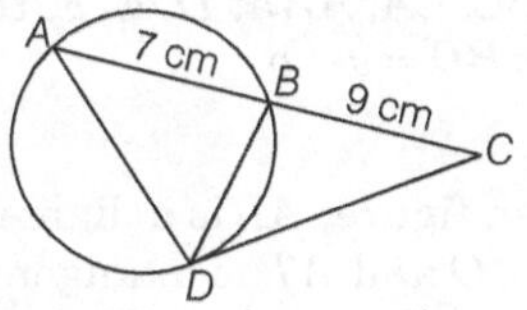

(i) In ΔACD and ΔDCB,

$\angle C = \angle C$ [common angle]

$\Rightarrow \quad \angle CDB = \angle BAD$ [angles in alternate segment]

$\therefore \quad \Delta ACD \sim \Delta DCB$ [by AA similarity criterion]

Hence proved.

(ii) Since, the chord AB and tangent at D intersect each other at point C.

$\therefore \quad AC \times BC = CD^2$ [By Theorem 6]

$\Rightarrow \quad 16 \times 9 = CD^2$

$\Rightarrow \quad CD^2 = 144 = (12)^2$

$\Rightarrow \quad CD = 12\text{cm}$ [taking positive square root]

Hence, the required length of $CD = 12\text{cm}$.

Example 45. In the given figure, PQ is a tangent to the circle at A. AB and AD are the bisectors of $\angle CAQ$ and $\angle PAC$. If $\angle BAQ = 30^\circ$, prove that

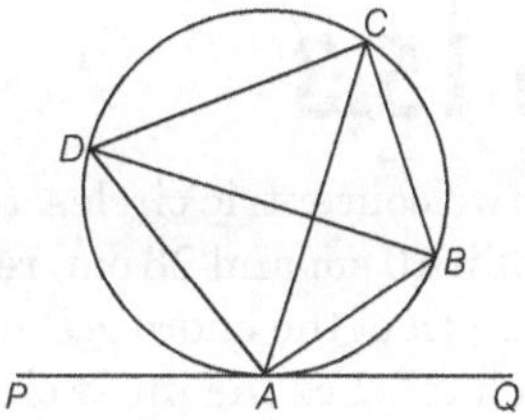

(i) BD is a diameter of the circle.

(ii) ABC is an isosceles triangle. **[ICSE 2017]**

Sol. Given, $\angle BAQ = 30^\circ$ and AB is the bisector of $\angle CAQ$.

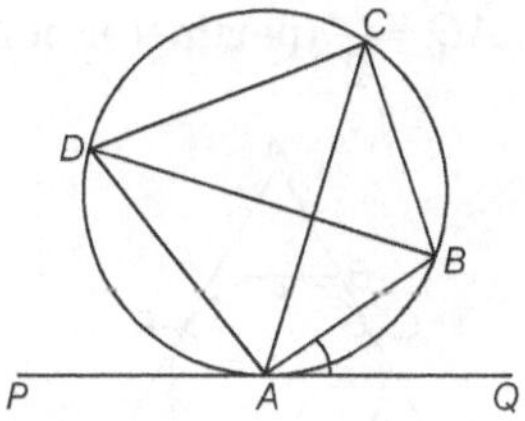

$\therefore \quad \angle CAB = 30^\circ$

$\therefore \quad \angle CAQ = 2\angle BAQ = 2 \times 30^\circ = 60^\circ$

$\because$ PAQ is a straight line.

$\therefore \quad \angle PAC + \angle CAQ = 180^\circ$

$\Rightarrow \quad \angle PAC = 180^\circ - \angle CAQ = 180^\circ - 60^\circ = 120^\circ$

Now, AD is bisector of $\angle PAC$.

$\therefore \quad \angle DAC = \frac{1}{2}\angle PAC = \frac{1}{2} \times 120^\circ = 60^\circ$

and $\angle DAB = \angle DAC + \angle CAB = 60^\circ + 30^\circ = 90^\circ$

(i) We know that, angle in a semi-circle is 90°, i.e. angle made by diameter to any point on the circle 90°.

$\therefore$ BD is a diameter of the circle. **Hence proved.**

(ii) We know that, if a chord is drawn through the point of contact of a tangent to a circle, then the angles made by the chord with the given tangent are respectively equal to the angle formed in the corresponding alternate segment.

$\therefore \quad \angle CDA = \angle CAQ$

$\Rightarrow \quad \angle CDA = 60^\circ$ [$\because \angle CAQ = 60^\circ$]

Here, $ABCD$ is cyclic quadrilateral.

$\therefore \quad \angle CDA + \angle CBA = 180^\circ$

[$\because$ sum of opposite angle of a cyclic quadrilateral is 180°]

$\therefore \quad \angle CBA = 180^\circ - \angle CDA = 180^\circ - 60^\circ = 120^\circ$

Now, in ΔABC, $\angle BCA + \angle CAB + \angle CBA = 180^\circ$

[by angle sum property of a triangle]

$\therefore \quad \angle BCA + 30^\circ + 120^\circ = 180^\circ$

$\Rightarrow \quad \angle BCA = 180^\circ - 150^\circ = 30^\circ$

Here, $\angle BCA = \angle CAB$

$\therefore$ ΔABC is an isosceles triangle. **Hence proved.**

Exercise 15.3

1. There are two concentric circles, each with centre O and of radii 10 cm and 26 cm, respectively. Find the length of the chord AB of the outer circle, which touches the inner circle at P.

2. A circle is touching the side BC of ΔABC at point P and touching AB and AC produced at Q and R, respectively.

Prove that $AQ = \frac{1}{2}$ (perimeter of ΔABC)

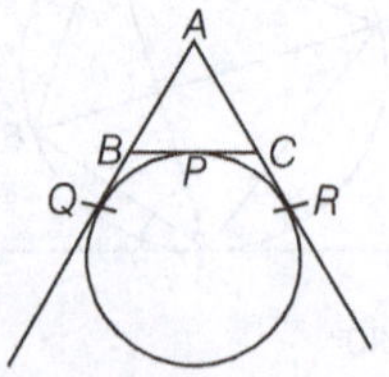

3. TA and TB are tangents to a circle with centre O from an external point T. OT intersects the circle at point P. Prove that TP bisects $\angle ATB$.

4. In the given figure, O is the centre of a circle of radius 5 cm, T is a point such that $OT = 13$ cm and OT intersects the circle at E. If AB is the tangent to the circle at E, then find the length of AB.

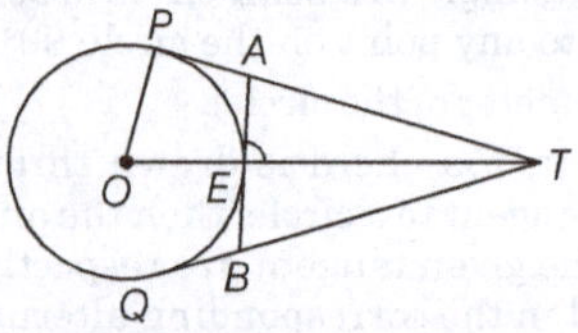

5. In the given figure, a circle is inscribed in a quadrilateral $ABCD$ in which $\angle B = 90°$. If $AD = 23$ cm, $AB = 29$ cm and $DS = 5$ cm, then find the radius of the circle.

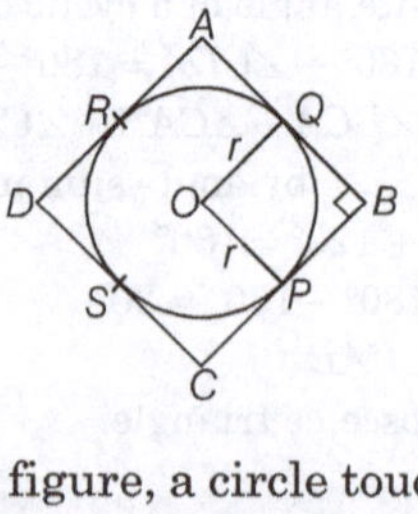

6. In the given figure, a circle touches all the four sides of a quadrilateral $ABCD$, whose three sides are $AB = 6$ cm, $BC = 7$ cm and $CD = 4$ cm. Find AD.

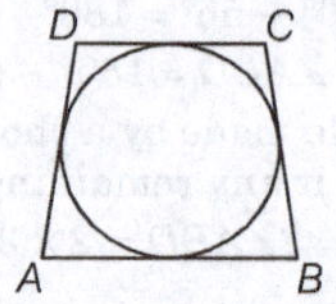

7. PA and PB are tangents drawn from an external point P to a circle with centre C. Prove that $\angle APB = 2\angle CAB$.

8. In the given figure, AB is a diameter of the circle with centre O. AP, BQ and PRQ are tangents. Prove that $\angle POQ = 90°$.

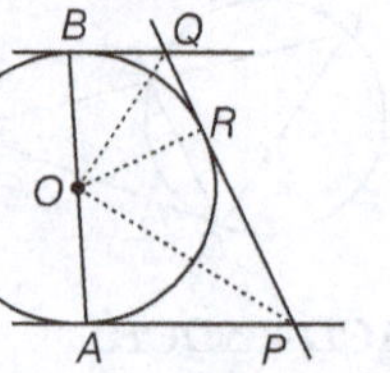

9. Let s denotes the semi-perimeter of ΔABC in which $BC = a$, $CA = b$, $AB = c$. If a circle touches the sides BC, CA, AB at D, E, F, respectively. Prove that $BD = s - b$.

10. In the given figure, AB is a diameter of a circle with centre O and AT is a tangent. If $\angle AOQ = 58°$, then find $\angle ATQ$.

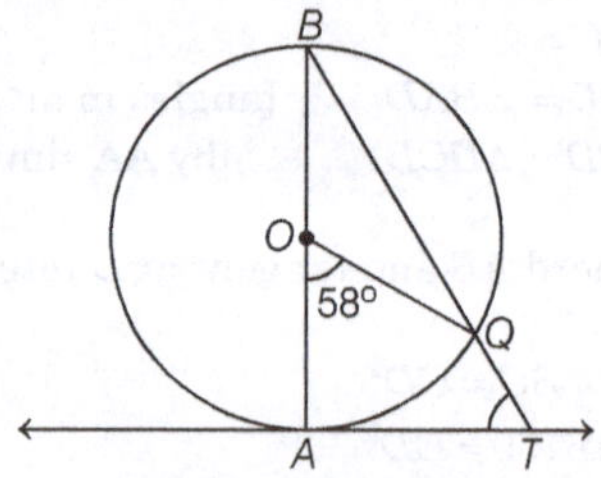

11. In the given figure, O is the centre of the circle and AB is a tangent at B. If $AB = 15$ cm and $AC = 7.5$ cm, then calculate the radius of the circle.

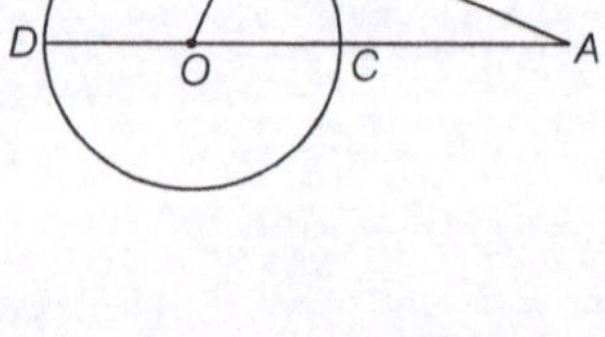

12. In the given figure, AB is a diameter of a circle with centre O and CP is the tangent to the circle at the point C.

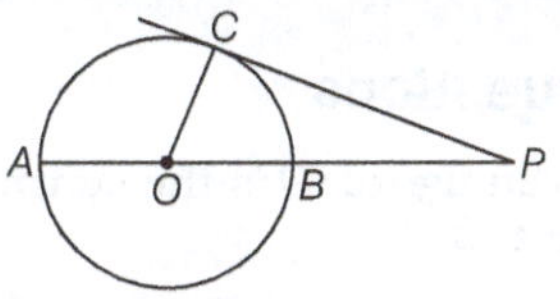

If $AP = 20$ cm and $CP = 10$ cm, then find the radius of the circle.

13. In the given figure, O is the centre of the circle and AB is a tangent to it at point B. If $\angle BDC = 65°$, find $\angle BAO$. **[ICSE 2010]**

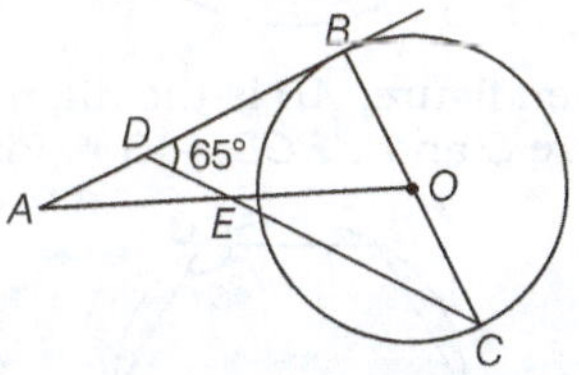

14. In the given figure, 'O' is the centre of the circle. CE is a tangent to the circle at A. If $\angle ABD = 26°$, then find **[ICSE 2023]**

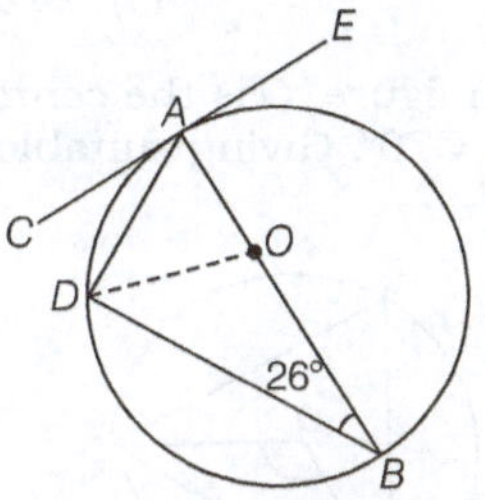

(a) $\angle BDA$ (b) $\angle BAD$
(c) $\angle CAD$ (d) $\angle ODB$

15. In the given figure, ABC is a triangle in which $AB = AC$. A circle through B touches AC at D and intersects AB at P. If D is the mid-point of AC, then show that $4\ AP = AB$.

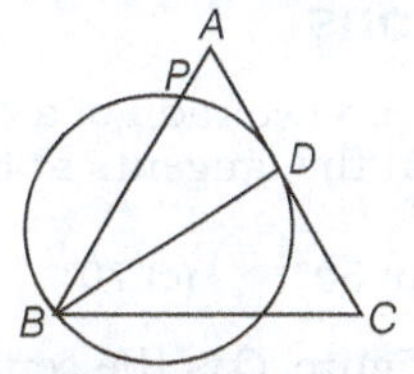

16. Two circles touch each other internally at the point P. QPR is a common tangent at P. If segments PAB and PCD meet the circles at points A, B, C and D (as shown in the given figure), then show that chord AC is parallel to the chord BD.

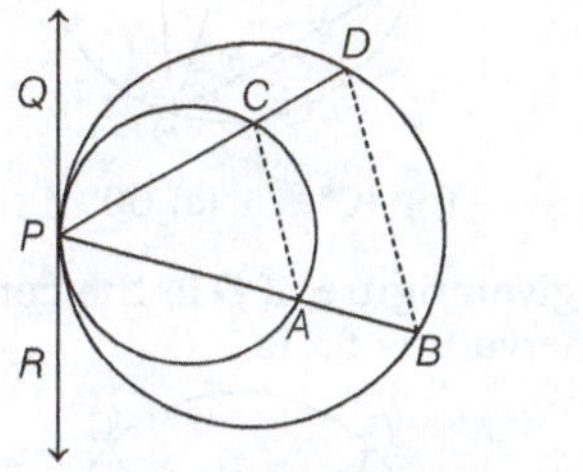

17. Prove that the opposite sides of a quadrilateral circumscribing a circle subtend supplementary angles at the centre of the circle.

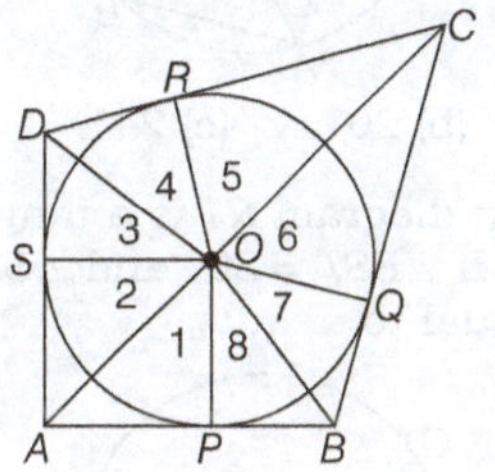

Chapter Practice

a. 1 Mark Questions

1. If angle between two radii of a circle is 130°, the angle between the tangents at the ends of the radii is

(a) 90° (b) 50° (c) 70° (d) 40°

2. In the given figure, O is the centre of the circle. If $\angle OAB = 40°$, then $\angle ACB$ is equal to

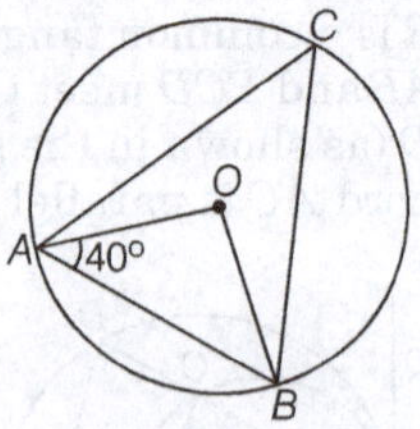

(a) 50° (b) 40° (c) 60° (d) 70°

3. In the given figure, if O is the centre of the circle then the value of x is

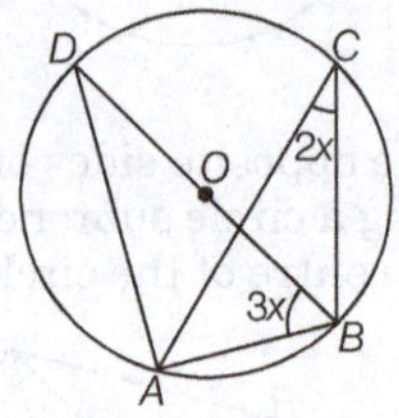

(a) 18° (b) 20° (c) 24° (d) 36°

4. In the given diagram RT is a tangent touching the circle at S. If $\angle PST = 30°$ and $\angle SPQ = 60°$, then $\angle PSQ$ is equal to **[ICSE 2023]**

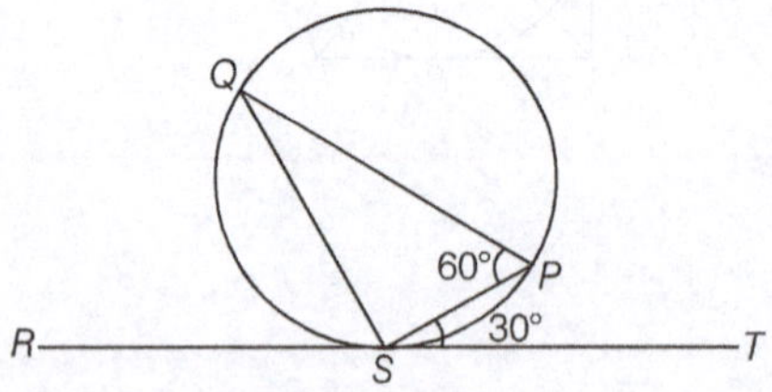

(a) 40° (b) 30° (c) 60° (d) 90°

5. In the given figure, PA is a tangent from an external point P to a circle with centre O. If $\angle POB = 115°$, then $\angle APO$ is

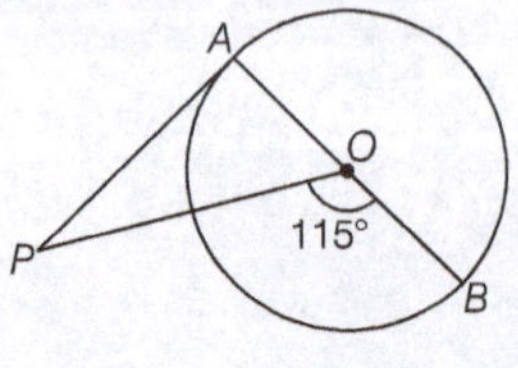

(a) 25° (b) 20° (c) 30° (d) 65°

b. 3 Marks Questions

6. In the given figure, O is the centre of a circle. Find the value of b.

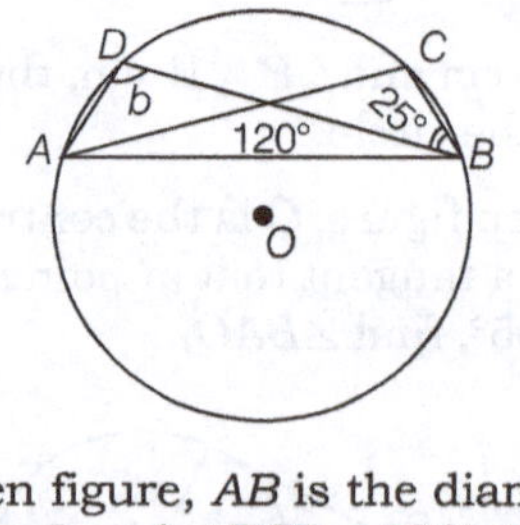

7. In the given figure, AB is the diameter of a circle with centre O and $\angle BCD = 130°$. Find

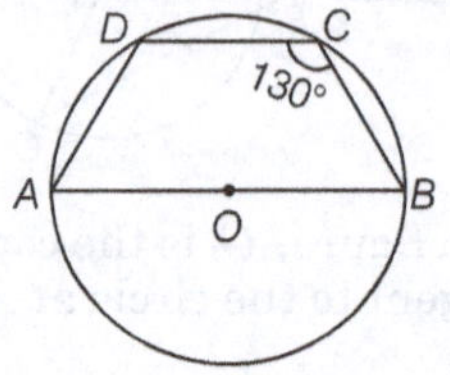

(i) $\angle DAB$ (ii) $\angle DBA$ **[ICSE 2012]**

8. In the given figure, O is the centre of the circle and $\angle DAE = 70°$. Giving suitable reasons, find the measure of

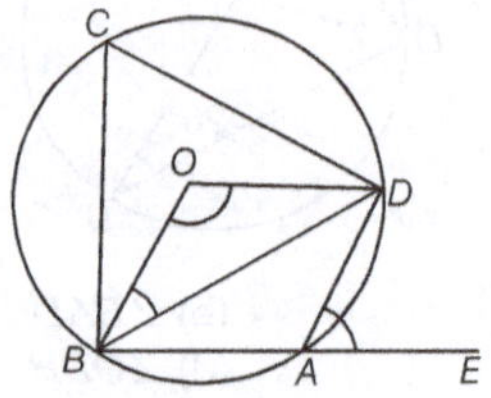

(i) $\angle BCD$

(ii) $\angle BOD$

(iii) $\angle OBD$ **[ICSE 2017]**

9. ABC is an equilateral triangle. A circle is drawn with centre A, so that it cuts AB and AC at points M and N, respectively. Prove that $BN = CM$.

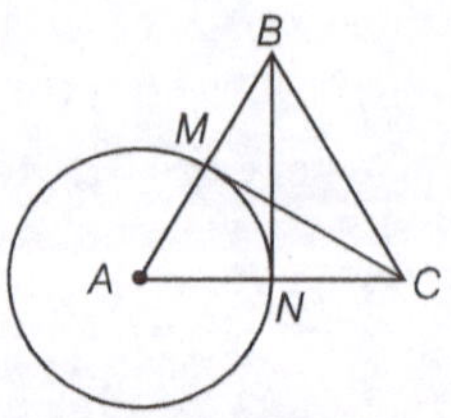

10. ABC is an isosceles triangle in which $AB = AC$. If D and E are the mid-points of AB and AC respectively, then prove that B, C, D and E are concyclic.

11. In the given figure, ABC, AEQ and CEP are straight lines. Show that $\angle APE$ and $\angle CQE$ are supplementary.

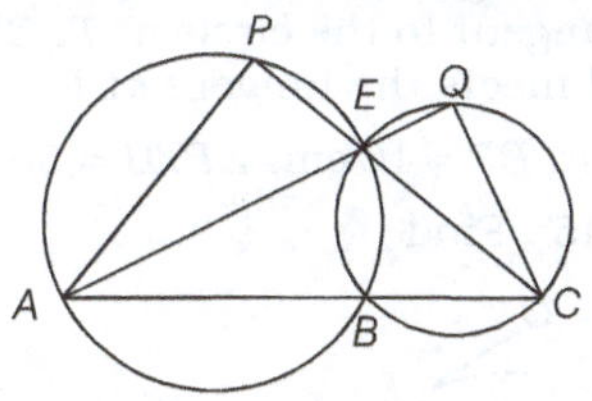

12. In the given figure, $\angle OPQ = 52°$, $\angle PQR = 110°$, then find

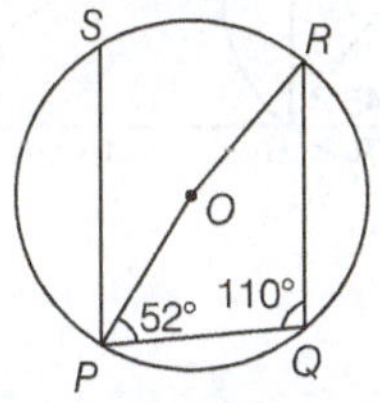

(i) $\angle PSR$
(ii) $\angle POR$
(iii) $\angle ORQ$

13. In the given figure, $\angle DAB = 105°$ and AB is parallel to CD.

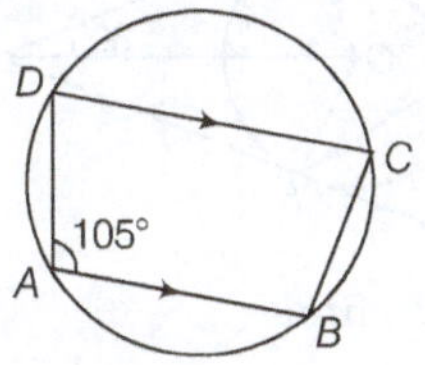

Find
(i) $\angle BCD$
(ii) $\angle ADC$
(iii) $\angle ABC$

14. Two circles intersect each other at P and Q. Through P, a straight line APB is drawn to meet the circles in A and B. Through Q, a straight line is drawn to meet the circles at C and D. Prove that AC is parallel to BD.

15. PQR is a right angled triangle with $PQ = 3$ cm and $QR = 4$ cm. A circle which touches all the sides of the triangle is inscribed in the triangle. Calculate the radius of the circle. **[2005]**

16. Two chords AB and CD of a circle intersect each other at P outside the circle. If $AB = 5$ cm, $BP = 3$ cm and $PD = 2$ cm, then find the value of CD.

17. Two chords AB and CD of a circle intersect each other at a point E inside the circle. If $AB = 9$ cm, $AE = 4$ cm and $ED = 6$ cm, then find CE.

C. 4 Marks Questions

18. If PA and PB are two tangents drawn from a point P to a circle with centre O touching it at A and B, then prove that OP is perpendicular bisector of AB.

19. In the given figure, O is the centre of circle and AB is a tangent to it at point B. If $\angle BDC = 65°$, then find $\angle BAO$.

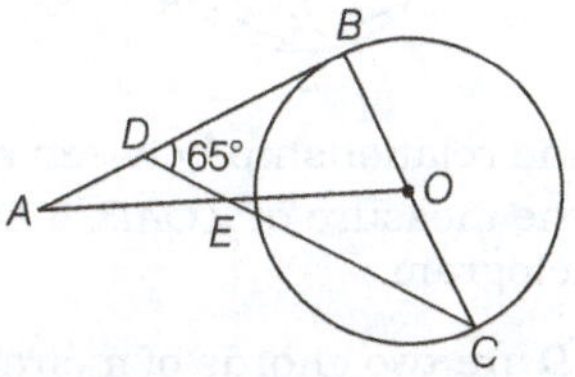

20. In the given figure, AB is diameter of a circle with centre O. AC and BD are perpendiculars on a line PQ. BD meets the circle at E. Prove that $AC = ED$.

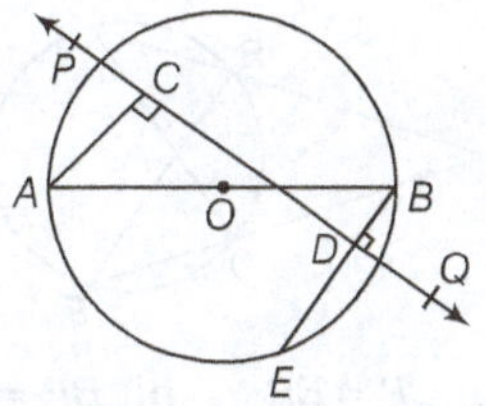

21. $ABCD$ is a cyclic quadrilateral. Sides AB and CD produced meet at a point E, whereas sides BC and AD produced meet at a point F. If $\angle DCF : \angle F : \angle E = 3 : 5 : 4$, then find the angles of the cyclic quadrilateral $ABCD$.

22. Find the length of the tangent drawn to a circle of radius 8 cm from a point which is at a distance of 10 cm from the centre of the circle.

23. Two circles of radii 5 cm and 3 cm are concentric. Calculate the length of a chord of the outer circle which touches the inner.

24. In the given figure, XP and XQ are tangents from X to the circle with centre O and R is a point on the circle. Prove that $XA + AR = XB + BR$.

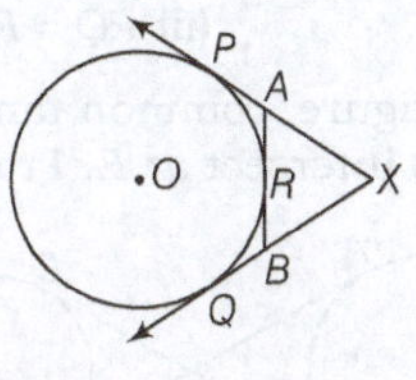

25. Let P be the mid-point of an arc APB of a circle. Prove that the tangent drawn at P will be parallel to the chord AB.

d. 6 Marks Questions

26. The given figure shows a circle with centre O. Given, $\angle AOC = a$ and $\angle ABC = b$.

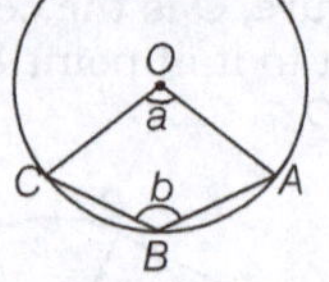

(i) Find the relationship between a and b.
(ii) Find the measure of $\angle OAB$, if $OABC$ is a parallelogram.

27. AB and CD are two chords of a circle, intersecting each other at P such that $AP = CP$. Show that $AB = CD$.

28. In the given figure, $AC = AE$.

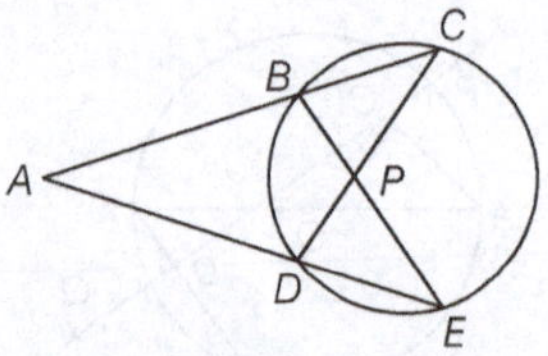

Show that (i) $CP = EP$ (ii) $BP = DP$

29. P and Q are centres of circles of radii 9 cm and 2 cm, respectively, $PQ = 17$ cm. R is the centre of a circle of radius x cm, which touches the above circles externally. Given that $\angle PRQ = 90°$, write an equation in x and solve it.

30. In the given figure, O is the centre of the circle, chord PQ is parallel and equal to the chord RS and QR is the diameter.

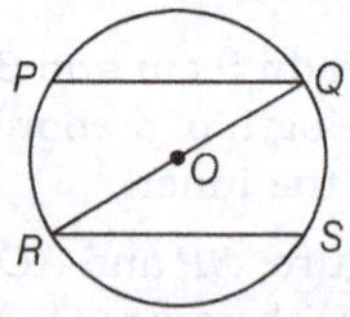

Prove that

(i) $\overset{\frown}{PR} = \overset{\frown}{QS}$ (ii) $\overset{\frown}{PQ} = \overset{\frown}{RS}$

31. In the given figure, common tangents AD and BC to two circles intersect at E. Prove that $AD = BC$.

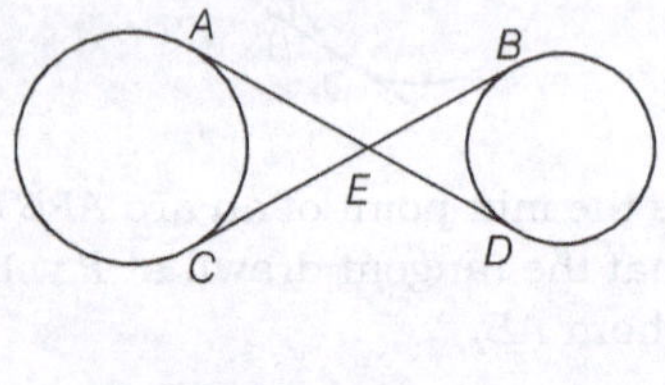

32. If the sides of a quadrilateral $ABCD$ touch a circle, then prove that $AB + CD = BC + AD$.

33. In the given figure, O is the centre of the circle. PQ is a tangent to the circle at T. Chord AB produced meets the tangent at P.

$AB = 9$ cm, $BP = 16$ cm, $\angle PTB = 50°$, $\angle OBA = 45°$. Find

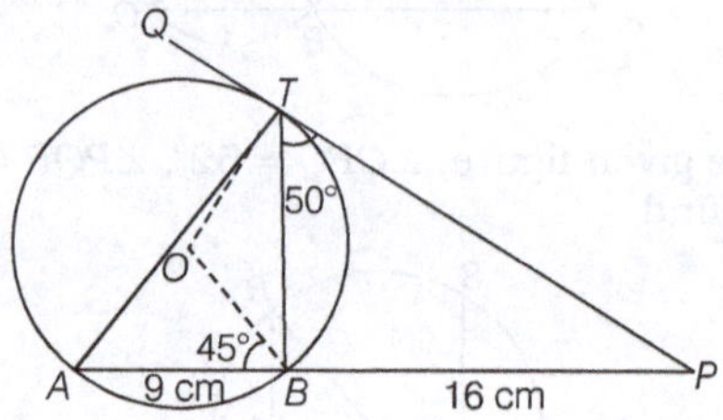

(i) length of PT
(ii) $\angle BAT$
(iii) $\angle BOT$
(iv) $\angle ABT$ **[ICSE 2023]**

34. In the given figure, O is the centre of the circle. Tangents at A and B meet at C.

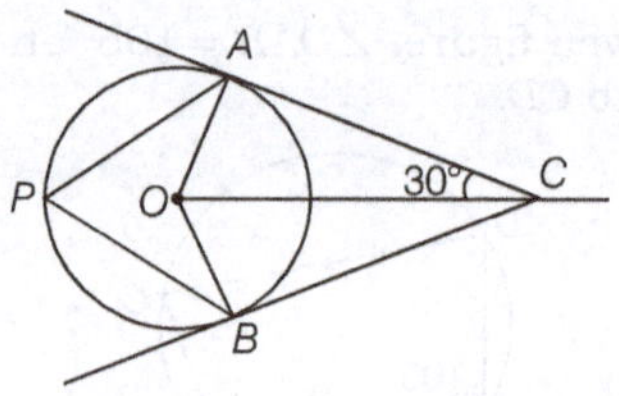

If $\angle ACO = 30°$, find
(i) $\angle BCO$
(ii) $\angle AOB$
(iii) $\angle APB$. **[ICSE 2011]**

35. In the given figure, a circle is inscribed in the quadrilateral $ABCD$. If $BC = 38$ cm, $QB = 27$ cm, $DC = 25$ cm and AD is perpendicular to DC, then find the radius of the circle.

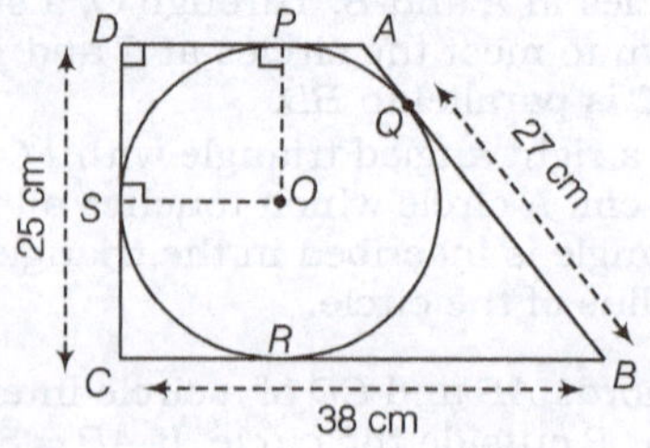

Hints and Answers

Exercise 15.1

1. (i) **Hint** The angle subtended by an arc at the centre is double the angle subtended by it at any point on the remaining part of the circle.

$$\angle ACO = \frac{1}{2}\angle AOB = \frac{1}{2} \times 110^\circ. \textbf{ Ans. } 55^\circ$$

(ii) **Hint** $OA = OC \Rightarrow \angle ACO = \angle CAO$ **Ans.** 55°

2. (i) Do same as Q. 1. **Ans.** 60°

(ii) **Hint** Reflex $\angle AOB = 360^\circ - 100^\circ = 260^\circ$

$\therefore \quad y = \frac{1}{2}$ reflex $\angle AOB \qquad$ **Ans.** 130°

(iii) **Hint** $\because$ Angle at centre $= 2 \times$ Angle at any point on the remaining part of circle

$\therefore\ \angle ABC = \frac{x}{2}$ and reflex $\angle AOC = (360^\circ - x)$

In quadrilateral $ABCO$,

$$\angle A + \angle B + \angle C + \angle O = 360^\circ$$

$$\Rightarrow 15^\circ + \frac{x}{2} + 15^\circ + (360^\circ - x) = 360^\circ$$

$$\Rightarrow 30^\circ - \frac{x}{2} = 0 \textbf{ Ans. } 60^\circ$$

(iv) **Hint** Do same as part (iii).

Ans. $140^\circ, 40^\circ$

(v) **Hint** $\because$ Angle at centre $= 2 \times$ Angle at any point on the remaining part of circle

$\therefore \quad y = \frac{1}{2} \times 240^\circ$ **Ans.** 120°

(vi) $\because$ Angle at centre $= 2 \times$ Angle at any point on the remaining part of circle

$\therefore \quad x = \frac{1}{2} \times 100 = 50^\circ$

and $\quad x = y \qquad$ [$\because$ angles in the same segment]

Ans. 50°

3. **Hint** Do same as example 10.

Ans. $\angle BOC = 120^\circ$

4. **Hint**

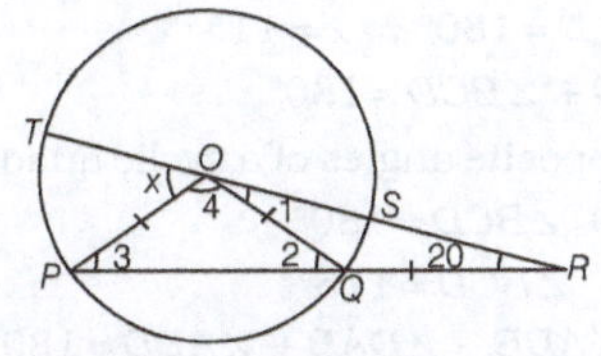

$$OP = OQ = QR$$

$\therefore \quad \angle 1 = \angle ORP$

$\Rightarrow \quad \angle 1 = 20^\circ$

Again, $\quad \angle 2 = \angle 1 + \angle ORP$

$\qquad\qquad = 20^\circ + 20^\circ = 40^\circ$

Also, $\quad OP = OQ$

$\Rightarrow \quad \angle 3 = \angle 2 = 40^\circ$

Now, $\quad \angle 2 + \angle 3 + \angle 4 = 180^\circ$

$\Rightarrow \quad 40^\circ + 40^\circ + \angle 4 = 180^\circ$

$\Rightarrow \quad \angle 4 = 100^\circ$

Again, $\quad x + \angle 1 + \angle 4 = 180^\circ$

Ans. $x = 60^\circ$

5. **Hint** $\angle ADB = \angle CBD = 32^\circ$

[$\because AD \parallel BC$, so alternate interior angles]

and $\quad \angle ODB = \angle OBD$

[$\because OB = OD$, so angles opposite to equal sides are equal]

(i) $\angle OBD = \angle ODB = \angle ADB$

(ii) $\angle AOB = 2 \times \angle ADB$

(iii) In ΔBOD, $\angle BOD = 180^\circ - (\angle OBD + \angle ODB)$

$\qquad = 180^\circ - (32^\circ + 32^\circ) = 116^\circ$

$\therefore \quad \angle BED = \frac{1}{2}\angle BOD$

Ans. (i) 32° (ii) 64° (iii) 58°

6. **Hint** Join BC

$\angle AOC = 2\angle ABC$ i.e. $\angle AOC = 2\angle EBC$ ...(i)

and $\angle BOD = 2\angle BCD$ i.e. $\angle BOD = 2\angle BCE$ ...(ii)

For $\angle ECB$,

$$\angle AEC = \angle EBC + \angle BCE$$

[exterior angles are equals to the sum of two interiro oppostie angles]

$\Rightarrow 2\angle AEC = 2\angle EBC + 2\angle BCE$

$\Rightarrow 2\angle AEC = \angle AOC + \angle BOD \qquad$ [using Eqs. (i) and (ii)]

Hence, $\angle AOC + \angle BOD = 2\angle AEC \qquad$ Hence proved.

7. **Hint** Reflex $\angle APB = 360^\circ - 60^\circ = 300^\circ$

$\angle AQB = \frac{1}{2} \cdot$ reflex $\angle APB$

[$\because$ angle at the centre = double the angle at any point on the remaining part of the circle]

$\Rightarrow \quad \angle AQB = \frac{1}{2} \times 300^\circ = 150^\circ$

$\Rightarrow \quad \angle ARB = \frac{1}{2} \times 150^\circ \quad$ **Ans.** 75°

8. **Hint** Given two congruent circles with centres O, O' and intersecting each others at points A and B.

AB is common chord.

$\angle AOB = \angle AO'B$ ...(i)

$\angle AOB = 2\angle APB$ ...(ii)

$\angle AO'B = 2\angle AQB$ ...(iii)

From Eqs. (i), (ii) and (iii), we get

$2\angle APB = 2\angle AQB$

$\Rightarrow \angle APB = \angle AQB$

$\Rightarrow \quad BP = BQ \qquad$ **Hence proved.**

9. **Hint**

(i) $\angle CAB = x$

$\angle COB = 2x$ (angle at the centre = double the angle at the remaining part of the circle)

(ii) $\angle OCD = \angle COB = 2x$

$\angle ODC = 2x$ [$OC = OD$, radii of same circle]

$\angle ODC = 180° - (2x + 2x)$

$= 180° - 4x$

(iii) $\angle DAC = \frac{1}{2}\angle DOC$

$= \frac{1}{2}(180 - 4x) = (90 - 2x)$

(iv) $\angle ACD = \angle CAB = x$

$\Rightarrow \angle ADC = 180° - (x - 90° - 2x) = (90° + x)$

10. Hint Angle at centre = 2 × Angle at any point on the remaining part of circle. Join OC.

$\therefore \quad \angle AOC = 2 \times \angle AEC = 2 \times 50° = 100°$

Since, $AB = BC$

$\therefore \quad \angle AOB = \angle BOC$

[$\because$ equal chords of a circle subtends equal angles at the centre]

$\Rightarrow \quad \angle AOC = \angle AOB + \angle BOC = 100°$

$\Rightarrow \angle AOB + \angle AOB = 100° \Rightarrow 2\angle AOB = 100°$

$\Rightarrow \quad \angle AOB = 50°$

Thus, $\angle AOB = \angle AEC = 50° \Rightarrow BO || CE$ Hence proved.

[$\because$ a pair of corresponding angles are equal]

11. (i) **Hint** AC and BD are chords of a circle that bisects each other.

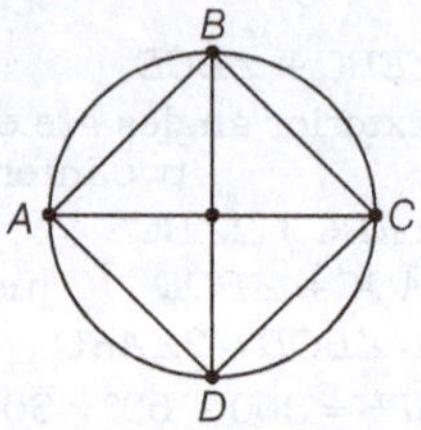

$\Rightarrow$ Both are passing through the centre of the circle.

$\Rightarrow$ Both are the diameter of the circle

Hence proved.

(ii) **Hint** AC and BD are diameters of the circle

$\therefore \angle ABC = 90°, \angle ADC = 90°,$

$\angle BAD = 90°$ and $\angle BCD = 90°$

$\Rightarrow ABCD$ is quadrilateral in which each angle is 90°.

$\Rightarrow ABCD$ is rectangle Hence proved.

12. Hint Join OB and OC.

Now, $\angle BOC = 2\angle BAC$

[$\because$ angle subtended by an arc at the centre = double the angle subtended by it at any point on the remaining part of the circle]

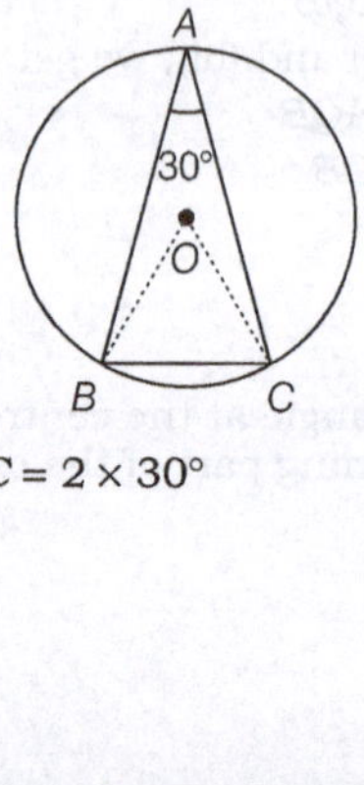

$\Rightarrow \quad \angle BOC = 2 \times 30°$

In ΔOBC, $OB = OC$ [radii of same circle]

$\therefore \quad \angle OCB = \angle OBC$

[$\because$ angles opposite to equal sides of a triangle are equal]

As the sum of angles of a triangle is 180°.

$\therefore \quad \angle OBC + \angle OCB + \angle BOC = 180°$

$\Rightarrow \Delta OBC$ is an equilateral triangle.

$\Rightarrow BC = OB$, i.e. BC is equal to the radius of circle.

13. Hint $\angle BEC$ is an exterior angle of ΔCDE.

$\therefore \quad \angle BEC = \angle ECD + \angle EDC$

[$\because$ exterior angle = sum of two interior opposite angles]

$\Rightarrow \quad 130° = 20° + \angle EDC$

Now, $\angle BAC = \angle BDC$

Ans. 110°

14. (i) **Hint** In ΔABD, $\angle ADB + \angle BAD + \angle ABD = 180°$

[by angle sum property of a triangle]

$\Rightarrow \angle ADB + 65° + 70° = 180° \Rightarrow \angle ADB = 45°$

From figure, $\angle ADC = \angle ADB + \angle BDC$

$= 45° + 45° = 90°$

Thus, an arc of a circle subtends a right angle, so the arc is a semi-circle.

$\Rightarrow AC$ is a diameter of the circle Hence proved.

(ii) **Hint** $\angle ACB = \angle ADB$

[$\because$ angles in same segment of a circle]

Ans. 45°

Exercise 15.2

1. Hint (i) $\angle BAD + \angle DCB = 180°$

[$\because$ sum of opposite angles of a cyclic quadrilateral is 180°]

Ans. 60°

(ii) **Hint** $\angle ADB = 90°$ [$\because AB$ is the diameter]

In ΔABD, $\angle BAD + \angle ADB + \angle DBA = 180°$

[by angle sum property of a triangle]

$\Rightarrow \quad 60° + 90° + \angle DBA = 180°$ **Ans.** 30°

2. Hint $\angle ABC + \angle ACB + \angle BAC = 180°$

$\Rightarrow \quad \angle ABC + 90° + 25° = 180° \Rightarrow \angle ABC = 65°$

$\because ABCD$ is a cyclic quadrilateral.

So, $\angle B + \angle D = 180° \Rightarrow x = 115°$

3. Hint $\angle BAD + \angle BCD = 180°$

[$\because$ sum of opposite angles of a cyclic quadrilateral is 180°]

$\Rightarrow \quad 65° + \angle BCD = 180°$

$\Rightarrow \quad \angle BCD = 115°$

In ΔADB, $\angle ADB + \angle DAB + \angle ABD = 180°$

[$\because$ angle sum property of a triangle]

$\Rightarrow \quad \angle ADB + 65° + 70° = 180°$

$\angle ACB = \angle ADB$

[$\because$ angle in the same segment are equal]

Here, $\angle ADC = \angle ADB + \angle BDC = 45° + 45° = 90°$

Since, angle in a semi-circle is 90°

$\therefore AC$ is diameter. Hence proved.

Ans. 45°

4. Hint $\angle ACD + \angle AED = 180°$ ...(i)

[$\because$ sum of opposite angles of a cyclic quadrilateral is 180°]

$\because$ AB is a diameter of circle.

$\therefore$ $\angle AEB = 90°$ [angle in a semi-circle] ...(ii)

On adding Eqs. (i) and (ii), we get the required value.

Ans. 270°

5. Hint

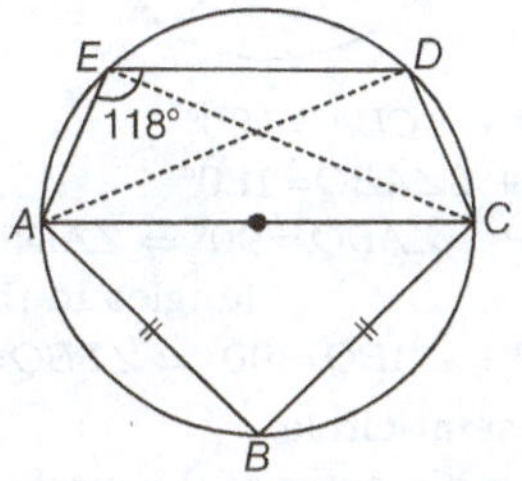

(i) $\angle AEC = 90°$ [$\because$ angle of semi-circle]

$\angle DEC = \angle AED - \angle AEC$

$= 118° - 90° = 28°$

(ii) $\angle DAC = \angle DEC = 28°$

$\angle BAC = \angle BCA$

AC is a diameter of the circle $\angle ABC = 90°$

$\Rightarrow$ $2\angle BAC = 90°$

$\angle BAC = 45°$

$\angle DAB = \angle DAC + \angle BAC$

$\angle DAB = 28° + 45° = 73°$

6. Hint

(i) $\angle QPS + \angle QRS = 180°$

Ans. $\angle QRS = 107°$

(ii) In ΔPQS,

$\angle SPQ + \angle PQS + \angle PSQ = 180°$

Now, in ΔQRS,

$\angle QSR + \angle SRQ + \angle RQS = 180°$

Ans. $\angle RQS = 43°$

(iii) Here, $\angle PRQ = \angle PSQ$

[since, angles in same segment are equal]

Ans. $\angle PRQ = 52°$

7. (i) **Hint** $\angle BOD = 2 \times \angle BAD$

[$\because$ angle at centre = 2 × angle at any point on the remaining part of circle]

(ii) **Hint** $\angle BCD + \angle BAD = 180°$

[$\because$ sum of a pair of opposite angles of a cyclic quadrilateral is 180°]

(iii) **Hint** Join OC. As equal chords of a circle subtend equal angles at the centre and chord BC = chord CD, then $\angle BOC = \angle COD \Rightarrow$ $\angle BOC = \frac{1}{2}\angle BOD$

(iv) **Hint** In ΔOBD, $OB = OD$ [$\because$ radii of same circle]

$\Rightarrow$ $\angle ODB = \angle OBD$

[$\because$ angle opposite to the equal sides are equal]

$\because$ $\angle OBD + \angle ODB + \angle BOD = 180°$

[by angle sum property of a triangle]

$\therefore$ $2\angle OBD + 150° = 180°$

Ans. (i) 150° (ii) 105° (iii) 75° (iv) 15°

8. (i) **Hint** $\angle BAD = \angle BCE$

[$\because$ exterior angle of a cyclic quadrilateral is equal to the opposite interior angle]

$\Rightarrow \angle BAC + \angle CAD = 80°$

$\Rightarrow$ $\angle CAD = 80° - \angle BAC$

Ans. 55°

(ii) **Hint** $\angle CBD = \angle CAD$

[$\because$ angles in the same segment are equal]

Ans. 55°

(iii) **Hint** $\angle BAD + \angle ADC = 180°$ [$\because AB \parallel DC$]

$\Rightarrow (\angle BAC + \angle DAC) + \angle ADC = 180°$

$\Rightarrow$ $25° + 55° + \angle ADC = 180°$ **Ans.** 100°

9. (i) **Hint** $\angle DAB + \angle DCB = 180°$

[$\because$ sum of a pair of opposite angles of cyclic quadrilateral is 180°]

Ans. 60°

(ii) **Hint** $\angle ADB = 90°$ [$\because$ angle in a semi-circle]

$\therefore$ $\angle DBA = 180° - (\angle ADB + \angle DAB)$ **Ans.** 30°

(iii) **Hint** $\angle BOD = 2 \times \angle DAB$

[$\because$ angle at centre = 2 × angle at any point on the remaining part of centre]

$OD = OB$ [radii]

$\Rightarrow$ $\angle ODB = \angle OBD$

[$\because$ angles opposite to equal sides]

$\therefore$ $\angle ODB = \frac{1}{2}(180° - \angle BOD)$

[by angle sum property of a triangle]

Since, $OD \parallel BC$

$\Rightarrow$ $\angle DBC = \angle ODB$ **Ans.** 30°

(iv) **Hint** $OA = OD$ [radii of same circle]

$\Rightarrow \angle ODA = \angle DAO = 60°$

In ΔBCD, $\angle BCD + \angle DBC + \angle CDB = 180°$

[angle sum property of triangle]

$\Rightarrow 120° + 30° + \angle CDB = 180° \Rightarrow \angle CDB = 30°$

$\therefore \angle ADC = \angle ODA + \angle ODB + \angle CDB$ **Ans.** 120°

Again, in ΔODA, $AO = OD$

$\Rightarrow$ $\angle OAD = \angle ODA = 60°$

[$\because$ angle opposite to equal sides]

$\therefore$ $\angle AOD = 180° - (60° + 60°) = 60°$

$\Rightarrow \Delta AOD$ is equilateral triangle. **Hence proved.**

10. (i) **Hint** $\angle AOB = 2 \times \angle APB$

[$\because$ angle at the centre = 2 × angle at any point on the remaining part of circle]

Ans. 150°

(ii) **Hint** First join BC.

$AOBC$ is a cyclic quadrilateral.

$\therefore$ $\angle AOB + \angle ACB = 180°$

$\Rightarrow$ $150° + \angle ACB = 180°$ **Ans.** 30°

(iii) **Hint** $\angle ADB = \angle ACB$

[$\because$ angles in the same segment]

Ans. 30°

11. Hint Since, $ABCE$ is cyclic quadrilateral, therefore

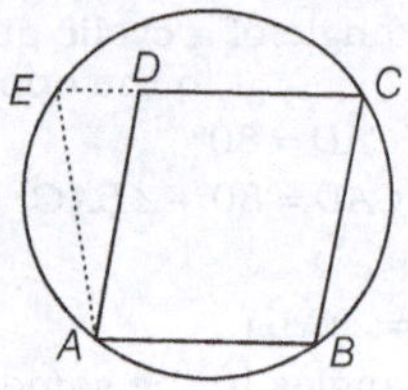

$\angle AED + \angle ABC = 180°$ ...(i)

[$\because$ sum of pair of opposite angles of a cyclic quadrilateral is 180°]

$\because \quad \angle ADE + \angle ADC = 180°$

[$\because$ EDC is a straight line]

$\Rightarrow \quad \angle ADE + \angle ABC = 180°$ ...(ii)

[$\because \angle ADC = \angle ABC$, opposite angles of a parallelogram]

From Eqs. (i) and (ii), we get

$\angle AED = \angle ADE$ **Hence proved.**

12. Hint Prove sum of opposite angles is 180°.

13. Since, SP is a bisector of $\angle RPT$.

$\therefore \quad \angle RPS = \angle TPS$ ...(i)

$\angle RPS = \angle RQS$ [angle in the same segment] ...(ii)

and $\angle TPS = \angle QRS$ ...(iii)

[exterior angle of a cyclic quadrilateral]

From Eqs. (i), (ii) and (iii), we get

$\angle QRS = \angle RQS$ **Hence proved.**

14. Hint We have, $\angle PAT = \angle PSB$ ...(i)

[$\because$ exterior angle of a cyclic quadrilateral is equal to the interior opposite angle]

and $\quad \angle PDT = \angle PSC$ ...(ii)

On adding Eqs. (i) and (ii), we get

$\angle PAT + \angle PDT = \angle PSB + \angle PSC$

But $\angle PSB + \angle PSC = 180°$ [linear pair axiom]

$\Rightarrow \angle PAT + \angle PDT = 180°$

15. Hint $AD = BC$ ...(i) [given]

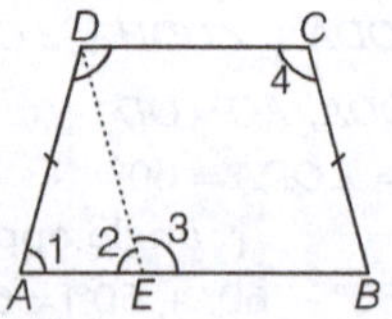

Draw $\quad DE \parallel CB$

$\Rightarrow \quad DE = BC$

[opposite sides of a parallelogram] ...(ii)

From Eqs. (i) and (ii), we get

$AD = DE$

$\Rightarrow \quad \angle 1 = \angle 2$

[$\because$ angles opposite to equal sides of triangle are equal]

Also, $\quad \angle 3 = \angle 4$

[$\because$ opposite angles of a parallelogram]

Now, $\quad \angle 2 + \angle 3 = 180°$ [by linear pair axiom]

$\therefore \quad \angle 1 + \angle 4 = 180°$ **Hence proved.**

16. Hint $ABCD$ is a cyclic quadrilateral.

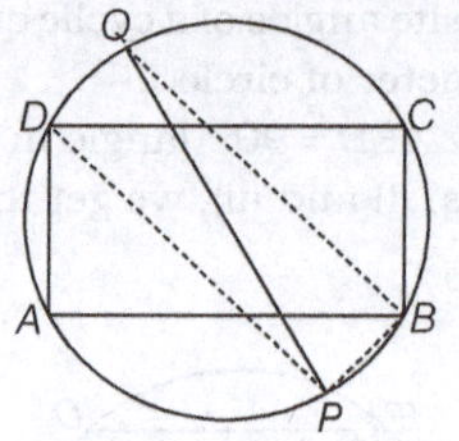

$\angle CDA + \angle CBA = 180°$

$\Rightarrow \quad 2\angle ADP + 2\angle ABQ = 180°$

$\Rightarrow \quad \angle ADP + \angle ABQ = 90° \Rightarrow \angle ADP = \angle ABP$

[angles in the same segment]

$\Rightarrow \quad \angle ABP + \angle ABQ = 90° \Rightarrow \angle PBQ = 90$

$\Rightarrow PBCQ$ is a semi-circle.

Hence, PQ is a diameter of the circle, because diameter of the circle subtends a right angle at the circumference. **Hence proved.**

17. Hint Join O to A, B, C, D and join A to C.

$AD = BC$ [given]

$\therefore \quad \angle AOD = \angle BOC$

[$\because$ equal chords of a circle subtends equal angles at the centre of the circle]

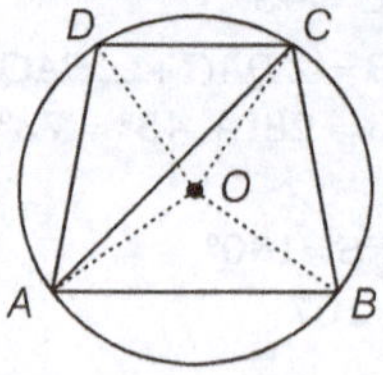

$\Rightarrow \quad 2\angle ACD = 2\angle BAC$

[$\because$ angle subtended by an arc at the centre is double the angle subtended by it at any other point on the remaining part of the circle]

or $\quad \angle ACD = \angle BAC$

But they are alternate interior angles.

$\therefore \quad AB \parallel DC$ **Hence proved.**

18. Let $ABCD$ be a cyclic quadrilateral in which $AB \parallel DC$.

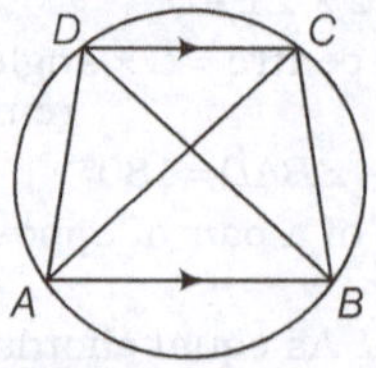

Then, $\angle A + \angle D = 180°$ [sum of cointerior angles] ...(i)

and $\angle D + \angle B = 180°$ ...(ii)

[$\because$ sum of opposite angles in a cyclic quadrilateral is 180°]

From Eqs. (i) and (ii), we get

$\angle A = \angle B$ ...(iii)

To show $\Delta ABC \cong \Delta BAD$ [by rule AAS]

By CPCT,

(i) $BC = AD$ (ii) $AC = BD$. **Hence proved.**

19. Hint Do same example 27

(ii) 6 (iii) 24

Exercise 15.3

1. **Hint** Radius of outer circle, $AO = 26$ cm and radius of inner circle, $AP = 10$ cm

In ΔACP, $AO^2 = AP^2 + OP^2$

[By Pythagoras Theorem] [$\because OP \perp AB$]

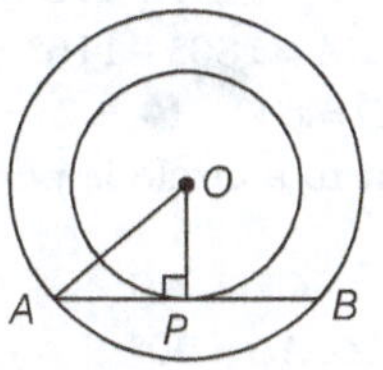

$\Rightarrow \quad 26^2 = AP^2 + 10^2$

$\Rightarrow \quad AP^2 = 576$

$\Rightarrow \quad AP = 24$ cm

$\therefore \quad AB = 2AP$ **Ans.** 48 cm

2. **Hint** $AQ = AR$ [tangents from A] ...(i)

$BP = QB$ [tangents from B] ...(ii)

$CP = CR$ [tangents from C] ...(iii)

$\therefore$ Perimeter of ΔABC

$= AB + BC + AC$

$= AB + BP + CP + AC$

$= AQ + AR$ [using Eqs. (ii) and (iii)]

$= 2AQ$ [using Eq. (i)]

Hence proved.

3. **Hint** To show that

$\Delta TOA \cong \Delta TOB$ [by SSS congruency rule]

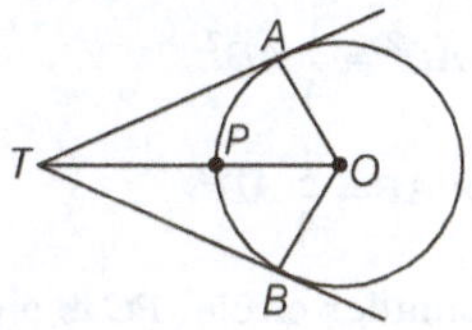

By CPCT, $\angle ATO = \angle BTO$

$\Rightarrow TP$ bisects $\angle ATB$. **Hence proved.**

4. **Hint** Since, $OP \perp PT$

In right angled ΔOPT,

$OT^2 = OP^2 + PT^2$ [by Pythagoras theorem]

$\Rightarrow \quad PT^2 = (13)^2 - (5)^2 = 169 - 25 = 144$

$\Rightarrow \quad PT = 12$ cm

Now, $OE + ET = 13$ cm

$\Rightarrow \quad ET = 13 - 5 = 8$ cm [$\because OE = 5$ cm]

Let $\quad AP = x \Rightarrow AT = 12 - x$

In right angled ΔAET,

$AT^2 = AE^2 + ET^2$

$AT^2 = PA^2 + ET^2$ [$\because PA = AE$]

$\Rightarrow \quad (12 - x)^2 = x^2 + (8)^2$

$\Rightarrow \quad x = \dfrac{10}{3}$

$\therefore \quad AB = 2AE$

$= 2x$

Ans. 20/3 cm

5. **Hint** We know that, the tangents drawn from an external point to a circle are equal.

$\therefore \quad AQ = AR,\ BP = BQ,\ CS = CP$ and $DR = DS$

Now, $DR = DS = 5$ cm

$AR = (AD - DR) = (23 - 5)$ cm $= 18$ cm

$\therefore \quad AQ = AR = 18$ cm

$BQ = (AB - AQ) = (29 - 18)$ cm $= 11$ cm

Since, tangent to a circle is perpendicular to the radius through the point of contact.

$\therefore \quad \angle OQB = \angle OPB = 90°$ and $\angle B = 90°$ [given]

$\Rightarrow \quad OQBP$ is a square $\Rightarrow OP = OQ = BQ$

Ans. 11cm

6. **Hint** Since, the tangents from an external point being equal.

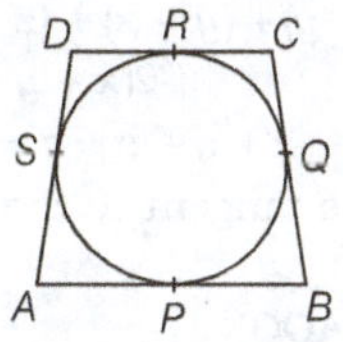

$\therefore \quad AP = AS,\ BP = BQ,\ CR = CQ$ and $DR = DS$

$\therefore \quad AP + BP + CR + DR = AS + BQ + CQ + DS$

$\Rightarrow (AP + BP) + (CR + DR) = (AS + DS) + (BQ + CQ)$

$\Rightarrow \quad AB + CD = AD + BC$

$\Rightarrow \quad AD = (AB + CD) - BC$

Ans. 3 cm

7. **Hint** $PA = PB \Rightarrow \angle PAB = \angle PBA = \theta$ (let)

In ΔPAB, $\angle PAB + \angle PBA + \angle APB = 180°$

[By angle sum property of a triangle]

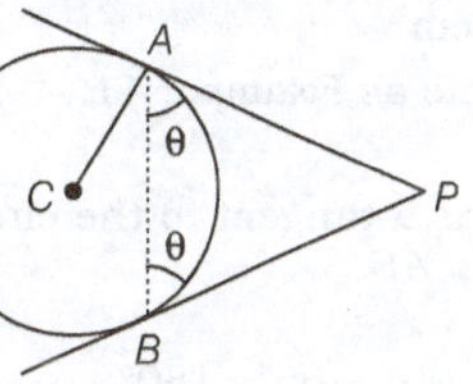

$\Rightarrow \quad \theta + \theta + \angle APB = 180°$

$\Rightarrow \quad \angle APB = 180° - 2\theta$ ...(i)

Now, $\angle CAB + \angle PAB = 90°$ [$\because$ tangent at a point to a circle is perpendicular to the radius]

$\Rightarrow \quad \angle CAB = 90° - \theta$ ...(ii)

From Eqs. (i) and (ii), we get

$\angle APB = 2\angle CAB$ **Hence proved.**

8. **Hint** In ΔOAP and ΔORP,

$PA = PR$ [tangents from point P]

$\Rightarrow \quad OA = OR$ [radii]

$\Rightarrow \quad OP = OP$ [common]

$\therefore \quad \Delta OAP \cong \Delta ORP$ [by SSS congruency rule]

By CPCT, $\angle AOP = \angle POR$ ...(i)

Similarly, $\angle BOQ = \angle ROQ$ ...(ii)

Now, $\angle AOP + \angle POR + \angle ROQ + \angle BOQ = 180°$

[$\because AOB$ is a straight line]

$\therefore \quad 2(\angle POR + \angle ROQ) = 180°$

9. Hint Since, tangent are drawn from an external point to the circle are equal length.

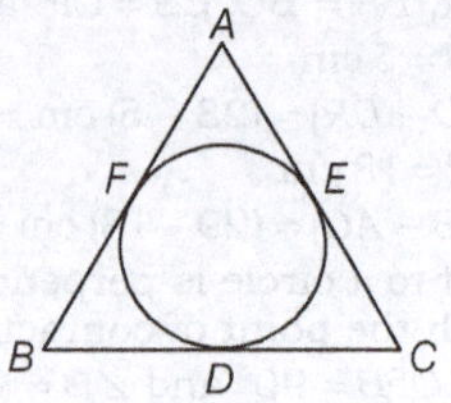

Let $BD = BF = x$

$CD = CE = y$ and $AE = AF = z$

Now, $BC + CA + AB = a + b + c$

$\Rightarrow (BD + DC) + (CE + EA) + (AF + FB) = a + b + c$

$\Rightarrow \quad (x + y) + (y + z) + (z + x) = a + b + c$

$\Rightarrow \quad 2(x + y + z) = 2s$

$\Rightarrow \quad x + y + z = s \Rightarrow x = s - (y + z)$

10. Hint Given, AT is tangent to the circle at A and OA is radius $OA \perp AT$.

$\angle ABQ = \frac{1}{2} \angle AOQ$

[$\because$ angle at centre of a circle = double the angle at any point on the remaining part of circle]

$\Rightarrow \angle ABQ = \frac{1}{2} \times 58°$

$\Rightarrow \angle ABT = 29°$

In ΔABT,

$\angle ATB + \angle ABT + \angle BAT = 180°$

$\angle ATB = 61°$

$\therefore \quad \angle ATQ = 61°$

11. Hint Do same as Example 41.

Ans. 11.25 cm

12. Hint Do same as Example 41.

Ans. 75 cm

13. Hint As AB is a tangent to the circle at B and OB is radius, $OB \perp AB$

In ΔBCD,

$\angle BCD + 90° + 65° = 180°$

$\Rightarrow \quad \angle BCE = 25°$

$\Rightarrow \quad \angle BOE = 2 \times 25° = 50°$

[angle at the centre = double the angle at the remaining part of circle]

$\therefore \quad \angle BOA = 50°$

In ΔBOA,

$\Rightarrow \angle BAO + 90° + 50° = 180°$ **Ans.** 40°

14. (i) $\because$ The angle formed by semi-circle is 90°.

Hence, $\angle BDA = 90°$

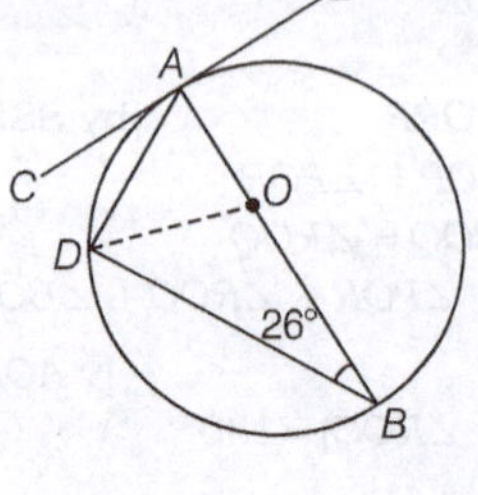

(ii) In ΔABD,

$\angle A + \angle B + \angle D = 180°$

[$\because$ sum of angles of a triangle is 180°]

$\Rightarrow \quad \angle A + 26° + 90° = 180°$

[$\because$ given $\angle B = 26°$ and $\angle BDA = 90°$]

$\Rightarrow \quad \angle A + 116° = 180°$

$\Rightarrow \quad \angle A = 180° - 116° = 64°$

Hence, $\angle BAD = 64°$

(iii) $\because$ The tangent to a circle is perpendicular to its diameter.

$\Rightarrow \quad CE \perp AB$

$\therefore \quad \angle CAB = 90°$

$\Rightarrow \quad \angle CAD + \angle DAB = 90°$ [$\because \angle CAB = \angle CAD + \angle DAB$]

$\Rightarrow \quad \angle CAD + 64° = 90°$ [$\because \angle DAB = 90° - 26° = 64°$]

$\Rightarrow \quad \angle CAD = 90° - 64° = 26°$

Hence, $\angle CAD = 26°$

(iv) In ΔODB,

$OD = OB$ [$\because$ OD and OB are radius]

So, ΔODB is isosceles triangle.

$\therefore \quad \angle OBD = \angle ODB$

$\therefore \quad \angle ODB = 26°$ [$\because$ given, $\angle OBD = 26°$]

15. Hint Since, chord PB and tangent at point D intersect each other at A.

$\therefore \quad AD^2 = AP \times AB$ ...(i)

Since, D is the mid-point of AC.

$\therefore \quad AD = \frac{1}{2} AC = \frac{1}{2} AB$ [$\because AB = AC$]

$\Rightarrow \quad AD^2 = \frac{1}{4} AB^2$

$\Rightarrow \quad AP \times AB = \frac{1}{4} AB^2$ [from Eq. (i)]

16. Hint For the smaller circle, PC is a chord and QPR is the tangent at the point P.

$\therefore \quad \angle QPC = \angle CAP$

[angle in alternate segment are equal]

For the bigger circle PD is a chord and QPR is the tangent at the point P.

$\angle QPC = \angle DBP$

$\angle CAP = \angle DBP$ [$\because$ corresponding angle]

Therefore, $AC \parallel BD$.

17. Hint $\angle COD + \angle AOD = 180°$

$\angle AOD + \angle BOC = 180°$

$\because \quad \Delta OAP \cong \Delta OAS$ [from SSS congruency]

$\therefore \quad \angle 1 = \angle 2$

$\angle 5 = \angle 6$

and $\quad \angle 7 = \angle 8$

But $\angle 1 + \angle 2 + \angle 3 + \angle 4 + \angle 5 + \angle 6 + \angle 7 + \angle 8 = 360°$

$\Rightarrow \quad 2(\angle 1 + \angle 4 + \angle 5 + \angle 8) = 360°$

$\Rightarrow \quad (\angle 1 + \angle 8) + (\angle 4 + \angle 5) = 180°$

$\Rightarrow \quad \angle AOB + \angle COD = 180°$

Similarly, $\angle BOC + \angle COD = 180°$

Chapter Exercise

1. Hint (b) Let O is centre of circle

$\angle POQ = 130°$

$\therefore \angle OPT = \angle OQT = 90°$

[radius is perpendicular to tangent]

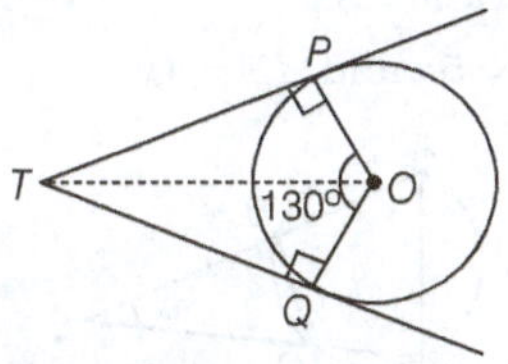

In quadrilateral $OPTQ$,

$\angle PTQ + \angle OPT + \angle OQT + \angle POQ = 360°$

$\Rightarrow \angle PTQ + 90° + 90° + 130° = 360°$

$\Rightarrow \angle PTQ = 50°$

2. Hint (a) In ΔOAB

$OA = OB$ [radii of circle]

$\Rightarrow \angle OAB = \angle OBA = 40°$

$\Rightarrow \angle AOB = 180° - (40 + 40) = 100°$

$\Rightarrow \angle ACB = \frac{1}{2} \angle AOB$

$\Rightarrow \angle ACB = \frac{1}{2} \times 100 = 50°$

3. Hint (a) In $\Delta OAB = \angle OBA = 3x$ [$\because OA = OB$]

In ΔOAB,

$\angle OAB + \angle OBA + \angle AOB = 180°$

$\Rightarrow 3x + 3x + 4x = 180°$

$\Rightarrow x = \frac{180°}{10}$

$\Rightarrow x = 18°$

4. (d) Given, $\angle PST = 30°$ and $\angle SPQ = 60°$

From alternate segment theorem

$\angle PQS = \angle PST = 30°$ ...(i)

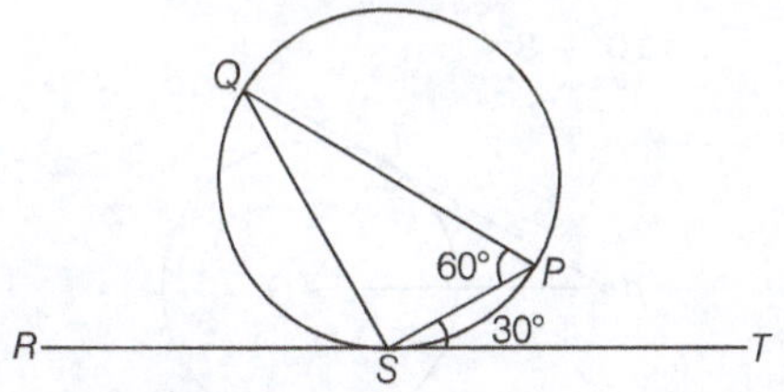

Now, in ΔPQS,

$\angle PQS + \angle PSQ + \angle SPQ = 180°$

$\Rightarrow 30° + \angle PSQ + 60° = 180°$

$\Rightarrow \angle PSQ = 180° - 60° - 30°$

$\Rightarrow \angle PSQ = 90°$

5. Hint (a) Here, $\angle OAP = 90°$

[$\because$ tangent at a point to a circle is perpendicular to the radius]

Now, $\angle AOP + \angle BOP = 180°$

$\Rightarrow \angle AOP + 115° = 180°$

and also, $\angle OAP + \angle AOP + \angle APO = 180°$

[angle sum property of triangle]

$\Rightarrow 90° + 65° + \angle APO = 180°$

$\Rightarrow \angle APO = 180° - 155° = 25°$

6. Hint $\because \angle ACB = 180° - (60° + 25°) = 95°$

$\therefore \angle ADB = b$

[$\because$ angles in the same segment are equal]

Ans. 95°

7. (i) **Hint** Now, $\angle DAB + \angle BCD = 180°$

[$\because$ sum of opposite angles of cyclic quadrilateral is 180°]

$\Rightarrow \angle DAB + 130° = 180°$ **Ans.** 50°

(ii) **Hint** $\angle ADB = 90°$ [$\because$ angle in semi-circle]

In ΔADB, $\angle DBA + \angle DAB + \angle ADB = 180°$

[by angle sum property of a triangle]

$\Rightarrow \angle DBA + 50° + 90° = 180°$ [from part (i)]

Ans. 40°

8. Hint $\angle DAB = 180° - \angle DAE$ [by linear pair axiom]

$= 180° - 70° = 110°$

(i) $\angle BCD + \angle DAB = 180°$

[$\because$ sum of opposite angles of cyclic quadrilateral is 180°]

(ii) $\angle BOD = 2\angle BCD = 2 \times 70° = 140°$

(iii) $\because OB = OD =$ Radius of circle

$\therefore \angle OBD = \angle ODB$ ...(i)

$\Rightarrow \angle OBD + \angle BDO + \angle DOB = 180°$

$\Rightarrow \angle OBD + \angle ODB + 140° = 180°$ [from part (ii)]

$\Rightarrow 2\angle OBD = 180° - 140° = 40°$

Ans. (i) 70° (ii) 140° (iii) 20°

9. Hint To show $\Delta BMC \cong \Delta CNB$ by CPCT, $BN = CM$

10. Hint Here, $AB = AC$

$\Rightarrow \angle ABC = \angle ACB$ ...(i)

$AD = AE$

[$\because D$ and E are the mid-points of AB and AC]

$\angle AED = \angle ADE$ ...(ii)

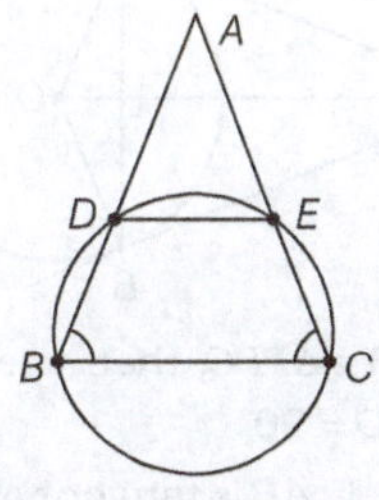

Now, $\angle A + \angle ABC + \angle ACB = 180°$

[by angle sum property of a triangle]

and $\angle A + \angle ADE + \angle AED = 180°$

$\Rightarrow \angle A + 2\angle ACB = 180°$ and $\angle A + 2\angle ADE = 180°$

[using Eqs. (i) and (ii)]

$\therefore \angle A + 2\angle ACB = \angle A + 2\angle ADE$

$\Rightarrow \angle ACB = \angle ADE$

$\Rightarrow \angle ECB = \angle ADE$

$\Rightarrow \angle ECB + \angle EDB = \angle ADE + \angle EDB = 180°$

11. Hint $\angle APC = \angle EBC$

[$\because$ exterior angle of a cyclic quadrilateral equals the opposite interior angle]

$\angle EBC + \angle EQC = 180^\circ$

[$\because$ sum of opposite angles of a cyclic quadrilateral is 180°]

$\therefore \quad \angle APC + \angle EQC = 180^\circ$

12. Hint Use property of cyclic quadrilateral.

Ans. (i) 70° (ii) 220° (iii) 58°

13. Hint Use property of cyclic quadrilateral and parallel lines.

Ans. (i) 75° (ii) 75° (iii) 105°

14. Hint Join PQ.

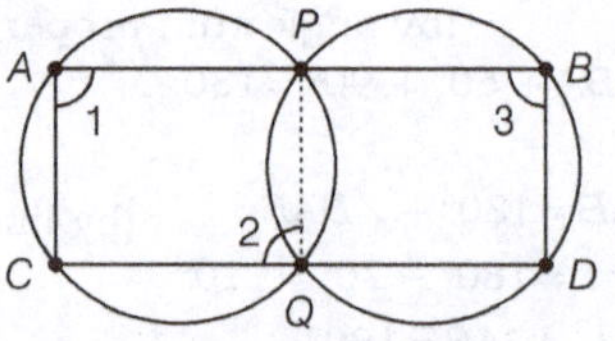

Here, $APQC$ is a cyclic quadrilateral.

$\therefore \quad \angle 1 + \angle 2 = 180^\circ$ ...(i)

Again, $BPQD$ is a cyclic quadrilateral.

$\therefore \quad \angle 2 = \angle 3$ ...(ii)

[$\because$ exterior angle of a cyclic quadrilateral equals the opposite interior angle]

From Eqs. (i) and (ii), we get

$\angle 1 + \angle 3 = 180^\circ$

15. Hint Do same as Example 37. **Ans.** 1 cm

16. Hint Do same as Example 39. **Ans.** 10 cm

17. Hint Do same as Example 39. **Ans.** $\frac{10}{3}$ cm

18. Hint Given, PA and PB are the two tangents from a point P lying outside the circle to the circle with centre O.

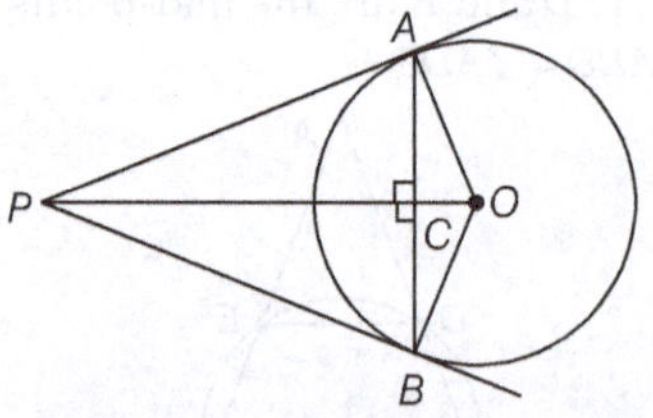

We show, $\Delta PAO \cong \Delta PBO$, then use CPCT.

19. Hint $\angle ABO = 90^\circ$

[$\because AB$ is tangent at point B to the circle]

In ΔBCD, $\angle DBC + \angle BCD + \angle CDB = 180^\circ$

[by angle sum property of triangle]

$\Rightarrow \quad 90^\circ + \angle BCD + 65^\circ = 180^\circ$

$\Rightarrow \quad \angle BCD = 25^\circ$

$\therefore \angle BOE = 2\angle BCE$

In ΔABO,

$\angle BAO = 180^\circ - (\angle ABO + \angle AOB)$

Ans. 40°

20. Hint Join AE

$\Rightarrow \quad \angle CDE = 90^\circ, \angle ACD = 90^\circ$

Also, $\quad \angle AED = 90^\circ$

$\Rightarrow ACDE$ is a rectangle.

$\therefore \quad AC = ED$ **Hence proved.**

21. Hint Here, $\angle DCF = 3x$

$\angle F = 5x$ and $\angle E = 4x$

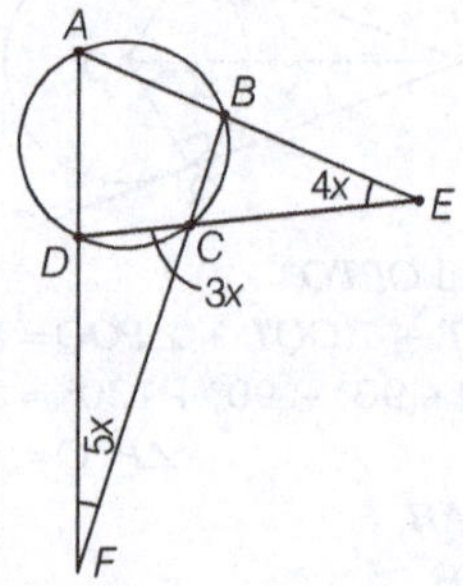

Now, $\quad \angle A = 3x$

[$\because$ exterior angle of cyclic quadrilateral equals the opposite interior angle]

$\angle ADC = 3x + 5x = 8x$

[$\because$ exterior angle of triangle equals the sum of two interior opposite angles]

In ΔADE, $\angle A + \angle D + \angle E = 180^\circ$

[by angle sum property of triangle]

$\Rightarrow \quad 3x + 8x + 4x = 180^\circ$

$\Rightarrow \quad 15x = 180^\circ$

$\Rightarrow \quad x = 12^\circ$

$\therefore \quad \angle A = 3x, \angle E = 4x$

$\angle C = 180 - \angle A, \angle D = 8x$

and $\quad \angle B = 180^\circ - \angle D$

Ans. $36^\circ, 144^\circ, 96^\circ, 84^\circ$

22. Hint $PO^2 = PT^2 + TO^2$

$\Rightarrow \quad PT^2 = PO^2 - TO^2$

$= 10^2 - 8^2$

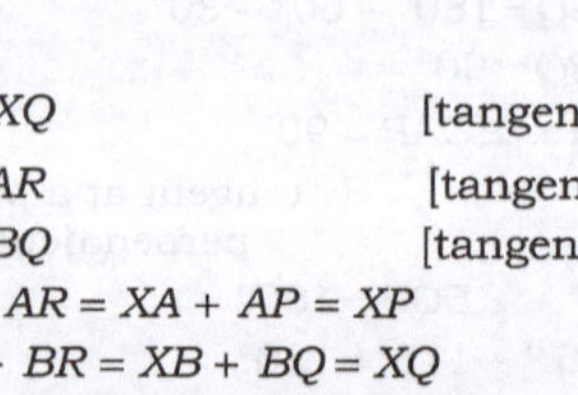

Ans. 6 cm

23. Hint Do same as Q. 1 of Topic Exercise 3.

Ans. 8 cm

24. Hint $XP = XQ$ [tangents from X]

$AP = AR$ [tangents from A] ...(i)

$BR = BQ$ [tangents from B]

Now, $XA + AR = XA + AP = XP$ ...(ii)

and $\quad XB + BR = XB + BQ = XQ$ ...(iii)

From Eqs. (i), (ii) and (iii), we get the result.

25. **Hint** Since, P is the mid-point of arc APB and $OP \perp MN$.

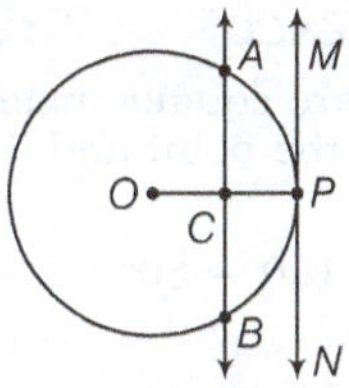

$\Rightarrow$ C is the mid-point of AB.

$\Rightarrow$ OC is the perpendicular bisector of AB.

26. (i) **Hint** Reflex $\angle COA = 360° - \angle COA = 360° - a$

Since, angle made by an arc at the centre of the circle = 2 × (angle made by the arc at any point on the remaining part)

$\therefore \quad 360° - a = 2b$

(ii) **Hint** Here, $OA = OC$ and $OABC$ is a parallelogram.

$\Rightarrow$ $OABC$ is a square.

Ans. (i) $a + 2b = 360°$ (ii) 90°

27. **Hint** $AP \times PB = PC \times PD$

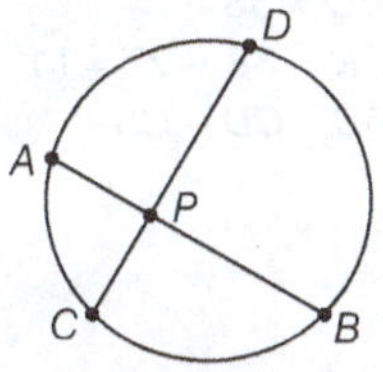

28. **Hint** From the figure, $AC \times AB = AE \times AD$

But $\quad AC = AE$ [given]

$\therefore \quad AB = AD$ ... (i)

Now, $\quad CB = AC - AB$ ...(ii)

and $\quad DE = AE - AD$ ...(iii)

From Eqs. (i), (ii) and (iii), we get

$CB = DE$

In ΔCBP and ΔDPE,

$\angle BPC = \angle DPE$ [vertically opposite angles]

$\Rightarrow \angle BCP = \angle DEP$ [angles in the same segment]

$CB = DE$ [proved above]

$\therefore \quad \Delta CBP \cong \Delta DPE$

$\Rightarrow \quad CP = EP$

and $\quad BP = DP$ [by CPCT]

29. **Hint** Given, P and Q are the centres of circles, whose radii are 9 cm and 2 cm, respectively.

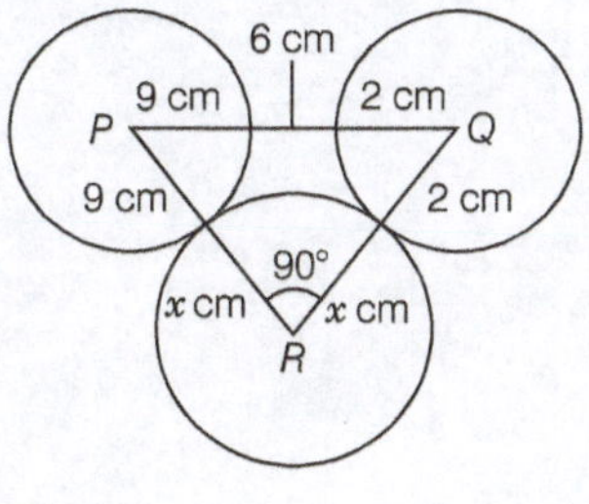

Also, $PQ = 17$ cm

A circle with centre R and radius x cm touches above circles.

$\therefore \quad PR = 9 + x$ cm and $QR = 2 + x$ cm

Given, ΔPRQ is a right angled triangle.

$\therefore \quad PQ^2 = PR^2 + QR^2$ [by Pythagoras theorem]

$\Rightarrow \quad (17)^2 = (9 + x)^2 + (2 + x)^2$

$\Rightarrow \quad (x - 6)(x + 17) = 0$

$\Rightarrow \quad x = -17$ and $x = 6$

$\therefore \quad x = 6$ cm [$\because$ radius cannot be negative]

30. Since, $PQ \parallel RS$ and $PQ = RS$

Join OP and OS.

(i) **Hint** $\angle PQR = \angle SRQ$ [$\because$ alternate angles]

Also, $\angle QOS = 2\angle SRQ$

and $\angle POR = 2\angle PQR$

$\Rightarrow \quad \angle POR = \angle QOS$

$\Rightarrow \quad \overset{\frown}{PR} = \overset{\frown}{QS}$

(ii) **Hint** $PQ = RS \quad \Rightarrow \overset{\frown}{PQ} = \overset{\frown}{RS}$

31. **Given** AD and BC are two common tangents of circles C_1 and C_2 (say).

To prove $AD = BC$

Proof Let F and G be the centres of the circles C_1 and C_2, respectively and join AF, FC, FB and FD, BG and GD.

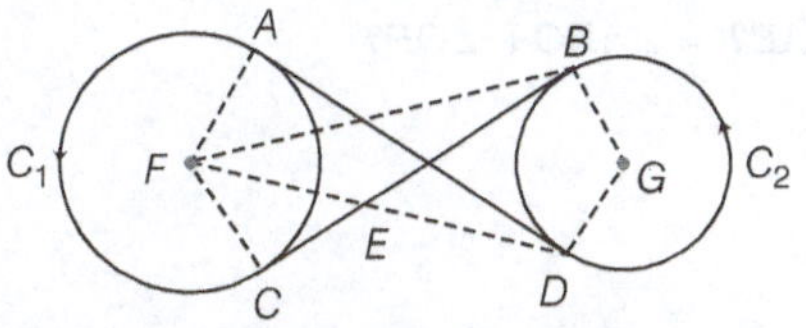

Now, tangents FB and FD are drawn from an external point F to the circle C_2.

$\therefore \quad FD = FB$ ...(i)

Since, the radius is perpendicular to the tangent at the point of contact.

$\therefore \quad AF \perp AD$ and $FC \perp BC$

$\Rightarrow \quad \angle FAD = \angle FCB = 90°$

In right angled ΔFAD and ΔFCB,

$AF = FC$ [radii of same circle]

$\angle A = \angle C = 90°$

and $\quad FD = FB$ [from Eq. (i)]

$\therefore \quad \Delta AFD \cong \Delta CFB$ [by SAS congruence rule]

Then, $\quad AD = BC$ [by CPCT]

32. **Hint** Do same as Example 33.

33. Given, O is the centre and PQ is a tangent to the circle T.

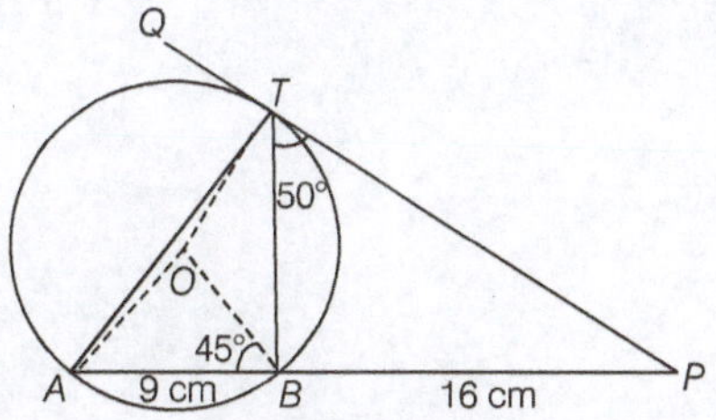

(i) We know,
$$PB \times AP = PT^2$$
$$\Rightarrow \quad 16 \times 25 = PT^2$$
$$\Rightarrow \quad PT = 4 \times 5$$
$$\Rightarrow \quad PT = 20 \text{ cm}$$
(ii) $\because$ Radius makes 90° at tangent, we have
$$\angle BTP = 50°$$
$$\Rightarrow \angle BTO = 90° - 50° = 40°$$
Also, $\angle OBT = 40°$ [$\because \Delta BOT$ is an isosceles triangle]
$\because \Delta AOB$ is isosceles triangle.
$$\therefore \quad \angle OAB = \angle OBA = 45°$$
$$\therefore \quad \angle AOB = 90°$$
Then, $\angle AOT = 360° - (90° + 100°)$ [$\because \angle BOT = 100°$]
$$= 170°$$
$OA = OT$ [both are radius]
$\therefore$ ΔAOT is isosceles triangle
$$\Rightarrow \quad \angle OAT = \angle OTA$$
$$= \frac{180° - 170°}{2} = 5°$$
Now, $\angle BAT = \angle OAT + \angle OAB$
$$= 5° + 45° = 50°$$
$$\Rightarrow \quad \angle BAT = 50°$$
(iii) $\angle BOT = 180° - (\angle TBO + \angle OTB)$
$$= 180° - 80° = 100°$$
$$\Rightarrow \quad \angle BOT = 100°$$
(iv) $\angle ABT = \angle ABO + \angle OBT$
$$= 45° + 40° = 85°$$
$$\Rightarrow \quad \angle ABT = 85°$$

34. (i) **Hint** $\angle BCO = \angle ACO$

[$\because$ tangents are equally inclined to the line joining the point and the centre of the circle]

Ans. 30°

(ii) **Hint** $\angle AOB = 180° - 60°$

Ans. 120°

(iii) **Hint** $\angle APB = \frac{1}{2} \angle AOB$

Ans. 60°

35. Hint Since, tangents to a circle is perpendicular to the radius through the point.

$\therefore$ $\angle OPD = \angle OSD = 90°$,
$\angle D = 90°$ and $PO = OS$

Therefore, $PQSD$ is square.

Since, tangents from an exterior point to a circle are equal in length.

$\therefore$ $BR = BQ$, $AQ = AP$ and $DP = DS$

Now, $BC = 38$ cm
$$\Rightarrow \quad CR + BR = 38$$
$$\Rightarrow \quad CR + BQ = 38 \quad [\because BR = BQ]$$
$$\Rightarrow \quad CR = 38 - 27 = 11$$
$$\because \quad DS = CD - CS$$

Ans. 14 cm

Olympiad Section

Brain Teasing Questions asked in Previous Olympiads

1 If P, Q, S and R are points on the circumference of a circle of radius r, such that PQR is an equilateral triangle and PS is a diameter of the circle. Then, the perimeter of the quadrilateral $PQSR$ will be

(a) $2\sqrt{3}r$ (b) $2r$
(c) $2(\sqrt{3}+1)r$ (d) $2\sqrt{3}+r$

2 In the given figure, if the chord ED is parallel to the diameter AC. Then, the measure of $\angle CED$ will be

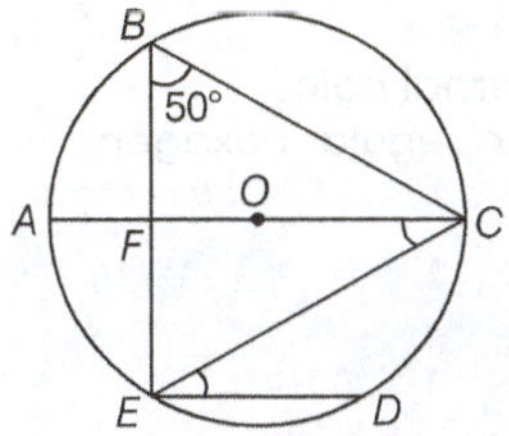

(a) 50° (b) 70°
(c) 40° (d) 30°

3 As shown in the figure, ΔPAB is formed by three tangents to circle with centre O and $\angle APB = 40°$. Then, the measure of $\angle AOB$ will be

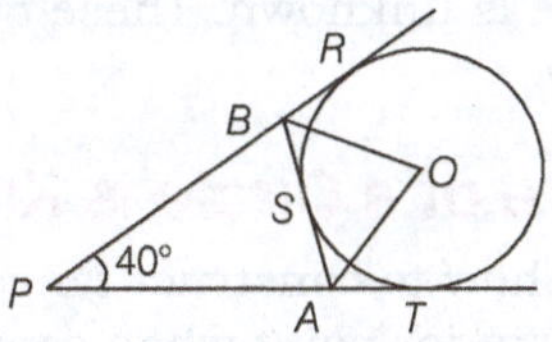

(a) 50° (b) 40°
(c) 80° (d) 70°

4 A, B and C are three points on a circle. The tangents at C meets BA produced at T. Given that $\angle ATC = 36°$ and $\angle ACT = 48°$. Then, the angle subtended by AB at the centre of the circle will be

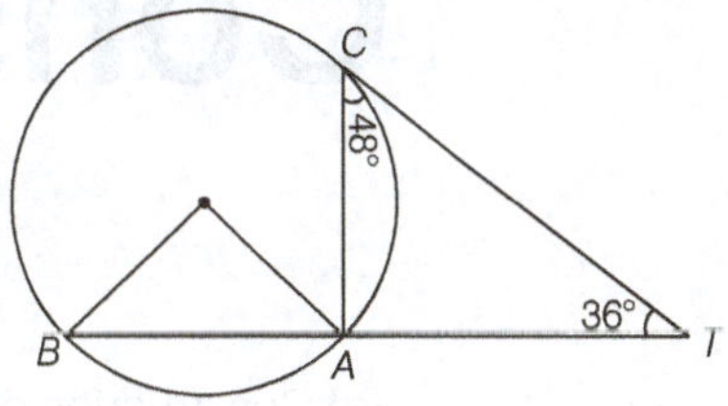

(a) 69° (b) 96°
(c) 72° (d) 82°

5 In the given figure, TBP and TCQ are tangents to the circle whose centre is O. Also, $\angle PBA = 60°$ and $\angle ACQ = 70°$. Then, $\angle BAC$ and $\angle BTC$ are respectively.

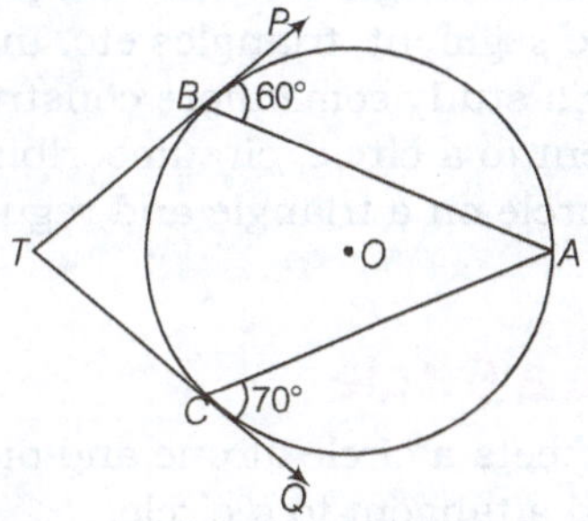

(a) 80°, 50° (b) 50°, 80°
(c) 60°, 50° (d) 70°, 80°

Answers

1. (c) **2.** (c) **3.** (d) **4.** (b) **5.** (b)

* *These questions may or may not be asked in the examination, have been given just for additional practice required for olympiads Scholarship Exams etc. For detailed explanations refer Page No. 493.*

CHAPTER

16

Constructions

SYLLABUS

(a) Construction of tangents to a circle from an external point.
(b) Circumscribing and inscribing a circle on a triangle and a regular hexagon.

In earlier classes, we have already studied construction by using a ruler and a pair of compasses to draw angle bisector and perpendicular bisector of line segment, triangles etc. In this chapter, we will study some more constructions, such as tangent to a circle, circumscribing and inscribing a circle on a triangle and regular hexagon.

Tangent to a Circle

A line which meets a circle at one and only one point, is called a tangent to a circle.

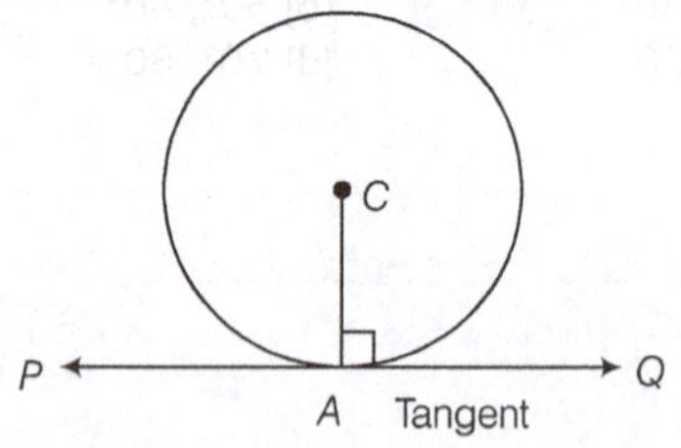

In the above figure, PQ is a tangent to a circle, as it meet the circle at only one point, i.e. A. Here, the point A at which the tangent line meets the circle, is called the **point of contact**.

Note The tangent is always perpendicular to the radius of the circle at the point of contact.

Construction of a Tangent to a Circle from an External Point

From an external point, only two tangents can be drawn. These tangents can be drawn in two ways, such as when centre of a circle is known and when centre of a circle is unknown. These two ways are explained below

When Centre of a Circle is Known

To understand, how to construct tangents to a given circle from an exterior point when centre of a circle is known, the following steps are given.

Step I Draw a circle with centre C and take a point A exterior to it.

Step II Join CA and draw the perpendicular bisector of CA. Let it meets CA at M, which is the mid–point of CA.

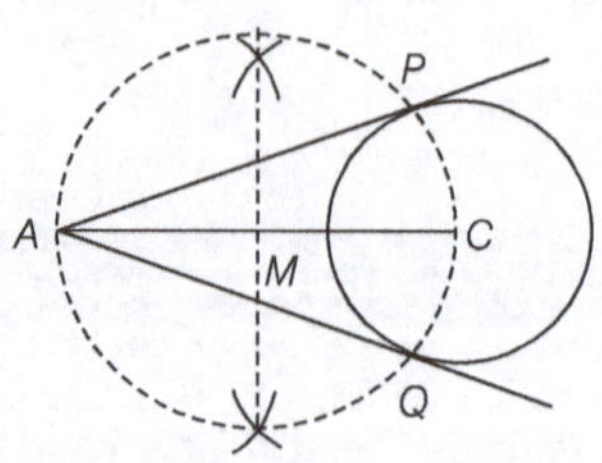

Step III Draw a dotted circle with centre M and radius $AM = MC$, which cuts the given circle at the points P and Q.

Step IV Now, join PA and QA.

Hence, PA and QA are the required tangents from exterior point A to the given circle.

Note We observe that the lengths of two tangents drawn from an exterior point of a circle are equal.

Example 1. Use ruler and compass only for answering this question.

Draw a circle of radius 4 cm. Mark the centre as O. Mark a point P outside the circle at a distance of 7 cm from the centre. Construct two tangents to the circle from the external point P. Measure and write down the length of any one tangent. [ICSE 2019]

Sol. Given, a circle of radius 4 cm and distance between the point and centre of a circle is 7 cm.

Steps of construction

(i) Draw a circle with centre O and radius 4 cm and take a point P outside the circle at a distance of 7 cm from its centre.

(ii) Join OP.

(iii) Draw a perpendicular bisector of OP, which intersects OP at (the mid-point) M.

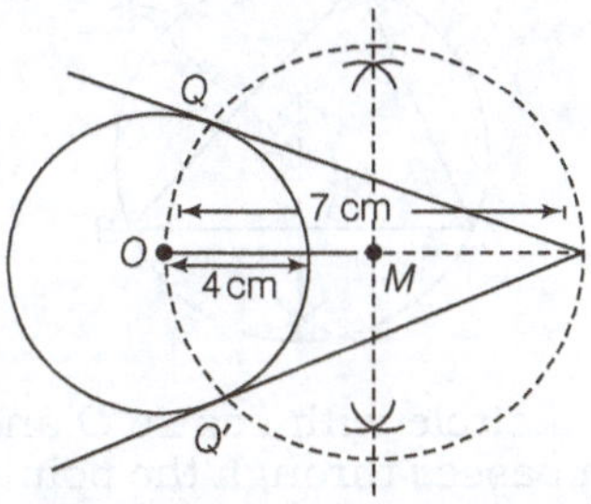

(iv) Taking M as centre and $OM = MP$ as radius, draw a dotted circle, which intersects the given circle at Q and Q'.

(v) Join PQ and PQ', which are the required tangents.

On measuring the length of tangent with the help of ruler, we get $PQ = PQ' = 5.7$ cm.

Example 2. Construct a tangents to a circle of radius 1.8 cm from a point on the concentric circle of radius 2.8 cm and measure its length.

Sol. Given, two concentric circles of radii 1.8 cm and 2.8 cm with common centre C.

Steps of construction

1. Draw two circles with common centre C and radii 1.8 cm and 2.8 cm.
2. Take a point A on the circumference of the outer circle and join CA.

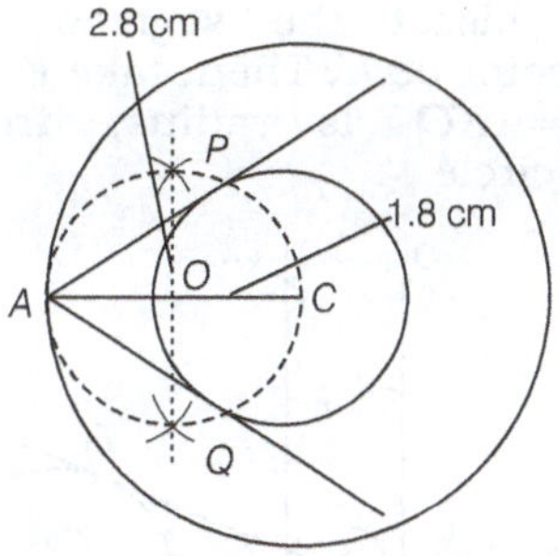

3. Now, draw the perpendicular bisector of CA. Let it meets CA at point O, which is the mid-point of CA.
4. Draw a dotted circle with centre O and radius $OC = OA$, which cuts inner circle at two points, say P and Q.
5. Join AP and AQ.

Hence, AP and AQ are the required tangents.

On measuring the lengths, we get $AP = AQ = 2.14$ cm

Example 3. Draw a circle of radius 7 cm. Draw a tangent to this circle making an angle of 30° with a line passing through the centre of the circle.

Sol. Given, a circle of radius 7 cm.

Steps of construction

1. Draw a circle with centre O and radius 7 cm.
2. Draw the diameter CA of this circle and produce it to B.
3. Construct an $\angle AOP$ (where, P is on the circumference) equal to the complement of 30°, i.e. equal to 60°.

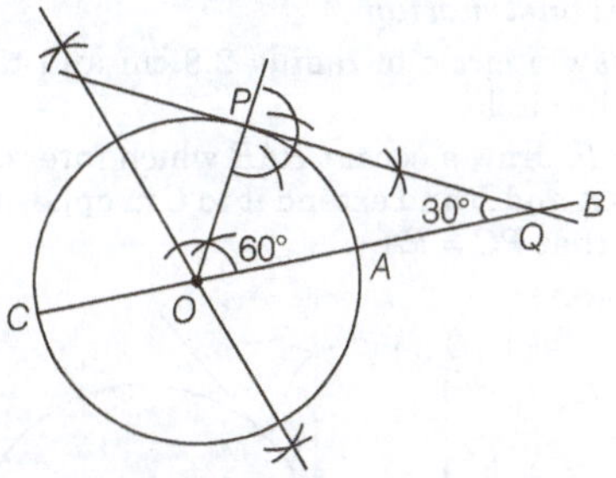

4. Draw perpendicular on OP at point P, which intersects OB at point Q.

Hence, PQ is the desired tangent, such that $\angle OQP = 30°$.

When Centre of a Circle is Unknown

To understand how to construct tangents to a given circle from an exterior point when centre of a circle is unknown, the following steps are given below

Step I Draw a circle of given radius and take a point P outside it.

Step II Through P, draw a line (i.e. secant) intersecting the given circle at points A and B respectively and produce it to C in opposite direction of AB such that $AP = CP$.

Step III Now, bisect the segment *CB*. Let its mid-point be *K*. Then, take *K* as centre and *KB* (= *KC*) as radius, draw a dotted semi-circle.

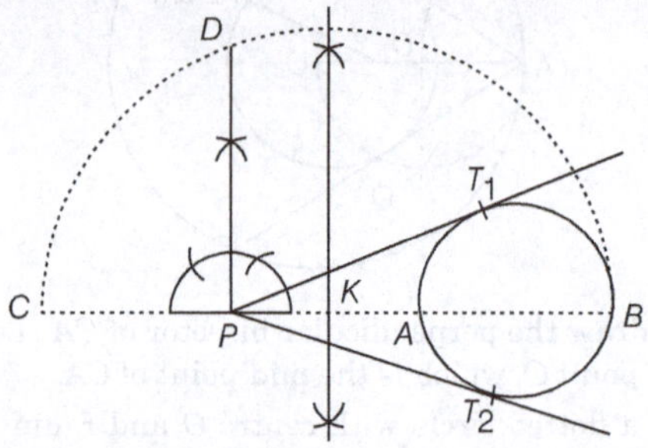

Step IV At point *P*, draw $PD \perp CB$ which cuts the semi-circle at point *D*.

Step V Take *P* as centre and *PD* as radius draw two arcs which intersect the given circle at points T_1 and T_2.

Step VI Join PT_1 and PT_2, which are the required tangents.

Example 4. Draw a circle of radius 2.8 cm. From an external point *P*, draw tangents to the circle without using the centre of the circle.

Sol. Given, a circle of radius 2.8 cm and we have to draw tangents without using the centre.

Steps of construction

1. First, draw a circle of radius 2.8 cm and take a point *P* outside the circle.
2. Through *P*, draw a secant *PAB* which intersects the circle at points *A* and *B* and extend it to *C* in opposite direction of *AB* such that *PC* = *PA*.

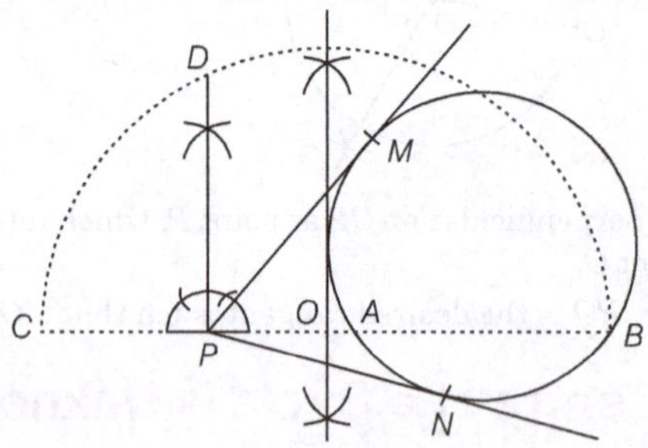

3. Now, bisect *BC* and take its mid-point as *O*. Draw a dotted semi-circle with centre *O* and radius *OB* (= *OC*).
4. Draw $PD \perp BC$ which intersects the semi-circle at point *D*.
5. With centre *P* and radius *PD* draw two arcs which intersects the given circle at points *M* and *N*.
6. Join *PM* and *PN*.

Thus, *PM* and *PN* are the required tangents to the given circle.

Circumscribed Circle of a Polygon

A circle passing through all the vertices of a polygon (triangle or hexagon) is called a circumscribed circle of the polygon, and its centre is called **circumcentre**.

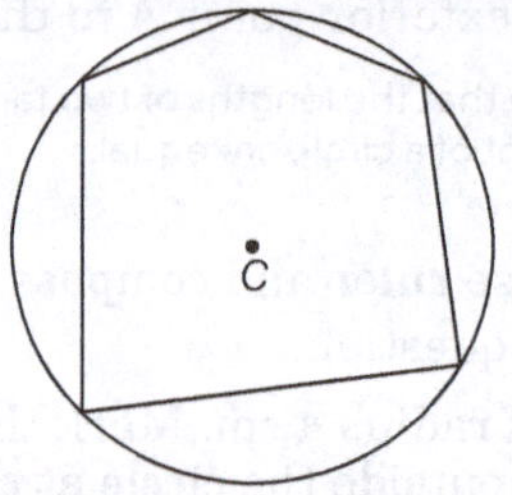

Construction of Circumcircle of a Triangle

To understand how to construct the circumscribed circle of a given triangle, the following steps are given below

Step I Draw a ΔABC with the given data.

Step II Draw the perpendicular bisectors of any two sides, say *AB* and *BC*. Let these bisectors meet at point *O*.

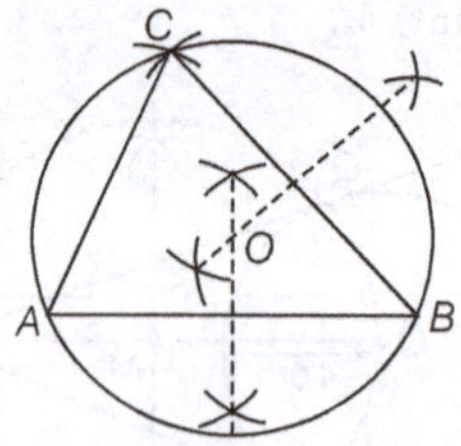

Step III Draw a circle with centre *O* and radius *OA*, which passes through the points *A*, *B* and *C*. It is the required circumcircle of ΔABC.

Note (i) The point *O* of the above construction is called the circumcentre of triangle.
(ii) The circumcentre of the triangle is always equidistant from the vertices of the triangle.

Example 5. Construct a ΔPQR, in which *PQ* = 6 cm, *PR* = 5.5 cm and $\angle Q = 60°$. Draw the circumcircle of ΔPQR. Also, write the steps of construction.

Sol. Given, *PQ* = 6 cm, *PR* = 5.5 cm and $\angle Q = 60°$.

Steps of construction

1. First, draw the base *PQ* = 6 cm.
2. Taking *Q* as centre, draw a ray *QX* making an angle of 60° with *PQ*.
3. Now, taking *P* as centre, draw an arc of 5.5 cm, which cuts *QX* at point *R*.
4. Join *PR*. Thus, *PQR* is the required triangle.

5. Draw the perpendicular bisectors of PQ and QR, which meet at point O.

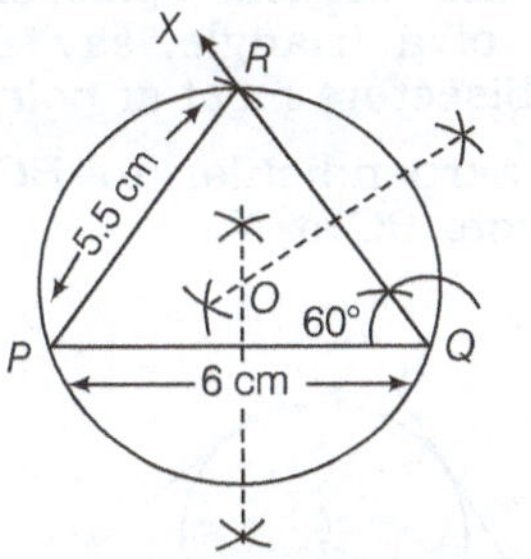

6. Draw a circle with centre O and radius OP, which passes through all the vertices of ΔPQR.
Hence, it is the required circumcircle of ΔPQR.

Example 6. Using ruler and compass construct a ΔABC where $AB = 3$ cm, $BC = 4$ cm and $\angle ABC = 90°$. Hence, construct a circle circumscribing the ΔABC. Measure and write down the radius of the circle. **[ICSE 2020]**

Sol. Given, $AB = 3$ cm, $BC = 4$ cm and $\angle ABC = 90°$

Steps of construction

(i) Draw a line segment $BC = 4$ cm
(ii) Make an angle of 90° at B and cut-off $AB = 3$ cm from it.
(iii) Join AC. Thus, ΔABC is the required triangle.
(iv) Draw the perpendicular bisectors of BC and AB, which meets at point O.
(v) Draw a circle with centre O and radius OA, which passes through the all vertices of ΔABC. Hence, it is the required circumcircle of ΔABC with radius 2.5 cm.

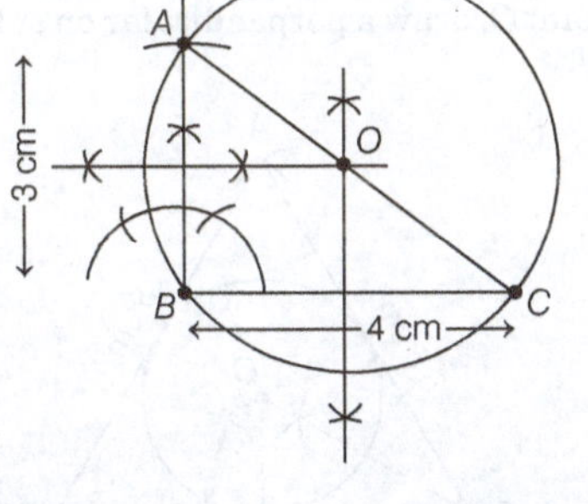

Example 7. Using a ruler and a pair of compasses only, construct a ΔABC, such that $AB = 5$ cm, $\angle ABC = 75°$ and the radius of the circumcircle of ΔABC is 3.5 cm. On the same diagram, construct a circle, touching AB at its middle point and also touching the side AC.

Sol. Given, in ΔABC, $AB = 5$ cm, $\angle ABC = 75°$ and radius of a circumcircle of ΔABC is 3.5 cm.

Steps of construction

1. Draw a line segment $AB = 5$ cm.
2. From point B, draw a ray BX, making $\angle ABX = 75°$.
3. Taking A and B as centres one-by-one, mark two arcs of radius 3.5 cm, which intersect at the point O.
4. Taking O as the centre and OB as radius, draw a circumcircle, which passes through the points A and B. It also intersects BX at point C. Join AC and BC.
Hence, ΔABC is the required triangle.

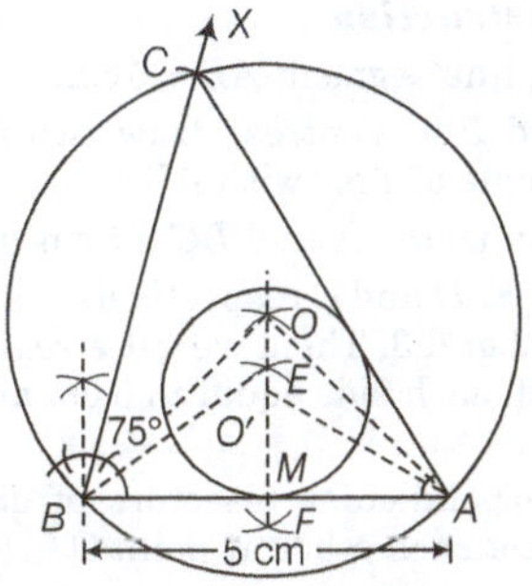

5. Draw perpendicular bisector EF of AB, which intersects AB at point M and draw an angle bisector of $\angle CAB$, which intersects EF at O'.
6. Taking O' as centre and $O'M$ as radius, draw a circle, which touches AB and AC.

Construction of a Circle Circumscribing a Given Regular Hexagon

To understand how to construct a circle about a given regular hexagon, the following steps are given below

Step I Construct a regular hexagon $ABCDEF$ with given data.

Step II Draw perpendicular bisectors of any two sides of regular polygon, say AB and BC. Let these bisectors intersect each other at O.

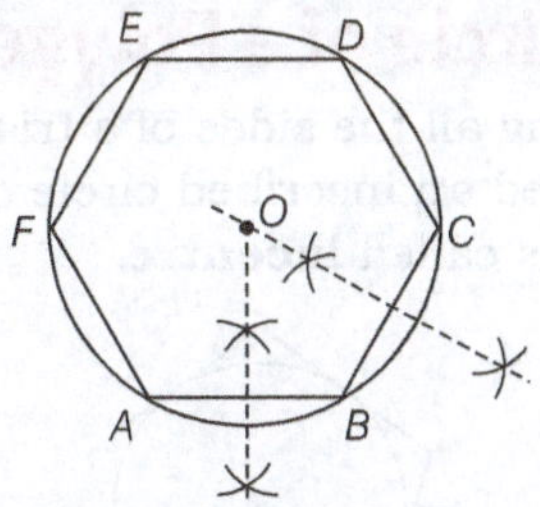

Step III Draw a circle with centre O and radius OA, which passes through all the vertices of the regular hexagon $ABCDEF$.
Hence, it is the required circle about the regular hexagon.

Note (i) Whenever a circle circumscribes a given regular hexagon, its radius is always equal to the length of the side of the regular hexagon.
(ii) Each interior angle of the regular hexagon = 120°, where n denotes the number of sides.

Example 8. Construct a regular hexagon of side 5 cm. Construct a circle circumscribing the hexagon. All traces of construction must be clearly shown. [ICSE 2015]

Sol. Given, each side of a regular hexagon is 5 cm.

We know that each interior angle of regular hexagon is 120°

Steps of construction

1. First, draw a line segment $AB = 5$ cm.
2. Taking A and B as centres, draw two rays AX and BY, making an angle of 120° with AB.
3. Cut $AF = 5$ cm from AX and $BC = 5$ cm from BY.
4. Now, take F, E, D and C respectively, as centres to repeat steps 2 and 3. Then, we get a regular hexagon $ABCDEF$ with each side equal to 5 cm and each angle equal to 120°.
5. Draw the perpendicular bisectors of sides AB and BC, which intersect each other at point O.
6. Draw a circle with O as centre and OA as radius, which passes through all the vertices of the regular hexagon $ABCDEF$.

Hence, $ABCDEF$ is the required circumcircle of the regular hexagon.

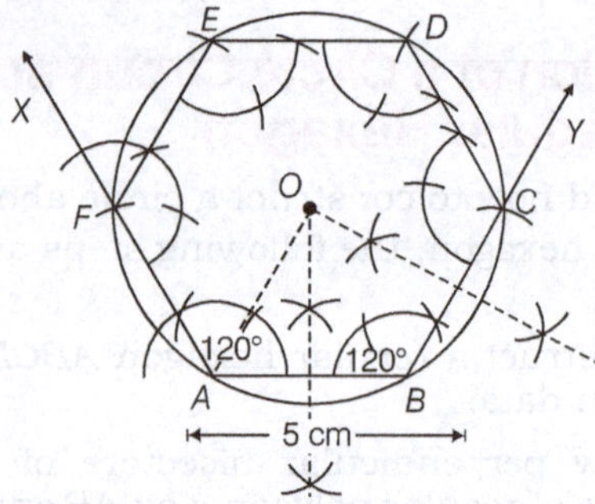

Inscribed Circle of a Polygon

A circle touching all the sides of a triangle or hexagon is called an inscribed circle of the polygon, and its centre is called **incentre**.

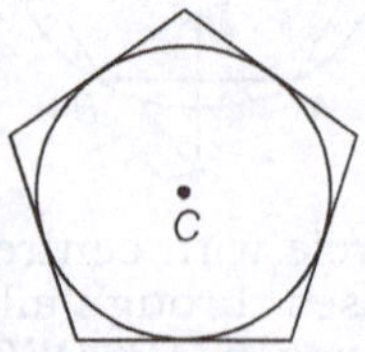

Construction of Incircle of a Triangle

To understand how to construct the inscribed circle of a given triangle, the following steps are given below

Step I Draw a ΔABC with the given data.

Step II Draw the internal bisectors of any two angles of a triangle, say $\angle B$ and $\angle C$. Let these bisectors meet at point I.

Step III Draw perpendicular to BC from I, which intersects BC at N.

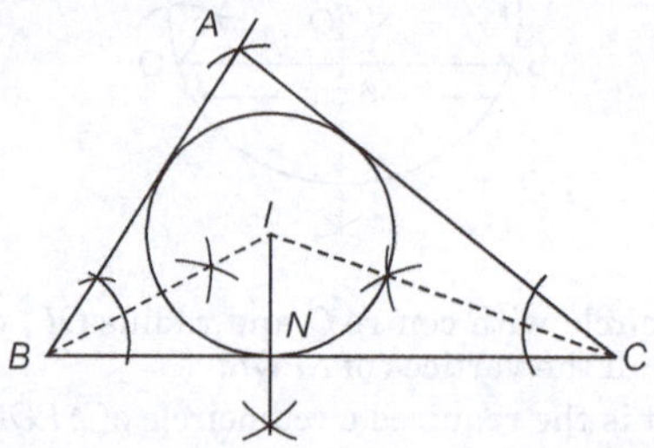

Step IV Now, draw a circle with centre I and radius NI, which touches all sides of ΔABC.

Hence, it is the required incircle of ΔABC.

Example 9. Construct a ΔABC with $BC = 6.5$ cm, $AB = 5.5$ cm and $AC = 5$ cm. Construct the incircle of the triangle. Measure and record the radius of the incircle. [ICSE 2014]

Sol. Given, $BC = 6.5$ cm, $AB = 5.5$ cm and $AC = 5$ cm.

Steps of construction

1. Draw the base $BC = 6.5$ cm.
2. Taking B and C as centres, draw two arcs of radius 5.5 cm and 5 cm respectively, which intersect each other at A.
3. Join AB and AC. Thus, ABC is the required triangle.
4. Now, draw the internal bisectors of $\angle B$ and $\angle C$. Let these bisectors meet at point O.
5. From point O, draw a perpendicular on side BC, which cuts BC at N.

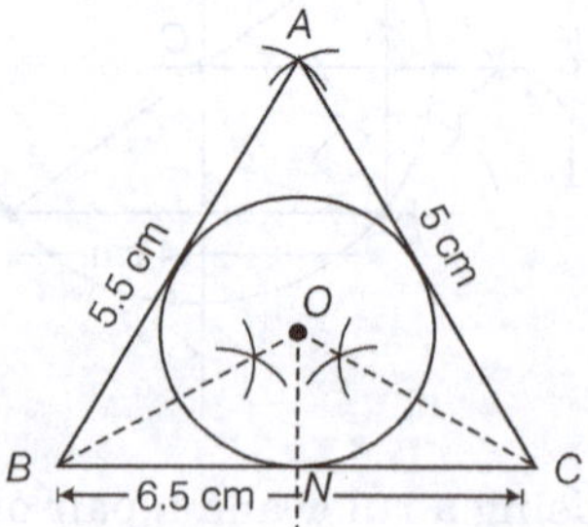

6. Taking O as centre and radius equal to ON, draw a circle which touches all the sides of the ΔABC.

Hence, it is the required incircle of ΔABC.

7. Measure ON, which is the required radius of the incircle, i.e. $ON = 1.55$ cm.

Example 10. Draw a right angled ΔABC with $AB = 4.5$ cm, $AC = 7.5$ cm and $\angle B = 90°$ and also draw its incircle.

Sol. Given, $AB = 4.5$ cm, $AC = 7.5$ cm and $\angle B = 90°$.

Steps of construction

1. First, draw the base $AB = 4.5$ cm.
2. Taking B as centre, draw a ray BD making an angle of 90° with AB.
3. Draw an arc with centre A and radius 7.5 cm, which cuts BD at C.
4. Join AC to obtain ΔABC.
5. Draw the internal bisectors of $\angle A$ and $\angle B$, which meet each other at O.
6. Draw a perpendicular to AB from O, which intersects AB at E.

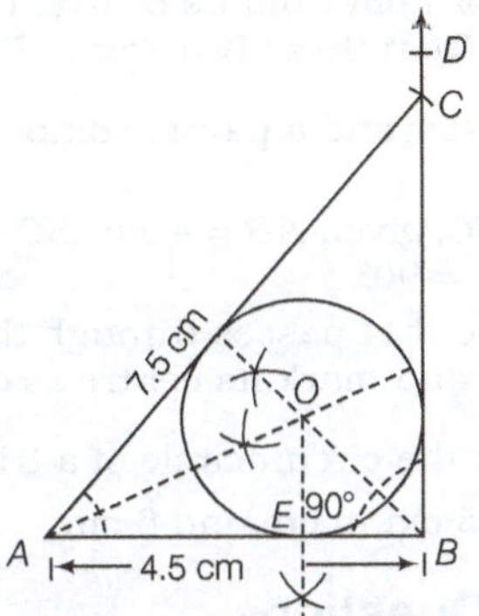

7. Now, draw a circle with centre O and radius OE, which touches all the sides of the ΔABC.

Hence, it is the required incircle of ΔABC.

Construction of a Circle Inscribing a Given Regular Hexagon

To understand how to construct a circle inscribing a given regular hexagon, the following steps are given below

Step I Construct a regular hexagon $ABCDEF$ with given data.

Step II Draw the internal bisectors of any two adjacent angles, say $\angle A$ and $\angle B$. Let these bisectors intersect each other at I.

Step III Draw perpendicular to AB from point I, which intersects AB at N.

Step IV Draw a circle with centre I and radius NI, which touches all the sides of regular hexagon $ABCDEF$.

Hence, it is the required incircle of regular hexagon.

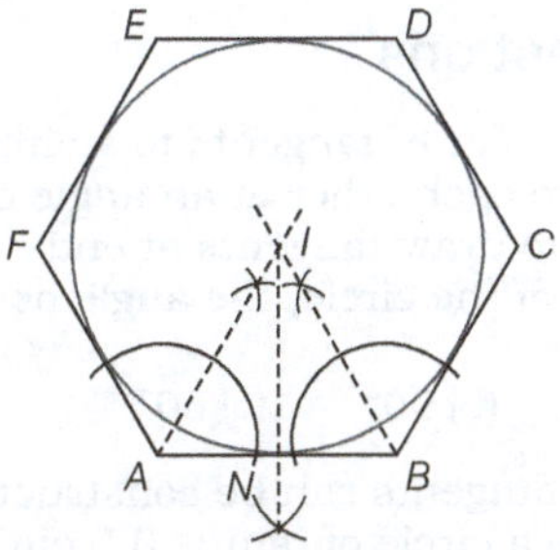

Example 11. Draw a regular hexagon of side 3 cm. Draw its incircle.

Sol. Given, each side of regular hexagon is 3 cm.

We know that each interior angle of a regular hexagon is 120°

Steps of construction

1. Draw a line segment $AB = 3$ cm.
2. Taking A and B as centres, draw two rays AX and BY, making an angle of 120° with AB.
3. Cut $AF = 3$ cm from AX and $BC = 3$ cm from BY. Now, take F, E, D and C respectively as centres to repeat steps 2, 3. Then, we get a required regular hexagon $ABCDEF$ with each side equal to 3 cm and each angle is equal to 120°.
4. Draw the internal bisectors of $\angle A$ and $\angle B$, which intersect each other at I.
5. Draw the perpendicular to AB from I, which intersects AB at M.
6. Draw a circle with centre I and radius IM, which touches all the sides of regular hexagon $ABCDEF$.

Hence, it is the required incircle of regular hexagon $ABCDEF$.

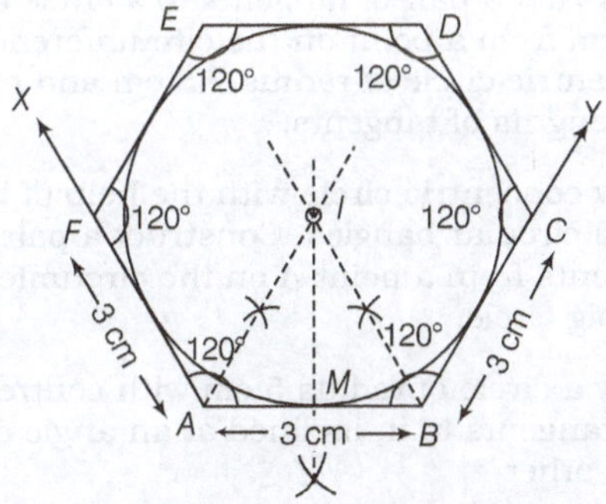

Chapter Practice

a. 1 Mark Questions

1. To draw a pair of tangents to a circle, which are inclined to each other at an angle of 60°, it is required to draw tangents at end points of those two radii of the circle, the angle between them should be
(a) 135° (b) 90° (c) 60° (d) 120°

2. A pair of tangents can be constructed from a point P to a circle of radius 3.5 cm, situated at a distance of 3 cm from the centre.
(a) True (b) False
(c) Can't determined (d) None of these

3. A pair of tangents can be constructed to a circle inclined at an angle of 170°.
(a) True (b) False
(c) Can't determined (d) None of these

b. 3 Marks Questions

4. Draw a circle of radius 3 cm, mark its centre as O. Take a point A at a distance of 8 cm from O. Construct a pair of tangents to this circle from point A.

5. Draw a circle of radius 6 cm. From a point 10 cm away from its centre, construct the pair of tangents to the circle and measure their lengths.

6. Construct tangents to a circle of radius 4.5 cm from a point on the circumference of the concentric circle of radius 6 cm.

7. Construct a pair of tangents to a circle of radius 5.5 cm from a point on the circumference of the concentric circle of radius 7.5 cm and measure the lengths of tangents.

8. Draw concentric circle with the help of big and small circular bangles. Construct a pair of tangents from a point A on the circumference of the big circle.

9. Draw a circle of radius 5 cm with centre. Draw two tangents to it, inclined at an angle of 60° to each other.

10. Draw a circle of radius 4.5 cm. Draw two tangents to this circle so that the angle between the tangents is 60°.

11. Draw a circle of radius 3.3 cm. From an external point Q, draw tangents to the circle without using the centre of the circle.

12. Draw a circle of radius 4 cm. Mark a point A outside the circle. Draw the tangents to the circle from point A, without using the centre of the circle.

13. The area of a circle is 154 cm^2. Draw this circle and take any point P on it. Without using its centre draw tangent at P to the circle.

14. Draw a circle of radius 3 cm. Take two points P and Q on one of its extended diameter each at a distance of 7 cm from its centre. Draw tangents to the circle from these two points P and Q.

15. Using a ruler and a pair of compasses only, construct
(i) a ΔABC, given $AB = 4$ cm, $BC = 6$ cm and $\angle ABC = 90°$.
(ii) a circle that passes through the points A, B and C and mark its centre as O.

16. Construct the circumcircle of a triangle whose sides are 5 cm, 6 cm and 8 cm.

c. 4/5 Marks Questions

17. Draw a triangle with sides 5.5 cm, 6 cm and 6.5 cm. Construct its circumcircle.

18. Construct a circumscribing circle of an equilateral triangle of side 4 cm.

19. Use a ruler and a pair of compasses to construct a ΔABC, in which $BC = 4.2$ cm, $\angle ABC = 60°$ and $AB = 5$ cm. Construct a circle of radius 2 cm to touch both the arms of $\angle ABC$ of ΔABC.

20. Construct a ΔABC, such that $BC = 4$ cm, $\angle C = 75°$ and radius of circumcircle of ΔABC is 3 cm.

21. Inscribe a circle of an equilateral triangle having side 2.5 cm.

22. Inscribe the equilateral triangle in the circle of radius 3.5 cm.

23. Construct a triangle with sides 6.1 cm, 7 cm and 8 cm. Draw its incircle.

24. ABC is a right angled triangle, right angled at B with $AB = 8$ cm and $BC = 6$ cm. Construct an inscribed circle which touches all the sides of the triangle.

25. Using a ruler and a pair of compasses only, construct a ΔABC with $BC = 6.4$ cm, $CA = 5.8$ cm and $\angle ABC = 60°$. Draw its incircle. Measure and record the radius of the incircle.

d. 6 Marks Questions

26. Construct a ΔABC, in which $AB = 5$ cm, $BC = 7$ cm and $AC = 6$ cm.
(i) Mark D, the mid-point of AB.
(ii) Construct the circle, which touches BC at C and passes through D.

27. Using ruler and compass construct a triangle ABC in which $AB = 6$ cm, $\angle BAC = 120°$ and $AC = 5$ cm. Construct a circle passing through A, B and C. Measure and write down the radius of the circle. **[ICSE 2023]**

28. Draw a line $AB = 5$ cm. Mark a point C on AB such that $AC = 3$ cm. Using a ruler and a compasses only, construct
(i) a circle of radius 2.5 cm, passing through A and C.
(ii) two tangents to the circle from the external point B. Measure and record the length of the tangents. **[ICSE 2016]**

29. Construct an $\angle PQR = 45°$. Mark a point S on QR, such that $QS = 4.5$ cm. Construct a circle to touch PQ at Q and also to passes through S.

30. Using a ruler and a pair of compasses only, construct
(i) a ΔABC, such that $AB = 6.5$ cm, $\angle A = 30°$ and $\angle B = 60°$.
(ii) in the same figure, draw a circle passing through the points A, B and C and mark its circumcentre as O.

31. Using a ruler and a pair of compasses only, construct
(i) a ΔEFG, such that $EF = 7$ cm, $\angle E = 45°$ and $\angle F = 75°$.
(ii) in the same figure, draw a circle which touches all the sides of the triangle.

32. Using a ruler and a compasses only, construct
(i) a ΔABC in which $AB = 3.5$ cm, $BC = 6$ cm and $\angle ABC = 120°$.
(ii) in the same diagram, draw a circle with BC as diameter. Find a point P on the circumference of the circle which is equidistant from AB and BC.
(iii) Measure $\angle BCP$. **[ICSE 2013]**

33. Construct a ΔABC in which base $BC = 6$ cm, $AB = 5.5$ cm and $\angle ABC = 120°$.
(i) Construct circle circumscribing the ΔABC.
(ii) Draw a cyclic quadrilateral $ABCD$, so that D is equidistant from B and C. **[ICSE 2012]**

34. Using ruler and compass only, construct a ΔABC such that $BC = 5$ cm and $AB = 6.5$ cm and $\angle ABC = 120°$.
(i) Construct a circumcircle of ΔABC.
(ii) Construct a cyclic quadrilateral $ABCD$, such that D is equidistant from AB and BC. **[ICSE 2018]**

35. Construct a regular hexagon of side 4 cm. Construct a circle circumscribing the hexagon. **[ICSE 2010]**

36. Construct a regular hexagon of side 6 cm and construct a circle in the regular hexagon. Mark its incentre as I.

Hints and Answers

1. (d) The angle between them should be 120° because in that case the figure formed by the intersection point of pair of tangent, the two end points of those two radii (at which tangents are drawn) and the centre of the circle is a quadrilateral.

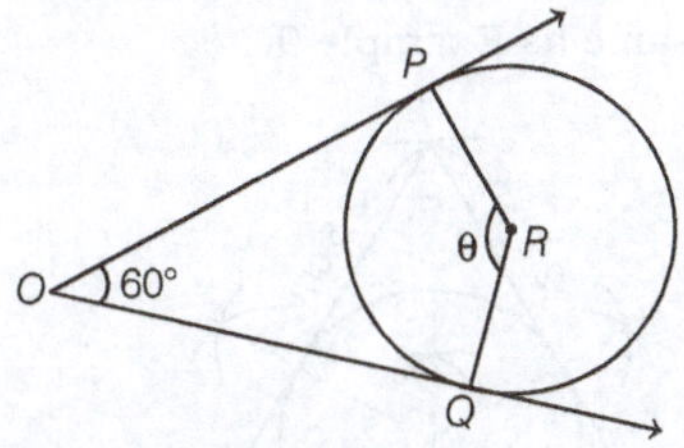

From figure, it is quadrilateral

$$\angle POQ + \angle PRQ = 180°$$ [∵ sum of opposite angles are 180°]

$$60° + \theta = 180°$$

$$\therefore \quad \theta = 120°$$

Hence, the required angle between them is 120°.

2. (b) False, since, the radius of the circle is 3.5 cm i.e. $r = 3.5$ cm and a point P is situated at a distance of 3 cm from the centre i.e. $d = 3$ cm

We see that, $r > d$

i.e. a point P lies inside the circle. So, no tangent can be drawn to a circle from a point lying inside it.

3. True

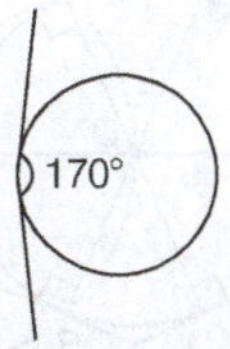

If the angle between the pair of tangents is always greater than 0° or less than 180°, then we can construct a pair of tangents to a circle.

Hence, we can draw a pair of tangents to a circle inclined at an angle of 170°.

4. Hint Do same as Example 1.

5. **Hint** Do same as Example 1.
Ans. 8 cm
6. **Hint** Do same as Example 2.
7. **Hint** Do same as Example 2.
Ans. 5.1 cm
8. **Hint** Do same as Example 2.
9. **Hint** Do same as Example 3.
10. **Hint**

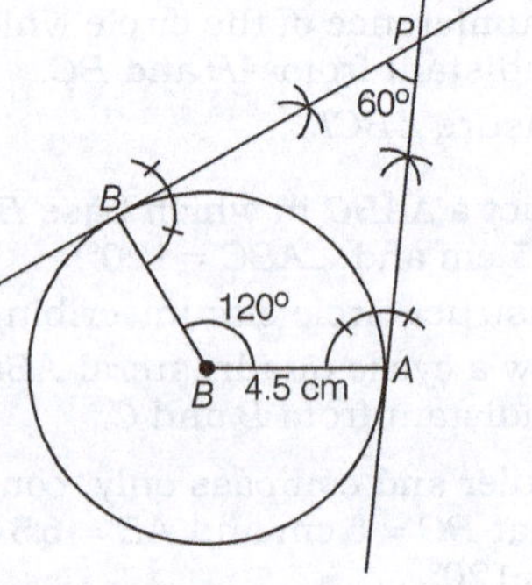

11. **Hint** Do same as Example 4.
12. **Hint** Do same as Example 4.
13. **Hint** ∴ Area of circle = πr^2
$r = 7$ cm

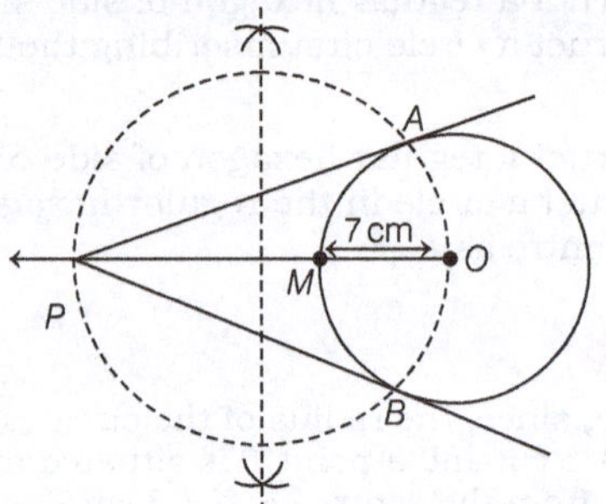

14. **Hint**

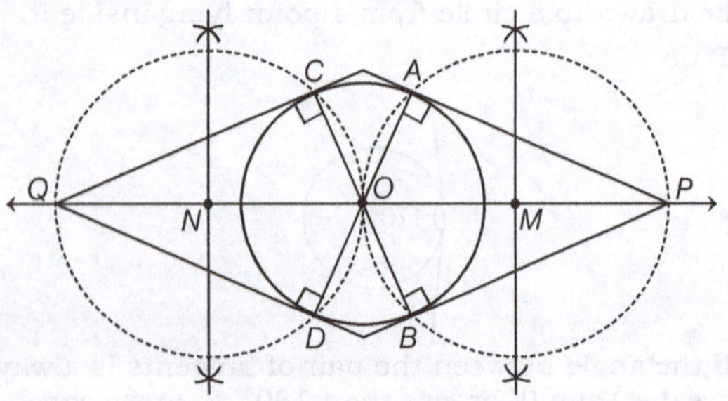

15. **Hint** Do same as Example 6.

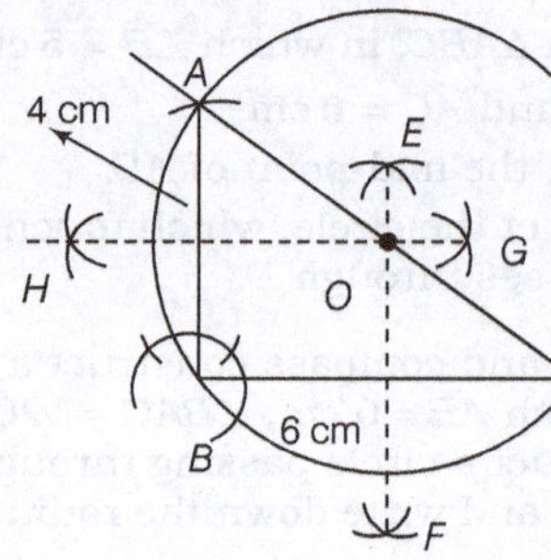

16. **Hint**

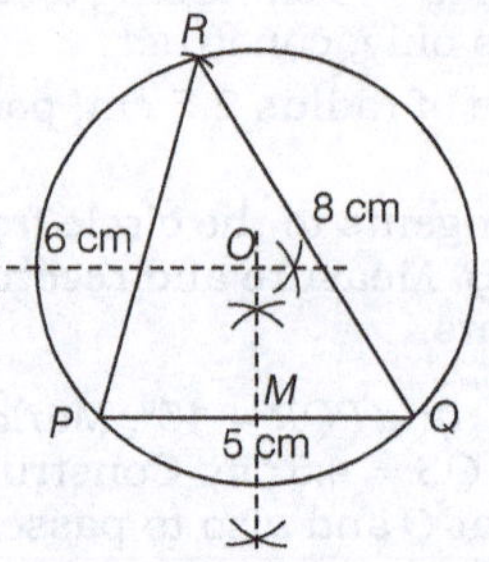

17. **Hint** Do same as Q. 16.
18. **Hint** Do same as Q. 16.
19. **Hint** Do same as Example 7.

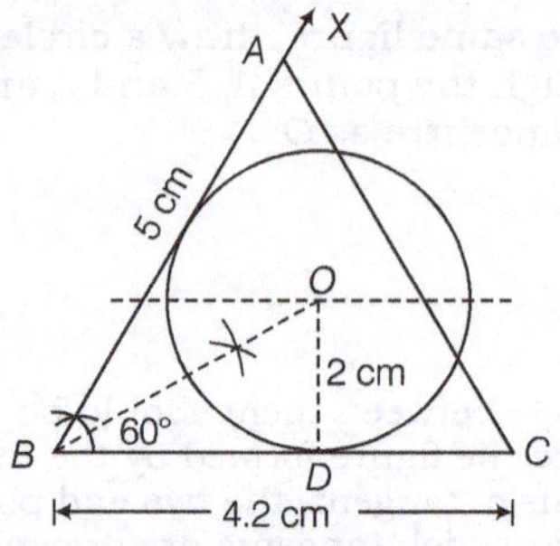

20. **Hint** Do same as Example 7.
21. **Hint** Do same as Example 9.

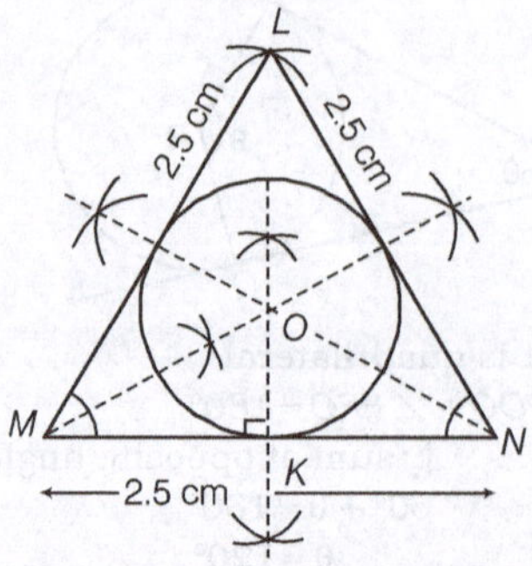

22. Hint Do same as Example 9.

23. Hint Do same as Example 9.

24. Hint Do same as Example 10.

25. Hint Do same as Example 10.

Ans. Radius of incircle = 1.5 cm

26. Hint

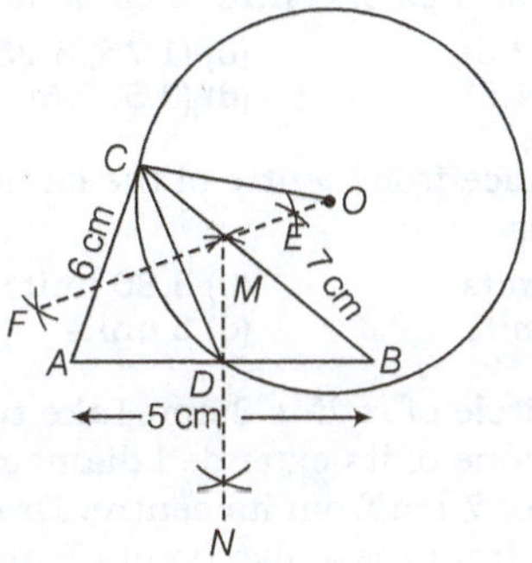

27. Given in ΔABC

$AB = 6$ cm, $\angle BAC = 120°$

and $AC = 5$ cm

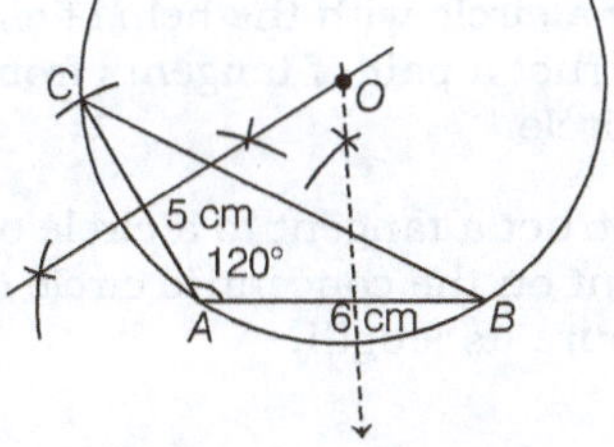

By measuring the length of the radius, we get it is 5.5 cm.

Ans. 5.5 cm

28. Hint

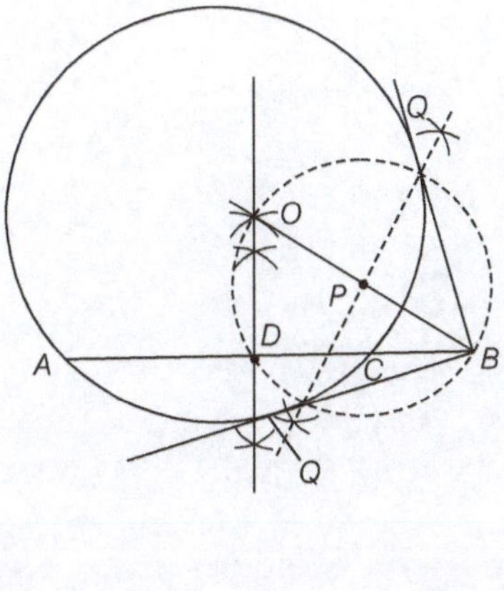

29. Hint

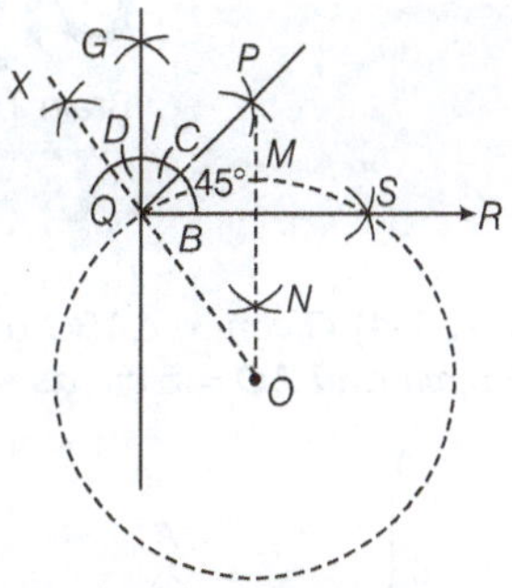

30. (i) **Hint** Do same as Example 5.

(ii) **Hint** Do same as Example 5.

31. (i) **Hint** Do same as Example 9.

(ii) **Hint** Do same as Example 9.

32. Hint

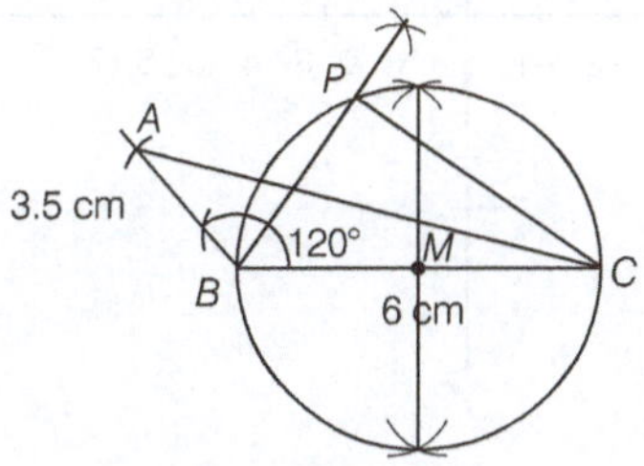

Ans. (iii) $\angle BCP = 30°$

33. Hint

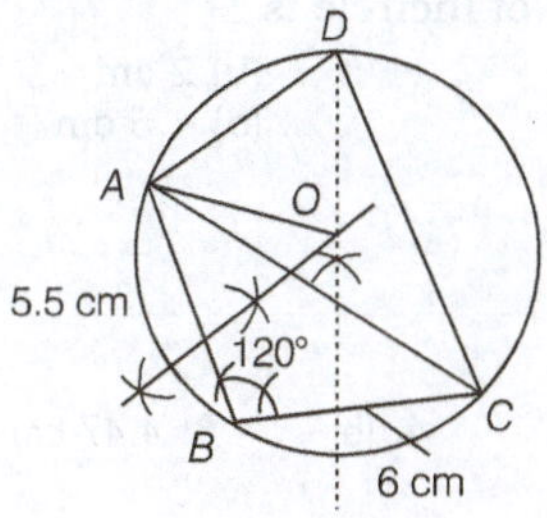

34. Hint

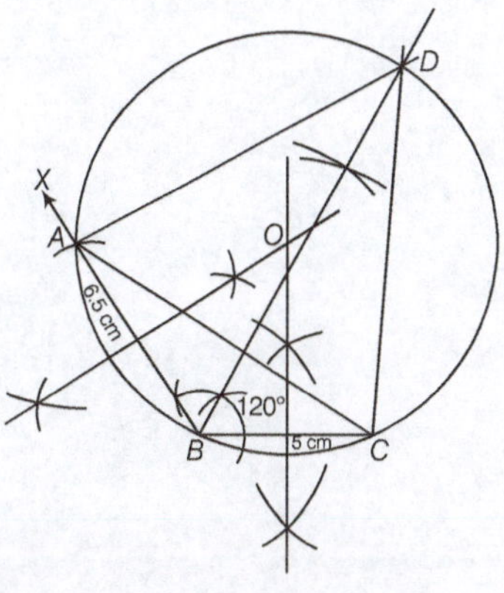

35. Hint Do same as Example 11.

36. Hint Do same as Example 11.

Olympiad Section

Brain Teasing Questions asked in Previous Olympiads

Directions (Q. Nos. 1-4) *Given, a ΔABC with $BC = 6.5$ cm, $AB = 5.5$ cm and $AC = 5$ cm as shown below*

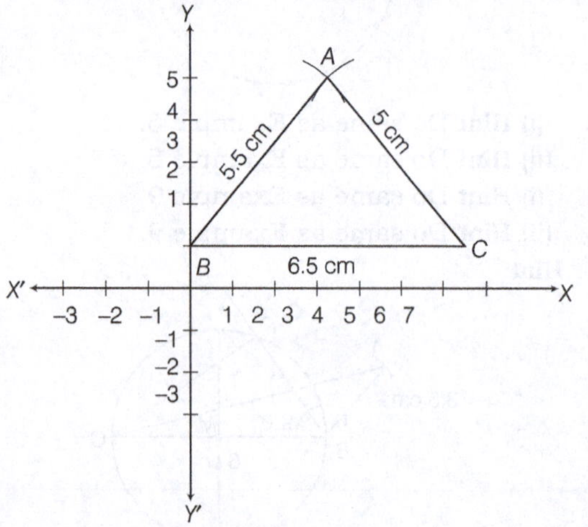

1 Construct a incircle of a ΔABC.

2 The radius of incircle is

(a) 1.5 cm (b) 2 cm
(c) 3 cm (d) 4.5 cm

3 The coordinates of centre of circle is

(a) (1.25, 2.5) (b) (1.75, 3.25)
(c) (3.25, 4.5) (d) (3.5, 2.5)

4 The distance from centre of the circle to vertex B of ΔABC is

(a) 1.50 units (b) 3.80 units
(c) 4.25 units (d) 5 units

5 Draw a circle of radius 3 cm. Take two points P and Q on one of its extended diameter, each at a distance of 7 cm from its centre. Draw tangents to the circle from these two points P and Q.

6 Let ABC be a right angled triangle, in which $AB = 6$ cm, $BC = 8$ cm, $\angle B = 90°$ and BD is the perpendicular from B on AC. The circle through B, C and D is drawn. Construct the tangents from A to this circle.

7 Draw a circle with the help of circular solid ring construct a pair of tangents from a point P outside the circle.

8 Construct a tangent to a circle of radius 4 cm from a point on the concentric circle of radius 6 cm and measure its length.

Answers

2. (a) **3.** (d) **4.** (b) **8.** 4.47 cm

* *These questions may or may not be asked in the examination, have been given just for additional practice required for olympiads Scholarship Exams etc. For detailed explanations refer Page No. 495.*

CHAPTER

17

Surface Area and Volume

SYLLABUS

• Area and volume of solids-Cylinder, cone and sphere

Three-dimensional solids-right circular cylinder and right circular cone : Area (total surface and curved surface) and Volume. Direct application problems including cost, Inner and Outer volume and melting and recasting method to find the volume or surface area of a new solid. Combination of solids included.

Note Problems on Frustum are not included.

In earlier classes, we have learnt to find the surface area and volume of some solid figures like; cuboid and cube. In this chapter, we will learn to find the surface area and volume of some new solid figures, like cylinder, cone and sphere.

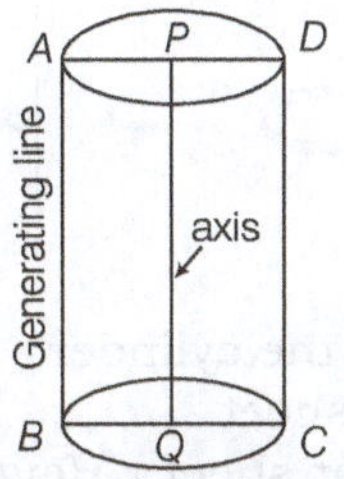

Surface Area and Volume of a Cylinder

Right Circular Cylinder

A right circular cylinder has two plane congruent circular ends parallel to each other and joined by a curved surface at right angles to both the ends.

e.g. A round glass jar, a circular oil container, a gas cylinder, a circular pillar of a hall, a piece of a circular pipe, etc., are all right circular cylinder.

In other words, a solid generated by the revolution of a rectangle about one of its sides which is kept fixed, is called a **right circular cylinder**. The fixed side of the rectangle about which it rotates, is called the **axis of the cylinder**.

In the figure, line *AB* when moving on the circumference of the circle *BC* generates a **right circular cylinder**. Here, the line *AB* is the generating line and *PQ* joining the centres of the circular base and top is called the **axis**. Also, circle *BC* is the **base** of the cylinder.

Important Terms Related to Right Circular Cylinder

There are various terms related to right circular cylinder, which are as follow

(i) **Base** Each of the circular ends on which the cylinder rests, is called its base.

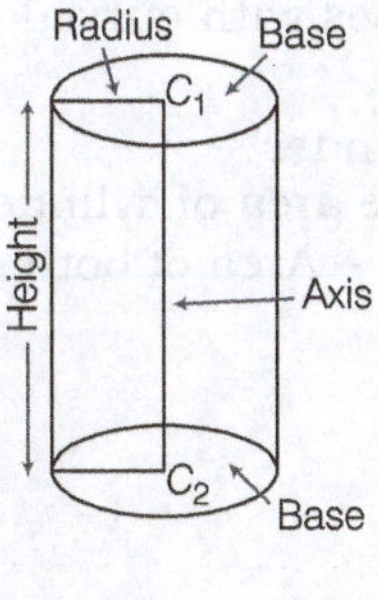

(ii) **Axis** The line segment joining the centres of two circular bases is called the axis of cylinder and the axis of cylinder is always perpendicular to the bases of it.

(iii) **Radius** The radius of circular bases is called the radius of cylinder (radius of both ends will be always same).

(iv) **Height** The length of the axis of the cylinder is called the height of the cylinder.

(v) **Lateral surface** The curved surface joining the two bases of a right circular cylinder is called its lateral surface.

Surface Area of a Right Circular Cylinder

We know that right circular cylinder is generated by revolution of a rectangular sheet about one of its side, so the area of the rectangular sheet gives us the curved surface area of the cylinder and length of the rectangular sheet is equal to the circumference of the circular base.

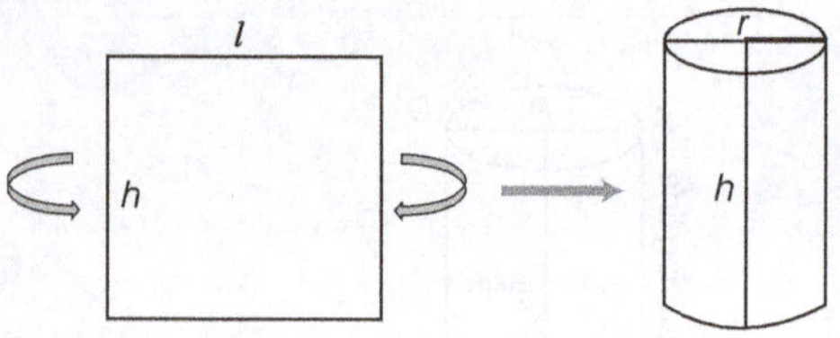

∴ Curved surface area of the cylinder
= Area of rectangular sheet
= Length of rectangular sheet × Height
= Circumference of the base of the cylinder × Height
[∵ Length of rectangular sheet = Circumference of the base]

∴ Curved surface area of cylinder = $2\pi rh$ sq units

where, circumference of the base of the cylinder = $2\pi r$, r is the radius of the base and h is the height of the cylinder.

Total Surface Area of a Right Circular Cylinder

For total surface area of a cylinder, we also take area of both circular bases with curved surface area of the cylinder. So,

Total surface area of cylinder
= Curved surface area of cylinder + Area of both circular ends

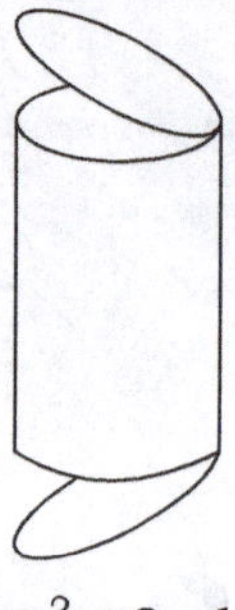

$= 2\pi rh + \pi r^2 + \pi r^2 = 2\pi rh + 2\pi r^2$

∴ TSA of cylinder = $2\pi r(h + r)$ sq units

where, r = radius of base and h = height of cylinder.

Surface Area of a Hollow Cylinder

A solid bounded by two coaxial cylinders of the same height and different radii is called a hollow cylinder.

Let a hollow cylinder whose external and internal radii are R and r, respectively with h as height. Then,

Surface area of each base = $\pi(R^2 - r^2)$ sq units

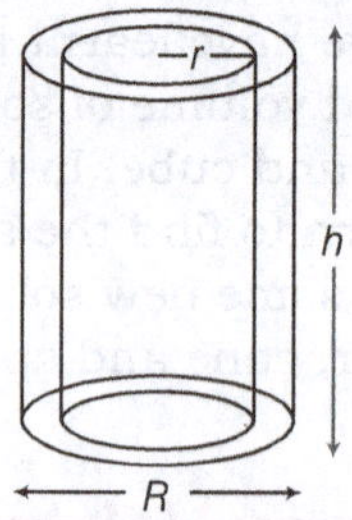

Curved surface area = External surface area + Internal surface area

$= 2\pi Rh + 2\pi rh$
$= 2\pi h(R + r)$ sq units

Curved surface area of hollow cylinder = $2\pi h(R + r)$ sq units

Total surface area = Curved surface area + 2(Surface area of each base)
$= 2\pi h(R + r) + 2\pi(R^2 - r^2)$

∴ TSA of hollow cylinder = $2\pi(R + r)(h + R - r)$ sq units

Example 1. The ratio between the curved surface area and the total surface area of a right circular cylinder is 1 : 3. Find the ratio between the height and radius of the cylinder.

Sol. Let radius of the cylinder = r and height = h.

Then, curved surface area = $2\pi rh$

and total surface area = $2\pi r(h+r)$

According to the question,

Curved surface area : Total surface area = 1 : 3

$$\therefore \quad \frac{2\pi rh}{2\pi r(h+r)} = \frac{1}{3}$$

$$\Rightarrow \quad \frac{h}{h+r} = \frac{1}{3}$$

$$\Rightarrow \quad 3h = h + r$$

$$\Rightarrow \quad 2h = r$$

$$\Rightarrow \quad \frac{h}{r} = \frac{1}{2} \quad \text{or} \quad h : r = 1 : 2$$

Hence, the required ratio between height and radius of the cylinder is 1 : 2.

Example 2. A rectangular sheet of paper 44 cm × 18 cm is rolled along its length and a cylinder is formed. Find the radius of the cylinder.

Sol. Given, measures of a rectangular sheet = 44 cm × 18 cm

Here, length = 44 cm and breadth = 18 cm

Let radius of the base of the cylinder be r.

On revolving it about its length, a cylinder is formed.

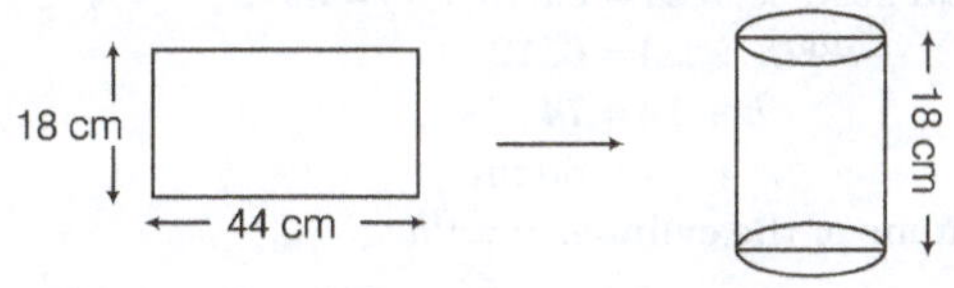

∴ Circumference of the base of the cylinder = Length of sheet

$$\Rightarrow \quad 2\pi r = 44$$

$$\Rightarrow \quad 2 \times \frac{22}{7} \times r = 44$$

$$\Rightarrow \quad r = \frac{44 \times 7}{2 \times 22} = 7$$

Hence, the radius of the cylinder is 7 cm.

Example 3. A cylindrical roller 2.5 m in length, 1.75 m in radius when rolled on a road was found to cover an area of 5500 m^2. How many revolutions did it make?

Sol. Given, length of cylindrical roller = 2.5 m = $\frac{5}{2}$ m,

and radius = 1.75 m = $\frac{7}{4}$ m

∴ Area covered by the roller in one revolution

= Curved surface area of roller

$$= 2\pi rh = \left(2 \times \frac{22}{7} \times \frac{7}{4} \times \frac{5}{2}\right) m^2$$

$$= \frac{55}{2} m^2$$

Let the number of revolutions made by the roller be n, then

Area covered in one revolution × n = Total area covered

$$\Rightarrow \quad \frac{55}{2} \times n = 5500 \Rightarrow n = 200$$

Hence, the number of revolutions made by the roller are 200.

Example 4. An iron pipe 20 cm long has exterior diameter equal to 25 cm. If the thickness of the pipe is 1 cm, then find the whole surface area of the pipe.

Sol. Given, length of the pipe (h) = 20 cm

and exterior diameter = 25 cm

Now, exterior radius (R) = $\frac{25}{2}$ = 12.5 cm

Thickness of the pipe = 1 cm

∴ Internal radius (r) = External radius − Thickness = 12.5 − 1 = 11.5 cm

Now, whole surface area of the pipe

= (External curved surface area) + (Internal curved surface area) + 2 (Area of the base of the pipe)

$$= 2\pi Rh + 2\pi rh + 2\pi(R^2 - r^2)$$

$$= 2\pi h(R + r) + 2\pi(R - r)(R + r) \quad [\because a^2 - b^2 = (a-b)(a+b)]$$

$$= 2\pi(R + r)(h + R - r)$$

$$= 2 \times \frac{22}{7} \times (12.5 + 11.5) \times (20 + 12.5 - 11.5)$$

$$= 2 \times \frac{22}{7} \times 24 \times 21 = 3168 \text{ cm}^2$$

Example 5. The cost of painting the outer curved surface of a cylinder at ₹ 1.50 per cm^2 is ₹ 660. If the height of the cylinder is 2 m. Then, find the curved surface of the base of cylinder.

Sol. Given, height of the cylinder = 2 m = 200 cm [∵ 1 m = 100 cm]

Total cost of painting = ₹ 660

and rate of painting the outer curved surface area of the cylinder = ₹ 1.50 per cm^2

∵ Total cost of painting = Curved surface area of cylinder × Rate of painting the curved surface area

⇒ 660 = Curved surface area × 1.50

$$\Rightarrow \text{Curved surface area} = \frac{660}{1.50} \text{ cm}^2$$

$$\Rightarrow \quad 2\pi rh = 440$$

[∵ curved surface area of cylinder = $2\pi rh$]

$$\Rightarrow \quad 2 \times \frac{22}{7} \times r \times 200 = 440$$

$$\Rightarrow \quad r = \frac{440 \times 7}{2 \times 22 \times 200} = \frac{35}{100} \text{ cm}$$

∴ Curved surface of the base of cylinder

= Circumference of the base of the cylinder

$$= 2\pi r = 2 \times \frac{22}{7} \times \frac{35}{100} = 2.2 \text{ cm}$$

Volume of a Right Circular Cylinder

We know that a right circular cylinder can be built up using circles of the same radius. Let h be the height and r be the radius of the right circular cylinder, then

Volume of the cylinder

= Measure of the space occupied by the cylinder

= Area of circular base × Height

$\therefore$ **Volume of the cylinder = $\pi r^2 h$ cu units**

Volume of a Hollow Cylinder

For volume of the material used for making a hollow cylinder will be obtain by subtracting the interior volume from exterior volume, i.e.

Volume of the material

= Exterior volume – Interior volume

$= \pi R^2 h - \pi r^2 h$

$\therefore$ **Volume of hollow cylinder = $\pi(R^2 - r^2)h$**

where, R and r are exterior and interior radii respectively, h is the height of that hollow cylinder.

Example 6. The circumference of the base of a cylindrical vessel is 132 cm and its height is 25 cm. Find the

(i) radius of the cylinder.

(ii) volume of cylinder. [use $\pi = 22/7$] **[ICSE 2018]**

Sol. Given, circumference of the base of a cylindrical vessel = 132 cm and height = 25 cm

(i) We know that base of a cylinder is in the shape of a circle.

$\therefore$ Circumference of the base of a cylinder = $2\pi r$

$\Rightarrow 2\pi r = 132 \Rightarrow 2\times\frac{22}{7}\times r = 132 \Rightarrow r = 3\times 7 \Rightarrow r = 21\text{ cm}$

(ii) Volume of cylinder $= \pi r^2 h = \frac{22}{7}\times 21\times 21\times 25$

$= 66\times 21\times 25 = 34650\text{ cm}^3$

Example 7. The sum of the radius of base and height of a right circular cylinder is 37 cm. If the total surface area of the solid cylinder is 1628 sq cm, then find volume of the cylinder.

Sol. Given, sum of base radius and height of a right circular solid cylinder = 37 cm

$r + h = 37$ ...(i)

Total surface area of cylinder $= 2\pi r(h + r) = 1628$

$2\times\frac{22}{7}\times r\times 37 = 1628 \Rightarrow r = 7$

From Eq. (i), $7 + h = 37 \Rightarrow h = 30$

Volume of the cylinder $= \pi r^2 h = \frac{22}{7}\times 7\times 7\times 30$

$= 4620\text{ cm}^3$

Hence, the volume of the cylinder = 4620 cm^3

Example 8. A cylindrical bucket of diameter 28 cm and height 12 cm is full of water. The water is emptied into a rectangular tub of length 66 cm and breadth 28 cm, then find the height of water rises in the tub.

Sol. Given, diameter of bucket = 28 cm

$\therefore$ Radius $(r) = \frac{28}{2} = 14\text{ cm}$

and height of water in bucket $(h) = 12\text{ cm}$

Volume of water in the bucket $= \pi r^2 h$

$= \frac{22}{7}\times 14\times 14\times 12 = 7392\text{ cu cm}$

Let h be the height of water rises in the tub.

Then, volume of water in the tub = $(66\times 28\times h)$ cu cm

According to the question,

Volume of water in bucket = Volume of water in tub

$\Rightarrow 7392 = 66\times 28\times h \Rightarrow h = \frac{7392}{66\times 28} = 4\text{ cm}$

Hence, the water rises to a height of 4 cm in the tub.

Example 9. The total surface area of a cylinder is 6512 cm^2 and the circumference of its base is 88 cm, find the volume of the cylinder.

Sol. Let h is the height and r be the radius of the given cylinder.

Circumference $= 2\pi r = 88\text{ cm}$

$= 2\times\frac{22}{7}\times r = 88$

$\Rightarrow r = 14\text{ cm}$

Total surface area $= 2\pi r(h + r) = 6512$

$\Rightarrow 88(h + 14) = 6512$

$\Rightarrow h + 14 = 74$

$\Rightarrow h = 60\text{ cm}$

Volume of the cylinder $= \pi r^2 h$

$= \frac{22}{7}\times(14)^2\times 60 = 36960\text{ cm}^3$

Example 10. A solid metallic sphere of radius 6 cm is melted and made into a solid cylinder of height 32 cm. Find the **[ICSE 2019]**

(i) radius of the cylinder.

(ii) curved surface area of the cylinder. [take $\pi = 3.1$]

Sol. Given, radius of sphere $(r) = 6\text{ cm}$

and height of cylinder $(h) = 32\text{ cm}$

According to the given condition,

(i) Volume of solid sphere = Volume of cylinder

$\Rightarrow \frac{4}{3}\pi r^3 = \pi R^2 h$

$\Rightarrow \frac{4}{3}(6)^3 = R^2\times(32)$

$\Rightarrow R^2 = \frac{4}{3}\times\frac{6\times 6\times 6}{32} = \frac{2\times 6\times 6}{8} = 3^2$

$\Rightarrow R = 3\text{ cm}$

Hence, the radius of cylinder is 3 cm.

(ii) Curved surface area of the cylinder $= 2\pi Rh$

$= 2\times 3.1\times 3\times 32$

$= 595.2\text{ cm}^2$

Example 11. 30 circular plates, each of radius 14 cm and thickness 3 cm are placed one above the another to form a cylindrical solid. Find

(i) the total surface area.

(ii) the volume of the cylinder so formed.

Sol. $\because$ Height of the cylinder formed, h

$= \text{Number of plates} \times \text{thickness of one plate}$

$= (30 \times 3)\text{ cm} = 90\text{ cm}$

And radius of each circular plate, $r = 14\text{ cm}$

(i) Total surface area of cylinder $= 2\pi r(h + r)$

$$= 2 \times \frac{22}{7} \times 14 \times (90 + 14) = (88 \times 104)\text{ cm}^2 = 9152\text{ cm}^2$$

(ii) Volume of the cylinder $= \pi r^2 h = \frac{22}{7} \times (14)^2 \times 90$

$$= 22 \times 28 \times 90$$
$$= 55440\text{ cm}^3$$

Example 12. The radius and the height of a cylinder are in the ratio 2 : 7. If the volume of the cylinder is 704 cm^3, then find the total surface area of the cylinder.

Sol. Given, radius and the height of a cylinder are the ratio 2 : 7. Let r (radius) $= 2x$ cm, and h(height) $= 7x$ cm

Volume of the cylinder $= \pi r^2 h$

$$704 = \frac{22}{7} \times (2x)^2 \times 7x$$

$\Rightarrow$ $88x^3 = 704$

$\Rightarrow$ $x^3 = 8$

$\Rightarrow$ $x = 2$

Radius of cylinder $= 2x$ cm $= 4$ cm and

height of cylinder $= 7x$ cm $= 14$ cm

Total surface area of the cylinder $= 2\pi r(h + r)$

$$= 2 \times \frac{22}{7} \times 4(14 + 4)\text{ cm}^2$$
$$= \frac{176}{7} \times 18\text{ cm}^2$$
$$= \frac{3168}{7}\text{ cm}^2$$
$$= 452\frac{4}{7}\text{ cm}^2$$

Hence, the total surface area is $452\frac{4}{7}$ cm^2.

Example 13. The difference between outside and inside surfaces of a cylindrical metallic pipe 14 cm and long is 44 cm^2. If the pipe is made of 88 cm^3 of metal. Find outer and inner radii of the pipe.

Sol. Let R cm and r cm be the external and internal radii of the metallic pipe, respectively.

Given, height/length of the pipe $(h) = 14$ cm

According to the question,

Outside surface area – Inside surface area $= 44\text{ cm}^2$

$\Rightarrow$ $2\pi Rh - 2\pi rh = 44$ [given]

$\Rightarrow$ $2 \times \frac{22}{7}(R - r) \times 14 = 44$

$\Rightarrow$ $R - r = \frac{1}{2}$ ...(i)

$\because$ Volume of the metal used for making the pipe $= 88\text{ cm}^3$

$$\pi(R^2 - r^2)h = 88$$

$\Rightarrow$ $\frac{22}{7} \times (R + r)(R - r) \times 14 = 88$ $[\because a^2 - b^2 = (a + b)(a - b)]$

$\Rightarrow$ $\frac{22}{7} \times (R + r) \times \frac{1}{2} \times 14 = 88$ [from Eq. (i)]

$\Rightarrow$ $R + r = \frac{88}{22}$

$\Rightarrow$ $R + r = 4$ ...(ii)

On adding Eqs. (i) and (ii), we get

$$R - r + R + r = \frac{1}{2} + 4 = 0.5 + 4 = 4.5$$

$\Rightarrow$ $2R = 4.5 \Rightarrow R = \frac{4.5}{2} = 2.25\text{ cm}$

On putting $R = 2.25$ cm in Eq. (ii), we get

$$r = 4 - 2.25 = 1.75\text{ cm}$$

Hence, the outer and inner radii of the pipe are 2.25 cm and 1.75 cm, respectively.

Example 14. A metal pipe has a bare (Internal diameter) of 5 cm. The pipe is 2 mm thick all round. Find the weight (in kg), of 2 m of the pipe, if 1 cm^3 of the metal weighs 7.7 g.

Sol. The thickness of the pipe all round $= 2\text{ mm} = \frac{2}{10}\text{ cm} = \frac{1}{5}\text{ cm}$

$[\because 1\text{ mm} = 10\text{ cm}]$

Internal radius (r) of the pipe $= \frac{1}{2} \times 5\text{ cm} = \frac{5}{2}\text{ cm}$

$\therefore$ External radius (R) of the pipe $= \left(\frac{5}{2} + \frac{1}{5}\right)\text{ cm} = \frac{27}{10}\text{ cm}$

Length of the pipe $= 2\text{ m} = 200\text{ cm}$ $[\because 1\text{ m} = 100\text{ cm}]$

$\therefore$ The volume of the metal $= \pi(R^2 - r^2)h$

$$= \frac{22}{7}\left[\left(\frac{27}{10}\right)^2 - \left(\frac{5}{2}\right)^2\right] \times 200\text{ cm}^3$$
$$= \frac{22}{7}\left(\frac{27}{10} + \frac{5}{2}\right)\left(\frac{27}{10} - \frac{5}{2}\right) \times 200\text{ cm}^3$$
$$= \frac{22}{7} \times \frac{52}{10} \times \frac{2}{10} \times 200\text{ cm}^3$$
$$= \frac{88 \times 52}{7}\text{ cm}^3$$

Since 1 cm^3 of metal weighs 7.7 g.

$\therefore$ The weight of the pipe $= \frac{88 \times 52}{7} \times 7.7\text{ g}$

$$= \frac{88 \times 52 \times 77}{7 \times 10 \times 1000}\text{ kg}$$

$\left[\because 1\text{g} = \frac{1}{1000}\text{kg}\right]$

$$= 5.0336\text{ kg}$$

Exercise 17.1

1. If radius and height of the cylinder are 2 cm and 14 cm, respectively. Then, find its
   (i) lateral surface area
   (ii) total surface area
   (iii) volume
2. If the curved surface area of a cylinder is 1760 cm^2 and its base radius is 14 cm. Then, find its height.
3. The curved surface area of a right circular cylinder is 660 cm^2 and base radius is 5 cm. Find its height.
4. Find the ratio between the total surface area of a cylinder to its curved surface area given that its height and radius are 7.5 cm and 3.5 cm.
5. The total surface area of a cylinder is 352 cm^2. If its height is 10 cm, then find the diameter of the base.
6. The heights of two cylinders are in the ratio 5 : 3 and their radii are in the ratio 2 : 3. Then, find the ratio of their curved surface area.
7. The area of the curved surface of a right circular cylinder is 4400 cm^2 and the circumference of its base is 110 cm. Find the height of the cylinder.
8. A cylinder is formed by rolling a sheet whose dimension is 8.8 cm $\times$ 2.8 cm. Find the radius of the cylinder.
9. A cylindrical container is to be made of tin sheet the height of the container is 1 m and its diameter is 70 cm. If the container is open at the top and the tin sheet costs ₹ 100 per m^2, find the cost of tin sheet for making the container.
10. A roadroller (in the shape of a cylinder) has a diameter 0.7 m and its width is 1.2 m. Find the least number of revolutions that the roller must make in order to level a playground of size 120 m by 44 m.
11. An iron pipe 10 cm long has exterior diameter equal to 15 cm. If the thickness of the pipe is 2 cm, then find the whole surface of the pipe.
12. The given figure shows a metal pipe 77 cm long. The inner diameter of a cross-section is 4 cm and the outer one is 4.4 cm.

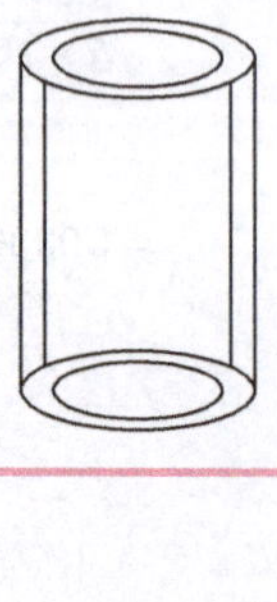

   Find its
   (i) inner curved surface area.
   (ii) outer curved surface area.
   (iii) total surface area.
13. If the diameter of the base and height of a cylinder are 6 cm and 14 cm, respectively. Then, find its volume.
14. A rectangular paper 11 cm by 8 cm can be exactly wrapped to cover the curved surface of a cylinder of height 8 cm. Find the volume of the cylinder.
15. The sum of the height and the radius of a solid cylinder is 35 cm and its total surface area is 3080 cm^2, find the volume of the cylinder.
16. The total surface area of a circular cylinder is 462 cm^2. If its curved surface area is one third of its total surface area, then find the volume of the cylinder.
17. It costs ₹ 2200 to point the inner curved surface of a cylindrical tank 10 m deep. If the rate of painting is ₹ 20 per m^2. Find the capacity of the tank.
18. The internal and external diameters of steel pipe of length 140 cm are 8 cm and 10 cm, respectively. Then, find the volume of steel.
19. A cylindrical tube open at both ends is made of metal. The internal diameter of the tube is 11.2 cm and its length is 21 cm. the metal thickness is 0.4 cm. Calculate the volume of the metal.
20. In a cylinder, if radius is halved and height is doubled, then find its volume.
21. Calculate the volume of a right circular cylinder with base radius 14 cm and height 14 cm.
22. The radius and the height of a cylinder are in the ratio 5 : 7 and its volume is 550 cm^3. Find its radius.
23. The height and the radius of the base of a cylinder are in the ratio 3 : 1. If its volume is 1029 π cm^3, then find the total surface area.
24. The cylindrical water tank of diameter 1.4 m and height 2.1 m is being fill by a pipe of diameter 3.5 cm through which water flows at the rate of 2 m/s. Calculate the time it takes to fill the tank.
25. A lead pencil consists of a cylinder of wood with a solid cylinder of graphite filled in the interior. The diameter of the pencil is 7 mm and the diameter of the graphite is 1 mm. If the length of the pencil is 14 cm, find the volume of the wood and that of the graphite.

Surface Area and Volume of a Cone

Right Circular Cone

If a right angled triangle is revolved about one of the two sides forming a right angle, keeping the other sides fixed in position, then the solid so obtained by revolving the line segments, is called a right circular cone.

In our daily life, we see many objects having conical shape; an ice–cream, conical tent, birthday cap, conical vessel etc.

Important Terms Related to Right Circular Cone

There are various terms related to right circular cone, which are as follow

(i) **Vertex** O is called the vertex of the cone.

(ii) **Axis** The fixed line OP is called the axis of the cone.

(iii) **Base** The circle ABC is called the base of the cone.

(iv) **Slant height** The length of the line segment joining the vertex O to any point on the circular edge of the base, is called the slant height of the cone. Here, $OA = OB$ are the slant heights of the cone.

(v) **Vertical angle** $\angle AOB$ is called the vertex angle of the cone.

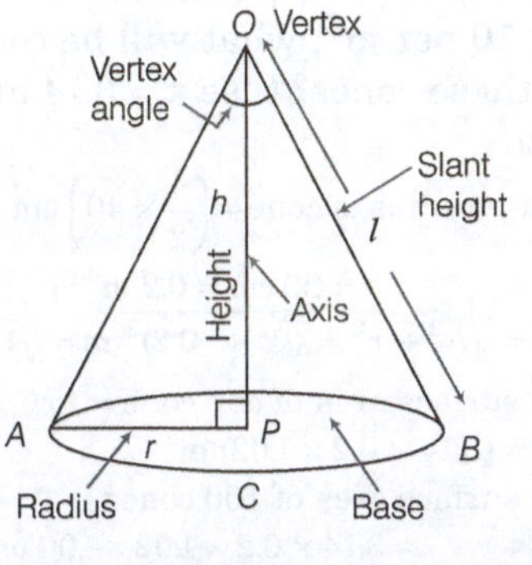

(vi) **Height** The length of the line segment joining the vertex to the centre of the base, is called the height of the cone. Here, OP is the height of the cone.

(vii) **Radius** The radius AP of the base circle is called the radius of the cone.

Curved Surface Area of a Cone

When a cone is cut along by any slant height and spread out on plane surface, it forms a shape of sector of a circle. The area of this sector is called curved surface area of the cone.

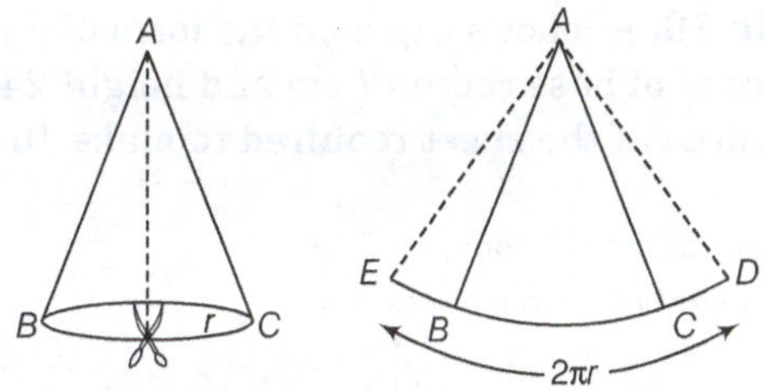

$\therefore$ **Curved surface area of a cone = πrl sq units**

where, r = radius of the base of a cone

and l = slant height of the cone, in which

$l = \sqrt{h^2 + r^2}$, here h = vertical height of the cone.

Surface Area of a Cone

If the base of the cone is to be closed, then a circular piece of paper of radius r is also required.

Surface (Total surface) area of a cone

= Curved surface area of a cone + Area of the base

$= \pi rl + \pi r^2$

$\therefore$ **SA (TSA) of a cone = $\pi r(l + r)$ sq units**

Volume of a Cone

The quantity of liquid contained in a cone, is called the volume of a cone.

$\therefore$ **Volume of a cone = $\frac{1}{3}\pi r^2 h$ cu units**

where, r is the radius and h is the height of a cone.

Example 15. A solid cone of radius 5 cm and height 7 cm is given. Calculate

(i) curved surface area of a cone.

(ii) volume of a cone. [take $\pi = 3.14$ and $\sqrt{74} = 8.6$]

(iii) total surface area of cone.

Sol. Given, radius of a cone, $r = 5$ cm

and height of a cone, $h = 7$ cm

(i) Curved surface area of a cone $= \pi rl$

$= 3.14 \times 5 \times \sqrt{5^2 + 7^2}$ $[\because l = \sqrt{r^2 + h^2}]$

$= 3.14 \times 5 \times \sqrt{25 + 49} = 3.14 \times 5 \times \sqrt{74}$

$= 15.7 \times 8.6 = 135.02 \text{ cm}^2$

(ii) Volume of a cone $= \frac{1}{3}\pi r^2 h = \frac{3.14}{3} \times (5)^2 \times 7$

$= \frac{549.5}{3} = 183.17 \text{ cm}^3$

(iii) Total surface area of cone $= \pi r(l + r)$

$= 3.14 \times 5(8.6 + 5) = 3.14 \times 5 \times 13.6 \text{ cm}^2$

$= 213.52 \text{ cm}^2$

Example 16. A joker's cap is in the form of a right circular cone of base radius 7 cm and height 24 cm. Find the area of the sheet required to make 10 such caps.

Sol. Given, radius of a cone, $r = 7$ cm

and height of a cone, $h = 24$ cm

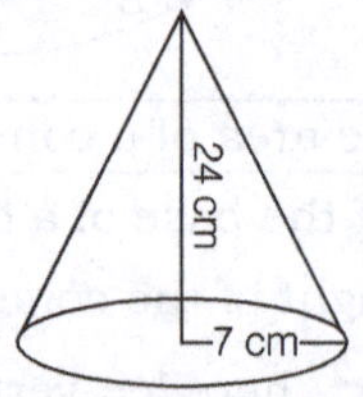

We know that, $l = \sqrt{h^2 + r^2} = \sqrt{(24)^2 + (7)^2}$

$= \sqrt{576 + 49} = \sqrt{625} = 25$ cm

$\therefore$ Curved surface area of a joker's cap

= Curved surface area of a cone $= \pi rl$

$= \frac{22}{7} \times 7 \times 25 = 22 \times 25 = 550 \text{ cm}^2$

$\because$ Sheet required to make 1 cap $= 550 \text{ cm}^2$

$\therefore$ Sheet required to make 10 such caps $= 550 \times 10$

$= 5500 \text{ cm}^2$

Example 17. How many square metres of canvas is required for a conical tent whose height is 7 m and the radius of the base is 24 m?

Sol. Here, height of cone $= h = 7$m and radius of base $= r = 24$m

Let l metre be the slant height of the cone, then

$l = \sqrt{h^2 + r^2} = \sqrt{(7)^2 + (24)^2}$

$= \sqrt{625} = 25$ m

Note, that a tent has only curved surface area of canvas required for a conical tent = curved surface area of the cone

$\pi rl = \frac{22}{7} \times 24 \times 25 \text{ m}^2$

$= \frac{13200}{7} \text{ m}^2$

$= 1885.71 \text{ m}^2$

Example 18. If the height of a cone is doubled, then find its increased volume in percentage.

Sol. Let r and h be the radius and height of a cone, respectively.

Then, original volume of a cone $= \frac{1}{3} \pi r^2 h = V$ (say)

New radius $= r$ and new height $= 2h$

Then, new volume of a cone

$= \frac{1}{3} \pi r^2 \times 2h = 2 \times \left(\frac{1}{3} \pi r^2 h\right) = 2V$

$\therefore$ Increase in volume $= 2V - V = V$

Increase percentage of volume

$= \left(\frac{\text{Increase in volume}}{\text{Original volume}} \times 100\right)\%$

$= \left(\frac{V}{V} \times 100\right)\% = 100\%$

Example 19. A semi-circular sheet of metal of diameter 28 cm is bent to form an open conical cup. Find the capacity of the cup. [take $\pi = 22/7$]

Sol. Given, diameter of a semi-circular sheet = 28 cm

$\therefore$ Radius of a semi-circular sheet, $r = \frac{28}{2} = 14$ cm

Let the radius of a conical cup be R.

Since, a semi-circular sheet of metal is bent to form an open conical cup.

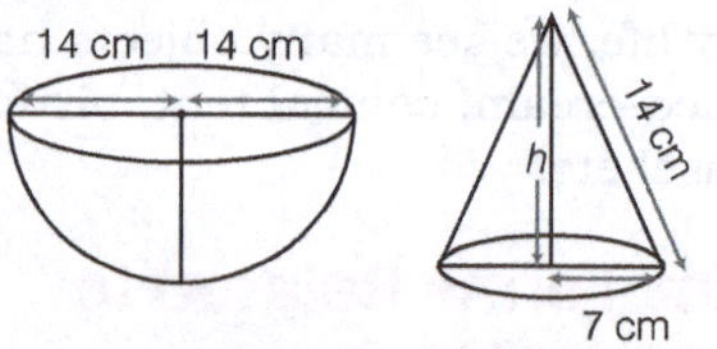

$\therefore$ Circumference of the base of a cone

= Circumference of a semi-circle

$\Rightarrow \quad 2\pi R = \pi r \Rightarrow 2\pi R = \pi \times 14 \Rightarrow R = 7$ cm

Now, $\quad h = \sqrt{l^2 - R^2} = \sqrt{14^2 - 7^2} \quad [\because l^2 = h^2 + R^2]$

$= \sqrt{196 - 49} = \sqrt{147} = 12.12$ cm

$\therefore$ Volume or capacity of conical cup

$= \frac{1}{3} \pi R^2 h = \frac{1}{3} \times \frac{22}{7} \times 7 \times 7 \times 12.12 = 622.16 \text{ cm}^3$

Hence, the capacity of an open conical cup is 622.16 cm^3.

Example 20. A bus stop is barricaded from the remaining part of the road, by using 100 hollow cones made of recycled cardboard. Each cone has a base diameter of 40 cm and height 1 m. If the outside of each of the cones is to be painted and the cost of painting is ₹ 10 per m^2, what will be the cost of painting all these cones? (use $\pi = 3.14$ and $\sqrt{1.04} = 1.02$).

Sol. Given, base radius of cone $= \left(\frac{1}{2} \times 40\right)$ cm

$= 20 \text{ cm} = 0.2$ m

$\because \quad l = \sqrt{h^2 + r^2} = \sqrt{1^2 + (0.2)^2} \text{ m} = \sqrt{1.04} = 1.02$ m

$\therefore$ Curved surface area of one cone $= \pi rl$

$= (3.14 \times 0.2 \times 1.02) \text{ m}^2$

$\therefore$ Curved surface area of 100 cones

$= 3.14 \times 0.2 \times 1.02 \times 100 \text{ m}^2$

Cost of painting of 100 cones = ₹ $3.14 \times 0.2 \times 102 \times 100 \times 10$

= ₹ 3.14×204 = ₹ 640.56

Example 21. Monika has a piece of canvas whose area is 551 m^2. She uses it to made conical tent with a base radius of 7 m. Assuming that all the stitching margins and the wastage incurred while cutting, amounts to approximately 1 m^2, then find the volume of the tent that can be made with it.

Sol. Let l m be the slant height and hm be the height of cone.

Here, base radius of cone = 7 m,

Total area of canvas $= 551 \text{m}^2$ and wastage $= 1 \text{m}^2$.

$\therefore$ The actual area of the conical tent

$= (551 - 1)\ m^2 = 550\ m^2$

Now, area of conical tent = curved surface area of cone $= \pi rl$

$\Rightarrow \quad \frac{22}{7} \times 7 \times l = 550 \Rightarrow l = 25\ m$

Also, $\quad l^2 = h^2 + r^2 \Rightarrow 25^2 = h^2 + 7^2$

$\Rightarrow \quad h^2 = 625 - 49 = 576 \Rightarrow h = 24\ m$

[taking positive square root]

$\therefore$ Volume of the conical tent

$= \frac{1}{3}\pi r^2 h = \frac{1}{3} \times \frac{22}{7} \times 7^2 \times 24 = (22 \times 7 \times 8) = 1232\ m^3$

Example 22. A conical tent is 10 m high and the radius of its base is 24 m. Find

(i) the slant height of the tent.

(ii) the cost of the canvas required to make the tent, if the cost of 1 m^2 canvas is ₹ 70.

(iii) the volume of air contained in the conical tent.

Sol. Given, height of a conical tent, $h = 10\ m$

and radius, $r = 24\ m$

(i) We know that, $l = \sqrt{r^2 + h^2} = \sqrt{(24)^2 + (10)^2}$

$= \sqrt{576 + 100} = \sqrt{676} = 26\ m$

Hence, the slant height of the tent is 26 m.

(ii) Canvas required to make the tent

= Curved surface area of the tent

$= \pi rl = \pi \times 24 \times 26 = 624\pi\ m^2$

$\because$ Cost of 1 m^2 canvas = ₹ 70

$\therefore$ Cost of $624\pi\ m^2$ canvas = ₹ $70 \times 624\pi$ = ₹ $70 \times 624 \times \frac{22}{7}$

= ₹ $10 \times 624 \times 22$ = ₹ 137280

Hence, the required cost of the canvas is ₹137280.

(iii) Volume of air contained in the conical tent

$= \frac{1}{3}\pi r^2 h = \frac{1}{3} \times \frac{22}{7} \times (24)^2 \times 10 = 6034.29\ m^3$

Example 23. The volume of a conical tent is 1232 m^3 and the area of the base floor is 154 m^2. Calculate

(i) radius of the floor. (ii) height of the tent.

(iii) length of the canvas required to cover this conical tent, if its width is 2 m. [take $\pi = 22/7$]

Sol. (i) Let the radius of conical tent be r.

$\because$ Area of base floor $= 154\ m^2$ [given]

$\Rightarrow \quad \pi r^2 = 154$

$\Rightarrow \quad \frac{22}{7} \times r^2 = 154 \Rightarrow r^2 = \frac{154 \times 7}{22}$

$\Rightarrow \quad r^2 = 49 \Rightarrow r = 7\ m$ [taking positive square root]

(ii) Let the height of conical tent be h.

$\because$ Volume of conical tent $= 1232\ m^3$

$\Rightarrow \quad \frac{1}{3}\pi r^2 h = 1232$

$\Rightarrow \quad \frac{1}{3} \times \frac{22}{7} \times 7 \times 7 \times h = 1232$

$\Rightarrow \quad h = \frac{1232 \times 3}{22 \times 7} \Rightarrow h = 24\ m$

(iii) Curved surface area of cone

= Area of the canvas required to cover conical tent

$\Rightarrow \quad \pi rl = \text{Length} \times \text{Width}$

$\Rightarrow \quad \frac{22}{7} \times 7 \times \sqrt{r^2 + h^2} = \text{Length} \times 2$ [$\because$ width = 2 m (given)]

$\Rightarrow \quad 22 \times \sqrt{(7)^2 + (24)^2} = \text{Length} \times 2$

$\therefore$ Length $= 11 \times \sqrt{625} = 11 \times 25 = 275\ m$

Example 24. A cloth having an area of 165 m^2 is shaped in the form of a conical tent of radius 5 m. How many students can sit in the tent, if a student, on an average, occupies $\frac{5}{7}\ m^2$ area on the ground?

Sol. Given, radius of the cone, $r = 5\ m$

$\therefore$ Floor area of the tent $= \pi r^2 = \left(\frac{22}{7} \times 5^2\right) = \frac{550}{7}\ m^2$

Let n be the number of students.

As each student, on an average, occupies $\frac{5}{7}\ m^2$ area.

$\therefore \quad \frac{5}{7} \times n = \frac{550}{7} \Rightarrow n = 110$

Hence, the number of students are 110.

Example 25. The height of a cone is 40 cm. A small cone is cut off at the top by a plane parallel to its base. If its volume be $\frac{1}{64}$ of the volume of the given cone, at what height above the base is the section cut?

Sol. Let OAB be the given cone of height 40 cm and base radius R cm. Let this cone be cut by the plane CND (parallel to the base plane AMB) to obtain the cone OCD with height h cm and the base radius r cm.

Then, $\Delta OND \sim \Delta OMB$.

$\therefore \quad \frac{ND}{MB} = \frac{ON}{OM} \Rightarrow \frac{r}{R} = \frac{h}{40}$ ...(i)

According to the question,

Volume of cone $OCD = \frac{1}{64} \times$ Volume of cone OAB

$\Rightarrow \quad \frac{1}{3}\pi r^2 h = \frac{1}{64} \times \frac{1}{3}\pi R^2 \times 40 \Rightarrow r^2 h = \frac{1}{64} R^2 \times 40$

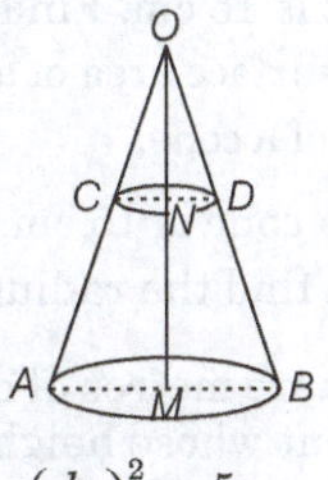

$\Rightarrow \quad \left(\frac{r}{R}\right)^2 = \frac{5}{8h} \Rightarrow \left(\frac{h}{40}\right)^2 = \frac{5}{8h}$ [using Eq. (i)]

$\Rightarrow \quad h^3 = \frac{40 \times 40 \times 5}{8} = 1000$

$\Rightarrow \quad h = 10\ cm$ [taking cube root]

Since, the height of the cone OCD is 10 cm.

Here, the section is cut at the height of (40 – 10) cm i.e. 30 cm from the base.

Example 26. A right angled triangle with sides 3 cm and 4 cm is made to revolve about its hypotenuse. Find the volume of the double cone so formed. [take $\pi = 22/7$]

Sol. Let ABC be a right angled triangle, right angled at A, having sides $AC = 3$ cm and $AB = 4$ cm.

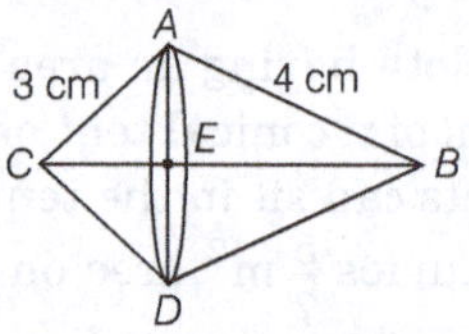

When we revolve a triangle about hypotenuse BC, then double cone is formed with common base AD.

In right angled ΔBAC,

$BC^2 = AC^2 + AB^2$ [using Pythagoras theorem]

$= 3^2 + 4^2 = 9 + 16 = 25$ cm

$\Rightarrow BC = 5$ cm [taking positive square root]

In ΔACE and ΔBCA,

$\angle CEA = \angle CAB = 90°$

and $\angle ACE = \angle BCA$ [common angles]

$\therefore \Delta ACE \sim \Delta BCA$ [by AA similarity axiom]

$$\Rightarrow \frac{CE}{AC} = \frac{AE}{AB} = \frac{AC}{BC} \Rightarrow \frac{CE}{3} = \frac{AE}{4} = \frac{3}{5}$$

$$\Rightarrow CE = \frac{9}{5} \text{ cm and } AE = \frac{12}{5} \text{ cm}$$

Now, $BE = BC - CE = 5 - \frac{9}{5} = \frac{25-9}{5} = \frac{16}{5}$ cm

Now, volume of double cone

= Volume of cone ACD + Volume of cone ABD

$$= \frac{1}{3}\pi r^2 h_1 + \frac{1}{3}\pi r^2 h_2 = \frac{1}{3}\pi r^2 (h_1 + h_2)$$

$$= \frac{1}{3} \times \frac{22}{7} \times \left(\frac{12}{5}\right)^2 \left(\frac{9}{5} + \frac{16}{5}\right)$$

$$\left[\because r = AE = \frac{12}{5}, h_1 = CE = \frac{9}{5} \text{ and } h_2 = BE = \frac{16}{5}\right]$$

$$= \frac{1}{3} \times \frac{22}{7} \times \frac{144}{25}\left(\frac{25}{5}\right)$$

$$= \frac{22 \times 48}{35} = 30.17 \text{ cm}^3$$

Exercise 17.2

1. If radius and height of a right circular cone be 3 cm and 21 cm, respectively, then find its
   (i) slant height (ii) curved surface area
   (iii) total surface area
   (iv) volume
2. Find the curved surface area of a right circular cone whose slant height is 10 cm and base radius is 7 cm.
3. Diameter of the base of a cone is 10.5 cm and its slant height is 10 cm. Find
   (i) the curved surface area of a cone.
   (ii) the surface area of a cone.
4. The radius of the base of a cone is 7cm and its vertical height is 15 cm. Find
   (i) the curved surface area of a cone.
   (ii) the volume of a cone.
5. The height of a cone is 15 cm. If its volume is 1570 cm^3, then find the radius of the base.
6. How many square metres of canvas is required for a conical tent whose height is 3.5 m and the radius of the base is 12 m?
7. The diameter of the base of a right circular cone is 10 cm and its slant height is 13 cm. Calculate
   (i) height of the cone.
   (ii) curved surface area of the cone.
   (iii) total surface area of the cone.
   (iv) the volume of the cone. [take $\pi = 3.14$]
8. Find the ratio of the curved surface areas of two cones, if the diameters of their bases are equal and slant heights are in the ratio 3 : 4.
9. The radius and the height of a cone are in the ratio 1 : 3 and its volume is 1078 cm^3. Find its diameter and the lateral surface area.
10. Two right circular cones X and Y are made, X having three times the radius of Y and Y having half the volume of X. Find the ratio of heights of X and Y.
11. A semi-circular thin sheet of metal of radius 7 cm is bent and an open conical cup is made. Find the capacity of the cup.
12. Find the length of canvas 2 m in width is required to make a conical tent 20 m in diameter and 42 m in slant height allowing 10% for folds and the stitching. Also, find the cost of the canvas at the rate of ₹ 80 per metre.
13. A bus stop is barricaded from the remaining part of the road, by using 50 hollow cones made of recycled cardboard. Each cone has a base diameter of 40 cm and height 1 m. If the outside of each of the cones is to be painted and the cost of painting is ₹ 12 per m^2, what will be the cost of painting all these cones? [use $\pi = 3.14$ and $\sqrt{1.04} = 1.02$]
14. A conical military tent is 5 m high and the diameter of the base is 24 m. Find the cost of canvas used in making this tent at the rate of ₹ 14 per m^2. [take $\pi = 22/7$]

15. A sector of a circle of radius 8 cm has an angle of 90°. It is rolled up, so that the two bounding radii are joined together to form a cone. Find
(i) the radius of the cone.
(ii) the total surface area of the cone.
(iii) the volume of the cone.

16. A tent in the form of a right circular cone is 3 m high and its base has a diameter of 14 m. If 100 men sleep in it, then find the average number of cubic metres of air space per man.

17. A ΔPQR, where $PQ = 9$ cm, $QR = 12$ cm and $PR = 15$ cm, is rotated about the side QR to trace out a cone. Find the total surface area of the cone.

18. A conical tent is to accommodate 77 persons. Each person must have $16\,m^3$ of air to breathe. Given, the radius of the tent as 7 m. Find the height of the tent and also its curved surface area. [ICSE 2017]

Surface Area and Volume of a Sphere

Sphere

A sphere is three–dimensional figure (solid figure), which is made up of all points in the space, which lie at a constant distance from a fixed point, called the **centre** of the sphere and the constant distance is called its **radius**.

In our daily life, we see many objects having spherical shape; cricket ball, round metallic ball, football etc.

Or

A sphere is a solid generated by the revolution of a circular lamina about any of its diameter is called a solid sphere.

(i) The centre of the circle revolved, is called the **centre** of the sphere.

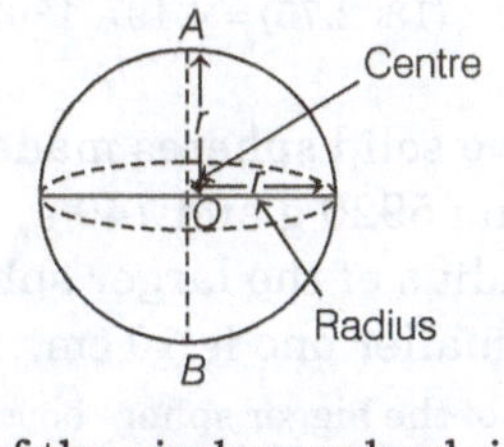

(ii) The radius of the circle revolved, is called the **radius** of the sphere.

(iii) A line segment through the centre of a sphere and intersecting the end–points on the sphere, is called the **diameter** of the sphere.

Surface Area and Volume of a Sphere

(i) Surface area of a sphere $= 4\pi r^2$ sq units

(ii) Volume of a sphere $= \frac{4}{3}\pi r^3$ cu units

where, r is the radius of the sphere.

Note In sphere, surface area and curved surface area both are same.

Example 27. Find the surface area and volume of a sphere having diameter 12 cm. [take $\pi = 22/7$]

Sol. Given, diameter of a sphere, $d = 12$ cm

Then, radius of a sphere, $r = \frac{d}{2} = \frac{12}{2} = 6$ cm

Now, surface area of a sphere $= 4\pi r^2 = 4 \times \frac{22}{7} \times (6)^2$

$= \frac{88}{7} \times 36$

$= \frac{3168}{7} = 452.57\text{ cm}^2$

and volume of a sphere $= \frac{4}{3}\pi r^3 = \frac{4}{3} \times \frac{22}{7} \times (6)^3$

$= \frac{88}{21} \times 216 = \frac{19008}{21}$

$= 905.14\text{ cm}^3$

Example 28. The volumes of two spheres are in the ratio 64 : 27. If the sum of their radii is 21 cm, then find their radii.

Sol. Let the radius of one sphere be r_1 and the radius of second sphere be r_2.

Given, ratio of volumes of two spheres $= \frac{64}{27}$

$\therefore \quad \frac{V_1}{V_2} = \frac{64}{27} \Rightarrow \frac{\frac{4}{3}\pi r_1^3}{\frac{4}{3}\pi r_2^3} = \frac{64}{27}$

$\left[\because \text{volume of a sphere} = \frac{4}{3}\pi r^3\right]$

$\Rightarrow \quad \left(\frac{r_1}{r_2}\right)^3 = \frac{64}{27} = \left(\frac{4}{3}\right)^3$

$\Rightarrow \quad \frac{r_1}{r_2} = \frac{4}{3}$ [taking cube root]

Again, let radius of one sphere, $r_1 = 4x$

and radius of second sphere, $r_2 = 3x$

Given, sum of radii = 21

$\therefore \quad 4x + 3x = 21$

$\Rightarrow \quad 7x = 21$

$\Rightarrow \quad x = 3$

Hence, the radius of first sphere $= 4x = 4 \times 3 = 12$ cm

and the radius of second sphere $= 3x = 3 \times 3 = 9$ cm

Example 29. The radius of a sphere is increased by 10%. Prove that the volume will be increased by 33.1%.

Sol. Let r (units) be the radius of the given sphere, then

Volume of sphere $= \frac{4}{3}\pi r^3$

New radius of sphere $= r + 10\%$ of $r = r + \frac{10}{100}r = \frac{11}{10}r$

Volume of new sphere $= \frac{4}{3}\pi\left(\frac{11}{10}r\right)^3 = \frac{4}{3}\pi \times \frac{1331}{1000}r^3$

$\therefore$ Increase in volume $= \frac{4}{3}\pi \times \frac{1331}{1000}r^3 - \frac{4}{3}\pi r^3$

$= \frac{4}{3}\pi r^3 (1.331 - 1)$

$= \frac{4}{3}\pi r^3 \times 0.331$

$\therefore$ Percentage increase in volume

$$= \left(\frac{\frac{4}{3}\pi r^3 \times 0.331}{\frac{4}{3}\pi r^3} \times 100\right)\% = 33.1\%$$

Example 30. Metal spheres, each of radius 2 cm, are packed into a rectangular box of internal dimensions 25 cm × 8 cm × 8 cm. When 16 sphere are packed the box is filled with preservative liquid. Find the volume of this liquid give your answer to the nearest integer. [use $\pi = 3.14$]

Sol. Capacity of box = internal volume of box

$= (25 \times 8 \times 8)\ cm^3 = 1600\ cm^3$

Radius of each sphere = 2 cm

Volume of 16 spheres $= \left(16 \times \frac{4}{3} \times 3.14 \times 2^3\right) cm^3$

$= 535.89\ cm^3$

$\therefore$ Volume of preservative liquid = Capacity of box − Volume of spheres

$= (1600 - 535.89)\ cm^3$

$= 1064.11\ cm^3$

$= 1064\ cm^3$ (to the nearest integers)

Spherical Shell (Hollow Sphere)

The solid enclosed between two concentric spheres is called a spherical shell.

Let r and R be the radii of inner and outer spheres. Then,

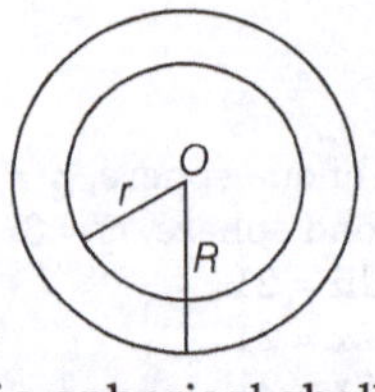

(i) Surface area of a spherical shell

$= 4\pi (R^2 + r^2)$ sq units

(ii) Volume of a spherical shell $= \frac{4}{3}\pi (R^3 - r^3)$ cu units

Example 31. The inner radius and thickness of a hollow spherical shell are 14 cm and 5 cm, respectively. Find the surface area of a spherical shell. [take $\pi = 3.14$]

Sol. Given, radius of the inner sphere, $r = 14$ cm

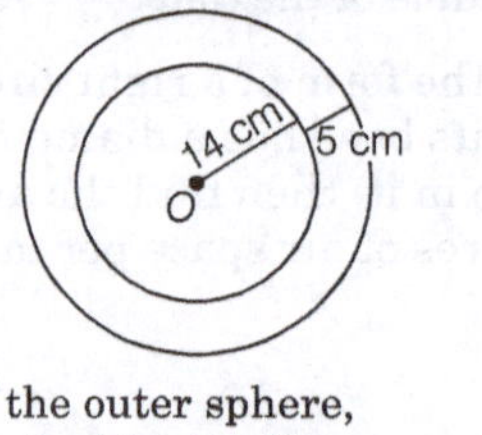

Then, radius of the outer sphere,

$R = r + 5 = 14 + 5 = 19$ cm

$\therefore$ Surface area of a spherical shell,

$S = 4\pi (R^2 + r^2) = 4 \times 3.14\ [(19)^2 + (14)^2]$

$= 12.56\ (361 + 196) = 12.56 \times 557 = 6995.92\ cm^2$

Example 32. The outer and inner diameters of a spherical shell are 27 cm and 21 cm, respectively. Find the volume of spherical shell. [take $\pi = 3.14$]

Sol. Given, outer diameter, $D = 27$ cm

and inner diameter, $d = 21$ cm

Then, outer radius, $R = \frac{D}{2} = \frac{27}{2} = 13.5$ cm

and inner radius, $r = \frac{d}{2} = \frac{21}{2} = 10.5$ cm

$\therefore$ Volume of a spherical shell $= \frac{4}{3}\pi (R^3 - r^3)$

$= \frac{4}{3}\pi\ [(13.5)^3 - (10.5)^3]$

$= \frac{4}{3} \times 3.14\ (2460.38 - 1157.63)$

$= \frac{12.56}{3} \times (1302.75) = 4.19 \times 1302.75 = 5458.52\ cm^3$

Example 33. Two solid spheres made of the same metal have weights 5920 g and 740 g, respectively. Determine the radius of the larger sphere, if the diameter of the smaller one is 10 cm.

Sol. Let the radius of the bigger sphere be r cm, then its volume $= \frac{4}{3}\pi r^3\ cm^3$

Radius of smaller sphere $= \frac{1}{2}$ of 10 cm = 5 cm

$\therefore$ Volume of smaller sphere $= \frac{4}{3}\pi (5)^3\ cm^3 = \frac{500\pi}{3}\ cm^3$

As the two spheres are made up of same metal, their volumes are proportional to their weights.

$\therefore \frac{\text{Volume of bigger sphere}}{\text{Volume of smaller sphere}} = \frac{\text{Weight of bigger sphere}}{\text{Weight of smaller sphere}}$

$\Rightarrow \frac{\frac{4}{3}\pi r^3}{\frac{500\pi}{3}} = \frac{5920}{740}$

$\Rightarrow r^3 = 1000 \Rightarrow r = 10$

Hence, the radius of the bigger sphere is 10 cm.

Hemisphere

A plane through the centre of a sphere divides the sphere into two equal parts, each part is called a hemisphere.

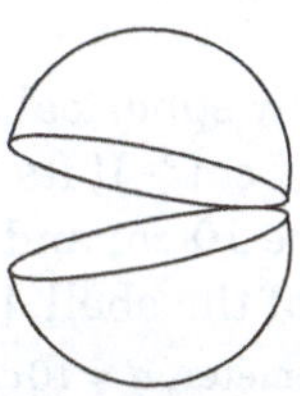

Let r be the radius of hemisphere. Then,

(i) Curved surface area of hemisphere $= 2\pi r^2$ sq units

(ii) Total surface area of hemisphere $= 3\pi r^2$ sq units

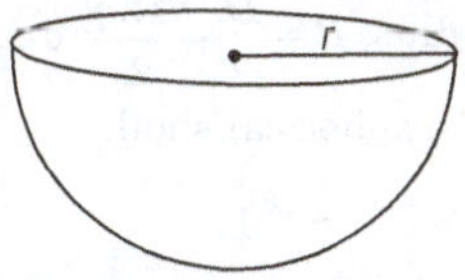

(iii) Volume of hemisphere $= \frac{2}{3}\pi r^3$ cu units

Note In hemisphere, surface area and curved surface area both area different.

Example 34. Find the curved and total surface area of a hemisphere of radius 10 cm. [take $\pi = 3.14$]

Sol. Given, radius of a hemisphere, $r = 10\,\text{cm}$

Then, curved surface area of a hemisphere

$$= 2\pi r^2 = 2 \times 3.14 \times (10)^2 = 6.28 \times 100 = 628\ \text{cm}^2$$

and total surface area of a hemisphere $= 3\pi r^2$

$$= 3 \times 3.14 \times (10)^2 = 9.42 \times 100 = 942\ \text{cm}^2$$

Example 35. Find the volume of a hemisphere, whose diameter is 14 cm. [take $\pi = 22/7$]

Sol. Given, diameter of a hemisphere, $d = 14\,\text{cm}$

Then, radius of a hemisphere, $r = \frac{d}{2} = \frac{14}{2} = 7\,\text{cm}$

Now, volume of a hemisphere $= \frac{2}{3}\pi r^3$

$$= \frac{2}{3} \times \frac{22}{7} \times (7)^3 = \frac{44}{3} \times 7^2$$

$$= \frac{2156}{3} = 718.67\ \text{cm}^3$$

Example 36. How many litres of milk can a hemispherical bowl of diameter 10.5 cm hold? [take $\pi = 22/7$]

Sol. Given, diameter of hemispherical bowl, $d = 10.5\,\text{cm}$

Then, radius, $r = \frac{d}{2} = \frac{10.5}{2} = 5.25\,\text{cm}$

Now, volume of a hemisphere $= \frac{2}{3}\pi r^3$

$$= \frac{2}{3} \times \frac{22}{7} \times 5.25 \times 5.25 \times 5.25 = \frac{6366.94}{21} = 303.1876\ \text{cm}^3$$

$\therefore$ Quantity of milk that hemispherical bowl can hold

$$= \frac{303.1876}{1000}\ \text{L} \qquad \left[\because 1\ \text{cm}^3 = \frac{1}{1000}\ \text{L}\right]$$

$$= 0.303\ \text{L (approx)}$$

Example 37. A hemispherical bowl made of brass has inner diameter 10.5 cm. Find the cost of tin plating it on the inside at the rate of ₹ 16 per 100 cm^2.

Sol. Given, inner diameter, $d = 10.5$ cm

Then, inner radius, $r = \frac{10.5}{2} = 5.25\,\text{cm}$

Curved surface area of hemispherical bowl of inner side

$$= 2\pi r^2 = 2 \times \frac{22}{7} \times (5.25)^2 = 2 \times \frac{22}{7} \times 5.25 \times 5.25$$

$$= 44 \times 0.75 \times 5.25 = 173.25\ \text{cm}^2$$

Since, the cost of tin plating on inside for 100 cm^2 is ₹ 16.

$\therefore$ Cost of tin plating on the inside for 173.25 cm^2

$$= \frac{16 \times 173.25}{100} = ₹\ 27.72$$

Example 38. A hemispherical dome of a building needs to be painted from outside. If the circumference of base of the dome is 17.6 m, find the cost of painting it at the rate of ₹ 10 per 100 cm^2.

Sol. Given, circumference of base $= 2\pi r = 17.6\,\text{m}$

$$2 \times \frac{22}{7} \times r = \frac{176}{10}$$

$$\Rightarrow \qquad r = \frac{14}{5}\ \text{m}$$

Curved surface area of dome

$$= 2\pi r^2 = \left[2 \times \frac{22}{7} \times \left(\frac{14}{5}\right)^2\right] \text{m}^2$$

$$= \frac{1232}{25}\ \text{m}^2$$

$$= \left(\frac{1232}{25} \times 100 \times 100\right) \text{cm}^2$$

$$\therefore \text{Cost of painting} = ₹\left(\frac{1232}{25} \times 100 \times 100 \times \frac{10}{100}\right)$$

$$= ₹\ 49280$$

Example 39. A dome of a building is in the form of a hemisphere. From inside, it was white washed at the cost of ₹ 498.96. If the cost of white-washing is ₹ 2 per m^2, then find

(i) inside surface area of the dome.

(ii) volume of the air inside the dome. [take $\pi = 22/7$]

Sol. Given, cost of white wash = ₹ 498.96

and cost of white-washing per square metre = ₹ 2

(i) Surface area of the dome

$$= \frac{\text{Cost of white wash}}{\text{Cost of white-washing per square metre}}$$

$$= \frac{498.96}{2} = 249.48\ \text{m}^2$$

Let r be the radius of the dome.

Then, surface area $= 249.48\ m^2$

$\Rightarrow \quad 2\pi r^2 = 249.48\ m^2$

$\Rightarrow 2 \times \frac{22}{7} \times r^2 = 249.48 \Rightarrow r^2 = \frac{249.48 \times 7}{44} \quad \Rightarrow r^2 = 39.69$

$\therefore \quad r = 6.3$ m [taking positive square root]

(ii) Volume of the air inside the dome $= \frac{2}{3}\pi r^3$

$= \frac{2}{3} \times \frac{22}{7} \times (6.3)^3 = 44 \times 2.1 \times 0.9 \times 6.3 = 523.908\ m^3$

Hemispherical Shell (Hollow Hemisphere)

The solid enclosed between two concentric hemispheres is called a hemispherical shell.

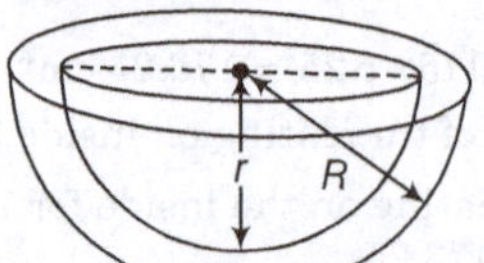

Let r and R be the radii of the inner and outer hemispheres. Then,

(i) Thickness of shell $= (R - r)$ units

(ii) Area of base $= \pi\ (R^2 - r^2)$ sq units

(iii) External curved surface area $= 2\pi R^2$ sq units

(iv) Internal curved surface area $= 2\pi r^2$ sq units

(v) Curved surface area of hemispherical shell

$= 2\pi\ (R^2 + r^2)$ sq units

(vi) Total surface area $= 2\pi R^2 + 2\pi r^2 + \pi(R^2 - r^2)$

$= 3\pi R^2 + \pi r^2 = \pi\ (3R^2 + r^2)$ sq units

(vii) Volume of a hemispherical shell

$= \frac{2}{3}\pi\ (R^3 - r^3)$ cu units

Example 40. A hollow spherical shell is made of a metal of density $5.6\ g / cm^3$. If its internal and external diameters are 10 cm and 12 cm respectively, then find the weight of the shell. [take $\pi = 3.14$]

Sol. Given, internal diameter, $d = 10$ cm

and external diameter, $D = 12$ cm

Then, internal radius, $r = \frac{d}{2} = \frac{10}{2} = 5$ cm

and external radius, $R = \frac{D}{2} = \frac{12}{2} = 6$ cm

Now, volume of a spherical shell,

$V = \frac{4}{3}\pi\ (R^3 - r^3)$

$= \frac{4}{3} \times 3.14\ (6^3 - 5^3)$

$= \frac{12.56}{3}(216 - 125) = \frac{12.56 \times 91}{3}$

$= \frac{1142.96}{3} = 380.99\ cm^3 \approx 381\ cm^3$

$\therefore$ Weight of the shell $= 5.6 \times V = 5.6 \times 381$

[$\because$ mass = density × volume]

$= 2133.6$ g $= 2.134$ kg [$\because$ 1 kg = 1000 g]

Exercise 17.3

1. If radius of a sphere is 21 cm, then find its
(i) surface area (ii) volume

2. Find the volume and surface area of a sphere of radius 4.2 cm. [take $\pi = 3.14$]

3. Find the radius of a sphere, whose surface area is $154\ cm^2$. [take $\pi = 22/7$]

4. Metal spheres, each of radius 2 cm are packed into a rectangular box of internal dimensions 16 cm × 8 cm × 8 cm. When 16 sphere are packed the box is filled with preservative liquid find the volume of this liquid give your answer to the nearest integer. (use $\pi = 3.14$)

5. The total surface area of a sphere is $616\ cm^2$. Find the radius and volume of the sphere. [take $\pi = 22/7$]

6. If volume and surface area of a sphere is numerically equal, then find its radius.

7. The diameter of the moon is approximately one-fourth of the diameter of the earth find the ratio of their surface areas.

8. Find the amount of water displaced by a solid spherical bowl of diameter 28 cm. [take $\pi = 22/7$]

9. The difference of the surface areas of two spheres is $3080\ cm^2$. If the radius of the larger sphere is 21 cm, then find the difference of their volumes.

10. The diameter of a sphere is decreased by 25%. By what percent does its curved surface area decrease?

11. Find the surface area and volume of a spherical shell, whose external and internal radii are 7 cm and 5 cm, respectively. [take $\pi = 3.14$]

12. If a sphere is inscribed in a cube, then find the ratio of the volume of the cube to the volume of the sphere.

13. A solid spherical ball of radius 6 cm is melted and recast into 64 identical spherical marbles. Find the radius of each marble.

14. If radius of a hemisphere be 42 cm, then find its
 (i) curved surface area
 (ii) total surface area
 (iii) volume

15. The radius of a hemispherical balloon increases from 6 cm to 12 cm as air is being pumped into it. Find ratio of the surface areas of the balloon in the two cases.

16. A hemispherical bowl is made of steel, 0.25 cm thick. The inner radius of the bowl is 5 cm. Find the outer curved surface area of the bowl. [take $\pi = 3.14$]

17. Find the volume, curved surface area and total surface area of a hemisphere of diameter 12.6 cm. [take $\pi = 22/7$]

18. A solid sphere and a solid hemisphere have the same total surface areas. Find the ratio of their volumes.

19. The internal and external diameters of a hollow hemispherical vessel are 14 cm and 21 cm, respectively. The cost of silver plating of 1 cm^2 of the surface is ₹ 0.40. Find the total cost of silver plating the vessel all over. [take $\pi = 3.14$]

Conversion of Solid and Combination of Two Solids

Conversion of Solid from One Shape to Another

When we come across objects which are converted from one shape to another or when a liquid which originally filled in one container of a particular shape is poured into another container of a different shape or size, the volume remains same, but the surface area may change.

e.g. Solid metallic sphere is melted and recast into more than one spherical balls or recast into a conical shape, the earth taken out by digging a well and spreading it uniformly around the well to form an embankment taking the shape of a cylindrical shell from its original shape of right circular cylinder, etc.

Example 41. Two solid spheres of radii 2 cm and 4 cm are melted and recast into a cone of height 8 cm. Find the radius of the cone so formed. **[ICSE 2015]**

Sol. Given, radii of spheres are $r_1 = 2\,\text{cm}$ and $r_2 = 4\,\text{cm}$.

$$\therefore \text{Volume of spheres} = \frac{4}{3}\pi r_1^3 + \frac{4}{3}\pi r_2^3$$

$$= \frac{4}{3}\pi(2^3 + 4^3) = \frac{4}{3}\pi(8+64)$$

$$= \frac{4}{3} \times \frac{22}{7} \times 72 = \frac{6336}{21}\text{ cm}^3$$

Since, these spheres recasted into a cone.

$\because$ Volume of spheres = Volume of cone

$$\therefore \quad \text{Volume of cone} = \frac{6336}{21}\text{ cm}^3 \qquad \text{[given]...(i)}$$

Also, height of a cone, $h = 8\,\text{cm}$

From Eq. (i), we get

$$\frac{1}{3}\pi r^2 h = \frac{6336}{21}$$

$$\Rightarrow \frac{1}{3} \times \frac{22}{7} \times r^2 \times 8 = \frac{6336}{21}$$

$$\Rightarrow r^2 = \frac{6336}{21} \times \frac{7}{22} \times \frac{3}{8} \Rightarrow r^2 = 36$$

$\therefore \quad r = 6\,\text{cm}$ [taking positive square root]

Hence, the radius of cone is 6 cm.

Example 42. How many shots each having diameter 3 cm can be made from a cuboidal lead solid of dimensions 9 cm × 11 cm × 12 cm?

Sol. Given, dimensions of cuboidal lead solid

$= 9\,\text{cm} \times 11\,\text{cm} \times 12\,\text{cm}$

$\therefore$ Volume of a cuboidal lead solid

$= 9 \times 11 \times 12 = 1188\text{ cm}^3$

[$\because$ volume of cuboid $= l \times b \times h$]

Also, diameter of a shot = 3 cm

$\therefore$ Radius of a shot, $r = \frac{3}{2} = 1.5\,\text{cm}$

Now, volume of a shot

$$= \frac{4}{3}\pi r^3 = \frac{4}{3} \times \frac{22}{7} \times (1.5)^3 = \frac{297}{21} = 14.143\text{ cm}^3$$

$\therefore$ Required number of shots

$$= \frac{\text{Volume of cuboidal lead solid}}{\text{Volume of a shot}} = \frac{1188}{14.143}$$

$= 84$ (approx)

Example 43. A metallic cone of base radius 8 cm and height 6.912 cm is melted down and shaped into a sphere without any loss of metal. Find the radius of the sphere. [take $\pi = 3.14$]

Sol. Given, radius of a cone, $r = 8\,\text{cm}$

and height of a cone, $h = 6.912\,\text{cm}$

$$\text{Now, volume of a cone} = \frac{1}{3}\pi r^2 h = \frac{1}{3} \times \pi \times (8)^2 \times 6.912$$

$$= \frac{442.368}{3}\pi\text{ cm}^3$$

Let r_1 be the radius of a sphere.
Then, according to the given condition,

Volume of cone = Volume of sphere

$$\Rightarrow \frac{442.368}{3}\pi = \frac{4}{3}\pi r_1^3$$

$$\Rightarrow \frac{442.368}{4} = r_1^3 \Rightarrow r_1^3 = 110.592$$

$$\therefore r_1 = 4.8\,\text{cm}$$

Hence, the radius of the sphere is 4.8 cm.

Example 44. How many solid spheres of diameter 6 cm are required to be melted to form a cylindrical solid of height 45 cm and diameter 4 cm?

Sol. Given, diameter of solid sphere, $d_1 = 6\,\text{cm}$

$\therefore$ Radius of sphere, $r_1 = \frac{6}{2} = 3\,\text{cm}$

Also, given diameter of cylinder, $d_2 = 4\,\text{cm}$

$\therefore$ Radius of cylinder, $r_2 = \frac{4}{2} = 2\,\text{cm}$

$\because$ Height of cylinder, $h = 45\,\text{cm}$ [given]

Let the required number of spheres be N.

$\therefore$ $N \times$ Volume of sphere = Volume of cylinder

$$\Rightarrow N \times \frac{4}{3}\pi r_1^3 = \pi r_2^2 h$$

$$\Rightarrow N \times \frac{4}{3}\pi \times (3)^3 = \pi \times (2)^2 \times 45$$

$$\therefore N = \frac{2 \times 2 \times 45}{4 \times 3 \times 3} = 5$$

Hence, the required number of solid spheres is 5.

Example 45. The surface area of a solid metallic sphere is 2464 cm^2. It is melted and recast into solid right circular cones of radius 3.5 cm and height 7 cm. Calculate **[ICSE 2014]**

(i) the radius of the sphere.
(ii) the number of cones recast. [take $\pi = 22/7$]

Sol. (i) Given, surface area of a sphere = 2464 cm^2

Let the radius of sphere be r cm.

Then, surface area of sphere = $4\pi r^2$

$$\therefore 2464 = 4\pi r^2$$

$$\Rightarrow r^2 = \frac{2464 \times 7}{4 \times 22}$$

$$\Rightarrow r^2 = 196$$

$$\Rightarrow r = \pm 14$$

$$\therefore r = 14\,\text{cm}$$

[taking positive square root, because radius cannot be negative]

Hence, the radius of sphere is 14 cm.

(ii) Also, given radius of cone, $r_1 = 3.5$ cm and height of cone, $h = 7$ cm

Volume of cone $= \frac{1}{3}\pi r_1^2 h = \frac{1}{3}\pi (3.5)^2 \times 7$

Now, volume of sphere $= \frac{4}{3}\pi r^3 = \frac{4}{3}\pi (14)^3$

$\therefore$ Number of cones recast

$$= \frac{\text{Volume of sphere}}{\text{Volume of cone}} = \frac{\frac{4}{3}\pi (14)^3}{\frac{1}{3}\pi (3.5)^2 \times 7}$$

$$= \frac{4 \times 14 \times 14 \times 14}{3.5 \times 3.5 \times 7} = \frac{3200}{25} = 128$$

Hence, the number of cones recast from solid metallic sphere is 128.

Example 46. A hemispherical bowl of diameter 7.2 cm is filled completely with chocolate sauce. This sauce is poured into an inverted cone of radius 4.8 cm. Find the height of the cone. [ICSE 2010]

Sol. Given, diameter of hemispherical bowl, $d = 7.2\,\text{cm}$

$\therefore$ Radius of hemispherical bowl,

$$r_1 = \frac{d}{2} = \frac{7.2}{2} = 3.6\,\text{cm}$$

Now, volume of hemispherical bowl $= \frac{2}{3} \times \pi r_1^3$

$$= \frac{2}{3} \times \pi \times (3.6)^3\ \text{cm}^3$$

Also, radius of cone, $r_2 = 4.8$ cm [given]

Let the height of cone be h cm.

$\therefore$ Volume of cone $= \frac{1}{3}\pi r_2^2 h = \frac{1}{3}\pi (4.8)^2 \times h\ \text{cm}^2$

Since, the chocolate sauce from hemispherical bowl is completely poured into an inverted cone.

$\therefore$ Volume of hemispherical bowl = Volume of cone

$$\Rightarrow \frac{2}{3}\pi \times (3.6)^3 = \frac{1}{3}\pi (4.8)^2 \times h$$

$$\Rightarrow 93.312 = 23.04\,h$$

$$\therefore h = \frac{93.312}{23.04} = 4.05\,\text{cm}$$

Hence, the height of the cone is 4.05 cm.

Combination of Two (or More) Solids

Sometimes, we have to find the curved surface area and volume of a solid, which is a combination of two (or more) solids. Then, for finding the surface area, we add the curved surface areas of individual solids and for finding the volume of this solid, we add the volumes of individual solids. e.g. A combined solid is formed by joining hemisphere and right circular cone.

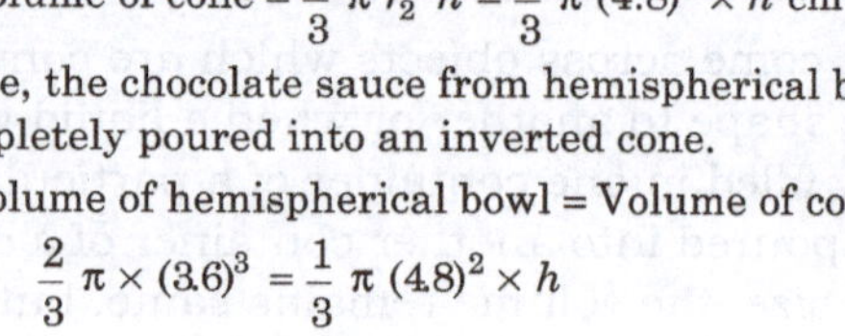

(i) Surface area of combined solid figure
= CSA of cone + CSA of hemisphere

(ii) Volume of combined solid figure
= Volume of cone + Volume of hemisphere

While calculating the surface area, we have not added the surface areas of the two individual solids, rather we have added curved surface area because some part of the surface area disappeared in the process of joining them. But this will not be in the case, when we calculate the volume.

Example 47. A circular side of hemisphere of radius 3 cm is kept on a rectangular sheet of dimensions 7 cm × 9 cm. Find the surface area of the combined figure.

Sol. Given, dimensions of rectangular sheet are $l = 7$cm, $b = 9$ cm and radius of hemisphere, $r = 3$ cm.

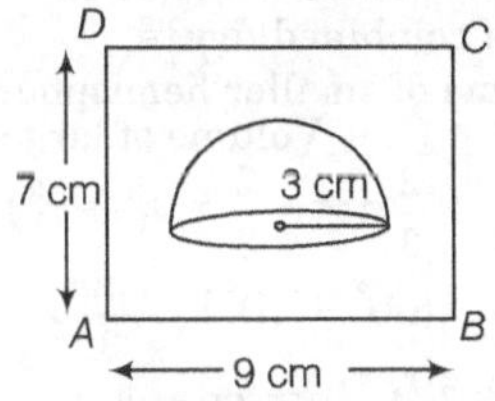

Now, area of rectangle $= l \times b = 9 \times 7 = 63 \text{ cm}^2$

and area of circular base of hemisphere $= \pi r^2$

$= 3.14 \times 3^2 = 3.14 \times 9 = 28.26 \text{ cm}^2$

$\therefore$ Surface area of the combined figure

= Area of rectangle – Area of circular base of hemisphere

$= 63 - 28.26 = 34.74 \text{ cm}^2$

Example 48. A toy is in the form of a cone mounted on a hemisphere with the same radius. The radius of the conical portion is 4 cm and its height is 3 cm. Calculate the surface area and volume of the toy. [take $\pi = 3.14$]

Sol. Given, toy is formed with combination of a cone and a hemisphere.

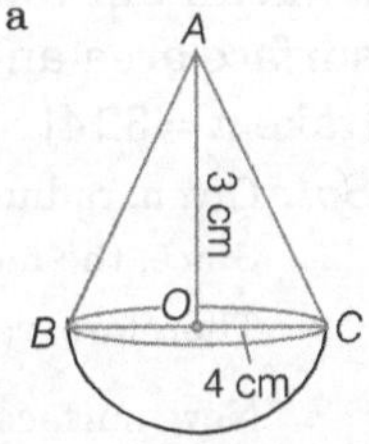

Here, radius of cone = radius of sphere

= 4 cm

and height of cone, $h = 3$ cm

Now, in right angled ΔAOC,

$AC = \sqrt{AO^2 + OC^2}$

[by Pythagoras theorem]

$= \sqrt{3^2 + 4^2} = \sqrt{9 + 16} = \sqrt{25} = 5$ cm

$\therefore$ Slant height of a cone, $l = AC = 5$ cm

Now, curved surface area of conical portion $= \pi r l$

$= 3.14 \times 4 \times 5 = 62.8 \text{ cm}^2$

and curved surface area of hemispherical portion

$= 2\pi r^2 = 2 \times 3.14 \times (4)^2$

$= 6.28 \times 16 = 100.48 \text{ cm}^2$

$\therefore$ Required surface area of toy

= Curved surface area of conical portion

+ Curved surface area of the hemispherical portion

$= 62.8 + 100.48 = 163.28 \text{ cm}^2$

Now, volume of conical portion $= \frac{1}{3}\pi r^2 h$

$= \frac{1}{3} \times 3.14 \times (4)^2 \times 3 = \frac{3.14 \times 16 \times 3}{3}$

$= 50.24 \text{ cm}^3$

and volume of hemispherical portion $= \frac{2}{3}\pi r^3$

$= \frac{2}{3} \times 3.14 \times (4)^3 = \frac{6.28 \times 64}{3} = \frac{401.92}{3} = 133.97 \text{ cm}^3$

$\therefore$ Required volume of toy = Volume of conical portion + Volume of hemispherical portion

$= 50.24 + 133.97$

$= 184.21 \text{ cm}^3$

Example 49. A sphere of radius 7 cm is mounted on the solid cone of radius 6 cm and height 8 cm. Find the volume of the combined solid. [take $\pi = 3.14$]

Sol. Given, radius of sphere, $r_1 = 7$ cm

Radius of cone, $r_2 = 6$ cm and height of cone, $h = 8$ cm

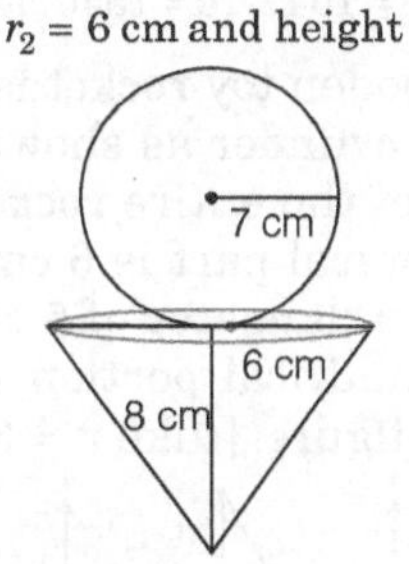

Now, volume of sphere

$= \frac{4}{3}\pi r_1^3 = \frac{4}{3} \times 3.14 \times (7)^3$

$= \frac{12.56}{3} \times 343$

$= \frac{4308.08}{3} = 1436.03 \text{ cm}^3$

and volume of cone $= \frac{1}{3}\pi r_2^2 h = \frac{1}{3} \times 3.14 \times (6)^2 \times 8$

$= \frac{3.14 \times 36 \times 8}{3}$

$= \frac{904.32}{3} = 301.44 \text{ cm}^3$

$\therefore$ Volume of combined two solids

= Volume of sphere + Volume of cone

$= 1436.03 + 301.44 = 1737.47 \text{ cm}^3$

Example 50. The following figure represents a solid consisting of a right circular cylinder with a hemisphere at one end and a cone at the other. Their common radius is 7 cm. The height of the cylinder and cone are each of 4 cm. Find the volume of the solid. **[ICSE 2018]**

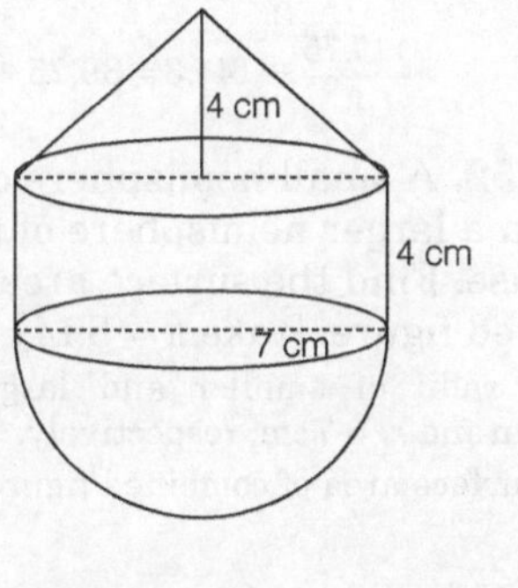

Sol. Given, common radius, $r = 7$ cm
and height of cone = height of cylinder, $h = 4$ cm
$\therefore$ Volume of solid = Volume of cone + Volume of cylinder + Volume of hemisphere

$$= \frac{1}{3}\pi r^2 h + \pi r^2 h + \frac{2}{3}\pi r^3$$
$$= \frac{1}{3}\pi r^2 (h + 3h + 2r)$$
$$= \frac{1}{3}\pi r^2 (4h + 2r)$$
$$= \frac{1}{3} \times \frac{22}{7} \times 7 \times 7 \times (16 + 14)$$
$$= \frac{1}{3} \times 22 \times 7 \times 30 = 22 \times 7 \times 10$$
$$= 154 \times 10 = 1540 \text{ cm}^3$$

Example 51. A wooden toy rocket is in the shape of a cone mounted on a cylinder as shown in the following figure. The height of the entire rocket is 26 cm, while the height of the conical part is 6 cm. The base of the conical portion has a diameter of 5 cm, while the base diameter of the cylindrical portion is 3 cm. Find the volume of the solid figure. [take $\pi = 3.14$]

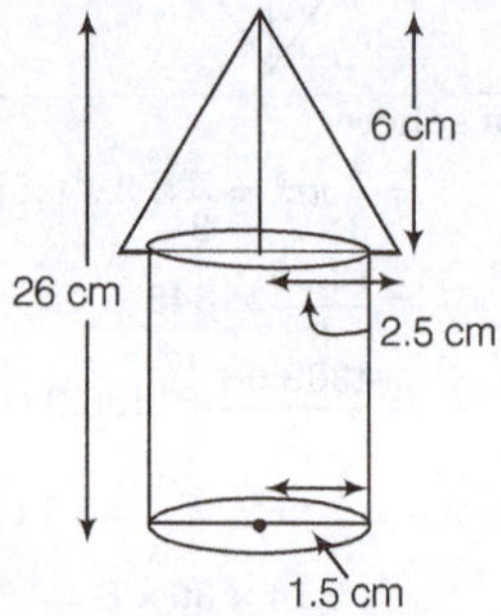

Sol. Given, diameter and height of the conical portion are $d_1 = 5$ cm and $h_1 = 6$ cm.
$\therefore$ Radius, $r_1 = \frac{5}{2} = 2.5$ cm
Also, given diameter and height of a cylindrical portion are $d_2 = 3$ cm, $h_2 = 26 - 6 = 20$ cm.
$\therefore$ Radius, $r_2 = \frac{3}{2} = 1.5$ cm
Now, volume of the solid figure
= Volume of a cone + Volume of a cylinder

$$= \frac{1}{3}\pi r_1^2 h_1 + \pi r_2^2 h_2$$
$$= \frac{3.14 \times (2.5)^2 \times 6}{3} + 3.14 \times (1.5)^2 \times 20$$
$$= \frac{117.75}{3} + 141.3 = 39.25 + 141.3 = 180.55 \text{ cm}^3$$

Example 52. A small hemisphere of radius 4 cm is mounted on a larger hemisphere of radius 7 cm with common base. Find the surface area and volume of the combined figure. [take $\pi = 3.14$]

Sol. Given, radii of smaller and larger hemispheres are $r_1 = 4$ cm and $r_2 = 7$ cm, respectively.
Now, surface area of combined figure
= Curved surface area of a smaller hemisphere
+ Curved surface area of larger hemisphere
+ (Area of circular base of larger hemisphere
− Area of circular base of smaller hemisphere)

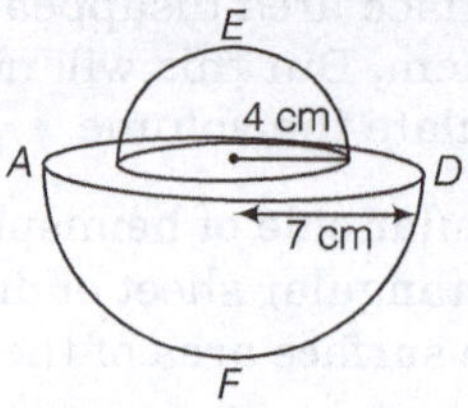

$$= 2\pi r_1^2 + 2\pi r_2^2 + [\pi r_2^2 - \pi r_1^2] = 3\pi r_2^2 + \pi r_1^2$$
$$= 3 \times 3.14 \times (7)^2 + 3.14 \times (4)^2$$
$$= 461.58 + 50.24 = 511.82 \text{ cm}^2$$

Now, volume of combined figure
= Volume of smaller hemisphere
+ Volume of larger hemisphere

$$= \frac{2}{3}\pi r_1^3 + \frac{2}{3}\pi r_2^3 = \frac{2}{3}\pi (r_1^3 + r_2^3)$$
$$= \frac{2}{3} \times 3.14 [(4)^3 + (7)^3] = \frac{6.28}{3} \times (64 + 343)$$
$$= \frac{6.28 \times 407}{3} = 851.99 \text{ cm}^3$$

Problems Related to Inner and Outer Solid Figures

In such types of problems, a cone or sphere or hemisphere etc., is given either inside or outside the another figure and we have to find inner and outer surface area or volume by using the given information according to the questions.

Example 53. In a solid hemisphere of radius 10 cm, a maximum volume of sphere is cut out. Find the surface area and volume of the remaining solid. [take $\pi = 3.14$]

Sol. Given, radius of hemisphere, $r_1 = 10$ cm
Since, the maximum sphere is cut out of diameter 10 cm.
Therefore, radius of the sphere, $r_2 = \frac{10}{2} = 5$ cm
Now, surface area of the hemisphere $= 3\pi r_1^2$
$= 3 \times 3.14 \times (10)^2 = 942 \text{ cm}^2$
and surface area of the sphere $= 4\pi r_2^2 = 4 \times 3.14 \times (5)^2$
$= 314 \text{ cm}^2$
$\therefore$ Surface area of the remaining solid
= Surface area of the hemisphere
+ Surface area of the sphere
$= 942 + 314 = 1256 \text{ cm}^2$

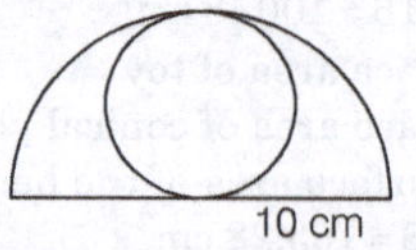

Now, volume of the hemisphere

$$= \frac{2}{3}\pi r_1^3 = \frac{2}{3} \times 3.14 \times (10)^3 = \frac{6280}{3} = 2093.33 \text{ cm}^3$$

and volume of the sphere

$= \frac{4}{3}\pi r_2^3 = \frac{4}{3} \times 3.14 \times (5)^3 = \frac{1570}{3} = 523.33 \text{ cm}^3$

∴ Volume of the remaining solid

= Volume of hemisphere − Volume of sphere

$= 2093.33 - 523.33 = 1570 \text{ cm}^3$

Example 54. **From a solid wooden cylinder of height 28 cm and diameter 6 cm, two conical cavities are hollowed out. The diameter of the cones are also of 6 cm and height 10.5 cm. Find the volume of the remaining solid.** $\left[\text{take } \pi = \frac{22}{7}\right]$ **[ICSE 2020]**

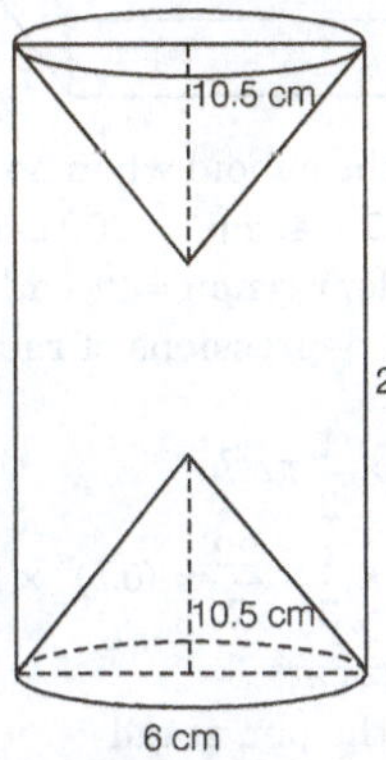

Sol. Given, height of solid wooden cylinder (H) is 28 cm and its diameter is 6 cm.

∴ Radius = 3 cm

Also, diameter of the cones are 6 cm

∴ Radius = 3 cm and height of cone (h) = 10.5 cm

Volume of the remaining solid

= Volume of solid wooden cylinder − 2 × Volume of each cone

$= \pi r^2 H - 2 \times \frac{1}{3}\pi r^2 h$

$= \pi r^2 \times 28 - 2 \times \frac{1}{3}\pi r^2 \times (10.5)$

$= \pi r^2\left[28 - \frac{2}{3} \times 10.5\right] = \frac{22}{7} \times 9\,[28 - 7]$

$= \frac{22 \times 9 \times 21}{7} = 594 \text{ cm}^3$

Example 55. **A solid cone of radius 5 cm and height 9 cm is melted and made into small cylinders of radius of 0.5 cm and height 1.5 cm. Find the number of cylinder so formed.**

Sol. Given, radius of a cone (R) = 5 cm

Height (H) = 9 cm and radius of the cylinder (r) = 0.5 cm

Height (h) = 1.5 cm

$\therefore \text{Number of cylinder} = \frac{\text{Volume of a cone}}{\text{Volume of a cylinder}}$

$= \frac{\frac{1}{3}\pi R^2 H}{\pi r^2 h} = \frac{R^2 H}{3r^2 h}$

$= \frac{(5)^2 \times 9}{3 \times (0.5)^2 \times 1.5} = 200$

Hence, the required number of cylinders formed are 200.

Example 56. **A conical vessel of radius 6 cm and height 8 cm is completely filled with water. A sphere is lowered into the water such that when it touches the sides, it is just immersed. What fraction of the water overflow?**

Sol. Given, radius of conical vessel, $r_1 = 6$ cm

and height, $h = 8$ cm

In a conical vessel, a sphere is immersed as shown in the figure.

In right angled ΔADB,

$AB^2 = AD^2 + DB^2$ [using Pythagoras theorem]

$= 8^2 + 6^2$ [∵ $AD = 8$ cm and $DB = 6$ cm, given]

$= 64 + 36 = 100$

$\Rightarrow AB = 10$ cm [taking positive square root] ... (i)

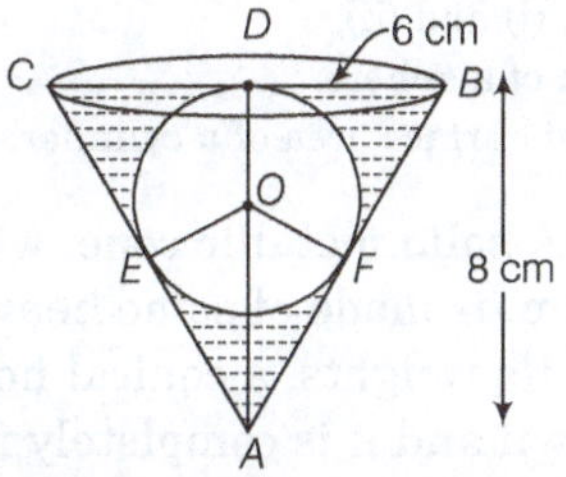

In the figure, BC is a tangent to the circle at point D and AB is a tangent to the circle at point F

∴ $BD = BF = 6$ cm

[∵ tangents drawn from an external point to the circle are equal in lengths]

Now, $AF = AB - BF = 10 - 6 = 4$ cm [from Eq. (i)]

Let r cm be the radius of the sphere. Then,

$OE = OF = r$ cm

Now, $AO = AD - OD = (8 - r)$ cm

In right angled ΔAFO,

$AO^2 = AF^2 + OF^2$ [using Pythagoras theorem]

$\Rightarrow (8 - r)^2 = 4^2 + r^2$

$\Rightarrow 64 + r^2 - 16r = 16 + r^2$

$\Rightarrow 48 = 16r \Rightarrow r = 3$ cm

Now, volume of sphere $= \frac{4}{3}\pi r^3 = \frac{4}{3}\pi \times (3)^3 = 36\pi \text{ cm}^3$

∴ The volume of water which overflows by immersing the sphere = Volume of sphere = $36\pi \text{ cm}^3$

Now, total volume of water in the cone before immersing the sphere = Volume of the cone $= \frac{1}{3}\pi r_1^2 h$

$= \frac{1}{3}\pi \times (6)^2 \times 8 = \pi \times 12 \times 8 = 96\pi \text{ cm}^3$

∴ Fraction of water which overflows by immersing the sphere $= \frac{\text{Volume of water overflows}}{\text{Total volume of water}} = \frac{36\pi}{96\pi} = \frac{3}{8}$

Example 57. In the given figure, a sphere is inscribed in a cylinder. Prove that the surface area of the sphere is equal to the curved surface area of the cylinder.

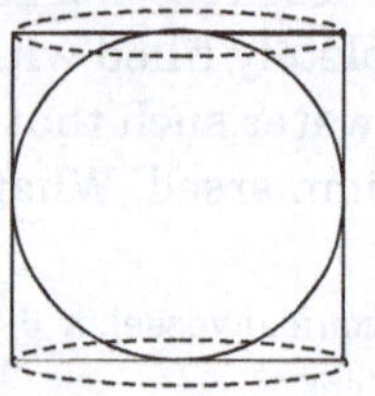

Sol. Let r be the radius of a sphere. Then, diameter of the sphere is $2r$. It is clear from the figure that radius and diameter of a sphere are equal to the radius and height of a cylinder, respectively.

Therefore, height of cylinder, $h = 2r$

Now, surface area of sphere $= 4\pi r^2$ ...(i)

and curved surface area of cylinder $= 2\pi rh$

$= 2\pi r \times 2r = 4\pi r^2$ ...(ii)

$\therefore$ From Eqs. (i) and (ii),

Surface area of a sphere

= Curved surface area of a cylinder **Hence proved.**

Example 58. A solid metallic cone, with radius 7 cm and height 12 cm, is made of some heavy metal *A*. In order to reduce its weights, a conical hole is made in the cone as shown and it is completely filled with a lighter metal *B*. The conical hole has a radius 4 cm and depth 3 cm. Calculate the ratio of the volume of metal *A* to the volume of the metal *B* in the solid. [take $\pi = 3.14$]

Sol. Given, radius and height of the cone of heavy metal *A* are $r_1 = 7\text{ cm}$ and $h_1 = 12\text{ cm}$, respectively.

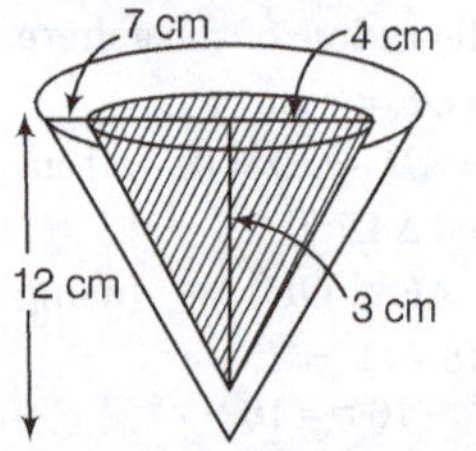

Also, radius and height (depth) of the cone of lighter metal *B* are $r_2 = 4\text{ cm}$ and $h_2 = 3\text{ cm}$.

Now, volume of a cone having metal *A*,

$$V_1 = \frac{1}{3}\pi r_1^2 h_1 = \frac{1}{3} \times 3.14 \times (7)^2 \times 12$$

$$= \frac{3.14 \times 49 \times 12}{3} = \frac{1846.32}{3} = 615.44\text{ cm}^3$$

And volume of a cone having metal *B*,

$$V_2 = \frac{1}{3}\pi r_2^2 h_2 = \frac{1}{3} \times 3.14 \times (4)^2 \times 3$$

$$= 3.14 \times 16 = 50.24\text{ cm}^3$$

$\therefore$ Ratio of the volume of metal *A* to the volume of the metal $B = \dfrac{V_1}{V_2} = \dfrac{615.44}{50.24} = \dfrac{61544}{5024} = \dfrac{7693}{628} = 7693 : 628$

Example 59. A pen stand made of wood is in the shape of a cuboid with four conical depressions and a cubical depression to hold the pens and pins, respectively. The dimensions of the cuboid are 10 cm, 5 cm and 4 cm. The radius of each of the conical depression is 0.5 cm and the depth is 2.1 cm. The edge of the cubical depression is 3 cm. Find the volume of the wood in the entire stand.

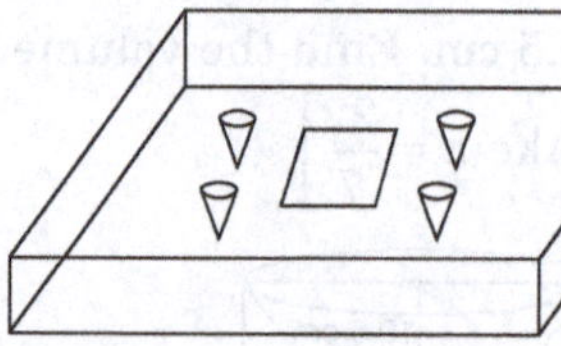

Sol. Volume of wood in the cuboid when no depressions.

Were made $= (10 \times 5 \times 4)\text{ cm}^3 = 200\text{ cm}^3$

Volume of cubical depression $= 3^3\text{ cm}^3 = 27\text{ cm}^3$

Volume of 4 conical depressions of radius 0.5 cm and depth 2.1 cm.

$$= 4 \times \frac{1}{3}\pi r^2 h$$

$$= 4 \times \frac{1}{3} \times \frac{22}{7} \times (0.5)^2 \times 2.1\text{ cm}^3$$

$$= 2.2\text{ cm}^3$$

Volume of wood in the pen stand

= Volume of cuboid

– Volume of cubical depression

– Volume of 4 conical depressions

$= (200 - 27 - 2.2)\text{ cm}^3 = 170.8\text{ cm}^3$

Example 60. A hemispherical depression is cut out from one face of a cubical wooden block, such that the diameter l of the hemisphere is equal to the edge of the cube. Determine the surface area of the remaining solid.

Sol. Given, side of the cube = diameter of the hemisphere = l

$\therefore$ Radius of the hemisphere $= \dfrac{l}{2}$

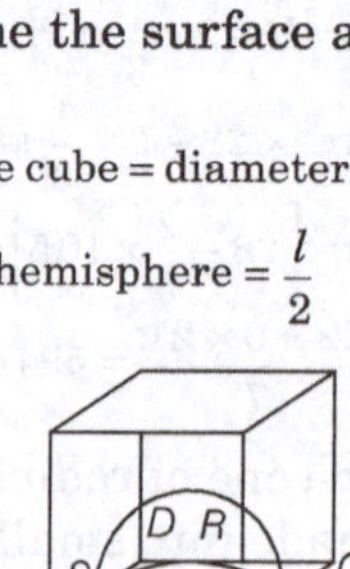

Now, required surface area of the remaining solid

= Area of one face *ABCD* of cube – Area of circle *PQRS*

+ Area of remaining five faces of cube

+ curved surface area of hemisphere

$$= l^2 - \pi\frac{l^2}{4} + 5l^2 + 2\pi\frac{l^2}{4} \quad \left[\because \text{radius of hemisphere} = \frac{l}{2}\right]$$

$$= 6l^2 + \frac{\pi l^2}{4} = \frac{l^2}{4}(\pi + 24)\text{ sq units}$$

Example 61. A hemispherical and a conical hole is scooped out of a solid wooden cylinder. Find the volume of the remaining solid where the measurements are as follows :

The height of the solid cylinder is 7 cm, radius of each of hemisphere, cone and cylinder is 3 cm. Height of cone is 3 cm. Give your answer correct to the nearest whole number. $\left[\text{take } \pi = \frac{22}{7}\right]$ **[ICSE 2019]**

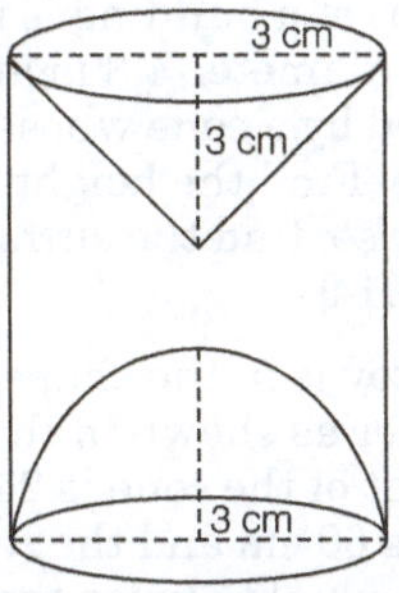

Sol. Given, for cylinder, $h_1 = 7\,\text{cm}$ and $r_1 = 3\,\text{cm}$

For hemisphere, $r_2 = 3\,\text{cm}$

For cone,

$r_3 = 3\,\text{cm}$ and $h_2 = 3\,\text{cm}$

Now, volume of cone,

$$V_1 = \frac{1}{3}\pi r_3^2 h_2 = \frac{1}{3} \times \frac{22}{7} \times (3)^2 \times 3 = \frac{22 \times 9}{7} = \frac{198}{7}\,\text{cm}^3$$

Volume of hemisphere, $V_2 = \frac{2}{3}\pi r_2^3$

$$= \frac{2}{3} \times \frac{22}{7} \times (3)^3 = \frac{44 \times 9}{7} = \frac{396}{7}\,\text{cm}^3$$

and volume of cylinder, $V_3 = \pi r_1^2 h_1$

$$= \frac{22}{7} \times (3)^2 \times 7 = \frac{1386}{7}\,\text{cm}^3$$

$\therefore$ Volume of remaining solid figure

= Volume of cylinder − Volume of hemisphere − Volume of cone

$$= V_3 - V_2 - V_1 = \frac{1386}{7} - \frac{396}{7} - \frac{198}{7} = \frac{792}{7} = 113\,\text{cm}^3$$

Exercise 17.4

1. A hollow sphere of internal and external radii 6 cm and 8 cm respectively, is melted and recast into small cones of base radius 2 cm and height 8 cm. Find the number of cones. **[ICSE 2012]**
2. A hollow sphere of internal and external diameters 4 cm and 8 cm respectively, is melted into a cone of base diameter 8 cm. Find the height of the cone.
3. A solid rectangular block of metal 49 cm × 44 cm × 18 cm is melted and formed into a solid sphere. Calculate the radius of the sphere.
4. A solid cone of radius 5 cm and height 8 cm is melted and recast into small spheres of radius 0.5 cm. Find the number of spheres formed. **[ICSE 2011]**
5. The surface area of a solid metallic sphere is 616 cm^2. It is melted and recast into smaller spheres of diameter 3.5 cm. How many such spheres can be obtained? [take $\pi = 22/7$]
6. A metallic disc in the shape of a right circular cylinder is of height 2.5 mm and base radius 12 cm. Metallic disc is melted and made into a sphere. Calculate the radius of the sphere.
7. A solid sphere of radius 15 cm is melted and recast into solid right circular cones of radius 2.5 cm and height 8 cm. Calculate the number of cones recast.
8. A certain number of metallic cones, each of radius 2 cm and height 3 cm are melted and recast into a solid sphere of radius 6 cm. Find the number of cones. **[ICSE 2016]**
9. The given block is made of two solids; a cone and a hemisphere. If the height and the base radius of the cone are 9 cm and 7 cm, respectively and the radius of the sphere is 5 cm, then find the volume of the block. [take $\pi = 3.14$]

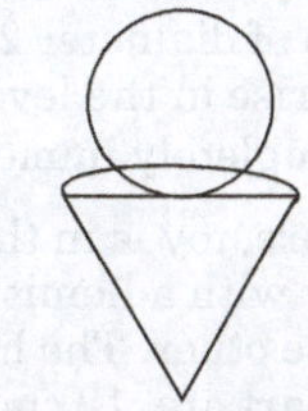

10. A small solid cone of radius 4 cm and having slant height 6 cm is mounted on a bigger solid cone of radius 6 cm and having slant height 10 cm with common base. Find the surface area of combined figure. [take $\pi = 3.14$]

11. In a solid hemisphere of radius 10 cm, a right cone of same radius is removed out. Find the volume and surface area of the remaining solid. [take $\pi = 3.14$ and $\sqrt{2} = 1.41$]

12. A pen stand made of wood is in the shape of a cuboid with four conical depressions to hold pens. The dimensions of the cuboid are 15 cm by 10 cm by 3.5 cm. The radius of each of the depression is 0.5 cm and the depth is 1.4 cm. Find the volume of the wood in the entire stand, correct to 2 decimal places.

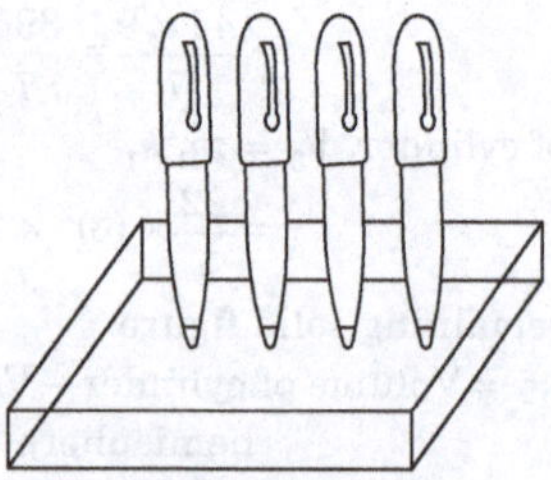

13. In the figure, it shows a metal container in the form of a cylinder surmounted by a hemisphere of the same radius. The internal height of the cylinder is 7 m and the internal radius is 3.5 m.

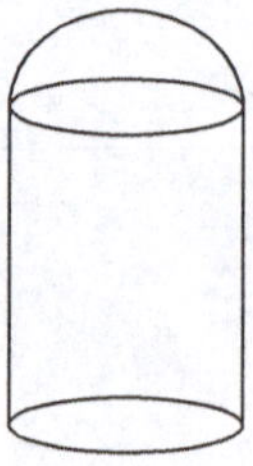

Calculate

(i) the total area of the internal surface, excluding the base (in m^2).

(ii) the internal volume of the container (in m^3).

14. A gulabjamun, contains sugar syrup approximately 30% of its volume. Find how much syrup would be found in 45 gulabjamuns, each shaped like a cylinder with two hemispherical ends with length 5 cm and diameter 2.8 cm. Give your answer correct to the nearest cubic centimetre.

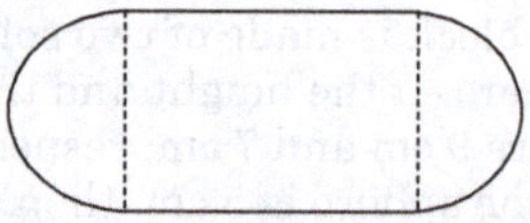

15. An iron sphere of diameter 12 cm is dropped into a cylindrical can of diameter 24 cm containing water. Find the rise in the level of water when the sphere is completely immersed.

16. In the given figure, toy is in the shape of a right circular cylinder with a hemisphere on one end and a cone on the other. The height and radius of the cylindrical part are 13 cm and 5 cm, respectively. The radii of the hemispherical and conical parts are the same as that of the cylindrical part. Calculate the surface area of the toy if height of the conical part is 12 cm.

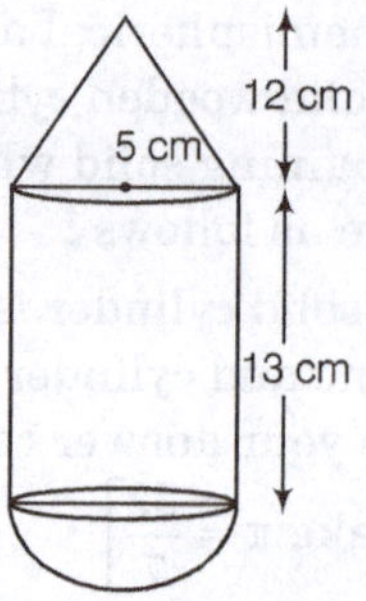

17. The interior of a building is in the form of a cylinder of diameter 4.3 m and 3.8 m height, surmounted by a cone whose vertical angle is a right angle. Find the height and slant height of the cone. Also, find the surface area of building. [take $\pi = 3.14$]

18. A wooden toy is in the shape of a cone mounted on a cylinder as shown in the following figure. If the height of the cone is 24 cm, the total height of the toy is 60 cm and the radius of the base of the cone is equal to twice the radius of the base of the cylinder is 10 cm, then find the total surface area of the toy. [take $\pi = 3.14$]

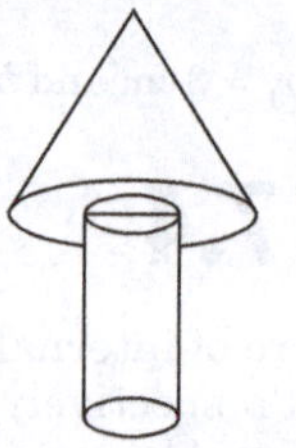

19. From a cuboidal solid metallic block of dimensions 15 cm × 10 cm × 5 cm, a cylindrical hole of diameter 7 cm is drilled out. Find the surface area of the remaining block.

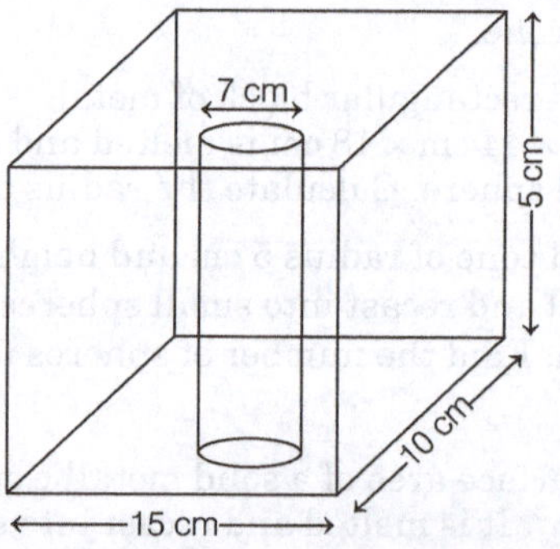

20. A cone of maximum size is carved out from a cube of edge 14 cm. Find the surface area of the cone and of the remaining solid left out after the cone carved out.

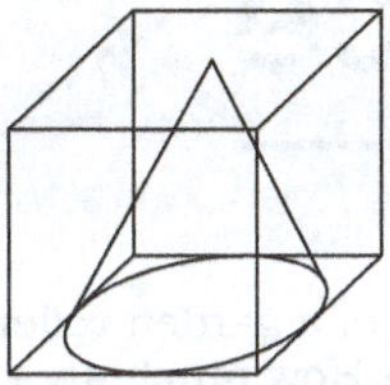

21. A container shaped like a right circular cylinder having diameter 12 cm and height 15 cm is full of ice-cream. The ice-cream is to be filled into cones of height 12 cm and diameter 6 cm, having a hemispherical shape on the top. Find the number of such cones which can be filled with ice-cream. [take $\pi = 22/7$]

22. In the given figure, from a solid sphere of radius 9 cm, a cone mounted on a hemisphere shape is carved out. The radius and height of a cone are 4 cm and 5 cm, respectively. Find the surface area of the remaining figure.

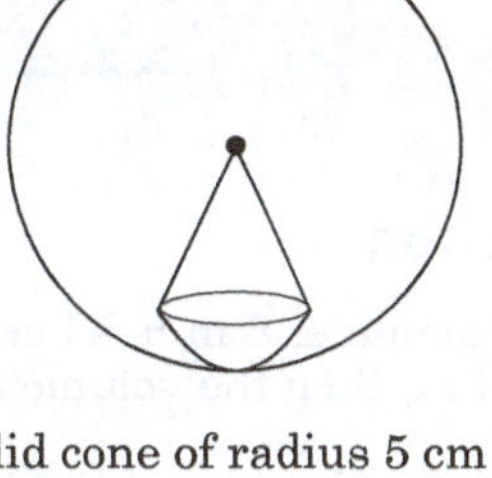

23. A small solid cone of radius 5 cm and slant height 7 cm is mounted on a bigger solid cone of radius 8 cm and slant height 12 cm with common base. Find the surface area and volume of the combined figure. [take $\pi = 3.14$]

24. A vessel in the form of an inverted cone is filled with water to the brim. Its height is 20 cm and diameter is 16.8 cm. Two equal solid cones are dropped in it, so that they are fully submerged. As a result, one-third of the water in the original cone overflows. What is the volume of each of the solid cones submerged?

Chapter Practice

a. 1 Mark Questions

1. If a well of diameter 8 m has been dug to the depth of 14 m, then the volume of the earth dug out is
(a) 352 m^3 (b) 704 m^3
(c) 1408 m^3 (d) 2816 m^3

2. Volume of a cylinder of height 3 cm is 48π. Radius of the cylinder is **[ICSE 2023]**
(a) 48 cm (b) 16 cm
(c) 4 cm (d) 24 cm

3. If two cylinders of same lateral surface have their radii in the ratio 4 : 9, then the ratio of their heights is
(a) 2 : 3 (b) 3 : 2
(c) 4 : 9 (d) 9 : 4

4. The volumes of two spheres are in the ratio 64 : 27. The ratio of their surface areas is
(a) 3 : 4 (b) 4 : 3
(c) 9 : 16 (d) 16 : 9

5. The radius of roller 100 cm long is 14 cm. The curved surface area of the roller is $\left[\text{take } \pi = \frac{22}{7}\right]$
(a) 13200 cm^2 (b) 15400 cm^2
(c) 4400 cm^2 (d) 8800 cm^2

6. A cubical ice-cream brick of edge 22 cm is to be distributed among some children by filling ice-cream cones of radius 2 cm and height 7 cm upto its brim. The number of children who will get the ice-cream cones is
(a) 163 (b) 263
(c) 363 (d) 463

7. The radii of two cylinders are in the ratio 2 : 3 and their heights are in the ratio 5 : 3. The ratio of their volumes is
(a) 10 : 17 (b) 20 : 27
(c) 17 : 27 (d) 20 : 37

b. 3 Marks Questions

8. The height of a right circular cylinder with lateral surface area 792 cm^2 is 21 cm. Find the diameter of its base.

9. The curved surface area of a right circular cylinder is 4400 cm^2. If the circumference of the base is 110 cm, then find the height of the cylinder.

10. The diameter of a garden roller is 1.4 m and it is 2 m long. How much area will it level in 5 revolutions?

11. A school provides milk to the students daily in a cylindrical glasses of diameter 7 cm. If the glass is filled with milk upto an height of 12 cm, then find how many litres of milk is needed to serve 1600 students?

12. The diameter of the roller 120 cm long is 84 cm. If it takes 500 complete revolutions to level a playground, then find the cost of levelling at the rate of 30 paise per m^2.

13. The pillars of a temple are cylindrically shaped. If each pillar has a circular base of radius 20 cm and height 10 m, how much concrete mixture would be required to build 14 such pillars?

14. The radius and the slant height of a cone are in the ratio of 4 : 7. If its curved surface area is 792 cm^2. Then, find the radius.

15. A cone and a cylinder are having equal base radius. Find the ratio of the heights of cone and cylinder, if their volumes are equal.

16. A temple is of shape right circular cylinder upto a height of 6 m and then becomes a right circular cone with a maximum height 30 m above the ground. Calculate the cost of painting the inner side of temple at the rate of ₹ 3 per m^2, if radius of base of temple is 7 m.

17. The height and base diameter of a conical tent is 16 m and 24 m, respectively. Find the cost of canvas required to make it at the rate of ₹ 210 per m^2.

18. How many metres of 5 m wide cloth will be required to make a conical tent, the radius of whose base is 3.5 m and height is 12 m?

19. Find the volume of a sphere which is equal to two-third of the volume of a cylinder whose height and diameter are equal to the diameter of the sphere.

20. The radius of a spherical balloon is inflated from 1.5 cm to 2.5 cm by pumping more air in it. Find the ratio of surface area of resulting balloon to the original balloon.

21. The radius of the base of a cone and the radius of a sphere are the same, each being 8 cm. Given that, the volume of these two solids are also the same. Calculate the slant height of the cone.

c. 4/5 Mark Questions

22. A vessel is in the form of an inverted cone. Its height is 8 cm and the radius of its top, which is open, is 5 cm. It is filled with water upto the brim. When lead shots, each of which is a sphere of radius 0.5 cm are dropped into the vessel, one-fourth of the water flow out. Find the number of lead shots dropped into the vessel.

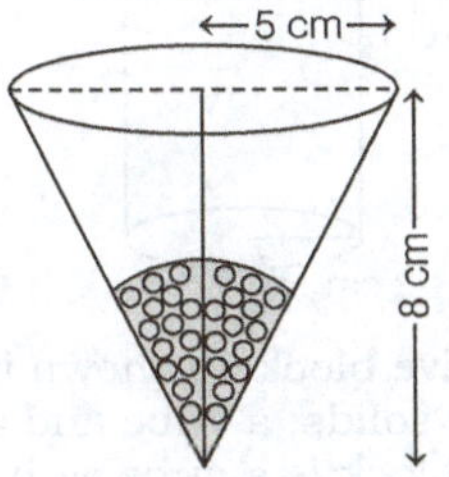

23. A hemi-spherical bowl of internal diameter 36 cm contains a liquid. This liquid is filled in cylindrical bottles of radius 3 cm and height 6 cm. How many bottles are required to empty the bowl?

24. A cone is filled of water poured into the hemisphere, which is also filled. The radius and height of a cone are 10 cm and 20 cm, respectively. Find the radius of the hemisphere.

25. How many spherical bullets can be made out of a solid cube of lead whose edge measures 44 cm, each bullet being 4 cm in diameter? [take $\pi = 22/7$]

26. Find the maximum volume of a cone, that can be carved out of a solid hemisphere of radius r.

27. The rainwater from a roof 22 m × 20 m drain into a conical vessel having diameter of base as 2 m and height 3.5 m. If the vessel is just full, then find the rainfall.

28. If a sphere is inscribed in a cube, then find the ratio of the volume of the cube to the volume of the sphere.

29. The water for a factory is stored in a hemispherical tank, whose internal diameter is 14 m. The tank contains 50 kL of water. Water is pumped into the tank to fill to its capacity. Calculate the volume of water pumped into the tank. [take $\pi = 22/7$]

30. A wooden article was made by scooping out a hemisphere from each end of a solid cylinder, as shown in figure. If the height of the cylinder is 10 cm and its base is of radius 3.5 cm,then find the total surface area of the article. [take $\pi = 22/7$]

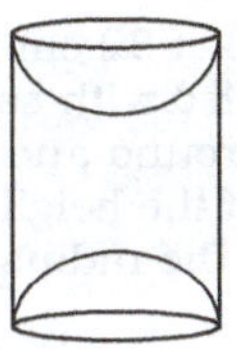

31. A storage oil tanker consists of a cylindrical portion 7m in diameter with two hemispherical ends of the same diameter. The oil tanker lying horizontally. If the total length of the tanker is 20 m, then find the capacity of the container.

32. A cylindrical beaker, whose base has a radius of 15 cm, is filled with water upto a height of 20 cm. A heavy iron spherical ball of radius 10 cm is dropped to submerge completely in water in the beaker. Find the increase in the level of water. [take $\pi = 3.14$]

33. The radii of the internal and external surfaces of a metallic spherical shell are 3 cm and 5 cm, respectively. It is melted and recast into a solid right circular cylinder of height $10\frac{2}{3}$ cm. Find the diameter of the base of the cylinder.

d. 6 Marks Questions

34. Circumference of the base of a cylinder, open at the top, is 132 cm. The sum of radius and height is 41 cm. Find the cost of polishing the outer surface area of cylinder at the rate ₹ 10 per dm^2 (decimetre). [take $\pi = 22/7$]

35. In the given figue, A sector of a circle of radius 9 cm and central angle of 120°. It is rolled up so that the two bounding radii are joined together to form a cone. Find

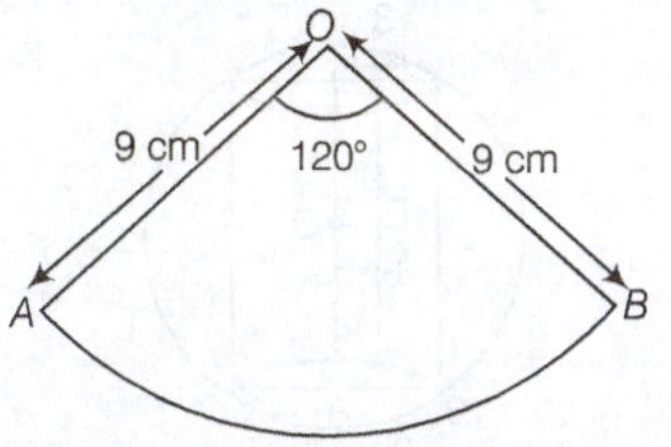

(i) the slant height of the cone.
(ii) the radius of the base of the cone.
(iii) the volume of the cone.
(iv) the total surface area of the cone.

36. The internal and external diameters of a hollow hemispherical vessel are 7cm and 14 cm, respectively. The cost of silver plating of 1 sq cm surface is ₹ 0.60. Find the total cost of silver plating the vessel all over.

37. A cylindrical bucket 32 cm hight and radius of base 18 cm, is filled with sand. This bucket is emptied on the ground and a conical heap of sand is formed. If the height of the conical heap is 24 cm, then find the radius and slant height of the heap.

38. A circular hall (i.e. cylindrical) has a hemispherical roof. The greatest height is equal to the inner diameter. Find the area of the floor, given that the capacity of the hall is 48510 m^3.

39. A medicine capsule is in the shape of a cylinder with two hemispheres stuck to each of its ends (see figure). The length of the entire capsule is 14 mm and the diameter of the capsule is 5 mm. Find the surface area of the figure. [take π = 22/7]

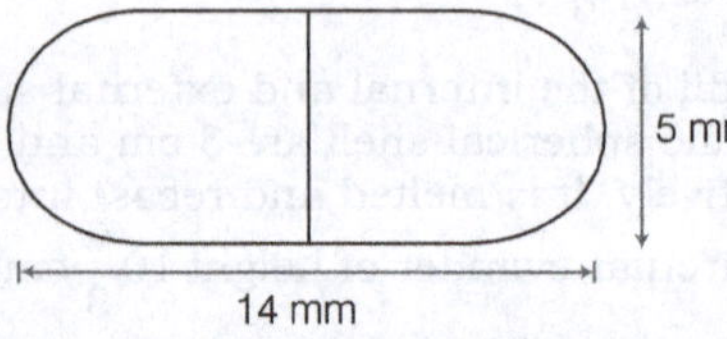

40. A rocket is in the form of a right circular cylinder closed at the lower end and surmounted by a cone with the same radius as that of the cylinder. The diameter and height of the cylinder are 6 cm and 12 cm, respectively. If the slant height of the conical portion is 5 cm, then find the total surface area and volume of the rocket. [take π = 3.14]

41. In the given figure, a sphere circumscribes a right cylinder whose height is 8 cm and radius of the base is 3 cm. Find the ratio of the volumes of the sphere and the cylinder.

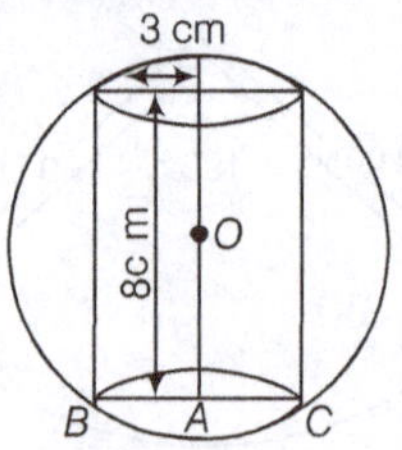

42. A metallic cylinder has radius 3 cm and height 5 cm. It is made of metal *A*. To reduce its weight, a conical hole is drilled in the cylinder as shown in the figure and it is completely filled with a lighter metal *B*. The conical hole has a radius of 3/2 cm and its depth is 8/9 cm. Calculate the ratio of the volume of the metal *A* to the volume of the metal *B* in the solid.

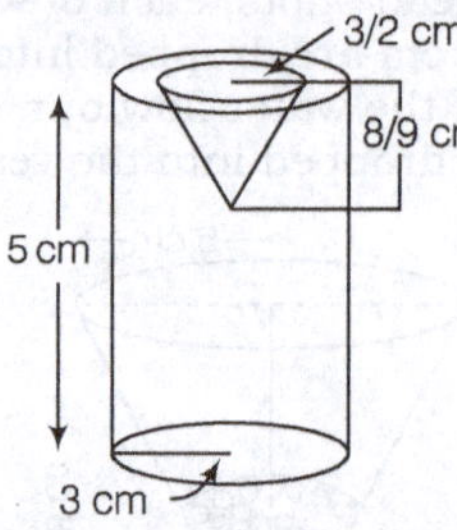

43. The decorative block as shown in the figure is made of two solids, a cube and a hemisphere. The base of the block is a cube with edge 5 cm and the hemisphere fixed on the top has a diameter of 4.2 cm, then find the total area to be painted.

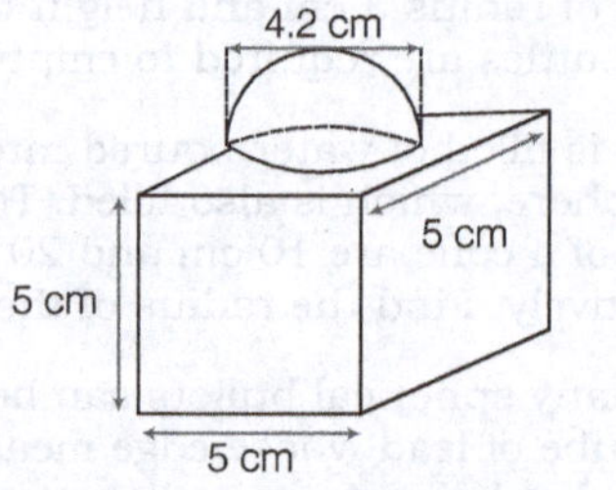

44. A solid is in the shape of a hemi-sphere of radius 7 cm, surmounted by a cone of height 4 cm. The solid is immersed completely in a cylindrical container filled with water to a certain height. If the radius of the cylinder is 14 cm, find the rise in the water level. **[ICSE 2023]**

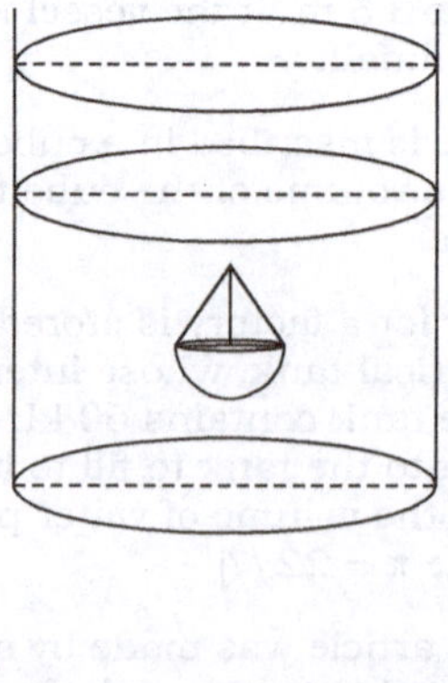

Hints and Answers

Exercise 17.1

1. **Hint**
   (i) Lateral surface area of cylinder $= 2\pi rh$
   Ans. 176 cm^2
   (ii) Total surface area of cylinder $= 2\pi r(r + h)$
   Ans. 201.14 cm^2
   (iii) Volume of cylinder $= \pi r^2 h$ **Ans.** 176 cm^3
2. **Hint** Curved surface area $= 2\pi rh = 1760$
   $\Rightarrow h = \dfrac{1760}{2\pi r}$ **Ans.** 20
3. **Hint** Do same as Q. 2. **Ans.** 21 cm
4. **Hint** Required ratio $= \dfrac{2\pi r(h + r)}{2\pi rh} = \dfrac{h + r}{h}$
   $= \dfrac{7.5 + 3.5}{7.5} = \dfrac{22}{15}$ **Ans.** 22 : 15
5. **Hint** Let the radius of cylinder be r.
   $2\pi r(h + r) = 352$
   $\Rightarrow 2 \times \dfrac{22}{7} \times r(10 + r) = 352$
   $\Rightarrow r(10 + r) = \dfrac{352 \times 7}{44} = 56$
   $\Rightarrow 10r + r^2 - 56 = 0$
   $\Rightarrow r(r + 14) - 4(r + 14) = 0$
   $\Rightarrow (r + 14)(r - 4) = 0$
   Either $r + 14 = 0$, then $r = -14$ which is not possible
   or $r - 4 = 0 \Rightarrow r = 4$
   diameter of cylinder $= 2r = 2 \times 4 = 8$ cm **Ans.** 8 cm
6. **Hint** Curved surface area $= 2\pi rh$
   $\therefore$ Required ratio $= \dfrac{2\pi \cdot 2r \cdot 5h}{2\pi \cdot 3r \cdot 3h}$ **Ans.** 10 : 9
7. **Hint** Circumference of base, $2\pi r = 110$
   and curved surface area, $2\pi rh = 4400$
   $\Rightarrow 110 \times h = 4400 \Rightarrow h = 40$ cm **Ans.** 40 cm
8. **Hint** Do same as Example 2. **Ans.** 1.4 cm
9. **Hint** Given, the height of circular cylinder = 1 m
   $\therefore$ Radius $= \dfrac{\text{Diameter}}{2} = \dfrac{70}{2} = 35$ cm
   $= \dfrac{35}{100}\text{ m} = \dfrac{7}{20}\text{ m}$
   The area of the tin sheet required for making the container = Curved surface area + Area of base
   $\Rightarrow 2\pi rh + \pi r^2 = \pi r(2h + r)$
   $= \dfrac{22}{7} \times \dfrac{7}{20}\left(2 \times 1 + \dfrac{7}{20}\right)\text{ m}^2$
   $= \dfrac{11}{10} \times \dfrac{47}{20}\text{ m}^2$
   $\therefore$ The cost of the tin sheet for making the container
   ₹ $\left(\dfrac{11}{10} \times \dfrac{47}{20} \times 100\right) =$ ₹ 258.50
   Ans. ₹ 258.50
10. **Hint** Do same as Example 3. **Ans.** 2000
11. **Hint** Do same as Example 4. **Ans.** 980.57 cm^2
12. **Hint**
    (i) Inner curved surface area $= 2\pi r_1 h$ $[\because r_1 = 2\text{ cm}]$
    Ans. 968 cm^2
    (ii) Outer curved surface area $= 2\pi r_2 h$ $[\because r_2 = 2.2\text{ cm}]$
    Ans. 1064.8 cm^2
    (iii) Total surface area $= 2\pi(r_1 + r_2)[h + r_2 - r_1]$
    Ans. 2038.08 cm^2
13. **Hint** Do same as Example 7. **Ans.** 396 cm^3
14. **Hint** Here, height $(h) = 8$ cm
    $\therefore$ Circumference of base
    = Length of sheet $\Rightarrow 2\pi r = 11$
    $\Rightarrow r = \dfrac{11 \times 7}{2 \times 22} = \dfrac{7}{4}$
    Now, volume $= \pi r^2 h = \dfrac{22}{7} \times \dfrac{7}{4} \times \dfrac{7}{4} \times 8$ **Ans.** 77 cm^3
15. **Hint** $r + h = 35$
    $2\pi r^2 + 2\pi rh = 3080$
    $r = 14$ cm
    $r + h = 35$
    $h = 21$
    $\therefore$ Volume of the cylinder $= \pi r^2 h$
    $= \dfrac{22}{7} \times 14 \times 14 \times 21$
    Ans. 12936 cm^3
16. **Hint** Let the height of the circular cylinder be h on and its radius be r cm.
    Total surface area = 462 cm^2
    $2\pi rh + 2\pi r^2 = 462$ (given) ...(i)
    Given, curved surface area $= \dfrac{1}{3}$ of total surface area.
    $2\pi rh = \dfrac{1}{3} \times 462$
    $2\pi rh = 154$ ...(ii)
    Put the value of $2\pi rh$ in Eq. (i), we get
    $154 + 2\pi r^2 = 462$
    $\Rightarrow 2 \times \dfrac{22}{7} \times r^2 = 308$
    $\Rightarrow r^2 = \dfrac{308 \times 7}{2 \times 22} \Rightarrow r = 7$
    Put the value of r in Eq. (ii), we get
    $2 \times \dfrac{22}{7} \times 7 \times h = 154$
    $\Rightarrow 44h = 154$
    $\Rightarrow h = \dfrac{7}{2}$
    $\therefore$ Volume of cylinder $= \pi r^2 h = \dfrac{22}{7} \times 7^2 \times \dfrac{7}{2}\text{ cm}^3$
    $= 539\text{ cm}^3$

17. Hint Inner curved surface area $= \frac{2200}{20}\ m^2$
$= 110\ m^2$.

$\because$ Curved surface area $= 2\pi rh$

$\Rightarrow\ 2 \times \frac{22}{7} \times r \times 10 = 110$ [$\because$ given deep, $h = 10$ m]

$\Rightarrow\ r = \frac{7}{4}$ m

$\because$ Capacity of the tank $= \pi r^2 h$

$= \frac{22}{7} \times \left(\frac{7}{4}\right)^2 \times 10$

$= 96.25\ m^2$

$= 96.25$ kL

[$\because 1\ m^3 = 1000$ L $= 1$ kL]

Ans. 96.25 kL

18. Hint Volume of steel = Volume of hollow cylinder

$= \frac{22}{7}[(5)^2 - (4)^2] \times 140$

Ans. 3960 cm^3

19. Hint External radius of tube

$(R) = 5.6 + 0.4 = 6$ cm

$\therefore$ Required volume of metal used

$\pi h(R^2 - r^2) = \frac{22}{7} \times 21[(6)^2 - (5.6)^2]$

$= 66(6 + 5.6)(6 - 5.6)\ cm^3$

$= 66 \times 11.6 \times 0.4\ cm^3$

$= 306.24\ cm^3$

20. Hint $\because$ Volume of cylinder $= \pi r^2 h$

$\therefore$ Volume of new cylinder $= \pi\left(\frac{r}{2}\right)^2 2h = \pi \frac{r^2}{2} h$

$= \frac{1}{2} \times$ Volume of cylinder

Ans. $\frac{1}{2}\pi r^2 h$

21. Hint Volume $= \pi r^2 h$ **Ans.** 8624 cm^3

22. Hint Let radius $= 5x$ and height $= 7x$

Then, $\pi r^2 h = 550 \Rightarrow \frac{22}{7}(5x)^2(7x) = 550$

$\Rightarrow\ x^3 = 1 \Rightarrow x = 1$ **Ans.** 5 cm

23. Hint Let height $= 3x$ and radius $= x$

Volume of cylinder $= \pi r^2 h = 1029\ \pi$

$x^2 \times 3x = 1029 \Rightarrow x = 7$

Height = 21 cm and radius = 7 cm

Total surface area $= 2\pi r(r + h)\ cm^3 = 1232\ cm^3$

24. Hint Height of water = 2.1 m = 210 cm

Radius of water tank $= \frac{1}{2} \times 1.4$ m $= 70$ cm

$\therefore$ Capacity (volume) of water tank $= \pi r^2 h$

$= \frac{22}{7} \times (70)^2 \times 210\ cm^3$

$= 22 \times 700 \times 210$

Radius of water pipe $= \frac{1}{2} \times 3.5$ cm $= \frac{7}{4}$ cm

Length of water delivered by the pipe in 1s

= 2 m = 200 cm

$\therefore$ Volume of water delivered by the pipe in 1s

$= \pi r^2 h$

$= \frac{22}{7} \times \left(\frac{7}{4}\right)^2 \times 200\ cm^3$

$= (77 \times 25)\ cm^3$

$\therefore$ Time consumed by the water pipe in filling the water tank

$= \frac{22 \times 700 \times 210}{77 \times 25} = 1680$s

$= \frac{1680}{60} = 28$ min

25. Hint Volume of hollow wood $= \pi h(R^2 - r^2)$

and volume of graphite $= \pi r^2 h$

Ans. 5.28 cm^3, 0.11 cm^3

Exercise 17.2

1. (i) **Hint** Slant height of a right circular cone,

$l = \sqrt{h^2 + r^2}$ **Ans.** 21.21 cm

(ii) **Hint** Curved surface area of a right circular cone $= \pi rl$ **Ans.** 199.98 cm^2

(iii) **Hint** Total surface area of cone $= \pi r(l + r)$

Ans. 228.27 cm^2

(iv) **Hint** Volume of cone $= \frac{1}{3}\pi r^2 h$ **Ans.** 198 cm^3

2. Hint Curved surface area of cone $= \pi rl$

Ans. 220 cm^2

3. Hint (i) CSA of cone $= \pi rl$ **Ans.** 165 cm^2

(ii) TSA of cone $= \pi r(l + r)$ **Ans.** 251.625 cm^2

4. Hint Do same as Example 15.

Ans. (i) 364.1 cm^2 (ii) 770 cm^3

5. Hint $\because$ Volume of the cone $= \frac{1}{3}\pi r^2 h$

$\Rightarrow\ 1570 = \frac{1}{3} \times \frac{22}{7}(15) \times r^2$

$\Rightarrow\ 1570 \times 3 \times \frac{7}{22} = 15r^2 \Rightarrow r^2 = 100$ **Ans.** 10 cm

6. Hint Do same as Example 17

Ans. 471.43 m^2 (approx.)

7. Hint Radius of the cone $= \frac{10}{2} = 5$ cm

(i) $h^2 = (13)^2 - (5)^2$ **Ans.** $h = 12$ cm

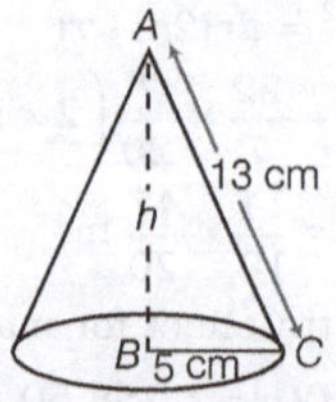

(ii) Curved surface area of the cone $= \pi rl$

Ans. 204.1 cm^2

(iii) Total surface area of the cone $= \pi r(l + r)$
Ans. 282.6 cm^2

(iv) Volume of the cone $= \frac{1}{3}\pi r^2 h$ **Ans.** 314 cm^3

8. Hint Let the slant heights of each cone be $3x$ and $4x$, respectively i.e. $l_1 = 3x$ and $l_2 = 4x$

$\therefore$ Radius of each cone $= \frac{d}{2}$

$\therefore$ Ratio of the curved surface areas

$$= \frac{\pi \times \left(\frac{d}{2}\right) \times 3x}{\pi \times \left(\frac{d}{2}\right) \times 4x}$$ **Ans.** 3 : 4

9. Hint Let $r = x$ and $h = 3x$

Volume of cone $= \frac{1}{3}\pi r^2 h$

Now, slant height $= \sqrt{h^2 + r^2}$

Lateral surface area $= \pi r l$

Ans. 14 cm, 487.08 cm^2

10. Hint Let the radius of cone Y be r, then the radius of cone X will be $3r$.

Let the volume of cone X be V, then volume of cone Y will be $\frac{V}{2}$. **Ans.** 2 : 9

11. Hint Do same as Example 19. **Ans.** 77.70 cm^3

12. Hint Let the length of canvas be x m.

Given, diameter of conical tent, $2r = 20$ m

$\Rightarrow$ Radius, $r = 10$ m

Also given slant height $= 42$ m $= l$ (say)

Then, area of canvas $= \pi r l$

and in folds and stitching $= 10\%$ of $[\pi r l]$

$$= 1320 \times \frac{10}{100} = 132 \text{ m}^2$$

$\Rightarrow$ The actual total area of the conical tent

$$= \frac{22}{7} \times 10 \times 42 + 132$$
$$= 1320 + 132 = 1452 \text{ m}^2$$

$\because$ Length $\times$ Width = Total actual area of tent

$x \times 2 = 1452$ [$\because$ given width = 2 m]

$\Rightarrow$ Length $= x = 726$ m

Also, total cost of the canvas at the rate of ₹ 80 per meter $= 80 \times 726 =$ ₹ 58080

Ans. 726 m, ₹ 58080

13. Hint Do same as Example 20.
Ans. ₹ 384.34 (approx.)

14. Hint Do same as Example 22 (ii). **Ans.** ₹ 6864

15. Hint A sector of a circle of radius 8 cm having an angle of 90°, is shown below

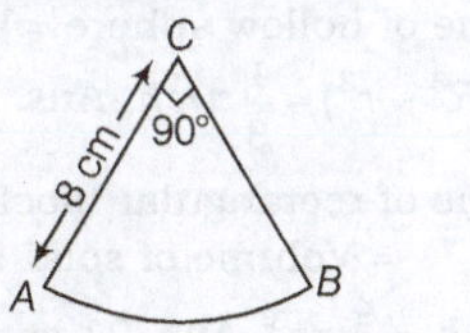

When we rolled up and joined the bounding radii, a conical shape is formed,

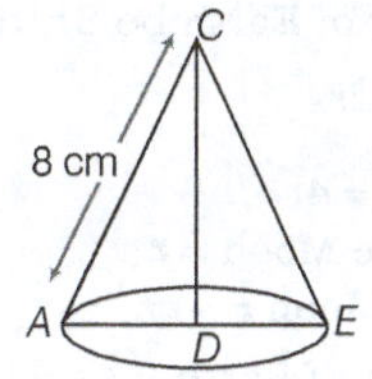

Now, length of an arc of the sector

$$= \frac{1}{4}(2\pi r) = \frac{1}{4}(2\pi \times 8) = 4\pi \text{ cm}$$

(i) **Hint** Let r be the radius of the cone.
Then, circumference of the circular base of the cone = Length of an arc of the sector

$\therefore$ $2\pi r = 4\pi$

Ans. $r = 2$ cm

(ii) **Hint** Total surface area of the cone $= \pi r(l + r)$.
Ans. 20π cm^2

(iii) **Hint** In right angled ΔADC,
Volume of a cone $= \frac{1}{3}\pi r^2 h$

Ans. $\frac{8\sqrt{15}}{3}\pi$ cm^3

16. Air occupied space = Volume of conical tent

$$= \frac{1}{3}\pi r^2 h$$

$\therefore$ Area space per man $= \dfrac{\frac{1}{3}\pi r^2 h}{100}$

Ans. 1.54 cm^3

17. Hint Do same as Example 26 and also use total surface area of cone $= \pi r(r + l)$ sq unit
Ans. 678.82 cm^2

18. Hint Volume of tent $= 77 \times 16 \text{ m}^3 = 1232 \text{ m}^3$ and Curved surface area $= \pi r l$
Ans. $h = 24$ m, CSA $= 550 \text{ m}^2$

Exercise 17.3

1. Hint

(i) Surface area of sphere $= 4\pi r^2$ **Ans.** 5544 cm^2

(ii) Volume of sphere $= \frac{4}{3}\pi r^3$ **Ans.** 38808 cm^3

2. Hint Do same as Example 27.
Ans. 310.18 cm^3, 221.56 cm^2

3. Hint Surface area of sphere $= 4\pi r^2$

$\Rightarrow 154 = 4 \times \frac{22}{7} r^2 \Rightarrow r^2 = \frac{49}{4}$ **Ans.** 3.5 cm

4. Hint Do same as Example 30. **Ans.** 488 cm^3

5. Hint TSA of sphere $= 4\pi r^2$

and volume of sphere $= \frac{4}{3}\pi r^3$

Ans. 7 cm, 1437.33 cm^3

6. Hint Volume of a sphere = Surface area of a sphere

$\Rightarrow \frac{4}{3}\pi r^3 = 4\pi r^2$ **Ans.** 3 units

7. Let the diameter of Earth be $8r$, then diameter of the Moon $= \frac{1}{4} \times 8r = 2r$

Radius of Earth $= 4r$
and radius of the Moon $= r$
Surface area of Moon $= 4\pi r^2$
and surface area of Earth $= 4\pi \times (4r)^2 = 64\pi r^2$

$\therefore \frac{\text{Surface area of Moon}}{\text{Surface area of Earth}} = \frac{4\pi r^2}{64\pi r^2} = \frac{1}{16}$

Hence, the required ratio is 1 : 16.

8. Hint Volume of spherical bowl $= \frac{4}{3}\pi r^3$

Ans. 11498.67 cm^3

9. Hint Difference of two spheres $= 4\pi R^2 - 4\pi r^2$

$\Rightarrow 3080 = 4 \times \frac{22}{7}[(21)^2 - r^2]$

$\Rightarrow \frac{3080 \times 7}{4 \times 22} = 441 - r^2 \Rightarrow r = 14$ cm

Now, difference of their volumes $= \frac{4}{3}\pi(R^3 - r^3)$

Ans. 27309.33 cm^3

10. Hint Let the radius of the sphere be r, then its diameter, $d = 2r$

New diameter, $d_1 = d - 25\%$ of d.

New radius, $r_1 = \frac{d_1}{2}$

Decrease in surface area,

S_1 = Original surface area – New surface area

$\because$ Decrease percentage $= \frac{S_1}{S} \times 100\%$

Ans. 43.75%

11. Hint Surface area of spherical shell

$= 4\pi(R^2 + r^2)$

Volume of spherical shell $= \frac{4}{3}\pi(R^3 - r^3)$

Ans. 929.44 cm^2, 912.69 cm^3

12. Let an edge of a cube be $2a$, then its volume

$= (2a)^3$
$= 8a^3$

As a sphere is inscribed in the cube, diameter of sphere $= 2a$

$\therefore$ Radius of sphere $= \frac{1}{2} \times 2a = a$

Volume of sphere $= \frac{4}{3}\pi a^3$

$\therefore \frac{\text{Volume of cube}}{\text{Volume of sphere}} = \frac{8a^3}{\frac{4}{3}\pi a^3} = \frac{6}{\pi}$

Ans. $6 : \pi$

13. Hint Let radius of each spherical marble be r cm.
According to the question,
Volume of 64 identical spherical marbles
= Volume of solid spherical ball of radius 6 cm

$\Rightarrow 64 \times \frac{4}{3}\pi r^3 = \frac{4}{3}\pi \times (6)^3$

$\Rightarrow 64 \times r^3 = 6^3$

$\Rightarrow r^3 = \left(\frac{6}{4}\right)^3$

$\Rightarrow r = \frac{6}{4} = 1.5$ cm

14. Hint

(i) Curved surface area of hemisphere $= 2\pi r^2$
Ans. 11088 cm^2

(ii) Total surface area of hemisphere $= 3\pi r^2$
Ans. 16632 cm^2

(iii) Volume of hemisphere $= \frac{2}{3}\pi r^3$
Ans. 155232 cm^3

15. Hint Ratio of surface areas of the balloon in two cases $= \frac{3\pi r_1^2}{3\pi r_2^2}$ **Ans.** 1 : 4

16. Hint Here outer, radius $= 5 + 0.25 = 5.25$ cm
Curved surface area of hemisphere bowl $= 2\pi r^2$
Ans. 173.09 cm^2

17. Hint Volume of hemisphere $= \frac{2}{3}\pi r^3$

curved surface area of hemisphere $= 2\pi r^2$
and total surface area $= 3\pi r^2$
Ans. 523.9 cm^3, 249.48 cm^2, 374.22 cm^2

18. Hint $\because$ Surface area of sphere $= 4\pi R^2$
Total surface area of hemisphere $= 3\pi r^2$
Given, $4\pi R^2 = 3\pi r^2$

$\therefore \frac{\text{Volume of sphere}}{\text{Volume of hemisphere}} = \frac{\frac{4}{3}\pi R^3}{\frac{2}{3}\pi r^3}$ **Ans.** $3\sqrt{3} : 4$

19. Hint Total surface area $= \pi(3R^2 + r^2)$
Total cost of silver plating the vessel all over
= ₹ 0.40 × Total surface area
Ans. ₹ 476.96

Exercise 17.4

1. Hint Volume of hollow sphere

$= \frac{4}{3}\pi(R^3 - r^3)$ [$\because R = 8$ cm, $r = 6$ cm]

Volume of cone $= \frac{1}{3}\pi r_1^2 h$ [$\because h = 8$ cm and $r_1 = 2$ cm]

$\therefore$ Number of cones $= \frac{\text{Volume of hollow spheres}}{\text{Volume of cone}}$

Ans. 37

2. Hint Volume of hollow sphere = Volume of cone

$\Rightarrow \frac{4}{3}\pi(R^3 - r^3) = \frac{1}{3}\pi r_1^2 h$ **Ans.** 14 cm

3. Hint Volume of rectangular block
= Volume of solid sphere

$\Rightarrow l \times b \times h = \frac{4}{3}\pi r^3$ **Ans.** 21 cm

4. **Hint** Number of spheres = $\frac{\text{Volume of cone}}{\text{Volume of each sphere}}$

Ans. 400

5. **Hint** Number of spheres = $\frac{\text{Volume of a sphere}}{\text{Volume of a smaller sphere}}$

Ans. 64

6. **Hint** Volume of right circular cylinder = Volume of sphere **Ans.** 3 cm

7. **Hint** Number of cones = $\frac{\text{Volume of a sphere}}{\text{Volume of each cone}}$

Ans. 270

8. **Hint** Number of cones = $\frac{\text{Volume of a sphere}}{\text{Volume of a small cone}}$

Ans. 72

9. **Hint** Do same as Example 49. **Ans.** 984.91 cm^3

10. **Hint**

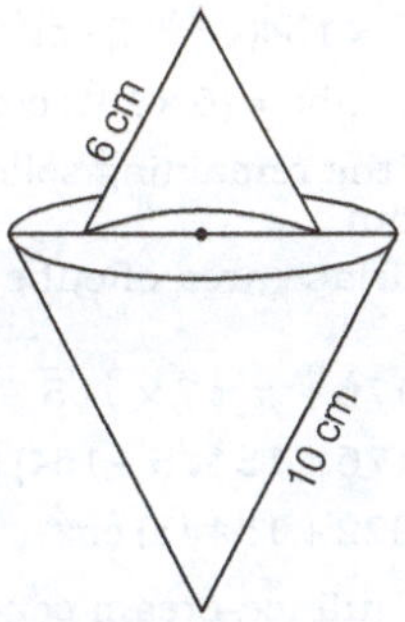

For small solid cone,
Radius, $r_1 = 4$ cm
Slant height, $l_1 = 6$ cm

$\Rightarrow$ Curved surface area = $\pi r_1 l_1$
$= \pi \times 4 \times 6 = 24\pi \text{ cm}^2$

For bigger solid cone,
Radius, $r_2 = 6$ cm
Slant height, $l_2 = 10$ cm
Curved surface area = $\pi r_2 l_2$
$= \pi \times 6 \times 10 = 60\pi \text{ cm}^2$

$\therefore$ Surface area of combine figure
$= \pi r_1 l_1 + \pi r_2 l_2 + \pi r_2^2 - \pi r_1^2$
$= 24\pi + 60\pi + 36\pi - 16\pi$
$= 104\pi = 104 \times 3.14$
$= 326.56 \text{ cm}^2$

Ans. 326.56 cm^2

11. **Hint** Volume of remaining solid
= Volume of hemisphere – Volume of cone

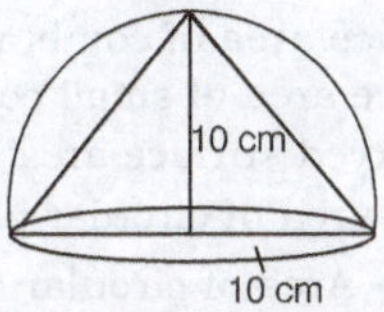

Surface area of remaining solid
= Curved surface area of hemisphere
+ Curved surface area of cone

Ans. 1046.67 cm^3; 1070.74 cm^2

12. **Hint** Volume of cuboid
$= 15 \times 10 \times 3.5 = 525 \text{ cm}^3$
$r = 0.5$ cm and $h = 1.4$ cm

Volume of one cavity = $\frac{1}{3}\pi r^2 h$
$= \frac{1}{3} \times \frac{22}{7} \times 0.5 \times 0.5 \times 1.4 = \frac{1.1}{3} \text{ cm}^3$

Volume of four depression
$= 4 \times \frac{1.1}{3} \text{ cm} = 1.467 \text{ cm}^3$

Volume of wood used in pen stand
$= (525 - 1.467) \text{ cm}^3$
$= 523.533 \text{ cm}^3 = 523.53 \text{ cm}^3$
(correct to two decimal places)

13. **Hint**

(i) Total area of the internal surface
= Curved surface area of hemisphere
+ Curved surface area of cylinder

Ans. 231 m^2

(ii) Volume of container = Volume of hemisphere
+ Volume of cylinder

Ans. 359.33 m^3

14. **Hint** Diameter = 2.8 cm and radius = 1.4 cm

Length (height) of the cylindrical part
$= 5 \text{ cm} - (1.4 + 1.4) \text{ cm} = 2.2 \text{ cm}$

Now, volume of the cylindrical part = $\pi r^2 h$

Volume of both the hemispherical ends
$= 2\left(\frac{2}{3}\pi r^3\right) = \frac{4}{3}\pi r^3$

Volume of gulabjamun
= Volume of cylinder
+ 2 × Volume of hemisphere
$= \frac{22}{7} \times (1.4)^2 \left(2.2 + \frac{5.6}{3}\right) \text{ cm}^3$
$= 25.05 \text{ cm}^3$

Volume of 45 gulabjamuns = (25.05 × 45)

Since, each gulabjamun contains sugar syrup approximately 30%.

$\left(25 \cdot 05 \times 45 \times \frac{30}{100}\right) \text{ cm}^3 = 338 \text{ cm}^3$

15. **Hint** Let the rise in the level of water be h.

Given, diameter of sphere = 12 cm

$\Rightarrow$ Radius, $r_1 = 6$ cm

$\Rightarrow$ Volume of the sphere = $\frac{4}{3}\pi r_1^3$
$= \frac{4}{3} \times 6 \times 6 \times 6 \times \pi = 288\pi$

$\because$ Volume of the sphere = Volume of rising part of cylindrical can

$\Rightarrow \quad 288\pi = \pi r_2^2 h_1 \Rightarrow 288\pi = \pi \times 144 \times h$

[where r_2 is the radius of cylindrical can]

$\Rightarrow \quad h = \frac{288\pi}{144\pi} = 2 \text{ cm} \quad [\because r_2 = 12 \text{ cm}]$

Ans. 2 cm

16. Hint Surface area of the toy

= Curved surface area of cone
+ Curved surface area of cylinder
+ Curved surface area of hemisphere

Ans. 770 cm^2

17. Hint In right angled ΔABC,

$$\sin 45° = \frac{BC}{AC} = \frac{2.15}{l} \Rightarrow l = 2.15 \times \sqrt{2}$$

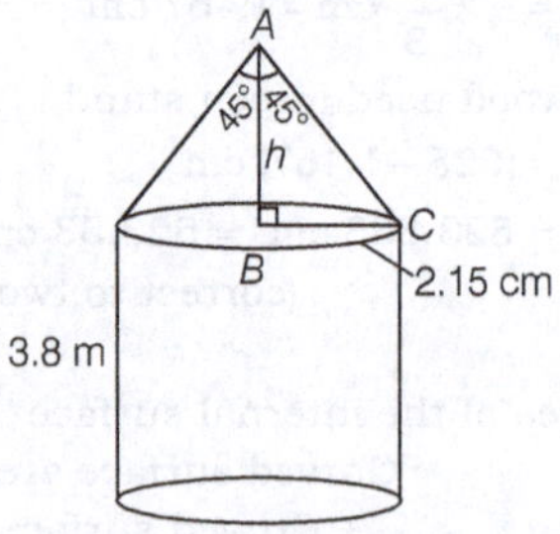

Also, $\angle BCA = 45°$

Here, ΔABC is an isosceles triangle.

$\therefore$ $AB = BC = 2.15$ m

$\therefore$ Surface area of building

= Curved surface area of cone
+ Curved surface area of cylinder

Ans. Height = 2.15 m, slant height = 3.04 m and surface area = 71.83 m^2

18. Hint Total surface area of toy

= Curved surface area of cone
+ Curved surface area of cylinder
+ [Area of circular base of cone
− Area of circular base of cylinder]

Ans. 2260.8 cm^2

19. Length of the cuboid, $l = 15$ cm

Breadth of cuboid, $b = 10$ cm

Height of cuboid, $h = 5$ cm

Diameter of cylinder = 7 cm

radius of cylinder, $r = \frac{7}{2}$ cm

Height of cylinder, $h = 5$ cm

Surface area of the cuboidal block

$= 2(lb + lh + bh)$

$= 2(15 \times 10 + 15 \times 5 + 10 \times 5)\ cm^3$

$= 2(150 + 75 + 50)\ cm^2 = 550\ cm^2$

Curved surface area of cylindrical hole $= 2\pi rh$

$= \left(2 \times \frac{22}{7} \times \frac{7}{2} \times 5\right) cm^2 = 110\ cm^2$

Area of two circular bases of cylindrical hole

$= \pi r^2 + \pi r^2 = 2\pi r^2$

$= \left(2 \times \frac{22}{7} \times \left(\frac{7}{2}\right)^2\right) cm^2 = 77\ cm^2$

$\therefore$ Required surface area

= Surface area of cuboidal block
+ CSA of cylindrical hole
− Area of two circular bases of cylindrical hole

$= 550\ cm^2 + 110\ cm^2 - 77\ cm^2$

$= 583\ cm^2$

20. Given, the cone of maximum size that is carved out from a cube of edge 14 cm will be of base radius 7 cm and the height 14 cm.

Slant height of cone $= \sqrt{h^2 + r^2}$

$= \sqrt{(14)^2 + (7)^2}$ cm

$= 7\sqrt{5}$ cm

Surface area of the cone = CSA of cone
+ Area of base of cone

$= (\pi \times 7 \times 7\sqrt{5} + \pi \times 7^2)\ cm^2$

$= \frac{22}{7} \times 49(\sqrt{5} + 1)\ cm^2$

$= 154(\sqrt{5} + 1)\ cm^2$

Surface area of cube $= (6 \times 14^2)\ cm^2 = 1176\ cm^2$

Surface area of the remaining solid left out after the cone is carved out

= Surface area of cube + CSA of cone
− Area of base of cone

$= (1176 + \pi \times 7 \times 7\sqrt{5} - \pi \times 7^2)\ cm^2$

$= (1176 + 154\sqrt{5} - 154)\ cm^2$

$= (1022 + 154\sqrt{5})\ cm^2$

21. Hint Volume of full ice-cream cone, V_1

= Volume of cone + Volume of hemisphere

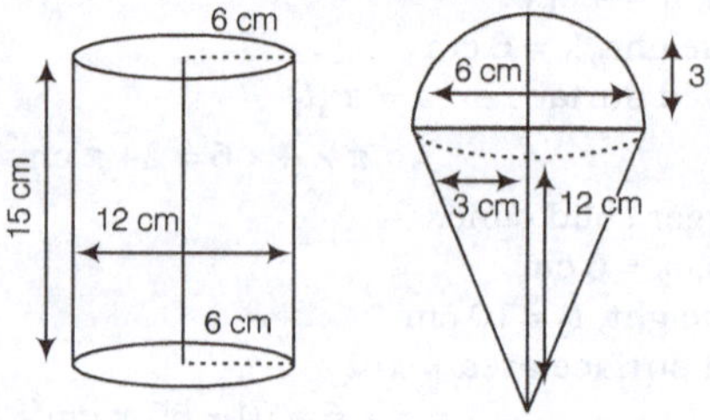

Number of cones

$= \frac{\text{Volume of cylinderical ice-cream container}}{V_1}$

Ans. 10

22. Hint Surface area of the remaining figure

= Surface area of the sphere
+ Curved surface area of cone
+ Curved surface area of hemisphere

Ans. 1198.22 cm^2

23. Hint Now, surface area of combined figure

= Curved surface area of small cone
+ Curved surface area of larger cone
+ (Area of circular base of larger cone
− Area of circular base of smaller cone)

and volume of combined figure

= Volume of smaller cone + Volume of larger cone

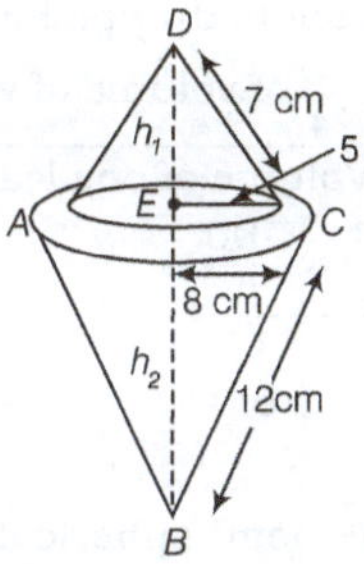

Ans. 727.31 cm^3

24. **Hint** Volume of water in conical vessel,

i.e. original volume $= \frac{1}{3}\pi r^2 h$

$\therefore$ Volume of water overflow $= \frac{1}{3} \times$ Original volume

Ans. 246.4 cm^3

Chapter Exercise

1. (b) **Hint** Given, height = 14 m

Radius $= \frac{8}{2} = 4$ m

$\therefore$ Volume of Earth $= \pi r^2 h$

$= \frac{22}{7} \times (4)^2 \times 14 = 704 \text{ m}^3$

2. (c) Given, height of cylinder $(h) = 3$ cm,

and volume of cylinder $(V) = 48\pi \text{ cm}^3$

Let the radius of the base of cylinder = r cm

$\because$ Volume of cylinder $= \pi r^2 h = 48\pi$

$\Rightarrow \quad \pi \times r^2 \times 3 = 48\pi$

$\Rightarrow \quad r^2 = \frac{48}{3} = 16$

$\Rightarrow \quad r = 4$ cm

3. (d) **Hint** Ratio in two cylinder same lateral surface area their radii is 4 : 9.

Let r_1 and r_2 be the radius of the first and second cylinder respectively and h_1, h_2 are their heights.

Let $r_1 = 4x$ and $r_2 = 9x$

$2\pi r_1 h_1 = 2\pi r_2 h_2$

$\Rightarrow \quad 2\pi \times 4x \times h_1 = 2\pi \times 9x \times h_2$

$\because \quad \frac{h_1}{h_2} = \frac{9x}{4x} = 9:4$

4. (d) **Hint** Volume of sphere $= \frac{4}{3}\pi r^3$

So, ratio of volume of sphere is $r_1^3 : r_2^3 = 64 : 27$

$\Rightarrow \quad r_1 : r_2 = 4 : 3$

Surface area of sphere $= 4\pi r^2$

So, ratio of surface area is $r_1^2 : r_2^2 = 16 : 9$

5. (d) **Hint** Given, radius of the roller = 14 cm

and length = 100 cm

We know that roller is looks like a cylinder.

$\therefore$ Radius of the cylinder $(r) = 14$ cm

and height (h) = Length of the roller = 100 cm

Thus, curved surface area of the roller

= Curved surface area of cylinder

$= 2\pi rh$

$= 2 \times \frac{22}{7} \times 14 \times 100$

$= 44 \times 200 = 8800 \text{ cm}^2$

6. (c) **Hint** Let the number of cones be n

$\because \quad n \times \frac{1}{3}\pi r^2 h = 22 \times 22 \times 22$

$\Rightarrow \quad n \times \frac{1}{3} \times \frac{22}{7} \times 2 \times 2 \times 7 = 22 \times 22 \times 22$

$\therefore \quad n = \left(22 \times 22 \times 22 \times \frac{3}{88}\right) = 363$

7. (b) **Hint** Let the radii of two cylinders be r_1 and r_2 and heights of two cylinders be h_1 and h_2.

We have, $\frac{r_1}{r_2} = \frac{2}{3}$ and $\frac{h_1}{h_2} = \frac{5}{3}$

$\therefore \quad \frac{\pi r_1^2 h_1}{\pi r_2^2 h_2} = \left(\frac{r_1}{r_2}\right)^2 \left(\frac{h_1}{h_2}\right)$

$= \left(\frac{2}{3}\right)^2 \left(\frac{5}{3}\right)$

$= \frac{4}{9} \times \frac{5}{3} = \frac{20}{27}$

8. **Hint** Lateral surface area of a right circular cylinder $= 2\pi rh$

Ans. 12 cm

9. **Hint** Curved surface area of right circular cylinder $= 2\pi rh = 4400 \text{ cm}^2$.

Also, given $2\pi r = 110$ cm

Ans. 40 cm

10. **Hint** Do same as Example 3. **Ans.** 44 m^2

11. **Hint** Volume of cylinderical glass $= \pi r^2 h$

Volume of milk needed to serve 1600 students $= 1600 \times \pi r^2 h$

Also, use $1 \text{ cm}^3 = \frac{1}{1000}$ L

Ans. 739.2 L

12. **Hint** Lateral surface area of the roller, S_1

= Lateral surface area of a cylinder $= 2\pi rh$

$\because$ Area covered in 1 revolution

= Lateral surface area of the roller $= S_1$

$\therefore$ Area covered in 500 revolutions $= 500 \times S_1$

Ans. ₹ 475.20

13. **Hint** Volume of each cylindrical shaped pillar $= \pi r^2 h$

Now, required concrete mixture to make 14 such pillars = Volume of one cylindrical pillar × 14

Ans. 17.6 m^3

14. **Hint** Let radius of a cone be $4x$ and slant height of a cone $= 7x$.

Now, curved surface area of a cone $= 792 \text{ cm}^2$

$\Rightarrow \quad \frac{22}{7} \times 4x \times 7x = 792 \Rightarrow x = 3$

Ans. 12 cm

15. **Hint** Volume of cone, $V_1 = \frac{1}{3}\pi r^2 h_1$
and volume of cylinder, $V_2 = \pi r^2 h_2$
$\because \quad V_1 = V_2$
Ans. $h_1 : h_2 = 3 : 1$

16. **Hint** Radius of base, $r = 7$ cm
Height of cylinder, $h = 6$ m
Curved surface area of cylinder $= 2\pi rh$
$$= 2 \times \frac{22}{7} \times 7 \times 6 = 264 \text{ m}^2$$
Now, height of cone $= 30 - 6 = 24$ m
Slant height, $l = \sqrt{r^2 + h^2}$
$$= \sqrt{7^2 + 24^2} \text{ m} \quad [\because \text{given, } r = 7 \text{ m}]$$
$$= 25 \text{ m}$$
Curved surface area of cone $= \pi rl$
$$= \frac{22}{7} \times 7 \times 25$$
$$= 550 \text{ m}^2$$
Total area to be painted
$$= (264 + 550) \text{ m}^2 = 814 \text{ m}^2$$
The cost of painting at the rate of ₹ 3 per m^2
$$= 3 \times 814 = ₹\, 2442$$
Ans. ₹ 2442

17. **Hint** Do same as Example 22 (i) and (ii).
Ans. ₹ 158400

18. **Hint** Slant height $(l) = \sqrt{h^2 + r^2}$
Now, curved surface area of the conical tent
= Curved surface area of a cone $= \pi rl$
$\because$ Length of cloth required to make conical tent
$$= \frac{\text{Curved surface area of conical tent}}{\text{Width of the cloth}}$$
Ans. 27.5 m

19. **Hint** Volume of sphere $= \frac{2}{3} \times$ Volume of cylinder
Ans. $\frac{4}{3}\pi r^3$

20. **Hint** Here $r_1 = 1.5$ cm, $r_2 = 2.5$ cm
$\because$ Ratio $= \frac{4\pi r_2^2}{4\pi r_1^2}$
Ans. 25 : 9

21. **Hint** Volume of sphere = Volume of cone
Ans. 33 cm

22. **Hint** Volume of one lead shot (which is a sphere of radius 0.5 cm) $= \frac{4}{3}\pi\left(\frac{1}{2}\right)^3 \text{ cm}^3$
$$= \frac{\pi}{6} \text{ cm}^3$$
Volume of water in the cone = Volume of the cone of height 8 cm and radius 5 cm
$$= \left(\frac{1}{3}\pi \times 5^2 \times 8\right) \text{cm}^3$$
$$= \frac{200}{3}\pi \text{ cm}^3$$
$\therefore$ Number of lead shots dropped into the vessel
$$= \frac{\frac{1}{4} \text{ of volume of water}}{\text{Volume of one lead shot}}$$
$$= \frac{\frac{1}{4} \times \frac{200}{3}\pi}{\frac{\pi}{6}}$$
Ans. 100

23. **Hint** Volume of the hemi-spherical bowl $= \frac{2}{3}\pi r^3$
and volume of the cylindrical bottle of radius 3 cm and height 6 cm = Volume of a cylinder
$$= \pi \times (3)^2 \times 6$$
$\therefore$ Required number of bottle to empty the bowl
$$= \frac{\text{Volume of the bowl}}{\text{Volume of one bottle}}$$
Ans. 72

24. **Hint** Volume of cone = Volume of the hemisphere
Ans. 10 cm

25. **Hint** Number of bullets
$$= \frac{\text{Volume of cube}}{\text{Volume of one spherical bullet}}$$
Ans. 2541

26. **Hint** For the maximum volume of cone carved out from the hemisphere, radius of the cone should be equal radius of hemisphere.
Volume of cone $= \frac{1}{3}\pi r^2 h = \frac{1}{3}\pi r^2 (r)$
Ans. $\frac{\pi r^3}{3}$

27. **Hint** Let the rainfall be x m.
Then, volume of water on the roof
= Volume of conical vessel
$\Rightarrow \quad 22 \times 20 \times x = \frac{1}{3}\pi r^2 h$ **Ans.** 0.83 cm

28. **Hint** Let the side of a cube be x.
Then, radius of the sphere, $r = \frac{x}{2}$
$\therefore \quad$ Ratio $= \frac{\text{Volume of the cube}}{\text{Volume of the sphere}}$
Ans. $6 : \pi$

29. **Hint** Water in the hemi-spherical tank = 50 kL
$$= 50 \times 1000 \text{ L} = 50 \text{ m}^3$$
Volume of water in the hemi-spherical tank
$$V_1 = \frac{2}{3}\pi r^3$$
$\therefore$ Volume of water pumped in the hemi-spherical tank
$$= V_1 - 50$$
Ans. 668.67 m

30. **Hint** Total surface area of the wooden article
= 2 × Curved surface area of the hemisphere
+ Curved surface area of cylinder
Ans. 374 cm^2

31. Hint Capacity of container = Volume of cylinder + 2(Volume of hemisphere)

Ans. 680.17 m^3

32. Hint Volume of cylinder,

$$V_1 = \pi r^2 h$$

and volume of spherical ball,

$$V_2 = \frac{4}{3}\pi r^3$$

When spherical ball is dropped in the cylinderical beaker, then total volume = $V_1 + V_2$

$$\Rightarrow \quad \pi r^2 h_1 = V_1 + V_2$$

Increase in the level of water = $h_1 - h$

Ans. 5.9 cm

33. Hint Volume of spherical shell = Volume of right circular cylinder

Ans. 7 cm

34. Hint Circumference of base of cylinder = $2\pi r$

Surface area of cylinder whose top is open,

$$S_1 = 2\pi rh + \pi r^2 \text{ (change into dm)}$$

∴ Total cost of polishing at the rate of ₹ 10 per dm^2 = ₹ $10 \times S_1$

Ans. ₹ 402. 60

35. Hint

(i) The slant height of the cone = Radius of the given sector of a circle.

Ans. 9 cm

(ii) Circumference of base of the cone = Length of arc of given sector whose central angle is 120°

$$\Rightarrow \quad 2\pi r = \frac{\theta}{360°} \times 2\pi r_1$$

Ans. $r = 3$ cm

(iii) Let h be the height of the cone, then

$$h = \sqrt{l^2 - r^2}$$

$$\therefore \text{ Volume of the cone} = \frac{1}{3}\pi r^2 h$$

Ans. $18\pi\sqrt{2}$ cm^3

(iv) Total surface area of the cone = Area of the given sector + Area of base of the cone

$$= \frac{\theta}{360°} \times \pi (r_1)^2 + \pi r^2$$

Ans. 36π cm^2

36. Hint Total surface area of hemisphere,

$$S = \pi(3R^2 + r^2)$$

∴ Cost of silver plating = $S \times$ ₹ 0.60

Ans. ₹ 300.3

37. Hint Volume of cylinderical bucket = Volume of cone

$$\Rightarrow \quad \pi r^2 h = \frac{1}{3}\pi r_1^2 h_1$$

Also, $\quad l = \sqrt{h^2 + r_1^2}$

Ans. Radius = 36 cm and slant height = $12\sqrt{13}$ cm

38. Hint Volume of hemisphere = $\frac{2}{3}\pi r^3$

and area of floor = πr^2 **Ans.** 1386 m

39. Hint Surface area of figure = 2 × Curved surface area of hemisphere + Curved surface area of cylinder

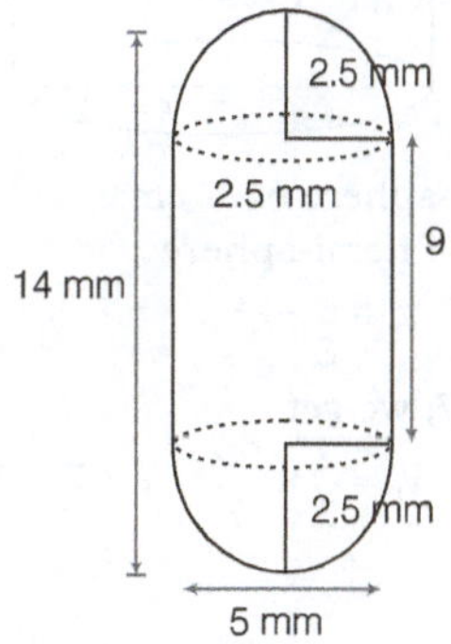

Ans. 220 mm^2

40. Hint In ΔAOC,

$$h_1 = \sqrt{5^2 - 3^2}$$

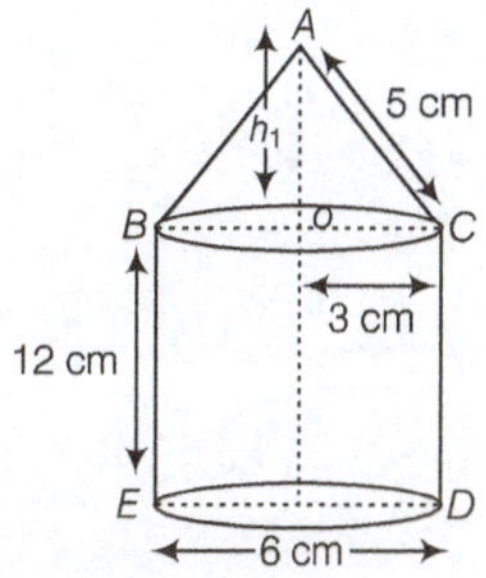

Total surface area of rocket = Curved surface area of cone + Curved surface area of cylinder

∴ Volume of rocket = Volume of cone + Volume of cylinder

Ans. 301.44 cm , 376.8 cm

41. Hint Ratio = $\frac{\text{Volume of sphere}}{\text{Volume of cylinder}}$

$$= \frac{\frac{4}{3}\pi r^3}{\pi r_1^2 h}$$

Ans. 125 : 54

42. Hint Ratio = $\frac{\text{Volume of metal } A}{\text{Volume of metal } B}$

Ans. 133 : 2

43. Hint Total area to be painted = Total surface area of cube − Base area of cube − Area of base of the hemisphere + Curved surfaced area of the hemisphere

Ans. 138.86 cm^2

44. Given,

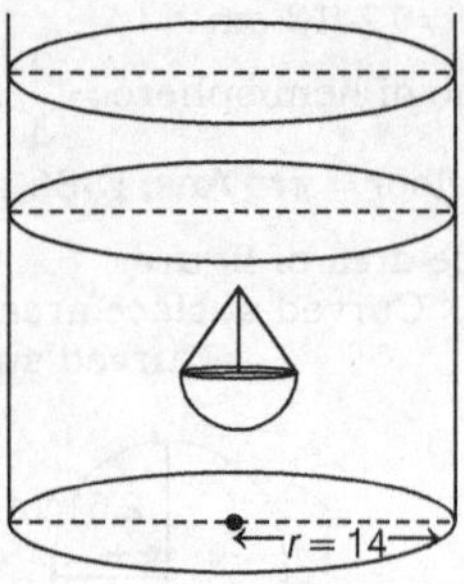

Radius of hemi-sphere $r = 7$ cm.

$\Rightarrow$ The volume of hemi-sphere

$$V_1 = \frac{2}{3}\pi r^3$$

On putting $r = 7$, we get

$$V_1 = \frac{2}{3} \times \frac{22}{7} \times 7 \times 7 \times 7 \qquad \left[\because \pi = \frac{22}{7}\right]$$

$$\Rightarrow \quad V_1 = 718.66 \text{ cm}^3$$

Now, volume of the cone

$$V_2 = \frac{1}{3}\pi r^2 h \Rightarrow V_2 = \frac{1}{3} \times \frac{22}{7} \times 7 \times 7 \times 4$$

[$\because$ Radius of hemi-sphere = Radius of cone]

[$\because$ given, cone's height (h) = 4 cm]

$$\Rightarrow \quad V_2 = \frac{22 \times 28}{3} = 205.33 \text{ cm}^3$$

$\therefore$ Total volume of solid, $V = V_1 + V_2$

$$V = 718.66 + 205.33 = 923.99 \text{ cm}^3$$

We know that the volume of water displaced is equal to the volume of the solid.

Let h cm rises water level.

The formula for the volume of a cylinder is

$$V = \pi r^2 h$$

On putting $r = 14$ (given) and $V = 923.99$, we get

$$923.99 = \frac{22}{7} \times 14 \times 14 \times h$$

$$\Rightarrow \quad h = 1.49 \text{ cm} \cong 1.5 \text{ cm}$$

Olympiad Section

Brain Teasing Questions asked in Previous Olympiads

1 A corn cob (see figure), shaped somewhat like a cone, has the radius of its broadest end as 2.1 cm and length as 20 cm. If each 1 cm^2 of the surface of the cob carries an average of four grains, then how many grains you would find on the entire cob? [Take $\pi = 22/7$]

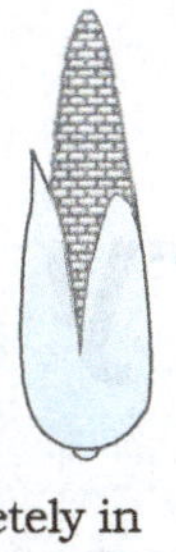

(a) 132 (b) 530 (c) 531 (d) 513

2 A sphere of radius a units is immersed completely in water contained in a right circular cone of semi-vertical angle 30°and water is drained off from the cone till its surface touches the sphere. Then, the volume of water remaining in the cone will be

(a) $\frac{5\pi}{3}a^3$ (b) $5\pi a^3$ (c) $\frac{\pi a^3}{3}$ (d) $\frac{5}{3}\pi a^2$

Directions (Q. Nos. 3-4) *A semi-circle is drawn, which is passing through the points* $A(3, 0)$, $B(0, 3)$ *and* $C(-3, 0)$. [Take $\pi = 3.14$]

3 When we rotate this figure along the side AC, then write the name of the figure formed and then the space occupied by this will be

(a) 113.40 cm^3 (b) 113.04 cm^3
(c) 114.03 cm^3 (d) 11.304 cm^3

4 When we rotate this figure along the side BO, then write the name of the figure formed and then the space occupied by this will be

(a) 56.52 cm^3 (b) 52.56 cm^3
(c) 50.52 cm^3 (d) 55.50 cm^3

5 A pen-stand made of wood is in the shape of a cuboid with four conical depressions to hold pens. The dimensions of the cuboid are 15 cm × 10 cm × 3.5 cm. The radius of each of the depressions is 0.5 cm and the depth is 1.4 cm. Then, the volume of wood in the entire stand (see the figure). [take $\pi = 22/7$]

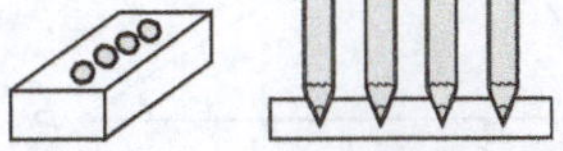

(a) 523.54 cm^3 (b) 523.45 cm^3
(c) 523 cm^3 (d) 532.45 cm^3

6 A hollow cone of radius 6 cm and height 8 cm is vertical standing at the origin, such that the vertex of the cone is at the origin. Some pipes are hanging around the circular base of the cone, such that they touch the surface of the graph paper. Then, the total surface area of the formed by the figure will be

(a) 484.98 cm^2 (b) 489.84 cm^2
(c) 948.84 cm^2 (d) None of these

7 A cone made of paper has height $3h$ and vertical angle 2α. It contains two other cones of height $2h$ and h and vertical angles 4α and 6α, respectively. Then, the ratio of the volumes of regions S and S_1 will be

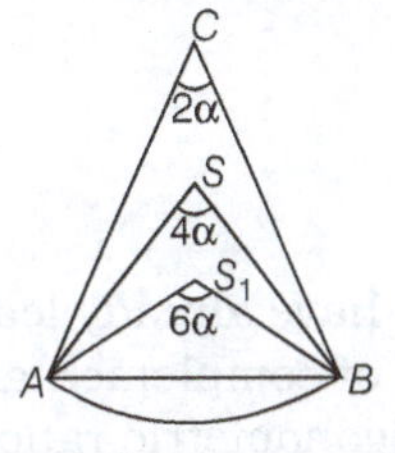

(a) $(8\tan^2\alpha - 27\tan^2 2\alpha) : (5\tan^2\alpha - \tan 3\alpha)$
(b) $(27\tan^2\alpha - 8\tan^2 2\alpha) : (8\tan^2 2\alpha - \tan^2 3\alpha)$
(c) $(25\tan^2\alpha - 7\tan^2 2\alpha) : (8\tan^2\alpha - \tan 3\alpha)$
(d) None of the above

8 A right isosceles triangle is shown below

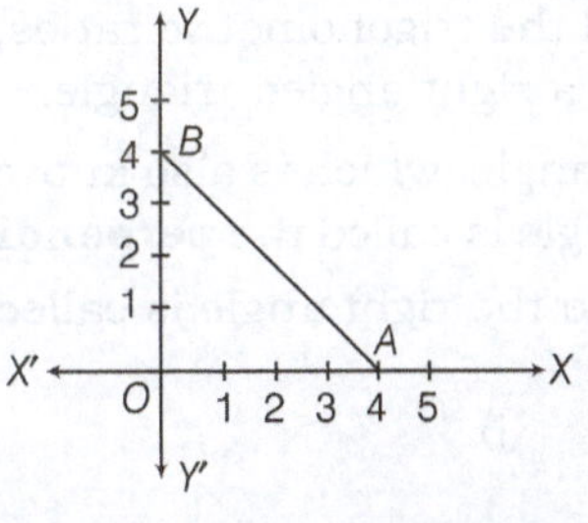

When we rotate a right angled triangle about the vertex O, then write the name of the formed figure and then the curved surface area of the formed figure will be

(a) 284.15 sq units (b) 254.15 sq units
(c) 215.84 sq units (d) 215.54 sq units

Answers

1. (c) **2.** (a) **3.** (b) **4.** (a) **5.** (a) **6.** (b) **7.** (b) **8.** (a)

* *These questions may or may not be asked in the examination, have been given just for additional practice required for olympiads Scholarship Exams etc. For detailed explanations refer Page No. 496.*

CHAPTER 18

Trigonometry Identities

SYLLABUS

- **Using Identities to solve/prove simple algebraic trigonometric expressions**

$$\sin^2 A + \cos^2 A = 1$$
$$1 + \tan^2 A = \sec^2 A$$
$$1 + \cot^2 A = \text{cosec}^2 A; \text{ for all } 0 \leq A \leq 90^\circ$$

In earlier class, we have already learnt about the various trigonometric ratios and their relations as well as trigonometric ratio of complementary angles. Now, we will establish some identities involving trigonometric ratios as well as trigonometric ratios of complementary angles.

Trigonometric Ratios

The ratios of the sides of a right angled triangle with respect to its acute angles, are called trigonometric ratios. Trigonometric ratios are also called **T-ratios**.

To understand the trigonometric ratios, first of all we will understand the concept of perpendicular, base and hypotenuse in a right angled triangle.

For any acute angle (which is also known as the **angle of reference**) in a right angled triangle, the side opposite to the acute angle is called the **perpendicular** (P), the side adjacent to this acute angle is called the **base** (B) and side opposite to the right angle is called the **hypotenuse** (H).

(i)

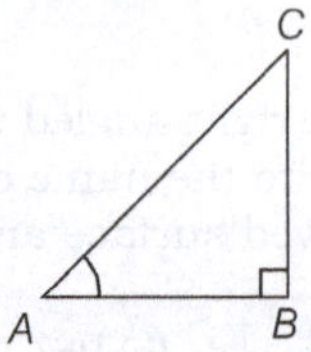

Angle of reference = $\angle A$
Perpendicular = BC
Base = AB
Hypotenuse = AC

(ii)

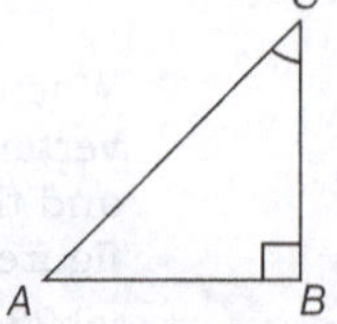

Angle of reference = $\angle C$
Perpendicular = AB
Base = BC
Hypotenuse = AC

(iii)

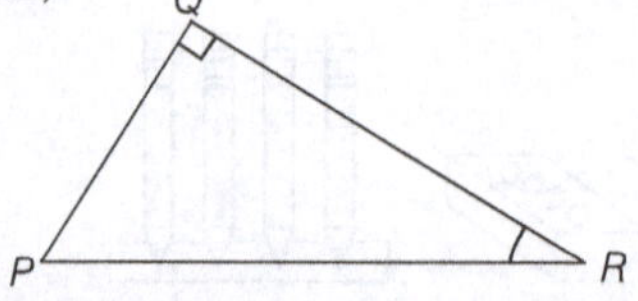

Angle of reference = $\angle R$
perpendicular = PQ
Base = QR
Hypotenuse = PR

Trigonometric ratios of $\angle A$ in right angled ΔABC are defined as follows

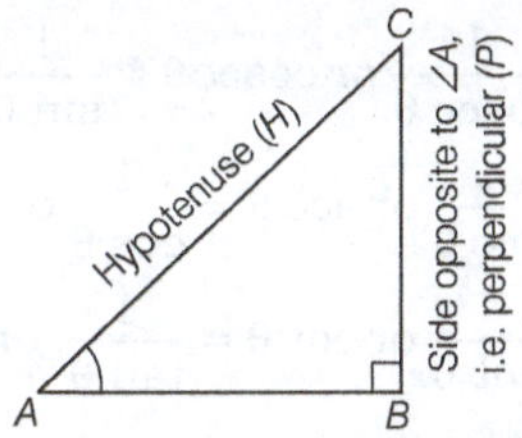

Side adjacent to $\angle A$, i.e. base (B)

(i) sine of $\angle A$ or $\sin A = \dfrac{\text{Side opposite to } \angle A}{\text{Hypotenuse}} = \dfrac{P}{H} = \dfrac{BC}{AC}$

(ii) cosine of $\angle A$ or $\cos A = \dfrac{\text{Side adjacent to } \angle A}{\text{Hypotenuse}} = \dfrac{B}{H} = \dfrac{AB}{AC}$

(iii) tangent of $\angle A$ or $\tan A = \dfrac{\text{Side opposite to } \angle A}{\text{Side adjacent to } \angle A} = \dfrac{P}{B} = \dfrac{BC}{AB}$

(iv) cosecant of $\angle A$ or cosec A

$= \dfrac{\text{Hypotenuse}}{\text{Side opposite to } \angle A} = \dfrac{H}{P} = \dfrac{AC}{BC}$

(v) secant of $\angle A$ or $\sec A = \dfrac{\text{Hypotenuse}}{\text{Side adjacent to } \angle A} = \dfrac{H}{B} = \dfrac{AC}{AB}$

(vi) cotangent of $\angle A$ or $\cot A = \dfrac{\text{Side adjacent to } \angle A}{\text{Side opposite to } \angle A} = \dfrac{B}{P} = \dfrac{AB}{BC}$

Similarly, trigonometric ratios of $\angle C$ in right angled ΔABC are as follows:

(i) $\sin C = \dfrac{AB}{AC}$ (ii) $\cos C = \dfrac{BC}{AC}$

(iii) $\tan C = \dfrac{AB}{BC}$ (iv) $\operatorname{cosec} C = \dfrac{AC}{AB}$

(v) $\sec C = \dfrac{AC}{BC}$ (vi) $\cot C = \dfrac{BC}{AB}$

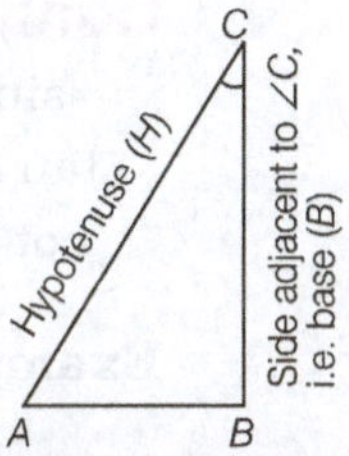

Side opposite to $\angle C$, i.e. perpendicular (P)

Note The symbol sin A is used as an abbreviation for 'the sine of $\angle A$' sin A is not the product of 'sin' and 'A'. 'sin' separated from 'A' has no meaning. This interpretation follows for other trigonometric ratios also.

A Popular Technique to Remember T-Ratios

sin θ↓	cos θ↓	tan θ↓
Pandit (P)	Badari (B)	Prasad (P)
Har (H)	Har (H)	Bholay (B)
cosec θ↑	sec θ↑	cot θ↑

Then, $\sin\theta = \dfrac{P}{H}$, $\cos\theta = \dfrac{B}{H}$, $\tan\theta = \dfrac{P}{B}$,

$\operatorname{cosec}\theta = \dfrac{H}{P}$, $\sec\theta = \dfrac{H}{B}$, $\cot\theta = \dfrac{B}{P}$

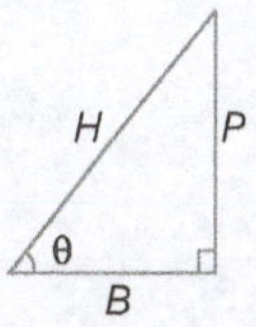

where, P is perpendicular, B is base and H is hypotenuse.

Example 1. If $\tan A = \dfrac{4}{3}$, then find the other trigonometric ratios of $\angle A$.

Sol. First, draw a ΔABC, right angled at B.

Given, $\tan A = \dfrac{4}{3} \Rightarrow \dfrac{\text{Perpendicular}}{\text{Base}} = \dfrac{4}{3}$

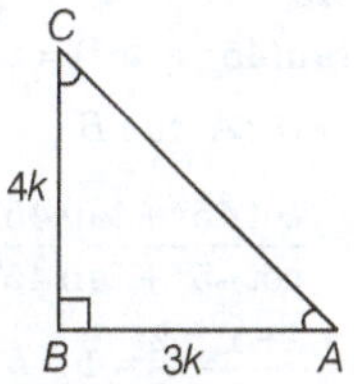

$\Rightarrow \quad \dfrac{BC}{AB} = \dfrac{4}{3} = k$ (say)

[where, k is any positive integer]

$\therefore \quad BC = 4k$ and $AB = 3k$

Using Pythagoras theorem in ΔABC, we have

$AC^2 = BC^2 + AB^2$

$\Rightarrow \quad AC^2 = (4k)^2 + (3k)^2 = 16k^2 + 9k^2$

$\Rightarrow \quad AC^2 = 25k^2 \Rightarrow AC = \sqrt{25k^2} = 5k$

[taking positive square root as side cannot be negative]

Now, $\sin A = \dfrac{BC}{AC} = \dfrac{4k}{5k} = \dfrac{4}{5}$,

$\cos A = \dfrac{AB}{AC} = \dfrac{3k}{5k} = \dfrac{3}{5}$

$\cot A = \dfrac{AB}{BC} = \dfrac{3k}{4k} = \dfrac{3}{4}$,

$\operatorname{cosec} A = \dfrac{AC}{BC} = \dfrac{5k}{4k} = \dfrac{5}{4}$

and $\sec A = \dfrac{AC}{AB} = \dfrac{5k}{3k} = \dfrac{5}{3}$

Example 2. If $\tan(A + B) = 1$, then find

(i) value of $(A + B)$

(ii) value of A, when B is $30°$

(iii) value of $\sin(A + B)$

Sol.

(i) $\tan(A + B) = 1$

$\Rightarrow \tan(A + B) = \tan 45°$

$\therefore \quad A + B = 45°$

(ii) $A + B = 45°$ ...(i)

$\Rightarrow \quad \angle B = 30°$ (given)

$\therefore \quad A + 30° = 45°$ [from Eq. (i)]

$\Rightarrow \quad A = 45° - 30°$

$\Rightarrow \quad A = 15°$

(iii) $A + B = 45°$

$\therefore \quad \sin(45°) = \dfrac{1}{\sqrt{2}}$

Example 3. If $\text{cosec}\, B = \sec A$, then find

(i) value of $\tan(A+B)$

(ii) Prove that $\dfrac{\cot A + \tan B}{\cot B + \tan A} = \cot A \tan B$

Sol. $\text{cosec}\, B = \sec A$

$A = B$ [$\because \text{cosec}\,\theta$ and $\sec\theta$ have equal value at $\theta = 45°$]

$\therefore \quad A = B = 45°$

(i) $\tan(A+B) = \tan(45° + 45°) = \tan 90° = \infty$

(ii) $\dfrac{\cot A + \tan B}{\cot B + \tan A} = \cot A \cdot \tan B$

$$\text{LHS} = \frac{\cot 45° + \tan 45°}{\cot 45° + \tan 45°} \quad [\because A = B = 45°]$$

$$= \frac{1+1}{1+1} = \frac{2}{2} = 1 \quad [\because \tan 45° = \cot 45° = 1]$$

$$\text{RHS} = \cot A \cdot \tan B = \cot 45° \tan 45° = 1 \times 1 = 1$$

$\text{LHS} = \text{RHS}$ **Hence proved.**

Example 4. If θ is an acute angle and $3\sin\theta = 4\cos\theta$, then find the value of $4\sin^2\theta - 3\cos^2\theta + 2$.

Sol. Given, equation is $3\sin\theta = 4\cos\theta$

$$\Rightarrow \quad \frac{\sin\theta}{\cos\theta} = \frac{4}{3} \Rightarrow \tan\theta = \frac{4}{3} \quad \text{...(i)}$$

Now, draw a right angled ΔABC, such that $\angle B = 90°$ and let $\angle A = \theta$.

From Eq. (i), we get

$$\tan\theta = \frac{4}{3} = \frac{\text{Perpendicular}}{\text{Base}} = \frac{BC}{AB}$$

$\therefore$ $BC = 4k$ and $AB = 3k$.

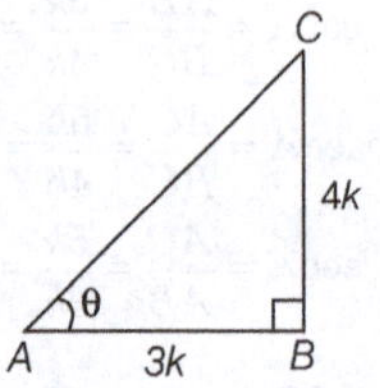

Using Pythagoras theorem, we have

$$AC^2 = AB^2 + BC^2$$

$$\Rightarrow \quad AC^2 = (3k)^2 + (4k)^2 = 9k^2 + 16k^2$$

$$\Rightarrow \quad AC^2 = 25k^2$$

$$\therefore \quad AC = 5k \quad \text{[taking positive square root]}$$

Now, $\sin\theta = \dfrac{\text{Perpendicular}}{\text{Hypotenuse}} = \dfrac{BC}{CA} = \dfrac{4k}{5k} = \dfrac{4}{5}$

and $\cos\theta = \dfrac{\text{Base}}{\text{Hypotenuse}} = \dfrac{AB}{CA} = \dfrac{3k}{5k} = \dfrac{3}{5}$

$$\therefore \quad 4\sin^2\theta - 3\cos^2\theta + 2 = 4\left(\frac{4}{5}\right)^2 - 3\left(\frac{3}{5}\right)^2 + 2$$

$$= 4\left(\frac{16}{25}\right) - 3\left(\frac{9}{25}\right) + 2$$

$$= \frac{64}{25} - \frac{27}{25} + 2$$

$$= \frac{64 - 27 + 50}{25} = \frac{87}{25} = 3\frac{12}{25}$$

Relations between Trigonometric Ratios

Reciprocal Relation

(i) $\sin\theta = \dfrac{1}{\text{cosec}\,\theta}$ or $\text{cosec}\,\theta = \dfrac{1}{\sin\theta}$ or $\sin\theta \cdot \text{cosec}\,\theta = 1$

(ii) $\cos\theta = \dfrac{1}{\sec\theta}$ or $\sec\theta = \dfrac{1}{\cos\theta}$ or $\cos\theta \cdot \sec\theta = 1$

(iii) $\tan\theta = \dfrac{1}{\cot\theta}$ or $\cot\theta = \dfrac{1}{\tan\theta}$ or $\tan\theta \cdot \cot\theta = 1$

Quotient Relation

(i) $\tan\theta = \dfrac{AB}{BC} = \dfrac{AB/AC}{BC/AC} = \dfrac{\sin\theta}{\cos\theta}$

(ii) $\cot\theta = \dfrac{BC}{AB} = \dfrac{BC/AC}{AB/AC} = \dfrac{\cos\theta}{\sin\theta}$

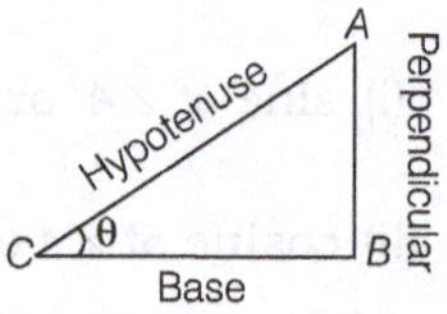

Example 5. Prove that $\dfrac{\sec A - 1}{\sec A + 1} = \dfrac{1 - \cos A}{1 + \cos A}$.

Sol. $\text{LHS} = \dfrac{\sec A - 1}{\sec A + 1} = \dfrac{(1/\cos A) - 1}{(1/\cos A) + 1}$ $\left[\because \sec\theta = \dfrac{1}{\cos\theta}\right]$

$$= \frac{1 - \cos A}{\cos A} \times \frac{\cos A}{1 + \cos A}$$

$$= \frac{1 - \cos A}{1 + \cos A} = \text{RHS}$$

Hence proved.

Trigonometric Ratios of Complementary Angles

$$\sin(90° - \theta) = \cos\theta, \quad \cos(90° - \theta) = \sin\theta$$

$$\tan(90° - \theta) = \cot\theta, \quad \text{cosec}(90° - \theta) = \sec\theta$$

$$\cot(90° - \theta) = \tan\theta, \quad \sec(90° - \theta) = \text{cosec}\,\theta$$

Example 6. Evaluate $\dfrac{\sin 70°}{\cos 20°} + \dfrac{\text{cosec}\, 36°}{\sec 54°} - \dfrac{2\cos 43° \ \text{cosec}\, 47°}{\tan 10° \tan 40° \tan 50° \tan 80°}$.

Sol. $\dfrac{\sin 70°}{\cos 20°} + \dfrac{\text{cosec}\, 36°}{\sec 54°} - \dfrac{2\cos 43° \ \text{cosec}\, 47°}{\tan 10° \tan 40° \tan 50° \tan 80°}$

$$= \frac{\sin(90° - 20°)}{\cos 20°} + \frac{\text{cosec}(90° - 54°)}{\sec 54°} - \frac{2\cos 43° \ \text{cosec}(90° - 43°)}{\tan(90° - 80°)\tan(90° - 50°)\tan 50° \tan 80°}$$

$$= \frac{\cos 20°}{\cos 20°} + \frac{\sec 54°}{\sec 54°} - \frac{2\cos 43° \sec 43°}{\cot 80° \cot 50° \tan 50° \tan 80°}$$

$\left[\because \sin(90° - \theta) = \cos\theta, \ \text{cosec}(90° - \theta) = \sec\theta \text{ and } \tan(90° - \theta) = \cot\theta\right]$

$$= 1 + 1 - \frac{2\cos 43° \cdot \dfrac{1}{\cos 43°}}{\dfrac{1}{\tan 80°} \cdot \tan 80° \cdot \dfrac{1}{\tan 50°} \cdot \tan 50°}$$

$\left[\because \tan\theta = \dfrac{1}{\cot\theta} \text{ and } \sec\theta = \dfrac{1}{\cos\theta}\right]$

$$= 2 - \frac{2 \cdot 1}{1 \cdot 1} = 2 - 2 = 0$$

Values of Trigonometric Ratios for Some Specific Angles

Angles	0° or 0	30° or $\frac{\pi}{6}$	45° or $\frac{\pi}{4}$	60° or $\frac{\pi}{3}$	90° or $\frac{\pi}{2}$
$\sin\theta$	0	1/2	$\frac{1}{\sqrt{2}}$	$\frac{\sqrt{3}}{2}$	1
$\cos\theta$	1	$\sqrt{3}/2$	$1/\sqrt{2}$	1/2	0
$\tan\theta$	0	$1/\sqrt{3}$	1	$\sqrt{3}$	∞
$\text{cosec}\,\theta$	∞	2	$\sqrt{2}$	$\frac{2}{\sqrt{3}}$	1
$\sec\theta$	1	$2/\sqrt{3}$	$\sqrt{2}$	2	∞
$\cot\theta$	∞	$\sqrt{3}$	1	$1/\sqrt{3}$	0

Here, ∞ = Undefined [not defined]

Example 7. Find the value of $\dfrac{\sin 30° + \tan 45° - \text{cosec}\,60°}{\sec 30° + \cos 60° + \cot 45°}$.

Sol. We have, $\dfrac{\sin 30° + \tan 45° - \text{cosec}\,60°}{\sec 30° + \cos 60° + \cot 45°}$

$$= \frac{\frac{1}{2} + 1 - \frac{2}{\sqrt{3}}}{\frac{2}{\sqrt{3}} + \frac{1}{2} + 1} = \frac{\frac{\sqrt{3} + 2\sqrt{3} - 4}{2\sqrt{3}}}{\frac{4 + \sqrt{3} + 2\sqrt{3}}{2\sqrt{3}}}$$

$\left[\because \sin 30° = \frac{1}{2}, \tan 45° = 1, \text{cosec}\,60° = \frac{2}{\sqrt{3}}, \sec 30° = \frac{2}{\sqrt{3}}, \cos 60° = \frac{1}{2} \text{ and } \cot 45° = 1\right]$

$$= \frac{3\sqrt{3} - 4}{4 + 3\sqrt{3}} = \frac{3\sqrt{3} - 4}{4 + 3\sqrt{3}} \times \frac{4 - 3\sqrt{3}}{4 - 3\sqrt{3}}$$

[by rationalising the denominator]

$$= \frac{12\sqrt{3} - 27 - 16 + 12\sqrt{3}}{(4)^2 - (3\sqrt{3})^2} \quad [\because (a+b)(a-b) = a^2 - b^2]$$

$$= \frac{24\sqrt{3} - 43}{16 - 27} = \frac{-(43 - 24\sqrt{3})}{-11}$$

$$= \frac{43 - 24\sqrt{3}}{11}$$

Example 8. If $\tan(3x + 30°) = 1$, then find the value of x.

Sol. We have, $\tan(3x + 30°) = 1$

$\Rightarrow \quad \tan(3x + 30°) = \tan 45° \quad [\because \tan 45° = 1]$

$\Rightarrow \quad 3x + 30° = 45°$

$\Rightarrow \quad 3x = 45° - 30° = 15° \Rightarrow x = 5°$

Exercise 18.1

1. If $\sin A = \frac{12}{13}$, then find the other trigonometric ratio of $\angle A$.
2. In the following figure, find $\tan P - \cot R$.

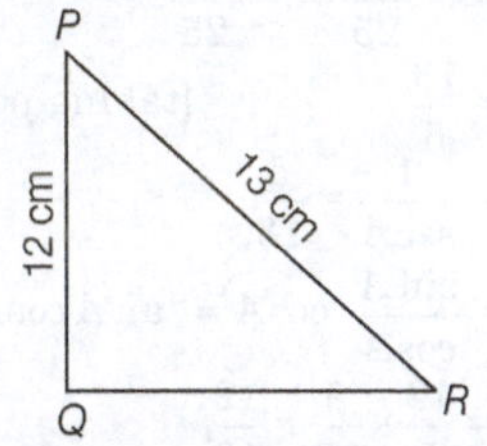

3. In a ΔPQR, right angled at Q, $PR + QR = 25$ cm and $PQ = 5$ cm. Determine the values of $\sin P$, $\cos P$ and $\tan P$.
4. If $m \cot A = n$, then find the value of $\dfrac{m \sin A - n \cos A}{n \cos A + m \sin A}$.
5. If $\angle A = \angle B = 45°$, then verify that $\sin(A + B) = \sin A \cos B + \cos A \sin B$.
6. Find the value of $\dfrac{5\cos^2 60° + 4\sec^2 30° - \tan^2 45°}{\sin^2 30° + \cos^2 30°}$.
7. If $A = 15°$, then find the value of $\dfrac{\sin 3A - 2\cos 4A}{\cos 3A + 2\sin 4A}$.
8. If A and B are acute angles such that $\sin A = \cos B$, prove that $(A + B) = 90°$.
9. If $\sin 3A = \cos(A - 26°)$, where $3A$ is an acute angle, then find the value of A.
10. If $\sec 5A = \text{cosec}(A + 30°)$, then find A.

Trigonometric Identities

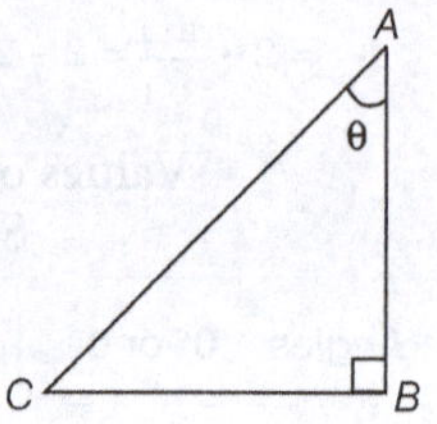

We know that an equation is called **identity** when it is true for all values of the variables involved. Similarly, an equation involving trigonometric ratios of an angle is called a trigonometric identity, if it is true for all values of the angle(s) involved. For any acute angle θ, we have three identities

(i) $\sin^2\theta + \cos^2\theta = 1$ (ii) $1 + \tan^2\theta = \sec^2\theta$ (iii) $\cot^2\theta + 1 = \text{cosec}^2\theta$

Note $\sin^2\theta = (\sin\theta)^2$ but $\sin\theta^2 \neq (\sin\theta)^2$. The same is true for all other trigonometric ratios.

Conversion of Trigonometric Ratios in Terms of Other Trigonometric Ratios

	$\sin\theta$	$\cos\theta$	$\tan\theta$	$\cot\theta$	$\sec\theta$	$\text{cosec}\,\theta$
$\sin\theta$	$\sin\theta$	$\sqrt{1-\cos^2\theta}$	$\frac{\tan\theta}{\sqrt{1+\tan^2\theta}}$	$\frac{1}{\sqrt{1+\cot^2\theta}}$	$\frac{\sqrt{\sec^2\theta-1}}{\sec\theta}$	$\frac{1}{\text{cosec}\,\theta}$
$\cos\theta$	$\sqrt{1-\sin^2\theta}$	$\cos\theta$	$\frac{1}{\sqrt{1+\tan^2\theta}}$	$\frac{\cot\theta}{\sqrt{1+\cot^2\theta}}$	$\frac{1}{\sec\theta}$	$\frac{\sqrt{\text{cosec}^2\theta-1}}{\text{cosec}\,\theta}$
$\tan\theta$	$\frac{\sin\theta}{\sqrt{1-\sin^2\theta}}$	$\frac{\sqrt{1-\cos^2\theta}}{\cos\theta}$	$\tan\theta$	$\frac{1}{\cot\theta}$	$\sqrt{\sec^2\theta-1}$	$\frac{1}{\sqrt{\text{cosec}^2\theta-1}}$
$\cot\theta$	$\frac{\sqrt{1-\sin^2\theta}}{\sin\theta}$	$\frac{\cos\theta}{\sqrt{1-\cos^2\theta}}$	$\frac{1}{\tan\theta}$	$\cot\theta$	$\frac{1}{\sqrt{\sec^2\theta-1}}$	$\sqrt{\text{cosec}^2\theta-1}$
$\sec\theta$	$\frac{1}{\sqrt{1-\sin^2\theta}}$	$\frac{1}{\cos\theta}$	$\sqrt{1+\tan^2\theta}$	$\frac{\sqrt{1+\cot^2\theta}}{\cot\theta}$	$\sec\theta$	$\frac{\text{cosec}\,\theta}{\sqrt{\text{cosec}^2\theta-1}}$
$\text{cosec}\,\theta$	$\frac{1}{\sin\theta}$	$\frac{1}{\sqrt{1-\cos^2\theta}}$	$\frac{\sqrt{1+\tan^2\theta}}{\tan\theta}$	$\sqrt{1+\cot^2\theta}$	$\frac{\sec\theta}{\sqrt{\sec^2\theta-1}}$	$\text{cosec}\,\theta$

Example 9. Write all the other trigonometric ratios of $\angle A$ in terms of $\sec A$.

Sol.

(i) We know that $\sin^2 A + \cos^2 A = 1$

$\Rightarrow \quad \sin^2 A = 1 - \cos^2 A$

$\Rightarrow \quad \sin A = \sqrt{1-\cos^2 A}$ [taking positive square root]

$= \sqrt{1 - \frac{1}{\sec^2 A}}$ $\left[\because \cos\theta = \frac{1}{\sec\theta}\right]$

$= \sqrt{\frac{\sec^2 A - 1}{\sec^2 A}} = \frac{\sqrt{\sec^2 A - 1}}{\sec A}$

(ii) $\cos A = \frac{1}{\sec A}$

(iii) We know that, $\sec^2 A - \tan^2 A = 1$

$\Rightarrow \quad \tan^2 A = \sec^2 A - 1$

$\therefore \quad \tan A = \sqrt{\sec^2 A - 1}$

[taking positive square root]

(iv) $\cot A = \frac{1}{\tan A} = \frac{1}{\sqrt{\sec^2 A - 1}}$ [using part (iii)]

(v) $\text{cosec}\, A = \frac{1}{\sin A} = \frac{\sec A}{\sqrt{\sec^2 A - 1}}$ [using part (i)]

Example 10. If A is an acute angle and $\tan A = 12/5$, then, find all other trigonometric ratios of $\angle A$ using trigonometric identities.

Sol. Given, $\tan A = \frac{12}{5} \Rightarrow \cot A = \frac{1}{\tan A} = \frac{5}{12}$

Now, $\sec^2 A = 1 + \tan^2 A = 1 + \left(\frac{12}{5}\right)^2$

$= \frac{25+144}{25} = \frac{169}{25}$

$\Rightarrow \quad \sec A = \frac{13}{5}$ [taking positive square root]

$\therefore \quad \cos A = \frac{1}{\sec A} = \frac{5}{13},$

$\sin A = \frac{\sin A}{\cos A} \cdot \cos A = \tan A \cos A$

$= \frac{12}{5} \times \frac{5}{13} = \frac{12}{13},$

$\text{cosec}\, A = \frac{1}{\sin A} = \frac{13}{12}$

Hence, $\sin A = \frac{12}{13}$, $\cos A = \frac{5}{13}$, $\cot A = \frac{5}{12}$,

$\sec A = \frac{13}{5}$ and $\text{cosec}\, A = \frac{13}{12}$.

Example 11. Evaluate the following.

(i) Prove the following identity:

$(\sin^2\theta - 1)(\tan^2\theta + 1) + 1 = 0$ **[ICSE 2023]**

(ii) $(1 + \tan\theta + \sec\theta)(1 + \cot\theta - \text{cosec}\,\theta)$

(iii) $(\sec A + \tan A)(1 - \sin A)$ **[ICSE 2018]**

Sol.

(i) LHS $= (\sin^2\theta - 1)(\tan^2\theta + 1) + 1$

By using Trigonometric identities, we have

$\sec^2\theta - \tan^2\theta = 1$ and $\sin^2\theta + \cos^2\theta = 1$

$\Rightarrow \quad \sec^2\theta = 1 + \tan^2\theta \quad$ ...(i)

and $\quad -\cos^2\theta = \sin^2\theta - 1 \quad$ ...(ii)

$$\text{LHS} = (\sin^2\theta - 1)(\tan^2\theta + 1) + 1$$
$$= -\cos^2\theta \times \sec^2\theta + 1$$
$$= -\cos^2\theta \times \frac{1}{\cos^2\theta} + 1$$
$$= -1 + 1 = 0 = \text{RHS}$$

(ii) We have, $(1 + \tan\theta + \sec\theta)(1 + \cot\theta - \csc\theta)$

$$= \left(1 + \frac{\sin\theta}{\cos\theta} + \frac{1}{\cos\theta}\right)\left(1 + \frac{\cos\theta}{\sin\theta} - \frac{1}{\sin\theta}\right)$$
$$\left[\because \tan A = \frac{\sin A}{\cos A}, \sec A = \frac{1}{\cos A}, \cot A = \frac{\cos A}{\sin A} \text{ and } \operatorname{cosec} A = \frac{1}{\sin A}\right]$$
$$= \left[\frac{(\cos\theta + \sin\theta) + 1}{\cos\theta}\right] \times \left[\frac{(\sin\theta + \cos\theta) - 1}{\sin\theta}\right]$$
$$= \frac{(\cos\theta + \sin\theta)^2 - 1^2}{\cos\theta\sin\theta} \quad [\because (a+b)(a-b) = a^2 - b^2]$$
$$= \frac{\cos^2\theta + \sin^2\theta + 2\cos\theta\sin\theta - 1}{\cos\theta\sin\theta} \quad [\because (a+b)^2 = a^2 + b^2 + 2ab]$$
$$= \frac{1 + 2\cos\theta\sin\theta - 1}{\cos\theta\sin\theta} \quad [\because \cos^2 A + \sin^2 A = 1]$$
$$= \frac{2\cos\theta\sin\theta}{\cos\theta\sin\theta} = 2$$

(iii) We have, $(\sec A + \tan A)(1 - \sin A)$

$$= \left(\frac{1}{\cos A} + \frac{\sin A}{\cos A}\right)(1 - \sin A) \quad \left[\because \sec\theta = \frac{1}{\cos\theta} \text{ and } \tan\theta = \frac{\sin\theta}{\cos\theta}\right]$$
$$= \frac{(1 + \sin A)(1 - \sin A)}{\cos A} = \frac{1 - \sin^2 A}{\cos A} \quad [\because (a+b)(a-b) = a^2 - b^2]$$
$$= \frac{\cos^2 A}{\cos A} = \cos A \quad [\because \sin^2\theta + \cos^2\theta = 1 \Rightarrow \cos^2\theta = 1 - \sin^2\theta]$$

Example 12. Prove that $\sqrt{\dfrac{\operatorname{cosec} A - 1}{\operatorname{cosec} A + 1}} + \sqrt{\dfrac{\operatorname{cosec} A + 1}{\operatorname{cosec} A - 1}} = 2\sec A.$

Sol. LHS $= \sqrt{\dfrac{\operatorname{cosec} A - 1}{\operatorname{cosec} A + 1}} + \sqrt{\dfrac{\operatorname{cosec} A + 1}{\operatorname{cosec} A - 1}}$

$$= \frac{(\sqrt{\operatorname{cosec} A - 1})(\sqrt{\operatorname{cosec} A - 1}) + (\sqrt{\operatorname{cosec} A + 1})(\sqrt{\operatorname{cosec} A + 1})}{(\sqrt{\operatorname{cosec} A + 1})(\sqrt{\operatorname{cosec} A - 1})}$$
$$= \frac{(\sqrt{(\operatorname{cosec} A - 1})^2 + (\sqrt{\operatorname{cosec} A + 1})^2}{\sqrt{(\operatorname{cosec} A + 1)(\operatorname{cosec} A - 1)}}$$
$$= \frac{(\operatorname{cosec} A - 1) + (\operatorname{cosec} A + 1)}{\sqrt{\operatorname{cosec}^2 A - 1}} \quad [\because (a+b)(a-b) = a^2 - b^2]$$
$$= \frac{2\operatorname{cosec} A}{\sqrt{\cot^2 A}} \quad [\because \operatorname{cosec}^2\theta = 1 + \cot^2\theta \Rightarrow \operatorname{cosec}^2\theta - 1 = \cot^2\theta]$$
$$= \frac{2\operatorname{cosec} A}{\cot A} = \frac{2}{\sin A} \times \frac{\sin A}{\cos A} \quad \left[\because \operatorname{cosec}\theta = \frac{1}{\sin\theta} \text{ and } \cot\theta = \frac{\cos\theta}{\sin\theta}\right]$$
$$= \frac{2}{\cos A} = 2\sec A \quad \left[\because \frac{1}{\cos\theta} = \sec\theta\right]$$
$$= \text{RHS}$$

Hence proved.

Example 13. Prove that

$$\frac{\sin A + \cos A}{\sin A - \cos A} + \frac{\sin A - \cos A}{\sin A + \cos A} = \frac{2}{\sin^2 A - \cos^2 A}.$$

Sol. LHS $= \dfrac{\sin A + \cos A}{\sin A - \cos A} + \dfrac{\sin A - \cos A}{\sin A + \cos A}$

$$= \frac{(\sin A + \cos A)^2 + (\sin A - \cos A)^2}{(\sin A - \cos A)(\sin A + \cos A)}$$
$$= \frac{[\sin^2 A + 2\sin A\cos A + \cos^2 A + \sin^2 A - 2\sin A\cos A + \cos^2 A]}{\sin^2 A - \cos^2 A}$$
$$[\because (a \pm b)^2 = a^2 \pm 2ab + b^2 \text{ and } (a-b)(a+b) = a^2 - b^2]$$
$$= \frac{2\sin^2 A + 2\cos^2 A}{\sin^2 A - \cos^2 A} = \frac{2(\sin^2 A + \cos^2 A)}{\sin^2 A - \cos^2 A}$$
$$= \frac{2}{\sin^2 A - \cos^2 A} \quad [\because \sin^2\theta + \cos^2\theta = 1]$$
$$= \text{RHS}$$

Hence proved.

Example 14. Prove that $\dfrac{\sin\theta - \cos\theta + 1}{\sin\theta + \cos\theta - 1} = \dfrac{1}{\sec\theta - \tan\theta}$, using the identity $\sec^2\theta = 1 + \tan^2\theta$.

Sol. LHS $= \dfrac{\sin\theta - \cos\theta + 1}{\sin\theta + \cos\theta - 1} = \dfrac{\dfrac{\sin\theta}{\cos\theta} - \dfrac{\cos\theta}{\cos\theta} + \dfrac{1}{\cos\theta}}{\dfrac{\sin\theta}{\cos\theta} + \dfrac{\cos\theta}{\cos\theta} - \dfrac{1}{\cos\theta}}$

[dividing numerator and denominator by $\cos\theta$]

$$= \frac{\tan\theta - 1 + \sec\theta}{\tan\theta + 1 - \sec\theta} \quad \left[\because \tan A = \frac{\sin A}{\cos A} \text{ and } \frac{1}{\cos A} = \sec A\right]$$
$$= \frac{(\tan\theta + \sec\theta) - 1}{(\tan\theta - \sec\theta) + 1} = \frac{[(\tan\theta + \sec\theta) - 1][\tan\theta - \sec\theta]}{[(\tan\theta - \sec\theta) + 1][\tan\theta - \sec\theta]}$$

[multiplying and dividing by $(\tan\theta - \sec\theta)$]

$$= \frac{(\tan\theta + \sec\theta)(\tan\theta - \sec\theta) - (\tan\theta - \sec\theta)}{(\tan\theta - \sec\theta + 1)(\tan\theta - \sec\theta)}$$
$$= \frac{(\tan^2\theta - \sec^2\theta) - (\tan\theta - \sec\theta)}{(\tan\theta - \sec\theta + 1)(\tan\theta - \sec\theta)} \quad [\because (a+b)(a-b) = a^2 - b^2]$$
$$= \frac{-1 - \tan\theta + \sec\theta}{(\tan\theta - \sec\theta + 1)(\tan\theta - \sec\theta)} \quad [\because \tan^2 A - \sec^2 A = -1]$$
$$= \frac{-(\tan\theta - \sec\theta + 1)}{(\tan\theta - \sec\theta + 1)(\tan\theta - \sec\theta)}$$
$$= \frac{-1}{\tan\theta - \sec\theta} = \frac{1}{\sec\theta - \tan\theta} = \text{RHS}$$

Hence proved.

Example 15. Show that $\sqrt{\dfrac{1-\cos A}{1+\cos A}} = \dfrac{\sin A}{1+\cos A}$. **[ICSE 2020, 2013]**

Sol. LHS $= \sqrt{\dfrac{1-\cos A}{1+\cos A}} \times \sqrt{\dfrac{1+\cos A}{1+\cos A}}$

[multiplying numerator and denominator by $\sqrt{1+\cos A}$]

$= \sqrt{\dfrac{(1-\cos A)(1+\cos A)}{(1+\cos A)^2}} = \dfrac{\sqrt{1^2-\cos^2 A}}{1+\cos A}$ $[\because (a-b)(a+b) = a^2 - b^2]$

$= \dfrac{\sqrt{\sin^2 A}}{1+\cos A}$ $[\because \sin^2\theta + \cos^2\theta = 1 \Rightarrow \sin^2\theta = 1-\cos^2\theta]$

$= \dfrac{\sin A}{1+\cos A} = \text{RHS}$

Example 16. Prove the following identities.

(i) $\sqrt{\sec^2\theta + \text{cosec}^2\theta} = \tan\theta + \cot\theta$ **[ICSE 2018]**

(ii) $\sec A(1-\sin A)(\sec A + \tan A) = 1$

Sol.

(i) LHS $= \sqrt{\sec^2\theta + \text{cosec}^2\theta}$

$= \sqrt{1+\tan^2\theta + 1 + \cot^2\theta}$

$[\because 1+\tan^2 A = \sec^2 A \text{ and } 1+\cot^2 A = \text{cosec}^2 A]$

$= \sqrt{\tan^2\theta + \cot^2\theta + 2}$

$= \sqrt{\tan^2\theta + \cot^2\theta + 2\tan\theta\cot\theta}$ $[\because \tan A \cdot \cot A = 1]$

$= \sqrt{(\tan\theta + \cot\theta)^2}$ $[\because a^2 + b^2 + 2ab = (a+b)^2]$

$= \tan\theta + \cot\theta = \text{RHS}$ **Hence proved.**

(ii) LHS $= \sec A(1-\sin A)(\sec A + \tan A)$

$= \left(\dfrac{1}{\cos A}\right)(1-\sin A)\left(\dfrac{1}{\cos A} + \dfrac{\sin A}{\cos A}\right)$

$= \dfrac{(1-\sin A)(1+\sin A)}{\cos^2 A} = \dfrac{1-\sin^2 A}{\cos^2 A} = \dfrac{\cos^2 A}{\cos^2 A}$

$[\because 1-\sin^2 A = \cos^2 A]$

$= 1 = \text{RHS}$ **Hence proved.**

Example 17. Prove that

$$\frac{\sin\theta - 2\sin^3\theta}{2\cos^3\theta - \cos\theta} = \tan\theta.$$ **[ICSE 2017]**

Sol. LHS $= \dfrac{\sin\theta - 2\sin^3\theta}{2\cos^3\theta - \cos\theta} = \dfrac{\sin\theta(1-2\sin^2\theta)}{\cos\theta(2\cos^2\theta - 1)}$

$= \dfrac{\sin\theta[1-2(1-\cos^2\theta)]}{\cos\theta(2\cos^2\theta-1)}$ $[\because \sin^2 A = 1-\cos^2 A]$

$= \dfrac{\sin\theta(1-2+2\cos^2\theta)}{\cos\theta(2\cos^2\theta-1)}$

$= \dfrac{\sin\theta(2\cos^2\theta-1)}{\cos\theta(2\cos^2\theta-1)} = \dfrac{\sin\theta}{\cos\theta}$

$= \tan\theta = \text{RHS}$ **Hence proved.**

Example 18. Prove the following identities, where the angles involved are acute angles for which the expressions are defined.

(i) $(\text{cosec}\,\theta - \cot\theta)^2 = \dfrac{1-\cos\theta}{1+\cos\theta}$

(ii) $\dfrac{\cos A}{1+\sin A} + \dfrac{1+\sin A}{\cos A} = 2\sec A$

Sol.

(i) LHS $= (\text{cosec}\,\theta - \cot\theta)^2$

$= \left(\dfrac{1}{\sin\theta} - \dfrac{\cos\theta}{\sin\theta}\right)^2$ $\left[\because \text{cosec}\,A = \dfrac{1}{\sin A} \text{ and } \cot A = \dfrac{\cos A}{\sin A}\right]$

$= \left(\dfrac{1-\cos\theta}{\sin\theta}\right)^2 = \dfrac{(1-\cos\theta)^2}{\sin^2\theta} = \dfrac{(1-\cos\theta)^2}{1-\cos^2\theta}$

$[\because \sin^2 A = 1-\cos^2 A]$

$= \dfrac{(1-\cos\theta)(1-\cos\theta)}{(1+\cos\theta)(1-\cos\theta)}$ $[\because a^2 - b^2 = (a+b)(a-b)]$

$= \dfrac{1-\cos\theta}{1+\cos\theta} = \text{RHS}$ **Hence proved.**

(ii) LHS $= \dfrac{\cos A}{1+\sin A} + \dfrac{1+\sin A}{\cos A} = \dfrac{\cos^2 A + (1+\sin A)^2}{(1+\sin A)\cos A}$

$= \dfrac{\cos^2 A + \sin^2 A + 1 + 2\sin A}{(1+\sin A)\cos A}$

$[\because (a+b)^2 = a^2 + b^2 + 2ab]$

$= \dfrac{1+1+2\sin A}{(1+\sin A)\cos A}$ $[\because \sin^2\theta + \cos^2\theta = 1]$

$= \dfrac{2+2\sin A}{(1+\sin A)\cos A} = \dfrac{2(1+\sin A)}{(1+\sin A)\cos A}$

$= \dfrac{2}{\cos A} = 2\sec A$ $\left[\because \dfrac{1}{\cos\theta} = \sec\theta\right]$

$= \text{RHS}$ **Hence proved.**

Example 19. Show that

$\dfrac{\cos A - \sin A + 1}{\cos A + \sin A - 1} = \text{cosec}\,A + \cot A$, using the identity $\text{cosec}^2 A = 1 + \cot^2 A$.

Sol. LHS $= \dfrac{\cos A - \sin A + 1}{\cos A + \sin A - 1} = \dfrac{\dfrac{\cos A}{\sin A} - \dfrac{\sin A}{\sin A} + \dfrac{1}{\sin A}}{\dfrac{\cos A}{\sin A} + \dfrac{\sin A}{\sin A} - \dfrac{1}{\sin A}}$

[dividing of numerator and denominator by $\sin A$]

$= \dfrac{\cot A - 1 + \text{cosec}\,A}{\cot A + 1 - \text{cosec}\,A}$ $\left[\because \dfrac{\cos\theta}{\sin\theta} = \cot\theta \text{ and } \dfrac{1}{\sin\theta} = \text{cosec}\,\theta\right]$

$= \dfrac{\cot A + \text{cosec}\,A - 1}{\cot A + 1 - \text{cosec}\,A} = \dfrac{(\cot A + \text{cosec}\,A) - (\text{cosec}^2 A - \cot^2 A)}{\cot A + 1 - \text{cosec}\,A}$

$[\because 1 = \text{cosec}^2\theta - \cot^2\theta]$

$= \dfrac{(\cot A + \text{cosec}\,A) - [(\text{cosec}\,A + \cot A)(\text{cosec}\,A - \cot A)]}{\cot A + 1 - \text{cosec}\,A}$

$[\because a^2 - b^2 = (a+b)(a-b)]$

$= \dfrac{(\cot A + \text{cosec}\,A)[1 - (\text{cosec}\,A - \cot A)]}{\cot A + 1 - \text{cosec}\,A}$

$= \dfrac{(\cot A + \text{cosec}\,A)(1 - \text{cosec}\,A + \cot A)}{(\cot A + 1 - \text{cosec}\,A)}$

$= \cot A + \text{cosec}\,A = \text{RHS}$

Example 20. Evaluate the following in terms of $\tan A$ and $\cot A$.

(i) $(\sin A + \text{cosec}\, A)^2 + (\cos A + \sec A)^2$

(ii) $(\text{cosec}\, A - \sin A)(\sec A - \cos A)$

Sol.

(i) We have, $(\sin A + \text{cosec} A)^2 + (\cos A + \sec A)^2$

$= \sin^2 A + \text{cosec}^2 A + 2\sin A \,\text{cosec} A + \cos^2 A + \sec^2 A + 2\cos A \sec A$ $[\because (a+b)^2 = a^2 + b^2 + 2ab]$

$= (\sin^2 A + \cos^2 A) + (1 + \cot^2 A) + 2\sin A \dfrac{1}{\sin A} + (1 + \tan^2 A) + 2\cos A \dfrac{1}{\cos A}$

$\left[\because \text{cosec}^2\theta = 1 + \cot^2\theta, \sec^2\theta = 1 + \tan^2\theta, \text{cosec}\,\theta = \dfrac{1}{\sin\theta} \text{ and } \sec\theta = \dfrac{1}{\cos\theta}\right]$

$= 1 + 1 + \cot^2 A + 2 + 1 + \tan^2 A + 2$ $[\because \sin^2\theta + \cos^2\theta = 1]$

$= 7 + \tan^2 A + \cot^2 A$

(ii) We have, $(\text{cosec} A - \sin A)(\sec A - \cos A)$

$= \left(\dfrac{1}{\sin A} - \dfrac{\sin A}{1}\right)\left(\dfrac{1}{\cos A} - \dfrac{\cos A}{1}\right)$ $\left[\because \text{cosec}\,\theta = \dfrac{1}{\sin\theta} \text{ and } \sec\theta = \dfrac{1}{\cos\theta}\right]$

$= \left(\dfrac{1 - \sin^2 A}{\sin A}\right)\left(\dfrac{1 - \cos^2 A}{\cos A}\right) = \dfrac{\cos^2 A}{\sin A} \times \dfrac{\sin^2 A}{\cos A}$

$= \cos A \sin A$ ...(i)

$= \dfrac{1}{\dfrac{1}{\cos A \sin A}} = \dfrac{1}{\left(\dfrac{\sin^2 A + \cos^2 A}{\cos A \sin A}\right)} = \dfrac{1}{\left(\dfrac{\sin A}{\cos A} + \dfrac{\cos A}{\sin A}\right)}$ $\left[\because \tan\theta = \dfrac{\sin\theta}{\cos\theta}, \cot\theta = \dfrac{\cos\theta}{\sin\theta}\right]$

$= \dfrac{1}{\tan A + \cot A}$ $[\because \sin^2\theta + \cos^2\theta = 1]$

Example 21. Evaluate the following in terms of $\sin A$.

(i) $(1 + \tan^2 A) + \left(1 + \dfrac{1}{\tan^2 A}\right)$ (ii) $\dfrac{\tan A + \sec A - 1}{\tan A - \sec A + 1}$

Sol.

(i) We have, $(1 + \tan^2 A) + \left(1 + \dfrac{1}{\tan^2 A}\right)$

$= \sec^2 A + (1 + \cot^2 A)$ $\left[\because 1 + \tan^2\theta = \sec^2\theta \text{ and } \dfrac{1}{\tan\theta} = \cot\theta\right]$

$= \sec^2 A + \text{cosec}^2 A$ $[\because 1 + \cot^2\theta = \text{cosec}^2\theta]$

$= \dfrac{1}{\cos^2 A} + \dfrac{1}{\sin^2 A} = \dfrac{\sin^2 A + \cos^2 A}{\cos^2 A \sin^2 A}$ $\left[\because \sec\theta = \dfrac{1}{\cos\theta} \text{ and } \text{cosec}\,\theta = \dfrac{1}{\sin\theta}\right]$

$= \dfrac{1}{\cos^2 A \sin^2 A}$ $[\because \sin^2\theta + \cos^2\theta = 1]$

$= \dfrac{1}{(1 - \sin^2 A)\sin^2 A} = \dfrac{1}{\sin^2 A - \sin^4 A}$

(ii) We have, $\dfrac{\tan A + \sec A - 1}{\tan A - \sec A + 1} = \dfrac{\tan A + \sec A - (\sec^2 A - \tan^2 A)}{\tan A - \sec A + 1}$ $[\because \sec^2\theta - \tan^2\theta = 1]$

$= \dfrac{(\tan A + \sec A) - (\sec A + \tan A)(\sec A - \tan A)}{\tan A - \sec A + 1}$ $[\because a^2 - b^2 = (a+b)(a-b)]$

$= \dfrac{(\tan A + \sec A)(1 - \sec A + \tan A)}{\tan A - \sec A + 1}$ [taking $\sec A + \tan A$ as common]

$= \tan A + \sec A$

$= \dfrac{\sin A}{\cos A} + \dfrac{1}{\cos A}$ $\left[\because \tan\theta = \dfrac{\sin\theta}{\cos\theta} \text{ and } \sec\theta = \dfrac{1}{\cos\theta}\right]$

$= \dfrac{\sin A + 1}{\cos A} = \dfrac{\sin A + 1}{\sqrt{1 - \sin^2 A}}$ $[\because \cos^2\theta = 1 - \sin^2\theta]$

Alternate Method

We have, $\dfrac{\dfrac{\sin A}{\cos A} + \dfrac{1}{\cos A} - 1}{\dfrac{\sin A}{\cos A} - \dfrac{1}{\cos A} + 1} = \dfrac{\dfrac{\sin A + 1 - \cos A}{\cos A}}{\dfrac{\sin A - 1 + \cos A}{\cos A}}$

$= \dfrac{\sin A + 1 - \cos A}{\sin A - 1 + \cos A} = \dfrac{\sin A + 1 - \cos A}{\sin A - 1 + \cos A} \times \dfrac{1 + \sin A}{1 + \sin A}$

[multiplying and dividing by $(1 + \sin A)$]

$= \dfrac{(\sin A + 1 - \cos A)(1 + \sin A)}{\sin A - 1 + \cos A + \sin^2 A - \sin A + \sin A \cos A}$

$= \dfrac{(\sin A + 1 - \cos A)(1 + \sin A)}{-1 + \cos A + (1 - \cos^2 A) + \sin A \cos A}$ $[\because \sin^2\theta = 1 - \cos^2\theta]$

$= \dfrac{(\sin A + 1 - \cos A)(1 + \sin A)}{\cos A - \cos^2 A + \sin A \cos A}$

$= \dfrac{(\sin A + 1 - \cos A)(1 + \sin A)}{\cos A(1 - \cos A + \sin A)}$

$= \dfrac{1 + \sin A}{\cos A} = \dfrac{\sin A + 1}{\sqrt{1 - \sin^2 A}}$

Example 22. Convert the following in terms of $\sec\theta$ and $\text{cosec}\,\theta$.

(i) $(\sin\theta + \cos\theta)(\tan\theta + \cot\theta)$ **[ICSE 2014]**

(ii) $\dfrac{\sin\theta \tan\theta}{1 - \cos\theta}$ **[ICSE 2006]**

Sol.

(i) We have, $(\sin\theta + \cos\theta)(\tan\theta + \cot\theta)$

$= (\sin\theta + \cos\theta)\left(\dfrac{\sin\theta}{\cos\theta} + \dfrac{\cos\theta}{\sin\theta}\right)$

$= (\sin\theta + \cos\theta)\dfrac{\sin^2\theta + \cos^2\theta}{\cos\theta \sin\theta}$

$= (\sin\theta + \cos\theta) \times \dfrac{1}{\cos\theta \sin\theta} = \dfrac{\cos\theta + \sin\theta}{\cos\theta \sin\theta}$ $[\because \sin^2 A + \cos^2 A = 1]$

$= \dfrac{\cos\theta}{\cos\theta \sin\theta} + \dfrac{\sin\theta}{\cos\theta \sin\theta} = \dfrac{1}{\sin\theta} + \dfrac{1}{\cos\theta}$

$= \text{cosec}\,\theta + \sec\theta$

(ii) We have, $\frac{\sin\theta\tan\theta}{1-\cos\theta}=\frac{\sin\theta\tan\theta}{1-\cos\theta}\times\frac{1+\cos\theta}{1+\cos\theta}$

$=\frac{\sin\theta\tan\theta\,(1+\cos\theta)}{1-\cos^2\theta}$

$=\frac{\sin\theta\tan\theta\,(1+\cos\theta)}{\sin^2\theta}$ $[\because \sin^2A+\cos^2A=1]$

$=\frac{\tan\theta\,(1+\cos\theta)}{\sin\theta}=\frac{\frac{\sin\theta}{\cos\theta}\times(1+\cos\theta)}{\sin\theta}$

$=\frac{1+\cos\theta}{\cos\theta}=\frac{1}{\cos\theta}+\frac{\cos\theta}{\cos\theta}=\sec\theta+1$

Example 23. Prove the following.

(i) $(\sec A-\cos A)(\tan A+\cot A)=\tan A\sec A$

(ii) $(\sin\theta+\cos\theta+1)(\sin\theta-1+\cos\theta)\sec\theta\,\mathrm{cosec}\,\theta=2$

Sol.

(i) LHS $=(\sec A-\cos A)(\tan A+\cot A)$

$=\left(\frac{1}{\cos A}-\cos A\right)\left(\frac{\sin A}{\cos A}+\frac{\cos A}{\sin A}\right)$

$=\left(\frac{1-\cos^2A}{\cos A}\right)\cdot\left(\frac{\sin^2A+\cos^2A}{\cos A\sin A}\right)=\frac{\sin^2A}{\cos A}\cdot\frac{1}{\cos A\sin A}$

$[\because \sin^2\theta+\cos^2\theta=1]$

$=\frac{\sin A}{\cos^2A}=\frac{\sin A}{\cos A}\cdot\frac{1}{\cos A}=\tan A\sec A=$ RHS

Hence proved.

(ii) LHS $=(\sin\theta+\cos\theta+1)(\sin\theta-1+\cos\theta)\sec\theta\,\mathrm{cosec}\,\theta$

$=(\sin\theta+\cos\theta+1)(\sin\theta+\cos\theta-1)\sec\theta\,\mathrm{cosec}\,\theta$

$=[(\sin\theta+\cos\theta)^2-1^2]\sec\theta\,\mathrm{cosec}\,\theta$

$[\because (a+b)(a-b)=a^2-b^2]$

$=(\sin^2\theta+\cos^2\theta+2\sin\theta\cos\theta-1)\sec\theta\,\mathrm{cosec}\,\theta$

$[\because (a+b)^2=a^2+b^2+2ab]$

$=(1+2\sin\theta\cos\theta-1)\sec\theta\,\mathrm{cosec}\,\theta$

$[\because \sin^2A+\cos^2A=1]$

$=2\sin\theta\cos\theta\times\frac{1}{\cos\theta}\times\frac{1}{\sin\theta}=2=$ RHS

Hence proved.

Example 24. Convert the following trigonometric identities into unity.

(i) $[\sin\theta(1+\tan\theta)+\cos\theta(1+\cot\theta)]\div(\sec\theta+\mathrm{cosec}\,\theta)$

(ii) $(1+\cot\theta-\mathrm{cosec}\,\theta)(1+\tan\theta+\sec\theta)\div2$

Sol.

(i) We have, $[\sin\theta(1+\tan\theta)+\cos\theta(1+\cot\theta)]\div(\sec\theta+\mathrm{cosec}\,\theta)$

$=\left[\sin\theta\left(1+\frac{\sin\theta}{\cos\theta}\right)+\cos\theta\left(1+\frac{\cos\theta}{\sin\theta}\right)\right]\times\left[\frac{1}{\sec\theta+\mathrm{cosec}\,\theta}\right]$

$=\left[\sin\theta\left(\frac{\cos\theta+\sin\theta}{\cos\theta}\right)+\cos\theta\left(\frac{\sin\theta+\cos\theta}{\sin\theta}\right)\right]\times\left[\frac{1}{\sec\theta+\mathrm{cosec}\,\theta}\right]$

$=(\cos\theta+\sin\theta)\left(\frac{\sin\theta}{\cos\theta}+\frac{\cos\theta}{\sin\theta}\right)\times\frac{1}{(\sec\theta+\mathrm{cosec}\,\theta)}$

$=\frac{(\cos\theta+\sin\theta)}{(\sec\theta+\mathrm{cosec}\,\theta)}\left(\frac{\sin^2\theta+\cos^2\theta}{\cos\theta\sin\theta}\right)$

$=\frac{(\cos\theta+\sin\theta)}{(\sec\theta+\mathrm{cosec}\,\theta)}\left(\frac{1}{\cos\theta\sin\theta}\right)$ $[\because \sin^2A+\cos^2A=1]$

$=\left[\frac{\cos\theta}{\cos\theta\sin\theta}+\frac{\sin\theta}{\cos\theta\sin\theta}\right]\times\left[\frac{1}{\sec\theta+\mathrm{cosec}\,\theta}\right]$

$=\frac{(\mathrm{cosec}\,\theta+\sec\theta)}{\mathrm{cosec}\,\theta+\sec\theta}=1$

(ii) We have, $\frac{(1+\cot\theta-\mathrm{cosec}\,\theta)\;(1+\tan\theta+\sec\theta)}{2}$

$=\frac{1}{2}\left(1+\frac{\cos\theta}{\sin\theta}-\frac{1}{\sin\theta}\right)\left(1+\frac{\sin\theta}{\cos\theta}+\frac{1}{\cos\theta}\right)$

$=\frac{1}{2}\left(\frac{\sin\theta+\cos\theta-1}{\sin\theta}\right)\left(\frac{\cos\theta+\sin\theta+1}{\cos\theta}\right)$

$=\frac{(\sin\theta+\cos\theta)^2-1}{2\sin\theta\cos\theta}$ $[\because (a-b)(a+b)=a^2-b^2]$

$=\frac{\sin^2\theta+\cos^2\theta+2\sin\theta\cos\theta-1}{2\sin\theta\cos\theta}$

$[\because (a+b)^2=a^2+b^2+2ab]$

$=\frac{1+2\sin\theta\cos\theta-1}{2\sin\theta\cos\theta}=\frac{2\sin\theta\cos\theta}{2\sin\theta\cos\theta}=1$

Example 25. Prove that

$$\frac{\sin A}{1+\cot A}-\frac{\cos A}{1+\tan A}=\sin A-\cos A$$

Sol. LHS $=\frac{\sin A}{1+\cot A}-\frac{\cos A}{1+\tan A}=\frac{\sin A}{1+\frac{\cos A}{\sin A}}-\frac{\cos A}{1+\frac{\sin A}{\cos A}}$

$=\frac{\sin^2A}{\sin A+\cos A}-\frac{\cos^2A}{\cos A+\sin A}$

$=\frac{\sin^2A-\cos^2A}{\sin A+\cos A}$

$=\frac{(\sin A+\cos A)(\sin A-\cos A)}{\sin A+\cos A}$

$[\because a^2-b^2=(a+b)(a-b)]$

$=\sin A-\cos A=$ RHS **Hence proved.**

Example 26. Prove the following identities.

(i) $\frac{\sec A+\tan A}{\mathrm{cosec}\,A+\cot A}=\frac{\mathrm{cosec}\,A-\cot A}{\sec A-\tan A}$

(ii) $\frac{\tan A}{1-\cot A}+\frac{\cot A}{1-\tan A}=1+\tan A+\cot A$

Sol.

(i) $\frac{\sec A+\tan A}{\mathrm{cosec}\,A+\cot A}=\frac{\mathrm{cosec}\,A-\cot A}{\sec A-\tan A}$

$(\sec A+\tan A)(\sec A-\tan A)=(\mathrm{cosec}\,A+\cot A)(\mathrm{cosec}\,A-\cot A)$

$\sec^2A-\tan^2A=\mathrm{cosec}^2A-\cot^2A$

$(1+\tan^2A)-\tan^2A=(1+\cot^2A)-\cot^2A$

$1=1$, LHS = RHS **Hence proved.**

(ii) $\text{LHS} = \dfrac{\tan A}{1-\cot A} + \dfrac{\cot A}{1-\tan A} = \dfrac{\frac{\sin A}{\cos A}}{1-\frac{\cos A}{\sin A}} + \dfrac{\frac{\cos A}{\sin A}}{1-\frac{\sin A}{\cos A}}$

$= \dfrac{\sin^2 A}{\cos A(\sin A - \cos A)} + \dfrac{\cos^2 A}{\sin A(\cos A - \sin A)}$

$= \dfrac{1}{\sin A - \cos A}\left(\dfrac{\sin^2 A}{\cos A} - \dfrac{\cos^2 A}{\sin A}\right)$

$= \dfrac{1}{\sin A - \cos A} \cdot \dfrac{\sin^3 A - \cos^3 A}{\cos A \sin A}$

$= \dfrac{(\sin A - \cos A)(\sin^2 A + \sin A\cos A + \cos^2 A)}{(\sin A - \cos A)\sin A\cos A}$

$[\because a^3 - b^3 = (a-b)(a^2+b^2+ab)]$

$= \dfrac{\sin^2 A + \sin A\cos A + \cos^2 A}{\sin A\cos A}$

$= \dfrac{\sin^2 A}{\sin A\cos A} + \dfrac{\sin A\cos A}{\sin A\cos A} + \dfrac{\cos^2 A}{\sin A\cos A}$

$= \dfrac{\sin A}{\cos A} + 1 + \dfrac{\cos A}{\sin A}$

$= \tan A + 1 + \cot A$

$= 1 + \tan A + \cot A = \text{RHS}$ **Hence proved.**

Example 27. Prove the following identities.

(i) $(\sec A - \sin A)(\operatorname{cosec} A + \cos A) = \sin^2 A\tan A + \cot A$

(ii) $(1 + \cot A + \tan A)(\sin A - \cos A) = \dfrac{\sec A}{\operatorname{cosec}^2 A} - \dfrac{\operatorname{cosec} A}{\sec^2 A}$

Sol.

(i) $\text{LHS} = (\sec A - \sin A)(\operatorname{cosec} A + \cos A)$

$= \left(\dfrac{1}{\cos A} - \sin A\right)\left(\dfrac{1}{\sin A} + \cos A\right)$

$= \left(\dfrac{1-\sin A\cos A}{\cos A}\right)\left(\dfrac{1+\sin A\cos A}{\sin A}\right)$

$= \dfrac{(1-\sin^2 A\cos^2 A)}{\sin A\cos A}$ $[\because (a-b)(a+b) = a^2 - b^2]$

$= \dfrac{\sin^2 A + \cos^2 A - \sin^2 A\cos^2 A}{\sin A\cos A}$ $[\because \sin^2\theta + \cos^2\theta = 1]$

$= \dfrac{\sin^2 A - \sin^2 A\cos^2 A + \cos^2 A}{\sin A\cos A}$

$= \dfrac{\sin^2 A(1-\cos^2 A) + \cos^2 A}{\sin A\cos A}$

$= \dfrac{\sin^2 A\sin^2 A + \cos^2 A}{\sin A\cos A} = \dfrac{\sin^4 A + \cos^2 A}{\sin A\cos A}$

$= \dfrac{\sin^4 A}{\sin A\cos A} + \dfrac{\cos^2 A}{\sin A\cos A} = \dfrac{\sin^3 A}{\cos A} + \dfrac{\cos A}{\sin A}$

$= \sin^2 A \cdot \dfrac{\sin A}{\cos A} + \cot A$

$= \sin^2 A \cdot \tan A + \cot A = \text{RHS}$ **Hence proved.**

(ii) $\text{LHS} = (1 + \cot A + \tan A)(\sin A - \cos A)$

$= \left(1 + \dfrac{\cos A}{\sin A} + \dfrac{\sin A}{\cos A}\right)(\sin A - \cos A)$

$= \left(\dfrac{\sin A\cos A + \cos^2 A + \sin^2 A}{\sin A\cos A}\right)(\sin A - \cos A)$

$= \dfrac{(\sin A - \cos A)(\sin^2 A + \cos^2 A + \sin A\cos A)}{\sin A\cos A}$

$= \dfrac{\sin^3 A - \cos^3 A}{\sin A\cos A}$ $[\because (a-b)(a^2+b^2+ab) = a^3 - b^3]$ ...(i)

and $\text{RHS} = \dfrac{\sec A}{\operatorname{cosec}^2 A} - \dfrac{\operatorname{cosec} A}{\sec^2 A} = \dfrac{\frac{1}{\cos A}}{\frac{1}{\sin^2 A}} - \dfrac{\frac{1}{\sin A}}{\frac{1}{\cos^2 A}}$

$= \dfrac{\sin^2 A}{\cos A} - \dfrac{\cos^2 A}{\sin A} = \dfrac{\sin^3 A - \cos^3 A}{\cos A\sin A}$ ...(ii)

From Eqs. (i) and (ii),

LHS = RHS **Hence proved.**

Example 28. Prove the following identities.

(i) $\tan^2\theta + \cot^2\theta + 2 = \sec^2\theta\operatorname{cosec}^2\theta$

(ii) $\sqrt{\sec^2\theta + \operatorname{cosec}^2\theta} = \tan\theta + \cot\theta$

Sol.

(i) $\text{LHS} = \tan^2\theta + \cot^2\theta + 2 = (1+\tan^2\theta) + (1+\cot^2\theta)$

$= \sec^2\theta + \operatorname{cosec}^2\theta$

$[\because 1+\tan^2 A = \sec^2 A \text{ and } 1+\cot^2 A = \operatorname{cosec}^2 A]$

$= \dfrac{1}{\cos^2\theta} + \dfrac{1}{\sin^2\theta} = \dfrac{\sin^2\theta + \cos^2\theta}{\cos^2\theta\sin^2\theta}$

$= \dfrac{1}{\cos^2\theta\sin^2\theta} = \dfrac{1}{\cos^2\theta} \cdot \dfrac{1}{\sin^2\theta}$ $[\because \sin^2 A + \cos^2 A = 1]$

$= \sec^2\theta\operatorname{cosec}^2\theta = \text{RHS}$ **Hence proved.**

(ii) $\text{LHS} = \sqrt{\sec^2\theta + \operatorname{cosec}^2\theta} = \sqrt{(1+\tan^2\theta) + (1+\cot^2\theta)}$

$= \sqrt{\tan^2\theta + \cot^2\theta + 2}$

$= \sqrt{\tan^2\theta + \cot^2\theta + 2\tan\theta\cot\theta}$ $[\because \tan A\cot A = 1]$

$= \sqrt{(\tan\theta + \cot\theta)^2}$

$= \tan\theta + \cot\theta = \text{RHS}$ **Hence proved.**

Example 29. Prove the following identities.

(i) $\sin^4\theta + \cos^4\theta = 1 - 2\sin^2\theta\cos^2\theta$

(ii) $\dfrac{1}{\operatorname{cosec}\theta - \cot\theta} - \dfrac{1}{\sin\theta} = \dfrac{1}{\sin\theta} - \dfrac{1}{\operatorname{cosec}\theta + \cot\theta}$

Sol.

(i) $\text{LHS} = \sin^4\theta + \cos^4\theta = (\sin^2\theta)^2 + (\cos^2\theta)^2$

$= (\sin^2\theta + \cos^2\theta)^2 - 2\cdot\sin^2\theta\cos^2\theta$

$[\because a^2 + b^2 = (a+b)^2 - 2ab]$

$= 1^2 - 2\sin^2\theta\cos^2\theta = 1 - 2\sin^2\theta\cos^2\theta$

$[\because \sin^2 A + \cos^2 A = 1]$

$= \text{RHS}$ **Hence proved.**

(ii) $\dfrac{1}{\operatorname{cosec}\theta - \cot\theta} - \dfrac{1}{\sin\theta} = \dfrac{1}{\sin\theta} - \dfrac{1}{\operatorname{cosec}\theta + \cot\theta}$

if $\dfrac{1}{\operatorname{cosec}\theta - \cot\theta} + \dfrac{1}{\operatorname{cosec}\theta + \cot\theta} = \dfrac{1}{\sin\theta} + \dfrac{1}{\sin\theta}$

$$\frac{(\text{cosec}\,\theta+\cot\theta)+(\text{cosec}\,\theta-\cot\theta)}{(\text{cosec}\,\theta-\cot\theta)(\text{cosec}\,\theta+\cot\theta)}=\frac{2}{\sin\theta}$$

$$\frac{2\,\text{cosec}\,\theta}{\text{cosec}^2\theta-\cot^2\theta}=2\,\text{cosec}\,\theta$$

$$\frac{2\,\text{cosec}\,\theta}{1}=2\,\text{cosec}\,\theta \qquad [\because \text{cosec}^2A-\cot^2A=1]$$

Hence proved.

Example 30. Prove the following identities.

(i) $\dfrac{1+\tan^2\theta}{1+\cot^2\theta}=\left(\dfrac{1-\tan\theta}{1-\cot\theta}\right)^2=\tan^2\theta$

(ii) $\sin^6\theta+\cos^6\theta+3\sin^2\theta\cos^2\theta=1$

Sol.

(i) We have, $\dfrac{1+\tan^2\theta}{1+\cot^2\theta}=\dfrac{\sec^2\theta}{\text{cosec}^2\theta}=\dfrac{1/\cos^2\theta}{1/\sin^2\theta}$

$$=\frac{1}{\cos^2\theta}\times\frac{\sin^2\theta}{1}=\left(\frac{\sin\theta}{\cos\theta}\right)^2=\tan^2\theta$$

Also, $\left(\dfrac{1-\tan\theta}{1-\cot\theta}\right)^2=\left(\dfrac{1-\dfrac{\sin\theta}{\cos\theta}}{1-\dfrac{\cos\theta}{\sin\theta}}\right)^2=\left(\dfrac{\dfrac{\cos\theta-\sin\theta}{\cos\theta}}{\dfrac{\sin\theta-\cos\theta}{\sin\theta}}\right)^2$

$$=\left(-\frac{\sin\theta-\cos\theta}{\cos\theta}\times\frac{\sin\theta}{\sin\theta-\cos\theta}\right)^2=\left(-\frac{\sin\theta}{\cos\theta}\right)^2$$

$$=(-\tan\theta)^2=\tan^2\theta$$

$\therefore\quad \dfrac{1+\tan^2\theta}{1+\cot^2\theta}=\left(\dfrac{1-\tan\theta}{1-\cot\theta}\right)^2=\tan^2\theta$ **Hence proved.**

(ii) LHS $=\sin^6\theta+\cos^6\theta+3\sin^2\theta\cos^2\theta$

$=(\sin^2\theta)^3+(\cos^2\theta)^3+3\sin^2\theta\cos^2\theta$

$=(\sin^2\theta+\cos^2\theta)^3-3\sin^2\theta\cos^2\theta(\sin^2\theta+\cos^2\theta)+3\sin^2\theta\cos^2\theta$

$[\because a^3+b^3=(a+b)^3-3ab(a+b)]$

$=(1)^3-3\sin^2\theta\cos^2\theta(1)+3\sin^2\theta\cos^2\theta$

$[\because \sin^2A+\cos^2A=1]$

$=1-3\sin^2\theta\cos^2\theta+3\sin^2\theta\cos^2\theta=1=$ RHS

Hence proved.

Example 31. Prove that $(\text{cosec}\,\theta-\sin\theta)(\sec\theta-\cos\theta)(\tan\theta+\cot\theta)=1$.

Sol. To prove,

$$(\text{cosec}\,\theta-\sin\theta)(\sec\theta-\cos\theta)(\tan\theta+\cot\theta)=1$$

$$\text{LHS}=\left(\frac{1}{\sin\theta}-\sin\theta\right)\left(\frac{1}{\cos\theta}-\cos\theta\right)\left(\frac{\sin\theta}{\cos\theta}+\frac{\cos\theta}{\sin\theta}\right)$$

$$=\left(\frac{1-\sin^2\theta}{\sin\theta}\right)\left(\frac{1-\cos^2\theta}{\cos\theta}\right)\left(\frac{\sin^2\theta+\cos^2\theta}{\sin\theta\cos\theta}\right)$$

$$=\frac{\cos^2\theta}{\sin\theta}\times\frac{\sin^2\theta}{\cos\theta}\left(\frac{1}{\sin\theta\cos\theta}\right)\qquad[\because \sin^2A+\cos^2A=1]$$

$=1=$ RHS **Hence proved.**

Example 32. If $1+\sin^2\theta=3\sin\theta\cos\theta$, then prove that $\tan\theta=1$ or $1/2$.

Sol. Given, $1+\sin^2\theta=3\sin\theta\cos\theta$

On dividing both sides by $\cos^2\theta$, we get

$$\frac{1}{\cos^2\theta}+\frac{\sin^2\theta}{\cos^2\theta}=3\frac{\sin\theta\cos\theta}{\cos^2\theta}$$

$\Rightarrow\quad \sec^2\theta+\tan^2\theta=3\tan\theta$

$\Rightarrow\quad (1+\tan^2\theta)+\tan^2\theta=3\tan\theta\quad[\because \sec^2A=1+\tan^2A]$

$\Rightarrow\quad 2\tan^2\theta-3\tan\theta+1=0$

$\Rightarrow\quad 2\tan^2\theta-2\tan\theta-\tan\theta+1=0$

[by factorisation method]

$\Rightarrow\quad 2\tan\theta(\tan\theta-1)-1(\tan\theta-1)=0$

$\Rightarrow\quad (\tan\theta-1)(2\tan\theta-1)=0$

$\Rightarrow\quad \tan\theta-1=0$ or $2\tan\theta-1=0$

$\Rightarrow\quad \tan\theta=1$ or $\tan\theta=\dfrac{1}{2}$

Example 33. If $\sin\theta+\cos\theta=\sqrt{3}$, then prove that $\tan\theta+\cot\theta=1$.

Sol. Given, $\sin\theta+\cos\theta=\sqrt{3}$

$\Rightarrow\quad (\sin\theta+\cos\theta)^2=(\sqrt{3})^2$ [squaring on both sides]

$\Rightarrow\quad \sin^2\theta+\cos^2\theta+2\sin\theta\cos\theta=3$

$[\because (a+b)^2=a^2+b^2+2ab]$

$\Rightarrow\quad 1+2\sin\theta\cos\theta=3\quad[\because \sin^2A+\cos^2A=1]$

$\Rightarrow\quad 2\sin\theta\cos\theta=2$

$\Rightarrow\quad \sin\theta\cos\theta=1$

$\Rightarrow\quad \sin\theta\cos\theta=\sin^2\theta+\cos^2\theta\quad[\because \sin^2A+\cos^2A=1]$

$\Rightarrow\quad 1=\dfrac{\sin^2\theta+\cos^2\theta}{\sin\theta\cos\theta}$

[dividing both sides by $\sin\theta\cos\theta$]

$\Rightarrow\quad 1=\dfrac{\sin^2\theta}{\sin\theta\cos\theta}+\dfrac{\cos^2\theta}{\sin\theta\cos\theta}$

$\Rightarrow\quad 1=\dfrac{\sin\theta}{\cos\theta}+\dfrac{\cos\theta}{\sin\theta}$

$\Rightarrow\quad 1=\tan\theta+\cot\theta$ **Hence proved.**

Example 34. If $\text{cosec}\,\theta-\sin\theta=\sqrt{5}$ and $\text{cosec}\,\theta$, $\sin\theta$ are positive, then show that $\text{cosec}\,\theta+\sin\theta=3$.

Sol. Given, $\text{cosec}\,\theta-\sin\theta=\sqrt{5}$

$\Rightarrow\quad (\text{cosec}\,\theta-\sin\theta)^2=(\sqrt{5})^2$ [squaring on both sides]

$\Rightarrow\quad \text{cosec}^2\theta+\sin^2\theta-2\,\text{cosec}\,\theta\sin\theta=5$

$[\because (a-b)^2=a^2+b^2-2ab]$

$\Rightarrow\quad \text{cosec}^2\theta+\sin^2\theta+2\,\text{cosec}\,\theta\sin\theta=5+4\,\text{cosec}\,\theta\sin\theta$

[adding $4\,\text{cosec}\,\theta\sin\theta$ on both sides]

$\Rightarrow\quad (\text{cosec}\,\theta+\sin\theta)^2=5+4\times1\quad[\because \text{cosec}\,A\sin A=1]$

$\Rightarrow\quad (\text{cosec}\,\theta+\sin\theta)^2=9$

$\Rightarrow\quad \text{cosec}\,\theta+\sin\theta=\pm3$ [taking square root]

But $\text{cosec}\,\theta>0$ and $\sin\theta>0$, so $\text{cosec}\,\theta+\sin\theta>0$.

$\therefore\quad \text{cosec}\,\theta+\sin\theta=3$ **Hence proved.**

Example 35. If $a \sin \theta + b \cos \theta = c$, then prove that $a \cos \theta - b \sin \theta = \pm \sqrt{a^2 + b^2 - c^2}$.

Sol. Given, $a \sin \theta + b \cos \theta = c$

$\Rightarrow (a \sin \theta + b \cos \theta)^2 = c^2$ [squaring on both sides]

$\Rightarrow a^2 \sin^2\theta + b^2 \cos^2\theta + 2ab \sin \theta \cos \theta = c^2$

$\Rightarrow a^2 (1 - \cos^2\theta) + b^2 (1 - \sin^2\theta) + 2ab \sin \theta \cos \theta = c^2$

[$\because \sin^2 A + \cos^2 A = 1$]

$\Rightarrow a^2 + b^2 - (a^2 \cos^2\theta + b^2 \sin^2\theta - 2ab \sin \theta \cos \theta) = c^2$

$\Rightarrow a^2 \cos^2\theta + b^2 \sin^2\theta - 2ab \sin \theta \cos \theta = a^2 + b^2 - c^2$

$\Rightarrow (a \cos \theta - b \sin \theta)^2 = a^2 + b^2 - c^2$

$\Rightarrow a \cos \theta - b \sin \theta = \pm \sqrt{a^2 + b^2 - c^2}$

Hence proved.

Example 36. If $a \cos \theta - b \sin \theta = x$ and $a \sin \theta + b \cos \theta = y$, then prove that $a^2 + b^2 = x^2 + y^2$.

Sol. Given, $a \cos \theta - b \sin \theta = x$ ...(i)

and $a \sin \theta + b \cos \theta = y$ ...(ii)

On adding the squares of Eqs. (i) and (ii), we get

$x^2 + y^2 = (a \cos \theta - b \sin \theta)^2 + (a \sin \theta + b \cos \theta)^2$

$\Rightarrow x^2 + y^2 = a^2 \cos^2\theta + b^2 \sin^2\theta - 2ab \cos \theta \sin \theta + a^2 \sin^2\theta + b^2 \cos^2\theta + 2ab \sin \theta \cos \theta$

[$\because (a \pm b)^2 = a^2 + b^2 \pm 2ab$]

$\Rightarrow x^2 + y^2 = a^2 \cos^2\theta + b^2 \sin^2\theta + a^2 \sin^2\theta + b^2 \cos^2\theta$

$\Rightarrow x^2 + y^2 = a^2 (\cos^2\theta + \sin^2\theta) + b^2 (\sin^2\theta + \cos^2\theta)$

$\Rightarrow x^2 + y^2 = a^2 + b^2$ [$\because \sin^2 A + \cos^2 A = 1$]

Hence proved.

Example 37. If $\tan \theta + \sec \theta = l$, then prove that $\sec \theta = \frac{l^2 + 1}{2l}$.

Sol. Given, $\tan \theta + \sec \theta = l$ ...(i)

We know that $\sec^2 \theta - \tan^2\theta = 1$

$\Rightarrow (\sec \theta + \tan \theta)(\sec \theta - \tan \theta) = 1$

[$\because a^2 - b^2 = (a + b)(a - b)$]

$\Rightarrow l(\sec \theta - \tan \theta) = 1$ [from Eq. (i)]

$\Rightarrow \sec \theta - \tan \theta = \frac{1}{l}$ ...(ii)

On adding Eqs. (i) and (ii), we get

$2 \sec \theta = l + \frac{1}{l}$

$\Rightarrow \sec \theta = \frac{l^2 + 1}{2l}$ **Hence proved.**

Example 38. If $\tan \theta + \sin \theta = m$ and $\tan \theta - \sin \theta = n$, then show that $(m^2 - n^2)^2 = 16\, mn$ or $(m^2 - n^2) = 4\sqrt{mn}$.

Sol. Given, $\tan \theta + \sin \theta = m$ ...(i)

and $\tan \theta - \sin \theta = n$ ...(ii)

On adding Eqs. (i) and (ii), we get

$2 \tan \theta = m + n$

$\Rightarrow \tan \theta = \frac{m + n}{2}$

$\therefore \cot \theta = \frac{1}{\tan \theta} = \frac{2}{m + n}$ ...(iii)

On subtracting Eq. (ii) from Eq. (i), we get

$2 \sin \theta = m - n$

$\Rightarrow \sin \theta = \frac{m - n}{2}$ ...(iv)

$\therefore \operatorname{cosec} \theta = \frac{1}{\sin \theta} = \frac{2}{m - n}$

We know that $\operatorname{cosec}^2\theta - \cot^2\theta = 1$

$\Rightarrow \left(\frac{2}{m - n}\right)^2 - \left(\frac{2}{m + n}\right)^2 = 1$ [from Eqs. (iii) and (iv)]

$\Rightarrow \frac{4}{(m - n)^2} - \frac{4}{(m + n)^2} = 1$

$\Rightarrow 4\left[\frac{1}{(m - n)^2} - \frac{1}{(m + n)^2}\right] = 1$

$\Rightarrow 4\left[\frac{(m + n)^2 - (m - n)^2}{(m - n)^2 (m + n)^2}\right] = 1$

$\Rightarrow 4\left[\frac{(m^2 + n^2 + 2mn) - (m^2 + n^2 - 2mn)}{(m - n)^2 (m + n)^2}\right] = 1$

[$\because (a \pm b)^2 = a^2 + b^2 \pm 2ab$]

$\Rightarrow 4\left[\frac{2mn + 2mn}{(m - n)^2 (m + n)^2}\right] = 1$

$\Rightarrow \frac{16mn}{[(m - n)(m + n)]^2} = 1$

$\Rightarrow \frac{16mn}{(m^2 - n^2)^2} = 1$

$\Rightarrow (m^2 - n^2)^2 = 16mn$ [$\because (a - b)(a + b) = a^2 - b^2$]

$\therefore (m^2 - n^2) = 4\sqrt{mn}$ [taking positive square root]

Hence proved.

Example 39. If $\operatorname{cosec} \theta = x + \frac{1}{4x}$, then prove that $\operatorname{cosec} \theta + \cot \theta = 2x$ or $\frac{1}{2x}$.

Sol. Given, $\operatorname{cosec} \theta = x + \frac{1}{4x}$ ...(i)

We know that $\cot^2\theta = \operatorname{cosec}^2\theta - 1$

$\Rightarrow \cot^2 \theta = \left(x + \frac{1}{4x}\right)^2 - 1$ [from Eq. (i)]

$\Rightarrow \cot^2\theta = x^2 + \frac{1}{16x^2} + 2x \cdot \frac{1}{4x} - 1$

[$\because (a + b)^2 = a^2 + b^2 + 2ab$]

$= x^2 + \frac{1}{16x^2} + \frac{1}{2} - 1 = x^2 + \frac{1}{16x^2} - \frac{1}{2}$

$= x^2 + \frac{1}{16x^2} - 2x \cdot \frac{1}{4x} = \left(x - \frac{1}{4x}\right)^2$

[$\because a^2 + b^2 - 2ab = (a - b)^2$]

$\Rightarrow \cot \theta = x - \frac{1}{4x}$ ...(ii)

or $\cot \theta = -\left(x - \frac{1}{4x}\right)$ ...(iii)

On adding Eqs. (i) and (ii), we get

$$\text{cosec}\,\theta + \cot\theta = 2x$$

Now, adding Eqs. (i) and (iii), we get

$$\text{cosec}\,\theta + \cot\theta = \frac{1}{2x}$$

Hence, $\text{cosec}\,\theta + \cot\theta = 2x$ or $\frac{1}{2x}$.

Example 40. Without using trigonometric tables, evaluate $\text{cosec}^2 57° - \tan^2 33° + \cos 44° \text{ cosec } 46° - \sqrt{2}\cos 45° - \tan^2 60°$. [ICSE2016]

Sol. We have, $\text{cosec}^2 57° - \tan^2 33° + \cos 44° \text{ cosec } 46° - \sqrt{2}\cos 45° - \tan^2 60°$

$= \text{cosec}^2 (90° - 33°) - \tan^2 33° + \cos(90° - 46°) \text{ cosec } 46° - \sqrt{2}\cos 45° - \tan^2 60°$

$= (\sec^2 33° - \tan^2 33°) + (\sin 46° \text{ cosec } 46°) - \sqrt{2}\cos 45° - \tan^2 60°$

[$\because \text{cosec}(90° - \theta) = \sec\theta$ and $\cos(90° - \theta) = \sin\theta$]

$= 1 + 1 - \sqrt{2} \times \frac{1}{\sqrt{2}} - (\sqrt{3})^2$

[$\because \sec^2\theta - \tan^2\theta = 1, \sin\theta \cdot \text{cosec}\,\theta = 1, \cos 45° = \frac{1}{\sqrt{2}}$ and $\tan 60° = \sqrt{3}$]

$= 2 - 1 - 3 = 2 - 4 = -2$

Example 41. Without using trigonometric tables evaluate $\sin^2 28° + \sin^2 62° + \tan^2 38° - \cot^2 52° + \frac{1}{4}\sec^2 30°$. [ICSE 2017]

Sol. We have, $\sin^2 28° + \sin^2 62° + \tan^2 38° - \cot^2 52° + \frac{1}{4}\sec^2 30°$

$= \sin^2 28° + \sin^2(90° - 28°) + \tan^2(90° - 52°) - \cot^2 52° + \frac{1}{4}\sec^2 30°$

$= \sin^2 28° + \cos^2 28° + \cot^2 52° - \cot^2 52° + \frac{1}{4}\sec^2 30°$

[$\because \sin(90° - \theta) = \cos\theta$ and $\tan(90° - \theta) = \cot\theta$]

$= 1 + 0 + \frac{1}{4}\sec^2 30°$ [$\because \sin^2\theta + \cos^2\theta = 1$]

$= 1 + \frac{1}{4}\left(\frac{2}{\sqrt{3}}\right)^2 = 1 + \frac{1}{4} \times \frac{4}{3} = 1 + \frac{1}{3} = \frac{4}{3}$ $\left[\because \sec 30° = \frac{2}{\sqrt{3}}\right]$

Example 42. Without using trigonometric tables, evaluate the following.

(i) $\frac{2}{3}\text{cosec}^2 58° - \frac{2}{3}\cot 58° \tan 32° - \frac{5}{3}\tan 13° \tan 37° \tan 45° \tan 53° \tan 77°$

(ii) $\left(\frac{\tan 20°}{\text{cosec } 70°}\right)^2 + \left(\frac{\cot 20°}{\sec 70°}\right)^2 + 2\tan 15° \tan 45° \tan 75°$

Sol.

(i) We have, $\frac{2}{3}\text{cosec}^2 58° - \frac{2}{3}\cot 58° \tan 32° - \frac{5}{3}\tan 13° \tan 37° \tan 45° \tan 53° \tan 77°$

$= \frac{2}{3}\text{cosec}^2 58° - \frac{2}{3}\cot 58° \tan(90° - 58°) - \frac{5}{3}\tan 13° \tan 37° \cdot 1 \cdot \tan(90° - 37°)\tan(90° - 13°)$

[$\because \tan 45° = 1$]

$= \frac{2}{3}\text{cosec}^2 58° - \frac{2}{3}\cot 58° \cot 58° - \frac{5}{3}\tan 13° \tan 37° \cot 37° \cot 13°$ [$\because \tan(90° - \theta) = \cot\theta$]

$= \frac{2}{3}(\text{cosec}^2 58° - \cot^2 58°) - \frac{5}{3}\tan 13° \cdot 1 \cdot \cot 13°$

[$\because \tan\theta \cot\theta = 1$]

$= \frac{2}{3} \cdot 1 - \frac{5}{3} \cdot 1 = \frac{2}{3} - \frac{5}{3} = -1$ [$\because \text{cosec}^2\theta - \cot^2\theta = 1$]

(ii) We have,

$\left(\frac{\tan 20°}{\text{cosec } 70°}\right)^2 + \left(\frac{\cot 20°}{\sec 70°}\right)^2 + 2\tan 15° \tan 45° \tan 75°$

$= \left(\frac{\tan 20°}{\text{cosec}(90° - 20°)}\right)^2 + \left(\frac{\cot 20°}{\sec(90° - 20°)}\right)^2 + 2\tan 15° \cdot 1 \cdot \tan(90° - 15°)$ [$\because \tan 45° = 1$]

$= \left(\frac{\tan 20°}{\sec 20°}\right)^2 + \left(\frac{\cot 20°}{\text{cosec } 20°}\right)^2 + 2\tan 15° \cot 15°$

[$\because \text{cosec}(90° - \theta) = \sec\theta, \sec(90° - \theta) = \text{cosec}\,\theta$ and $\tan(90° - \theta) = \cot\theta$]

$= \left(\frac{\sin 20°}{\cos 20°} \cdot \cos 20°\right)^2 + \left(\frac{\cos 20°}{\sin 20°} \cdot \sin 20°\right)^2 + 2 \cdot 1$

[$\because \tan\theta \cdot \cot\theta = 1$]

$= \sin^2 20° + \cos^2 20° + 2 = 1 + 2 = 3$ [$\because \sin^2\theta + \cos^2\theta = 1$]

Exercise 18.2

1. If $2\sin^2\theta - \cos^2\theta = 2$, then find the value of θ, when θ lies in first quadrant.
2. If $7\tan\theta = 4$, then find the value of $\frac{7\sin\theta - 3\cos\theta}{7\sin\theta + 3\cos\theta}$.
3. If $A = 30°$ and $B = 60°$, then verify that $\sin(A + B) = \sin A \cos B + \cos A \sin B$.
4. Prove that
   (i) $\sec A(1 - \sin A)(\sec A + \tan A) = 1$
   (ii) $\frac{\cos A}{1 + \sin A} + \tan A = \sec A$
   (iii) $\frac{\sin\theta}{1 - \cot\theta} + \frac{\cos\theta}{1 - \tan\theta} = \cos\theta + \sin\theta$
   (iv) $\frac{\tan^2\theta}{(\sec\theta - 1)^2} = \frac{1 + \cos\theta}{1 - \cos\theta}$
5. If $\cos A + \cos^2 A = 1$, then find the value of $\sin^2 A + \sin^4 A$.

6. Show that $\frac{\cos A}{1-\tan A}+\frac{\sin A}{1-\cot A}=\sin A+\cos A$. **[ICSE 2015, 03]**

7. Prove that $\frac{\sin A}{1+\cos A}+\frac{1+\cos A}{\sin A}=2\operatorname{cosec} A$. **[ICSE 2009, 04]**

8. Prove that $\sqrt{\frac{\sec A+\tan A}{\sec A-\tan A}}\cdot\sqrt{\frac{\operatorname{cosec} A-1}{\operatorname{cosec} A+1}}=1$.

9. Prove that $\frac{\sin\theta}{\cot\theta+\operatorname{cosec}\theta}=2+\frac{\sin\theta}{\cot\theta-\operatorname{cosec}\theta}$.

10. Prove that
$$\frac{\sin A}{1-\cos A}=\operatorname{cosec} A+\cos A.$$ **[ICSE 2016]**

11. Prove that $\sec^2 A-\left(\frac{\sin^2 A-2\sin^4 A}{2\cos^4 A-\cos^2 A}\right)=1$.

12. If $\tan\theta=\frac{1}{\sqrt{3}}$, then evaluate $\frac{\operatorname{cosec}^2\theta-\sec^2\theta}{\operatorname{cosec}^2\theta+\sec^2\theta}$.

13. Show that $\frac{\tan\theta}{1-\cot\theta}+\frac{\cot\theta}{1-\tan\theta}=1+\sec\theta\operatorname{cosec}\theta$.

14. Prove that
$$2\sec^2\theta-\sec^4\theta-2\operatorname{cosec}^2\theta+\operatorname{cosec}^4\theta=\cot^4\theta-\tan^4\theta.$$

15. Prove that $\frac{\operatorname{cosec}\theta+\cot\theta}{\operatorname{cosec}\theta-\cot\theta}$
$$=1+2\cot^2\theta+2\operatorname{cosec}^2\theta\cos\theta.$$

16. Prove that
$$\left(\frac{1}{\sec^2\theta-\cos^2\theta}+\frac{1}{\operatorname{cosec}^2\theta-\sin^2\theta}\right)\sin^2\theta\cos^2\theta=\frac{1-\sin^2\theta\cos^2\theta}{2+\sin^2\theta\cos^2\theta}.$$

17. Prove that $\frac{1}{(\sec x-\tan x)}-\frac{1}{\cos x}$
$$=\frac{1}{\cos x}-\frac{1}{\sec x+\tan x}.$$

18. Simplify $\frac{\tan 28^\circ}{\cot 62^\circ}+\frac{1}{\sqrt{3}}(\tan 20^\circ\cdot\tan 60^\circ\cdot\tan 70^\circ)$.

19. Find the value of
$$\frac{\sin^2 22^\circ+\sin^2 68^\circ}{\cos^2 22^\circ+\cos^2 68^\circ}+\sin^2 63^\circ+\cos 63^\circ\sin 27^\circ$$

20. Without using trigonometric tables, evaluate the following.
$$\cos^2 26^\circ+\cos 64^\circ\sin 26^\circ+\frac{\tan 36^\circ}{\cot 54^\circ}.$$ **[ICSE 2012]**

21. Find the value of
$$\sec\theta\operatorname{cosec}(90^\circ-\theta)-\tan\theta\cot(90^\circ-\theta)+\frac{\sin^2 55^\circ+\sin^2 35^\circ}{\tan 10^\circ\tan 20^\circ\tan 60^\circ\tan 70^\circ\tan 80^\circ}.$$

22. Prove that
$$\frac{\sin^2 40^\circ+\sin^2 50^\circ}{\cos^2 20^\circ+\cos^2 70^\circ}+\tan 10^\circ\tan 20^\circ\tan 60^\circ\tan 70^\circ\tan 80^\circ=1+\sqrt{3}.$$

23. Evaluate $\frac{\sec^2(90^\circ-\theta)-\cot^2\theta}{2(\sin^2 25^\circ+\sin^2 65^\circ)}+\frac{2\cos^2 60^\circ\tan^2 28^\circ\tan^2 62^\circ}{\sin 30^\circ\cos 60^\circ}$.

24. If $\operatorname{cosec}\theta-\sin\theta=m$ and $\sec\theta-\cos\theta=n$, then prove that $(m^2n)^{2/3}+(mn^2)^{2/3}=1$.

25. If $\sec\theta=x+\frac{1}{4x}$, then find the value of $\sec\theta+\tan\theta$.

26. If $\frac{\cos\alpha}{\cos\beta}=m$ and $\frac{\cos\alpha}{\sin\beta}=n$, then show that
$$(m^2+n^2)\cos^2\alpha=m^2n^2.$$

27. If $\operatorname{cosec} A-\cot A=q$, show that $\frac{q^2-1}{q^2+1}+\cos A=0$.

28. If $\operatorname{cosec}\theta+\cot\theta=p$, then prove that
$$\cos\theta=\frac{p^2-1}{p^2+1}.$$

29. If $x=r\sin A\cos B$, $y=r\sin A\sin B$ and $z=r\cos A$, then show that $x^2+y^2+z^2=r^2$.

30. If $\tan\theta+\frac{1}{\tan\theta}=2$, then find the value of
$$\cot^2\theta+\frac{1}{\cot^2\theta}.$$

31. If $\sin^6 A+\cos^6 A+3\sin^2 A\cdot\cos^2 A+4=k$, then find the value of k.

32. Prove that
$$\cot^2 A\left(\frac{\sec A-1}{1+\sin A}\right)+\sec^2 A\left(\frac{\sin A-1}{1+\sec A}\right)=0.$$

Chapter Practice

a. 1 Mark Questions

1. $(\text{cosec}^2\theta - 1)(1 - \sec^2\theta)$ is equal to

(a) 1 (b) $\sin^2\theta$
(c) -1 (d) $\,^{2}\theta$

2. $\dfrac{1+\tan^2\theta}{1+\cot^2\theta}$ is equal to

(a) $\sin^2\theta$ (b) $\tan^2\theta$
(c) $2\sin^2\theta$ (d) $2\tan^2\theta$

3. $(1+\sin A)(1-\sin A)$ is equal to **[ICSE 2023]**

(a) $\text{cosec}^2 A$ (b) $\sin^2 A$
(c) $\sec^2 A$ (d) $\cos^2 A$

4. If θ is an acute angle of right triangle, then the value of $\sin\theta\cos(90^\circ-\theta)+\cos\theta\sin(90^\circ-\theta)$ is

(a) 0 (b) $2\sin\theta\cos\theta$
(c) 1 (d) $2\sin^2\theta$

5. The value of $\cos 65^\circ \sin 25^\circ + \sin 65^\circ \cos 25^\circ$ is

(a) 0 (b) 1 (c) 2 (d) 4

6. The value of $3\tan^2 26^\circ - 3\,\text{cosec}^2 64^\circ$ is

(a) 0 (b) 3 (c) -3 (d) -1

b. 3 Marks Questions

7. If $4\cos^2\theta = 3$, then find the value of θ in 1st quadrant.

8. If $\tan\theta = \dfrac{20}{21}$, then prove that $\dfrac{1-\sin\theta+\cos\theta}{1+\sin\theta+\cos\theta} = \dfrac{3}{7}$.

9. With the help of following figure, find the value of

(i) $\sec^2\theta + \tan^2\theta$. (ii) $\text{cosec}^2\theta - \cot^2\theta$.

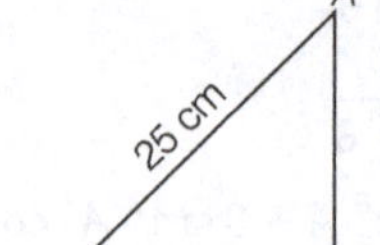

10. If $2\sin\theta - 1 = 0$, then prove that $\sec\theta + \tan\theta = \sqrt{3}$.

11. If $\sin\theta = \dfrac{1}{2}$, then prove that $3\cos\theta - 4\cos^3\theta = 0$.

12. In right angled ΔACB, $\angle C = 90^\circ$, $AB = 29$ units and $BC = 21$ units. If $\angle ABC = \theta$, then find $\cos^2\theta - \sin^2\theta$ and $\sin^2\theta + \cos^2\theta$.

13. If $\sin\theta + \cos\theta = \sqrt{2}\sin(90^\circ - \theta)$, show that $\cot\theta = \sqrt{2}+1$.

14. Find an acute angle θ, when $\dfrac{\cos\theta - \sin\theta}{\cos\theta + \sin\theta} = \dfrac{1-\sqrt{3}}{1+\sqrt{3}}$.

15. If $\tan\theta = \cot(30^\circ + \theta)$, then find the value of θ.

16. If $7\sin^2\theta + 3\cos^2\theta = 4$, $0^\circ \le \theta \le 90^\circ$, then find the value of θ.

17. Prove that $(\tan\theta + 2)(2\tan\theta + 1) = 5\tan\theta + 2\sec^2\theta$.

18. If $\cot\theta = \dfrac{15}{8}$, then find the value of $\dfrac{(2+2\sin\theta)(1-\sin\theta)}{(1+\cos\theta)(2-2\cos\theta)}$.

19. If $4x = \text{cosec}\,\theta$ and $\dfrac{4}{x} = \cot\theta$, then find the value of $4\left(x^2 - \dfrac{1}{x^2}\right)$.

20. If $\sin A + \sin^2 A = 1$, then find the value of $\cos^2 A + \cos^4 A$.

21. Prove that $\dfrac{1}{1+\sin\theta} + \dfrac{1}{1-\sin\theta} = 2\sec^2\theta$.

[ICSE Semester II 2022]

22. If $\sqrt{3}\tan\theta = 3\sin\theta$, then find the value of $\sin^2\theta - \cos^2\theta$.

23. If $\tan A = \sqrt{2} - 1$, then prove that $\dfrac{\tan A}{1+\tan^2 A} = \dfrac{\sqrt{2}}{4}$.

24. If $\tan\theta = 1$ and $\sin\phi = \dfrac{1}{\sqrt{2}}$, then find the value of $\cos(\theta+\phi)$, where θ and ϕ are both acute angles.

25. If $A + B = 90^\circ$, then prove that

$$\sqrt{\frac{\tan A \tan B + \tan A \cot B}{\sin A \sec B} - \frac{\sin^2 B}{\cos^2 A}} = \tan A.$$

26. Prove that $1 + \dfrac{\tan^2\theta}{1+\sec\theta} = \sec\theta$.

[ICSE Semester II 2022]

27. Prove that

$$\frac{(1+\sin\theta)^2 + (1-\sin\theta)^2}{2\cos^2\theta} = \sec^2\theta + \tan^2\theta.$$

[ICSE Semester II 2022]

c. 4 Marks Questions

28. Prove that

(i) $\dfrac{\sin\theta}{1-\cos\theta} = \operatorname{cosec}\theta + \cot\theta$.

(ii) $(\operatorname{cosec}A - \sin A)(\sec A - \cos A)\sec^2 A = \tan A$. [ICSE 2011]

29. Prove that $\dfrac{\sin^4\theta + \cos^4\theta}{1 - 2\sin^2\theta\cdot\cos^2\theta} = 1$.

30. Simplify $\dfrac{\sin^3\theta + \cos^3\theta}{\sin\theta + \cos\theta} + \sin\theta\cos\theta$.

31. Prove the following identities

(i) $\tan^4 A + \tan^2 A = \sec^4 A - \sec^2 A$

(ii) $\dfrac{\cos^2 A + \tan^2 A - 1}{\sin^2 A} = \tan^2 A$

32. If $7\sin^2 A + 3\cos^2 A = 4$, then prove that $\tan A = \dfrac{1}{\sqrt{3}}$.

33. If $\cos\theta + \sin\theta = \sqrt{2}\cos\theta$, then prove that $\cos\theta - \sin\theta = \sqrt{2}\sin\theta$.

34. In ΔABC, show that $\sin^2\dfrac{A}{2} + \sin^2\dfrac{B+C}{2} = 1$.

35. If $\cot\theta = 3x - \dfrac{1}{12x}$, then show that

$\cot\theta + \operatorname{cosec}\theta = 6x$ or $-\dfrac{1}{6x}$.

36. If A, B and C are interior angles of ΔABC, then show that $\tan^2\left(\dfrac{B+C}{2}\right) = \left(-1 + \operatorname{cosec}^2\dfrac{A}{2}\right)$.

37. If $\sec\theta + \tan\theta = a$, then show that $\dfrac{a^2-1}{a^2+1} = \sin\theta$.

38. If $x = a\sec A\cos B$, $y = b\sec A\sin B$ and $z = c\tan A$, show that $\dfrac{x^2}{a^2} + \dfrac{y^2}{b^2} - \dfrac{z^2}{c^2} = 1$.

39. Prove that $\sqrt{\sec^2\theta + \operatorname{cosec}^2\theta} = \tan\theta + \cot\theta$.

40. Eliminate θ from the following equations.

(i) $x = a\sec\theta$ and $y = b\tan\theta$

(ii) $x = k + a\cos\theta$ and $y = h + b\sin\theta$

41. If $\sec\theta + \tan\theta = m$ and $\sec\theta - \tan\theta = n$, then prove that $mn = 1$

42. If $p = m\operatorname{cosec}\theta + n\cot\theta$ and $q = m\cot\theta + n\operatorname{cosec}\theta$, then prove that $p^2 - q^2 = m^2 - n^2$.

43. If $\dfrac{\cos\alpha}{\cos\beta} = m$ and $\dfrac{\cos\alpha}{\sin\beta} = n$, then

show that $(m^2 + n^2)\cos^2\beta = n^2$

44. Show that $2(\cos^4 60° + \sin^4 30°) - (\tan^2 60° + \cot^2 45°) + 3\sec^2 30° = \dfrac{1}{4}$.

45. If $\alpha + \beta = 90°$, then prove that

$\sqrt{\cos\alpha\operatorname{cosec}\beta - \cos\alpha\sin\beta} = \sin\alpha$.

46. Evaluate the following.

(i) $\dfrac{\sin^2 17° + \sin^2 73°}{\cos^2 63° + \cos^2 27°}$

(ii) $\sin 35°\cos 55° + \cos 35°\sin 55°$

47. If $\dfrac{1}{x}\left(\dfrac{\sin^2 5° + \sin^2 85°}{\cos^2 5° + \cos^2 85°}\right) - \dfrac{3}{4} = 1$, then find the value of x.

48. Evaluate $\dfrac{\cot(90° - \theta)\sin(90° - \theta)}{\sin\theta} + \dfrac{\cot 40°}{\tan 50°} - (\cos^2 20° + \cos^2 70°)$.

49. In each case, given below, find the value of angle A, where $0° \le A \le 90°$

(i) $\sin(90° - 3A)\cdot\operatorname{cosec} 42° = 1$

(ii) $\cos(90° - A)\cdot\sec 78° = 1$

50. Prove that $\cos\theta\sin\theta - \dfrac{\sin\theta\cos(90° - \theta)\cos\theta}{\sec(90° - \theta)} - \dfrac{\cos\theta\sin(90° - \theta)\sin\theta}{\operatorname{cosec}(90° - \theta)} + \operatorname{cosec}(90° - \theta) = \dfrac{1}{\cos\theta}$.

d. 6 Marks Questions

51. If $\sec A = \dfrac{17}{8}$, then show that

$\dfrac{3 - 4\sin^2 A}{4\cos^2 A - 3} = \dfrac{3 - \tan^2 A}{1 - 3\tan^2 A}$.

52. Prove that $(1 + \tan A\tan B)^2 + (\tan A - \tan B)^2 = \sec^2 A\sec^2 B$.

53. If $\sqrt{3}\cot^2\theta - 4\cot\theta + \sqrt{3} = 0$, then find the value of $\tan^2\theta + \cot^2\theta$.

54. If $\sin\theta + 2\cos\theta = 1$, then prove that $2\sin\theta - \cos\theta = 2$.

55. If $1 + \cos^2\theta = 3\sin\theta\cos\theta$, then prove that $\tan\theta = 1$ or 2.

56. Prove that $\left(\tan\theta + \dfrac{1}{\cos\theta}\right)^2 + \left(\tan\theta - \dfrac{1}{\cos\theta}\right)^2 = 2\left(\dfrac{1 + \sin^2\theta}{1 - \sin^2\theta}\right)$.

57. Prove that $\dfrac{(1 + \cot\theta + \tan\theta)(\sin\theta - \cos\theta)}{\sec^3\theta - \operatorname{cosec}^3\theta} = \sin^2\theta\cos^2\theta$.

58. Show that $(\sin^8 A - \cos^8 A)$
$$= (2\sin^2 A - 1)(1 - 2\sin^2 A\cos^2 A).$$

59. If $\sin\theta + \cos\theta = p$ and $\sec\theta + \operatorname{cosec}\theta = q$, then prove that $q(p^2 - 1) = 2p$.

60. If $x = r\cos A\cos B$, $y = r\cos A\sin B$ and $z = r\sin A$, then show that $x^2 + y^2 + z^2 = r^2$

61. Prove that $l^2m^2(l^2 + m^2 + 3) = 1$, if
$$\operatorname{cosec}\theta - \sin\theta = l \text{ and } \sec\theta - \cos\theta = m.$$

62. If $\tan A = a\tan B$ and $\sin A = b\sin B$, then prove that $\cos^2 A = \dfrac{b^2 - 1}{a^2 - 1}$.

63. If $a\cos\theta - b\sin\theta = c$, then prove that
$$a\sin\theta + b\cos\theta = \pm\sqrt{a^2 + b^2 - c^2}.$$

64. Evaluate
$$\frac{\cos^2 35° + \cos^2 55°}{\operatorname{cosec}^2 15° - \tan^2 75°} + \sqrt{3}(\tan 13° \tan 23° \tan 30° \tan 67° \tan 77°).$$

65. Evaluate $\dfrac{\sec^2(90° - \theta) - \cot^2\theta}{2(\sin^2 25° + \sin^2 65°)} - \dfrac{2\sin^2 30° \tan^2 32° \cdot \tan^2 58°}{2(\sec^2 33° - \cot^2 57°)}$.

Hints and Answers

Exercise 18.1

1. Hint Do same as Example 1.

Ans. $\sin A = \dfrac{12}{13}$, $\cos A = \dfrac{5}{13}$, $\cot A = \dfrac{5}{12}$, $\tan A = \dfrac{12}{5}$, $\sec A = \dfrac{13}{5}$, $\operatorname{cosec} A = \dfrac{13}{12}$

2. Hint $QR = \sqrt{25} = 5$ cm[using]

$$\tan P = \frac{QR}{PQ} = \frac{5}{12}$$

and $\cot R = \dfrac{QR}{PQ} = \dfrac{5}{12}$

Ans. 0

3. Hint Let $QR = x$ and $PR = y$.

In right angled ΔPQR, we have

$QR^2 + PQ^2 = PR^2$ [using Pythagoras theorem]

$\Rightarrow \quad x^2 + (5)^2 = y^2$

$\Rightarrow \quad x^2 + 25 = (25 - x)^2$ [from Eq. (i)]

$\therefore \quad x = \dfrac{600}{50} = 12 = QR$

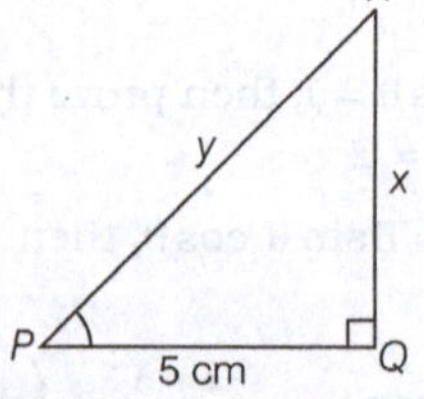

Ans. $\sin P = \dfrac{QR}{PR} = \dfrac{12}{13}$,

$\cos P = \dfrac{PQ}{PR} = \dfrac{5}{13}$

$\tan P = \dfrac{QR}{PQ} = \dfrac{12}{5}$

4. Hint $\tan A = \dfrac{m}{n}$ and $\dfrac{m\sin A - n\cos A}{n\cos A + m\sin A} = \dfrac{m \cdot \dfrac{\sin A}{\cos A} - n}{n + m \cdot \dfrac{\sin A}{\cos A}}$

Ans. $\dfrac{m^2 - n^2}{m^2 + n^2}$

5. Hint Now, LHS $= \sin(A + B) = \sin(45° + 45°)$
$= \sin 90°$

and RHS $= \sin A\cos B + \cos A\sin B$
$= \sin 45° \cos 45° + \cos 45° \sin 45°$

$\therefore$ LHS = RHS

6. Hint Substitute the values $\cos 60° = \dfrac{1}{2}$,

$\sec 30° = \dfrac{2}{\sqrt{3}}$, $\tan 45° = 1$, $\sin 30° = \dfrac{1}{2}$

and $\cos 30° = \sqrt{3}$ into the given expression.

Ans. $\dfrac{67}{12}$.

7. Hint $\dfrac{\sin 3A - 2\cos 4A}{\cos 3A + 2\sin 4A} = \dfrac{\sin 3\times 15° - 2\cos 4\times 15°}{\cos 3\times 15° + 2\sin 4\times 15°}$

Ans. $\dfrac{1-\sqrt{2}}{1+\sqrt{6}}$

8. Hint $\sin A = \cos B \Rightarrow \sin A = \sin(90° - B)$

$\Rightarrow \quad A = 90° - B$

$\therefore \quad A + B = 90°$

9. Hint $\cos(90° - 3A) = \cos(A - 26°)$

Since, $(90° - 3A)$ and $(A - 26°)$ both are acute angles.

$\therefore \quad 90° - 3A = A\ 26°$

Ans. 29°

10. Hint $\sec 5A = \sec[90° - (A + 30°)]$

[$\because \sec(90° - \theta) = \operatorname{cosec}\theta$]

$\Rightarrow \sec 5A = \sec(60° - A)$

Ans. 10°

Exercise 18.2

1. **Hint** $2\sin^2\theta - (1-\sin^2\theta) = 2 \Rightarrow 3\sin^2\theta = 3$

$\Rightarrow \quad \sin\theta = \pm 1$

But θ lies in 1st quadrant.

$\therefore \sin\theta = 1$ **Ans.** $\theta = \frac{\pi}{2}$

2. **Hint** Divide each term of numerator and denominator of the given expression by $\cos\theta$ and then put $\tan\theta = \frac{4}{7}$. **Ans.** $\frac{1}{7}$

3. **Hint** $\sin(A+B) = \sin(30^\circ + 60^\circ) = \sin 90^\circ = 1$

and $\sin A\cos B + \cos A\sin B = \sin 30^\circ \cos 60^\circ + \cos 30^\circ \sin 60^\circ$

$= \frac{1}{2}\times\frac{1}{2} + \frac{\sqrt{3}}{2}\times\frac{\sqrt{3}}{2}$

4. (i) **Hint** Put $\sec A = \frac{1}{\cos A}$, $\tan A = \frac{\sin A}{\cos A}$

and $\quad 1-\sin^2 A = \cos^2 A$

(ii) **Hint** Put $\tan A = \frac{\sin A}{\cos A}$ and $\sin^2 A + \cos^2 A = 1$

(iii) **Hint** Put $\cot\theta = \frac{\cos\theta}{\sin\theta}$ and $\tan\theta = \frac{\sin\theta}{\cos\theta}$

(iv) **Hint** Put $\tan^2\theta = \sec^2\theta - 1$ in LHS of the given expression and use $\sec\theta = \frac{1}{\cos\theta}$.

5. **Hint** $\cos A = 1 - \cos^2 A$

$\Rightarrow \quad \cos A = \sin^2 A.$

Put $\sin^4 A = \cos^2 A$

Ans. 1

6. **Hint** Substitute $\tan A = \frac{\sin A}{\cos A}$ and $\cot A = \frac{\cos A}{\sin A}$

7. **Hint** LHS $= \frac{\sin A}{1+\cos A} + \frac{1+\cos A}{\sin A}$

$= \frac{\sin^2 A + (1+\cos A)^2}{(1+\cos A)\sin A}$

$= \frac{(\sin^2 A + \cos^2 A) + 1 + 2\cos A}{(1+\cos A)\sin A}$

$= \frac{2(1+\cos A)}{(1+\cos A)\sin A}$

8. **Hint** Put $\sec A = \frac{1}{\cos A}$, $\tan A = \frac{\sin A}{\cos A}$

and $\operatorname{cosec} A = \frac{1}{\sin A}$ in LHS.

9. **Hint** Put $\cot\theta = \frac{\cos\theta}{\sin\theta}$ and $\operatorname{cosec}\theta = \frac{1}{\sin\theta}$ in both sides and simplify both sides separately.

10. **Hint** LHS $= \frac{\sin A}{1-\cos A} = \frac{\sin A}{1-\cos A} \times \frac{1+\cos A}{1+\cos A}$

Applying $\sin^2\theta + \cos^2\theta = 1$, $\operatorname{cosec}\theta = \frac{1}{\sin\theta}$

and $\cot\theta = \frac{\cos\theta}{\sin\theta}$

11. **Hint** $\sec^2 A - \frac{\sin^2 A(1-2\sin^2 A)}{\cos^2 A(2\cos^2 A - 1)}$

$= \sec^2 A - \frac{\tan^2 A[(1-2(1-\cos^2 A)]}{(2\cos^2 A - 1)}$

12. **Hint** $\frac{\operatorname{cosec}^2\theta - \sec^2\theta}{\operatorname{cosec}^2\theta + \sec^2\theta} = \frac{\frac{1}{\sin^2\theta} - \frac{1}{\cos^2\theta}}{\frac{1}{\sin^2\theta} + \frac{1}{\cos^2\theta}}$

$= \frac{\cos^2\theta - \sin^2\theta}{\sin^2\theta + \cos^2\theta} = \cos^2\theta - \sin^2\theta$

Also, $\tan\theta = \frac{1}{\sqrt{3}} \Rightarrow \theta = 30^\circ$ **Ans.** $\frac{1}{2}$

13. **Hint** Put $\tan\theta = \frac{\sin\theta}{\cos\theta}$ and $\cot\theta = \frac{\cos\theta}{\sin\theta}$

14. **Hint** $(\operatorname{cosec}\theta - 2\operatorname{cosec}\theta) - (\sec\theta - 2\sec\theta)$

$= (\operatorname{cosec}^4\theta - 2\operatorname{cosec}^2\theta + 1) - (\sec^4\theta - 2\sec^2\theta + 1)$

$= (\operatorname{cosec}^2\theta - 1)^2 - (\sec^2\theta - 1)^2$

Put $\sec^2\theta = \tan^2\theta + 1$ and $\operatorname{cosec}^2\theta = \cot^2\theta + 1$.

15. **Hint** Use $\operatorname{cosec}\theta = \frac{1}{\sin\theta}$ and $\cot\theta = \frac{\cos\theta}{\sin\theta}$

16. **Hint** LHS

$= \left[\frac{1}{\frac{1}{\cos^2\theta} - \cos^2\theta} + \frac{1}{\frac{1}{\sin^2\theta} - \sin^2\theta}\right]\sin^2\theta\cos^2\theta$

$= \left[\frac{\cos^2\theta}{1-\cos^4\theta} + \frac{\sin^2\theta}{1-\sin^4\theta}\right]\sin^2\theta\cos^2\theta$

$= \left[\frac{\cos^2\theta}{(1+\cos^2\theta)(1-\cos^2\theta)} + \frac{\sin^2\theta}{(1-\sin^2\theta)(1+\sin^2\theta)}\right] \times \sin^2\theta\cos^2\theta$

$= \left[\frac{\cos^2\theta}{(1+\cos^2\theta)\sin^2\theta} + \frac{\sin^2\theta}{\cos^2\theta(1+\sin^2\theta)}\right] \times \sin^2\theta\cos^2\theta$

17. **Hint** Put $\sec x = \frac{1}{\cos x}$ and $\tan x = \frac{\sin x}{\cos x}$ and then simplify both sides separately.

18. **Hint** $\frac{\tan 28^\circ}{\cot 62^\circ} \times \frac{\sqrt{3}}{\tan 20^\circ \tan 60^\circ \tan 70^\circ}$

$= \frac{\cot 62^\circ}{\cot 62^\circ} \times \frac{\sqrt{3}}{\tan 20^\circ \times \sqrt{3} \times \cot 20^\circ}$ **Ans.** 1

19. **Hint** Use $\sin(90^\circ - \theta) = \cos\theta$, $\cos(90^\circ - \theta) = \sin\theta$ and $\sin^2\theta + \cos^2\theta = 1$. **Ans.** 2

20. **Hint** Use complementary angles formula and also use identity $\sin^2 A + \cos^2 A = 1$. **Ans.** 2

21. **Hint** $\frac{\sec\theta\sec\theta - \tan\theta\tan\theta + \sin^2(90^\circ - 35^\circ) + \sin^2 35^\circ}{\tan 10^\circ \tan 20^\circ \tan 60^\circ \tan(90^\circ - 20^\circ)\tan(90^\circ - 10^\circ)}$

$= \frac{\sec^2\theta - \tan^2\theta + \cos^2 35^\circ + \sin^2 35^\circ}{\tan 10^\circ \tan 20^\circ (\sqrt{3}) \cot 20^\circ \cot 10^\circ}$

Ans. $\frac{2}{\sqrt{3}}$

22. **Hint** Using complementary angle formulae and identity $\sin^2 A + \cos^2 A = 1$.

23. **Hint** We have, $\dfrac{\sec^2(90° - \theta) - \cot^2\theta}{2(\sin^2 25° + \sin^2 65°)} + \dfrac{2\cos^2 60° \tan^2 28° \tan^2 62°}{\sin 30° \cos 60°}$

$$= \frac{\text{cosec}^2\theta - \cot^2\theta}{2[\sin^2(90° - 65°) + \sin^2 65°]} + \frac{2\cos 60° \tan^2(90° - 62°)\tan^2 62°}{\sin 30°}$$

$$= \frac{1}{2(\cos^2 65° + \sin^2 65°)} + \frac{2\cdot\frac{1}{2}\cot^2 62° \tan^2 62°}{1/2}$$

Ans. 5/2

24. **Hint** Given, $\text{cosec}\,\theta - \sin\theta = m$; $\sec\theta - \cos\theta = n$

$$\Rightarrow \frac{1}{\sin\theta} - \sin\theta = m \text{ and } \frac{1}{\cos\theta} - \cos\theta = n$$

$$\Rightarrow \frac{1 - \sin^2\theta}{\sin\theta} = m \text{ and } \frac{1 - \cos^2\theta}{\cos\theta} = n$$

$$\Rightarrow \frac{\cos^2\theta}{\sin\theta} = m \text{ and } \frac{\sin^2\theta}{\cos\theta} = n$$

Now, determine $(m^2 n)^{2/3}$ and $(mn^2)^{2/3}$.

25. **Hint** $\sec\theta = x + \dfrac{1}{4x}$

$$\Rightarrow \sec^2\theta = x^2 + \left(\frac{1}{4x}\right)^2 + 2\cdot x\cdot\frac{1}{4x}$$

$$\Rightarrow \sec^2\theta - 1 = x^2 + \frac{1}{16x^2} - \frac{1}{2}$$

$$\Rightarrow \tan^2\theta = \left(x - \frac{1}{4x}\right)^2$$

$$\Rightarrow \tan\theta = \pm\left(x - \frac{1}{4x}\right)$$ **Ans.** $2x, 1/2x$

26. **Hint** $\cos\beta = \dfrac{\cos\alpha}{m}$ and $\sin\beta = \dfrac{\cos\alpha}{n}$

Determine $(m^2 + n^2)\cos\alpha$ and m^2n^2.

Use $\cos^2\beta + \sin^2\beta = 1$

27. **Hint** Substitute $\text{cosec}\,A - \cot A = q$ into $\dfrac{q^2 - 1}{q^2 + 1} + \cos A = 0$ and simplify to get the result.

28. Given, $\text{cosec}\,\theta + \cot\theta = p$ ...(i)

We know that $\text{cosec}^2\theta - \cot^2\theta = 1$

$\Rightarrow (\text{cosec}\,\theta + \cot\theta)(\text{cosec}\,\theta - \cot\theta) = 1$

$[\because a^2 - b^2 = (a + b)(a - b)]$

$\Rightarrow p(\text{cosec}\,\theta - \cot\theta) = 1$ [from Eq. (i)]

$\Rightarrow \text{cosec}\,\theta - \cot\theta = \dfrac{1}{p}$ ...(ii)

On adding Eqs. (i) and (ii), we get

$2\,\text{cosec}\,\theta = p + \dfrac{1}{p} \Rightarrow \text{cosec}\,\theta = \dfrac{p^2 + 1}{2p}$ ...(iii)

On subtracting Eq. (ii) from Eq. (i), we get

$$2\cot\theta = p - \frac{1}{p}$$

$\Rightarrow \cot\theta = \dfrac{p^2 - 1}{2p}$ ...(iv)

On dividing Eq. (iv) by Eq. (iii), we get

$$\frac{\cot\theta}{\text{cosec}\,\theta} = \frac{p^2 - 1}{p^2 + 1}$$

$$\Rightarrow \cos\theta = \frac{p^2 - 1}{p^2 + 1}$$

$\left[\because \dfrac{\cot A}{\text{cosec}\,A} = \dfrac{\cos A \times \sin A}{\sin A} = \cos A\right]$

Hence proved.

29. **Hint** Put the values of x, y and z in LHS and simplify it.

30. **Hint** $\left(\tan\theta + \dfrac{1}{\tan\theta}\right)^2 = (2)^2$

$$\Rightarrow \tan^2\theta + \frac{1}{\tan^2\theta} + 2 = 4$$

Now, put $\tan\theta = \dfrac{1}{\cot\theta}$, we get the required result.

Ans. 2

31. **Hint** LHS $= (\sin^2 A + \cos^2 A)^3 - 3\sin^2 A\cos^2 A$

$(\sin^2 A + \cos^2 A) + 3\sin^2 A\cos^2 A + 4$

$= 1 + 4 = 5$ **Ans.** $k = 5$

32. **Hint** Put $\cot A = \dfrac{\cos A}{\sin A}$ and $\sec A = \dfrac{1}{\cos A}$

Chapter Exercise

1. (c) Given, $(\text{cosec}^2\theta - 1)(1 - \sec^2\theta)$

$= \cot^2\theta \times (-\tan^2\theta)$

$[\because \text{cosec}^2 A - \cot^2 A = 1, \because \sec^2 A - \tan^2 A = 1]$

$= -1$ $[\tan A \cdot \cot A = 1]$

2. (b) $\dfrac{1 + \tan^2\theta}{1 + \cot^2\theta} = \dfrac{1 + \tan^2\theta}{\text{cosec}^2\theta}$ $[\because 1 + \cot^2 A = \text{cosec}^2 A]$

$= \dfrac{\sec^2\theta}{\text{cosec}^2\theta} = \tan^2\theta$

3. (d) Given, $(1 + \sin A)(1 - \sin A)$

$= 1^2 - \sin^2 A$ $[\because a^2 - b^2 = (a + b)(a - b)]$

$= 1 - \sin^2 A$

$[\because \sin^2 A + \cos^2 A = 1 \Rightarrow 1 - \sin^2 A = \cos^2 A]$

$= \cos^2 A$

4. (c) $\sin\theta\sin\theta + \cos\theta\cos\theta$

$[\because \sin(90° - A) = \cos A \text{ and } \cos(90° - A) = \sin A]$

$= \sin^2\theta + \cos^2\theta = 1$

5. (b) $\cos 65° \sin 25° + \sin 65° \cos 25°$

$= \sin(65° + 25°)$

$= \sin 90°$

$[\because \sin(A + B) = \sin A\cos B + \cos A\sin B]$

$= 1$

6. (c) Given, $3\tan^2 26° - 3\,\text{cosec}^2 64°$

$= 3\tan^2(90 - 64°) - 3\,\text{cosec}^2 64°$

$= 3\cot^2 64° - 3\,\text{cosec}^2 64°$

$= -3$ $\quad [\because \text{cosec}^2\theta - \cot^2\theta = 1]$

7. Hint $\cos\theta = \pm\dfrac{\sqrt{3}}{2}$

In first quadrant, we have $\cos\theta = \dfrac{\sqrt{3}}{2}$

Ans. 30°

8. Hint $\sin\theta = \dfrac{20}{29}$ and $\cos\theta = \dfrac{21}{29}$

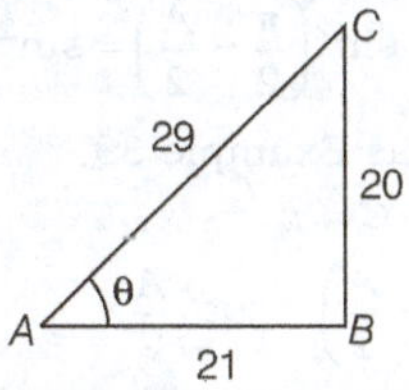

9. Hint $AB = \sqrt{(25)^2 - (24)^2} = \sqrt{49} = 7$

(i) $\sec^2\theta + \tan^2\theta = \left(\dfrac{25}{24}\right)^2 + \left(\dfrac{7}{24}\right)^2$

(ii) $\text{cosec}^2\theta - \cot^2\theta = \left(\dfrac{25}{7}\right)^2 - \left(\dfrac{24}{7}\right)^2$

Ans. (i) $\dfrac{337}{288}$ (ii) 1

10. Hint $\sin\theta = \dfrac{1}{2}$ and $\cos\theta = \sqrt{1 - \sin^2\theta} = \sqrt{1 - \dfrac{1}{4}} = \dfrac{\sqrt{3}}{2}$

$\therefore \sec\theta = \dfrac{2}{\sqrt{3}}$ and $\tan\theta = \dfrac{1}{\sqrt{3}}$

11. Hint $\cos\theta = \sqrt{1 - \sin^2\theta} = \sqrt{1 - \dfrac{1}{4}} = \dfrac{\sqrt{3}}{2}$

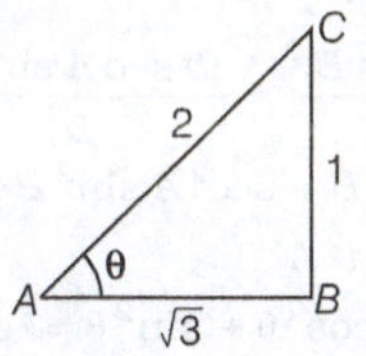

12. Hint In ΔACB, $\cos\theta = \dfrac{21}{29}$

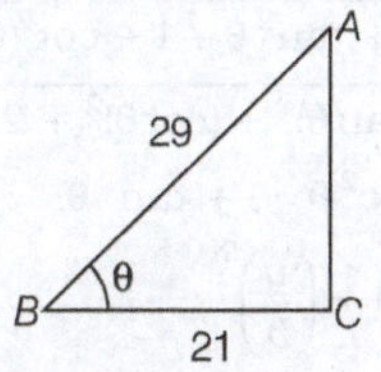

$\therefore \sin\theta = \sqrt{1 - \cos^2\theta} = \sqrt{1 - \left(\dfrac{21}{29}\right)^2} = \dfrac{20}{29}$

Ans. $\dfrac{41}{841}$, 1

13. Hint $\sin\theta + \cos\theta = \sqrt{2}\sin(90° - \theta)$

$\Rightarrow \dfrac{\sin\theta}{\sin\theta} + \dfrac{\cos\theta}{\sin\theta} = \sqrt{2}\left(\dfrac{\cos\theta}{\sin\theta}\right)$

$\Rightarrow 1 + \cot\theta = \sqrt{2}\cot\theta$

$\Rightarrow \sqrt{2} + 1 = \cot\theta$

14. Hint On dividing numerator and denominator of LHS by $\cos\theta$, we get

$$\frac{1 - \tan\theta}{1 + \tan\theta} = \frac{1 - \sqrt{3}}{1 + \sqrt{3}}$$

On comparing both sides, we get

$$\tan\theta = \sqrt{3}$$

Ans. 60°

15. Hint We have, $\tan\theta = \cot(30° + \theta)$

$\Rightarrow \cot(90° - \theta) = \cot(30° + \theta)$

$\Rightarrow 90° - \theta = 30° + \theta$

Ans. $\theta = 30°$

16. Hint $7\sin^2\theta + 3\cos^2\theta = 4$

$4\sin^2\theta + 3\sin^2\theta + 3\cos^2\theta = 4$

$\Rightarrow 4\sin^2\theta = 4 - 3 \quad [\because \sin^2 A + \cos^2 A = 1]$

$\Rightarrow \sin^2\theta = \dfrac{1}{4}$

$\Rightarrow \sin\theta = \pm\dfrac{1}{\sqrt{2}}$

$\theta = 45°$

17. Hint LHS $= 2\tan^2\theta + 5\tan\theta + 2$

Put $\tan^2\theta = \sec^2\theta - 1$

18. Hint $\dfrac{(2 + 2\sin\theta)(1 - \sin\theta)}{(1 + \cos\theta)(2 - 2\cos\theta)} = \dfrac{2(1 - \sin^2\theta)}{2(1 - \cos^2\theta)} = \dfrac{\cos^2\theta}{\sin^2\theta}$

Ans. 225 / 64

19. Hint $4x = \text{cosec}\,\theta \Rightarrow x = \dfrac{\text{cosec}\,\theta}{4}$

and $\dfrac{4}{x} = \cot\theta \Rightarrow \dfrac{1}{x} = \dfrac{\cot\theta}{4}$

Now, $4\left(x^2 - \dfrac{1}{x^2}\right) = 4\left[\left(\dfrac{\text{cosec}\,\theta}{4}\right)^2 - \left(\dfrac{\cot\theta}{4}\right)^2\right]$

Ans. 1/4

20. Hint $\sin A = 1 - \sin^2 A = \cos^2 A$. **Ans.** 1

21. Hint LHS $= \dfrac{1}{1 + \sin\theta} + \dfrac{1}{1 - \sin\theta}$

$= \dfrac{1 - \sin\theta + 1 + \sin\theta}{1 - \sin^2\theta}$

22. Hint $\sqrt{3}\tan\theta = 3\sin\theta$

$\Rightarrow \cos\theta = \dfrac{1}{\sqrt{3}}$ and $\sin\theta = \sqrt{1 - \cos^2\theta} = \sqrt{1 - \dfrac{1}{3}} = \sqrt{\dfrac{2}{3}}$

Ans. $\dfrac{1}{3}$

23. Hint Put $\tan A = \sqrt{2} - 1$ in LHS and simplify it.

24. Hint $\tan\theta = 1 \Rightarrow \theta = 45°$ and $\sin\phi = \dfrac{1}{\sqrt{2}} \Rightarrow \phi = 45°$

$\therefore \cos(\theta + \phi) = \cos(45° + 45°)$ **Ans.** 0

25. Given, $A + B = 90° \Rightarrow B = 90° - A$

Now, $\text{LHS} = \sqrt{\dfrac{\tan A \tan B + \tan A \cot B}{\sin A \sec B} - \dfrac{\sin^2 B}{\cos^2 A}}$

$= \sqrt{\dfrac{\tan A \tan(90° - A) + \tan A \cot(90° - A)}{\sin A \sec(90° - A)} - \dfrac{\sin^2(90° - A)}{\cos^2 A}}$

26. Hint $\text{LHS} = 1 + \dfrac{\tan^2\theta}{1 + \sec\theta}$

$= 1 + \dfrac{\sec^2\theta - 1}{1 + \sec\theta}$ $[\because \tan^2\theta = \sec^2\theta - 1]$

$= 1 + \dfrac{(\sec\theta + 1)(\sec\theta - 1)}{(1 + \sec\theta)}$

$[\because a^2 - b^2 = (a + b)(a - b)]$

27. Hint $\text{LHS} = \dfrac{(1 + \sin\theta)^2 + (1 - \sin\theta)^2}{2\cos^2\theta}$

$= \dfrac{1 + \sin^2\theta + 2\sin\theta + 1 + \sin^2\theta - 2\sin\theta}{2\cos^2\theta}$

$[\because (a \pm b)^2 = a^2 + b^2 \pm 2ab]$

$= \dfrac{2(1 + \sin^2\theta)}{2\cos^2\theta} = \dfrac{1 + \sin^2\theta}{\cos^2\theta}$

$= \dfrac{1}{\cos^2\theta} + \dfrac{\sin^2\theta}{\cos^2\theta}$

28. (i) **Hint** $\text{LHS} = \dfrac{\sin\theta}{1 - \cos\theta} = \dfrac{\sin\theta(1 + \cos\theta)}{(1 - \cos\theta)(1 + \cos\theta)}$

(ii) **Hint** Put $\operatorname{cosec} A = \dfrac{1}{\sin A}$,

$\sec A = \dfrac{1}{\cos A}$ and use identity $\sin^2 A + \cos^2 A = 1$.

29. Hint Using the formula,

$a^2 + b^2 = (a + b)^2 - 2ab$

$\text{LHS} = \dfrac{(\sin^2\theta + \cos^2\theta)^2 - 2\sin^2\theta\cos^2\theta}{1 - 2\sin^2\theta\cos^2\theta}$

30. Hint Using the formula,

$a^3 + b^3 = (a + b)(a^2 + b^2 - ab)$

$\text{LHS} = \dfrac{(\sin\theta + \cos\theta)(\sin^2\theta + \cos^2\theta - \sin\theta\cos\theta)}{\sin\theta + \cos\theta} + \sin\theta\cos\theta$

$= 1 - \sin\theta\cos\theta + \sin\theta\cos\theta$ **Ans.** 1

31. Hint

(i) $\text{LHS} = \tan^2 A(\tan^2 A + 1)$

$= (\sec^2 A - 1)\sec^2 A = \text{RHS}$

(ii) $\text{LHS} = \dfrac{\tan^2 A - (1 - \cos^2 A)}{\sin^2 A} = \dfrac{\tan^2 A}{\sin^2 A} - \dfrac{\sin^2 A}{\sin^2 A}$

$= \sec^2 A - 1 = \tan^2 A = \text{RHS}$

32. Hint Put $\sin A = \dfrac{\tan A}{\sqrt{1 + \tan^2 A}}$

and $\cos A = \dfrac{1}{\sqrt{1 + \tan^2 A}}$ in given equation and simplify it.

33. Hint $(\cos\theta + \sin\theta)^2 = (\sqrt{2}\cos\theta)^2$

$\Rightarrow \cos^2\theta + \sin^2\theta + 2\sin\theta\cos\theta = 2\cos^2\theta$

$\Rightarrow 2\cos^2\theta - \cos^2\theta + \sin^2\theta - 2\sin\theta\cos\theta$

$= \sin^2\theta + \sin^2\theta$

$[\because$ adding $\sin^2\theta$ on both sides$]$

$\Rightarrow \cos^2\theta + \sin^2\theta - 2\sin\theta\cos\theta = 2\sin^2\theta$

$\Rightarrow (\cos\theta - \sin\theta)^2 = (\sqrt{2}\sin\theta)^2$

34. Hint Consider, $A + B + C = \pi \Rightarrow B + C = \pi - A$

$\text{LHS} = \sin^2\dfrac{A}{2} + \sin^2\left(\dfrac{\pi - A}{2}\right)$

$= \sin^2\dfrac{A}{2} + \sin^2\left(\dfrac{\pi}{2} - \dfrac{A}{2}\right) = \sin^2\dfrac{A}{2} + \cos^2\dfrac{A}{2}$

35. Hint Do same as Example 39.

36. Hint $\because A + B + C = \pi$

$\text{LHS} = \tan^2\left(\dfrac{\pi}{2} - \dfrac{A}{2}\right) = \cot^2\dfrac{A}{2}$

37. Hint $\dfrac{a^2 - 1}{a^2 + 1} = \dfrac{(\sec\theta + \tan\theta)^2 - 1}{(\sec\theta + \tan\theta)^2 + 1}$

$= \dfrac{\sec^2\theta + \tan^2\theta + 2\sec\theta\tan\theta - 1}{\sec^2\theta + \tan^2\theta + 2\sec\tan\theta + 1}$

$= \dfrac{(\sec^2\theta - 1) + \tan^2\theta + 2\sec\theta\tan\theta}{\sec^2\theta + (\tan^2\theta + 1) + 2\sec\theta\tan\theta}$

$= \dfrac{2\tan^2\theta + 2\sec\theta\tan\theta}{2\sec^2\theta + + 2\sec\theta\tan\theta}$

$= \dfrac{2\tan\theta}{2\sec\theta}$

$= \dfrac{\sin\theta}{\cos\theta} \times \cos\theta$

$= \sin\theta$ **Hence proved.**

38. Hint LHS $\dfrac{x^2}{a^2} + \dfrac{y^2}{b^2} - \dfrac{z^2}{c^2}$

$= \dfrac{(a\sec A\cos B)^2}{a^2} + \dfrac{(b\sec A\sin B)^2}{b^2} - \dfrac{(c\tan A)^2}{c^2}$

$= \sec^2 A\cos^2 B + \sec^2 A\sin^2 B - \tan^2 A$

$= \sec^2 A - \tan^2 A$

$[\because \cos^2\theta + \sin^2\theta = 1$ and $\sec^2\theta - \tan^2\theta = 1]$

$= 1$ RHS

39. Hint $\text{LHS} = \sqrt{\sec^2\theta + \operatorname{cosec}^2\theta}$

$= \sqrt{1 + \tan^2\theta + 1 + \cot^2\theta}$

$= \sqrt{(\tan\theta)^2 + (\cot\theta)^2 + 2\tan\theta\cot\theta}$

40. (i) **Hint** Use $\sec^2\theta = 1 + \tan^2\theta$.

Ans. $\left(\dfrac{x}{a}\right)^2 = 1 + \left(\dfrac{y}{b}\right)^2$

(ii) **Hint** $\cos\theta = \dfrac{x - k}{a}$ and $\sin\theta = \dfrac{y - h}{b}$

Ans. $\left(\dfrac{x - k}{a}\right)^2 + \left(\dfrac{y - h}{b}\right)^2 = 1$

41. Hint $(\sec\theta + \tan\theta)(\sec\theta - \tan\theta) = mn$

$mn = 1$ $[\because \sec^2 A - \tan^2 A = 1]$

42. **Hint** Do same as Example 36.

43. **Hint** Taking LCM we get

$$\left(\frac{\cos^2\alpha\sin^2\beta+\cos^2\alpha\cos^2\beta}{\cos^2\beta\sin^2\beta}\right)\cdot\cos^2\beta$$

$$=\frac{\cos^2\alpha(\sin^2\beta+\cos^2\beta)}{\sin^2\beta}=n^2$$

LHS = RHS **Hence proved.**

44. **Hint** Put $\cos 60^\circ=\frac{1}{2}$, $\sin 30^\circ=\frac{1}{2}$, $\tan 60^\circ=\sqrt{3}$, $\cot 45^\circ=1$ and $\sec 30^\circ=\frac{2}{\sqrt{3}}$

45. **Hint** LHS $=\sqrt{\cos\alpha\,\text{cosec}\,(90^\circ-\alpha)-\cos\alpha\sin(90^\circ-\alpha)}$

$=\sqrt{\cos\alpha\sec\alpha-\cos\alpha\cos\alpha}$

$=\sqrt{1-\cos^2\alpha}$

$=\sqrt{\sin^2\alpha}$

46. **Hint** $\sin(90^\circ-\theta)=\cos\theta$

and $\cos(90^\circ-\theta)=\sin\theta$

Then, $\sin 17^\circ=\sin(90^\circ-73^\circ)=\cos 73^\circ$

(i) $\frac{\sin^2(90^\circ-73^\circ)+\sin^2 73^\circ}{\cos^2 63^\circ+\cos^2(90^\circ-63^\circ)}=\frac{\cos^2 73^\circ+\sin^2 73^\circ}{\cos^2 63^\circ+\sin^2 63^\circ}$

$[\because \sin^2\theta+\cos^2\theta=1]$

Ans. 1

(ii) Do as same part (i). **Ans.** 1

47. **Hint** Use $\sin(90^\circ-\theta)=\cos\theta$, $\cos(90^\circ-\theta)=\sin\theta$

and $\sin^2\theta+\cos^2\theta=1$ **Ans.** $\frac{4}{7}$

48. **Hint** $\frac{\tan\theta\cos\theta}{\sin\theta}+\frac{\tan 50^\circ}{\tan 50^\circ}-(\cos^2 20^\circ+\sin^2 20^\circ)$

$=1+1-1$ $[\because \cot(90^\circ-\theta)=\tan\theta, \sin(90^\circ-\theta)=\cos\theta$ and $\cos(90^\circ-\theta)=\sin\theta]$

Ans. 1

49. **Hint**

(i) $\sin(90^\circ-3A)=\frac{1}{\text{cosec}\,42^\circ}$

$\sin(90^\circ-3A)=\sin 42^\circ$ $\left[\because \sin\theta=\frac{1}{\text{cosec}\,\theta}\right]$

$A=16^\circ$

(ii) $\cos(90^\circ-A)=\frac{1}{\sec 78^\circ}$

$90^\circ-A=78^\circ$ $\left[\because \cos\theta=\frac{1}{\sec\theta}\right]$

$A=12^\circ$

Ans. (i) 16° (ii) 12°

50. **Hint** LHS $=\cos\theta\sin\theta-\frac{\sin\theta\sin\theta\cos\theta}{\text{cosec}\theta}-\frac{\cos\theta\cos\theta\sin\theta}{\sec\theta}+\sec\theta$

$=\cos\theta\sin\theta-\sin^3\theta\cos\theta-\cos^3\theta\sin\theta+\sec\theta$

$=\cos\theta\sin\theta-\sin\theta\cos\theta(\sin^2\theta+\cos^2\theta)+\sec\theta$

51. **Hint** Here, $\sin A=\frac{15}{17}$, $\tan A=\frac{15}{8}$ and $\cos A=\frac{8}{17}$

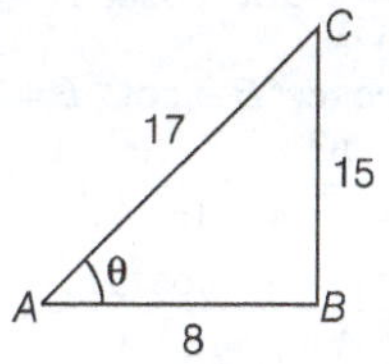

[by using Pythagoras theorem]

52. **Hint** LHS $=1+\tan^2 A\tan^2 B+2\tan A\tan B+\tan^2 A+\tan^2 B-2\tan A\tan B$

$=\tan^2 A(1+\tan^2 B)+1(1+\tan^2 B)$

$=(1+\tan^2 B)(1+\tan^2 A)$

53. **Hint** Given, equation is quadratic in terms of $\cot\theta$.

So, find the roots, i.e. $\cot\theta=\frac{1}{\sqrt{3}}$ and $\cot\theta=\sqrt{3}$.

Ans. $\frac{10}{3}$

54. **Hint** $(\sin\theta+2\cos\theta)^2=1^2$

$\Rightarrow$ $\sin^2\theta+4\cos^2\theta+4\sin\theta\cos\theta=1$

$\Rightarrow$ $\sin^2\theta+4(1-\sin^2\theta)+4\sin\theta\cos\theta=\cos^2\theta+\sin^2\theta$

$\Rightarrow$ $4\sin^2\theta+\cos^2\theta-4\sin\theta\cos\theta=4$

55. **Hint** Put $\sin\theta=\frac{\tan\theta}{\sqrt{1+\tan^2\theta}}$;

$\cos\theta=\frac{1}{\sqrt{1+\tan^2\theta}}$

56. **Hint** Put $\tan\theta=\frac{\sin\theta}{\cos\theta}$

57. **Hint** LHS $=\frac{\left(1+\frac{\cos\theta}{\sin\theta}+\frac{\sin\theta}{\cos\theta}\right)(\sin\theta-\cos\theta)}{\frac{1}{\cos^3\theta}-\frac{1}{\sin^3\theta}}$

$=\frac{(\cos\theta\sin\theta+1)(\sin\theta-\cos\theta)}{(\sin^3\theta-\cos^3\theta)\sin\theta\cos\theta}(\sin^3\theta\cos^3\theta)$

$[\because \sin^2 A+\cos^2 A=1]$

$=\frac{(\cos\theta\sin\theta+1)(\sin\theta-\cos\theta)\cdot\sin^2\theta\cos^2\theta}{(\sin\theta-\cos\theta)(\sin^2\theta+\sin\theta\cos\theta+\cos^2\theta)}$

$[\because a^3-b^3=(a-b)(a^2+ab+b^2)]$

$=\sin^2\theta\cos^2\theta$

58. **Hint** $(\sin^8 A-\cos^8 A)=[(\sin^4 A)^2-(\cos^4 A)^2)]$

$=(\sin^4 A+\cos^4 A)(\sin^4 A-\cos^4 A)$

$=[(\sin^2 A+\cos^2 A)^2-2\sin^2 A\cos^2 A]$

$[\because a^2+b^2=(a+b)^2-2ab]$

$\times(\sin^2 A+\cos^2 A)(\sin^2 A-\cos^2 A)$

$=(1-2\sin^2 A\cos^2 A)(\sin^2 A-\cos^2 A)$

59. **Hint** Substitute the values of p and q in LHS.

60. **Hint** $x^2+y^2+z^2$

$=r^2\cos^2 A\cos^2 B+r^2\cos^2 A\sin^2 B+r^2\sin^2 A$

LHS = RHS **Hence proved.**

61. **Hint** Put the values of l and m in the given equation.

62. **Hint** $\cot B = \frac{a}{\tan A}$ and $\operatorname{cosec} B = \frac{b}{\sin A}$

We know that $\operatorname{cosec}^2 B - \cot^2 B = 1$

$$\Rightarrow \quad \frac{b^2}{\sin^2 A} - \frac{a^2}{\tan^2 A} = 1$$

$$\Rightarrow \quad \frac{b^2}{\sin^2 A} - \frac{a^2 \cos^2 A}{\sin^2 A} = 1$$

$$\Rightarrow \quad b^2 - a^2 \cos^2 A = \sin^2 A$$

$$\Rightarrow \quad b^2 - a^2 \cos^2 A = 1 - \cos^2 A$$

63. **Hint** Do same as Example 35.

64. **Hint** $\frac{\cos^2 35° + \sin^2 35°}{\operatorname{cosec}^2 15° - \cot^2 15°} + \sqrt{3}\left(\tan 13° \tan 23° \times \frac{1}{\sqrt{3}} \times \cot 23° \cot 13°\right)$

Ans. 2

65. **Hint** $\frac{\operatorname{cosec}^2\theta - \cot^2\theta}{2(\sin^2 25° + \cos^2 25°)} - \frac{2 \times \frac{1}{4} \times \tan^2 32° \times \cot^2 32°}{2(\sec^2 33° - \tan^2 33°)} = \frac{1}{2} - \frac{1}{4}$

Ans. $\frac{1}{4}$

Olympiad Section

Brain Teasing Questions asked in Previous Olympiads

1 If $\sin\alpha$ and $\cos\alpha$ are the roots of the equation $px^2 + qx + r = 0$, then the value of $p^2 - q^2 + 2rp$ is

(a) 1 (b) -1
(c) 0 (d) None of these

2 In ΔABC right angled at B, if $BC = 5$ cm and $AC - AB = 1$ cm, then the value of $\dfrac{\cos^2 C}{1 - \sin C}$ is

(a) $\dfrac{12}{13}$ (b) $\dfrac{13}{12}$
(c) $\dfrac{25}{13}$ (d) $\dfrac{13}{25}$

3 If $\operatorname{cosec}\theta - \sin\theta = x^3$ and $\sec\theta - \cos\theta = y^3$, then the value of $x^2y^2(x^2 + y^2)$ is

(a) 0 (b) 1
(c) 2 (d) 3

4 If $T_n = \sin^n\theta + \cos^n\theta$, then the value of $\dfrac{T_3 - T_5}{T_1}$ is

(a) $\sin^2\theta\cos^2\theta$ (b) $\dfrac{\cos^2\theta}{\sin^2\theta}$
(c) $\sin^2\theta - \cos^2\theta$ (d) $\cos^3\theta + \sin^2\theta$

5 If $\sin\theta + \sin^2\theta = 1$, then the value of $\cos^{12}\theta + 3\cos^{10}\theta + 3\cos^8\theta + \cos^6\theta + 2\cos^4\theta + 2\cos^2\theta - 2$ is

(a) 0 (b) 1
(c) 2 (d) 3

6 The value of the expression $1 - \dfrac{\sin^2 y}{1+\cos y} + \dfrac{1+\cos y}{\sin y} - \dfrac{\sin y}{1-\cos y}$ is

(a) 0 (b) 1
(c) $\sin y$ (d) $\cos y$

7 If $(\sec A + \tan A)(\sec B + \tan B)(\sec C + \tan C) = (\sec A - \tan A)(\sec B - \tan B)(\sec C - \tan C) = x$, then the value(s) of x is/are

(a) ± 1 (b) 0
(c) ± 2 (d) 1

8 If $f(x) = \cos^2 x + \sec^2 x$, then $f(x)$

(a) ≥ 1 (b) ≤ 1
(c) ≥ 2 (d) ≤ 2

9 If ABC is a right angled triangle, then find the relation between $\tan\left(\dfrac{A-B-C}{2}\right)$ and $-\tan\left(\dfrac{A+B-C}{2}\right)$.

(a) Equal (b) Unequal
(c) Sum of these equal to 1
(d) None of these

10 If $a\sec\theta + b\tan\theta + c = 0$ and $p\sec\theta + q\tan\theta + r = 0$, then $(br - qc)^2 - (pc - ar)^2$ is equal to

(a) $(ap - bq)^2$ (b) $(aq - bp)^2$
(c) $(ap - bq)$ (d) $(aq - bp)$

Answers

1. (c) **2.** (c) **3.** (b) **4.** (a) **5.** (b) **6.** (d) **7.** (a) **8.** (c) **9.** (b) **10.** (b)

* *These questions may or may not be asked in the examination, have been given just for additional practice required for olympiads Scholarship Exams etc. For detailed explanations refer Page No. 498.*

CHAPTER

19

Heights and Distances

SYLLABUS

- **Solving 2-D problems involving angles of elevation and depression using trigonometric tables.**

Note Cases involving more than two right angled triangles excluded.

Measuring of heights and distances is the important application of Trigonometry. Sometimes, we need to find the height of different objects like tower, building, tree, etc., distance of a ship from a light-house, width of river and angle subtended by any object at a given point, etc., it is difficult to measure them directly. In this chapter, we will study the use of trigonometry in measuring the heights and distances of such cases.

Important Terms Related to Heights and Distances

In solving problems related to heights and distances of various objects, we need to define few terms as discussed below

Line of Sight

The line of sight is the line drawn from the eye of an observer to the point in the object viewed by the observer.

Angle of Elevation

The angle of elevation of an object viewed, is the angle formed by the line of sight with the horizontal, when it is above the horizontal level, i.e. the case when we raise our head to look at object.

Let P be the position of the object above the horizontal line OA and O be the eye of the observer. Then, OP is the **line of sight** and $\angle AOP$ is called **angle of elevation**, because the observer has to elevate (raise) his/her line of sight from the horizontal OA to see the object P.

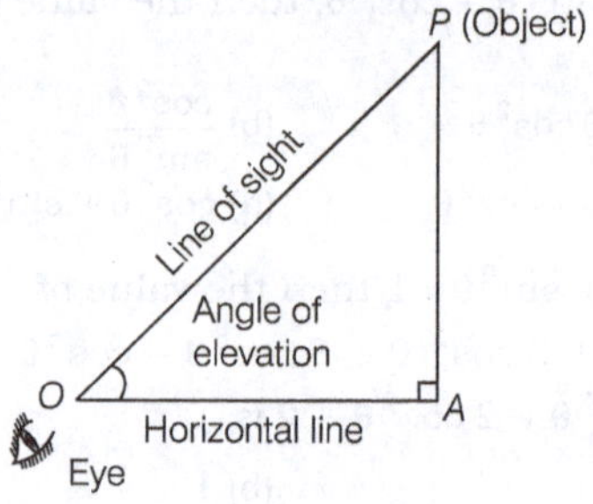

Some important points about angle of elevation are given below

(i) A plane level parallel to Earth's surface is called the horizontal plane level and a line drawn parallel to horizontal plane is called a horizontal line.

(ii) If the observer moves towards the perpendicular line (tower/building), then angle of elevation increases and if the observer moves away from the perpendicular line (tower/building), then angle of elevation decreases.

(iii) If the height of tower is doubled and the distance between the observer and foot of the tower is also doubled, then the angle of elevation remains same.

(iv) If the angle of elevation of Sun, above a tower decreases, then the length of shadow of a tower increases and *vice-versa*.

Angle of Depression

The angle of depression of an object viewed, is the angle formed by the line of sight with the horizontal, when it is below the horizontal level, i.e. the case when we lower our head to look at the object.

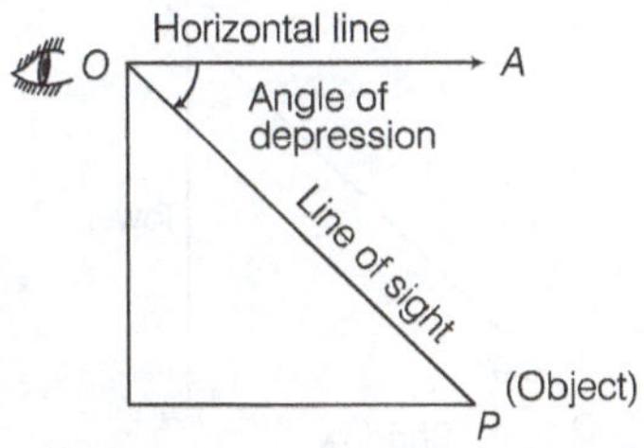

Let P be the position of the object below the horizontal level OA and O be the eye of the observer. Then, OP is the **line of sight** and $\angle AOP$ is called an **angle of depression**, because the observer has to depress (lower) his/her line of sight from the horizontal OA to see the object P.

Some important points about angle of depression are given below

(i) The angle of elevation of a point P as seen from a point O is always equal to the angle of depression of O as seen from P.

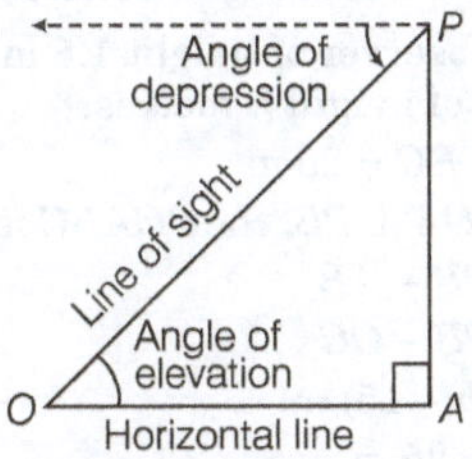

(ii) The angles of elevation and depression are always acute angles.

(iii) In solving problems, observer is represented by a point and object is represented by a line segment or a point.

Problems Based on Heights and Distances

We can solve different types of problems related to heights and distances by applying trigonometric ratios in right angled triangle formed with the help of given information. e.g. The height of a tower or a tree can be determined without climbing over it, width of a river can be measured without crossing it.

It can be easily understood with the help of following examples.

Example 1. Find the angular elevation of the Sun, when the shadow of 10 m long pole is $10\sqrt{3}$ m.

Sol. Let BC be the pole, AB be its shadow and the angle of elevation of the Sun be θ.

Then, $\angle BAC = \theta$, $\angle ABC = 90°$,

$AB = 10\sqrt{3}$ m

and $BC = 10$ m

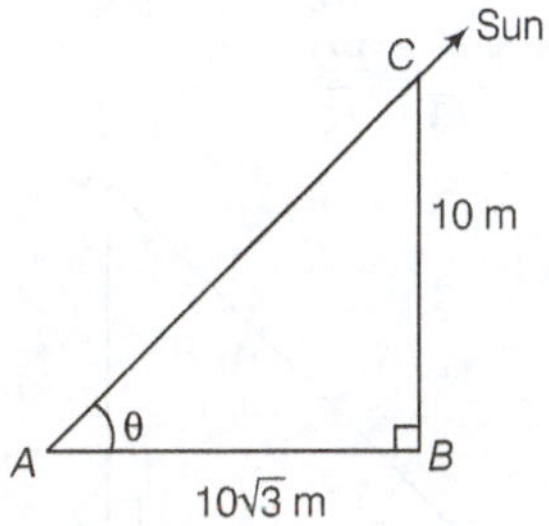

In right angled ΔABC,

$$\tan\theta = \frac{\text{Perpendicular}}{\text{Base}} = \frac{BC}{AB}$$

$$\Rightarrow \tan\theta = \frac{10}{10\sqrt{3}} \quad \text{[given]}$$

$$\Rightarrow \tan\theta = \frac{1}{\sqrt{3}}$$

$$\Rightarrow \tan\theta = \tan 30° \quad \left[\because \tan 30° = \frac{1}{\sqrt{3}}\right]$$

$$\therefore \theta = 30°$$

Hence, the angular elevation of the Sun is 30°.

Example 2. A tower is 200 m high. Find the angle of elevation of its top from a point $200\sqrt{2}$ m away from its top.

Sol. Let height of the tower be $AB = 200$ m and the distance between its top and a point be $AC = 200\sqrt{2}$ m.

Also, let $\angle ACB = \theta$.

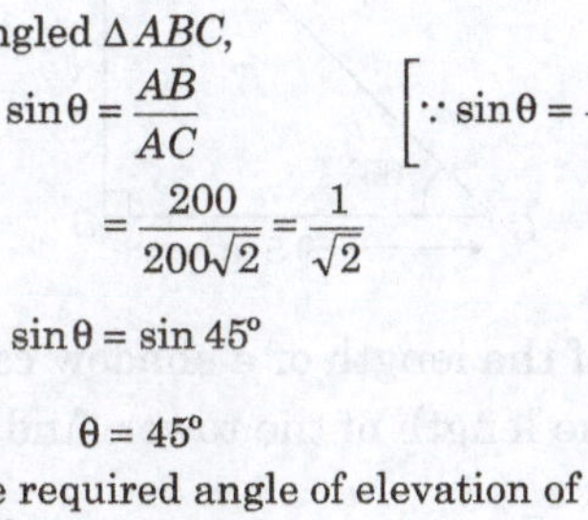

In right angled ΔABC,

$$\sin\theta = \frac{AB}{AC} \quad \left[\because \sin\theta = \frac{\text{perpendicular}}{\text{hypotenuse}}\right]$$

$$= \frac{200}{200\sqrt{2}} = \frac{1}{\sqrt{2}}$$

$$\Rightarrow \sin\theta = \sin 45° \quad \left[\because \sin 45° = \frac{1}{\sqrt{2}}\right]$$

$$\therefore \theta = 45°$$

Hence, the required angle of elevation of its top from a point is 45°.

Example 3. From a point 15 m away from the foot of a tower, the angle of elevation of the top of the tower is 30°. Find the height of the tower.

Sol. From the figure, $RQ = 15\,\text{m}$ and $\angle PRQ = 30°$.

In right angled ΔPQR, we have

$$\tan 30° = \frac{PQ}{RQ} \qquad \left[\because \tan\theta = \frac{\text{perpendicular}}{\text{base}}\right]$$

$$\Rightarrow \quad \frac{1}{\sqrt{3}} = \frac{PQ}{15} \qquad \left[\because \tan 30° = \frac{1}{\sqrt{3}}\right]$$

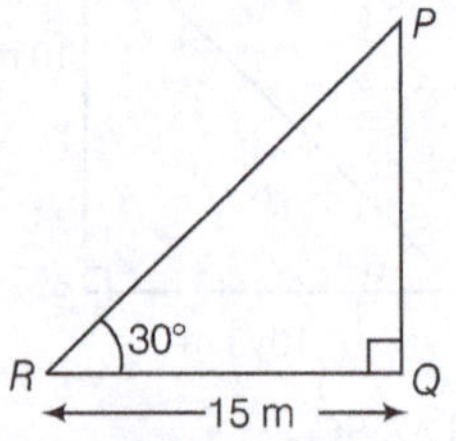

$$\Rightarrow \quad PQ = \frac{15}{\sqrt{3}} \times \frac{\sqrt{3}}{\sqrt{3}} = \frac{15\sqrt{3}}{3} \qquad \text{[rationalising]}$$

$$\therefore \quad PQ = 5\sqrt{3} = 5 \times 1.732 = 8.66\ \text{m}$$

Hence, the height of the tower is 8.66 m.

Example 4. The angle of elevation of a ladder leaning against a wall is 60° and the foot of the ladder is 9.5 m away from the wall. Find the length of the ladder.

Sol. Let BC be the horizontal ground and AC be the ladder leaning against the wall AB.

Then, $\angle ABC = 90°$, $\angle ACB = 60°$

and $BC = 9.5\ \text{m}$

In right angled ΔABC, we have

$$\cos 60° = \frac{BC}{AC} \qquad \left[\because \cos\theta = \frac{\text{base}}{\text{hypotenuse}}\right]$$

$$\Rightarrow \quad \frac{1}{2} = \frac{9.5}{AC} \qquad \left[\because \cos 60° = \frac{1}{2}\right]$$

$$\Rightarrow \quad AC = 9.5 \times 2$$

$$\therefore \quad AC = 19\ \text{m}$$

Hence, the length of the ladder is 19 m.

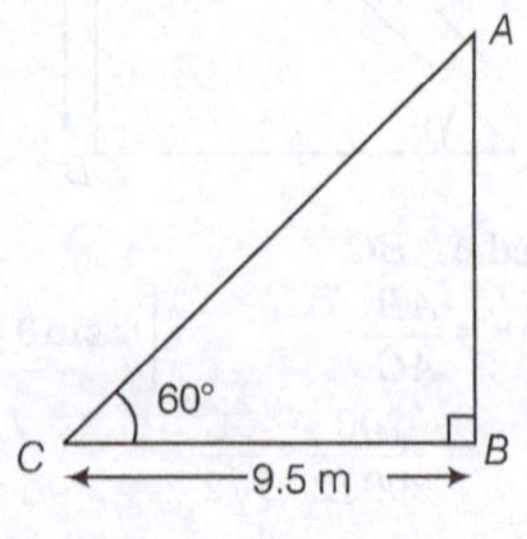

Example 5. If the length of a shadow cast by a tower be $\frac{1}{\sqrt{3}}$ times the length of the tower, find the angle of elevation of the Sun.

Sol. Let AP be the tower, then

Shadow of the tower $= OA = \frac{1}{\sqrt{3}} AP$ [$\because$ given]

Let the angle of elevation of the Sun $\angle AOP = \theta$

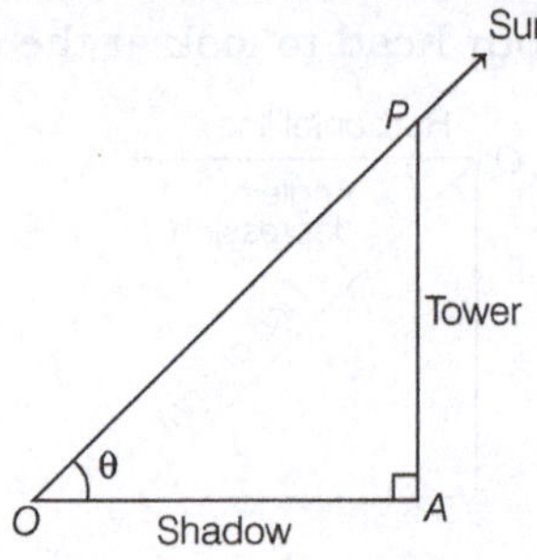

From right-angled ΔOAP, we get

$$\tan\theta = \frac{AP}{OA} \text{ but } OA = \frac{1}{\sqrt{3}} AP$$

$$\Rightarrow \quad \tan\theta = \frac{AP}{\frac{1}{\sqrt{3}} AP} = \frac{\sqrt{3}}{1} = \tan 60°$$

$$\Rightarrow \quad \theta = 60°$$

Hence, the angle of elevation of the Sun is 60°.

Example 6. A man 1.5 m tall is 25 m away from a pole. The angle of elevation of the top of the pole from his eye is 45°. Find the height of the pole.

Sol. Let OC be an observer of height 1.5 m which is 25 m away from a pole PB of height h metres.

$OC = 1.5\ \text{m}$ and $BC = 25\ \text{m}$.

From O, draw $OA \perp PB$, then $OABC$ is a rectangle.

$$PA = PB - AB$$

$$\Rightarrow \quad PA = PB - OC \qquad [\because OC = AB]$$

$$= (h - 1.5)\ \text{m}$$

and $OA = BC = 25\ \text{m}$

Given, angle of elevation $\angle AOP = 45°$

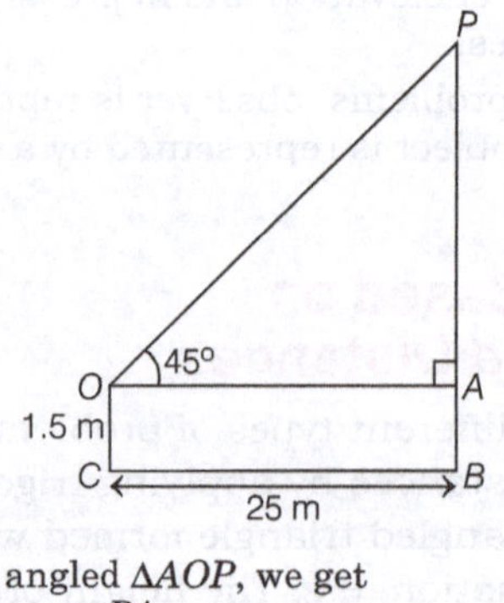

From right angled ΔAOP, we get

$$\tan 45° = \frac{PA}{OA}$$

$$\Rightarrow \quad 1 = \frac{h - 1.5}{25}$$

$$\Rightarrow \quad 25 = h - 1.5 \Rightarrow h = 26.5$$

Hence, the height of the pole is 26.5 m.

Example 7. From the top of the building 86 m high, the angle of depression of a point on the level ground is 45°. Calculate the distance of the point from the foot of the building.

Sol. Given, $PQ = 86$ m and $\angle PRQ = 45°$

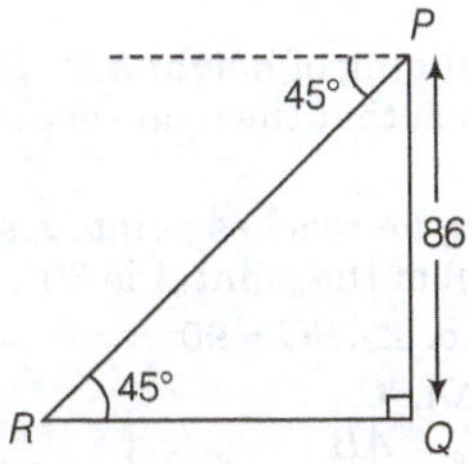

In right angled ΔPQR, we have

$$\tan 45° = \frac{PQ}{QR} \quad \left[\because \tan\theta = \frac{\text{perpendicular}}{\text{base}}\right]$$

$$\Rightarrow \quad 1 = \frac{86}{QR} \quad [\because \tan 45° = 1]$$

$$\therefore \quad QR = 86 \text{ m}$$

Hence, the distance of a point from the foot of the building is 86 m.

Example 8. A security officer observes an enemy boat, from an observation tower at a height of 180 m above sea level, to be at an angle of depression of 29°.

(i) Calculate, to the nearest metre, the distance of the boat from the foot of the observation tower.

(ii) After some time, it is observed that the boat is 200 m from the foot of the observation tower. Calculate the new angle of depression.

Sol.

(i) Let B be the boat and AC be the observation tower. In right angled ΔACB, $\tan 29° = \dfrac{AC}{BC}$

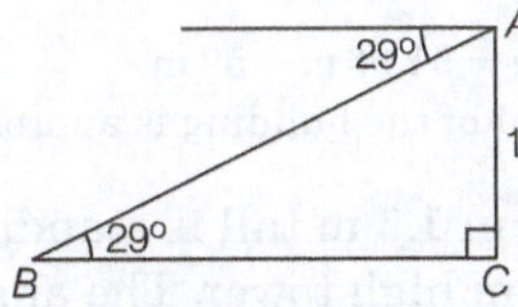

$$\Rightarrow \quad 0.5543 = \frac{180}{BC}$$

$$\therefore \quad BC = \frac{180}{0.5543} = 325\text{m (App.)}$$

(ii) Let D be the new position of the boat and θ be the new angle of depression.

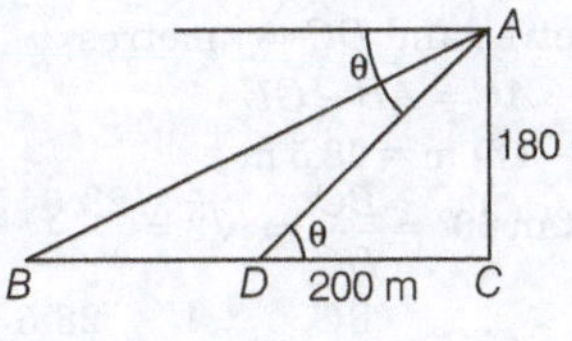

$$\therefore \quad \tan\theta = \frac{AC}{DC}$$

$$= \frac{180}{200} = 0.9000$$

$$= \tan 41° 59'$$

$$\therefore \quad \theta = 41° 59'$$

Example 9. In a violent storm, a tree got bent by the wind. The top of the tree meets the ground at an angle of 30°, at a distance of 30 m from the root. At what height from the bottom, did the tree get bent? What was the original height of the tree?

Sol. Let AB be the original height of the tree, which has got bent at a point C. After getting bent, let the part CB take the position CD, meeting the ground at D.

Then, $AD = 30$ m, $\angle ADC = 30°$, $\angle DAC = 90°$ and $CD = CB$.

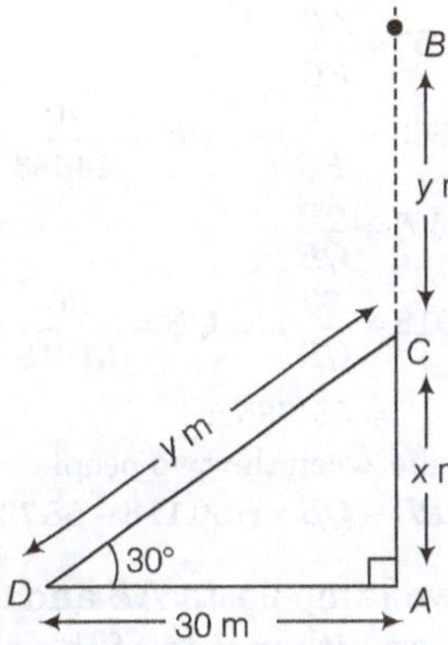

Let $AC = x$ m and $CD = CB = y$ m.

In right angled ΔDAC, we have

$$\tan 30° = \frac{AC}{AD} \quad \left[\because \tan\theta = \frac{\text{perpendicular}}{\text{base}}\right]$$

$$\Rightarrow \quad \frac{1}{\sqrt{3}} = \frac{x}{30} \quad \left[\because \tan 30° = \frac{1}{\sqrt{3}}, AC = x \text{ and } AD = 30 \text{ m}\right]$$

$$\Rightarrow \quad x = 30 \times \frac{1}{\sqrt{3}} \times \frac{\sqrt{3}}{\sqrt{3}} = 10\sqrt{3} \text{ m}$$

[by rationalising] ...(i)

$$\text{and} \quad \sec 30° = \frac{CD}{AD} \quad \left[\because \sec\theta = \frac{\text{hypotenuse}}{\text{base}}\right]$$

$$\Rightarrow \quad \frac{2}{\sqrt{3}} = \frac{y}{30} \quad \left[\because \sec 30° = \frac{2}{\sqrt{3}}, CD = y \text{ and } AD = 30 \text{ m}\right]$$

$$\Rightarrow \quad y = 30 \times \frac{2}{\sqrt{3}} \times \frac{\sqrt{3}}{\sqrt{3}} = 20\sqrt{3} \text{ m}$$

[by rationalising] ...(ii)

Since, $AB = AC + CB$

$\therefore \quad AB = x + y = 10\sqrt{3} + 20\sqrt{3}$ [from Eqs. (i) and (ii)]

$= 30\sqrt{3}$ m

Hence, the tree got bent at a height of $10\sqrt{3}$ m from the ground and the original height of the tree was $30\sqrt{3}$ m.

Example 10. Two people standing on the same side of a tower in a straight line with it, measure the angles of elevation of the top of the tower as 25° and 50° respectively. If the height of the tower is 70 m, find the distance between the two people.

Sol. According to the given statement, the figure will be as shown alongside in which AB is the tower so $AB = 70$ m and P and Q be the positions of two people, such that $\angle APB = 25°$ and $\angle AQB = 50°$

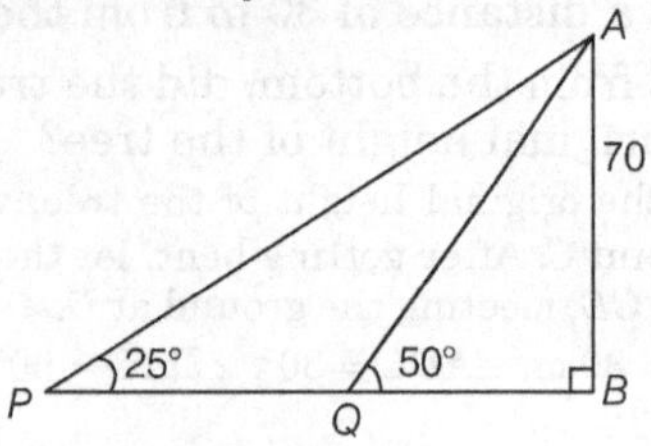

In ΔAPB, $\tan 25° = \dfrac{AB}{PB}$

$\Rightarrow \quad 0.4663 = \dfrac{70}{PB}$ i.e., $PB = \dfrac{70}{0.4663}$ m $= 150{\cdot}118$ m

In ΔAQB, $\tan 50° = \dfrac{AB}{QB}$

$\Rightarrow \quad 1.1918 = \dfrac{70}{QB}$ i.e., $QB = \dfrac{70}{1.1918}$ m

$= 58{\cdot}735$ m

$\therefore$ The distance between the two people

$PQ = PB - QB = (150.118 - 58.735)$ m $= 91.383$ m

Example 11. Two lamp posts AB and CD each of height 100 m are on either side of the road. P is a point on the road between the two lamp posts. The angles of elevation of the top of the lamp posts from the point P are 60° and 40°. Find the distances PB and PD. [given, tan 40° = 0.84] **[ICSE Semester II 2022]**

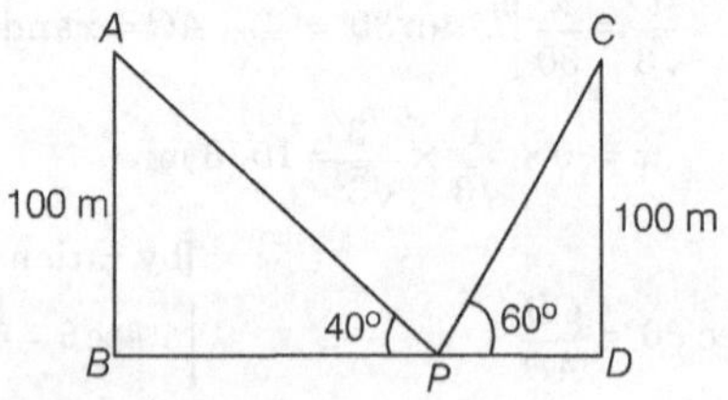

Sol. Given, $AB = CD = 100$ m

In ΔABP, $\tan 40° = \dfrac{AB}{BP}$

$\Rightarrow \quad 0.84 = \dfrac{100}{BP}$ $\quad [\because \tan 40° = 0.84]$

$\Rightarrow \quad BP = \dfrac{100}{0.84} \Rightarrow BP = 119.04$ m

In ΔCDP,

$\tan 60° = \dfrac{CD}{PD} \Rightarrow \sqrt{3} = \dfrac{100}{PD}$

$\Rightarrow \quad PD = \dfrac{100}{1.7}$ $\quad [\because \sqrt{3} = 1.7]$

$\Rightarrow \quad PD = 58.8$ m

Example 12. A man observes the angle of elevation of the top of a building to be 30°. He walks towards it in a horizontal line through its base. On covering 60 m, the angle of elevation changes to 60°. Find the height of the building correct to the nearest metres. **[ICSE 2011]**

Sol. Let AB be the building of height h m. Initially, the man is at the point C, such that the angle of elevation of the point A is 30°.

On walking 60 m, he reaches point D, such that the angle of elevation of the point A is 60°.

Also, $AB \perp CB$, i.e. $\angle ABC = 90°$

In right angled ΔABC,

$\tan 30° = \dfrac{AB}{BC}$ $\quad \left[\because \tan\theta = \dfrac{\text{perpendicular}}{\text{base}}\right]$

$\Rightarrow \quad \dfrac{1}{\sqrt{3}} = \dfrac{h}{BC}$ $\quad \left[\because \tan 30° = \dfrac{1}{\sqrt{3}}\right]$

$\Rightarrow \quad BC = h\sqrt{3}$ m $\quad$ ...(i)

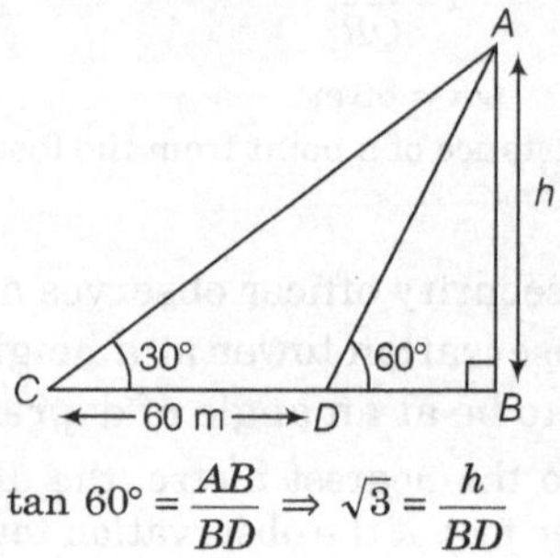

In ΔABD, $\tan 60° = \dfrac{AB}{BD} \Rightarrow \sqrt{3} = \dfrac{h}{BD}$

$\Rightarrow \quad BD = \dfrac{h}{\sqrt{3}}$ m $\quad$ ...(ii)

Now, $\quad BC - BD = CD$

$\Rightarrow \quad \sqrt{3}h - \dfrac{h}{\sqrt{3}} = 60$ $\quad$ [from Eqs. (i) and (ii)]

$\Rightarrow \quad 3h - h = 60\sqrt{3}$

$\Rightarrow \quad h = \dfrac{60\sqrt{3}}{2} = 30 \times 1.732$ $\quad [\because \sqrt{3} = 1.732]$

$\therefore \quad h = 51.96 \text{ m} \approx 52$ m

Hence, the height of the building is approximately 52 m.

Example 13. A man 1.5 m tall is standing at some distance from a 30 m high tower. The angle of elevation from his eye to the top of the tower increase from 30° to 60° as he walks towards the tower. Find the distance he walked towards the tower.

Sol. Let AB be the tower and GE represent the man when the angle of elevation is 30° and DF be the position of man when the angle of elevation is 60°.

Let $GD = x$ metres and $DC = y$ metres

$BC = AB - AC = AB - GE$

$= (30 - 1.5)$ m $= 28.5$ m

From ΔBDC, $\tan 60° = \dfrac{BC}{DC} \Rightarrow \sqrt{3} = \dfrac{28.5}{y}$ $\quad$ ...(i)

From ΔBGC, $\tan 30° = \dfrac{BC}{GC} \Rightarrow \dfrac{1}{\sqrt{3}} = \dfrac{28.5}{x + y}$ $\quad$ ...(ii)

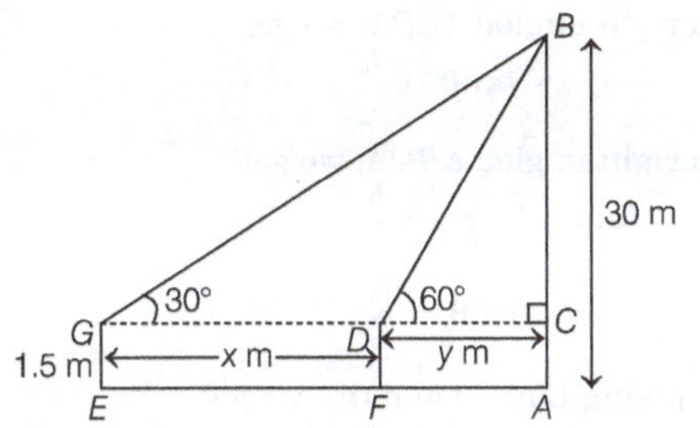

From Eqs. (i) and (ii), we get

$$\sqrt{3} \times \frac{\sqrt{3}}{1} = \frac{28.5}{y} \times \frac{x+y}{28.5}$$

$$\Rightarrow \quad 3 = \frac{x+y}{y}$$

$$\Rightarrow \quad 3y = x + y$$

$$\Rightarrow \quad x = 2y$$

$$\Rightarrow \quad x = 2 \times \frac{28.5}{\sqrt{3}} \quad \text{[from Eq. (i)]}$$

$$\Rightarrow \quad x = \frac{57}{\sqrt{3}}$$

$$\Rightarrow \quad x = 19\sqrt{3}$$

$$\Rightarrow \quad x = 19 \times 1.732 = 32.908 \text{ m}$$

Distance walked by the man towards tower is 32.9 m (approx).

Example 14. The length of the shadow of a vertical pole on level ground increases by 10 m, when the altitude of the Sun changes from 45° to 30°. Calculate the height of the pole, correct to two decimal places.

Sol. Let AB be the vertical pole. BC be its shadow when the sun's altitude is 45°, i.e. $\angle ACB = 45°$.

When the sun's altitude changes to 30°, the length of the shadow is BD and $\angle ADB = 30°$.

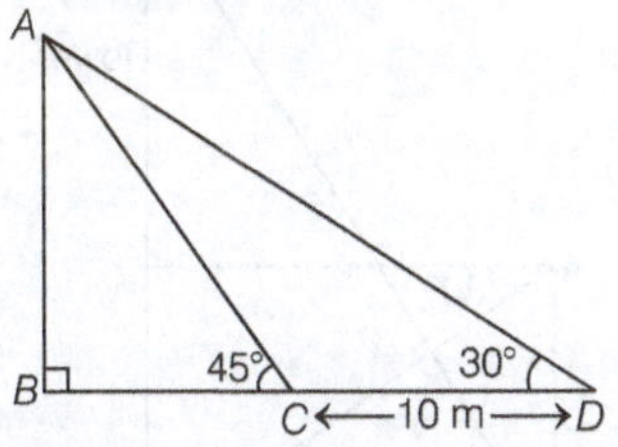

Clearly, $DC = 10$ m

In ΔABC,

$$\tan 45° = \frac{AB}{BC}$$

$$\Rightarrow \quad 1 = \frac{AB}{BC}$$

$$\Rightarrow \quad BC = AB$$

In ΔABD,

$$\tan 30° = \frac{AB}{BD}$$

$$\Rightarrow \quad \frac{1}{\sqrt{3}} = \frac{AB}{BD}$$

$$\Rightarrow \quad BD = AB\sqrt{3}$$

Since $\quad BD - BC = DC$

$$AB\sqrt{3} - AB = 10 \quad [\because BC = AB \text{ and } BD = AB\sqrt{3}]$$

$$AB(\sqrt{3} - 1) = 10$$

$$\Rightarrow \quad AB = \frac{10}{\sqrt{3}-1} = \frac{10}{\sqrt{3}-1} \times \frac{\sqrt{3}+1}{\sqrt{3}+1}$$

$$= \frac{10(1.732 + 1)}{3 - 1}$$

$$= \frac{2.732 \times 10}{2} = \frac{27.32}{2}$$

$$AB = 13.66 \text{ m}$$

Example 15. The angle of elevation of the top of an unfinished tower from a point distant 120 m from its base is 45°. How much higher must the tower be raised, so that its angle of elevation from the same point may be 60°?

Sol. Given, $PQ = 120$ m, $\angle SPQ = 60°$ and $\angle RPQ = 45°$

In ΔSQP, we have

$$\tan 60° = \frac{SQ}{PQ} \quad \left[\because \tan\theta = \frac{\text{perpendicular}}{\text{base}}\right]$$

$$\Rightarrow \quad \sqrt{3} = \frac{SQ}{120} \quad [\because \tan 60° = \sqrt{3}]$$

$$\Rightarrow \quad SQ = 120\sqrt{3} \text{ m} \quad \text{...(i)}$$

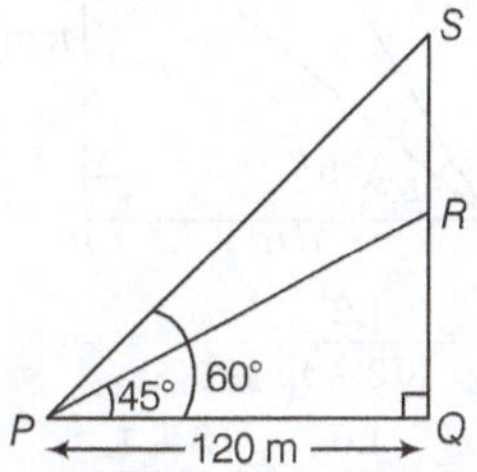

In ΔRQP, we have

$$\tan 45° = \frac{RQ}{PQ}$$

$$\Rightarrow \quad 1 = \frac{RQ}{120} \quad [\because \tan 45° = 1]$$

$$\Rightarrow \quad RQ = 120 \text{ m} \quad \text{...(ii)}$$

Now, the height to be raised

$$= SQ - RQ$$

$$= 120\sqrt{3} - 120 \quad \text{[from Eqs. (i) and (ii)]}$$

$$= 120(\sqrt{3} - 1)$$

$$= 120(1.732 - 1) \quad [\because \sqrt{3} = 1.732]$$

$$= 120 \times 0.732$$

$$= 87.84 \text{ m}$$

Hence, the height to be raised is 87.84 m.

Example 16. A statue, 1.6 m tall, stands on the top of a pedestal. From a point on the ground, the angle of elevation of the top of the statue is 60° and from the same point the angle of elevation of the top of the pedestal is 45°. Find the height of the pedestal.

Sol. Let PQ be the pedestal and QR be the statue which stands on the top of pedestal, and O be the point of observation on the ground, $QR = 1.6$ m.

Let $PQ = h$ metres and $OP = d$ metres.
Given, $\angle POQ = 45°$ and $\angle POR = 60°$
From right angled ΔOPQ, we get

$$\tan 45° = \frac{PQ}{OP}$$

$$\Rightarrow \quad 1 = \frac{h}{d} \Rightarrow d = h \quad \text{...(i)}$$

From right angled ΔOPR, we get

$$\tan 60° = \frac{PR}{OP}$$

$$\Rightarrow \quad \sqrt{3} = \frac{h + 1.6}{d}$$

$$\Rightarrow \quad \sqrt{3}d = h + 1.6$$

$$\Rightarrow \quad \sqrt{3}h - h = 1.6 \quad \text{[using Eq. (i)]}$$

$$\Rightarrow \quad (\sqrt{3} - 1)\, h = 1.6$$

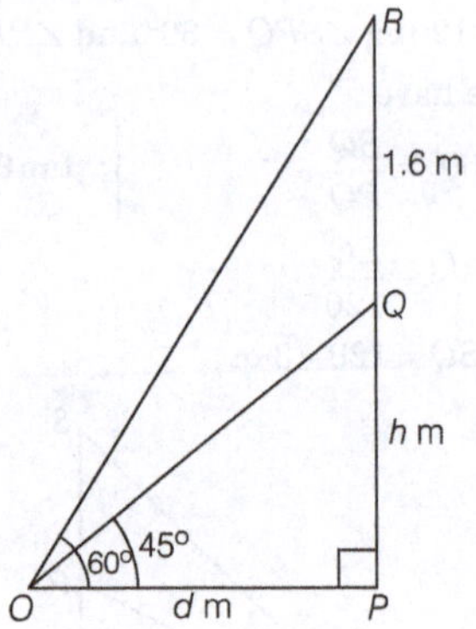

$$\Rightarrow \quad h = \frac{1.6}{\sqrt{3} - 1}$$

$$\Rightarrow \quad h = \frac{1.6}{\sqrt{3} - 1} \times \frac{\sqrt{3} + 1}{\sqrt{3} + 1}$$

$$= \frac{1.6}{2}(\sqrt{3} + 1) = (0.8)(\sqrt{3} + 1)$$

$$= 0.8 \times (1.732 + 1)$$

$$= 0.8 \times 2.732 = 2.19 \text{ m (approx)}$$

Hence, the height of the pedestal = 2.19 m (approx)

Example 17. **The angles of elevation of the top of a tower from two points P and Q at distance of x and y respectively from the base and in the same straight line with it are complementary. Prove that the height of the tower is $\sqrt{xy}$.**

Sol. Let AB be the tower of height h (units).
$AP = x$ and $QA = y$
As the angles of elevation are complementary, if $\angle APB = \theta°$, then $\angle AQB = 90° - \theta°$.

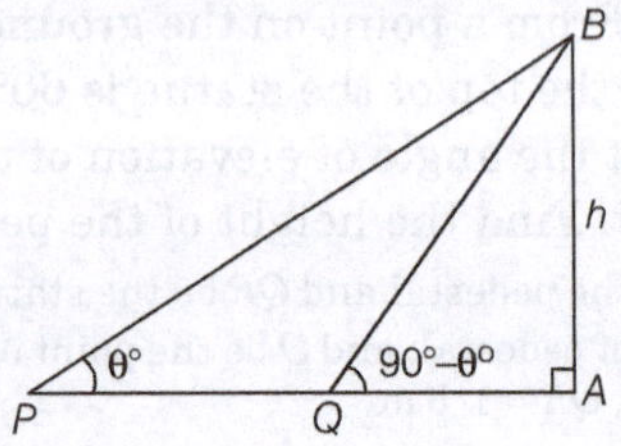

From right angled ΔBPA, we get

$$\tan\theta° = \frac{h}{x} \quad \text{...(i)}$$

From right angled ΔBQA, we get

$$\tan(90° - \theta°) = \frac{h}{y}$$

$$\Rightarrow \quad \cot\theta° = \frac{h}{y} \quad \text{...(ii)}$$

Multiplying Eqs. (i) and (ii), we get

$$\tan\theta° \cot\theta° = \frac{h}{x} \times \frac{h}{y}$$

$$\Rightarrow \quad 1 = \frac{h^2}{xy}$$

$$\Rightarrow \quad h^2 = xy \Rightarrow h = \sqrt{xy} \quad [\because h > 0]$$

Hence, the height of the tower is $\sqrt{xy}$ units.

Example 18. **The angle of elevation of the top of a tower at the foot of a building is 60° and the angle of depression from the top of the building of the foot of the tower is 30°. If the building is 50 m high, find the height of the tower.**

Sol. Let AB be the building and CD be the tower $AB = 50$ m (given).
The angles of elevation and depression are shown in the figure.
Then, $\angle CBD = 60°$ and $\angle ADB = 30°$.
From right angled ΔCDB,

$$\tan 60° = \frac{CD}{BD}$$

$$\Rightarrow \quad \sqrt{3} = \frac{CD}{BD} \quad \text{...(i)}$$

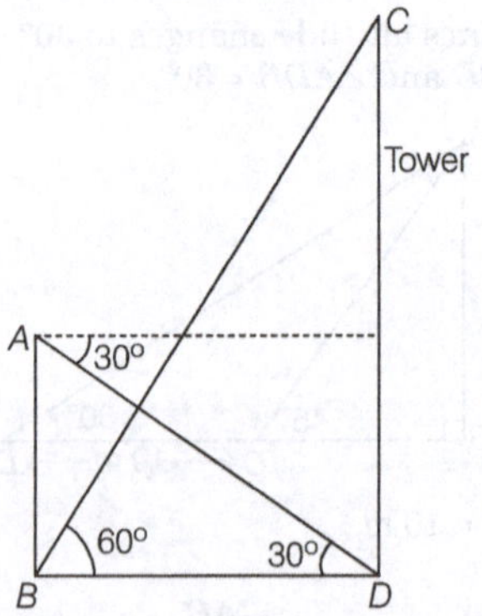

From right angled ΔABD,

$$\tan 30° = \frac{AB}{BD} \Rightarrow \frac{1}{\sqrt{3}} = \frac{AB}{BD} \quad \text{...(ii)}$$

Dividing Eq. (i) by Eq. (ii), we get

$$\sqrt{3} \times \frac{\sqrt{3}}{1} = \frac{CD}{BD} \times \frac{BD}{AB}$$

$$\Rightarrow \quad 3 = \frac{CD}{AB}$$

$$\Rightarrow \quad CD = 3AB$$

$$\Rightarrow \quad CD = (3 \times 50) \text{ m} = 150 \text{ m}$$

Hence, the height of the tower is 150 m.

Example 19. As observed from the top of a 80 m tall light-house, the angles of depression of two ships on the same side of the light-house in horizontal line with its base are 30° and 40°, respectively. Find the distance between the two ships. Give your answer correct to the nearest metres. **[ICSE 2012]**

Sol. Given, height of a light-house, $AB = 80$ m.

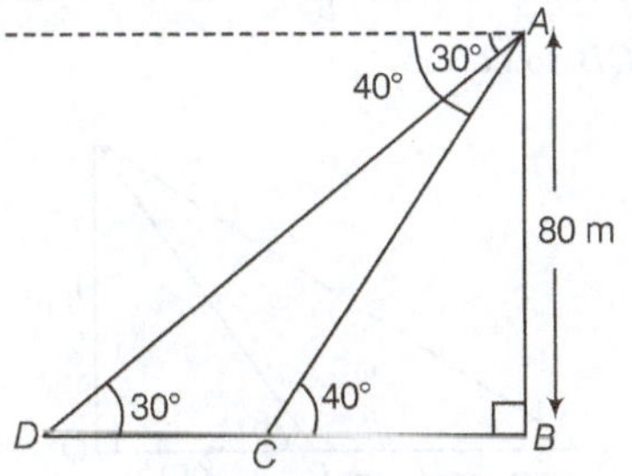

Let C and D be the positions of two ships, such that $\angle ADB = 30°$ and $\angle ACB = 40°$.

In right angled ΔABC, we have

$$\tan 40° = \frac{AB}{BC} \quad \left[\because \tan\theta = \frac{\text{perpendicular}}{\text{base}}\right]$$

$$\Rightarrow \tan(90° - 50°) = \frac{80}{BC}$$

$$\Rightarrow \cot 50° = \frac{80}{BC} \quad [\because \tan(90° - \theta) = \cot\theta]$$

$$\Rightarrow BC = \frac{80}{\cot 50°} = 80 \times \tan 50° \quad \left[\because \frac{1}{\cot\theta} = \tan\theta\right]$$

$$= 80 \times 1.1918$$

[from natural tangent table, $\tan 50° = 1.1918$]

$$\therefore BC = 95.34 \text{ m} \quad \text{...(i)}$$

In right angled ΔABD, we have

$$\tan 30° = \frac{AB}{BD} \Rightarrow \frac{1}{\sqrt{3}} = \frac{80}{DC + BC} \quad \left[\because \tan 30° = \frac{1}{\sqrt{3}}\right]$$

$$\Rightarrow DC + 95.34 = 80 \times \sqrt{3} \quad \text{[from Eq. (i)]}$$

$$\Rightarrow DC = 80 \times 1.732 - 95.34$$

$$\therefore DC = 138.56 - 95.34 = 43.22 \text{ m}$$

Hence, the distance between two ships is 43.22 m.

Example 20. An aeroplane at an altitude of 1500 m finds that two ships are sailing towards it in the same direction. The angles of depression as observed from the aeroplane are 45° and 30°, respectively. Find the distance between the two ships. **[ICSE 2016]**

Sol. Let the distance between two ships be $DC = x$ m and height of the aeroplane from the ground is $AB = 1500$ m

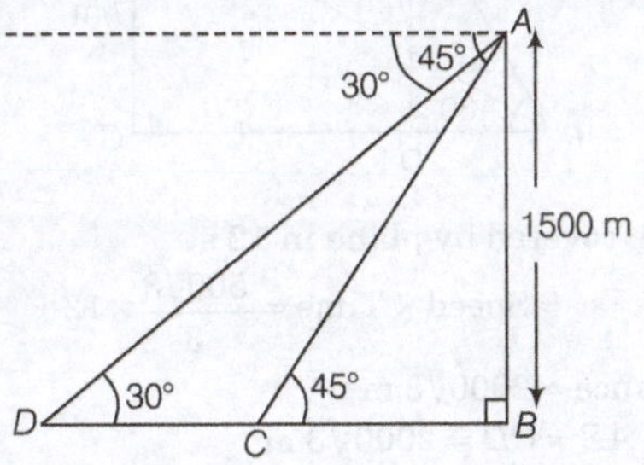

In right angled ΔABC,

$$\tan 45° = \frac{AB}{BC} \quad \left[\because \tan\theta = \frac{\text{perpendicular}}{\text{base}}\right]$$

$$\Rightarrow 1 = \frac{1500}{BC} \quad [\because \tan 45° = 1]$$

$$\Rightarrow BC = 1500 \text{ m}$$

In right angled ΔABD,

$$\tan 30° = \frac{AB}{BD} = \frac{AB}{BC + DC} = \frac{1500}{1500 + x}$$

$$\Rightarrow \frac{1}{\sqrt{3}} = \frac{1500}{1500 + x} \quad \left[\because \tan 30° = \frac{1}{\sqrt{3}}\right]$$

$$\Rightarrow 1500 + x = 1500\sqrt{3}$$

$$\therefore x = 1500(\sqrt{3} - 1)$$

$$= 1500 \times (1.732 - 1)$$

$$= 1500 \times 0.732 = 1098 \text{ m}$$

Hence, the distance between the two ships is 1098 m.

Example 21. A man on the top of a vertical observation tower observes a car moving at a uniform speed coming directly towards it. If it takes 12 min for the angle of depression to change from 30° to 45°, how soon after this will the car reach the observation tower?

Sol. Let PQ be the tower and R be the initial position of the car. After 12 min, the car reaches the position S.

Clearly, $\angle PRQ = 30°$ and $\angle PSQ = 45°$.

Let the speed of the car be x m/min and it will take t min to reach the observation tower.

$$\therefore RS = 12x \text{ m} \quad \text{[Since, distance = time × speed]}$$

and $SQ = tx$ m

In ΔPQS, $\frac{h}{tx} = \tan 45° = \frac{h}{tx} \Rightarrow 1 = \frac{h}{tx}$

$$\therefore h = tx$$

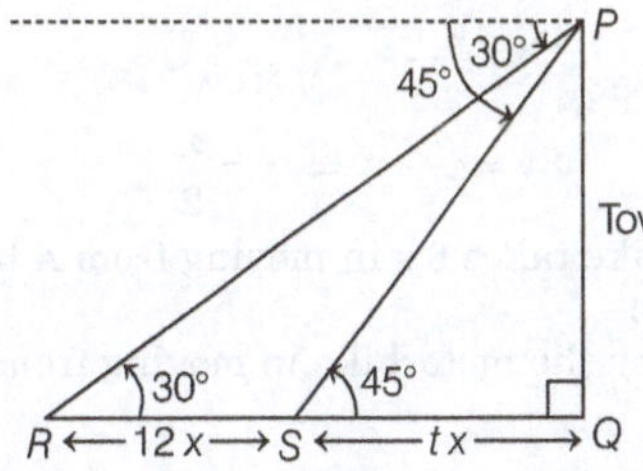

In ΔPRQ, $\frac{h}{12x + tx} = \tan 30°$

$$\Rightarrow \frac{tx}{(12 + t)x} = \frac{1}{\sqrt{3}} \quad [\text{Since } h = tx]$$

$$\therefore \sqrt{3}\,t = 12 + t$$

$$\Rightarrow \sqrt{3}\,t - t = 12$$

$$\Rightarrow t(\sqrt{3} - 1) = 12$$

$$\Rightarrow t = \frac{12}{\sqrt{3} - 1}$$

$$= \frac{12}{1.732 - 1} = \frac{12}{0.732} \quad [\because \sqrt{3} = 1.732]$$

$$= 16.39 \text{ min}$$

Example 22. A straight highway leads to the foot of a tower. A man standing at the top of the tower observes a motorbike at an angle of depression of 30°, which is approaching the foot of the tower with a uniform speed. Six seconds later, the angle of depression of the motorbike is found to be 60°. Find the time taken by the motorbike to reach the foot of the tower from this point.

Sol. Let NP be the tower of height h m.

Let A be the position of the motorbike when its angle of depression (as seen from P) is 30° and 6 s later, let the motorbike be at the point B when its angle of depression is 60°.

Let AB be x m and BN be y m.

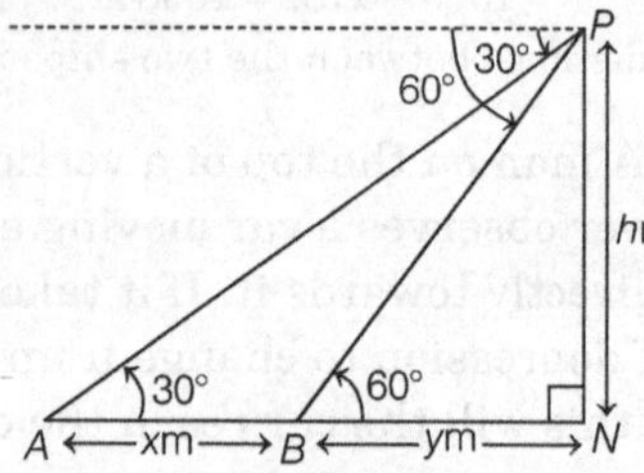

From ΔPAN, $\tan 30° = \frac{NP}{AN}$

$$\Rightarrow \quad \frac{1}{\sqrt{3}} = \frac{h}{x+y} \quad \text{...(i)}$$

From ΔPBN, $\tan 60° = \frac{NP}{BN}$

$$\Rightarrow \quad \sqrt{3} = \frac{h}{y} \quad \text{...(ii)}$$

On dividing Eq. (ii) by Eq. (i), we get

$$\sqrt{3} \times \frac{\sqrt{3}}{1} = \frac{h}{y} \times \frac{x+y}{h}$$

$$\Rightarrow \quad 3 = \frac{x+y}{y}$$

$$\Rightarrow \quad 3y = x + y \Rightarrow y = \frac{x}{2}$$

As the motorbike takes 6 s in moving from A to B i.e., to cover x metres.

$\therefore$ Time taken by the motorbike in moving from B to N i.e., $\frac{x}{2}$ metres.

$$= \frac{6}{2} \text{ s} = 3 \text{ s}$$

Hence, the time taken by the motorbike to reach the foot of tower is 3 s.

Example 23. From a point on the ground, the angle of elevation of the top of a vertical tower is found to be such that its tangent is $\frac{3}{5}$. On walking 50 m towards the tower, the tangent of the new angle of elevation of the top of the tower is found to be $\frac{4}{5}$. Find the height of the tower.

Sol. Let PQ be the tower whose height is h m. A be the first point of observation such that if the angle of elevation of the top of the tower at point A is α, then $\tan\alpha = \frac{3}{5}$.

Let B be the other point of observation obtained on moving 50 m towards the tower (i.e., AB = 50 m) such that if the angle of elevation of the top of the tower at point B is β, then $\tan\beta = \frac{4}{5}$.

Assume QB to be x m.

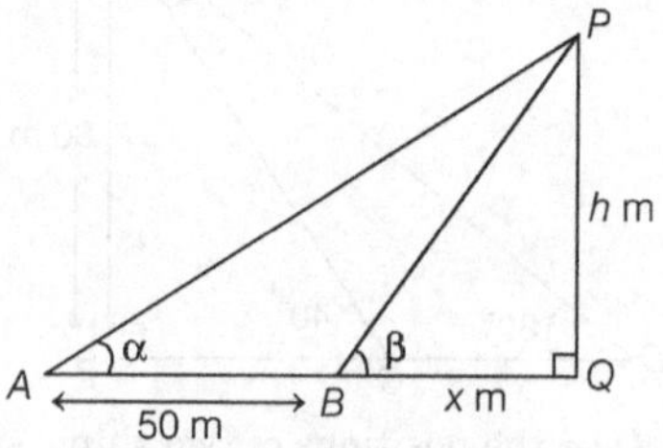

In ΔPAQ, $\tan\alpha = \frac{PQ}{AQ} \Rightarrow \frac{3}{5} = \frac{h}{x+50}$

$$\Rightarrow \quad 5h = 3x + 150 \quad \text{...(i)}$$

In ΔPBQ, $\tan\beta = \frac{PQ}{BQ}$

$$\Rightarrow \quad \frac{4}{5} = \frac{h}{x}$$

$$\Rightarrow \quad 5h = 4x \quad \text{...(ii)}$$

On solving Eqs. (i) and (ii), we get

$$x = 150 \text{ and } h = 120$$

$\therefore$ The height of the tower is 120 m.

Example 24. The angle of elevation of an aeroplane from a point P on the ground is 60°. After 12 s from the same point P, the angle of elevation of the same plane changes to 30°. If the plane is flying horizontally at a speed of $600\sqrt{3}$ km/h, then find the height at which the plane is flying.

Sol. Let A be the position of plane, when the angle of elevation from point P on the ground is 60° and B be the position of plane, when the angle of elevation is 30°.

Given, speed of plane = $600\sqrt{3}$ km/h

$$= \frac{600\sqrt{3} \times 1000}{60 \times 60} = \frac{500\sqrt{3}}{3} \text{ m/s} \left[\because 1 \text{ km/h} = \frac{1000}{60 \times 60} \text{ m/s}\right]$$

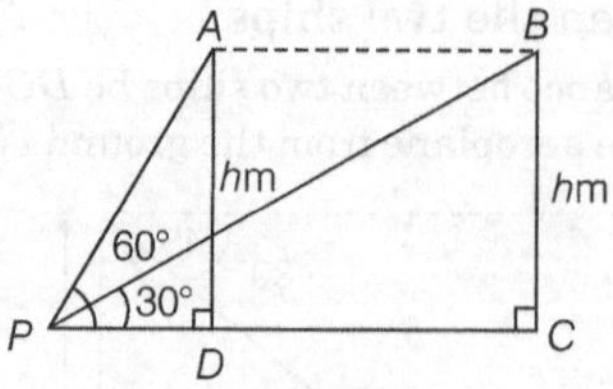

Distance covered by plane in 12 s

$$= \text{Speed} \times \text{Time} = \frac{500\sqrt{3}}{3} \times 12$$

$\Rightarrow$ Distance = $2000\sqrt{3}$ m

$$\therefore \quad AB = CD = 2000\sqrt{3} \text{ m}$$

Let the height of plane (AD) be h m and PD be x m.

In right angled ΔADP,

$$\tan 60° = \frac{AD}{PD} \quad \left[\because \tan\theta = \frac{\text{perpendicular}}{\text{base}}\right]$$

$$\Rightarrow \frac{\sqrt{3}}{1} = \frac{h}{x} \quad [\because \tan 60° = \sqrt{3}]$$

$$\Rightarrow h = \sqrt{3}x$$

$$\Rightarrow x = \frac{h}{\sqrt{3}} \quad \text{...(i)}$$

In right angled ΔBCP,

$$\tan 30° = \frac{BC}{PC} \Rightarrow \frac{1}{\sqrt{3}} = \frac{BC}{PD+CD} \quad \left[\because \tan 30° = \frac{1}{\sqrt{3}}\right]$$

$$\Rightarrow \sqrt{3}h = x + 2000\sqrt{3} \quad \left[\because \begin{array}{l} AD = BC = h \text{ m}, \\ PD = x \text{ m and} \\ AB = CD = 2000\sqrt{3} \text{ m}\end{array}\right]$$

$$\Rightarrow \sqrt{3}h = \frac{h}{\sqrt{3}} + 2000\sqrt{3} \quad \text{[from Eq. (i)]}$$

$$\Rightarrow \sqrt{3}h - \frac{h}{\sqrt{3}} = 2000\sqrt{3} \Rightarrow \frac{3h-h}{\sqrt{3}} = 2000\sqrt{3}$$

$$\Rightarrow \frac{2h}{\sqrt{3}} = 2000\sqrt{3}$$

$$\Rightarrow h = \frac{2000\sqrt{3}\times\sqrt{3}}{2} = 3000 \text{ m}$$

Hence, the height of plane is 3000 m or 3 km.

Example 25. The horizontal distance between two towers is 120 m. The angle of elevation of the top and angle of depression of the bottom of the first tower as observed from the second tower are 30° and 24°, respectively. Find the heights of the two towers.

Sol. Let the heights of towers CD and AB be h m and $(h + h')$ m, respectively.

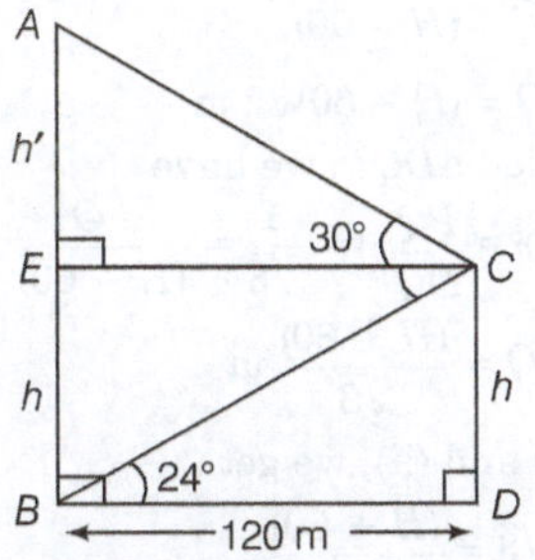

Join CA, CB, BD and draw $CE \perp AB$.

Then, $BD = EC = 120$ m

In right angled ΔBDC,

$$\tan 24° = \frac{CD}{BD} = \frac{h}{120} \quad \left[\because \tan\theta = \frac{\text{perpendicular}}{\text{base}}\right]$$

$$\Rightarrow h = 120 \tan 24° = 120 \times 0.445 = 53.4 \text{ m}$$

In right angled ΔAEC, $\tan 30° = \dfrac{h'}{120}$

$$\Rightarrow h' = 120 \tan 30° = 120 \times 0.577 = 69.24 \text{ m}$$

Hence, height of tower $AB = h + h'$

$$= 53.4 + 69.24 = 122.64 \text{ m}$$

and height of tower $CD = h = 53.4$ m

Example 26. A man standing on the deck of a ship, which is 10 m above the water level, observes the angle of elevation of the top of the hill as 60° and the angle of depression of the base of the hill as 30°. Find the distance of the hill from the ship and the height of the hill.

Sol. Let AB and CD be the deck and hill respectively.

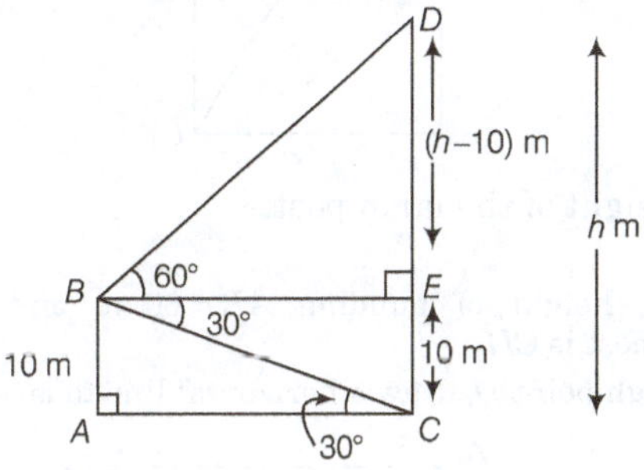

Let the man be at B.

Then, $AB = 10$ m.

Again, let $BE \perp CD$ and $AC \perp CD$.

Then, $\angle EBD = 60°$

and $\angle EBC = \angle BCA = 30°$

$CE = AB = 10$ m

Let $CD = h$ m.

Then, $ED = (h - 10)$ m

In right angled ΔBED, we have

$$\cot 60° = \frac{BE}{ED} \quad \left[\because \cot\theta = \frac{\text{base}}{\text{perpendicular}}\right]$$

$$\Rightarrow \frac{1}{\sqrt{3}} = \frac{BE}{(h-10)} \quad \left[\because \cot 60° = \frac{1}{\sqrt{3}}\right]$$

$$\Rightarrow BE = \frac{(h-10)}{\sqrt{3}} \text{ m} \quad \text{...(i)}$$

In right angled ΔCAB, we have

$$\cot 30° = \frac{AC}{AB}$$

$$\Rightarrow \sqrt{3} = \frac{AC}{10} \quad [\because \cot 30° = \sqrt{3}]$$

$$\Rightarrow AC = 10\sqrt{3} \text{ m} \quad \text{...(ii)}$$

But, $BE = AC$

$$\therefore \frac{(h-10)}{\sqrt{3}} = 10\sqrt{3} \quad \text{[from Eqs. (i) and (ii)]}$$

$$\Rightarrow (h - 10) = 30$$

$$\Rightarrow h = 40 \text{ m}$$

Hence, the distance of the ship from the hill is $10\sqrt{3}$ m and the height of the hill is 40 m.

Example 27. In the following figure, from the top of a building $AB = 60$ m high, the angles of depression of the top and bottom of a vertical lamp-post CD are observed to be 30° and 60°, respectively. Find

(i) the horizontal distance observed between AB and CD.

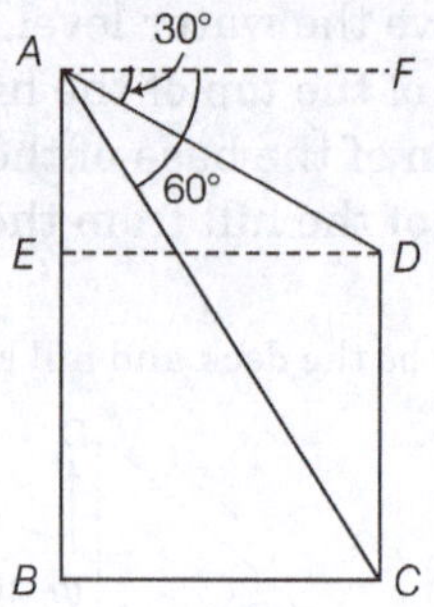

(ii) the height of the lamp-post.

Sol.

(i) Given, height of building $AB = 60$ m and height of lamp-post is CD.

Through point D, draw a horizontal line to meet AB at E.

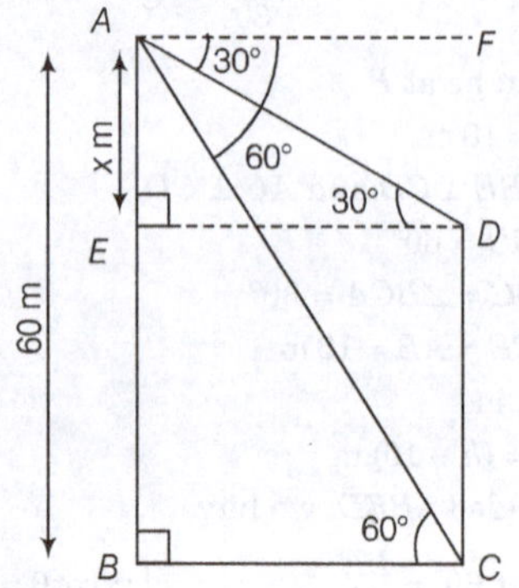

Here, $\angle FAD = \angle EDA = 30°$

and $\angle FAC = \angle BCA = 60°$ [alternate angles]

In right angled ΔABC, we have

$$\tan 60° = \frac{AB}{BC} \quad \left[\because \tan\theta = \frac{\text{perpendicular}}{\text{base}}\right]$$

$$\Rightarrow \sqrt{3} = \frac{60}{BC} \quad [\because \tan 60° = \sqrt{3}]$$

$$\Rightarrow BC = \frac{60}{\sqrt{3}} = \frac{60}{\sqrt{3}} \times \frac{\sqrt{3}}{\sqrt{3}} = \frac{60\sqrt{3}}{3} \quad \text{[rationalising]}$$

$$\therefore BC = 20\sqrt{3}\text{ m} \quad \text{...(i)}$$

Hence, the horizontal distance between AB and CD is $20\sqrt{3}$ m.

(ii) Let $AE = x$ m.

In right angled ΔAED, we have

$$\tan 30° = \frac{AE}{ED}$$

$$\Rightarrow \frac{1}{\sqrt{3}} = \frac{x}{20\sqrt{3}} \quad \left[\because \tan 30° = \frac{1}{\sqrt{3}} \text{ and } BC = ED = 20\sqrt{3}\text{ m}\right]$$

$$\therefore x = \frac{20\sqrt{3}}{\sqrt{3}} = 20\text{ m}$$

Now, height of the lamp-post,

$$CD = AB - AE$$

$$= 60 - 20 = 40\text{ m} \quad [\because AE = x = 20\text{ m}]$$

Hence, the height of the lamp-post is 40 m.

Example 28. **The angle of elevation of a cloud from a point 60 m above a lake is 30° and the angle of depression of the reflection of the cloud in the lake is 60°. Find the height of the cloud.**

Sol. Let AB be the surface of the lake and P be a point vertically above A, such that $AP = 60$ m.

Again, let C be the position of the cloud and D be its reflection in the lake.

Let the height of the cloud be H m.

Then, $BC = BD = H$ m

Draw $PQ \perp CD$.

Then, $\angle QPC = 30°$, $\angle QPD = 60°$,

$BQ = AP = 60$ m,

$CQ = (H - 60)$ m

and $DQ = (H + 60)$ m

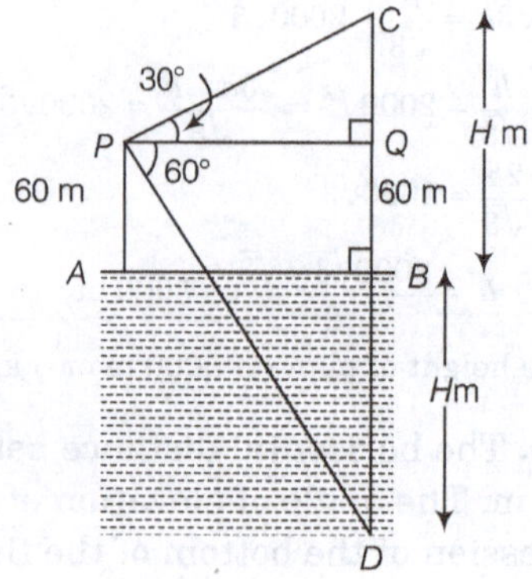

In right angled ΔCQP, we have

$$\cot 30° = \frac{PQ}{CQ} \quad \left[\because \cot\theta = \frac{\text{base}}{\text{perpendicular}}\right]$$

$$\Rightarrow \sqrt{3} = \frac{PQ}{(H - 60)} \quad [\because \cot 30° = \sqrt{3}]$$

$$\Rightarrow PQ = (H - 60)\sqrt{3}\text{ m} \quad \text{...(i)}$$

In right angled ΔDQP, we have

$$\cot 60° = \frac{PQ}{DQ} \Rightarrow \frac{1}{\sqrt{3}} = \frac{PQ}{(H + 60)} \quad \left[\because \cot 60° = \frac{1}{\sqrt{3}}\right]$$

$$\Rightarrow PQ = \frac{(H + 60)}{\sqrt{3}}\text{ m} \quad \text{...(ii)}$$

From Eqs. (i) and (ii), we get

$$(H - 60)\sqrt{3} = \frac{(H + 60)}{\sqrt{3}}$$

$$\Rightarrow 3H - 180 = H + 60 \Rightarrow 2H = 240$$

$$\therefore H = 120\text{ m}$$

Hence, the height of the cloud is 120 m.

Example 29. **From a window A, 10 m above the ground, the angle of elevation of the top C of a tower is $x°$, where $\tan x° = \frac{5}{2}$; and the angle of depression of the foot D of the tower is $y°$, where $\tan y° = \frac{1}{4}$. Calculate the height CD (in metres) of the tower.**

Sol. Given, $\tan x° = \frac{5}{2}$ and $\tan y° = \frac{1}{4}$ ...(i)

Draw $AE \perp CD$ and $BD \perp CD$.

Then, $BD = 10$ m, $\angle CAE = x°$

and $\angle DAE = \angle ADB = y°$ [alternate angles]

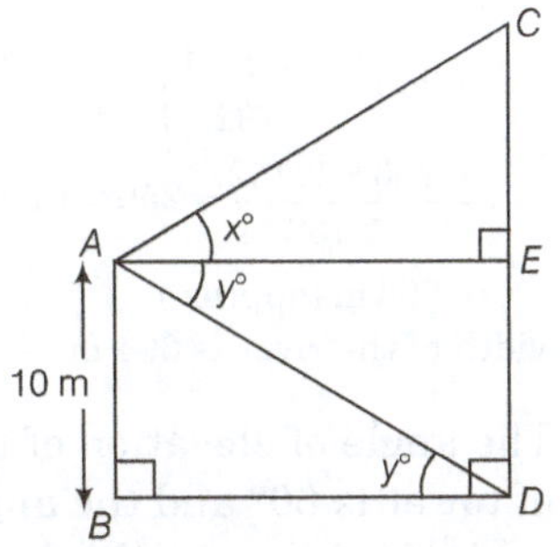

In ΔAEC, we have

$$\tan x° = \frac{CE}{AE} \quad \left[\because \tan\theta = \frac{\text{perpendicular}}{\text{base}}\right]$$

[from Eq. (i)]

$$\Rightarrow \frac{5}{2} = \frac{CE}{AE} \quad ...(ii)$$

In ΔABD, we have

$$\tan y° = \frac{AB}{BD}$$

$$\Rightarrow \frac{1}{4} = \frac{10}{AE} \quad [\because \text{from Eq. (i) and } BD = AE]$$

$$\Rightarrow AE = 40 \text{ m}$$

On putting the value of $AE = 40$ in Eq. (ii), we get

$$\Rightarrow \frac{5}{2} = \frac{CE}{40} \Rightarrow CE = \frac{40 \times 5}{2} = 100 \text{ m}$$

Now, $CD = CE + DE = CE + AB$ [$\because AB = DE$]

$= 100 + 10 = 110$ m [$\because AB = 10$ m, $CE = 100$ m]

$\therefore$ $CD = 110$ m

Hence, the height of the tower is 110 m.

Example 30. Two pillars of equal heights stand on either side of a road, which is 150 m wide. At a point on the road between the pillars, the angles of elevation of the tops of the pillars are 60° and 30°. Find the height of each pillar and the position of the point on the road.

Sol. Let AB and CD be the given pillars and O be the point of observation on the road AC. Then, $\angle AOB = 60°$, $\angle COD = 30°$, $\angle OAB = 90°$, $\angle OCD = 90°$ and $AC = 150$ m

Let $AB = CD = h$ m and $OA = x$ m

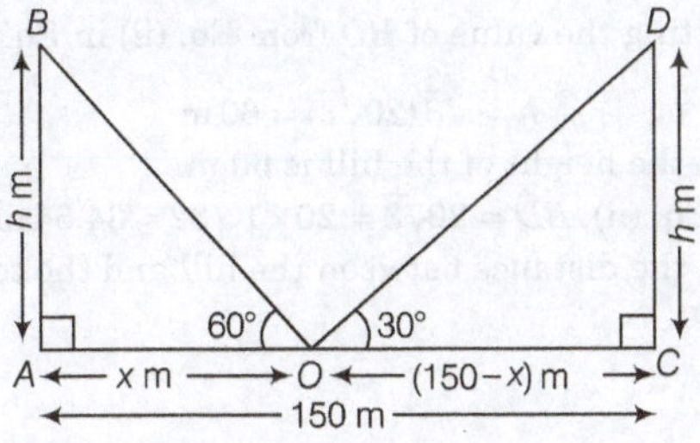

Then, $OC = (150 - x)$ m

In right angled ΔOAB, we have

$$\tan 60° = \frac{AB}{OA} \quad \left[\because \tan\theta = \frac{\text{perpendicular}}{\text{base}}\right]$$

$$\Rightarrow \sqrt{3} = \frac{h}{x} \Rightarrow h = \sqrt{3}x \quad [\because \tan 60° = \sqrt{3}] \quad ...(i)$$

In right angled ΔOCD, we have

$$\tan 30° = \frac{CD}{OC} \Rightarrow \frac{1}{\sqrt{3}} = \frac{h}{(150 - x)} \quad \left[\because \tan 30° = \frac{1}{\sqrt{3}}\right]$$

$$\Rightarrow h = \frac{(150 - x)}{\sqrt{3}} \quad ...(ii)$$

From Eqs. (i) and (ii), we get

$$\sqrt{3}x = \frac{(150 - x)}{\sqrt{3}}$$

$$\Rightarrow 3x = (150 - x)$$

$$\Rightarrow 4x = 150$$

$$\Rightarrow x = \frac{150}{4} = \frac{75}{2}$$

$$\Rightarrow x = 37.5 \text{ m}$$

On putting $x = \frac{75}{2}$ in Eq. (i), we get

$$h = \frac{75\sqrt{3}}{2} \text{ m}$$

Hence, the height of each pillar is $\frac{75\sqrt{3}}{2}$ m and the point of observation is 37.5 m away from the first pillar AB.

Example 31. A fire at a building B is reported on telephone to two fire stations F_1 and F_2 10 km apart from each other. F_1 observes that the fire is at an angle of 50° from it and F_2 observes that it is at an angle of 45° from it. Which station should send its team and how much distance it has to travel?

Sol. Let $AF_2 = x$ km, then $AF_1 = (10 - x)$ km

In ΔF_1BF_2, clearly $\angle F_1 > \angle F_2$

[$\because$ side opposite to greater angle of a triangle is smaller]

$\therefore$ F_1 should send their team.

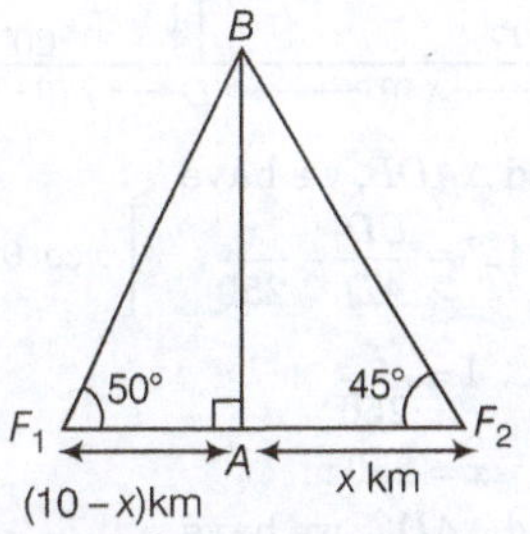

In right angled ΔBAF_2,

$$\tan 45° = \frac{AB}{AF_2} \quad \left[\because \tan\theta = \frac{\text{perpendicular}}{\text{base}}\right]$$

$$\Rightarrow 1 = \frac{AB}{AF_2} \quad [\because \tan 45° = 1]$$

$$\Rightarrow AB = AF_2 = x \text{ km}$$

In right angled ΔBAF_1,

$$\tan 50° = \frac{AB}{AF_1}$$

$\Rightarrow$ $\tan 50° = \frac{x}{10-x}$

$\Rightarrow$ $x = (10-x) \times 1.1918$

$\Rightarrow$ $x = 11.918 - 1.1918x$

$\Rightarrow$ $2.1918x = 11.918$

$\Rightarrow$ $x = \frac{11.918}{2.1918} = 5.44 \text{ km}$

$\Rightarrow$ $F_1A = 10 - x = 10 - 5.44 = 4.56 \text{ km}$

and $\sec 50° = \frac{F_1B}{F_1A}$ $\left[\because \sec\theta = \frac{\text{hypotenuse}}{\text{base}}\right]$

$\Rightarrow$ $\frac{1}{\cos 50°} = \frac{F_1B}{4.56}$

$\Rightarrow$ $F_1B = \frac{4.56}{0.6428} = 7.094 \text{ km}$

Hence, the team from F_1 has to travel 7.094 km.

Example 32. An aeroplane at an altitude of 250 m observes the angles of depression of two boats on the opposite banks of a river to be 45° and 60°, respectively. Find the width of the river. Write the answer correct to the nearest whole number.

Sol. Given, the height of aeroplane is $AD = 250$ m.

Let B and C be the positions of the boats, such that the angles of depression of two boats are 45° and 60°, respectively.

So, $\angle ABD = 45°$ and $\angle ACD = 60°$.

Let the distances of boats from the foot of perpendicular be $BD = x$ m and $DC = y$ m.

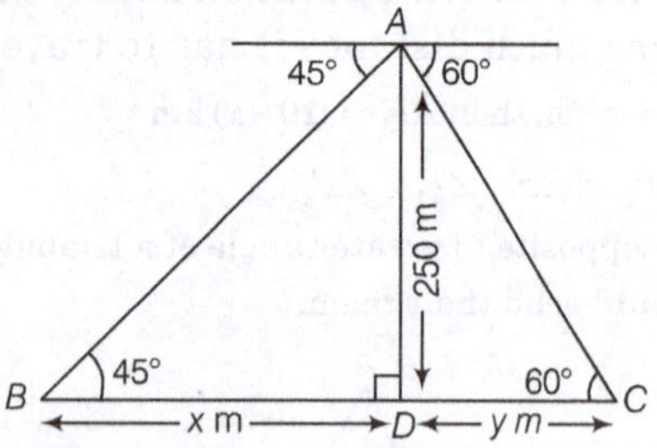

In right angled ΔADB, we have

$$\cot 45° = \frac{BD}{AD} = \frac{x}{250} \quad \left[\because \cot\theta = \frac{\text{base}}{\text{perpendicular}}\right]$$

$\Rightarrow$ $1 = \frac{x}{250}$ $[\because \cot 45° = 1]$

$\Rightarrow$ $x = 250$ m

In right angled ΔADC, we have

$$\cot 60° = \frac{DC}{AD} = \frac{y}{250}$$

$\Rightarrow$ $\frac{1}{\sqrt{3}} = \frac{y}{250}$ $\left[\because \cot 60° = \frac{1}{\sqrt{3}}\right]$

$\Rightarrow$ $y = \frac{250}{\sqrt{3}}$ m

Now, width of the river, $BC = BD + DC = x + y$

$$= 250 + \frac{250}{\sqrt{3}} = 250\left(1 + \frac{1}{\sqrt{3}}\right)$$

$$= 250\left(\frac{\sqrt{3}+1}{\sqrt{3}}\right)$$

$$= 250\left(\frac{1.732+1}{1.732}\right) \quad [\because \sqrt{3} = 1.732]$$

$$= \frac{250 \times 2.732}{1.732} = 250 \times 1.577 = 394.25 \text{ m}$$

$= 394$ m (approx.)

Hence, the width of the river is 394 m.

Example 33. The angle of elevation of the top of a hill at the foot of tower is 60° and the angle of elevation of the top of tower from the foot of hill is 30°. If the tower is 20 m high, then find

(i) the height of the hill.

(ii) the distance between the hill and the tower.

Sol. Let AB (= h m) be the height of the hill and CD (= 20 m) be the height of the tower.

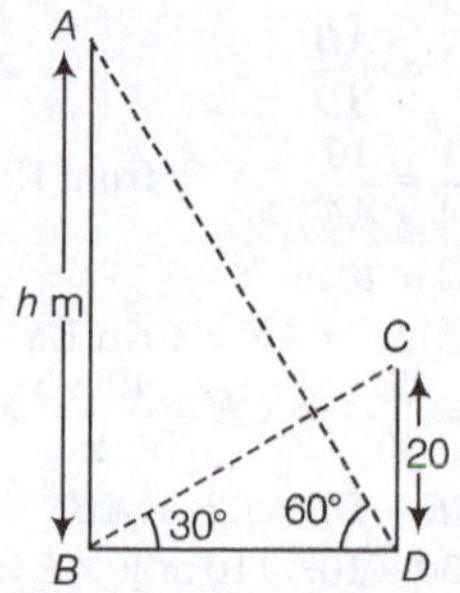

Then, $\angle ADB = 60°$ and $\angle CBD = 30°$ [given]

In right angled ΔABD,

$$\tan 60° = \frac{AB}{BD} \quad \left[\because \tan\theta = \frac{\text{perpendicular}}{\text{base}}\right]$$

$\Rightarrow$ $\sqrt{3} = \frac{h}{BD}$ $[\because \tan 60° = \sqrt{3}]$

$\Rightarrow$ $h = \sqrt{3}\,BD$ ...(i)

In right angled ΔCDB,

$$\tan 30° = \frac{CD}{BD}$$

$\Rightarrow$ $\frac{1}{\sqrt{3}} = \frac{20}{BD}$ $\left[\because \tan 30° = \frac{1}{\sqrt{3}}\right]$

$\Rightarrow$ $BD = 20\sqrt{3}$ m ...(ii)

(i) On putting the value of BD from Eq. (ii) in Eq. (i), we get

$$h = \sqrt{3}(20\sqrt{3}) = 60 \text{ m}$$

Hence, the height of the hill is 60 m.

(ii) From Eq. (ii), $BD = 20\sqrt{3} = 20 \times 1.732 = 34.64$ m

Hence, the distance between the hill and the tower is 34.64 m.

Example 34. A girl standing on the ground finds a bird flying at a distance of 200 m from her at an elevation of 60°. A man standing on the roof of 40 m high building, finds the angle of elevation of the same bird to be 30°. The girl and the man are on opposite sides of the bird. Find the distance of the bird from the man, correct to nearest metres.

Sol. Given, $AB = 200\text{ m}$, $FC = ED = 40\text{ m}$, $\angle ABC = 60°$ and $\angle AEF = 30°$.

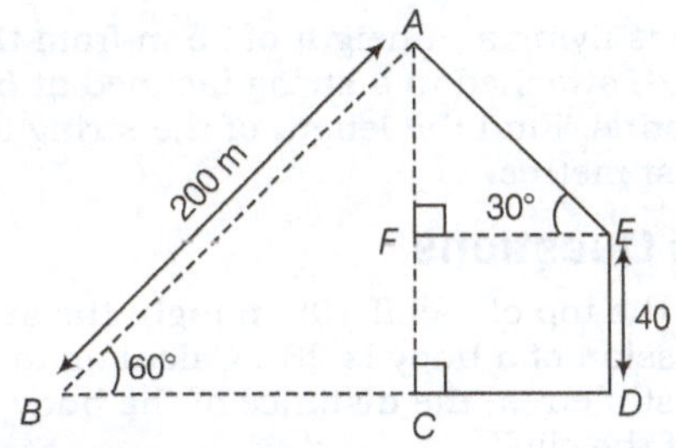

In right angled ΔACB, we have

$$\sin 60° = \frac{AC}{AB} \quad \left[\because \sin\theta = \frac{\text{perpendicular}}{\text{hypotenuse}}\right]$$

$$\Rightarrow \frac{\sqrt{3}}{2} = \frac{AC}{200} \quad \left[\because \sin 60° = \frac{\sqrt{3}}{2}\right]$$

$$\Rightarrow AC = \frac{200\sqrt{3}}{2} = 100\sqrt{3}$$

$$= 100 \times 1.732 \quad [\because \sqrt{3} = 1.732]$$

$$\therefore AC = 173.2\text{ m}$$

Now, $AF = AC - FC$

$$= 173.2 - 40 = 133.2\text{ m} \quad \ldots\text{(i)}$$

In right angled ΔAFE, we have

$$\sin 30° = \frac{AF}{AE}$$

$$\Rightarrow \frac{1}{2} = \frac{133.2}{AE} \quad \left[\sin 30° = \frac{1}{2} \text{ and from Eq. (i)}\right]$$

$$\Rightarrow AE = 133.2 \times 2 = 266.4\text{ m}$$

$$\therefore AE = 266\text{ m (approx.)}$$

Hence, the bird is 266 m away from the man.

Example 35. A 1.4 m tall boy spots a balloon moving with the wind in a horizontal line at a height of 91.4 m from the ground. The angle of elevation of the balloon from the eyes of the boy at that instant is 60°. After some time, the angle of elevation reduces to 30°. Find the distance travelled by the balloon during that interval. (take $\sqrt{3} = 1\cdot732$.)

Sol. Let AB represent the boy 1.4 m tall and P, Q be the two positions of the balloon when the angles of elevation observed from the point A are 60° and 30°, respectively. Through A, draw a horizontal line AX, BY represents ground.

From P, draw $PM' \perp BY$ to meet AX at M; and from Q, drawn $QN' \perp BY$ to meet AX at N.

$$MP = M'P - MM' = M'P - AB$$
$$= 91.4\text{ m} - 1.4\text{ m} = 90\text{ m}$$

Then, $NQ = MP = 90\text{ m}$ [$\because PMNQ$ forms a rectangle]

Let PQ be y m, then

$$MN = PQ = y\text{ m}.$$

Let AM be x m, then

$$AN = AM + MN = (x + y)\text{ m}$$

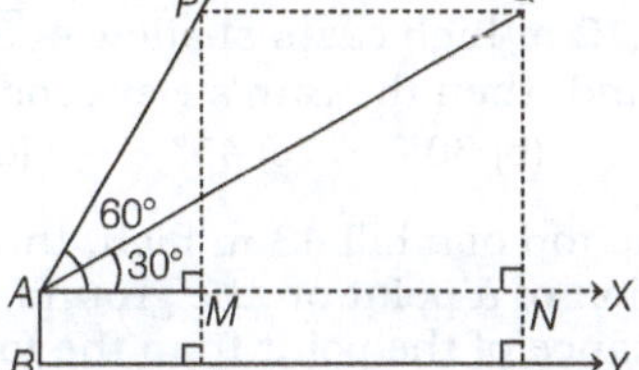

In right angled ΔAMP,

$$\angle PAM = 60°$$

$$\therefore \tan 60° = \frac{MP}{AM}$$

$$\Rightarrow \sqrt{3} = \frac{90}{x} \quad \ldots\text{(i)}$$

In right angled ΔANQ,

$$\angle QAN = 30°$$

$$\therefore \tan 30° = \frac{NQ}{AN}$$

$$\Rightarrow \frac{1}{\sqrt{3}} = \frac{90}{x + y} \quad \ldots\text{(ii)}$$

Dividing Eq. (i) by Eq. (ii), we get

$$\sqrt{3} \times \frac{\sqrt{3}}{1} = \frac{90}{x} \times \frac{x + y}{90}$$

$$\Rightarrow 3 = \frac{x + y}{x}$$

$$\Rightarrow 3x = x + y$$

$$\Rightarrow y = 2x \quad \ldots\text{(iii)}$$

From Eq. (i),

$$x = \frac{90}{\sqrt{3}} = 30\sqrt{3}$$

From Eq. (iii),

$$y = 2 \times 30\sqrt{3} = 60\sqrt{3}$$
$$= 60 \times 1.732 = 103.92$$

Hence, the distance travelled by the balloon during the interval is 103·92 m.

Chapter Practice

a. 1 Mark Questions

1. A ladder 28 m long rests against a wall. If the foot of the ladder is 14 m from the wall, then the angle of elevation is
(a) 30° (b) 45° (c) 60° (d) 75°

2. A kite is flying at a height of $20\sqrt{3}$ m from the ground level, attached to a string inclined 60° to the horizontal, then the string length is
(a) $40\sqrt{3}$ m (b) $30\sqrt{3}$ m (c) 40 m (d) 30 m

3. A tower 12 m high casts shadow $4\sqrt{3}$ m long on the ground, then the Sun's elevation is
(a) 15° (b) 30° (c) 45° (d) 60°

4. From the top of a hill 43 m high, the angle of depression of a point on the ground level is 30°. The distance of the point from the foot of the building is
(a) $43\sqrt{3}$ m (b) 129 m (c) 43 m (d) 86 m

5. In ΔPQR, $\angle P = 30°$ and $\angle Q = 90°$. If $PR = 4$ cm, then its area is
(a) 2 cm (b) 3 cm (c) $2\sqrt{2}$ cm (d) $4\sqrt{2}$ cm

6. A lighthouse is 80 m high. The angle of elevation of its top from a point 80 m away from its foot along the same horizontal line is **[ICSE Semester II 2022]**
(a) 60° (b) 45° (c) 30° (d) 90°

b. 3 Marks Questions

7. What is the angle of elevation of the Sun, when the length of the shadow of a tree is equal to its vertical height?

8. The height of a tree is $\sqrt{3}$ times the length of its shadow. Find the angle of elevation of the Sun.

9. If the length of a shadow casted by a pole is $1/\sqrt{3}$ times the length of the pole, then find the angle of elevation of the Sun.

10. A tower is $100\sqrt{3}$ m high. Find the angle of elevation of its top from a point $100\sqrt{6}$ m away from its top.

11. The angle of elevation of the top of a tower from a point on the ground at a distance of 160 m from its foot, is found to be 60°. Find the height of the tower.

12. A vertical pole stands on the level ground. From a point on the ground, 25 m away from the foot of the pole, the angle of elevation of its top is found to be 60°. Find the height of the pole.

13. A ladder is placed along a wall, such that its upper end is resting against vertical wall. The foot of the ladder is 2.4 m away from the wall and the ladder is making an angle of 68° with the ground. Find the height, upto which the ladder reaches.

14. A kite is flying at a height of 75 m from the level ground, attached to a string inclined at 60° to the horizontal. Find the length of the string to the nearest metres.

c. 4 Marks Questions

15. From the top of a cliff 108 m high, the angle of depression of a buoy is 28°. Calculate to the nearest metres, the distance of the buoy from the foot of the cliff.

16. A man standing on the top of a building observing a flag 9 m away from the building such that the angle of depression of the flag to be 28°. Find the height of the building.

17. From the top of a light-house 100 m high, the angle of depression of the ship is observed as 36°. Find the distance of a ship from the foot of the light-house.

18. The height of a tree is 10 m. It is bent by the wind in such a way that its top touches the ground and makes an angle of 60° with the ground. At what height from the bottom, did the tree get bent? [take $\sqrt{3} = 1.732$]

19. In the following figure, not drawn to scale, AB is a tower. The angle of depression of C from A is α, where $\tan \alpha = 2/5$ and $BC = 200$ m. Calculate the height of the tower AB.

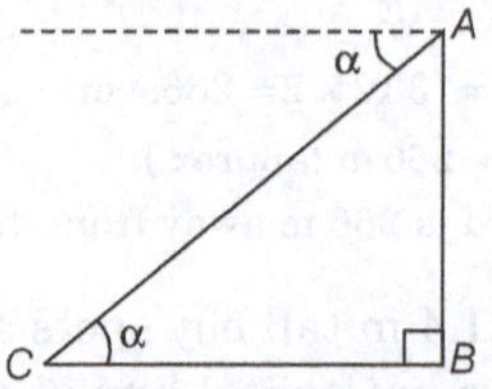

20. A man observes the angle of elevation of the top of the tower to be 45°. He walks towards it in a horizontal line through its base. On covering 20 m the angle of elevation changes to 60°. Find the height of the tower correct to 2 significant figures.

21. A person, standing on the bank of a river, observes that the angle subtended by a tree on the opposite bank is 60°. When he moves 50 m away from the bank, he finds that the angle of elevation to be 30°. Find the height of the tree and the breadth of the river.

22. Two climbers are at points A and B on a vertical cliff face. To an observer C, 40 m from the foot of the cliff, on the level ground, A is at an elevation of 48° and B of 57°. What is the distance between the climbers?

23. Two poles AB and PQ are standing opposite each other on either side of a road 200 m wide. From a point R between them on the road, the angles of elevation of the top of the poles AB and PQ are 45° and 40°, respectively. If height of $AB = 80$ m, then find the height of PQ correct to the nearest metre. **[ICSE 2020]**

24. Two persons are standing on the opposite sides of a tower. They observe the angles of elevation of the top of the tower to be 30° and 38°, respectively. Find the distance between them, if the height of the tower is 50 m.

25. The angles of depression of two ships A and B as observed from the top of a light-house 60 m high are 60° and 45°, respectively. If two ships are on the opposite sides of the light-house, then find the distance between the two ships. Give your answer correct to the nearest whole number. **[ICSE 2017]**

d. 6 Marks Questions

26. An observe on the top of a cliff, 200 m above the sea-level, observes the angle of depression of the two ships to be 45° and 30°, respectively. Find the distance between the ships, if the ships are

(i) on the same side of the cliff,

(ii) on the opposite sides of the cliff.

27. An observer 1.2 m tall and standing 28.2 m away from the tower. If the angle of elevation of the top of the tower from his eye is 60°, then what is the height of the tower?

28. The angle of elevation from a point P of the top of tower QR, 50 m high is 60° and that of the tower PT from a point Q is 30°. Find the height of the tower PT, connect to the nearest metre. **[ICSE 2018]**

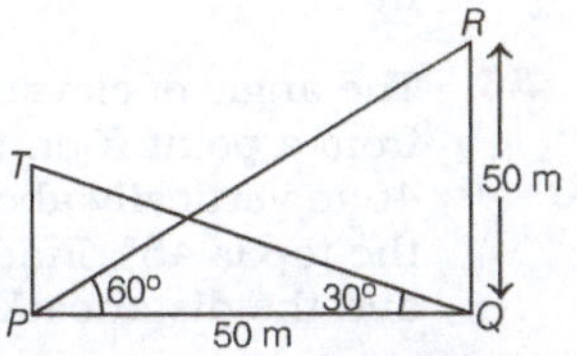

29. The angle of elevation of a jet plane from a point A on the ground is 60°. After a flight of 15 s, the angle of elevation changes to 30°. If the jet plane is flying horizontally at a constant height of $1500\sqrt{3}$ m, then find the speed of the jet plane.

30. A 1.2 m tall girl spots a balloon moving with the wind in a horizontal line at a height of 88.2 m from the ground. The angle of elevation of the balloon from the eyes of the girl at any instant is 60°. After sometime, the angle of elevation reduces to 30°. Find the distance travelled by the balloon during the interval.

31. The shadow of a vertical tower on level ground increases by 10 m, when the altitude of the Sun changes from angle of elevation 45° to 30°. Find the height of the tower, correct to one place of decimal. [take $\sqrt{3} = 1.732$]

32. The horizontal distance between two towers is 60 m. The angle of depression of the top of the first tower, when seen from the top of the second tower, is 30°. If the height of the second tower is 90 m, then find the height of the first tower.

33. A TV tower stands vertically on a bank of a river. From a point on the other bank directly opposite the tower, the angle of elevation of the top of the tower is 60°. From a point 20 m away this point on the same bank, the angle of elevation of the top of the tower is 30°. Find the height of the tower and width of the river.

34. A vertical pole and a vertical tower are on the same level ground. From the top of the pole, the angle of elevation of the top of the tower is 60° and the angle of depression of the foot of the tower is 30°. Find the height of the tower, if the height of the pole is 20 m.

35. A statue 1.46 m tall, stands on the top of a pedestal. From a point on the ground, the angle of elevation of the top of the statue is 60° and from the same point, the angle of elevation of the top of the pedestal is 45°. Find the height of the pedestal. [take $\sqrt{3} = 1.732$]

36. A man on the deck of a ship, 16 m above the water level, observes that the angles of elevation and depression respectively, of the top and bottom of a cliff are 60° and 30°. Calculate the distance of the cliff from the ship.

37. The angles of elevation and depression of the top and the bottom of a tower from the top of a building, 60 m high, are 30° and 60°, respectively. Find the difference between the height of the building and tower and the distance between them (use $\sqrt{3} = 1.732$).

38. The angle of elevation of a stationary cloud from a point 25 m above a lake is 30° and the angle of depression of its reflection in the lake is 60°. What is the height of the cloud above that lake-level?

39. The angle of elevation of a bird from a point 50 m above a lake is 30° and the angle of depression of its reflection in the lake is 60°. Find the height of the bird.

40. At the foot of a mountain, the angle of elevation of its summit is 45°. After ascending 1000 m towards the mountain up a slope of 30° inclination, the elevation is found to be 60°. Find the height of the mountain.

41. From the top of a hill, the angles of depression of two consecutive kilometre stones due East are found to be 30° and 45°. Find the height of the hill and the distance of two stones from the foot of the hill. **[2007]**

42. From the top of a tower 100 m high a man observes the angles of depression of two ships A and B, on opposite sides of the tower as 45° and 38° respectively. If the foot of the tower and the ships are in the same horizontal line find the distance between the two ships A and B to the nearest metre. **[ICSE 2023]**

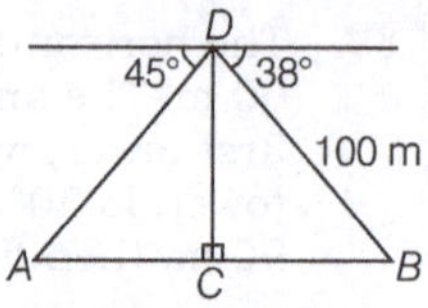

(use mathematical tables for this question.)

43. From the top of a church spire 96 m high, the angles of depression of two vehicles on road, at the same level as the base of the spire and on the same side of it, are α and β, where $\tan \alpha = 3/4$ and $\tan \beta = 1/3$. Calculate the distance between the vehicles.

44. From two points A and B on the same side of a building, the angles of elevation of the top of the building are 30° and 60°, respectively. If the height of the building is 10 m, then find the distance between A and B, correct to two decimal places.

45. A man on the top of a hill observes a truck at an angle of depression $x°$, where $\tan x° = \dfrac{1}{\sqrt{5}}$ and sees that it is moving towards the base of the hill. 10 min later, the angle of depression of the truck is found to be $y°$, where $\tan y° = \sqrt{5}$. Assuming that the truck moves at a uniform speed, determine how much more time it will take to reach the base of the tower?

46. A woman on a cliff observes a boat at an angle of depression of 30°, which is approaching the shore to the point immediately beneath the observer with a uniform speed. 6 min later, the angle of depression of the boat is found to be 60°. Find the time taken by the boat to reach the shore.

47. From the top of a tower, the angles of depression of two objects on the same side of the tower are found to be α and β ($\alpha > \beta$), respectively. If the distance between the objects is a m, then show that the height of the tower is

$$h = \frac{a \tan \alpha \tan \beta}{\tan \alpha - \tan \beta} \text{ m.}$$

48. The angle of elevation of a jet plane from a point A on the ground is 60°. After a flight of 30 s, the angle of elevation changes to 30°. If the jet plane is flying at a constant height of $3600\sqrt{3}$ m, then find the speed of the jet plane.

49. A bird is perched on the top of a tree 20 m high and its angle of elevation from a point on the ground is 45°. The bird flies-off horizontally straight away from the observe and in 1 s, the angle of elevation of the bird reduces to 30°. Find the speed of the bird.

50. An aeroplane when flying at a height of 4000 m from the ground, passes vertically above another aeroplane at an instant, when the angles of the elevation of the two planes from the same point on the ground are 60° and 45°, respectively. Find the vertical distance between the aeroplanes at that instant.

51. The radius of a circle is given as 15 cm and chord AB subtends an angle of 131° at the centre C of the circle, using trigonometry. Calculate

(i) the length of AB.

(ii) the distance of AB from the centre C.

52. The angle of elevation of a stationary cloud from a point 25 m above a lake is 30° and the angle of depression of its reflection in the lake is 60°. What is the height of the cloud above that lake-level?

53. A boy standing on the ground finds a bird flying at a distance of 100 m from him at an elevation of 30°. A girl standing on the roof of 20 m high building, finds the angle of elevation of the same bird to be 45°. The boy and the girl are on opposite sides of the bird. Find the distance of the bird from the girl.

54. The angle of elevation of the top of a hill at the foot of a tower is 60° and the angle of elevation of the top of the tower from the foot of hill is 30°. If the tower is 50 m high, then find the height of the hill.

55. The angle of elevation of the top B of a tower AB from a point X on the ground is 60°. At a point Y, 40 m vertically above X, the angle of elevation of the top is 45°. Find the height of the tower AB and the distance XB.

56. A vertical tower stand on a horizontal plane and is surmounted by a vertical flagstaff of height "h". At a point on the plane, the angle of elevation of the bottom of the flagstaff is α and that of the top of flagstaff is β. Prove that the height of the tower is $\dfrac{h \tan \alpha}{\tan \beta - \tan \alpha}$.

57. In the given figure, $PQRS$ is a cubical box with each edge 1 m and $\angle B = 30°$. Calculate length of board (AB).

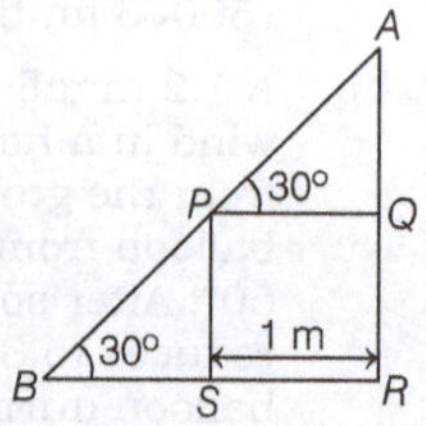

Hints and Answers

1. (c) **Hint** $\cos\theta = \frac{14}{28} = \frac{1}{2}$

Ans. 60°

2. (c) **Hint**

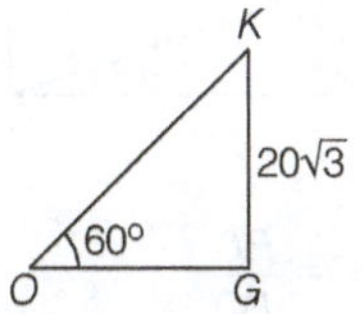

Ans. 40 m

3. (d) **Hint**

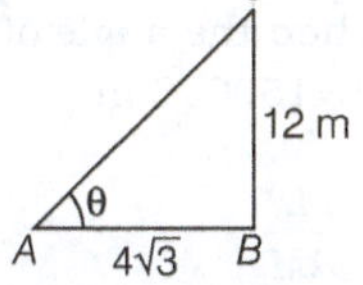

Ans. 60°

4. (a) **Hint**

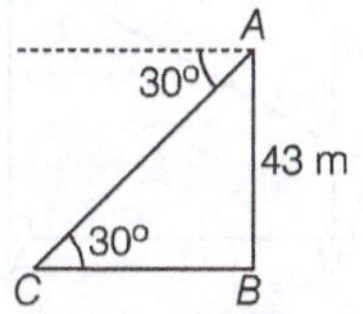

Ans. $43\sqrt{3}$ m

5. (a) **Hint** $\sin 30° = \frac{PQ}{PR}$

Ans. 2 cm

6. (b) Let AB be the given lighthouse and $\angle C = x$.

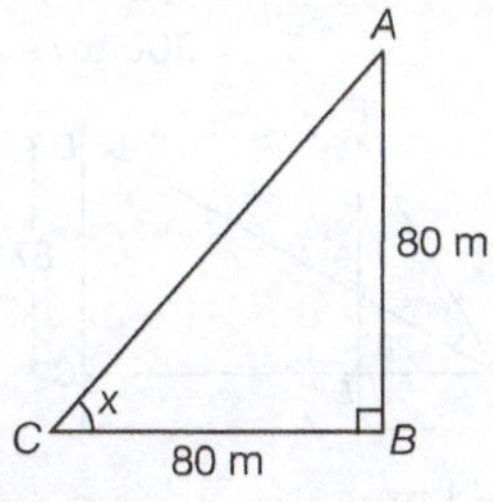

Given, $AB = 80$ m

and $CB = 80$ m

$\therefore \quad \tan x = \frac{AB}{BC} \Rightarrow \tan x = \frac{80}{80}$

$\Rightarrow \quad \tan x = 1$

$\Rightarrow \quad \tan x = \tan 45° [\because \tan 45° = 1]$

$\Rightarrow \quad x = 45°$

Hence the required angle of elevation of its top from a point is 45°.

7. **Hint** Do same as Example 1. **Ans.** 45°

8. **Hint** Do same as Example 1. **Ans.** 60°

9. **Hint** Let AB be the pole and BC be its shadow.

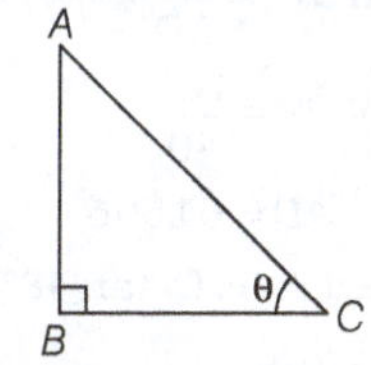

Then, $BC = \frac{1}{\sqrt{3}} AB \Rightarrow \frac{BC}{AB} = \frac{1}{\sqrt{3}}$ **Ans.** 60°

10. **Hint** Do same as Example 2. **Ans.** 45°

11. **Hint** Do same as Example 3.

Ans. 277.12 m

12. **Hint** Do same as Example 3. **Ans.** 43.3 m

13. **Hint** Do same as Example 4.

Ans. 5.94 m

14. **Hint** Let AB (= 75 m) be the height of kite from the ground and $\angle ACB = 60°$.

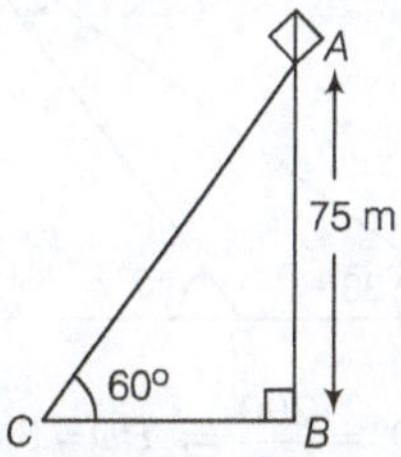

Also, let length of the string be AC.

Now, in ΔABC,

$$\sin 60° = \frac{AB}{AC}$$

$$\Rightarrow \quad \frac{\sqrt{3}}{2} = \frac{75}{AC}$$

Ans. 87 m (approx.)

15. **Hint** Do same as Example 7. **Ans.** 203 m

16. **Hint** Do same as Example 7. **Ans.** 4.785 m

17. **Hint** Do same as Example 7. **Ans.** 137.65 m

18. **Hint** Do same as Example 9. **Ans.** 4.64 m

19. **Hint** In the given ΔABC,

$$\tan\alpha = \frac{AB}{BC} \Rightarrow \frac{2}{5} = \frac{AB}{200}$$ **Ans.** 80 m

20. **Hint** Do same as Example 12. **Ans.** 47 m

21. **Hint** Do same as Example 12. **Ans.** 43.3 m, 25 m

22. **Hint** Here, $CD = 40$ m, $\angle ACD = 57°$ and $\angle BCD = 48°$

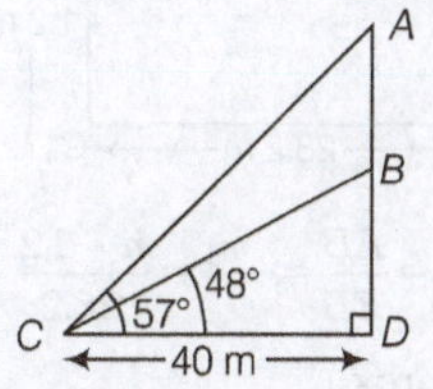

Let distance between the climbus A and B

$$= AD - BD \quad \text{...(i)}$$

Now, in right angled ΔADC,

$$\tan 57° = \frac{AD}{CD}$$

$$\Rightarrow \quad 1.5399 = \frac{AD}{40}$$

$$\Rightarrow \quad AD = 61.596$$

and in right angled $\Delta\, BDC$, $\tan 48° = \dfrac{BD}{CD}$

$$\Rightarrow \quad 1.1106 = \frac{BD}{40} \Rightarrow BD = 44.424$$

On substituting AD and BD in Eq. (i), we get the required result. **Ans.** 17.17 m

23. Hint Do same as Example 30. **Ans.** 101 m

24. Hint Do same as Example 31. **Ans.** 150.6 m

25. Hint Do same as Example 32. **Ans.** 94

26. Hint In ΔABC, $\tan 45° = \dfrac{200}{BC}$

$$\Rightarrow \quad BC = 200 \text{ m}$$

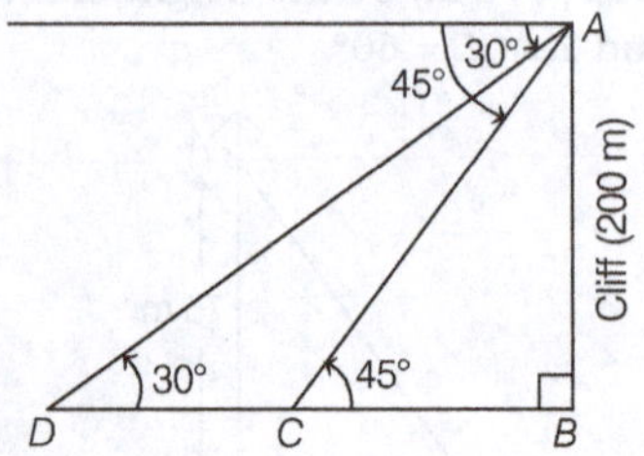

In ΔABD, $\tan 30° = \dfrac{200}{BD} \Rightarrow BD = 346.4$ m

$\therefore$ Distance between the ships

$$= CD = BD - BC = 146 \cdot 4 \text{ m}$$

(ii) The distance between the ships

$$= CD = BD + BC = 546.4 \text{ m}$$

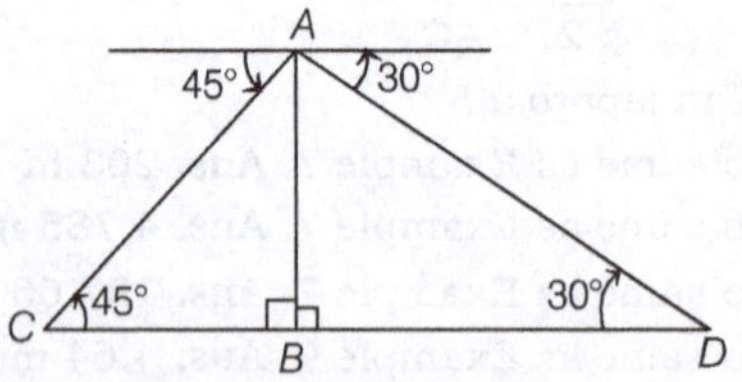

27. Hint In right angled ΔABE,

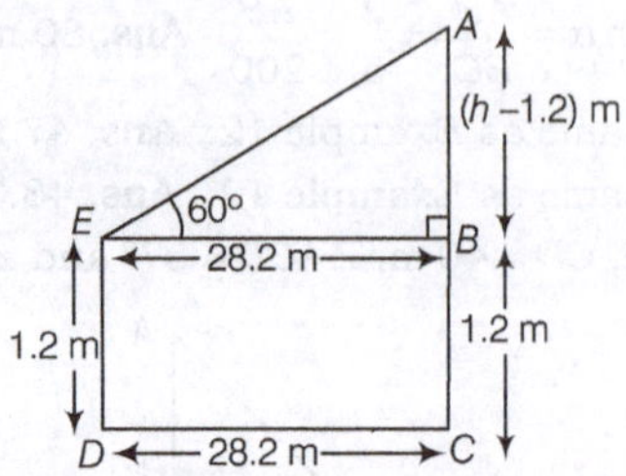

$$\tan 60° = \frac{AB}{EB} \Rightarrow \sqrt{3} = \frac{h - 1.2}{28.2}$$

Ans. 50 m (approx.)

28. Hint In ΔPQR,

$$\tan 60° = \frac{QR}{PQ} \Rightarrow \sqrt{3} = \frac{50}{PQ} \Rightarrow PQ = 28.86 \text{ m}$$

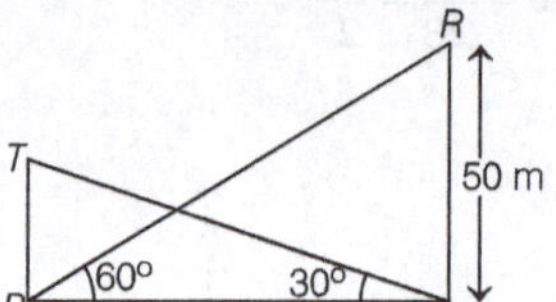

Similarly in PQT,

$$\tan 30° = \frac{PT}{PQ}$$

Ans. $PT = 16.66$ m

29. Hint Let P be the position of the jet plane when its elevation from a point A on the ground is 60° and Q be its position when the angle of elevation is 30°.

Given, $MP = NQ = 1500\sqrt{3}$ m

In ΔAMP,

$$\tan 60° = \frac{MP}{AM}$$

$$\Rightarrow \quad AM = 1500 \text{ m}$$

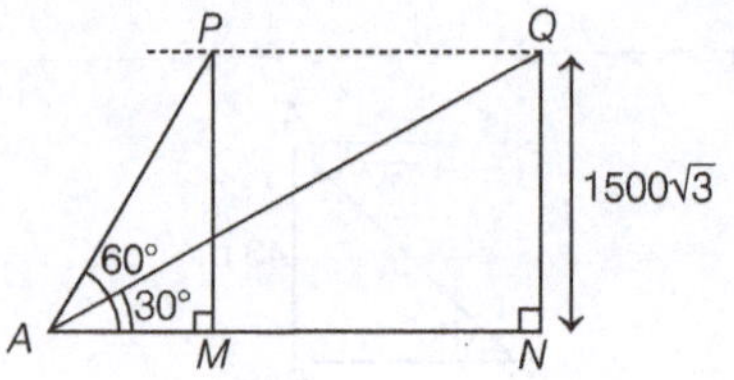

In ΔANQ,

$$\tan 30° = \frac{NQ}{AN}$$

$$\Rightarrow \quad AN = 4500 \text{ m}$$

$$\therefore \quad PQ = MN = AN - AM = 3000 \text{ m}$$

$\therefore$ The speed of the plane $= \dfrac{3000}{15}$ m/s

$$= 200 \text{ m/s} = 720 \text{ km/h}$$

30. Hint

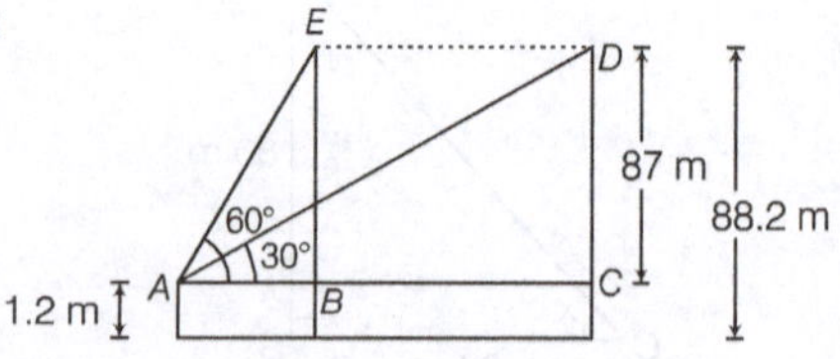

Ans. $BC = 58\sqrt{3}$ m

31. Hint In right angled ΔABC, $\tan 45° = \dfrac{AB}{CB} = \dfrac{h}{x}$

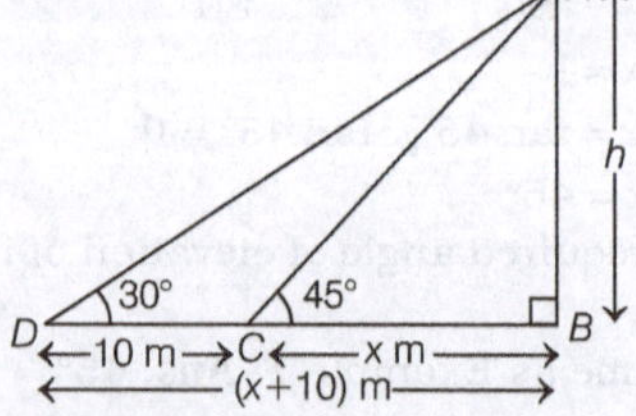

and in right angled $\Delta\, ABD$,

$$\tan 30^\circ = \frac{AB}{BD}$$

$$\Rightarrow \quad \frac{1}{\sqrt{3}} = \frac{h}{x+10}$$

Ans. 13.66 m

32. Hint $\tan 30^\circ = \frac{ED}{CD} = \frac{90-h}{60}$

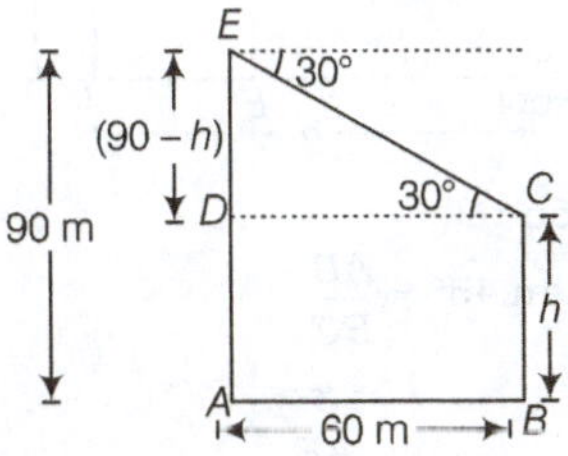

Ans. 55.36 m

33. Hint Do same as Example 12.

Ans. $10\sqrt{3}$ m, 10 m

34. In ΔABD, $\tan 60^\circ = \frac{AD}{BD} \Rightarrow BD = \frac{x}{\sqrt{3}}$ ...(i)

In ΔEBD, $\tan 30^\circ = \frac{DE}{BD} \Rightarrow BD = 20\sqrt{3}$ ...(ii)

From Eqs (i) and (ii), we get

$$x = 60$$

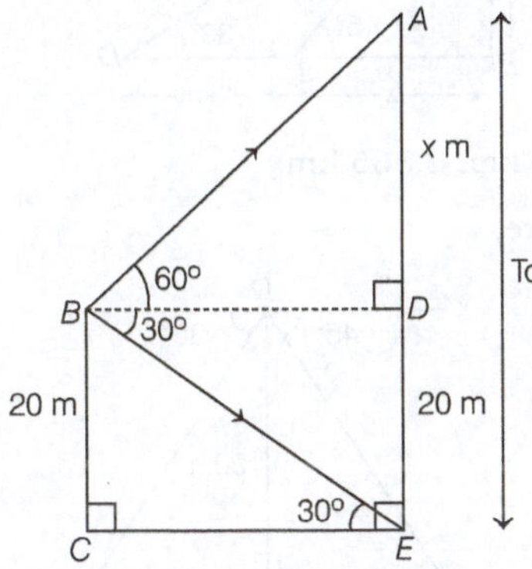

$\therefore$ Height of the tower = AE = 80 m

35. Hint

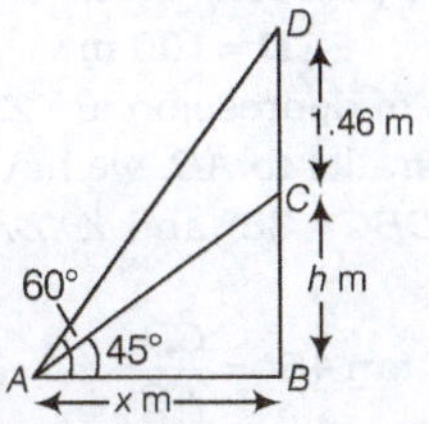

$$\tan 45^\circ = \frac{BC}{AB}$$

$$\tan 60^\circ = \frac{DB}{AB}$$

$$\sqrt{3} = \frac{1.46+h}{h}$$

Ans. 2 m

36. Hint

$$\tan 60^\circ = \frac{h}{x}$$

$$\tan 30^\circ = \frac{16}{x}$$

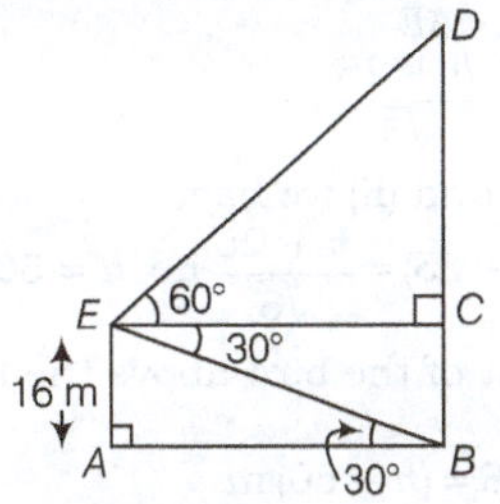

Ans. 27.7 m

37. Hint ΔABD, $\tan 60^\circ = \frac{AB}{BD}$

$$\Rightarrow \quad BD = \frac{60}{\sqrt{3}} \text{ m} = 20\sqrt{3} \text{ m} = 34.64 \text{ m}$$

From right ΔCAN,

$$\tan 30^\circ = \frac{CN}{AN}$$

$$\Rightarrow \quad \frac{1}{\sqrt{3}} = \frac{CN}{BD}$$

$$\frac{1}{\sqrt{3}} = \frac{CN}{20\sqrt{3}}$$

CN = 20 m and BD = 34.64 m

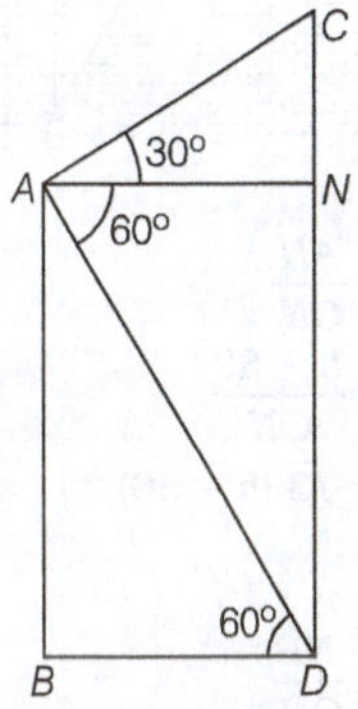

Ans. 20 m, 34.64 m

38. Hint As shown in figure $\angle CAE = 30^\circ$

$\angle DAE = 60^\circ$, $CE = CF - EF = (h - 25)$ m

and $DE = DF + EF = (h + 25)$ m

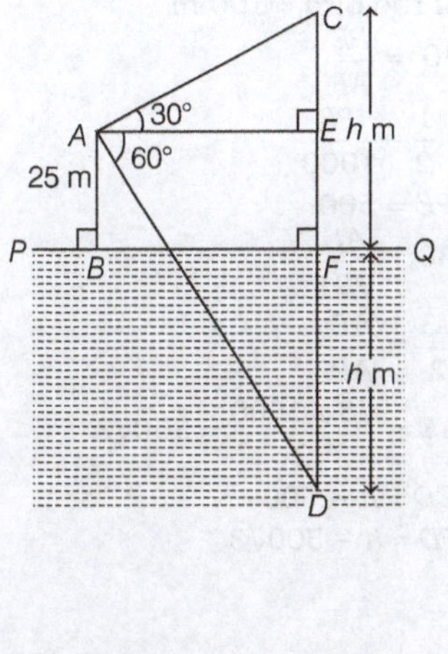

Clearly, $\tan 30^\circ = \dfrac{CE}{AE}$

$\Rightarrow \quad AE = \sqrt{3}(h-25)$ ...(i)

And, $\tan 60^\circ = \dfrac{DE}{AE}$

$\Rightarrow \quad AE = \dfrac{h+25}{\sqrt{3}}$ ...(ii)

From Eqs. (i) and (ii) we have

$\sqrt{3}(h-25) = \dfrac{h+25}{\sqrt{3}}$ i.e. $h = 50$

39. Let the height of the bird above the lake level be h m, then

$AB = (h-50)$ m

and $NB = (h+50)$ m

$\angle AON = 30^\circ$

and $\angle BON = 60^\circ$

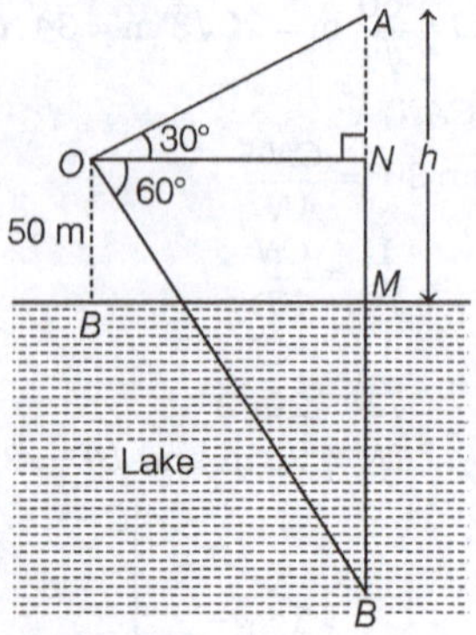

In ΔOAN,

$\tan 30^\circ = \dfrac{AN}{ON}$

$\Rightarrow \quad \dfrac{1}{\sqrt{3}} = \dfrac{h-50}{ON}$

$\Rightarrow \quad ON = \sqrt{3}(h-50)$ ...(i)

In ΔOBN,

$\tan 60^\circ = \dfrac{NB}{ON}$

$\Rightarrow \quad \sqrt{3} = \dfrac{h+50}{ON}$

$\Rightarrow \quad \sqrt{3} \times \sqrt{3}(h-50) = h+50$ [from Eq. (i)]

$\Rightarrow \quad h = 100$

$\therefore$ Height of the bird = 100 m

40. Hint $\sin 30^\circ = \dfrac{PE}{AP}$

$\dfrac{1}{2} = \dfrac{PE}{1000}$

$PE = 500$

$\cos 30^\circ = \dfrac{AE}{AP}$

$\dfrac{\sqrt{3}}{2} = \dfrac{AE}{AP}$

$AE = \dfrac{\sqrt{3} \times 1000}{2} = 500\sqrt{3}$

$CD = h - 500$

$PD = h - 500\sqrt{3}$

$\tan 60^\circ = \dfrac{CD}{PD}$

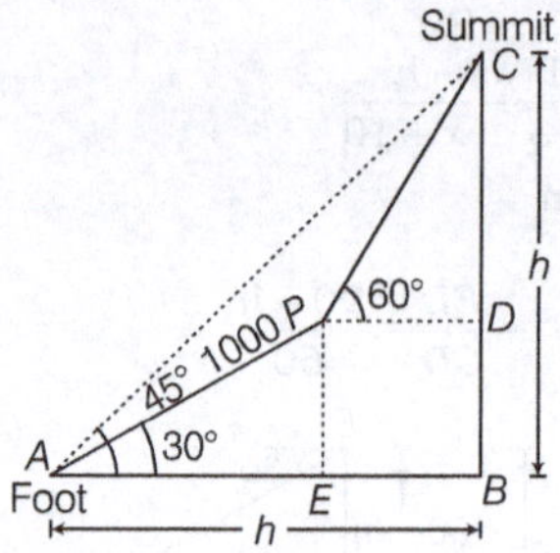

Ans. $h = 1366$ m

41. Hint $\tan 45^\circ = \dfrac{AB}{BC}$

$h = x$ ...(i)

$\tan 30^\circ = \dfrac{AB}{BD}$

$x + 1000 = x\sqrt{3}$ ...(ii)

After solving Eqs. (i) and (ii)

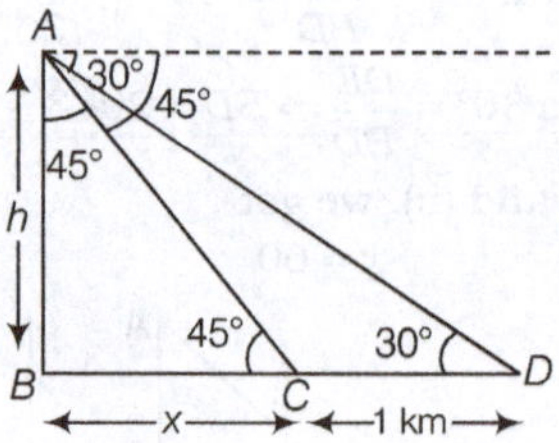

Ans. 1.365 km, 2.365 km

42. In the figure,

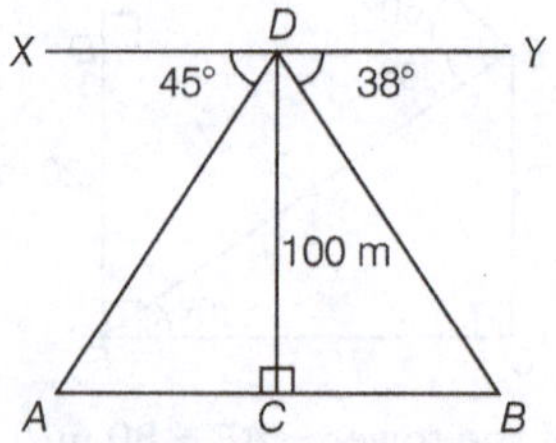

A and B are the positions of the ship A and ship B.

$CD = 100$ m

and the angles of depression are $\angle XDA$ and $\angle YDB$.

Since, XY is parallel to AB, we have

$\angle YDB = \angle DBC = 38^\circ$ and $\angle XDA = \angle DAC = 45^\circ$

[Alternate angles]

In right ΔACD, $\tan 45^\circ = \dfrac{CD}{AC}$

$\Rightarrow \quad 1 = \dfrac{100}{AC} \Rightarrow AC = 100$ m

In right ΔBCD, $\tan 38^\circ = \dfrac{CD}{CB}$

$0.781 = \dfrac{100}{BC} \Rightarrow BC = 128.04$

Now, $AB = AC + BC = 100 + 128.04 = 228.04$ m

Hence, distance between the ships is 228.04 m

43. Do same as Example 19. **Ans.** 160 m

44. Do same as Example 19.
Ans. 11.55 m

45. Do same as Example 21.
Ans. 150 s

46. Do same as Example 21.
Ans. 3 min

47. Hint

In ΔDAB, $\tan\alpha = \dfrac{AD}{AB} = \dfrac{h}{x}$ ...(i)

In ΔDAC, $\tan\beta = \dfrac{DA}{AC} = \dfrac{h}{x+a}$ ...(ii)

By solving Eqs. (i) and (ii)

$$h = \frac{a\tan\alpha\tan\beta}{\tan\alpha - \tan\beta}\text{ m}$$

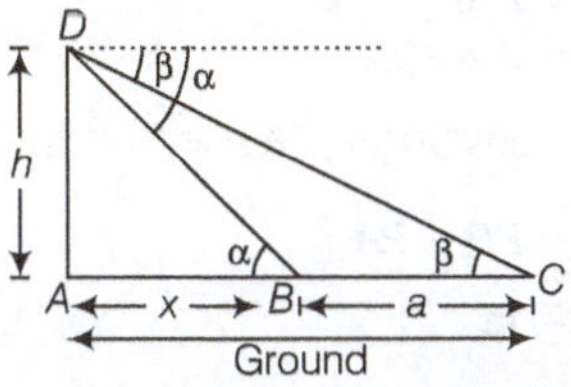

48. Hint

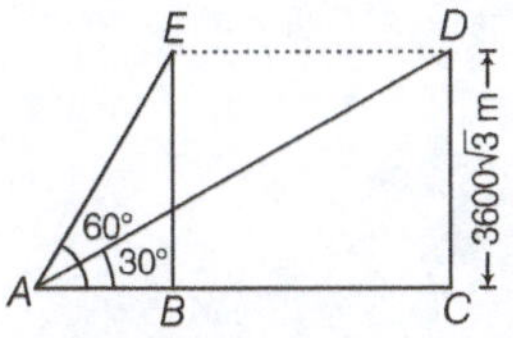

Further, solve as Example 24. **Ans.** 864 km/h

49. Hint Do same as Q. 30. **Ans.** $20(\sqrt{3}-1)$ m/s

50. Hint $\tan 60° = \dfrac{BD}{BA}$

$\tan 45° = \dfrac{CB}{BA}$

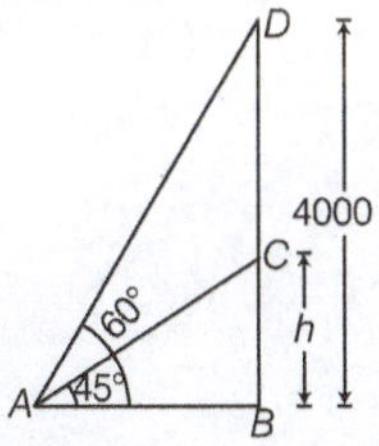

Ans. 1690.53 m

51. Hint Draw $OC \perp AB$

Then, $AO = OB$ and $AC = BC = 15$ cm

Also, $\angle ACO = \angle BCO = \dfrac{131°}{2}$

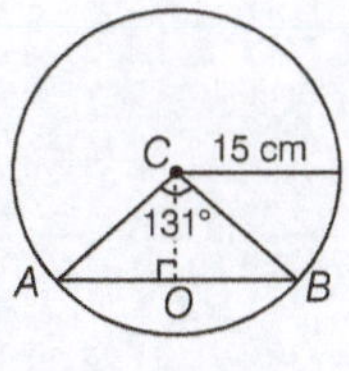

(i) Now, in right angled ΔAOC,

$$\sin\frac{131°}{2} = \frac{OA}{AC} \Rightarrow OA = 0.91\times 15 = 13.65$$

$\therefore$ $AB = 2OA$

(ii) In right angled ΔAOC,

$$\cos\frac{131°}{2} = \frac{OC}{AC} \Rightarrow OC = 0.415\times 15$$

Ans. (i) 27.3 cm (ii) 6.23 cm

52. Hint Do same as Example 28. **Ans.** 50 m

53. Hint In ΔPBN, $\sin 30° = \dfrac{NP}{BP}$

$\Rightarrow$ $NP = 50$ m

$\therefore$ $CP = NP - NC = NP - AG = 30$ m

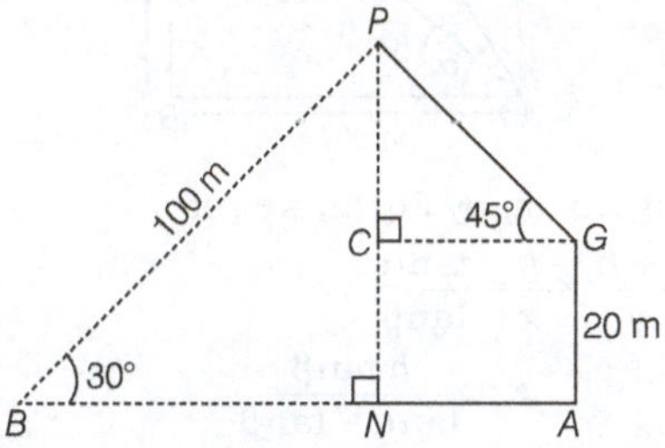

In ΔPCG, $\sin 45° = \dfrac{CP}{GP}$

$\Rightarrow$ $GP = 30\sqrt{2}$ m $= 42.426$ m $= 42.43$ m

54. Hint $\tan 30° = \dfrac{AB}{AC}$

$\tan 60° = \dfrac{DC}{AC}$ (Futher solve as Example 33)

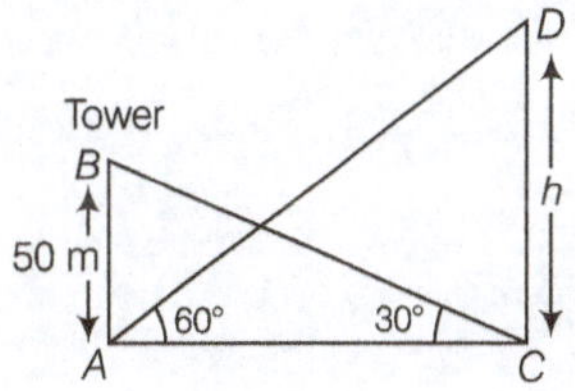

Ans. 150 m

55. Hint

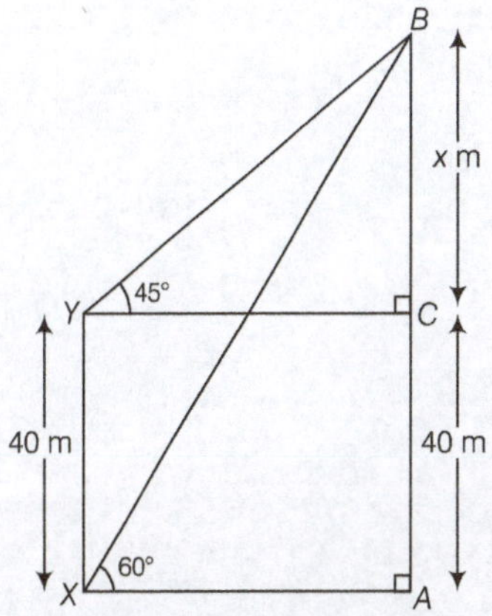

Ans. $AB = 20(\sqrt{3}+3)$ m, $BX = 109.282$ m

56. Hint In right angled ΔABC, $\frac{x}{y} = \tan\beta$ ...(i)

In right angled ΔABD, $\frac{x+h}{y} = \tan\alpha$ ...(ii)

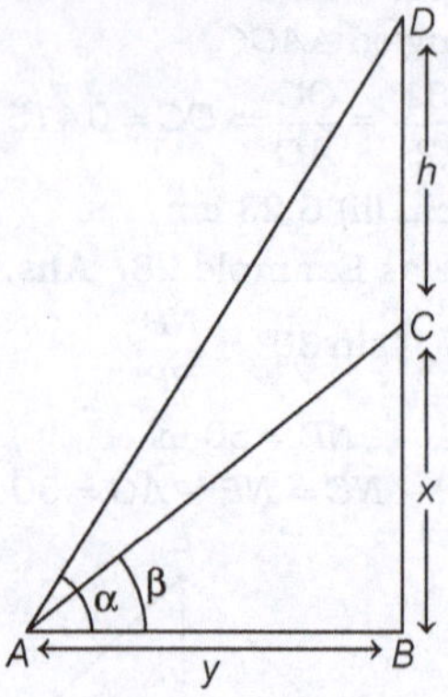

Dividing Eq. (ii) by Eq. (i), we get

$$\frac{x+h}{y} \times \frac{y}{x} = \frac{\tan\alpha}{\tan\beta}$$

$$\Rightarrow \quad x = \frac{h\tan\beta}{\tan\alpha - \tan\beta}$$

57. Hint

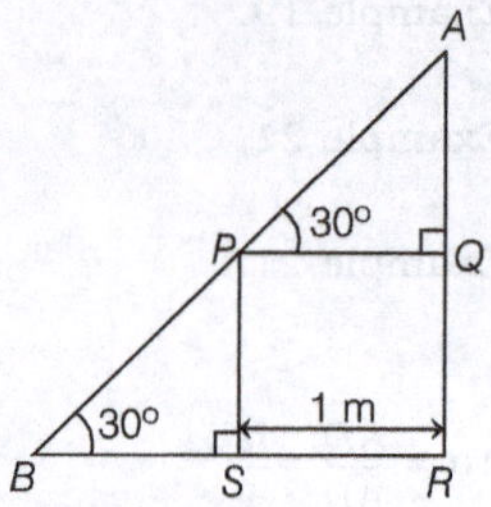

$PQ = QR = RS = PS = 1\text{ m}$

$\angle B = \angle P = 30°$ [corresponding $\angle S$]

In right angled ΔBSP,

$$\frac{PS}{PB} = \sin 30°$$

$\Rightarrow \quad PB = 2\text{ m}$

In right angled ΔPQA,

$$\frac{PQ}{AP} = \cos 30° \Rightarrow AP = \frac{2\sqrt{3}}{3}\text{ m}$$

$AB = PB + PA$

Ans. $\frac{6+2\sqrt{3}}{3}$ m

Olympiad Section

Brain Teasing Questions asked in Previous Olympiads

1 A tower stands at the centre of a circular park. If A and B are two points on the boundary of the park, such that $AB = a$ m subtends an angle of 60° at the foot of the tower and the angle of elevation of the top of the tower from A or B is 30°, then the height of the tower is

(a) $\sqrt{3}\,a$ m (b) $a/\sqrt{3}$ m (c) $\frac{\sqrt{3}}{a}$ m (d) None of these

Directions (Q.Nos. 2- 4) *In the given figure, from the top of a building AB, 60 m high, the angles of depression of the top and the bottom of a vertical lamp-post CD are observed to be 30° and 60°, respectively.*

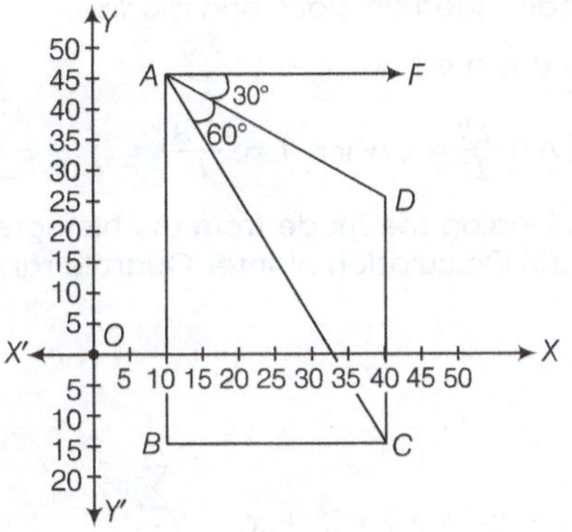

2 Find the horizontal distance between BA and CD.

(a) $60\sqrt{3}$ m (b) $40\sqrt{3}$ m (c) $20\sqrt{3}$ m (d) $10\sqrt{3}$ m

3 Find the height of the lamp-post CD.

(a) 60 m (b) 40 m (c) 20 m (d) 10 m

4 Find the radius of the circle, if Y-axis and AB are the tangent to the circle.

(a) 20 m (b) 15 m (c) 10 m (d) 5 m

5 First, plot the points $A(2, 4)$, $B(6, 4)$, $C(6, 2)$ and $D(2, 2)$ and join all adjacent points. A pole BE of height h is standing on point B. If angle of elevation of the top of a pole from point A is 30°, then the total area formed by the figure is

(a $8(\sqrt{3}+1)$ m^2 (b) $8(\sqrt{3}-1)$ m^2

(c) $\frac{8(\sqrt{3}+1)}{\sqrt{3}}$ m^2 (d) $\frac{8(\sqrt{3}-1)}{\sqrt{3}}$ m^2

6 If the angle of elevation of a cloud from a point h m above a lake is α and angle of depression of its reflection in the lake is β, then the height of the cloud is

(a) $\frac{h(\tan\beta + \tan\alpha)}{\tan\beta - \tan\alpha}$ m (b) $\frac{h(\tan\beta - \tan\alpha)}{\tan\beta + \tan\alpha}$ m

(c) $\frac{h\tan\beta + \tan\alpha}{\tan\beta - \tan\alpha}$ m (d) $\frac{h\tan\beta - \tan\alpha}{\tan\beta + \tan\alpha}$ m

7 A ladder rests against a vertical wall at an inclination α to the horizontal. If its foot is pulled away from the wall through a distance p, so that its upper end slides at distance q down the wall and the ladder makes an angle β to the horizontal, then $\frac{\cos\beta - \cos\alpha}{\sin\alpha - \sin\beta}$ is equal to

(a) q/p (b) p/q (c) pq (d) $1/pq$

8 A spherical balloon of radius r subtends an angle θ at the eye of the observer. If the angle of elevation of its centre is ϕ, then the height of the centre of balloon is

(a) $r\sin\phi / 2\cos\theta$ (b) $r\sin\phi\ \text{cosec}\theta$

(c) $r\sin\phi\ \text{cosec}\theta/2$ (d) None of these

9 ABC is a triangular park with $AB = AC = 100$ m. A clock tower is situated at the mid-point of BC. The angles of elevation of the top of the tower at A and B are α and β respectively, where $\cot\alpha = 3.2$ and $\text{cosec}\,\beta = 2.6$. Then, the height of the tower is

(a) 625 m (b) 25 m (c) 60 m (d) 100 m

10 The angle of elevation of the top of a tower (i.e. East) from a point A due South of it, is α, where $\tan\alpha = 6$ and that from B due West of it, is β, where $\tan\beta = 0.75$. If h is the height of the tower, then $AB = \lambda h$. Then, λ^2 is

(a) 65/36 (b) 36/65

(c) 16/9 (d) 9/16

11 The base of a cliff is circular. From the extremities of a diameter of the base, angles of elevation of the top of the cliff are 30° and 60°, respectively. If the height of the cliff is 500 m, then the diameter of the base of the cliff will be

(a) 2000 m (b) $\frac{2000}{\sqrt{3}}$ m

(c) $2000\sqrt{3}$ m (d) $\frac{500}{\sqrt{3}}$ m

Answers

1. (b)	2. (c)	3. (b)	4. (d)	5. (c)	6. (a)
7. (b)	8. (c)	9. (b)	10. (a)	11. (b)	

** These questions may or may not be asked in the examination, have been given just for additional practice required for olympiads Scholarship Exams etc. For detailed explanations refer Page No. 499.*

CHAPTER

20

Statistics

SYLLABUS

Statistics–basic concepts, Mean, Median, Mode. Histograms and Ogive.

(a) Computation of (I) Measures of Central Tendency : Mean*, Median class and modal class for continuous grouped data. (ii) *Mean by any method Direct : $\frac{\Sigma fd}{\Sigma f}$

Short-cut : $A+\frac{\Sigma fd}{\Sigma f}$, where $d = x - A$ Step-deviation : $A + \frac{\Sigma ft}{\Sigma f} \times i$, where $t = \frac{x-A}{i}$

(b) Graphical Representation. Histograms and Less than Ogive. (I) Finding the mode from the histogram, the upper quartile, lower Quartile and median etc. from the ogive. (ii) Calculation of inter Quartile range.

Statistics is the study of collection, presentation analysis and interpretation of numerical data.

In the previous class, we have studied the classification of given data into ungrouped and grouped frequency distribution, representation of data (such as bar graphs, histograms, frequency polygon) and mean, median, for the ungrouped data.

In this chapter, we will study the measures of central tendency, i.e. mean, median and mode, from ungrouped data to that of grouped data along with graphical representation of data.

Mean of Grouped Data

Mean or Arithmetic Mean or Average

The arithmetic mean of a set of observations is obtained by dividing the sum of the values of all observations by the total number of observations.

Thus, the mean of n observations $x_1, x_2, x_3, \ldots, x_n$, is defined as

$$\text{Mean } (\bar{x}) = \frac{x_1 + x_2 + x_3 + \ldots + x_n}{n} = \frac{\sum_{i=1}^{n} x_i}{n}$$

where, the Greek letter 'Σ' (sigma) means 'Summation.'

Let $x_1, x_2, \ldots, x_n$ be n observations with respective frequencies $f_1, f_2, \ldots, f_n$. This means observation x_1 occurs f_1 times, x_2 occurs f_2 times and so on.

Then, sum of the values of all the observations

$$= f_1x_1 + f_2x_2 + \ldots + f_nx_n = \sum_{i=1}^{n} f_ix_i$$

$$\text{Total number of observations} = f_1 + f_2 + \ldots + f_n = \sum_{i=1}^{n} f_i$$

$$\therefore \text{ Mean } (\bar{x}) = \frac{\sum_{i=1}^{n} f_ix_i}{\sum_{i=1}^{n} f_i}$$

It can also be written as $\bar{x} = \frac{\Sigma fx}{\Sigma f}$

Note $\bar{x}$ is read as 'x bar'.

Example 1. The mean of the numbers 6, y, 7, x, 14 is 8. Express y in terms of x.

Sol. Given, the mean of the numbers 6, y, 7, x, 14 is 8

$$\therefore \quad \frac{6+y+7+x+14}{5} = 8$$

$$\Rightarrow \quad 27 + x + y = 40$$

$$\Rightarrow \quad x + y = 40 - 27 = 13$$

$$\Rightarrow \quad y = 13 - x$$

Example 2. The mean height of 8 students is 152 cm. Two more students of heights 142 cm and 152 cm join the group. What is the new mean height?

Sol. Mean height of 8 students

$$= \frac{\text{Sum of height of 8 students}}{8}$$

$$\therefore \quad 152 \text{ cm} = \frac{\text{Sum of height of 8 students}}{8}$$

$\Rightarrow$ Sum of height of 8 students = 1216 cm

Now, two more students of heights 142 cm and 152 cm join the group.

$\therefore$ Sum of heights of 10 students = 1216 + 142 + 152 = 1510 cm

$$\therefore \text{ New mean height} = \frac{\text{Sum of height of 10 students}}{10} = \frac{1510}{10} = 151 \text{ cm}$$

Example 3. Find the mean of the following data.

x	10	30	50	70	89
f	7	8	10	15	10

Sol. Table for given data is

x_i	f_i	$f_i x_i$
10	7	70
30	8	240
50	10	500
70	15	1050
89	10	890
Total	$\Sigma f_i = 50$	$\Sigma f_i x_i = 2750$

Here, $\Sigma f_i = 50$ and $\Sigma f_i x_i = 2750$

$$\therefore \quad \text{Mean } (\bar{x}) = \frac{\Sigma f_i x_i}{\Sigma f_i} = \frac{2750}{50} = 55$$

Hence, mean of the given data is 55.

Example 4. The mean of the following data is 14. Find the value of k.

x	5	10	15	20	25
f	7	k	8	4	5

Sol. Table for the given data is

x_i	f_i	$f_i x_i$
5	7	35
10	k	$10k$
15	8	120
20	4	80
25	5	125
Total	$\Sigma f_i = k + 24$	$\Sigma f_i x_i = 10k + 360$

Here, $\Sigma f_i = k + 24$ and $\Sigma f_i x_i = 10k + 360$

Given, mean = 14

$$\therefore \quad \frac{\Sigma f_i x_i}{\Sigma f_i} = 14$$

$$\Rightarrow \quad \frac{10k + 360}{k + 24} = 14$$

$$\Rightarrow \quad 10k + 360 = 14(k + 24)$$

$$\Rightarrow \quad 10k + 360 = 14k + 336$$

$$\Rightarrow \quad 14k - 10k = 360 - 336$$

$$\Rightarrow \quad 4k = 24$$

$$\Rightarrow \quad k = \frac{24}{4} = 6$$

Method of Calculating Mean of Grouped Data

To calculate the mean of grouped data, we have following three methods

1. Direct method
2. Assumed mean or shortcut method
3. Step-deviation method

The process of finding the mean by these methods are given below

1. Direct Method

In this method, we find the class marks of each class interval. These class marks would serve as the representative of whole class and are denoted by x_i. In general, for the ith class interval, we have the frequency f_i corresponding to the class mark x_i.

Example 5. The marks obtained by 30 students of Class X of a certain school in a Mathematics paper consisting of 100 marks are presented in table below

Class interval	10-25	25-40	40-55	55-70	70-85	85-100
Number of students	2	3	7	6	6	6

Find the mean of the marks obtained by the students.

Sol. The class marks for each class are given below

For 10-25, $x_1 = \dfrac{10 + 25}{2} = \dfrac{35}{2} = 17.5$

For 25-40, $x_2 = \frac{25+40}{2} = \frac{65}{2} = 32.5$

For 40-55, $x_3 = \frac{40+55}{2} = \frac{95}{2} = 47.5$

For 55-70, $x_4 = \frac{55+70}{2} = \frac{125}{2} = 62.5$

For 70-85, $x_5 = \frac{70+85}{2} = \frac{155}{2} = 77.5$

For 85-100, $x_6 = \frac{85+100}{2} = \frac{185}{2} = 92.5$

Now, the table for the given data is

Class interval	Frequency (f_i)	x_i	$f_i x_i$
10-25	2	17.5	35.0
25-40	3	32.5	97.5
40-55	7	47.5	332.5
55-70	6	62.5	375.0
70-85	6	77.5	465.0
85-100	6	92.5	555.0
Total	$\Sigma f_i = 30$		$\Sigma f_i x_i = 1860.0$

On putting the values of $\Sigma f_i x_i$ and Σf_i in the formula

$\bar{x} = \frac{\Sigma f_i x_i}{\Sigma f_i}$, we get $\bar{x} = \frac{1860.0}{30} = 62$

Hence, the mean marks obtained by the students are 62.

Example 6. Calculate the mean of the following distribution.

Class interval	0-10	10-20	20-30	30-40	40-50	50-60
Frequency	8	5	12	35	24	16

[ICSE 2015]

Sol. The table for given data is

Class interval	Class marks (x_i)	Frequency (f_i)	$f_i x_i$
0-10	5	8	40
10-20	15	5	75
20-30	25	12	300
30-40	35	35	1225
40-50	45	24	1080
50-60	55	16	880
Total		$\Sigma f_i = 100$	$\Sigma f_i x_i = 3600$

$$\therefore \quad \text{Mean} = \frac{\Sigma f_i x_i}{\Sigma f_i} = \frac{3600}{100} = 36$$

Example 7. If the mean of the following distribution is 24, find the value of 'a'.

Marks	0-10	10-20	20-30	30-40	40-50
Number of students	7	a	8	10	5

[ICSE 2018]

Sol.

Marks	Mid value (x)	Number of students (f)	$f \cdot x$
0-10	5	7	35
10-20	15	a	$15a$
20-30	25	8	200
30-40	35	10	350
40-50	45	5	225
Total		$\Sigma f = 30 + a$	$\Sigma f \cdot x = 810 + 15a$

$$\because \quad \text{Mean} = \frac{\Sigma fx}{\Sigma f}$$

$$\therefore \quad 24 = \frac{810 + 15a}{30 + a}$$

$$\Rightarrow \quad 24(30 + a) = 810 + 15a$$

$$\Rightarrow \quad 720 + 24a = 810 + 15a$$

$$\Rightarrow \quad 24a - 15a = 810 - 720$$

$$\Rightarrow \quad 9a = 90 \Rightarrow a = \frac{90}{9} = 10$$

Hence, the required value of a is 10.

2. Assumed Mean or Shortcut Method

The cases in which numerical values of x_i and f_i are large and computation of product of x_i and f_i becomes tedious and time consuming, assumed mean method is used. In this method, first of all, one among x_i's is chosen as the assumed mean denoted by 'A'. After that, the difference d_i between A and each of the x_i's,

i.e. $d_i = x_i - A$ is calculated.

Then, arithmetic mean is given by

$$\bar{x} = A + \frac{\Sigma f_i d_i}{\Sigma f_i}, \text{ where } d_i = x_i - A.$$

It can also be written as $\bar{x} = A + \frac{\Sigma fd}{\Sigma f}$, where

$d = x - A$.

Note We may take A to be that x_i which lies in the middle of $x_1, x_2, \ldots, x_n$.

Example 8. The following table gives the percentage distribution of female teachers in the primary schools of rural areas of various states and union territories of India

Percentage of female teachers	Number of states/UT
15-25	6
25-35	11
35-45	7
45-55	4
55-65	4
65-75	2
75-85	1

Find the mean percentage of female teachers by assumed mean method.

Sol. The class marks for each class are given below

For 15-25, $x_1 = \frac{15+25}{2} = \frac{40}{2} = 20$

For 25-35, $x_2 = \frac{25+35}{2} = \frac{60}{2} = 30$

For 35-45, $x_3 = \frac{35+45}{2} = \frac{80}{2} = 40$

For 45-55, $x_4 = \frac{45+55}{2} = \frac{100}{2} = 50$

For 55-65, $x_5 = \frac{55+65}{2} = \frac{120}{2} = 60$

For 65-75, $x_6 = \frac{65+75}{2} = \frac{140}{2} = 70$

For 75-85, $x_7 = \frac{75+85}{2} = \frac{160}{2} = 80$

Here, 50 lies in the centre of 20 , 30, ..., 80.

$\therefore$ Let $A = 50$.

Now, $d_1 = 20 - 50 = -30$, $d_2 = 30 - 50 = -20$

$d_3 = 40 - 50 = -10$, $d_4 = 50 - 50 = 0$

$d_5 = 60 - 50 = 10$, $d_6 = 70 - 50 = 20$, $d_7 = 80 - 50 = 30$

Now, let us make the following table

Percentage of female teachers	Class marks (x_i)	Number of States/UT (f_i)	$d_i = x_i - A$	$f_i d_i$
15-25	20	6	− 30	− 180
25-35	30	11	− 20	− 220
35-45	40	7	− 10	− 70
45-55	50	4	0	0
55-65	60	4	10	40
65-75	70	2	20	40
75-85	80	1	30	30
Total		$\Sigma f_i = 35$		$\Sigma f_i d_i = -360$

Here, $A = 50$, $\Sigma f_i d_i = -360$ and $\Sigma f_i = 35$

On putting these values in the formula $\bar{x} = A + \frac{\Sigma f_i d_i}{\Sigma f_i}$, we get

$$\bar{x} = 50 + \frac{(-360)}{35} = 50 - \frac{360}{35} = 50 - 10.29 = 39.71$$

Hence, the required mean percentage of female teachers is 39.71.

Example 9. Find the mean of the following frequency distribution using assumed mean method.

Class	2-8	8-14	14-20	20-26	26-32
Frequency	6	3	12	11	8

Sol. The table for the given data is

Class	Frequency (f_i)	x_i	$d_i = x_i - A$	$f_i d_i$
2-8	6	5	$5 - 17 = -12$	$6(-12) = -72$
8-14	3	11	$11 - 17 = -6$	$3(-6) = -18$
14-20	12	$17 = A$	$17 - 17 = 0$	$12 \times 0 = 0$
20-26	11	23	$23 - 17 = 6$	$11 \times 6 = 66$
26-32	8	29	$29 - 17 = 12$	$8 \times 12 = 96$
Total	$\Sigma f_i = 40$			$\Sigma f_i d_i = 72$

Here, $A = 17$, $\Sigma f_i = 40$ and $\Sigma f_i d_i = 72$

$$\therefore \quad \text{Mean } (\bar{x}) = A + \frac{\Sigma f_i d_i}{\Sigma f_i}$$

$$= 17 + \frac{72}{40} = 17 + 1.8$$

$$= 18.8$$

Example 10. Calculate the mean of the distribution given below using the shortcut method.

Marks	11-20	21-30	31-40	41-50	51-60	61-70	71-80
Number of students	2	6	10	12	9	7	4

[ICSE 2014]

Sol. The table for the given data is

Marks	Number of students (f_i)	Mid-value (x_i)	$d_i = x_i - A$	$f_i d_i$
11-20	2	15.5	−30	− 60
21-30	6	25.5	−20	−120
31-40	10	35.5	−10	−100
41-50	12	$45.5 = A$	0	0
51-60	9	55.5	10	90
61-70	7	65.5	20	140
71-80	4	75.5	30	120
Total	$\Sigma f_i = 50$			$\Sigma f_i d_i = 70$

Here, $A = 45.5$, $\Sigma f_i = 50$ and $\Sigma f_i d_i = 70$

By using shortcut method,

$$\text{Mean marks} = A + \frac{\Sigma f_i d_i}{\Sigma f_i} = 45.5 + \frac{70}{50}$$

$$= 45.5 + 1.4 = 46.9$$

Hence, the mean marks of the given distribution is 46.9.

3. Step-deviation Method

Step-deviation method is used in the cases, where the deviation from the assumed mean are multiples of a common number. If the values of d_i for each class is a multiple of h (say), the calculation becomes simpler by taking $u_i = \frac{d_i}{h} = \frac{x_i - A}{h}$.

Generally, the value of h is equal to the difference between upper and lower class limits of a class or the difference between two consecutive class marks. The arithmetic mean is given by

$$\overline{x} = A + \left(\frac{\Sigma f_i u_i}{\Sigma f_i}\right) \times h, \text{ where } u_i = \frac{x_i - A}{h}.$$

(i) The assumed mean method and step deviation method are just simplified forms of the direct method.

(ii) If the given data is discontinuous, there is no need to convert it into continuous data, while finding the mean. Because mid value x_i of each class interval would be same either class interval is continuous or not continuous.

Example 11. Find the mean of the following data by using step-deviation method.

Class	10-20	20-30	30-40	40-50	50-60	60-70
Frequency	4	28	15	20	17	16

Sol. Here, class width, $h = 20 - 10 = 10$.

Now, let the assumed mean, $A = 35$.

Then, the table for the given data is

Class	x_i	f_i	$u_i = \frac{x_i - A}{h}$	$f_i u_i$
10-20	$\frac{10+20}{2} = 15$	4	$\frac{15-35}{10} = \frac{-20}{10} = -2$	−8
20-30	$\frac{20+30}{2} = 25$	28	$\frac{25-35}{10} = \frac{-10}{10} = -1$	−28
30-40	$\frac{30+40}{2} = 35 = A$	15	$\frac{35-35}{10} = \frac{0}{10} = 0$	0
40-50	$\frac{40+50}{2} = 45$	20	$\frac{45-35}{10} = \frac{10}{10} = 1$	20
50-60	$\frac{50+60}{2} = 55$	17	$\frac{55-35}{10} = \frac{20}{10} = 2$	34
60-70	$\frac{60+70}{2} = 65$	16	$\frac{65-35}{10} = \frac{30}{10} = 3$	48
Total		$\Sigma f_i = 100$		$\Sigma f_i u_i = 66$

Here, $\Sigma f_i u_i = 66$, $\Sigma f_i = 100$, $A = 35$ and $h = 10$

$$\therefore \text{ Mean } (\overline{x}) = A + \left(\frac{\Sigma f_i u_i}{\Sigma f_i}\right) \times h$$

$$= 35 + \frac{66}{100} \times 10$$

$$= 35 + \frac{660}{100}$$

$$= 35 + 6.6 = 41.6$$

Example 12. The data on the number of patients attending a hospital in a month are given below. Find the average (mean) number of patients attending the hospital in a month by using step-deviation method. Take the assumed mean as 45. Give your answer correct to 2 decimal places. **[ICSE 2019]**

Number of patients	10-20	20-30	30-40	40-50	50-60	60-70
Number of days	5	2	7	9	2	5

Sol. Given, assumed mean, $A = 45$

and class width, $h = 20 - 10 = 10$

The table for the given data is

Class	x_i	f_i	$u_i = \frac{x_i - A}{h}$	$f_i u_i$
10-20	$\frac{10+20}{2} = 15$	5	$\frac{15-45}{10} = -3$	−15
20-30	$\frac{20+30}{2} = 25$	2	$\frac{25-45}{10} = -2$	−4
30-40	$\frac{30+40}{2} = 35$	7	$\frac{35-45}{10} = -1$	−7
40-50	$\frac{40+50}{2} = 45$	9	$\frac{45-45}{10} = 0$	0
50-60	$\frac{50+60}{2} = 55$	2	$\frac{55-45}{10} = 1$	2
60-70	$\frac{60+70}{2} = 65$	5	$\frac{65-45}{10} = 2$	10
Total		$\Sigma f_i = 30$		$\Sigma f_i u_i = -14$

Here, $\Sigma f_i u_i = -14$, $\Sigma f_i = 30$, $A = 45$ and $h = 10$

$$\therefore \text{ Mean } (\overline{x}) = A + \frac{\Sigma f_i u_i}{\Sigma f_i} \times h$$

$$= 45 + \frac{(-14)}{30} \times (10)$$

$$= 45 - \frac{14}{3} = \frac{135 - 14}{3} = \frac{121}{3} = 40.33$$

Example 13. Calculate the mean of the following distribution using step-deviation method.

Marks	0-10	10-20	20-30	30-40	40-50	50-60
Number of students	10	9	25	30	16	10

[ICSE 2017]

Sol. Let the assumed mean A be 25 and $h = 10$.

Class intervals	Mid values (x_i)	Frequency (f_i)	$d_i = x_i - 25$	$u_i = \frac{x_i - A}{h}$	$f_i u_i$
0-10	5	10	−20	−2	−20
10-20	15	9	−10	−1	−9
20-30	25 = A	25	0	0	0
30-40	35	30	10	1	30
40-50	45	16	20	2	32
50-60	55	10	30	3	30
Total		$N = \Sigma f_i = 100$			$\Sigma f_i u_i = 63$

Here, $A = 25$, $h = 10$, $\Sigma f_i = 100$ and $\Sigma f_i u_i = 63$

$$\therefore \text{ Mean} = A + \left\{\frac{\Sigma f_i u_i}{\Sigma f_i}\right\} \times h$$

$$= 25 + \frac{63}{100} \times 10$$

$$= 25 + \frac{63}{10}$$

$$= \frac{250 + 63}{10}$$

$$= 31.3$$

Selection of Method for Calculating the Mean

The value of mean obtained by all the three methods is the same. So, the choice of method to be used depends on the numerical values of x_i and f_i.

(i) If x_i and f_i are sufficiently small, then we use the direct method.

(ii) If x_i and f_i are numerically large numbers, then we can use assumed mean method or shortcut method.

(iii) If the class sizes are unequal and x_i are numerically large, we can still apply the step-deviation method by taking h to be a suitable divisor of all the d_i's.

Example 14. In a class test, marks obtained by 120 students are given in the following frequency distribution. If it is given that mean is 59, then find the missing frequencies x and y.

Marks	Number of students
0-10	1
10-20	3
20-30	7
30-40	10
40-50	15
50-60	x
60-70	9
70-80	27
80-90	18
90-100	y

Sol. Let the assumed mean, $A = 55$ and width of class interval, $h = 10$.

The table for the given data is

Marks	Class mark (x_i)	Number of students (f_i)	$u_i = \frac{x_i - A}{h}$	$f_i u_i$
0-10	5	1	−5	−5
10-20	15	3	−4	−12
20-30	25	7	−3	−21
30-40	35	10	−2	−20
40-50	45	15	−1	−15
50-60	55 = A	x	0	0
60-70	65	9	1	9
70-80	75	27	2	54
80-90	85	18	3	54
90-100	95	y	4	$4y$
Total		$N = \Sigma f_i = 90 + x + y$		$\Sigma f_i u_i = 44 + 4y$

Here, $N = 90 + x + y = 120$

$\Rightarrow \quad x + y = 30$ ...(i)

$\because \quad$ Mean = 59 [given]

$$\Rightarrow \quad A + \left(\frac{\Sigma f_i u_i}{N}\right) \times h = 59$$

$$\Rightarrow \quad 55 + \left(\frac{44 + 4y}{120}\right) \times 10 = 59$$

$$\Rightarrow \quad \frac{11 + y}{3} = 4 \Rightarrow 11 + y = 12 \Rightarrow y = 1$$

On putting the value of y in Eq. (i), we get

$$x + 1 = 30 \Rightarrow x = 29$$

Hence, $x = 29$ and $y = 1$.

Exercise 20.1

1. The mean of 9 variates is 11. If eight of them are 7, 12, 9, 14, 21, 3, 8 and 15, find the 9th variate.

2. The mean of the following data is 16. Find the value of f.

Marks	5	10	15	20	25
Number of students	3	7	f	9	6

3. Find the mean of the following distribution by direct method.

Class interval	0-10	10-20	20-30	30-40	40-50
Number of workers	7	10	15	8	10

4. Find the mean of the following data by direct method.

Class	25-35	35-45	45-55	55-65	65-75
Frequency	6	10	8	12	4

5. The table below shows the daily expenditure on food of 50 households in a locality

Daily expenditure (in ₹)	0-100	100-200	200-300	300-400	400-500
Number of workers	6	9	15	12	8

Find the mean daily expenditure on food by direct method.

6. If the mean of given data is 50, find the value of p.

Class interval	0-20	20-40	40-60	60-80	80-100
Frequency	17	28	32	p	19

7. Find the missing frequency for the given frequency distribution table, if the mean of the distribution is 18.

Class interval	11-13	13-15	15-17	17-19	19-21	21-23	23-25
Frequency	3	6	9	13	f	5	4

8. Calculate the mean of the following data.

Class	4-7	8-11	12-15	16-19
Frequency	5	4	9	10

9. Find the mean of the following frequency distribution by assumed mean method.

Class	25-30	30-35	35-40	40-45	45-50	50-55	55-60
Frequency	14	22	16	6	5	3	4

10. The data on number of patients attending a hospital in a month are given below

Number of patients	0-10	10-20	20-30	30-40	40-50	50-60	60-70
Number of days	4	4	7	20	12	8	5

Find the average number of patients attending the hospital by using assumed mean method.

11. Using assumed mean method, find the mean of the following frequency distribution.

Class	63-65	66-68	69-71	72-74	75-77
Frequency	4	3	7	8	3

12. Find the mean of the following distribution by step-deviation method. **[ICSE 2013]**

Class interval	20-30	30-40	40-50	50-60	60-70	70-80
Frequency	10	6	8	12	5	9

13. Find the mean of the following data by using step-deviation method.

Class	0-20	20-40	40-60	60-80	80-100
Frequency	17	28	32	24	19

14. The monthly pocket money of students of a class is given in the following frequency distribution

Pocket money (in ₹)	100-125	125-150	150-175	175-200	200-225
Number of students	14	8	12	5	11

Find the mean of pocket money using step-deviation method.

15. Calculate the mean of the scores of 20 students in a Mathematics test.

Marks	10-20	20-30	30-40	40-50	50-60
Number of students	2	4	7	6	1

16. If the mean of the distribution is 33.2 and the sum of all frequencies is 100, then find the missing frequencies f_1 and f_2.

Class	6-14	14-22	22-30	30-38	38-46	46-54	54-62	62-70
Frequency	11	21	f_1	15	14	8	f_2	6

Median of Grouped Data

Median

Median is defined as the middle-most or the central observation, when the observations are arranged either in ascending or descending order of their magnitudes.

Median divides the arranged series into two equal parts, i.e. 50% of the observations lie below the median and the remaining are above the median.

Let n be the total number of observations and let they are arranged in ascending or descending order.

Median of the data depends on the number of observations (n).

Case I If n is odd, then

$$\text{Median} = \text{Value of } \left(\frac{n+1}{2}\right)\text{th observation}$$

e.g. If five girls of different heights are made to stand in a row, in descending order of their heights, then the height of the third girl from either end is median height. Since, $n = 5$ is odd.

$\therefore$ Median $= \left(\frac{n+1}{2}\right)$th observation $= \frac{5+1}{2}$

$= \frac{6}{2} = 3$rd observation

Case II If n is even, then

$$\text{Median} = \text{Mean of the values of } \left(\frac{n}{2}\right)\text{th and } \left(\frac{n}{2}+1\right)\text{th observations}$$

$$= \frac{1}{2} \times \text{Value of } \left[\left(\frac{n}{2}\right)\text{th} + \left(\frac{n}{2}+1\right)\text{th}\right] \text{observations}$$

e.g. If six girls of different heights are made to stand in a row, in descending order of their heights, then the mean height of third and fourth girl from either end is the median height.

Since, $n = 6$ is even.

So, $\frac{n}{2} = \frac{6}{2} = 3$rd observation

and $\left(\frac{n}{2}+1\right) = \frac{6}{2}+1 = \frac{6+2}{2} = 4$th observation

$\therefore$ Median = Mean of 3rd and 4th observations

Example 15. Find the median of the first ten prime numbers.

Sol. First ten prime numbers in ascending order are 2, 3, 5, 7, 11, 13, 17, 19, 23 and 29.

Here, $n = 10$ (even)

$\therefore$ Median $= \frac{1}{2} \times$ Value of $\left[\left(\frac{n}{2}\right)\text{th} \quad \left(\frac{n}{2}+1\right)\text{th}\right]$ observation

$= \frac{1}{2} \times$ Value of $\left[\left(\frac{10}{2}\right)\text{th} + \left(\frac{10}{2}+1\right)\text{th}\right]$ observation

$= \frac{1}{2}$[Value of 5th observation + Value of 6th observation]

$= \frac{1}{2}(11+13) = \frac{24}{2} = 12$

Example 16. The mean of the following numbers is 68. Find the value of x.

45, 52, 60, x, 69, 70, 26, 81 and 94

Hence, estimate the median. **[ICSE 2016]**

Sol. Given, mean $(\bar{y}) = 68$

$\therefore \quad \bar{y} = \frac{\Sigma y}{n} = \frac{\text{Sum of the observations}}{\text{Number of observations}}$

$\Rightarrow \quad 68 = \frac{[45+52+60+x+69+70+26+81+94]}{9}$

$\Rightarrow \quad 68 = \frac{497+x}{9} \Rightarrow 497 + x = 612$

$\therefore \quad x = 612 - 497 = 115$

Now, for the median, we have to write the given data in ascending order 26, 45, 52, 60, 69, 70, 81, 94, 115

Here, $n = 9$ (odd)

$\therefore$ Median $= \left(\frac{n+1}{2}\right)$th term $= \left(\frac{10}{2}\right) = 5$th term $= 69$

Cumulative Frequency

The frequency of an observation in a data refers to how many times that observation occur in the data. Cumulative frequency of a class is defined as the sum of all frequencies up to the given class. The cumulative frequency is usually observed by constructing a cumulative frequency table.

Formation of cumulative frequency table can be understood with the help of an example which is given below

Example 17. The set of data given below shows the ages of participants in a certain summer camp. Draw a cumulative frequency table for the data.

Age (in years)	10	11	12	13	14	15
Frequency	3	18	13	12	7	27

Sol. The cumulative frequency of first observation is the same as its frequency, since there is no frequency before it.

Now, the cumulative frequency table is

Age (in years)	Frequency	Cumulative frequency (*cf*)
10	3	3
11	18	$3+18=21$
12	13	$21+13=34$
13	12	$34+12=46$
14	7	$46+7=53$
15	27	$53+27=80$

Cumulative Frequency Distribution

Cumulative frequency distribution is of two types

(i) Less than type (ii) More than type

Formation of these two distributions can be understood with the help of an example.

Example 18. Consider a grouped frequency distribution of marks obtained, out of 100, by 58 students, in a certain examination, as follows

Marks	Number of students
0-10	5
10-20	7
20-30	4
30-40	2
40-50	3
50-60	6
60-70	7
70-80	9
80-90	8
90-100	7

Form the cumulative frequency distribution of less than type and more than type.

Sol. **Cumulative frequency distribution of the less than type** Here, the number of students who have scored marks less than 10 are 5. The number of students who have scored marks less than 20 includes the number of students who have scored marks from 0-10 as well as the number of students who have scored marks from 10-20.

Thus, the total number of students with marks less than 20 is $5+7$, i.e. 12. So, the cumulative frequency of the class 10-20 is 12.

Similarly, on computing the cumulative frequencies of the other classes, i.e. the number of students with marks less than 30, less than 40, ..., less than 100, we get the distribution which is called the cumulative frequency distribution of the less than type.

Marks obtained	Number of students (Cumulative frequency)
Less than 10	5
Less than 20	$5+7=12$
Less than 30	$12+4=16$
Less than 40	$16+2=18$
Less than 50	$18+3=21$
Less than 60	$21+6=27$
Less than 70	$27+7=34$
Less than 80	$34+9=43$
Less than 90	$43+8=51$
Less than 100	$51+7=58$

Here, 10, 20, 30,..., 100 are the upper limits of the respective class intervals.

Cumulative frequency distribution of the more than type For this type of distribution, we make the table for the number of students with scores, more than or equal to 0, more than or equal to 10, more than or equal to 20 and so on. From the question, we observed that all 58 students have scored marks more than or equal to 0.

There are 5 students scoring marks in the interval 0-10, it shows that there are $58-5=53$ students getting more than or equal to 10 marks. In the same manner, the number of students scoring 20 marks or above $=53-7=46$ students, scoring 30 or above $=46-4=42$ students and so on.

Similarly, computing the cumulative frequencies of the other classes, i.e. the number of students with marks more than or equal to 40, more than or equal to 50,..., we get the distribution which is called the cumulative frequency distribution of the more than type.

Marks obtained	Number of students (Cumulative frequency)
More than or equal to 0	58
More than or equal to 10	$58-5=53$
More than or equal to 20	$53-7=46$
More than or equal to 30	$46-4=42$
More than or equal to 40	$42-2=40$
More than or equal to 50	$40-3=37$
More than or equal to 60	$37-6=31$
More than or equal to 70	$31-7=24$
More than or equal to 80	$24-9=15$
More than or equal to 90	$15-8=7$

Here, 0, 10, 20, 30,..., 90 are the lower limits of the respective class intervals.

Example 19. The following distribution gives the daily income of 50 workers of a factory

Daily income (in ₹)	100-120	120-140	140-160	160-180	180-200
Number of workers	12	14	8	6	10

Write the above distribution as 'less than type' cumulative frequency distribution.

Sol. We construct a cumulative frequency distribution of the less than type as follows

Daily income (in ₹)	Number of workers	Cumulative frequency (*cf*)
Less than 120	12	12
Less than 140	14	$12+14=26$
Less than 160	8	$26+8=34$
Less than 180	6	$34+6=40$
Less than 200	10	$40+10=50$

Example 20. The following distribution gives cumulative frequencies of 'more than type'

Marks obtained (More than or equal to)	5	10	15	20
Number of students (Cumulative frequency)	30	23	8	2

Change the above data into a continuous grouped frequency distribution.

Sol. Given distribution is the more than type distribution. Here, we observe that, all 30 students have obtained marks more than or equal to 5. Further, since 23 students have obtained score more than or equal to 10. So, $30-23=7$ students lie in the class 5-10. Similarly, we can find the other classes and their corresponding frequencies. Now, we construct the continuous grouped frequency distribution as

Class (Marks obtained)	Number of students
5-10	$30-23=7$
10-15	$23-8=15$
15-20	$8-2=6$
More than or equal to 20	2

Median for Discrete Data

A set of observations $x_1, x_2, x_3, \ldots, x_n$ with respective frequencies $f_1, f_2, f_3, \ldots, f_n$ is known as discrete data.

Method to find the Median of Discrete Data

Firstly, we arrange the data in the ascending or descending order of x_i, then we find the cumulative frequencies of all the observations. Let n be the total number of observations (sum of frequencies), then median of the data depends on the number of observations (n).

If n is odd, then

$$\text{Median} = \text{Value of } \left(\frac{n+1}{2}\right)\text{th observation}$$

If n is even, then

$$\text{Median} = \text{Mean of } \left(\frac{n}{2}\right)\text{th and } \left(\frac{n}{2}+1\right)\text{th observation}$$

$$= \frac{1}{2} \times \text{Value of} \left[\left(\frac{n}{2}\right)\text{th} + \left(\frac{n}{2}+1\right)\text{th}\right] \text{observation}$$

Here, for the value of observation, first look at the cumulative frequency just greater than (and nearest to) the position of required observations. Then, determine the corresponding value of the observation.

Example 21. Find the median of the following data.

Marks obtained	20	29	28	42	19	35	51
Number of students	3	4	5	7	9	2	3

Sol. Let us arrange the data in ascending order of x_i and make a cumulative frequency table.

Marks obtained (x_i)	Number of students (f_i)	Cumulative frequency (*cf*)
19	9	9
20	3	$9+3=12$
28	5	$12+5=17$
29	4	$17+4=21$
35	2	$21+2=23$
42	7	$23+7=30$
51	3	$30+3=33$

Here, $n = 33$ (odd)

$\therefore$ Median = Value of $\left(\frac{n+1}{2}\right)$th observation

= Value of $\left(\frac{33+1}{2}\right)$th observation

= Value of 17th observation

Since, the corresponding value of 17th observation of cumulative frequency in x_i is 28.

Hence, the median is 28.

Example 22. Obtain the median for the following frequency distribution.

x	1	2	3	4	5	6	7	8	9
y	8	10	11	16	20	25	15	9	6

Sol. Here, the given data is in ascending order of x_i.

The cumulative frequency table for the given data is

x_i	f_i	cf
1	8	8
2	10	18
3	11	29
4	16	45
5	20	65
6	25	90
7	15	105
8	9	114
9	6	120

Here, $n = 120$ (even)

$\therefore$ Median

$$= \frac{1}{2}\left[\text{Value of}\left\{\left(\frac{n}{2}\right)\text{th} + \left(\frac{n}{2}+1\right)\text{th}\right\}\text{observation}\right]$$

$$= \frac{1}{2}\left[\text{Value of}\left\{\left(\frac{120}{2}\right)\text{th} + \left(\frac{120}{2}+1\right)\text{th}\right\}\text{observation}\right]$$

$$= \frac{1}{2}[\text{Value of 60th observation + Value of 61th observation}]$$

Both 60th and 61th observations lie in the cumulative frequency 65 and its corresponding value of x is 5.

$$\therefore \text{Median} = \frac{1}{2}(5 + 5) = 5$$

Median for Grouped Data

In a grouped data, we may not find the middle observation by looking at the cumulative frequencies, since the middle observation will be some value in a class interval, so it is necessary to find the value inside a class that divides the whole distribution into two halves.

For this, we find the cumulative frequencies of all the classes and $n/2$, where n = number of observations. Now, locate the class whose cumulative frequency is greater than (and nearest to) $n/2$ and this class is called the **median class.** After finding the median class, use the following formula for calculating the median.

$$\text{Median} = l + \left\{\frac{(n/2) - cf}{f}\right\} \times h$$

where, l = lower limit of median class

n = number of observations

cf = cumulative frequency of the class preceding the median class

f = frequency of the median class

and h = class width (assuming class sizes to be equal).

Example 23. 200 surnames were randomly picked up from a local telephone directory and the frequency distribution of the number of letters in English alphabets in the surnames was obtained as follows

Number of letters	0-5	5-10	10-15	15-20	20-25
Number of surnames	20	60	80	32	8

Find the median of the above data.

Sol. The cumulative frequency table of given data is

Number of letters	Number of surnames (f_i)	Cumulative frequency (cf)
0-5	20	20
5-10	60	20 + 60 = 80 (cf)
10-15	80 = f	80 + 80 = 160
15-20	32	160 + 32 = 192
20-25	8	192 + 8 = 200
Total	$n = 200$	

Here, $n = 200 \Rightarrow \frac{n}{2} = \frac{200}{2} = 100$

Since, the cumulative frequency just greater than 100 is 160 and the corresponding class interval is 10-15.

$\therefore$ Median class = 10-15, $l = 10$, $cf = 80$, $h = 5$ and $f = 80$

Now, median $= l + \left\{\frac{\frac{n}{2} - cf}{f}\right\} \times h$

$$= 10 + \left\{\frac{100 - 80}{80}\right\} \times 5 = 10 + \left(\frac{20}{80}\right) \times 5$$

$$= 10 + 1.25 = 11.25$$

Example 24. A survey regarding the heights (in cm) of 51 boys of class X of a school was conducted and the following data was obtained

Heights (in cm)	Number of boys
Less than 140	4
Less than 145	11
Less than 150	29
Less than 155	40
Less than 160	46
Less than 165	51

Find the median height.

Sol. To calculate the median height, we need to convert the given data in the continuous grouped frequency distribution.

Given distribution is of less than type and 140, 145, 150,...,165 gives the upper limits of the corresponding class intervals. So, the classes should be below 140, 140-145, 145-150, ..., 160-165.

Clearly, the frequency of class interval below 140 is 4, since there are 4 boys with height less than 140. For the frequency of class interval 140-145 subtract the number of boys having height less than 140 from the number of boys having height less than 145.

Thus, the frequency of class interval 140-145 is 11 − 4 = 7. Similarly, we can calculate the frequencies of other class intervals and get the following table

Class interval	Frequency	Cumulative frequency (*cf*)
Below 140	4	4
140-145	11 − 4 = 7	11
145-150	29 − 11 = 18	29
150-155	40 − 29 = 11	40
155-160	46 − 40 = 6	46
160-165	51 − 46 = 5	51

Here, $n = 51 \Rightarrow \frac{n}{2} = \frac{51}{2} = 25.5$

Since, the cumulative frequency just greater than 25.5 is 29 and the corresponding class interval is 145-150.

$\therefore$ Median class = 145 − 150

Now, $l = 145$, $f = 18$, $cf = 11$ and $h = 5$

$$\therefore \quad \text{Median} = l + \left\{\frac{\frac{n}{2} - cf}{f}\right\} \times h$$

$$= 145 + \left\{\frac{25.5 - 11}{18}\right\} \times 5$$

$$= 145 + \frac{72.5}{18} = 145 + 4.03$$

$$= 149.03$$

Example 25. Find the missing frequencies in the following frequency distribution table, if $n = 100$ and median is 32.

Marks obtained	0-10	10-20	20-30	30-40	40-50	50-60	Total
Number of students	10	?	25	30	?	10	100

Sol. Given, median = 32 and $n = \Sigma f = 100$

Let f_1 and f_2 be the frequencies of the class interval 10-20 and 40-50, respectively.

Since, sum of frequencies = 100

$\therefore 10 + f_1 + 25 + 30 + f_2 + 10 = 100$

$\Rightarrow \quad f_1 + f_2 = 100 - 75$

$\Rightarrow \quad f_1 + f_2 = 25$

$\Rightarrow \quad f_2 = 25 - f_1 \quad$ ...(i)

Now, the cumulative frequency table for given distribution is

Class interval	Frequency (*f*)	Cumulative frequency (*cf*)
0-10	10	10
10-20	f_1	$10 + f_1$
20-30	25	$35 + f_1$ (*cf*)
30-40	$30 = f$	$65 + f_1$
40-50	f_2	$65 + f_1 + f_2$
50-60	10	$75 + f_1 + f_2$
Total	$n = f_1 + f_2 + 75$	

Here, $n = 100 \Rightarrow \frac{n}{2} = 50$

Given, median = 32, which belongs to the class 30-40.

So, the median class is 30 − 40.

Then, $l = 30$, $h = 10$, $f = 30$ and $cf = 35 + f_1$

$$\therefore \quad \text{Median} = l + \left\{\frac{\frac{n}{2} - cf}{f}\right\} \times h$$

$$\Rightarrow \quad 32 = 30 + \left\{\frac{50 - 35 - f_1}{30}\right\} \times 10$$

$$\Rightarrow \quad 32 - 30 = \frac{15 - f_1}{3} \Rightarrow 2 \times 3 = 15 - f_1$$

$$\Rightarrow \quad f_1 = 15 - 6 = 9$$

On putting the value of f_1 in Eq. (i), we get

$$f_2 = 25 - 9 = 16$$

Hence, the missing frequencies are $f_1 = 9$ and $f_2 = 16$.

Quartiles

Quartiles of a ranked set of data values are the three points that divide the data set into four equal groups, each group comprising a quarter of the data.

Lower (First) Quartile

The lower (first) quartile is the median of the lower half of the data set. It is denoted by Q_1.

$$\text{Lower quartile, } Q_1 = \begin{cases} \frac{n+1}{4} \text{ th observation, if } n \text{ is odd} \\ \frac{n}{4} \text{ th observation, if } n \text{ is even} \end{cases}$$

Upper (Third) Quartile

The upper (third) quartile is the median of the upper half of a data set. It is denoted by Q_3.

$$\text{Upper quartile, } Q_3 = \begin{cases} \frac{3(n+1)}{4} \text{ th observation, if } n \text{ is odd} \\ \frac{3n}{4} \text{ th observation, if } n \text{ is even} \end{cases}$$

Inter Quartile Range

The difference between the upper quartile (Q_3) and the lower quartile (Q_1) is called the inter quartile range.

Thus, the inter quartile range = $Q_3 - Q_1$

and the semi-inter quartile range = $\frac{Q_3 - Q_1}{2}$.

Note (i) The middle quartile (Q_2) is called the median.

(ii) The semi-inter quartile range is also known as quartile deviation.

Example 26. From the following data, compute the lower, middle, upper and Inter quartile range.

Age (in years)	20	30	40	50	60	70	80
Number of members	3	61	132	153	140	51	3

Sol. The cumulative frequency table is as given below

Age (in years)	Number of members	Cumulative frequency (*cf*)
20	3	3
30	61	64
40	132	196
50	153	349
60	140	489
70	51	540
80	3	543
	$n = 543$	

Lower Quartile

We have, $\frac{n+1}{4} = \frac{543+1}{4} = \frac{544}{4} = 136$

The cumulative frequency just greater than $\frac{n+1}{4}$ is 196 and the corresponding value of the variable is 40.

$\therefore$ Q_1 = Lower Quartile = 40 yr

Middle Quartile (Median)

We have, $\frac{n+1}{2} = \frac{543+1}{2} = \frac{544}{2} = 272$

Cumulative frequency just greater than $\frac{n+1}{2}$ is 349 and the corresponding value of the variable is 50.

$\therefore$ Q_2 = Middle Quartile = 50 yr

Upper Quartile

We have, $\frac{3(n+1)}{4} = \frac{3 \times (543+1)}{4} = \frac{3 \times 544}{4} = 408$

Cumulative frequency just greater than $\frac{3(n+1)}{4}$ is 489 and the corresponding value of the variable is 60.

$\therefore$ Q_3 = Upper Quartile = 60 yr

Inter quartile range = $Q_3 - Q_1 = 60 - 40 = 20$ yr.

Exercise 20.2

1. The median of the observations 11, 12, 14, $(x-2), (x+4), (x+9)$, 32, 38 and 47 arranged in ascending order is 24. Find the value of x and hence find the mean. [ICSE 2013]

2. Write the frequency distribution table for the following data.

Marks	Below 10	Below 20	Below 30	Below 40	Below 50	Below 60
Number of students	0	15	20	30	35	40

3. Given below is a cumulative frequency distribution of 'more than type'

Marks	Number of students
More than or equal to 60	11
More than or equal to 50	23
More than or equal to 40	43
More than or equal to 30	58
More than or equal to 20	72
More than or equal to 10	82

Change the above data into a continuous grouped frequency distribution.

4. The number of students absent in a school was recorded everyday for 147 days and the raw data was presented in the form of the following frequency table

Number of students	Number of days
5	1
6	5
7	11
8	14
9	16
10	13
11	10
12	70
13	4
15	1
18	1
20	1

Find the median of the above data.

5. Find the median of the following frequency distribution.

x	1	2	3	4	5	6	7	8	9	10
y	2	3	6	8	16	12	10	13	9	15

6. Calculate the median from the following distribution.

Class	5-10	10-15	15-20	20-25	25-30	30-35	35-40	40-45
Frequency	5	6	15	16	5	4	2	2

7. The maximum bowling speed (in km/h) of 33 players at a cricket coaching centre are given below

Speed (in km/h)	85-100	100-115	115-130	130-145
Number of players	11	9	8	5

Calculate the median bowling speed.

8. Find the median for the following data.

Height (in cm) [Less than]	120	140	160	180	200
Number of students	12	26	34	40	50

9. The weights (in kg) of 45 students of a class are given in the following distribution table. Determine the value of weight x which is such that the number of students having weight less than x kg is same as the number of students having weight more than x kg.

Weight (in kg)	Cumulative frequency
Below 45	5
Below 50	11
Below 55	15
Below 60	22
Below 65	38
Below 70	45

10. Compute the median marks for the following data.

Marks	Number of students
0 and above	50
10 and above	46
20 and above	40
30 and above	20
40 and above	10
50 and above	3
60 and above	0

11. If the median of the following frequency distribution is 24, then find the missing frequency x.

Age (in years)	0-10	10-20	20-30	30-40	40-50
Number of persons	5	25	x	18	7

12. If the median of the following frequency distribution is 35, then find the value of x.

Class interval	0-10	10-20	20-30	30-40	40-50	50-60	60-70
Frequency	2	3	x	6	5	3	2

13. If the median of the following distribution is 58 and the sum of all the frequencies is 140. Find the values of x and y.

Variable	15-25	25-35	35-45	45-55	55-65	65-75	75-85	85-95
Frequency	8	10	x	25	40	y	15	7

14. If the median of the number of patients attending a hospital is 36, then find the missing frequencies f_1 and f_2 in the following frequency distribution, when it is given that total number of days is 100.

Number of patients	0-10	10-20	20-30	30-40	40-50	50-60	60-70
Number of days	5	12	f_1	f_2	15	11	14

15. During Medical check up of 200 students of school, their weights were recorded as follows

Weight (in kg)	30-39	40-49	50-59	60-69	70-79	80-89
Number of students	5	22	63	74	30	6

Find the median weight of students.

16. The daily wages (in rupees) of 19 workers are 41, 21, 38, 27, 31, 45, 23, 26, 29, 30, 28, 25, 35, 42, 47, 53, 29, 31, 35. Find
(i) the median
(ii) lower quartile
(iii) upper quartile
(iv) inter quartile range

17. From the following frequency distribution, find
(i) the median
(ii) lower quartile
(iii) upper quartile
(iv) inter quartile range

Variate	15	18	20	22	25	27	30
Frequency	4	6	8	9	7	8	6

Mode of Grouped Data

Mode

The observation, which occurs most frequently among the given observations, i.e. the value of the observation having maximum frequency is called mode. e.g. Mode of the numbers 2, 3, 4, 4, 6, 6, 6, 6, 7 and 9 is 6 because it is repeated maximum number of times, i.e. 4 times.

Sometimes, it is possible that more than one value may have the same maximum frequency. In this situation, the data is said to be **multimodal**. Grouped data can also be multimodal but here we will discuss the problems having single mode only. In case of ungrouped data, the mode is the observation with maximum frequency.

Example 27. In a class of 72 students, marks obtained by the students in a class test (out of 10) are given below

Marks obtained (Out of 10)	1	2	3	4	6	7	9	10
Number of students	3	5	12	18	23	8	2	1

Find the mode of the data.

Sol. The mode of the given data is 6 as it has the maximum frequency, i.e. 23.

Modal Class

In a grouped frequency distribution, it is not possible to determine the mode by looking at the frequencies. So, here we first locate a class with the maximum frequency. This class is called modal class. e.g.

Class interval	0-10	10-20	20-30	30-40	40-50	50-60
Number of students	2	9	14	20	22	8

Here, the highest frequency is of the class 40-50, which is 22. Hence, the modal class is 40-50.

Mode of Grouped Data

In grouped data, mode is a value lies in the modal class and it is given by the formula,

$$\text{Mode} = l + \left\{\frac{f_1 - f_0}{2f_1 - f_0 - f_2}\right\} \times h$$

where, l = lower limit of the modal class

h = size of the class intervals (assuming all class sizes to be equal)

f_1 = frequency of the modal class

f_0 = frequency of the class preceding the modal class

f_2 = frequency of the class succeeding the modal class

(i) Mode can also be calculated for a grouped data with unequal class sizes.

(ii) Mode can be less, equal or more than the mean of the data.

(iii) It depends upon the situation whether we have to calculate mean or mode. Since, mean is used to find the average value of data and mode is used to find the value having maximum frequency. e.g. If we are interested in finding the average marks obtained by the students, then mean is required and if we are interested in finding the average of the marks obtained by most of the students then mode is required.

Example 28. An NGO working for welfare of cancer patients, maintained its records as follows

Age of patients (in years)	0-20	20-40	40-60	60-80
Number of patients	35	315	120	50

Find the mode.

Sol. Here, the maximum frequency is 315 and the class corresponding to this frequency is 20-40. So, the modal class is 20-40.

Age of patients (in years)	0-20	20-40	40-60	60-80
Number of patients	$35 = f_0$	$315 = f_1$	$120 = f_2$	50

$\therefore\ l = 20, f_1 = 315, f_0 = 35, f_2 = 120$ and $h = 20$

$$\text{Now, mode} = l + \left(\frac{f_1 - f_0}{2f_1 - f_0 - f_2}\right) \times h$$

$$= 20 + \frac{315 - 35}{2 \times 315 - 35 - 120} \times 20$$

$$= 20 + \frac{280}{475} \times 20 = 20 + 11.79 = 31.79$$

Hence, the average age of maximum number of patients is 31.79.

Example 29. If the mode of the following series is 54, then find the value of f.

Class interval	0-15	15-30	30-45	45-60	60-75	75-90
Frequency	3	5	f	16	12	7

Sol. Here, the given mode is 54, which lies between 45-60. Therefore, the modal class is 45-60.

$\therefore\ l = 45, f_1 = 16, f_0 = f, f_2 = 12$ and $h = 15$

$$\because \quad \text{Mode} = l + \left(\frac{f_1 - f_0}{2f_1 - f_0 - f_2}\right) \times h$$

$$\therefore \quad 54 = 45 + \left(\frac{16 - f}{32 - f - 12}\right) \times 15$$

$$\Rightarrow \quad 9 = \frac{16 - f}{20 - f} \times 15$$

$$\Rightarrow \quad 9(20 - f) = 15(16 - f) \Rightarrow 180 - 9f = 240 - 15f$$

$$\Rightarrow \quad 6f = 240 - 180 = 60 \Rightarrow f = 10$$

Hence, the required value of f is 10.

Relationship between Mean, Median and Mode

There is an empirical relationship between the three measures of central tendency, which is given by

$$\text{Mode} = 3(\text{Median}) - 2(\text{Mean})$$

or $\text{Mean} = \dfrac{3\,(\text{Median}) - \text{Mode}}{2}$ or $\text{Median} = \dfrac{\text{Mode} + 2\,(\text{Mean})}{3}$

(i) The mean is the most frequently used measure of central tendency, because it takes into account all the observations and lies between the extremes. Extreme values in the data affect the mean.

(ii) In problems, where individual observations are not important and we wish to find out a typical observation, the median is more appropriate. e.g. finding average wage in a country etc.

(iii) In situations, which require establishing the most frequent value or most popular item, the mode is the best choice. e.g. finding the most popular TV programme being watched, etc.

Example 30. If median = 137 units and mean = 137.05 units, then find the mode.

Sol. Given, median = 137 units and mean = 137.05 units

We know that,

$$\begin{aligned}\text{Mode} &= 3\,(\text{Median}) - 2(\text{Mean})\\ &= 3(137) - 2(137.05)\\ &= 411 - 274.10\\ &= 136.90\end{aligned}$$

Hence, the value of mode is 136.90 units.

Exercise 20.3

1. Find the mode of the given data.

Marks	0-20	20-40	40-60	60-80
Frequency	15	6	18	10

2. For the following data, find the mode.

Class	1-3	3-5	5-7	7-9	9-11
Frequency	14	16	4	4	2

3. The following table shows the age distribution of cases of a certain disease admitted during a year in a particular hospital

Age (in years)	Number of cases
0-10	5
10-20	8
20-30	7
30-40	12
40-50	28
50-60	20
60-70	10
70-80	10

Find the average age for which maximum case occurred.

4. The weight of coffee in 70 packets are shown in the following table

Weight (in grams)	Number of packets
200-201	12
201-202	26
202-203	20
203-204	9
204-205	2
205-206	1

Determine the modal weight.

5. The mode of the following data is 36. Find the missing frequency x in it.

Class	0-10	10-20	20-30	30-40	40-50	50-60	60-70
Frequency	8	10	x	16	12	6	7

6. The monthly consumption of electricity of some consumers is given below as a distribution

Monthly consumption (in units)	Number of consumers
90-120	20
120-150	15
150-180	x
180-210	75
210-240	50

Find the missing frequency (x), if mode of distribution is given to be 200 units.

7. Some surnames were picked up from a local telephone directory and the frequency distribution of the number of letters of the English alphabets was obtained as follows

Number of letters	1-4	4-7	7-10	10-13	13-16	16-19
Number of surnames	10	25	35	x	12	8

If it is given that mode of the distribution is 8, then find the missing frequency (x).

8. Find the mode of the following data.

Class interval	0-9	10-19	20-29	30-39	40-49	50-59
Frequency	12	15	21	17	19	6

9. Given below is the frequency distribution of the heights of players in a school

Height (in cm)	Number of students
160-163	18
164-167	116
168-171	142
172-175	129
176-179	80
180-183	15

10. On sports day of a school, agewise participation of students is shown in the following distribution

Age (in years)	5-7	7-9	9-11	11-13	13-15	15-17	17-19
Number of students	x	15	18	30	50	48	x

Find the mode of the data. Also, find missing frequencies when sum of frequencies is 181.

11. In a certain distribution, mean and median are 9.5 and 10, respectively. Find the mode of the distribution, using an empirical relation?

12. Mode and mean of a data are $12k$ and $15k$, respectively. Find the median of the data.

Graphical Representation

Histogram

A histogram is the graphical representation of a grouped frequency distribution in exclusive form with continuous classes in the form of rectangles with class intervals as bases and the corresponding frequencies as heights. There is no gap between any two consecutive rectangles.

Example 31. Represent the following frequency distribution by means of a histogram.

Marks	10-20	20-30	30-40	40-50	50-60	60-70	70-80
Number of students	7	11	9	13	16	4	2

Sol. We represent the class intervals along the X-axis on a suitable scale and the corresponding frequencies along the Y-axis on a suitable scale. We construct rectangles with class intervals as bases and the corresponding frequencies as heights. Thus, we obtain a histogram as shown below

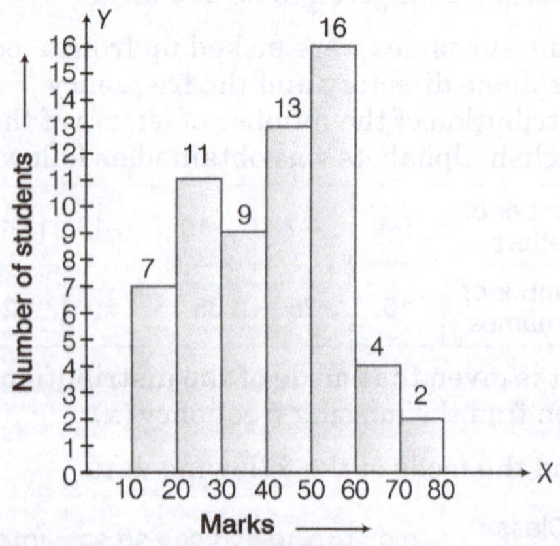

Example 32. The histogram adjacent represents the scores obtained by 25 students in a Mathematics mental test. Use the data to

(i) frame a frequency distribution table.

(ii) calculate mean.

(iii) determine the modal class. **[ICSE 2016]**

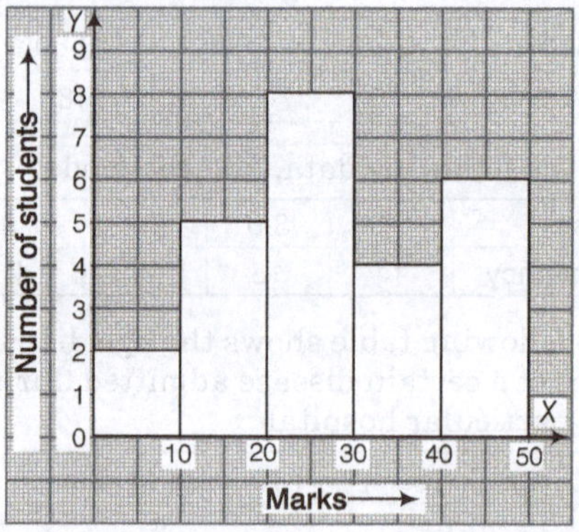

Sol. (i) From the given histogram, it is clear that the frequency of each class would be height of rectangle corresponding to each class. Therefore, the frequency distribution table is as follows

Scores	Number of students
0-10	2
10-20	5
20-30	8
30-40	4
40-50	6
Total	25

(ii) To calculate mean, we have following table

Class	f_i	Class mark (x_i)	$f_i x_i$
0-10	2	5	10
10-20	5	15	75
20-30	8	25	200
30-40	4	35	140
40-50	6	45	270
Total	$\Sigma f_i = 25$		$\Sigma f_i x_i = 695$

$$\therefore \text{ Mean } (\bar{x}) = \frac{\Sigma f_i x_i}{\Sigma f_i} = \frac{695}{25} = 27.8$$

(iii) We know that in a frequency distribution, the class which have maximum frequency is called modal class.

$\therefore$ Modal class is 20-30.

[$\because$ class 20-30 has frequency 8, which is maximum amongst all given frequencies]

Calculation of Mode from Histogram

In a continuous frequency distribution, the mode can be determined from the histogram of the given (continuous) frequency distribution.

Method to Determine the Mode

Following steps are used to determine the mode

Step I Draw histogram for the given data.

Step II Inside the highest rectangle (which represents the class with maximum frequency, i.e. modal class), draw two straight lines from the corners of the rectangles on both sides of the highest rectangle to the opposite corners of the highest rectangle.

Step III Through the point of intersection of the two straight lines drawn in Step II, draw a vertical line to meet the X-axis at the point M (say). The variate at the point M is the required mode.

Note If in a problem, frequency distribution is discontinuous, first convert it into continuous distribution and then find the mode as explained above.

Example 33. Use a graph paper for this question, the daily pocket expenses of 200 students in a school are given below.

Pocket expenses (in ₹)	0-5	5-10	10-15	15-20	20-25	25-30	30-35	35-40
Number of students (Frequency)	10	14	28	42	50	30	14	12

Draw a histogram representing the above distribution and estimate the mode from the graph. **[ICSE 2014]**

Sol. In the highest rectangle, draw two straight lines AC and BD which intersect at P. Through point P, draw a vertical line to meet the X-axis at N. The abscissa of the point represents 21. Hence, the required mode is 21.

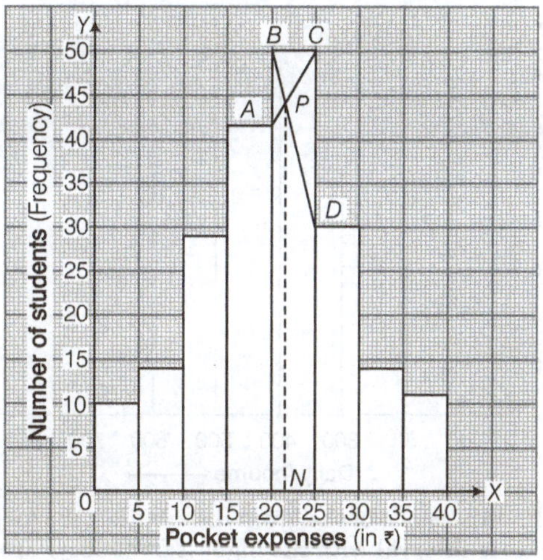

Example 34. The following distribution gives the daily wages of 60 workers of a factory.

Daily income (in ₹)	Number of workers (f)
200-300	6
300-400	10
400-500	14
500-600	16
600-700	10
700-800	4

Use graph paper to answer this question.

Take 2 cm = ₹ 100 along one axis and 2 cm = 2 workers along the other axis.

Draw a histogram and hence find the mode of the given distribution. **[ICSE 2023]**

Sol.

Class of daily income	Lower income	Upper daily income	Number of workers/ frequency
200-300	200	300	6
300-400	300	400	10
400-500	400	500	14
500-600	500	600	16
600-700	600	700	10
700-800	700	800	4

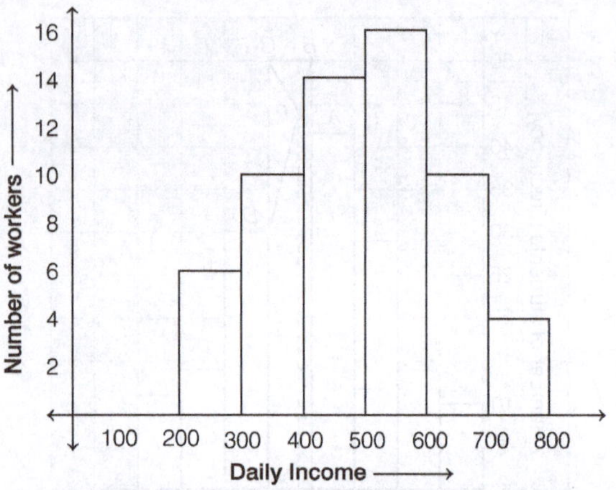

To find the mode of the given distribution, we look for the class interval with the highest frequency. From the histogram, we can see that the class interval 500-600 has the highest frequency of 16. Therefore, the mode of the given distribution of ₹500 – ₹600.

$$\text{Mode} = L + \left(\frac{f_1 - f_0}{2f_1 - f_0 - f_2}\right) \times h$$

Here, $L = 500$, $f_1 = 16$, $f_0 = 14$ and $f_2 = 10$

$$\text{Mode} = 500 + \left(\frac{16 - 14}{2 \times 16 - 14 - 10}\right) \times 100$$

$$\text{Mode} = 525$$

An Ogive Curve

The term 'ogive' is pronounced as 'ojeev' and is derived from the word ogee. An ogive is a shape consisting of a concave arc flowing into a convex arcs. So, forming an *S*-shaped curve with vertical ends.

Graphical representation of cumulative frequency distribution is of two types, less than type ogive and more than type ogive. The process of graphical representation of less than type cumulative frequency distribution are given below.

Less Than Type Ogive

It is the graph drawn between the upper limits and cumulative frequencies of a distribution. Here, we mark the points with upper limit as *x*-coordinate and corresponding cumulative frequency as *y*-coordinate and join them by a free hand smooth curve. This type of graph is cumulated upward.

Example 35. The following table gives the height of trees

Height (Less than)	7	14	21	28	35	42	49	56
Number of trees	26	57	92	134	216	287	341	360

Draw 'less than ogive'.

Sol. Given distribution is cumulative frequency distribution of less than type.

Now, we mark the upper limits along *X*-axis and cumulative frequencies along *Y*-axis, on the graph paper. Then, plot the points (7, 26), (14, 57), (21, 92), (28, 134), (35, 216), (42, 287), (49, 341) and (56, 360). Join all these points by a freehand smooth curve to obtain an ogive of less than type.

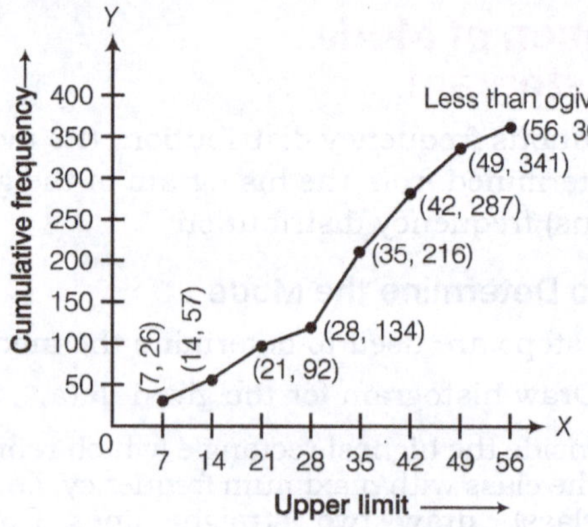

Median and Quartiles from Ogives

In a continuous frequency distribution, the median and the quartiles (lower and upper) can be estimated from the ogive of the given (continuous) frequency distribution.

Method to Determine the Median and Quartiles

Step I Construct cumulative frequency table. Let n be the sum of frequencies.

Step II Draw ogive for the given distribution.

Step III

(a) **To find the median** (M_e) Locate a point along *Y*-axis representing frequency equal to $n/2$. Through this point, draw a horizontal line to meet the ogive and through this point of the ogive, draw a vertical line to meet the *X*-axis at the point *M* (say). The variate at the point *M* is the required median. The class in which the median lies is called the **median class**.

(b) **To find the lower quartile** (Q_1) Locate a point along *Y*-axis representing frequency equal to $n/4$. Through this point, draw a horizontal line to meet the ogive and through this point of the ogive, draw a vertical line to meet the *X*-axis at the point *N*(say). The variate at the point *N* is the required lower quartile.

(c) **To find the upper quartile** (Q_3) Locate a point along *Y*-axis representing frequency equal to $\frac{3n}{4}$.

Now, proceed as in Step III (b) to find the required upper quartile.

Example 36. The weight of 50 workers is given below.

Weight (in kg)	50-60	60-70	70-80	80-90	90-100	100-110	110-120
Number of workers	4	7	11	14	6	5	3

Draw an ogive of the given distribution using a graph sheet. Take 2 cm = 10 kg on one axis and 2 cm = 5 workers along the other axis. Use a graph to estimate the following.

(i) The upper and lower quartiles.

(ii) If weighing 95 kg and above is considered overweight, then find the number of workers who are overweight. **[ICSE 2015]**

Sol. The cumulative frequency table for the continuous distribution is shown below

Weight (in kg)	50-60	60-70	70-80	80-90	90-100	100-110	110-120
Frequency (*f*)	4	7	11	14	6	5	3
Cumulative frequency (*cf*)	4	11	22	36	42	47	50

On the graph paper, we plot the following points $A(60, 4)$, $B(70, 11)$, $C(80, 22)$, $D(90, 36)$, $E(100, 42)$, $F(110, 47)$ and $G(120, 50)$, join all these points by a free hand drawing.

The required ogive is shown on the graph paper given below

Take width of two large square boxes = 10 kg on X-axis and take width of two large square boxes = 5 workers on Y-axis.

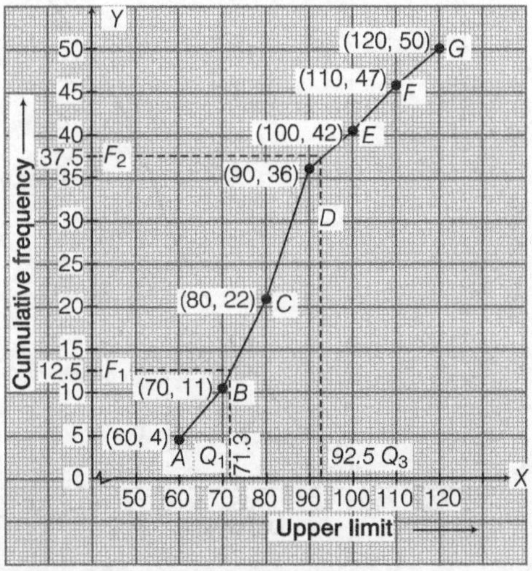

(i) **Lower quartile** $n = 50$, so $\frac{n}{4} = \frac{50}{4} = 12.5$

Taking point F_1 on Y-axis representing frequency = 12.5 and corresponding value of X-axis is 71.3.

$\therefore$ $Q_1 = 71.3$

Upper quartile $n = 50$, so $\frac{3n}{4} = \frac{3 \times 50}{4} = \frac{150}{4} = 37.5$

Taking point F_2 on Y-axis representing frequency = 37.5 and corresponding value of X-axis is 92.5.

$\therefore$ $Q_3 = 92.5$

(ii) On the ogive, the point $(95, y)$ corresponds to $y = 40$. So, cf is 40. Therefore, the number of variates above 95 kg is $50 - 40 = 10$.

Example 37. The marks obtained by 100 students in a Mathematics test are given below

Marks	Number of students
0-10	3
10-20	7
20-30	12
30-40	17
40-50	23
50-60	14
60-70	9
70-80	6
80-90	5
90-100	4

Draw an ogive for the given distribution on a graph sheet. (use a scale of 2 cm = 10 units on both axes). Use the ogive to estimate the

(i) median. (ii) lower quartile.

(iii) number of students who obtained more than 85% marks in the test.

(iv) number of students who did not pass in the test, if the pass percentage was 35. **[ICSE 2014]**

Sol. The cumulative frequency table for the given continuous distribution is given below

Marks	Number of students	Cumulative frequency (*cf*)
0-10	3	3
10-20	7	10
20-30	12	22
30-40	17	39
40-50	23	62
50-60	14	76
60-70	9	85
70-80	6	91
80-90	5	96
90-100	4	100

On the graph paper, we plot the following points A (10, 3), B (20, 10), C (30 , 22), D (40, 39), E (50, 62), F (60, 76), G (70, 85), H (80, 91), I (90, 96) and V(100, 100). Join all these points by a free hand drawing. The required ogive is shown on the graph paper given below

Here, number of students $(n) = 100$, which is even.

(i) Let P be the point on Y-axis representing frequency $= \frac{n}{2} = \frac{100}{2} = 50$.

Through P, draw a horizontal line to meet the ogive at point Q. Through Q, draw a vertical line to meet the X-axis at T. The abscissa of the point T represents 43 marks. Hence, the median marks is 43.

(ii) Let R be the point on Y-axis representing frequency $= \frac{n}{4} = \frac{100}{4} = 25$

Through R, draw a horizontal line to meet the ogive at point S. Through S, draw a vertical line to meet the X-axis at N. The abscissa of the point N represents 31 marks. Hence, the lower quartile = 31 marks.

Take width of two large boxes = 10 units on both axis.

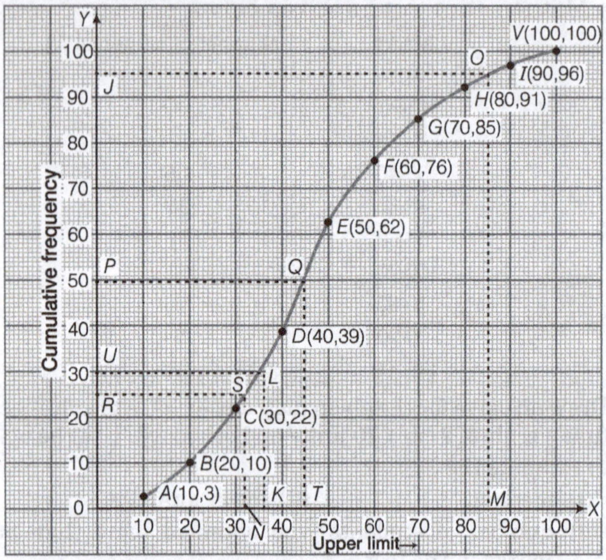

(iii) 85% marks = 85% of 100 = 85 marks.

Let the point M on X-axis represents 85 marks.

Through M, draw a vertical line to meet the ogive at the point O. Through O draw a horizontal line to meet the Y-axis at point J. The ordinate of point J represents 95 students.

∴ Number of students who obtained more than 85% in the test = 100 − 95 = 5

(iv) 35% marks = 35% of 100 = 35

Let the point K on X-axis represents 35 marks.

Through K, draw a vertical line to meet the ogive at the point L. Through L, draw a horizontal line to meet the Y-axis at point U. The ordinate of point U represents 30 students on Y-axis. Hence, the number of students, who did not pass in the test is 30.

Note If the student solve all the results directly, then they do not get full marks.

Example 38. The daily wages of 80 workers in a project are given below.

Wages (in ₹)	400-450	450-500	500-550	550-600	600-650	650-700	700-750
Number of workers	2	6	12	18	24	13	5

Use a graph paper to draw an ogive for the above distribution. (Use a scale of 2 cm = ₹ 50 on X-axis and 2 cm = 10 workers on Y-axis). Use your ogive to estimate

(i) the median wage of the workers.

(ii) the lower quartile wage of workers.

(iii) the number of workers who earn more than ₹ 625 daily. [ICSE 2017]

Sol. Let us first prepare the following cumulative frequency table

Wages (in ₹)	Number of workers	Cumulative frequency
400-450	2	2
450-500	6	8
500-550	12	20
550-600	18	38
600-650	24	62
650-700	13	75
700-750	5	80

In order to draw an ogive for the given distribution, we assume a class 350-400 before the first class interval with zero frequency.

Now, we mark the upper class limits (including the imagined class) along X-axis and the cumulative frequency along Y-axis on the following scale.

2 cm = ₹ 50 on X-axis, 2 cm = 10 workers on Y-axis

On the scale, we plot the points (400, 0), (450, 2), (500, 8), (550, 20), (600, 38), (650, 62), (700, 75) and (750, 80) with the help of following graph.

Join all these points by a free hand drawing the required ogive is shown on the graph.

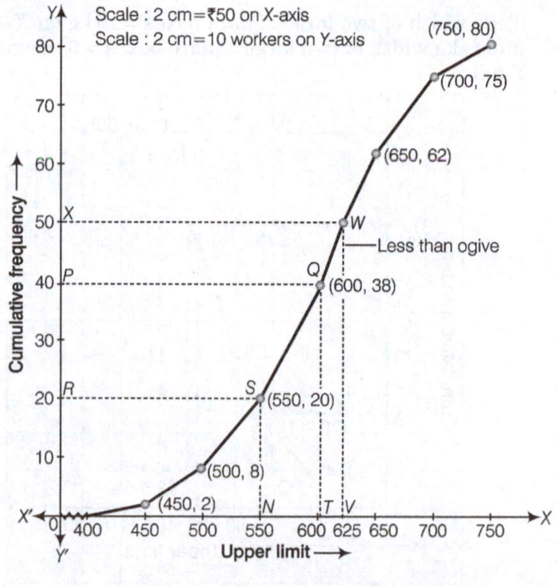

(i) Let P be the point on Y-axis representing frequency

$$= \frac{n}{2} = \frac{80}{2} = 40$$

Through point P, draw a horizontal line to meet the ogive at point Q. Through Q draw a vertical line to meet the X-axis at T. The abscissa of the point T represents ₹ 605 wages.

Hence, the median marks is ₹ 605.

(ii) Let R be the point on Y-axis representing frequency

$= \frac{n}{4} = \frac{80}{4} = 20$

Through R, draw a horizontal line to meet the ogive at S. Through S, draw a vertical line to meet the X-axis at N. The abscissa of the point N represents ₹ 550 wages. Hence, the lower quartile = ₹ 550

(iii) The number of workers who earn more than ₹ 625 are $80 - 50 = 30$ (according to graph).

Example 39. Use graph paper for this question. The marks obtained by 120 students in an English test are given below **[ICSE 2019]**

Marks	Number of students
0-10	5
10-20	9
20-30	16
30-40	22
40-50	26
50-60	18
60-70	11
70-80	6
80-90	4
90-100	3

Draw the ogive and hence, estimate

(i) the median marks.

(ii) the upper quartile marks.

(iii) the number of students who did not pass the test, if the pass percentage was 50.

Sol. The cumulative frequency table for the given continuous distribution is given below

Marks	Number	Cumulative frequency (*cf*)
0-10	5	5
10-20	9	14
20-30	16	30
30-40	22	52
40-50	26	78
50-60	18	96
60-70	11	107
70-80	6	113
80-90	4	117
90-100	3	120
Total	120	

On the graph paper, we plot the following points $A(10, 5)$, $B(20, 14)$, $C(30, 30)$, $D(40, 52)$, $E(50, 78)$, $F(60, 96)$, $G(70, 107)$, $H(80, 113)$, $I(90, 117)$, $J(100, 120)$. Join all these points by a free hand drawing.

The required ogive is shown on the graph paper, which is given below

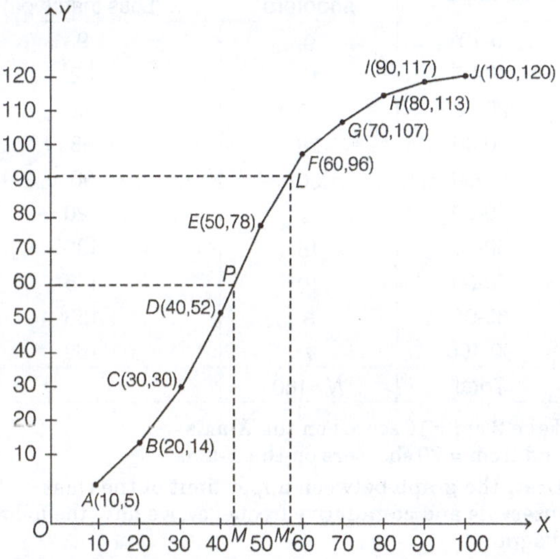

(i) Here, $n = 120$

Now, $\frac{n}{2} = \frac{120}{2} = 60$

Taking point 60 on Y-axis, draw a horizontal line parallel to X-axis, which intersect the curve at point P. Now, draw a line parallel to Y-axis from point P, which meets the X-axis at M.

∴ The distance of point M from O is 43, which is the required median marks.

(ii) Here, $n = 120$

For upper quartile, $\frac{3n}{4} = \frac{3 \times 120}{4} = 90$

Taking point 90 on Y-axis, draw a horizontal line parallel to X-axis, which meets the curve at point L. Further draw a line at point L parallel to Y-axis, which meets the X-axis at point M'. Hence, the distance from origin to the point M' is 57, which is the required upper quartile marks.

(iii) The number of students, who did not pass the test is 78.

Example 40. The table shows the distribution of the scores obtained by 160 shooters in a shooting competition. Use a graph sheet and draw an ogive for the distribution. [Take 2 cm = 10 scores on the X-axis and 2 cm = 20 shooters on the Y-axis].

Scores	0-10	10-20	20-30	30-40	40-50	50-60	60-70	70-80	80-90	90-100
Number of shooters	9	13	20	26	30	22	15	10	8	7

Use your graph to estimate the following.

(i) The median

(ii) The inter quartile range

(iii) The number of shooters who obtained a score of more than 85%. **[ICSE 2016]**

Sol. The table is as follows

Scores	Number of shooters	Cumulative frequency (Less than type)
0-10	9	9
10-20	13	22
20-30	20	42
30-40	26	68
40-50	30	98
50-60	22	120
60-70	15	135
70-80	10	145
80-90	8	153
90-100	7	160
Total	$N = 160$	

Take 2 cm = 10 scores on the X-axis and 2 cm = 20 shooters on the Y-axis.

Draw the graph between upper limit of the class intervals and cumulative frequency, we have the following diagram

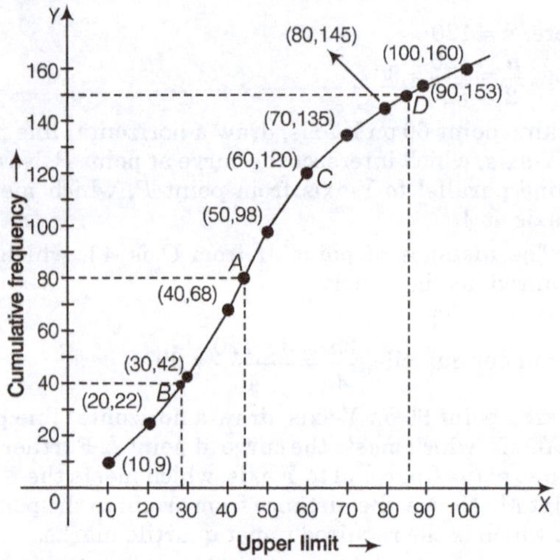

$\therefore \quad \frac{n}{2} = \frac{160}{2} = 80$

(i) Draw a line $y = 80$, parallel to X-axis which cuts the graph at point A. Draw perpendicular from point A on the X-axis. This line, where cuts the X-axis, will be median.

$\therefore$ From the graph, we see that the perpendicular line meets X-axis at $x = 44$.

$\therefore$ Median = 44

(ii) Now, to find first quartile $\frac{n}{4} = \frac{160}{4} = 40$

Draw a line $y = 40$, parallel to X-axis which cuts the ogive at point B. Draw a perpendicular line from point B on the X-axis which cuts the X-axis at $x = 29$.

$\therefore$ First quartile (Q_1) = 29

To find third quartile $\frac{3n}{4} = \frac{160 \times 3}{4} = 120$

Draw a line $y = 120$, parallel to X-axis, which cuts the ogive at point C. Now, draw a perpendicular line from point C on the X-axis which cuts the X-axis at $x = 60$.

$\therefore$ Third quartile (Q_3) = 60

$\therefore$ Inter quartile range = $Q_3 - Q_1 = 60 - 29 = 31$

(iii) Draw a line $x = 85$, parallel to Y-axis, which cuts the ogive at point D. Now, draw a line from point O, parallel to X-axis which cuts Y-axis at $y = 148$.

$\therefore$ Number of shooters above 85% = 160 − 148 = 12

Example 41. 40 students enter for a game of shot-put competition. The distance thrown (in metres) is recorded below **[ICSE 2020]**

Distance (in m)	12-13	13-14	14-15	15-16	16-17	17-18	18-19
Number of students	3	9	12	9	4	2	1

Use a graph paper to draw an ogive for the above distribution.

Use a scale of 2 cm = 1 m on one axis and 2 cm = 5 students on the other axis.

Hence, using your graph find

(i) the median

(ii) upper quartile

(iii) number of students who cover a distance which is above $16\frac{1}{2}$ m.

Sol. The cumulative frequency table for the continuous distribution is shown below

Distance	12-13	13-14	14-15	15-16	16-17	17-18	18-19
Number of students	3	9	12	9	4	2	1
Cumulative frequency (cf)	3	12	24	33	37	39	40

On the graph paper, we plot the following points $A(13, 3)$, $B(14, 12)$, $C(15, 24)$, $D(16, 33)$, $E(17, 37)$, $F(18, 39)$ and $G(19, 40)$. Join all these points by a free hand drawing. The required ogive is shown on the graph paper given below.

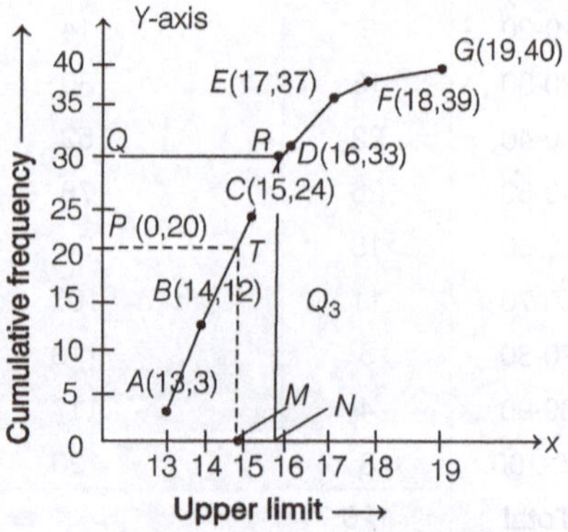

(i) For, median $\frac{n}{2} = \frac{40}{2} = 20$

Take a point P on Y-axis representing 20. Through P, draw a line PT parallel to X-axis which meets the ogive at T.

Draw TM perpendicular to X-axis, meeting X-axis at M. The abscissa of M, is 14.7 which is the required median.

(ii) Upper quartile, $\frac{3n}{4} = \frac{3 \times 40}{4} = 30$

Taking point Q on Y-axis representing frequency = 30 Through Q, draw a line QR parallel to X-axis, which meets the ogive at R. Draw RN perpendicular to X-axis, meeting X-axis at N. The abscissa of N is 15.67 which is required upper Quartile.

(iii) Number of students who cover a distance which is above $16\frac{1}{2}$ m are $40 - 35 = 5$ (according to graph)

Exercise 20.4

1. For the following frequency distribution draw a histogram. Hence, calculate the mode.

Class	0-5	5-10	10-15	15-20	20-25	25-30
Frequency	2	7	18	10	8	5

2. Draw a Histogram for the given data, using a graph paper.

Weekly wages (in ₹)	Number of people
3000-4000	4
4000-5000	18
5000-6000	9
6000-7000	6
7000-8000	7
8000-9000	2
9000-10000	4

Estimate the mode from the graph.

3. Draw a histogram from the following frequency distribution and find the mode from the graph.

Class	0-5	5-10	10-15	15-20	20-25	25-30
Frequency	2	5	18	14	8	5

[ICSE 2013]

4. Find the mode of following data, using a histogram.

Class	0-10	10-20	20-30	30-40	40-50
Frequency	5	12	20	9	4

5. The following table shows the expenditure of 60 boys on books.

Expenditure (in ₹)	20-25	25-30	30-35	35-40	40-45	45-50
Number of students	4	7	23	18	6	2

Find the mode of their expenditure.

6. Using a graph paper draw a histogram for the given distribution showing the number of runs scored by 50 batsman. Estimate the mode of the data. [ICSE 2018]

Runs scored	Number of batsman
3000-4000	4
4000-5000	18
5000-6000	9
6000-7000	6
7000-8000	7
8000-9000	2
9000-10000	4

7. The marks of 200 students in a test are given below

Marks %	10-19	20-29	30-39	40-49	50-59	60-69	70-79	80-89
Number of students	7	11	20	46	57	37	15	7

Draw the histogram and find the mode.

8. Draw a histogram for the distributions and estimate the mode from the graph.

Marks %	30-39	40-49	50-59	60-69	70-79	80-89	90-99
Number of students	14	26	40	92	114	78	36

9. Find the mode of the following frequency distribution by drawing a histogram.

Mid-values	12	18	24	30	36	42	48
Frequency	20	12	8	24	16	8	12

10. Find the median for the following distribution graphically.

Class interval	0-10	10-20	20-30	30-40	40-50
Frequency	5	7	10	8	5

11. Estimate the median for the given data by drawing ogive.

Class	0-10	10-20	20-30	30-40	40-50
Frequency	4	9	15	14	8

12. A frequency distribution of lengths of sticks in a bundle is given below

Class mark (in cm)	5	15	25	35	45	55	65
Frequency	10	17	12	9	11	18	7

Prepare a classified frequency distribution. Display it by an ogive and use it to find the median length of the sticks.

13. Use graph paper for this question.
A survey regarding height (in cm) of 60 boys belonging to class 10 of a school was conducted. The following data was recorded

Height (in cm)	Number of boys
135-140	4
140-145	8
145-150	20
150-155	14
155-160	7
160-165	6
165-170	1

Taking 2 cm = height of 10 cm along one axis and 2 cm = 10 boys along the other axis draw an ogive of the above distribution. Use the graph to estimate the following.

(i) the median (ii) lower quartile

(iii) if above 158 cm is considered as the tall boys of the class. Find the number of boys in the class who are tall. **[ICSE 2018]**

14. Use graph paper to answer this question.
During a medical checkup of 60 students in a school, weights were recorded as follows: **[ICSE 2023]**

Weight (in kg)	Number of Students
28-30	2
30-32	4
32-34	10
34-36	13
36-38	15
38-40	9
40-42	5
42-44	2

Taking 2 cm = 2 kg along one axis and 2 cm = 10 students along the other axis draw an ogive. Use your graph to find the

(i) median

(ii) upper quartile

(iii) number of students whose weight is above 37 kg.

15. The marks obtained by 200 students in an examination are given below.

Marks	Number of students
0-10	5
10-20	11
20-30	10
30-40	20
40-50	28
50-60	37
60-70	40
70-80	29
80-90	14
90-100	6

Draw an ogive for the given distribution taking 2 cm = 10 marks on one axis and 2 cm = 20 students on the other axis. Using the graph, determine

(i) the median marks.

(ii) the number of students who failed, if minimum marks required to pass is 40.

(iii) if scoring 85 and more marks is considered as grade one, find the number of students who secured grade one in the examination. **[ICSE 2011]**

16. The marks obtained by 120 students in a test are given below.

Marks	Number of students
0-10	5
10-20	9
20-30	16
30-40	22
40-50	26
50-60	18
60-70	11
70-80	6
80-90	4
90-100	3

Draw an ogive for the given distribution on a graph sheet.
Use suitable scale for ogive to estimate

(i) the median.

(ii) the number of students who obtained more than 75% marks in the test.

(iii) the number of students who did not pass the test, if minimum marks required to pass is 40. **[ICSE 2013, 12]**

17. Attempt this question on graph paper.

Age (in years)	5-15	15-25	25-35	35-45	45-55	55-65	65-75
Number of casualties	6	10	15	13	24	8	7

(i) Construct the 'less than' cumulative frequency curve for the above data, using 2 cm = 10 yr, on one axis and 2 cm = 10 casualties on the other.

(ii) From your graph determine (a) median (b) lower quartile.

18. From the following cumulative frequency table, draw ogive and then use it to find

Marks (Less than)	10	20	30	40	50	60	70	80	90	100
Cumulative frequency	5	24	37	40	42	48	70	77	79	80

(i) median (ii) lower quartile
(iii) upper quartile.

19. The weights of 60 boys are given in the following distribution table

Weight (in kg)	37	38	39	40	41
Number of boys	10	14	18	12	6

Find the

(i) median (ii) lower quartile
(iii) upper quartile (iv) inter quartile range.

20. The following distribution represents the height of 160 students of a school

Height (in cm)	Number of students
140-145	12
145-150	20
150-155	30
155-160	38
16-165	24
165-170	16
170-175	12
175-180	8

Draw an ogive for the given distribution taking 2 cm = 5 cm of height on one axis and 2 cm = 20 students on the other axis. Using the graph, determine

(i) the median height.
(ii) the inter quartile range.
(iii) the number of students, whose height is above 172 cm **[ICSE 2012]**

21. The monthly income of a group of 320 employees in a company is given below.

Monthly income	Number of employees
6000-7000	20
7000-8000	45
8000-9000	65
9000-10000	95
10000-11000	60
11000-12000	30
12000-13000	5

Draw an ogive of the given distribution on a graph sheet taking 2 cm = ₹ 1000 on one axis and 2 cm = 50 employees on the other axis. From the graph determine

(i) the median wage.
(ii) the number of employees whose income is below ₹ 8500.
(iii) if the salary of a senior employee is above ₹ 11500, then find the number of senior employees in the company.
(iv) the upper quartile. **[ICSE 2010]**

Chapter Practice

a. 1 Mark Questions

1. If the arithmetic mean of the following distribution is 47, then the value of p is

Class interval	0-20	20-40	40-60	60-80	80-100
Frequency	8	15	20	p	5

(a) 10 (b) 11
(c) 13 (d) 12

2. The time (in seconds) taken by 150 atheletes to run a 110 m hurdle race are tabulated below

Time (in seconds)	13.8-14	14-14.2	14.2-14.4	14.4-14.6	14.6-14.8	14.8-15
Frequency	2	4	5	71	48	20

The number of atheletes who complete the race in less than 14.6s is
(a) 11 (b) 71
(c) 82 (d) 130

3. For the following distribution

Marks	Number of students
Below 10	3
Below 20	12
Below 30	27
Below 40	57
Below 50	75
Below 60	80

The modal class is
(a) 10-20 (b) 20-30
(c) 30-40 (d) 50-60

4. Consider the following distribution

Marks obtained	Number of students
More than or equal to 0	63
More than or equal to 10	58
More than or equal to 20	55
More than or equal to 30	51
More than or equal to 40	48
More than or equal to 50	42

The frequency of the class 30-40 is
(a) 3 (b) 4 (c) 48 (d) 51

5. For the following distribution

Marks	Number of students	Marks	Number of students
Below 10	3	Below 40	57
Below 20	12	Below 50	75
Below 30	28	Below 60	80

The modal class is
(a) 0-20 (b) 20-30
(c) 30-40 (d) 50-60

6. A student noted the number of cars passing through a spot on a road for 100 periods each of 3 min and summarised in the table given below

Number of cars	Frequency
0-10	7
10-20	14
20-30	13
30-40	12
40-50	20
50-60	11
60-70	15
70-80	8

Then, the mode of the data is
(a) 34.7 (b) 44.7
(c) 54.7 (d) 64.7

7. Which of the following cannot be determined graphically for a grouped frequency distribution? **[ICSE 2023]**
(a) Median (b) Mode
(c) Quartiles (d) Mean

8. The modal class of a given distribution always corresponds to the **[ICSE Semester II 2022]**
(a) interval with highest frequency
(b) interval with lowest frequency
(c) the first interval
(d) the last interval

9. The median class for the given distribution is **[ICSE Semester II 2022]**

Class Interval	0-10	10-20	20-30	30-40
Frequency	2	4	3	5

(a) 0-10 (b) 10-20
(c) 20-30 (d) 30-40

b. 3 Marks Questions

10. The marks obtained by 12 students in a monthly test are 11, 19, 7, 13, 18, 21, 9, 5, 20, 17, 16, 21. Find

(i) the mean of their marks.

(ii) the mean of their marks, when the marks of each student are increased by 3.

11. In a class test, the mean of marks scored by a class of 40 students was calculated as 18.2. Later on, it was detected that the marks of one student was wrongly copied as 21 instead of 29. Find the correct mean.

12. If $\bar{x}$ is the mean of the ten natural numbers, $x_1, x_2, x_3, \dots x_{10}$, show that :

$(x_1 - \bar{x}) + (x_2 - \bar{x}) + (x_3 - \bar{x}) + \dots + (x_{10} - \bar{x}) = 0$

13. The mean of eleven observations is 65. If the mean of first six observations is 63 and that of last six observation is 66; find the sixth observation.

14. Calculate the mean for the following distribution.

Pocket money (in ₹)	60	70	80	90	100	110	120
Number of students	2	6	13	22	24	10	3

15. The table below gives the distribution of villages under different heights from sea level in a certain region. Compute the mean height of the region.

Heights (in m)	200	600	1000	1400	1800	2200
Number of villages	142	265	560	271	89	16

16.

Category	A	B	C	D	E	F	G
Wages (in ₹ per day)	50	60	70	80	90	100	110
Number of workers	2	4	8	12	10	6	8

If the number of workers in each category is doubled, what would be the new mean wage?

17. Marks obtained by 40 students in a short assessment are given below, where *a* and *b* are missing data.

Marks	5	6	7	8	9
Number of students	6	*a*	16	13	*b*

If the mean of the distribution is 7.2, find *a* and *b*.

18. The mean of the following data is 16. Calculate the value of *f*.

Marks	5	10	15	20	25
Number of students	3	7	*f*	9	6

19. Calculate the mean of the following frequency distribution. **[ICSE Semester II 2022]**

Class Interval	5-15	15-25	25-35	35-45	45-55
Frequency	2	6	4	8	4

20. The mean of the following distribution is 50. Find the unknown frequency. **[ICSE Semester II 2022]**

Class Interval	0-20	20-40	40-60	60-80	80-100
Frequency	6	*f*	8	12	8

21. The mean of the following distribution is 23.4. Find the value of *p*.

Class intervals	0-8	8-16	16-24	24-32	32-40	40-48
Frequency	5	3	10	*p*	4	2

22. The following table gives the marks scored by a set of students in an examination. Calculate the mean of the distribution by using the short cut method. **[ICSE 2023]**

Marks	0-10	10-20	20-30	30-40	40-50	50-60
Number of students (*f*)	3	8	14	9	4	2

23. The following are the marks obtained by 70 boys in a class test

Marks	30-40	40-50	50-60	60-70	70-80	80-90	90-100
Number of boys	10	12	14	12	9	7	6

Calculate the mean by

(i) shortcut method.

(ii) step-deviation method.

24. A study of the yield of 150 tomato plants resulted in the following record.

Tomatoes per plant	1-5	6-10	11-15	16-20	21-25
Number of plants	20	50	46	22	12

Calculate the mean of the number of tomatoes per plant.

c. 4/5 Marks Questions

25. Using the information given in the following histogram, calculate the mean correct to one decimal place.

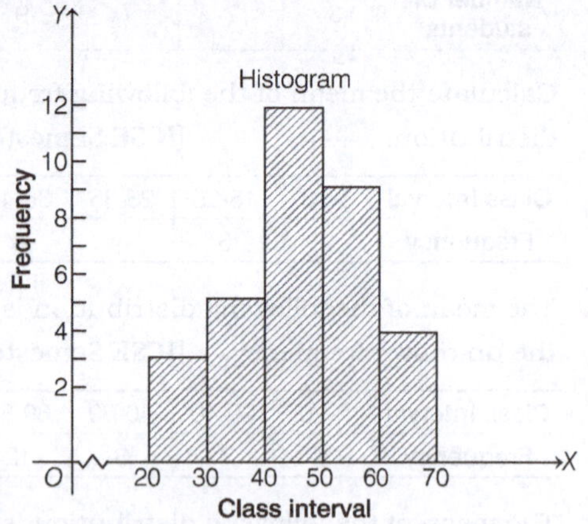

26. Marks obtained by 100 students in an examination are given below

Marks	0-10	10-20	20-30	30-40	40-50	50-60
Number of students	5	15	20	28	20	12

Draw a histogram for the given data using a graph paper and find the mode.

Take 2 cm = 10 marks along one axis and 2 cm = 10 students along the other axis.

[ICSE Semester II 2022]

27. Marks obtained by 40 students in an examination are given below

Marks	10-20	20-30	30-40	40-50	50-60	60-70
Number of students	3	8	14	9	4	2

Using graph paper an ogive and estimate the median marks. Take 2 cm = 10 marks along one axis and 2 cm = 5 students along the other axis.

[ICSE Semester II 2022]

28. The contents of 100 match boxes were checked to determine the number of matches they contained.

Number of matches	35	36	37	38	39	40	41
Number of boxes	6	10	18	25	21	12	8

(i) Calculate, correct to two decimal place, the mean number of matches per box.

(ii) Determine, how many extra matches would have to be added to the total contents of the 100 boxes to bring the mean up to exactly 39 matches?

29. Consider the following distribution of daily wages of 50 workers of a factory.

Daily wages (in ₹)	100-120	120-140	140-160	160-180	180-200
Number of workers	12	14	8	6	10

Find the mean daily wages of the workers of the factory by using an appropriate method.

30. Apply step-deviation method to find the arithmetic mean of the following frequency distribution.

Variate (x)	5	10	15	20	25	30	35	40	45	50
Frequency (f)	20	43	75	67	72	45	39	9	8	6

31. The mean of the following frequency distribution is 25.8 and the sum of all the frequencies is 50. Find the values of p and q.

Class	0-10	10-20	20-30	30-40	40-50
Frequency	7	p	15	q	10

32. The following table gives the life-time in days of 100 electricity tubes of a certain make.

Life-time (in days)	Number of tubes
Less than 50	8
Less than 100	23
Less than 150	55
Less than 200	81
Less than 250	93
Less than 300	100

Find the mean life-time of electricity tubes.

33. Find the mean marks of students from the following cumulative frequency distribution.

Marks	Number of students	Marks	Number of students
0 and above	80	60 and above	28
10 and above	77	70 and above	16
20 and above	72	80 and above	10
30 and above	65	90 and above	8
40 and above	55	100 and above	0
50 and above	43		

34. From the following data,
25, 10, 40, 88, 45, 60, 77, 36, 18, 95, 56, 65, 70, 38 and 83. Find

(i) median (ii) upper quartile

(iii) inter quartile range.

35. Find the mean, median and mode of the following distribution.

8, 10, 7, 6, 10, 11, 6, 13, 10

36. A boy scored the following marks in various class tests during a term, each test being marked out of 20.

15, 17, 16, 7, 10, 12, 14, 16, 19, 12, 16

(i) What are his modal marks?

(ii) What are his median marks?

(iii) What are his mean marks?

37. Find the mean, median and mode of the following marks obtained by 16 students in a class test, marked out of 10 marks.

0, 0, 2, 2, 3, 3, 3, 4, 5, 5, 5, 5, 6, 6, 7, 8

38. Find the mode and median of the following frequency distribution. **[ICSE 2012]**

x	10	11	12	13	14	15
f	1	4	7	5	9	3

39. In a class of 40 students, marks obtained by the students in a class test (out of 10) are given below

Marks	1	2	3	4	5	6	7	8	9	10
Number of students	1	2	3	3	6	10	5	4	3	3

Calculate the following for the given distribution.

(i) Median (ii) Mode

40. The marks obtained by 30 students in a class assessment of 5 marks is given below

Marks	0	1	2	3	4	5
Number of students	1	3	6	10	5	5

Calculate the mean, median and mode of the above distribution. **[ICSE 2015]**

41. Draw a histogram to represent the following data and estimate the mode from the graph.

Marks obtained	0-10	10-20	20-30	30-40	40-50	50-60
Number of students	4	10	6	8	5	9

42. Construct a histogram for the frequently distribution and estimate the mode from the graphs.

Class interval	1-10	11-20	21-30	31-40	41-50
Frequency	11	23	30	20	16

43. Draw a histogram for the following data and estimate the mode from the graph.

Class marks	12.5	17.5	22.5	27.5	32.5	37.5
Frequency	7	12	20	28	8	11

44. Construct a frequency distribution table and a cumulative frequency curve (ogive) for the following distribution.

Marks obtained	Less than 10	Less than 20	Less than 30	Less than 40	Less than 50
Number of students	8	22	48	60	75

45. Construct an ogive for the following distribution by less than method.

Cost of living	Under 140	Under 150	Under 160	Under 170	Under 180	Under 190	Under 200
Cumulative frequency	0	4	12	30	42	48	52

46. The marks obtained by 15 students in a class test are 12, 14, 07, 9, 23, 11, 8, 13, 11, 19, 16, 24, 17, 3 and 20. Find

(i) the mean of their marks.

(ii) the mean of their marks when the marks of each student are increased by 4.

(iii) the mean of their marks when 2 marks are deducted from the marks of each student.

d. 6 Marks Questions

47. Find the upper quartile, lower quartile, inter quartile range and semi-inter quartile range for the frequency distribution.

Variate	10	11	12	13	14	15	16	17	18	19	20
Frequency	1	2	3	1	2	4	2	1	1	2	1

48. (i) Using step-deviation method, calculate the mean marks of the following distribution.

Class interval	50-55	55-60	60-65	65-70	70-75	75-80	80-85	85-90
Frequency	5	20	10	10	9	6	12	8

(ii) State the modal class.

49. The marks of 10 students of a class in an examination arranged in ascending order is as follows

13, 35, 43, 46, x, $x+4$, 55, 61, 71, 80

If the median marks is 48, find the value of x. Hence, find the mode of the given data. **[ICSE 2017]**

50. The monthly profits (in rupees) of 100 shops are distributed as follows

Profit (in ₹)	0-100	100-200	200-300	300-400	400-500	500-600
Number of shops	13	18	27	20	17	6

Find the modal value graphically and check this value by direct calculation.

51. By drawing an ogive, estimate the median for the following frequency distribution.

Weight (kg)	10-15	15-20	20-25	25-30	30-35
Number of boys	11	25	12	5	2

52. The table given below shows the monthly salary of some employees of a company, if lowest salary being ₹ 6500.

Salary (in ₹)	Under 7000	Under 7500	Under 8000	Under 8500	Under 9000	Under 9500	Under 10000
Number of employees	10	18	22	25	17	10	8

(i) Use the table to form its cumulative frequency curve.
Take 2 cm = ₹ 500, starting the origin at ₹ 6500 on the X-axis and 2 cm = 10 employees on the Y-axis.
(ii) Use the graph to write down the median salary in rupees.

53. Using a graph paper, draw an ogive for the following distribution that shows a record of the weight in kilograms of 200 students.

Weight	40-45	45-50	50-55	55-60	60-65	65-70	70-75	75-80
Frequency	5	17	22	45	51	31	20	9

Use your ogive to estimate the following.
(i) The percentage of students weighing 55 kg or more.
(ii) The weight above which the heaviest 30% of the students fall.
(iii) The number of students who are
(a) underweight and (b) overweight, if 55.70 kg is considered as standard weight.

54. Draw an ogive of the following distribution and use it to find

Class interval	0-10	10-20	20-30	30-40	40-50	50-60	60-70
Frequency	20	35	15	40	13	17	10

(i) the median.
(ii) the lower quartile.
(iii) the upper quartile.
(iv) the inter quartile range.
(v) the semi-inter quartile range.

55. Attempt this question on graph paper. Marks obtained by 200 students in examination are given below

Marks	Number of students
0-10	5
10-20	10
20-30	14
30-40	21
40-50	25
50-60	34
60-70	36
70-80	27
80-90	16
90-100	12

Draw an ogive for the given distribution, taking 2 cm = 10 marks on one axis and 2 cm = 20 students on the other axis. From the graph, find
(i) the median.
(ii) the upper quartile.
(iii) number of students scoring above 65 marks.
(iv) if 10 students qualify for merit scholarship, find the minimum marks required to qualify.

56. The table below shows the distribution of the scores obtained by 120 shooters in a shooting competition.

Scores obtained	Number of shooters
0-10	5
10-20	9
20-30	16
30-40	22
40-50	26
50-60	18
60-70	11
70-80	6
80-90	4
90-100	3

Using a graph sheet, draw an ogive for the distribution.
Use your ogive to estimate
(i) the median.
(ii) the inter quartile range.
(iii) the number of shooters who obtained more than 75% scores.

57. The daily wages of 160 workers in a building project are given below.

Wages (in ₹)	0-10	10-20	20-30	30-40	40-50	50-60	60-70	70-80
Number of workers	12	20	30	38	24	16	12	8

Using a graph paper, draw an ogive for the above distribution.
Use your ogive to estimate
(i) the median wage of the workers.
(ii) the upper quartile wage of the workers.
(iii) the lower quartile wage of the workers.
(iv) the percentage of workers, who earn more than ₹ 45 a day.

Hints and Answers

Exercise 20.1

1. Given, the mean of 9th variates is 11.
Let 9th variate = x

$$\text{Mean} = \frac{x+7+12+9+14+21+3+8+15}{9}$$

$$11 = \frac{x+89}{9}$$

$\therefore x = 99 - 89 = 10$

2. **Hint** Do same as Example 4. **Ans.** $f = 15$

3. **Hint**

Class interval	Class marks (x_i)	Number of workers (f_i)	$f_i x_i$
0-10	5	7	35
10-20	15	10	150
20-30	25	15	375
30-40	35	8	280
40-50	45	10	450
Total		$\Sigma f_i = 50$	$\Sigma f_i x_i = 1290$

$\therefore \quad \text{Mean } (\bar{x}) = \frac{\Sigma f_i x_i}{\Sigma f_i} = \frac{1290}{50}$

Ans. 25.8

4. **Hint** Do same as Q. 3. **Ans.** 49.5
5. **Hint** Do same as Q. 3. **Ans.** 264
6. **Hint** Do same as Example 7. **Ans.** $p = 24$
7. **Hint** Do same as Example 7. **Ans.** $f = 8$
8. **Hint** Here, class interval are not continuous. But it does not affect mid-values (x_i).
So, we will solve it without making it continuous.

Class	Class marks (x_i)	Frequency (f_i)	$f_i x_i$
4-7	5.5	5	27.5
8-11	9.5	4	38
12-15	13.5	9	121.5
16-19	17.5	10	175
Total		$\Sigma f_i = 28$	$\Sigma f_i x_i = 362$

$\therefore \quad \text{Mean } (\bar{x}) = \frac{\Sigma f_i x_i}{\Sigma f_i} = \frac{362}{28}$

Ans. 12.93

9. **Hint** Do same as Example 9. **Ans.** 36.85
10. **Hint** Do same as Example 9. **Ans.** 37.66
11. **Hint** Here, class interval are not continuous.
We can solve it without making it continuous.

Class	Class marks (x_i)	Frequency (f_i)	$d_i = x_i - 70$	$f_i d_i$
63-65	64	4	−6	−24
66-68	67	3	−3	−9
69-71	70 = A	7	0	0
72-74	73	8	3	24
75-77	76	3	6	18
Total		$\Sigma f_i = 25$		$\Sigma f_i d_i = 9$

$\therefore \text{ Mean } (\bar{x}) = A + \frac{\Sigma f_i d_i}{\Sigma f_i} = 70 + \frac{9}{25}$

Ans. 70.36

12. **Hint** Do same as Example 11. **Ans.** 49.6
13. **Hint** Do same as Example 13. **Ans.** 50
14. **Hint** Do same as Example 13. **Ans.** ₹ 158
15. **Hint** Do same as Example 13.
Ans. 35
16. **Hint** Do same as Example 14.
Ans. $f_1 = 16, f_2 = 9$

Exercise 20.2

1. **Hint** Here, number of observations, $n = 9$, which is odd.
So, we use the formula,

$$\text{Median} = \left(\frac{n+1}{2}\right)\text{th observation} = 5\text{th observation}$$

$\Rightarrow \quad 24 = x + 4 \qquad [\because \text{median} = 24, \text{given}]$

$$\therefore \text{Mean} = \frac{11+12+14+x-2+x+4+x+9+32+38+47}{9}$$

$$= \frac{165+3x}{9}$$

Ans. 20 and 25

2.

Marks	Number of students
10-20	15
20-30	20 − 15 = 5
30-40	30 − 20 = 10
40-50	35 − 30 = 5
50-60	40 − 35 = 5

3. **Hint** Do same as Example 20.
Ans.

Marks	Number of students
10-20	10
20-30	14
30-40	15
40-50	20
50-60	12
60 or more	11

4. **Hint** Do same as Example 21. **Ans.** 12
5. **Hint** Do same as Example 22. **Ans.** 6.5
6. **Hint** Do same as Example 23. **Ans.** 20.47
7. **Hint** Do same as Example 23. **Ans.** 109.72 km/h
8. **Hint** Do same as Example 24. **Ans.** 138.57 cm
9. **Hint** Here, we are required to find median weight of students and do same as Example 24. **Ans.** 60.16 kg
10. **Hint** To find median marks, we convert the given data into continuous grouped frequency distribution

Marks	Number of students	Cumulative frequency (*cf*)
0-10	$50-46=4$	4
10-20	$46-40=6$	10
20-30	$40-20=20$	30
30-40	$20-10=10$	40
40-50	$10-3=7$	47
50-60	$3-0=3$	50

Here, $\frac{n}{2}=\frac{50}{2}=25$

$\therefore$ Median class = 20-30

Now, median $= l+\frac{\frac{n}{2}-cf}{f}\times h = 20+\frac{25-10}{20}\times 10$

Ans. 27.5

11. **Hint**

Age (in years)	Number of persons	Cumulative frequency (*cf*)
0-10	5	5
10-20	25	30
20-30	x	$30+x$
30-40	18	$48+x$
40-50	7	$55+x$

Since, the median is 24. Therefore, the median class is 20-30.

$$\therefore \quad \text{Median} = l+\left(\frac{\frac{n}{2}-cf}{f}\right)\times h$$

$$\Rightarrow 24 = 20+\frac{\frac{55+x}{2}-30}{x}\times 10$$

$$\Rightarrow \quad 4=\frac{x-5}{2x}\times 10$$

$$\Rightarrow 8x = 10x-50$$

$$\Rightarrow \quad x=\frac{50}{2}=25$$ **Ans.** $x=25$

12. **Hint** Do same as Q. 11.
Ans. $x=5$
13. **Hint** Do same as Example 25.
Ans. $x=15,\ y=20$
14. **Hint** Do same as Example 25.
Ans. $f_1=18,\ f_2=25$
15. **Hint** Convert the given distribution into continuous grouped frequency distribution and then find the median.
Ans. 60.85 kg
16. **Hint**

(i) Median $=\left(\frac{n+1}{2}\right)$th term $=\left(\frac{19+1}{2}\right)$th $=10$th term

(ii) Lower Quartile $(Q_1)=\frac{n+1}{4}=\frac{20}{4}=5$th term

(iii) Upper Quartile $(Q_3)=3\left(\frac{n+1}{4}\right)$th term $=3\times 5$th $=15$th term

(iv) Inter Quartile Range $=(Q_3-Q_1)$

Ans. (i) 31 (ii) 27 (iii) 41 (iv) 14

17. **Hint**

Variate	Frequency	Cumulative frequency (*cf*)
15	4	4
18	6	10
20	8	18
22	9	27
25	7	34
27	8	42
30	6	48

Ans. (i) 22 (ii) 20 (iii) 27 (iv) 7

Exercise 20.3

1. **Hint** Do same as Example 28. **Ans.** 52
2. **Hint** Do same as Example 28. **Ans.** 3.28
3. **Hint** Do same as Example 28. **Ans.** 46.67
4. **Hint** Do same as Example 28. **Ans.** 201.7 g
5. **Hint** Do same as Example 29. **Ans.** $x=10$
6. **Hint** Do same as Example 29. **Ans.** $x=25$
7. **Hint** Do same as Example 29. **Ans.** $x=15$

8. **Hint** Here, the given frequency distribution is not continuous.
So, first we make it continuous by subtracting 0.5 from lower limit and adding 0.5 to upper limit.

Class interval	Continuous class interval	Frequency
0-9	−0.5 - 9.5	12
10-19	9.5 - 19.5	15
20-29	19.5 - 29.5	21 (Modal class)
30-39	29.5 - 39.5	17
40-49	39.5 - 49.5	19
50-59	49.5 - 59.5	6

$\therefore \quad l = 19.5,\ f_1 = 21,\ f_0 = 15,\ f_2 = 17$ and $h = 10$

Now, mode $= 19.5 + \dfrac{21-15}{42-15-17} \times 10$

Ans. 25.5

9. **Hint** Do same as Q. 8.
Ans. 170.17

10. **Hint** Here, the maximum frequency is 50. So, the modal class is 13-15.
$\therefore\ l = 13,\ f_1 = 50,\ f_0 = 30,\ f_2 = 48$ and $h = 2$

Now, mode $= 13 + \dfrac{50-30}{100-30-48} \times 2$

$= 13 + \dfrac{20}{22} \times 2$

Since, sum of frequencies $= 181$

$\therefore \quad x + 15 + 18 + 30 + 50 + 48 + x = 181$

Ans. 14.82; 10

11. **Hint** Do same as Example 30. **Ans.** 11

12. **Hint** Median $= \dfrac{\text{Mode} + 2(\text{Mean})}{3}$

$= \dfrac{12k + 2 \times 15k}{3} = \dfrac{42k}{3}$

Ans. 14 k

Exercise 20.4

1. **Hint** Do same as Example 33. **Ans.** 13
2. **Hint** Do same as Example 33.
Ans. Mode = 5428.57
3. **Hint** Do same as Example 33. **Ans.** 14
4. **Hint** Do same as Example 33. **Ans.** 24
5. **Hint** Do same as Example 33. **Ans.** 34
6. **Hint** Do same as Example 33. **Ans.** 4600
7. **Hint** Do same as Example 34. **Ans.** 53.5
8. **Hint** Do same as Example 34. **Ans.** 73

9. **Hint** Here, mid-values of the class-intervals are given. So, we find class limits by subtracting and adding $\dfrac{h}{2}$ to the mid values, where $h = 18 - 12 = 6$.
The continuous frequency distribution obtained from the given distribution is as follows

Class intervals	9-15	15-21	21-27	27-33	33-39	39-45	45-51
Frequency	20	12	8	24	16	8	12

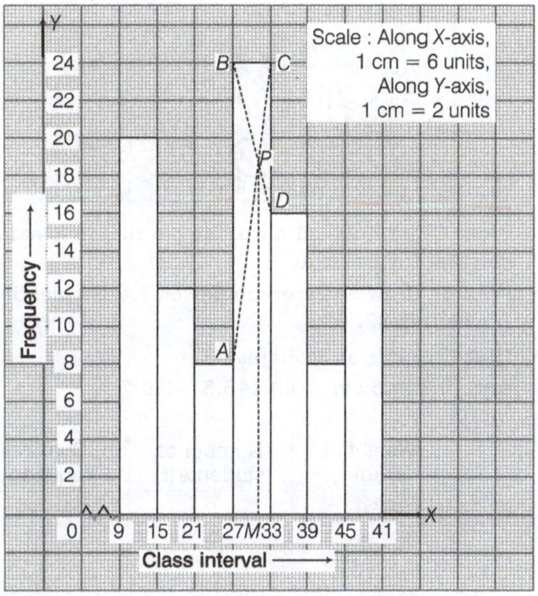

Ans. 30.9

10. **Hint** Do same as Example 37 (i). **Ans.** 26
11. **Hint** Do same as Example 37 (i). **Ans.** 28
12.

Class mark (in cm)	Class interval	Frequency	Cumulative frequency (cf)
5	0-10	10	10
15	10-20	17	27
25	20-30	12	39
35	30-40	9	48
45	40-50	11	59
55	50-60	18	77
65	60-70	7	84

Here, $\quad N = 84$

$\Rightarrow \quad \dfrac{N}{2} = \dfrac{84}{2} = 42$

Scale : Along X-axis, 1 cm = 10 units and along Y-axis, 1 cm = 10 units

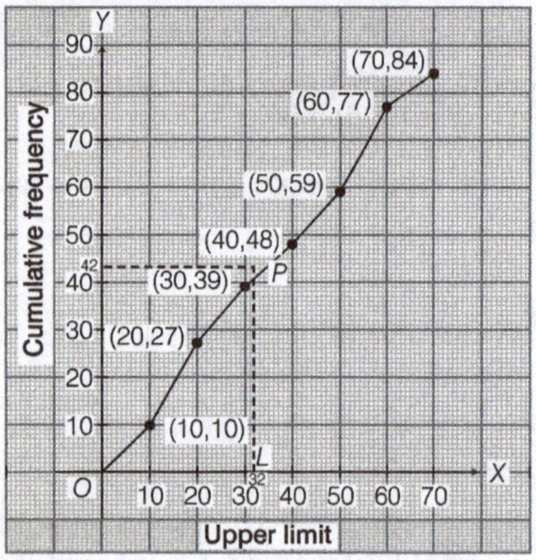

From 42 on Y-axis draw a line parallel to X-axis meeting the curve at P.

From P, draw a perpendicular on X-axis meeting it at L, which is 32.

13. **Hint** Do same as Example 37.

Ans. (i) 149.5 cm (ii) 145.5 (iii) 7

14. (i)

Weight (in kg)	Number of students (f)	Cumulative frequency (cf)
28-30	2	2
30-32	4	6
32-34	10	16
34-36	13	29
36-38	15	44
38-40	9	53
40-42	5	58
42-44	2	60
Total	60	

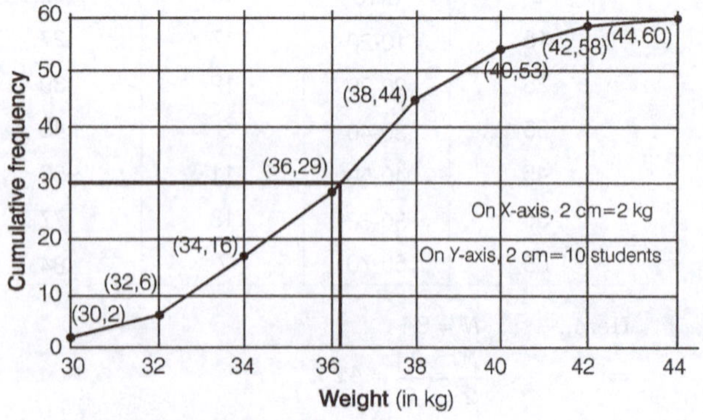

Using the graph drawn, we get

$$\text{Median} = \left(\frac{n}{2}\right)\text{th term, where } n = 60$$

$$= \left(\frac{60}{2}\right)\text{th term} = 30\text{th term} = 36.4$$

(ii)

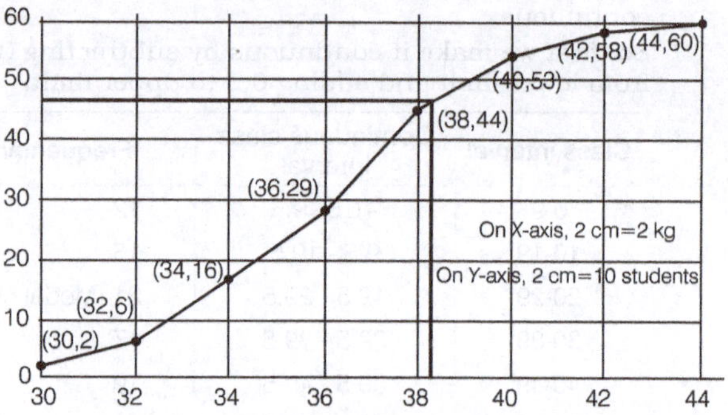

$$\therefore \text{Upper quartile} = \left(\frac{3n}{4}\right)\text{th term}$$

$$= \left(\frac{3 \times 60}{4}\right)\text{th term} \qquad [\because n = 60]$$

$$= 45\text{th term} = 38.2$$

(iii)

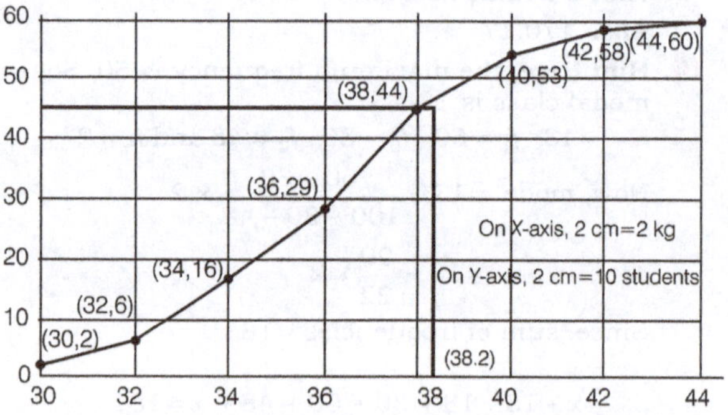

The number of students whose weight is above 37 kg is

Total number of students – The cumulative frequency at the weight of 37 kg

= 60 – 36 = 24 students

Therefore, the number of students whose weight is above 37 kg is 24 students.

15. **Hint** Do same as Example 37 (i), (iii) and (iv).

Take two large boxes on X-axis as 10 marks and take two large boxes on Y-axis as 20 students.

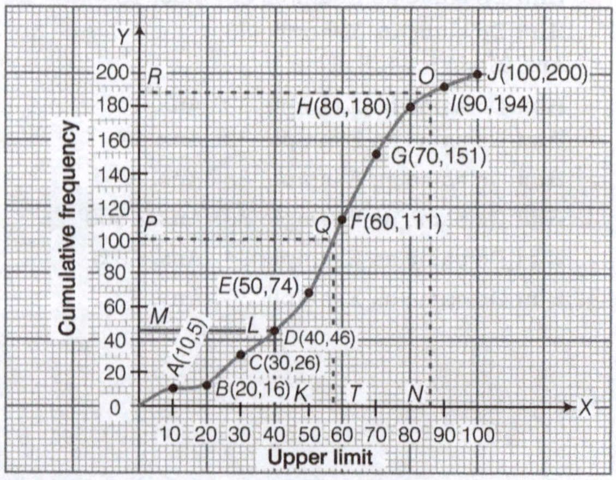

(i) **Hint** Here, $n = 200$, which is even. **Ans.** 57

(ii) **Hint** The minimum marks required to pass is 40, let the point K on X-axis represents 40 marks. Through K, draw a vertical line to meet the ogive at the point L. Through L, draw a horizontal line to meet the Y-axis at point M. The ordinate of point M represents 46 students on Y-axis. Hence, the number of students who failed is 46, if minimum marks required to pass is 40.

Ans. 46

(iii) **Hint** Scoring 85 and more marks is considered as grade one.

Let point N on X-axis represents 85 marks. Through N, draw a vertical line to meet the ogive at the point O. Through O draw a horizontal line to meet the Y-axis at point R. The ordering of point P represents 190 marks.

$\therefore$ Number of students who secured grade one in the examination $= 200 - 190 = 10$.

Ans. 10

16. **Hint** Do same as Example 37.

Ans. (i) 43.5 marks (ii) 10 students (iii) 52 students

17. **Hint** Do same as Example 40.

Ans. (ii) (a) 43 (b) 29

18. **Hint** Do same as Example 40.

Ans. (i) 40 (ii) 18 (iii) 66

19. **Hint** Do same as Example 40.

Ans. (i) 39 (ii) 38 (iii) 40 (iv) 2

20. **Hint** Do same as Example 40.

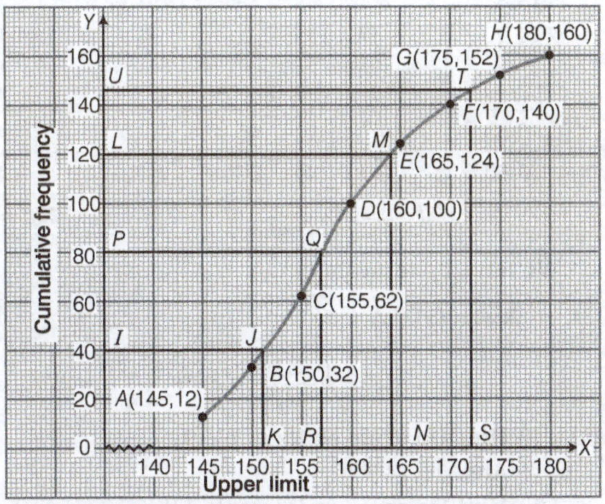

Ans. (i) 157.3 (ii) 172 cm (iii) 13

21. **Hint** Do same as Example 40.

Ans. (i) ₹ 15.70 (ii) ₹ 95 (iii) ₹ 20 (iv) ₹ 10200

Chapter Exercise

1. (d)

2. (c)

3. (c)

4. (a)

5. (c)

6. (b)

7. (d)

8. (a)

9. (c)

Class Interval	Class mark (x)	f	Cumulative Frequency
0-10	5	2	2
10-20	15	4	6
20-30	25	3	9
30-40	35	5	14
		$N = 14$	

$\therefore$ Here, $N = 14$

Then, $\frac{N}{2} = \frac{14}{2} = 7$

$\Rightarrow$ 7 is nearest to cumulative frequency 9.

So, median class is 20-30.

10. (i) **Hint** Mean of marks

$$= \frac{\text{Sum of marks of all students}}{\text{Number of students}} = \frac{177}{12}$$

Ans. 14.75

(ii) **Hint** When the marks of each student are increased by 3, then the sum of their marks increases by 12×3, i.e. by 36.

$\therefore$ New sum of marks of all students $= 177 + 36 = 213$

$$\therefore \text{New mean of marks} = \frac{\text{New sum of marks}}{\text{Number of students}} = \frac{213}{12}$$

Ans. 17.75

Note The new mean of marks also increases by 3.

11. **Hint** Let $x_1, x_2, x_3, x_4 \dots x_{40}$ marks

Scored by a class of 40 students.

According to the question,

$x_1 + x_2 + \dots + x_{40} - 21 + 29 = 18.2 \times 40 - 21 + 29$

$$\Rightarrow \frac{x_1 + x_2 + \dots x_{40}}{40} = \frac{18.2 \times 40 + 8}{40}$$

Ans. 18.4.

12. **Hint** $(x_1 - \bar{x}) + (x_2 - \bar{x}) + (x_3 - \bar{x}) + \dots + (x_{10} - \bar{x})$

$= (x_1 + x_2 + \dots + x_{10}) - (\bar{x} + \bar{x} + \dots + 10 \text{ times})$

$$= \left[\left(\frac{x_1 + x_2 + \dots + x_{10}}{10}\right) \times (10)\right] - 10\,\bar{x}$$

13. **Hint** Sum of 11 observation $= 65 \times 11 = 715$

Sum of first 6 observation $= 63 \times 6 = 378$

Sum of last 6 observation $= 66 \times 6 = 396$

Total of 12th observation $= 774$

Sixth observation $= 774 - 715 = 59$

Ans. 59

14. **Hint** Do same as Example 3. **Ans.** ₹ 92.75

15. **Hint** Do same as Example 3. **Ans.** 984.51

16. **Hint**

Category	Wages (in ₹)	Number of workers	fx
A	50	2	100
B	60	4	240
C	70	8	560
D	80	12	960
E	90	10	900
F	100	6	600
G	110	8	880
		$\Sigma f = 50$	$\Sigma fx = 4240$

$\therefore$ Mean $= \dfrac{\Sigma f_i x_i}{\Sigma f_i} = \dfrac{8480}{100} = 84.80 = 85$

Ans. 85

17. **Hint**

Marks (x_i)	Number of students (f_i)	$f_i x_i$
5	6	30
6	a	$6a$
7	16	112
8	13	104
9	b	$9b$
Total	$\Sigma f_i = 35 + a + b$	$\Sigma f_i x_i = 246 + 6a + 9b$

$\therefore \quad 40 = 35 + a + b \quad [\because \Sigma f_i = 40]$

$\Rightarrow \quad a + b = 5 \quad \ldots(i)$

$\Rightarrow \quad 7.2 = \dfrac{246 + 6a + 9b}{40} \quad [\because \bar{x} = 7.2]$

$\Rightarrow \quad 2a + 3b = 14 \quad \ldots(ii)$

Ans. 1 and 4

18. **Hint** Do same as Example 4.

Ans. $f = 15$

19.

Class Interval	Class mark (x_i)	f_i	$x_i f_i$
5-15	10	2	20
15-25	20	6	120
25-35	30	4	120
35-45	40	8	320
45-55	50	4	200
		$\Sigma f_i = 24$	$\Sigma x_i f_i = 780$

Now, mean $= \dfrac{\Sigma x_i f_i}{\Sigma f_i}$

$= \dfrac{780}{24} = 32.5$

20.

Class Interval	Class mark (x_i)	f_i	$x_i f_i$
0-20	10	6	60
20-40	30	f	$30f$
40-60	50	8	400
60-80	70	12	840
80-100	90	8	720
		$\Sigma f_i = 34 + f$	$\Sigma f_i x_i = 2020 + 30f$

Here, $\Sigma f_i = 34 + f$

and $\Sigma f_i x_i = 2020 + 30f$

Given, $\bar{x} = 50$

$\because \quad$ Mean, $\bar{x} = \dfrac{\Sigma f_i x_i}{\Sigma f_i}$

$\therefore \quad 50 = \dfrac{2020 + 30f}{34 + f}$

$\Rightarrow \quad 1700 + 50f = 2020 + 30f$

$\Rightarrow \quad 20f = 320$

$\Rightarrow \quad f = 16$

21. **Hint** Do same as Example 7. **Ans.** 16

22.

Marks	Number of student (frequency) f	Mid-value (x)	$d = x - A = x - 35$, $A = 35$	$f \times d$
0-10	3	5	− 30	− 90
10-20	8	15	− 20	− 160
20-30	14	25	− 10	− 140
30-40	9	35 = A	0	0
40-50	4	45	10	40
50-60	2	55	20	40
	$\Sigma f = n = 40$			$\Sigma fd = -310$

We have by formula,

Mean $(\bar{x}) = A + \dfrac{\Sigma fd}{n}$

$= 35 + \dfrac{(-310)}{40} = 35 + \dfrac{(-31)}{4} = 27.25$

23. (i) **Hint** Do same as Example 9.

Ans. 61.14

(ii) **Hint** Do same as Example 11.

Ans. 61.14

24. **Hint** We shall use step deviation method. Construct the table as under, taking assumed mean $A = 13$.

Here, h (width of each class) = 5.

Now, further proceed as Example 10.

Ans. 11.534

Note The frequency distribution is discontinuous.

$\left(\dfrac{\text{Upper limit + Lower limit}}{2}\right)$

25. **Hint** $A = 45$

Class interval	Frequency	Class mark (x_i)	$d_i = x_i - A$	$f_i d_i$
20-30	3	25	– 20	– 60
30-40	5	35	– 10	– 50
40-50	12	45	0	0
50-60	9	55	10	90
60-70	4	65	20	80

Apply assumed mean method,

$$\bar{x} = A + \frac{\Sigma f_i d_i}{\Sigma f_i}$$

Ans. 46.8

26. Take along X-axis 2 cm = 10 marks and along Y-axis 2 cm = 10 students

The histogram representing the given frequency distribution is shown below

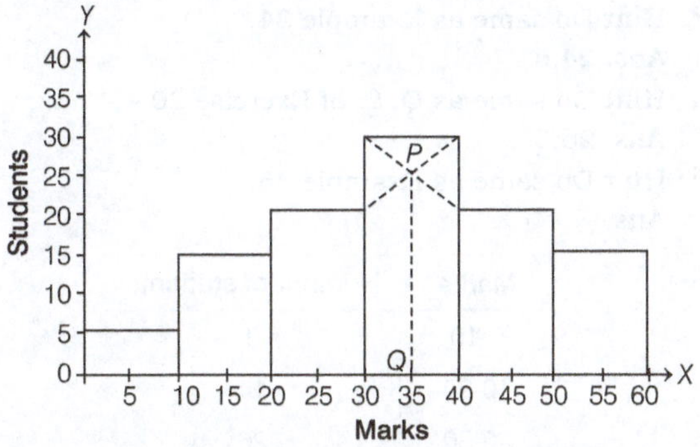

∴ Modal class is 30-40.

Two lines segments drawn diagonally in the modal class bar intersect at point P and the perpendicular drawn from P on X-axis meets Xaxis at Q.

Hence, the value of mode is 35.

27.

Marks	Number of students	Cumulative frequency (cf)
10-20	3	3
20-30	8	11
30-40	14	25
40-50	9	34
50-60	4	38
60-70	2	40

On the graph paper, we plot the following points $A(20, 3)$, $B(30, 11)$, $C(40, 25)$, $D(50, 34)$, $E(60, 38)$ and $F(70, 40)$.

Join all these points by a free hand drawing. The required ogive is shown on the graph paper given below.

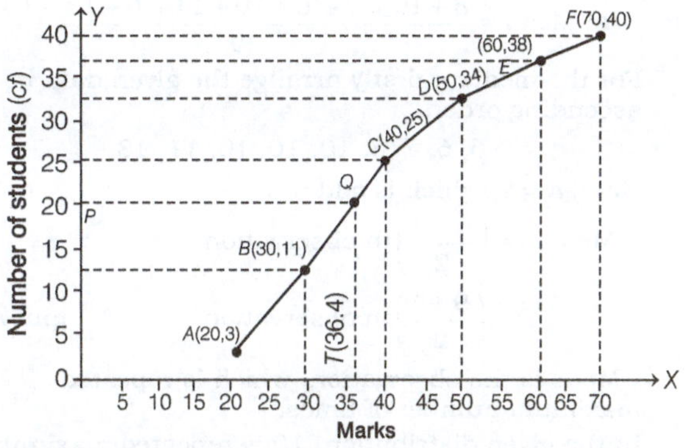

Here, number of students $(n) = 40$

∴ Let P be the point on Y-axis representing frequency $= \frac{n}{2} = \frac{40}{2} = 20$.

Through P, draw a horizontal line to meet the ogive at point Q. Through Q draw a vertical line to meet the X-axis at T. The abscissa of the point T represents 36.4 marks.

Hence, median marks is 36.4.

28. **Hint**

Number of matchsticks (x_i)	Number of boxes (f_i)	$f_i x_i$
35	6	210
36	10	360
37	18	666
38	25	950
39	21	819
40	12	480
41	8	328
	$\Sigma f_i = 100$	$\Sigma f_i x_i = 3813$

$$\therefore \text{ Mean} = \frac{\Sigma f_i x_i}{\Sigma f_i} = \frac{3813}{100}$$

Number of extra matches $= 39 \times 100 - 38.13 \times 100$

Ans. (i) 38.13 (ii) 87

29. **Hint** Do same as Example 11. **Ans.** 145.20

30. **Hint** Here, $h = 10 - 5 = 5$ and do same as Example 11. **Ans.** 22.214

31. **Hint** Do same as Example 14. **Ans.** $p = 10$ and $q = 18$

32. **Hint** Convert into the class intervals and their corresponding frequencies. Do same as Example 11. **Ans.** 142

33. **Hint** Convert into the class intervals and their corresponding frequencies and do same as Example 11. **Ans.** 51.75 marks

34. (i) **Hint** Median $= \left(\frac{n+1}{2}\right)$th observation. **Ans.** 56

(ii) **Hint** Upper quartile $= \left(\frac{3(n+1)}{4}\right)$th observation.

Ans. 77

(iii) **Hint** For inter quartile range $= Q_3 - Q_1$.

Ans. 41

35. Hint Mean $= \frac{8+10+7+6+10+11+6+13+10}{9}$

For the median, firstly arrange the given data in ascending order.

6, 6, 7, 8, 10, 10, 10, 11, 13

Here, $n = 9$, which is odd.

$\therefore$ Median $= \left(\frac{n+1}{2}\right)$th observation

$= \left(\frac{9+1}{2}\right)$th observation [put $n = 9$]

$\because$ Mode is the observation, which is repeated maximum number of times.

In the given distribution, 10 is repeated maximum number of times.

Ans. Mean = 9; median = 10 and mode = 10

36. Hint Do same as Q. 35.

Ans. (i) 16 (ii) 15 (iii) 14

37. Hint Do same as Q. 35. **Ans.** 4, 4.5, 5

38. The table for cumulative frequency is shown below

x	f	cf
10	1	1
11	4	5
12	7	12
13	5	17
14	9	26
15	3	29
Total	$n = 29$	

Here, $n = 29$, which is odd.

$\therefore$ Median $= \left(\frac{n+1}{2}\right)$th observation

$= 15$th observation

We know that mode is the highest occurring frequency of an observation.

From the table, we see that highest frequency is 9 and corresponding observation is 14.

Median = 13 and Mode = 14

39. Hint

Marks (x)	Number of students (f)	Cumulative Frequency (cf)
1	1	1
2	2	3
3	3	6
4	3	9
5	6	15
6	10	25
7	5	30
8	4	34
9	3	37
10	3	40
Total	$\Sigma f_i = 40$	

(i) Here, $N = 40$, which is even.

$\therefore$ Median $= \frac{\left[\left(\frac{40}{2}\right)\text{th} + \left(\frac{40}{2}+1\right)\text{th}\right]\text{term}}{2}$

$= \frac{(20\text{ th} + 21\text{ th})}{2}$ term

$= \frac{6+6}{2} = 6$

(ii) It is clear from the table that highest number of students is 10, i.e. it has highest frequency 10. And corresponding value of 10 is 6.

Hence, the mode is 6.

Ans. (i) Median = 6,
(ii) Mode = 6

40. Hint For mean marks, do same as Example 3.
For median, do same as Example 21.
For modal class, do same as Example 27.

Ans. (i) 3 (ii) 3 (iii) 3

41. Hint Do same as Example 33.
Ans. 16

42. Hint Do same as Example 34.
Ans. 24.6

43. Hint Do same as Q. 9. of Exercise 20.4.
Ans. 26.5

44. Hint Do same as Example 35.
Ans.

Marks	Number of students
0-10	8
10-20	14
20-30	26
30-40	12
40-50	15

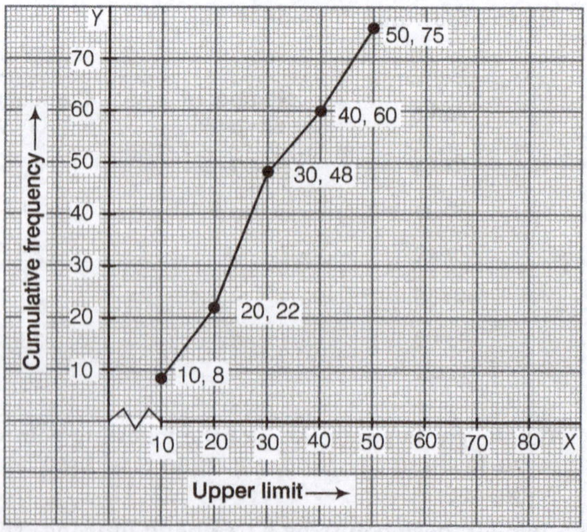

45. Hint Use scale : Along X-axis, 1 cm = 10 units and Y-axis, 1 cm = 5 units

Ans.

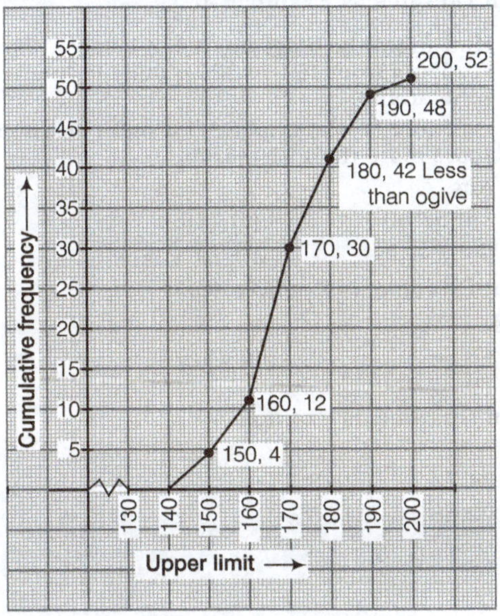

46. Hint Do same as Q. 10

Ans. (i) 13.8 (ii) 17.8 (iii) 11.8

47. Hint Do same as Example 26.

Ans. 16, 12, 4, 2

48. Hint (i) Do same as Example 13.

Ans. (i) 69 (ii) 55-60

49. Hint Here, number of observations = 10 (even)

$$\therefore \text{Median} = \frac{\text{Value of } \left(\frac{10}{2}\right)\text{th observation} + \text{Value of } \left(\frac{10}{2} + 1\right)\text{th observation}}{2}$$

$$= \frac{\text{Value of 5th observation} + \text{Value of 6th observation}}{2}$$

$$= \frac{x + x + 4}{2} = \frac{2x + 4}{2} = x + 2$$

$\because$ Median = 48 [given]

$\therefore$ $x + 2 = 48$

$\Rightarrow$ $x = 46$

$\therefore$ 5th observation = 46

and 6th observation = $x + 4 = 46 + 4 = 50$

Now, the given data is

13, 35, 43, 46, 46, 50, 55, 61, 71, 80.

Since, 46 appear maximum number of times.

Ans. $x = 46$, mode = 46

50. Hint Do same as Example 33.

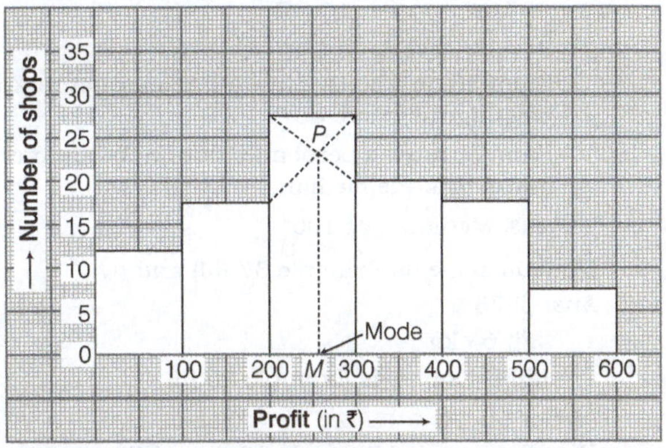

Direct calculation We observe that the class 200-300 has the maximum frequency. Therefore, 200-300 is the modal class, such that

$l = 200$, $h = 100$, $f = 27$, $f_1 = 18$ and $f_2 = 20$

$$\therefore \text{Mode} = l + \frac{f - f_1}{2f - f_1 - f_2} \times h$$

$$= 200 + \frac{27 - 18}{54 - 18 - 20} \times 100$$

Ans. Mode = 256, the value of mode is same by both method, i.e. mathematically and graphically.

51. Hint Do same as Example 37 (i).

Ans. 18.4

52. Hint Do same as Example 37 (i).

(i) Take two large baxes on X-axis = 500 and take two large boxes on Y-axis = 10 employees

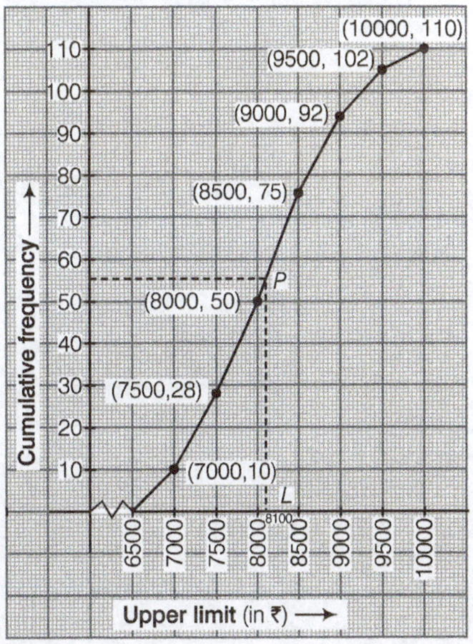

(ii) **Hint** Here, $N = 110$

$\Rightarrow \quad \frac{N}{2} = \frac{110}{2} = 55$

From 55 on Y-axis, draw a line parallel to X-axis meeting the curve at P.

From P, draw a perpendicular on X-axis meeting it at L. L is the median.

Ans. Median = ₹ 8100

53. Hint Do same as Example 37 (iii) and (iv).

Ans. (i) 78%

(ii) 65 kg

(iii) Do same as Example 36 (ii).

Ans. 150

54. Hint Do same as Example 40 (i) and (ii).

Ans. (i) 32.5

(ii) 14.5

(iii) 41

(iv) 26.5

(v) **Hint** Semi-inter quartile range,

$$L = \frac{Q_3 - Q_1}{2} = \frac{41 - 14.5}{2} = \frac{26.5}{2}$$

Ans. 13.25

55. Hint Do same as Example 40.

(iv) **Hint** From the diagram, it can be seen that students from 191 to 200 qualify for merit scholarship.

∴ Students who qualifies for merit scholarship score more than 91 marks.

Ans.

(i) 57.30 (ii) 71.80

(iii) 72 (iv) 92

56. Hint Do same as Example 40.

Ans.

(i) 43 (ii) 26.7

(iii) 10

57. Hint Do same as Example 40.

Ans.

(i) 34.73 (ii) 48.33

(iii) 22.66 (iv) 30%

Olympiad Section

Brain Teasing Questions asked in Previous Olympiads

1 Mean of a certain number of observations is m. If each observation is divided by $x(x \neq 0)$ and increased by y, then the mean of new observation is

(a) $\frac{m + xy}{x}$ (b) $\frac{m + xy}{y}$

(c) $\frac{m - xy}{x}$ (d) $\frac{m - xy}{y}$

2 If $x < y < 2x$, then the median and mean of x, y and $2x$ are 27 and 33, respectively. The mean of x and y is

(a) 25 (b) 25.1

(c) 25.2 (d) 25.5

3 In a colony, the average age of the boys is 14 yr and the average age of the girls is 17 yr. If the average age of the children in the colony is 15 yr, then the ratio of number of boys to that of girls is

(a) 1 : 2 (b) 2 : 1

(c) 1 : 1 (d) None of these

4 In a class of 20 students, 10 boys brought 11 books each and 6 girls brought 13 books each. Remaining students brought atleast one book each and no two students brought the same number of books. If the average number of books brought in the class is a positive integer, then the minimum number of books brought by the remaining students is

(a) 18 (b) 16 (c) 14 (d) 12

5 The mean expenditure of a person from Monday to Wednesday is ₹ 250 and the mean expenditure from Wednesday to Friday is ₹ 400. If he spend is ₹ 300 on Wednesday, then the mean expenditure of the person from Monday to Friday is

(a) ₹ 300 (b) ₹ 310

(c) ₹ 320 (d) ₹ 330

6 Observe the data given in three sets

P : 3, 5, 9, 12, x, 7, 2

Q : 8, 2, 1, 5, 7, 9, 3

R : 5, 9, 8, 3, 2, 7, 1

If the ratio between P's and Q's means is 7 : 5, then the ratio between P's and R's means is

(a) 5 : 7 (b) 6 : 7

(c) 7 : 5 (d) 7 : 6

7 If the ratio of mode and median of a certain data is 6 : 5, then the ratio of its mean and median is

(a) 10 : 9 (b) 9 : 10

(c) 10 : 8 (d) 8 : 10

8 If the range of 15, 14, x, 25, 30 and 35 is 23. Then, the least possible value of x is

(a) 8 (b) 10

(c) 12 (d) 14

Answers

1. (a) **2.** (d) **3.** (b) **4.** (d) **5.** (d) **6.** (c) **7.** (b) **8.** (c)

* *These questions may or may not be asked in the examination, have been given just for additional practice required for olympiads Scholarship Exams etc. For detailed explanations refer Page No. 502.*

CHAPTER

21

Probability

SYLLABUS

• Random experiments, Sample space, Events, definition of probability, Simple problems on single events.

In our daily life, we come across many statements having words 'probably, doubt, most probably, chances', etc., which involve an element of uncertainty.

e.g. (i) Most probably, it will rain today.

(ii) There is a 50–50 chance of India winning a toss in today's match.

Here, in statement (i), we are predicting rain today based on our past experience, when it was rained under similar conditions. Similar prediction is made in statement (ii).

The uncertainty or certainty of an even can be measured in terms of numbers varying from 0 to 1 by means of probability. In this chapter, we will study the concept of probability as a measure of certainty or uncertainty.

Some Basic Terms

To understand probability we need to understand some basic terms related to it, which are discussed below

Experiment

An operation which produce some well–defined outcomes, is called an experiment e.g. Tossing of a coin, throwing a die, etc.

Random Experiment

An experiment, when repeated under identical conditions, do not produce the same outcome every time, but the outcomes produced is one out of the several possible outcomes is known as a random (or probabilistic) experiment.

e.g. Tossing a fair coin is a random experiment because if we toss a coin, then either a head or a tail will come up. But if we toss a coin again and again, then the outcome each time will not be the same. Here, head and tail are called **outcomes**.

Sample Space

A set of all possible outcomes of an experiment is called a sample space. It is denoted by S. Each element of a sample space is called **sample point**.

e.g. When a die is thrown, then sample space for this experiment is $S = \{1, 2, 3, 4, 5, 6\}$.

Example 1. What is the resulting sample space, if

(i) one coin is tossed?

(ii) two coins are tossed simultaneously?

(iii) three coins are tossed simultaneously?

Sol.

(i) When a coin is tossed, then possible outcomes are H and T.

$\therefore$ Sample space, $S = \{H, T\}$

(ii) When two coins are tossed, then possible outcomes are (HH), (HT), (TH) and (TT).

∴ Sample space, $S = \{(HH), (HT), (TH), (TT)\}$

(iii) When three coins are tossed, then possible outcomes are (HHH), (HHT), (HTH), (THH), (THT), (TTH), (HTT) and (TTT).

∴ Sample space, $S = \{(HHH), (HHT), (HTH), (THH), (THT), (TTH), (HTT), (TTT)\}$

Example 2. What is the resulting sample space, if

(i) one die is rolled?

(ii) two dice is rolled?

Sol.

(i) When a die is rolled, then possible outcomes are 1, 2, 3, 4, 5 and 6.

∴ Sample space = {1, 2, 3, 4, 5, 6}

(ii) When two dice are rolled, then possible outcomes are (1, 1), (1, 2), (1, 3), (1, 4), (1, 5), (1, 6) and so on.

∴ Sample space = {(1, 1), (1, 2), (1, 3), (1, 4), (1, 5), (1, 6), (2, 1), (2, 2), (2, 3), (2, 4), (2, 5), (2, 6), (3, 1), (3, 2), (3, 3), (3, 4), (3, 5), (3, 6), (4, 1), (4, 2), (4, 3), (4, 4), (4, 5), (4, 6), (5, 1), (5, 2), (5, 3), (5, 4), (5, 5), (5, 6), (6, 1), (6, 2), (6, 3), (6, 4), (6, 5), (6, 6)}

Event

A possible outcome or combination of outcomes is called an **event**. In other words, a subset of a sample space associated with a random experiment, is called an event. It is denoted by capital letters, like E, F, etc.

e.g. Getting head in the toss of a coin is an event.

If E is an event of getting head in the toss of a coin, then $E = \{H\}$.

Occurrence of an Event

An event E associated to a random experiment is said to be occur (or happen) in a trial, if the outcome of trial is one of the outcomes that favours E.

e.g. If a die is rolled and the outcome of a trial is 4, then we can say that each of the following events has happened (or occurred)

(i) getting a number greater than 2.

(ii) getting an even number.

(iii) getting a number less than 5.

Favourable Outcomes

The outcomes which ensure the occurrence of an event are called favourable (desired) outcomes to the event.

e.g. The favourable outcomes to the occurrence of an even number, when a die is thrown, are 2, 4 and 6.

Equally Likely Outcomes

The outcomes of a random experiment are said to be equally likely, when each outcome is as likely to occur as the other, i.e. when we have no reason to believe that one is more likely to occur than the other.

e.g. When a die is thrown, all the six outcomes, i.e. 1, 2, 3, 4, 5 and 6 are equally likely to appear. So, the outcomes 1, 2, 3, 4, 5 and 6 are equally likely outcomes.

Types of Events

There are various types of events are given below

Elementary Event

An event having only one (favourable) outcome from the sample space is called an elementary event. e.g. In tossing a coin, the sample space $S = \{H, T\}$, so there are exactly two elementary events, namely $\{H\}$ and $\{T\}$.

Compound Event

A collection of two or more elementary events associated with an experiment is called compound event.

In other words, an event which has more than one (favourable) outcomes from the sample space, is called compound event. e.g. In the random experiment of tossing two coins simultaneously, the sample space, $S = \{HH, HT, TH, TT\}$ and if we define the event E as getting exactly one head, then it is a collection of elementary events (or outcomes) HT and TH, i.e. $E = \{HT, TH\}$, which is a compound event.

Complement of an Event

Let E be an event associated with an sample space S, then complement of E is the set of all those sample points of the sample space which are not in E and it is denoted by E' or $\overline{E}$.

In set form, $\overline{E}$ is written as $\{n : n \in S, n \notin E\}$. Also, E and $\overline{E}$ are called complementary events of each other.

e.g. In the random experiment of throwing a die, the sample space $S = \{1, 2, 3, 4, 5, 6\}$ and if we define the event E as getting the multiple of 3, then the complement of E, i.e. $\overline{E} = \{1, 2, 4, 5\}$.

Sure Event

An event, which is sure to occur, is called a sure event or a certain event. e.g. When we throw a die, then the event of getting a number less than 7 is a sure event.

Impossible Event

An event, which is impossible to occur, is called an impossible event. In other words, the events, which are unreliable or unlogical, are considered as impossible events.

e.g. In throwing a die, there are only six possible outcomes 1, 2, 3, 4, 5 and 6. Then, the event of getting a number less than 1 is an impossible event.

Example 3. Which of the following cannot be the probability of an event?

(i) $\frac{3}{5}$ (ii) 2.7 (iii) 43% (iv) – 0.6 (v) $2\frac{1}{2}$

Sol. (i) $\frac{3}{5}$ is lies between 0 to 1. An event which is possible.

(ii) 2.7 is greater than 1. An event which is impossible.

(iii) 43% is lies between 0 to 1. An event which is possible.

(iv) – 0.6 is less than 1, it is impossible.

(v) $2\frac{1}{2}$ is greater than 1, it is impossible.

Probability

If E is an event that happen when an experiment is performed, then the probability of the event $P(E)$ is given by

$$P(E) = \frac{\text{Number of outcomes favourable to } E}{\text{Total number of possible outcomes}}$$

e.g. When a die is thrown, then there are six possible outcomes. So, sample space, $S = \{1, 2, 3, 4, 5, 6\}$ and total number of outcomes is 6. Let E be the event of getting 4, then favourable outcome is only one, i.e. 4.

So, probability of getting 4,

$$P(E) = \frac{\text{Number of outcomes favourable to } E}{\text{Total number of possible outcomes}} = \frac{1}{6}$$

Important Results Related to Probability

(i) The probability of happening of an event (E) always varies from 0 to 1.

(ii) The sum of all the probabilities of all possible outcomes of an experiment is 1.

(iii) Probability of an impossible event is zero.

(iv) Probability of a sure event is 1.

(v) $P(E) + P(\overline{E}) = 1$ where, E represents the occurrence of an event and $\overline{E}$ represents the non–occurrence of an event.

In other words, let E and $\overline{E}$ are complementary events.

Then, $P(E) + P(\overline{E}) = 1$

or $P(\overline{E}) = 1 - P(E)$

or $P(E) = 1 - P(\overline{E})$

Different Types of Problems Based on Single Event

There are different types of problems in which we need to find the probability of an single event. To solve these problems, we required the sample space related to given problem and favourable outcomes, related to given event which depend on the object/coin/die, etc., given in the problem. Let us discuss to find the probability for the problems of the following types

Type I Problems Based on Tossing a Coin

A coin has two sides, head (H) and tail (T). If we toss one coin or more than one coin, then

(i) Sample space of one coin = $\{H, T\}$

(ii) Sample space of two coins

$= \{(H, T), (T, H), (H, H), (T, T)\}$

(iii) Sample space of three coins

$= \{(H, H, H), (H, H, T), (H, T, H), (T, H, H), (H, T, T), (T, H, T), (T, T, H), (T, T, T)\}$

Now, if given problem is related to tossing one or more than one (i.e. 2 or 3) coins simultaneously, then we can easily understand to find its probability with the help of following examples

Note (i) When we take a coin, we assume that it is to be 'fair'. Since, it is symmetrical, so there is no reason for it to come down more often on one side than the other. This property of the coin is said to be unbiased.

(ii) **Random toss of a coin** It is a phrase, which means that the coin, is allowed to fall freely without any bias or interference.

Example 4. Two unbiased coins are tossed simultaneously. Find the probability of getting (i) one head (ii) two tails (iii) exactly one tail (iv) atleast one head.

Sol. Here, two coins are tossed simultaneously.

So, sample space, $S = \{(H, T), (T, H), (H, H), (T, T)\}$

$\therefore$ Total number of possible outcomes = 4

(i) Let E_1 be the event of getting one head. Then, favourable outcomes related to E_1 are (H,T) and (T,H).

$\therefore$ Number of outcomes favourable to $E_1 = 2$

So, $P(E_1) = \dfrac{\text{Number of outcomes favourable to } E_1}{\text{Total number of possible outcomes}}$

$= \dfrac{2}{4} = \dfrac{1}{2}$

(ii) Let E_2 be the event of getting two tails. Then, favourable outcomes related to E_2 are (T,T).

$\therefore$ Number of outcomes favourable to $E_2 = 1$.

So, $P(E_2) = \dfrac{1}{4}$.

(iii) Let E_3 be the event of getting exactly one tail. Then, favourable outcomes related to E_3 are (T,H) and (H,T).

$\therefore$ Number of outcomes favourable to $E_3 = 2$

So, $P(E_3) = \dfrac{2}{4} = \dfrac{1}{2}$.

(iv) Let E_4 be the event of getting atleast one head. Then, favourable outcomes related to E_4 are (H,T), (T,H) and (H,H).

$\therefore$ Number of outcomes favourable to $E_4 = 3$

So, $P(E_4) = \dfrac{3}{4}$.

Example 5. Three unbiased coins are tossed together. Find the probability of getting

(i) all heads.
(ii) two heads.
(iii) one head.
(iv) atleast two heads.

Sol. Here, three coins are tossed simultaneously.

So, sample space,

$S = \{HHH, HHT, HTH, THH, HTT, THT, TTH, TTT\}$

$\therefore$ Total number of possible outcomes = 8

(i) Let E_1 = Event of getting all heads = $\{HHH\}$

Then, number of outcomes favourable to $E_1 = 1$

$\therefore P$ (getting all heads) = $P(E_1)$

$= \dfrac{\text{Number of outcomes favourable to } E_1}{\text{Total number of possible outcomes}} = \dfrac{1}{8}$

(ii) Let E_2 = Event of getting two heads

$= \{HHT, THH, HTH\}$

Then, number of outcomes favourable to $E_2 = 3$

$\therefore$ P (getting two heads) = $P(E_2) = \dfrac{3}{8}$

(iii) Let E_3 = Event of getting one head = $\{HTT, THT, TTH\}$

Then, number of outcomes favourable to $E_3 = 3$

$\therefore P$ (getting one head) = $P(E_3) = \dfrac{3}{8}$

(iv) Let E_4 = Event of getting atleast two heads

$= \{HHT, HTH, THH, HHH\}$

Then, number of outcomes favourable to $E_4 = 4$

$\therefore$ P (getting atleast two heads) = $P(E_4) = \dfrac{4}{8} = \dfrac{1}{2}$

Type II Problems Based on Throwing a Die

A die has six faces marked with 1, 2, 3, 4, 5 and 6. If we have more than one die, then all dice are considered as distinct, if not otherwise stated. If we throw one (or two) die (or dice), then

(i) Sample space of a die = {1, 2, 3, 4, 5, 6}

(ii) Sample space of two dice

$$= \begin{Bmatrix} (1,1), (1,2), (1,3), (1,4), (1,5), (1,6) \\ (2,1), (2,2), (2,3), (2,4), (2,5), (2,6) \\ (3,1), (3,2), (3,3), (3,4), (3,5), (3,6) \\ (4,1), (4,2), (4,3), (4,4), (4,5), (4,6) \\ (5,1), (5,2), (5,3), (5,4), (5,5), (5,6) \\ (6,1), (6,2), (6,3), (6,4), (6,5), (6,6) \end{Bmatrix}$$

To solve such type of problems, we can understand easily with the help of following examples.

Example 6. A die is tossed once. Find the probability of getting

(i) a number 4. (ii) a number greater than 4.
(iii) a number less than 4. (iv) an even number.
(v) a number greater than 6.

Sol. When a die is tossed once, then sample space,

$S = \{1, 2, 3, 4, 5, 6\}$.

So, the total number of possible outcomes = 6

(i) Let E_1 = Event of getting a number 4.

Then, the number of outcomes favourable to $E_1 = 1$

$\therefore P$ (getting a number 4) = $P(E_1)$

$= \dfrac{\text{Number of outcomes favourable to } E_1}{\text{Total number of possible outcomes}} = \dfrac{1}{6}$

(ii) Let E_2 = Event of getting a number greater than 4, i.e. 5 and 6.

Then, the number of outcomes favourable to $E_2 = 2$

$\therefore$ P (getting a number greater than 4) = $P(E_2) = \dfrac{2}{6} = \dfrac{1}{3}$

(iii) Let E_3 = Event of getting a number less than 4, i.e. 1, 2 and 3.

Then, the number of outcomes favourable to $E_3 = 3$

$\therefore P$ (getting a number less than 4) = $P(E_3) = \dfrac{3}{6} = \dfrac{1}{2}$

(iv) Let E_4 = Event of getting an even number, i.e. 2, 4 and 6.

Then, the number of outcomes favourable to $E_4 = 3$

$\therefore$ P(getting an even number) = $P(E_4) = \dfrac{3}{6} = \dfrac{1}{2}$

(v) Let E_5 = Event of getting a number greater than 6.

Then, the number of outcomes favourable to $E_5 = 0$

$\therefore$ P (getting a number greater than 6) = $P(E_5) = \dfrac{0}{6} = 0$

Note In this experiment, getting a number greater than 6 is an impossible event.

Example 7. Two dice are thrown simultaneously. Find the probability of getting an even number on one die and a multiple of 3 on the other die.

Sol. When two dice are thrown, so sample space,

$$S=\begin{Bmatrix} (1,1),(1,2),(1,3),(1,4),(1,5),(1,6) \\ (2,1),(2,2),(2,3),(2,4),(2,5),(2,6) \\ (3,1),(3,2),(3,3),(3,4),(3,5),(3,6) \\ (4,1),(4,2),(4,3),(4,4),(4,5),(4,6) \\ (5,1),(5,2),(5,3),(5,4),(5,5),(5,6) \\ (6,1),(6,2),(6,3),(6,4),(6,5),(6,6) \end{Bmatrix}$$

$\therefore$ Total number of possible outcomes = 36.

Let E be the event of getting an even number on one die and a multiple of 3 on the other die.

Here, even numbers are 2, 4 and 6 and multiples of 3 are 3 and 6.

So, outcomes favourable to E are {(2, 3), (4, 3), (6, 3), (2, 6), (4, 6), (6, 6), (3, 2), (3, 4), (3, 6), (6, 2) and (6, 4)}

$\therefore$ Number of outcomes favourable to E = 11.

Now, required probability,

$$P(E)=\frac{\text{Number of outcomes favourable to } E}{\text{Total number of possible outcomes}}=\frac{11}{36}$$

Type III Problems Based on Playing Cards

A deck of playing cards consists of 52 cards out of which 26 are black cards and other 26 are red cards, where red cards consist of 13 cards of heart (♥), 13 cards of diamond (♦) and black cards consist of 13 cards of spades (♠) and 13 cards of club (♣).

Thus, 52 playing cards are divided into four parts (called suits) of 13 cards each, namely heart, diamond, spades and club.

Also, 13 cards in each suit are ace, king, queen, jack, 10, 9, 8, 7, 6, 5, 4, 3 and 2.

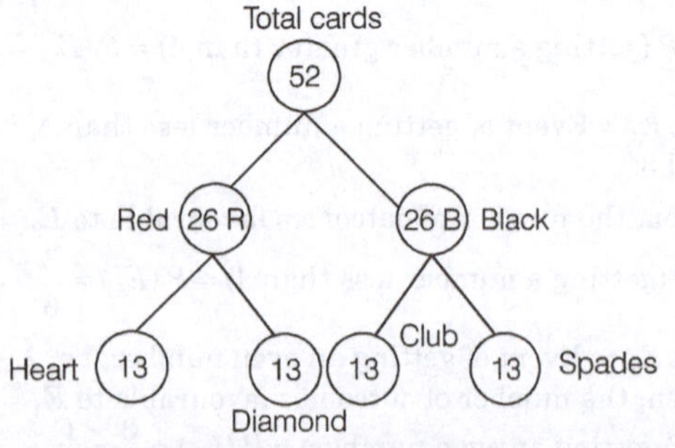

Tree diagram of playing cards

Face cards King, Queen and Jack are called face cards.

So, total face cards = 12

To solve such type of problem, we can understand easily with the help of following examples

Example 8. A card is drawn from a well-shuffled pack of 52 playing cards. Find the probability that the card drawn is

(i) a diamond. (ii) an ace or a queen. (iii) Jack of heart.

Sol. The total number of cards in one pack of cards is 52.

$\therefore$ Total number of possible outcomes = 52.

(i) Let E_1 = Event of drawing a diamond card.

$\therefore$ Number of outcomes favourable to E_1 = 13

So, P (drawing a diamond card)

$$P(E_1)=\frac{\text{Number of outcomes favourable to } E_1}{\text{Total number of possible outcomes}}$$

$$\Rightarrow \quad P(E_1)=\frac{13}{52}=\frac{1}{4}$$

(ii) Let E_2 = Event of drawing an ace or a queen card.

$\therefore$ Number of outcomes favourable to E_2 = 4 + 4 = 8

So, P (drawing an ace or a queen) $= P(E_2)=\frac{8}{52}=\frac{2}{13}$

(iii) Let E_3 = Event of drawing a jack of heart.

$\therefore$ Number of outcomes favourable to E_3 = 1

So, P (drawing a jack of heart) $= P(E_3)=\frac{1}{52}$.

Example 9. One card is drawn from a well-shuffled deck of 52 cards. Find the probability of getting

(i) a king of red colour. (ii) a face card.

(iii) a red face card. (iv) the queen of diamonds.

Sol. Total number of cards in one deck of cards is 52.

$\therefore$ Total number of possible outcomes = 52

(i) Let E_1 = Event of getting a king of red colour.

$\therefore$ Number of outcomes favourable to E_1 = 2

[$\because$ there are four kings in a deck, in which two are red and two are black]

Hence, $P(E_1)=\frac{\text{Number of outcomes favourable to } E_1}{\text{Total number of possible outcomes}}$

$=\frac{2}{52}=\frac{1}{26}$

(ii) Let E_2 = Event of getting a face card.

Then, number of outcomes favourable to E_2 = 12

[$\because$ in a deck of cards, there are 12 face cards, namely, 4 kings, 4 jacks and 4 queens]

Hence, $P(E_2)=\frac{12}{52}=\frac{3}{13}$.

(iii) Let E_3 = Event of getting a red face card.

Then, number of outcomes favourable to E_3 = 6

[$\because$ in a deck of cards, there are 12 face cards in which 6 red and 6 black]

Hence, $P(E_3)=\frac{6}{52}=\frac{3}{26}$.

(iv) Let E_4 = Event of getting the queen of diamonds.

Then, number of outcomes favourable to E_4 = 1

[$\because$ in a deck of cards, there are 13 diamond cards, in which there is only one queen]

Hence, $P(E_4)=\frac{1}{52}$.

Type IV Problems Based on Selection of an Object from a Bag/Box

In these types of problems, we need to find the probability of selecting an item/object such as ball, marble, orange, bulb, etc., from a bag/box which have these items/objects in more than one colour/type.

This type of problem can easily understand with the help of following examples

Example 10. Three bags containing 10 orange, 10 green and 10 red balls, respectively are mixed together in one large bag. If one of the ball is taken out at random without looking into the bag, then what is the probability that it is (i) orange or green (ii) not orange?

Sol. Given, number of orange balls = 10

Number of green balls = 10

and number of red balls = 10

Since, all balls are mixed in one large bag.

So, total number of balls in large bag = 10 + 10 + 10 = 30

$\therefore$ Total number of possible outcomes = 30

(i) Let E be the event of selecting an orange or green ball. Since, there are 10 orange and 10 green balls, out of which one can be select in 20 ways.

Then, number of outcomes favourable to E = 20

$\therefore$ P (getting orange or green ball) = $P(E)$

$$= \frac{\text{Number of outcomes favourable to } E}{\text{Total number of possible outcomes}} = \frac{20}{30} = \frac{2}{3}$$

(ii) Let F be the event of selecting a ball which is not orange. Since, there are 10 green and 10 red balls, so one ball which is not orange can be select in 20 ways.

Then, number of outcomes favourable to F = 20

$\therefore$ P (getting not orange ball) = $P(F) = \frac{20}{30} = \frac{2}{3}$

Example 11. A bag contains 5 white, 2 red and 3 black balls. A ball is drawn at random. What is the probability that the ball drawn is a red ball? **[ICSE Semsester II 2022]**

Sol. Given, number of white balls = 5

Number of red balls = 2

and number of black balls = 3

Total number of balls in the bag = 5 + 2 + 3 = 10

Number of red balls = 2

$\therefore$ Probability of getting a red ball

$$= \frac{\text{Number of favourable outcomes}}{\text{Total number of outcomes}}$$

$$= \frac{2}{10} = \frac{1}{5}$$

Example 12. There are 25 discs numbered 1 to 25. They are put in a closed box and shaken thoroughly. A disc is drawn at random from the box. Find the probability that the number on the disc is

(i) an odd number.

(ii) divisible by 2 and 3 both.

(iii) a number less than 16. **[ICSE 2019]**

Sol. (i) Total number of discs in a box, $n(S) = 25$

Odd number of discs,

$$E = \{1, 3, 5, 7, 9, 11, 13, 15, 17, 19, 21, 23, 25\}$$

$\therefore$ $n(E) = 13$

$\therefore$ Probability of getting odd number $= \frac{n(E)}{n(S)} = \frac{13}{25}$

(ii) Number divisible by 2 and 3 i.e. 6,

$$E_1 = \{6, 12, 18, 24\}$$

$\therefore$ $n(E_1) = 4$

$\therefore$ Probability of getting the number divisible by 2 and 3

$$= \frac{n(E_1)}{n(S)} = \frac{4}{25}$$

(iii) Number less than 16, $E_2 = \{1, 2, ..., 15\}$

$\therefore$ $n(E_2) = 15$

$\therefore$ Probability of getting a number less than 16

$$= \frac{n(E_2)}{n(S)} = \frac{15}{25} = \frac{3}{5}$$

Example 13. A bag contains 5 white balls, 6 red balls and 9 green balls. A ball is drawn at random from the bag. Find the probability that the ball drawn is

(i) a green ball. (ii) a white or a red ball.

(iii) neither a green ball nor a white ball. **[ICSE 2015]**

Sol. Given, a bag contains 5 white balls, 6 red balls and 9 green balls.

$\therefore$ Total number of possible outcomes = 5 + 6 + 9 = 20

(i) Let G be the event of getting a green ball.

Then, number of outcomes favourable to G = 9

$\therefore$ Probability of drawing a green ball $= P(G) = \frac{9}{20}$

(ii) Let F be the event of getting a white or a red ball.

Then, number of outcomes favourable to F = 5 + 6 = 11

$\therefore$ Probability of drawing a white or red ball

$$= P(F) = \frac{11}{20}$$

(iii) Let E be the event of getting neither a green ball nor a white ball, i.e. getting a red ball.

Then, number of outcomes favourable to E = 6

$\therefore$ Probability of drawing neither a green ball nor a white ball

$$= P(E) = \frac{6}{20} = \frac{3}{10}$$

Type V Problems Based on Geometry

In this type of problems, a geometrical figure is given to us and we have to find the probability that, a given element lies inside the small part of the geometrical figure. For this, we first find the area/volume of both geometrical figures (small and big) separately and then find the required probability by taking area/volume of small part as number of favourable outcomes and area/volume of whole part as total number of possible outcomes.

To solve such type of problem, we can understand easily with the help of following example

Example 14. A missing helicopter is reported to have crashed somewhere in the rectangular region shown in figure. What is the probability that it crashed inside the lake shown in the figure?

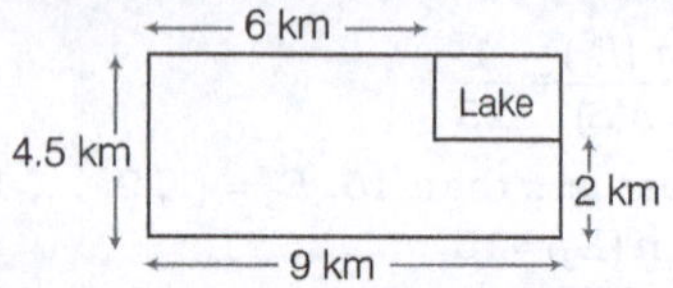

Sol. Here, the helicopter is equally likely to crash anywhere in the region. The given geometrical figure is a rectangle and its small part, i.e. lake is also a rectangle.

For rectangular region,

Length = 9 km and Breadth = 4.5 km

$\therefore$ Area of entire rectangular region,

where the helicopter can crash $= 4.5 \times 9 = 40.5\ \text{km}^2$

For rectangular lake,

Length = 9 − 6 = 3 km

Breadth = 4.5 − 2 = 2.5 km

$\therefore$ Area of the lake $= 2.5 \times 3 = 7.5\ \text{km}^2$

Hence, probability that helicopter crashed inside the lake

$$= \frac{\text{Area of the lake}}{\text{Area of entire rectangular region, where the helicopter can crash}}$$

$$= \frac{7.5}{40.5} = \frac{75}{405} = \frac{5}{27}$$

Type VI Miscellaneous Problems

Sometimes, the given problem is not of the type I to V which are discussed before. To solve these problems, first find the possible outcomes for these problems very carefully and then find the outcomes favourable to the given event for which we want to find the probability. Now, use the definition of probability, i.e. to calculate the required probability.

Probability

$$= \frac{\text{Number of outcomes favourable to the given event}}{\text{Total number of possible outcomes}}$$

Example 15. Two players Neha and Shivani play a tennis match. It is known that the probability of Neha winning the match is 0.62. What is the probability of Shivani winning the match?

Sol. Let E and F denote the events that Neha and Shivani win the match, respectively. It is clear that, if Neha wins the match, then Shivani losses the match and if Shivani wins the match, then Neha losses the match. Thus, E and F are complementary events.

$$\therefore \quad P(E) + P(F) = 1$$

Since, probability of Neha's winning the match,

i.e. $P(E) = 0.62$

$\therefore$ Probability of Shivani's winning the match,

$$P(F) = P\,(\text{Neha losses the match})$$
$$= 1 - P(E) \quad [\because P(E) + P(F) = 1]$$
$$= 1 - 0.62 = 0.38$$

Example 16. 12 defective pens are accidentally mixed with 132 good ones. It is not possible to just look at a pen and tell whether or not it is defective. One pen is taken out at random from this lot. Determine the probability that the pen taken out is a good one.

Sol. Total number of pens = 12 defective pens + 132 good pens = 144 pens

$\therefore$ Total number of possible outcomes = 144

Let E be the event of selecting a good pen.

Then, number of outcomes favourable to $E = 132$

$\therefore$ Probability of selecting a good pen, $P(E) = \dfrac{132}{144} = \dfrac{11}{12}$

Example 17. A lot consists of 48 mobile phones of which 42 are good, 3 have only minor defect and 3 have major defect. Varnika will buy a phone, if it is good but the trader will only buy a mobile, if it has no major defect. One phone is selected at random from the lot. What is the probability that it is

(i) acceptable to Varnika?

(ii) acceptable to the trader?

Sol. Given, total number of mobile phones is 48.

So, number of possible outcomes = 48

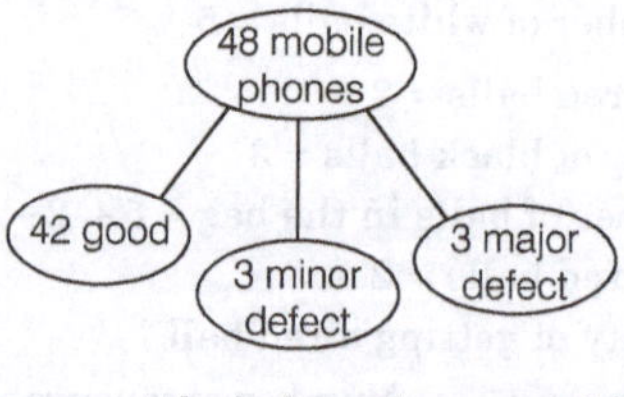

(i) Let E_1 be the event that phone is acceptable to Varnika, i.e. E_1 be the event of getting a good phone.

$\therefore$ Number of outcomes favourable to $E_1 = 42$

Hence, probability that phone is acceptable to Varnika,

$$P(E_1) = \frac{42}{48} = \frac{7}{8}$$

(ii) Let E_2 be the event that phone is acceptable to the trader, i.e. E_2 be the event of getting a good phone or a phone with minor defect.

$\therefore$ Number of outcomes favourable to E_2

= Number of good phones + Number of phone with minor defect

$= 42 + 3 = 45$

Hence, probability that phone is acceptable to the trader,

$$P(E_2) = \frac{45}{48} = \frac{15}{16}$$

Example 18. Savita and Hamida are friends. What is the probability that both will have

(i) the same birthday?

(ii) different birthdays? (ignoring a leap year)

Sol. There are 365 days in a year, so Savita's birthday can be at any day of 365 days in the year.

Similarly, Hamida's birthday can be at any day of 365 days in the year.

So, total number of possible outcomes $= 365 \times 365$

(i) If both have same birthday, then the number of outcomes favourable for their birthday = 365

$\therefore$ P (Savita and Hamida have same birthday)

$$= \frac{365}{365 \times 365} = \frac{1}{365}$$

(ii) P (Savita and Hamida have different birthdays)

$= 1 - P$ (Savita and Hamida have same birthday)

$[\because P(E) + P(\bar{E}) = 1]$

$$= 1 - \frac{1}{365} = \frac{364}{365}$$

Example 19. An integer is chosen between 0 and 100. What is the probability that it is

(i) divisible by 7? (ii) not divisible by 7?

Sol. The total number of integers between 0 and 100 is 99.

$\therefore$ Total number of possible outcomes = 99

(i) Let E_1 = Event of choosing an integer which is divisible by 7

$= \{7, 14, 21, 28, 35, 42, 49, 56, 63, 70, 77, 84, 91, 98\}$

Then, number of outcomes favourable to $E_1 = 14$

Hence, required probability $= P(E_1) = \frac{14}{99}$

(ii) Let E_2 = Event of choosing an integer which is not divisible by 7.

Then, number of outcomes favourable to

$E_2 = 99 - 14 = 85$

$\therefore$ Required probability $= P(E_2) = \frac{85}{99}$

Example 20. A game of numbers has cards marked with 11, 12, 13,..., 40. A card is drawn at random. Find the probability that the number on the card drawn is

(i) a perfect square

(ii) divisible by 7 **[ICSE 2016]**

Sol. Given cards marked with number

11, 12, 13, 14, ..., 40.

Total number of cards = 30

$\therefore$ Total number of possible outcomes = 30

(i) A perfect square number = {16, 25, 36}

$\therefore$ Number of outcomes favourable to event = 3

So, required probability $= \frac{3}{30} = \frac{1}{10}$

(ii) Number divisible by 7 = {14, 21, 28, 35}

$\therefore$ Number of outcomes favourable to event = 4

So, required probability $= \frac{4}{30} = \frac{2}{15}$

Example 21. A box contains 17 cards numbered, 1, 2, 3, ... , 17 and are mixed thoroughly. A card is drawn at random from the box. Find the probability that the number on the card is

(i) odd (ii) even

(iii) prime (iv) divisible by 3

(v) divisible by 3 and 2 both

(vi) divisible by 3 or 2

Sol. The cards are mixed thoroughly and a card is drawn at random from the box, means that all the outcomes are equally likely. As the box contains 17 cards, total number of possible outcomes = 17

(i) Let E be the event of getting 'the number on the card is odd'. Then, the outcomes favourable to E are 1, 3, 5, 7, 9, 11, 13, 15, 17.

$\therefore$ Number of outcomes favourable to $E = 9$

$\therefore$ P (drawing card is odd) $= P(E) = \frac{9}{17}$

(ii) Let F be the event of getting 'the number on the card is even'. Then, the outcomes favourable to F are 2, 4, 6, 8, 10, 12, 14, 16.

$\therefore$ Number of outcomes favourable to $F = 8$

$\therefore$ P (drawing card is even) $= P(F) = \frac{8}{17}$

(iii) Let G be the event of getting 'the number on the card is prime'. Then, the outcomes favourable to the event are 2, 3, 5, 7, 11, 13, 17.

$\therefore$ Number of outcomes favourable to $G = 7$

$\therefore$ P (drawing card is prime) $= P(G) = \frac{7}{17}$

(iv) Let H be the event of getting 'the number on the card is divisible by 3'. Then, the outcomes favourable to the event are 3, 6, 9, 12, 15.

$\therefore$ Number of outcomes favourable to $H = 5$

$\therefore$ P (drawing card is divisible by 3) $= P(H) = \frac{5}{17}$

(v) Let I be the event of getting 'the number on the card is divisible by 3 and 2 both'. Then, the outcomes favourable to the event are 6 and 12.

$\therefore$ Number of outcomes favourable to $I = 2$

$\therefore$ P (drawing card is divisible by 3 and 2 both)

$$= P(I) = \frac{2}{17}$$

(vi) Let J be the event of getting 'the number on the card is divisible by 3 or 2'. Then, the outcomes favourable to the event are 2, 3, 4, 6, 8, 9, 10, 12, 14, 15, 16.

$\therefore$ Number of outcomes favourable to $J = 11$

$\therefore$ P (drawing card is divisible by 3 or 2)

$$= P(J) = \frac{11}{17}$$

Example 22. A letter of the word 'SECONDARY' is selected at random. What is the probability that the letter selected is not a vowel? **[ICSE Semester II 2022]**

Sol. Given, total number of letters in the word 'SECONDARY' $= 9$

Total number of consonant present in the given word = 6

So, probability of the letter selected is not a vowel in the given word $= \frac{6}{9} = \frac{2}{3}$

Example 23. Each of the letters of the word 'AUTHORIZES' is written on identical circular disc and put in a bag. They are well shuffled. If a disc is drawn at random from the bag, what is the probability that the letter is

(i) a vowel?

(ii) one of the first 9 letters of the English alphabet which appears in the given word?

(iii) one of the last 9 letters of the English alphabet which appears in the given word? **[ICSE 2020]**

Sol. Given, word 'AUTHORIZES' so, total number of identical circular discs = 10

(i) Here vowels are A, U, O, I, E

Total number of vowel = 5

$\therefore$ Required probability

$$= \frac{5}{10} = \frac{1}{2}$$

(ii) One of the first 9 letters of the English alphabet which appears in the given word are A, H, I, E

$\therefore$ Required probability

$$= \frac{4}{10} = \frac{2}{5}$$

(iii) One of the last 9 letters of the English alphabets which appears in the given word are U, T, R, Z, S

$\therefore$ Required probability

$$= \frac{5}{10} = \frac{1}{2}$$

Example 24. Sixteen cards are labelled as *a, b, c,..., m, n, o, p*. They are put in a box and shuffled. A boy is asked to draw a card from the box. What is the probability that the card drawn is

(i) a vowel?

(ii) a consonant?

(iii) none of the letters of the word 'median'? **[ICSE 2017]**

Sol. Total number of cards = 16

$\therefore$ Total number of possible outcomes = 16

Clearly, the cards labelled a, e, i, o are vowels and rest 12 are consonant.

(i) There are 4 ways of drawing a vowel card.

$\therefore$ Number of outcomes favourable to event = 4

So, probability of drawing a vowel card $= \frac{4}{16} = \frac{1}{4}$

(ii) There are 12 ways of drawing a consonant card.

$\therefore$ Number of outcomes favourable to event = 12

So, probability of drawing a consonant card $= \frac{12}{16} = \frac{3}{4}$

(iii) Number of cards not labelled with letters of the word median $= 16 - 6 = 10$

Then, number of ways of drawing a card not labelled with letters of the word median = 10

$\therefore$ Number of outcomes favourable to event = 10

So, probability of drawing a card not labelled with letters of the word median $= \frac{10}{16} = \frac{5}{8}$

Example 25. If 65% of the population have black eyes, 25% have brown eyes and the remaining have blue eyes, then what is the probability that a person selected at random has

(i) blue eyes? (ii) brown or black eyes?

(iii) neither blue nor brown eyes?

Sol. Given, 65% of the population have black eyes, 25% have brown eyes and the remaining $(100 - 65 - 25)\%$, i.e. 10% have blue eyes.

Let the total number of people be 100, then 65 have black eyes, 25 have brown eyes and 10 have blue eyes. Therefore, the sample space of the experiment has 100 equally likely outcomes.

$\therefore$ Total number of possible outcomes = 100

(i) Let the event be 'have blue eyes'. As 10 people have blue eyes.

So, the number of outcomes favourable to the event 'have blue eyes' = 10.

$$\therefore P\text{ (blue eyes)} = \frac{10}{100} = \frac{1}{10}$$

(ii) Let the event be 'have brown or black eyes'.

Then, number of persons who have brown or black eyes

$$= 25 + 65 = 90$$

So, the number of outcomes favourable to the event 'have brown or black eyes' = 90.

$$\therefore P\text{(brown or black eyes)} = \frac{90}{100} = \frac{9}{10}$$

(iii) The event 'have neither blue nor brown eyes' mean have black eyes.

Thus, number of persons who have neither blue nor brown eyes = Number of persons who have black eyes = 65

So, the number of outcomes favourable to the event 'have neither blue nor brown eyes' = 65

$$\therefore P\text{ (neither blue nor brown eyes)} = \frac{65}{100} = \frac{13}{20}$$

Example 26. A child's game has 8 triangles of which 3 are blue and rest are red, and 10 squares of which 6 are blue and rest are red. If one piece is lost at random, then find the probability that it is a

(i) triangle.
(ii) square.
(iii) square of blue colour.
(iv) triangle of red colour.

Sol. A child's game has 8 triangular pieces and 10 squared pieces.

So, total number of pieces in the game = 8 + 10 = 18.
One piece is lost at random means that all pieces are equally likely to be lost.
Therefore, the sample space of the experiment has 18 equally likely outcomes.

∴ Total number of possible outcomes = 18

(i) Number of triangular pieces = 8

$$\therefore \quad P\text{ (triangle)} = \frac{8}{18} = \frac{4}{9}$$

(ii) Number of squared pieces = 10

$$\therefore \quad P\text{ (square)} = \frac{10}{18} = \frac{5}{9}$$

(iii) Number of blue squared pieces = 6

$$\therefore \quad P\text{ (square of blue colour)} = \frac{6}{18} = \frac{1}{3}$$

(iv) Number of red coloured triangular pieces
= Total number of triangular pieces − Blue coloured triangular pieces
= 8 − 3 = 5

$$\therefore \quad P\text{(triangle of red colour)} = \frac{5}{18}$$

Example 27. In a musical chair game, the person playing the music has been advised to stop playing the music at any time within 2 min after she starts playing. What is the probability that the music will stop within the first half-minute after starting?

Sol. Since, the music is stopped at any time within 2 min. So, the possible outcomes are all real numbers (representing minute) between 0 and 2 which are represented on the number line.

Let E be the event that the music is stopped within the first half-minute. Then, outcomes favourable to E are points on the number line from 0 to $\frac{1}{2}$.

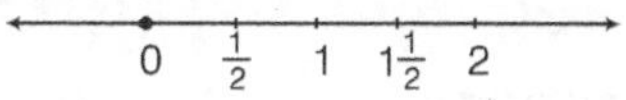

Here, all the outcomes are equally likely.

∴ Total number of possible outcomes
= Total distance from 0 to 2 = 2

∵ Number of outcomes favourable to E
= Distance from 0 to $\frac{1}{2} = \frac{1}{2}$

Now, required probability $= P(E) = \frac{1/2}{2} = \frac{1}{4}$.

Example 28. Three-digit numbers are made using the digits 4, 5, 9 (without repetition). If a number among them is selected at random, then what is the probability that the number will

(i) be a multiple of 5?
(ii) be a multiple of 9?
(iii) end with 9?

Sol. Here, three-digit numbers made from the digits 4, 5, 9 (without repetition) are 459, 495, 549, 594, 945, 954.

∴ Sample space, S = {459, 495, 549, 594, 945, 954}
The sample space has 6 equally likely outcomes.
∴ Total number of possible outcomes = 6

(i) Let E be the event of getting a multiple of 5, then E = {495, 945}.
So, number of outcomes favourable to E = 2
∴ $P(E) = P$ (a multiple of 5) $= \frac{2}{6} = \frac{1}{3}$

(ii) Let F be the event of getting a multiple of 9.
∵ All the six numbers are divisible by 9.
So, number of outcomes favourable to F = 9
∴ P (a multiple of 9) $= \frac{6}{6} = 1$

(iii) Let G be the event of getting the number end with 9.
Since, the numbers that end with 9 are 459, 549.
So, number of outcomes favourable to G = 2
∴ P (end with 9) $= \frac{2}{6} = \frac{1}{3}$

Chapter Practice

a. 1 Mark Questions

1. The probability of getting a number divisible by 3 in throwing a dice is

(a) $\frac{1}{6}$ (b) $\frac{1}{3}$ (c) $\frac{1}{2}$ (d) $\frac{2}{3}$

2. Two unbiased coins are tossed simultaneously then the probability of getting no head is $\frac{A}{B}$, then $(A+B)^2$ is equal to

(a) 1 (b) 4 (c) 5 (d) 25

3. A letter is chosen at random from all the letters of the English alphabets. The probability that the letter chosen is a vowel, is **[ICSE 2023]**

(a) $\frac{4}{26}$ (b) $\frac{5}{26}$ (c) $\frac{21}{26}$ (d) $\frac{5}{24}$

4. If a number x is chosen at random from the numbers $-2, -1, 0, 1, 2$. Then, the probability that $x^2 < 2$ is

(a) $\frac{2}{5}$ (b) $\frac{4}{5}$ (c) $\frac{1}{5}$ (d) $\frac{3}{5}$

5. Tickets numbered from 1 to 20 are mixed up together and then a ticket is drawn at random, then the probability that the ticket has a number which is a multiple of 3 or 7, is

(a) $\frac{2}{5}$ (b) $\frac{3}{5}$ (c) $\frac{4}{5}$ (d) $\frac{1}{5}$

6. Ramesh buys a fish from a shop for his aquarium. The shopkeeper takes out one fish at random a tank containing 5 male fish and 9 female fish. Then, the probability that the fish taken out is a male fish, is

(a) $\frac{5}{13}$ (b) $\frac{5}{14}$ (c) $\frac{6}{13}$ (d) $\frac{7}{13}$

7. A number x is selected from the numbers 1,2,3 and then a second number y is randomly selected from the numbers 1,4,9, then the probability that the product xy of the two numbers will be less than 9 is

(a) $\frac{3}{7}$ (b) $\frac{4}{9}$ (c) $\frac{5}{9}$ (d) $\frac{7}{9}$

8. A bag contains 3 red and 2 blue marbles. If a marble is drawn at random, then the probability of drawing a blue marble is

(a) $\frac{1}{5}$ (b) $\frac{2}{5}$ (c) $\frac{3}{5}$ (d) $\frac{4}{5}$

9. A bag contains 8 red balls and some blue balls. If the probability of drawing a blue ball is three times of a red ball, then the number of blue balls in the bag

(a) 12 (b) 18 (c) 24 (d) 36

10. There are 1000 sealed envelopes in a box, 10 of them contain a cash prize of ₹ 100 each, 100 of them contain a cash prize of ₹ 50 each and 200 of them contain a cash prize of ₹ 10 each and rest do not contain any cash prize. If they are well-shuffled and an envelope is picked up out, then the probability that the envelope contains no cash prize is

(a) 0.65 (b) 0.69 (c) 0.54 (d) 0.57

11. Two dice are thrown together. The probability that sum of the two numbers will be a multiple of 4, is

(a) $\frac{1}{2}$ (b) $\frac{1}{3}$ (c) $\frac{1}{8}$ (d) $\frac{1}{4}$

b. 3 Marks Questions

12. In a simultaneous toss of two coins, find the probability of exactly one head.

13. A coin is tossed two times. Find the probability of getting atmost one head.

14. Two coins are tossed once. Find the probability of getting

(i) 2 heads.

(ii) atleast 1 tail. **[ICSE 2012]**

15. In a game, the entry fee is ₹5. The game consists of tossing a coin 3 times. If one or two heads show, Sweta gets her entry fee back. If she tosses 3 heads, she receives double the entry fee. Otherwise, she will loss. For tossing a coin three times, find the probability that she

(i) losses the entry fee.

(ii) gets double entry fee.

(iii) just gets her entry fee.

16. Three different coins are tossed together. Find the probability of getting

(i) exactly two heads.

(ii) atleast two heads.

(iii) atleast two tails.

17. A die is thrown once. Find the probability of getting an even number less than 5.

18. If a die is thrown, what is the probability of getting a number less than 3 and greater than 2?

19. If two dice are thrown, then find the probability of getting an odd number on one and multiple of 3 on other die.

20. A die is thrown once. Find the probability of getting a number which is not a factor of 36.

21. Two dice are thrown at the same time. Find the probability that the sum of the two numbers appearing on the top of the dice is more than 9.

22. A child has a die whose six faces shows the letters as given below

A	B	C	D	E	F

The die is thrown once. What is the probability of getting

(i) *A*? (ii) *D*?

23. A die is thrown once. Find the probability of getting
   (i) a prime number.
   (ii) a number lying between 2 and 6.
   (iii) an odd number.

24. A die has its six faces marked 0, 1, 1, 1, 6, 6. Two such dice are thrown together and the total score is recorded.
   (i) How many different scores are possible?
   (ii) What is the probability of getting a total of 7?

25. Two dice are thrown at the same time and the product of numbers appearing on them is noted. Find the probability that the product is less than 9.

26. Two dice are thrown simultaneously. What is the probability that the sum of the numbers appearing on the dice, is
   (i) 7? (ii) not a prime number?
   (iii) 1?

27. Two dice are thrown together. Find the probability that the product of the numbers on the top of the dice is
   (i) 6 (ii) 12 (iii) 7

28. A pair of dice is thrown once. Find the probability of getting
   (i) doublet of prime numbers.
   (ii) a doublet of odd numbers.

29. From a pack of 52 playing cards, whose numbers are multiples of 3 are removed. A card is now drawn at random. What is the probability that the card drawn is
   (i) a face card (king, jack or queen)?
   (ii) an even numbered red card? **[ICSE 2011]**

30. A card is drawn from a well-shuffled pack of 52 cards. Find the probability that the card drawn is neither a red card nor a queen.

31. The king queen and jack of clubs are removed from a deck of 52 playing cards and then well-shuffled. Now, one card is drawn at random from the remaining cards. Find the probability of getting a card of
   (i) a heart (ii) a king

32. One card is drawn from a pack of 52 cards, each of the 52 cards being equally likely to be drawn. Find the probability that the card drawn is
   (i) a red king.
   (ii) '2' of spade.
   (iii) '10' of a black suit.

33. Cards marked with numbers 5 to 75 are placed in a box and mixed thoroughly. One card is drawn from the box. Find the probability that the number on the card is odd.

34. A box contains some black balls and 30 white balls. If the probability of drawing a black ball is two-fifth of a white ball, then find the number of black balls in the box. **[ICSE 2013]**

35. A bag contains 25 cards, numbered through 1 to 25. A card is drawn at random. What is the probability that the number on the card drawn is **[ICSE 2023]**
   (i) a multiple of 5
   (ii) a perfect square
   (iii) a prime number?

36. A bag contains 2 green, 3 red and 4 black balls. A ball is taken out of the bag at random. Find the probability that the selected ball is
   (i) not green (ii) not black

37. Box *A* contains 25 slips of which 19 are marked ₹ 1 and other are marked ₹ 5. Box *B* contains 50 slips of which 45 are marked ₹ 1 and others are marked ₹ 13. Slips of both boxes are put into a third box and reshuffled. A slip is drawn at random. What is the probability that it is marked other than ₹ 1?

38. A box contains a certain number of balls. Some of these balls are marked *A*, some are marked *B* and the remainings are marked *C*. When a ball is drawn at random from the box $P(A) = \frac{1}{3}$ and $P(B) = \frac{1}{4}$. If there are 40 balls in the box which are marked *C*, find the number of balls in the box.

39. In a box contain 40 electric rods in which 30 are goods, 4 have minor defect and 6 have major defect Anita will buy a electric rod, if it is good but the trader will only buy a electric rod, if it has no major defect. If one electric rod is selected at random from the lot, then what is the probability that it is
(i) acceptable to Anita?
(ii) acceptable to the trader?

40. There are 100 cards in a bag on which numbers from 1 to 100 are written. A card is taken out from the bag at random. Find the probability that the number on the selected card
(i) is divisible by 9 and is a perfect square.
(ii) is a prime number greater than 80.

41. A bag contains 24 balls of which x are red, $2x$ are white and $3x$ are blue. A ball is selected at random. What is the probability that it is
(i) not red?
(ii) white?

42. An urn contains 10 red balls, 6 blue balls and 4 green balls. Three balls are drawn, one-by-one, without replacement. Find the probability that
(i) first ball is red
(ii) second ball is red
(iii) third ball is green

43. A bag contains 18 balls out of which x balls are red.
(i) If one ball is drawn at random from the bag, what is the probability that it is red ball?
(ii) If 2 more red balls are put in the bag, the probability of drawing a red ball will be 9/8 times that of probability of red ball coming in part (i). Find the value of x.

44. A jar contains 81 balls each of which is red, white or orange. The probability of selecting a red ball is $\frac{2}{3}$ and that of white is $\frac{1}{9}$. How many orange balls does the jar contain.

45. A rectangle of dimension 2 cm × 4 cm is drawn in one of the corner of square of side 10 cm and shaded as shown in the adjoining figure. A point is selected at random from the interior of square $ABCD$. What is the probability that the point will be chosen from the shaded part?

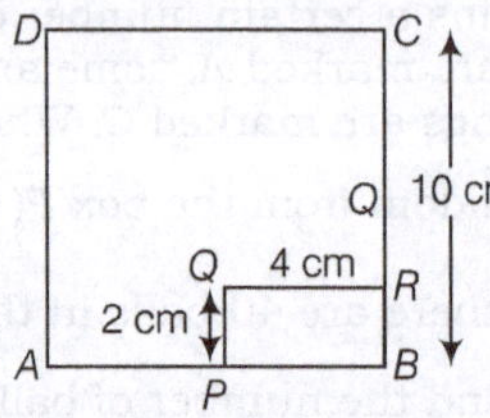

46. A circle with diameter 20 cm is drawn somewhere on a rectangular piece of paper with length 40 cm and width 30 cm. This paper is kept horizontal on table top and a dice, very small in size, is dropped on the rectangular paper without seeing towards it. If the dice falls and lands on the paper only, find the probability that it will fall and land
(i) inside the circle (ii) outside the circle

47. A number is chosen from 1 to 100. Find the probability that it is a prime number.

48. The probability of getting a rotten egg from a lot of 400 eggs is 0.035. Find the number of rotten eggs in the lot.

49. A single letter is selected at random from the word 'PROBABILITY'. Find the probability that it is a vowel.

50. A letter of English alphabet is chosen at random. Determine the probability that the letter is a consonant.

51. A letter is chosen at random from the English alphabet. What is the probability that it is a letter of the word 'RAMANUJAN'?

52. Rajesh chooses a data at random in December for a party (see the following figure).

December						
M	T	W	T	F	S	S
		1	2	3	4	5
6	7	8	9	10	11	12
13	14	15	16	17	18	19
20	21	22	23	24	25	26
27	28	29	30	31		

Find the probability that he chooses
(i) a Wednesday (ii) a Friday
(iii) a Thursday or a Saturday

53. Find the probability of having 53 Sunday in
(i) a non-leap year
(ii) a leap year

54. Find the probability that a non-leap year selected at random will contain 53 Friday.

55. Two friends were born in the year 2000. What is the probability that they have the same birthday?

56. A school has five houses A, B, C, D and E. A class has 23 students, 4 from house A, 8 from house B, 5 from house C, 2 from house D and rest from house E. A single student is selected at random to be the class monitor. Find the probability that the selected students is not from A, B and C.

c. 4/5 Marks Questions

57. The probability of guessing the correct answer to certain question is $p/12$. If the probability of not guessing the correct answer to same question is $3/4$, then find the value of p.

58. A girl calculates that the probability of her winning the first prize in a lottery is 0.08. If 6000 tickets are sold, then how many tickets has she bought?

59. Malini buys a fish from a shop for her aquarium. The shopkeeper takes out one fish at random from a tank containing 5 male fish and 8 female fish. What is the probability that the fish taken out is a male fish?

60. A book contain 85 pages. A page is chosen at random. What is the probability that
(i) the sum of the digits on the page is 8?
(ii) the sum of the digits on the page is 9?

61. Cards marked with numbers 1, 2, 3, 4, ..., 20 are well-shuffled and a card is drawn at random. What is the probability, that the number of the cards is
(i) a prime number?
(ii) divisible by 3?
(iii) a perfect square? **[ICSE 2010]**

62. A piggy bank contains hundred 50 paise coins, fifty ₹ 1 coins, twenty ₹ 2 coins and ten ₹ 5 coins. If it is equally likely that one of the coins will fall out when the bank is turned upside down, then what is the probability that the coin
(i) will be a 50 paise coin?
(ii) will not be a ₹ 5 coin?

63. From a group of 2 boys and 2 girls, two children are selected at random. List the possible outcomes. Find the probability that one boy and one girl are selected.

64. An integer is chosen between 0 and 100. What is the probability that it is
(i) divisible by 8?
(ii) not divisible by 8?

65. A carton of 24 bulbs contains 6 defective bulbs. One bulb is drawn at random. What is the probability that the bulb is not defective? If the bulb selected is defective and it is not replaced and a second bulb is selected at random from the rest, then what is the probability that the second bulb is defective?

66. A number x is selected from the numbers 2, 3, 4 and then a second number y is randomly selected from 1, 4, 9. What is the probability that the product xy of the two numbers will be less than 12?

67. A number is selected at random from first 50 natural numbers. Find the probability that it is a multiple of 3 and 4.

68. In a musical chairs game, a person has been advised to stop playing the music at any time within 40 seconds after its start. What is the probability that the music will stop within the first 15 seconds?

69. A number is selected from the numbers 2, 3, 3, 5, 5, 5, 7, 7, 7, 7, 9, 9, 9, 9, 9 at random. Find the probability that the number selected is
(i) their median (ii) their mode

70. A carton consists of 100 shirts of which 88 are good, 8 have minor defect and 4 have major defect. Jimmy, a trader, will only accept the shirts which are good but Sujata, another trader, will only reject the shirts which have major defect. One shirt is drawn at random from the carton. What is the probability that it is acceptable to
(i) Jimmy? (ii) Sujata?

71. A game of chance consists of an arrow which comes to rest pointing at one of the regions 1, 2 or 3. O is the centre of the circle, $OC \perp AB$.

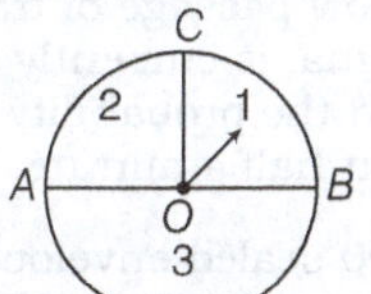

Find the probability that
(i) arrow is resting on 3.
(ii) arrow is resting on 1.
(iii) arrow is not resting on 2.

d. 6 Marks Questions

72. A die has six faces marked by the given numbers as shown below

1 2 3 −1 −2 −3

The die is thrown once. What is the probability of getting
(i) a positive integer?
(ii) an integer greater than −3?
(iii) the smallest integer? **[ICSE 2014]**

73. Two dice are thrown simultaneously. Find the probability of getting
(i) an even number as the sum.
(ii) the sum as a prime number.
(iii) a total of atleast 10.
(iv) a doublet of even number.
(v) a multiple of 2 on one die and a multiple of 3 on the other.
(vi) same number on both dice i.e. a doublet.
(vii) a multiple of 3 as the sum.

74. The king, queen and jack of clubs are removed from a deck of 52 playing cards and then well-shuffled. One card is selected from the remaining cards. Find the probability of getting

(i) a heart (ii) a king
(iii) a club (iv) the '10' of hearts

75. All the three face cards of spades are removed from a well-shuffled pack of 52 cards. A card is drawn at random from the remaining pack. Find the probability of getting

(i) a black face card
(ii) a queen
(iii) a black card
(iv) a spade

76. A bag contains white, black and red balls only. A ball is drawn at random from the bag. The probability of getting a white ball is 3/10 and that of a black ball is 2/5. Find the probability of getting a red ball. If the bag contains 20 black balls, then find the total number of balls in the bag.

77. A traffic signal displays green light for two minutes to allow passage of traffic on a particular road. If the signal is currently displaying green light, then find the probability that it will turn red within the next half a minute.

78. There are 1000 sealed envelopes in a box, 10 of them contain a cash prize of ₹ 100 each, 100 of them contain a cash prize of ₹ 50 each and 200 of them contain a cash prize of ₹ 10 each and rest do not contain any cash prize. If they are well-shuffled and an envelope is picked up out, what is the probability that it contains no cash prize?

79. A number x is selected at random from the numbers 1, 4, 9, 16 and another number y is selected at random from the numbers 1, 2, 3, 4. Find the probability that the value of xy is more than 16.

80. Cards bearing numbers 2, 4, 6, 8, 10, 12, 14, 16, 18 and 20 are kept in a bag. A card is drawn at random from the bag. Find the probability of getting a card which is

(i) a prime number
(ii) a number divisible by 4
(iii) a number that is a multiple of 6
(iv) an odd number **[ICSE 2018]**

81. A game consists of spinning an arrow which comes to rest pointing at one of the numbers 1, 2, 3, 4, 5, 6, 7, 8, 9, 10, 11, 12; as shown below.

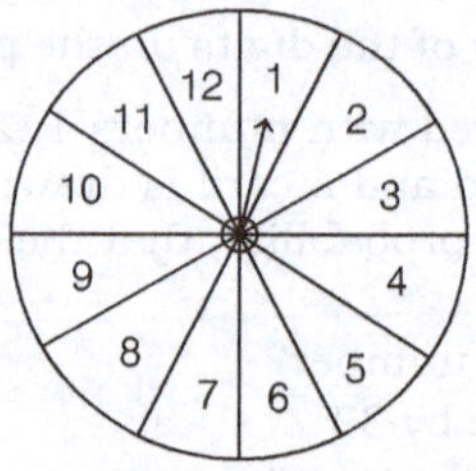

If the outcomes are equally likely, find the probability that the pointer will point at :

(i) 6
(ii) an even number
(iii) a prime number
(iv) a number greater than 8
(v) a number less than or equal to 9
(vi) a number between 3 and 11

Hints and Answers

1. (b) In a dice, 3 and 6 are divisible by 3.
So, the probability of getting a number divisible by 3

$$= \frac{2}{6} = \frac{1}{3}$$

2. (d) If two unbiased coins are tossed simultaneously we obtain possible outcomes.

HH, HT, TH, TT

∴ Total number of outcomes = 4
No head is obtained if the event *TT* occurs.
∴ Number of favourable outcomes = 1

$$\therefore \text{Required probality} = \frac{1}{4}$$

$$\text{But, given probability} = \frac{A}{B}$$

So, $A = 1$ and $B = 4$

Therefore, $(A + B)^2 = (1 + 4)^2$
$= (5)^2 = 25$

3. (b) We know,
The number of English alphabets = 26
The number of vowels in English alphabets = 5
∴ The probability that the letter chosen is a vowel

$$= \frac{\text{The number of vowels in English alphabets}}{\text{The number of English alphabets}}$$

$$= \frac{5}{26}$$

4. (d) Clearly, number x can take any one of the five given values.
So, total number of possible outcomes = 5. We observe that $x^2 < 2$ when x takes any one of the following three values − 1, 0 and 1.
So, favourable number of elementary events = 3

Hence, $P(x^2 < 2) = \frac{3}{5}$

5. (a) Out of 20 tickets numbered from 1 to 20, one can be chosen in 20 ways. So, total number of possible outcomes associated with the given random experiment is 20. Out of 20 tickets numbered 1 to 20, tickets bearing numbers which are multiple of 3 or 7 are 3, 6, 7, 9, 12, 14, 15 and 18.

$\therefore$ Favourable number of elementary events = 8

Hence, the required probability $= \frac{8}{20} = \frac{2}{5}$

6. (b) There are 14 = (5 + 9) fish out of which one can be chosen in 14 ways.

$\therefore$ Total numbers of possible outcomes = 14

There are 5 male fish so, a male fish can be chosen in 5 ways.

$\therefore$ Favourable number of elementary events = 5

Hence, the required probability $= \frac{5}{14}$

7. (c) Number x can be selected in three ways and corresponding to each such way there are three ways of selecting number y.

Therefore, two numbers can be selected in 9 ways as listed below

(1, 1), (1,4), (1,9), (2, 1), (2, 4), (2,9), (3,1), (3,4), (3,9)

So, total numbers of possible outcomes = 9

The product xy will be less than 9, if x and y are chosen in one of the following ways

(1, 1), (1,4), (2, 1), (2, 4), (3,1)

$\therefore$ Favourable number of elementary events = 5

Hence, the required probability $= \frac{5}{9}$

8. (b) There are 5 marbles in the bag. Out of these 5 marbles one can be choose in 5 ways.

$\therefore$ Total number of possible outcomes = 5

Since the bag contains 2 blue marbles. Therefore one blue marble can be drawn in 2 ways.

$\therefore$ Favourable number of elementary events = 2

Hence, P (getting a blue marble) $= \frac{2}{5}$

9. (c) Let there be x blue balls in the bag.

$\therefore$ Total number of balls in the beg = $(8 + x)$

Now, P_1 = Probability of drawing a blue ball

$$= \frac{x}{8+x}$$

and P_2 = Probability of drawing a red ball

$$= \frac{8}{8+x}$$

It is given that,

$$P_1 = 3P_2$$

$$\Rightarrow \frac{x}{8+x} = 3 \times \frac{8}{(8+x)}$$

$$\Rightarrow \frac{x}{8+x} = \frac{24}{8+x} \Rightarrow x = 24$$

Hence, there are 24 blue balls in the bag.

10. (b) Total number of envelopes in the box = 1000

Number of envelopes containing cash prize

$$= 10 + 100 + 200 = 310$$

Number of envelopes containing no cash prize

$$= 1000 - 310 = 690$$

$\therefore$ Required probability $= \frac{690}{1000} = 0.69$

11. (d) Here, total number of possible outcomes = 36

Let P = event of sum of two numbers will be a multiple of 4.

So, P = {(3,1), (2,2), (1,3), (6,2), (5,3), (4,4), (3, 5), (2, 6), (6, 6)}

Number of favourable outcomes = 9

$\therefore P$ (sum of two numbers will be multiple of 4)

$$= \frac{9}{36} = \frac{1}{4}$$

12. **Hint** Here, the number of possible outcomes = 4

Let E be the event of getting exactly one head

So, E would consist of two outcomes, namely HT and TH.

$\therefore$ Number of outcomes favourable to $E = 2$ **Ans.** 1/2

13. **Hint** Let E = Event of getting atmost one head

= {(HT), (TH), (TT)} **Ans.** 3/4

14. **Hint**

(i) Favourable outcomes for getting 2 heads is HH.

$\therefore$ Number of outcomes favourable to given event = 1 **Ans.** $\frac{1}{4}$

(ii) Favourable outcomes for getting atleast 1 tail are HT, TH and TT.

$\therefore$ Number of outcomes favourable to given event = 3 **Ans.** 3/4

15. **Hint** Total number of possible outcomes = 8

(i) She tosses tail three times i.e. TTT. **Ans.** $\frac{1}{8}$

(ii) She tosses heads three times i.e. HHH. **Ans.** $\frac{1}{8}$

(iii) Sweta gets heads one or two times i.e. event of getting HTT, THT, TTH, HHT, HTH or THH.

Ans. 3/4

16. **Hint** When three coins are tossed together, all possible outcomes are HHH, HHT, HTH, THH, HTT, THT, TTH and TTT.

$\therefore$ Total number of possible outcomes = 8

(i) The favourable outcomes of getting exactly 2 heads are HHT, HTH and THH. **Ans.** 3/8

(ii) The event of getting atleast two heads, i.e. HHT, HTH, THH or HHH. **Ans.** $\frac{1}{2}$

(iii) Do same as part (ii). **Ans.** $\frac{1}{2}$

17. **Hint** Total number of possible outcomes = 6

There are two even numbers, 2 and 4, which is less than 5.

$\therefore$ Number of outcomes favourable to given event = 2

Ans. 1/3

18. **Hint** There is no such number lies on a die which is less than 3 and greater than 2. **Ans.** 0

19. **Hint** Do same as Example 7. **Ans.** $\frac{11}{36}$

20. **Hint** Total number of possible outcomes = 6
The factors of 36 are 1, 2, 3, 4, 6, 9, 12, 18, 36.
Here, we see that 5 is not a factor of 36.
Ans. 1/6

21. **Hint** Let E be the event of getting the sum of the numbers appearing on the top of the two dice is more than 9. Then, the favourable outcomes are (4, 6), (5, 5), (6, 4), (5, 6), (6, 5) and (6, 6).

∴ Number of favourable outcomes to $E = 6$

Ans. $\frac{1}{6}$

22. **Hint**

(i) Let E_1 be the event of getting a letter A.
Number of outcomes favourable to $E_1 = 1$
Ans. $\frac{1}{6}$

(ii) Let E_2 be the event of getting a letter D.
Number of outcomes favourable to $E_2 = 1$ **Ans.** 1/6

23. **Hint**

(i) Let E_1 be the event of getting a prime number.
Then, $E_1 = \{2, 3, 5\}$ **Ans.** 1/2

(ii) Let E_2 be the event of getting a number.
Lying between 2 and 6. Then, $E_2 = \{3, 4, 5\}$
Ans. 1/2

(iii) Let E_3 be the event of getting an odd number.
Then, $E_3 = \{1, 3, 5\}$ **Ans.** 1/2

24. **Hint**

(i) Here are following different scores are possible :
$(0, 0) = 0$; $(0, 1) = 1$
$(0, 6) = 6$; $(1, 1) = 2$
$(1, 6) = 7$ **Ans.** 6

(ii) To obtain a score of 7, one dice must show 1 and one dice must show 6.

Probability of getting $1 = \frac{3}{6} = \frac{1}{2}$

Probability of getting $6 = \frac{2}{3} = \frac{1}{3}$

∴ Probability of getting a total of 7

$= \frac{1}{2} \times \frac{1}{3} + \frac{1}{3} \times \frac{1}{2} = \frac{1}{3}$ **Ans.** $\frac{1}{3}$

25. **Hint** The favourable events are (1, 1), (1, 2), (1, 3), (1, 4), (1, 5), (1, 6), (2, 2), (2, 3), (2, 4), (2, 1), (3, 1), (4, 1), (5, 1), (6, 1), (3, 2), (4, 2).
Ans. $\frac{4}{9}$

26. **Hint** Total number of possible outcomes = 36

(i) The event of getting a sum of numbers is seven
= {(1, 6), (2, 5), (3, 4), (6, 1), (5, 2), (4, 3)}
Ans. 1/6

(ii) The event of getting a sum of number is not prime i.e. 4, 6, 8, 9, 10, 12
= {(1, 3), (3, 1), (2, 2), (1, 5), (5, 1), (2, 4), (4, 2), (3, 3), (2, 6), (6, 2), (3, 5), (5, 3), (4, 4), (3, 6), (6, 3), (4, 5), (5, 4), (4, 6), (6, 4), (5, 5), (6, 6)}
Ans. $\frac{7}{12}$

(iii) No such a pair exist, in which sum of numbers is 1.
Ans. 0

27. **Hint** Total number of possible outcomes = 36

(i) Favourable outcomes are (1, 6), (2, 3), (3, 2) and (6, 1). **Ans.** $\frac{1}{9}$

(ii) Favourable outcomes are (2, 6), (3, 4), (4, 3) and (6, 2). **Ans.** $\frac{1}{9}$

(iii) Product of the numbers on the top of the dice cannot be 7. So, its probability is zero.
Ans. 0

28. **Hint** Total number of possible outcomes
$= 6 \times 6 = 36$

(i) Doublets of prime numbers are (2, 2), (3, 3) and (5, 5). They are three in numbers.
Ans. $\frac{1}{12}$

(ii) Doublets of odd numbers are (1, 1), (3, 3) and (5, 5). They are three in number.
Ans. $\frac{1}{12}$

29. **Hint** Total number of cards in a pack = 52
Multiples of 3 in each suit are 3, 6 and 9.
We know that in a pack of cards, there are four suits.
Number of remove cards $= 3 \times 4 = 12$
Total number of cards left $= 52 - 12 = 40$

(i) Number of favourable cards $= 3 \times 4 = 12$ **Ans.** $\frac{3}{10}$

(ii) Even numbered red cards
$= 2 \times$ even number in each red card i.e.
$\{2, 4, 8, 10\} = 2 \times 4 = 8$
[since, there are two suits of red cards]
Number of favourable cards = 8 **Ans.** $\frac{1}{5}$

30. **Hint** Total number of red cards
= 26 (including 2 queens)
Total number of queen cards is 4, out of which 2 are black queen cards and 2 are red queen cards.
Total number of red cards and queen cards
$= 26 + 2 = 28$
Let E be the event of getting neither red nor a queen card, then
Number of outcomes favourable to $E = 52 - 28 = 24$
Ans. $\frac{6}{13}$

31. **Hint** Total number of left card in a pack = 49

(i) Number of heart card in a pack = 13

(ii) Number of king card in a pack = 3

Ans. (i) 13/49 (ii) 3/49

32. **Hint** Out of 52 cards, one card can be drawn in 52 ways. So, total number of possible outcomes = 52

(i) The number of red king in a pack of card is 2.

Ans. $\frac{1}{26}$

(ii) Only one card exist in spade which shows number 2.

Ans. $\frac{1}{52}$

(iii) There are two suits of black cards, namely spades and clubs. Each suit contains one card bearing number 10.

$\therefore$ Total number of outcomes favourable to the given event = 2

Ans. 1/26

33. **Hint** Total number of possible outcomes = 71

Let E = Event of getting an odd number from 5 to 75, i.e. event of getting = 5, 7, 9, 11, ..., 75 **Ans.** 36/71

34. **Hint** Let number of black balls be x.

So, total number of balls = $x + 30$

Now, probability of drawing a white ball = $\frac{30}{x+30}$

and probability of drawing a black ball = $\frac{x}{x+30}$

According to the question,

Probability of drawing a black ball

$= \frac{2}{5}$ (Probability of drawing a white ball)

Ans. 12

35. (i) Cards which are multiple of 5 are

5, 10, 15, 20, 25

$\therefore$ Probability that the drawn card is a multiple of 5 is P_1

$$P_1 = \frac{\text{Number of card multiples of 5}}{\text{Total number of cards}}$$

$$\Rightarrow \quad P_1 = \frac{5}{25} \Rightarrow P_1 = \frac{1}{5}$$

(ii) $\therefore$ Perfect squares in 1 to 25 are 1, 4, 9, 16, 25.

Let probability of drawn card is a perfect square is P_2

$$P_2 = \frac{\text{Number of perfect squares}}{\text{Total numbers of cards}}$$

$$\Rightarrow \quad P_2 = \frac{5}{25} = \frac{1}{5}$$

(iii) $\therefore$ Prime numbers in 1 to 25 and

2, 3, 5, 7, 11, 13, 17, 19, 23

Let probability of drawn card is a prime number is P_3

$$\Rightarrow \quad P_3 = \frac{\text{Number of primes}}{\text{Total numbers of cards}}$$

$$\Rightarrow \quad P_3 = \frac{9}{25}$$

36. **Hint** Total number of balls = 9

(i) Number of outcomes favourable to the given event = 7 **Ans.** 7/9

(ii) Number of outcomes favourable to the given event = 5 **Ans.** 5/9

37. **Hint** Total number of slips in third box

= 25 + 50 = 75

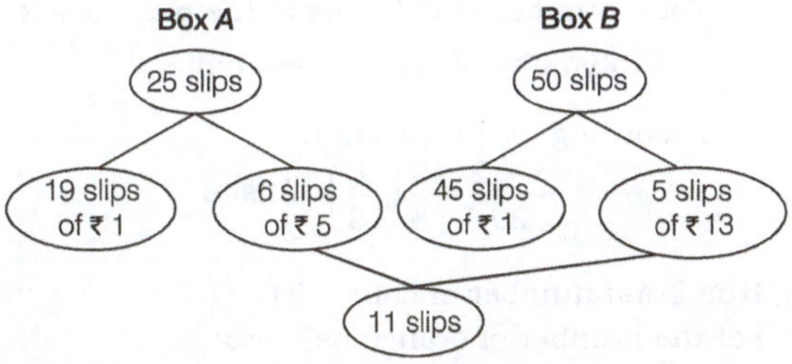

From the chart, it is clear that there are 11 slips which are marked other than ₹ 1. **Ans.** $\frac{11}{75}$

38. **Hint** Let the total number of ball be x.

$$P(A) + P(B) + P(C) = 1$$

$$P(C) = 1 - \left[\frac{1}{3} + \frac{1}{4}\right] = \frac{5}{12}$$

$$\therefore \quad \frac{5}{12} = \frac{40}{\text{Number of possible outcomes}}$$

Ans. There are total 96 balls in the box.

39. **Hint** Do same as Example 17. **Ans.** (i) $\frac{3}{4}$ (ii) $\frac{17}{20}$

40. **Hint** Number of all possible outcomes = 100

(i) Let E_1 be the event of getting a number which is divisible by 9 and is a perfect square.

Then, outcomes favourable to E_1 are $3^2, 6^2, 9^2$. **Ans.** 3/100

(ii) Let E_2 be the event of getting a prime number greater than 80.

Then, outcomes favourable to E_2 are 83, 89 and 97.

Ans. $\frac{3}{100}$

41. **Hint** Total number of balls in a bag = 24

Number of red balls = x

Number of white balls = $2x$

Number of blue balls = $3x$

$\therefore$ $x + 2x + 3x = 24$ **Ans.** (i) 5/6 (ii) 1/3

42. **Hint** Total number of balls in urn

= 10 + 6 + 4 = 20

(i) P (first ball is red) $= \frac{10}{20} = \frac{1}{2}$

(ii) Now, left ball in urn = 20 − 1 = 19

P (second ball is red) $= \frac{9}{19}$

(iii) Now, total number of ball in urn = 19 − 1 = 18

P (third ball is green) $= \frac{4}{18}$

43. Hint

(i) Total number of balls, in the bag = 18
and total number of red balls in the bag = x
Ans. $\frac{x}{18}$

(ii) Now, 2 red balls are added to the bag.
$\therefore$ Total balls in the bag = 18 + 2 = 20
Total number of red balls in the bag = $x + 2$
$\therefore$ Probability of drawing red ball = $\frac{x+2}{20}$
According to the question,
$$\frac{x+2}{20} = \frac{9}{8}\left(\frac{x}{18}\right)$$ **Ans.** 8

44. Hint Total number of balls = 81
Let the number of orange ball be x.
According to the question,
$$1 - \frac{2}{3} - \frac{1}{9} = \frac{x}{81}$$ **Ans.** 18

45. Hint P (point will be chosen from the shaded part)
$= \frac{\text{Area of the rectangle } PQRB}{\text{Area of the square } ABCD}$ **Ans.** 0.08

46. Hint (i) P (falling inside circle) $= \frac{\text{Area of circle}}{\text{Area of rectangle}}$

(ii) P (falling outside circle) $= \frac{\text{Area outside the circle}}{\text{Area of rectangle}}$

Ans. (i) 0.262 (ii) 0.738

47. Hint Total number of possible outcomes = 100
Let E be the event of getting a prime number i.e. event of getting 2, 3, 5, 7, 11, 13, 17, 19, 23, 29, 31, 37, 41, 43, 47, 53, 59, 61, 67, 71, 73, 79, 83, 89 or 97
Ans. 1/4

48. Hint Number of rotten eggs
= Total number of eggs × $P(E)$.
Ans. 14

49. Hint There are three vowels and one is repeated. So, number of outcomes favourable to the given event = 4. **Ans.** $\frac{4}{11}$

50. Hint We know that in English alphabet, there are 26 letters (5 vowels + 21 consonants).
So, total number of possible outcomes = 26
Let E = Event of choosing a consonant,
i.e. choosing t, v, w, x, y or z **Ans.** 21/26

51. Hint Number of possible outcomes = 26
Letters in the word 'RAMANUJAN' are
R, A, M, N, U, J. **Ans.** 3/13

52. Hint (i) There are 5 Wednesday on the given calender.
(ii) There are 5 Friday on the given calender.
(iii) Event of selection of a Thursday or a Saturday
= {2, 9, 16, 23, 30, 4, 11, 18, 25} = 9

Ans. (i) $\frac{5}{31}$ (ii) $\frac{5}{31}$ (iii) $\frac{9}{31}$

53. Hint

(i) In non-leap year, there are 365 days, out of which 364 days make 52 weeks and in each week there is one Sunday.
Therefore, we have to find probability of having a Sunday on the remaining 1 day. Now, that 1 day can be Monday, Tuesday, Wednesday, Thursday, Friday, Saturday and Sunday. **Ans.** 1/7

(ii) In a leap year, there are 366 days, out of which 364 days make 52 weeks and in each week there is one Sunday. Therefore, we have to find the probability of having a Sunday on one of the remaining 2 days.
Now, the 2 days can be (Sunday, Monday) or (Monday, Tuesday) or (Tuesday, Wednesday) or (Wednesday, Thursday) or (Thursday, Friday) or (Friday, Saturday) or (Saturday, Sunday). Note that Sunday occurs 2 times in these 7 pairs.
Ans. $\frac{2}{7}$

54. Hint Non-leap year contains 365 days, in which 52 weeks and one day extra. **Ans.** 1/7

55. Hint Total number of days in the year 2000
= 366 [$\because$ year 2000 is a leap year]
Total number of ways in which two friends may have their birthday = 366 × 366
Number of ways in which two friends have same birthday = 366 **Ans.** $\frac{1}{366}$

56. Hint Total number of students = 23
$\therefore$ Total number of possible outcomes = 23
Number of students in houses A, B and C
= 4 + 8 + 5 = 17
$\therefore$ Remaining students = 23 − 17 = 6
Thus, number of outcomes favourable to the given event = 6 **Ans.** $\frac{6}{23}$

57. Hint We know that $1 - P(E) = P(\overline{E}) \Rightarrow 1 - \frac{p}{12} = \frac{3}{4}$
Ans. $p = 3$

58. Hint Let she bought x tickets.
Then, probability of her winning the first prize
$$\frac{x}{6000} = 0.08$$
Ans. 480

59. Hint Let E be the event of getting a male fish. As there are 5 male fish in the tank, the number of outcomes favourable to E = 5
Ans. 5/13

60. Hint

(i) Let E = Event of getting the sum of the digits on the page is 8 = {17, 26, 35, 44, 53, 62, 71}
Then, the number of outcomes favourable to E = 7
Ans. 7/85

(ii) Let E = Event of getting the sum of the digits on the page is 9 = {18, 27, 36, 45, 54, 63, 72, 81}
Then, the number of outcomes favourable to E = 8
Ans. $\frac{8}{85}$

61. Hint Total number of cards = 20

$\therefore$ Total number of possible outcomes = 20

(i) Prime numbers are 2, 3, 5, 7, 11, 13, 17 and 19.

$\therefore$ Number of favourable cards = 8 **Ans.** $\frac{2}{5}$

(ii) Numbers divisible by 3 are 3, 6, 9, 12, 15 and 18.

$\therefore$ Number of favourable cards = 6 **Ans.** $\frac{3}{10}$

(iii) Perfect square numbers are 1, 4, 9 and 16.

$\therefore$ Number of favourable cards = 4 **Ans.** $\frac{1}{5}$

62. Hint

(i) Total number of coins

= 100 + 50 + 20 + 10 = 180 **Ans.** 5/9

(ii) Number of coins, which are not of ₹ 5

= 180 − 10 = 170 **Ans.** 17/18

63. Hint Let the 2 boys and 2 girls be denoted by B_1, B_2, G_1 and G_2, respectively.

$\therefore$ The total possible outcomes are

B_1B_2, B_1G_1, B_1G_2, B_2G_1, B_2G_2 and G_1G_2.

$\therefore$ Total number of possible outcomes = 6

If one boy and one girl are selected, then favourable outcomes are B_1G_1, B_1G_2, B_2G_1 and B_2G_2.

Ans. 2/3

64. Hint The numbers divisible by 8 are 8, 16, 24, 32, 40, 48, 56, 64, 72, 80, 88, 96.

Ans. (i) $\frac{4}{33}$ (ii) $\frac{29}{33}$

65. Hint Number of not defective bulb = 18

$\therefore$ Probability of not defective bulb = $\frac{18}{24}$

If in first selection, defective bulb is not replaced, then in the second selection, total number of bulbs left 23 and number of defective balls left 5.

Ans. 3/4 and 5/23

66. Hint Two numbers can be selected in 9 ways.

(4, 1), (2, 1), (2, 4), (3, 1)

Ans. $\frac{4}{9}$

67. Hint The multiples of 3 and 4 are 12, 24, 36, 48.

Ans. $\frac{2}{25}$

68. Hint The favourable results = 0 sec to 15 sec and the total result = 0 sec to 40 sec

So, we can say,

The favourable outcomes = 15 and the total number of outcomes = 40

Ans. $\frac{3}{8}$

69. Hint

(i) Median of the numbers is 7.

$\therefore$ Number of outcomes favourable to the given event = 4 **Ans.** $\frac{4}{15}$

(ii) Mode = 9

$\therefore$ Number of outcomes favourable to the given event = 5 **Ans.** $\frac{1}{3}$

70. Hint

(i) Favourable outcomes for Jimmy acceptable = 88

(ii) Favourable outcomes for Sujata acceptable = 88 + 8 = 96

Ans. (i) 0.88 (ii) 0.96

71. Hint Total angle made by the circle at O is 360°.

Angle subtended by region 1 at O = 90°

Angle subtended by region 2 at O = 90°

Angle subtended by region 3 at O = 180°

Ans. (i) 1/2 (ii) 1/4 (iii) 3/4

72. Hint Total number of possible outcomes = 6

(i) Positive integers are 1, 2 and 3.

$\therefore$ Number of outcomes favourable to the given event = 3

Ans. $\frac{1}{2}$

(ii) Integers greater than −3 are 1, 2, 3, −1 and −2.

$\therefore$ Number of outcomes favourable to the given event

= Number of integers greater than −3 = 5

Ans. $\frac{5}{6}$

(iii) Smallest integer is −3 only.

$\therefore$ Number of outcomes favourable to the given event = 1

Ans. $\frac{1}{6}$

73. Hint Total number of possible outcomes = 36

(i) The event of getting an even number as the sum are 2, 4, 6, 8, 10 and 12.

$\therefore$ Number of outcomes favourable to the given event = 18

Ans. $\frac{1}{2}$

(ii) The event of getting the sum as a prime number are 2, 3, 5, 7 and 11.

$\therefore$ Number of outcomes favourable to the given event = 15

Ans. $\frac{5}{12}$

(iii) The event of getting a total of atleast 10 are 10, 11 and 12.

$\therefore$ Number of outcomes favourable to the given event = 6

Ans. $\frac{1}{6}$

(iv) ∴ Number of outcomes favourable to the given event, i.e. event of getting a doublet of even number = 3

Ans. $\frac{1}{12}$

(v) ∴ Number of outcomes favourable to the given event, i.e. event of getting a multiple of 2 on one die and a multiple of 3 on the other = 11

Ans. $\frac{11}{36}$

(vi) Let A_6 be the event of getting the same number on both dice.

∴ Number of outcomes favourable to the given event = 6.

Ans. $\frac{1}{6}$

(vii) Number of outcomes favourable to the given event, i.e. events of getting a multiple of 3 as the sum,

i.e. event of getting the sum 3, 6, 9 and 12 = 12

Ans. $\frac{1}{3}$

74. Hint After removing king, queen and jack of clubs from a deck of 52 playing cards, there are 49 cards left in the deck.

∴ Total number of possible outcomes = 49

(i) Here, number of outcomes favourable to the given event = 13 **Ans.** 13/49

(ii) Here, number of outcomes favourable to the given event = 3 **Ans.** 3/49

(iii) After removing king, queen and jack of clubs only 10 clubs cards are left in the deck.

Here, number of outcomes favourable to the given event = 10 **Ans.** 10/49

(iv) Number of outcomes favourable to the given event = 1 **Ans.** $\frac{1}{49}$

75. Hint Total number of left card in a pack = 49

(i) Remaining number of black face cards in a pack = 3

Ans. $\frac{3}{49}$

(ii) Remaining number of queen cards in a pack = 3

Ans. 3/49

(iii) Remaining number of black cards in a pack = 23

Ans. 23/49

(iv) Remaining number of spade cards in a pack = 10

Ans. $\frac{10}{49}$

76. Hint Probability of getting a red ball

$= 1 - [P(\text{white ball}) + P(\text{black ball})]$

$= 1 - \frac{3}{10} - \frac{2}{5} = \frac{3}{10}$

Now, let the number of balls in the bag be x.

and probability of getting a black ball

$= \frac{20}{x} \Rightarrow \frac{2}{5} = \frac{20}{x}$

Ans. 50

77. Hint Total number of minutes = 2

Outcomes favourable to the given event = $\frac{1}{2}$ **Ans.** $\frac{1}{4}$

78. Hint Number of envelopes containing cash prize

$= 10 + 100 + 200 = 310$

Number of envelopes containing no cash prize

$= 1000 - 310 = 690$ **Ans.** 0.69

79. Hint Two numbers can be selected in 16 ways as listed below

(1, 1), (1, 2), (1, 3), (1, 4), (4, 1), (4, 2), (4, 3), (4, 4), (9, 1), (9, 2), (9, 3), (9, 4), (16, 1), (16, 2), (16, 3) and (16, 4)

∴ Total number of possible outcomes = 16

Now, the product of xy will be more than 16, if x and y are chosen in one of the following ways

(9, 2), (9, 3), (9, 4), (16, 2), (16, 3) and (16, 4)

∴ Number of outcomes favourable to the given event = 6

Ans. $\frac{3}{8}$

80. Hint Total number of outcomes = 10

(i) Number of favourable outcomes (prime numbers) = 1

Ans. $\frac{1}{10}$

(ii) Number of favourable outcomes (numbers divisible by 4) = 5

Ans. $\frac{1}{2}$

(iii) Number of favourable outcomes (numbers which is a multiple of 6) = 3

Ans. $\frac{3}{10}$

(iv) Number of favourable outcomes (odd numbers) = 0

Ans. 0

81. Hint Total number of possible outcomes = 12

Ans. (i) $\frac{1}{12}$ (ii) $\frac{1}{2}$ (iii) $\frac{5}{12}$ (iv) $\frac{1}{3}$

(v) $\frac{3}{4}$ (vi) $\frac{7}{12}$

Olympiad Section

Brain Teasing Questions asked in Previous Olympiads

1 The probability that the minute hand lies from 5 to 15 min in the wall clock, is

(a) $\frac{1}{6}$ (b) $\frac{5}{6}$ (c) $\frac{1}{5}$ (d) $\frac{1}{10}$

Directions (Q.Nos. 2-4) The diameters of circles (in mm) drawn on a table are given below

Diameters	14–20	21–27	28–34	35–41	42–48
Number of circles	3	5	8	11	7

2 If a circle is chosen at random, then the probability that chosen circle has diameter less than 28.

(a) $\frac{4}{17}$ (b) $\frac{17}{4}$ (c) $\frac{15}{2}$ (d) $\frac{13}{5}$

3 If a circle is chosen at random, then find the probability that chosen circle has radius lying between 14 to 17.

(a) $\frac{15}{2}$ (b) $\frac{4}{17}$ (c) $\frac{17}{4}$ (d) $\frac{19}{4}$

4 If a circle is chosen at random, then find the probability that chosen circle has diameter above 50.

(a) $\frac{17}{4}$ (b) $\frac{4}{17}$ (c) 0 (d) $\frac{15}{2}$

5 A square of side 5 cm is drawn in the interior of another square of side 10 cm and shaded as shown in the figure below

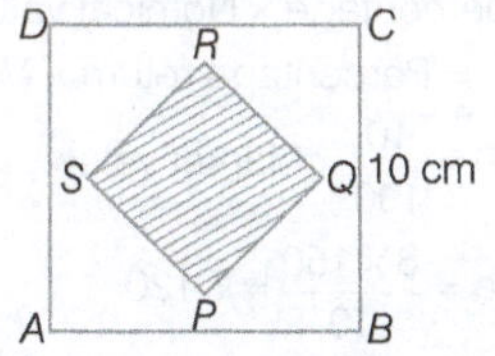

A point is selected at random from the interior of square *ABCD*. The probability that the point will be chosen from the shaded part is

(a) 0.05 (b) 0.10
(c) 0.25 (d) 0.30

6 Suppose you drop a die at random on the rectangular region shown in the figure. The probability that it will land inside the circle of diameter 1m, is

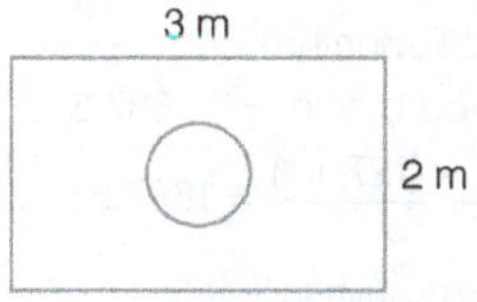

(a) $\frac{\pi}{4}$ (b) $\frac{\pi}{24}$
(c) $\frac{\pi}{6}$ (d) $\frac{\pi}{2}$

7 In the given figure, points *A*, *B*, *C* and *D* are the centres of four circles that each have a radius of length one unit. If a point is selected at random from the interior of square *ABCD*, then the probability that the point will be chosen from the shaded region, is

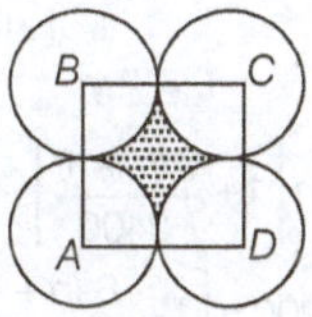

(a) $\frac{4-\pi}{2}$ (b) $\frac{4-\pi}{4}$
(c) $\frac{4+\pi}{2}$ (d) None of these

Answers

1. (a) **2.** (a) **3.** (b) **4.** (c) **5.** (c) **6.** (b) **7.** (b)

* *These questions may or may not be asked in the examination, have been given just for additional practice required for olympiads Scholarship Exams etc. For detailed explanations refer Page No. 503.*

Solutions to Olympiad Section

Chapter 2 Banking

1. *(a)* Given, number of instalments (n) = 15 months,

amount of each instalment (P) = ₹ 500

and interest (I) = ₹ 300

Now, as $I = \frac{Prn(n+1)}{2400}$

$\therefore\quad r = \frac{2400\,I}{Pn(n+1)}$

$= \frac{2400 \times 300}{500 \times 15 \times 16} = 6\%$

2. *(b)* Let the time period be T yr.

Then, T yr $= 12T$ months

$\because$ Interest received by him = ₹ 1687.5

$\therefore\quad \frac{900 \times 7.5 \times 12T \times (12T+1)}{2400} = 1687.5 \quad \left[\because I = \frac{Prn(n+1)}{2400}\right]$

$\Rightarrow\quad \frac{9(T)(12T+1)(7.5)}{2} = 1687.5$

$\Rightarrow\quad T(12T+1) = \frac{1687.5 \times 2}{9 \times 7.5} = 50$

$\Rightarrow\quad 12T^2 + T - 50 = 0$

$\Rightarrow\quad 12T^2 - 24T + 25T - 50 = 0$

$\Rightarrow\quad 12T(T-2) + 25(T-2) = 0$

$\Rightarrow\quad (12T+25)(T-2) = 0$

$\Rightarrow\quad T = \frac{-25}{12}$ or 2

[$\because$ time cannot be negative]

$\therefore\quad T = 2$ yr

3. *(a)* We have, $MV = Pn\left[1 + \frac{r(n+1)}{2400}\right]$

$\therefore\quad 12440 = 1200\,n\left[1 + \frac{8(n+1)}{2400}\right]$

$\Rightarrow\quad 12440 = 1200n\left(\frac{2400 + 8n + 8}{2400}\right)$

$\Rightarrow\quad 24880 = 8n^2 + 2408n$

$\Rightarrow\quad n^2 + 301n - 3110 = 0$

$\Rightarrow\quad n = -311$ or 10

$\Rightarrow\quad n = 10$ months

4. *(c)* We know that,

$MV = Pn\left[1 + \frac{r(n+1)}{2400}\right]$

$\therefore\quad 9390 = P \times 12\left(1 + \frac{8 \times 13}{2400}\right)$

$\Rightarrow\quad 9390 = P \times 12\left(\frac{2400 + 104}{2400}\right)$

$\Rightarrow\quad 9390 = P \times \frac{2504}{200}$

$\Rightarrow\quad \frac{9390 \times 200}{2504} = P$

$\Rightarrow\quad P = ₹\,750$

5. *(b)* We know that, $I = \frac{Prn(n+1)}{2400}$

$\therefore$ Interest earned by Ravi

$= \frac{400 \times 9 \times 24 \times 25}{2400} = ₹\,900$

and interest earned by Sonu

$= \frac{400 \times 12 \times 30 \times 31}{2400} = ₹\,1860$

Hence, option (b) is correct.

Chapter 03 Shares and Dividends

1. *(a)* (i) Percentage return $= \left(\frac{\text{Dividend}}{\text{Investment}} \times 100\right)\%$

$= \left(\frac{10}{120} \times 100\right)\% = 8\frac{1}{3}\%$

(ii) Percentage return $= \left(\frac{\text{Dividend}}{\text{Investment}} \times 100\right)\%$

$= \left(\frac{9}{110} \times 100\right)\% = 8\frac{18}{99}\% = 8\frac{2}{11}\%$

Since, $8\frac{1}{3}\% > 8\frac{2}{11}\%$, therefore part (i) is better.

2. *(d)* Number of shares $= \frac{\text{Total investment}}{\text{Market value of one share}}$

$= \frac{125X}{X + \frac{25}{100}X} = \frac{125X}{\left(\frac{5X}{4}\right)}$

$= 125X \times \frac{4}{5X} = 100$

3. *(b)* $\because$ Dividend percentage × Nominal value

= Percentage return × Market value

$\therefore\quad \frac{8}{100} \times 150 = \frac{10}{100} \times$ Market value

$\Rightarrow\quad$ Market value $= \frac{8 \times 150}{10} = ₹\,120$

4. *(a)* From the given data, 400 shares can be purchased with an investment of ₹ 25000.

$\therefore$ Market value of each share $= ₹\left(\frac{25000}{400}\right) = ₹\,62.50$

5. *(d)* $\because$ Dividend × Face value = Market value × Rate of return

$\therefore\quad \frac{x}{100} \times 110 = 100 \times \frac{y}{100}$

$\Rightarrow\quad \frac{x}{y} = \frac{100}{110} = \frac{10}{11}$

$\Rightarrow\quad x : y = 10 : 11$

6. *(a)* Number of shares bought by Ms. Neelam

$= \frac{27000}{90} = 300$

$\Rightarrow$ Dividend earned on 300 shares

$$= 300 \times \frac{10}{100} \times 100 = ₹3000$$

Money received by selling these 300 shares

$$= 300 \times 110 = ₹33000$$

$\Rightarrow$ Earning of Ms. Neelam

$$= 33000 + 3000 - 27000 = ₹9000$$

Number of shares bought by Mr. Ram

$$= \frac{\text{Total investment}}{\text{Market value}}$$

$$= \frac{30000}{120} = 250$$

$\Rightarrow$ Dividend earned on 250 shares

$$= 250 \times \frac{8}{100} \times 150 = ₹3000$$

Money received by selling these 250 shares

$$= 250 \times 110 = ₹27500$$

$\therefore$ Earning of Mr. Ram = 27500 + 3000 − 30000 = ₹500

7. *(c)* Jindal Electronics

Investment = ₹54000, Dividend = 18%, Face value = ₹200,

Percentage return = 16%

$\because$ Market price × Percentage return = Face value × Dividend

$\Rightarrow$ Market price × 16 = 200 × 18

$$\therefore \text{Market price} = \frac{200 \times 18}{16} = ₹225$$

$$\text{Number of shares} = \frac{\text{Investment}}{\text{Market price}} = \frac{54000}{225} = 240$$

Annual income = Number of shares

$$\times \text{Nominal value} \times \frac{\text{Rate of dividend}}{100}$$

$$= 240 \times 200 \times \frac{18}{100} = ₹8640$$

Number of shares = 240, Market price = ₹275

Sale proceeds = 240 × 275 = ₹66000

Golmal Entertainment

Investment = Amount received = ₹66000

Dividend = 24%

Face value = ₹100

Annual income = Number of shares

$$\times \text{Nominal value} \times \frac{\text{Rate of dividend}}{100}$$

$$\Rightarrow 10560 = \text{Number of shares} \times 100 \times \frac{24}{100}$$

[$\because$ Annual income = 8640 + 1920 = ₹ 10560]

$$\text{Number of shares} = 10560 \times \frac{1}{100} \times \frac{100}{24} = 440$$

Market price of one share

$$= \frac{\text{Investment}}{\text{Number of shares}}$$

$$= \frac{66000}{440} = ₹150$$

8. *(d)* Let the man invests ₹ x in each company.

For company X

Nominal value of each share = ₹ 100

Market value of each share

$$= ₹\,100 + 20\% \text{ of } ₹\,100 = ₹\,120$$

$$\therefore \text{Number of shares bought} = \frac{x}{120}$$

and dividend on each share = 5% of ₹ 100 = ₹ 5 [$\because$ rate = 5%]

$$\Rightarrow \text{Total dividend} = 5 \times \frac{x}{120} = ₹\,\frac{x}{24}$$

For company Y

Nominal value of each share = ₹ 100

Market value of each share = ₹ 100 − 10% of ₹ 100

$$= ₹\,90$$

$$\therefore \text{Number of shares bought} = \frac{x}{90}$$

and dividend on each share = 7% of ₹ 100 = ₹ 7 [$\because$ rate = 7%]

$$\Rightarrow \text{Total dividend} = 7 \times \frac{x}{90} = ₹\,\frac{7x}{90}$$

Given, sum of dividends (returns) from both the companies is ₹ 1290.

$$\therefore \quad \frac{x}{24} + \frac{7x}{90} = 1290$$

On solving, we get $x = 10800$

Since, the man invests ₹ 10800 in each of the two companies.

$\therefore$ Man invests in all companies

$$= 2 \times 10800 = ₹\,21600$$

Chapter 4 Linear Inequations

1. *(c)* We have, $(x+1)^2 - (x-1)^2 < 6$

$$\Rightarrow (x^2 + 1 + 2x) - (x^2 + 1 - 2x) < 6$$

[$\because (a \pm b)^2 = a^2 + b^2 \pm 2ab$]

$$\Rightarrow 4x < 6$$

$$\Rightarrow x < \frac{6}{4}$$

$$\Rightarrow x < \frac{3}{2}$$

$$\Rightarrow x \in \left(-\infty, \frac{3}{2}\right)$$

2. *(d)* Since, $|x|$ is always non-negative.

$$\therefore \quad a - |x| \le a$$

So, the maximum value of $23 - |2x + 3|$ is 23.

3. *(d)* We have, $\frac{1}{5+3x} \le 0$.

This is possible, when $5 + 3x < 0$

$$\Rightarrow 3x < -5 \Rightarrow x < -\frac{5}{3}$$

$$\Rightarrow x \in \left(-\infty, -\frac{5}{3}\right)$$

4. *(c)* Given inequation is $\left|\frac{2}{x-4}\right| > 1, x \ne 4$

$$\Rightarrow 1 < \frac{2}{x-4} \text{ or } \frac{2}{x-4} < -1 \quad \text{[splitting the inequation]}$$

Consider $\frac{2}{x-4} > 1$. If $x - 4 > 0$.

Then, $2 > x - 4$ [multiplying by $(x-4)$ on both sides]

$$\Rightarrow x < 6$$

So, $4 < x < 6$

If $x - 4 < 0$. Then, $2 < x - 4$

[multiplying by $(x - 4)$ both sides]

$\Rightarrow \quad x > 6$

But, $x < 4$ and $x > 6$ is not possible simultaneously.

Consider $\dfrac{2}{x-4} < -1$

If $x - 4 < 0$. Then, $2 > -(x - 4)$

[multiplying by $(x - 4)$ both sides]

$\Rightarrow \quad 2 > -x + 4 \Rightarrow -x < -2 \Rightarrow x > 2$

So, $2 < x < 4$.

If $x - 4 > 0$. Then, $2 < -(x - 4)$

[multiplying by $(x - 4)$ on both sides]

$\Rightarrow \quad 2 < -x + 4 \Rightarrow -x > -2 \Rightarrow x < 2$

But, $x < 2$ and $x > 4$ is not possible simultaneously. The required solution set is $\{x : x \in (2, 4) \cup (4, 6), x \in R\}$.

5. *(a)* Given inequation is $|x + 1| + |x| > 3$

Put $x + 1 = 0 \Rightarrow x = -1$ and $x = 0$.

So, we will consider three intervals $(-\infty, -1)$, $(-1, 0)$ and $(0, \infty)$.

***Case* I** When $-\infty < x < -1$, then $|x + 1| = -(x + 1)$ and $|x| = -x$.

$\therefore \quad |x + 1| + |x| > 3 \Rightarrow -(x + 1) - x > 3$

$\Rightarrow \quad -x - 1 - x > 3 \Rightarrow -2x - 1 > 3$

$\Rightarrow \quad -2x - 1 + 1 > 3 + 1$ [adding 1 both sides]

$\Rightarrow \quad -2x > 4 \Rightarrow \dfrac{-2x}{-2} < \dfrac{4}{-2}$ [dividing both sides by -2]

$\Rightarrow \quad x < -2$

***Case* II** When $-1 \le x < 0$, then $|x + 1| = x + 1$ and $|x| = -x$.

$\therefore \quad |x + 1| + |x| > 3$

$\Rightarrow \quad x + 1 - x > 3$

$\Rightarrow$ $1 > 3$, which is not possible.

***Case* III** When $0 \le x < \infty$, then $|x + 1| = x + 1$ and $|x| = x$.

$\therefore \quad |x + 1| + |x| > 3 \Rightarrow x + 1 + x > 3$

$\Rightarrow \quad 2x + 1 > 3 \Rightarrow 2x + 1 - 1 > 3 - 1$

[subtracting 1 from both sides]

$\Rightarrow \quad 2x > 2 \Rightarrow \dfrac{2x}{2} > \dfrac{2}{2}$ [dividing both sides by 2]

$\Rightarrow \quad x > 1$

On combining results of the above cases, we get

$x < -2$ or $x > 1$

$\therefore \quad x \in (-\infty, -2) \cup (1, \infty)$

6. *(d)* Given, $-2\dfrac{2}{3} \le x + \dfrac{1}{3} \le 3\dfrac{1}{3}$

$\Rightarrow \quad \dfrac{-8}{3} \le x + \dfrac{1}{3} \le \dfrac{10}{3}$

$\dfrac{-8}{3} \times 3 \le \left(x + \dfrac{1}{3}\right)3 \le \dfrac{10}{3} \times 3$ [multiplying by 3 in each term]

$\Rightarrow \quad -8 \le 3x + 1 \le 10$

$\Rightarrow -8 - 1 \le 3x + 1 - 1 \le 10 - 1$

[subtracting 1 from each term]

$\Rightarrow \quad -9 \le 3x \le 9$

$\Rightarrow \quad \dfrac{-9}{3} \le \dfrac{3x}{3} \le \dfrac{9}{3}$ [dividing by 3 each term]

$\Rightarrow \quad -3 \le x \le 3$

Since, $x \in R$.

$\therefore$ Range of x is $[-3, 3]$.

Representation of range of x on the number line is given as

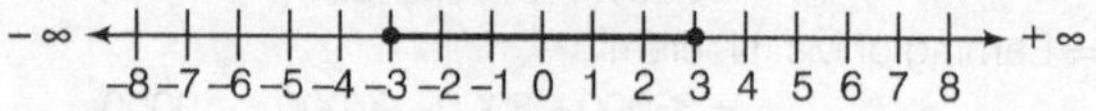

Now, consider the following figure

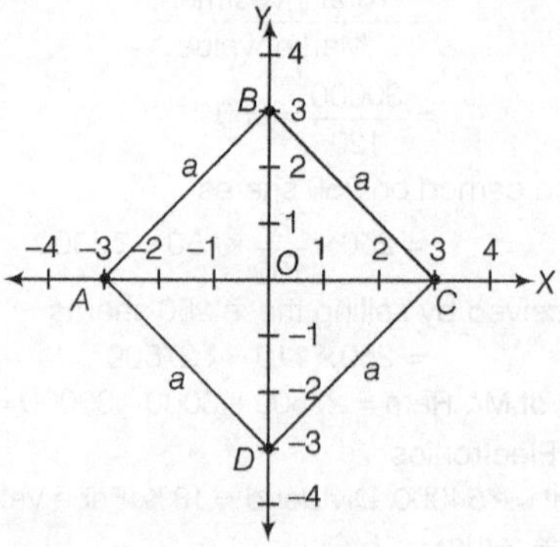

Here, $AC = 6$ units, which is a diagonal of square.

Let side of a square $ABCD$ be a.

In right angled ΔABC,

$$AC^2 = AB^2 + BC^2$$

$\Rightarrow \quad 6^2 = a^2 + a^2$

$\Rightarrow \quad 36 = 2a^2$

$\Rightarrow \quad a^2 = 18$

Now, area of a square $ABCD = (\text{Side})^2 = a^2 = 18$ sq units

7. *(b)* Given system of linear inequations is $-2 < 2x - 6$ or $-2x + 5 \ge 13$.

Consider $\quad -2 < 2x - 6$

$\Rightarrow \quad -2 + 6 < 2x - 6 + 6$ [adding 6 both sides]

$\Rightarrow \quad 4 < 2x$

$\Rightarrow \quad 2 < x$ [dividing both sides by 2] ...(i)

or $\quad -2x + 5 \ge 13$

$\Rightarrow -2x + 5 + 2x \ge 13 + 2x$ [adding $2x$ on both sides]

$\Rightarrow \quad 5 \ge 13 + 2x \Rightarrow 5 - 13 \ge 13 + 2x - 13$

[subtracting 13 from both sides]

$\Rightarrow \quad -8 \ge 2x$

$\Rightarrow \quad \dfrac{-8}{2} \ge \dfrac{2x}{2}$ [dividing both sides by 2]

$\Rightarrow \quad -4 \ge x$ ...(ii)

From Eqs. (i) and (ii), we get the solution set is $\{x : x > 2$ or $x \le -4, x \in R\}$.

The representation of solution set on the number line is

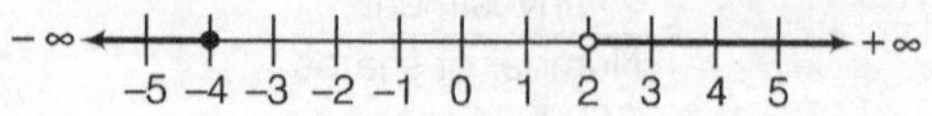

When we shift the origin at the position 1, then the solution set will be $\{x : x + 1 > 2$ or $x + 1 \le -4, x \in R\}$

or $\quad \{x : x > 1$ or $x \le -5, x \in R\}$.

8. *(a)* The number line P on Y-axis and number line Q on X-axis is shown below

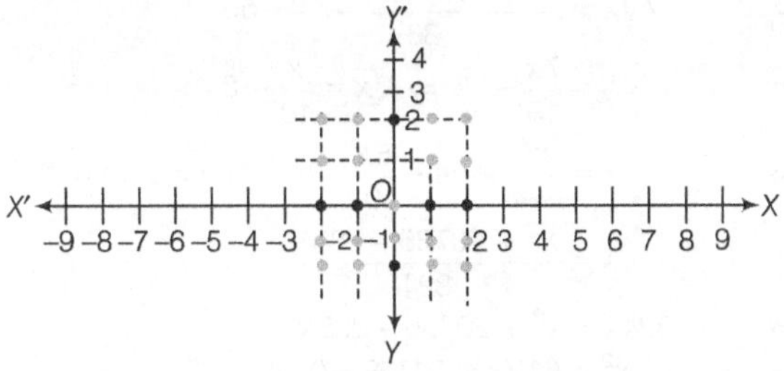

In the graph, the dotted points show all the pairs of coordinate axes.

Thus, the coordinates are (0, 0), (1, 0), (2, 0), (1, 1), (2, 1), (1, 2), (2, 2), (0, 1), (0, 2), (−1, 0), (−2, 0), (−1, 1), (−2, 1), (−1, 2), (−2, 2), (−1, −1), (−2, −1), (−1, −2), (−2, −2) (0, −1), (0, −2), (1, −1), (2, −1), (1, −2), (2, −2).

Hence, the number of all pairs of coordinates of the solution set is 25.

Chapter 5 Quadratic Equations in One Variable

1. *(c)* We have, $x^2 + kx + 1 = 0$

On comparing it with $ax^2 + bx + c = 0$, we get

$$a = 1, b = k \text{ and } c = 1$$

For the linear factors, $D \geq 0$

$\Rightarrow \quad b^2 - 4ac \geq 0$

$\Rightarrow \quad k^2 - 4 \times 1 \times 1 \geq 0$

$\Rightarrow \quad (k^2 - 2^2) \geq 0$

$\Rightarrow \quad (k-2)(k+2) \geq 0$

$\therefore \quad k \geq 2 \text{ or } k \leq -2$

2. *(b)* Given equation is

$$2\sin\theta + \frac{3}{\sin\theta} + 7 = 0$$

$\Rightarrow \quad 2\sin^2\theta + 3 + 7\sin\theta = 0$

$\Rightarrow \quad 2\sin^2\theta + 7\sin\theta + 3 = 0$

$\Rightarrow \quad 2\sin^2\theta + 6\sin\theta + \sin\theta + 3 = 0$ [splitting the middle term]

$\Rightarrow 2\sin\theta(\sin\theta + 3) + 1(\sin\theta + 3) = 0$

$\Rightarrow \quad (2\sin\theta + 1)(\sin\theta + 3) = 0$

$\Rightarrow \quad 2\sin\theta + 1 = 0 \text{ and } \sin\theta + 3 = 0$

But we know that, $\sin\theta$ lies between −1 and 1.

$\therefore \quad \sin\theta = -\frac{1}{2}$

Hence, the root of given equation is $-\frac{1}{2}$.

3. *(a)* Given equation is

$$x^2(a^2 + b^2) + 2x(ac + bd) + (c^2 + d^2) = 0$$

On comparing it with $Ax^2 + Bx + C = 0$, we get

$$A = (a^2 + b^2), B = 2(ac + bd)$$

and $\quad C = c^2 + d^2$

Now, discriminant, $D = B^2 - 4AC$

$= 4(ac + bd)^2 - 4(a^2 + b^2)(c^2 + d^2)$

$= 4[(ac + bd)^2 - (a^2 + b^2)(c^2 + d^2)]$

$= 4(a^2c^2 + b^2d^2 + 2acbd - a^2c^2 - a^2d^2 - b^2c^2 - b^2d^2)$

$= 4(2acbd - a^2d^2 - b^2c^2)$

$= -4(a^2d^2 + b^2c^2 - 2adbc) = -4(ad - bc)^2$

Clearly, when $ad \neq bc$, then $(ad - bc)^2 > 0$

$\Rightarrow \quad -4(ad - bc)^2 < 0 \Rightarrow \quad D < 0$

Hence, the given equation has no real roots.

4. *(d)* Let P be the initial production (2 yr ago) and the increase in production every year be x%. Then, production at the end of first year $= P + \frac{Px}{100} = P\left(1 + \frac{x}{100}\right)$

Production at the end of second year

$$= P\left(1 + \frac{x}{100}\right) + \frac{Px}{100}\left[\left(1 + \frac{x}{100}\right)\right]$$

$$= P\left(1 + \frac{x}{100}\right)\left(1 + \frac{x}{100}\right) = P\left(1 + \frac{x}{100}\right)^2$$

Since, the production is doubled in last two years.

$\therefore \quad P\left(1 + \frac{x}{100}\right)^2 = 2P \Rightarrow \left(1 + \frac{x}{100}\right)^2 = 2$

$\Rightarrow \quad (100 + x)^2 = 2 \times (100)^2 \Rightarrow 10000 + x^2 + 200x = 20000$

$\Rightarrow \quad x^2 + 200x - 10000 = 0$

On comparing it with $ax^2 + bx + c = 0$, we get

$$a = 1, b = 200 \text{ and } c = -10000$$

By quadratic formula, $x = \frac{-b \pm \sqrt{b^2 - 4ac}}{2a}$

$\therefore \quad x = \frac{-200 \pm \sqrt{(200)^2 + 40000}}{2}$

$= -100 \pm 100\sqrt{2} = 100(-1 \pm \sqrt{2})$

$= 100(-1 + 1.414)$

[$\because$ percentage cannot be negative]

$= 100(0.414) = 41.4$

Hence, the required percentage is 41.4%.

5. *(a)* As the CP of x articles is ₹ 1200.

$\therefore$ CP of one article $= ₹\frac{1200}{x}$

As the selling price of each article is ₹ 2 more than its CP.

$\therefore$ SP of each article $= ₹\left(\frac{1200}{x} + 2\right)$

Since, 10 articles were damaged, therefore

Number of articles left for selling $= x - 10$

$\therefore$ SP of all articles (worth selling) $= ₹(x - 10)\left(\frac{1200}{x} + 2\right)$

As the trader earns a net profit of ₹ 60.

$\therefore \quad (x - 10)\left(\frac{1200}{x} + 2\right) = 1200 + 60$

$\Rightarrow \quad (x - 10)\left(\frac{1200 + 2x}{x}\right) = 1260$

$\Rightarrow \quad (x - 10)(1200 + 2x) = 1260x$

$\Rightarrow 1200x + 2x^2 - 12000 - 20x - 1260x = 0$

$\Rightarrow \quad 2x^2 - 80x - 12000 = 0$

$\Rightarrow \quad x^2 - 40x - 6000 = 0$

[dividing both sides by 2]

$\Rightarrow \quad x^2 - 100x + 60x - 6000 = 0$ [splitting the middle term]

$\Rightarrow \quad x(x-100)+60(x-100)=0$

$\Rightarrow \quad (x-100)(x+60)=0$

$\Rightarrow \quad x=100 \text{ or } x=-60$

$\therefore \quad x=100$

[∵ number of articles cannot be negative]

6. *(b)* Given equations are $x^2+2cx+ab=0$ ...(i)

and $x^2-2(a+b)x+a^2+b^2+2c^2=0$ ...(ii)

On comparing above equations with $A_1x^2+B_1x+C_1=0$ and $A_2x^2+B_2x+C_2=0$ respectively, we get

$A_1=1, B_1=2c, C_1=ab$

and $A_2=1, B_2=-2(a+b), C_2=a^2+b^2+2c^2$

Let D_1 and D_2 be the discriminants of Eqs. (i) and (ii), respectively.

Then, $D_1=(2c)^2-4\times1\times ab$ [∵ $D=B^2-4AC$]

$=4c^2-4ab=4(c^2-ab)$

and $D_2=[-2(a+b)]^2-4\times1\times(a^2+b^2+2c^2)$

$=4(a+b)^2-4(a^2+b^2+2c^2)$

$=4(a^2+b^2+2ab-a^2-b^2-2c^2)$

$=4(2ab-2c^2)=-8(c^2-ab)$

Since, the roots of Eq. (i) are real and unequal.

$\therefore \quad D_1>0 \Rightarrow 4(c^2-ab)>0$

$\Rightarrow \quad c^2-ab>0 \Rightarrow -8(c^2-ab)<0$ [∵ $A>0 \Rightarrow -A<0$]

$\Rightarrow \quad D_2<0$

Hence, roots of Eq. (ii) are not real.

7. *(a)* We have, $p^2x^2+(p^2-q^2)x-q^2=0$

On comparing it with $ax^2+bx+c=0$, we get

$a=p^2, b=p^2-q^2$ and $c=-q^2$

Now, discriminant, $D=b^2-4ac$

$=(p^2-q^2)^2-4\times p^2\times(-q^2)$

$=(p^2-q^2)^2+4p^2q^2$

$=p^4+q^4-2p^2q^2+4p^2q^2$

$=p^4+q^4+2p^2q^2=(p^2+q^2)^2>0$

So, the given equation has real roots, which are given by

$$\alpha=\frac{-b+\sqrt{D}}{2a}=\frac{-(p^2-q^2)+\sqrt{(p^2+q^2)^2}}{2p^2}$$

$$=\frac{-p^2+q^2+p^2+q^2}{2p^2}=\frac{2q^2}{2p^2}=\frac{q^2}{p^2}$$

and $$\beta=\frac{-b-\sqrt{D}}{2a}=\frac{-(p^2-q^2)-\sqrt{(p^2+q^2)^2}}{2p^2}$$

$$=\frac{-p^2+q^2-(p^2+q^2)}{2p^2}=\frac{-p^2+q^2-p^2-q^2}{2p^2}=\frac{-2p^2}{2p^2}=-1$$

Hence, the required roots are $\frac{q^2}{p^2}$ and -1.

8. *(d)* Let the total number of Saras birds be x.

Then, number of Saras birds moving in lotus plants $=\frac{x}{4}$

Number of Saras birds moving on a hill $=\frac{x}{9}+\frac{x}{4}+7\sqrt{x}$

Number of Saras birds sitting on the Bakula trees = 56

According to the question,

$$\frac{x}{4}+\frac{x}{9}+\frac{x}{4}+7\sqrt{x}+56=x$$

$$\Rightarrow \quad 7\sqrt{x}=x-\frac{x}{4}-\frac{x}{9}-\frac{x}{4}-56$$

$$\Rightarrow \quad 7\sqrt{x}=\frac{36x-9x-4x-9x}{36}-56$$

$$\Rightarrow \quad 7\sqrt{x}=\frac{7x}{18}-56 \Rightarrow \sqrt{x}=\frac{x}{18}-8$$

$$\Rightarrow \quad x=\frac{x^2}{324}+64-\frac{8x}{9}$$ [squaring on both sides]

$$\Rightarrow \quad x=\frac{x^2+20736-288x}{324}$$

$\Rightarrow \quad 324x=x^2+20736-288x$

$\Rightarrow \quad x^2-612x+20736=0$

$\Rightarrow \quad x^2-36x-576x+20736=0$ [splitting the middle term]

$\Rightarrow \quad x(x-36)-576(x-36)=0$

$\Rightarrow \quad (x-36)(x-576)=0$

$\Rightarrow \quad x-36=0 \text{ or } x-576=0$

$\Rightarrow \quad x=576 \text{ or } x=36$

Here, $x=36$ is not possible, because if there are only 36 birds, then 56 cannot be on the trees.

Thus, total number of Saras birds is 576.

Chapter 6 Ratio and Proportion

1. *(d)* In order to compare the price of coffee with that of tea, we must find the cost of the same quantity of each of them. Let us find the cost of 1 kg of each of the two items.

We have, cost of 100 g of coffee = ₹ 24

Cost of 1 g of coffee = ₹ $\left(\frac{24}{100}\right)$

$\Rightarrow$ Cost of 1000 g of coffee = ₹ $\left(\frac{24}{100}\times1000\right)$ = ₹ 240

$\therefore$ Cost of 1 kg of coffee = ₹ 240 [∵ 1 kg = 1000 g]

It is given that, the cost of 1 kg of tea is ₹ 80.

$\therefore$ Ratio of price of coffee to that of tea

= Cost of 1 kg of coffee : Cost of 1 kg of tea

= ₹ 240 : ₹ 80 = 240 : 80 = 3 : 1

2. *(a)* Given, $(x^2+y^2):(x^2+y^2+xy)$

According to the question,

$$\frac{x^2+y^2-2xy}{x^2+y^2+xy-2xy}=\frac{x^2-y^2}{1}$$

$$\Rightarrow \quad \frac{(x-y)^2}{x^2+y^2-xy}=\frac{(x-y)(x+y)}{1}$$

[∵ $(a-b)^2=a^2+b^2-2ab$]

$$\Rightarrow \quad \frac{(x-y)}{x^2+y^2-xy}=(x+y)$$

$\Rightarrow \quad x-y=(x+y)(x^2+y^2-xy)$

$\Rightarrow \quad x-y=x^3+y^3$

$\Rightarrow \quad x-x^3=y^3+y$

$\Rightarrow \quad x(1-x^2)=y(y^2+1)$

$$\Rightarrow \quad \frac{x}{y}=\frac{1+y^2}{1-x^2}$$

$\therefore \quad x:y=(1+y^2):(1-x^2)$

3. *(d)* We have, $15 \times 42 = 630$ and $18 \times 35 = 630$

$\therefore \quad 15 \times 42 = 18 \times 35 \quad \ldots(i)$

$\Rightarrow$ First term = 15 , fourth term = 42, second term = 18 and third term = 35

Hence, $\quad 15 : 18 :: 35 : 42$

We can also write Eq. (i) as $15 \times 42 = 35 \times 18$

$\Rightarrow$ First term = 15, fourth term = 42, second term = 35 and third term = 18

Hence, $\quad 15 : 35 :: 18 : 42$

Again, Eq. (i) can also be written as

$$42 \times 15 = 18 \times 35$$

$\Rightarrow$ First term = 42, fourth term = 15, second term = 18 and third term = 35

Hence, $\quad 42 : 18 :: 35 : 15$

Finally, Eq. (i) can be written as

$$42 \times 15 = 35 \times 18$$

$\Rightarrow$ First term = 42, fourth term = 15, second term = 35 and third term = 18

Hence, $\quad 42 : 35 :: 18 : 15$

Thus, the required proportions are

$15 : 18 :: 35 : 42$, $15 : 35 :: 18 : 42$, $42 : 18 :: 35 : 15$ and $42 : 35 :: 18 : 15$.

Hence, required number of proportions are 4.

4. *(b)* Given, $\dfrac{x+y}{a^3-b^3} = \dfrac{y+z}{b^3-c^3} = \dfrac{z+x}{c^3-a^3} = k$ (let)

$\therefore \quad x + y = k(a^3 - b^3) \quad \ldots(i)$

$y + z = k(b^3 - c^3) \quad \ldots(ii)$

and $\quad z + x = k(c^3 - a^3) \quad \ldots(iii)$

On adding Eqs. (i), (ii) and (iii), we get

$x + y + y + z + z + x = k(a^3 - b^3) + k(b^3 - c^3) + k(c^3 - a^3)$

$\Rightarrow \quad 2x + 2y + 2z = k(a^3 - b^3 + b^3 - c^3 + c^3 - a^3)$

$\Rightarrow \quad 2(x + y + z) = k \times 0$

$\Rightarrow \quad 2(x + y + z) = 0$

$\therefore \quad x + y + z = 0 \quad [\because 2 \neq 0]$

5. *(a)* Given, $\dfrac{3k+4l+6m+7n}{3k+4l-6m-7n} = \dfrac{3k-4l+6m-7n}{3k-4l-6m+7n}$

$\Rightarrow \dfrac{(3k+4l)+(6m+7n)}{(3k+4l)-(6m+7n)} = \dfrac{(3k-4l)+(6m-7n)}{(3k-4l)-(6m-7n)}$

$\Rightarrow \dfrac{2(3k+4l)}{2(6m+7n)} = \dfrac{2(3k-4l)}{2(6m-7n)}$

[applying componendo and dividendo]

$\Rightarrow \dfrac{3k+4l}{3k-4l} = \dfrac{6m+7n}{6m-7n}$

$\Rightarrow \dfrac{2(3k)}{2(4l)} = \dfrac{2(6m)}{2(7n)}$

[applying componendo and dividendo]

$\Rightarrow \dfrac{k}{4l} = \dfrac{2m}{7n}$

$\Rightarrow \dfrac{k}{2m} = \dfrac{4l}{7n}$

6. *(b)* Given, *a*, *b*, *c* and *d* are in proportion.

$\therefore \quad \dfrac{a}{b} = \dfrac{c}{d}$

On applying componendo and dividendo, we get

$$\frac{a+b}{a-b} = \frac{c+d}{c-d}$$

On cubing both sides, we get

$$\left(\frac{a+b}{a-b}\right)^3 = \left(\frac{c+d}{c-d}\right)^3$$

$\Rightarrow \dfrac{a^3+3a^2b+3ab^2+b^3}{a^3-3a^2b+3ab^2-b^3} = \dfrac{c^3+3c^2d+3cd^2+d^3}{c^3-3c^2d+3cd^2-d^3}$

$\Rightarrow \dfrac{(a^3+3ab^2)+(3a^2b+b^3)}{(a^3+3ab^2)-(3a^2b+b^3)} = \dfrac{(c^3+3cd^2)+(3c^2d+d^3)}{(c^3+3cd^2)-(3c^2d+d^3)}$

$\Rightarrow \dfrac{a^3+3ab^2}{3a^2b+b^3} = \dfrac{c^3+3cd^2}{3c^2d+d^3}$

[applying componendo and dividendo property]

7. *(c)* Given, $\dfrac{a}{b} = \dfrac{c}{d} = \dfrac{e}{f} = \dfrac{121}{125}$

$\Rightarrow \dfrac{3a}{3b} = \dfrac{4c}{4d} = \dfrac{9e}{9f} = \dfrac{121}{125}$

We know that,

$$\text{Each ratio} = \frac{\text{Sum of antecedents}}{\text{Sum of consequents}} = \frac{3a+4c+9e}{3b+4d+9f}$$

$\Rightarrow \dfrac{121}{125} = \dfrac{3a+4c+9e}{3b+4d+9f} \quad \left[\because \text{each ratio} = \dfrac{121}{125}\right]$

8. *(b)* Given equation is $\dfrac{x}{1} = \dfrac{\sqrt[3]{m+1}+\sqrt[3]{m-1}}{\sqrt[3]{m+1}-\sqrt[3]{m-1}}$

On applying componendo and dividendo, we get

$$\frac{x+1}{x-1} = \frac{(\sqrt[3]{m+1}+\sqrt[3]{m-1})+(\sqrt[3]{m+1})-\sqrt[3]{m-1}}{(\sqrt[3]{m+1}+\sqrt[3]{m-1})-(\sqrt[3]{m+1})-\sqrt[3]{m-1}}$$

$\Rightarrow \dfrac{x+1}{x-1} = \dfrac{2(\sqrt[3]{m+1})}{2(\sqrt[3]{m-1})} \Rightarrow \dfrac{x+1}{x-1} = \dfrac{\sqrt[3]{m+1}}{\sqrt[3]{m-1}}$

On cubing both sides, we get

$$\frac{(x+1)^3}{(x-1)^3} = \frac{m+1}{m-1}$$

Again, applying componendo and dividendo, we get

$$\frac{(x+1)^3+(x-1)^3}{(x+1)^3-(x-1)^3} = \frac{m+1+m-1}{m+1-(m-1)}$$

$\Rightarrow \dfrac{x^3+1^3+3x^2\times1+3x\times1^2+(x^3-1^3-3x^2\times1+3x\times1^2)}{x^3+1^3+3x^2\times1+3x\times1^2-(x^3-1^3-3x^2\times1+3x\times1^2)} = \dfrac{2m}{2}$

$\Rightarrow \dfrac{2x^3+6x}{6x^2+2} = \dfrac{m}{1}$

$\Rightarrow \dfrac{2(x^3+3x)}{2(3x^2+1)} = \dfrac{m}{1}$

$\Rightarrow \quad x^3 + 3x = 3mx^2 + m$

$\Rightarrow \quad x^3 - 3mx^2 + 3x = m$

Chapter 8 Matrices

1. *(a)* Given quadratic equation is $x^2 + x - 6 = 0$

$\Rightarrow \quad x^2 + 3x - 2x - 6 = 0$ [by splitting the middle term]

$\Rightarrow \quad x(x+3) - 2(x+3) = 0$

$\Rightarrow \quad (x+3)(x-2) = 0$

$\Rightarrow \quad x = -3, 2$

Also, given $\beta > \alpha$.

$\therefore$ We take $\beta = 2$ and $\alpha = -3$

$$\text{Now, } \begin{bmatrix} 0 & \alpha \\ \alpha & \beta \end{bmatrix}\begin{bmatrix} \beta+1 & 0 \\ -\beta & \alpha \end{bmatrix} = \begin{bmatrix} 0-\alpha\beta & 0+\alpha^2 \\ \alpha\beta+\alpha-\beta^2 & 0+\alpha\beta \end{bmatrix}$$

$$= \begin{bmatrix} -(-3)(2) & (-3)^2 \\ (-3)(2)-3-(2)^2 & (-3)(2) \end{bmatrix}$$

$$= \begin{bmatrix} 6 & 9 \\ -6-3-4 & -6 \end{bmatrix}$$

$$= \begin{bmatrix} 6 & 9 \\ -13 & -6 \end{bmatrix}$$

2. *(a)* From option (a), we have

$$A = \begin{bmatrix} 2 & 2 \\ 2 & 2 \end{bmatrix} \text{ and } B = \begin{bmatrix} 1 & 1 \\ -1 & -1 \end{bmatrix}$$

Then, $A \neq O, B \neq O$

$$\text{Now, } \quad AB = \begin{bmatrix} 2 & 2 \\ 2 & 2 \end{bmatrix}\begin{bmatrix} 1 & 1 \\ -1 & -1 \end{bmatrix}$$

$$= \begin{bmatrix} 2\times1+2(-1) & 2\times1+2(-1) \\ 2\times1+2(-1) & 2\times1+2(-1) \end{bmatrix} = \begin{bmatrix} 0 & 0 \\ 0 & 0 \end{bmatrix} = O$$

3. *(a)* Given, $A = \begin{bmatrix} 3 & 1 \\ -1 & 2 \end{bmatrix}$

$$\text{Now, } \quad A^2 = A \cdot A = \begin{bmatrix} 3 & 1 \\ -1 & 2 \end{bmatrix}\begin{bmatrix} 3 & 1 \\ -1 & 2 \end{bmatrix}$$

$$= \begin{bmatrix} 9-1 & 3+2 \\ -3-2 & -1+4 \end{bmatrix} = \begin{bmatrix} 8 & 5 \\ -5 & 3 \end{bmatrix}$$

$$\therefore A^4 = A^2 \cdot A^2 = \begin{bmatrix} 8 & 5 \\ -5 & 3 \end{bmatrix}\begin{bmatrix} 8 & 5 \\ -5 & 3 \end{bmatrix} = \begin{bmatrix} 64-25 & 40+15 \\ -40-15 & -25+9 \end{bmatrix}$$

$$= \begin{bmatrix} 39 & 55 \\ -55 & -16 \end{bmatrix}$$

$$\text{Now, } \quad A^5 = A^4 \cdot A = \begin{bmatrix} 39 & 55 \\ -55 & -16 \end{bmatrix}\begin{bmatrix} 3 & 1 \\ -1 & 2 \end{bmatrix}$$

$$= \begin{bmatrix} 117-55 & 39+110 \\ -165+16 & -55-32 \end{bmatrix} = \begin{bmatrix} 62 & 149 \\ -149 & -87 \end{bmatrix}$$

4. *(b)* Since, $A + B$ is defined, therefore both A and B are of the same type.

Suppose that both A and B are of order $m \times n$.

Also, AB is defined.

Thus, the number of columns in the pre-factor A must be equal to the number of rows in the post-factor B, i.e. $n = m$

Hence, both A and B are of order $n \times n$, i.e. A and B are square matrices of the same type.

5. *(c)* We have, $A = \begin{bmatrix} 3 & 0 \\ 0 & 3 \end{bmatrix} = 3\begin{bmatrix} 1 & 0 \\ 0 & 1 \end{bmatrix} = 3I$

$\therefore \quad A^n = (3I)^n = 3^n I^n = 3^n I$

[$\because I^n = I$, for all natural numbers n]

$$= 3^n \begin{bmatrix} 1 & 0 \\ 0 & 1 \end{bmatrix}$$

6. *(b)* We have, $\begin{bmatrix} a^x \\ a^{-x} \end{bmatrix}[1 \quad 2] = \begin{bmatrix} p & a^{-2} \\ q & \log_2 2 \end{bmatrix}$

$$\Rightarrow \begin{bmatrix} a^x & 2a^x \\ a^{-x} & 2a^{-x} \end{bmatrix} = \begin{bmatrix} p & a^{-2} \\ q & 1 \end{bmatrix} \quad \left[\because \log_2 2 = \frac{\log 2}{\log 2} = 1\right]$$

On comparing the corresponding elements both sides, we get

$\Rightarrow \quad a^x = p$ ...(i)

$\Rightarrow \quad 2a^x = a^{-2}$ ...(ii)

$\Rightarrow \quad a^{-x} = q$ ...(iii)

and $\quad 2a^{-x} = 1$ ...(iv)

On multiplying Eqs. (ii) and (iv), we get

$4a^{x-x} = a^{-2}$

$\Rightarrow \quad 4a^0 = a^{-2} \Rightarrow 4 = a^{-2} \Rightarrow 4 = \frac{1}{a^2}$

$\Rightarrow \quad a^2 = \frac{1}{4} \Rightarrow a = \frac{1}{2}$ [$\because a > 0$]

Now, $\quad a^{p-q} = a^{a^x - a^{-x}}$ [from Eqs. (i) and (iii)]

$= a^{\frac{1}{2}a^{-2} - \frac{1}{2}} = a^{2-\frac{1}{2}}$ [from Eqs. (ii) and (iv)]

$= a^{\frac{1}{2}\cdot 4 - \frac{1}{2}}$ [$\because a^{-2} = 4$]

$= \left(\frac{1}{2}\right)^{3/2} = 2^{-3/2}$

7. *(a)* We have, $A = \begin{bmatrix} 5 & 5 \\ 0 & 0 \end{bmatrix}\begin{bmatrix} 0 & 0 \\ 5 & 5 \end{bmatrix} = \begin{bmatrix} 25 & 25 \\ 0 & 0 \end{bmatrix} = \begin{bmatrix} 5^2 & 5^2 \\ 0 & 0 \end{bmatrix}$

$$\therefore \quad A^2 = A \cdot A = \begin{bmatrix} 5^2 & 5^2 \\ 0 & 0 \end{bmatrix}\begin{bmatrix} 5^2 & 5^2 \\ 0 & 0 \end{bmatrix}$$

$$= \begin{bmatrix} 5^4 & 5^4 \\ 0 & 0 \end{bmatrix}$$

$\vdots \quad \vdots$

$$A^n = \begin{bmatrix} 5^{2n} & 5^{2n} \\ 0 & 0 \end{bmatrix}$$

$$\text{Thus, } \begin{bmatrix} 5^{2n} & 5^{2n} \\ 0 & 0 \end{bmatrix} = \begin{bmatrix} 5^{200} & 5^{200} \\ 0 & 0 \end{bmatrix}$$

$\Rightarrow \quad 5^{2n} = 5^{200}$

$\Rightarrow \quad 2n = 200$

$\Rightarrow \quad n = 100$

8. *(c)* Let $A = \begin{bmatrix} 7 & -6 \\ 8 & -7 \end{bmatrix}$.

$$\text{Then, } A^2 = \begin{bmatrix} 7 & -6 \\ 8 & -7 \end{bmatrix}\begin{bmatrix} 7 & -6 \\ 8 & -7 \end{bmatrix} = \begin{bmatrix} 1 & 0 \\ 0 & 1 \end{bmatrix} = I$$

$$\therefore \quad \begin{bmatrix} 7 & -6 \\ 8 & -7 \end{bmatrix}^{2017} = A^{2017} = A^{2016} \cdot A$$

$= (A^2)^{1008} \cdot A = I^{2008} \cdot A = I \cdot A$ [$\because I^{1008} = I$]

$$= A = \begin{bmatrix} 7 & -6 \\ 8 & -7 \end{bmatrix}$$

Chapter 9 Arithmetic and Geometric Progression

1. (c) Let the five integers be $a-2d, a-d, a, a+d, a+2d$.

Then, we have

$(a-2d)+(a-d)+a+(a+d)+(a+2d)=10020$

$\Rightarrow \quad 5a=10020$

$\Rightarrow \quad a=2004$

Now, as smallest possible value of d is 1.

$\therefore$ Smallest possible value of $a+2d=2004+2=2006$

2. (b) Let $S=1+(1+2)+(1+2+3)+(1+2+3+4)+\ldots+(1+2+3+\ldots+20)$

$=1+3+6+10+15+21+28+36+45+55+66+78+91+105+120+136+153+171+190+210$

$=1540 \quad \left[\because 1+2+3+\ldots+n=\frac{n(n+1)}{2}\right]$

3. (a) Given, $S_{11}=33$

$\Rightarrow \quad \frac{11}{2}(2a+10d)=33 \quad \left[\because S_n=\frac{n}{2}[2a+(n-1)d]\right]$

$\Rightarrow \quad a+5d=3$

i.e. $a_6=3 \Rightarrow a_4=2$

[$\because$ alternate terms are integers and the given sum is possible]

4. (b) Let $S=(45^2-43^2)+(44^2-42^2)+(43^2-41^2)+(42^2-40^2)+\ldots$upto 15 terms

$=(45+43)(45-43)+(44+42)(44-42)+(43+41)(43-41)+(42+40)(42-40)+\ldots$upto 15 terms

$[\because a^2-b^2=(a-b)(a+b)]$

$=(45+43)2+(44+42)2+(43+41)2+(42+40)2+\ldots$upto 15 terms

$=2[\{45+44+43+\ldots$upto 15 terms$\}+\{43+42+41+\ldots$upto 15 terms$\}]$

$=2\times\left[\frac{15}{2}\{2\times45+(15-1)(-1)\}+\frac{15}{2}\{2\times43+(15-1)(-1)\}\right]$

$\left[\because S_n=\frac{n}{2}\{2a+(n-1)d\}\right]$

$=2\left[\frac{15}{2}(76)+\frac{15}{2}(72)\right]$

$=15(76+72)$

$=15\times148=2220$

Hence, the sum of the given series is 2220.

5. (c) Given point is $A(3, 4)$. The x-coordinate of A is 3. Since, the common difference is 2.

$\therefore$ x-coordinates of the point before A is $(3-2)$, i.e. 1 and after A is $(3+2)$, i.e. 5.

$\Rightarrow D(1, 4)$ and $B(5, 4)$ are the required points.

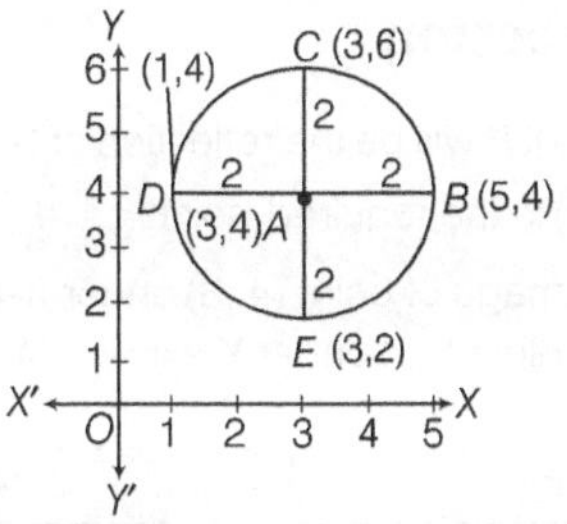

The y-coordinate of A is 4.

Since, the common difference is 2.

$\therefore$ y-coordinates of the point above A is $(4+2)$, i.e. 6 and below A is $(4-2)$, i.e. 2.

$\Rightarrow C(3, 6)$ and $E(3, 2)$ are the required points.

A circle shown in the figure having centre $A(3,4)$ and passing through the points B, C, D and E.

Clearly, radius of circle is, $AB=5-3=2$ units

$\therefore$ Area of circle $=\pi r^2=3.14\times(2)^2=3.14\times4$

$=12.56$ sq units

6. (b) Given, a, b, c and d are in GP.

$\therefore \quad \frac{b}{a}=\frac{c}{b}=\frac{d}{c}=r$ (say)

$\Rightarrow \quad b=ar, c=br, d=cr$

$\Rightarrow \quad b=ar, c=(ar)r, d=(br)r$

$\Rightarrow \quad b=ar, c=ar^2, d=br^2$

$\Rightarrow \quad b=ar, c=ar^2, d=(ar)r^2=ar^3 \quad \ldots$(i)

Now, consider

$(a^2+b^2+c^2)(b^2+c^2+d^2)$

$=(a^2+a^2r^2+a^2r^4)(a^2r^2+a^2r^4+a^2r^6)$

$=a^2(1+r^2+r^4)a^2r^2(1+r^2+r^4)$

$=a^4r^2(1+r^2+r^4)^2=[a^2r(1+r^2+r^4)]^2$

$=(a^2r+a^2r^3+a^2r^5)^2$

$=(a\cdot ar+ar\cdot ar^2+ar^2\cdot ar^3)^2$

$=(ab+bc+cd)^2$ [from Eq. (i)]

7. (d) Let A be the first term and R be the common ratio of the given GP.

Then, $\quad a=p$th term $\Rightarrow a=AR^{p-1}$

$\Rightarrow \quad \log a=\log A+(p-1)\log R \quad \ldots$(i)

$b=q$th term $\Rightarrow b=AR^{q-1}$

$\Rightarrow \quad \log b=\log A+(q-1)\log R \quad \ldots$(ii)

$c=r$th term $\Rightarrow c=AR^{r-1}$

$\Rightarrow \quad \log c=\log A+(r-1)\log R \quad \ldots$(iii)

Now, consider $(q-r)\log a+(r-p)\log b+(p-q)\log c$

$=(q-r)\{\log A+(p-1)\log R\}+(r-p)\{\log A+(q-1)\log R\}+(p-q)\{\log A+(r-1)\log R\}$

[from Eqs. (i), (ii) and (iii)]

$=\log A\{(q-r)+(r-p)+(p-q)\}+\log R\{(p-1)(q-r)+(q-1)(r-p)+(r-1)(p-q)\}$

$=(\log A)0+\{p(q-r)+q(r-p)+r(p-q)-(q-r)-(r-p)-(p-q)\}\log R$

$=(\log A)0+(\log R)0=0$

Chapter 10 Reflection

1. *(b)* Clearly, point P will be the reflection of $(-3, 2)$ in the X-axis. Thus, $(-3, -2)$ is the required point.

2. *(a)* Since, the image of point $(4, 3)$ under X-axis is $(4, -3)$ and the image of point $(4, 3)$ under Y-axis is $(-4, 3)$.

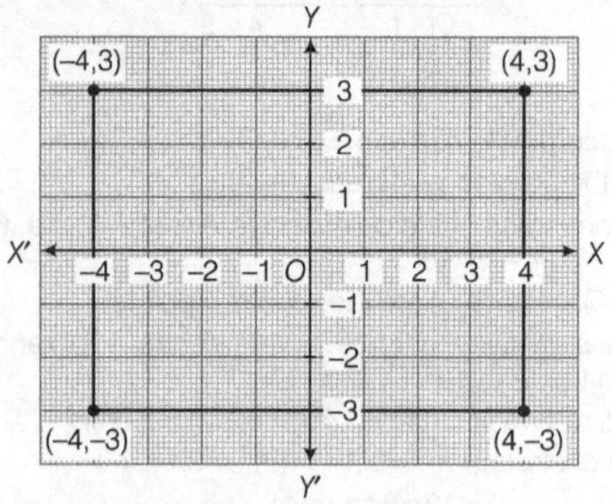

$\therefore$ Other two vertices of the rectangle are $(4, -3)$ and $(-4, 3)$.

3. *(c)* Since, the image of any point (x, y) under X-axis is $(x, -y)$.

$\therefore$ Coordinate of $M \equiv (4, 5)$

Since, the image of any point (x, y) under Y-axis is $(-x, y)$.

$\therefore$ Coordinate of $M'' \equiv (-4, 5)$

Since, the image of any point (x, y) under origin is $(-x, -y)$.

$\therefore$ Coordinate of $M''' \equiv (4, -5)$

4. *(a)* $\because$ Image of $(-8, 5)$ under origin $\equiv (8, -5)$

and image of $(8, -5)$ under X-axis $\equiv (8, 5)$

$\therefore$ $h = 8$ and $k = 5$

5. *(b)* We know that a point is invariant when the line of reflection passing through it.

$\because$ $(3, -2)$ lie on $y = -2$.

$\therefore$ $(3, -2)$ is the required point.

Chapter 11 Section and Mid-Point Formulae

1. *(c)* When we rotate the line PQ in anti-clockwise direction at an angle of 270°, then the new coordinates of point Q will be at R, which touches the X-axis at $(2, 0)$.

Hence, the coordinates of R are $(2, 0)$.

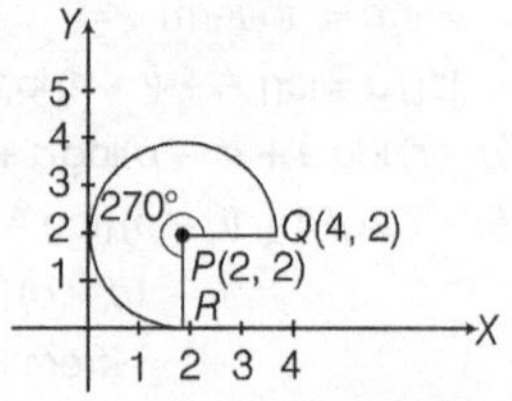

Now, $PQ = \sqrt{(4-2)^2 + (2-2)^2} = \sqrt{2^2 + 0} = 2$ units

$\left[\because \text{distance} = \sqrt{(x_2 - x_1)^2 + (y_2 - y_1)^2}\right]$

Area of the figure $= \frac{3}{4}\pi r^2 = \frac{3}{4} \times 3.14 \times 4 = 9.42$ sq units

2. *(d)* Let the vertices of a triangle be $A(x_1, y_1), B(x_2, y_2)$ and $C(x_3, y_3)$.

Again, let coordinates of P be (h, k).

Since, G is the centroid of a ΔABC.

$\therefore$ Coordinates of $G = \left(\frac{x_1 + x_2 + x_3}{3}, \frac{y_1 + y_2 + y_3}{3}\right)$.

Let $P(h, k)$ be a point in the plane.

Now, $PA^2 = (x_1 - h)^2 + (y_1 - k)^2$

$\left[\because \text{distance} = \sqrt{(x_2 - x_1)^2 + (y_2 - y_1)^2}\right]$

$= x_1^2 + h^2 - 2x_1 h + y_1^2 + k^2 - 2y_1 k$

$PB^2 = (x_2 - h)^2 + (y_2 - k)^2$

$= x_2^2 + h^2 - 2x_2 h + y_2^2 + k^2 - 2y_2 k$

and $PC^2 = (x_3 - h)^2 + (y_3 - k)^2$

$= x_3^2 + h^2 - 2x_3 h + y_3^2 + k^2 - 2y_3 k$

Now, $GA^2 = \left(x_1 - \frac{x_1 + x_2 + x_3}{3}\right)^2 + \left(y_1 - \frac{y_1 + y_2 + y_3}{3}\right)^2$

$= \left(\frac{2x_1 - x_2 - x_3}{3}\right)^2 + \left(\frac{2y_1 - y_2 - y_3}{3}\right)^2$

$= \frac{1}{9}\left[\begin{array}{l} 4x_1^2 + x_2^2 + x_3^2 - 4x_1x_2 + 2x_2x_3 - 4x_1x_3 \\ + 4y_1^2 + y_2^2 + y_3^2 - 4y_1y_2 + 2y_2y_3 - 4y_1y_3 \end{array}\right]$

$[\because (a + b + c)^2 = a^2 + b^2 + c^2 + 2ab + 2bc + 2ca]$

Similarly,

$GB^2 = \frac{1}{9}\left[\begin{array}{l} x_1^2 + 4x_2^2 + x_3^2 - 4x_1x_2 + 2x_1x_3 - 4x_2x_3 \\ + y_1^2 + 4y_2^2 + y_3^2 - 4y_1y_2 + 2y_1y_3 - 4y_2y_3 \end{array}\right]$

and $GC^2 = \frac{1}{9}\left[\begin{array}{l} x_1^2 + x_2^2 + 4x_3^2 + 2x_1x_2 - 4x_1x_3 \\ \quad - 4x_2x_3 + y_1^2 + y_2^2 + 4y_3^2 \\ \quad + 2y_1y_2 - 4y_2y_3 - 4y_1y_3 \end{array}\right]$

Also, $GP^2 = \left(h - \frac{x_1 + x_2 + x_3}{3}\right)^2 + \left(k - \frac{y_1 + y_2 + y_3}{3}\right)^2$

$= h^2 + \left(\frac{x_1 + x_2 + x_3}{3}\right)^2 - 2h\left(\frac{x_1 + x_2 + x_3}{3}\right)$

$+ k^2 + \left(\frac{y_1 + y_2 + y_3}{3}\right)^2 - 2k\left(\frac{y_1 + y_2 + y_3}{3}\right)$

$\Rightarrow 3GP^2 = 3h^2 + \frac{1}{3}(x_1 + x_2 + x_3)^2 - 2h(x_1 + x_2 + x_3)$

$+ 3k^2 + \frac{1}{3}(y_1 + y_2 + y_3)^2 - 2k(y_1 + y_2 + y_3)$

Now, $PA^2 + PB^2 + PC^2 = 3(x_1^2 + x_2^2 + x_3^2)$

$+ 3(y_1^2 + y_2^2 + y_3^2) - 2h(x_1 + x_2 + x_3)$

$+ 3h^2 + 3k^2 - 2k(y_1 + y_2 + y_3)$

Similarly, $GA^2 + GB^2 + GC^2 + 3GP^2$

$= 3(x_1^2 + x_2^2 + x_3^2) + 3(y_1^2 + y_2^2 + y_3^2)$

$+ 3h^2 + 3k^2 - 2k(y_1 + y_2 + y_3)$

$\therefore PA^2 + PB^2 + PC^2 = GA^2 + GB^2 + GC^2 + 3GP^2$

3. *(b)* When we rotate the given graph at an angle of 180°, then the new graph is shown below

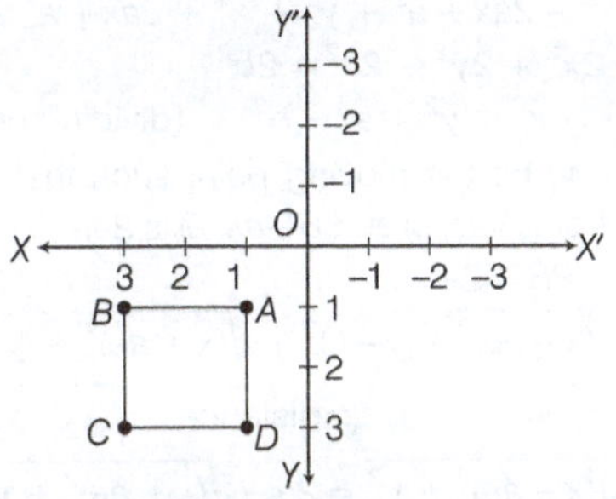

Thus, the new coordinates will be remain same, i.e. $A(1, 1)$, $B(3, 1)$, $C(3, 3)$ and $D(1, 3)$.

We know that in a square, the diagonals bisect each other.

$\therefore$ Mid-point of $BD = \left(\frac{3+1}{2}, \frac{1+3}{2}\right)$

$= \left(\frac{4}{2}, \frac{4}{2}\right) = (2, 2)$

4. *(c)* Let the third vertex of an equilateral triangle be (x, y).

Then, vertices of triangles are $A(-4, 3)$, $B(4, 3)$ and $C(x, y)$.

We know that in equilateral triangle, the angle between two adjacent sides is 60° and all three sides are equal.

$\therefore \quad AB = BC = CA$

$\Rightarrow \quad AB^2 = BC^2 = CA^2 \quad \text{...(i)}$

Now, taking first two terms, $AB^2 = BC^2$

$\Rightarrow (4+4)^2 + (3-3)^2 = (x-4)^2 + (y-3)^2$

$\left[\because \text{distance} = \sqrt{(x_2 - x_1)^2 + (y_2 - y_1)^2}\right]$

$\Rightarrow \quad 64 + 0 = x^2 + 16 - 8x + y^2 + 9 - 6y$

$[\because (a-b)^2 = a^2 + b^2 - 2ab]$

$\Rightarrow x^2 + y^2 - 8x - 6y = 39 \quad \text{...(ii)}$

Now, taking first and third terms, $AB^2 = CA^2$

$\Rightarrow \quad (4+4)^2 + (3-3)^2 = (-4-x)^2 + (3-y)^2$

$\Rightarrow \quad 64 + 0 = 16 + x^2 + 8x + 9 + y^2 - 6y$

$\Rightarrow \quad x^2 + y^2 + 8x - 6y = 39 \quad \text{...(iii)}$

On subtracting Eq. (ii) from Eq. (iii), we get

$$\begin{array}{r} x^2 + y^2 + 8x - 6y = 39 \\ x^2 + y^2 - 8x - 6y = 39 \\ - \quad - \quad + \quad + \quad - \\ \hline 16x = 0 \\ \hline \end{array}$$

$\Rightarrow \quad x = 0$

Now, putting the value of x in Eq. (ii), we get

$0 + y^2 - 0 - 6y = 39$

$\Rightarrow \quad y^2 - 6y - 39 = 0$

$\therefore \quad y = \frac{6 \pm \sqrt{(-6)^2 - 4(1)(-39)}}{2 \times 1}$

$\left[\text{by quadratic formula, } x = \frac{-b \pm \sqrt{b^2 - 4ac}}{2a}\right]$

$= \frac{6 \pm \sqrt{36 + 156}}{2} = \frac{6 \pm \sqrt{192}}{2}$

$= \frac{6 \pm 2\sqrt{48}}{2} = 3 \pm \sqrt{48}$

$= 3 \pm 4\sqrt{3} = 3 + 4\sqrt{3} \quad \text{or} \quad 3 - 4\sqrt{3}$

So, the points of third vertex are $(0, 3 + 4\sqrt{3})$ or $(0, 3 - 4\sqrt{3})$.

But given that, the origin lies in the interior of the ΔABC and the x-coordinate of third vertex is zero. Then, y-coordinate of third vertex should be negative.

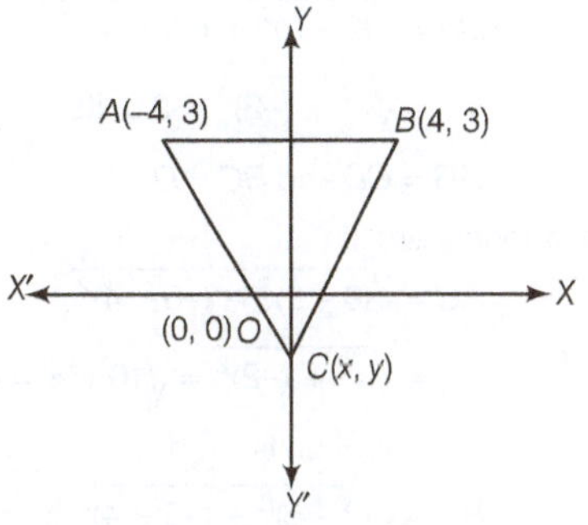

Hence, the required coordinates of third vertex are

$C(0, 3 - 4\sqrt{3}) \quad [\because C \neq (0, 3 + 4\sqrt{3})]$

5. *(b)* Given points $A(2, 4)$, $B(6, 4)$, $C(6, 6)$ and $D(2, 6)$ plotting on a graph paper, is shown below

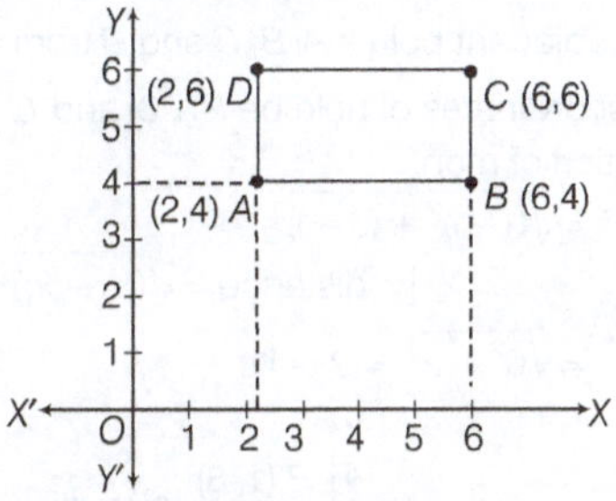

When we rotate only the axes at an angle of 90° in anti-clockwise direction, the new axes are shown below

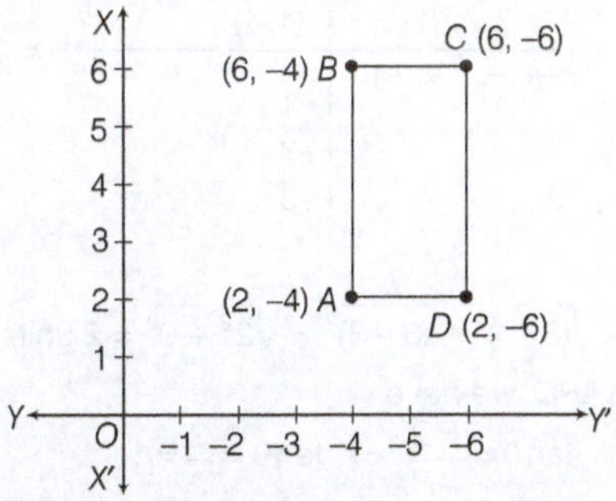

Here, we see that, in first quadrant, y-coordinates will be negative.

$\therefore$ The new coordinates of A, B, C and D are respectively

$A(2, -4)$, $B(6, -4)$, $C(6, -6)$ and $D(2, -6)$.

Now, $\quad AB = \sqrt{(6-2)^2 + (-4+4)^2}$

$= \sqrt{4^2 + 0^2} = 4$ units

$[\because \text{distance} = \sqrt{(x_2 - x_1)^2 + (y_2 - y_1)^2}]$

$BC = \sqrt{(6-6)^2 + (-6+4)^2}$

$= \sqrt{(0)^2 + (-2)^2} = 2$ units

$CD = \sqrt{(2-6)^2 + (-6+6)^2}$

$= \sqrt{(-4)^2 + 0^2} = 4$ units

and $DA = \sqrt{(2-2)^2 + (-6+4)^2}$

$= \sqrt{0^2 + (-2)^2} = 2$ units

$\therefore$ $AB = CD$ and $BC = DA$

Now, the diagonals are

$AC = \sqrt{(6-2)^2 + (-6+4)^2}$

$= \sqrt{4^2 + (-2)^2} = \sqrt{16+4} = \sqrt{20}$

$= 2\sqrt{5}$ units

and $BD = \sqrt{(2-6)^2 + (-6+4)^2}$

$= \sqrt{(-4)^2 + (-2)^2} = \sqrt{16+4} = \sqrt{20}$

$= 2\sqrt{5}$ units

$\therefore$ $AC = BD$

Hence, the adjacent points A, B, C and D from a rectangle.

6. *(a)* Given, coordinates of pole be $P(1, 3)$ and $Q(3, 3)$ and $A(1, 1)$ be the position of man.

(i) Now, $AP = \sqrt{(1-1)^2 + (3-1)^2}$

$[\because \text{distance} = \sqrt{(x_2 - x_1)^2 + (y_2 - y_1)^2}]$

$= \sqrt{0^2 + 2^2} = 2$ units

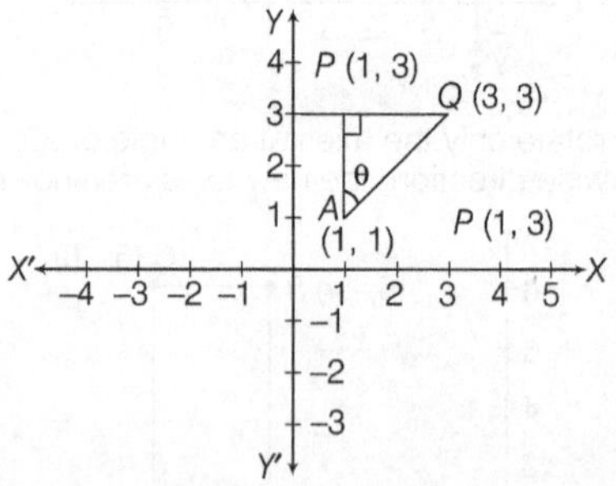

and $PQ = \sqrt{(3-1)^2 + (3-3)^2} = \sqrt{2^2 + 0^2} = 2$ units

Now, in ΔAPQ, we have

$\tan\theta = \dfrac{PQ}{AP} \Rightarrow \tan\theta = \dfrac{2}{2} = 1$

$\Rightarrow \theta = 45°$ $[\because \tan 45° = 1]$

(ii) When we shift the origin at (1, 1), then the angle will remain same, i.e. $\theta = 45°$.

7. *(d)* Let $P(x, y)$ be the moving point.

Let given two fixed points be $A(a, 0)$ and $B(-a, 0)$.

According to the given condition,

$PA^2 + PB^2 = 2b^2$

$\Rightarrow (x-a)^2 + (y-0)^2 + (x+a)^2 + (y-0)^2 = 2b^2$ [by distance formula]

$\Rightarrow x^2 - 2ax + a^2 + y^2 + x^2 + 2ax + a^2 + y^2 = 2b^2$

$\Rightarrow 2x^2 + 2y^2 + 2a^2 = 2b^2$

$\Rightarrow x^2 + y^2 + a^2 = b^2$ [dividing both sides by 2]

8. *(c)* Let $P(x, y)$ be the moving point such that the sum of its distances from $A(ae, 0)$ and $B(-ae, 0)$ is $2a$.

Then, $PA + PB = 2a$

$\Rightarrow \sqrt{(x-ae)^2 + (y-0)^2} + \sqrt{(x+ae)^2 + (y-0)^2} = 2a$

$[\because \text{distance} = \sqrt{(x_2 - x_1)^2 + (y_2 - y_1)^2}]$

$\Rightarrow \sqrt{(x-ae)^2 + y^2} = 2a - \sqrt{(x+ae)^2 + y^2}$

$\Rightarrow (x-ae)^2 + y^2 = 4a^2 + (x+ae)^2 + y^2 - 4a\sqrt{(x+ae)^2 + y^2}$ [squaring on both sides]

$\Rightarrow x^2 + a^2e^2 - 2xae = 4a^2 + x^2 + a^2e^2 + 2xae - 4a\sqrt{(x+ae)^2 + y^2}$

$\Rightarrow -4aex - 4a^2 = -4a\sqrt{(x+ae)^2 + y^2}$

$\Rightarrow (ex + a) = \sqrt{(x+ae)^2 + y^2}$

$\Rightarrow (ex + a)^2 = (x + ae)^2 + y^2$ [again, squaring on both sides]

$\Rightarrow e^2x^2 + 2aex + a^2 = x^2 + a^2e^2 + 2aex + y^2$

$\Rightarrow x^2(1-e^2) + y^2 = a^2(1-e^2)$

$\Rightarrow \dfrac{x^2}{a^2} + \dfrac{y^2}{a^2(1-e^2)} = 1$

$\therefore \dfrac{x^2}{a^2} + \dfrac{y^2}{b^2} = 1$, where $b^2 = a^2(1-e^2)$

Chapter 12 Equation of a Straight Line

1. *(b)* Let the vertices of ΔABC be $A(-1, 3)$, $B(2, -1)$ and $C(0, 0)$.

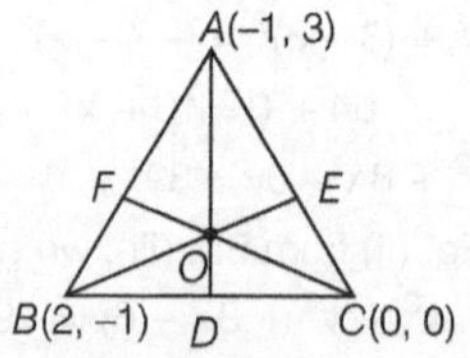

Let AD, BE and CF be the altitudes and $O(h, k)$ be the orthocentre of ΔABC.

$\because$ $AO \perp BC$

$\therefore$ Slope of line $AO \times$ Slope of line $BC = -1$

$\Rightarrow \dfrac{k-3}{h+1} \times \left(\dfrac{0+1}{0-2}\right) = -1$ $[\because m_1 \times m_2 = -1]$

$\Rightarrow \dfrac{k-3}{h+1} = 2 \Rightarrow 2h - k + 5 = 0$ ...(i)

Also, $BO \perp AC$

$\therefore$ Slope of line $BO \times$ Slope of line $AC = -1$

$\dfrac{k+1}{h-2} \times \dfrac{3-0}{-1-0} = -1$ $[\because m_1 \times m_2 = -1]$

$$\Rightarrow \quad \frac{k+1}{h-2} \times (-3) = -1$$

$$\Rightarrow \quad h - 2 = 3k + 3$$

$$\Rightarrow \quad h - 3k - 5 = 0 \qquad \text{...(ii)}$$

On solving Eqs. (i) and (ii), we get

$$\frac{h}{5+15} = \frac{k}{5+10} = \frac{1}{-6+1}$$

$$\Rightarrow \quad \frac{h}{20} = \frac{k}{15} = \frac{1}{-5}$$

$$\therefore \quad h = -4 \text{ and } k = -3$$

Hence, the orthocentre is $(-4, -3)$.

2. *(a)* The equation of the line parallel to Y-axis at a distance 3 units to the left of Y-axis, is $x = -3$.

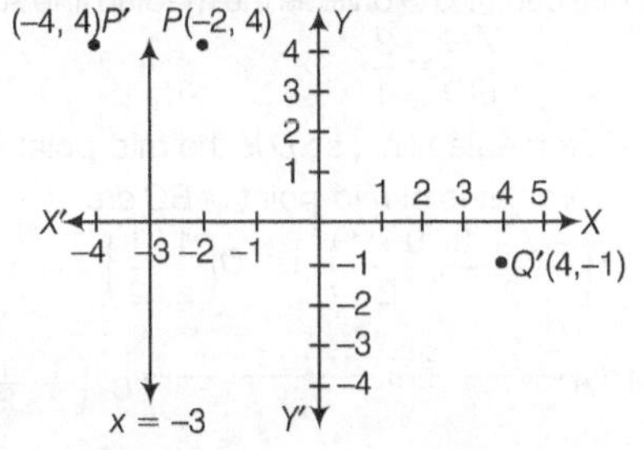

We know that reflection of the point (x, y) in the line $x = a$ is $(-x + 2a, y)$. Therefore, the reflection of the point $P(-2, 4)$ in the line $x = -3$ is the point $P'(-(-2) + 2 \times (-3), 4)$, i.e. $P'(-4, 4)$.

Since, $Q'(4, -1)$ is the image of the point Q in the origin. Therefore, the coordinates of the point Q are $(-4, 1)$.

Now, the equation of a line $P'Q$ passing through $P'(-4, 4)$ and $Q(-4, 1)$ is

$$y - 4 = \frac{1-4}{-4+4}(x+4)$$

$$\Rightarrow \quad y - 4 = \frac{-3}{0}(x+4)$$

$$\Rightarrow \quad 0 = -3(x+4)$$

$$\Rightarrow \quad x + 4 = 0$$

3. *(d)* Equation of the line passing through (3, 2) having slope $\frac{3}{4}$ is given by

$$y - 2 = \frac{3}{4}(x - 3) \qquad [\because y - y_1 = m(x - x_1)]$$

$$\Rightarrow \quad 4y - 3x + 1 = 0 \qquad \text{...(i)}$$

Let (h, k) be the required point on the line, such that distance between (h, k) and (3, 2) is 5.

Then, $\quad (h-3)^2 + (k-2)^2 = 25 \qquad \text{...(ii)}$

Also, point (h, k) lies on the line.

$$\therefore \quad 4k - 3h + 1 = 0 \qquad \text{[from Eq. (i)]...(iii)}$$

$$\Rightarrow \quad k = \frac{3h-1}{4} \qquad \text{...(iv)}$$

On putting the value of k in Eq. (ii) and simplifying, we get

$$25h^2 - 150h - 175 = 0$$

$$\Rightarrow \quad h^2 - 6h - 7 = 0$$

$$\Rightarrow \quad (h+1)(h-7) = 0$$

$$\Rightarrow \quad h = -1, 7$$

On putting these values of h in Eq. (iv), we get

$$k = -1 \text{ and } k = 5$$

Therefore, the coordinates of the required points are either $(-1, -1)$ or $(7, 5)$.

4. *(c)* Let the incident ray strike X-axis at the point A, whose coordinates be $(x, 0)$. From the figure, the slope of the reflected ray is given by

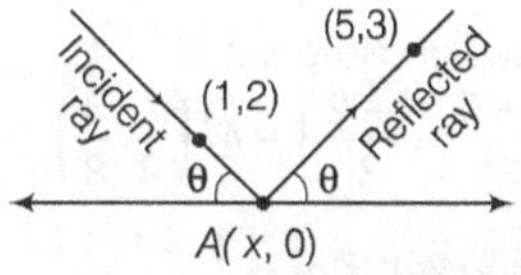

$$\tan\theta = \frac{3}{5-x} \qquad \text{...(i)}$$

Again, the slope of the incident ray is given by

$$\tan(\pi - \theta) = \frac{-2}{x-1} \Rightarrow -\tan\theta = \frac{-2}{x-1}$$

$$\Rightarrow \quad \tan\theta = \frac{2}{x-1} \qquad [\because \tan(\pi - \theta) = -\tan\theta] \text{...(ii)}$$

On solving Eqs. (i) and (ii), we get

$$\frac{3}{5-x} = \frac{2}{x-1}$$

$$\Rightarrow \quad 3x - 3 = 10 - 2x \Rightarrow x = \frac{13}{5}$$

Therefore, the required coordinates of the point A are $\left(\frac{13}{5}, 0\right)$.

5. *(d)* Let the equation of the line be $\frac{x}{a} + \frac{y}{b} = 1$. $\qquad$ ...(i)

Since, it passes through the point $(3, -2)$.

$$\therefore \quad \frac{3}{a} - \frac{2}{b} = 1 \qquad \text{...(ii)}$$

The line (i) cuts the coordinate axes at $A(a, 0)$ and $B(0, b)$. Let $P(h, k)$ be the mid-point of the portion AB.

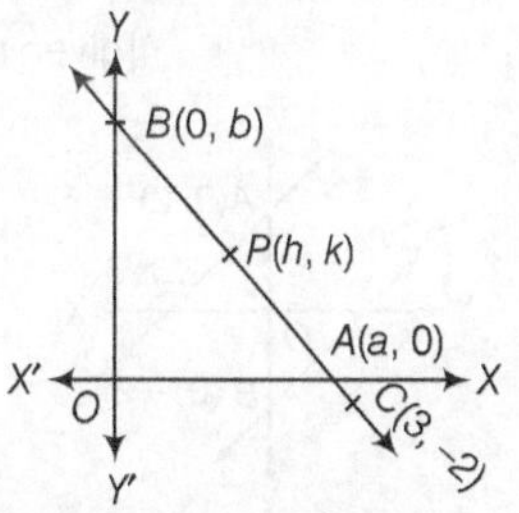

Then,

$$h = \frac{a+0}{2} \text{ and } k = \frac{0+b}{2}$$

$$\Rightarrow \quad a = 2h \text{ and } b = 2k$$

On substituting the values of a and b in Eq. (ii), we get

$$\frac{3}{2h} - \frac{2}{2k} = 1$$

Hence, the locus of $P(h, k)$ is $\frac{3}{2x} - \frac{1}{y} = 1$ or $3y - 2x = 2xy$.

6. *(a)* Let PQ be the mirror line. Given, image of point $A(2, 1)$ with respect to the line PQ is $A'(5, 2)$. Since, image line is the perpendicular bisector of the mirror line. So, mid-point (M) of AA' lies on PQ.

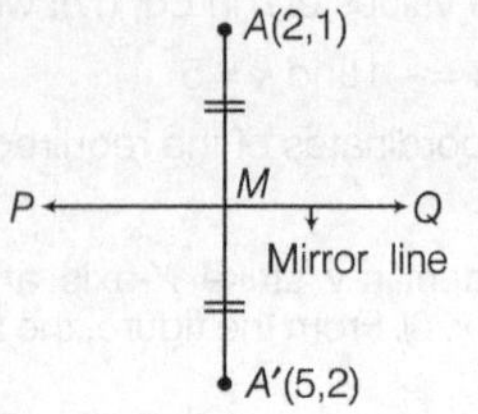

Now, coordinates of mid-point of

$$AA' = M\left(\frac{2+5}{2}, \frac{1+2}{2}\right) = M\left(\frac{7}{2}, \frac{3}{2}\right)$$

Now, slope of line AA' is $m_1 = \frac{2-1}{5-2} = \frac{1}{3}$ $\left[\because \text{slope} = \frac{y_2 - y_1}{x_2 - x_1}\right]$

Let the slope of a mirror line PQ be m_2.

Since, PQ is perpendicular to AA'.

$$\therefore \quad m_1 \times m_2 = -1$$

$$\Rightarrow \quad \frac{1}{3} \times m_2 = -1 \Rightarrow m_2 = -3$$

Now, equation of the mirror line PQ, which is passing through $M\left(\frac{7}{2}, \frac{3}{2}\right)$ and having slope $m_2 = -3$, is

$$y - \frac{3}{2} = -3\left(x - \frac{7}{2}\right)$$

$$\Rightarrow \quad \left(\frac{2y-3}{2}\right) = -3\left(\frac{2x-7}{2}\right)$$

$$\Rightarrow \quad 2y - 3 = -3(2x - 7)$$

$$\Rightarrow \quad 2y - 3 = -6x + 21$$

$$\Rightarrow \quad 6x + 2y - 24 = 0$$

$$\Rightarrow \quad 3x + y - 12 = 0 \quad \text{[dividing both sides by 2]}$$

7. *(b)* Since, $m = \tan\theta = \tan\frac{2\pi}{3}$

$$= \tan\left(\pi - \frac{\pi}{3}\right) = -\tan\frac{\pi}{3} = -\sqrt{3}$$

[given $\tan(\pi - \theta) = -\tan\theta$]

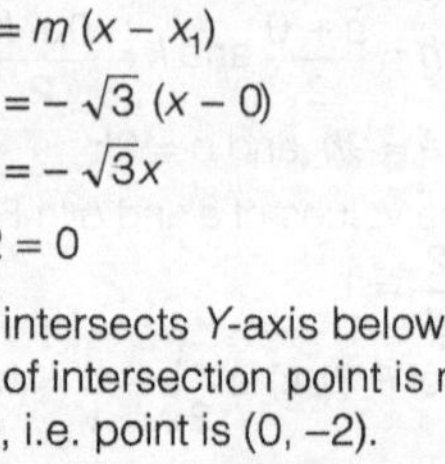

Hence, the equation of line AC passing through the point $A(0, 2)$ is $y - y_1 = m(x - x_1)$

$$\Rightarrow \quad y - 2 = -\sqrt{3}(x - 0) \quad [\because x_1 = 0, y_1 = 2]$$

$$\Rightarrow \quad y - 2 = -\sqrt{3}x$$

$$\Rightarrow \quad \sqrt{3}x + y - 2 = 0$$

Also, the line BD intersects Y-axis below origin. It means that the y-coordinate of intersection point is negative and x-coordinate is 0, i.e. point is $(0, -2)$.

Hence, equation of line passing through the point $B(0, -2)$ and parallel to AC is

$$y + 2 = -\sqrt{3}(x - 0) \quad [\because y - y_1 = m(x - x_1)]$$

$$\Rightarrow \quad \sqrt{3}x + y + 2 = 0$$

8. *(a)* Let third vertex of a ΔABC be $A(x_1, y_1)$.

Given vertices and centroid of a ΔABC are $B(-2, 0)$, $C(3, 1)$ and $G(1, 5)$.

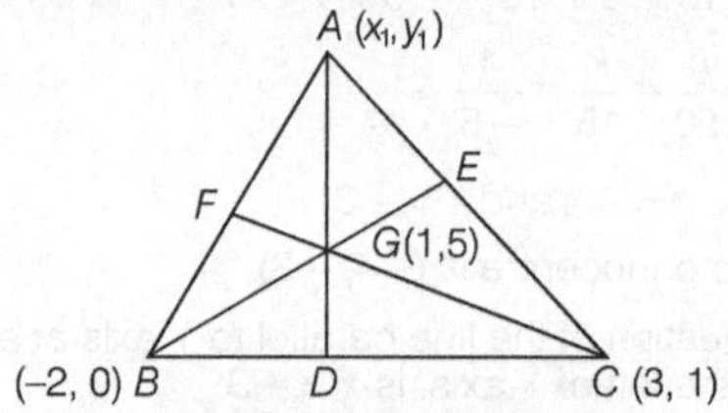

We know that centroid G divides the median line AD into 2 : 1,

i.e. $\frac{AG}{GD} = \frac{2}{1}$

Since, AD is a median line, so D is the mid-point of BC.

Now, the coordinates of mid-point of BC are

$$D\left(\frac{-2+3}{2}, \frac{0+1}{2}\right), \text{ i.e. } D\left(\frac{1}{2}, \frac{1}{2}\right)$$

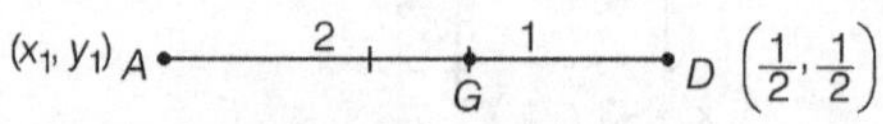

Now, using the internal division formula,

$$\text{Coordinates of } G = \left(\frac{2 \times \frac{1}{2} + 1 \times x_1}{2+1}, \frac{2 \times \frac{1}{2} + 1 \times y_1}{2+1}\right)$$

$$\Rightarrow \quad (1, 5) = \left(\frac{1 + x_1}{3}, \frac{1 + y_1}{3}\right)$$

On equating the x and y-coordinates of both sides, we get

$$1 = \frac{1 + x_1}{3} \text{ and } 5 = \frac{1 + y_1}{3}$$

$$\Rightarrow \quad 3 = 1 + x_1 \text{ and } 15 = 1 + y_1$$

$$\therefore \quad x_1 = 2 \text{ and } y_1 = 14$$

Thus, the coordinates of A are $(2, 14)$.

Now, the equation of side AB, which is passing through $A(2, 14)$ and $B(-2, 0)$, is

$$y - 14 = \frac{0 - 14}{-2 - 2}(x - 2)$$

$$\Rightarrow \quad y - 14 = \frac{-14}{-4}(x - 2)$$

$$\Rightarrow \quad 2y - 28 = 7x - 14$$

$$\Rightarrow \quad 2y - 7x = 28 - 14$$

$$\Rightarrow \quad 2y - 7x = 14 \Rightarrow 7x - 2y + 14 = 0$$

Now, the equation of side AC, which is passing through $A(2, 14)$ and $C(3, 1)$, is

$$y - 14 = \frac{1 - 14}{3 - 2}(x - 2)$$

$$\Rightarrow \quad y - 14 = \frac{-13}{1}(x - 2)$$

$$\Rightarrow \quad y - 14 = -13x + 26 \Rightarrow 13x + y - 40 = 0$$

Chapter 13 Similarity

1. (b) Given, height of boy (BC) = 90 cm = 0.9 m

Height of lamp-post (PQ) = 3.6 m

Speed of boy = 1.2 m/s

Time taken = 6 s

$\therefore$ Distance moved by boy (CQ) = Speed × Time

$= 1.2 \times 6 = 7.2$ m

Let length of shadow be $AC = x$ cm

In ΔABC and ΔAPQ,

$\angle ACB = \angle AQP$ [each 90°]

and $\angle BAC = \angle PAQ$ [common angle]

$\therefore$ $\Delta ABC \sim \Delta APQ$ [by AA similarity criterion]

Then, $\dfrac{AC}{AQ} = \dfrac{BC}{PQ}$

$\Rightarrow \dfrac{x}{x+7.2} = \dfrac{0.9}{3.6}$ [$\because AQ = AC + CQ = x + 7.2$]

$\Rightarrow \dfrac{x}{x+7.2} = \dfrac{1}{4}$

$\Rightarrow 4x = x + 7.2 \Rightarrow 4x - x = 7.2$

$\Rightarrow 3x = 7.2$

$\therefore x = \dfrac{7.2}{3} = 2.4$

2. (c) Given $AM : MC = 3 : 4$

$BP : PM = 3 : 2$ and $BN = 12$ cm

Draw MR parallel to CN which meets AB at the point R.

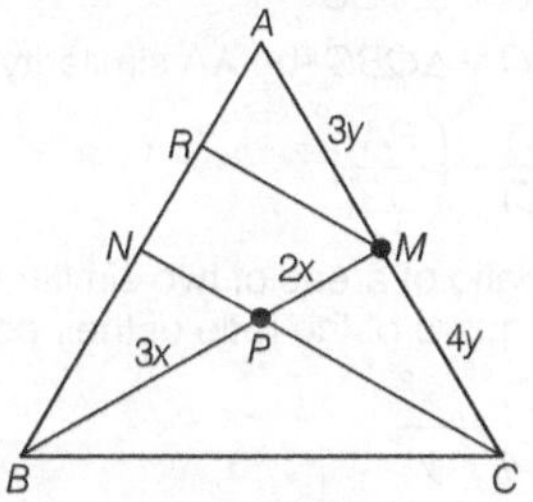

Consider ΔBMR. In this, we have

$PN \parallel MR$ [by construction]

$\therefore$ By BPT, $\dfrac{BN}{NR} = \dfrac{BP}{PM} \Rightarrow \dfrac{12}{NR} = \dfrac{3}{2}$

$\Rightarrow NR = 8$ cm

Now, consider ΔANC, $RM \parallel NC$ [by construction]

$\therefore$ By BPT, $\dfrac{AR}{RN} = \dfrac{AM}{MC} \Rightarrow \dfrac{AR}{8} = \dfrac{3}{4} \Rightarrow AR = 6$ cm

Thus, $AN = AR + RN = 6 + 18 = 14$ cm

3. (c) Given $AB = 8$ cm and $BC = 6$ cm

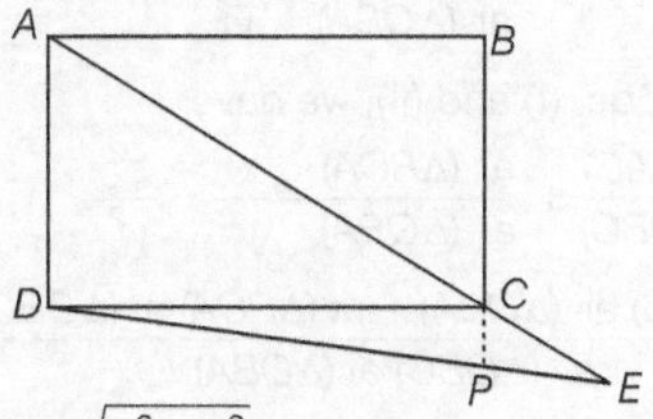

$\therefore AC = \sqrt{8^2 + 6^2} = 10$ cm

Also, given $AC : CE = 2 : 1$

Now, produce BC to meet DE at the point P as CP is parallel to AD,

$\Delta ECP \sim \Delta EAD$ ...(i)

$\Rightarrow \dfrac{CP}{AD} = \dfrac{CE}{AE} \Rightarrow \dfrac{CP}{6} = \dfrac{1}{3}$ ...(ii)

$\Rightarrow CP = 2$ cm

Also, ΔCPD is a right triangle.

$\therefore DP = \sqrt{CD^2 + CP^2}$

$= \sqrt{68} = 2\sqrt{17}$ cm

But $DP = PE = 2:1$ [from Eq.(i)]

$\therefore PE = \sqrt{17}$ cm

Thus, $DE = DP + PE = 2\sqrt{17} + \sqrt{17} = 3\sqrt{17}$ cm

4. (a) In ΔABC, we have $DE \parallel BC$

Now, in ΔADE and ΔABC, we have

$\angle A = \angle A$ [common angle]

$\angle ADE = \angle ABC$ [corresponding angles]

and $\angle AED = \angle ACB$ [corresponding angles]

$\therefore \Delta ADE \sim \Delta ABC$ [by AAA similarity criterion]

$\Rightarrow \dfrac{AD}{AB} = \dfrac{DE}{BC}$ ...(i)

We have, $\dfrac{AD}{DB} = \dfrac{5}{4}$ [$\because$ if two triangles are similar, then their corresponding sides are proportional]

$\Rightarrow \dfrac{DB}{AD} = \dfrac{4}{5}$ [given]

$\Rightarrow \dfrac{DB}{AD} + 1 = \dfrac{4}{5} + 1$ [adding 1 both sides]

$\Rightarrow \dfrac{DB + AD}{AD} = \dfrac{9}{5}$

$\Rightarrow \dfrac{AB}{AD} = \dfrac{9}{5} \Rightarrow \dfrac{AD}{AB} = \dfrac{5}{9}$

$\therefore \dfrac{DE}{BC} = \dfrac{5}{9}$ [from Eq. (i)]

In ΔDFE and ΔCFB, we have

$\angle 1 = \angle 3$ [alternate interior angles]

$\angle 2 = \angle 4$ [vertically opposite angles]

Therefore, by AA similarity criterion, we have

$\Delta DFE \sim \Delta CFB$

$\Rightarrow \dfrac{\text{ar}(\Delta DFE)}{\text{ar}(\Delta CFB)} = \dfrac{DE^2}{BC^2} = \left(\dfrac{5}{9}\right)^2 = \dfrac{25}{81}$

[by areas of similar triangles theorem]

5. (c) In ΔBMC and ΔEMD, we have

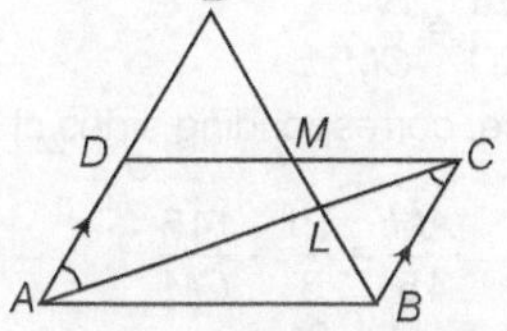

$\angle BMC = \angle EMD$ [vertically opposite angles]

$\Rightarrow MC = MD$ [$\because M$ is the mid-point of CD]

$\Rightarrow \quad \angle MCB = \angle MDE$ [alternate angles]

So, by AAS congruence criterion, we have

$$\Delta BMC \cong \Delta EMD$$

$\Rightarrow \quad BC = ED$

[$\because$ corresponding parts of congruent triangles are equal]

In ΔAEL and ΔCBL, we have

$\angle ALE = \angle CLB$ [vertically opposite angles]

and $\angle EAL = \angle BCL$ [alternate angles]

So, by AA criterion of similarity, we have

$$\Delta AEL \sim \Delta CBL$$

$\Rightarrow \quad \dfrac{AE}{BC} = \dfrac{EL}{BL} = \dfrac{AL}{CL}$

[$\because$ if two triangles are similar, then their corresponding sides are proportional]

On taking first two terms, we get

$$\frac{EL}{BL} = \frac{AE}{BC} = \frac{AD + DE}{BC}$$

$$= \frac{BC + BC}{BC} = \frac{2BC}{BC} = 2$$

[$\because AD = BC$ as sides opposite to parallelogram and $DE = BC$, proved above]

$\Rightarrow \quad EL = 2BL$ ...(i)

Now, $\dfrac{\text{ar}(\Delta AEL)}{\text{ar}(\Delta CBL)} = \left(\dfrac{EL}{BL}\right)^2$

[$\because$ ratio of areas of two similar triangles is equal to the square of the ratio of their corresponding sides]

$= \left(\dfrac{2BL}{BL}\right)^2 = (2)^2$ [from Eq. (i)]

$\Rightarrow \quad \dfrac{\text{ar}(\Delta AEL)}{\text{ar}(\Delta CBL)} = 4$

$\Rightarrow \quad \text{ar}(\Delta AEL) = 4\ \text{ar}(\Delta CBL)$

6. *(a)* Given figure can be redrawn as

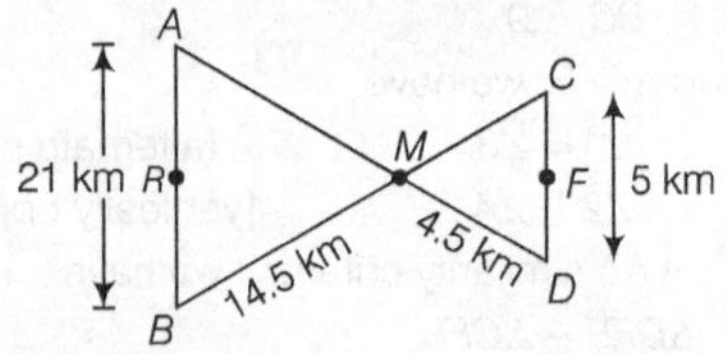

In ΔBAM and ΔCDM,

$\angle BAM = \angle CDM$ [alternate interior angles as $AB \| CD$]

$\angle ABM = \angle DCM$ [alternate interior angles]

and $\angle AMB = \angle DMC$ [vertically opposite angles]

$\therefore \quad \Delta BAM \sim \Delta CDM$ [by AAA similarity criterion]

So, $\dfrac{AM}{DM} = \dfrac{BA}{CD} = \dfrac{BM}{CM}$

[since, corresponding sides of similar triangles are proportional]

$\therefore \quad \dfrac{AM}{4.5} = \dfrac{21}{5} = \dfrac{14.5}{CM}$

Now, consider $\dfrac{AM}{4.5} = \dfrac{21}{5}$

$\Rightarrow \quad AM = \dfrac{21 \times 4.5}{5} = 21 \times 0.9 = 18.9 \text{ km}$

and consider $\dfrac{21}{5} = \dfrac{14.5}{CM}$

$\Rightarrow \quad CM = \dfrac{5 \times 14.5}{21} = 3.45 \text{ km}$

There are four routes which Radhika may follow to reach friend's house, are given below

1st route $R \to A \to M \to C \to F$

Total distance $= RA + AM + MC + CF$
$= 10.5 + 18.9 + 3.45 + 2.5$
$= 35.35$ km

2nd route $R \to B \to M \to D \to F$

Total distance $= RB + BM + MD + DF$
$= 10.5 + 14.5 + 4.5 + 2.5 = 32$ km

3rd route $R \to A \to M \to D \to F$

Total distance $= RA + AM + MD + DF$
$= 10.5 + 18.9 + 4.5 + 2.5 = 36.4$ km

4th route $R \to B \to M \to C \to F$

Total distance $= RB + BM + MC + CF$
$= 10.5 + 14.5 + 3.45 + 2.5 = 30.95$ km

Hence, the shortest distance which Radhika has to travel is 30.95 km.

7. *(b)* Given PA, QB and RC are perpendicular to AC.

In ΔPAC and ΔQBC, we have

$\angle PCA = \angle QCB$ [common angle]

$\angle PAC = \angle QBC$ [each 90°]

$\therefore \quad \Delta PAC \sim \Delta QBC$ [by AA similarity criterion]

Now, $\dfrac{\text{ar}(\Delta PAC)}{\text{ar}(\Delta QBC)} = \left(\dfrac{PA}{QB}\right)^2$

[$\because$ ratio of areas of two similar triangles is equal to square of the ratio of their corresponding sides]

$\Rightarrow \quad \dfrac{\text{ar}(\Delta PAC)}{\text{ar}(\Delta QBC)} = \dfrac{x^2}{y^2}$ ...(i)

Similarly, in ΔRCA and ΔQBA, we have

$\angle RCA = \angle QBA$ [each 90°]

$\angle RAC = \angle QAB$ [common angle]

$\therefore \quad \Delta RCA \sim \Delta QBA$ [by AA similarity criterion]

Now, $\dfrac{\text{ar}(\Delta RCA)}{\text{ar}(\Delta QBA)} = \left(\dfrac{RC}{QB}\right)^2$

[$\because$ ratio of areas of two similar triangles is equal to the square of the ratio of their corresponding sides]

$\Rightarrow \quad \dfrac{\text{ar}(\Delta RCA)}{\text{ar}(\Delta QBA)} = \dfrac{z^2}{y^2}$ ...(ii)

On adding Eqs. (i) and (ii), we have

$$\frac{\text{ar}(\Delta PAC)}{\text{ar}(\Delta QBC)} + \frac{\text{ar}(\Delta RCA)}{\text{ar}(\Delta QBA)} = \frac{x^2}{y^2} + \frac{z^2}{y^2}$$

$$\Rightarrow \frac{\text{ar}(\Delta PAC)\ \text{ar}(\Delta QBA) + \text{ar}(\Delta RCA)\ \text{ar}(\Delta QBC)}{\text{ar}(\Delta QBC)\ \text{ar}(\Delta QBA)} = \frac{x^2 + z^2}{y^2}$$

8. *(a)* Given $ABCD$ is a trapezium. Diagonals AC and BD intersect at O.

$\therefore \quad PQ \parallel AB \parallel DC$

To prove $\quad PO = QO$

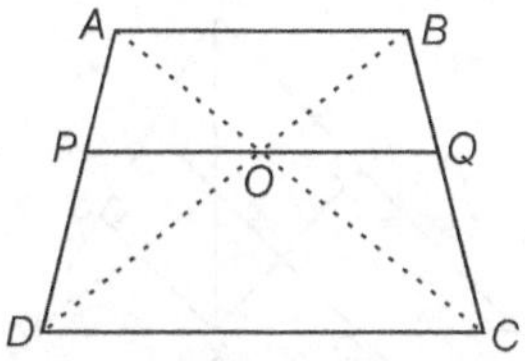

Proof In ΔABD and ΔPOD,

$PO \parallel AB$ [$\because PQ \parallel AB$]

$\angle ADB = \angle PDO$ [common angle]

$\angle ABD = \angle POD$ [corresponding angles]

$\therefore \quad \Delta ABD \sim \Delta POD$ [by AA similarity critorion]

Then, $\quad \dfrac{OP}{AB} = \dfrac{PD}{AD}$ ...(i)

In ΔABC and ΔOQC, $OQ \parallel AB$ [$\because PQ \parallel AB$]

$\angle ACB = \angle OCQ$ [common angle]

and $\quad \angle BAC = \angle QOC$ [corresponding angles]

$\therefore \quad \Delta ABC \sim \Delta OQC$ [by AA similarity criterion]

Then, $\quad \dfrac{OQ}{AB} = \dfrac{QC}{BC}$ ...(ii)

Now, in ΔADC, $OP \parallel DC$

$\therefore \quad \dfrac{AP}{PD} = \dfrac{OA}{OC}$ ...(iii)

[by basic proportionality theorem]

In ΔABC, $\quad OQ \parallel AB$

$\therefore \quad \dfrac{BQ}{QC} = \dfrac{OA}{OC}$ ...(iv)

[by basic proportionality theorem]

From Eqs. (iii) and (iv),

$$\frac{AP}{PD} = \frac{BQ}{QC}$$

On adding 1 to both sides, we get

$$\frac{AP}{PD} + 1 = \frac{BQ}{QC} + 1$$

$\Rightarrow \quad \dfrac{AP + PD}{PD} = \dfrac{BQ + QC}{QC}$

$\Rightarrow \quad \dfrac{AD}{PD} = \dfrac{BC}{QC}$

$\Rightarrow \quad \dfrac{PD}{AD} = \dfrac{QC}{BC}$ [reciprocal the terms]

$\Rightarrow \quad \dfrac{OP}{AB} = \dfrac{OQ}{AB}$ [from Eqs. (i) and (ii)]

$\Rightarrow \quad OP = OQ$

9. *(d)* Given $\angle LPQ = \angle QRP$

and $\quad \angle RPM = \angle RQP$

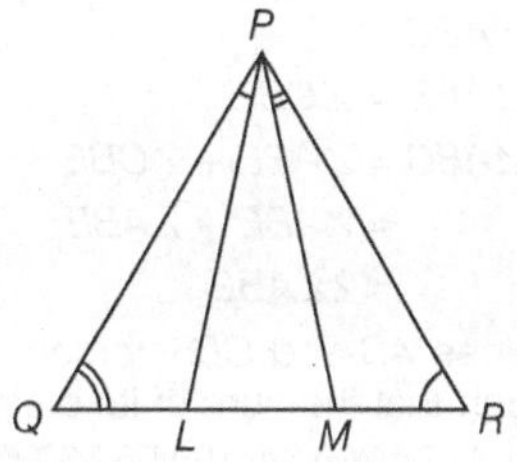

In ΔPQL and ΔRPM, $\angle LPQ = \angle MRP$ [$\because \angle LPQ = \angle QRP$, given]

and $\quad \angle LQP = \angle RPM$ [$\because \angle RQP = \angle RPM$, given]

$\therefore \quad \Delta PQL \sim \Delta RPM$ [by AA similarity criterion]

Since, $\quad \Delta PQL \sim \Delta RPM$

$\therefore \quad \dfrac{QL}{PM} = \dfrac{PL}{RM} \Rightarrow QL \times RM = PL \times PM$

In ΔPQL and ΔRQP,

$\angle PQL = \angle RQP$ [common angle]

and $\quad \angle QPL = \angle QRP$ [given]

$\therefore \quad \Delta PQL \sim \Delta RQP$ [by AA similarity criterion]

Then, $\quad \dfrac{PQ}{QR} = \dfrac{QL}{PQ}$

$\Rightarrow \quad PQ^2 = QR \times QL$

Chapter 14 Locus

1. *(a)* Given A quadrilateral $ABCD$ in which $AB = BC$ and PE and QE are right bisectors of AD and CD respectively, such that they meet at E.

To prove BE bisects $\angle ABC$.

Construction Join AE, DE and CE.

Proof Since, PE is the right bisector of AD and E lies on it.

$\therefore \quad AE = ED$ ...(i)

[$\because$ points on the right bisector of line segment are equidistant from the ends of the segment]

Also, QE is the right bisector of CD and E lies on it.

$\therefore \quad ED = EC$ ...(ii)

From Eqs. (i) and (ii), we get

$AE = EC$ ...(iii)

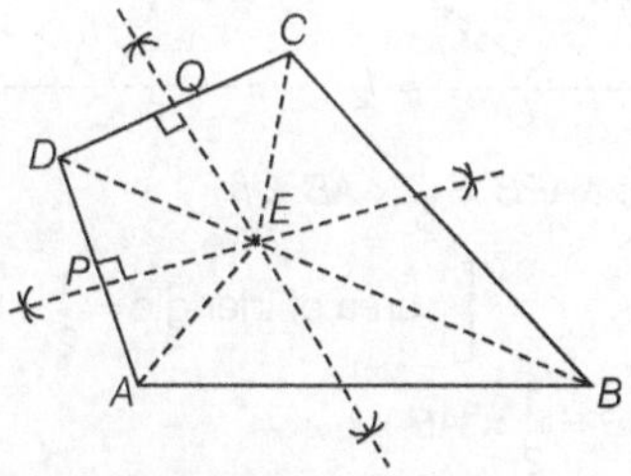

Now, in ΔABE and ΔCBE, we have

$AB = BC$ [given]

$BE = BE$ [common]

and $\quad AE = EC$ [from Eq. (iii)]

So, by SSS criterion of congruence, we have

$\Delta ABE \cong \Delta ACE$

$\Rightarrow \quad \angle ABE = \angle CBE$

$\Rightarrow$ BE bisects $\angle ABC$

$\therefore \quad \angle ABE = \angle CBE$ ...(iv)

Now, $\angle ABC = \angle ABE + \angle CBE$

$= \angle ABE + \angle ABE$ [from Eq. (iv)]

$= 2\angle ABE$

2. *(d)* Given Two lines AB and CD intersecting at O and P is a moving point such that the sum of its distances from AB and CD is constant, i.e. it always remains same.

Construction Draw $PL \perp AB$ and $PM \perp CD$.

Proof We have to find the locus of P, when it is given that $PL + PM = k$ constant.

Draw $EF \| AB$ at a distance k from AB. Suppose EF meets CD at G. Join GP and produce LP to meet EF at N.

Now, $EF \| AB$ at a distance k from it.

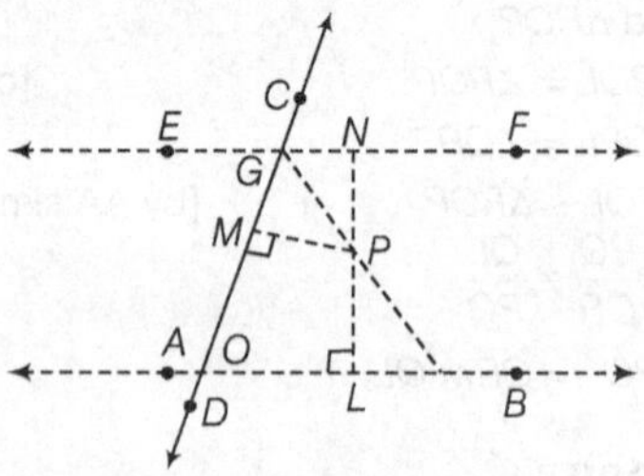

$\therefore$ LN = Distance between AB and EF.

$\Rightarrow \quad LN = k$

$\therefore \quad PL + PM = LN$ [$\because PL + PM = k$ (given)]

$\Rightarrow \quad PL + PM = PL + PN$

$\Rightarrow \quad PM = PN$

$\Rightarrow$ P is equidistant from CD and EF.

$\Rightarrow$ P lies on the bisector of $\angle FGO$.

3. *(a)* Given a ΔPAB, in which AB is the base and h is the height of the vertex P of the triangle. Take a point Q on the other side of AB at a distance of h from AB. Join PB and BQ.

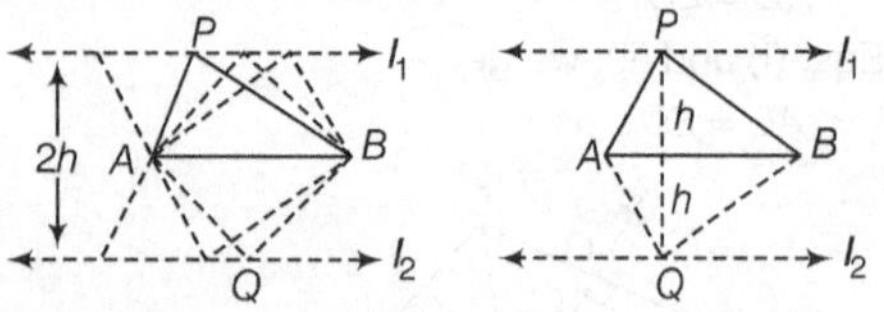

Now, area of $\Delta APB = \frac{1}{2} \times AB \times h$ ...(i)

$\left[\because \text{area of triangle} = \frac{1}{2} \times \text{base} \times \text{altitude}\right]$

Area of $\Delta AQB = \frac{1}{2} \times AB \times h$ ...(ii)

From Eqs. (i) and (ii), we get

Area of ΔAPB = Area of ΔAQB

The areas of the two triangles remain the same for the same base AB and altitude h.

Hence, the lines l_1 and l_2 drawn from P and Q parallel to AB at a height of h, are the loci of the vertex of triangle.

4. *(c)* Given a ΔABC, in which AX is a bisector of $\angle BAC$ meeting BC at X. Also, PQ is a perpendicular bisector of AC, which meets AX at Y and AC at T.

Draw $XR \perp AB$ and $XS \perp AC$. Join YC also.

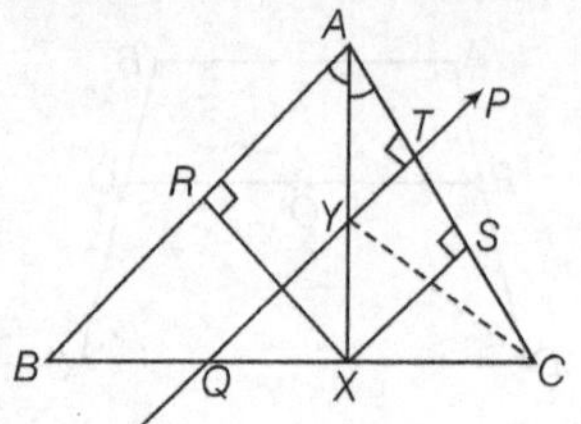

I. In ΔARX and ΔASX,

$AX = AX$ [common side]

$\angle XAR = \angle XAS$ [given]

$\angle XRA = \angle XSA$ [each 90°]

$\therefore \quad \Delta ARX \cong \Delta ASX$ [SAA congruency]

$\therefore \quad XR = XS$ [by CPCT]

II. In ΔYTA and ΔYTC,

$TA = TC$ [given]

$\angle YTA = \angle YTC$ [each 90°]

$YT = YT$ [common side]

$\therefore \quad \Delta YTA \cong \Delta YTC$ [SAS congruency]

$\therefore \quad YA = YC$ [by CPCT]

Thus, Y is equidistant from A and C.

5. *(b)* Steps of construction

1. Draw $AC = 5$ cm.
2. From A, draw an arc of radius 4.2 cm and from C, draw an arc of radius 6.3 cm, so that both arcs intersect at B.
3. Join AB and BC. Thus, ABC is the required triangle.
4. Draw perpendicular bisector PD of BC, which meets AC at D.

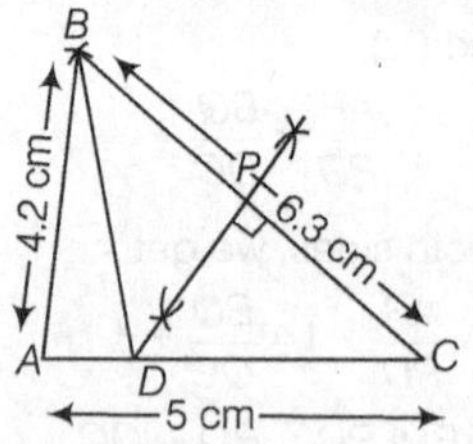

5. Join DB. Measure DB and DC.

$\therefore DB = DC = 4.3$ cm

Thus, D is equidistant from B and C.

Now, we have to prove this result.

In ΔDPB and ΔDPC,

$\angle DPB = \angle DPC$ [each 90°]

$BP = PC$ [$\because DP$ is perpendicular bisector of BC]

$DP = DP$ [common side]

$\therefore \quad \Delta DPB \cong \Delta DPC$ [SAS congruency]

$\therefore \quad DB = DC$ [by CPCT]

Thus, D is equidistant from B and C.

6. (a) Steps of construction

1. Draw a line segment $QR = 4.5$ cm.
2. Draw $QX \perp QR$.
3. From R, draw an arc of radius 8 cm, which intersects QX at P.
4. Now, join PR.

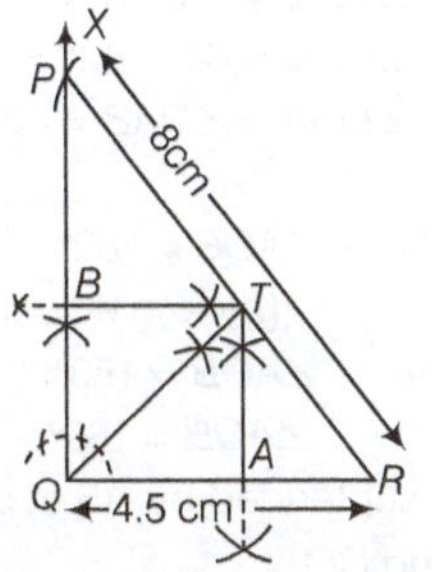

5. Draw bisector QT of $\angle Q$, which meets PR at T.
6. From T, draw $TA \perp QR$ and $TB \perp QP$.
7. Measure TA and TB.

Thus, $TA = TB = 2.8$ cm

Now, we have to prove $TA = TB$.

In ΔTAQ and ΔTBQ,

$TQ = TQ$ [common side]

$\angle TQA = \angle TQB$ [$\because QT$ is bisector of $\angle AQB$]

$\angle TAQ = \angle TBQ$ [each 90°]

$\therefore \Delta TAQ \cong \Delta TBQ$ [SAA congruency]

$\therefore TA = TB$ [by CPCT]

Thus, T is equidistant from PQ and QR.

7. (c) Steps of construction

1. Draw a line segment $BC = 6.4$ cm.
2. At B, draw $\angle XBC = 75°$ and cut $AB = 5$ cm from BX.
3. Join AC.
4. Draw perpendicular bisector of BC; and also bisector of $\angle ACB$, so that both lines intersect at P.
5. Measure PB, PC, PQ and PR.

$\therefore PB = PC = 3.4$ cm

and $PQ = PR = 1.2$ cm

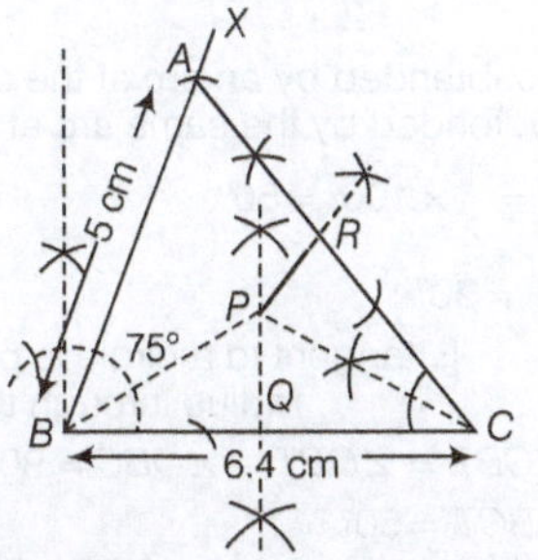

In ΔPBQ and ΔPCQ,

$BQ = CQ$ [$\because PQ$ is perpendicular bisector of BC]

$\angle BQP = \angle CQP$ [each 90°]

$PQ = PQ$ [common side]

$\therefore \Delta PBQ \cong \Delta PCQ$ [SAS congruency]

$\therefore PB = PC$ [by CPCT] ...(i)

In ΔPQC and ΔPRC,

$PC = PC$ [common side]

$\angle PCQ = \angle PCR$ [$\because PC$ is bisector of $\angle ACB$]

$\angle PQC = \angle PRC$ [each 90°]

$\Delta PQC \cong \Delta PRC$ [SAA congruency]

$\therefore PQ = PR$ [by CPCT] ...(ii)

From Eqs. (i) and (ii), it is clear that P is equidistant from B and C; and also equidistant from AC and BC.

Chapter 15 Circles

1. (c) As PQR is an equilateral triangle, hence PS will be perpendicular to QR and will divide it into 2 equal parts.

Since, $\angle P$ and $\angle S$ will be supplementary, so

$\angle S = 120°$ and $\angle QSA = \angle RSA = 60°$.

Now, $PA = PQ \cos 30°$ and $OA = OQ \sin 30° = \frac{r}{2}$

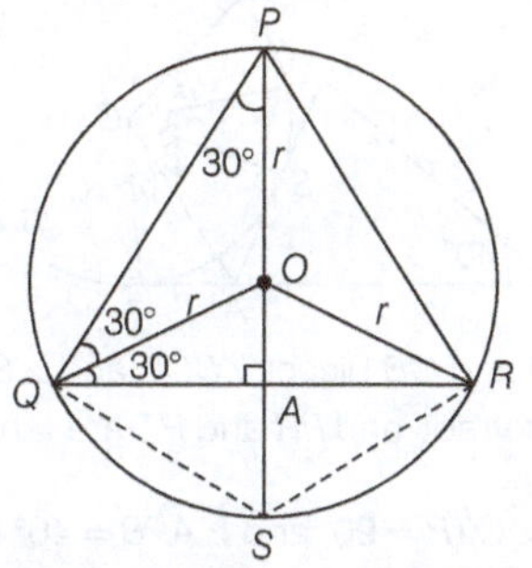

$\Rightarrow AS = OA = \frac{r}{2}$ and $PA = PO + OA = r + \frac{r}{2}$

Hence, $PQ = \frac{PA}{\cos 30°} = \frac{r + \frac{r}{2}}{\frac{\sqrt{3}}{2}} = \sqrt{3}r$

In ΔQAS, $AS = QS \cos 60° \Rightarrow QS = \frac{r/2}{1/2} = r$

Since, $AQ = AR$, AS is common and $\angle QAS = \angle RAS = 90°$

So, $QS = RS$.

$\therefore$ Perimeter of $PQSR = 2(PQ + QS) = 2(\sqrt{3} + 1)r$

2. (c) Join AE, AB and CD.

Then, $\angle CBE = \angle CAE$

[$\because$ angles in the same segment are equal]

$\Rightarrow \angle CAE = \angle 1 = 50°$ [$\because \angle CBE = 50°$] ... (i)

and $\angle AEC = 90°$ ...(ii)

[$\because$ angle in a semi-circle]

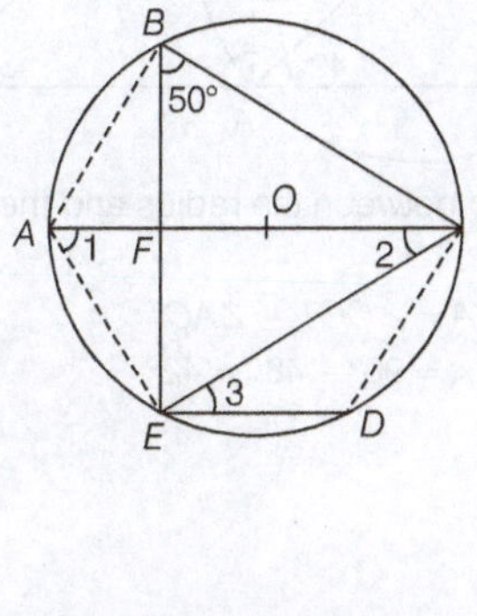

Now, in ΔAEC,

$$\angle 1 + \angle AEC + \angle 2 = 180^\circ$$

[by angle sum property of a triangle]

$\therefore$ $50^\circ + 90^\circ + \angle 2 = 180^\circ$

$\Rightarrow$ $\angle 2 = 40^\circ$ ...(iii)

Also, $ED \parallel AC$ [given]

$\therefore$ $\angle 2 = \angle 3$ [alternate angles]

$\therefore$ $40^\circ = \angle 3$, i.e. $\angle 3 = 40^\circ$

Hence, $\angle CED = 40^\circ$.

3. *(d)* AS and AT are two tangents from A, so $AT = AS$.

Join O and S.

Since, AB is tangent at S and OS is radius.

$\Rightarrow$ $OS \perp AB$ and $OS = OT$

BS and BR are two tangents from B. So, $BS = BR$. Since, OS and OR are radius of the same circle.

$\Rightarrow$ $OS = OR$

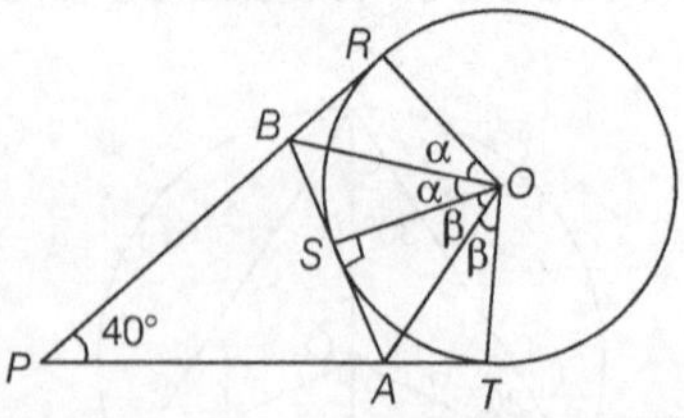

Therefore, OA and OB bisect $\angle SOT$ and $\angle SOR$.

OR and OT are radii and PR and PT are tangent at R and T, respectively.

So, $\angle ORP = \angle OTP = 90^\circ$ and $\angle APB = 40^\circ = \angle TPR$

In quadrilateral $PROT$,

$$\angle ORP + \angle TPR + \angle OTP + \angle ROT = 360^\circ$$

[by angle sum property of a quadrilateral]

$\Rightarrow 90^\circ + 40^\circ + 90^\circ + \angle ROT = 360^\circ \Rightarrow \angle ROT = 140^\circ$

Let $\angle SOR = 2\alpha$ and $\angle SOT = 2\beta$ and OB and OA are respective bisectors, so $\angle ROB = \angle BOS = \alpha$ and $\angle SOA = \angle AOT = \beta$.

Then, $\angle AOB = \angle BOS + \angle SOA = \alpha + \beta$

$\Rightarrow \angle ROT = \angle SOR + \angle SOT = 2\alpha + 2\beta = 2(\alpha + \beta) = 140^\circ$

$\Rightarrow$ $\alpha + \beta = 70^\circ = \angle AOB$. So, $\angle AOB = 70^\circ$.

4. *(b)* Let O be centre of the circle. Join OC.

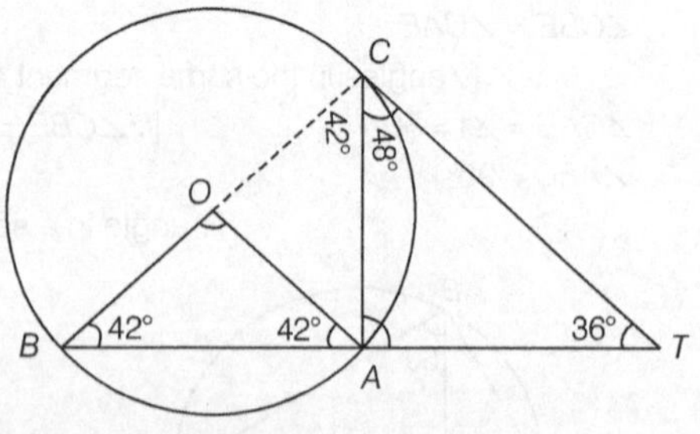

Since, the angle between the radius and the tangent is 90°, i.e. $\angle OCT = 90^\circ$.

$\therefore$ $\angle OCA = \angle OCT - \angle ACT$

$= 90^\circ - 48^\circ = 42^\circ$

and $OA = OC = OB$ [radii of the same circle]

$\Rightarrow$ $\angle OAC = \angle OCA = 42^\circ$

[$\because$ angle opposite to equal sides are equal]

In ΔACT, exterior $\angle CAB = \angle ACT + \angle CTA$

$\Rightarrow$ $\angle CAB = 48^\circ + 36^\circ = 84^\circ$

$\therefore$ $\angle OAB = \angle CAB - \angle OAC$

$\Rightarrow$ $\angle OAB = 84^\circ - 42^\circ = 42^\circ$

$\therefore$ $\angle OBA = \angle OAB = 42^\circ$

In ΔAOB,

$$\angle OBA + \angle OAB + \angle AOB = 180^\circ$$

[by angle sum property of a triangle]

$\Rightarrow$ $42^\circ + 42^\circ + \angle AOB = 180^\circ$

$\Rightarrow$ $\angle AOB = 180^\circ - 84^\circ = 96^\circ$

Hence, the angle subtended by AB at centre is 96°.

5. *(b)* Join BC, BO and CO.

Clearly, $\angle OBP = 90^\circ$

[$\because$ tangent to a circle is perpendicular to the radius through the point of contact]

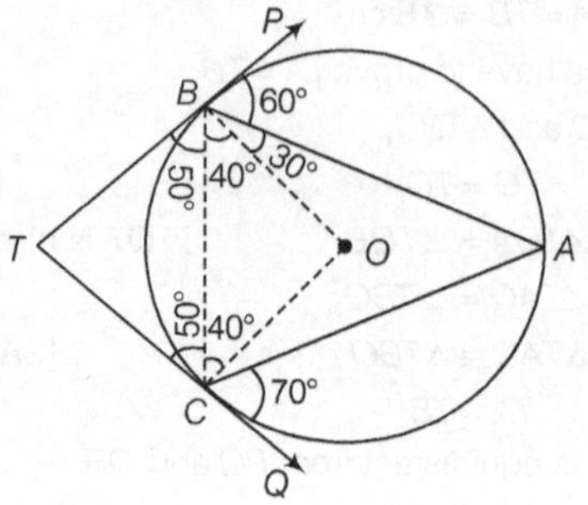

$\therefore$ $\angle OBA = 90^\circ - 60^\circ = 30^\circ$

Now, $\angle ACQ = \angle CBA$ [angles in the alternate segment]

$\therefore$ $\angle CBA = 70^\circ$ [alternate segments theorem]

$\therefore$ $\angle OBC = \angle CBA - \angle OBA = 70^\circ - 30^\circ = 40^\circ$

In ΔOBC, $OB = OC$

$\therefore$ $\angle OBC = \angle OCB$ [$\because \angle OBC = 40^\circ$]

$\therefore$ $\angle BOC = 180^\circ - (40^\circ + 40^\circ) = 100^\circ$

Again, $\angle BAC = \frac{1}{2}\angle BOC$

[$\because$ angle subtended by an arc at the centre is double the angle subtended by the same arc at the circumference]

$\Rightarrow$ $\angle BAC = \frac{1}{2} \times 100^\circ = 50^\circ$

Again, $\angle OBT = 90^\circ$

[$\because$ tangent to a circle is perpendicular to the radius through the point of contact]

$\therefore$ $\angle CBT = \angle OBT - \angle OBC = 90^\circ - 40^\circ = 50^\circ$

Similarly, $\angle BCT = 50^\circ$

In ΔBCT, $\angle BTC = 180^\circ - (\angle CBT + \angle BCT)$

$= 180^\circ - (50^\circ + 50^\circ) = 80^\circ$

Hence, $\angle BAC = 50^\circ$ and $\angle BTC = 80^\circ$.

Chapter 16 Constructions

Solutions (Q.Nos. 1-4)

1. ***Steps of construction***

1. Now, draw the internal bisectors of $\angle B$ and $\angle C$. Let these bisectors meet at point E.
2. From point E, draw a perpendicular on side BC, which cuts BC at N.

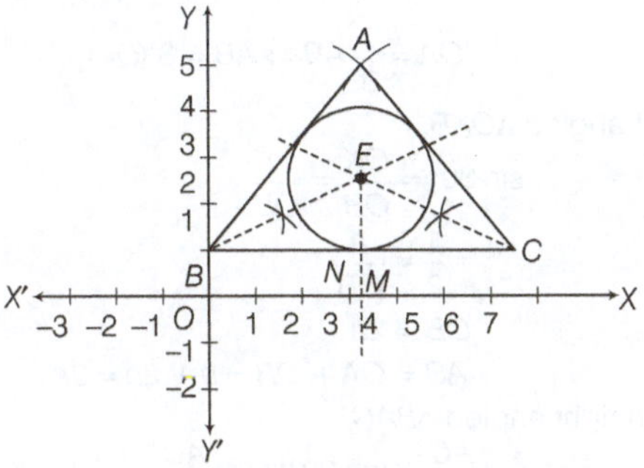

3. Taking E as centre and radius equal to EN, draw a circle, which touches all the sides of the ΔABC. Thus, it is the required incircle.

2. *(a)* Now, measure of radius, $r = EN = 1.5$ cm.

3. *(d)* Then, x-coordinate of E is $OM = 3.5$

and y-coordinate of E is $ME = MN + NE$

$= 1 + 1.5 = 2.5$

Hence, coordinates of E are (3.5, 2.5).

4. *(b)* Here, coordinates of B (0, 1)

Required distance, $BE = \sqrt{(3.5-0)^2 + (2.5-1)^2}$

$= \sqrt{12.25 + 2.25} = \sqrt{14.5} = 3.80$ units

5. Given, two points P and Q on the extended diameter of a circle with radius 3 cm, such that its distance from the centre equal to 7 cm.

We have to construct the tangents to the circle from the given points P and Q.

Steps of construction

1. Draw a circle of radius 3 cm with centre O.
2. Produce its diameter on both sides and take points P and Q on this diameter, such that $OP = OQ = 7$ cm.
3. Bisect OP and OQ. Let E and F be the mid-points of OP and OQ, respectively.

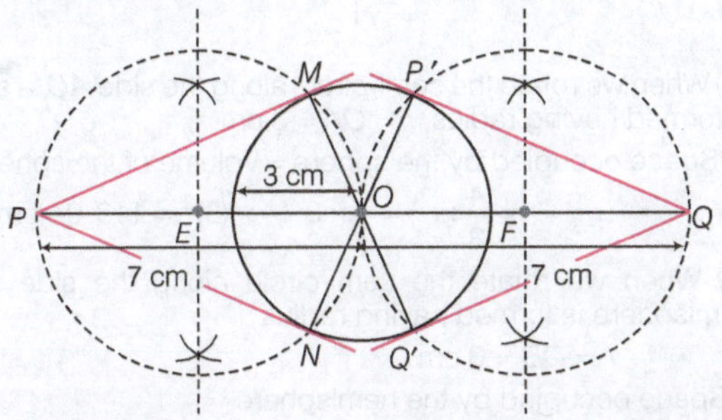

4. Now, taking E as centre and OE as radius, draw a circle, which intersects the given circle at two points M and N. Again, taking F as centre and OF as radius, draw a circle, which intersects the given circle at two points P' and Q'.
5. Join PM, PN, QP' and QQ'. These are the required tangents from P and Q to the given circle.

6. Given, ABC is a right angled triangle, in which $AB = 6$ cm, $BC = 8$ cm, $\angle B = 90°$ and BD is perpendicular to AC. Then, $\angle ADB = \angle CDB = 90°$.

Steps of construction

1. Draw the line segments $AB = 6$ cm and $BC = 8$ cm, such that they perpendicular to each other. Join AC. Thus, ΔABC is the given right angled triangle.
2. Draw $BD \perp AC$.
3. Taking the mid-point F of BC as centre and draw a circle with radius 4 cm, passing through B, C and D.
4. Now, join AF and bisect it. Let mid-point of AF be O.

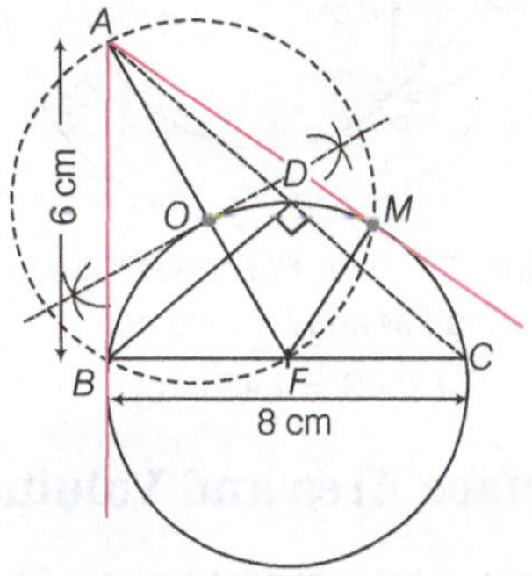

5. Taking O as centre and OA as radius and draw a circle, which intersects the given circle (which passes through B,C and D) at B and M.
6. Now, join AB and AM, which are the required tangents.

7. ***Steps of construction***

1. First, draw a circle with the help of given circular solid ring and then draw two non-parallel chords AB and CD.
2. Draw perpendicular bisectors of AB and CD, which intersect each other at point O. Then, O is centre of the circle.
3. Now, take a point P outside the circle and join OP.
4. Draw bisector of OP. Let its mid-point be M.

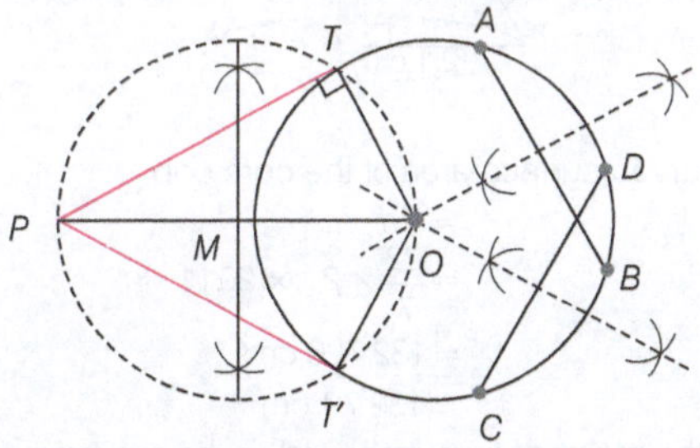

5. Taking M as centre and MP as radius, draw a dotted circle which intersect the given circle at T and T'.
6. Join PT and PT'.

   Then, PT and PT' are the required pair of tangents drawn to the circle from P.

8. Given, two concentric circles of radii 4 cm and 6 cm with common centre O.

Here, we have to draw two tangents to inner circle C_1 from a point on the outer circle C_2.

Steps of construction

1. Draw two concentric circles C_1 and C_2 with common centre O and radii 4 cm and 6 cm, respectively.
2. Take any point P on outer circle C_2 and join OP.
3. Draw the bisector of OP, which bisect OP at M'.
4. Taking M' as centre and OM' as radius, draw a dotted circle which cuts the inner circle C_1 at two points M and P'.

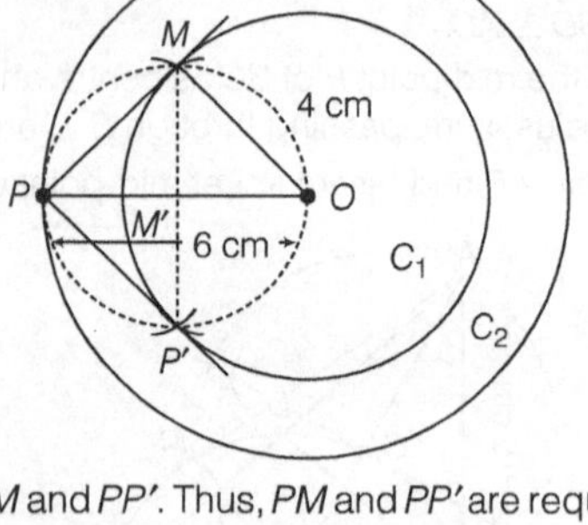

5. Join PM and PP'. Thus, PM and PP' are required tangents. On measuring PM and PP', we get

$$PM = PP' = 4.47 \text{ cm}$$

Chapter 17 Surface Area and Volume

1. *(c)* Given, radius of the broadest end, $r = 2.1$ cm and length, $h = 20$ cm.

Let l be the slant height of the conical corn cob.

Then, $l = \sqrt{r^2 + h^2} = \sqrt{(2.1)^2 + (20)^2}$

$= \sqrt{4.41 + 400} = \sqrt{404.41} = 20.11$ cm

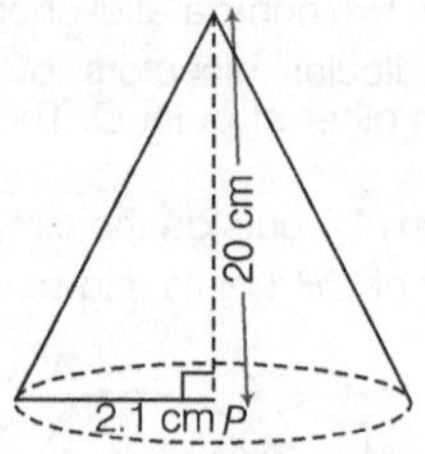

Now, curved surface area of the corn cob

$= \pi r l$

$= \frac{22}{7} \times 2.1 \times 20.11$

$= 132.726 \text{ cm}^2$

$= 132.73 \text{ cm}^2$

Since, the grains of corn are found on the curved surface of the corn cob.

So, total number of grains on the corn cob = Curved surface area of the corn cob × Number of grains of corn on 1 cm^2

$= 132.73 \times 4 = 530.92$

So, there would be approximately 531 grains of corn on the entire cob.

2. *(a)* Let radius of sphere be a, i.e. $OK = OA = a$.

Then, the centre O of a sphere will be centroid of the ΔBCD.

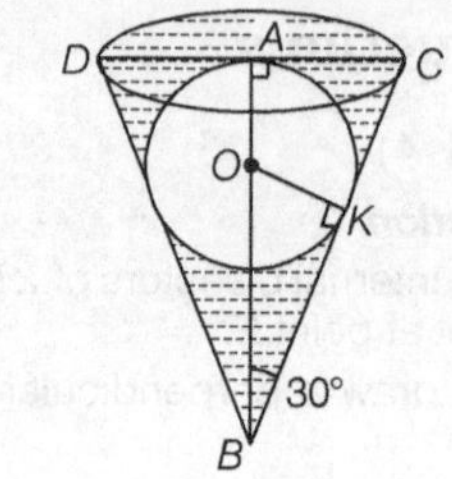

$\therefore \quad OA = \frac{1}{3} AB \Rightarrow AB = 3\,(OA)$

In right angled ΔOKB,

$$\sin 30° = \frac{OK}{OB} = \frac{a}{OB}$$

$\Rightarrow \quad \frac{1}{2} = \frac{a}{OB}$

$\Rightarrow \quad OB = 2a$

Now, $\quad AB = OA + OB = a + 2a = 3a$

Now, in right angled ΔBAC,

$$\frac{AC}{AB} = \tan 30° \Rightarrow \frac{AC}{AB} = \frac{1}{\sqrt{3}}$$

$\Rightarrow \quad AC = \frac{AB}{\sqrt{3}} = \frac{3a}{\sqrt{3}}$

$\therefore \quad AC = \sqrt{3}a$ units

Now, volume of a cone $BCD = \frac{1}{3}\pi (AC)^2 \times AB$

$= \frac{1}{3}\pi (a\sqrt{3})^2 \times 3a = 3\pi a^3$

and volume of a sphere $= \frac{4}{3}\pi a^3$

$\therefore$ Volume of water remaining in the cone

= Volume of the cone BCD − Volume of a sphere

$= 3\pi a^3 - \frac{4}{3}\pi a^3 = \frac{5\pi}{3} a^3$ cu units

Solutions (Q. Nos. 3-4) A semi-circle passing through $A(3, 0)$, $B(0, 3)$ and $C(-3, 0)$ as shown in the figure.

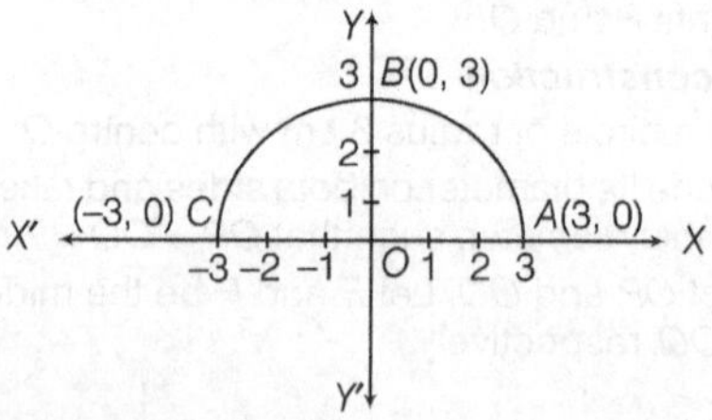

3. *(b)* When we rotate the semi-circle along the side AC, a sphere is formed having radius, $r = OA = 3$ cm

$\therefore$ Space occupied by the sphere = Volume of the sphere

$= \frac{4}{3}\pi r^3 = \frac{4}{3} \times 3.14 \times (3)^3 = 113.04 \text{ cm}^3$

4. *(a)* When we rotate the semi-circle along the side BO, a hemisphere is formed having radius

$r = OB = 3$ cm

$\therefore$ Space occupied by the hemisphere

= Volume of the hemisphere

$= \frac{2}{3}\pi r^3 = \frac{2}{3} \times 3.14 \times (3)^3$

$= 56.52 \text{ cm}^3$

5. *(a)* Given, length of cuboid, $l = 15$ cm,

breadth of cuboid, $b = 10$ cm

and height of cuboid, $h = 3.5$ cm

$\therefore$ Volume of the cuboid $= l \times b \times h$

$= 15 \times 10 \times 3.5 = 525 \text{ cm}^3$

Also, radius of a conical depression, $r = 0.5$ cm

and height of a conical depression, $h = 1.4$ cm

$\therefore$ Volume of one conical depression $= \frac{1}{3} \pi r^2 h$

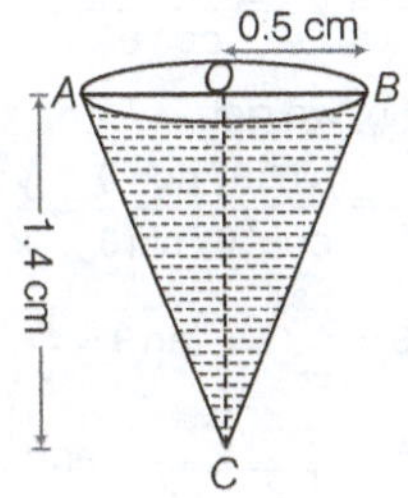

$= \frac{1}{3} \times \frac{22}{7} \times 0.5 \times 0.5 \times 1.4$

$= \frac{22}{3} \times \frac{1}{2} \times \frac{1}{2} \times \frac{2}{10} = \frac{11}{30} \text{ cm}^3$

Now, volume of 4 conical depressions

$= 4 \times$ Volume of one conical depression $= 4 \times \frac{11}{30} = \frac{22}{15} \text{ cm}^3$

$\therefore$ Volume of wood in the pen-stand

= Volume of the cuboid − Volume of 4 conical depressions

$= 525 - \frac{22}{15} = 525 - 1.46$

$= 523.54 \text{ cm}^3$

6. *(b)* According to the given information, a shape of figure is shown below

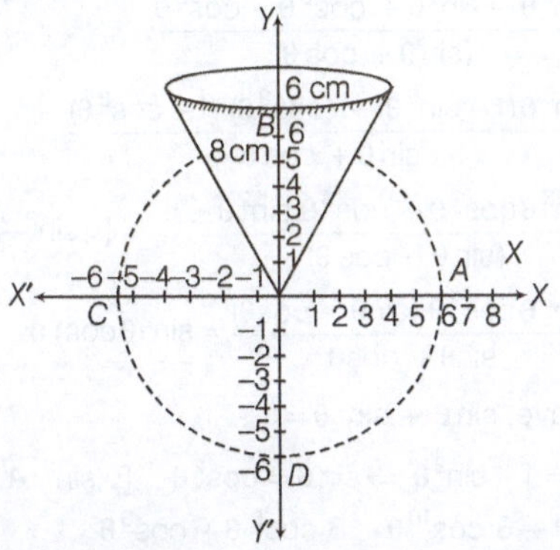

When the hanging pipes touches the surface paper, a circular shape *ABCD* is formed on the graph paper. The size of circle *ABCD* is equal to the size of circular base of the cone.

$\therefore$ Radius of the circle *ABCD* is 6 cm.

Hence, the coordinates of *A*, *B*, *C* and *D* are (6, 0), (0, 6), (–6, 0) and (0, –6), respectively.

The figure formed in the given information is cylindrical in outer surface and conical in the inner surface.

Now, total surface area of the figure

= Curved surface area of the cylinder

+ Curved surface area of the cone

$= 2\pi rh + \pi rl = \pi r(2h + l)$

$= \pi r(2h + \sqrt{r^2 + h^2})$

$= 3.14 \times 6\,(2 \times 8 + \sqrt{6^2 + 8^2})$

$= 18.84(16 + \sqrt{36 + 64})$

$= 18.84(16 + \sqrt{100}) = 18.84\,(16 + 10)$

$= 18.84 \times 26 = 489.84 \text{ cm}^2$

7. *(b)* Let V_1, V_2 and V_3 be the volumes of the cones *CAB*, C_1AB and C_2AB, respectively.

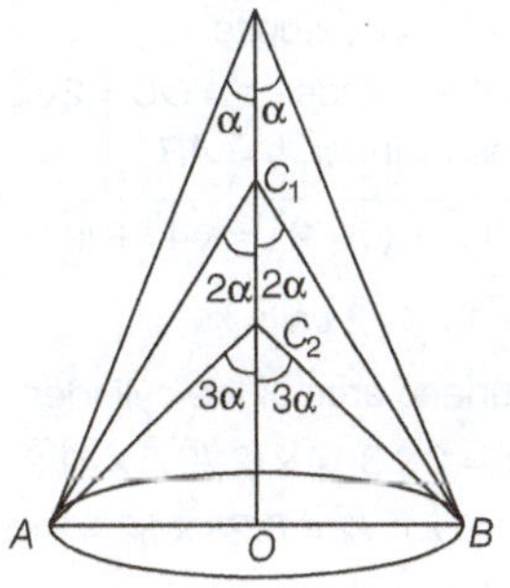

For cone *CAB*, we have

$CO = 3h$

In ΔCOA, $\tan\alpha = \frac{OA}{OC} = \frac{OA}{3h}$

$\Rightarrow \quad OA = 3h \tan\alpha$

$\therefore$ Volume, $\quad V_1 = \frac{1}{3}\pi\,(3h \tan\alpha)^2 \times 3h \quad$ [$\because$ radius $= 3h \tan\alpha$]

$\Rightarrow \quad V_1 = \frac{27}{3}\pi h^3 \tan^2\alpha$

For cone C_1AB, we have

$C_1O = 2h$

In ΔC_1AO, $\tan 2\alpha = \frac{OA}{OC_1} = \frac{OA}{2h}$

$\Rightarrow \quad OA = 2h \tan 2\alpha$

$\therefore$ Volume, $V_2 = \frac{1}{3}\pi\;\;2h \tan 2\alpha)^2 \times 2h \quad$ [$\because$ radius $= 2h \tan 2\alpha$]

$\Rightarrow \quad V_2 = \frac{8}{3}\pi h^3 \tan^2 2\alpha$

For cone C_2AB, we have $C_2O = h$

In ΔC_2OA, $\tan 3\alpha = \frac{OA}{OC_2} = \frac{OA}{h}$

$\Rightarrow \quad OA = h \tan 3\alpha$

$\therefore$ Volume, $V_3 = \frac{1}{3}\pi\,(h \tan 3\alpha)^2 \times h \quad$ [$\because$ radius $= h \tan 3\alpha$]

$\Rightarrow \quad V_3 = \frac{1}{3}\pi h^3 \tan^2 3\alpha$

Now, $V_1 - V_2 = \frac{27}{3}\pi h^3 \tan^2\alpha - \frac{8}{3}\pi h^3 \tan^2 2\alpha$

$= \frac{\pi h^3}{3}(27 \tan^2\alpha - 8 \tan^2 2\alpha)$

and $V_2 - V_3 = \frac{8}{3}\pi h^3 \tan^2 2\alpha - \frac{1}{3}\pi h^3 \tan^2 3\alpha$

$= \frac{\pi h^3}{3}(8 \tan^2 2\alpha - \tan^2 3\alpha)$

$\therefore$ Required ratio $= (V_1 - V_2) : (V_2 - V_3)$

$= (27 \tan^2\alpha - 8 \tan^2 2\alpha) : (8 \tan^2 2\alpha - \tan^2 3\alpha)$

8. *(a)* When we rotate a right triangle about the origin *O*, a cylinder is formed. To determine the radius, first draw a perpendicular line from origin to the side *AB*, which bisects it. So, *C* is the mid-point of *AB*. Thus, the coordinate of *C* is $\left(\frac{0+4}{2}, \frac{4+0}{2}\right)$, i.e. (2, 2)

Now, $OC = \sqrt{(2-0)^2 + (2-0)^2}$

[$\because$ distance between two points $= \sqrt{(x_2 - x_1)^2 + (y_2 - y_1)^2}$]

$= \sqrt{2^2 + 2^2} = 2\sqrt{2}$ units

Here, radius of the cylinder, $r = OC = 2\sqrt{2}$ units

and height of the cylinder, $h = AB$

$= \sqrt{(4-0)^2 + (0-4)^2} = \sqrt{4^2 + 4^2}$

$= 4\sqrt{1+1} = 4\sqrt{2}$ units

Now, curved surface area of the cylinder

$= 2\pi rh = 2 \times 3.14 \times (2\sqrt{2})^2 \times 4\sqrt{2}$

$= 6.28 \times 8 \times 4\sqrt{2} = 6.28 \times 32 \times 1.414$

$= 284.15$ sq units

Chapter 18 Trigonometric Identities

1. *(c)* Since, $\sin\alpha$ and $\cos\alpha$ are the roots of the equation

$$px^2 + qx + r = 0$$

$\therefore \quad \sin\alpha + \cos\alpha = -\dfrac{q}{p}$

and $\quad p\sin^2\alpha + q\sin\alpha + r = 0 \quad$ ...(i)

or $\quad p\cos^2\alpha + q\cos\alpha + r = 0 \quad$ ...(ii)

On adding Eqs. (i) and (ii), we get

$$p(\sin^2\alpha + \cos^2\alpha) + q(\sin\alpha + \cos\alpha) + 2r = 0$$

$\Rightarrow \quad p + q\left(-\dfrac{q}{p}\right) + 2r = 0 \quad [\because \sin^2 A + \cos^2 A = 1]$

$\Rightarrow \quad p^2 - q^2 + 2rp = 0$

2. *(c)* In right angled ΔABC,

$AC^2 = BC^2 + AB^2$ [by using Pythagoras theorem]

$\Rightarrow AC^2 - AB^2 = BC^2$

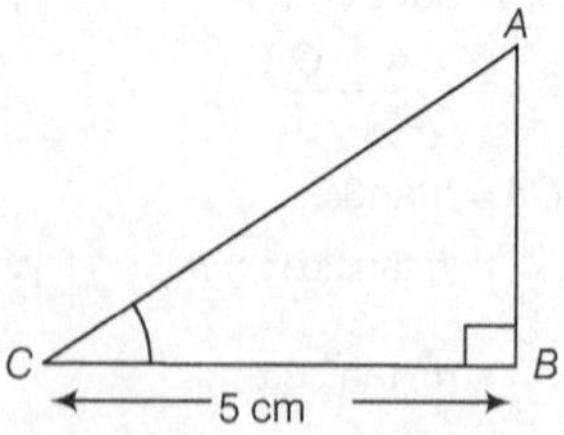

$\Rightarrow \quad (AC + AB)(AC - AB) = (5)^2$

$\Rightarrow \quad (AC + AB)(1) = 25$

[$\because AC - AB = 1$ cm, given]

$\Rightarrow \quad AC + AB = 25$ and $AC - AB = 1$

On solving above equations, we get

$AC = 13$ and $AB = 12$

Now, in ΔABC, $\sin C = \dfrac{AB}{AC} = \dfrac{12}{13}$

$\therefore \quad \dfrac{\cos^2 C}{1 - \sin C} = \dfrac{1 - \sin^2 C}{1 - \sin C} = \dfrac{(1 - \sin C)(1 + \sin C)}{1 - \sin C}$

$= 1 + \sin C = 1 + \dfrac{12}{13} = \dfrac{13 + 12}{13} = \dfrac{25}{13}$

3. *(b)* We have, $\operatorname{cosec}\theta - \sin\theta = x^3$

$\Rightarrow \quad \dfrac{1}{\sin\theta} - \sin\theta = x^3$

$\Rightarrow \quad \dfrac{1 - \sin^2\theta}{\sin\theta} = x^3 \Rightarrow \dfrac{\cos^2\theta}{\sin\theta} = x^3 \quad$ ...(i)

and $\quad \sec\theta - \cos\theta = y^3 \quad$ ...(ii)

$\Rightarrow \quad \dfrac{1 - \cos^2\theta}{\cos\theta} = y^3 \Rightarrow \dfrac{\sin^2\theta}{\cos\theta} = y^3$

From Eqs. (i) and (ii), we get

$$\frac{y^3}{x^3} = \frac{\sin^2\theta/\cos\theta}{\cos^2\theta/\sin\theta} \Rightarrow \frac{y^3}{x^3} = \frac{\sin^3\theta}{\cos^3\theta}$$

$\Rightarrow \quad \tan^3\theta = \dfrac{y^3}{x^3} \Rightarrow \tan\theta = \dfrac{y}{x}$

$\therefore \quad \sin\theta = \dfrac{y}{\sqrt{x^2 + y^2}}$ and $\cos\theta = \dfrac{x}{\sqrt{x^2 + y^2}}$

$\left[\because \sin\theta = \dfrac{\tan\theta}{\sqrt{1 + \tan^2\theta}} \text{ and } \cos\theta = \dfrac{1}{\sqrt{1 + \tan^2\theta}}\right]$

Now, putting the values of $\sin\theta$ and $\cos\theta$ in Eq. (i), we get

$$x^3 = \frac{x^2/(\sqrt{x^2 + y^2})^2}{y/\sqrt{x^2 + y^2}}$$

$\Rightarrow \quad x^3 y\sqrt{x^2 + y^2} = x^2 \Rightarrow xy\sqrt{x^2 + y^2} = 1$

$\Rightarrow \quad x^2y^2(x^2 + y^2) = 1 \quad$ [squaring on both sides]

4. *(a)* Given, $T_n = \sin^n\theta + \cos^n\theta$. ...(i)

Now, $\dfrac{T_3 - T_5}{T_1} = \dfrac{\sin^3\theta + \cos^3\theta - \sin^5\theta - \cos^5\theta}{\sin\theta + \cos\theta}$ [from Eq. (i)]

$= \dfrac{\sin^3\theta - \sin^5\theta + \cos^3\theta - \cos^5\theta}{(\sin\theta + \cos\theta)}$

$= \dfrac{\sin^3\theta(1 - \sin^2\theta) + (\cos^3\theta)(1 - \cos^2\theta)}{\sin\theta + \cos\theta}$

$= \dfrac{\sin^3\theta\cos^2\theta + \cos^3\theta\sin^2\theta}{(\sin\theta + \cos\theta)} \quad [\because \sin^2 A + \cos^2 A = 1]$

$= \dfrac{\sin^2\theta\cos^2\theta(\sin\theta + \cos\theta)}{\sin\theta + \cos\theta} = \sin^2\theta\cos^2\theta$

5. *(b)* We have, $\sin\theta + \sin^2\theta = 1$

$\Rightarrow \sin\theta = 1 - \sin^2\theta \Rightarrow \sin\theta = \cos^2\theta \quad [\because \sin^2 A + \cos^2 A = 1]$

$\therefore \cos^{12}\theta + 3\cos^{10}\theta + 3\cos^8\theta + \cos^6\theta + 2\cos^4\theta + 2\cos^2\theta - 2$

$= (\cos^{12}\theta + 3\cos^{10}\theta + 3\cos^8\theta + \cos^6\theta) + 2(\cos^4\theta + \cos^2\theta - 1)$

$= (\cos^4\theta)^3 + 3\cos^6\theta(\cos^4\theta + \cos^2\theta) + (\cos^2\theta)^3 + 2(\cos^4\theta + \cos^2\theta - 1)$

$= (\cos^4\theta + \cos^2\theta)^3 + 2(\cos^4\theta + \cos^2\theta - 1)$

$[\because (a+b)^3 = a^3 + b^3 + 3ab(a+b)]$

$= (\sin^2\theta + \cos^2\theta)^3 + 2(\sin^2\theta + \cos^2\theta - 1)$

$[\because \cos^2\theta = \sin\theta \Rightarrow \cos^4\theta = \sin^2\theta]$

$= (1)^3 + 2(1 - 1) = 1 \quad [\because \sin^2 A + \cos^2 A = 1]$

6. *(d)* Given expression can be written as

$$\frac{1+\cos y-\sin^2 y}{1+\cos y}+\frac{(1-\cos^2 y)-\sin^2 y}{\sin y(1-\cos y)}$$

$$=\frac{\cos y(1+\cos y)}{1+\cos y}+\frac{1-1}{\sin y(1-\cos y)}$$

$$=\cos y+0=\cos y$$

7. *(a)* We have, $(\sec A+\tan A)(\sec B+\tan B)(\sec C+\tan C)$

$$=(\sec A-\tan A)(\sec B-\tan B)(\sec C-\tan C)$$

On multiplying both sides by

$(\sec A-\tan A)(\sec B-\tan B)(\sec C-\tan C)$, we get

$(\sec A+\tan A)(\sec B+\tan B)(\sec C+\tan C)$

$$\times(\sec A-\tan A)(\sec B-\tan B)(\sec C-\tan C)$$

$$=(\sec A-\tan A)^2(\sec B-\tan B)^2(\sec C-\tan C)^2$$

$$\Rightarrow (\sec^2 A-\tan^2 A)(\sec^2 B-\tan^2 B)(\sec^2 C-\tan^2 C)$$

$$=(\sec A-\tan A)^2(\sec B-\tan B)^2(\sec C-\tan C)^2$$

$$\Rightarrow 1\times1\times1=[(\sec A-\tan A)(\sec B-\tan B)(\sec C-\tan C)]^2$$

$[\because \sec^2\theta-\tan^2\theta=1]$

$$\Rightarrow (\sec A-\tan A)(\sec B-\tan B)(\sec C-\tan C)=\pm 1$$

8. *(c)* Given, $f(x)=\cos^2 x+\sec^2 x=\cos^2 x+\sec^2 x-2+2$

[adding and subtracting 2]

$=\cos^2 x+\sec^2 x-2\cos x\cdot\sec x+2$ $[\because \cos x\cdot\sec x=1]$

$=(\cos x-\sec x)^2+2$ $[\because a^2+b^2-2ab=(a-b)^2]$

We know that square of any equation is always greater than equal to zero.

$\therefore$ $f(x)\geq 2$

9. *(b)* Given, ABC is a right angled triangle.

So, the sum of the angles of a triangle is 180°.

$\therefore$ $A+B+C=180°$ ...(i)

Now, $\tan\left(\frac{A-B-C}{2}\right)=\tan\left[\frac{A-(180°-A)}{2}\right]$ [from Eq. (i)]

$$=\tan\left(\frac{2A-180°}{2}\right)=\tan(A-90°)$$

$$=\tan[-(90°-A)]$$

$=-\tan(90°-A)$ $[\because \tan(-\theta)=-\tan\theta]$

$=-\cot A$ $[\because \tan(90°-A)=\cot A]$ ...(ii)

and $-\tan\left(\frac{A+B-C}{2}\right)=-\tan\left(\frac{180°-C-C}{2}\right)$ [from Eq. (i)]

$=-\tan(90°-C)=\cot C$ ...(iii)

From Eq. (ii) and Eq. (iii), we get

$$\tan\left(\frac{A-B-C}{2}\right)\neq-\tan\left(\frac{A+B-C}{2}\right)$$

10. *(b)* We have,

$$a\sec\theta+b\tan\theta+c=0$$

and $p\sec\theta+q\tan\theta+r=0$

On solving these two equations for $\sec\theta$ and $\tan\theta$ by cross-multiplication, we get

$$\frac{\sec\theta}{br-qc}=\frac{\tan\theta}{cp-ar}=\frac{1}{aq-bp}$$

$$\Rightarrow \sec\theta=\frac{br-cq}{aq-bp}\text{ and }\tan\theta=\frac{cp-ar}{aq-bp}$$

Now, $\sec^2\theta-\tan^2\theta=1$

$$\Rightarrow \left(\frac{br-cq}{aq-bp}\right)^2-\left(\frac{cp-ar}{aq-bp}\right)^2=1$$

$$\Rightarrow (br-cq)^2-(cp-ar)^2=(aq-bp)^2$$

Chapter 19 Heights and Distances

1. *(b)* Let $OC=h$ m be the height of the tower at the centre of the circular park.

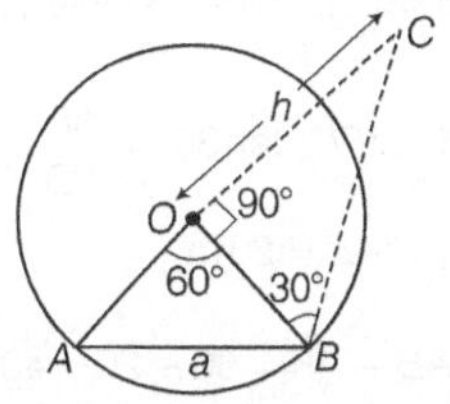

Given, $AB=a$ and $\angle AOB=60°$.

Also, $OA=OB$ [same radius of a circle]

$\therefore$ $\angle OAB=\angle OBA$ ...(i)

We know that, sum of all angles in a triangle is 180°.

$\therefore$ $\angle AOB+\angle OAB+\angle OBA=180°$

$\Rightarrow$ $60°+\angle OAB+\angle OAB=180°$ [from Eq. (i)]

$\Rightarrow$ $60°+2\angle OAB=180°$

$\Rightarrow$ $2\angle OAB=120°$

$\Rightarrow$ $\angle OAB=60°$

$\therefore$ $\angle OAB=\angle OBA=60°$ [from Eq.(i)]

Hence, ΔOAB is an equilateral triangle.

$\Rightarrow$ $OA=AB=OB=a$

In right angled ΔCOB,

$$\tan 30°=\frac{OC}{OB}\Rightarrow\frac{1}{\sqrt3}=\frac{h}{a}\Rightarrow h=\frac{a}{\sqrt3}\text{ m}$$

Hence, height of the tower is $a/\sqrt3$ m.

Solutions (Q. Nos. 2-4) In the given figure, draw ED perpendicular to the line AB.

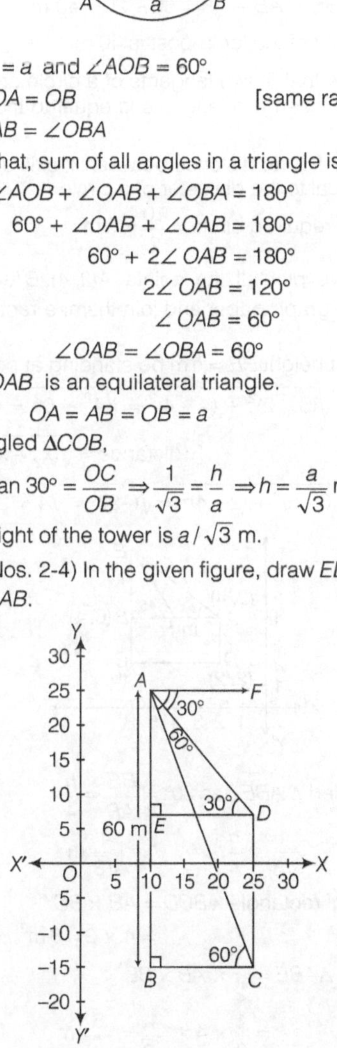

From the figure,

$\angle FAD=\angle EDA=30°$ [alternate angles]

and $\angle FAC=\angle ACB=60°$ [alternate angles]

2. *(c)* In right angled ΔABC, $\tan 60° = \dfrac{AB}{BC}$

$$\Rightarrow \quad \sqrt{3} = \frac{60}{BC}$$

$$\Rightarrow \quad BC = \frac{60}{\sqrt{3}} \times \frac{\sqrt{3}}{\sqrt{3}}$$

$$\Rightarrow \quad BC = \frac{60\sqrt{3}}{3} = 20\sqrt{3} \text{ m}$$

Hence, the horizontal distance between BA and CD is $20\sqrt{3}$ m.

3. *(b)* In right angled ΔAED, $\tan 30° = \dfrac{AE}{ED}$

$$\Rightarrow \quad \frac{1}{\sqrt{3}} = \frac{AE}{20\sqrt{3}} \Rightarrow AE = 20 \text{ m}$$

Now, $CD = BE = AB - AE = 60 - 20 = 40$ m

Hence, height of the lamp-post is 40 m.

4. *(d)* We know that, if two tangents of a circle are parallel, then distance between two tangents is equal to the diameter of a circle.

In the above figure, distance between Y-axis and AB is 10 m, which is equal to the diameter of a circle.

$\therefore$ Radius of required circle $= \dfrac{10}{2} = 5$ m

5. *(c)* When we plot all the points $A(2, 4)$, $B(6, 4)$, $C(6, 2)$ and $D(2, 2)$ on a graph paper and join them, a rectangle $ABCD$ is formed.

Let a pole of height $BE = h$ m be standing at point B.

Now, $AB = \sqrt{(6-2)^2 + (4-4)^2} = \sqrt{4^2 + 0^2} = 4$ m

$$\left[\because \text{distance} = \sqrt{(x_2 - x_1)^2 + (y_2 - y_1)^2}\right]$$

and $BC = \sqrt{(6-6)^2 + (2-4)^2} = \sqrt{(-2)^2} = \sqrt{4} = 2$ m

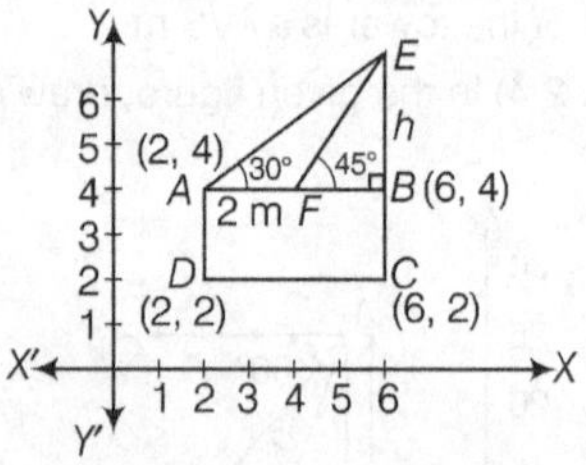

In right angled ΔABE, $\tan 30° = \dfrac{BE}{AB} = \dfrac{h}{4}$

$$\Rightarrow \quad \frac{1}{\sqrt{3}} = \frac{h}{4} \Rightarrow h = \frac{4}{\sqrt{3}} \text{ m}$$

Now, area of rectangle $ABCD = AB \times BC$

$$= 4 \times 2 = 8 \text{ m}^2$$

and area of $\Delta ABE = \dfrac{1}{2} \times AB \times BE$

$$= \frac{1}{2} \times 4 \times \frac{4}{\sqrt{3}} = \frac{8}{\sqrt{3}} \text{ m}^2$$

$\therefore$ Total area of the figure = Area of rectangle $ABCD$ + Area of ΔABE

$$= 8 + \frac{8}{\sqrt{3}} = \frac{8(\sqrt{3}+1)}{\sqrt{3}} \text{ m}^2$$

6. *(a)* Let AB be the surface of the lake and P be a point of observation, such that $AP = h$ m.

Let C be the position of the cloud and C' be its reflection in the lake. Then, $CB = C'B$.

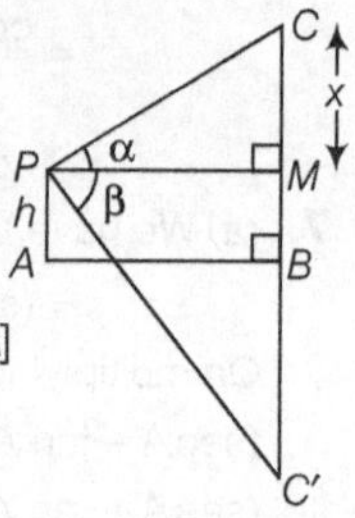

Let $PM \perp CB$.

Then, $\angle CPM = \alpha$ and $\angle MPC' = \beta$.

Let $CM = x$

Then, $CB = CM + MB = x + h$

$= CM + PA$ $\quad [\because MB = PA]$

In right angled ΔCMP,

$$\tan\alpha = \frac{CM}{PM}$$

$$\Rightarrow \quad \tan\alpha = \frac{x}{AB} \quad [\because PM = AB]$$

$$\Rightarrow \quad x = AB \cdot \tan\alpha$$

$$\Rightarrow \quad AB = \frac{x}{\tan\alpha}$$

$$\Rightarrow \quad AB = x\cot\alpha \quad \left[\because \tan\alpha = \frac{1}{\cot\alpha}\right] \quad \text{...(i)}$$

Again, in right angled $\Delta PMC'$,

$$\tan\beta = \frac{C'M}{PM}$$

$$\Rightarrow \quad \tan\beta = \frac{x + 2h}{AB} \quad [\because C'M = C'B + BM = x + h + h = x + 2h]$$

$$\Rightarrow \quad AB = \frac{x + 2h}{\tan\beta}$$

$$\Rightarrow \quad AB = (x + 2h)\cot\beta \quad \left[\because \tan\beta = \frac{1}{\cot\beta}\right] \quad \text{...(ii)}$$

From Eqs. (i) and (ii), we get

$$x\cot\alpha = (x + 2h)\cot\beta$$

$$\Rightarrow \quad x\cot\alpha = x\cot\beta + 2h\cot\beta$$

$$\Rightarrow \quad x(\cot\alpha - \cot\beta) = 2h\cot\beta$$

$$\Rightarrow \quad x\left(\frac{1}{\tan\alpha} - \frac{1}{\tan\beta}\right) = \frac{2h}{\tan\beta}$$

$$\Rightarrow \quad x\left(\frac{\tan\beta - \tan\alpha}{\tan\alpha \cdot \tan\beta}\right) = \frac{2h}{\tan\beta}$$

$$\therefore \quad x = \frac{2h \cdot \tan\alpha}{\tan\beta - \tan\alpha} \quad \text{...(iii)}$$

Hence, the height of the cloud, $CB = x + h$

$$= \left(\frac{2h \cdot \tan\alpha}{\tan\beta - \tan\alpha}\right) + h \quad \text{[from Eq. (iii)]}$$

$$= \left(\frac{2h \cdot \tan\alpha + h\tan\beta - h\tan\alpha}{\tan\beta - \tan\alpha}\right) = \frac{h(\tan\alpha + \tan\beta)}{\tan\beta - \tan\alpha} \text{ m}$$

7. *(b)* Let $BC = h$ m be the height of the wall and $AC = l$ m be the length of the ladder, which rests against a vertical wall at $\angle BAC = \alpha$.

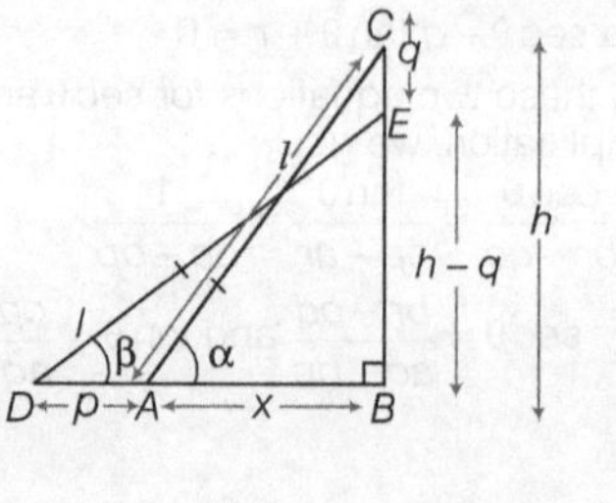

We have to prove that $\dfrac{\cos\beta - \cos\alpha}{\sin\alpha - \sin\beta} = \dfrac{p}{q}$.

When the ladder pulled away from the wall, its new position will be $DE = l$ m and $AD = p$ m.

Let $AB = x$ and $EC = q$.

In right angled ΔABC,

$$\sin\alpha = \frac{BC}{AC} = \frac{h}{l} \text{ and } \cos\alpha = \frac{AB}{AC} = \frac{x}{l}$$

In right angled ΔEBD,

$$\sin\beta = \frac{BE}{DE} = \frac{BC - EC}{DE} = \frac{h-q}{l}$$

and $$\cos\beta = \frac{BD}{DE} = \frac{AB + DA}{DE} = \frac{p+x}{l}$$

Now, $$\frac{\cos\beta - \cos\alpha}{\sin\alpha - \sin\beta} = \frac{\frac{p+x}{l} - \frac{x}{l}}{\frac{h}{l} - \frac{h-q}{l}} = \frac{p+x-x}{h-(h-q)} = \frac{p}{q}$$

8. *(c)* Let A be the eye of the observer and O be the centre of the balloon.

Given, $OP = r$, $\angle PAQ = \theta$ and $\angle OAB = \phi$.

Let height of the centre of balloon be $OB = h$ m

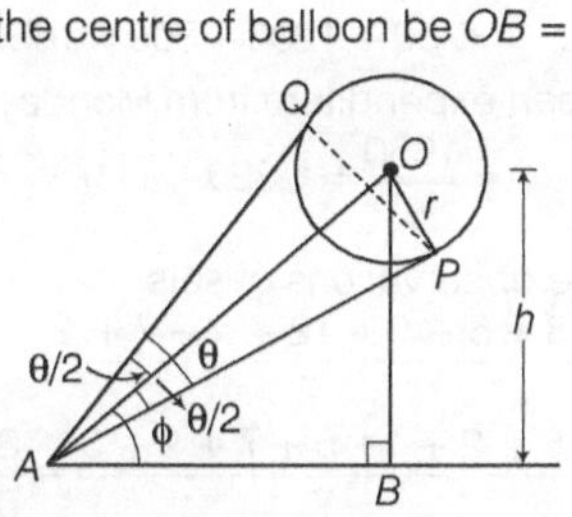

In right angled ΔOAP, $\angle OPA = 90°$

[$\because$ radius is perpendicular to the tangent]

$$\Rightarrow \quad \sin\frac{\theta}{2} = \frac{OP}{OA} = \frac{r}{OA} \quad \ldots(i)$$

and in right angled ΔOBA,

$$\sin\phi = \frac{OB}{OA} = \frac{h}{OA} \quad \ldots(ii)$$

From Eqs. (i) and (ii), we get

$$\frac{\sin\phi}{\sin\frac{\theta}{2}} = \frac{\frac{h}{OA}}{\frac{r}{OA}} = \frac{h}{r} \Rightarrow h = \frac{r\sin\phi}{\sin\frac{\theta}{2}}$$

$$\Rightarrow \quad h = r\sin\phi \operatorname{cosec}\frac{\theta}{2}$$

Hence, the height of the centre of balloon is $r\sin\phi \operatorname{cosec}\dfrac{\theta}{2}$.

9. *(b)* Let OP be the clock tower of height h m, standing at the mid-point O of side BC of ΔABC.

Given, $\alpha = \angle PAO$ and $\beta = \angle PBO$.

$\because \quad \cot\alpha = 3.2$ and $\operatorname{cosec}\beta = 2.6$

$\therefore \quad \cot\beta = \sqrt{\operatorname{cosec}^2\beta - 1} = \sqrt{(2.6)^2 - 1}$

$= \sqrt{6.76 - 1} = \sqrt{5.76} = 2.4$

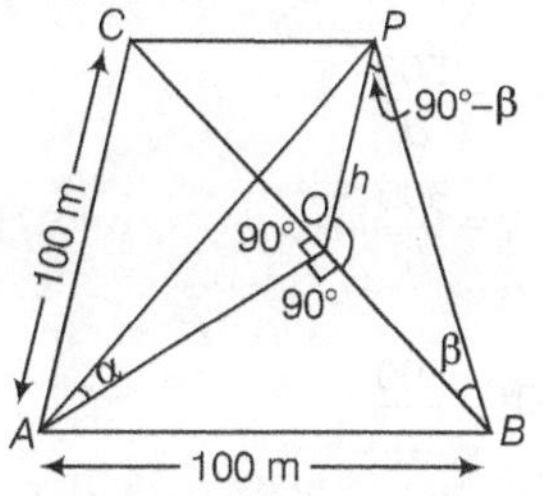

In right angled ΔPOA and ΔPOB, we have

$$AO = h\cot\alpha = 3.2h$$

and $$BO = h\cot\beta = 2.4h$$

In right angled ΔAOB, $AB^2 = OA^2 + OB^2$

$$\Rightarrow \quad 100^2 = (3.2h)^2 + (2.4h)^2$$

$$\Rightarrow \quad 100^2 = 16h^2$$

$$\Rightarrow \quad h^2 = \frac{10000}{16} = 625$$

$$\therefore \quad h = 25 \text{ m}$$

[taking positive square root as side cannot be negative]

Hence, the height of the tower is 25 m.

10. *(a)* In right angled ΔAOP, we have

$$\tan\alpha = \frac{OP}{OA} = \frac{h}{OA}$$

Since, $\tan\alpha = 6$

$$\therefore \quad OA = \frac{h}{6} \quad \ldots(i)$$

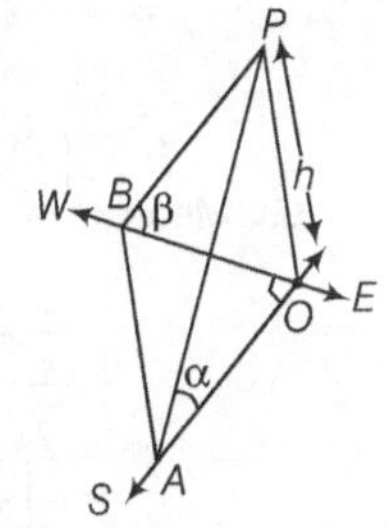

Also, in right angled ΔBOP, we have

$$\tan\beta = \frac{OP}{OB} = \frac{h}{OB}$$

Since, $\tan\beta = 0.75$

$$\therefore \quad OB = \frac{h}{0.75} = \frac{4h}{3} \quad \ldots(ii)$$

Now, in right angled ΔAOB, we have

$$OA^2 + OB^2 = AB^2$$

$$\Rightarrow \quad AB^2 = \frac{h^2}{36} + \frac{16h^2}{9} \quad \text{[from Eqs. (i) and (ii)]}$$

$$\Rightarrow \quad \lambda^2h^2 = h^2\left(\frac{1+64}{36}\right) \quad [\because AB = \lambda h]$$

$$\Rightarrow \quad \lambda^2 = \frac{65}{36}$$

11. *(b)* According to the given information, we have the following figure

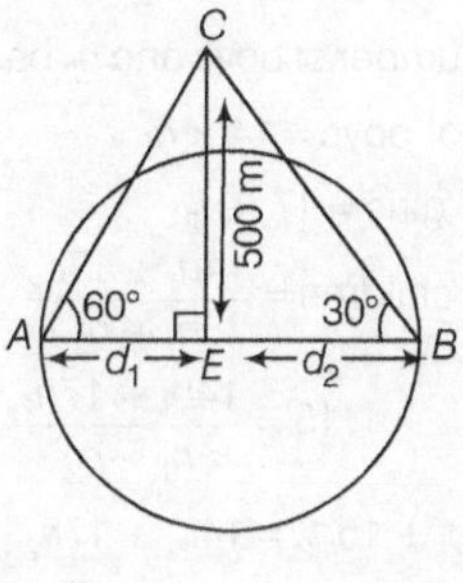

In ΔAEC,

$$\tan 60^\circ = \frac{500}{d_1}$$

$$\Rightarrow \quad d_1 = \frac{500}{\sqrt{3}} \text{ m} \quad [\because \tan 60^\circ = \sqrt{3}] \quad \text{...(i)}$$

and in ΔBEC,

$$\tan 30^\circ = \frac{500}{d_2}$$

$$\Rightarrow \quad d_2 = 500\sqrt{3} \text{ m} \quad \left[\because \tan 30^\circ = \frac{1}{\sqrt{3}}\right] \quad \text{...(ii)}$$

$\therefore$ Required diameter,

$$AB = d_1 + d_2$$

$$= \frac{500}{\sqrt{3}} + 500\sqrt{3} \quad \text{[from Eqs. (i) and (ii)]}$$

$$= \frac{2000}{\sqrt{3}} \text{ m}$$

Chapter 20 Statistics

1. *(a)* Let the observations are $x_1, x_2, x_3, x_4, \dots, x_n$. Now, if we divide each observation by x and increased each observation by y, then the observations become

$$\frac{x_1}{x} + y, \frac{x_2}{x} + y, \frac{x_3}{x} + y, \dots, \frac{x_n}{x} + y.$$

$$\therefore \quad \text{Mean} = \frac{\left(\frac{x_1}{x} + y\right) + \left(\frac{x_2}{x} + y\right) + \dots + \left(\frac{x_n}{x} + y\right)}{n}$$

$$= \frac{\frac{1}{x}(x_1 + x_2 + \dots + x_n) + ny}{n}$$

$$= \frac{1}{x}\left(\frac{x_1 + x_2 + \dots + x_n}{n}\right) + y$$

$$= \frac{1}{x}m + y = \frac{m + xy}{x} \quad [\because \text{mean of } x_1, x_2, \dots, x_n \text{ is } m]$$

2. *(d)* As x, y and $2x$ are in ascending order, therefore median is y.

$$\Rightarrow \quad y = 27$$

Also, $\quad \text{mean} = \dfrac{x + y + 2x}{3} = 33$

$$\Rightarrow \quad \frac{3x + 27}{3} = 33 \Rightarrow x = 24$$

$$\therefore \text{Mean of } x \text{ and } y = \frac{x + y}{2} = \frac{24 + 27}{2} = \frac{51}{2} = 25.5$$

3. *(b)* Let n_1 be the number of boys and n_2 be the number of girls.

Then, total ages of boys $= 14 \times n_1$

and total ages of girls $= 17 \times n_2$

Now, average of children $= \dfrac{14n_1 + 17n_2}{n_1 + n_2}$

$$\Rightarrow \quad 15 = \frac{14n_1 + 17n_2}{n_1 + n_2}$$

$$\Rightarrow \quad 15n_1 + 15n_2 = 14n_1 + 17n_2$$

$$\Rightarrow \quad n_1 = 2n_2 \Rightarrow \frac{n_1}{n_2} = \frac{2}{1}$$

or $\quad n_1 : n_2 = 2 : 1$

4. *(d)* Given, 10 boys brought 11 books each, therefore total number of books brought by 10 boys $= 10 \times 11 = 110$

Also, as 6 girls brought 13 books each.

$\therefore$ Total number of books brought by 6 girls $= 6 \times 13 = 78$

Clearly, the remaining number of students $= 4$

Now, let the number of books brought by 4 students be x.

Then, $x \geq 10$

[$\because$ no two students brought the same number of books]

Thus, the average number of books brought in the class

$$= \frac{x + 78 + 110}{20}$$

It is given that, average number of books brought in the class is a positive integer, therefore the minimum value of x is 12.

5. *(d)* Sum of expenditure from Monday to Wednesday

$$= 250 \times 3 = ₹\,750$$

Sum of expenditure from Wednesday to Friday

$$= 400 \times 3 = ₹\,1200$$

$\because$ Expenditure on Wednesday $= ₹\,300$

$\therefore$ Expenditure from Monday to Friday

$$= 750 + 1200 - 300 = 1650$$

Hence, the mean expenditure from Monday to Friday

$$= \frac{1650}{5} = ₹\,330$$

6. *(c)* Mean of the observations of sets

$$P = \frac{3 + 5 + 9 + 12 + x + 7 + 2}{7} = \frac{38 + x}{7}$$

$$Q = \frac{8 + 2 + 1 + 5 + 7 + 9 + 3}{7} = \frac{35}{7} = 5$$

and $\quad R = \dfrac{5 + 9 + 8 + 3 + 2 + 7 + 1}{7} = \dfrac{35}{7} = 5$

$\therefore$ Ratio of means of sets P and $Q = 7 : 5$ [given]

Let P's mean $= 7y$ and Q's mean $= 5y$.

$$\Rightarrow \quad 5y = 5$$

$$\Rightarrow \quad y = 1$$

$\therefore$ Q's mean $= 5$

Now, P's mean $= 7y$

$$\Rightarrow \quad \frac{38 + x}{7} = 7 \times 1 \Rightarrow 38 + x = 48 \Rightarrow x = 11$$

$\therefore$ Mean of P : Mean of $R = 7y : 5 = 7 \times 1 : 5 = 7 : 5$

7. *(b)* We know that,

$$\text{Mode} = 3\,\text{Median} - 2\,\text{Mean}$$

On dividing both sides by median, we get

$$\frac{\text{Mode}}{\text{Median}} = 3 - 2\frac{\text{Mean}}{\text{Median}}$$

$$\Rightarrow \quad \frac{6}{5} = 3 - 2\frac{\text{Mean}}{\text{Median}} \quad \left[\because \frac{\text{mode}}{\text{median}} = \frac{6}{5}, \text{given}\right]$$

$$\Rightarrow \quad \frac{6}{5} - 3 = -2\frac{\text{Mean}}{\text{Median}}$$

$$\Rightarrow \quad \frac{6 - 15}{5} = -2\frac{\text{Mean}}{\text{Median}}$$

$$\Rightarrow \quad \frac{-9}{5} = -2\frac{\text{Mean}}{\text{Median}}$$

$$\Rightarrow \quad \frac{\text{Mean}}{\text{Median}} = \frac{9}{10}$$

8. *(c)* Let the least possible value of x be n. Then,

Range = Maximum value – Minimum value

$\Rightarrow \quad 23 = 35 - n$

$\Rightarrow \quad n = 35 - 23 = 12$

Hence, the least value of x is 12.

Chapter 21 Probability

1. *(a)* In a wall clock, the minute hand cover the 60 min in one complete round.

$\therefore$ Total number of possible outcomes = 60

The minute hand cover the time from 5 to 15 min,

Number of outcomes favourable to E

= Distance from 5 to 15 min = 10

$\therefore$ Required probability $= \frac{10}{60} = \frac{1}{6}$

Solution (Q.Nos. 2-4) Total number of circles = 34

$\therefore$ Total number of possible outcomes = 34

2. *(a)* Number of circles having diameter less than 28.

Thus, number of outcomes favourable to $E = 3 + 5 = 8$

[$\because$ number of circles having diameter 14 – 20 = 3 and 21 – 27 = 5]

$\therefore \quad P(E) = \frac{8}{34} = \frac{4}{17}$

3. *(b)* Number of circles having radius lying between 14 to 17.

Thus, number of outcomes favourable to $F = 8$

$\therefore \quad P(F) = \frac{8}{34} = \frac{4}{17}$

4. *(c)* Number of circles having diameter above 50.

Thus, number of outcomes favourable to $G = 0$

$\therefore \quad P(G) = \frac{0}{34} = 0$

5. *(c)* Area of the square $ABCD = (BC)^2 = 10^2 = 100\text{ cm}^2$

and area of the square $PQRS = (\text{Side})^2 = (5)^2$ [$\because$ side = 5 cm, given]

$= 25\text{cm}^2$

$\therefore$ P (that the point will be chosen from the shaded part)

$= \frac{\text{Area of the square } PQRS}{\text{Area of the square } ABCD} = \frac{25}{100} = 0.25$

6. *(b)* Area of rectangle $= 3 \times 2 = 6\text{m}^2$

$E = \text{Area of circle} = \pi\left(\frac{1}{2}\right)^2 = \frac{\pi}{4}\text{m}^2$

$\left[\because \text{diameter} = 1\text{m} \Rightarrow \text{radius} = \frac{1}{2}\text{m and area of circle} = \pi r^2\right]$

$\therefore$ Probability that the die land inside the circle

$= \frac{\text{Area of circle}}{\text{Area of rectangle}} = \frac{\pi / 4}{6} = \frac{\pi}{24}$

7. *(b)* Since, radius of each of the given circles is 1 unit.

$\therefore$ Side of square $ABCD = 1 + 1 = 2$ units

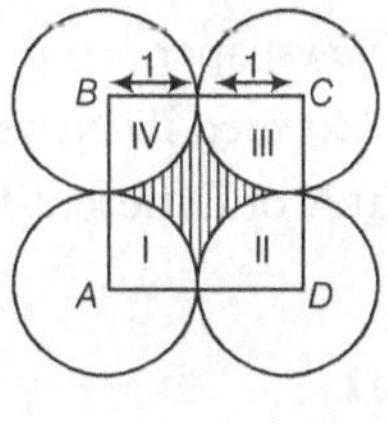

Now, area of square $= 2^2 = 4$ sq units

Clearly, area of shaded region = area of square – area of quadrant I – area of quadrant II – area of qudrant III – area of quadrant IV

$= 4 - 4 \times$ area of a quadrant

$= 4 - 4 \times \frac{\pi(1)^2}{4}$ $\left[\because \text{area of a quadrant} = \frac{1}{4}\pi r^2\right]$

$= 4 - \pi$

$\therefore$ Required probability

$= \frac{\text{Area of shaded region}}{\text{Area of square}} = \frac{4 - \pi}{4}$

Internal Assessment of Practical Work

Project 1

Topic

Comparative newspaper coverage of different items

1. Introduction
2. Importance of Newspaper
3. Different Items Covered by Newspaper
4. Comparative Study of Different Items
5. Conclusion

1. Introduction

Newspaper is defined as 'a printed paper or publication, reporting local or general news, or printed editorial comment, announcement, miscellaneous, reading matter, commercial advertising, classical advertising, legal advertising and other notices and comment on public news'.

Each newspaper tries to establish its identity and win the loyalty of its readers through a combination of words, pictures, cartoons, presentations, techniques and exclusive news stories. Newspaper also contains public grievances and reflects public opinion.

In India, newspapers have undeniably a vital role to play and an important duty to perform both as voice of people and a builder of public opinion.

It is believed that not more than 17% people in India read newspapers. Young men mostly read the sports news and film reviews, the traders and other business-minded people fix themselves to the commercial pages which provides them the latest market quotations of shares, stock, etc.

2. Importance of Newspaper

Newspaper performs its true role as a guardian of the public interest, a watch dog and a source of all kinds of information.

Newspapers give us all types of news about our country and the world. All the government policies are published by the newspapers. Newspapers not only give us the latest news but also publish advertisements for jobs and many other things.

People of all profession need newspaper. Engineers, doctors, scientists, professors and other professionals need them to know the day to day developments in their respective fields.

Newspapers give us knowledge about many things of the past and present. Without these, people cannot get knowledge and news about the country and the world. Thus, in our society, newspapers are very important.

3. Different Items Covered by Newspapers

(i) Local News
(ii) State News
(iii) National News
(iv) International News
(v) Political News
(vi) Sports News
(vii) Classified News
(viii) Business News
(ix) Educational News
(x) Entertainment News

4. Comparative Study of Different Items of a News

Sports News

(i) **Headline of Main Sports News** (Cricket News) News on the match played on 26.02.2015 between India and South Africa.

	Newspaper	Date	Headline
a	The Hindu	23.10.2015	India won the match against South Africa by 6 wickets
b	The Times of India	23.10.2015	Virat Kohli made another century
c	The Indian Express	23.10.2015	India *vs* South Africa : Virat Kohli lead Indian Cricket Team

(ii) Presentation of News

	Newspaper	Headline
a	The Hindu	Presents this news very exclusively and in details.
b	The Times of India	Present this news in short.
c	The Indian Express	Presents this news effectively and in a remarkable manner.

(iii) Pictures of News

	Newspaper	Headline
a	The Hindu	Highlights the picture of Indian batsman Kohli who celebrates his century against South Africa during the fourth ODI in Chennai in coloured mode.
b	The Times of India3	Also presents the picture of Indian bastman (Virat Kohli, Dhoni) in coloured mode.
c	The Indian Express	Presents the picture of Virat Kohli and AB de villiers in coloured mode.

(iv) Views of Experts about the News

	Newspaper	Headline
a	The Hindu	Kohli said he knew he would have to push himself more than usual given the conditions he was batting in.
b	The Times of India	Virat Kohli should be allowed to bat No. 3 said Sunil Gavaskar
c	The Indian Express	Aakash Chopra a sports critic says that "Duminy's absence has meant that SA forced to go with Morris and not Abbott picked a bowel for his batting huge toss to win for India"

(v) Format of the News

	Newspaper	Headline
a	The Hindu	Presents the news in a simple way in three or four small columns with pictures.
b	The Times of India	Presents the news in good manner with the extended views of experts in four columns.
c	The Indian Express	Presents the news at almost full sports page with some small and big pictures in three column.

5. Conclusion

So, we can say that newspaper plays very important role in the society. By comparing the news of some item in different news papers, we can judge the truthfulness and standard of that news and can choose the correct and genuine newspaper for reading.

Project 2

Topic

Survey of various types of Bank Accounts, rates of interest offered

Table for Contents

1. Types of Bank Accounts
2. Calculation of Interest
3. Prevailing Rate of Interest by State Bank of India
4. Prevailing Rate of Interest by Bank of Baroda.

1. Types of Bank Accounts

Bank is an institution, which attracts money on deposits for the purpose of lending to trade, industry, etc. Receiving deposits from the public is an important function of a commercial bank. A bank provides the facility to open different kinds of deposit accounts with various facilities to suit the needs of various customers or depositors.

There are mainly five types of accounts which a person can open with a bank

(i) **Fixed or Time Deposit Account** Fixed deposit account is one where money is deposited for a fixed period and is not supposed to be withdrawn before the expiry of the commit period. This period usually varies from 15 days to five years. The rate of interest allowed on such accounts generally increases with the period of deposit. This account is also known as "Term Deposit Account".

This is the most suitable form of accepting deposits for a commercial bank.

Banks allow a higher rate of interest to attract such deposits. Customers deposit their money in such account with a view to earn interest as well as to withdraw the same on the expiry of the period of the deposit.

(ii) **Savings Bank Deposit Account** This is an account into which small savings are deposited into bank by the customers. This account is meant for the benefit of middle class and low-income group people. Any person with a minimum specific deposit can open a Saving Bank Deposit Account.

The special feature of this account is deposits can be made for any number of times in a week but withdrawals can be made only once or twice a week. Banks, to discourage the habit of frequent withdrawals, impose restrictions on withdrawals.

(iii) **Current Deposit Account or Current Account** It is one in which money can be deposited and withdrawn at any time during the working hours without giving any notice to the bank. This account may be defined as running account between a banker and a customer. Current accounts suit the requirements of businessmen, companies, corporations, institutions, firms, etc.

It is also known as "Open Account".

Since customers can deposit money into or withdraw money from their current accounts whenever they like.

(iv) **Recurring Deposit Account** This is a special type of bank accounts, in which a depositor deposits fixed amount every month for a fixed period of time. At the end of the period depositor gets all the principal sum, alongwith the interest earned during that period.

(v) **Flexible Accounts** These accounts combine the characteristics and benefits of savings account and fixed deposit accounts. In such accounts a fixed deposit account is opened for the maturity periods available and a savings account is also opened. The amount in fixed deposit account is treated as units of ₹1000 each. In case of customer needs money in excess of balance in the savings account, the requisite amount will be transferred out of fixed deposit account in units of ₹1000 each along with interest payable on the amount.

2. Calculation of Interest

Calculating Interest on a Savings Bank Account

To calculate the interest on a savings account proceed as under

(i) Interest for the month is calculated on the minimum balance between the 10th day and the last day of the month.

(ii) Convert the minimum balance of each month as a multiple of ₹10. No interest is paid up to ₹ 5.

(iii) Add all these balances. However, if the same balance continues for n months then multiply this balance by n, rather than writing it n times and then adding.

(iv) Find the simple interest on this sum for one month.

(v) If the interest is less than ₹ 1, neglect it.

(vi) No interest is paid for the month in which the account is closed. e.g. A page from savings bank passbook of Mr. Brar is given below

Date, Year 2006	Particulars	Withdrawals (in ₹)	Deposits (in ₹)	Balance (in ₹)
Jan 1	B/F			3142.35
Jan 1	By Salary	...	2718.50	5860.85
Jan 6	To self	2500.00	...	3360.85
Jan 13	To cheque	255.00	...	3105.85
Feb 3	By salary	...	2805.40	5911.25
March 2	By salary	...	2805.40	8716.65
March 10	To self	3000.00	...	5716.65
April 4	By salary	...	2805.40	8522.05
April 23	To cheque	2625.00	...	5897.05
May 5	By salary	...	3060.70	8957.75
May 8	To self	5000.00	...	3957.75
May 13	By cash	...	650.00	4607.75

Mr. Brar closes his account in the period ending May, 2006. Calculate the interest earned for this period if the rate of interest is 5%.

Sol.

Month	Minimum balance between 10th and last day	Qualifying amount for interest
Jan	3105.85	3110
Feb	5911.25	5910
March	5716.65	5720
April	5897.05	5900
May	3957.75	3960
Total		**₹ 24600**

Principal for one month = ₹ 24600,

Time $= \frac{1}{12}$ yr, Rate = 5% per annum

$$\therefore \text{ Interest} = \frac{P \times R \times T}{100} = \frac{24600 \times 5 \times 1}{100 \times 12} = ₹102.50$$

(i) Calculating Interest on a Recurring Deposit Account

e.g. Aman has a recurring deposit account of ₹2500 per month for a period of 6 yr. What interest will he get at the time of maturity if the rate of interest is 11.5% per annum?

Sol. Equivalent principal for one month = ₹ 2500

Time = 6 yr (72 months), Rate of interest = 11.5% per annum

$$\text{Interest} = \frac{xI \times (x+1)}{2} \times \frac{r}{100} \times \frac{1}{12}$$

[where, I = monthly instalment, x = number of months, r = rate of interest]

$$\therefore \text{Interest} = \frac{2500 \times 72 \times (72+1)}{2} \times \frac{11.5}{100} \times \frac{1}{12} = ₹62962.50$$

3. Prevailing Rates of Interest by State Bank of India : Fixed Deposit

Duration (in years)	Rate of interest
6 Months	5%
1-2 yr	5.5%
3-5 yr	5.75%
Above 5 yr	6.25%

Recurring Deposit = 5.5 %

Savings Account = 3.5 % per annum

4. Prevailing Rates of Interest by Bank of Baroda : Fixed Deposit

Duration	Rate of interest
7-14 days	3.75%
15-19 days	4.25%
30-45 days	4.50%
76-89 days	4.70%
90-179 days	5.00%
180 days-9 months	5.25%
9 months-1 yr	5.50%
1-2 yr	5.75%
2-5 yr	6.00%
5 yr and above	6.25%
Senior Citizens Extra	0.50%

Recurring Deposit = 5.75%

Savings Account = 3.5%

Project 3

Topic

Planning a Home Budget

1. Introduction
2. Monthly income of family
3. Monthly expenditure of family
4. Family size
5. Bar graph
6. Pie chart
7. Savings
8. Pie chart
9. Conclusion

1. **Introduction** A home budget is a snapshot of income and expenses, usually expressed over a period of one month. After adding up all of the sources of income, you can calculate total amount available to spend.

2. **Monthly Income of Family**

I. Father → (Mr. Amit Chhabra)

Income from salary	₹ 65000
Income from other sources	₹ 10000
Deductions (GPF, LIC, etc.)	₹ 10000
Taxes	₹ 15000
Total income	₹ 50000

II. Mother → (M/s Sunita Chhabra)

Income from salary	₹ 20000
Deductions (GPF, LIC etc.)	₹ 3000
Taxes	₹ 4000
Total income	₹ 13000

Grand total income of family

= ₹ 50000 + ₹ 13000 = 63000

3. **Monthly Expenditure of Family**

Category	Expenditure (in ₹)
House Maintainance	4000
Grocery + fruits + vegetables	12000
Milk	5000
Electricity + water	2500
Conveyance	1000
Clothing	2500
Education	5000
Entertainment	2000
Automobiles	2000
Telephone + Mobile	2000

Category	Expenditure (in ₹)
Home helpers	1500
Repairs	500
Cable + Internet connection	500
Travelling	2000
Laundary	500
Shopping	2500
Stationery	500
Medical	3000
Grand total	₹ 53000

$\therefore$ Monthly expenditure = ₹ 53000

4. **Family Size** Our income and expenditure are totally depend on the size of family. Family size varies from family-to-family. The general family size is as follows:

   Father $\rightarrow$ One (Mr. Amit Chhabra)

   Mother $\rightarrow$ One (M/s Sunita Chhabra)

   Children $\rightarrow$ Two (Pawan and Sheena)

   Total members of family $\rightarrow$ Four

5. **Bar Graph Comparing all the Expenses**

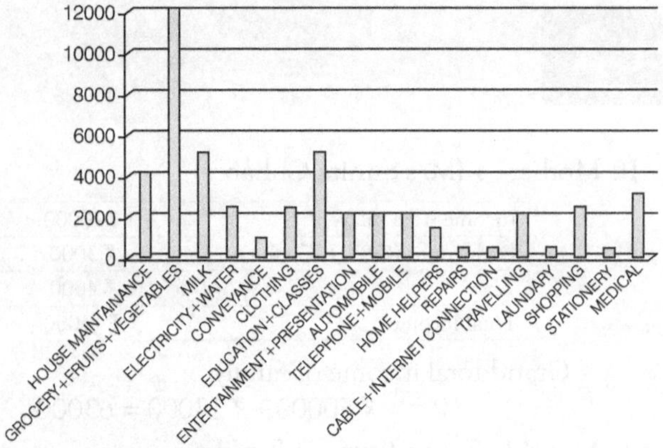

6. **Pie Chart Comparing all the Expenses**

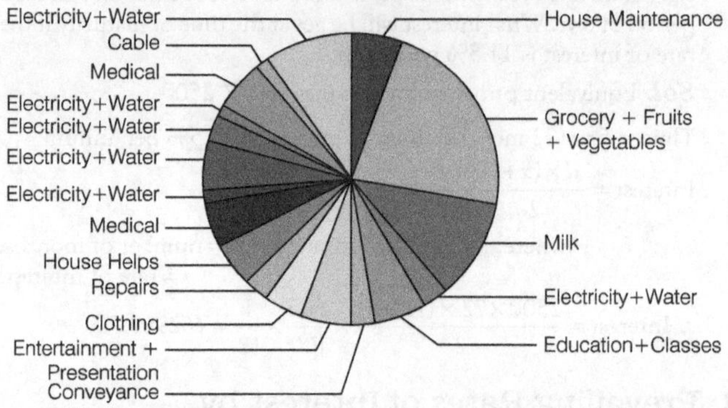

7. **Savings** Some saving is important for the better future of the family. This saving can be helpful at the time of requirement or need. So, every family make saving according to their need and reach.

   Total savings = Total income – Total expenditure

   = ₹ 63000 – ₹ 51000 = ₹ 12000

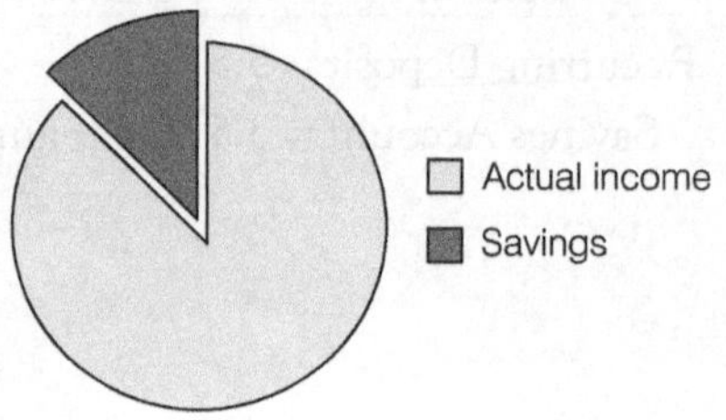

Conclusion

From the above we conclude that planning a Home-Budget is an essential for a family with the help of this planning, we can actuals estimate that how much we should spend on different elements.

Project 4

Topic

Conduct a survey in your locality to study the mode of conveyance/prices of various essential commodities favourite sports. Represent the data, using a bar graph/ histogram and estimate the mode.

1. Mode of conveyance
2. Prices of various essential commodities
3. Favourite sports

1. Mode of Conveyance

(i) **Introduction** In our locality people use various type of mode of conveyance such as bicycle rickshaw, two wheeler, three wheeler, four- wheeler, local bus, local train and etc for doing their day-to-day work.

On the basis of their work age and financial conditions they use various types of modes of conveyance.

(ii) **Description** The percentage (%) of various types of modes of conveyance used by the people of our locality are given as

Mode of conveyance	Percentage of people
Bicycle	5%
Rickshaw	5%
Two wheeler	30%
Three wheeler	5%
Four Wheeler	25%
Local bus	20%
Local train	10%

Representation of the above data using bar graph is given as

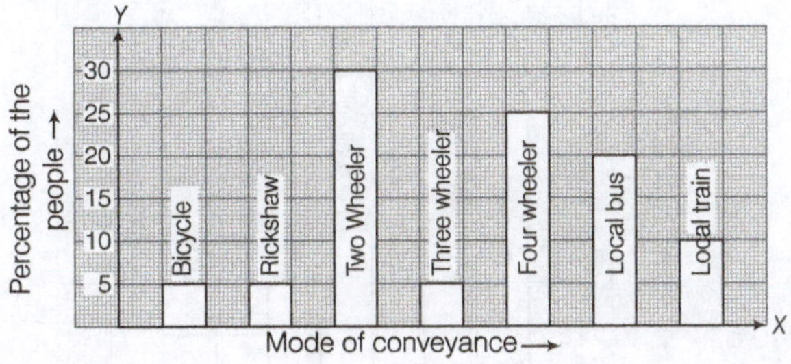

The number of people used various types of modes of conveyance according to their age are given as below

Let take sample of 100 people.

Age group (in years)	Mode of conveyance	Number of people
15-20	Bicycle	5
20-25	Rickshaw	5
25-30	Two wheeler	30
30-35	Three wheeler	5
35-40	Four wheeler	25
40-45	Local bus	20
45-50	Local train	10

Representation of the above data using histogram is given as

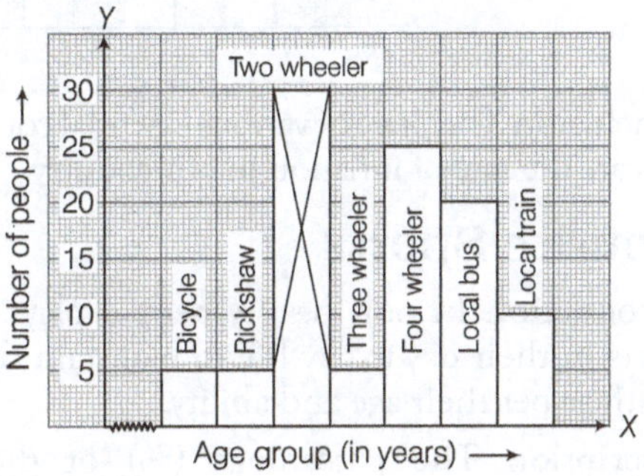

(iii) **Conclusion** Mode = 27 yr

2. Prices of Various Essential Commodities

(i) **Introduction** In our locality people use various essential commodities in their daily life to fulfil their daily needs. On the basis of their essential commodities.

(ii) **Description** The price of various essential commodities used by people of our locality are given as

Essential Commodities	Price per kg /litre (in ₹)
Salt	10
Sugar	30
Tea leaf	40
Milk	50
Spices	100
Wheat	30
Vegetable	70
Rice	50
Pluses	130
Fruits	100

Representation of above data using bar graph is given as

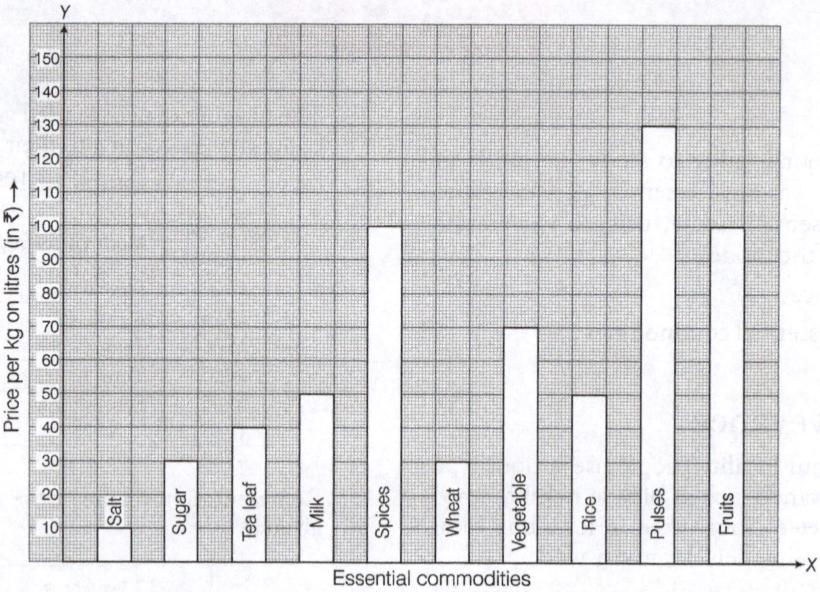

(iii) **Conclusion** The price of various essential commodities indicate the rate of inflation in our country.

3. Favourite Sports

(i) **Introduction** In our locality people plays different sports in their day-to-day life to maintain their good health as per their age and ability.

(ii) **Description** The percentage (%) of the people playing different sports in their day-to-day life are given as

Favourite sports	Percentage (%) of people
Cricket	30%
Basketball	10%
Badminton	15%
Football	15%
Hockey	10%
Skating	5%
Volleyball	5%
Swimming	10%

Representation of above data using bar graph is given as

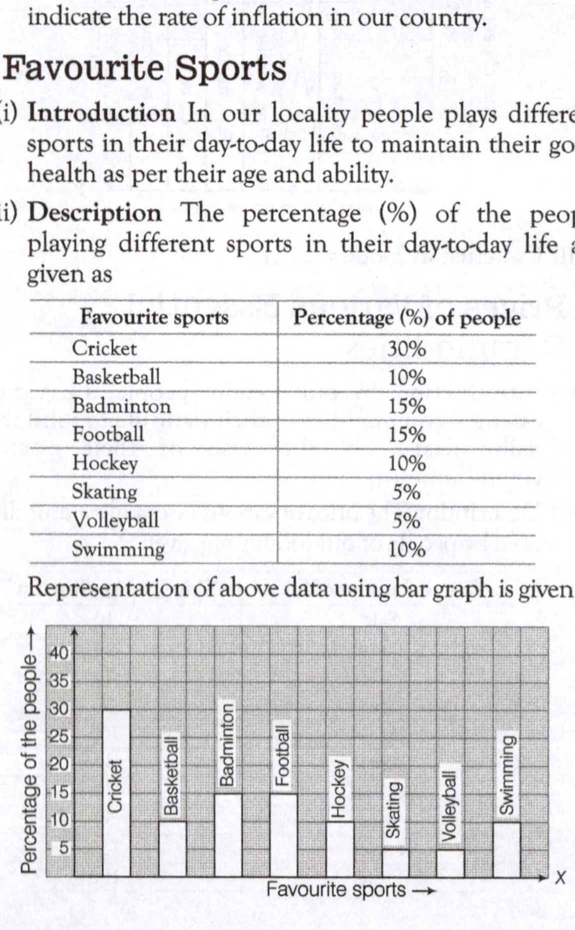

The number of people, play various sports as per their age are given below. Let us take as sample of 100 people

Age group (in years)	Favourite sports	Number of people
5-10	Cricket	30
10-15	Basketball	10
15-20	Badminton	15
20-25	Football	15
25-30	Hockey	10
30-35	Skating	5
35-40	Volleyball	5
40-45	Swimming	10

Representation of above data using histogram on the graph paper is given as

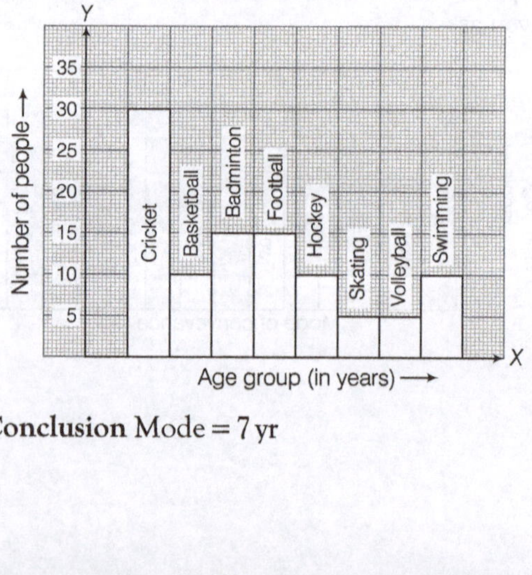

(iii) **Conclusion** Mode = 7 yr

Project 5

Topic

To use a Newspaper to Study and Report on Shares and Dividends

Important Points

1. Introduction
2. Business news
3. Meaning of shares and dividends
4. Discussion of various shares and dividends of different companies.
5. Comparative study of shares of different companies.
6. Comparative study of profit on sale/purchase of shares of different companies.
7. Conclusion

Now, do same as Project 1.

Project 6

Topic

Set up a dropper with ink in it vertical at a height say 20 cm above a horizontally placed sheet of plain paper. Release one ink drop; observe the pattern, if any, on the paper. Vary the vertical distance and repeat. Discover any pattern of relationship between the vertical height and the ink drop observed.

1. **Material used** Ink, dropper, plain paper sheet, scale.
2. **Procedure** Place a plain paper sheet horizontally and fill the dropper with ink, now release one ink drop from dropper on the sheet from different heights at different places.
3. **Observation** We see circular shapes of released drop of ink on the paper sheet and observe that "As the height of dropper increases then the size of circular shapes also increases," as shown in figure.

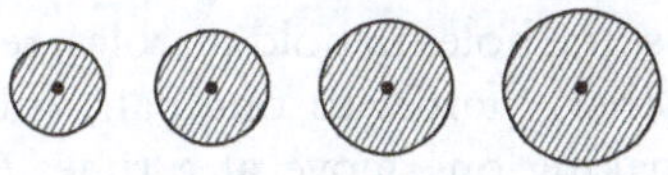

Radius	1 cm	2 cm	3 cm	4 cm
Height of dropper	10 cm	20 cm	30 cm	40 cm

4. **Conclusion** Radius of circular shapes (R) is directly proportional to the height of dropper (H) above the paper sheet.

Project 7

Topic

You are provided (or you construct a model as shown) three vertical sticks (size of a pencil) stuck to a horizontal board. You should also have discs of varying sizes with holes (like a doughnut). Start with one disc; place it on (in) stick A. Transfer it to another stick (B or C); this is one move (m). Now try with two discs placed in A such that the large disc is below and the smaller disc is above (number of discs $n = 2$). Now transfer them one at a time in B or C to obtain similar situation (larger disc below). How many moves? Try with more discs ($n = 1, 2, 3$, etc.) and generalise.

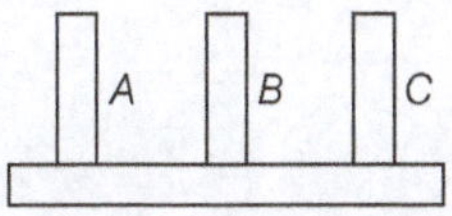

1. **Material used** Three vertical sticks, horizontal board, discs of varying size having holes.
2. **Procedure**

***Case* I** Stuck three vertical sticks on a horizontal board 30 cm apart. Now start with one disc, place it on (in) stick A.

Transfer it to another stick B of C.

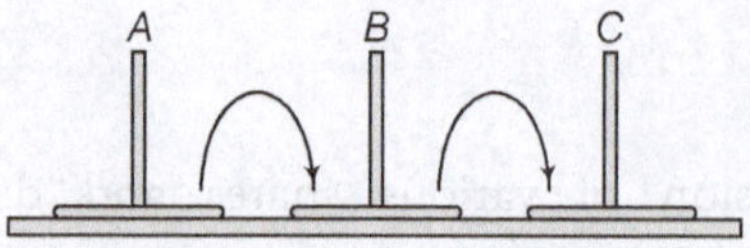

***Case* II** Now try with two discs placed in A such that the larger disc is below and the smaller disc is above. Now, transfer them one at a time in B or C to obtain similar situation.

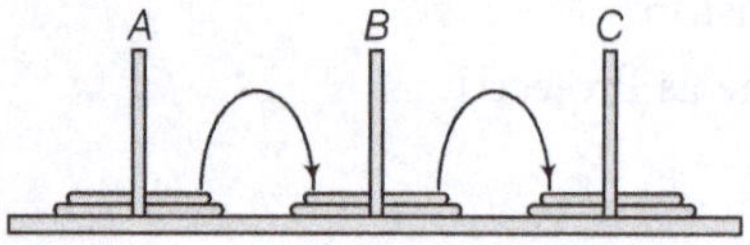

***Case* III** Similarly, try this experiment with three, four, etc, discs to obtain similar situation.

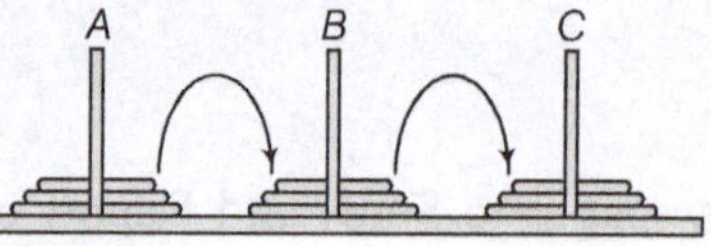

3. **Observation**

Number of discs	1	2	3	4
Number of moves	2	4	6	8

4. **Conclusion** Number of moves of disc = 2 × Number of disc used.

Project 8

Topic

The board has some holes to hold marbles, red on one side and blue on other. Start with one pair. Interchange the positions by making one move at a time. A marble can jump, over another to fill the hole behind. The move (m) equal 3. Try with 2($n=2$) and more. Find relationship between n and m.

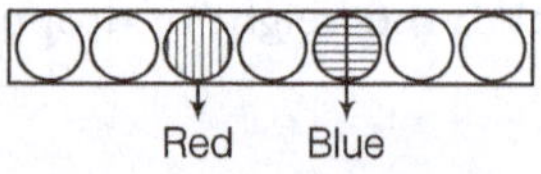

1. **Material used** Card board having holes, red and blue marbles.
2. **Procedure** Set a card board having seven holes horizontally and then fill the holes by using red and blue marbles, as red one side and the blue on the other side. Now interchange the positions by making one move, at a time in any manner.

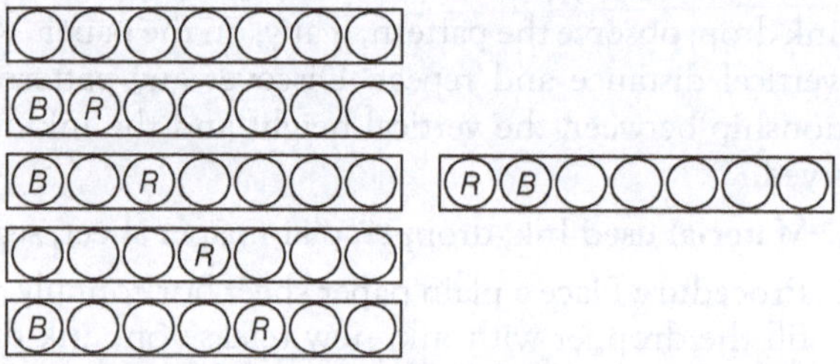

3. **Calculations** Now count the number of moves (m). So, $m = {}^7P_2 = 7 \times 6 = 42$. When $n = 2$ $n \rightarrow$ (number of marbles)
4. **Conclusion** $m = {}^qP_n$ where m = Number of moves, q = Number of holes, n = Number of marbles.

Project 9

Topic

Take a square sheet of paper of side 10 cm four small squares are to be cut from the corners of the square sheet and then paper folded at the cuts to form an open box. What should be the size of the squares cut so that the volume of the open box is maximum?

1. **Material used** Pencil, square sheet of paper of side 20 cm, a pair of scissors, scale.
2. **Procedure**

(i) Take a square sheet of paper of side 20 cm.

(ii) Cut small squares from the corners of the squares sheet say 'x' cm and then the paper folder at the cuts to form an open box as shown in the following figures.

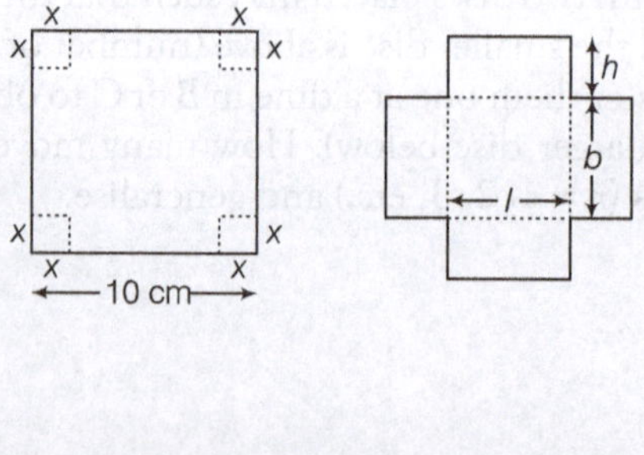

3. **Observation** In this way, we find different open box of different volume by taking the different values of x

Calculation $V = l \times b \times h$

where, V = volume of the square box,

l = length of the square box,

b = breadth of the square box,

and h = height of the square box.

Let $h = x$ cm and each side of square = 20 cm.

For different cases, we have different volume which are given as

S.No.	$h = x$ cm	l (in cm)	b (in cm)	V (in cm) $[V = l \times b \times h]$
1.	1	18	18	324
2.	$\frac{5}{3}$	$\frac{50}{3}$	$\frac{50}{3}$	$\frac{50}{3} \times \frac{50}{3} \times \frac{50}{3} = 462.96$
3.	2	16	16	512
4.	3	11	11	363

For $x = 2$ cm the volume of the open box is maximum.

4. **Conclusion** From the above we conclude that the volume of the open box is totally depend on the value of x.

Project 10

Topic

Take an open box, four sets of marbles (ensuring that marbles in each set are of same size) and some water. By placing the marbles and water in the box, attempt to answer the question do larger marbles or smaller marbles occupy more volume in a given space?

1. **Material used** An open box, four sets of marbles, some water.
2. **Procedure** Take an open box and put the set of marbles and some water into the box. (Set of marbles has 4 marbles of diameter 2 cm each). Repeat the experiment with other set of marbles of different size.
3. **Observation**

(i) Larger marbles occupy more volumes in a given space.

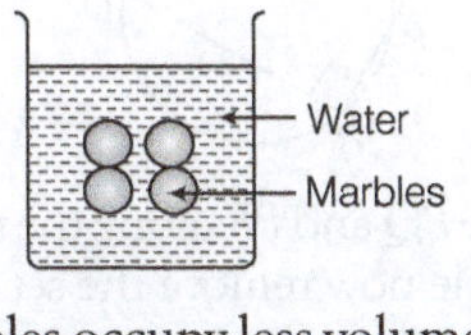

(ii) Smaller marbles occupy less volumes in a given space.

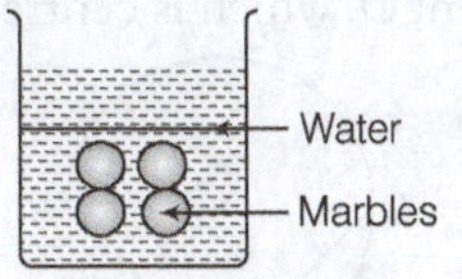

(iii) If the number of marbles, and size of marbles are different, then volumes occupied may by same.

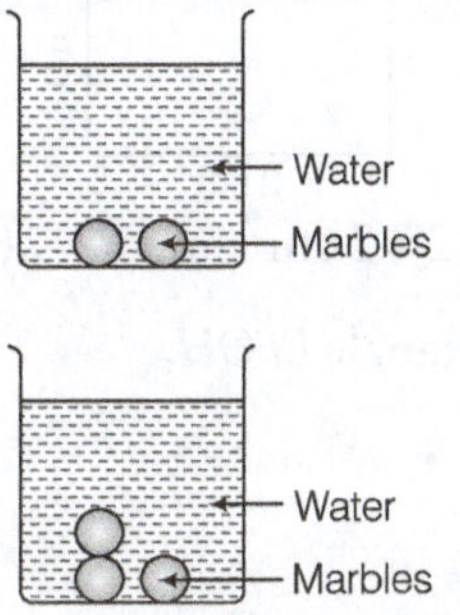

(iv) If the number of marbles is different, then volume occupied by marbles is also different.

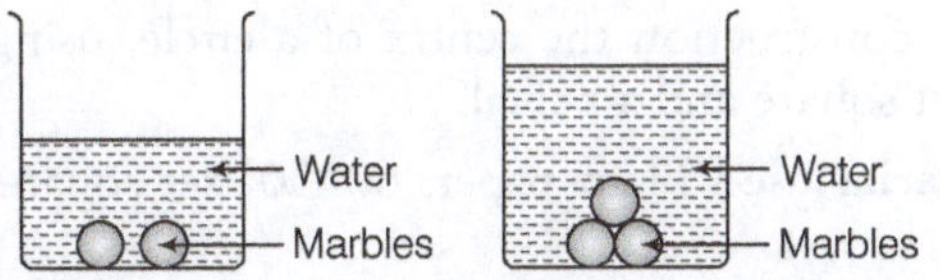

4. **Conclusion**

(i) If the number of marbles is same, then volume occupied by marbles is directly proportional to the size of marble.

(ii) If the size of marbles is same, then volume occupied by marbles is directly proportional to the number of marbles.

Project 11

Topic

An eccentric artist says that the best paintings have the same area as their perimeter (numerically). Let us not argue whether such sizes increase the viewers appreciation, but only try and find what sides (in integers only) a rectangle must have if its area and perimeter are to be equal (note : there are only two rectangles).

1. **Introduction** An eccentric artist says that the best paintings have the same area as their perimeter in case of rectangles.
2. **Procedure** Draw different rectangles of different dimensions as

***Case* I** In rectangle *ABCD*,

$$A = l \times b, P = 2(l + b)$$

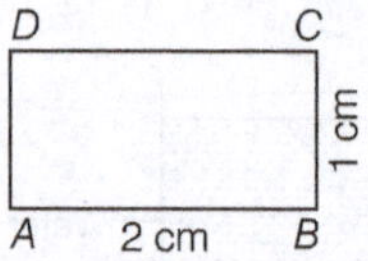

$\Rightarrow \quad A = 1 \times 2 = 2\,\text{cm}^2$ and $P = 2(1+2) 6\,\text{cm}$

***Case* II** In rectangle *EFGH*,

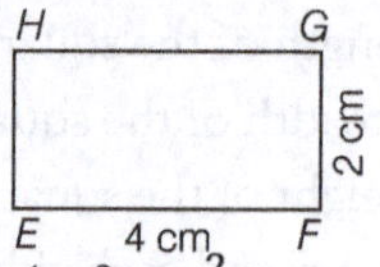

$$A = 2 \times 4 = 8\,\text{cm}^2$$

$$P = 2(2+4) = 12\,\text{cm}$$

***Case* III** In rectangle *PQRS*,

$$A = 3 \times 6 = 18\,\text{cm}^2$$

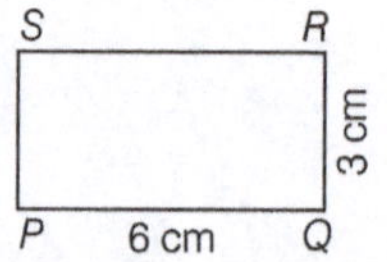

$$P = 2(3+6) = 18\,\text{cm}$$

Here, we observe that in the third case area and perimeter is same.

3. **Conclusion** Hence, if length of the rectangle is 6 cm and breadth of rectangle is 3 cm, then area and perimeter will be same numerically.

Project 12

Topic

Find by construction the centre of a circle, using only a 60-30 set square and a pencil.

1. **Material used** Plain paper, 60°-30° set square, pencil etc.
2. **Procedure**
   (i) Draw a circle of any radius.
   (ii) Now, put 60°-30° set square on the circle as

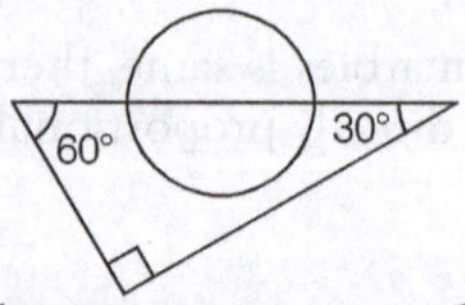

   (iii) Now, move the set square upward so as to bring one corner of set square at the circumference of the cirlce as

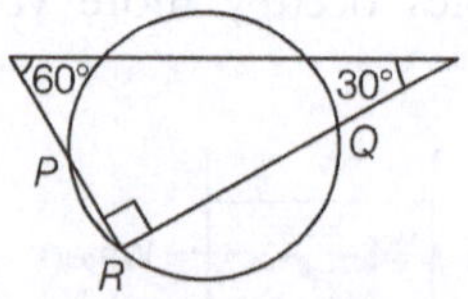

   (iv) Draw the line *PQ* and *PR* along the sides of set square as chords of circle now remove the set square.
   (v) Draw perpendicular bisector of *PQ* and *PR* which meet at a point O, which is centre of the circle

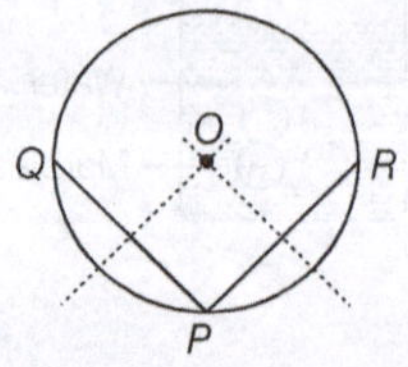

3. **Conclusion** O is the required centre of the given circle.

Project 13

Topic

Various types of 'Cryptarithm'.

A cryptarithmetic is a type of mathematical puzzle in which the digits are replaced by letters of the alphabet or other symbols. To find the solution you have to find the original digits. Making and solving such puzzles are called **cryptarithmetic.**

1. **Let us understand the rules to solve such problems**

Each letter or symbol represents only one digit throughout the problem.

When letters are replaced by their digits, the resultant arithmetical operation must be correct.

Numbers must not begin with a zero.

There must be only one solution to the problem.

2. **We follow the following steps to solve such problems**

Step I Write the problems in columns, leaving gaps in between letters for writing trial numbers.

Step II A good hint to find zero or 9 is to look for columns containing two or three identical letters.

Look at these additions

$$\begin{array}{r} ***A \\ +***A \\ \hline ***A \end{array} \qquad \begin{array}{r} ***B \\ +***A \\ \hline ***B \end{array}$$

The columns $A+A=A$ and $B+A=B$ indicate that A = zero. In math this is called the "additive identity property of zero" ; it says that you add "0" to anything and it does not change, therefore it stays the same. Now, look at those same additions in the body of the cryptarithm.

$$\begin{array}{r} *A** \\ +*A** \\ \hline *A** \end{array} \qquad \begin{array}{r} *B** \\ +*A** \\ \hline *B** \end{array}$$

In these cases, we may have A = zero or A = 9. It depends whether or not "carry 1" is received from the previous column. In other words, the "9" mimics zero every time it gets a carry-over of "1".

Step III Look for 1 in addition or subtraction, observe left hand digits. If single, they are probably 1.

e.g. (i)
$$\begin{array}{r} B*** \\ +A*** \\ \hline A**** \end{array}$$

In this example A can only be 1 as it has been carried over from the previous column. This means that whenever an addition of p digits gives a total of, $p+1$ digits the left hand digit of the total must be 1.

e.g. (ii)
$$\begin{array}{r} B*** \\ -B*** \\ \hline ***** \end{array}$$

In this example, $B=1$ e.g. (iii)
$$\begin{array}{r} 1BA \\ +AA2 \\ \hline B75 \end{array}$$

Here, $A+2=5 \Rightarrow A=5-2=3$

$B+A=7 \Rightarrow B+3=7$

$\Rightarrow B=7-3=4 \Rightarrow B=4$ and $1+A=B$

$\Rightarrow \quad 1+A=4 \Rightarrow A=4-1=3$

Thus, $\begin{array}{r} 1BA \\ +AA2 \\ \hline B75 \end{array}$ is $\begin{array}{r} 143 \\ +332 \\ \hline 475 \end{array}$

3 SAMPLE QUESTION PAPERS

SAMPLE QUESTION PAPER 1

A HIGHLY SIMULATED SAMPLE QUESTION PAPER FOR ICSE CLASS X

MATHEMATICS

GENERAL INSTRUCTIONS

1. Attempt **all questions** from **Section A** and **any 4 questions** from **Section B**.
2. All working, including rough work, must be clearly shown and must be done on the same sheet as the rest of the answer.
3. Omission of essential working will result in loss of marks.
4. The intended marks for questions or parts of questions are given in brackets [ ].

Time : 2.5 Hrs **Max. Marks : 80**

Section A [40 *Marks*]

(Attempt all questions from this section)

1. Choose the correct answers to the questions from the given options. [15]

(i) The first terms of an AP, whose first term is 4 and common difference is –6, are • ***Understanding***

(a) 4, – 10, – 16, – 22 (b) 4, 10, 16, 22
(c) 4, – 2, – 8, – 14 (d) 4, 2, 8, 14

(ii) If $(x-2)$ is a factor of $x^3+2x^2-kx+10$, then k is • ***Evaluation***

(a) –13 (b) 13
(c) 12 (d) –12

(iii) Abhay invested ₹ 8000 with interest rate of 5% for 2 yr, then simple interest is • ***Application***

(a) ₹ 400 (b) ₹ 600
(c) ₹ 800 (d) ₹ 1000

(iv) The marked price of an article is ₹ 12000. The discount on the article is 10%, then the amount paid by the customer is • ***Application***

(a) ₹ 11000 (b) ₹ 10000
(c) ₹ 10500 (d) ₹ 10800

(v) **Assertion (A)** The sum of first 8 terms of an AP 3, 5, 7, 9 ...... is 80.

Reason (R) The sum of first n terms of an AP is given by $S_n=\frac{n}{2}[2a+(n-1)d]$. • ***Understanding***

(a) Both A and R are correct and R is the correct explanation of A.
(b) Both A and R are correct but R is not the correct explanation of A.
(c) A is false, R is true.
(d) A is true, R is false.

(vi) If $A=\begin{bmatrix}2&7\\6&3\end{bmatrix}$ and $B=\begin{bmatrix}1&5\\8&4\end{bmatrix}$, then $2A+B$ is • ***Analysis***

(a) $\begin{bmatrix}4&12\\20&7\end{bmatrix}$ (b) $\begin{bmatrix}4&12\\22&7\end{bmatrix}$
(c) $\begin{bmatrix}5&19\\20&10\end{bmatrix}$ (d) $\begin{bmatrix}4&17\\22&11\end{bmatrix}$

(vii) **Assertion** (A) A die is thrown. Probability of getting an even number is $\frac{1}{2}$.

Reason (R) $P(E)+P(\text{not } E)=1$

(a) Both A and R are correct and R is the correct explanation of A.
(b) Both A and R are correct but R is not the correct explanation of A.
(c) A is false, R is true.
(d) A is true, R is false.

(viii) $(1+\text{cosec}\,\theta)(\text{cosec}\,\theta)$ is equal to • ***Understanding***

(a) $\cot^2\theta$ (b) $\text{cosec}^2\theta$
(c) $\sin^2\theta$ (d) $-\cot^2\theta$

(ix) The printed price of an article is ₹ 9000. If the rate of GST is 15%, then GST charge is • ***Application***

(a) ₹ 1500 (b) ₹ 1350
(c) ₹ 1080 (d) ₹ 900

(x) If $\begin{bmatrix} 5 & 0 \\ 0 & -8 \end{bmatrix}\begin{bmatrix} x \\ y \end{bmatrix} = \begin{bmatrix} 4 & 5 \\ -2 & 4 \end{bmatrix}$, the value of x and y respectively are • *Evaluation*

(a) 9, – 3 (b) –9, 3 (c) –9, – 3 (d) 9, 3

(xi) The solution set for the inequation $9x + 4 < 39$, $x \in W$ is • *Analysis*

(a) {1, 2, 3, 4} (b) {0, 1, 2, 3}
(c) {0, 1, 2, 3, 4} (d) {1, 2, 3}

(xii) In ΔPQR, if $ST \| QR$, $\frac{PS}{SQ} = \frac{3}{5}$ and $PR = 28$ cm, then PT is • *Understanding*

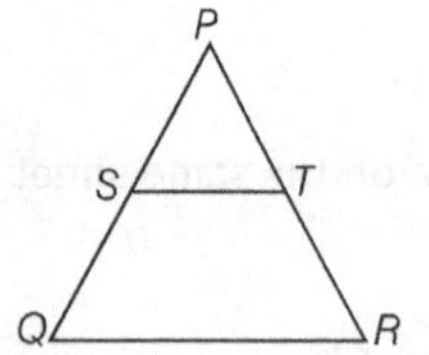

(a) 2.5 cm (b) 10.5 cm
(c) 5 cm (d) 3.4 cm

(xiii) In the given figure, if $\Delta ADB \sim \Delta ADC$, then find the value of p is • *Analysis*

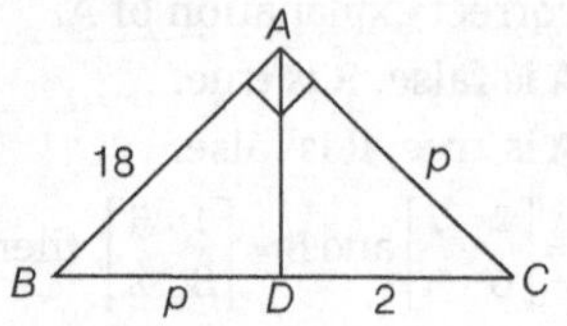

(a) 6 cm (b) 9 cm (c) 3 cm (d) 4 cm

(xiv) The radius of roller 200 m long is 21 cm curved surface of the roller is (in cm) • *Application*

(a) 13200 (b) 8800
(c) 26400 (d) 24400

(xv) **Statement I** $1 - \tan^2\theta = \sec^2\theta$

Statement II $\frac{\sin^2\theta - \sin\theta\cos\theta}{\cos^2\theta - \sin\theta\cos\theta} = -\tan\theta$ • *Understanding*

(a) only I is correct (b) only II is correct
(c) Both are correct (d) Neither I nor II.

2. (i) Factorise $9z^3 - 27z^2 - 100z + 300$, if it is given that $(3z + 10)$ is a factor of it. • *Understanding* [4]

(ii) Mr. Kumar has recurring deposite account for 2 yr at 10% per annum. If he receives ₹ 1900 as interest, then find the value of monthly instalment paid by him. • *Application* [4]

(iii) A retailer buys an bicycle at a discount of 15% on the printed price from a wholesaler. He marks up the price by 10% on the printed price but due to competition in the market, he allows a discount of 5% on the market price to a buyer. If the rate of GST is 12% and the buyer pays ₹468.16 for the article inclusive of tax (under GST), find • *Application*

(a) the printed price of the article.
(b) the profit percentage of the retailer. [4]

3. (i) Find three consecutive largest positive integers, such that the sum of one-third of first, one-fourth of second and one-fifth of third is atmost 20. • *Understanding* [4]

(ii) Find the common difference of an AP whose first term is $\frac{1}{2}$ and 8th term is $\frac{17}{6}$. Also, write its 4th term. • *Understanding* [4]

(iii) Two circles intersect at P and Q. A straight line through P meets the circles in A and B. Prove that $QA = QB$. • *Analysis* [5]

Section B

[40 *Marks*]

(Attempt any four questions from this section)

4. (i) Show that $\frac{\tan\theta}{1-\cot\theta} + \frac{\cot\theta}{1-\tan\theta} = 1 + \tan\theta + \cot\theta$ $= 1 + \sec\theta \, \mathrm{cosec}\theta$. • *Understanding* [3]

(ii) Let a, b, c and d be non-zero real numbers. Find the values of x and y in the following.

$$\begin{bmatrix} ax + by & 0 \\ 0 & cx + dy \end{bmatrix} = \begin{bmatrix} a-b & 0 \\ 0 & c-d \end{bmatrix}$$

• *Evaluation* [3]

(iii) Find the values of k for which the equation $x^2 + 5kx + 16 = 0$ has no real roots. • *Evaluation* [4]

5. (i) A family has 3 children. Find the probability that the family has • *Understanding*

(a) atleast one girl child.
(b) atmost one girl child.
(c) exactly one girl child.
(d) no girl child. [3]

(ii) Following is the distribution of IQ of 100 students. Find the median IQ.

IQ	Number of students
55-64	1
65-74	2
75-84	9
85-94	22
95-104	33
105-114	22
115-124	8
125-134	2
135-144	1

• *Analysis* [3]

(iii) Metal spheres, each of radius 2 cm, are packed into a rectangular box of internal dimension 16 cm × 8 cm × 8 cm. When 16 spheres are packed, the box is filled with preservative liquid. Find the volume of this liquid.

$\left[\text{take, } \pi = \frac{669}{213}\right]$ • *Application* [4]

6. (i) If the pth and q^{th} terms of a GP are q and p respectively then show that its $(p+q)^{th}$ term is $\left(\frac{q^p}{p^q}\right)^{\frac{1}{p-q}}$. • *Understanding* [5]

(ii) Using a graph paper, plot the points $A(6, 4)$ and $B(0, 4)$. • *Application*

(a) Reflect A and B in the origin to get the images A' and B'.

(b) Write the coordinates of A' and B'.

(c) State the geometrical name for the figure $ABA'B'$. [5]

7. (i) In the given figure, $\angle ABC = 69°$ and $\angle ACB = 31°$. Find $\angle BDC$. • *Understanding*

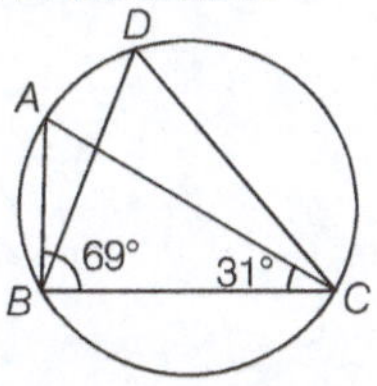

[3]

(ii) A right circular cylinder just encloses a sphere of radius r (see the figure). Find the • *Application*

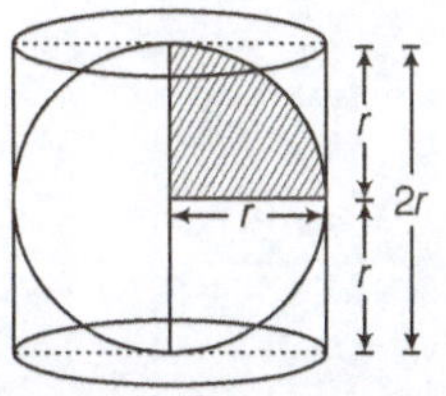

(a) surface area of the sphere.

(b) curved surface area of the cylinder.

(c) ratio of the areas obtained in (i) and (ii). [3]

(iii) If the mean of the following distribution is 7.5, find the missing frequency 'f'.

Variable	5	6	7	8	9	10	11	12
Frequency	20	17	f	10	8	6	7	6

• *Analysis* [4]

8. (i) If $\frac{\cos\alpha}{\cos\beta} = m$ and $\frac{\cos\alpha}{\sin\beta} = n$, then show that $(m^2 + n^2)\cos^2\beta = n^2$. • *Understanding* [3]

(ii) Find the equation of the diagonals of a rectangle, whose sides are $x = -1$, $x = 4$, $y = -1$ and $y = 2$. • *Understanding* [3]

(iii) If $a : b :: c : d$, then show that $(4a + 5b) : (4a - 5b) :: (4c + 5d) : (4c - 5d)$. • *Analysis* [4]

9. (i) If $x = \frac{\sqrt{a^2+b^2} + \sqrt{a^2-b^2}}{\sqrt{a^2+b^2} - \sqrt{a^2-b^2}}$, then show that $b^2x^2 - 2a^2x + b^2 = 0$. • *Understanding* [3]

(ii) Draw a circle of diameter 9 cm. Mark a point at a distance of 7.5 cm from the centre of the circle. Draw tangents to the given circle from this exterior point. Measure the length of each tangent. • *Application* [3]

(iii) Find the mode of the following frequency distribution by drawing a histogram.

Mid-values	12	18	24	30	36	42	48
Frequency	20	12	8	24	16	8	12

• *Analysis* [4]

10. (i) In parallelogram $ABCD$, E is a point on AB, CE intersects the diagonal BD at O and $EF \parallel BC$. If $AE : EB = 2 : 3$, then find • *Application*

(a) $EF : AD$.

(b) ar (ΔBEF) : ar (ΔABD).

(c) ar (ΔABD) : ar (Trapezium $AEFD$).

(d) ar (ΔFEO) : ar (ΔOBC). [3]

(ii) The surface areas of a sphere and a cube are equal. Prove that their volumes are in the ratio $1 : \sqrt{\frac{\pi}{6}}$. • *Application* [3]

(iii) If the coordinates of the mid-points of the sides of a triangle are (1, 2), (0, – 1) and (2, – 1), then find the coordinates of its vertices. • *Understanding* [4]

ANSWERS

1. (i) (c) (ii) (b) (iii) (c) (iv) (d) (v) (a)
(vi) (c) (vii) (b) (viii) (d) (ix) (b) (x) (d)
(xi) (b) (xii) (b) (xiii) (a) (xiv) (c) (xv) (b)

2. (i) $(3z+10)(3z-10)(z-3)$
(ii) ₹ 760 (iii) (a) ₹ 400 (b) $22\frac{16}{17}\%$

3. (i) 24, 25, 26 (ii) $d=\frac{1}{3}, a_4=\frac{3}{2}$

4. (ii) $x=1, y=-1$ (iii) $-\frac{8}{5}<k<\frac{8}{5}$

5. (i) (a) $\frac{7}{8}$ (b) $\frac{1}{2}$ (c) $\frac{3}{8}$ (d) $\frac{1}{8}$
(ii) 99.35 (iii) 487.96 cm^3 (approx.)

6. (ii) (b) $A'(-6,-4)$ and $B'(0,-4)$
(c) Parallelogram

7. (i) 80° (ii) (a) $4\pi r^2$ (b) $4\pi r^2$ (c) 1 : 1
(iii) $f=16$

8. (ii) $3x+5y-7=0$, $5y-3x+2=0$

9. (ii) 6 cm (iii) 30.9

10. (i) (a) 3 : 5 (b) 9 : 25 (c) 25 : 16 (d) 9 : 25
(iii) (1, − 4), (3, 2), (−1, 2)

SAMPLE QUESTION PAPER 2

A HIGHLY SIMULATED SAMPLE QUESTION PAPER FOR ICSE CLASS X

MATHEMATICS

GENERAL INSTRUCTIONS See the Sample Question Paper 1.

Section A [40 *Marks*]

(Attempt all questions from this section)

1. Choose the correct answers to the questions from the given options. [15]

(i) If $(x + 2)$ is a factor of the polynomial $x^3 - kx^2 - 5x + 6$, then the value of k is • ***Evaluation***

(a) 1 (b) 2 (c) 3 (d) – 2

(ii) If $A = \begin{bmatrix} 5 & 10 \\ 3 & -4 \end{bmatrix}$ and $I = \begin{bmatrix} 1 & 0 \\ 0 & 1 \end{bmatrix}$, then AI is equal to • ***Understanding***

(a) $\begin{bmatrix} 1 & 0 \\ 0 & 1 \end{bmatrix}$ (b) $\begin{bmatrix} 5 & 10 \\ -3 & 4 \end{bmatrix}$

(c) $\begin{bmatrix} 5 & 10 \\ 3 & -4 \end{bmatrix}$ (d) $\begin{bmatrix} 15 & 15 \\ -1 & -1 \end{bmatrix}$

(iii) In the given figure, O is the centre of the circle. $\angle DAE = 70°$. Then, $\angle BCD$ is • ***Evaluation***

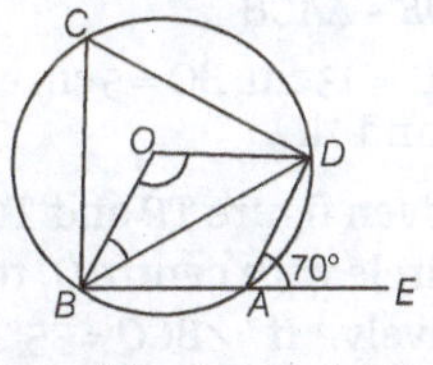

(a) 35° (b) 70° (c) 140° (d) 90°

(iv) The median class for the given distribution is

Class Interval	0-10	10-20	20-30	30-40
Frequency	2	4	3	5

• ***Analysis***

(a) 0-10 (b) 10-20
(c) 20-30 (d) 30-40

(v) The value of k for which the following equation has equal roots. • ***Evaluation***

$$x^2 + 4kx + (k^2 - k + 2) = 0$$

(a) $\frac{2}{3}, -1$ (b) $-\frac{2}{3}, -1$ (c) $\frac{2}{3}, 1$ (d) $-\frac{2}{3}, 1$

(vi) $\frac{\sin\theta}{1+\cos\theta}$ is equal to • ***Understanding***

(a) $\cot\theta - \text{cosec}\theta$ (b) $\text{cosec}\theta - \cot\theta$
(c) $\sec\theta - \tan\theta$ (d) $\tan\theta - \sec\theta$

(vii) The selling price of a shirt excluding GST is ₹ 800. If the rate of GST is 12%, then the total price of the shirt is • ***Application***

(a) ₹ 704 (b) ₹ 96 (c) ₹ 896 (d) ₹ 848

(viii) The modal class of a given distribution always corresponds to the • ***Analysis***

(a) interval with highest frequency
(b) interval with lowest frequency
(c) the first interval
(d) the last interval

(ix) **Assertion (A)** The probability of getting a number divisible by 3 in throwing a dice is $\frac{1}{3}$.

Reason (R) Probability of an event $E = \frac{\text{Favourable outcomes}}{\text{Total number of outcomes}}$ • ***Analysis***

(a) Both A and R are correct but R is not the correct explanation of A.
(b) Both A and R are correct and R is the correct explanation of A.
(c) A is true, R is false.
(d) A is false, R is true.

(x) **Statement I** The terms $a + 2d, a + d, a, (a - d), (a - 2d)$ are in AP. Whose common difference is $(-d)$.

Statement II The sum of n terms of a GP is $S_n = \frac{n}{2}[a + l]$ • ***Analysis***

(a) Only I is correct
(b) Only II is correct
(c) Both are correct
(d) Neither I nor II are correct

(xi) $A(1, 4), B(4, 1), C(x, 4)$ are the vertices of ΔABC. If the centroid of the triangle is $G(4, 3)$, then x is equal to • ***Evaluation***
(a) 2 (b) 1 (c) 7 (d) 4

(xii) The volume of a conical tent is $462\ m^3$ and the area of the base is $154\ m^2$. The height of the cone is • ***Application***
(a) 15 m (b) 12 m (c) 9 m (d) 24 m

(xiii) If $\Delta ABC \sim \Delta PQR$ and $AB = 2$, $BC = x$, $PQ = 3$, $QR = 9$, then x is equal to • ***Application***
(a) 6 (b) 2/3 (c) 3/2 (d) 4

(xiv) Mohit opened a Recurring Deposit Account in a bank for 2 yr. He deposits ₹ 1000 every month and receives ₹ 25500 on maturity. The interest he earned in 2 yr is • ***Application***
(a) ₹ 13500 (b) ₹ 3000
(c) ₹ 24000 (d) ₹ 1500

(xv) **Assertion** (A) If $\frac{4}{x} > \frac{3}{y}$ then $\frac{x}{4} > \frac{y}{3}$.

Reason (R) If $x > y$ then $\frac{1}{x} < \frac{1}{y}$ and if $x < y$ then $\frac{1}{x} > \frac{1}{y}$. • ***Analysis***

(a) (A) is true, (R) is false.
(b) (A) is false, (R) is true.
(c) Both (A) and (R) are true and (R) is the correct reason for (A).
(d) Both (A) and (R) are true and (R) is the incorrect reason for (A).

2. (i) Use the factor theorem to factorise the following expression
$2x^3 + x^2 - 13x + 6$ • ***Understanding*** [4]

(ii) Katrina opened a Recurring Deposit Account with a nationalised bank for a period of 2 yr. If the bank pays interest at the rate of 6% per annum and the monthly instalment is ₹ 1000, find the • ***Application***
(a) interest earned in 2 yr
(b) matured value [4]

(iii) In the given figure, $\angle DBC = 58°$. BD is a diameter of the circle. Calculate • ***Analysis***

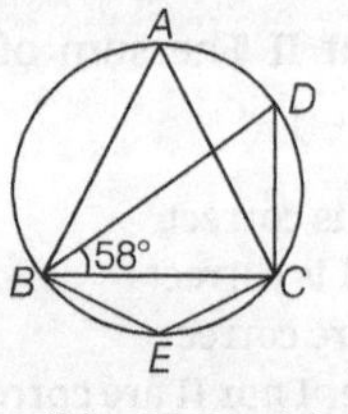

(a) $\angle BDC$ (b) $\angle BEC$ (c) $\angle BAC$ (d) $\angle BCD$ [4]

3. (i) Find the value of the constants a and b, if $(x - 2)$ and $(x + 3)$ are both factors of the expression $x^3 + ax^2 + bx - 12$. • ***Evaluation*** [4]

(ii) Prove that
$$\frac{\operatorname{cosec}\theta + \cot\theta}{\operatorname{cosec}\theta - \cot\theta} = 1 + 2\cot^2\theta + 2\operatorname{cosec}^2\theta\cos\theta$$
• ***Understanding*** [4]

(iii) Use a graph paper for this question taking (1 cm = 1 unit) along both the X and Y axes
(a) Plot the points $A(0,5), B(2,5), C(5,2), D(5,-2), E(2,-5)$ and $F(0,-5)$.
(b) Reflect the points B, C, D and E on the Y-axis and name them respectively, as B', C', D' and E'.
(c) Write the coordinates of B', C', D' and E'.
(d) Name the figure formed by $BCDEE'D'C'B'$.
• ***Analysis*** [5]

Section B
[40 *Marks*]

(Attempt any four questions from this section)

4. (i) If $A = \begin{bmatrix} 3 & 0 \\ 5 & 1 \end{bmatrix}$ and $B = \begin{bmatrix} -4 & 2 \\ 1 & 0 \end{bmatrix}$, then find $A^2 - 2AB + B^2$. • ***Evaluation*** [3]

(ii) $\angle ABC$ is a right angled triangle with $\angle ABC = 90°$. D is any point on AB and DE is perpendicular to AC. Prove that

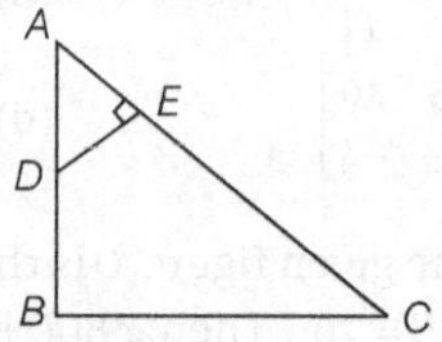

(a) $\Delta ADE \sim \Delta ACB$ • ***Understanding***
(b) If $AC = 13$ cm, $BC = 5$ cm and $AE = 4$ cm, find DE and AD. • ***Application*** [3]

(iii) In the given figure TP and TQ are two tangents to the circle with centre O, touching at A and C respectively. If $\angle BCQ = 55°$ and $\angle BAP = 60°$, find • ***Application*** [4]

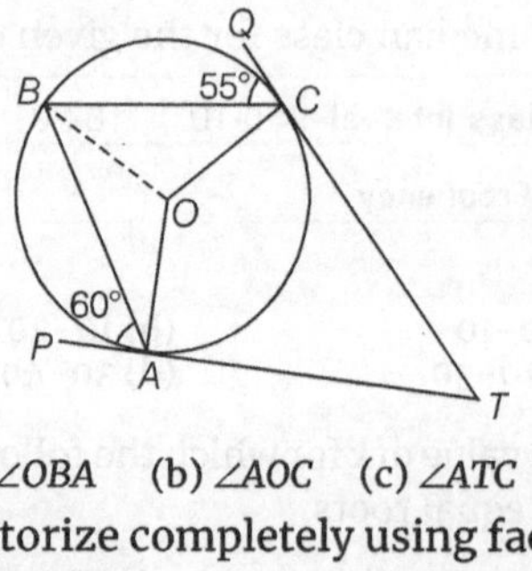

(a) $\angle OBA$ (b) $\angle AOC$ (c) $\angle ATC$ (d) $\angle OBC$

5. (i) Factorize completely using factor theorem
(a) $2x^3 - x^2 - 13x - 6$ (b) $2x^2 - 11x + 5$
• ***Understanding*** [3]

(ii) Use graph paper for this question.

The marks obtained by 120 students in an English test are given below :

Marks	Number of Students
0-10	5
10-20	9
20-30	16
30-40	22
40-50	26
50-60	18
60-70	11
70-80	6
80-90	4
90-100	3

Draw the ogive and hence, estimate

(a) the median marks.

(b) the number of students who did not pass the test, if the pass percentage was 50.

• *Analysis* [3]

(iii) The eight term of an AP is half its second term and the eleventh term exceeds one-third of its fourth term by 1. Find the 15th term.

• *Understanding* [4]

6. (i) The frequency distribution of scores obtained by 230 candidates in a medical entrance test is a follows

Scores	Number of Candidates
400-450	20
450-500	35
500-550	40
550-600	32
600-650	24
650-700	27
700-750	18
750-800	24

(a) Write the above distribution as 'less than type' cumulative frequency distribution.

(b) Draw a cumulative frequency curve to represent the above data. • *Analysis* [5]

(ii) The line through $P(5, 3)$ intersects Y-axis at Q.

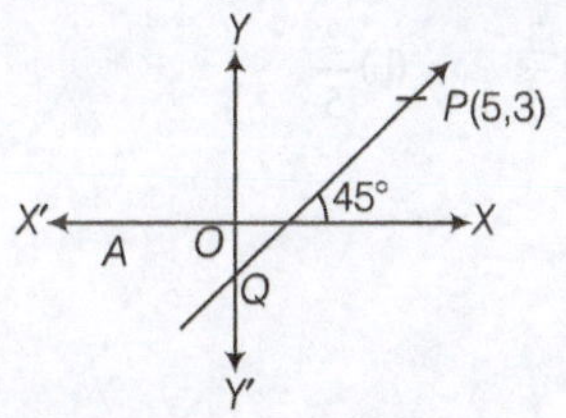

(a) Write the slope of the line

(b) Write the equation of the line

(c) Find the coordinates of Q. • *Application* [5]

7. (i) Cards marked with numbers 1, 2, 3, 4..., 20 are well shuffled and a card is drawn at random. What is the probability that the number of the card is

(a) a prime number ?

(b) divisible by 3 ?

(c) a perfect square ? • *Understanding* [3]

(ii) The speed of an express train is x km/h and the speed of an ordinary train is 12 km/h less than that of the express train. If the ordinary train takes one hour more than the express train to cover a distance of 240 km, then find the speed of the express train. • *Application* [3]

(iii) A hemi-spherical and a conical hole is scooped out of a solid wooden cylinder. Find the volume of the remaining solid where the measurements are as follows. The height of the solid cylinder is 7 cm, radius of each of hemi-sphere, cone and cylinder is 3 cm. Height of cone is 3 cm. Give your answer correct to the nearest whole number.

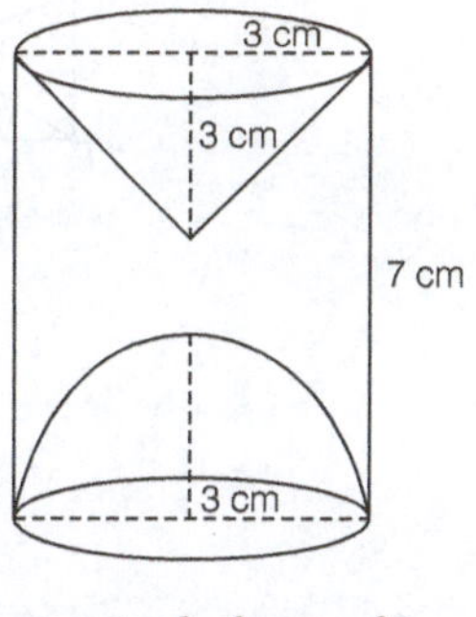

$\left[\text{take } \pi = \frac{22}{7}\right]$ • *Application* [4]

8. (i) If the mean of the following distribution is 24, find the value of 'a'. • *Evaluation* [3]

Marks	0-10	10-20	20-30	30-40	40-50
Number of students	7	a	8	10	5

(ii) The numbers $k+3$, $k+2$, $3k-7$ and $2k-3$ are in proportion. Find

(a) The value of k.

(b) The value of $k^2 + 2k + 5$ where k is a positive integer.

• *Evaluation* [3]

(iii) Use ruler and compass only for answering this question.

Draw a circle of radius 4 cm. Mark the centre as O. Mark a point P outside the circle at a distance of 7 cm from the centre. Construct two tangents to the circle from the external point P. Measure and write the down the length of any one tangent. • *Application* [4]

9. (i) If $\frac{3x+5y}{3x-5y}=\frac{7}{3}$, then find

(a) $x:y$

(b) $(x+y):(3x+7y)$ • *Understanding* [3]

(ii) How many terms of an AP $20, 19\frac{1}{3}, 18\frac{2}{3}, \ldots$ must be taken, so that their sum is 300 ? • *Understanding* [3]

(iii) The angle of elevation from a point P of the top of the tower QR, 50 m high is 60° and that of the tower PT from a point Q is 30°. Find the height of the tower PT, correct to the nearest metre. • *Application* [4]

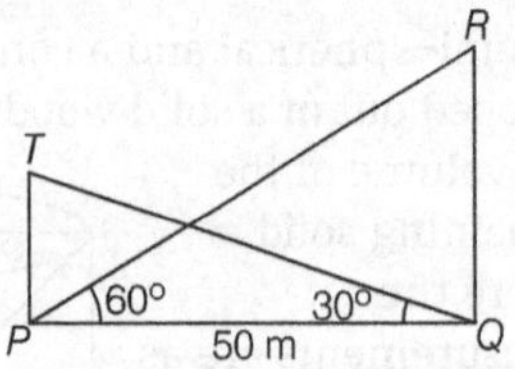

10. (i) Sandeep purchased a digital camera for ₹ 25488, which includes 10% rebate on the list price and 18% tax (under GST) on the remaining price. Find the marked price of the digital camera. • *Application* [3]

(ii) Solve the following equation, write down the solution set and represent it on the real number line.

$$-2+10x \leq 13x+10 < 24+10x,\ x \in Z$$

• *Analysis* [3]

(iii) In the given figure, ABC is a triangle. DE is parallel to BC and $\frac{AD}{BD}=\frac{3}{2}$.

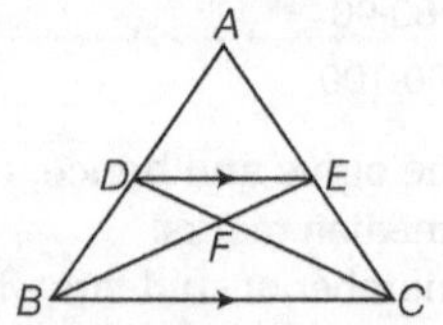

(a) Determine the ratio of $\frac{AD}{AB}$ and $\frac{DE}{BC}$.

(b) Prove that ΔDEF is similar to ΔCBF. Also, find $\frac{EF}{FB}$. • *Analysis* [4]

ANSWERS

1. (i) (b) (ii) (c) (iii) (b) (iv) (c) (v) (a)
(vi) (b) (vii) (c) (viii) (a) (ix) (b) (x) (a)
(xi) (c) (xii) (c) (xiii) (a) (xiv) (a) (xv) (b)

2. (i) (a) $f(x)=(x-2)(2x-1)(x+3)$
(b) $(x-5)(2x-1)$
(ii) (a) ₹1500 (b) ₹ 25500
(iii) (a) 32° (b) 148° (c) 32° (d) 90°

3. (i) $a=3, b=-4$
(ii) (c) $B'(-2,5), C'(-5,2), D'(-5,-2), E(-2,-5)$
(d) Octagon

4. (i) $\begin{bmatrix} 4 & -16 \\ 32 & -7 \end{bmatrix}$
(ii) (b) $AD=4.33$ cm and $DE=1.66$ cm
(iv) (a) 30° (b) 130° (c) 50° (d) 30°

5. (i) $f(x)=(x-2)(3x-1)(x+3)$
(ii) (a) 43 (b) 78
(iii) $a_{15}=3$

6. (ii) (a) 1 (b) $y=x-2$ (c) $(0,-2)$

7. (i) (a) $\frac{2}{5}$ (b) $\frac{3}{10}$ (c) $\frac{1}{5}$
(ii) 60 km/h
(iii) 113 cm^3

8. (i) 10 (ii) (a) $-1, 5$ (b) 40

9. (i) (a) 25:6 (b) 31 : 117 (ii) 25, 36
(iii) 16.66 m

10. (i) ₹ 24000
(ii) $\{-4,-3,-2,-1,0,1,2,3,4\}$

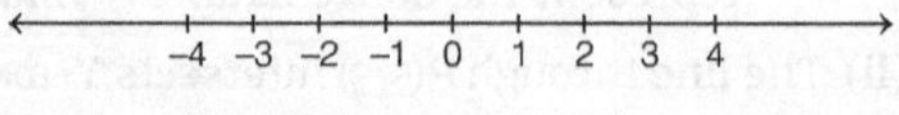

(iii) (a) $\frac{3}{5}$ (b) $\frac{3}{5}$

SAMPLE QUESTION PAPER 3

A HIGHLY SIMULATED SAMPLE QUESTION PAPER FOR ICSE CLASS X

MATHEMATICS

GENERAL INSTRUCTIONS See the Sample Question Paper 1.

Section A [40 *Marks*]

(Attempt all questions from this section)

1. Choose the correct answers to the questions from the given options. [15]

(i) The sum of 10 terms of an AP, whose nth term is given by $a_n = 3 + 4n$ • ***Evaluation***

(a) 250 (b) 500
(c) 430 (d) 215

(ii) If $A = \begin{bmatrix} 3 & 5 \\ 1 & 4 \end{bmatrix}$, $B = \begin{bmatrix} 2 & 4 \\ 0 & 3 \end{bmatrix}$ and $C = \begin{bmatrix} 1 & -1 \\ 2 & 1 \end{bmatrix}$, then $5A - BC$ is equal to • ***Understanding***

(a) $\begin{bmatrix} -5 & -23 \\ 1 & 17 \end{bmatrix}$ (b) $\begin{bmatrix} 5 & 23 \\ 1 & 17 \end{bmatrix}$
(c) $\begin{bmatrix} -2 & 8 \\ -3 & 3 \end{bmatrix}$ (d) $\begin{bmatrix} 5 & 23 \\ -1 & 17 \end{bmatrix}$

(iii) In the following figure, if $\Delta ADB \sim \Delta ADC$, then the value of p is • ***Analysis***

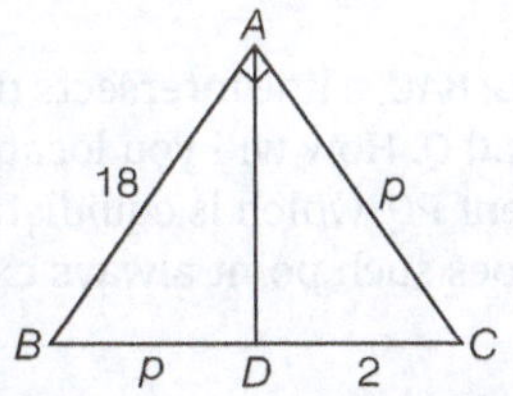

(a) 12 cm (b) 6 cm
(c) 3 cm (d) 4 cm

(iv) The radius of roller 100 cm long is 14 cm. The curved surface area of the roller is $\left[\text{take } \pi = \frac{22}{7}\right]$ • ***Application***

(a) 13200 cm² (b) 15400 cm²
(c) 4400 cm² (d) 8800 cm²

(v) If 70, 75, 80 and 85 are the first four terms of an AP, then the 10th term is • ***Evaluation***

(a) 35 (b) 25 (c) 115 (d) 105

(vi) **Assertion (A)** The price of article excluding tax is known as Market Price.

Reason (R) The reduction in price of object given by shopkeeper to customer, is known as discount. • ***Analysis***

(a) Both A and R are true and R is the correct explanation of A.
(b) Both A and R are true but R is not the correct explanation of A.
(c) A is false, R is true
(d) R is false, A is true

(vii) **Assertion (A)** If 5 is a root of $x^2 - 9x + 8 = 0$ the other root is $\frac{8}{5}$.

Reason (R) The product of the roots of quadratic equation is given as products of roots $= \frac{\text{constant term}}{\text{Coefficient of } x^2}$. • ***Analysis***

(a) Both A and R are true and R is the correct explanation of A.
(b) Both A and R are true but R is not the correct explanation of A.
(c) A is false, R is true
(d) R is false, A is true

(viii) The sum of the first 20 terms of an AP 2, 4, 6, 8 .... is • ***Understanding***

(a) 400 (b) 840
(c) 420 (d) 800

(ix) A car covers a distance of 400 km at a certain speed. Had the speed been 12 km/h more, the time taken for the journey would have been 1 h 40 min less ? The original speed of the car is • ***Application***

(a) 60 km/h (b) 48 km/h
(c) 72 km/h (d) 36 km/h

(x) If $\begin{bmatrix} 0 & -4 \\ 2 & 0 \end{bmatrix}\begin{bmatrix} x \\ y \end{bmatrix} = \begin{bmatrix} 12 \\ -8 \end{bmatrix}$, the value of x and y respectively are • *Evaluation*

(a) $-3, 4$ (b) $3, -4$
(c) $4, -3$ (d) $4, 3$

(vi) **Statement I** $(1+\cos\theta)(1-\cos\theta) = \tan^2\theta$

Statement II $\sec\theta - \tan\theta = \dfrac{1}{\sec\theta + \tan\theta}$ • *Analysis*

(a) Only I is correct (b) Only II is correct
(c) Both are correct (d) Neither I nor II

(xii) In the given figure $\angle NMQ = \angle POQ = 75°$ and $OQ = 3$ cm and $MO = 2$ cm, then $QN:QP$ is • *Understanding*

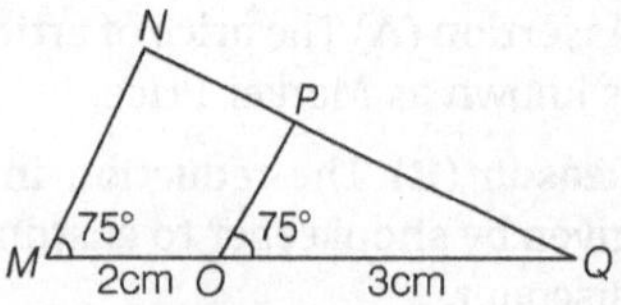

(a) 3:2 (b) 5:2 (c) 2:3 (d) 5:3

(xiii) The printed price of an article is ₹ 4080. If the rate of GST is 12%, then GST charged is • *Application*

(a) ₹ 408 (b) ₹ 489.6 (c) ₹ 480 (d) ₹ 612

(xiv) The mean proportional between 4 and 16 is • *Understanding*

(a) 12 (b) 8 (c) 10 (d) 64

(xv) The solution set for the inequation $3x + 9 \le 18$, $x \in W$ is • *Understanding*

(a) {1, 2, 3} (b) {1, 2, 3, 4, 5, 6}
(c) {0, 1, 2, 3} (d) {0, 1, 2, 3, 4, 5, 6, 7, 8, 9}

2. (i) Find the number of terms in the AP

$$18, 15\frac{1}{2}, 13, \ldots, -47.$$ • *Evaluation* [4]

(ii) If A is the solution set of $5x - 4 \ge 6$, $x \in R$ and B is the solution set of $5 - x > 1$, $x \in R$, then find $A \cap B$ and $A' \cap B$. • *Analysis* [4]

(iii) Prove that $\dfrac{(1+\cot A + \tan A)(\sin A - \cos A)}{\sec^3 A - \operatorname{cosec}^3 A} = \sin^2 A \cos^2 A$. • *Understanding* [4]

3. (i) In the adjoining figure, line APB meets the X-axis at A and Y-axis at B. P is the point $(-4, 2)$ and $AP : PB = 1 : 2$. Write down the coordinates of A and B. • *Analysis* [4]

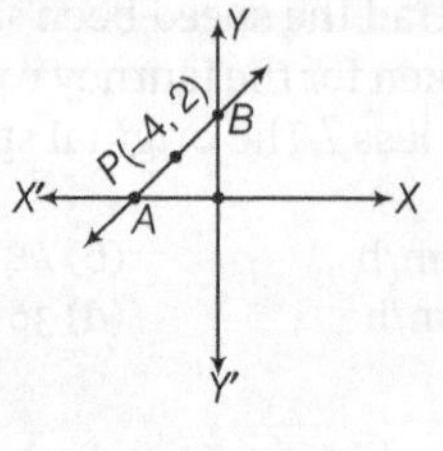

(ii) If $A = \begin{bmatrix} \sec 60° & \cos 90° \\ -3\tan 45° & \sin 90° \end{bmatrix}$ and $B = \begin{bmatrix} 0 & \cot 45° \\ -4\sin 30° & 3\sin 90° \end{bmatrix}$, then find

(a) A^2 (b) BA • *Evaluation* [4]

(iii) A shopkeeper in Rajasthan buys an article at the printed price of ₹ 50000 from a wholesaler in Delhi. The shopkeeper sells the article to a consumer in Rajasthan at a profit of 25% on the basic cost price. If the rate of GST is 18%, find

(a) the price of the article inclusive of tax (under GST) at which the shopkeeper bought it.

(b) the amount of tax (under GST) paid by the shopkeeper to Government. • *Application* [5]

Section B

[40 *Marks*]

(Attempt any four questions from this section)

4. (i) In a right angled ΔABC, right angled at B, the perpendicular BD on the hypotenuse AC is drawn. Prove that $AC \times CD = (BC)^2$. • *Understanding* [3]

(ii) Let $A(6, 4)$ and $B(2, 12)$ be two given points. Find the slope of a line • *Understanding* [3]

(a) parallel to AB.

(b) perpendicular to AB.

(iii) Apply step-deviation method to find the AM of the following frequency distribution.

Variate (x)	5	10	15	20	25	30	35	40	45	50
Frequency (f)	20	43	75	67	72	45	39	9	8	6

• *Analysis* [4]

5. (i) Given $\angle BAC$, a line intersects the arms of $\angle BAC$ in P and Q. How will you locate a point on line segment PQ, which is equidistant from AB and AC? Does such point always exist? • *Analysis* [3]

(ii) Veena has a cumulative deposit account of ₹ 400 per month at 10% per annum simple interest. If she gets ₹ 30100 at the time of maturity, then find the total time for which the account was held. • *Application* [3]

(iii) A piece of cloth costs ₹ 200. If the piece was 5 m longer and each metre of cloth cost ₹ 2 less, then the cost of the piece would have remain unchanged. How long is the piece and what is the original rate per metre? • *Application* [4]

6. (i) In the given figure, A, B, C and D, E, F are two sets of collinear points. Prove that $AD \parallel CF$.

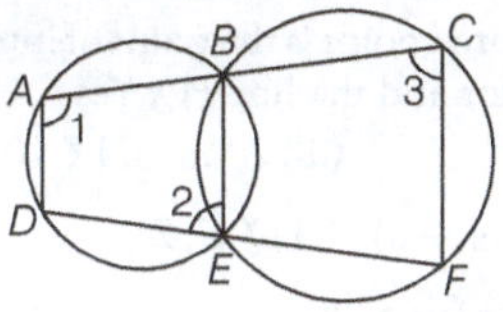

• *Understanding* [5]

(ii) Use graph paper to answer the following questions.

(a) Plot the points $P(4,6)$ and $Q(1,2)$.

(b) P' is the image of P when reflected in X-axis.

(c) Q' is the image of Q when reflected in the line PP'.

(d) Give the geometrical name for the figure $PQP'Q'$. • *Application* [5]

7. (i) Internal and external diameters of a hollow hemi-spherical vessel are 24 cm and 25 cm, respectively. The cost to paint 1 cm^2 the surface is ₹ 0.05. Find the total cost to paint the vessel all over. [use $\pi = 22/7$] [3]

(ii) Find α and β, if $x+1$ and $x+2$ are factors of $x^3+3x^2-2\alpha x+\beta$. • *Evaluation* [3]

(iii) Prove that

$2(\sin^6\theta+\cos^6\theta)-3(\sin^4\theta+\cos^4\theta)+1=0$.

• *Understanding* [4]

8. (i) A bag contains 5 white and 7 red balls. One ball is drawn at random. What is the probability that ball drawn is white? • *Understanding* [3]

(ii) Find the annual income derived from

(a) 260, ₹ 100 shares paying 15 % dividend.

(b) 750, ₹ 20 shares paying 25 % dividend.

• *Understanding* [3]

(iii) In the given figure, PT is tangent to the circle at P and QR is a diameter of the circle. If $\angle RPT = 50°$, find $\angle QRP$. • *Analysis* [4]

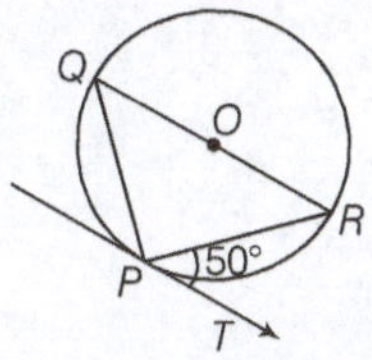

9. (i) A tower subtends an angle α at a point A in the plane of its base and the angle of depression of the foot of the tower at a point b m just above A is β. Prove that the height of the tower is $b\tan\alpha\cot\beta$. • *Application* [3]

(ii) If AB and CD are two chords which, when produced meet at P and if $AP = CP$, show that $AB = CD$. • *Application* [3]

(iii) The monthly profits in rupees of 100 shops are distributed as follows

Profit (in ₹)	Number of shops
0-100	13
100-200	18
200-300	27
300-400	20
400-500	16
500-600	6

Find the modal value graphically. *Analysis* [4]

10. (i) Draw the cumulative frequency curve for the following frequency distribution by less than method.

Marks	Number of students
0-10	7
10-20	10
20-30	23
30-40	51
40-50	6
50-60	3

• *Analysis* [3]

(ii) The third term of a GP is 4. Find the product of first five terms. • *Understanding* [3]

(iii) Two points P and Q have the coordinates (3, 2) and (7, 6), respectively. Find the

(a) gradient of PQ.

(b) equation of the perpendicular bisector of PQ.

(c) value of k for which $(-2, k)$ lies on PQ.

• *Application* [6]

ANSWERS

1. (i) (a) (ii) (d) (iii) (b) (iv) (d) (v) (c)
(vi) (b) (vii) (b) (viii) (a) (ix) (b) (x) (c)
(xi) (b) (xii) (d) (xiii) (b) (xiv) (b) (xv) (c)

2. (i) 27 (ii) $A \cap B = [2, 4)$ and $A' \cap B = (-\infty, 2)$

3. (i) $A(-6, 0)$ and $B(0, 6)$

(ii) (a) $A^2 = \begin{bmatrix} 4 & 0 \\ -9 & 1 \end{bmatrix}$ (b) $BA = \begin{bmatrix} 3 & 1 \\ -13 & 3 \end{bmatrix}$

(iii) (a) ₹ 59000 (b) ₹ 2250

4. (ii) (a) -2 (b) $\frac{1}{2}$ (iii) 22.2

5. (i) Required point is the point of intersection of the angle bisector and the line PQ, Yes
(ii) 5 yr (iii) 20 m and ₹ 10 per m

6. (ii) (b) $P'(4, -6)$ (c) $Q'(7, 2)$
(d) $PQP'Q'$ is a kite.

7. (i) ₹ 96.28 (ii) $\alpha = -1, \beta = 0$

8. (i) $\frac{5}{12}$ (ii) (a) ₹ 3900 (b) ₹ 3750 (iii) 40°

9. (iii) 256 (approx.)

10. (ii) (a) 1 (b) $x + y = 9$ (c) -3

ICSE
Specimen Paper

ICSE Specimen Paper

Mathematics (Code 51)

Class 10

General Instructions

1. Answers to this paper must be written on the paper provided separately.
2. You will not be allowed to write during the first 15 minutes. This time is to be spent in reading the question paper.
3. The time given at the head of this paper is the time allowed for writing the answers.
4. Attempt all questions from Section A and any 4 questions from Section B.
5. All working, including rough work, must be clearly shown and must be done on the same sheet as the rest of the answer.
6. Omission of essential working will result in loss of marks.
7. The intended marks for questions or parts of questions are given in bracket [ ].
8. Mathematical tables are provided.

- No. of Questions : 10
- No. of Sections : 2
- Time Alloted : 2 Hr. 30 min
- Max. Marks : 80

Section A [40 *Marks*]

(Attempt all questions from this section)

1. Choose the correct answers to the questions from the given options. [15]

(Do not copy the questions, write the correct answers only.)

(i) A polynomial in x is divided by $(x - a)$ and for $(x - a)$ to be a factor of this polynomial, then the remainder should be • *Analysis*

(a) $-a$ (b) 0 (c) a (d) $2a$

(ii) Radha deposited ₹ 400 per month in a recurring deposit account for 18 months.
The qualifying sum of money for the calculation of interest is • *Application*

(a) ₹ 3600 (b) ₹ 7200
(c) ₹ 68400 (d) ₹ 136800

(iii) In the given figure, AC is a diameter of the circle. $AP = 3$ cm and $PB = 4$ cm and $QP \perp AB$. If the area of ΔAPQ is 18 cm^2, then the area of shaded portion $QPBC$ is • *Understanding & Analysis*

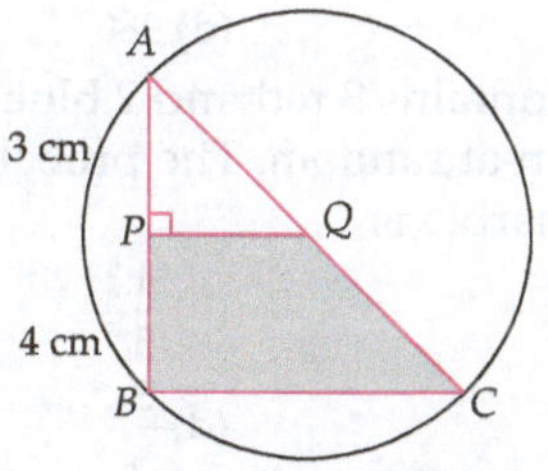

(a) 32 cm^2 (b) 49 cm^2
(c) 80 cm^2 (d) 98 cm^2

(iv) In the given diagram, O is the centre of the circle and PT is a tangent. The value of x is • *Application*

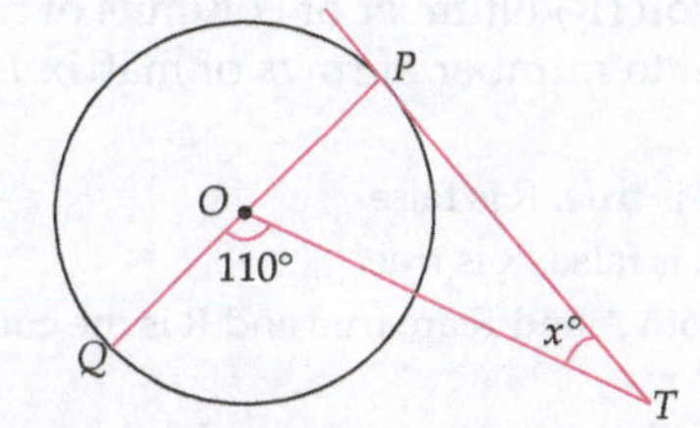

(a) 20° (b) 40° (c) 55° (d) 70°

(v) In the given diagram, the length of PR is
• *Application*

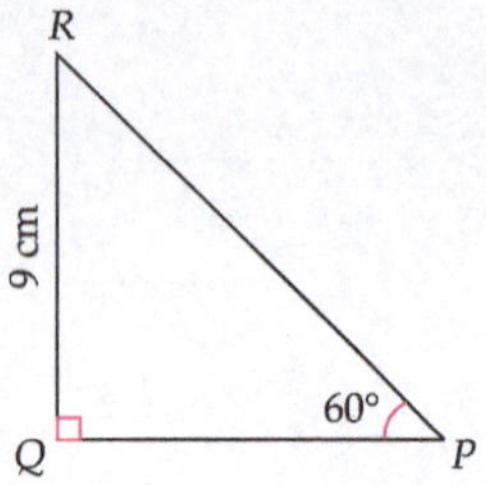

(a) $3\sqrt{3}$ cm (b) $6\sqrt{3}$ cm
(c) $9\sqrt{3}$ cm (d) 18 cm

(vi) A solid sphere is cut into two identical hemispheres.
Statement I The total volume of two hemispheres is equal to the volume of the original sphere.
Statement II The total surface area of two hemispheres together is equal to the surface area of the original sphere.
Which of the following is valid? • *Analysis*
(a) Both the statements are true.
(b) Both the statements are false.
(c) Statement I is true and Statement II is false.
(d) Statement I is false and Statement II is true.

(vii) Given that the sum of the squares of the first seven natural numbers is 140, then their mean is
• *Understanding & Evaluation*
(a) 20 (b) 70
(c) 280 (d) 980

(viii) A bag contains 3 red and 2 blue marbles. A marble is drawn at random. The probability of drawing a black marble is • *Application*
(a) 0 (b) $\frac{1}{5}$
(c) $\frac{2}{5}$ (d) $\frac{3}{5}$

(ix) If $A=[3 \; -2]$ and $B=\begin{bmatrix} -1 & 4 \\ 2 & 0 \end{bmatrix}$
Assertion (A) Product AB of two matrices A and B is possible.
Reason (R) Number of columns of matrix A is equal to number of rows of matrix B.
• *Analysis*
(a) A is true, R is false.
(b) A is false, R is true.
(c) Both A and R are true and R is the correct reason for A.
(d) Both A and R are true but R is incorrect reason for A.

(x) A mixture of paint is prepared by mixing 2 parts of red pigments with 5 parts of the base.
Using the given information in the following table, find the values of a, b and c to get the required mixture of paint.

Parts of red pigment	2	4	b	6
Parts of base	5	a	12.5	c

• *Application & Evaluation*
(a) $a=10, b=10, c=10$ (b) $a=5, b=2, c=5$
(c) $a=10, b=5, c=10$ (d) $a=10, b=5, c=15$

(xi) An article which is marked at ₹ 1200 is available at a discount of 20% and the rate of GST is 18%. The amount of SGST is
• *Analysis & Evaluation*
(a) ₹ 216.00 (b) ₹ 172.80
(c) ₹ 108.00 (d) ₹ 86.40

(xii) The sum of money required to buy 50, ₹ 40 shares at 38.50 is • *Application*
(a) ₹ 1920 (b) ₹ 1924
(c) ₹ 1925 (d) ₹ 1952

(xiii) The roots of quadratic equation $x^2-1=0$ are
• *Analysis & Evaluation*
(a) 0 (b) 1 (c) -1 (d) ± 1

(xiv) Which of the following equation represents a line equally inclined to the axes?
• *Analysis & Evaluation*
(a) $2x-3y+7=0$ (b) $x-y=7$
(c) $x=7$ (d) $y=-7$

(xv) Given $x+2 \le \frac{x}{3}+3$ and x is a prime number.
The solution set for x is
• *Understanding & Analysis*
(a) ϕ (b) {0}
(c) {1} (d) {0, 1}

2. (i) While factorising a given polynomial, using remainder and factor theorems, a student finds that $(2x+1)$ is a factor of $2x^3+7x^2+2x-3$. [4]
(a) Is the student's solution correct stating that $(2x+1)$ is a factor of the given polynomial?
(b) Give a valid reason for your answer.
Also, factorise the given polynomial completely.
• *Analysis & Application*

(ii) A line segment joining $P(2,-3)$ and $Q(0,-1)$ is cut by the X-axis at the point R. A line AB cuts the Y-axis at $T(0, 6)$ and is perpendicular to PQ at S. Find the [4]
(a) equation of line PQ.
(b) equation of line AB.
(c) coordinates of points R and S.
• *Analysis & Evaluation*

(iii) In the given figure, AC is the diameter of the circle with centre O and CD is parallel to BE. $\angle AOB = 80°$ and $\angle ACE = 20°$. Calculate [4]

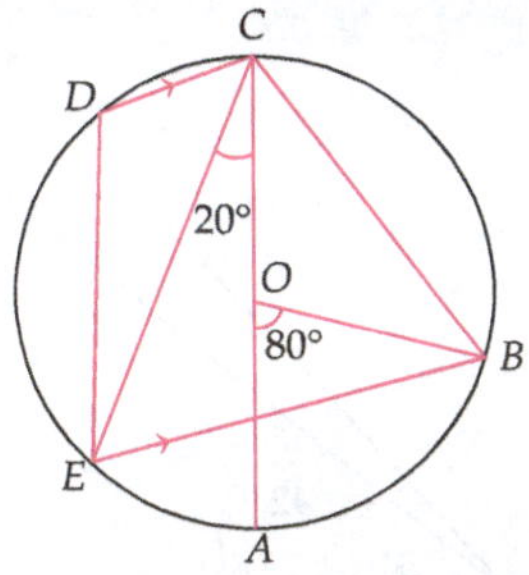

(a) $\angle BEC$ (b) $\angle BCD$
(c) $\angle CED$ • *Analysis & Evaluation*

3. (i) In a Geometric Progression (GP), the first term is 24 and the fifth term is 8. Find the ninth term of the GP. • *Analysis & Evaluation* [4]

(ii) In the given diagram, a tilted right circular cylindrical vessel with base diameter 7 cm contains a liquid. When placed vertically, the height of the liquid in the vessel is the mean of two heights shown in the diagram.

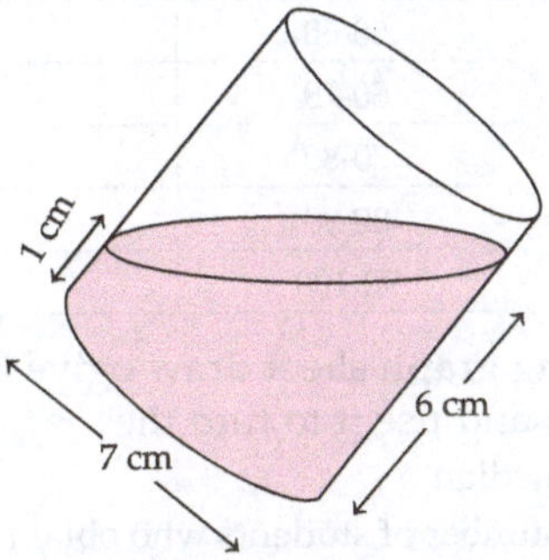

Find the area of wet surface, when the cylinder is placed vertically on a horizontal surface. (use $\pi = \frac{22}{7}$).
• *Application & Evaluation* [4]

(iii) Study the graph and answer each of the following: • *Analysis & Application* [5]

(a) Write the coordinates of points A, B, C and D.

(b) Given that point C is the image of point A. Name and write the equation of the line of reflection.

(c) Write the coordinates of the image of the point D under reflection in Y-axis.

(d) What is the name given to a point whose image is the point itself?

(e) On joining the points A, B, C, D and A in order, a figure is formed. Name of the closed figure.

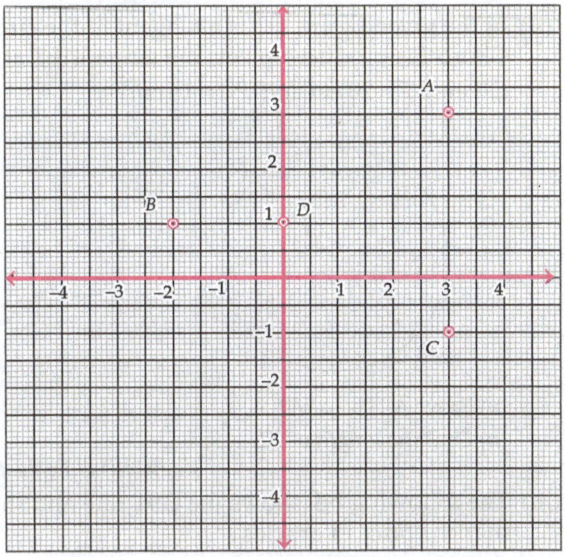

Section B [40 *Marks*]

(Attempt any four questions from this section)

4. (i) A man buys 250, ₹ 10 shares each at ₹ 12.50. If the rate of dividend is 7%, find the

(a) dividend he receives annually.

(b) percentage return on his investment.
• *Application & Evaluation* [3]

(ii) Solve the following inequation, write the solution set and represent it on the real number line $5x - 21 < \frac{5x}{7} - 6 \le -3\frac{3}{7} + x, x \in R$.
• *Evaluation* [3]

(iii) Prove the following trigonometry identity
$(\sin\theta + \cos\theta)(\operatorname{cosec}\theta - \sec\theta) = \operatorname{cosec}\theta \cdot \sec\theta - 2\tan\theta$
• *Application & Analysis* [4]

5. (i) In the given figure (drawn not to scale), chords AD and BC intersect at P, where $AB = 9$ cm, $PB = 3$ cm and $PD = 2$ cm.
• *Application & Evaluation* [3]

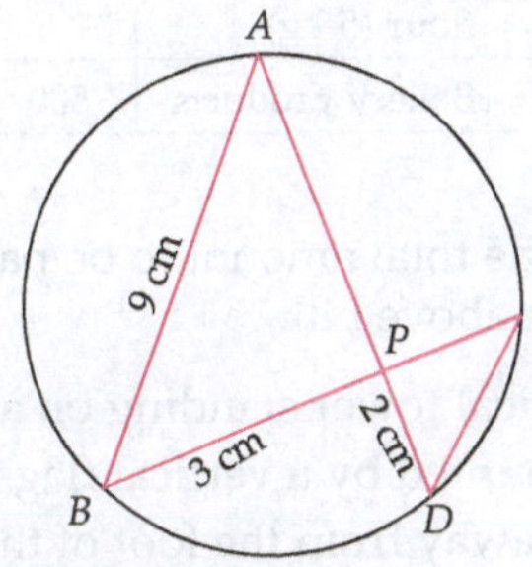

(a) Prove that $\Delta APB \sim \Delta CPD$.

(b) Find the length of CD.

(c) Find ar ΔAPB : ar ΔCPD.

(ii) Mr. Sameer has a recurring deposit account and deposits ₹ 600 per month for 2 yr. If he gets ₹ 15600 at the time of maturity, find the rate of interest earned by him. • *Application & Evaluation* [3]

(iii) Using step-deviation method, find mean for the following frequency distribution

Class	0-15	15-30	30-45	45-60	60-75	75-90
Frequency	3	4	7	6	8	2

• *Application & Evaluation*

6. (i) Find the coordinates of the centroid P of the ΔABC, whose vertices are $A(-1, 3)$, $B(3, -1)$ and $C(0, 0)$. Hence, find the equation of a line passing through P and parallel to AB. • *Analysis & Evaluation* [3]

(ii) In the given figure, PT is a tangent to the circle. Chord BA produced meets the tangent PT at P. Given $PT = 20$ cm and $PA = 16$ cm.

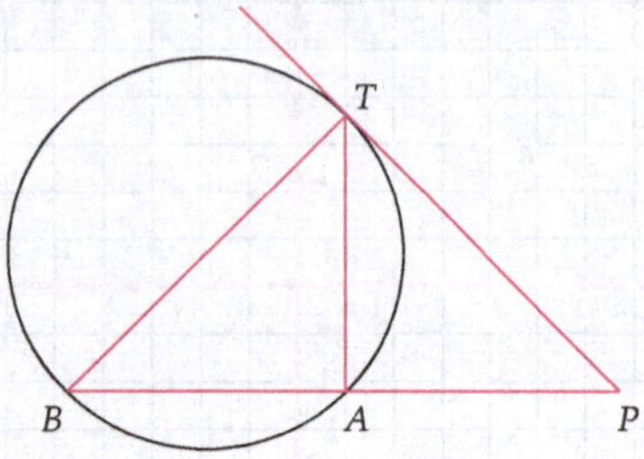

(a) Prove $\Delta PTB \sim \Delta PAT$

(b) Find the length of AB.

• *Analysis & Evaluation* [3]

(iii) The following bill shows the GST rate and the marked price of articles [4]

Rajdhani Departmental Store

S.No.	Items	Marked Price	Discount	Rate of GST
(a)	Dry fruits (1 kg)	₹ 1200	₹ 100	12%
(b)	Packed wheat flour (5 kg)	₹ 286	Nil	5%
(c)	Bakery products	₹ 500	10%	12%

• *Application & Evaluation*

Find the total amount to be paid (including GST) for the above bill.

7. (i) A vertical tower standing on a horizontal plane is surmounted by a vertical flagstaff. At a point 100m away from the foot of the tower, the angle of elevation of the top and bottom of the flagstaff are 54° and 42°, respectively. Find the height of the flagstaff. • *Application & Evaluation* [5]

Give your answer correct to nearest metre.
[Use tan 42° = 0.9004 and tan 54° = 1.3764]

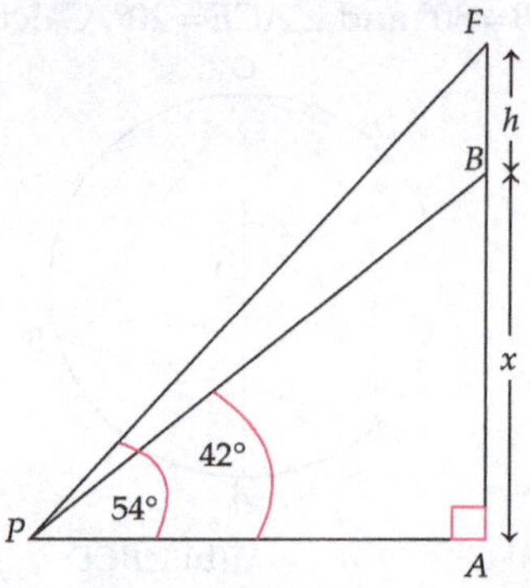

(ii) The marks of 200 students in a test were recorded as follows [5]

Marks%	Number of students
0-10	5
10-20	7
20-30	11
30-40	20
40-50	40
50-60	52
60-70	36
70-80	15
80-90	9
90-100	5

Using graph sheet draw ogive for the given data and use it to find the

(a) median

(b) number of students who obtained more than 65% marks.

(c) number of students who did not pass if the pass percentage was 35.

• *Application, Analysis & Evaluation*

8. (i) In a TV show, a contestant opts for video call a friend life line to get an answer from three of his friends, named Amar, Akbar and Anthony. The question which he asks from one of his friends has four options. Find the probability that [3]

(a) Akbar is chosen for the call.

(b) Akbar could not give the correct answer.

• *Analysis & Evaluation*

(ii) If x, y and z are in continued proportion, then prove that

$$\frac{x}{y^2 \cdot z^2} + \frac{y}{z^2 \cdot x^2} + \frac{z}{x^2 \cdot y^2} = \frac{1}{x^3} + \frac{1}{y^3} + \frac{1}{z^3}$$

• *Application & Analysis* [3]

(iii) A manufacturing company prepares spherical ball bearings, each of radius 7 mm and mass 4 gm. These ball bearings are packed into boxes. Each box can have maximum of 2156 cm^3 of ball bearings. Find the [4]

(a) maximum number of ball bearings that each box can have.

(b) mass of each box of ball bearings in kg.

(use $\pi = \frac{22}{7}$) • *Analysis, Application & Evaluation*

9. (i) The table given below shows the runs scored by a cricket team during the overs of a match. [3]

Overs	Runs scored
20-30	37
30-40	45
40-50	40
50-60	60
60-70	51
70-80	35

Use graph sheet for this question.

Take 2 cm = 10 overs along one axis and 2 cm = 10 runs along the other axis.

(a) Draw a histogram representing the above distribution.

(b) Estimate the modal runs scored.

• *Application & Evaluation*

(ii) An Arithmetic Progression (AP) has 3 as its first term. The sum of the first 8 terms is twice the sum of the first 5 terms. Find the common difference of the AP. • *Analysis & Analysis* [3]

(iii) The roots of equation $(q-r)x^2 + (r-p)x + (p-q) = 0$ are equal. Prove that $2q = p + r$, that is, p, q and r are in AP. • *Application & Analysis* [4]

10. (i) A car travels a distance of 72 km at a certain average speed of x km per hour and then travels a distance of 81 km at an average speed of 6 km per hour more than its original average speed. If it takes 3 h to complete the total journey, then form a quadratic equation and solve it to find its original average speed.

• *Analysis, Application & Evaluation* [3]

(ii) Given matrix, $X = \begin{bmatrix} 1 & 1 \\ 8 & 3 \end{bmatrix}$ and $I = \begin{bmatrix} 1 & 0 \\ 0 & 1 \end{bmatrix}$, prove that $X^2 = 4X + 5I$. • *Application & Evaluation* [3]

(iii) Use ruler and compasses for the following question taking a scale of 10 m = 1 cm. A park in a city is bounded by straight fences AB, BC, CD and DA.

Given that $AB = 50$ m, $BC = 63$ m, $\angle ABC = 75°$. D is a point equidistant from the fences AB and BC. If $\angle BAD = 90°$, construct the outline of the park $ABCD$. Also, locate a point P on the line BD for the flag post which is equidistant from the corners of the park A and B.

• *Analysis & Creativity*

Explanations

1. (i) (b) Let $p(x)$ be a polynomial.

$\therefore p(x)$ is divided by $(x - a)$.

Also, $(x - a)$ is a factor of $p(x)$.

By Remainder theorem, $x - a = 0 \Rightarrow x = a$

$\Rightarrow p(a) = 0$

Hence, remainder will be zero.

(ii) (c) Given, money deposited by Radha = 400 per month.

Number of months, $n = 18$

$\therefore$ Qualifying sum $= P \times n \times \left(\frac{n+1}{2}\right)$

$$= 400 \times 18 \times \frac{(18+1)}{2}$$

$$= 400 \times 9 \times 19 = 7600 \times 9$$

$$= ₹\ 68400$$

(iii) (c) In given figure,

$AP = 3$ cm, $PB = 4$ cm

and $QP \perp AB$

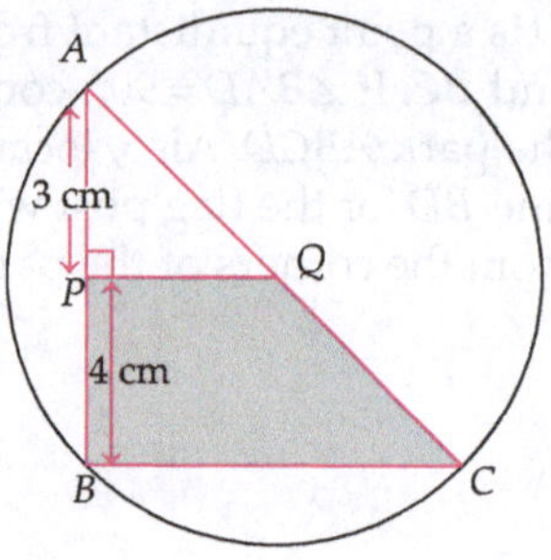

Area of $\Delta APQ = 18\text{ cm}^2$

We know that the angle at the circumference in a semi-circle is 90°.

Therefore, $\angle B = 90°$

In ΔABC and ΔAPQ,

$\angle APQ = \angle ABC$ [each 90°]

$\angle PAQ = \angle BAC$ [common]

$\therefore \quad \Delta ABC \cong \Delta APQ$ [AA similarity]

Now, $\frac{\text{ar }(\Delta ABC)}{\text{ar }(\Delta APQ)} = \left(\frac{AB}{AP}\right)^2$

$\Rightarrow \quad \frac{\text{ar }(\Delta ABC)}{18} = \left(\frac{7}{3}\right)^2$

$\Rightarrow \quad \text{ar }(\Delta ABC) = \frac{49}{9} \times 18 = 98\text{ cm}^2$

$\therefore \quad \text{ar }(QPBC) = \text{ar }(\Delta ABC) - \text{ar }(\Delta APQ)$

$$= 98 - 18 = 80\text{ cm}^2$$

(iv) (a) In the given figure,

by exterior angle property,

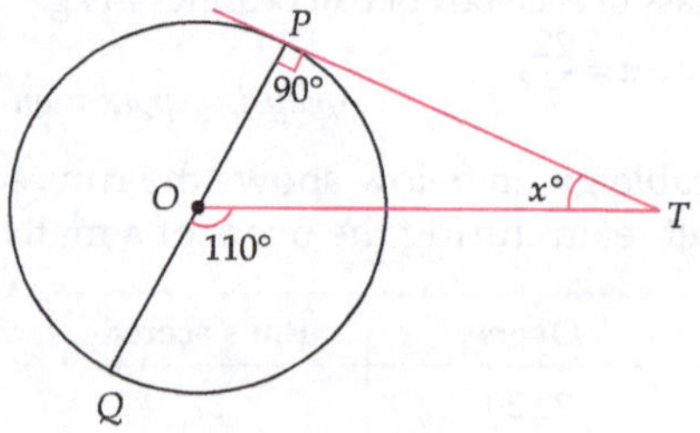

$\angle QOT = \angle OPT + \angle PTO$

$\Rightarrow 110° = 90° + x°$

$\Rightarrow \quad x = 110° - 90° = 20°$

(v) (b) In the given figure,

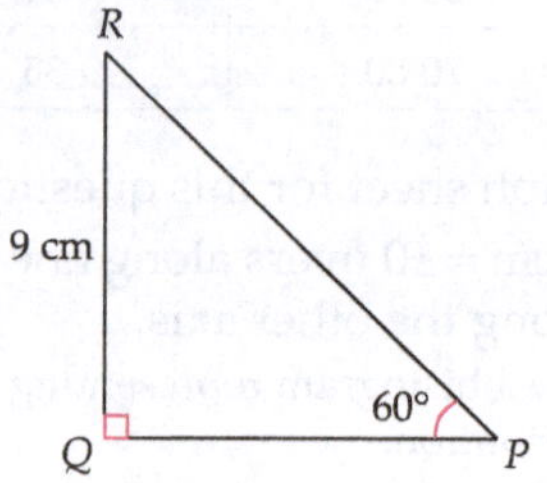

$$\sin 60° = \frac{RQ}{PR}$$

$\Rightarrow \quad PR = \frac{9}{\sin 60°} = \frac{9 \times 2}{\sqrt{3}}$ $\left[\because \sin 60° = \frac{\sqrt{3}}{2}\right]$

$$= \frac{\sqrt{3} \times \sqrt{3} \times 3 \times 2}{\sqrt{3}} = 6\sqrt{3}\text{ cm}$$

$\therefore \quad PR = 6\sqrt{3}$ cm

(vi) (c) **Statement I**

The volume of original sphere $= \frac{4}{3}\pi r^3$

The volume of hemisphere $= \frac{2}{3}\pi r^3$

$\because$ Solid sphere is cut into two identical hemispheres.

$\therefore$ Volume of original solid sphere

= 2 × Volume of hemispherical solid

$$= 2 \times \frac{2}{3}\pi r^3 = \frac{4}{3}\pi r^3$$

So, statement I is true.

Statement II

Surface area of sphere $= 4\pi r^2$

Total surface area of hemisphere $= 3\pi r^2$

∵ Solid sphere is cut into two identical hemisphere.

∴ Total surface area of two hemisphere

$= 3\pi r^2 + 3\pi r^2 = 6\pi r^2 \neq 4\pi r^2$

So, statement II is false.

(vii) (a) Given, the sum of first seven natural numbers is 140.

$\therefore \text{Mean} = \dfrac{\text{Sum of first seven natural numbers}}{7}$

$= \dfrac{140}{7} = 20$

(viii) (a) Given, number of red marbles $n(R) = 3$,

number of blue marbles $n(B) = 2$

and number of black marbles $= 0$

Total number of marbles, $n = n(R) + n(B) + 0$

$= 3 + 2 = 5$

∴ The probability of drawing a black marble

$= \dfrac{\text{Number of favourable outcomes}}{\text{Total number of outcomes}} = \dfrac{0}{5} = 0$

(ix) (c) We have,

$A = [3 \; -2]$ and $B = \begin{bmatrix} -1 & 4 \\ 2 & 0 \end{bmatrix}$

The order of matrix A is 1×2

and the order of matrix B is 2×2.

Here, the number of columns in A is equal to the number of rows in matrix B. Therefore, their product AB is possible.

Hence, both A and R are true and R is the correct explanation for A.

(x) (d) Here, the table is given below.

Parts of red pigment	2	4	b	6
Parts of base	5	a	12.5	c

∵ A mixture of paints is prepared by mixing as

$\dfrac{\text{Part of red pigment}}{\text{Part of base}} = \dfrac{2}{5}$

From table,

$\dfrac{2}{5} = \dfrac{4}{a} = \dfrac{b}{12.5} = \dfrac{6}{c}$

I II III IV

On taking I and II, we get

$\dfrac{2}{5} = \dfrac{4}{a} \Rightarrow a = 10$

On taking I and III, we get

$\dfrac{2}{5} = \dfrac{b}{12.5} \Rightarrow b = 5$

Now, on taking I and IV, we get

$\dfrac{2}{5} = \dfrac{6}{c} \Rightarrow c = 15$

Hence, $a = 10$, $b = 5$ and $c = 15$.

(xi) (d) Given, marked price of an article = ₹ 1200

Rate of discount = 20% and rate of GST = 18%

Now, rate of SGST $= \dfrac{1}{2} \times$ Rate of GST

$= \dfrac{1}{2} \times 18\% = 9\%$

∵ Discount = 1200 × 20% = ₹ 240

∴ Discounted price = ₹ 1200 − ₹ 240 = ₹ 960

Hence, the amount of SGST = 9% of 960

$= \dfrac{9}{100} \times 960$

= 9.6 × 9 = ₹ 86.40

(xii) (c) Given, number of shares = 50

Value of each share = ₹ 40

Total value of 50 shares = 50 × 40 = ₹ 2000

∴ Share buy at ₹ 38.50.

∴ Required money = ₹ 2000 − 50 × (40 − 38.50)

= ₹ 2000 − 50 × 1.5

= ₹ 2000 − 75 = ₹ 1925

(xiii) (d) Given, $x^2 - 1 = 0$

$\Rightarrow \quad x^2 = 1 \Rightarrow x = \pm 1$

Hence, the roots of the quadratic equation are ± 1.

(xiv) (b) From option (b), we have,

$x - y = 7 \Rightarrow y = x - 7$

On comparing with $y = mx + c$, we get

$m = 1$ and $c = -7$

$\because m = \tan\theta$

$\therefore \tan\theta = 1 \Rightarrow \tan\theta = \tan\left(\dfrac{\pi}{4}\right)$

$\left[\because \tan\left(\dfrac{\pi}{4}\right) = 1\right]$

$\therefore \quad \theta = \dfrac{\pi}{4}$

Hence, line $x - y = 7$ equally inclined to the axes.

(xv) (a) Given, $x + 2 \leq \dfrac{x}{3} + 3$,

where x is a prime number.

$x - \dfrac{x}{3} \leq 3 - 2$

$\Rightarrow \quad \dfrac{3x - x}{3} \leq 3 - 2$

$\Rightarrow \quad \dfrac{2x}{3} \leq 1$

$\Rightarrow \quad 2x \leq 3$

$\Rightarrow \quad x \leq \dfrac{3}{2}$ or $x \leq 1.5$

There is no prime number which is less than or equal to 1.5.

Hence, the solution set is ϕ.

2. (i) (a) Given polynomial is $2x^3+7x^2+2x-3$

Let $f(x)=2x^3+7x^2+2x-3$

We know that if $(2x+1)$ is factor of above polynomial, than $2x+1=0 \Rightarrow x=\frac{-1}{2}$ will satisfies the given polynomial.

So, $f\left(-\frac{1}{2}\right)=2\left(-\frac{1}{2}\right)^3+7\left(-\frac{1}{2}\right)^2+2\left(-\frac{1}{2}\right)-3 \neq 0$

Hence, $(2x+1)$ is not a factor of $f(x)$.

(b) We have, $f(x)=2x^3+7x^2+2x-3$

On patting $x=\frac{1}{2}$ in above polynomial, we get

$$f\left(\frac{1}{2}\right)=2\left(\frac{1}{2}\right)^3+7\left(\frac{1}{2}\right)^2+2\left(\frac{1}{2}\right)-3=0$$

$\therefore 2x-1$ is a factor of $f(x)$.

$$
\begin{array}{r|l}
 & x^2+4x+3 \\
2x-1 & 2x^3+7x^2+2x-3 \\
 & \underline{2x^3-x^2} \\
 & \,\,\,8x^2+2x \\
 & \underline{8x^2-4x} \\
 & 6x-3 \\
 & \underline{6x-3} \\
 & 0
\end{array}
$$

Therefore, $f(x)=(2x-1)(x^2+4x+3)$

$\Rightarrow \quad f(x)=(2x-1)(x+2)(x+1)$

(ii) (a) Given, $P(2,-3)$ and $Q(0,-1)$.

Here, $x_1=2, y_1=-3, x_2=0$ and $y_2=-1$.

The slope of line segment joining the point P and Q is

$$m=\frac{y_2-y_1}{x_2-x_1}=\frac{-1+3}{0-2}=\frac{2}{-2}=-1$$

$\therefore$ The equation of line PQ is

$y-y_1=m(x-x_1)$

$\Rightarrow \quad y+3=-1(x-2)$

$\Rightarrow \quad y+3=-x+2$

$\Rightarrow \quad x+y+1=0$ ...(i)

(b) Since, the line AB is perpendicular to the line PQ.

$\therefore$ Slope of line $AB=-\frac{1}{m}$,

where m is the slope of PQ.

Let M is the slope of AB, then

$M=-(-1)=1$

Also, the line AB passes through the point $(0, 6)$.

$\therefore$ The equation of line AB is

$y-y_1=M(x-x_1)$

$\Rightarrow \quad y-6=1(x-0)$ $[\because y_1=6, x_1=0]$

$\Rightarrow \quad y-6=x$

$\Rightarrow x-y+6=0$ ...(ii)

(c) Since, the line PQ cuts the X-axis at R.

At X-axis, $y=0$

On putting $y=0$ in Eq. (i), we get

$x+0+1=0 \Rightarrow x=-1$

Thus, the coordinates of point R are $(-1, 0)$.

On adding Eqs. (i) and (ii), we get

$2x+7=0 \Rightarrow x=-\frac{7}{2}$

From, Eq. (i), $\frac{-7}{2}+y+1=0$

$\Rightarrow y=\frac{5}{2}$

Thus, the coordinates of point S are $\left(\frac{-7}{2},\frac{5}{2}\right)$.

(iii) In the given figure,

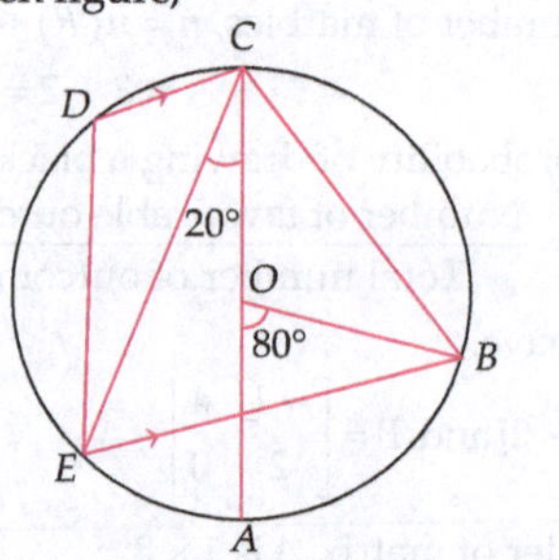

AC is the diameter with centre O.

$CD \parallel BE$

$\angle AOB=80°$ and $\angle ACE=20°$

(a) From the figure,

$\angle BOC+\angle AOB=180°$

$\Rightarrow \quad \angle BOC+80°=180°$

$\Rightarrow \angle BOC=180°-80°=100°$

Since, angle at centre is twice the angle in remaining segment.

$\therefore \quad \angle BEC=\frac{1}{2}\times\angle BOC=\frac{1}{2}\times 100°=50°$

(b) In ΔBOC,

$\angle BOC=100°$

$\angle OBC=\angle OCB=x$

[$\because OB=OC$, radius of the circle]

Now, $\angle BOC+\angle OBC+\angle OCB=180°$

$\Rightarrow \quad 100+x+x=180°$

$\Rightarrow \quad 2x=80°$

$\Rightarrow \quad x=40°$

$\because \quad \angle DCE=\angle BEC=50°$ [alternate angles]

$\therefore \quad \angle BCD=\angle BCO+\angle OCE+\angle DCE$

$=40°+20°+50°=110°$

(c) In ΔEBC,

$\angle BEC=50°$,

$\angle ECB=20°+40°=60°$

and $\angle EBC=\angle EBO+\angle OBC$

$=\angle EBO+40°$

Now, $\angle BEC + \angle ECB + \angle EBC = 180°$

$\Rightarrow \quad 50° + 60° + \angle EBO + 40° = 180°$

$\Rightarrow \quad \angle EBO = 180° - 150° = 30°$

Thus, $\quad \angle EBC = 30° + 40° = 70°$

In quadrilateral $EBCD$,

$\angle B + \angle D = 180° \Rightarrow \angle D = 180° - 70° = 110°$

Now, in ΔECD,

$\angle CED + \angle EDC + \angle DCE = 180°$

$\Rightarrow \quad \angle CED + 110° + 50° = 180°$

$\Rightarrow \quad \angle CED = 180° - 160° = 20°$

3. (i) Given, the first term of GP, $a = 27$

and fifth term, $a_5 = 8$

Let r be the common ratio of GP.

Then, $a_5 = 8 \Rightarrow ar^4 = 8 \qquad [\because a_n = ar^{n-1}]$

$\Rightarrow \quad 24r^4 = 8 \Rightarrow r^4 = \left(\frac{1}{3}\right)$

Now, $a_9 = ar^8 = 24(r^4)^2 = 24 \times \left(\frac{1}{3}\right)^2 = 24 \times \frac{1}{3 \times 3} = \frac{8}{3}$

Hence, the ninth term of GP is $\frac{8}{3}$.

(ii) Given, diameter of the base of cylindrical vessel, $d = 7$ cm

$\therefore$ Radius of the base of vessel, $r = \frac{d}{2} = \frac{7}{2}$ cm

and height of the water = mean of two heights

$= \frac{1}{2}(1 + 6) = \frac{7}{2}$ cm

Thus, area of wet surface $= \pi r^2 + 2\pi rh$

$= \pi r\,[r + 2h] = \frac{22}{7} \times \frac{7}{2}\left[\frac{7}{2} + 2 \times \frac{7}{2}\right]$

$= 11\,[3.5 + 7] = 11 \times 10.5 = 115.5\ \text{cm}^2$

(iii) (a) According to the graph,

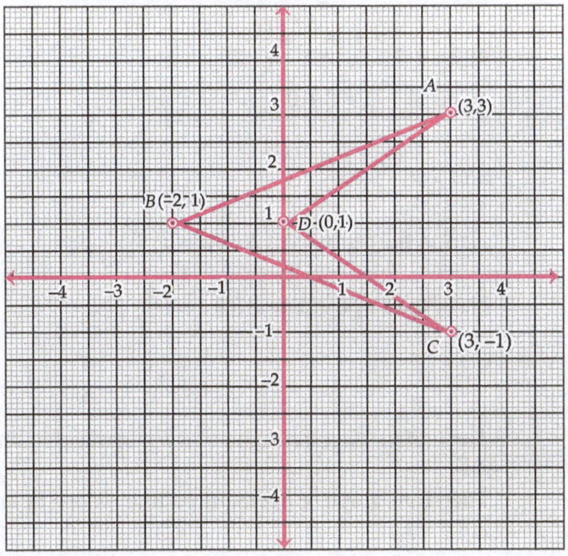

the coordinates of point A are $(3, 3)$,

the coordinates of point B are $(-2, 1)$,

the coordinates of point C are $(3, -1)$ and

the coordinates of point D are $(0, 1)$.

(b) If point C is the image of point A. Then, the name of the line of reflection is BD

and the equation of the line of reflection is $y = 1$.

(c) Since, the point D lies on Y-axis.

Therefore, the image of point D under the reflection of Y-axis remains same.

i.e. image of $D(0, 1) = (0, 1)$.

(d) The point whose image is the point itself is called invariant point.

(e) After joining the points A, B, C, D and A in order, we get a concave quadrilateral or arrowhead. (as shown in figure).

4. (i) Given, number of shares = 250

Original value of share = ₹ 10

Rate of dividend = 7%

(a) Annual dividend $= 250 \times 10 \times \frac{7}{100} =$ ₹ 175

(b) Percentage return on his investment $= \frac{7 \times 10}{12.5}$

$= 5.6\%$

(ii) We have, $5x - 21 < \frac{5x}{7} - 6 \le -3\frac{3}{7} + x,\ x \in R$.

On taking $5x - 21 < \frac{5x}{7} - 6$, we get

$5x - \frac{5x}{7} < 21 - 6$

$\Rightarrow \quad \frac{30}{7}x < 15 \Rightarrow x < \frac{7}{2} \qquad \ldots(i)$

Now, on taking $\frac{5x}{7} - 6 \le -3\frac{3}{7} + x$, we get

$3\frac{3}{7} - 6 \le x - \frac{5x}{7}$

$\Rightarrow \quad \frac{24}{7} - 6 \le \frac{2x}{7}$

$\Rightarrow \quad \frac{-18}{7} \le \frac{2x}{7}$

$\Rightarrow \quad x \ge -9 \qquad \ldots(ii)$

On combining Eqs. (i) and (ii), we get

$-9 \le x < \frac{7}{2}$

Hence, $\left\{x : -9 \le x < \frac{7}{2},\ x \in R\right\}$

Representation on number line

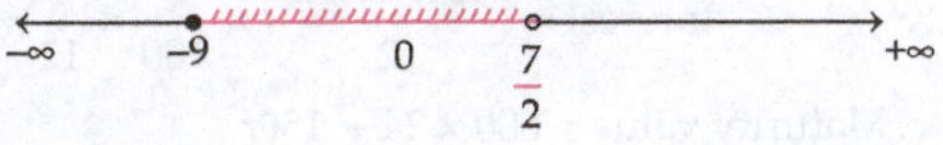

(iii) LHS = (sin θ + cos θ) (cosec θ − sec θ)

$$=(\sin\theta+\cos\theta)\left(\frac{1}{\sin\theta}-\frac{1}{\cos x}\right)$$

$$=(\sin\theta+\cos\theta)\left(\frac{\cos\theta-\sin\theta}{\sin\theta\cdot\cos\theta}\right)$$

$$=\frac{\cos^2\theta-\sin^2\theta}{\sin\theta\cdot\cos\theta}=\frac{1-2\sin^2\theta}{\sin\theta\cdot\cos\theta}$$

$$=\frac{1}{\sin\theta\cdot\cos\theta}-\frac{2\sin^2\theta}{\sin\theta\cdot\cos\theta}$$

= cosec θ·sec θ − 2 tan θ = RHS **Hence proved.**

5. (i) In the given figure,

$AB = 9$ cm, $PB = 3$ cm and $PD = 2$ cm

(a) In ΔAPB and ΔCPD,

$\angle ABP = \angle DCP$ [angles on same segment of AC]

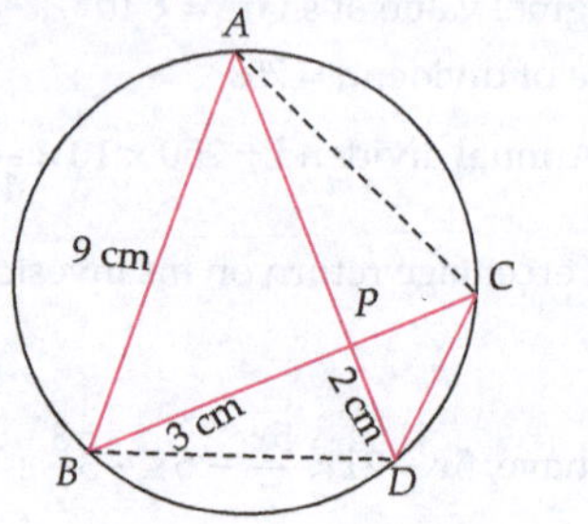

$\angle ABP = \angle CDP$ [angles on same segment]

$\therefore$ $\Delta ABP \sim \Delta CPD$ [AA similarity]

(b) Since, $\Delta ABP \sim \Delta CPD$

Therefore, $\frac{AB}{CD}=\frac{BP}{PD}$

$\Rightarrow$ $\frac{9}{CD}=\frac{3}{2}$

$\Rightarrow$ $CD=\frac{9\times 2}{3}=6$ cm

(c) Since, $\Delta APB \simeq \Delta CPD$

Therefore, $\frac{\text{ar}(\Delta APB)}{\text{ar}(\Delta CPD)}=\frac{BP^2}{PD^2}=\left(\frac{3}{2}\right)^2=\frac{9}{4}$

Hence, ar(ΔAPB) : ar(ΔCPD) = 9 : 4.

(ii) Given, Sameer deposits amount of ₹ 600/month.

Time = 2 yr = 2 × 12 = 24 months.

Maturity amount = ₹ 15600

$\because$ Qualifying sum $=\frac{600\times 24\times 25}{2}$ $\left[\because A=\frac{P\times n(n+1)}{2}\right]$

$= 7500 \times 24 = 180000$

$\because$ Interest $=\frac{600\times 24\times 25}{2}\times\frac{r}{100}\times\frac{1}{12}=150r$

$\therefore$ Maturity value = 600 × 24 + 150r

$\Rightarrow$ $15600 = 14400 + 150r$

$\Rightarrow$ $150r = 15600 - 14400$

$\Rightarrow$ $r=\frac{1200}{150}=8\%$

Hence, the rate of interest is 8%.

5. (iii) The frequency table is given below.

Class	x	$u=\frac{d}{i}$	f	fu
0-15	7.5	− 3	3	− 9
15-30	22.5	− 2	4	− 8
30-45	37.5	− 1	7	− 7
45-60	52.5	0	6	0
60-75	67.5	1	7	8
75-90	82.5	2	2	4
			Σf =30	Σfu = − 12

Mean $= A+\frac{\Sigma fu}{\Sigma f}\times i = 52.5+\frac{-12}{30}\times 15$

$= 52.5 - 6 = 46.50$

6. (i) Given, the coordinates of the vertices of ΔABC are $A(-1, 3)$, $B(3, -1)$ and $C(0, 0)$.

Let $P(x, y)$ be the centroid of the ΔABC.

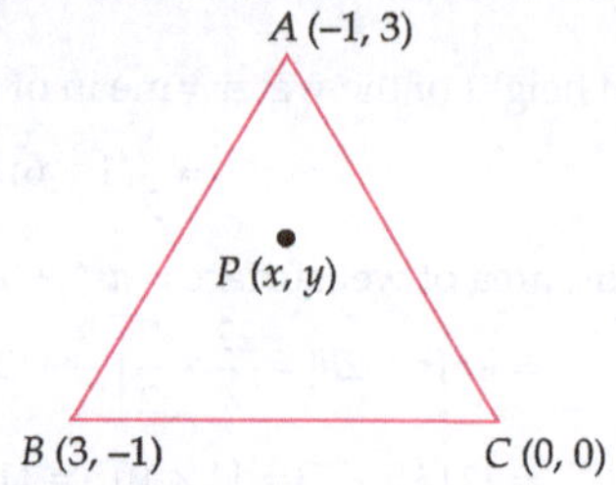

Then, $x=\frac{x_1+x_2+x_3}{3}$

and $y=\frac{y_1+y_2+y_3}{3}$

$\Rightarrow$ $x=\frac{-1+3+0}{3}=\frac{2}{3}$

and $y=\frac{3-1+0}{3}=\frac{2}{3}$

Hence, the centroid of ΔABC is $P\left(\frac{2}{3},\frac{2}{3}\right)$.

Now, the slope of line $AB=\frac{y_2-y_1}{x_2-x_1}$

$\Rightarrow$ $m=\frac{-1-3}{3+1}=-\frac{4}{4}=-1$

The line passing through point P is parallel to line AB.

Therefore, slope of the required line = slope of line $AB = -1$

Now, the equation of line passing through $P\left(\frac{2}{3}, \frac{2}{3}\right)$ is

$$y - \frac{2}{3} = -1\left(x - \frac{2}{3}\right)$$

$$\Rightarrow \quad y - \frac{2}{3} = -x + \frac{2}{3} \Rightarrow x + y = \frac{4}{3}$$

or $\quad 3x + 3y = 4$

which is required equation of line.

(ii) (a) From the given figure,

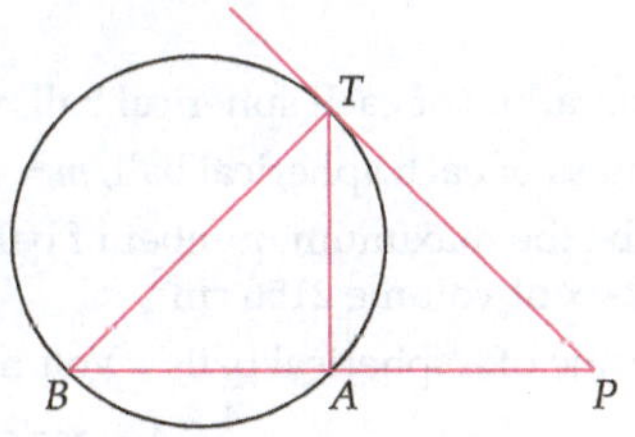

$PT = 20$ cm, $PA = 16$ cm

In ΔPTB and ΔPAT,

$\angle PTA = \angle PBT$ [alternate segment theorem]

$\angle TPA = \angle BPT$ [common]

$\therefore \quad \Delta PTB \sim \Delta PAT$ [by AA similarity]

Hence proved.

(b) We have,

$PT = 20$ cm, $PA = 16$ cm

We know that

$$PT^2 = PA \times PB$$

$$\Rightarrow \quad (20)^2 = 16 \times (16 + AB)$$

$$\Rightarrow \quad 400 = 16 \times (16 + AB)$$

$$\Rightarrow \quad 400 - 256 = 16AB \Rightarrow 144 = 16AB$$

$$\Rightarrow \quad AB = 9 \text{ cm}$$

(iii) Bill is shown below.

Rajdhani Departmental Store

S.No.	Item	Marked Price	Discount Price	GST	Tax
1.	Dry fruits (1 kg)	₹ 1200	₹ 1100	12%	$\frac{12 \times 1100}{100}$ = ₹ 132
2.	Wheat flour	₹ 286	₹ 286	5%	$\frac{5 \times 286}{100}$ = ₹ 14.30
3.	Bakery products	₹ 500	₹ 450	12%	$\frac{12 \times 450}{100}$ = ₹ 54
Total			₹ 1836		₹ 200.30
Grand Total		₹ 2036.30			

7. (i) Let h be the height of the flagstaff and x be the height of tower as shown in the figure.

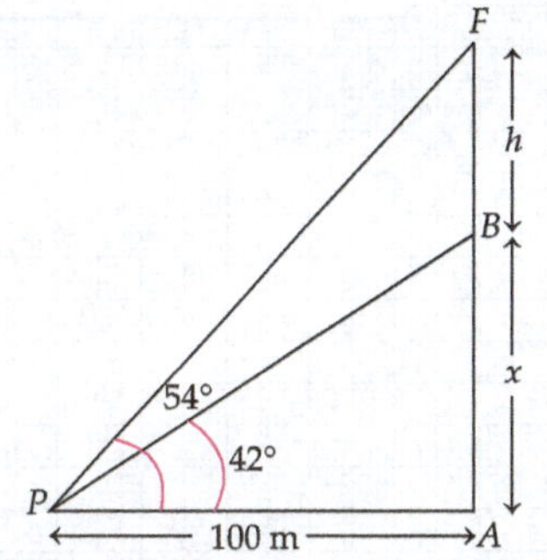

In ΔBPA,

$$\tan 42° = \frac{x}{100}$$

$$\Rightarrow \quad 0.9004 = \frac{x}{100} \qquad [\because \tan 42° = 0.9004]$$

$$\Rightarrow \quad x = 90.04 \text{ m}$$

In ΔPAF,

$$\tan 54° = \frac{h + x}{100}$$

$$\Rightarrow \quad 1.3764 = \frac{h + x}{100} \qquad [\because \tan 54° = 1.3764]$$

$$\Rightarrow \quad h + x = 137.64$$

$$\Rightarrow \quad h = 137.64 - x$$

$$= 137.64 - 90.04$$

$$= 47.60 \text{ m}$$

$$\approx 48 \text{ m.}$$

Hence, the height of the flagstaff is 48 m.

(ii) The cumulative frequency table is given below.

Marks (%)	f	cf
0-10	5	5
10-20	7	12
20-30	11	23
30-40	20	43
40-50	40	83
50-60	52	135
60-70	36	171
70-80	15	186
80-90	09	195
90-100	05	200
Total	$\Sigma f = 200$	

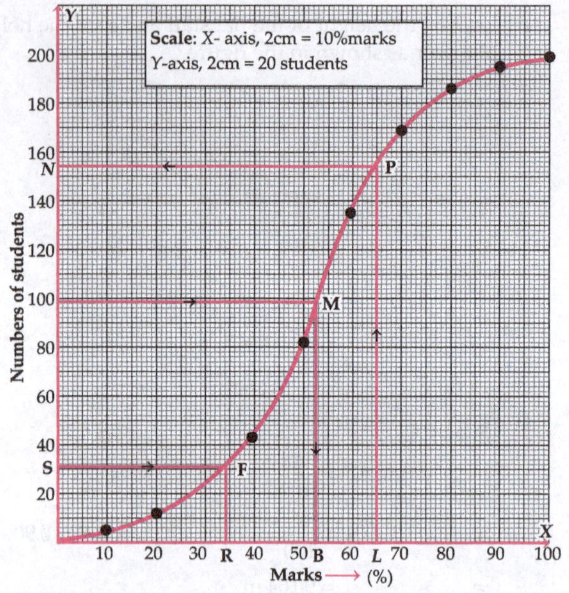

(a) Here, $\Sigma f = 200$

$$\Rightarrow \frac{N}{2} = \frac{200}{2} = 100$$

Therefore, median = 100th term

Locate 100 on Y-axis and draw a horizontal line parallel to X-axis. Intersecting the ogive at point M. From point M, we draw a vertical line perpendicular to the X-axis meeting it at B. The value of point B on X-axis is 53.

Hence, the median of data is 53.

(b) Locate a point L on X-axis at 65% and draw a vertical line from L intersect the ogive at P. From point P draw a horizontal line parallel to X-axis to intersect the Y-axis at point N. The value of point N is 154.

Thus, the number of students who got more than 65% is $200 - 154 = 46$ students.

(c) Locate a point R at 35% on X-axis and draw a vertical line intersecting ogive at F, then from point F draw a horizontal line parallel to X-axis, which intersects Y-axis at point S. The value of S is 31.

Hence, the number of students who failed is 31.

8. (i) (a) Number of friends = 3 (Amar, Akbar and Anthony).

The probability that Akbar is chosen for the call

$$= \frac{\text{Number of favaourable outcomes}}{\text{Total number of outcomes}} = \frac{1}{3}$$

(b) Each question has four options in which one option is correct and rest of them are incorrect.

Total number of outcomes = 4

$\therefore$ The probability that Akbar could not give the correct answer

$$= \frac{\text{Number of favourable outcomes}}{\text{Total number of outcomes}} = \frac{3}{4}$$

(ii) Since, x, y and z are in continued proportion

i.e. $$\frac{x}{y} = \frac{y}{z} \Rightarrow y^2 = xz \quad \text{...(i)}$$

Taking LHS

$$\frac{x}{y^2z^2} + \frac{y}{z^2x^2} + \frac{z}{x^2y^2} = \frac{x}{(xz)z^2} + \frac{y}{(y^2)^2} + \frac{z}{x^2 \times xz}$$

[using (i)]

$$= \frac{1}{z^3} + \frac{y}{y^4} + \frac{1}{x^3} = \frac{1}{x^3} + \frac{1}{y^3} + \frac{1}{z^3} = \text{RHS}$$

Hence proved.

(iii) Given, radius of each spherical ball, $r = 7$ mm

and mass of each spherical ball, $m = 4$ gm

Let n be the maximum number of balls bearing in each box of volume 2156 cm^3.

$\therefore$ Volume of n spherical balls = Volume of the box

$$\Rightarrow n \times \frac{4}{3}\pi r^3 = 2156$$

$$\Rightarrow n \times \frac{4}{3} \times \frac{22}{7} \times \left(\frac{7}{10}\right)^3 = 2156$$

$$\Rightarrow n \times \frac{4}{3} \times \frac{22}{7} \times \frac{7}{10} \times \frac{7}{10} \times \frac{7}{10} = 2156$$

$$\Rightarrow n = \frac{2156 \times 3 \times 7 \times 10 \times 10 \times 10}{4 \times 22 \times 7 \times 7 \times 7}$$

$$\Rightarrow n = 1500$$

(b) Mass of each box

= Mass of each ball × Number of balls

= 4 × 1500 gm

= 6000 gm = 6 kg

9. (i) (a) The histogram for the given data is given below.

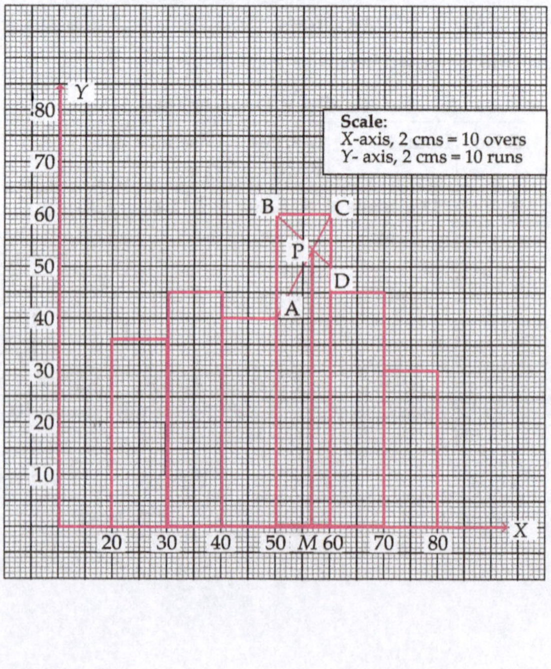

(b) The heighest frequency is 60.

Then, the corresponding model class is 50-60.

From the histogram, join the points A to C and B to D. From the intersection of AC and BD i.e. from point P, draw a vertical line perpendicular to X-axis meeting at point M.

The value of the point M is 57.

Hence, the modal runs is 57.

(ii) Given, the first term of AP, $a = 3$

Let d be the common difference of AP.

According to the question, $S_8 = 2S_5$

$$\frac{8}{2}[2(3)+(8-1)d] = 2\times\frac{5}{2}[2(3)+(5-1)d]$$

$$\Rightarrow \quad 4(6+7d) = 5(6+4d)$$

$$\Rightarrow \quad 24+28d = 30+20d$$

$$\Rightarrow \quad 8d = 6 \Rightarrow d = \frac{6}{8}$$

$$\therefore \quad d = \frac{3}{4}$$

Hence, the common difference of AP is $\frac{3}{4}$.

(iii) Given, $(q-r)x^2 + (r-p)x + p - q = 0$ ...(i)

On comparing Eq. (i) with $Ax^2 + Bx + C = 0$, we get

$A = q - r$, $B = r - p$ and $C = p - q$

$\because$ The roots of the equation are equal.

$\therefore B^2 - 4AC = 0$

$$\Rightarrow (r-p)^2 - 4(q-r)(p-q) = 0$$

$$\Rightarrow \quad r^2 + p^2 - 2pr = 4(pq - q^2 - pr + qr)$$

$$\Rightarrow \quad r^2 + p^2 - 2pr = 4pq - 4q^2 - 4pr + 4qr$$

$$\Rightarrow \quad r^2 + p^2 - 2pr + 4pr = 4pq - 4q^2 + 4qr$$

$$\Rightarrow \quad r^2 + p^2 + 2pr = 4[q(p+r) - q^2]$$

$$\Rightarrow (r+p)^2 - 4q(p+r) + 4q^2 = 0$$

$$\Rightarrow \quad [(r+p) - 2q]^2 = 0$$

$$[\because a^2 - 2ab + b^2 = (a-b)^2]$$

$$\Rightarrow \quad (r+p) - 2q = 0 \Rightarrow 2q = r + p$$

i.e. p, q and r are in AP. **Hence proved.**

10. (i) Let x be the original average speed of car.

Time taken to travel a distance of 72 km $= \frac{72}{x}$ h

and time taken to travel a distance of 81 km at a speed of $(x+6)$ km/h $= \left(\frac{81}{x+6}\right)$ h

According to the question,

total time taken to complete the journey = 3

$$\Rightarrow \quad \frac{72}{x} + \frac{81}{x+6} = 3$$

$$\Rightarrow \quad \frac{24}{x} + \frac{27}{x+6} = 1$$

$$\Rightarrow \quad 24(x+6) + 27x = x(x+6)$$

$$\Rightarrow \quad 51x + 144 = x^2 + 6x$$

$$\Rightarrow \quad x^2 - 45x - 144 = 0$$

$$\Rightarrow x^2 - 48x + 3x - 144 = 0$$

$$\Rightarrow x(x-48) + 3(x-48) = 0 \Rightarrow (x-48)(x+3) = 0$$

If $x - 48 = 0 \Rightarrow x = 48$

and if $x + 3 = 0 \Rightarrow x = -3$ (not possible)

Hence, the original speed of car is 48 km/h.

(ii) Given, $X = \begin{bmatrix} 1 & 1 \\ 8 & 3 \end{bmatrix}, I = \begin{bmatrix} 1 & 0 \\ 0 & 1 \end{bmatrix}$

$$\because \quad X^2 = X \cdot X = \begin{bmatrix} 1 & 1 \\ 8 & 3 \end{bmatrix}\begin{bmatrix} 1 & 1 \\ 8 & 3 \end{bmatrix}$$

$$= \begin{bmatrix} 1+8 & 1+3 \\ 8+24 & 8+9 \end{bmatrix} = \begin{bmatrix} 9 & 4 \\ 32 & 17 \end{bmatrix}$$

$$\text{and } 4X = 4\begin{bmatrix} 1 & 1 \\ 8 & 3 \end{bmatrix} = \begin{bmatrix} 4 & 4 \\ 32 & 12 \end{bmatrix}$$

$$5I = 5\begin{bmatrix} 1 & 0 \\ 0 & 1 \end{bmatrix} = \begin{bmatrix} 5 & 0 \\ 0 & 5 \end{bmatrix}$$

$$\because 4X + 5I = \begin{bmatrix} 4 & 4 \\ 32 & 12 \end{bmatrix} + \begin{bmatrix} 5 & 0 \\ 0 & 5 \end{bmatrix}$$

$$= \begin{bmatrix} 4 & 4 \\ 32 & 12 \end{bmatrix} + \begin{bmatrix} 5 & 0 \\ 0 & 5 \end{bmatrix} = \begin{bmatrix} 9 & 4 \\ 32 & 17 \end{bmatrix} = X^2$$

Hence, $X^2 = 4X + 5I$

Hence proved.

(iii) **Construction** Scale 10 m = 1 cm

1. Draw a line segment $AB = 5$ cm.
2. With the help of ruler and compass draw a ray by making an angle of 75° at point B.
3. Cut $BC = 6.3$ cm
4. Draw a ray AX making an angle of 90° at point A.
5. Draw a ray BX' making an angle of 45° at point B. Which cuts the ray AX at point D.
6. Joint D to C.
7. Draw the bisector of line segment AB. Which cuts the ray BX' at point P.

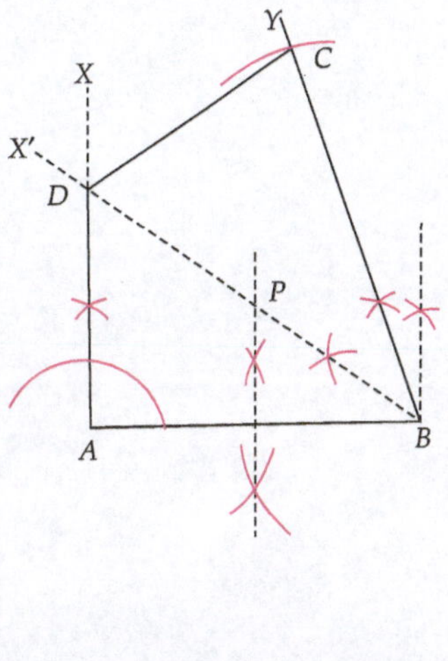

ICSE
QUESTION PAPER 2024
&
QUESTION PAPER 2025

QUESTION PAPER 2024

A HIGHLY SIMULATED Sample Question Paper for ICSE Class X

Mathematics (Fully solved)

GENERAL INSTRUCTIONS

1. Answers to this paper must be written on the paper provided separately.
2. You will not be allowed to write during the first 15 minutes. This time is to be spent in reading the question paper.
3. The time given at the head of this paper is the time allowed for writing the answers.
4. Attempt all **questions** from **Section A** and **any 4 questions** from **Section B.**
5. All working, including rough work, must be clearly shown and must be done on the same sheet as the rest of the answer.
6. Omission of essential working will result in loss of marks.
7. The intended marks for questions or parts of questions are given in bracket [ ].
8. Mathematical tables are provided.

Time : 2.5 Hrs **Max. Marks : 80**

Section A [40 *Marks*]

(Attempt all questions from this section)

1. Choose the correct answers to the questions from the given options. [15]

(Do not copy the questions, write the correct answers only.)

(i) For an Intra-state sale, the CGST paid by a dealer to the Central government is ₹ 120. If the marked price of the article is ₹ 2000, then the rate of GST is

(a) 6% (b) 10%

(c) 12% (d) 16.67%

(ii) What must be subtracted from the polynomial $x^3 + x^2 - 2x + 1$, so that the result is exactly divisible by $(x - 3)$?

(a) – 31 (b) – 30

(c) 30 (d) 31

(iii) The roots of the quadratic equation $px^2 - qx + r = 0$ are real and equal, if

(a) $p^2 = 4qr$ (b) $q^2 = 4pr$

(c) $-q^2 = 4pr$ (d) $p^2 > 4qr$

(iv) If matrix $A = \begin{bmatrix} 2 & 2 \\ 0 & 2 \end{bmatrix}$ and $A^2 = \begin{bmatrix} 4 & x \\ 0 & 4 \end{bmatrix}$, then the value of x is

(a) 2 (b) 4

(c) 8 (d) 10

(v) The median of the following observations arranged in ascending order is 64. Find the value of x.

27, 31, 46, 52, x, $x + 4$, 71, 79, 85, 90

(a) 60 (b) 61

(c) 62 (d) 66

(vi) Points $A(x,y)$, $B(3, -2)$ and $C(4, -5)$ are collinear. The value of y in terms of x is

(a) $3x - 11$ (b) $11 - 3x$

(c) $3x - 7$ (d) $7 - 3x$

(vi) The given table shows the distance covered and the time taken by a train moving at a uniform speed along a straight track.

Distance (in m)	60	90	y
Time (in sec)	2	x	5

The values of x and y are

(a) $x = 4, y = 150$ (b) $x = 3, y = 100$
(c) $x = 4, y = 100$ (d) $x = 3, y = 150$

(viii) The 7 term of the given Arithmetic Progression (AP)

$\frac{1}{a}, \left(\frac{1}{a}+1\right), \left(\frac{1}{a}+2\right)$.... is

(a) $\left(\frac{1}{a}+6\right)$ (b) $\left(\frac{1}{a}+7\right)$ (c) $\left(\frac{1}{a}+8\right)$ (d) $\left(\frac{1}{a}+7^7\right)$

(ix) The sum invested to purchase 15 shares of a company of nominal value ₹ 75 available at a discount of 20% is

(a) ₹ 60 (b) ₹ 90
(c) ₹ 1350 (d) ₹ 900

(x) The circumcentre of a triangle is the point which is

(a) at equal distance from the three sides of the triangle.
(b) at equal distance from the three vertices of the triangle.
(c) the point of intersection of the three medians.
(d) the point of intersection of the three altitudes of the triangle.

(xi) **Statement I** $\sin^2\theta + \cos^2\theta = 1$

Statement II $\operatorname{cosec}^2\theta + \cot^2\theta = 1$

Which of the following is valid?

(a) only I (b) only II
(c) Both I and II (d) Neither I nor II

(xii) In the given diagram, PS and PT are the tangents to the circle. $SQ \parallel PT$ and $\angle SPT = 80°$. The value of $\angle QST$ is

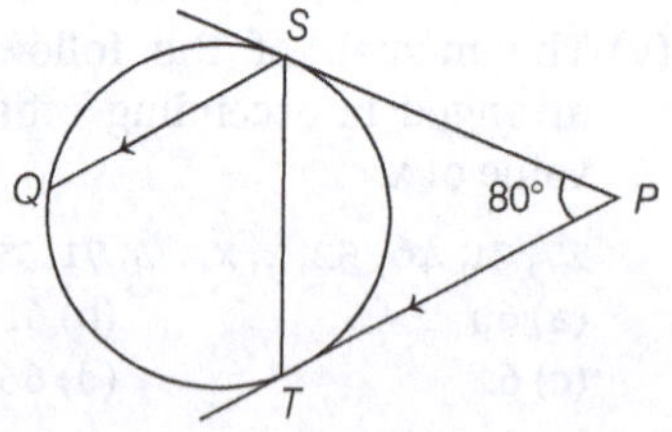

(a) 140° (b) 90°
(c) 80° (d) 50°

(xiii) **Assertion (A)** A die is thrown once and the probability of getting an even number is $\frac{2}{3}$.

Reason (R) The sample space for even numbers on a die is {2, 4, 6}

(a) A is true but R is false.
(b) A is false but R is true.
(c) Both A and R are true.
(d) Both A and R are false.

(xiv) A rectangular sheet of paper of size 11 cm × 7 cm is first rotated about the side 11 cm and then about the side 7 cm to form a cylinder, as shown in the diagram. The ratio of their curved surface areas is

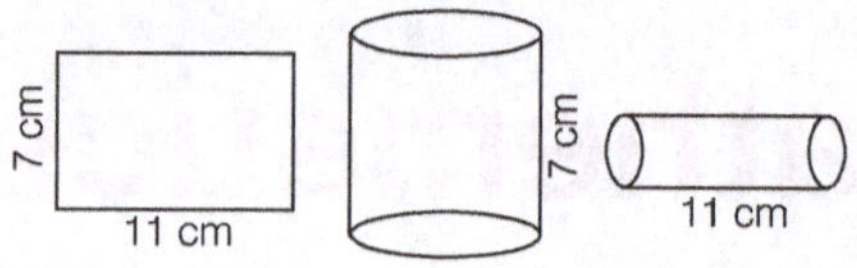

(a) 1 : 1 (b) 7 : 11
(c) 11: 7 (d) $\frac{11\pi}{7} : \frac{7\pi}{11}$

(xv) In the given figure, $\Delta ABC \sim \Delta PQR$. If AD and PS are bisectors of $\angle BAC$ and $\angle QPR$ respectively, then

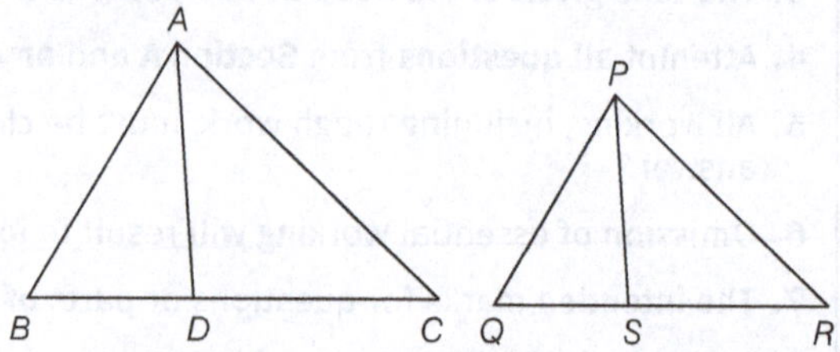

(a) $\Delta ABC \sim \Delta PQS$ (b) $\Delta ABD \sim \Delta PQS$
(c) $\Delta ABD \sim \Delta PSR$ (d) $\Delta ABC \sim \Delta PSR$

2. (i) If $A = \begin{bmatrix} x & 0 \\ 1 & 1 \end{bmatrix}, B = \begin{bmatrix} 4 & 0 \\ y & 1 \end{bmatrix}$ and $C = \begin{bmatrix} 4 & 0 \\ x & 1 \end{bmatrix}$, then find the values of x and y, if $AB = C$. [4]

(ii) A solid metallic cylinder is cut into two identical halves along its height (as shown in the figule). The diameter of the cylinder is 7 cm and the height is 10 cm. Find

(a) the total surface area (both the halves).
(b) the total cost of painting the two halves at the rate of ₹ 30 per cm² $\left[\text{Use } \pi = \frac{22}{7}\right]$ [4]

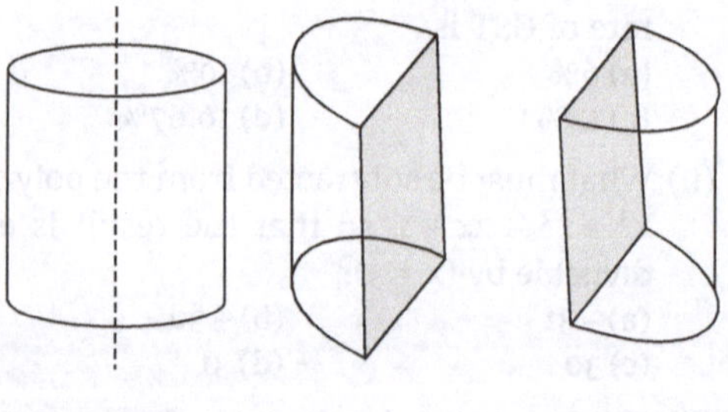

(iii) 15, 30, 60, 120... are in GP (Geometric Progression).

(a) Find the n term of this GP in terms of n.
(b) How many terms of the above GP will give the sum 945? [4]

3. (i) Factorise : $\sin^3\theta + \cos^3\theta$

Hence, prove the following identity:

$$\frac{\sin^3\theta + \cos^3\theta}{\sin\theta + \cos\theta} + \sin\theta\cos\theta = 1$$

[4]

(ii) In the given diagram, O is the centre of the circle. PR and PT are two tangents drawn from the external point P and touching the circle at Q and S respectively. MN is a diameter of the circle. Given $\angle PQM = 42^\circ$ and $\angle PSM = 25^\circ$.

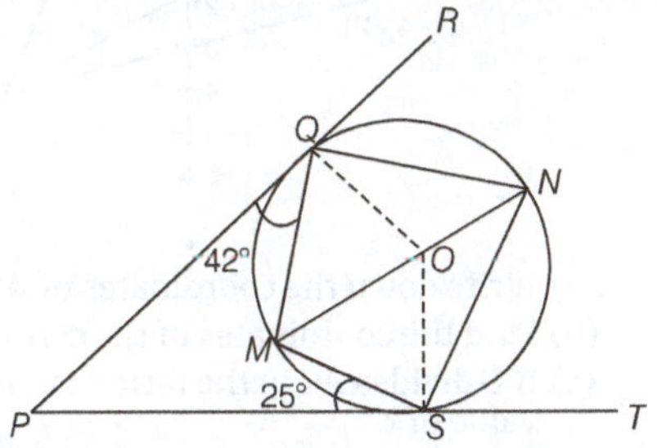

Find

(a) $\angle OQM$ (b) $\angle QNS$

(c) $\angle QOS$ (d) $\angle QMS$ [4]

(iii) Use graph sheet for this question.

Take 2 cm = 1 unit along the axes.

(a) Plot $A(0, 3)$, $B(2, 1)$ and $C(4, -1)$.

(b) Reflect point B and C in Y-axis and name their images as B' and C' respectively. Plot and write coordinates of the points B' and C'.

(c) Reflect point A in the line BB' and name its images as A'.

(d) Plot and write coordinates of point A'.

(e) Join the points $ABA'B'$ and give the geometrical name of the closed figure so formed. [5]

Section B [40 *Marks*]

(Attempt any four questions from this section)

4. (i) Suresh has a recurring deposit account in a bank. He deposits ₹ 2000 per month and the bank pays interest at the rate of 8% per annum. If he gets ₹ 1040 as interest at the time of maturity, find in years total time for which the account was held. [3]

(ii) The following table gives the duration of movies in minutes.

Duration (in minutes)	100-110	110-120	120-130	130-140	140-150	150-160
Number of movies	5	10	17	8	6	4

Using step-deviation method, find the mean duration of the movies. [3]

(iii) $\dfrac{(a+b)^3}{(a-b)^3} = \dfrac{64}{27}$

(a) Find $\dfrac{a+b}{a-b}$.

(b) Hence using properties of proportion, find $a : b$. [4]

5. (i) The given graph with a histogram represents the number of plants of different heights grown in a school campus. Study the graph carefully and answer the following questions

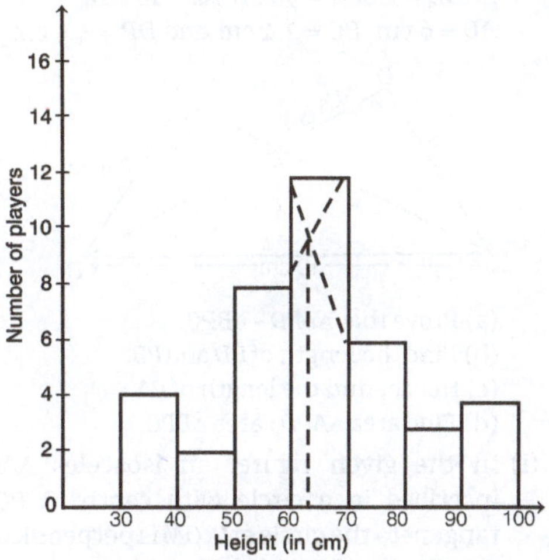

(a) Make a frequency table with respect to the class boundaries and their corresponding frequencies.

(b) State the modal class.

(c) Identify and note down the mode of the distribution.

(d) Find the number of plants whose height range is between 80 cm to 90 cm. [5]

(ii) The angle of elevation of the top of a 100 m high tree from two points A and B on the opposite side of the tree are 52° and 45° respectively. Find the distance AB to the nearest metre.

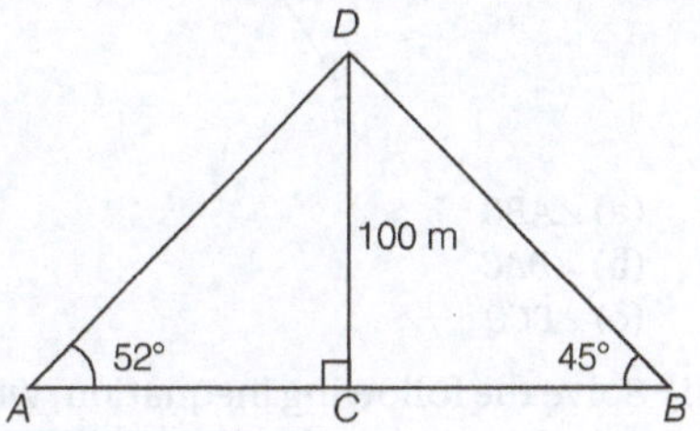

[5]

6. (i) Solve the following quadratic equation for x and give your answer correct to three significant figures $2x^2 - 10x + 5 = 0$
(Use mathematical tables if necessary) [3]

(ii) The n term of an Arithmetic Progression (AP) is given by the relation $T_n = 6(7 - n)$.
Find
(a) its first term and common difference.
(b) sum of its first 25 terms. [3]

(iii) In the given figure, ΔADB and ΔACB are two right angled triangles with $\angle ADB = \angle BCA = 90°$. If $AB = 10$ cm, $AD = 6$ cm, $BC = 2.4$ cm and $DP = 4.5$ cm.

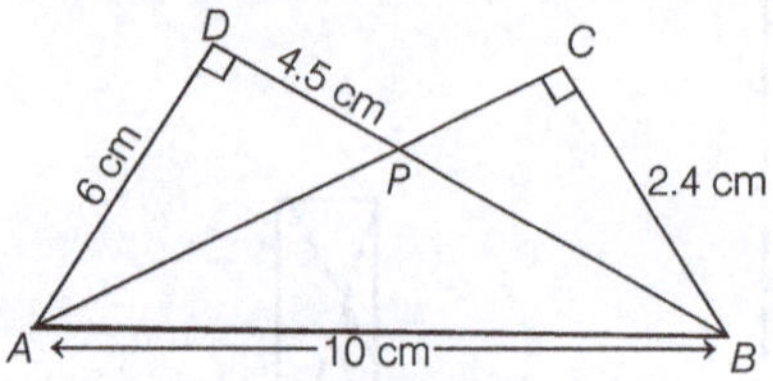

(a) Prove that $\Delta APD \sim \Delta BPC$.
(b) Find the length of BD and PB.
(c) Hence, find the length of PA.
(d) Find area ΔAPD : area ΔBPC. [4]

7. (i) In the given figure, an isosceles ΔABC is inscribed in a circle with centre O. PQ is a tangent to the circle at C, OM is perpendicular to chord AC and $\angle COM = 65°$.
Find

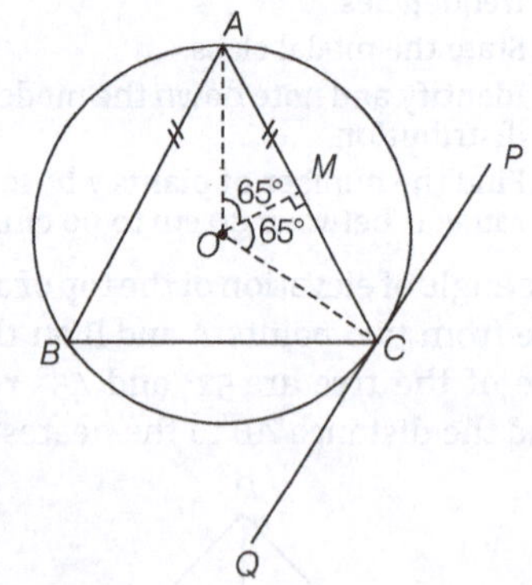

(a) $\angle ABC$
(b) $\angle BAC$
(c) $\angle BCQ$ [3]

(ii) Solve the following inequation, write down the solution set and represent it on the real number line.

$$-3 + x \le \frac{7x}{2} + 2 < 8 + 2x,\ x \in I$$ [3]

(iii) In the given figure, ABC is a triangle, where $B(4, -4)$ and $C(-4, -2)$. D is a point on AC.

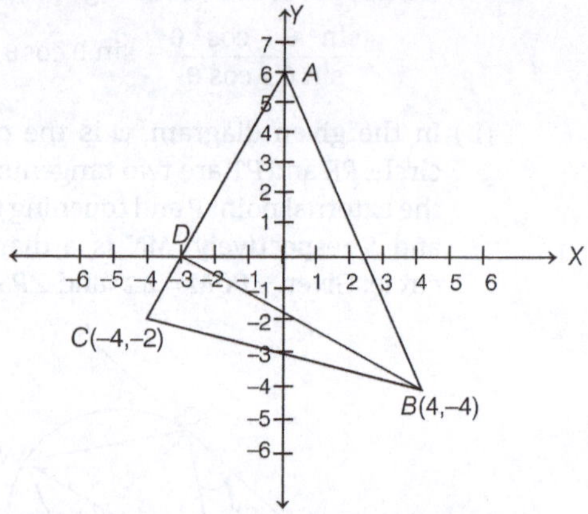

(a) Write down the coordinates of A and D.
(b) Find the coordinates of the centroid of ΔABC.
(c) If D divides AC in the ratio $k:1$, then find the value of k.
(d) Find the equation of the line BD. [4]

8. (i) The polynomial $3x^3 + 8x^2 - 15x + k$ has $(x - 1)$ as a factor. Find the value of k. Hence, the factorise the resulting polynomial completely. [3]

(ii) The following letters A, D, M, N, O, S, U, Y of the English alphabet are written on separate cards and put in a box. The cards are well shuffled and one card is drawn at random. What is the probability that the card drawn is a letter of the word
(a) MONDAY?
(b) which does not appear in MONDAY?
(c) which appears both in SUNDAY and MONDAY? [3]

(iii) Oil is stored in a spherical vessel occupying 3/4 of its full capacity. Radius of this spherical vessel is 28 cm. This oil is then poured into a cylindrical vessel with a radius of 21 cm. Find the height of the oil in the cylindrical vessel (correct to the nearest cm).
$\left[\text{Take } \pi = \frac{22}{7}\right]$

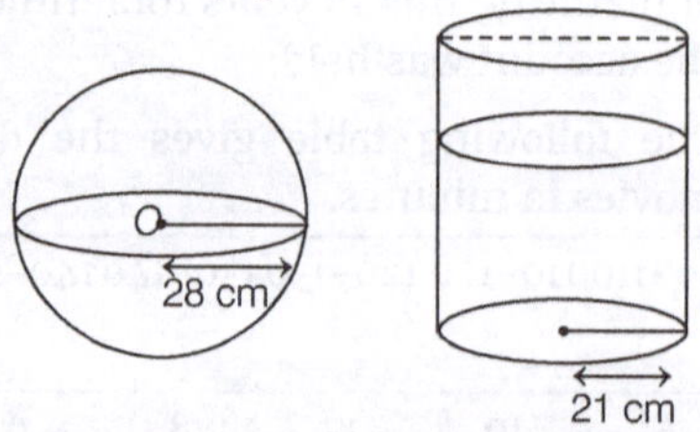

[4]

9. (i) The figure shows a circle of radius 9 cm with O as the centre. The diameter AB produced meets the tangent PQ at P. If $PA = 24$ cm, then find the length of tangent PQ.

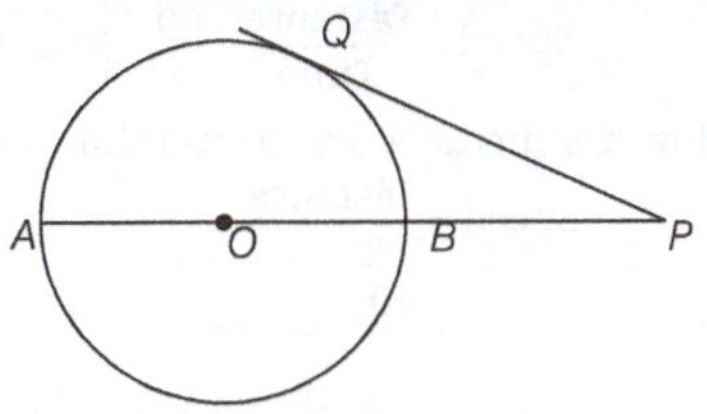

[3]

(ii) Mr. Gupta invested ₹ 3300 in buying ₹ 100 shares of a company at 10% premium. The dividend declared by the company is 12%. Find
(a) the number of shares purchased by him.
(b) his annual dividend. [3]

(iii) A life insurance agent found the following data for distribution of ages of 100 policy holders

Age (in years)	Policy Holders (frequency)	Cumulative frequency
20-25	2	2
25-30	4	6
30-35	12	18
35-40	20	38
40-45	28	66
45-50	22	88
50-55	8	96
55-60	4	100

On a graph sheet draw an ogive using the given data. Take 2 cm = 5 yr along one axis and 2 cm = 10 policy holders along the other axis.

Use your graph to find
(a) the median age.
(b) number of policy holders whose age is above 52 yr. [4]

10. (i) Rohan bought the following eatables for his friends

Soham Sweet Mart: Bill

S. No.	Item	Price	Quantity	Rate of GST
1	Laddu	₹ 500 per kg	2 kg	5%
2	Pastries	₹ 100 per piece	12 pieces	18%

Calculate
(a) Total GST paid.
(b) Total bill amount including GST. [3]

(ii) (a) If the lines $kx - y + 4 = 0$ and $2y = 6x + 7$ are perpendicular to each other, then find the value of k.
(b) Find the equation of a line parallel to $2y = 6x + 7$ and passing through $(-1, 1)$. [3]

(iii) Use ruler and compass to answer this question. Construct $\angle ABC = 90°$, where $AB = 6$ cm, $BC = 8$ cm.
(a) Construct the locus of points equidistant from B and C.
(b) Construct the locus of points equidistant from A and B.
(c) Mark the point which satisfies both the conditions (a) and (b) as O. Construct the locus of points keeping a fixed distance OA from the fixed point O.
(d) Construct the locus of points which are equidistant from BA and BC. [4]

SOLUTIONS

1. (i) (a) Given, marked price of article = ₹ 2000

CGST paid by dealer to government = ₹ 120

$\therefore$ Rate of GST $= \frac{120}{2000} \times 100 = 6\%$

(ii) (d) Given, $p(x) = x^3 + x^2 - 2x + 1$

By Remainder theorem,

If $(x-3)$ is a factor of $p(x)$, then remainder will be $p(3)$.

$\because \quad p(3) = 3^3 + 3^2 - 2 \times 3 + 1$

$= 27 + 9 - 6 + 1 = 31$

$\therefore$ 31 must be subtracted from $p(x)$, so that the result is divisible by $(x-3)$.

(iii) (b) Given, $px^2 - qx + r = 0$

$\because$ The roots are real and equal.

$\therefore \quad b^2 - 4ac = 0$

$\Rightarrow \quad (-q)^2 - 4 \times p \times r = 0 \Rightarrow q^2 = 4pr$

(iv) (c) Given, $A = \begin{bmatrix} 2 & 2 \\ 0 & 2 \end{bmatrix}$ and $A^2 = \begin{bmatrix} 4 & x \\ 0 & 4 \end{bmatrix}$

$\therefore \quad A^2 = A \times A$

$\Rightarrow \quad \begin{bmatrix} 4 & x \\ 0 & 4 \end{bmatrix} = \begin{bmatrix} 2 & 2 \\ 0 & 2 \end{bmatrix}\begin{bmatrix} 2 & 2 \\ 0 & 2 \end{bmatrix}$

$\Rightarrow \quad \begin{bmatrix} 4 & x \\ 0 & 4 \end{bmatrix} = \begin{bmatrix} 4 & 8 \\ 0 & 4 \end{bmatrix}$

By the definition of equality of two matrices, we get $x = 8$

(v) (c) Given observations are

27, 31, 46, 52, x, $x+4$, 71, 79, 85, 90

and median = 64

Number of observations = 10 (even number)

$\therefore \quad \text{Median} = \dfrac{\frac{10}{2}\text{th term} + \left(\frac{10}{2}+1\right)\text{th term}}{2}$

$\Rightarrow \quad 64 = \dfrac{5\text{th term} + 6\text{th term}}{2}$

$\Rightarrow \quad 128 = x + x + 4$

$\Rightarrow \quad 2x = 124 \Rightarrow x = 62$

(vi) (d) Given points are

$A(x, y)$, $B(3, -2)$ and $C(4, -5)$

Since, the points are collinear, therefore the area of triangle formed by these points will be zero.

$\therefore \quad \frac{1}{2}\sqrt{x(-2+5) + 3(-5-y) + 4(y+2)} = 0$

On squaring both sides, we get

$3x - 15 - 3y + 4y + 8 = 0$

$\Rightarrow \quad 3x + y - 7 = 0$

or $\quad y = 7 - 3x$

(vii) (d) Given table

Distance (in m)	60	90	y
Time (sec)	2	x	5

$\because$ Speed of train is uniform.

For distance = 60 m and time = 2 sec

$\text{Speed} = \frac{\text{Distance}}{\text{Time}} = \frac{60}{2} = 30 \text{ m/sec}$

Now, for distance = 90 m and time = x sec

$\text{Speed} = \frac{\text{Distance}}{\text{Time}}$

$\Rightarrow \quad 30 = \frac{90}{x} \Rightarrow x = 3$

Also, $30 = \frac{y}{5} \Rightarrow y = 150$

Hence, $x = 3$ and $y = 150$

(viii) (a) Given AP,

$\frac{1}{a}, \left(\frac{1}{a}+1\right), \left(\frac{1}{a}+2\right)$....

Here, first term $= \frac{1}{a}$

and common difference $(d) = \frac{1}{a} + 1 - \frac{1}{a} = 1$

$\therefore$ 7 term $= \frac{1}{a} + (7-1) \times 1 \quad [\because A_n = a + (n-1)d]$

$= \frac{1}{a} + 6$

(ix) (d) Given, number of shares = 15

Nominal value per share = ₹ 75

Rate of discount = 20%

$\therefore$ Invested sum $= 15 \times 75 \times \frac{4}{5} =$ ₹ 900

(x) (b) The circle that passes through all the vertices of a triangle is called the circumcircle of the triangle. The centre of the circumcircle is called circumcentre.

Hence, the circumcentre of a triangle is equidistant from its vertices.

(xi) (a) **Statement I** $\sin^2\theta + \cos^2\theta = 1$

which is true.

Statement II $\text{cosec}^2\theta + \cot^2\theta = 1$

which is false.

(xii) (d) In the given figure, PS and PT are the tangents to the circle, $\angle SPT = 80°$ and $SQ \parallel PT$ as shown in the figure.

We know that the tangents drawn from an external point to the circle are of equal length.

$\therefore \quad PT = PS$

$\angle PTS = \angle PST = x$ (let)

In ΔPST, $\angle P + \angle PTS + \angle PST = 180°$

$\Rightarrow \quad 80 + x + x = 180°$

$\Rightarrow \quad x = 50°$

Now, $QS \parallel PT$,

$\angle QST = \angle PTS \quad$ [alternate angles]

$\Rightarrow \quad \angle QST = 50°$

(xiii) (b) **Assertion (A)** When a die thrown once, then the possible outcomes are 6

i.e. $S=\{1, 2, 3, 4, 5, 6\}$

Even number $=\{2, 4, 6\}$

$\therefore$ Favourable outcomes $=3$

Thus, the probability of getting an even number

$$=\frac{\text{Number of favourable outcomes}}{\text{Total number of outcomes}}$$

$$=\frac{3}{6}=\frac{1}{2}$$

So, Assertion is false but Reason is true.

(xiv) (a) Dimensions of rectangular sheet are 11×7.

Case I When sheet rotated about the side 11 cm.

Then, curved surface area, $S_1=2\pi rh$

$$=2\pi\times\frac{11}{2}\times 7$$

$$=77\pi \text{ cm}^2$$

Case II When sheet rotated about the side 7 cm.

Then, curved surface area, $S_2=2\pi rh$

$$=2\pi\times\frac{7}{2}\times 11$$

$$=77\pi$$

So, $S_1:S_2=77\pi:77\pi=1:1$

(xv) (b) In the given figure, $\Delta ABC\sim\Delta PQR$.

$\angle ABC=\angle PQR$ [corresponding angles] ...(i)

$\angle BAC=\angle QPR$ [corresponding angles]

$\Rightarrow \frac{1}{2}\angle BAC=\frac{1}{2}\angle QPR$ ...(ii)

Now, AD and PS are angle bisectors of $\angle BAC$ and $\angle QPR$ respectively.

Thus, in ΔABD and ΔPQS

$\angle ABD=\angle PQS$ [from Eq. (i)]

$\angle BAD=\angle QPS$ [from Eq. (ii)]

$\angle BDA=\angle QSP$

Thus, $\Delta ABD\sim\Delta PQS$ [by AAA similarity]

2. (i) We have, $A=\begin{bmatrix}x & 0\\ 1 & 1\end{bmatrix}$, $B=\begin{bmatrix}4 & 0\\ y & 1\end{bmatrix}$ and $C=\begin{bmatrix}4 & 0\\ x & 1\end{bmatrix}$

$\because$ $AB=C$

$$\Rightarrow \begin{bmatrix}x & 0\\ 1 & 1\end{bmatrix}\begin{bmatrix}4 & 0\\ y & 1\end{bmatrix}=\begin{bmatrix}4 & 0\\ x & 1\end{bmatrix}$$

$$\Rightarrow \begin{bmatrix}4x & 0\\ 4+y & 1\end{bmatrix}=\begin{bmatrix}4 & 0\\ x & 1\end{bmatrix}$$

By the definition of equality of matrices, we get

$4x=4 \Rightarrow x=1$

and $4+y=x$

$\Rightarrow 4+y=1 \Rightarrow y=1-4=-3$

Hence, $x=1$ and $y=-3$

(ii) Given, the diameter of cylinder $=7$ cm

Radius of cylinder $(r)=\frac{7}{2}$ cm

and height of cylinder $(h)=10$ cm

(a) Total surface area (both the halves)

$$=2[\pi rh+\pi r^2+r\times h]$$

$$=2\left[\frac{22}{7}\times\frac{7}{2}\times 10+\frac{22}{7}\times\frac{49}{4}+\frac{7}{2}\times 10\right]$$

$$=\frac{2}{2}[220+77+70]=367 \text{ cm}^2$$

(b) Total surface area of two halves $=367 \text{ cm}^2$

Cost of painting $=$ ₹ 30 per cm^2

$\therefore$ Total cost of painting $=$ ₹ $367\times 30=$ ₹ 11010

(iii) Given, 15, 30, 60, 120, ... are in GP.

(a) We have, first term $(a)=15$

Common ratio $(r)=\frac{30}{15}=2$

$\therefore$ n term $=ar^{n-1}=15\cdot 2^{n-1}=\frac{15}{2}\times 2^n$

$$=7.5\times 2^n$$

(b) Let sum of n terms will give the sum 945.

We know that

$$S_n=\frac{a(r^n-1)}{r-1}, r>1$$

$$\Rightarrow 945=\frac{15(2^n-1)}{2-1}$$

$$\Rightarrow 63=2^n-1$$

$$\Rightarrow 2^n=64=2^6 \Rightarrow n=6$$

3. (i) We have,

$$\sin^3\theta+\cos^3\theta$$

$\because$ Using the identity

$$a^3+b^3=(a+b)(a^2+b^2-ab)$$

$\therefore \sin^3\theta+\cos^3\theta$

$$=(\cos\theta+\sin\theta)(\cos^2\theta+\sin^2\theta-\sin\theta\cos\theta)$$

$\Rightarrow \sin^3\theta+\cos^3\theta=(\cos\theta+\sin\theta)(1-\sin\theta\cos\theta)$

which is the required factor form.

$$\Rightarrow \frac{\sin^3\theta+\cos^3\theta}{\sin\theta+\cos\theta}=1-\sin\theta\cos\theta$$

Hence, $\frac{\sin^3\theta+\cos^3\theta}{\sin\theta+\cos\theta}+\sin\theta\cos\theta=1$

Hence proved.

(ii) In the given figure, PR and PT are two tangents drawn from the external point P.

$\angle PQM=42°$ and $\angle PSM=25°$

(a) In the given figure,

$OQ=OS=OM$ [radii of the circle]

We know that

$OQ\perp PR$

$\therefore \angle OQP=90°$

$\Rightarrow \angle OQM+\angle PQM=90°$

$\Rightarrow \angle OQM=90°-42°=48°$

(b) In ΔOQM,

$OQ=OM$ [radii of circle]

$\therefore \angle OQM=\angle OMQ=48°$ [from part (a)]

In ΔOMS,

$OS \perp PT$

$\angle OSM = 90° - 25° = 65°$

$\because \quad OM = OS \quad$ [radii of circle]

$\therefore \quad \angle OSM = \angle OMS = 65°$

So, $\angle QMS = \angle OMQ + \angle OMS = 48° + 65° = 113°$

Since, $QMSN$ is a cyclic quadrilateral. Therefore,

$\angle QNS = 180° - \angle QMS = 180° - 113° = 67°$

(c) In ΔOQM,

$\angle OQM = 48, \angle OMQ = 48°$

$\therefore \quad \angle QOM = 180° - 48° - 48° = 84°$

and in ΔOMS,

$\angle OMS = \angle OSM = 65°$

$\therefore \quad \angle MOS = 180° - 65° - 65° = 50°$

$\therefore \quad \angle QOS = \angle QOM + \angle MOS = 84° + 50° = 134°$

(d) From part (b),

$\angle QMS = 113°$

(iii) (a)

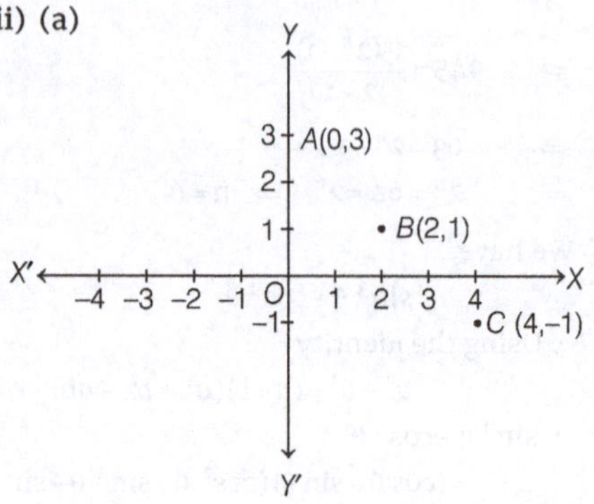

(b)

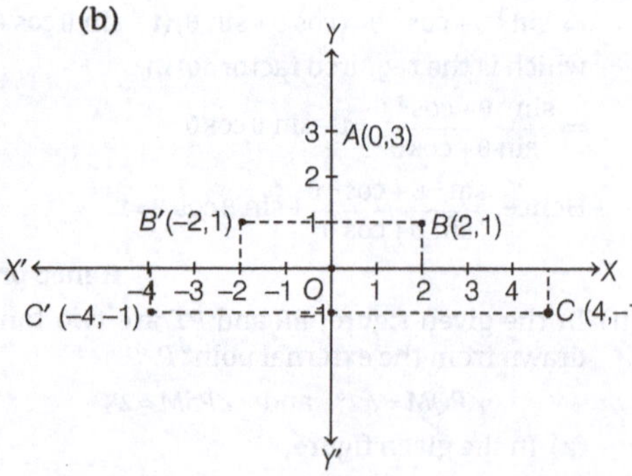

(c)

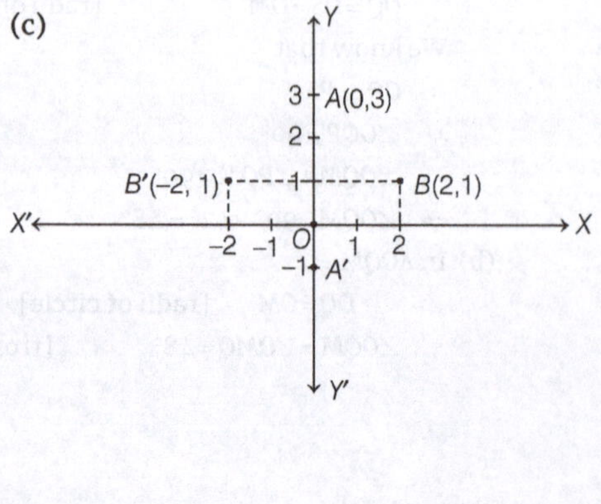

(d)

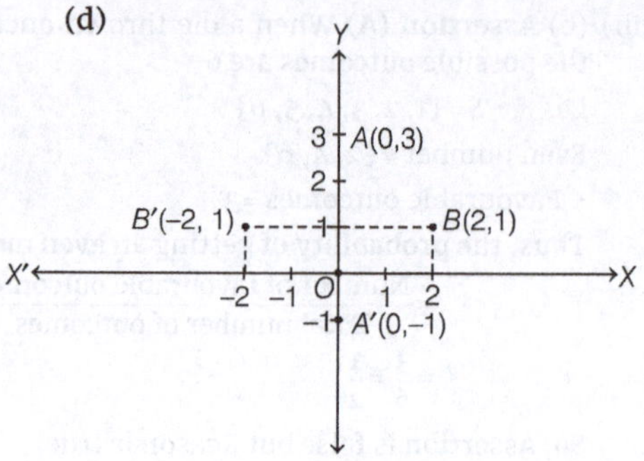

(e)

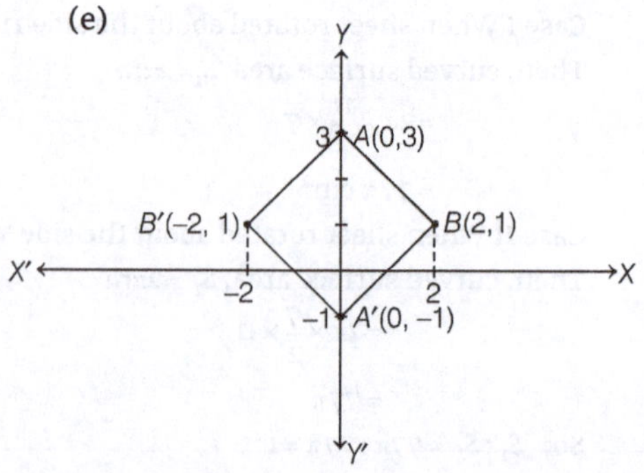

$\therefore$ By joining the points $AB\,A'B'$, we get the square.

4. (i) Given, amount deposited by Suresh

$= ₹\,2000$ per month

Rate of interest paid by bank = 8% per annum

Amount of interest = ₹ 1040

$\therefore \quad \text{Interest } (I) = \dfrac{Pn(n+1)}{2 \times 12} \times \dfrac{r}{100}$

$1040 = \dfrac{2000 \times n(n+1)}{24} \times \dfrac{8}{100}$

$\Rightarrow \quad \dfrac{1040 \times 3}{20} = n(n+1)$

$\Rightarrow \quad 52 \times 3 = n(n+1) \Rightarrow 156 = n(n+1)$

$\Rightarrow \quad 12(12+1) = n(n+1)$

On comparing, we get

$n = 12$ months

Hence, the time is 1 yr.

(ii) The table for the given data

Interval	Frequency (f_i)	Mid-value (x_i)	$u_i = \dfrac{x_i - A}{h}$	$f_i u_i$
100-110	5	105	−3	−15
110-120	10	115	−2	−20
120-130	17	125	−1	−17
130-140	8	135 = A	0	0
140-150	6	145	1	6
150-160	4	155	2	8
	$\Sigma f_i = 50$			$\Sigma f_i u_i = -38$

Here, $\Sigma f_i = 50$, $\Sigma f_i u_i = -38$, $A = 135$ and $h = 10$

Using step-deviation method,

$$\text{Mean} = A + \frac{\Sigma f_i u_i}{\Sigma f_i} \times h$$

$$= 135 + \left(\frac{-38}{50} \times 10\right)$$

$$= 135 - 7.6 = 127.4$$

Hence, the mean duration of the movies is 127.4 min.

(iii) (a) Given, $\frac{(a+b)^3}{(a-b)^3} = \frac{64}{27}$

On taking cube root of both sides, we get

$$\frac{a+b}{a-b} = \frac{4}{3}$$

(b) Now, we have

$$\frac{a+b}{a-b} = \frac{4}{3}$$

By componendo and dividendo rule, we get

$$\frac{a+b+a-b}{a+b-a+b} = \frac{4+3}{4-3}$$

$\Rightarrow$ $$\frac{2a}{2b} = \frac{7}{1}$$

or $$a : b = 7 : 1$$

5. (i) (a) The frequency table is given below.

Interval	30-40	40-50	50-60	60-70	70-80	80-90	90-100
Frequency	4	2	8	12	6	3	4

(b) The heighest frequency (in above table) is 12.

$\therefore$ Modal class = 60-70

(c) The histogram is given as

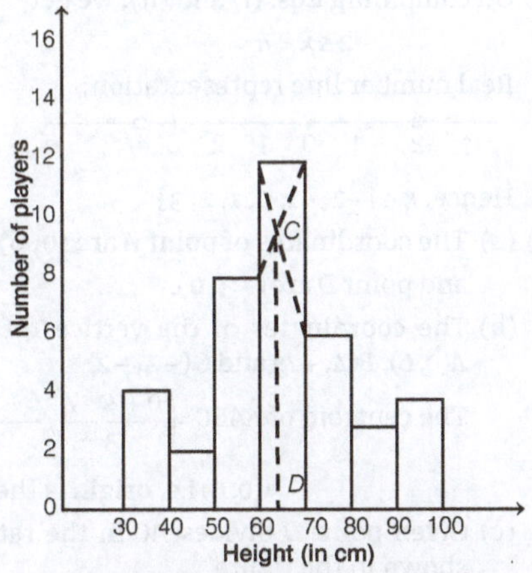

Here, line CD intersects the X-axis at $x = 64$.

So, the mode of the data is 64.

(d) From the histogram, the number of plants whose height range is between 80 cm to 90 cm is 3.

(ii) The given figure is

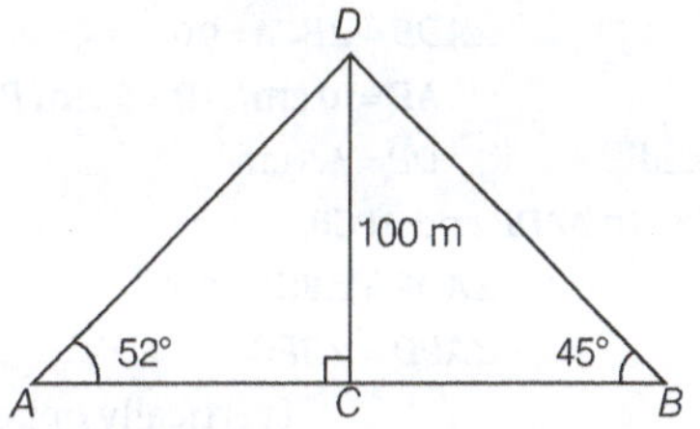

The height of tree $CD = 100$ m

In ΔACD,

$$\tan 52° = \frac{CD}{AC}$$

$\therefore$ $$AC = 100 \times \cot 52° \quad \text{...(i)}$$

In ΔDCB,

$$\tan 45° = \frac{CD}{CB}$$

$\therefore$ $$CB = 100 \text{ m}$$

Now, distance $AB = AC + CB$

$$= 100 \times \cot 52° + 100$$
$$= 100 \times 0.7813 + 100$$
$$= 78.13 + 100$$
$$= 178.13 \approx 178 \text{ m}$$

Hence, the distance AB is 178 m approximately.

6. (i) The given equation is

$$2x^2 - 10x + 5 = 0$$

On comparing with $ax^2 + bx + c = 0$, we get

$$a = 2, b = -10 \text{ and } c = 5$$

Now, using quadratic formula, we have

$$x = \frac{-b \pm \sqrt{b^2 - 4ac}}{2a} = \frac{10 \pm \sqrt{100 - 40}}{2 \times 2}$$

$$= \frac{10 \pm 2\sqrt{15}}{4} = \frac{5 \pm \sqrt{15}}{2}$$

So, $x = \frac{5+\sqrt{15}}{2}$ and $\frac{5-\sqrt{15}}{2}$

Hence, $x = 4.436$ and 0.564

(ii) Given, n term of an AP is $T_n = 6(7-n)$

(a) For first term,

On putting $n = 1$, we get

$$T_1 = 6(7-1) = 6 \times 6 = 36$$

and second term, $T_2 = 6(7-2) = 6 \times 5 = 30$

Now, common difference $(d) = T_2 - T_1$

$$= 30 - 36 = -6$$

(b) The sum of first 25 terms

$$S_{25} = \frac{25}{2}[2 \times 36 + (25-1) \times (-6)]$$

$$\left[\because S_n = \frac{n}{2}[2a + (n-1)d]\right]$$

$$= 25[36 - 72] = 25 \times (-36) = -900$$

Hence, the sum of first 25 terms is -900.

(iii) Given,

$\angle ADB = \angle BCA = 90°$

$AB = 10\text{ cm}, AD = 6\text{ cm}, BC = 2.4\text{ cm}$

and $DP = 4.5\text{ cm}$

(a) In ΔADP and ΔPCB,

$\angle ADP = \angle BCP = 90°$

$\angle APD = \angle BPC$ [vertically opposite angles]

So, by AA similarity criterion,

$\Delta APD \sim \Delta BPC$

(b) We have, $\Delta APD \sim \Delta BPC$

$\Rightarrow \quad \frac{6}{2.4} = \frac{4.5}{CP}$

$\Rightarrow \quad CP = 1.8\text{ cm}$

Now, in ΔBCP

Using Pythagoras theorem, we get

$BC^2 + CP^2 = PB^2$

$\Rightarrow \quad (2.4)^2 + (1.8)^2 = PB^2$

$\Rightarrow \quad PB^2 = 5.76 + 3.24 = 9$

$\Rightarrow \quad PB = 3\text{ cm}$

Hence, $BD = DP + PB = 4.5 + 3 = 7.5\text{ cm}$

(c) We know that

$\Delta ADP \sim \Delta BCP$

Therefore, $\frac{AD}{CB} = \frac{AP}{BP}$

$\Rightarrow \quad \frac{6}{2.4} = \frac{AP}{3} \Rightarrow AP = \frac{18}{2.4} = 7.5\text{ cm}$

Hence, the length of $PA = 7.5$ cm

(d) We know that

$\Delta APD \sim \Delta BPC$,

Then, $\frac{\text{ar}(\Delta APD)}{\text{ar}(\Delta BPC)} = \left(\frac{AD}{BC}\right)^2$

$= \left(\frac{6}{2.4}\right)^2 = \left(\frac{5}{2}\right)^2 = \frac{25}{4}$

Hence, ar ΔAPD : ar $\Delta BPC = 25 : 4$

7. (i) In the given figure,

$OM \perp AC$

and $\angle COM = 65°$

(a) We have,

$\angle COM = 65°$

$\because \quad OC = OA$ [radii of circle]

Since $OM \perp AC$

Therefore,

$AM = MC$

$\angle AOM = 65°$

Now, $\angle AOC = 65° + 65° = 130°$

$\therefore \quad \angle ABC = \frac{1}{2}\angle AOC = \frac{1}{2} \times 130° = 65°$

(b) In ΔABC,

$AB = AC$ [given]

Then, $\angle ABC = \angle ACB = 65°$ [from part (a)]

By angle sum property, we have

$\angle A + \angle B + \angle C = 180°$

$\Rightarrow \quad 65° + \angle BAC + 65° = 180°$

$\Rightarrow \quad \angle BAC = 180° - 130° = 50°$

(c) In ΔOMC,

$\angle COM = 65°$ and $\angle OMC = 90°$

$\therefore \quad \angle OCM = 90° - 65° = 25°$

$\because \quad \angle ACB = 65°$

$\therefore \quad \angle OCB = 65° - 25° = 40°$

Since, OC is perpendicular to PQ, therefore

$\angle OCQ = 90°$

$\Rightarrow \quad \angle OCB + \angle BCQ = 90°$

$\Rightarrow \quad \angle BCQ = 90° - 40°$

$\therefore \quad \angle BCQ = 50°$

(ii) Given,

$-3 + x \le \frac{7x}{2} + 2 < 8 + 2x, x \in I$

First we take,

$-3 + x \le \frac{7x}{2} + 2$

$\Rightarrow \quad -3 - 2 \le \frac{7x}{2} - x$

$\Rightarrow \quad -5 \le \frac{5x}{2}$

$\Rightarrow \quad x \ge -2$ ...(i)

and now, $\frac{7x}{2} + 2 < 8 + 2x$

$\Rightarrow \quad \frac{7x}{2} - 2x < 8 - 2 \Rightarrow \frac{3}{2}x < 6$

$\Rightarrow \quad x < 4$ ...(ii)

On combining Eqs. (i) and (ii), we get

$-2 \le x < 4$

Real number line representation,

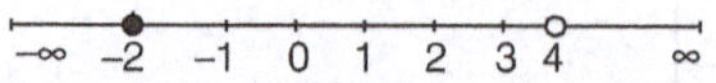

Hence, $x \in \{-2, -1, 0, 1, 2, 3\}$

(iii) (a) The coordinates of point A are $(0, 6)$ and point D are $(-3, 0)$.

(b) The coordinates of the vertices of ΔABC are $A(0, 6)$, $B(4, -4)$ and $C(-4, -2)$

The centroid of $\Delta ABC = \left(\frac{0 + 4 - 4}{3}, \frac{6 - 4 - 2}{3}\right)$

$= (0, 0)$ i.e. origin is the centroid

(c) Given point D divides AC in the ratio $k : 1$, as shown in the figure

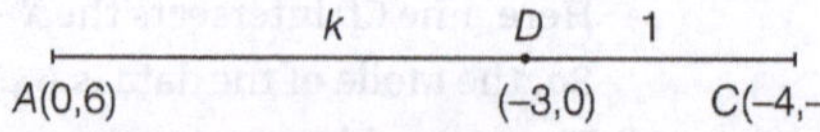

So, $(-3, 0) \equiv \left(\frac{-4k + 0}{k + 1}, \frac{-2k + 6}{k + 1}\right)$

On comparing the y-coordinate both sides, we get

$$\frac{-2k+6}{k+1}=0$$

$\Rightarrow \quad 2k=6 \Rightarrow k=3$

(d) The line BD passes through the points $(4, -4)$ and $(-3, 0)$.

The equation of line BD is

$$y+4=\frac{0+4}{-3-4}(x-4)$$

$\Rightarrow \quad -7y-28=4x-16$

$\Rightarrow \quad 4x+7y+12=0$

which is the required equation of line BD.

8. (i) Let $p(x)=3x^3+8x^2-15x+k$

Since, $(x-1)$ is a factor of $p(x)$, therefore by factor theorem $p(1)=0$

$\Rightarrow \quad 3(1)^3+8(1)^2-15(1)+k=0$

$\Rightarrow \quad 3+8-15+k=0$

$\Rightarrow \quad k=4$

Given, $(x-1)$ is a factor of $p(x)$.

$$x-1)3x^3+8x^2-15x+4(3x^2+11x-4$$
$$3x^3-3x^2$$
$$-\quad +$$
$$11x^2-15x+4$$
$$11x^2-11x$$
$$-\quad +$$
$$-4x+4$$
$$-4x+4$$
$$+\quad -$$
$$0$$

we get, $3x^2+11x-4$ which is a quadratic polynomial.

$3x^2+11x-4=3x^2+12x-x-4$

$=3x(x+4)-1(x+4)$

$=(x+4)(3x-1)$

Hence, $3x^3+8x^2-15x+4=(x-1)(x+4)(3x-1)$

(ii) Given, letters are

A, D, M, N, O, S, U, Y

Total number of letters = 8

(a) The number of letters in word 'MONDAY = 6

Number of favourable outcomes = 6

$\therefore$ Probability that the card drawn is a letter of the word "Monday"

$$=\frac{\text{Number favourable outcomes}}{\text{Total number of outcomes}}=\frac{6}{8}=\frac{3}{4}$$

(b) The letters which do not appear in MONDAY are S and U.

$\therefore$ Probability that the card drawn is a letter which does not appear in 'MONDAY' $=\frac{2}{8}=\frac{1}{4}$

(c) Number of letters which appear in MONDAY and SUNDAY = 4

$\therefore$ Probability that the card drawn is a letter which appear in both (SUNDAY and MONDAY)

$$=\frac{4}{8}=\frac{1}{2}$$

(iii) Given, radius of spherical vessel $(r_1)=28$ cm

$\because$ Volume of oil in spherical vessel $(V)=\frac{4}{3}\pi(28)^3\times\frac{3}{4}$

$$=\pi\times(28)^3 \text{ cm}^3$$

Since, the oil is poured into a cylindrical vessel.

The radius of vessel (cylindrical) $(r_2)=21$ cm

Let h be the height of oil in cylindrical vessel.

Therefore,

Volume of oil = Volume of oil in cylindrical vessel

$\Rightarrow \quad (28)^3\times\pi=\pi\times(21)^2\times h$

$\Rightarrow \quad h=\frac{(28)^3}{(21)^3}=\left(\frac{4}{3}\right)^3=\frac{64}{27}=2.37\text{ cm}$

Hence, the height of the oil in cylindrical vessel is 2.37 cm.

9. (i) Given, radius of circle = 9 cm

and $PA=24$ cm

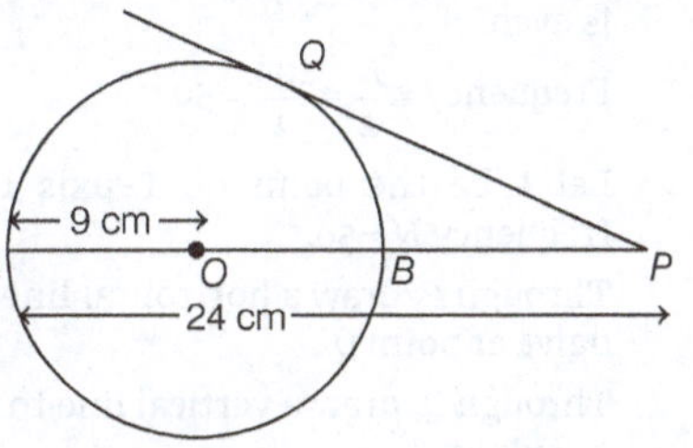

From the figure,

$AB=2\times9=18$ cm

$PB=AP-AB=24-18=6$ cm

Now, we know that

$PA\times PB=PQ^2$

$\Rightarrow \quad PQ^2=6\times24=144$

$\therefore \quad PQ=12$ cm

Hence, the length of tangent is 12 cm.

(ii) Given, invested amount = ₹ 3300

Value for each share = ₹ 100 = Nominal value

Rate of premium = 10%

Dividend declared by the company = 12%

(a) Market value of one share

$$=100+\frac{10}{100}\times100=100+10=₹\ 110$$

Number of shares

$$=\frac{\text{Money invested}}{\text{Market value for each share}}=\frac{3300}{110}=30$$

(b) Annual dividend = Number of shares × Rate of dividend × Nominal value

$=30\times12\%\times100$

$=₹\ 3600$

(iii) (a) From the given table,

On the graph paper, we plot the following points $A(25, 2)$, $B(30, 6)$, $C(35, 18)$, $D(40, 38)$, $D(45, 66)$, $F(50, 88)$, $G(55, 96)$ and $H(60, 100)$

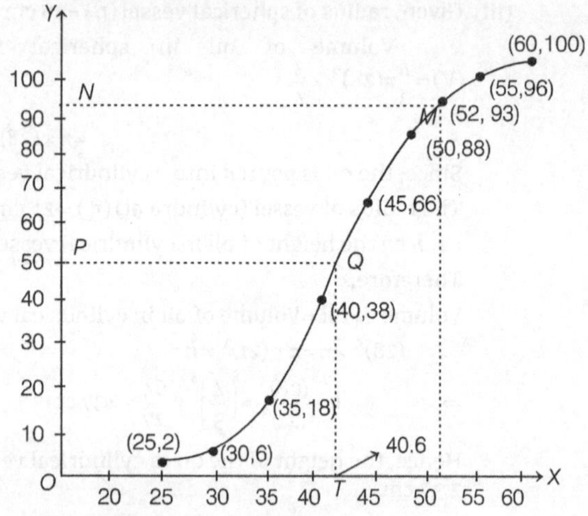

Join all these points by a free hand curve.

Here, the number of policy holder = 100 which is even.

$$\text{Frequency} = \frac{N}{2} = \frac{100}{2} = 50$$

Let P be the point on Y-axis representing frequency $N = 50$.

Through P, draw a horizontal line to meet the ogive at point Q.

Through Q, draw a vertical line to meet the X-axis at T.

$\therefore$ Median = 40.6

(b) On drawing a line $x = 52$ parallel to Y-axis which cuts ogive at point (52, 93)

$\therefore$ Number of policy holders whose age is above 52 yr $= 100 - 93 = 7$

10. (i) (a) Price of Laddu = ₹ 500 per kg

Price for 2 kg laddus $= 2 \times 500 =$ ₹ 1000

Rate of GST on laddu = 5%

$$\text{GST} = ₹\,1000 \times \frac{5}{100} = ₹\,50$$

Cost of laddus = ₹ 1000 + ₹ 50 = ₹ 1050

Also, price of pastries = ₹ 100 per piece

Price for 12 pieces $= 12 \times 100 =$ ₹ 1200

Rate of GST = 18%

$$\text{GST} = \frac{1200 \times 18}{100} = ₹\,216$$

Cost of pastries = ₹ 1200 + ₹ 216 = ₹ 1416

Total GST paid = ₹ 50 + ₹ 216 = ₹ 266

(b) Total bill amount = Cost of laddus with GST + Cost of pastries with GST

= ₹ 1050 + ₹ 1416 = ₹ 2466

(ii) (a) Given, $kx - y + 4 = 0$ ...(i)

and $2y = 6x + 7$ ...(ii)

From Eq. (i), we get

$$y = kx + 4$$

On comparing with $y = mx + c$, we get

Slope of Eq. (i), $m_1 = k$

and from Eq. (ii),

$$y = 3x + \frac{7}{2}$$

On comparing with $y = mx + c$, we get

Slope of Eq. (ii) $m_2 = 3$

Since, line (i) and line (ii) are perpendicular.

Therefore,

$$m_1 \times m_2 = -1$$

$$\Rightarrow \quad k \times 3 = -1 \text{ or } k = -\frac{1}{3}$$

(b) Let $6x - 2y + \lambda = 0$ be the equation of line parallel to $2y = 6x + 7$, passing through $(-1, 1)$.

Then, $6 \times (-1) - 2 \times 1 + \lambda = 0$

$\Rightarrow \quad -6 - 2 + \lambda = 0$

$\Rightarrow \quad \lambda = 8$

Hence, the equation of line is $6x - 2y + 8 = 0$

or $\quad 2y = 6x + 8$

(iii) Given $\angle ABC = 90°$, $AB = 6$ cm and $BC = 8$ cm.

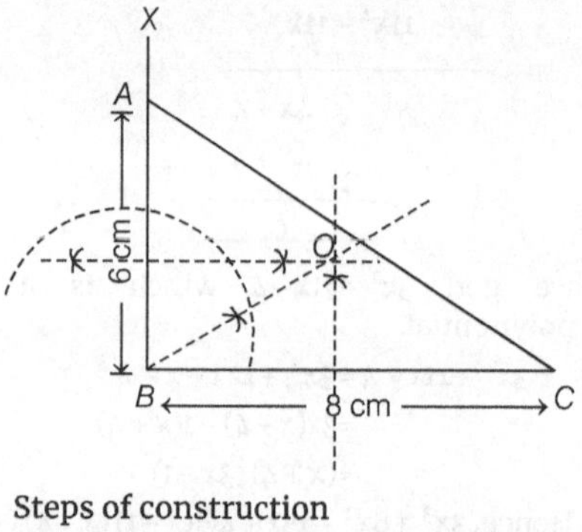

Steps of construction

(i) **Step I** Draw a line segment $BC = 8$ cm.

Step II From point B, draw $\angle ABC = 90°$.

Step III Taking radius 6 cm, with B as a centre cut $BA = 6$ cm from BX.

Step IV Join A to C which is the required ΔABC.

(a) Draw perpendicular bisector of BC which is the required locus of points equidistant from B and C.

(b) Draw perpendicular bisector of AB which is the required locus of points equidistant from A and B.

(c) The intersection of perpendicular bisector of BC and AB is O which is the required point.

(d) Draw the angle bisector of $\angle ABC$ which is the locus of points which are equidistant from BA and BC.

QUESTION PAPER 2025

A HIGHLY SIMULATED Sample Question Paper for ICSE Class X

Mathematics (Fully solved)

GENERAL INSTRUCTIONS

1. Answers to this paper must be written on the paper provided separately.
2. You will not be allowed to write during the first 15 minutes. This time is to be spent in reading the question paper.
3. The time given at the head of this paper is the time allowed for writing the answers.
4. Attempt all **questions** from **Section A** and **any 4 questions** from **Section B.**
5. All working, including rough work, must be clearly shown and must be done on the same sheet as the rest of the answer.
6. Omission of essential working will result in loss of marks.
7. The intended marks for questions or parts of questions are given in bracket [ ].
8. Mathematical tables are provided.

Time : 2.5 Hrs **Max. Marks : 80**

Section A

[40 *Marks*]

(Attempt all questions from this section)

1. Choose the correct answer to the question from the given options. [15]

(Do not copy the questions, write the correct answer only.)

(i) The given quadratic equation $3x^2 + \sqrt{7}x + 2 = 0$ has

(a) two equal real roots
(b) two distinct real roots
(c) more than two real roots
(d) no real roots

(ii) Mr. Anuj deposits ₹ 500 per month for 18 months in a recurring deposit account at a certain rate. If he earns ₹ 570 as interest at the time of maturity, then his matured amount is

(a) ₹ $(500 \times 18 + 570)$
(b) ₹ $(500 \times 19 + 570)$
(c) ₹ $(500 \times 18 \times 19 + 570)$
(d) ₹ $(500 \times 9 \times 19 + 570)$

(iii) Which of the following cannot be the probability of any event?

(a) $\frac{5}{4}$ (b) 0.25 (c) $\frac{1}{33}$ (d) 67%

(iv) The equation of the line passing through origin and parallel to the line $3x + 4y + 7 = 0$ is

(a) $3x + 4y + 5 = 0$ (b) $4x - 3y - 5 = 0$
(c) $4x - 3y = 0$ (d) $3x + 4y = 0$

(v) If $A = \begin{bmatrix} 0 & 1 \\ 1 & 0 \end{bmatrix}$, then A^2 is equal to

(a) $\begin{bmatrix} 1 & 1 \\ 0 & 0 \end{bmatrix}$ (b) $\begin{bmatrix} 0 & 0 \\ 1 & 1 \end{bmatrix}$

(c) $\begin{bmatrix} 1 & 0 \\ 0 & 1 \end{bmatrix}$ (d) $\begin{bmatrix} 0 & 1 \\ 1 & 0 \end{bmatrix}$

(vi) In the given diagram, chords AC and BC are equal. If $\angle ACD = 120°$, then $\angle AEC$ is

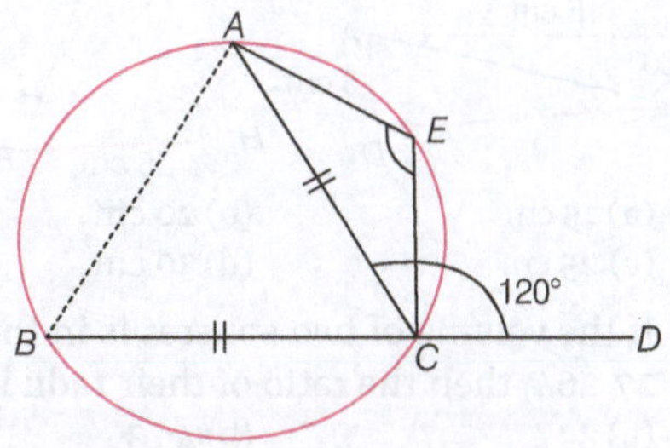

(a) 30° (b) 60°
(c) 90° (d) 120°

(vii) The factor common to the two polynomials $x^2 - 4$ and $x^3 - x^2 - 4x + 4$ is

(a) $(x + 1)$ (b) $(x - 1)$
(c) $(x + 2)$ (d) $(x - 2)$

(viii) A man invested in a company paying 12% dividend on its share. If the percentage return on his investment is 10%, then the shares are

(a) at par
(b) below par
(c) above par
(d) cannot be determined

(ix) **Statement I** The point which is equidistant from three non-collinear points D, E and F is the circumcentre of the ΔDEF.

Statement II The incentre of a triangle is the point where the bisector of the angles intersects.

(a) Both the Statements are true
(b) Both the Statements are false
(c) Statement I is true and Statement II is false
(d) Statement I is false and Statement II is true

(x) **Assertion** (A) If $\sin^2 A + \sin A = 1$, then $\cos^4 A + \cos^2 A = 1$.

Reason (R) $1 - \sin^2 A = \cos^2 A$

(a) (A) is true, (R) is false
(b) (A) is false, (R) is true
(c) Both (A) and (R) are true and (R) is the correct reason for (A)
(d) Both (A) and (R) are true and (R) is the incorrect reason for (A)

(xi) In the given diagram $\Delta ABC \sim \Delta EFG$. If $\angle ABC = \angle EFG = 60°$, then the length of the side FG is

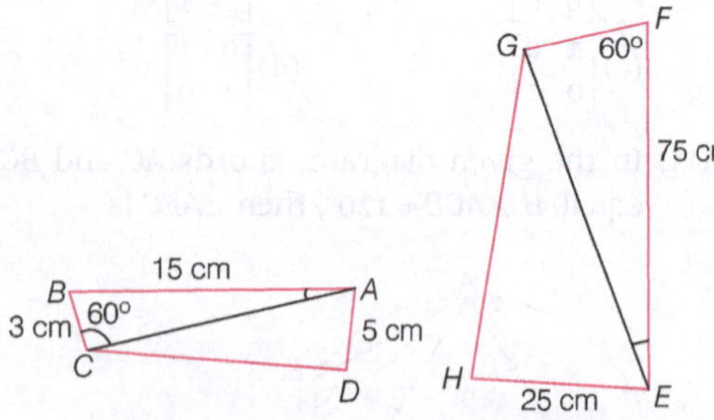

(a) 15 cm (b) 20 cm
(c) 25 cm (d) 30 cm

(xii) If the volume of two spheres is in the ratio 27 : 64, then the ratio of their radii is

(a) 3 : 4 (b) 4 : 3
(c) 9 : 16 (d) 16 : 9

(xiii) The marked price of an article is ₹ 1375. If the CGST is charged at a rate of 4%, then the price of the article including GST is

(a) ₹ 55 (b) ₹ 110
(c) ₹ 1430 (d) ₹ 1485

(xiv) The solution set for $0 < -\frac{x}{3} < 2, x \in Z$ is

(a) $\{-5, -4, -3, -2, -1\}$
(b) $\{-6, -5, -4, -3, -2, -1\}$
(c) $\{-5, -4, -3, -2, -1, 0\}$
(d) $\{-6, -5, -4, -3, -2, -1, 0\}$

(xv) **Assertion** (A) The mean of first 9 natural numbers is 4.5.

Reason (R) Mean

$$= \frac{\text{Sum of all the observations}}{\text{Total number of observations}}$$

(a) (A) is true, (R) is false
(b) (A) is false, (R) is true
(c) Both (A) and (R) are true and (R) is the correct reason for (A)
(d) Both (A) and (R) are true and (R) is the incorrect reason for (A)

2. (i) Solve the following quadratic equation $2x^2 - 5x - 4 = 0$. [4]

Give your answer correct to three significant figures.

(Use mathematical tables for this question)

(ii) Mrs. Rao deposited ₹ 250 per month in a recurring deposit account for a period of 3 yr. She received ₹ 10110 at the time of maturity. Find

(a) the rate of interest.

(b) how much more interest Mrs. Rao will receive if she had deposited ₹ 50 more per month at the same rate of interest and for the same time.

(iii) In ΔABC, $\Delta ABC = 90°$, $AB = 20$ cm, $AC = 25$ cm, DE is perpendicular to AC such that $\angle DEA = 90°$ and $DE = 3$ cm as shown in the given figure.

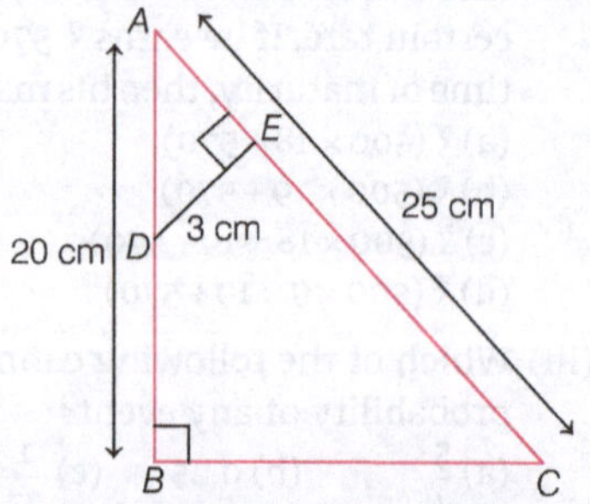

(a) Prove that $\Delta ABC \sim \Delta AED$.

(b) Find the lengths of BC, AD and AE.

(c) If $BCED$ represents a plot of land on a map whose actual area on ground is 576 m^2, then find the scale factor of the map.

3. (i) Use ruler and compass for the following construction. Construct a ΔABC, where $AB = 6$ cm, $AC = 4.5$ cm and $\angle BAC = 120°$. Construct a circle circumscribing the ΔABC. Measure and write down the length of the radius of the circle.

(ii) If $A = \begin{bmatrix} 1 & 2 \\ 3 & 4 \end{bmatrix}$, $B = \begin{bmatrix} 2 & 1 \\ 4 & 2 \end{bmatrix}$ and $C = \begin{bmatrix} -5 & 1 \\ 7 & -4 \end{bmatrix}$. [4]

Find

(a) $A + C$ (b) $B(A + C)$

(c) $5B$ (d) $B(A + C) - 5B$

(iii) In the given graph $ABCD$ is a parallelogram [5]

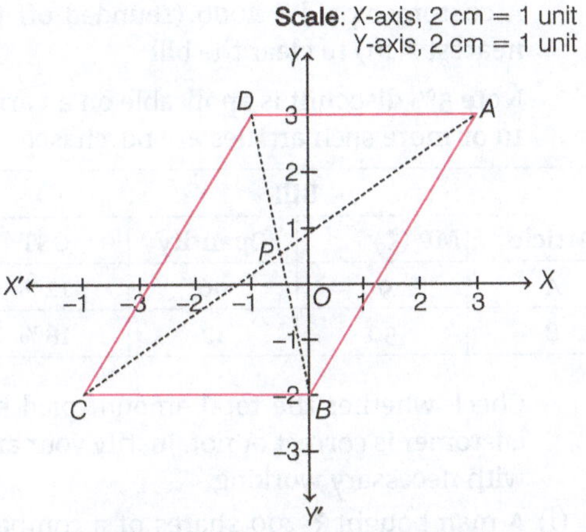

Using the graph, answer the following

(a) write down the coordinates of A, B, C and D.

(b) calculate the coordinates of P, the point of intersection of the diagonals AC and BD.

(c) find the slope of sides CB and DA, and verify that they represent parallel lines.

(d) find the equation of the diagonal AC.

Section B [40 *Marks*]

(Attempt any four questions from this section)

4. (i) Solve the following inequation, write the solution set and represent it on the real number line. [3]

$$2x - \frac{5}{3} < \frac{3x}{5} + 10 \le \frac{4x}{5} + 11;\ x \in R$$

(ii) The first term of an Arithmetic Progression (AP) is 5, the last term is 50 and their sum is 440. Find [3]

(a) the number of terms

(b) common difference

(iii) Prove that $\dfrac{(\cot A + \tan A - 1)(\sin A + \cos A)}{\sin^3 A + \cos^3 A} = \sec A \cdot \operatorname{cosec} A$

5. (i) Using properties of proportion, find the value of x [3]

$$\frac{6x^2 + 3x - 5}{3x - 5} = \frac{9x^2 + 2x + 5}{2x + 5};\ x \ne 0$$

(ii) Its is given that $(x - 2)$ is a factor of polynomial $2x^3 - 7x^2 + kx - 2$. Find

(a) the value of k

(b) hence, factorise the resulting polynomial completely.

(iii) A solid wooden capsule is shown in Figure 1. The capsule is formed of a cylindrical block and two hemispheres.

Find the sum of total surface area of the three parts as shown in Figure 2. Given, the radius of the capsule is 3.5 cm and the length of the cylindrical block is 14 cm.

$\left(\text{Use } \pi = \dfrac{22}{7}\right)$

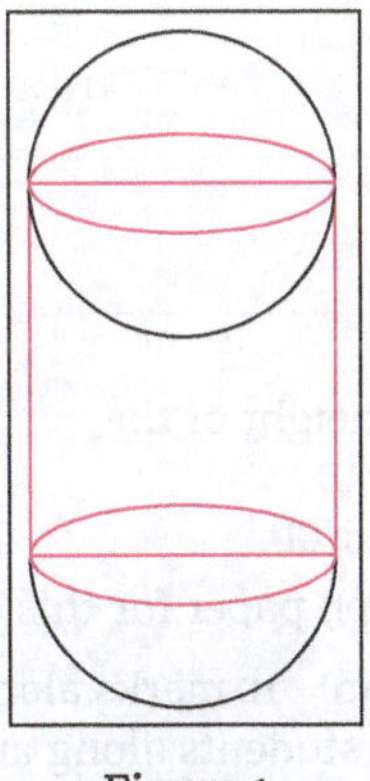

Figure 1

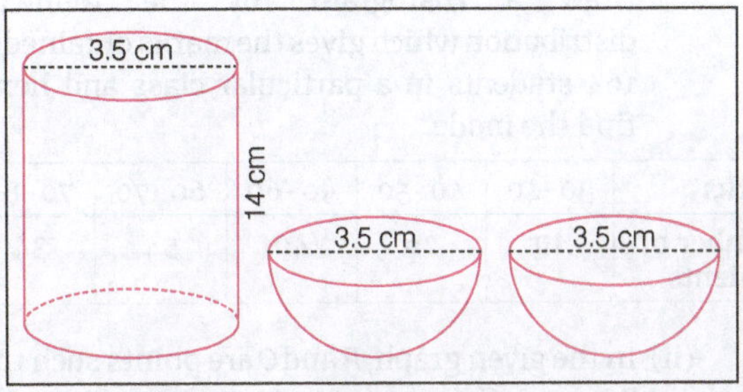

Figure 2

6. (i) Use a graph paper for this question taking 2 cm = 1 unit along both axes. [5]

(a) Plot $A(1, 3)$, $B(1, 2)$ and $C(3, 0)$.

(b) Reflect A and B on the X-axis and name their images as E and D, respectively. Write down their coordinates.

(c) Reflect A and B through the origin and name their images as F and G respectively.

(d) Reflect A, B and C on the Y-axis and name their images as J, I and H, respectively.

(e) Join all the points $A, B, C, D, E, F, G, H, I$ and J in order and name the closed figure so formed.

(ii) In the given diagram, AB is a vertical tower 100 m away from the foot of a 30 storied building CD. The angles of depression from the points C and E, (E being the mid-point of CD), are 35° and 14° respectively.

(Use mathematical table for the required values rounded off correct to two places of decimals only)

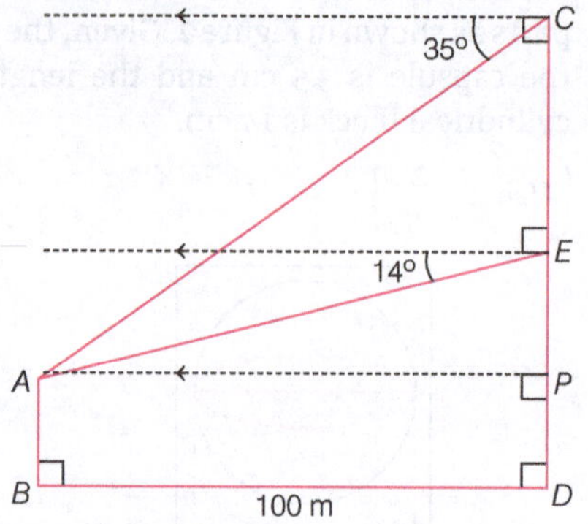

Find the height of the

(a) tower AB

(b) building CD

7. (i) Use a graph paper for this question.

(Take 2 cm = 10 marks along one axis and 2 cm = 10 students along another axis).

Draw a Histogram for the following distribution which gives the marks obtained by 164 students in a particular class and hence find the mode.

Marks	30-40	40-50	50-60	60-70	70-80
Number of Students	10	26	40	54	34

(ii) In the given graph, P and Q are points such that PQ cuts off intercepts of 5 units and 3 units along the X-axis and Y-axis, respectively. Line RS is perpendicular to PQ and passes through the origin. Find the

(a) coordinates of P and Q

(b) equation of line RS

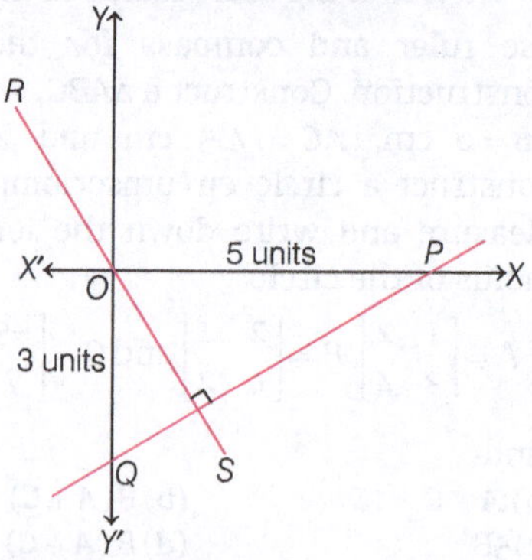

(iii) Refer to the given bill.

A customer paid ₹ 2000 (rounded off to the nearest ₹ 10) to clear the bill.

Note 5% discount is applicable on an article if 10 or more such articles are purchased.

Bill			
Article	MP (₹)	Quantity	GST
A	190	06	12%
B	50	12	18%

Check whether the total amount paid by the customer is correct or not. Justify your answer with necessary working.

8. (i) A man bought ₹ 200 shares of a company at 25% premium. If he received a return of 5% on his investment. Find the [3]

(a) market value

(b) dividend percent declared

(c) number of shares purchased, if annual dividend is ₹ 1000.

(ii) For the given frequency distribution, find the [3]

(a) mean, to the nearest whole number

(b) median

x	10	11	12	13	14	15	16
f	3	2	2	6	3	5	3

(iii) Mr. and Mrs. Das were travelling by car from Delhi to Kasauli for a holiday. Distance between Delhi and Kasauli is approximately 350 km (via NH 152D). Due to heavy rain they had to slow down. The average speed of the car was reduced by 20 km/h and time of the journey increased by 2 h. Find

(a) the original speed of the car.

(b) with the reduced speed, the number of hours they took to reach their destination.

9. (i) A hollow sphere of external diameter 10 cm and internal diameter 6 cm is melted and made into a solid right circular cone of height 8 cm. Find the radius of the cone so formed. [3]

$\left[\text{Use } \pi = \frac{22}{7}\right]$

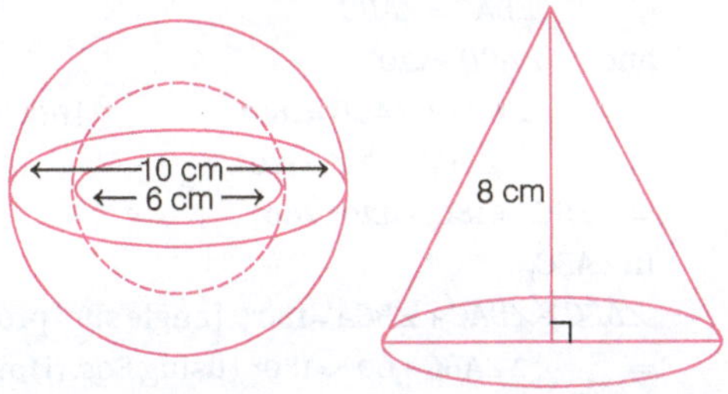

(ii) Ms. Sushmita went to a fair and participated in a game. The game consisted of a box having number cards with numbers from 01 to 30. The three prizes were as per the given table [3]

Prize	Number on the card drawn at random is a
Wall Clock	perfect square
Water Bottle	even number which is also a multiple of 3
Purse	prime number

Find the probability of winning a

(a) Wall Clock

(b) Water Bottle

(c) Purse

(iii) X, Y, Z and C are the points on the circumference of a circle with centre O. AB is a tangent to the circle at X and ZY = XY. Given $\angle OBX = 32°$ and $\angle AXZ = 66°$.

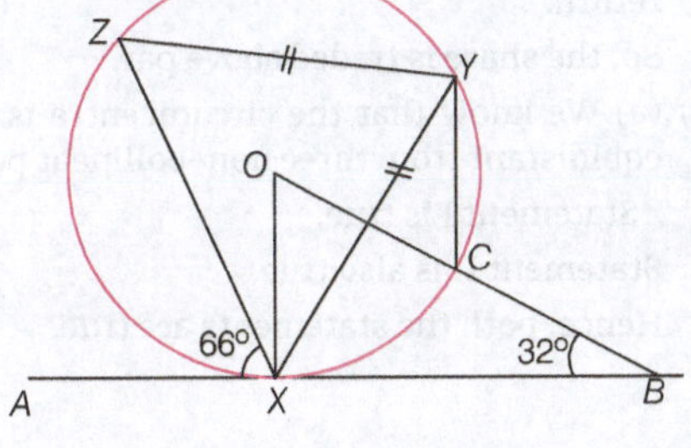

Find

(a) $\angle BOX$ (b) $\angle CYX$

(c) $\angle ZYX$ (d) $\angle OXY$

10. (i) If 1701 is the nth term of the Geometric Progression (GP) 7, 21, 63, ..., find [3]

(a) the value of n.

(b) hence find the sum of the n terms of the GP.

(ii) In the given diagram O is the centre of the circle. Chord SR produced meets the tangent XTP at P. [3]

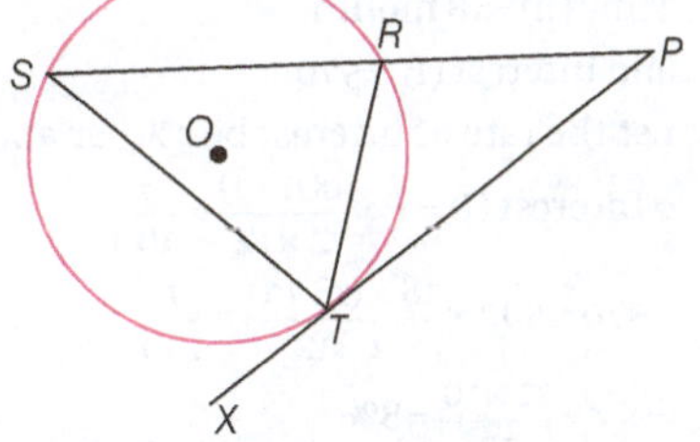

(a) Prove that $\Delta PTR \sim \Delta PST$

(b) Prove that $PT^2 = PR \times PS$

(c) If $PR = 4$ cm and $PS = 16$ cm, find the length of the tangent PT.

(iii) The given graph represents the monthly salaries (in ₹) of workers of a factory

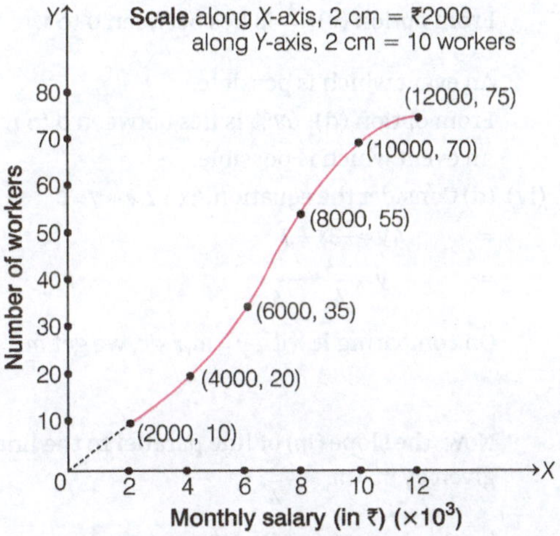

Using graph answer the following

(a) the total number of workers

(b) the median class

(c) the lower-quartile class

(d) number of workers having monthly salary more than or equal to ₹ 6000 but less than ₹ 10000.

SOLUTIONS

1. (i) (d) Given, quadratic equation is $3x^2+\sqrt{7}x+2=0$

On comparing it with $ax^2+bx+c=0$, we get

$a=3, b=\sqrt{7}$ and $c=2$

Now, discriminant, $D=b^2-4ac$

$$=(\sqrt{7})^2-4\times3\times2$$
$$=7-24=-17<0$$

$\therefore$ The roots of given quadratic equation are not real.

(ii) (a) Given, money deposited per month $(P)=$ ₹ 500

Time $(n)=18$ months

and interest $(I)=570$

Let the rate of interest be r% per annum

$\because$ Interest $(I)=P\times\dfrac{n(n+1)}{2\times12}\times\dfrac{r}{100}$

$\therefore 570=500\times\dfrac{18\times(18+1)}{2\times12}\times\dfrac{r}{100}$

$\Rightarrow r=\dfrac{12\times10}{15}=8\%$

Now, maturity value $=P\times n+I$

$=$ ₹ $(500\times18+570)$

(iii) (a) From option (a), $\frac{5}{4}$ is not lies between 0 to 1. An event which is not possible.

From option (b), 0.25 is lies between 0 to 1. An event which is possible.

From option (c), $\frac{1}{33}$ is lies between 0 to 1. An event which is possible.

From option (d), 67% is lies between 0 to 1. An event which is possible.

(iv) (d) Consider the equation, $3x+4y+7=0$ ...(i)

$\Rightarrow 4y=-3x-7$

$\Rightarrow y=\dfrac{-3}{4}x-\dfrac{7}{4}$

On comparing it with $y=m_1x+c$, we get $m_1=-\dfrac{3}{4}$ ...(ii)

Now, the slope (m) of line parallel to the line (i) is given by $m=m_1=-\dfrac{3}{4}$.

i.e. the slope of required line $=m=-\dfrac{3}{4}$ ...(iii)

Hence, the equation of line passing through origin (0,0) and having slope $-\frac{3}{4}$ is

$$y-0=-\frac{3}{4}(x-0)$$

$\Rightarrow y=\dfrac{-3}{4}x$

$\Rightarrow 4y=-3x$

$\Rightarrow 3x+4y=0$, which is the required equation.

(v) (c) Given, $A=\begin{bmatrix}0&1\\1&0\end{bmatrix}$

$\because A^2=A\cdot A=\begin{bmatrix}0&1\\1&0\end{bmatrix}\begin{bmatrix}0&1\\1&0\end{bmatrix}$

$=\begin{bmatrix}0\times0+1\times1 & 0\times1+1\times0\\1\times0+0\times1 & 1\times1+0\times0\end{bmatrix}$

$=\begin{bmatrix}1&0\\0&1\end{bmatrix}$

(vi) (d) In the given figure,

Chords AC and BC are equal

$\therefore \Delta ABC$ is a isosceles triangle.

$\therefore \angle BAC=\angle ABC$ ...(i)

and $\angle ACD=120°$ [given]

$\because \angle BCA+\angle ACD=180°$ [linear pair]

$\Rightarrow \angle BCA+120°=180°$

$\Rightarrow \angle BCA=180°-120°=60°$ ...(ii)

In ΔABC,

$\angle ABC+\angle BAC+\angle BCA=180°$ [angle sum property]

$\Rightarrow 2\angle ABC+60°=180°$ [using Eqs. (i) and (ii)]

$\Rightarrow \angle ABC=60°$

Since, $ABCE$ is a cyclic quadrilateral

$\therefore \angle ABC+\angle AEC=180°$ [sum of opposite angles]

$\Rightarrow 60°+\angle AEC=180°$

$\Rightarrow \angle AEC=120°$

*(vii) (c), (d) We have, two polynomials x^2-4 and x^3-x^2-4x+4

By factorisation,

$x^2-4=x^2-2^2$

$=(x+2)(x-2)$ [$\because a^2-b^2=(a+b)(a-b)$]

and $x^3-x^2-4x+4=x^2(x-1)-4(x-1)$

$=(x-1)(x^2-4)$

$=(x-1)(x^2-2^2)$

$=(x-1)(x+2)(x-2)$

Therefore, common factors are $(x+2)$ and $(x-2)$.

Hence, option (c) and (d) are correct.

(viii) (c) We have,

Dividend $=12\%$

Return on investment $=10\%$

Since, the dividend is greater than the expected return.

So, the share is traded above par.

(ix) (a) We know that the circumcentre is the point equidistant from three non-collinear points.

$\therefore$ Statement I is true.

Statement II is also true.

Hence, both the statements are true.

(x) (c) Given, $\sin^2 A + \sin A = 1$ ...(i)

$\Rightarrow \sin A = 1 - \sin^2 A$

$\Rightarrow \sin A = \cos^2 A$ ...(ii)

Now, $\cos^4 A + \cos^2 A = 1$

LHS $= \cos^4 A + \cos^2 A$

$= (\cos^2 A)^2 + \cos^2 A$

$= (\sin A)^2 + \sin A$ [using Eq. (ii)]

$= \sin^2 A + \sin A$

$= 1$ [using Eq. (i)]

= RHS

Hence, both (A) and (R) are true and (R) is the correct reason for (A).

(xi) (a) In the given diagram, we have

$\Delta ABC \sim \Delta EFG$

and $\angle EFG = 60°$

$\therefore \angle ABC = \angle EFG = 60°$

Also given, side $AB = 15$ cm, $BC = 3$ cm

Side $EF = 75$ cm

Since, $\Delta ABC \sim \Delta EFG$, so the corresponding sides are proportional.

Therefore, $\frac{AB}{EF} = \frac{BC}{FG}$

$\Rightarrow \frac{15}{75} = \frac{3}{FG}$

$\Rightarrow FG = \frac{3 \times 75}{15} \Rightarrow FG = 15$ cm

(xii) (a) The volume of sphere having radius r_1,

$V_1 = \frac{4}{3}\pi r_1^3$

and volume of sphere having radius r_2,

$V_2 = \frac{4}{3}\pi r_2^3$

$\because$ Given that $\frac{V_1}{V_2} = \frac{27}{64}$

$\therefore \frac{\frac{4}{3}\pi r_1^3}{\frac{4}{3}\pi r_2^3} = \frac{27}{64} = \frac{r_1^3}{r_2^3} = \frac{3^3}{4^3}$

$\Rightarrow \left(\frac{r_1}{r_2}\right)^3 = \left(\frac{3}{4}\right)^3$

$\therefore \frac{r_1}{r_2} = \frac{3}{4}$

$\therefore r_1 : r_2 = 3 : 4$

(xiii) (d) Given that

Market price = ₹ 1375

CGST rate = 4%

Since, GST includes both CGST and SGST

$\therefore$ The total GST rate = 4% + 4% = 8%

$\therefore$ Price including GST $= 1375 + \frac{8}{100} \times 1375$

$= 1375 + 110 =$ ₹ 1485

(xiv) (a) We have, inequality

$0 < -\frac{x}{3} < 2, x \in Z$

$\therefore 0 < -\frac{x}{3}$ and $-\frac{x}{3} < 2$

[splitting into two inequations]

Consider, $0 < -\frac{x}{3} \Rightarrow 0 \times (-3) > -\frac{x}{3} \times (-3)$

[multiplying by −3 on both sides, inequality sign changed]

$\Rightarrow 0 > x$ ...(i)

$\Rightarrow x < 0$

Consider, $-\frac{x}{3} < 2$

$\Rightarrow -\frac{x}{3} \times (-3) > 2 \times (-3)$

[multiplying by −3 on both sides, inequality sign changed]

$\Rightarrow x > -6$ ...(ii)

Since, $x \in Z$

$\therefore x \in \{-5, -4, -3, -2, -1\}$ [using Eqs. (i) and (ii)]

$\therefore$ The required solution set for given inequalities is $\{-5, -4, -3, -2, -1\}$

(xv) (b) First 9 natural numbers are 1, 2, 3, ..., 9.

Sum $= \frac{9(9+1)}{2}$ $\left[\because \text{sum of } n \text{ natural numbers} = \frac{n(n+1)}{2}\right]$

$= 45$

$\because$ Mean $= \frac{\text{Sum of all the observations}}{\text{Total number of observations}}$

$\therefore$ Mean $= \frac{45}{9} = 5$

Hence, (A) is false, (R) is true.

2. (i) Given, equation is $2x^2 - 5x - 4 = 0$

On comparing it with $ax^2 + bx + c = 0$, we get

$a = 2, b = -5$ and $c = -4$

On substituting the values of a, b and c in quadratic formula $x = \frac{-b \pm \sqrt{b^2 - 4ac}}{2a}$, we get

$x = \frac{-(-5) \pm \sqrt{(-5)^2 - 4(2)(-4)}}{2(2)}$

$= \frac{5 \pm \sqrt{25 + 32}}{4} = \frac{5 \pm \sqrt{57}}{4}$

$\Rightarrow x = \frac{5 + \sqrt{57}}{4} = \frac{5 + 7.55}{4} = 3.14$

[taking +ve sign]

or $x = \frac{5 - \sqrt{57}}{4} = \frac{5 - 7.55}{4} = -0.638$ [taking −ve sign]

Hence, solution for the given quadratic equation to three significant is 3.14 or − 0.638.

(ii) Given, monthly deposit = ₹ 250

Period = 3 yr

$\therefore$ Total deposit = $250 \times 12 \times 3 =$ ₹ 9000

and maturity value = ₹ 10110 [given]

Interest received = Total maturity amount − Total deposited amount

$= 10110 - 9000 =$ ₹ 1110

Formula for maturity value of a recurring deposit

$$M = P \times n + \frac{P \times n(n+1) \times r}{2 \times 12 \times 100}$$

Where, M = Maturity value

P = Monthly deposit

n = number of months

r = rate of interest per annum

$$\therefore \quad 10110 = 250 \times 36 + \frac{250 \times 36 \times 37 \times r}{2 \times 12 \times 100}$$

$$\Rightarrow 10110 - 9000 = \frac{250 \times 36 \times 37 \times r}{2 \times 12 \times 100}$$

$$\Rightarrow \quad 1110 = \frac{125 \times 3 \times 37 \times r}{100}$$

$$\Rightarrow \quad r = \frac{1110 \times 100}{125 \times 3 \times 37} = \frac{111000}{13875}$$

$$\Rightarrow \quad r = 8\%$$

(a) The rate of interest = 8% per annum

(b) Since, she deposited ₹ 50 more per month.

$\therefore$ Monthly deposit = ₹ 250 + ₹ 50 = ₹ 300

We have, period = 3 yr, rate of interest = 8%

Formula for interest of a recurring deposit,

$$I = \frac{P \times n(n+1) \times r}{2 \times 12 \times 100}$$

$$\therefore \quad I = \frac{300 \times 36 \times 37 \times 8}{2 \times 12 \times 100}$$

$$= 3 \times 3 \times 37 \times 4 = 1332$$

$\therefore$ Interest = ₹ 1332

$\therefore$ Extra interest earned = 1332 − 1110 = ₹ 222

(iii) Given that

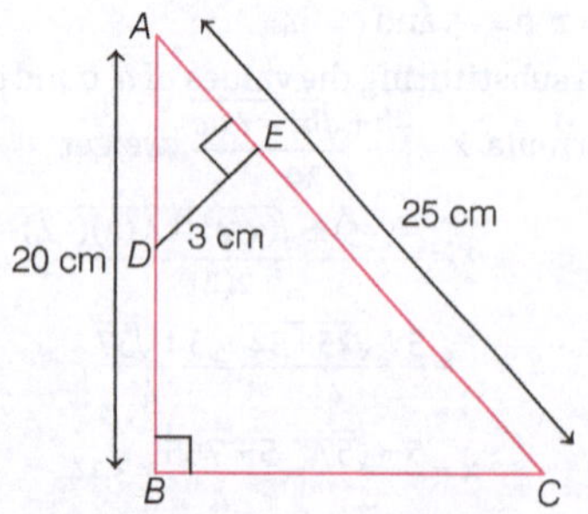

In ΔABC,

$\angle ABC = 90°$, $AB = 20$ cm, $AC = 25$ cm

Since, DE is perpendicular to AC.

$\therefore \quad \angle DEA = 90°$

Also given $DE = 3$ cm

(a) In ΔABC and ΔAED,

$\angle ABC = \angle DEA$ [each 90°]

$\angle BAC = \angle EAD$ [$\angle A$ is common]

$\therefore \quad \Delta ABC \sim \Delta AED$ [by AA similarity]

Hence proved

(b) In right angled ΔABC,

$AC^2 = AB^2 + BC^2$ [by Pythagoras theorem]

$\Rightarrow \quad (25)^2 = (20)^2 + (BC)^2$

$\Rightarrow \quad (BC)^2 = 625 - 400 = 225$

$\Rightarrow \quad BC = 15$ cm

Since, $\Delta ABC \sim \Delta AED$

$$\therefore \quad \frac{AB}{AE} = \frac{AC}{AD}$$ [sides are proportional in similar triangles]

$$\Rightarrow \quad \frac{20}{AE} = \frac{25}{AD} \quad ...(i)$$

and $\frac{BC}{ED} = \frac{AC}{AD} \Rightarrow \frac{15}{3} = \frac{25}{AD}$

[the sides are proportional in similar triangle and given $DE = 3$ cm]

$$\Rightarrow \quad AD = \frac{3 \times 25}{15}$$

$$\Rightarrow \quad AD = 5 \text{ cm}$$

From Eq. (i), we get

$$\frac{20}{AE} = \frac{25}{5} \Rightarrow AE = \frac{20 \times 5}{25}$$

$$\Rightarrow \quad AE = 4 \text{ cm}$$

Hence, the length of BC, AD and AE are 15 cm, 5 cm and 4 cm, respectively.

(c) We have, the actual area of plot $BCED = 576 \text{ m}^2$

$$\because (\text{Scale factor})^2 = \frac{\text{Area on map}}{\text{Actual area on ground}}$$

From the given figure, the area of $BCED$ on the map

= Area of ΔABC − Area of ΔAED

$$= \frac{1}{2}(BC \times AB) - \frac{1}{2}(DE \times AE)$$

[$\because$ area of right angled triangle $= \frac{1}{2}$(base × height)]

$$= \frac{1}{2}(15 \times 20) - \frac{1}{2}(3 \times 4)$$

$$= 150 - 6 = 144 \text{ m}^2$$

$$\therefore \quad (\text{Scale factor})^2 = \frac{144}{5760000}$$

[$\because 1 \text{ m}^2 = 10000 \text{ cm}^2$]

$$\therefore \quad \text{Scale factor} = \sqrt{\frac{144}{5760000}}$$

$$= \frac{12}{2400} = 0.005$$

$\therefore$ Scale factor of the map is 0.005.

3. (i) Given, $AB = 6$ cm, $AC = 4.5$ cm and $\angle BAC = 120°$

Steps of construction

Step I Draw a line segment $AB = 6$ cm

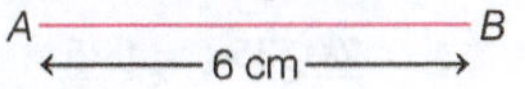

Step II Draw a measure of angle 120° at A i.e. $BAX = 120°$

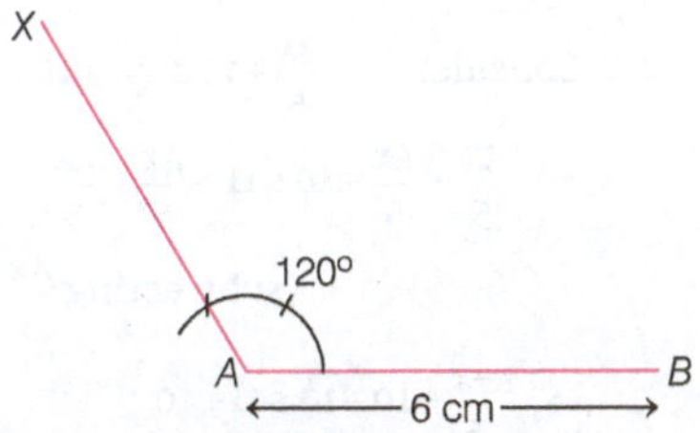

Step III Take a distance $AC = 4.5$ cm and cut an arc from AX and mark point C, then join BC.

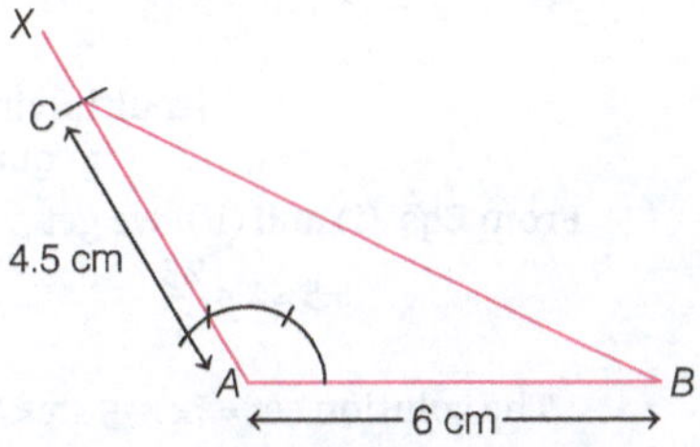

Step IV Draw the perpendicular bisector of AB, AC and mark O as the intersecting point of these perpendicular bisectors.

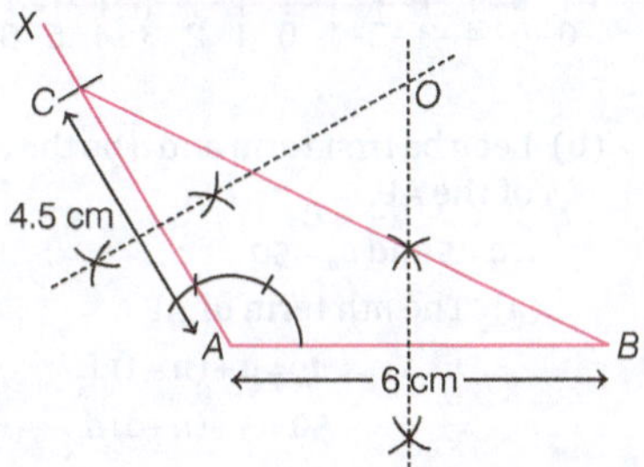

Step V Draw a circle with radius OC and centre O by joining OC.

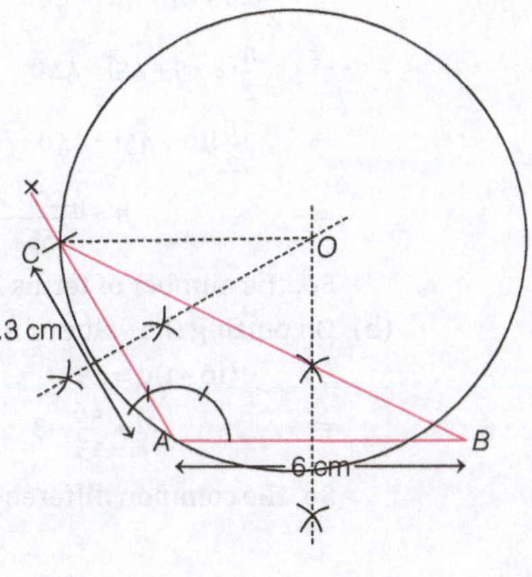

The circle passing through A, B and C is required.

On measuring, radius $OC = 5$ cm

(ii) Given, $A = \begin{bmatrix} 1 & 2 \\ 3 & 4 \end{bmatrix}$, $B = \begin{bmatrix} 2 & 1 \\ 4 & 2 \end{bmatrix}$ and $C = \begin{bmatrix} -5 & 1 \\ 7 & -4 \end{bmatrix}$

(a) $A + C = \begin{bmatrix} 1 & 2 \\ 3 & 4 \end{bmatrix} + \begin{bmatrix} -5 & 1 \\ 7 & -4 \end{bmatrix}$

$= \begin{bmatrix} -4 & 3 \\ 10 & 0 \end{bmatrix}$

(b) $B(A + C)$

$= \begin{bmatrix} 2 & 1 \\ 4 & 2 \end{bmatrix} \begin{bmatrix} -4 & 3 \\ 10 & 0 \end{bmatrix}$ [using part (a)]

$= \begin{bmatrix} 2 & 6 \\ 4 & 12 \end{bmatrix}$

(c) $5B = 5\begin{bmatrix} 2 & 1 \\ 4 & 2 \end{bmatrix}$

$= \begin{bmatrix} 10 & 5 \\ 20 & 10 \end{bmatrix}$

(d) $B(A + C) - 5B$

$\because$ From part (b), we have

$$B(A + C) = \begin{bmatrix} 2 & 6 \\ 4 & 12 \end{bmatrix} \quad \text{...(i)}$$

and from part (c), we have

$$5B = \begin{bmatrix} 10 & 5 \\ 20 & 10 \end{bmatrix} \quad \text{...(ii)}$$

$\therefore B(A + C) - 5B = \begin{bmatrix} 2 & 6 \\ 4 & 12 \end{bmatrix} - \begin{bmatrix} 10 & 5 \\ 20 & 10 \end{bmatrix}$

$= \begin{bmatrix} -8 & 1 \\ -16 & 2 \end{bmatrix}$

[using Eqs. (i) and (ii)]

(iii) In the given graph, we have $ABCD$ is a parallelogram.

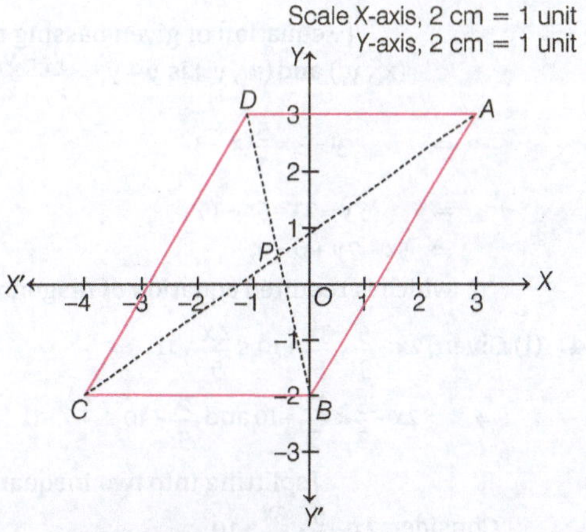

(a) From the graph,

The coordinates of $A = (3, 3)$

The coordinates of $B = (0, -2)$

The coordinates of $C = (-4, -2)$

The coordinates of $D = (-1, 3)$

(b) We know that the intersection point of the diagonals of a parallelogram is the mid-point of both diagonal

$\therefore$ Mid-point of diagonal AC,

$$P=\left(\frac{3+(-4)}{2}, \frac{3+(-2)}{2}\right)$$

$$=\left(-\frac{1}{2}, \frac{1}{2}\right)$$

Mid-point of diagonal BD,

$$P=\left(\frac{0+(-1)}{2}, \frac{-2+3}{2}\right)$$

$$=\left(-\frac{1}{2}, \frac{1}{2}\right)$$

Hence, the coordinate of point P which is the intersection point of diagonal AC and BD is $\left(-\frac{1}{2}, \frac{1}{2}\right)$.

(c) Slope of side CB,

$$m_{CB}=\frac{-2-(-2)}{-4-0} \qquad \left[\because m=\frac{y_2-y_1}{x_2-x_1}\right]$$

$$=0$$

Slope of side DA,

$$m_{DA}=\frac{3-(3)}{(-1)-(3)} \qquad \left[\because m=\frac{y_2-y_1}{x_2-x_1}\right]$$

$$=0$$

Since, both slopes are equal.

Hence, sides CB and DA represent parallel lines.

(d) We have, two points

$A(3, 3)$ and $C(-4, -2)$

$\therefore$ Equation of diagonal AC

$$= y-3=\frac{(-2)-3}{-4-3}(x-3)$$

[$\because$ equation of given passing through (x_1, y_1) and (x_2, y_2) is $y-y_1=\frac{y_2-y_1}{x_2-x_1}(x-x_1)$]

$$\Rightarrow \quad y-3=\frac{5}{7}(x-3)$$

$$\Rightarrow \quad 7y-21=5x-15$$

$$\Rightarrow \quad 5x-7y+6=0,$$

which is required equation of diagonal AC.

4. (i) Given, $2x-\frac{5}{3}<\frac{3x}{5}+10\le\frac{4x}{5}+11$

$$\Rightarrow \quad 2x-\frac{5}{3}<\frac{3x}{5}+10 \text{ and } \frac{3x}{5}+10\le\frac{4x}{5}+11$$

[splitting into two inequations]

Consider, $2x-\frac{5}{3}<\frac{3x}{5}+10$

$$\Rightarrow \quad 2x-\frac{3x}{5}-\frac{5}{3}<\frac{3x}{5}-\frac{3x}{5}+10$$

[subtracting $\frac{3x}{5}$ from both sides]

$$\Rightarrow \quad \frac{10x-3x}{5}-\frac{5}{3}+\frac{5}{3}<10+\frac{5}{3}$$

[adding $\frac{5}{3}$ from both sides]

$$\Rightarrow \quad \frac{7x}{5}<\frac{35}{3}\Rightarrow x<\frac{25}{3} \qquad \text{...(i)}$$

[multiplying both sides by $\frac{5}{7}$]

Consider, $\frac{3x}{5}+10\le\frac{4x}{5}+11$

$$\Rightarrow \quad \frac{3x}{5}-\frac{4x}{5}+10\le 11+\frac{4x}{5}-\frac{4x}{5}$$

[subtracting $\frac{4x}{5}$ from both sides]

$$\Rightarrow \quad \frac{-x}{5}+10-10\le 11-10$$

[subtracting 10 from both sides]

$$\Rightarrow \quad -\frac{x}{5}\le 1\Rightarrow x\ge -5 \qquad \text{...(ii)}$$

[multiplying both sides by -5, inequality sign changed]

From Eqs. (i) and (ii), we get

$$-5\le x<\frac{25}{3}$$

$\therefore$ The solution set $=\{x: -5\le x<\frac{25}{3}, x\in R\}=\left[-5, \frac{25}{3}\right)$

Representation of the solution set on the number line is shown by dark line.

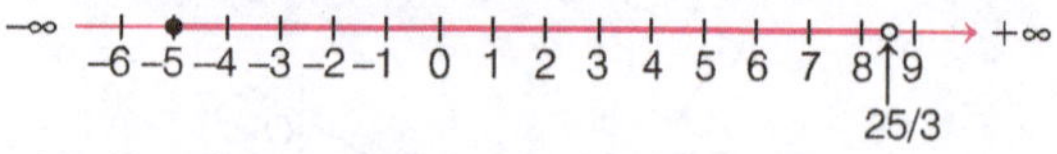

(ii) Let a be first term and d be the common difference of the AP.

$\therefore a=5$ and $a_n=50$

(a) The nth term of AP,

$$a_n=a+(n-1)d$$

$$\Rightarrow \quad 50=5+(n-1)d$$

$$\Rightarrow \quad (n-1)d=50-5=45 \qquad \text{...(i)}$$

Now, $S_n=440$ [given]

$$\therefore \quad \frac{n}{2}[2a+(n-1)d]=440$$

$$\Rightarrow \quad \frac{n}{2}[2\times 5+45]=440 \qquad \text{[from Eq. (i)]}$$

$$\Rightarrow \quad \frac{n}{2}[10+45]=440$$

$$\Rightarrow \quad n=\frac{440\times 2}{55}=16$$

So, the number of terms is 16.

(b) On putting the value of n in Eq. (i), we get

$$(16-1)d=45$$

$$\Rightarrow \quad d=\frac{45}{15}=3$$

So, the common difference is 3.

(iii) $\text{LHS} = \dfrac{(\cot A + \tan A - 1)(\sin A + \cos A)}{\sin^3 A + \cos^3 A}$

$= \dfrac{\left(\dfrac{\cos A}{\sin A} + \dfrac{\sin A}{\cos A} - 1\right)(\sin A + \cos A)}{(\sin A + \cos A)(\sin^2 A + \cos^2 A - \sin A \cdot \cos A)}$

$\left[\because \cot\theta = \dfrac{\cos\theta}{\sin\theta}, \tan\theta = \dfrac{\sin\theta}{\cos\theta} \text{ and } (a^3 + b^3) = (a+b)(a^2 + b^2 - ab)\right]$

$= \dfrac{(\cos^2 A + \sin^2 A - \sin A \cos A)(\sin A + \cos A)}{(\sin A \cdot \cos A)(\sin A + \cos A)(1 - \sin A \cos A)}$

$[\because \sin^2\theta + \cos^2\theta = 1]$

$= \dfrac{1}{\sin A \cdot \cos A}$

$= \sec A \cdot \operatorname{cosec} A$

$\left[\because \dfrac{1}{\sin\theta} = \operatorname{cosec}\theta \text{ and } \dfrac{1}{\cos\theta} = \sec\theta\right]$

= RHS **Hence proved.**

5. (i) We have, $\dfrac{6x^2 + 3x - 5}{3x - 5} = \dfrac{9x^2 + 2x + 5}{2x + 5}; x \neq 0$

Applying componendo and dividendo rule, we get

$\dfrac{(6x^2 + 3x - 5) + (3x - 5)}{(6x^2 + 3x - 5) - (3x - 5)} = \dfrac{9x^2 + 2x + 5) + (2x + 5)}{(9x^2 + 2x + 5) - (2x + 5)}$

$\Rightarrow \dfrac{6x^2 + 6x - 10}{6x^2} = \dfrac{9x^2 + 4x + 10}{9x^2}$

$\Rightarrow 9x^2[6x^2 + 6x - 10] = 6x^2[9x^2 + 4x + 10]$

$\Rightarrow 54x^4 + 54x^3 - 90x^2 = 54x^4 + 24x^3 + 60x^2$

$\Rightarrow 54x^3 - 24x^3 - 90x^2 - 60x^2 = 0$

$\Rightarrow 30x^3 - 150x^2 = 0$

$\Rightarrow x^2(30x - 150) = 0$

Here, $x^2 = 0$ or $30x - 150 = 0$

Since, $x \neq 0$ [given]

So, $30x - 150 = 0$

$\Rightarrow 30x = 150$

$\Rightarrow x = \dfrac{150}{30} = 5$

Hence, the value of x is 5.

(ii) Given, $(x - 2)$ is a factor of the polynomial

$2x^3 - 7x^2 + kx - 2 = f(x)$ (say)

(a) Then we have, by factor theorem

$f(2) = 0$

As $x - 2 = 0$

$\Rightarrow x = 2$

On substituting $x = 2$ in given polynomial equation,

$2(2)^3 - 7(2)^2 + k \times 2 - 2 = 0$

$\Rightarrow 16 - 28 + 2k - 2 = 0 \Rightarrow -14 + 2k = 0$

$\Rightarrow 2k = 14$

$\Rightarrow k = \dfrac{14}{2} = 7$

(b) Let divide $f(x)$ by $(x - 2)$ using long division method,

$$
\begin{array}{r l}
 & 2x^2 - 3x + 1 \\
(x-2) \big) & 2x^3 - 7x^2 + 7x - 2 \\
 & 2x^3 \mp 4x^2 \\
\hline
 & -3x^2 + 7x - 2 \\
 & -3x^2 \pm 6x \\
 & + \quad - \\
\hline
 & x - 2 \\
 & x - 2 \\
 & - \quad + \\
\hline
 & 0
\end{array}
$$

The other factors of $f(x)$ are the factors of $2x^2 - 3x + 1$.

Now, factorise $2x^2 - 3x + 1$

$\Rightarrow 2x^2 - 2x - x + 1$

$\Rightarrow 2x(x - 1) - 1(x - 1)$

$\Rightarrow (2x - 1)(x - 1)$

Hence, $2x^3 - 7x^2 + 7x - 2$

$= (x - 2)(2x - 1)(x - 1)$

(iii) Given, radius of the cylinder = 3.5 cm

and length of the cylindrical block = 14 cm

$\therefore$ The surface area of the cylinder $= 2\pi rh$

$= 2 \times \dfrac{22}{7} \times 3.5 \times 14 = \dfrac{2156}{7} = 308 \text{ cm}^2$

and surface area of the two hemisphere

$= 2 \times 3\pi r^2 = 6 \times \dfrac{22}{7} \times (3.5)^2$

$= \dfrac{1617}{7} = 231 \text{ cm}^2$

Now, the sum of total surface area of three parts = Surface area of cylinder + Surface area of two hemispheres

$= 308 + 231 = 539 \text{ cm}^2$

Hence, the total surface area of capsule is 539.

6. (i) (a) We can plot the given points on the graph paper as follows

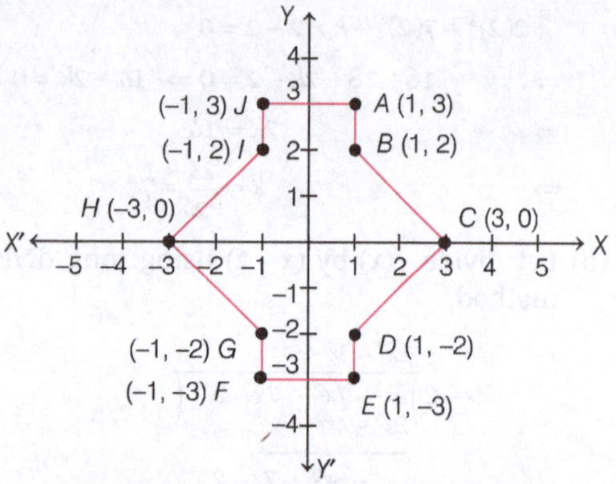

(b) When points $A(1, 3)$ and $B(1, 2)$ are reflected in X-axis then the image of points $A(1, 3)$ and $B(1, 2)$ are $E(1, -3)$ and $D(1, -2)$, respectively.

(c) When points $A(1, 3)$ and $B(1, 2)$ are reflected through the origin then the image of points $A(1, 3)$ and $B(1, 2)$ are $F(-1, -3)$ and $Q(-1, -2)$ respectively.

(d) When points $A(1, 3)$, $B(1, 2)$ and $C(3, 0)$ are reflected through the Y-axis then the image of points $A(1, 3)$, $B(1, 2)$ and $C(3, 0)$ are $J(-1, 3)$, $I(-1, 2)$ and $H(-3, 0)$, respectively.

(e) Join all the points $A, B, C, D, E, F, G, H, I$ and J in order and the closed figure so formed is decagon.

(ii) Given, $BD = AP = 100\,\text{m}$, $\angle EAP = 14°$ and $\angle CAP = 35°$

(a) In ΔEPA, we have

$$\tan 14° = \frac{PE}{AP} \quad \left[\because \tan\theta = \frac{\text{perpendicular}}{\text{base}}\right]$$

$$\Rightarrow \quad 0.2493 = \frac{PE}{100}$$

$[\because \tan 14° = 0.2493$ and $AP = 100\,\text{m}]$

$$\Rightarrow \quad PE = 0.2493 \times 100 = 24.93\,\text{m}$$

In ΔAPC, we have

$$\tan 35° = \frac{PC}{AP} \Rightarrow 0.7002 = \frac{PC}{100}$$

$[\because \tan 35° = 0.7002$ and $AP = 100\,\text{m}]$

$$\Rightarrow \quad PC = 0.7002 \times 100 = 70.02\,\text{m}$$

Now, $PC = PE + CE$

$$\Rightarrow \quad CE = PC - PE = 70.02 - 24.93 = 45.09\,\text{m}$$

Since, E is the mid-point of CD.

$$\therefore \quad CE = ED$$

$$\Rightarrow \quad 45.09 = EP + PD \quad [\because ED = PE + PD]$$

$$\Rightarrow \quad 45.09 = 24.93 + PD$$

$$\Rightarrow \quad PD = 45.09 - 24.93 = 20.16\,\text{m}$$

$$\because \quad AP \parallel BD$$

$$\therefore \quad AB = PD = 20.16\,\text{m}$$

So, height of the tower AB is 20.16 m.

(b) $\because CD = CE + PE + PD$

$\therefore CD = 45.09 + 24.93 + 20.16 = 90.18\,\text{m}$

Hence, the height of building CD is 90.18 m.

7. (i)

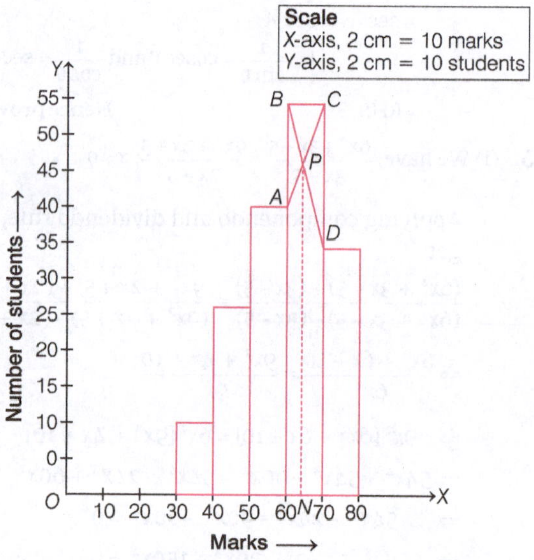

In the highest rectangle, draw two straight lines AC and BD which intersect at P. Through point P, draw a vertical line to meet the X-axis at N. The abscissa of the point N represents 64 (approx.). Hence, the required mode is 64 (approx.).

(ii) (a) P and Q are points such that PQ cuts off intercepts of 5 units and 3 units along the X-axis and Y-axis, respectively.

$\therefore$ The coordinates of P and Q are $(5, 0)$ and $(0, -3)$, respectively.

(b) Slope of line $PQ = \dfrac{y_2 - y_1}{x_2 - x_1} = \dfrac{-3-0}{0-5} = \dfrac{3}{5}$

Let m be the slope of line RS, then

$$\frac{3}{5} \times m = -1 \Rightarrow m = -\frac{5}{3}$$

[$\because$ both lines PQ and RS are perpendicular to each other, so $m_1 m_2 = -1$]

Now, equation of a line RS passes through $(0,0)$ having slope $-\frac{5}{3}$ is $y-0=-\frac{5}{3}(x-0)$

[$\because$ equation of a line passes through a point (x_1, y_1) and has a slope m is $y-y_1=m(x-x_1)$]

$$\Rightarrow \quad 3y+5x=0$$

(iii) The total cost of article A without GST

$= 190\times 6 = ₹\ 1140$

GST on article A

$= 12\%$ of $1140 = \frac{12}{100}\times 1140 = ₹\ 136.8$

The total cost of article B without GST

$= 50\times 12 = ₹\ 600$

Since, 12 articles of B are purchased.

$\therefore$ 5% discount is applicable on article B.

Discount on article B = 5% of ₹ 600

$= \frac{5}{100}\times 600 = ₹\ 30$

$\therefore$ Total cost of article B after discount $= 600-30$

$= ₹570$

GST on article B = 18% of ₹570

$= \frac{18}{100}\times 570 = ₹\ 102.60$

Now, total cost of article A including GST

$= 1140+136.80 = ₹\ 1276.80$

and total cost of article B including GST

$= 570+102.60$

$= ₹\ 672.60$

$\therefore$ Total bill amount $= 1276.80+672.60$

$= ₹\ 1949.40$

So, the actual bill amount is ₹ 1949.40

Rounding off ₹ 1949.40 to the nearest ₹ 10 gives ₹ 1950.

$\because$ The customer paid ₹ 2000, which in more than ₹1950.

$\therefore$ The total amount paid by the customer is not correct.

8. (i) (a) Given, face value of one share = ₹ 200 and premium = 25%

$\therefore$ Market value of one share = Face value + Premium

$= ₹\ 200 + ₹\left(200\times\frac{25}{100}\right)$

$= ₹\ 200 + ₹\ 50 = ₹\ 250$

(b) We know that

Dividend percentage × Face value

= Rate of return × Market value

$\Rightarrow$ Dividend percentage $\times 200 = 5\% \times 250$

$\Rightarrow$ Dividend percentage $= \frac{5\times 2.50}{200}\%$

$= 6.25\%$

(c) Given, annual dividend = ₹ 1000

Dividend on one share $= \frac{6.25}{100}\times 200$

$= ₹\ 12.5$

$\therefore$ Number of shares $= \frac{\text{Annual dividend}}{\text{Dividend per share}}$

$= \frac{1000}{12.5} = 80$

So, the number of shares is 80.

(ii) (a) Table for given data is

x_i	f_i	$x_i f_i$
10	3	30
11	2	22
12	2	24
13	6	78
14	3	42
15	5	75
16	3	48
Total	$\Sigma f_i = 24$	$\Sigma f_i x_i = 319$

Here, $\Sigma f_i = 24$ and $\Sigma f_i x_i = 319$

$\therefore$ Mean $(\bar{x}) = \frac{\Sigma f_i x_i}{\Sigma f_i} = \frac{319}{24}$

$= 13.29 \approx 13$

So, the mean of the given data is 13.

(b) The cumulative frequency of first observation is the same as its frequency, since there is no frequency before it.

Now, the cumulative frequency table is

x	f	Cumulative frequency (cf)
10	3	3
11	2	5
12	2	7
13	6	13
14	3	16
15	5	21
16	3	24

Here, $n = 24$ (even)

$\therefore$ Median $= \frac{1}{2} \times$ value of $\left[\left(\frac{n}{2}\right)\text{th} + \left(\frac{n}{2}+1\right)\text{th}\right]$ observation

$= \frac{1}{2} \times$ value of $\left[\left(\frac{24}{2}\right)\text{th} + \left(\frac{24}{2}+1\right)\text{th}\right]$ observation

$= \frac{1}{2} \times$ value of [12th + 13th] observation

Both 12th and 13th observations lie in the cumulative frequency 13 and its corresponding value of x_i is 13.

$\therefore$ Median $= \frac{1}{2} \times (13+13) = \frac{1}{2} \times 26 = 13$

Hence, the median is 13.

(iii) (a) Given, distance between Delhi and kasauli $= 350$ km

Let x km/h be the original speed of the car and t be the original time.

According to the question,

$$x = \frac{350}{t} \quad \text{...(i)}$$

$\left[\because \text{speed} = \frac{\text{distance}}{\text{time}}\right]$

and $(x-20) = \frac{350}{(t+2)}$

$\Rightarrow (x-20)(t+2) = 350$ ...(ii)

On substituting $t = \frac{350}{x}$ from Eq. (i) in Eq. (ii), we get

$$(x-20)\left[\frac{350}{x}+2\right] = 350$$

$\Rightarrow 350 + 2x - \frac{7000}{x} - 40 - 350 = 0$

$\Rightarrow 2x^2 - 7000 - 40x = 0$

$\Rightarrow x^2 - 20x - 3500 = 0$

$\Rightarrow x^2 - 70x + 50x - 3500 = 0$ [by splitting method]

$\Rightarrow x(x-70) + 50(x-70) = 0$

$\Rightarrow (x-70)(x+50) = 0$

$\Rightarrow x = 70$ or $x = -50$

$\because$ Speed cannot be negative.

$\therefore x = 70$ km/h

Hence, the original speed of the car is 70 km/h.

(b) On putting the value of x in Eq. (i), we get

$$t = \frac{350}{70} = 5\text{ h}$$

$\therefore$ With reduced speed, the number of hours they took to reach their destination $= 5 + 2 = 7$

9. (i) Given, external diameter of hollow sphere $= 10$ cm

$\therefore$ External radius $(r_1) = \frac{10}{2} = 5$ cm

and internal diameter of hollow sphere $= 6$ cm

$\therefore$ Internal radius $(r_2) = \frac{6}{2} = 3$ cm

$\therefore$ Volume of hollow sphere $= \frac{4}{3}\pi(r_1^3 - r_2^3)$

$= \frac{4}{3}\pi[5^3 - 3^3]$

$= \frac{4}{3}\pi[125 - 27]$

$= \frac{392\pi}{3}$ cm^3 ...(i)

Let r be the radius and h be the height of the cone.

$\because$ The hollow sphere recasted into a cone.

$\because$ Volume of cone = Volume of hollow sphere.

$\therefore \frac{1}{3}\pi r^2 h = \frac{392\pi}{3}$ [from Eq. (i)]

$\Rightarrow \frac{1}{3} \times \pi \times r^2 \times 8 = \frac{392\pi}{3}$ [$\because h = 8$ cm]

$\Rightarrow r^2 = \frac{392}{8} = 49$

$\therefore r = 7$ [taking positive square root]

Hence, the radius of the cone is 7 cm.

(ii) Given, the game consisted of a box having number cards with numbers from 01 to 30.

$\therefore$ Total numbers from 1 to 30 = 30

(a) The perfect squares from 1 to 30 are 1, 4, 9, 16, 25.

$\therefore$ Total number of perfect squares numbers = 5

$\therefore$ Probability of winning a wall clock

$= \frac{5}{30} = \frac{1}{6}$

(b) Even numbers which is also a multiple of 3 from 1 to 30 are 6, 12, 18, 24 and 30.

$\therefore$ Total number of even numbers which is also a multiple of 3 = 5

$\therefore$ Probability of winning a water bottle $= \frac{5}{30} = \frac{1}{6}$

(c) The prime numbers from 1 to 30 are 2, 3, 5, 7, 11, 13, 17, 19, 23 and 29.

$\therefore$ Total number of prime numbers = 10

$\therefore$ Probability of winning a purse

$= \frac{10}{30} = \frac{1}{3}$

(iii) Given, $ZY = XY$, $\angle OBX = 32°$ and $\angle AXZ = 66°$

(a) Here, $\angle OXB = \angle OXA = 90°$

[tangent is perpendicular to the radius at the point of contact]

In ΔOXB, we have

$\angle OXB + \angle XOB + \angle OBX = 180°$

[by angle sum property of a triangle]

$\Rightarrow \quad 90° + \angle BOX + 32° = 180$

$\Rightarrow \quad \angle BOX = 180° - 122° = 58°$

(b) Since, angle subtended by an arc at the centre is twice the angle subtended at the remaining part of the circumference of the circle.

$\therefore \quad \angle CYX = \frac{1}{2} \times \angle COX = \frac{1}{2} \times 58° = 29°$

(c) From alternate segment theorem

$\angle ZYX = \angle ZXA = 66°$

(d) Now, $\angle OXZ = \angle OXA - \angle ZXA$

$= 90° - 66° = 24°$

Since, $\quad ZY = XY$

$\therefore \quad \angle YZX = \angle YXZ$

[angles opposite to equal sides are equal]

In ΔXYZ,

$\angle YZX + \angle YXZ + \angle XYZ = 180°$

[by angle sum property of a triangle]

$\Rightarrow \quad 2\angle YXZ + 66° = 180°$

$\Rightarrow \quad 2\angle YXZ = 114°$

$\Rightarrow \quad \angle YXZ = \frac{114°}{2} = 57°$

Now, $\angle OXY = \angle YXZ - \angle OXZ$

$= 57° - 24° = 33°$

10. (i) Given, geometric progression is 7, 21, 63, ...

Here, first term, $a = 7$

Common ratio, $r = \frac{21}{7} = 3$

Also given, nth term of GP $= 1701$

(a) $\therefore T_n = a \cdot r^{n-1} = 1701$

$\Rightarrow \quad 7(3)^{n-1} = 1701$

$\Rightarrow \quad (3)^{n-1} = \frac{1701}{7} = 243$

$\Rightarrow \quad (3)^{n-1} = (3)^5$

$\therefore \quad n - 1 = 5$

$\Rightarrow \quad n = 6$

(b) We know that

Sum of n terms of GP, $S_n = \frac{a(r^n - 1)}{r - 1}, r > 1$

$\Rightarrow \quad S_n = \frac{7(3^6 - 1)}{3 - 1}$

$\Rightarrow \quad S_n = \frac{7(729 - 1)}{2}$

$\Rightarrow \quad S_n = \frac{7 \times 728}{2} = 7 \times 364 = 2548$

Hence, the sum of n terms of the given GP is 2548.

(ii) (a) Given, O is the centre of the circle XTP is a tangent to the circle at T.

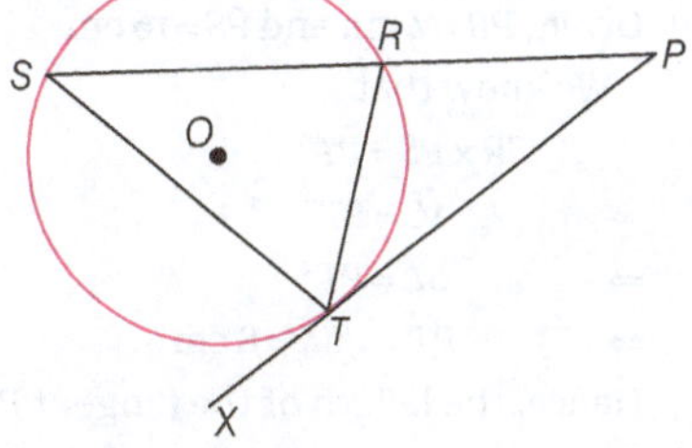

In ΔPTR and ΔPST,

$\angle P = \angle P$ [common angle]

$\Rightarrow \quad \angle PTR = \angle RST$ [angles in alternate segment]

$\therefore \quad \Delta PTR \sim \Delta PST$ [by AA similarity]

Hence proved.

(b) **Given** Let SR be the chord of a circle with centre O and tangent to the circle at T meets the chord SR produced at P.

To prove $PT^2 = PR \times PS$

Constructions Draw $OM \perp SR$ and join RO, SO, OP and OT.

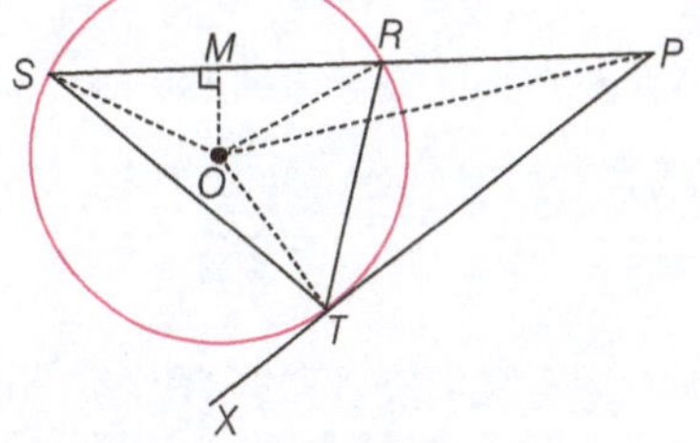

Proof Here, $RM = MS$ ...(i)

[$\because$ perpendicular from the centre bisect the chord]

Now, $PR \times PS = (PM - RM)(PM + MS)$

$= (PM - RM)(PM + RM)$

[from Eq. (i)]

$\Rightarrow \quad PR \times PS = PM^2 - RM^2$

[$\because (a-b)(a+b) = a^2 - b^2$]

$= PM^2 - [RO^2 - OM^2]$

[by Pythagoras theorem, in ΔRMO, $RM^2 = RO^2 - OM^2$]

$= PM^2 - RO^2 + OM^2$

$= PM^2 + OM^2 - RO^2 = PO^2 - RO^2$

[by Pythagoras theorem in ΔPMO, $PM^2 + OM^2 = PO^2$]

$= PO^2 - OT^2$

[$\because RO = OT$, radii of the same circle]

$= PT^2$ [by Pythagoras theorem, in ΔPTO, $PO^2 - OT^2 = PT^2$]

$\therefore$ $PR \times PS = PT^2$ **Hence proved.**

(c) Given, $PR = 4$ cm and $PS = 16$ cm

$\because$ We know that

$PR \times PS = PT^2$

$\Rightarrow 4 \times 16 = PT^2$

$\Rightarrow 64 = PT^2$

$\Rightarrow PT = \sqrt{64} = 8$ cm

Hence, the length of the tangent PT is 8 cm.

(iii) (a) From the given graph it is clear that the total number of workers is represented by the highest value of the Y-axis.

In graph, the highest point is at (12000, 75).

Therefore, the total number of workers is 75.

(b) Let P be the point on Y-axis representing frequency $= \frac{n}{2} = \frac{75}{2} = 37.5$

Through P draw a horizontal line to meet the ogive at point Q. Through Q draw vertical line to meet the X-axis at T.

The abscissa of point T represent ₹ 6250.

Therefore, the median class is 6000–8000.

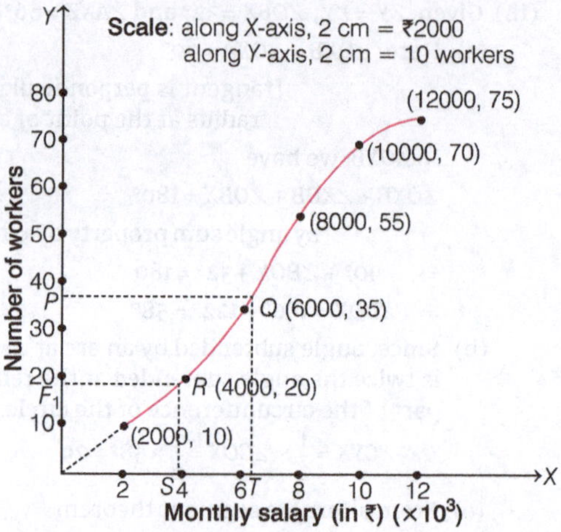

(c) **Lower quartile** Here, $n = 75$, so $\frac{n}{4} = \frac{75}{4} = 18.75$

Taking point F_1 on Y-axis representing frequency $= 18.75$

Through F_1, draw a horizontal line to meet the ogive at R. Through R, draw a vertical line to meet the X-axis at S.

The abscissa of point S represents ₹ 3750.

$\therefore Q_1 = 3750$

Hence, the lower quartile class is 2000–4000.

(d) From the graph,

the numbers of worker at ₹ 6000 and ₹ 10000 are 35 and 70, respectively

$\therefore$ Number of workers having salary more than or equal to ₹ 6000 but less than ₹ 10000 $= 70 - 35 = 35$